THE AMERICAN JOURNEY

A History of the United States

VOLUME I

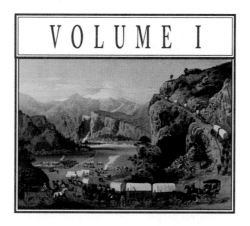

DAVID GOLDFIELD

CARL ABBOTT

VIRGINIA DEJOHN ANDERSON

JO ANN E. ARGERSINGER

PETER H. ARGERSINGER

WILLIAM L. BARNEY

ROBERT M. WEIR

Prentice Hall, Upper Saddle River, New Jersey 07458

Library of Congress Cataloging-in-Publication Data

The American Journey : a history of the United States / David
    Goldfield . . . [et. at]. — Combined ed.
        p.   cn.
    Includes bibliographical references and index.
    ISBN 0-13-652033-2
    1. United States—History.   I. Goldfield, David R., (date)
E178.1.A4925   1998
973—dc21   97-29756
                                                             CIP

Editorial director: Charlyce Jones Owen
Editorial/production supervision: Jenny Moss and Joe Scordato
Development editors: David Chodoff and Gerald Lombardi
Marketing manager: Sheryl Adams
Editorial assistant: Holly Brown
Copy editor: Bruce Emmer
Creative director: Leslie Osher
Design director: Carole Anson
Interior and cover designer: Carole Anson
Photo editor: Lorinda Morris-Nantz
Photo researcher: Kathy Ringrose
Fact checker: Ann Hofstra Grogg
Manufacturing manager: Nick Sklitsis
Manufacturing buyer: Lynn Pearlman
Line art coordinator: Michele Giusti
Cartographer: CARTO-GRAPHICS with shaded relief
    from Mountain High Maps®, Digital Wisdom, Inc.
Cover art: Travel by Ox-drawn Covered Wagons.
    Source: The Bancroft Library

This book was set in 10.5/12 New Baskerville Roman by
TSI Graphics and was printed and bound by Von Hoffman Press, Inc.
The cover was printed by The Lehigh Press, Inc.

© 1998 by Prentice-Hall, Inc.
A Simon & Schuster Company
Upper Saddle River, NJ 07458

Printed in the United States of America
10 9 8 7 6 5 4 3 2 1

ISBN 0-13-031766-7

Prentice Hall International (UK) Limited, *London*
Prentice-Hall of Australia Pty. Limited, *Sydney*
Prentice-Hall Canada Inc., *Toronto*
Prentice-Hall Hispanoamericana, S.A., *Mexico*
Prentice-Hall of India Private Limited, *New Delhi*
Prentice-Hall of Japan, Inc., *Tokyo*
Simon & Schuster Asia Pte. Ltd., *Singapore*
Editora Prentice-Hall do Brasil, Ltda., *Rio de Janeiro*

FOR OUR STUDENTS, WHO HELPED US WRITE THIS BOOK.

BRIEF CONTENTS

CONTENTS

1

WORLDS APART   1

2

TRANSPLANTATION 1600-1685   33

3

THE CREATION OF NEW WORLDS   61

4

CONVERGENCE AND CONFLICT
1660s-1763   91

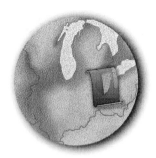

7

THE FIRST REPUBLIC
1776-1789   193

8

A NEW REPUBLIC AND THE
RISE OF PARTIES
1789-1800   225

9

THE TRIUMPH AND COLLAPSE OF JEFFERSONIAN REPUBLICANISM
1800-1824   255

10

THE JACKSONIAN ERA
1824-1845   285

11

Industrial Change and Urbanization
1820-1850 315

12

The Way West   345

13

SLAVERY AND THE OLD SOUTH
1800-1860 375

14

REFORMING ANTEBELLUM SOCIETY
1815-1850 403

15

THE POLITICS OF SECTIONALISM 1846-1861   431

16

BATTLE CRIES AND FREEDOM SONGS: THE CIVIL WAR, 1861-1863   469

17

The Union Preserved: The Civil War, 1863-1865   503

WE THE PEOPLE, 1789-1865   526

18

Reconstruction, 1865-1877   529

American Views

MAPS

FIGURES AND TABLES

SUMMARY TABLES

PREFACE

The personal journeys that led each of us to *The American Journey* began in the classroom with our students. We wrote this book for them. Responding to the many American history textbooks we have subjected them to over the years, our students have let us know what they liked and disliked, what they found difficult and what they grasped easily, what they skipped and what they devoured, what stories resonated with their own experiences and what seemed unconnected to them and their world.

But if we wrote this book to appeal to our students, we also wrote it to engage their minds. We wanted to avoid academic trendiness, particularly the restricting categories that have divided the discipline of history over the past twenty years or so. We believe that the distinctions involved in the debates about multiculturalism and identity, between social and political history, between the history of the common people and the history of the elite, are unnecessarily confusing.

What we seek is integration—to combine political and social history, to fit the experience of particular groups into the broader perspective of the American past, to give voice to minor and major players alike because of their role in the story we have to tell.

What is that story? A principal theme of *The American Journey* is the emergence of distinctively American ideals and the way the conflict between those ideals and reality has shaped the nation's development. At best, that conflict has broadened the understanding and application of American ideals to more and more formerly excluded people. This is not to say that American history is a heroic tale of constant improvement. Many conflicts over the meaning of our ideals have been resolved, if at all, only after great struggle. The United States is a diverse nation not always comfortable with its diversity but confronted—in the words of its founding documents, particularly the Declaration of Independence—with ideals that set a higher standard than its people might otherwise set for themselves. We remind the readers, our students, in four "We the People" essays placed at strategic junctures in the text, what those ideals are and how and why we are or are not making progress in fulfilling them. You might call the essays the "reality checks" for this text, taking stock of where we stood at four crucial periods in our history.

APPROACH

In telling our story, we had some definite ideas about what we might include and emphasize that other texts do not—information we felt that the current and next generations of students will need to know about our past to function best in a new society. We wanted to present that information in a clear, engaging style in such a way that it would stick with students after the course is over.

CHRONOLOGICAL ORGANIZATION A strong chronological backbone supports the book. We have found that jumping back and forth in time, as some American history textbooks do, confuses students. They abhor dates but need to know the sequence of events in history. A chronological presentation is the best way to be sure they do.

GEOGRAPHICAL LITERACY We also want students to be geographically literate. We expect them to know not only what happened in American history but where it happened as well, for physical locations and spatial relationships were often important in shaping historical events. *The American Journey* has more than 110 maps, all numbered and called out in the text. They are an integral part of our story.

COVERAGE OF THE SOUTH AND WEST The South and the West play significant roles in this text. American history is too often written from a northeastern perspective, at least when it comes to discussing cities, economic development, and reform. But the South and West were developing in their own ways throughout American history, and they remain important keys to the emerging character of the nation as a whole.

POINT OF VIEW *The American Journey* presents a balanced overview of the American past. But "balanced" does not mean bland. We do not shy away from definite positions on controversial issues, such as the nature of early contacts between Native Americans and Europeans, why the political crisis of the 1850s ended in a bloody Civil War, and how Populism and its followers fit into the American political spectrum. If students and instructors disagree, that's great; discussion and dissent are important catalysts for understanding and learning.

RELIGION Nor do we shy away from some topics that play relatively minor roles in other texts, like religion. Historians are often uncomfortable writing about religion and tend to slight its influence. This text stresses the importance of religion in American society both as a source of strength and as a reflection of some its more troubling aspects.

Historians write mostly for one another. That's too bad. We need to reach out and expand our audience. An American history text is a good place to start. Our students are not just our future historians but, more important, our future. Let their American journey begin!

FEATURES OF THE TEXT

The American Journey offers an array of features and pedagogical tools designed to make American history accessible to students.

- ❖ The **"Student Tool Kit"** that follows this preface helps students get the most out of the text and its features. It introduces students to key conventions of historical writing, and it explains how to read maps, graphs, and tables.

- ❖ An **outline** and a list of **key topics** give students a succinct overview of each chapter.

- ❖ Each chapter begins with an engaging **opening story** that highlights important themes.

- ❖ The **"American Views"** box in each chapter contains a relevant primary source document. Taken from letters, diaries, newspapers, government papers, and other sources, these bring the people of the past and their concerns vividly alive. An *introduction* and *prereading questions* relate the documents to the text and direct students' attention to important issues.

- ❖ **Summary tables** in each chapter provide an overview of complex issues.

- ❖ Chapter **chronologies** help students build a framework of key events.

- ❖ **Key terms** are highlighted within each chapter and defined in an end-of-book **glossary.**

- ❖ Chapter **review questions** help students review the material in a chapter and relate it to broader themes.

- ❖ Lists of **key readings** and **additional sources** at the end of each chapter direct interested students to further information about the subject of the chapter.

- ❖ **"Where to Learn More"** sections describe historical sites students can visit to gain a deeper understanding of the events discussed in the chapter.

- ❖ Four **"We the People"** essays focus on the relationship between American ideals and American reality at critical junctures in the nation's history—after the ratification of the Constitution, after the Civil War, after World War I, and at the present.

- ❖ Abundant **maps, charts,** and **graphs** help students understand important events and trends. The *topographical detail* in many of the maps helps students understand the influence of geography on history.

- ❖ **Illustrations** and **photographs,** tied to the text with detailed captions, provide a visual dimension to history.

SUPPLEMENTARY INSTRUCTIONAL MATERIALS

The American Journey comes with an extensive package of supplementary print and multimedia materials for both instructors and students.

Print Supplements

The *Instructor's Resource Manual,* prepared by JoAnne Carpenter, Florida Community College at Jacksonville, contains chapter outlines, detailed chapter overviews, activities, discussion questions, readings, and information on audiovisual resources.

The *Test Item File,* written by Tom DePalma, William Rainey Harper College, offers a menu of multiple-choice, true-false, essay, and map questions for each chapter. A collection of blank maps can be photocopied and used for map testing or other class exercises.

The *Prentice Hall Custom Test,* a commercial-quality computerized test management program, available for DOS, Windows, and Macintosh environments, allows instructors to select items from the *Test Item File* and design their own exams.

A *Transparency Pack* provides instructors with full-color transparency acetates of all the maps, charts, and graphs in the text for use in the classroom.

A two-volume *Study Guide,* prepared by Edward Lee, Winthrop University, provides students with a brief overview of each chapter, a list of chapter objectives, study exercises, multiple-choice, short answer, and essay questions. In addition, each chapter includes two to three pages of specific map questions and exercises.

The American Journey: Documents in U.S. History (Volumes I and II) provides five additional primary and secondary source documents—with prereading and postreading questions—for each chapter of the textbook.

Reading Critically about History, prepared by Rose Wassman, DeAnza College, provides students with helpful strategies for reading a history textbook. This brief guide, when packaged with *The American Journey,* is available free to students.

Understanding and Answering Essay Questions, prepared by Mary L. Kelley, San Antonio College, suggests helpful analytical tools for understanding different types of essay questions and provides precise guidelines for preparing well-crafted essay answers. This brief guide, when packaged with *The American Journey,* is available free to students.

Themes of the Times is a newspaper supplement prepared jointly for students by Prentice Hall and the premier news publication, *The New York Times.* Issued twice a year, it contains recent articles pertinent to  American history. These articles connect the classroom to the world. For information about a reduced-rate subscription to *The New York Times,* call toll-free: (800) 631-1222.

Retrieving the American Past: A Customized U.S. History Reader, an on-demand history database written and developed by leading historians and educators, offers fifty-two compelling modules on topics in American history, such as "Women on the Frontier", "The Salem Witchcraft Scare", "The Age of Industrial Violence", and "Native American Societies, 1870–1995". Approximately thirty-five pages in length, each module includes an introduc-tion, several primary documents and secondary sources, follow-up questions, and recommendations for further reading. By deciding which modules to include and the order in which they will appear, instructors can compile the reader they want to use. Instructor-originated material, including other readings and exercises, can be incorporated. Contact your local Prentice Hall representative for more information about this exciting custom publishing option.

Multimedia Supplements

History on the Internet, adapted by John Paul Rossi, Pennsylvania State University, Erie, is a brief guide that provides students with clear strategies for navigating the Internet and the World Wide Web. Exercises within and at the end of the chapters allow students to practice searching for the myriad resources available to the student of history. This 96-page supplementary book, when packaged with *The American Journey,* is free to students.

The American Journey, Interactive Edition, is a multimedia CD-ROM created by Zane Publishing, a leader in the field of multimedia, using the company's exclusive *Power CD*® technology. It features self-playing multimedia presentations, historical photographs with captions, interactive study questions to strengthen the student's understanding of U.S. history, additional interactive essay review questions, the complete *Webster's New World Dictionary, Third College Edition,* and the complete text of *The American Journey.* With *The American Journey, Interactive Edition,* the past has never been so vibrant, so accessible, and so interesting.

Powerpoint U.S. History is a collection of the maps, charts and graphs, summary tables, and other useful lecture material from the text on disk for use with Microsoft Powerpoint.™ The material can be used in lectures, for slide shows, or printed as transparency acetates.

The American Journey World Wide Web Companion Study Guide (www.prenhall.com/goldfield) works in tandem with the text to help students use the World Wide Web to enrich their understanding of American history. Featuring chapter objectives, study questions, new updates, labeling exercises, and much more, it links the text with related material available on the Internet.

Acknowledgments

We would like to thank the reviewers whose thoughtful and often detailed comments helped shape *The American Journey:*

Joseph Adams, Saint Louis Community College
David Aldstadt, Houston Community College
Janet Allured, McNeese State University
Tyler Anbinder, George Washington University
Michael Batinski, Southern Illinois University
Michael Bellesiles, Emory University
Eugene Berwanger, Colorado State University
Terry Bilhartz, Sam Houston State University
Fred Blue, Youngstown State University
Eric J. Bolsteri, University of Texas at Arlington
Charles Bolton, University of Arkansas at Little Rock
James Bradford, Texas A & M University
Michael Bradley, Motlow State Community College
Henry William Brands, Texas A & M University
Neal Brooks, Essex Community College
Richard Brown, University of Connecticut
Tom Bryan, Alvin Community College
Randolph Campbell, University of North Texas
Dale Carnagey, Blinn College
E. Wayne Carp, Pacific Lutheran University
David Castle, Ohio University, Eastern Campus
Andrew Cayton, Miami University
Bill Cecil-Fronsman, Washburn University
John Chalberg, Normandale Community College
Myles Clowers, San Diego City College
David Conrad, Southern Illinois University
William Corbett, Northeastern State University
Robert Cray, Montclair State College
Richard Crepeau, University of Central Florida
Samuel Crompton, Holyoke Community College
Gilbert Cruz, Glendale Community College
Light T. Cummins, Austin College
Eugene Demody, Cerritos College
Joseph Devine, Stephen F. Austin State University
Donald Dewey, California State University
Leonard Dinnerstein, University of Arizona
Marvin Dulaney, University of Texas at Arlington
Leflett Easley, Campbell University
Iris Engstrand, University of San Diego
Robin Fabel, Auburn University
Jay Fell, University of Colorado
Nancy Gabin, Purdue University
Scott Garrett, Paducah Community College
Marilyn Geiger, Washburn University
George Gerdow, Northeastern Illinois University
Gerald Ghelfi, Rancho Santiago College
Louis Gimelli, Eastern Michigan University

James Goode, Grand Valley State University
Gregory Goodwin, Bakersfield College
Ralph Goodwin, East Texas State University
Robert Greene, Morgan State University
Mark Grimsley, Ohio State University
Ira Gruber, U.S. Military Academy
Harland Hagler, University of North Texas
Steve Haley, Shelby State Community College
Gwendolyn Hall, Rutgers University
Timothy D. Hall, Central Michigan University
David Hamilton, University of Kentucky
Joe Hapak, Moraine Valley Community College
Ronald Hatzenbuchler, Idaho State University
David G. Hogan, Heidelberg College
Alfred Hunt, SUNY Purchase
John Ingham, University of Toronto
Priscilla Jackson-Evans, Longview Community College
Donald Jacobs, Northeastern University
Frederick Jaher, University of Illinois
John Johnson, University of Northern Iowa
Wilbur Johnson, Rock Valley College
Yvonne Johnson, Central Missouri State University
Yasuhide Kawashima, University of Texas at El Paso
Joseph E. King, Texas Tech University
Gene Kirkpatrick, Tyler Junior College
Lawrence Kohl, University of Alabama at Tuscaloosa
Michael Krenn, University of Miami
Michael Krutz, Southeastern Louisiana University
Robert LaPorte, North Texas University
Armand LaPotin, SUNY Oneonta
John LaSaine, University of Georgia
Bryan LeBeau, Creighton University
Martin Leff, University of Illinois, Urbana-Champaign
Ed Lukes, Hillsborough Community College
Leo Lyman, Victor, Valley College
Ronald McArthur, Atlantic Community College
Donald McCoy, University of Kansas
David McFadden, Fairfield University
Gerald MacFarland, University of Massachusetts
Thomas McLuen, Spokane Falls Community College
Peter C. Mancell, University of Kansas
Norman Markowitz, Rutgers University
Frank Marmolejo, Irvine Valley College
James Matray, New Mexico State University
Karen Miller, Oakland University
Otis Miller, Belleville Area College
Worth Robert Miller, Southwest Missouri State University
Timothy Morgan, Christopher Newport University
Christopher Moss, University of Texas at Arlington
Harmon Mothershead, Northwest Missouri State University
Benjamin Newcomb, Texas Technological University

Elizabeth Nybakken, Mississippi State University
Colleen O'Connor, San Diego Mesa College
Chris Padgett, Weber State University
David Parker, Kennesaw State College
Peggy Pascoe, University of Utah
Christopher Phillips, Emporia State University
Thomas L. Powers, University of South Carolina, Sumter
Kay Pulley, Trinity Valley Community College
Norman Raiford, Greenville Technical College
John Rector, Western Oregon State University
Thomas C. Reeves, University of Wisconsin, Parkside
Gary Reichard, Florida Atlantic University
Joseph Reidy, Howard University
Ronald Reitvald, California State University, Fullerton
Howard Rock, Florida International University
Hal Rothman, University of Nevada, Las Vegas
Richard Sadler, Weber State University
Henry Sage, Northern Virginia Community College, Alexandria
Bufford Satcher, University of Arkansas at Pine Bluff
Sandra Schackel, Boise State University
Michael Schaller, University of Arizona
Dale Schmitt, East Tennessee State University
Ronald Schultz, University of Wyoming
Rebecca Shoemaker, Indiana State University
Frank Siltman, U.S. Military Academy
David Sloan, University of Arkansas
J.B. Smallwood, University of North Texas
Sherry Smith, University of Texas at El Paso
Kenneth Stevens, Texas Christian University
William Stockton, Johnson County Community College
Mark Summers, University of Kentucky
William Tanner, Humbolt State University
Quintard Taylor, University of Oregon
Emily Teipe, Fullerton College
Frank Towers, Clarion University
Paula Trekel, Allegheny College
Stanley Underal, San Jose University
Andrew Wallace, Northern Arizona University
Harry Ward, University of Richmond
Ken Weatherbie, Del Mar College
Stephen Webre, Louisiana Tech University
Edward Weller, San Jacinto College, South
Michael Welsh, University of Northern Colorado
James Whittenberg, College of William and Mary
Brian Wills, Clinch Valley Community College
John Wiseman, Frostburg State University
James Woods, Georgia Southern University
Mark Wyman, Illinois State University
Neil York, Brigham Young University
William Young, Johnson County Community College
Nancy Zen, Central Oregon Community College

All of us are grateful to our families, friends, and colleagues for their support and encouragement. Jo Ann and Peter Argersinger would like in particular to thank Pamela Fesmire and Rosalie Radcliffe; Virginia Anderson thanks Kim Gruenwald, Ruth Helm, Eric Hinderaker, and Chidiebere Nwaubani; and David Goldfield thanks Frances Glenn and Jason Moscato. Jim Miller, Sylvia Mallory, and Sally Constable played key roles in the book's inception and initial development.

Finally, we would like to acknowledge the members of our Prentice Hall family. They are not only highly competent professionals but also pleasant people. We regard them with affection and appreciation. None of us would hesitate to work with this fine group again. We would especially like to thank David Chodoff, senior development editor, and Gerald Lombardi for their marvelous alchemy with our prose; Charlyce Jones Owen, editorial director, who organized her team and our social functions flawlessly; Alison Pendergast, senior manager for new media marketing and development, and Sheryl Adams, marketing manager, whose creative and informed marketing strategies demonstrated an appreciation for historical scholarship as well as the history textbook market; Carole Anson, art director, and Leslie Osher, creative design director, whose creativity is evident in this book's design and layout; Jenny Moss, project manager, for her efficient handling of the production process and her beyond-the-call-of-duty work on maps; Alice Thiede, who generated those maps and the other line art in the book; Bruce Emmer, copy editor; Ann Grogg, fact checker; Michelle Giusti, line art coordinator; Kathy Ringrose, Barbara Salz, and Francelle Carapetyan for their photo research; Susanna Lesan, editor in chief for development, for ensuring that the book had the developmental resources it needed; Nick Sklitsis, manufacturing manager, Lynn Pearlman, manufacturing buyer, and Jan Stephan, managing editor, who kept the whole team on schedule; and Phil Miller, president of Prentice Hall's Humanities and Social Sciences division, who had the good sense to let his staff run with this book.

DG
CA
VDJA
JEA
PHA
WLB
RMW

ABOUT THE AUTHORS

David Goldfield received his Ph.D. in history from the University of Maryland. Since 1982, he has been Robert Lee Baily Professor of History at the University of North Carolina in Charlotte. He is the author or editor of eleven books on various aspects of southern and urban history. Two of his works—*Cotton Fields and Skyscrapers: Southern City and Region, 1607 to 1980* (1982) and *Black, White, and Southern: Race Relations and Southern Culture, 1940 to the Present* (1990)—received the Mayflower Award for Nonfiction. Both books were also nominated for the Pulitzer Prize in history. When he is not writing or teaching, Goldfield applies the historical craft to history museum exhibits, federal voting rights cases, and local planning and policy issues. He is currently working on a book that asks the question: Why is the South different?

Carl Abbott is a Professor of Urban Studies and Planning at Portland State University. He taught previously in the history departments at the University of Denver and Old Dominion University and held visiting appointments at Mesa College in Colorado and George Washington University. He holds degrees in history from Swarthmore College and the Unversity of Chicago. He specializes in the history of cities and the American West and serves as co-editor of the *Pacific Historical Review*. His books include: *The New Urban America: Growth and Politics in Sunbelt Cities* (1981, 1987), *The Metropolitan Frontier: Cities in the Modern American West* (1993), and *Planning a New West: The Columbia River Gorge National Scenic Area* (1997).

Virginia DeJohn Anderson is Associate Professor of History at the University of Colorado at Boulder. She received her B.A. from the University of Connecticut. As the recipient of a Marshall Scholarship, she earned an M.A. degree at the University of East Anglia in Norwich, England. Returning to the United States, she received her A.M. and Ph.D. degrees from Harvard University. She is the author of *New England's Generation: The Great Migration and the Formation Of Society and Culture in the Seventeenth Century* (1991) and several articles on colonial history, which have appeared in such journals as the *William and Mary Quarterly* and the *New England Quarterly*.

Jo Ann E. Argersinger received her Ph.D. from George Washington University and is Provost and Professor of History at The University of Maryland Baltimore County (UMBC). A recipient of fellowships from the Rockefeller Foundation and the National Endowment for the Humanities, she is a historian of social, labor, and business policy. Her publications include *Toward a New Deal in Baltimore: People and Government in the Great Depression* (1988) and *The Making of a Union: Men, Women, and the Amalgamated Clothing Workers* (1998).

Peter H. Argersinger received his Ph.D. from the University of Wisconsin and is Presidential Research Professor of History at the University of Maryland Baltimore County (UMBC). He has won several fellowships and the Binkey-Stephenson Award from the Organization of American Historians. Among his books on American political and rural history are *Populism and Politics* (1974); *Structure, Process, and Party* (1992); and *The Limits of Agrarian Radicalism* (1995).

William L. Barney is Professor of History at the University of North Carolina at Chapel Hill. A native of Pennsylvania, he received his B.A. from Cornell University and his M.A. and Ph.D. from Columbia University. He has published extensively on nineteenth-century U.S. history and has a particular interest in the Old South and the coming of the Civil War. Among his publications are: *The Road to Secession* (1972), *The Secessionist Impulse* (1974), *Flawed Victory* (1975), *The Passage of the Republic* (1987), and *Battleground for the Union* (1989).

Robert M. Weir is a Distinguished Professor of History at the University of South Carolina. He received his B.A. in English from Pennsylvania State University, his M.A. in American Culture and his Ph.D. in History from Case Western Reserve University. He has taught at the University of Houston and, as a visiting professor, at the University of Southampton in the United Kingdom. His articles have won prizes from the Southeastern Society for the Study of the Eighteenth Century and the *William and Mary Quarterly*. Among his publications are *Colonial South Carolina: A History* and *"The Last of American Freemen": Studies in the Political Culture of the Colonial and Revolutionary South*. His current research deals with the Southern defense of slavery in the Revolutionary era.

STUDENT TOOL KIT

In writing history, historians use various tools such as maps, tables, and graphs to help their readers understand the past. This book contains many of these tools. What follows is a simple explanation of how to use the historians' tools that are in this book.

TEXT

The text itself, whether a biography of George Washington, an article on the Civil War, or a survey of American history such as this one, is the historian's basic tool for discussing the past. Historians write about the past in two ways, narration and analysis, and this book contains both types of writing. Narration is the story line of history. It tells what happened in the past, who did it, and where and when it occurred. Most of the text of this book is narration. Narration is also used to describe how people in the past lived, how they spent their daily lives, and even, when the historical evidence allows, what they thought, felt, feared, or desired. Analysis tells you *why* historians think events in the past happened the way they did. Analysis offers an explanation for the narrative, for the story of history. In this book, you will find narration and analysis interwoven in each chapter.

      This book also contains a number of features that are designed to help you study history. Each chapter begins with a short list of *Key Topics* that highlights the most important points that will be made in the chapter. Each chapter ends with a brief *Conclusion* section that puts the subject of the chapter in the broader perspective of U.S. history. Both the *Key Topics* and the *Conclusion* are study aids. You can use them to help you review your understanding of the text itself.

MAPS

Most of the chapters in this book contain maps. Maps are important historical tools. They show how geography has affected history and can concisely summarize complex relationships and events. You need to know how to "read" a map to absorb the information it has to offer. To help you understand how to do this, let's look at an example, Map 5-1 from Chapter 5. The map shows the British colonies on the eastern seaboard of North America in 1763,

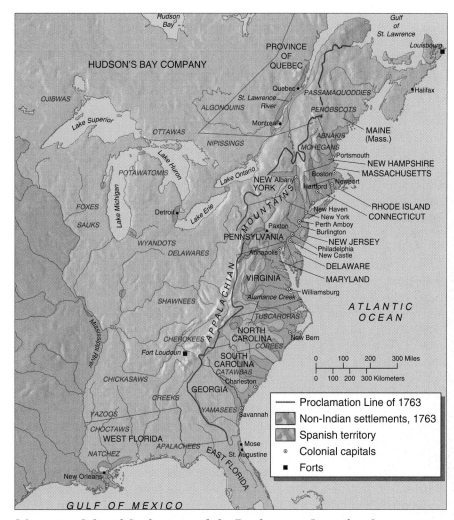

Map 5-1 Colonial Settlement and the Proclamation Line of 1763
This map depicts the regions claimed and settled by the major groups competing for territory in eastern North America. With the Proclamation Line of 1763 positioned along the crest of the Appalachian Mountains, the British government tried to stop the westward migration of settlers under its jurisdiction, and thereby limit conflict with the Indians. The result, however, was frustration and anger on the part of land-hungry settlers.

about twelve years before the American Revolution. It has three features to help you read it: a caption, a legend, and a scale. The caption is a paragraph of text that explains the historical significance of the map, that is, the point it is designed to make. Here the caption tells us that in 1763, the British government attempted to restrict colonial settlement to the eastern side of the Appalachian Mountains so that the colonists would not come into conflict with the Indian tribes who lived west of the mountains or had earlier been pushed there. Colonial frustration with this policy contributed to the outbreak of the American Revolution.

The legend and the scale appear at the lower right of the map. The legend tells you what the symbols on the map mean. Using it, we see that the solid line stretching along the Appalachian Mountains from Maine to Georgia represents the Proclamation Line of 1763—the line meant to restrict colonial settlement. Colonial capitals are marked with a dot in a circle, and forts with a black square. Spanish territory west of the Mississippi River is colored orange; territory settled by Europeans is colored green. The map also shows the lands inhabited by Indian tribes—Algonquins, Mohegans, Delawares, Creeks, and others. Note that these territories are not bounded by the solid lines the way the colonies are. The tribal lands of Native Americans did not have formal boundaries mapped out by surveyors. The scale tells us that 7/8 inch on the map represents 300 miles (about 480 kilometers) on the ground. You can use this information to estimate the distance between points on the map.

The map also shows us the topography of the region—its mountains, rivers, and lakes. This helps us understand how geography influenced history in this case. You can see, for example, that the Appalachian Mountains divide the eastern seaboard from the rest of the continent. The mountains obstructed colonial migration to the west for a long time. By running the Proclamation Line along the Appalachians, the British hoped to use this natural barrier to separate Indians and colonists. Note how small the green areas, the areas of European settlement, are, relative to the immense size of North America. Note also how the map shows that the Europeans tended to settle near the coasts and along rivers and across plains.

GRAPHS

Historians use graphs to make comparisons and summarize trends. Comparisons can be between groups of people, regions of the country, products, time periods—whatever focuses the reader's attention on an important historical development. Various types of graphs are used in this book, including pie charts, line graphs, and bar graphs. The names denote the way the graphs are drawn to make comparisons. All show the numbers of some significant factor, such as people, goods, or prices, at a given time or how they fluctuated over a given period. Figure 3-1 on page 64, for example, is a line graph that shows the dramatic decline in the population of four Native American groups during the colonial period. Figure 3-4 on page 86 is a pie chart—so called because it looks like a pie cut into slices. It shows the ethnic origins of the non-Indian population of the thirteen colonies at the start of the American Revolution. Figure 4-2 on page 114 is a bar chart that compares the growth in population of the four major colonial regions.

All graphs in the book are numbered by chapter and within each chapter. Thus the first graph in Chapter 3 is numbered Figure 3-1, the second Figure 3-2, and so on.

SUMMARY TABLES

Tables summarize information by organizing it into columns and rows. The *Summary Tables* in this text are a special feature designed to help you understand some important aspect of a chapter. The Summary Table on page 118 in Chapter 4, for example, summarizes information about the various colonial wars that were fought in North America between 1689 and 1763. Besides listing the wars by name, it allows you to compare how long each war lasted and what the results of each war were.

CHRONOLOGIES

Each chapter has a *Chronology*, a list of the key events discussed in the chapter arranged in chronological order, that is, according to the date on which they happened. The word *chronology* comes from the ancient Greek word for "time," *chronos*. A chronology is like a historical calendar, giving the dates of important events. The chronology in Chapter 2 on page 37 lists the dates of key events in the colonization of North America from 1603 to 1681. Chronologies can help you understand when important events occurred and their relationship to one another.

PRIMARY SOURCE DOCUMENTS

Our knowledge of the past comes from many sources. These include artworks like paintings, drawings, and sculptures as well as material artifacts like buildings and tools. Historians find most of their information, however, in written records, original documents that have survived from the past. These include government publications, letters, diaries, newspapers—whatever people wrote or printed, including many private documents never intended for publication. Each chapter in the book contains a feature called *American Views* with a selection from a primary source document. Each begins with a brief introduction followed by several questions to help you think about the selection. Within the documents themselves—as well as in other quoted material throughout the text—you will often encounter two types of punctuation with which you may not be familiar: ellipsis points and brackets. Points of ellipsis—three dots . . . —indicate that words have been edited out to save space or remove irrelevant material. This is often done when reprinting original documents. Brackets [ ] are printed around words or sentences that the authors of this book have added to the documents to clarify or improve your understanding. Brackets tell you that the words within them have been added, just as ellipsis points tell you that words have been left out.

RECOMMENDED READING, ADDITIONAL SOURCES, AND WHERE TO LEARN MORE

At the end of each chapter are two lists of books that you can read to deepen your knowledge of what was discussed in the chapter. *Recommended Reading* is annotated—that is, the authors of this text explain what is important about each of these books. *Additional Sources* is a longer list of books about each of the major topics covered in the chapter. The section called *Where to Learn More* lists historical sites and museums where you can go to gain a deeper understanding of the events discussed in the chapter.

GLOSSARY

Significant historical terms are emphasized with **heavy type** throughout the text. These are listed alphabetically and defined in the *Glossary* at the end of the book.

1 WORLDS APART

Pacific Ocean

Caho[la]

Santa Fe

Acoma
Pueblo

Tenochtitlán/
Mexico City

[G]ulf of Mexico

Tenochtitlán/
Mexico City

British Settlements

French Settlements

Spanish Settlements

0   400 miles

0   600 km

N
W   E
S

Quebec

Albany

Boston
Plymouth

New York

Philadelphia

Jamestown
Roanoke Island

Charleston

Atlantic Ocean

Caribbean Sea

KEY TOPICS

❖ Native American, West African, and European society on the eve of contact
❖ The reasons for Europe's impulse to global exploration
❖ The Spanish, French, and English experiences in America in the sixteenth century
❖ Consequences of contact between the Old and New Worlds

*B*y October 11, 1492, the three tiny ships had been sailing westward for more than five weeks. Over 3,000 miles of empty ocean separated them from their last landfall, in the Canary Islands off the coast of North Africa. Several times sailors had claimed to see land, but their sightings proved only mirages. Just the day before, frustration and fear drove officers and crew to threaten their admiral with mutiny unless they turned back for Spain. The admiral, Christopher Columbus, still confident that he could reach Asia and its riches by sailing west across the Atlantic, asked for two or three more days. His men, whose yearning for home mingled with hope that their long voyage might yet prove successful, agreed. Scouring sea and sky for signs, they saw floating branches and flying birds but still no land. Surely tomorrow night they would turn around.

Then, two hours after midnight on October 12, one of the sailors peered into the moonlight and shouted, "Land! Land!" In the pale light of dawn, a sliver of white sand beach indeed appeared. As the ships drew closer, the men thought they could smell the rich spices of the Orient. They searched the horizon for the golden-roofed temples about which they had heard so much. What they did not know was that this land was not the Orient. It was an island lying near two vast continents still invisible to them and about whose existence they had not the slightest inkling.

No one knows exactly where Columbus landed, but many historians believe it was an island in the Bahamas known to its inhabitants as Guanahani and now called Watling Island. Instead of a Chinese city, Columbus's landing party found a village of small wooden houses clustered around a central plaza. When the villagers first saw the strangers, who carried large banners that flapped in the breeze, they fled into the jungle. They soon emerged, however, bringing parrots and balls of cotton thread to trade for red caps and glass beads. Remarking on their nakedness and few possessions, Columbus judged these people—part of a group called the Tainos—"a people very poor in everything," although he noticed that a few of them wore gold nose ornaments. What the Tainos thought of Columbus and his men will never be known.

Thus began one of the most momentous encounters in human history. Columbus claimed the island as a possession of the monarchs of Spain and, grateful for his safe arrival, renamed it San Salvador (Holy Savior). Still convinced that he was near Asia, he did not realize he had found what was soon to be called the New World. At first, of course, it was new only to Europeans ignorant of its existence, not to the people whose ancestors had lived there for thousands of years. The far-reaching consequences of Columbus's voyage, however, would ultimately bring together people who had previously lived in worlds apart—Native American, African, and European—to forge a world that was new in fact as well as name.

Different Worlds

The New World that emerged after 1492 reflected the experience of the people who built it. Improving economic conditions in the fifteenth and early sixteenth centuries spurred Europeans to turn outward, seeking new opportunities for trade in overseas exploration and settlement. Spain, Portugal, France, and England, competing for political, economic, and religious domination within Europe, carried their conflict over into the Americas. Native Americans drew upon their familiarity with the land and its resources, their long-established patterns of political and religious authority, and their well-developed systems of trade and warfare to deal with the European newcomers. Africans were brought to the New World by Europeans intent on expansion. Before Columbus set out across the Atlantic, Portuguese vessels had sailed down the west coast of Africa, bringing back African gold and slaves. When faced with a need for labor in the New World, Europeans turned to the West African slave market they had already known for half a century.

This woodcut, which first appeared on the cover of a pamphlet in 1493, may be the first European drawing of Columbus's arrival in America. King Ferdinand of Spain sits on the left, directing Columbus and his three ships to an island. The nearly naked native peoples (depicted as being larger than the Europeans) appear to flee from the ships.

Native American Societies before 1492

Convinced that he had landed in the East Indies, Columbus called the people he met *indios*. His error is preserved in the word *Indian,* used by Europeans to identify the original inhabitants of the two American continents. (The word *America* itself derives from the name of another Italian explorer, Amerigo Vespucci.) In their own languages, many native groups called themselves "the original people" or "the true men."

By 1492, the continents of North and South America had been inhabited for a very long time—estimates range from 15,000 to 50,000 years. The human population of the two continents may have been as high as 70 million—nearly equal to the population of Europe at that time—with only 7 million or so living north of the Rio Grande in what is now the United States and Canada. These people belonged to hundreds of groups, each with its own language or dialect, history, and way of life. They varied from nomadic hunters in the Arctic to members of the complex imperial society centered in the Aztec capital of Tenochtitlán, one of the largest cities in the world in the year Columbus sailed.

Thousands of years ago, when much of the earth's water was frozen in the glaciers of the last ice age, the sea level was lower. Siberia and Alaska, now separated by the Bering Strait, were connected by a great land bridge. The first Americans were nomadic hunters from Siberia who probably came in three waves across this bridge. They gradually ranged southward and eastward. Within a few thousand years, their descendants had spread throughout North and South America.

These early hunters, whom archaeologists call **Paleo-Indians,** traveled in small bands, tracking and killing mammoths, bison, and other large game. Unaccustomed to the presence of humans, these animals were often easy prey. But Paleo-Indians were also resourceful hunters who crafted sharp stone points for their spears. Their efficiency may in fact have led to overhunting. Archaeological evidence shows that by around 9000 B.C., mammoths, mastodons, and other large animals had become extinct in the Americas. Climatic change also hastened the animals' disappearance. Around 12,000 years ago, the world's climate began to grow warmer, turning grasslands into deserts and reducing the animals' food supply. This meant that humans too had to find other food sources.

With a warmer climate, the American environment changed in important ways that affected human subsistence. Melting glaciers raised the sea level, created coastal marshes, and filled the Great Lakes and inland rivers. In the continent's interior, forests with many varieties of trees and bushes replaced grasslands and stands of evergreens. The largest animals had disappeared, but many smaller creatures roamed the land and swam in rivers and lakes. Deserts appeared in much of the West, with sparser plant and animal life.

Between roughly 8000 B.C. and 1500 B.C.—what archaeologists call the **Archaic** period—Indians adapted to regional environments, learning to use local resources efficiently. Indians living along North America's northeast coast, for instance, became proficient fishermen who took small boats out onto the North Atlantic to catch swordfish and perhaps even whales. In the Southwest, people hunted desert-dwelling mammals and birds and gathered various nuts, seeds, and roots.

More efficient food collection led to other changes in the Archaic period. Populations grew, and people began living in larger communities, some with a hundred or more residents. These villages had recognized leaders, but the rest of the inhabitants were not divided into social classes. Men and women, however, began to assume more specialized roles. Men did most of the hunting and fishing, activities that often required travel. Women remained closer to home, gathering and preparing wild plant foods and caring for children. Each group probably made

CHRONOLOGY

c. 50,000–15,000 B.C.	Ancestors of Native Americans cross Bering land bridge.
c. 10,000–9000 B.C.	Paleo-Indians expand through the Americas.
c. 9000 B.C.	Extinction of large land mammals in North America.
c. 8000–1500 B.C.	Archaic Indian era.
c. 5000 B.C.	Beginnings of agriculture in Mesoamerica.
c. 1500 B.C.	Earliest mound-building culture begins.
c. 500 B.C.–A.D. 400	Adena-Hopewell mound-building culture.
c. A.D. 700–1600	Rise of West African empires.
c. 900	First mounds built at Cahokia. Anasazi expansion.
c. 1000	Spread of Islam in West Africa.
c. 1000–1500	Last mound-building culture, the Mississippian.
c. 1290s	Anasazi dispersal into smaller pueblos.
1400–1600	Renaissance in Europe.
1430s	Beginnings of Portuguese slave trade in West Africa.

1492	Christopher Columbus's first voyage. End of *reconquista* in Spain.
1494	Treaty of Tordesillas.
1497	John Cabot visits Nova Scotia and Newfoundland.
1497–1499	Vasco da Gama sails around Africa to reach India.
1517	Protestant Reformation begins in Germany.
1519–1521	Hernán Cortés conquers the Aztec empire.
1532–1533	Francisco Pizarro conquers the Inca empire.
1534–1542	Jacques Cartier explores eastern Canada for France.
1542–1543	Roberval's failed colony in Canada.
1540–1542	Coronado explores southwestern North America.
1558	Elizabeth I becomes queen of England.
1565	Spanish establish outpost at St. Augustine in Florida.
1560s–1580s	English renew attempts to conquer Ireland.
1587	Founding of "Lost Colony" of Roanoke.
1598	Spanish found colony at New Mexico.

the tools it used, with men carving fishhooks and arrowheads and women making such items as bone needles and baskets.

Archaic Indians also collected local nonfood resources, including rocks, shells, and bones. They fashioned goods from these materials and traded them with other peoples, sometimes hundreds of miles away. At Indian Knoll, in western Kentucky, archaeologists have found copper from the Great Lakes area and shells from as far away as the Gulf of Mexico. Competition for control of lands where desirable materials could be found may have sparked conflict between peoples. Three bodies buried around 5000 B.C. in northwestern Alabama had stone arrowheads embedded in their backbones or ribcages, clear evidence of violent death.

Ideas as well as goods circulated among Archaic Indian peoples. Across the continent, human burials became more elaborate, suggesting that ideas

about death and the afterlife passed between groups. Bodies might be wrapped in woven mats or cloths, and the deceased's personal possessions were often placed in the grave. Certain valuable trade goods, such as exotic shell beads and animal figurines, have been found in some graves, perhaps indicating that such objects had spiritual significance.

Many Indian peoples flourished by hunting and gathering, but near the end of the Archaic period, some groups made a further adaptation when they began farming. The development of agriculture appears to have occurred independently in various parts of the world. People in the Middle East began farming around 9000 B.C. A few thousand years later, farming appeared in Southeast Asia, China, India's Indus Valley, Mexico, and Peru. Archaeologists speculate that agriculture first developed in areas where population growth threatened to outrun the supply of game and wild plants. Women, with their expertise in gathering wild plants, were probably the world's first farmers.

Agriculture in the Americas began around 5000 B.C., when the people of southern Mexico started raising an ancient type of maize, or corn. At first, farming supplemented a diet still largely dependent on hunting and gathering. But agriculture gradually became more widespread. In addition to maize, the main crop in both South and North America, farmers in Mexico, Central America, and the Peruvian Andes learned to cultivate many other crops. These include manioc, peppers, beans, pumpkins, squash, avocados, sweet and white potatoes (native to the Peruvian highlands), and tomatoes. Mexican farmers also grew cotton. Maize and bean cultivation spread from Mexico in a wide arc to the north and east. Peoples in what is now the southwestern United States began farming between 1500 and 500 B.C., and by A.D. 200, farmers tilled the soil in present-day Georgia and Florida.

Wherever agriculture took hold, important social changes followed. Populations grew, since farming produced a more secure food supply than hunting and gathering. Permanent villages appeared as farmers settled near their fields. In places such as central Mexico, agriculture eventually sustained the populations of large cities. Trade in agricultural surpluses flowed through existing networks of exchange and may have created new links. In many Indian societies, women's status improved because of their role as the principal farmers. Specialized craft workers made technological and artistic advances in producing pottery and baskets to store harvested grains. Even religious beliefs and practices reflected the centrality of farming. In describing the origins of their people, Pueblo Indians of the Southwest compared their emergence from the underworld to a maize plant sprouting from the earth.

By 1492, the peoples of North America had developed many distinctive ways of life. Despite their diversity, certain generalizations can be made about societies that developed within broad regions, or **culture areas** (see Map 1-1). Within each area, inhabitants shared basic patterns of subsistence and social organization, largely reflecting the natural environment to which they had adapted.

Throughout the North and West, Indians prospered without adopting agriculture. In the challenging environment of the Arctic and Subarctic, small nomadic bands moved seasonally to fish, follow game, and, in the brief summers, gather wild berries. Far to the north, Eskimos and Aleuts hunted whales, walruses, seals, and other sea mammals. Further inland, the Crees and other peoples followed migrating herds of caribou and moose. Northern peoples fashioned tools and weapons of bone and ivory, clothing and boats from animal skins, and houses of whalebones and hides or blocks of sod or snow. Many of their rituals and songs celebrated the hunt and the spiritual connection between humans and the animals on which they depended.

Along the Northwest Coast and Columbia River Plateau, regions of abundant resources, people developed a settled way of life without agriculture. With rivers teeming with salmon and other fish and forests full of game and edible plants, these were some of the most densely populated areas of North America. Among groups like the Kwakiutls and Chinooks, extended families lived in large communal houses constructed of cedar planks. These were often located in villages of several hundred people, where chiefs ruled over lower-ranking individuals. Rulers displayed their prominence most conspicuously during potlatches, or ceremonies in which they gave away or destroyed food, blankets, beads, and other possessions.

Women were the principal farmers in most Native American societies, growing corn, beans, and other crops that made up most of their food supply. This sixteenth-century French engraving shows Indian men preparing the soil for cultivation and Indian women sowing seeds in neat rows.

Map 1-1   North American Culture Areas, c. 1500
*Over the course of centuries, Indian peoples in North America developed distinctive cultures
suited to the environments in which they lived. Inhabitants of each culture area shared basic
patterns of subsistence, craft work, and social organization. Most, but not all, Indian peoples
combined farming with hunting and gathering.*

Craftsmen used the region's plentiful wood supply to
make many items, including distinctive religious
masks and memorial poles carved with images of
supernatural beings.

Farther south, in present-day California,
hunter-gatherers lived in smaller villages of perhaps
one hundred people. A single chief often led several
villages. These settlements usually adjoined oak

groves, where Indians gathered acorns. Preparing the nuts was time-consuming, for they had to be ground into meal, leached with water to remove bitter acid, and then cooked. To protect their access to this important food, chiefs and villagers vigorously defended their territorial claims to the oak groves. Elsewhere, in the foothills of the Sierras, Indians periodically set fire to thick underbrush to hasten the growth of new shoots that would attract deer and other game.

Small nomadic bands in the Great Basin, where the climate was warm and dry, lived in caves and rock shelters, surviving on the region's limited resources. Shoshone hunters captured antelope in corrals and trapped small game, such as groundhogs, squirrels, and rabbits. In present-day Utah and western Colorado, Utes hunted elk, bison, and mountain sheep and fished in mountain streams. Women gathered pinyon nuts, seeds, and wild berries. In hard times, people ate rattlesnakes, horned toads, and insects. They celebrated whenever food was plentiful and urged religious leaders to seek supernatural help when starvation loomed.

Mesoamerica, the birthplace of agriculture in North America, extends from central Mexico into Central America. A series of complex, literate, urban cultures emerged in this region beginning around 1200 B.C. Among the earliest was that of the Olmecs, who flourished on Mexico's Gulf Coast from about 1200 to 400 B.C. The Olmecs and other early Mesoamerican peoples built cities featuring large pyramids, developed religious practices that included human sacrifice, and devised calendars and writing systems. Two of the most prominent Mesoamerican civilizations to follow the Olmecs were that of the Mayans in the Yucatán and Guatemala and that of Teotihuacán in central Mexico.

Mayan civilization reached its greatest glory between about A.D. 150 and 900 in the southern Yucatán, creating Mesoamerica's most advanced writing and calendrical systems and developing a sophisticated mathematics that included the concept of zero. The Mayans of the southern Yucatán suffered a decline after 900, but there were still many thriving Mayan centers in the northern Yucatán in 1492. The great city of Teotihuacán dominated central Mexico from the first century to the eighth century A.D. and influenced much of the rest of Mesoamerica through trade and conquest.

Some two hundred years after the fall of Teotihuacán, the Toltecs, a warrior people, rose to prominence, dominating central Mexico from about 900 to 1100. In the wake of the Toltec collapse, the Aztecs, another warrior people, migrated from the north into the Valley of Mexico and built a great empire that soon controlled much of Mesoamerica.

The magnificent Aztec capital, Tenochtitlán, was a city of great plazas, broad avenues, magnificent temples and palaces, ball courts, busy marketplaces, and well-regulated residential neighborhoods. Built on islands in the middle of Lake Texcoco, it was connected to the mainland by four broad causeways. In 1492, Tenochtitlán was home to some 200,000 people, making it one of the largest cities in the world at the time.

The great pyramid in Tenochtitlán's principal temple complex was the center of Aztec religious life. Here Aztec priests sacrificed human victims— by cutting open their chests and removing their still-beating hearts—to offer to the gods. Human sacrifice had been part of the Mesoamerican religion since the time of the Olmecs. People believed that such ceremonies pleased the gods and prevented them from destroying the earth. The Aztecs, however, practiced sacrifice on a much larger scale than ever before. Hundreds, even thousands, of victims died in ceremonies that sometimes lasted for days.

Aztec culture expanded through continuous military conquest, driven by a quest for sacrificial victims and for wealth in the form of tribute payments of gold, food, and handcrafted goods. But as the empire grew, it became increasingly vulnerable to internal division. Neighboring peoples hated the Aztecs and submitted to them out of fear. With a powerful ally to lead them, they would readily turn on their overlords and bring the empire down.

Native societies emerging north of Mexico shared certain characteristics with those of Mesoamerica. The introduction of a drought-resistant type of maize (probably from Mexico) into the desert Southwest in 400 B.C. enabled a series of cultures to develop. Beginning about 300 B.C., the Hohokams settled in southern Arizona, eventually building permanent villages of several hundred people. Substantial harvests of beans, corn, and squash (sometimes two a year), watered by a complex system of canals, fed Hohokam villagers. In large communities, inhabitants built ball courts similar to those found in Mexico. Artisans wove cotton cloth and made goods reflecting Mesoamerican artistic styles out of shell, turquoise, and clay. Extensive trade networks linked the Hohokams to peoples as far away as California and Mexico. Their culture endured for over a thousand years, then disappeared mysteriously by 1450.

Beginning about A.D. 1, the Anasazis (their name is Navajo for "ancient alien ones") settled where the borders of present-day Colorado, Utah, Arizona, and New Mexico meet. They gradually adopted agriculture, adding first maize to a diet of wild foods and later beans and squash. Scarce rainfall, routed through

Acoma Pueblo has perched atop this 300-foot-tall mesa since the twelfth century. Now used mainly for ceremonial purposes, Acoma was once a thriving Anasazi village.

works of roads carried people and goods between villages. Artisans crafted intricate baskets and distinctive black-on-white painted pottery for use and trade. By the late 1200s, however, Anasazi culture collapsed, probably due to drought and invasion. People abandoned the large towns, many dispersing into smaller villages along the Rio Grande.

The Pueblo peoples of the Southwest, including the Hopis and Zunis, are the descendants of the Anasazis. In 1492, many lived in large communal dwellings in permanent villages (*pueblo* is the Spanish word for "village"). Pueblo men did most of the farming, tilling irrigated fields of corn, beans, squash, and sunflowers. Regular public ceremonies reinforced a sense of village identity. Religious rituals directed prayers to the gods for enough rain for the all-important harvest.

The Great Plains of the continent's interior were much less densely settled than the desert Southwest. Scattered villages of Mandans, Pawnees, and other groups clung to tree-lined rivers. Women raised corn, squash, beans, and sunflowers and gathered wild plants for food and medicine. Men hunted bison, whose skin and bones were used for clothing, shelter, and tools. Plains Indians moved frequently, seeking more fertile land or better hunting. Wherever they went, they continued to trade skins, food, and obsidian (a volcanic glass used for tools and weapons) with other native peoples.

dams and hillside terraces, watered the crops. By 900, Anasazi villagers lived in distinctive multistoried stone houses, often perched high on mesas or carved into steep canyon walls. They included special rooms, or **kivas,** for religious ceremonies. The largest communal dwelling, Pueblo Bonito in New Mexico's Chaco Canyon, covered 3 acres and contained 650 to 800 rooms to house about 1,200 people.

Anasazi culture reached its peak around the eleventh century. Unusually plentiful rainfall encouraged population growth and village expansion. Net-

The introduction of agriculture transformed native societies in the Eastern Woodlands, a vast territory extending from the Mississippi Valley to the Atlantic seaboard. As early as 2500 B.C., Indians in present-day Missouri and Kentucky grew pumpkins to supplement game and wild plant foods. Peoples in the Ohio Valley were growing corn by 300 B.C. Agriculture did not dominate Woodlands Indian subsistence, however, until about A.D. 700.

As agriculture spread, several "mound-building" societies—named for the large earthworks their members constructed—developed in the Ohio and Mississippi Valleys. The oldest flourished in Louisiana between 1500 and 700 B.C. By 1000 B.C., its main city of five thousand residents served as the center of an extensive trade in quartz, copper, crystal, and other valuable materials. Another mound-building culture, the Adena-Hopewell, appeared in the Ohio Valley between 500 B.C. and A.D. 400. Its members lived in small villages spread over a wide area. They built hundreds of mounds, often in the shapes of humans, birds, and serpents. Most were grave sites, where people were buried with valuable goods. Many burial objects were made from materials obtained through long-distance trade, including Wyoming obsidian, Lake Superior copper, and Florida conch shells.

The last mound-building culture, the Mississippian, emerged between 1000 and 1500 in the Mississippi Valley. Mississippian farmers raised enough maize, squash, and beans to support sizable populations and major urban centers. One of the largest cities was Cahokia, located on the Mississippi River across from present-day St. Louis. By 1250, Cahokia, the largest city north of Mexico, had perhaps thirty thousand residents, making it about the same size as medieval London. Its central feature was a 100-foot-high mound, the world's largest earthwork.

Cahokia dominated the Mississippian culture, but numerous other Mississippian towns, some with hundreds or thousands of residents, dotted the Woodlands region, linked by extensive trade networks. Artisans crafted distinctive styles of pottery and sculpture, often for religious uses. In major towns, religious ceremonies were conducted in large temples built atop platform mounds. Powerful chiefs, thought to be related to the sun, dominated these communities. When a chief died, his wife and servants were killed in order to accompany him to the afterlife.

Mississippian culture began to decline in the thirteenth century. Food shortages and warfare drove people from the great cities into the countryside. Elements of Mississippian culture survived among dispersed Woodlands people, particularly methods of maize and bean agriculture. By 1492,

Woodlands Indians lived part of the year in villages where women tilled lands that men had cleared. Twice a year, after crops were planted and again after the harvest, villagers separated into small family groups and dispersed into the forest. Men went off to hunt, while women and children foraged for wild plants. Although the large cities of the Mississippian era had disappeared, Woodlands Indians maintained long-distance trade links throughout the region, with such precious goods as copper, shell beads, and pearls passing among groups.

Woodlands villages generally contained several extended families headed by a chief who inherited his position but ruled with the advice of a council of elders. The southern Woodlands region was more densely populated than the northern, largely because the warmer southern climate provided a longer growing season and more abundant wild foods. Traces of Mississippian culture lasted longer in the southern Woodlands as well. In 1492, Natchez Indians living along the lower Mississippi still erected buildings on low mounds in their towns.

The Caribbean islanders whom Columbus first encountered likewise descended from ancient cultures. Around 5000 B.C., certain mainland peoples began moving to the islands. Ancestors of the Tainos probably came from what is now Venezuela. The Guanahatabeys of western Cuba originated in Florida, and the Caribs of the easternmost islands moved from Brazil's Orinoco Valley. Surviving at

The Adena people, who flourished in the Ohio and Mississippi Valleys between 500 B.C. and A.D. 400, often built giant earthen mounds shaped like humans and animals. This Great Serpent Mound in southern Ohio, the largest known effigy earthwork, extends over 1,300 feet. Often used as grave sites, many mounds contained buried goods that attested to the Indians' participation in long-distance trade.

In 1585, the Englishman John White sketched this composite picture of the Algonquian village of Secoton, located in the Eastern Woodlands region of North America in what is now North Carolina. Its details reveal many features of Eastern Woodlands life, including cornfields at different stages of ripeness, easily assembled bark dwellings, an outdoor place of worship (the "place of solemne prayer"), ceremonial dancing, and a tomb for the dead ("the Tombe of their Herounds").

first by hunting and gathering, island peoples began farming perhaps in the first century A.D. They raised manioc, sweet potatoes, maize, squash, beans, peppers, peanuts, and pineapple on clearings made in the tropical forests. Canoes carried trade goods throughout the Caribbean, as well as to Mesoamerica and coastal South America.

By 1492, as many as 4 million people may have inhabited the Caribbean islands. Powerful chiefs ruled over villages, conducted war and diplomacy, and controlled the distribution of food and other goods obtained as tribute from villagers. Island

societies were divided into several ranks. An elite group aided the chief and supplied religious leaders. Below them were a large class of ordinary farmers and fishermen and a lower class of servants who worked for the elites. Elite islanders were easily recognized by their fine clothing, bright feather headdresses, and golden ear and nose ornaments—items that eventually attracted European visitors' attention.

Long before 1492, North America had witnessed centuries of dynamic change. Populations grew and spread across thousands of miles of territory. People adapted to many different environments, some of which tested their ability to survive. Farmers developed new varieties of essential food plants. Empires rose and fell. Large cities flourished and disappeared. People traded goods over vast distances. They formed alliances with trading partners and warred with groups who refused to trade. Because their histories have largely been preserved in oral traditions and archaeological evidence rather than written documents, they are less distinct, but no less real, than those of the Europeans whom they would soon meet.

Cultural Perceptions and Misperceptions

Indian and European societies had developed differently in isolation from one another. Misunderstandings inevitably arose when such dissimilar peoples encountered each other for the first time. Even simple transactions had unexpected results. When Columbus showed swords to the Tainos, for example, "they took them by the edge and through ignorance cut themselves" because they had never seen metal weapons. Similarly, French explorers choked when they tried to smoke unfamiliar Iroquois tobacco, which tasted, one of them reported, like "powdered pepper."

Many misunderstandings, however, had far graver consequences for the outcome of the encounter. Each group struggled to understand the strange behavior and customs of the other. Europeans usually decided that native practices were not just different from their own but inferior. Indians doubtless felt the same about European practices, but their opinions were rarely recorded.

Religious differences were the hardest to reconcile. Seeing no churches or recognizable religious practices among the Tainos, Columbus wrote, "I do not detect in them any religion." His comment revealed the influence of his own Christian background. Christian Europeans worshiped one God in an organized church led by trained priests. They preserved their religious traditions in a written bible. Most Indians, however, believed in a variety of gods. They considered nature itself to be sacred and understood certain beings, including plants, animals, and stars, to possess spiritual powers. Indians living north of Mexico preserved religious beliefs through oral traditions, not in writing. Their religious leaders performed ceremonies that mediated between the human and spiritual worlds. Europeans, however, thought that these men were magicians or even witches. They assumed that Indians worshiped the devil and insisted that they adopt Christianity. In the face of this demand, many native peoples doubtless shared the opinion voiced by some Iroquois: "We do not know that God, we have never seen him, we know not who he is."

Europeans also disapproved of the relative equality of men and women they observed among some Native American peoples. Reasoning from their own experience, Europeans assumed that men were naturally superior to women and should dominate them. But in North America, Europeans encountered female rulers among the Wampanoags and Powhatans and learned that among groups such as the Hurons, women helped select chiefs. They found that many Indian societies, including the Pueblos, Hurons, and Iroquois, were **matrilineal;** that is, they traced descent through the mother's family line instead of the father's, as Europeans did. In these matrilineal societies, newly married couples went to live with the wife's family. Children inherited property from their mother's brother, not their father. Rulers succeeded to their positions through their mother's family line.

In most Indian societies, women were the principal farmers. Men cleared the fields, but women planted and harvested the crops. They also prepared food, cared for children, made clothing and baskets, carried burdens, and, in some regions, broke down, transported, and reassembled shelters when villages changed location. Europeans, who came from a society in which men did most agricultural work, thought that Indian women lived "a most slavish life." Misjudging the importance of Indian men's role as hunters and warriors, Europeans scorned them as lazy husbands who wasted their time "gambling, sleeping, singing, dancing, smoking or going to feasts." Such confusion worked both ways, of course. Massachusetts Indians ridiculed English men "for spoiling good working creatures" because they did not send their wives into the fields. Observing some English women sewing, native men called them "lazy squaws."

Such basic misunderstandings fed tensions between Indians and Europeans in the centuries after 1492. But the ultimate source of conflict between them was the intention of the Europeans to dominate the lands they discovered. Encounters that often began in peace rarely ended that way. Columbus reported that at first the Tainos "became so much our friends that it was a marvel." Within three days of his arrival in America, however, he announced his intention "not to pass by any island of which I did not take possession" and soon speculated on the possibility of enslaving Indians. Native peoples everywhere would challenge European claims to possession of their lands and resist European attempts at domination.

West African Societies

Once Europeans learned of Columbus's feat, many followed his lead in exploring what they soon realized was not Asia after all. Yet in the three centuries after 1492, fully six out of seven people who crossed the Atlantic to the Americas were not Europeans but Africans, the vast majority of whom arrived as slaves. Most came from West Africa, and like the inhabitants of North America or Europe, they belonged to many different ethnic groups, each with its own language and culture (see Map 1-2). Thus the Wolof peoples of the Sudan differed from the Yorubas of the Guinea coast as much as the Iroquois from the Pueblos or the English from the Spanish.

In 1492, Timbuktu, with a population of perhaps seventy thousand, was one of the greatest cities in West Africa. Located on the Niger River, the flourishing commercial metropolis was the seat of the powerful Songhai empire. Sunni Ali sat on the throne, ruling the empire with the support of a strong army and efficient bureaucrats. The city was a center of trade as well as government. A visitor in 1526 described Timbuktu's busy streets lined with "shops of artificers and merchants, and especially of such as weave linen and cotton cloth," and reported—with some exaggeration—that the inhabitants "are exceeding rich."

The Songhai empire was only the latest in a series of powerful states to develop in the western Sudan, the vast plain that lies south of the arid Sahara. One of the earliest, Ghana, rose to prominence in the eighth century and dominated West Africa for nearly three hundred years. Another, Mali, emerged around 1200 and fell in the early fifteenth century. Songhai, the largest and wealthiest, emerged around 1450, dominating the Sudan until it fell to a Moroccan invasion in 1591. Equivalently large empires did not appear in coastal West Africa, although the Asante, Dahomey, Oyo, and Bini kingdoms there grew to be quite powerful. Other coastal peoples, such as the Mendes and Ibos, were decentralized, living in autonomous villages where all adult males participated in making decisions.

Geographical as well as political differences marked the inland and coastal regions. In the vast grasslands of the Sudan, people raised cattle and cultivated millet and sorghum. In the 1500s, European

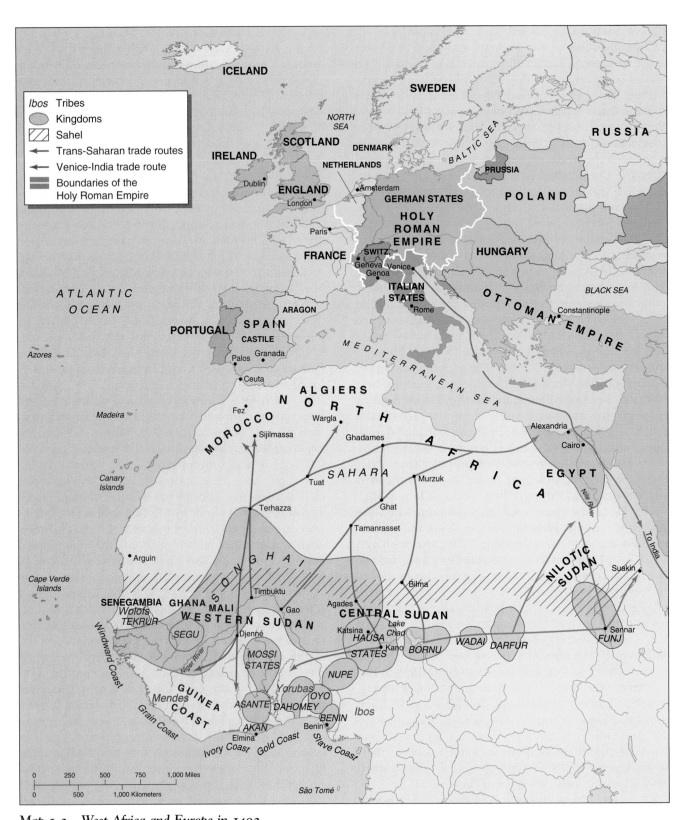

Map 1-2   West Africa and Europe in 1492
Before Columbus's voyage, Europeans knew little about the world beyond the Mediterranean basin and the coast of West Africa. Muslim merchants from North Africa largely controlled European traders' access to African gold and other materials.

visitors introduced varieties of Asian rice, which soon became another important crop. On the coast—where rain falls nearly every day—people grew yams, bananas, and various kinds of beans and peas in forest clearings. They also kept sheep, goats, and poultry.

West Africans were skilled artisans and particularly fine metalworkers. Smiths in Benin produced intricate bronze sculptures, and those from Asante designed distinctive miniature gold weights. West African smiths also used their skills to forge weapons, attesting to the frequent warfare between West African states.

Complex trade networks linked inland and coastal states, and long-distance commercial connections tied West Africa to southern Europe and the Middle East. For centuries, mines in the area of present-day Guinea and Mali produced tons of gold each year. West African merchants exchanged gold with traders from North Africa for salt, a commodity so rare in West Africa that it was sometimes literally worth its weight in gold. In addition to gold, North African merchants bought pepper, leather, and ivory. The wealth generated by this trans-Saharan trade contributed to the rise of the Songhai and earlier empires.

Most West Africans, however, were farmers, not merchants. A daily round of work, family duties, and worship defined their lives. West African men and women shared agricultural tasks, with children also contributing their labor. Men generally prepared fields for planting, while women cultivated the crops, harvested them, and dried grain for storage. Men also hunted and, in the grassland regions, herded cattle. Women in the coastal areas owned and cared for other kinds of livestock, including goats and sheep. West African women regularly traded goods, including the crops they grew, in local markets. In 1495, a Muslim African leader commented disapprovingly on the "free mixing of men and women in the markets and streets" in Timbuktu and other cities.

Family connections helped define each person's place in society. West Africans emphasized not only ties between parents and children but also those linking aunts, uncles, cousins, and grandparents. Groups of families often formed clans that further extended an individual's kin ties. Most clans were **patrilineal**—tracing descent through the father's line—but some (including the Akans and Ibos) were matrilineal. Matrilineal practices did not necessarily raise women's status above that of men. But to a North African–born Muslim unfamiliar with matrilineal families, it appeared that women in them received "more respect than the men."

Religious beliefs magnified the powerful influence of family on African life. Africans believed that their ancestors acted as mediators between the worlds of the living and the dead. Families held elaborate funerals for deceased members to ensure their passage into the realm of the spirits. Such rituals helped keep the memory of ancestors alive for younger generations.

West Africans worshiped a supreme being and several subordinate deities. In other respects, their beliefs resembled Native American religions. West Africans, like Indians, believed that the gods often sent spirits to speak to people. They performed rituals to ensure the goodwill of the spiritual forces that suffused the natural world. Like Native American priests who mediated between the human and spirit worlds, West African medicine men and women provided protection against evil spirits and sorcerers. Religious ceremonies took place in sacred places—often near water—but not in buildings that Europeans recognized as churches. And like the Indians, West Africans preserved their faith through oral traditions.

Islam began to take root in West Africa around the eleventh century, probably introduced by Muslim traders from North Africa. By the fifteenth century, the cities of Timbuktu and Djenné had become centers of Islamic learning, attracting students from as far away as southern Europe. Some African rulers began keeping records in Arabic and enforcing Islamic law, but most West Africans probably retained traditional religious beliefs and practices.

Before the fifteenth century, Europeans knew little about Africa beyond its Mediterranean coast, which had been part of the Islamic world since the eighth century. Spain, much of which had been subject to Islamic rule before 1492, had stronger ties to North Africa than most of Europe. But Christian merchants from other European lands had also traded for centuries with Muslims in the North African ports. When stories of West African gold reached the ears of European traders, they tried to move deeper into the continent. But they encountered powerful Muslim merchants intent on monopolizing the gold trade.

The kingdom of Portugal, eager to expand its trade to support a spendthrift nobility, sought in the early fifteenth century to circumvent this Muslim monopoly. In 1415, Portuguese forces conquered Ceuta in Morocco and gained a foothold on the continent. Portuguese mariners gradually explored the West African coast, establishing trading posts along the way. Portuguese merchants exchanged horses, clothing, wine, lead, iron, and steel for African gold, grain, animal skins, cotton, pepper, and camels.

Located in Djenné, Mali, this massive mosque, made of sun-hardened mud, dates from the fourteenth century. At that time, Djenné prospered as a center of trade and Islamic learning.

By the 1430s, the Portuguese had discovered perhaps the greatest source of wealth they could extract from Africa—slaves. Slavery had long been a part of West African society. African law made land available to anyone willing to cultivate it—provided that no one else was using the same plot—and the possession of a large labor force to work the land became the principal means to wealth. People became slaves in various ways. Some Africans lost their freedom as punishment for crime, but the majority of slaves were captured in war. Slave raids into neighboring territories were a regular feature of African life.

Slaves enriched their masters in a number of ways. Masters sold some slaves directly, tapping into a well-developed internal trade. Merchants from the Sahara frequently trekked to West Africa to exchange horses for slaves, and West Africans traded laborers among themselves. Most slaves, however, worked at a variety of tasks for their owners. Many labored more or less independently as farmers, producing surplus crops for their masters. Some rulers acquired female slaves to serve as wives or concubines but also as workers. One Italian visitor to the small state of Warri reported in 1656 that its ruler had many slave wives who wove cloth for sale. Powerful Sudanese rulers employed large numbers of slaves as bureaucrats and soldiers, rewarding them for loyal service with good treatment and, occasionally, freedom.

Europeans who observed African slaves' relative freedom and variety of employment often concluded that slaves in Africa were "slaves in name only." Slavery in Africa was not necessarily a permanent status and did not automatically apply to the slaves' children. European purchasers of African slaves generally treated them much more harshly. Slavery became even more oppressive as it developed in the Americas, making the lives of unwilling African immigrants more difficult than ever.

Western Europe on the Eve of Discovery

When Columbus sailed from the Spanish port of Palos in 1492, he left a continent recovering from the devastating disease and warfare of the fourteenth century and about to embark on the devastating religious conflicts of the sixteenth. Between 1337 and 1453, England and France had exhausted each other in a series of conflicts known as the Hundred Years' War. And between 1347 and 1351, an epidemic known as the **Black Death** (probably the pneumonic form of bubonic plague) wreaked havoc on a European population already suffering from persistent malnutrition. Perhaps a third of all Europeans died, with results that were felt for more than a century.

The plague left Europe with far fewer workers than before, but the survivors learned to be more efficient. Farmers selected only the most fertile land to till, and artisans adopted labor-saving techniques to increase productivity. Metalworkers, for instance, built larger furnaces with huge bellows driven by water power. Shipbuilders redesigned vessels with steering mechanisms that could be managed by smaller crews. Innovations in banking, accounting, and insurance also fostered economic recovery.

By 1500, Europe had a stronger, more productive economy than ever before, but not everyone prospered equally. In parts of England, France,

Sweden, and the German states, peasants and workers rebelled against the propertied classes. These protests grew not from the workers' desperation but from a desire to protect their improving economic fortunes. They did not want to see their rising wages eaten up by higher rents and taxes.

In some parts of Europe, economic improvement encouraged an extraordinary cultural movement known as the **Renaissance**—a "rebirth" of interest in the classical civilizations of ancient Greece and Rome. The Renaissance originated in the city-states of Italy, where a prosperous and educated urban class promoted learning and artistic expression. Wealthy townspeople joined princes in becoming patrons of the arts, offering financial support to numerous painters, sculptors, architects, writers, and musicians.

Renaissance culture gradually spread from the Italian cities to other regions. The daily lives of most Europeans, however, remained untouched by intellectual and artistic developments. Most of Europe's people were peasants, engaged in an annual round of agricultural labor. Within peasant families, men did most of the heavy field work, while women helped at planting and harvest time and cared for children, livestock, and the household. The economic recovery after the Black Death brought prosperity to some families, but the lives of many remained hard. Crop failures and disease often brought great suffering to villages and towns.

European states were hierarchical, with their populations divided into fairly rigid classes. Monarchs stood at the top of society. Just below were the aristocrats, who, along with the royal family, dominated government and owned most of the land, receiving rents and labor services from peasants and rural artisans. Next, in descending order, came prosperous gentry families, independent landowners, and, at the bottom, landless peasants and laborers.

European society was also **patriarchal,** with men dominating political and economic life. Europe's rulers were, with few exceptions, men, and men controlled the Catholic Church. Inheritance was patrilineal, and only men could own property. According to an ideal perhaps not always upheld, even the poorest man should be "as a king in his own house," ruling over his wife, children, and servants.

By the end of the fifteenth century, after more than a hundred years of incessant conflict, a measure of stability had returned to the countries about to embark on overseas expansion. Ferdinand and Isabella of Spain, Louis XI of France, and Henry VII of England successfully asserted royal authority over their previously fragmented realms, creating strong state bureaucracies to control political rivals.

They gave special trading privileges to merchants to gain their support, creating links that would later prove important in financing overseas expeditions. At the same time, Spain and Portugal negotiated an end to a long-running dispute about the succession to the throne of Castile, one of Spain's largest kingdoms.

The consolidation of military power went hand in hand with the strengthening of political authority. Portugal developed a strong navy to defend its seaborne merchants. Louis XI of France commanded a standing army, and Ferdinand of Spain created a palace guard to use against potential opponents. Before overseas expansion began, European monarchs exerted military force to extend their authority closer to home. Louis XI and his successors used warfare and intermarriage with ruling families of nearby provinces to expand French influence. In the early sixteenth century, England's Henry VIII sent soldiers to conquer Ireland. And the Spain of 1492 was forged from the successful conclusion of the *reconquista* ("reconquest") of territory from Muslim control.

Muslim invaders from North Africa first entered Spain in 711 and ruled much of the Iberian peninsula (which now includes Spain and Portugal) for centuries. Beginning in the mid-eleventh century, Christian armies embarked on a long effort to reclaim the region. By 1450, only the southern tip of Spain remained under Muslim control. After the marriage of Ferdinand of Aragon and Isabella of Castile in 1469 united Spain's two principal kingdoms, their combined forces completed the *reconquista*. Granada, the last Muslim stronghold, fell in 1492, shortly before Columbus set out on his first voyage.

Even as these rulers sought to unify their realms, religious conflicts began to tear Europe apart. For more than a thousand years, Catholic Christianity had united western Europeans in one faith. All Christians believed that God sent his only son, Jesus Christ, to suffer crucifixion, die, and rise from the dead in order to redeem humans from sin and give them eternal life. The Catholic Church built on this faith included an elaborate hierarchy of clergy, ranging upward from parish priests to bishops, archbishops, and cardinals, culminating in Christ's representative on earth, the pope. It also supported monastic orders whose members often lived and prayed apart from society.

By the sixteenth century, the Catholic Church had accumulated enormous wealth and power. The pope wielded influence not only as a spiritual leader but also as the political ruler of parts of Italy. The church owned considerable property throughout Europe. Many Christians, especially in northern Europe, began to criticize the worldliness of the popes and the church itself for corruption, abuse of power, and betrayal of the legacy of Christ.

In 1517, a German monk, Martin Luther, invited open debate on a set of propositions critical of official church practices and doctrines. Luther believed that the church had become too insistent on the performance of good works, such as charitable donations or other actions intended to please God. He called for a return to what he understood to be the purer practices and beliefs of the early church, emphasizing that salvation came not by good deeds but only by faith in God. With the help of the newly invented printing press, his ideas spread widely, inspiring a challenge to the Catholic Church that has come to be called the **Reformation.**

When the church refused to compromise, Luther and other critics withdrew to form their own religious organizations. Luther emphasized the direct, personal relationship of God to the individual believer. He urged people to take responsibility for their own spiritual growth by reading the Bible, which he translated for the first time into German. What started as a religious movement, however, quickly acquired an important political dimension.

Sixteenth-century Germany was a fragmented region of small kingdoms and principalities jealous of their independence. They were officially part of the **Holy Roman Empire,** but only loosely so, and many German princes were wary of efforts by the Catholic empire to assert its authority. Realizing that religious protest reinforced their claims to independence, many princes supported Luther for both spiritual and secular reasons. When the Holy Roman Empire under Charles V (who was also king of Spain) tried to silence them, the reformist princes protested. From that point on, these princes—and all Europeans who supported religious reform—became known as "Protestants."

The Protestant movement took a more radical turn under the influence of the French reformer John Calvin, who emphasized the doctrine of **predestination.** Calvin maintained that an all-powerful and all-knowing God chose at the moment of creation which humans would be saved and which would be damned. Each person's fate is thus foreordained, or predestined, by God, although we cannot know our fate during our lifetimes. Good Calvinists, however, struggled to behave as God's chosen, continually searching their souls for evidence of divine grace.

Calvin founded a religious community consistent with his principles at Geneva, a Swiss city-state near the French border. Men who claimed to be "saints," or God's chosen people, led the city's government. They drove out nonbelievers, subjected all citizens to a rigid discipline, and made Geneva the center of Protestant reform in Europe. But neither

Martin Luther (1483–1546), a German monk, sparked the Protestant Reformation with his criticisms of the worldliness of the Catholic Church. By the end of Luther's life, religious conflicts divided Europe as never before.

Lutherans nor Calvinists could contain the powerful Protestant impulse. In succeeding years, other groups formed, split, and split again, increasing Europe's religious fragmentation.

From Germany and Geneva the Protestant Reformation spread to France, the Netherlands, England, and Hungary. The new religious ideas particularly interested literate city-dwellers, such as merchants and skilled artisans, who were attracted to Protestant writings as well as the sermons of Protestant preachers. Peasants adopted the new ideas more slowly, although German peasants, claiming Luther as inspiration, staged an unsuccessful revolt against their masters in 1524. Luther disavowed them, however, and supported the German princes in their brutal suppression of the revolt.

The Reformation addressed spiritual needs that the Catholic Church had left unfulfilled, but it also fractured the religious unity of western Europe and spawned a century of warfare unprecedented in its bloody destructiveness. Protestants fought Catholics in France and the German states. Popes initiated a "Counter-Reformation," intending to strengthen the Catholic Church—in part by internal reform and in part by persecuting its opponents and reimposing religious conformity in Europe. Europe thus fragmented into warring camps just at the moment when Europeans were coming to terms with their discovery of America and seeking ways to exploit its wealth.

Contact

Religious fervor, political ambition, and the desire for wealth propelled European nations into overseas expansion as well as conflict at home. Portugal, Spain, France, and England competed to establish footholds on other continents in an intense scramble for riches and dominance. The success of these early endeavors was a reflection of Europe's prosperity and a series of technological breakthroughs that enabled its mariners to navigate beyond familiar waters.

By the end of the sixteenth century, Spain had emerged as the apparent winner among the European competitors for New World dominance. Its astonishingly wealthy empire included vast territories in Central and South America. The conquerors of this empire attributed their success to their military superiority and God's approval of their imperial ambitions. In reality, it was the result of a complex set of interactions with native peoples as well as an unanticipated demographic catastrophe.

The Lure of Discovery

The potential rewards of overseas exploration captured the imaginations of a small but powerful segment of European society. Most people, busy making a living, cared little about distant lands. But certain princes and merchants anticipated spiritual and material benefits from voyages of discovery. The spiritual advantages included making new Christian converts and blocking Islam's expansion—a Christian goal that dated back to the eleventh-century Crusades against the Muslims in the Middle East and continued with the *reconquista*. On the material side, the voyages would contribute to Europe's prosperity by increasing trade.

Merchants especially sought access to Asian spices like pepper, cinnamon, ginger, and nutmeg that added interest to an otherwise monotonous diet and helped preserve certain foods. Wealthy Europeans paid handsomely for small quantities of spices, making it worthwhile to transport them great distances. By serving rich dishes fragrant with cinnamon and cloves, hosts advertised their prosperity to their guests. But the overland spice trade—and the trade in other luxury goods such as silk and furs—spanned thousands of miles, involved many middlemen, and was controlled at key points by Muslim merchants. One critical center was Constantinople, the bastion of Christianity in the eastern Mediterranean. When it fell to the Ottomans—the Muslim rulers of Turkey—in 1453, Europeans feared that caravan routes to Asia would be disrupted. This encouraged merchants to turn westward and seek alternate routes.

The reorientation of European trade benefited western Italian cities such as Genoa as well as Portugal and Spain, whose ports gave access to the Mediterranean and the Atlantic Ocean. Mariners ventured farther into ocean waters, seeking direct access to the African gold trade. Some hoped to sail around Africa and chart a sea route to Asia. But had it not been for a set of technological developments that reduced the risks of ocean sailing, such lengthy voyages into unexplored areas would have been impossible.

Ocean voyages required sturdier ships than those that plied the Mediterranean. Because ocean-going mariners traveled beyond sight of coastal features, they also needed reliable navigational tools. In the early fifteenth century, Prince Henry of Portugal, excited by the idea of overseas discovery, sponsored the efforts of shipbuilders, mapmakers, and other workers to solve these practical problems.

By 1500, enterprising artisans had made several important advances. Iberian shipbuilders perfected the caravel, a ship whose narrow shape and steering rudder suited it for ocean travel. Ship designers combined square sails (good for speed) with triangular "lateen" sails, which increased maneuverability. Two Arab inventions—the magnetic compass and the astrolabe (which allowed mariners to determine their position in relation to a star's known location in the sky)—gained popularity among European navigators. As sailors acquired practical experience on the high seas, mapmakers recorded their observations of landfalls, wind patterns, and ocean currents.

After Portugal's conquest of the Moroccan city of Ceuta in 1415, its mariners slowly worked their way along Africa's western coast, establishing trading posts where they exchanged European goods for gold, ivory, and slaves (see Map 1-3). Bartolomeu Días reached the southern tip of Africa in 1488. Eleven years later, Vasco da Gama brought a Portuguese fleet around Africa to India, opening a sea route to Asia. These initiatives gave Portugal a virtual monopoly on Far Eastern trade for some time.

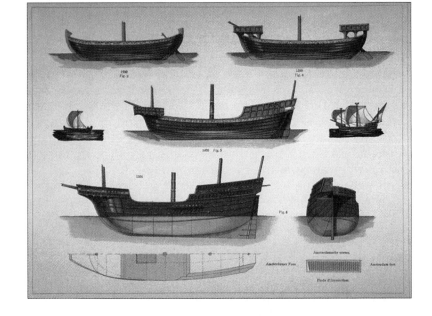

Before Europeans could safely navigate the Atlantic, they needed larger and more maneuverable ships. This drawing illustrates the evolution of sailing vessels from the late Middle Ages to the fifteenth century. Technological improvements included larger hulls, more masts, and new arrangements of sails.

The new trade routes gave strategic importance to the islands that lie in the Atlantic off the west coast of Africa and Europe. Spain and Portugal vied for control of the Canary Islands, located 800 miles southwest of the Iberian peninsula. Spain eventually prevailed in 1496 by defeating the islands' inhabitants. Portugal acquired Madeira and the Cape Verde Islands, along with a set of tiny islands off Africa's Guinea Coast.

Sugar, like Asian spices, commanded high prices in Europe, so the conquerors of the Atlantic islands began to cultivate sugar cane on them, on large plantations worked by slave labor. In the Canaries, the Spanish first enslaved the native inhabitants. When disease and exhaustion reduced their numbers, the Spanish brought in African slaves, often purchased from Portuguese traders. On uninhabited islands, the Europeans imported African slaves from the start. São Tomé and the other small islands off the Guinea Coast eventually became important way stations in the transatlantic slave trade.

These island societies, in which a small European master class dominated a much larger population of native peoples or imported African slaves, were to provide a model for Spain's and Portugal's later exploitation of their American colonies. Even as early as 1494, Christopher Columbus wrote to Ferdinand and Isabella of Spain to suggest that Caribbean islanders could be sold as slaves in order to cover the costs of exploration. He found the inhabitants to be "a people very savage and suitable for the purpose, and well made and of very good intelligence." They "will be better than any other slaves," he went on, "and their inhuman-

ity they will immediately lose when they are out of their own land."

Christopher Columbus

Columbus's proposal revealed him to be very much a man of his time. Born in Genoa in 1451, he later lived in Portugal and Spain and as a young man visited Africa's Guinea Coast and Madeira. He was thus thoroughly familiar with slavery and would have regarded the enslavement of Caribbean islanders as an extension of established practice.

Columbus was not the first European to believe that he could reach Asia by sailing westward. The idea developed logically during the fifteenth century as mariners gained knowledge and experience from their exploits in the Atlantic and around Africa. Columbus himself may have gained valuable experience on a voyage to Iceland. He also read widely in geographical treatises and paid close attention to the stories and rumors that circulated among mariners.

Most Europeans knew that the world was round, but most also scoffed at the idea of a westward voyage to Asia, believing that it would take so long, it would exhaust any ship's supplies. Columbus's confidence that he could make the voyage grew from a mathematical error. He mistakenly calculated the earth's circumference as 18,000 (rather than 24,000) miles and so concluded that Asia lay just 3,500 miles west of the Canary Islands. Columbus first sought financial support from the king of Portugal, whose advisers disputed his calculations and warned him that he would starve at sea before reaching Asia. Undaunted, he turned to Portugal's rival, Spain.

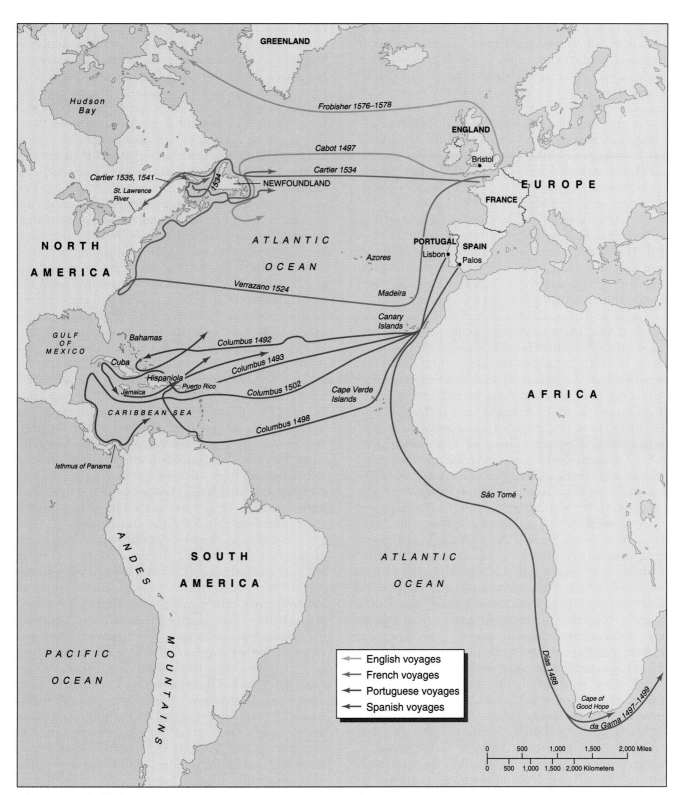

Map 1-3   European Voyages of Discovery in the Atlantic in the Fifteenth and Sixteenth Centuries
During the fifteenth and sixteenth centuries, Europeans embarked on voyages of discovery that carried them to both Asia and the Americas. Portugal dominated the ocean trade with Asia for most of this period. In the New World, reports of Spain's acquisition of vast wealth soon led France and England to attempt to establish their own territorial claims.

Columbus tried to convince Ferdinand and Isabella that his plan suited Spain's national goals. If he succeeded, Spain could grow rich from Asian trade, send Christian missionaries to Asia (a goal in keeping with the religious ideals of the *reconquista*), and perhaps enlist the Great Khan of China as an ally in the long struggle with Islam. If he failed, the "enterprise of the Indies" would cost little. The Spanish monarchs nonetheless kept Columbus waiting nearly seven years—until 1492, when the last Muslim stronghold at Granada fell to Spanish forces—before they gave him their support.

After thirty-three days at sea, Columbus and his men reached the Bahamas (see Map 1-3 on page 19). They spent four months exploring the Caribbean and visiting several islands, including Hispaniola (now the site of Haiti and the Dominican Republic) and Cuba. Although puzzled not to find the fabled cities of China or Japan, Columbus believed that he had reached Asia. Three more voyages, between 1493 and 1504, however, failed to yield clear evidence of an Asian landfall or samples of Asian riches. Columbus reported that the islands he encountered contained "great mines of gold and other metals" and spices in abundance, yet all he brought back to Isabella and Ferdinand were strange plants and animals, some gold ornaments, and several kidnapped Taino Indians.

Obsessed with the wealth he had promised himself and others, Columbus and his men turned violent, sacking the villages of Tainos and Caribs and demanding tribute in gold. But Caribbean gold reserves, found mainly on Hispaniola, Puerto Rico, and Cuba, were not extensive. The Spanish forced native gangs to pan rivers for the precious nuggets. Dissatisfied with the meager results, Columbus sought other sources of wealth. His plan to enslave islanders was a desperate attempt to show that the Indies could yield a profit. It earned him a sharp rebuke from Queen Isabella, who, at least initially, opposed the enslavement of people she considered to be new Spanish subjects. This royal fastidiousness was short-lived, however. Within thirty years of Columbus's first voyage, Spanish exploitation of native labor had brought the populations of many Caribbean islands close to extinction.

Columbus died in Spain in 1506, still convinced he had found Asia. What he had done was to set in motion a process that would transform both sides of the Atlantic. It would eventually bring wealth to many Europeans and immense suffering to Native Americans and Africans.

Spanish Conquest and Colonization

Of all European nations, Spain was best suited to take advantage of Columbus's discovery. Its experience with the *reconquista* gave it both a religious justification for conquest (bringing Christianity to nonbelievers) and an army of seasoned soldiers—**conquistadores**—eager to seek their fortunes in America now that the last Muslims had been expelled from Spain. In addition, during the *reconquista* and the conquest of the Canary Islands, Spain's rulers had developed efficient techniques for controlling newly conquered lands that could be applied to New World colonies.

The Spanish first consolidated their control of the Caribbean, establishing island outposts on Cuba, Puerto Rico, and Jamaica (see Map 1-4). The conquistadores were more interested in finding gold and slaves than in creating permanent settlements. Leaving a trail of destruction, they attacked Taino and Carib villages and killed or captured the inhabitants. By 1524, the Tainos had all but died out; the Caribs survived on more isolated islands until the eighteenth century. Spanish soldiers then ventured to the mainland. Juan Ponce de León led an expedition to Florida in 1513. In that same year, Vasco Núñez de Balboa arrived in Central America, crossing the isthmus of Panama to the Pacific Ocean.

In 1519, Hernán Cortés led a force of six hundred men to the coast of Mexico. "I and my companions," he declared, "suffer from a disease of the heart which can be cured only with gold." By 1521, Cortés and his men had conquered the powerful Aztec empire. The Spanish soldiers also discovered riches beyond their wildest dreams. They "picked up the gold and fingered it like monkeys," reported one Aztec witness. They were "transported by joy, as if their hearts were illumined and made new."

The swift, decisive Spanish victory depended on several factors. In part, the Spanish enjoyed certain technological advantages. Their guns and horses often enabled them to overwhelm larger groups of Aztec foot soldiers armed with spears and wooden swords edged with obsidian. But technology alone cannot account for the conquest of a vastly more numerous enemy, capable of absorbing far higher losses in combat.

Cortés benefited from two other factors. First, he exploited divisions within the Aztec empire. The Spanish acquired indispensable allies among subject Indians who resented Aztec domination, tribute demands, and seizure of captives for religious sacrifice. Cortés led only six hundred Spanish soldiers but eventually gained 200,000 Indian allies eager to throw off Aztec rule.

A second and more important factor was disease. One of Cortés's men was infected with smallpox, which soon devastated the native population. European diseases had been unknown in the Americas, and Indians lacked resistance to them. Historians estimate that nearly 40 percent of the inhabitants of central Mexico died of smallpox within a year. Other diseases

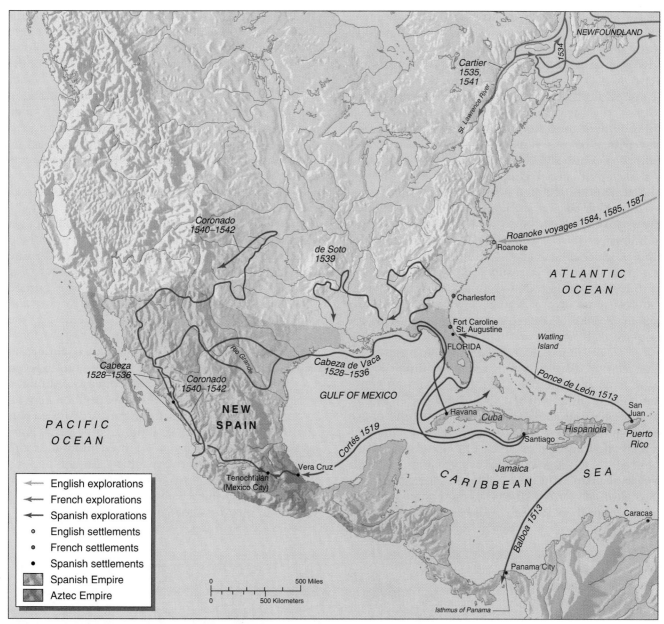

Map 1-4 *Spanish, English, and French Settlements in North America in the Sixteenth Century*
By the end of the sixteenth century, only Spain had established permanent settlements in North America. French outposts in Canada and at Fort Caroline, as well as the English settlement at Roanoke, failed to thrive. European rivalries for North America, however, would intensify after 1600.

followed, including typhus, measles, and influenza. By 1600, the population of Mexico may have declined from over 15 million to less than a million people.

Aztec society and culture collapsed in the face of appalling mortality. "The illness was so dreadful," one survivor recalled, "that no one could walk or move. The sick were so utterly helpless that they could only lie on their beds like corpses, unable to move their limbs or even their heads. . . . If they did move their bodies, they screamed with pain." The

epidemic ravaged families, wiped out whole villages, and destroyed traditional political authority. Early in their bid to gain control of the Aztec empire, the Spanish seized Moctezuma, the Aztec king, and eventually put him to death. They did not have to kill his successor, however, for he died of disease less than three months after gaining the throne.

In 1532, Francisco Pizarro and 180 men, following rumors of even greater riches than those of Mexico, discovered the Inca empire high in the

Peruvian Andes. The Spaniards arrived at a moment of weakness for the empire. A few years before, the Inca ruler had died, probably from smallpox, and civil war had broken out between two of his sons. The victor, Atahualpa, was on his way from the empire's northern provinces to claim his throne in Cuzco, the Inca capital, when Pizarro intercepted him. Pizarro took Atahualpa hostage, and despite receiving a colossal ransom—a roomful of gold and silver—had him killed. The Spaniards then captured Cuzco, eventually extended control over the whole empire, and established a new capital at Lima.

By 1550, Spain's New World empire extended from the Caribbean through Mexico to Peru. It was administered from Spain by the Council of the Indies, which enacted laws for the empire and supervised an elaborate bureaucracy charged with their enforcement. The council aimed to project royal authority into every village in New Spain in order to maintain political control and extract as much wealth as possible from the land and its people.

For more than a century, Spanish ships crossed the Atlantic carrying seemingly limitless treasure from the colonies. Gold, jewels, and immense amounts of silver enriched Spanish coffers. To extract this wealth, the colonial rulers subjected the native inhabitants of New Spain to compulsory tribute payments and forced labor. Tens of thousands of Indians toiled in silver mines in Peru and Bolivia and on sugar plantations in the Caribbean. When necessary, Spaniards imported African slaves to supplement a native labor force ravaged by disease and exhaustion.

The desire for gold eventually lured Spaniards farther into North America. In 1528, an expedition to Florida ended in disaster when the Spanish intruders provoked an attack by Apalachee Indians. Most of the Spanish survivors eventually perished, but Álvar Núñez Cabeza de Vaca and three other men (including an African slave) escaped from their captors and managed to reach Mexico after a grueling eight-year journey. In a published account of his ordeal, Cabeza de Vaca insisted that the interior of North America contained a fabulously wealthy empire.

This report inspired other Spaniards to seek the treasures that had eluded its author. In 1539, Hernán de Soto—who tried unsuccessfully to get Cabeza de Vaca to serve as a guide—led an expedition from Florida to the Mississippi River. Along the way, the Spaniards harassed Creeks, Cherokees, Choctaws, and other groups. They demanded provisions, burned villages, and captured native women to be servants and concubines. De Soto, who reportedly enjoyed "the sport of hunting Indians on horseback," ordered natives who resisted him to be mutilated, thrown to dogs, or burned alive. He and his men also exposed the Indians to deadly European diseases. Although weakened by native resistance, the expedition kept up its rampage for three years, turning toward Mexico only after de Soto died in 1542. In these same years, Francisco Vásquez de Coronado led three hundred troops on an equally destructive expedition through present-day Arizona, New Mexico, and Colorado on a futile search for the mythical Seven Cities of Cíbola, rumored to contain hoards of gold and precious stones.

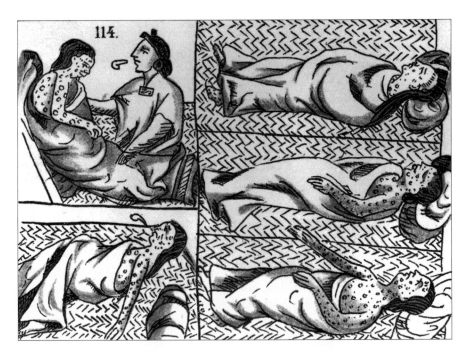

Smallpox wreaked havoc among Native Americans who lacked biological resistance to European diseases. This drawing by Aztec illustrators shows Aztec victims of a smallpox epidemic that struck Tenochtitlán in 1520. Historians estimate that up to 40 percent of the population of central Mexico died within a year. This catastrophic decline weakened the Aztecs' ability to resist the Spanish conquest of their land.

The failure to find gold and silver halted the Spanish attempt to extend their empire to the north. By the end of the sixteenth century, they maintained just two precarious footholds north of Mexico. One was at St. Augustine, on Florida's Atlantic coast. Founded in 1565, this fortified outpost served as a naval base to defend Spanish treasure fleets from raids by English and French privateers. The other settlement was located far to the west in what is now New Mexico. Juan de Oñate, on a futile search for silver mines, claimed the region for Spain in 1598. He and his men occupied a Pueblo village, renamed it San Gabriel, and proceeded to antagonize the area's inhabitants. In one surprise attack, the Spaniards destroyed the ancient town at Acoma, killing or enslaving most of the residents. Having earned the enmity of the Pueblo people—astonishing even his own superiors with his brutality—Oñate barely managed to keep his tiny colony together.

Oñate's cruelty was scarcely unusual. Almost from the start of the conquest, the conquistadores' bloody tactics aroused some protest back in Spain. The Indians' most eloquent advocate was Bartolomé de Las Casas, a Dominican priest shamed by his own role (as a layman) in the conquest of Hispaniola. In 1516, the Spanish king appointed him to the newly created office of Protector of the Indians, but his efforts had little effect. To publicize the horrors he saw, Las Casas wrote *In Defense of the Indians,* including graphic descriptions of native sufferings. Instead of eliciting Spanish reforms, however, his work inspired Protestant Europeans to create the "Black Legend," an exaggerated story according to which a fanatical Catholic Spain sought to spread its control at any cost (see "American Views: The Debate between Bartolomé de Las Casas and Juan Ginés de Sepúlveda" on page 26).

Meanwhile, the vast riches of Central and South America glutted Spain's treasury. Between 1500 and 1650, an estimated 181 tons of gold and 16,000 tons of silver were shipped from the New World to Spain, making it the richest and most powerful state in Europe (see Figure 1-1). But this influx of American treasure had unforeseen consequences that would soon undermine Spanish predominance.

In 1492, the Spanish crown, determined to impose religious conformity after the *reconquista,* expelled from Spain all Jews who refused to become Christians. The refugees included many leading merchants who had contributed significantly to Spain's economy. The remaining Christian merchants, now awash in American riches, saw no reason to invest in new trade or productive enterprises that might have sustained the economy once the flow of New World treasure diminished. As a result, Spain's economy eventually stagnated.

Compounding the problem, the flood of American gold and silver inflated prices throughout Europe, hurting both workers, whose wages failed to rise as fast, and aristocrats, who were dependent on fixed rents from their estates. Most damaging of all, Spain's monarchs wasted their American wealth fighting expensive wars against their European enemies that ultimately only weakened the nation. By 1600, some disillusioned Spaniards were arguing that the conquest had brought more problems than benefits to their country.

The Columbian Exchange

Spain's long-term economic decline was just one of many consequences of the conquest of the New World. The arrival of Europeans in America set in motion a whole series of changes. In the long run, the biological consequences of contact—what one historian has called the **Columbian exchange**—proved to be the most momentous (see the summary table "The Columbian Exchange").

The most catastrophic result of the exchange was the exposure of Native Americans to Old World diseases. Europeans and Africans, long exposed to these diseases, had developed some immunity to them. Native Americans, never exposed to them, had not. The Black Death of 1347–1351, Europe's worst epidemic, killed perhaps a third of its population. Epidemics of smallpox, measles, typhus, and influenza

Indian artists recorded the arrival of mounted Spanish soldiers with this painting on a rock wall in Canyon del Muerto, Arizona. Horses were just one of several domesticated animals brought by the Spanish to the Americas.

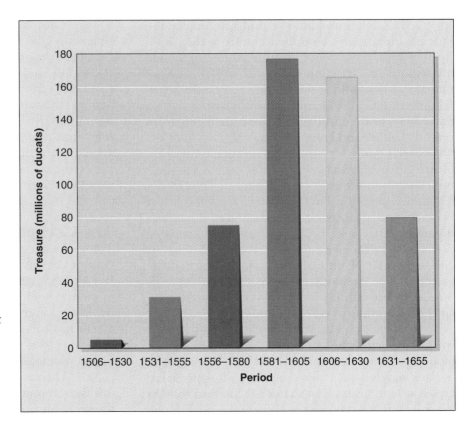

Figure 1-1   Value of New World Treasure Imported into Spain, 1506–1655
During the sixteenth and early seventeenth centuries, Spain was the only European power to reap great wealth from North America. The influx of New World treasure, however, slowed the development of Spain's economy in the long run. [Note: A ducat was a gold coin.]
Source: *Adapted from J. H. Elliott,* Imperial Spain, 1469–1716 *(1964), p. 175.*

struck Native Americans with far greater force, killing half, and sometimes as much as 90 percent, of the people in communities exposed to them. The only American disease to infect the Old World was syphilis, which appeared in Spain just after Columbus returned from his first voyage. Though its effects were far less catastrophic than those of the diseases Europeans brought to America, syphilis was painful, debilitating, and often fatal.

Another important aspect of the Columbian exchange was the introduction of Old World livestock to the New World, a process that began when Columbus brought horses, sheep, cattle, pigs, and goats with him on his second voyage in 1493. Native Americans had few domesticated animals and initially marveled at these large beasts. The animals, however, created problems for native peoples. With few natural predators to limit their numbers, livestock populations boomed in the New World, competing with native mammals, such as bison, for good grazing. Moreover, the Indians' unfamiliarity with the use of horses in warfare often gave mounted European soldiers a decisive military advantage.

But for some native groups, the introduction of European livestock created opportunities. Yaquis, Pueblos, and other peoples in the American Southwest began to raise cattle and sheep. By the eighteenth century, Plains Indians, including the Arapa-

hos, Sioux, Nez Percé, and Comanches, had not only adopted horses but also become exceptionally skilled riders. The men found it much easier to hunt buffalo on horseback than on foot, and the women valued horses as beasts of burden.

European ships carried unintentional passengers as well. The black rat, a carrier of disease, arrived on the first voyages. So did insects, including honeybees, previously unknown in the New World. Ships also brought weeds such as thistles and dandelions, whose seeds were often embedded in hay for animal fodder.

Europeans brought a variety of seeds and plant cuttings in order to grow familiar foods. Columbus's men planted wheat, chickpeas, melons, onions, and a variety of fruit trees on Caribbean islands. Although they optimistically reported that crops "sprouted in three days and were ready to eat by the twenty-fifth day," they—and later colonists— often found that European plants did not always fare well, at least not everywhere in the New World. As a result, Europeans learned to cultivate native foods, such as corn, tomatoes, squash, beans, and potatoes, as well as nonfood plants such as tobacco and cotton. They carried many of these plants back to Europe, enriching Old World diets with new foods. By the late seventeenth century, potatoes had become the mainstay of the Irish diet. And through-

SUMMARY

THE COLUMBIAN EXCHANGE

	From Old World to New World	From New World to Old World
Diseases	Smallpox, measles, plague, typhus, influenza, yellow fever, diphtheria, scarlet fever	Syphilis
Animals	Horses, cattle, pigs, sheep, goats, donkeys, mules, black rats, honeybees, cockroaches	Turkeys
Plants	Wheat, sugar, barley, coffee, rice, dandelion and other weeds	Maize, beans, peanut, potato, sweet potato, manioc, squash, papaya, guava, tomato, avocado, pineapple, chili pepper, cocoa

Source: *Adapted from Alfred Crosby Jr.*, The Columbian Exchange: Biological and Cultural Consequences of 1492 *(1972)*.

out Europe, new foods contributed to a sharp rise in population—which, in time, swelled the numbers of Europeans eager to leave their overcrowded communities for the New World.

Competition for a Continent

Spain's New World bonanza attracted the attention of other European states eager to share in the wealth. Portugal soon acquired its own profitable piece of South America. In 1494, the pope resolved the conflicting claims of Portugal and Spain with the **Treaty of Tordesillas.** The treaty drew a north-south line approximately 1,100 miles west of the Cape Verde Islands. Spain received all lands west of the line, while Portugal held sway to the east. This limited Portugal's New World empire to Brazil, where settlers followed the precedent of the Atlantic island colonies and established sugar plantations worked by slave labor. But the treaty also protected Portugal's

claims in Africa and Asia, which lay east of the line.

France and England, of course, rejected the papal grant of the Western Hemisphere to Spain and Portugal. Their initial challenges to Spanish dominance in the New World, however, proved quite feeble. Domestic troubles—largely sparked by the Protestant Reformation—distracted the two countries from the pursuit of empire. By the close of the sixteenth century, both France and England insisted on their rights to New World lands, but neither had created a permanent settlement to support its claim.

Early French Efforts in North America

France was a relative latecomer to New World exploration. In 1494, French troops invaded Italy, beginning a long and ultimately unsuccessful war with the Holy Roman Empire. Preoccupied with European affairs, France's rulers paid little attention to America. But when news of Cortés's exploits in Mexico arrived in the 1520s, King Francis I wanted his own New World empire to enrich France and block further Spanish expansion.

In 1524, Francis sponsored a voyage by Giovanni da Verrazano, an Italian navigator, who mapped the North American coast from present-day South Carolina to Maine. During the 1530s and 1540s, the French mariner Jacques Cartier made three voyages in search of rich mines to rival those of Mexico and Peru. He explored the St. Lawrence River up to what is now Montreal, hoping to discover a water route through the continent to Asia (what came to be called the Northwest Passage). His second voyage, in 1535, nearly ended in disaster. Unaware of the harshness of Canadian winters, he and his crew almost froze to death and suffered from scurvy, a disease caused by a lack of vitamin C. Many men died, and the rest survived only because the Iroquois showed them how to make a vitamin-rich concoction of boiled white cedar needles and bark.

On his third voyage, in 1541, Cartier was to serve under the command of a nobleman, Jean-

American Views

THE DEBATE BETWEEN BARTOLOMÉ DE LAS CASAS AND JUAN GINÉS DE SEPÚLVEDA

In 1550, in response to criticism of Spanish colonial tactics, the Spanish king called a special council to decide if it was lawful to wage war on Indians before preaching to them, in order to make them more submissive converts to Christianity. The council summoned Juan Ginés de Sepúlveda and Bartolomé de Las Casas to debate the issue. Sepúlveda, a noted classical scholar who had never visited America, argued that warfare was indeed just and that Indians were fit only to be Spanish slaves. Las Casas, the well-known defender of the Indians, insisted that the Indians' humanity demanded gentler treatment from the Spanish. In the end, this debate only polarized the issue even more. The council members began arguing among themselves and reached no decision. These extracts illustrate the two sides of the argument.

❖ **What are the main points of disagreement?**

❖ **Do the views of Sepúlveda and Las Casas share any common elements?**

❖ **What, according to the Spanish, were essential features of civilized society?**

❖ **Why were the Spanish so intent on converting the Indians?**

Sepúlveda's position

In prudence, talent, virtue, and humanity they are as inferior to thé Spaniards as children to adults, women to men, as the wild and cruel to the most meek, as the prodigiously intemperate to the continent and temperate, that I have almost said, as monkeys to men.

[The Indians] not only lack culture but do not even know how to write, [they] keep no records of their history except certain obscure and vague reminiscences of some things put down in certain pictures, and [they] do not have written laws but only barbarous institutions and customs. . . . And don't think that before the arrival of the Chris-

François de la Rocque, sieur de Roberval, who was commissioned by the king to establish a permanent settlement in Canada. Troubles in recruiting colonists delayed Roberval, who—when he finally set sail in 1542—ended up taking convicts as his settlers. In the meantime, Cartier had sailed ahead, gathered samples of what he thought were gold and diamonds, and returned to France without Roberval's permission.

This first attempt to found a permanent French colony failed miserably. Roberval's expedition was poorly organized, and his cruel treatment of the convicts provoked several uprisings. The Iroquois, suspicious of repeated French intrusions on their lands, saw no reason to help them. A year after they arrived in Canada, Roberval and the surviving colonists were back in France. Their return coincided with news that the gold brought back by Cartier was iron pyrite (fool's gold) and the diamonds were worthless quartz crystals.

Disappointed with their Canadian expeditions, the French made a few brief forays to the south, establishing outposts in what is now South Carolina in 1562 and Florida in 1564. They soon abandoned the Carolina colony (though not before the starving settlers resorted to cannibalism), and Spanish forces captured the Florida fort. Then, back in France, a prolonged civil war broke out between Catholics and Protestants. Renewed interest in colonization would have to await the return of peace at home.

tians they were living in quiet. . . . On the contrary they were making war continuously and ferociously against each other with such rage that they considered their victory worthless if they did not satisfy their monstrous hunger with the flesh of their enemies. . . . [Yet] these Indians are so cowardly and timid, that they scarcely withstand the appearance of our soldiers and often many thousands of them have given ground, fleeing like women before a very few Spaniards, who did not even number a hundred.

Las Casas's position

From the fact that the Indians are barbarians it does not necessarily follow that they are incapable of government and have to be ruled by others, except to be taught about the Catholic faith and to be admitted to the holy sacraments. They are not ignorant, inhuman, or bestial. Rather, long before they had heard the word Spaniard, they had properly organized states, wisely ordered by excellent laws, religion, and custom. They cultivated friendship and, bound together in common fellowship, lived in populous cities in which they wisely administered the affairs of both peace and war justly and equitably, truly governed by laws which at very many points surpass ours. . . .

The Indians are our brothers, and Christ has given his life for them. Why, then, do we persecute them with such inhuman savagery when they do not deserve such treatment? . . . [They] will embrace the teaching of the gospel, as I well know, for they are not stupid or barbarous but have a native sincerity and are simple, moderate, and meek, and, finally, such that I do not know whether there is any people readier to receive the gospel.

Source: *Lewis Hanke*, All Mankind Is One: A Study of the Disputation between Bartolomé de Las Casas and Juan Ginés de Sepúlveda in 1550 on the Intellectual and Religious Capacity of the American Indians *(1974), pp. 84, 85, 76.*

English Attempts in the New World

The English were quicker than the French to stake a claim to the New World but no more successful at colonization. In 1497, King Henry VII sent John Cabot, an Italian mariner, to explore eastern Canada on England's behalf. But neither Henry nor his wealthier subjects would invest the funds necessary to follow up on Cabot's discoveries. For nearly half a century, English contact with America was limited to the seasonal voyages of fishermen who lived each summer in Newfoundland, fished offshore, and returned in autumn with ships full of cod.

The lapse in English activity in the New World stemmed from religious troubles at home. Between 1534 and 1558, England changed its official religion several times. King Henry VIII, who had once defended the Catholic Church against its critics, took up the Protestant cause when the pope refused to annul his marriage to Catherine of Aragon. In 1534, Henry declared himself the head of a separate Church of England and seized the Catholic Church's English property. Since many English people sympathized with the Protestant cause, there was relatively little opposition to Henry's actions. But in 1553, Mary—daughter of the spurned Catherine of Aragon—became queen and tried to bring England back to Catholicism. She had nearly three hundred Protestants burned at the stake for their beliefs (earning her the nickname "Bloody Mary"), and many others went into exile in Europe.

After Mary's brief but destructive reign, which ended with her death in 1558, her half-sister Elizabeth, a committed Protestant, became queen. Elizabeth ruled for forty-five years (1558–1603), restoring Protestantism as the state religion, bringing stability to the nation, and renewing England's interest in the New World. She and her subjects saw colonization not only as a way to gain wealth and political advantage but also as a Protestant crusade against Catholic domination.

England's first target for colonization, however, was not America but Ireland. Located less than 60 miles west of England and populated by Catholics, Ireland threatened to become a base from which Spain or another Catholic power might invade England. Henry VIII had tried, with limited success, to bring the island under English control in the 1530s and 1540s. Elizabeth renewed the attempt in the 1560s and 1570s with a series of brutal expeditions that destroyed Irish villages and slaughtered the inhabitants. Several veterans of these campaigns later took part in New World colonization and drew on their Irish experience for guidance.

Two aspects of that experience were particularly important. First, the English transferred their assumptions about Irish "savages" to native Americans. Englishmen in America frequently observed similarities between Indians and the Irish. "When they [the Indians] have their apparel on they look like Irish," noted one Englishman. "The natives of New England," he added, "are accustomed to build their houses much like the wild Irish." Because the English held the "wild Irish" in contempt, these observations encouraged them to scorn the Indians. When Indians resisted their attempts at conquest, the English recalled the Irish example, claiming that native "savagery" required brutal suppression.

Second, the Irish experience influenced English ideas about colonial settlement. English conquerors set up "plantations" surrounded by palisades on seized Irish lands. These plantations were meant to be civilized outposts in a savage land. Their aristocratic owners imported Protestant tenants from England and Scotland to farm the land. Native Irish people, considered too wild to join proper Christian communities, were excluded. English colonists in America followed this precedent when they established plantations that separated English and native peoples.

Sir Humphrey Gilbert, a notoriously cruel veteran of the Irish campaigns, became fascinated with the idea of New World colonization. He composed a treatise to convince Queen Elizabeth to support such an endeavor. The queen, who counted

Gilbert among her favorite courtiers, authorized several exploratory voyages, including Martin Frobisher's three trips in 1576–1578 in search of the Northwest Passage to Asia. Frobisher failed to find the elusive passage and sent back shiploads of glittering ore that proved to be fool's gold. Elizabeth had better luck in allowing privateers, such as John Hawkins and Francis Drake, to raid Spanish ships and New World ports for gold and silver. The plunder taken during these raids enriched both the sailors and their investors—one of whom was the queen herself.

Meanwhile, Gilbert continued to promote New World settlement, arguing that it would increase England's trade and provide a place for the nation's unemployed people. Like many of his contemporaries, Gilbert believed that England's "surplus" population threatened social order. The population was indeed growing, and economic changes often made it difficult for people to support themselves. Many landlords, for instance, had been converting farmland into sheep pastures. They hoped to profit from the wool trade, but their decision threw tenant families off the land. Gilbert suggested offering free land in America to English families willing to emigrate.

In 1578, Gilbert received permission to set up a colony anywhere along the North American coast. It took him five years to organize an expedition to Newfoundland, which he claimed for England. After sailing southward seeking a more favorable site for a colony, Gilbert headed home, only to be lost at sea during an Atlantic storm. The impetus for English colonization did not die with him, however, for his half-brother, Sir Walter Raleigh (another veteran of the Irish wars), immediately took up the cause.

In 1584, Raleigh sent an expedition to find a suitable location for a colony. Learning that the Carolina coast seemed promising, Raleigh sent men in 1585 to build a settlement on Roanoke Island. Most colonists were soldiers fresh from Ireland who refused to grow their own food, insisting that the Roanoke Indians should feed them. When the local chief, Wingina, organized native resistance, they killed him. Eventually, the colonists, disappointed not to have found gold or precious stones and exhausted by a harsh winter, returned to England in 1586.

Two members of these early expeditions, however, left a more positive legacy. Thomas Hariot studied the Roanoke and Croatoan Indians and identified plants and animals in the area, hoping that some might prove to be profitable commodities. John White drew maps and painted a series of watercolors depicting the natives and the coastal landscape. (Two of White's paintings appear in this chap-

The English artist John White took particular care to record the daily practices of Carolina-area Indians. This painting shows both the natives' daytime method of fishing with nets and spears, and also their nighttime practice of fishing with a fire in a canoe. To the left is a woven weir, another means of catching fish. In addition, White drew local animals, including a catfish, hermit crab and other water creatures, as well as such birds as pelicans, swans, and ducks.

ter, one here and one on page 10.) When Raleigh tried once more, in 1587, to found a colony, he chose White to be its leader.

This attempt also failed. The ship captain dumped the settlers—who, for the first time, included women and children—on Roanoke Island so that he could pursue Spanish treasure ships. White waited until his granddaughter, Virginia Dare (the first English child born in America), was safely born and then sailed to England for supplies. But the outbreak of war with Spain delayed his return for three years. Spain had gathered an immense fleet to invade England, and all English ships were needed for defense. Although England defeated the Armada in 1588, White could not obtain a relief ship for Roanoke until 1590.

White found the colony deserted. Digging through the ruins of the village, he found "my books torn from the covers, the frames of some of my pictures and Maps rotten and spoiled with rain." He also saw the word CROATOAN carved on a post and assumed that the colonists had moved to nearby Croatoan Island. But bad weather prevented him from searching there. For years, English and Spanish mariners reported seeing white people along the coast of Chesapeake Bay. But no Roanoke colonists were ever found. They may have moved to the mainland and intermarried with local Indians. One historian has speculated that they survived until 1607 when Powhatan Indians, angered by the appearance of more English settlers, killed them. The actual fate of the "Lost Colony" at Roanoke will probably never be known.

At this point, Raleigh gave up on North America and turned his attention to his Irish plantations. But England's interest in colonization did not wane. In 1584, Richard Hakluyt had aroused enthusiasm for America by writing the "Discourse of Western Planting" for the queen and her advisers. He argued that England would prosper from the expansion of trade and the sale of New World commodities. Once the Indians were civilized, Hakluyt added, they would eagerly purchase English goods. Equally important, England could plant "sincere religion" (that is, Protestant Christianity) in the New World and prevent the power of "the Spanish king from flowing over all the face . . . of America."

Hakluyt's arguments fired the imaginations of many people, and the defeat of the Spanish Armada only emboldened England to challenge Spain's New World dominance. The experience of Roanoke should have tempered that enthusiasm, illustrating the problems as well as benefits of colonization. The colony's fate underscored the need for adequate funding, the unsuitability of soldiers as colonists, and the need to maintain good relations with the Indians. But the English were slow to learn these lessons; when they resumed colonization efforts in 1607, they repeated Roanoke's mistakes, with disastrous results for the people involved. As it was, the sixteenth century ended with no permanent English settlement in the New World.

Conclusion

Dramatic changes occurred in North America during the century after Columbus's first voyage. Europeans, eager for wealth and power, came by the thousands to a continent that just a hundred years earlier they had not dreamed existed. Africans came in even greater numbers to the Caribbean, Mexico, and Brazil, forced to labor for white masters in unfamiliar lands. In many parts of the Americas, native peoples encountered white and black strangers whose presence disturbed—and sometimes destroyed—their accustomed ways of life.

And yet conditions in North America in 1600 bore clearer witness to the past than to the future. Only Spain had established North American colonies, and its New World dominance seemed secure. And even Spain had struggled to expand north of Mexico. Its outposts in Florida and New Mexico staked claims to territory that Spain did not really control. Virtually the entire continent north of the Rio Grande remained firmly in Indian hands. Except in Mexico and the Caribbean, Europeans had merely touched the continent's shores—often only briefly. When natives and newcomers met, the encounter was often disastrous for the Indians, who died in great numbers from European diseases and warfare. Even so, in 1600, native peoples (even in Mexico) still greatly outnumbered European and African immigrants. The next century, however, brought powerful challenges both to native control and to the Spanish monopoly of settlement.

Review Questions

1. Compare men's and women's roles in Native American, West African, and European societies. What were the similarities and differences? How did differences between European and Native American gender roles lead to misunderstandings?

2. Many of the first European colonizers in North America were military veterans. What impact did this have on their relations with Indian peoples?

3. Why did Spain so quickly become the dominant colonial power in North America? What advantages did it enjoy over France and England?

4. What role did religion play in early European efforts at overseas colonization? Did religious factors always encourage colonization, or did they occasionally interfere with European expansion?

Recommended Reading

Hassig, Ross. *Mexico and the Spanish Conquest* (1994). A brief account of Cortés's expedition, focusing on the military aspects of the Spanish conquest.

Josephy, Alvin M., Jr. *America in 1492: The World of the Indian Peoples before the Arrival of Columbus* (1991). A collection of essays describing the wide variety of Indian cultures in North America prior to contact with Europeans.

Leon-Portillo, Miguel. *The Broken Spears: The Aztec Account of the Conquest of Mexico* (1962). Reprints of translated Indian chronicles, providing a moving account of the Aztec experience of the Spanish conquest.

Parry, J. H. *The Age of Reconnaissance* (1963). A comprehensive account of European exploration and the rise of overseas empires.

Phillips, William D., Jr., and Phillips, Carla Rahn. *The Worlds of Christopher Columbus* (1992). A judicious biography of Columbus that places him firmly in the context of fifteenth-century European culture.

Thornton, John. *Africa and Africans in the Making of the Atlantic World, 1400–1680* (1992). A thorough examination of the causes and consequences of the movement of Africans throughout the Atlantic world and the rise of the slave trade.

Additional Sources

Native American Cultures

Clendinnen, Inga. *Aztecs: An Interpretation* (1991).

Fagan, Brian M. *The Great Journey: The Peopling of Ancient America* (1987).

Fiedel, Stuart J. *Prehistory of the Americas*, 2d ed. (1992).

Jennings, Francis. *The Founders of America: How Indians Discovered the Land, Pioneered in It, and Created Great Classical Civilizations . . .* (1993).

Rouse, Irving. *The Tainos: Rise and Decline of the People Who Greeted Columbus* (1992).

Russell, Howard S. *Indian New England before the Mayflower* (1980).

West African Society

Bohannan, Paul, and Curtin, Philip. *Africa and Africans*, 3d ed. (1988).

Fage, J. D. *A History of West Africa: An Introductory Survey*, 4th ed. (1969).

Olaniyan, Richard, ed. *African History and Culture* (1982).

Europe in the Age of Discovery

Bainton, Roland H. *Here I Stand: A Life of Martin Luther* (1955).

Braudel, Fernand. *The Mediterranean and the Mediterranean World in the Age of Philip II*, 2d ed. (1966; English trans., 1972).

Burckhardt, Jacob. *The Civilization of the Renaissance in Italy* (1958).

Cipolla, Carlo M. *Before the Industrial Revolution: European Society and Economy, 1100–1700* (1976).

Cipolla, Carlo M. *Guns, Sails, and Empire: Technological Innovation and the Early Phases of European Expansion, 1400–1700* (1965).

Elliott, J. H. *Imperial Spain, 1469–1716* (1964).

Lewis, Bernard. *Cultures in Conflict: Christians, Muslims, and Jews in the Age of Discovery* (1995).

Morison, Samuel Eliot. *The European Discovery of America: The Northern Voyages, A.D. 500–1600* (1971).

Morison, Samuel Eliot. *The European Discovery of America: The Southern Voyages, A.D. 1492–1616* (1974).

Quinn, David Beers. *The Elizabethans and the Irish* (1966).

Rice, Eugene F., Jr. *The Foundations of Early Modern Europe, 1460–1559* (1970).

Scammell, G. V. *The First Imperial Age: European Overseas Expansion, c. 1400–1715* (1989).

Conquest and Colonization

Andrews, Kenneth R. *Trade, Plunder, and Settlement: Maritime Enterprise and the Genesis of the British Empire, 1480–1630* (1984).

Crosby, Alfred W., Jr. *The Columbian Exchange: Biological and Cultural Consequences of 1492* (1972).

Eccles, W. J. *France in America*, rev. ed. (1990).

Elliott, J. H. *The Old World and the New, 1492–1650* (1970).

Kupperman, Karen Ordahl. *Roanoke: The Abandoned Colony* (1984).

Meinig, D. W. *The Shaping of America*, Vol. 1: *Atlantic America, 1492–1800* (1986).

Weber, David J. *The Spanish Frontier in North America* (1992).

Where to Learn More

❖ **Chillicothe, Ohio.** The Mound City Group National Monument: This site preserves a prehistoric Indian burial site. The holdings in the museum include excavated grave goods from burial mounds dating from 200 B.C. to A.D. 500. There is also a library with research materials on prehistoric Native American culture.

❖ **Washington, Connecticut.** American Indian Archaeological Institute: With both a museum and library materials, the institute preserves artifacts of Eastern Woodlands Indians and has a special collection of Algonquin baskets.

❖ **Acoma Pueblo, New Mexico.** Adobe pueblo built on a 350-foot-high mesa; site of early contact between Pueblo Indians and Spanish soldiers. Contains San Estevan del Rey Mission, built 1629–1642. Site mainly used for ceremonial purposes, and travelers should obtain permission before visiting.

❖ **St. Augustine, Florida.** Founded in 1565, St. Augustine is the site of the first permanent Spanish settlement in North America. Today the restored community resembles a Spanish colonial town, with narrow, winding streets and seventeenth- and eighteenth-century buildings. The site also contains the restored Castillo de San Marcos, now a national park. The Historic St. Augustine Preservation Board owns and administers several historic house museums and offers programs in living history and craft exhibits.

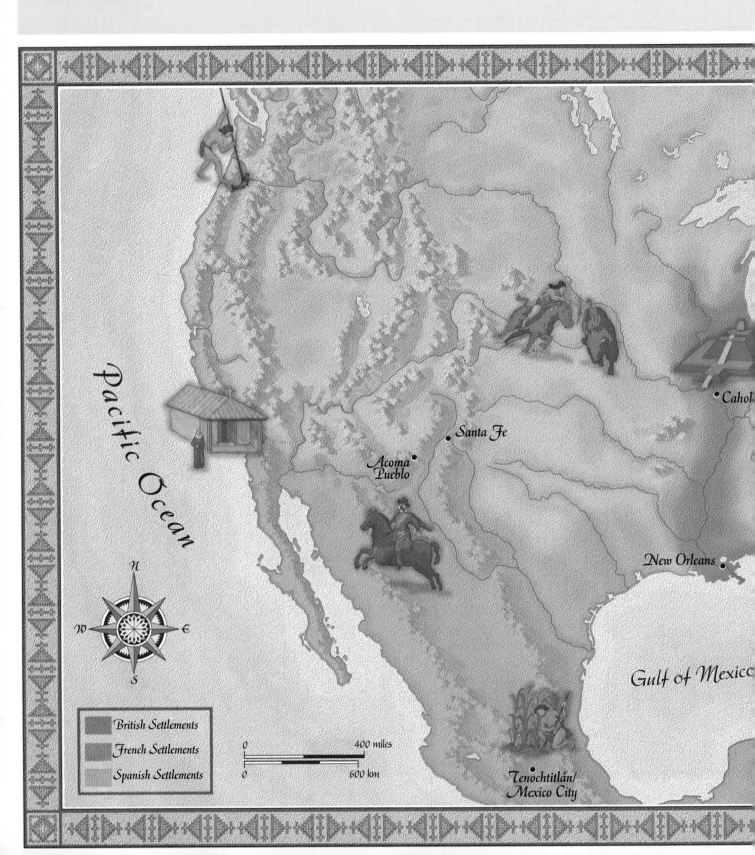

Pacific Ocean

Cahok

Santa Fe

Acoma
Pueblo

New Orleans

Gulf of Mexico

N
W   E
S

British Settlements
French Settlements
Spanish Settlements

0   400 miles
0   600 km

Tenochtitlán/
Mexico City

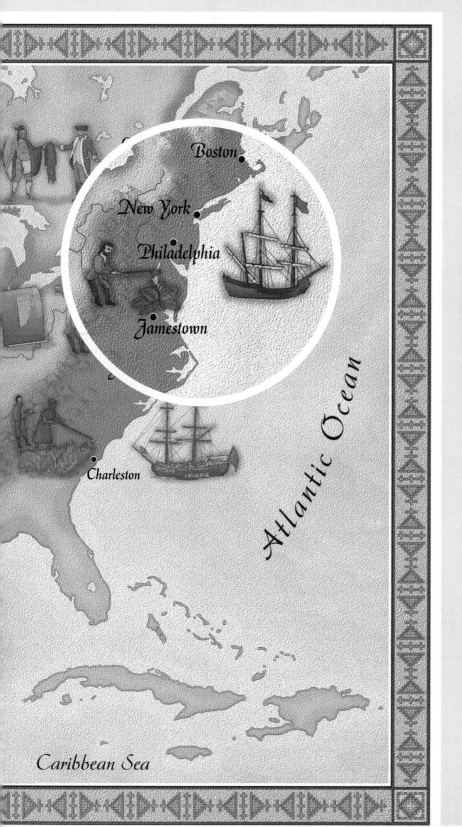

Boston

New York

Philadelphia

Jamestown

Charleston

Atlantic Ocean

Caribbean Sea

CHAPTER OUTLINE

KEY TOPICS

❖ Development of New France
❖ Diversity of English colonies in the seventeenth century
❖ Growth of staple crop economies in the southern and Caribbean colonies
❖ Role of religion in the founding of colonies
❖ Creation of biracial slave societies in the West Indies and Carolina

𝒞aptain John Smith wrote his brief book, *A Description of New England,* under difficult circumstances. It was the summer of 1615, and he was being held captive aboard a French pirate ship. Smith had left England with a crew of thirty sailors, bound for the northeast coast of North America, where they planned to set up a colony. They had not gone far before being seized by the pirates, who justified their action by accusing Smith of participating in an earlier English raid on a French settlement in Maine. When Smith boarded the pirate ship to bargain for their release, his crew escaped, leaving the captain stranded. With little else to occupy him during months of captivity, Smith composed his book promoting colonization of the region he named "New England" as a challenge to rival colonies in New Spain and New France.

Smith eventually made it back to England and published his book in 1616. By then, England and France had joined Spain as founders of New World colonies. Smith's work (no less than his experience with the pirates) testified to the intensifying rivalry among European nations for control of North America. His book emphasized the vast wealth of Spain's empire and scolded Protestant Englishmen for allowing Spanish Catholics to spread their faith among the natives. The Spanish king, Smith declared, scarcely knew "one halfe Quarter of those Territories" he claimed, and so the English "neede not greatly feare his furie" if they expanded their own settlements.

John Smith's name is usually associated with the founding of Virginia, England's first permanent colony in North America, in 1607. After a brief stint as Virginia's leader, Smith was ousted in 1609 by disgruntled colonists. Back in England, he developed a plan to set up a rival colony in New England. But he never returned to America after his ill-fated voyage of 1615, and New England settlement began in 1620 without him. Even so, Smith's thwarted plans illustrated an important feature of English colonization in North America.

The seventeenth century saw not only increased rivalry among European nations for New World territory but also competition among groups of English colonists. The English king—unlike French and Spanish monarchs—exercised little direct control over his American colonies. James I and his successors preferred instead to grant land to trading companies or prominent individuals who would then plant new settlements. This policy led to the founding of at least two dozen English colonies on the North American mainland and in the Caribbean before 1700. Some lasted only a few decades, but all attested to vigorous English expansion. Because the process lacked centralized direction, and because the experiences of colonists in different regions varied so widely, the result was an English empire united more in name than in reality.

The French in North America

The English raid on the French settlement in Maine—for which the French pirates held John Smith accountable—was indeed a devastating affair. But although it virtually wiped out the tiny outpost, it left French influence in the area scarcely diminished. The economic base of France's New World empire, known as New France, was the fur trade, which depended more on the control of waterways and alliances with Indians than on the occupation of land. The Maine outpost disappeared, but French trade continued to flourish.

If French explorers avoided what was to become New England to the south, it was less because of English resistance than because the region lacked New France's source of wealth. The focus of the French colony was the St. Lawrence River, which provided access to a vast interior populated by an abundance of beavers and by Indian peoples eager for trade. Because of its emphasis on the fur trade rather than extensive settlement, New France's population grew slowly in the seventeenth century. Its few, scattered villages were

This portrait, which appeared in John Smith's Description of New England, *boldly proclaimed him to be "Admiral" of the region. A restless adventurer, Smith served as a mercenary soldier in Hungary and Turkey and then grew fascinated with the New World. He served briefly as a leader in early Virginia, and later as a publicist for New England colonization.*

linked as closely to their Indian neighbors as to each other.

The Development of New France

As we saw in Chapter 1, French efforts to found American colonies in the late sixteenth century ended in failure. Preoccupied with religious conflict at home, the French government temporarily lost interest in the New World. But French fishermen, drawn to the rich fishing grounds of the Grand Banks, continued to visit the Newfoundland coast. Setting up frames onshore to dry their catch, they met Indians with furs to trade for European goods. The French quickly realized they were on to a good thing; the already strong market

for furs in Europe soon expanded dramatically as broad-brimmed beaver fur hats became fashionable.

Once it was clear that a profit could be made in Canada, France's interest revived. To strengthen their claim to the region (and make some money for themselves), French kings sold exclusive trading rights to merchants willing to set up outposts in Canada. But because these outposts had to be supplied, at great expense, from France, many merchants lost money on them. To succeed, the merchants needed to bring farmers to New France to produce food and other supplies for the traders.

Quebec, organized in 1608 by Samuel de Champlain, was the first permanent French settlement in Canada (see Map 2-1). Located more than 130 miles up the St. Lawrence and perched precariously between steep cliffs and the river, it was inhabited for its first two decades by only a few dozen settlers dependent on France for supplies. Thereafter, efforts to recruit colonists to New France intensified, and French Jesuits—members of a Catholic religious order founded during the Counter-Reformation—sent missionaries to convert the Indians. In 1642, Montreal was founded as a religious and commercial center.

By 1700, New France had about fifteen thousand settlers. Many of them enjoyed a better life than

Map 2-1   New France, c. 1650

By 1650, New France contained a number of thinly populated settlements along the St. Lawrence River Valley and the eastern shore of Lake Huron. Most colonists lived in Quebec and Montreal; other sites served mainly as fur-trading posts and Jesuit missions to the Huron Indians.

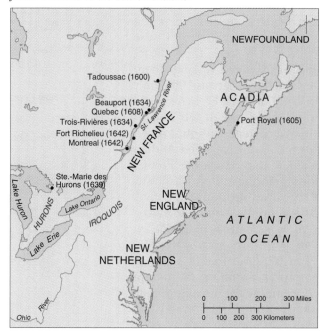

peasants back in France. One observer reported that "if they are the least inclined to work," immigrants could expect to prosper in Canada. Colonists generally lived in sturdier houses, enjoyed a better diet, and paid lower taxes than their relatives back home. They could acquire land to pass on to their children with an ease that French peasants could only envy. Despite these advantages, however, few French people moved to North America, and two-thirds of those who did eventually returned to France. Canada's fifteen thousand settlers in 1700 amounted to less than 7 percent of the number of English colonists in mainland North America that same year (see Figure 2-1).

Several factors accounted for this reluctance to emigrate, not least of which was Canada's reputation as a distant and inhospitable place. "Canada has always been regarded as a country at the end of the world," admitted one colonial official. Rumors about frigid winters and surprise Indian attacks circulated among French peasants and villagers. In addition, the government required prospective settlers to be Catholic (although Protestants could reside in Canada temporarily), reducing the pool from which they could be drawn.

In any case, few could pay their own way to America. Most settlers were sponsored, some by the government but most by employers who paid their passage in return for three years of labor in the colony. Those who completed their terms of service received land, but because most were young men eager to marry and raise children to help them farm, this often failed to keep them in Canada. As late as 1666, only one out of three French settlers was female, which left half of the young men without French brides. Some married Indian women (a practice the French king came to support as a way to "civilize" the natives). Others found brides from among the female orphans—called *filles du Roi*, or "king's girls"—that the French government paid to send to Canada in an attempt to remedy the sexual imbalance. (Rumors abounded that the *filles du Roi* were simply

prostitutes lured from the streets of Paris and other cities, but most were poor Frenchwomen who did find Canadian husbands.) Most young men, however, chose to go home to France. By 1700, the imbalance between men and women in Canada had all but disappeared. Nonetheless, Canada's settler population never approached that of England's North American colonies.

The Fur Trade

Problems with recruiting settlers did not, in the end, limit New France's prosperity, for fur traders, not settlers, determined the colony's success. Furs were an ideal commodity—light, easy to transport, and very profitable. For the French, at least, the fur trade was also not very hard work. It was Indians who trapped the beavers, prepared the skins, and carried them from the interior to French trading posts. French traders paid for the pelts with such goods as axes, knives, metal pots, and glass beads. The furs were then loaded on ships and sent to France. Transporting settlers to Canada was far less profitable, and merchants justified their reluctance to do so by claiming that too many settlers would displace beavers and the Indians who hunted them.

Figure 2-1   *European Populations of New France (Quebec) and English Colonies in 1650 and 1700*

Although New France's population grew rapidly between 1650 and 1700, it remained only a tiny fraction of the population of England's North American colonies. By 1700, English colonists on the mainland outnumbered New France's inhabitants by a factor of about 16 to 1.

Source: *Data from John J. McCusker and Russell R. Menard,* The Economy of British America, *1607–1789 (1985).*

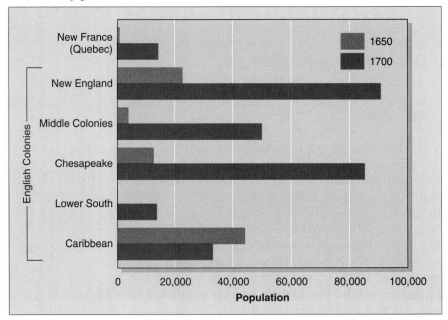

CHRONOLOGY

1603–1625 James I reigns as king of England.

1607 Founding of English colonies at Jamestown and Sagadahoc.

1608 Establishment of French colony at Quebec.

1619 Virginia's House of Burgesses meets for the first time.

1620 Founding of Plymouth Colony in New England.

Mayflower Compact signed.

1620s Tobacco boom in Virginia.

1624 Dutch found colony of New Netherlands.

1625 Virginia becomes a royal colony.

Fort Amsterdam founded.

1625–1649 Charles I reigns as king of England.

1627 English colony at Barbados founded.

1630 Massachusetts Bay Colony founded.

1630–1642 Great Migration to New England.

1634 Lord Baltimore (Cecilius Calvert) founds proprietary colony of Maryland.

1635–1636 Roger Williams banished from Massachusetts, founds Providence, Rhode Island.

1637 Anne Hutchinson banished from Massachusetts.

Pequot War.

1638 New Haven colony founded.

1640s Sugar cultivation and slavery established in West Indies.

1642–1660 English Civil War and Interregnum.

1649 Maryland's Act for Religious Toleration.

1660 Charles II restored to English throne; reigns until 1685.

1663 Founding of Carolina colony.

1664 New Netherlands conquered by the English, becomes New York.

New Jersey established.

1673 French explorers reach the Mississippi River.

1681 Founding of Pennsylvania.

The Indians understood trade as part of a broader process of alliance that involved the exchange of gifts and mutual military assistance. As a result, the fur trade drew the French deeply into the rivalries among Indian groups. When Champlain approached the Hurons for trade, they insisted that the French agree to help them fight the Iroquois. By becoming Huron allies, the French acquired Iroquois enemies. Thereafter the security of the colony depended on the ability of its governors to handle delicate diplomatic relations with the Indians.

To manage French interests in North America, the king and his advisers created an impressive colonial bureaucracy. Beginning in 1663, the colony was placed under the rule of a governor and ***intendant***, both of them royal appointees who in turn appointed several lesser officials. Because their affairs were controlled by appointed officials, New France's settlers never developed institutions of self-government as English colonists did. The king also insisted on a strong military force to protect the colony from attack by Indian enemies or European rivals. He ordered the construction of forts and sent several companies of professional soldiers—a much greater investment in defense than English kings would provide for their colonies until the middle of the eighteenth century.

Yet royal control in New France was hardly absolute. Colonial officials disobeyed orders from France when it suited them. Even though instructions from Paris prohibited westward expansion—officials feared creating an empire so far-flung that it would be impossible to defend—the *intendant* in Quebec allowed explorers to move inland. By the 1670s, French traders and missionaries had reached the Mississippi River, and in 1681–1682, Robert, sieur de La Salle, followed it to the Gulf of Mexico, claiming the entire river valley (which he named Louisiana in honor of King Louis XIV) for France. Scores of independent fur traders, known as ***coureurs de bois*** ("woods runners"), roamed the forests, living and trading among the Indians there. This expansion of French influence alarmed the English, who had founded colonies along the Atlantic seaboard and feared a growing French presence in the west.

Since Indians expected their trading partners to also be military allies, Europeans were often drawn into native conflicts. This illustration, from Samuel de Champlain's 1613 description of the founding of New France, shows him joining his Huron allies in an attack on the Iroquois.

English Settlement in the Chesapeake

Following the Roanoke colony's disappearance after 1587, twenty years passed before the English again attempted to settle in America. When they did, in 1607, it was in the lower Chesapeake Bay region. The new settlement, Jamestown, at first seemed likely to share Roanoke's dismal fate. But it endured, eventually developing into the prosperous colony of Virginia. The reason for Virginia's success was an American plant—tobacco—that commanded good prices from European consumers. Tobacco also underlay the economy of a neighboring colony, Maryland, founded by English settlers on the northern and eastern shores of Chesapeake Bay, and had a profound influence on the development of Chesapeake society.

The Ordeal of Early Virginia

In 1606, a group of English merchants, convinced that they could succeed where others had failed, petitioned King James I for a charter incorporating two companies to attempt New World settlement. One, the London, or **Virginia**, **Company**, included merchants from the City of London; the other, the **Plymouth Company**, included merchants from England's western ports.

James I agreed to issue a charter granting the companies two tracts of land along the mid-Atlantic coast but refrained from investing any money himself in such a risky enterprise. These **joint-stock companies** sold shares to investors (who expected a profit in return) to raise money for colonization.

Three small ships carried 104 settlers, all men, to the mouth of the Chesapeake Bay in May 1607 (see Map 2-2). On a peninsula about 50 miles up a river they named the James, in honor of their king, the colonists built a fortified settlement they called Jamestown. Hoping to earn quick profits for the company's investors, they immediately began searching for gold and exploring the James in search of the Northwest Passage to Asia. But Jamestown was no Mexico. All they found was disappointment and suffering. The swampy land around the settlement was a perfect breeding area for malarial mosquitoes and parasites carrying other diseases. Spending all their time in search of riches, the settlers neglected to plant crops, and their food supplies dwindled. By January 1608, only thirty-eight of them were still alive.

After the disastrous first year, the colony's governing council turned to Captain John Smith for leadership. Just 28 years old, Smith was a seasoned adventurer who had fought against Spain in the Netherlands and the Ottomans in Hungary. He imposed military discipline on Jamestown's settlers, forming them into work gangs and decreeing that "he that will not worke shall not eate." His high-handed methods revived the colony but antagonized certain settlers who believed that their social status exempted them from manual labor and who bristled at taking orders from a man of lower social rank. When a gunpowder explosion wounded Smith in 1609 and forced him to return to England, his enemies had him replaced as leader.

Once again, the colony nearly disintegrated. Shiploads of new settlers arrived, only to die of disease and starvation. Of the five hundred people in Jamestown in the autumn of 1609, just sixty remained alive by the spring of 1610—some of whom survived only by eating their dead companions. Facing financial ruin, company officials back in England tried to conceal the state of the colony. They reorganized the company twice and sent more settlers, including glassmakers, winegrowers, and silkmakers in a desperate effort to

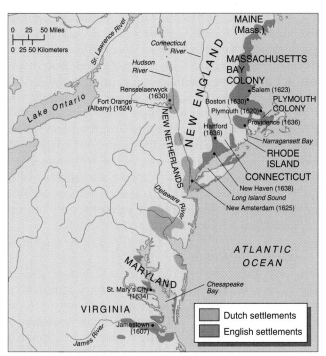

Map 2-2 *English and Dutch Mainland Colonies in North America, c. 1655*
Early English colonies clustered in two areas of the Atlantic seaboard—New England and the Chesapeake Bay. Between them lay Dutch New Netherlands, with settlements stretching up the Hudson River. The Dutch also acquired territory at the mouth of the Delaware River in 1655 when they seized a short-lived Swedish colony located there.

find a marketable colonial product. They experimented with harsh military discipline, instructing governors to enforce a legal code—the *Lawes Divine, Morall and Martiall*—that prescribed the death penalty for offenses as trivial as swearing or killing a chicken. When it became clear that such severity discouraged immigration, the company tried more positive inducements.

The first settlers had been expected to work together in return for food and other necessities; only the company's stockholders were supposed to share in the colony's profits. With no profits forthcoming, the company offered more substantial benefits to settlers. Governors began assigning small plots of land to colonists who finished their terms of service to the company. In 1616, the company instituted the **headright system**, giving 50 acres to anyone who paid his own way to Virginia and an additional 50 for each person (or "head") he brought with him.

In 1619, three other important developments occurred. That year, the company began transporting women to Virginia to become wives for planters and induce them to stay in the colony. It also sent over the first African slaves to Virginia. In addition, the company created the first legislative body in English America, the **House of Burgesses**, setting a prece-

dent for the establishment of self-government in other English colonies. Landowners elected representatives to the House of Burgesses, which, subject to the approval of the company, made laws for Virginia. In 1621 the *Lawes Divine, Morall and Martiall* gave way to a code based on English common law.

Despite these changes, the settlers were still unable to earn the company a profit, and life in the colony barely improved. To make things worse, the headright system expanded English settlement beyond Jamestown. This strained the already tense relations between the English and the Indians into whose lands they had intruded.

When the English arrived in 1607, they planted their settlement in the heart of territory ruled

Powhatan's first meeting with John Smith followed the rules of Indian formality. Smith was conducted down a long building made of bark and saplings. Powhatan sat at the far end, bedecked with "many Chaynes of great Pearles about his neck" and covered with raccoon skins. Several of Powhatan's wives and councilors sat before him, and "40 or 50 of the tallest men his Country doth afford" stood guard outside.

by the Indian leader Powhatan, who was then at the peak of his power. Chief of a confederacy of about thirty tribes with some fourteen thousand people, including 3,200 warriors, Powhatan had little to fear at first from the struggling English outpost. After an initial skirmish with English soldiers, he sent gifts of food, assuming that by accepting the gifts, the colonists acknowledged their dependence on him. Further action against the settlers seemed unnecessary, since they seemed fully capable of destroying themselves.

This conclusion was premature. Armed colonists began to seize corn from Indian villages whenever the natives refused to supply it voluntarily. During one raid in 1609, John Smith held a pistol to the chest of Opechancanough, Powhatan's younger brother, until the Indians ransomed him with loads of corn. Protesting that the English came "to invade my people and possesse my Country," Powhatan laid siege to Jamestown and tried to starve the colony to extinction. The colony was saved only by the timely arrival of reinforcements from England, but war with the Indians continued until 1614.

The marriage of the colonist John Rolfe to Pocahontas, Powhatan's daughter, helped seal the peace in 1614. Pocahontas had briefly been held captive by the English during the war and had been instructed in English manners and religion by Rolfe. Sent to negotiate with Powhatan in the spring of 1614, Rolfe asked the chief for his daughter's hand. Powhatan gave his consent, and Pocahontas—baptized in the Church of England and renamed Rebecca—became Rolfe's wife.

Powhatan died in 1618, and Opechancanough succeeded him as chief. Still harboring intense resentment against the English, the new chief made plans to retaliate against them. Pocahontas had died on a trip to England in 1617, severing the tie between his family and the English. With new settlers arriving each year and the ranks of his warriors depleted by the ravages of European diseases, he could not wait long to act. Early in the morning on March 22, 1622, hundreds of Indian men traveled to the scattered English settlements, as if they meant to visit or trade. Instead they attacked the unsuspecting colonists, killing 347 by the end of the day—more than one-fourth of the English population.

Opechancanough assumed that the survivors would flee to England, but instead they gathered to plot revenge. Believing that "now we have just cause to destroy them by all meanes possible," English forces struck at native villages, killing the inhabitants and burning cornfields. During peace talks held in April 1623, the English served poisoned wine to their enemies, killing two hundred more. During the ensuing nine years of war, the English treated the Indians with a ferocity that recalled their earlier subjugation of the Irish.

Although Opechancanough's attack failed to dislodge the colonists, it destroyed the Virginia Company. Economic activity ceased as settlers retreated to fortified garrisons. The company went bankrupt, and a royal commission investigating the 1622 surprise attack was shocked to discover that nearly ten times more colonists had died from starvation and disease than at the hands of Indians. King James had little choice but to dissolve the company in 1624 and Virginia became a royal colony the following year. The settlers continued to enjoy a measure of self-government through the House of Burgesses, but now the king chose the colony's governor and council, and royal advisers monitored its affairs.

Tobacco Colony

Ironically, the demise of the Virginia Company helped the colony succeed. In their search for a marketable product, some settlers had begun growing tobacco after 1610. Europeans had acquired a taste for tobacco in the late sixteenth century when the Spanish brought samples from the West Indies and Florida. Initially expensive, it became popular among wealthy consumers. The high price appealed to Virginians, but they found that native Virginia leaf was of poor quality. John Rolfe began experimenting with seeds from Trinidad, which did much better. The first cargo of Virginia-grown tobacco arrived in England in 1617 and sold at a highly profitable 3 shillings per pound.

Following Rolfe's success, settlers immediately planted tobacco everywhere—even in the streets of Jamestown. Company officials, unwilling to base the colony's economy on a single crop, especially one that many people (including King James) considered to be an unhealthy indulgence, tried to restrict annual production to 100 pounds per colonist. Colonists, busy "rooting in the ground about Tobacco like Swine" as one observer reported, ignored these restrictions. But it was only after company rule ended that tobacco planting really surged.

Between 1627 and 1669, tobacco exports climbed from 250,000 pounds to more than 15 million pounds. As the supply grew, the price plunged from 13 pence in 1624 to a mere penny in the late 1660s, where it remained for the next half century. What had once been a luxury product thus became affordable for Europeans of average means. Now thoroughly dependent on tobacco for their livelihood, the only way colonists could compensate for falling prices was to grow even more, pushing exports to England to more than 20 million pounds by the late 1670s (see Figure 2-2).

Tobacco shaped nearly every aspect of Virginia society, from patterns of settlement to the recruitment of colonists. Planters scrambled to claim lands near

This eighteenth-century label for Virginia tobacco depicts an Indian smoker on the right. To the left is an African slave. For most of the seventeenth century, white indentured servants predominated among Virginia's laborers, but a transition to African slaves began to occur in the 1680s.

navigable rivers so that ships could easily reach their plantations and carry their crops to market. As a result, the colonists dispersed across the countryside instead of gathering in towns. People settled, one governor wrote, wherever "a choice veine of rich ground invited them, and further from neighbours the better." Colonists competed to produce the biggest and best crop and get it to market the fastest, hoping to enjoy even a small price advantage over everyone else.

The key to success was to control a large labor force. Tobacco kept workers busy nine months of the year. Planters sowed seeds in the early spring, transplanted seedlings a few weeks later, and spent the summer pinching off the tops of the plants (so they would produce larger leaves) and removing worms. After the harvest, the leaves were "cured"—dried in ventilated sheds—and packed in large barrels. During the winter, planters cleared and fenced more land and made barrels for next year's crop. Working on his

own, one planter could tend two thousand plants, which yielded about 500 pounds of cured tobacco. Early on, when the price was high, this supplied a comfortable income. But as the price plummeted, planters could keep up only by producing more tobacco, and to do that, they urgently needed help.

To secure that help, the planters turned to England, importing thousands of **indentured servants**, or contract workers, who agreed to a fixed term of labor, usually four to seven years, in exchange for free passage to Virginia. The master provided food, shelter, clothing, and, at the end of the term of service, "freedom dues" paid in corn and clothing. Between 1625 and 1640, an estimated one thousand or more indentured servants arrived each year. Some were orphans; others were condemned criminals given a choice between execution and transportation to Virginia. The vast majority, however, came from the ranks of England's unemployed, who emigrated in hopes of "bettering their condition in a Growing Country."

Most found such hopes quickly dashed. Servants died in alarming numbers from disease, and those who survived faced years of backbreaking labor. Masters squeezed as much work out of them as possible with long hours and harsh discipline. Some servants died from mistreatment. Richard Price beat his servant, Endymion Inleherne, for "being a common runaway and one that did use to feign himself sick" so severely that the young man died. A jury refused to charge Price with murder, reasoning that Inleherne deserved punishment and Price had not intended to kill him. Few masters matched Price's cruelty, but because the courts (administered by masters) favored masters' authority over servants' rights, those who did generally escaped prosecution.

New obstacles faced servants who managed to survive their terms of indenture. For every ex-servant who made it into the ranks of Virginia landholders, dozens died in poverty. To prevent them from becoming economic rivals and further glutting the tobacco market, established planters avoided selling good land to freed servants, particularly after tobacco prices hit bottom in the 1660s. Many ex-servants could find farms only in parts of the colony that were less suitable for tobacco cultivation and more vulnerable to Indian attack. Forced to choose between eking a "poor living with hard labor out of the ground in a terrible Wilderness" or giving up all hope for ownership and either becoming tenants or laborers, ex-servants were a discontented group. In 1675, their discontent would flare into rebellion (discussed in Chapter 3).

By 1660, no one doubted that Virginia would survive, but few could have predicted how much it would differ from England. Because of their

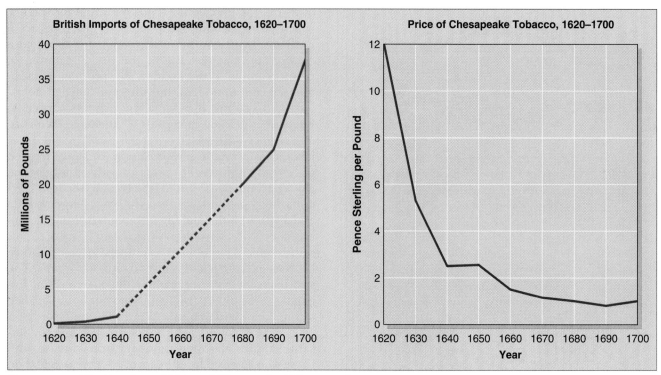

Figure 2-2   The Supply and Price of Chesapeake Tobacco, 1620–1700
*Tobacco cultivation dominated the economy of the Chesapeake region throughout the
seventeenth century. As planters brought more and more land under cultivation, the amount
of tobacco exported to Britain shot up and the price plummeted. (As the dashed line indicates,
no data on tobacco imports are available for the years 1650–1670.)*
Source: *Data from Russell R. Menard, "The Tobacco Industry in the Chesapeake Colonies, 1617–1730:
An Interpretation," Research in Economic History, 5 (1980), app.*

labor needs, masters favored young men in their teens and twenties as indentured servants, importing three or four times as many of them as women. As a result, Virginia's population in the seventeenth century was overwhelmingly young and male. Even in 1700, Virginia probably had three English men for every two women. Thus many free male servants found that marriage was as remote a possibility as landownership. Unlike Canadian men, very few Virginians chose Indian wives. John Rolfe's union with Pocahontas was one of only three English-Indian marriages recorded in seventeenth-century Virginia.

Few marriages meant few children. Population growth was further slowed because servants could not marry until their indentures were completed. Many men were already in their thirties when they married, usually to women in their early twenties. Older couples had fewer children than younger couples would have had. Disease also struck with depressing regularity. Few colonists lived past 50, and many of their offspring died young. Children who survived had usually lost one or both parents by the time they reached adulthood. The experience of the Chowning family was scarcely unusual. When Robert Chowning (just 15 when he lost

his own father) died in 1698, he left seven children ranging in age from 14 to 2. His eldest son, in turn, left six children under the age of 14 when he died in 1721.

Such conditions strained family ties but did not destroy them. Surviving spouses remarried quickly, often to a widow or widower with children, creating complex households with stepparents and half-brothers and half-sisters. Widows attracted great interest because they controlled property left to them by their husbands, assuming the normally male responsibility of managing estates for their children's benefit. When she remarried, a widow tried to choose a new spouse wisely, for he would generally take over management of the property that the children of her first marriage would inherit.

The slow rate of natural increase meant that population growth in Virginia resulted mostly from immigration. Even so, the number of settlers rose from about 2,500 in 1630 to 21,000 in 1660, thanks to the demand for indentured servants. This larger population was less vulnerable to Indian attacks. Opechancanough launched another raid in 1644 that killed nearly five hundred colonists, but this had a far less devastating effect than his attack of 1622 because the settler population had grown so much and now outnumbered the Indians.

If the balance of power had shifted to the colonists by midcentury, their lives were still far from easy. Some settlers acquired large estates and grew wealthy from the labor of indentured servants tilling their tobacco fields. Others, cultivating small land-holdings or renting plots from more successful colonists, grew just enough food to survive and as much tobacco as they could manage. But even the most successful settlers, investing every penny of profit in labor and land, lived under quite primitive conditions.

Early colonial dwellings were often no larger than 16 by 20 feet, with one or two rooms. Only at the end of the seventeenth century did prosperous planters begin to construct grander houses with as many as ten rooms. The poorest settlers slept on the floor on straw mattresses and had few other furnishings. In some counties, fewer than half of poor residents owned tables, and many had no chairs or benches to sit on. Even among middling planters, amenities were few: bedsheets, tablecloths, brass cookware, curtains. Rich planters owned more goods, though often of poor quality. In 1655, for instance, William Brocas, a prominent colonial official, owned "a parcell of old hangings, very thin and much worn"; seven chairs, "most of them unusefull"; and seven guns, "most unfixt." Servants and poor colonists had no choice but to accept crude living conditions. Their more fortunate neighbors tolerated discomfort in order to invest in family estates where their descendants might live in greater luxury.

Maryland

Virginia's success encouraged the English to consider further colonization of the Chesapeake Bay region. In 1632, King Charles I granted 10 million acres of land north of the bay to the nobleman George Calvert, Lord Baltimore. Unlike Virginia, which was founded by a joint-stock company, Maryland was a **proprietary colony**—the sole possession of Calvert and his heirs. They owned all the land, which they could divide up as they pleased, and had the right to set up the colony's government.

Calvert, who was Catholic, intended Maryland to be a refuge for others of his faith. When Queen Elizabeth's accession ensured that England would be a Protestant nation, Catholics became a disadvantaged minority. They paid double taxes, could not worship in public or hold political office, and could not send their children to universities. In Maryland, Calvert wanted Catholic colonists to enjoy economic and political power. He intended to divide the land into manors—large private estates like those of medieval England—and distribute them to wealthy Catholic friends. These manor lords would live on rents col-

lected from tenant farmers, hold the most important governmental offices, and run their own law courts.

Calvert died before settlement began, and it was the sad fate of his son, Cecilius, to see his father's plans unravel. The majority of colonists, who began arriving in 1634, were Protestants who despised Catholics. Refusing to live as tenants on Catholic estates, they claimed land of their own—a process that accelerated after 1640, when Maryland adopted a head-right system like Virginia's as a way to recruit settlers.

Maryland's problems intensified when civil war broke out in England in 1642. For years, political and religious disputes had divided the nation. Charles I, who became king in 1625, clashed with Protestants who called for further reform of the Church of England. He also antagonized many government leaders by dissolving Parliament in 1629 and ruling on his own for eleven years. Needing funds to suppress a rebellion in Scotland in 1640, however, Charles was forced to recall Parliament, which quickly turned against him. Both king and Parliament recruited armies and went to war in 1642. Parliamentary forces triumphed, and in 1649, they executed Charles. For the next decade, England was governed as a protectorate, not a monarchy. Oliver Cromwell, a general, ruled until his death in 1658. His son, Richard, proved an inept successor, however, and in 1660 a group of army officers invited Charles's exiled son to accept the throne.

During the 1640s and 1650s, Maryland Protestants took advantage of the upheaval in England to contest the Calverts' control of the colony. To pacify them, Cecilius Calvert established a legislature, assuming that Protestants would dominate the elective lower house while he could appoint Catholics to the upper house, or council. In 1649, Calvert also approved the **Act for Religious Toleration**, the first law in America to call for freedom of worship for all Christians, but even this measure brought no peace. The Protestant majority, supported during the 1650s by Cromwell and Parliament, continued to resist Catholic political influence, at one point passing a law that prohibited Catholics from voting.

Instead of the peaceful Catholic refuge Calvert intended, Maryland soon resembled neighboring Virginia. Its settlers raised tobacco and imported as many indentured servants as possible. Because Maryland initially provided former servants with 50 acres of land, more of them than in Virginia made it into the ranks of landholders. As in Virginia, however, economic opportunity diminished after 1660 when the price of tobacco dropped. Maryland's settlers enjoyed more peaceful relations with the Indians among whom they settled than Virginians had, but they fought intensely among themselves. Throughout the seventeenth century, Protestants kept up their opposition to the proprietor's control of land and political power and resisted all attempts by Catholics to govern the colony that was supposed to have been theirs.

The Founding of New England

The first English attempt to settle the northeastern coast of North America, what would soon be called New England, was a miserable failure. In 1607, the same year that the Virginia Company founded Jamestown, the Plymouth Company sent two ships with 120 Englishmen (and one Indian captive from an earlier raid) to found a colony at the mouth of the Sagadahoc River in present-day Maine. The would-be colonists alienated the Abenaki Indians who lived there, suffered through a harsh winter, and abandoned their settlement the next summer. But English explorers and fishermen continued to visit New England, among them John Smith, who published his book extolling its virtues as a site for colonization in 1616. Not long after, the English renewed their efforts to settle New England.

Six colonies appeared in the region between 1620 and 1640, settled by thousands of people troubled by religious, political, and economic upheavals in England. The society these settlers created differed markedly from the one developing in the Chesapeake—not least of all in the absence of significant Indian opposition. Between 1616 and 1618—just before any of these colonies was founded—a terrible epidemic swept through coastal New England, killing up to 90 percent of the Indians living there. The devastated survivors were unable to prevent the encroaching English from building towns where their villages had once stood.

The Pilgrims and Plymouth Colony

Plymouth Colony, the first of the New England settlements, was founded in 1620. Its origins lay in religious disputes that had plagued England since the late sixteenth century. Most of Queen Elizabeth's subjects approved of her efforts to keep England a Protestant nation, but some reformers believed that she had not sufficiently rid the Church of England of Catholic practices. The enemies of these reformers, ridiculing them for wanting to purify the Church of England (or **Anglican** Church) of all corruption, called them **Puritans**.

Following the doctrine of predestination taught by John Calvin and other Protestant reformers, English Puritans believed in an all-powerful God who, at the moment of Creation, had determined which humans would be saved and which would be damned. They held that salvation came through faith alone, not good works, and urged believers to seek a direct, personal relationship with God. The centerpiece of their spiritual life was conversion: the transforming experience that occurred when individuals felt the stirrings of grace in their souls and began to hope that they were among the saved. Those who experienced conversion were considered **saints** and acquired new strength to live godly lives.

Puritans objected to Anglican practices that, they felt, interfered with conversion and the believer's relationship with God. They rejected the Book of Common Prayer, which regulated Anglican worship, insisting that ministers should pray from the heart and preach from the Bible. They objected when Anglican clergy wore rich vestments that set them apart from ordinary Christians. And they objected to any church organization above the level of individual congregations, seeing no need for bishops and archbishops. But what they hated most of all about the Anglican Church was that anyone could be a member. Puritans believed that everyone should attend church services, but they wanted church membership—which conferred the right to partake in the Lord's Supper, or communion—to be limited to saints who had experienced conversion.

Puritans thus insisted on further reform. Elizabeth and the rulers who followed her—who as monarchs were the "supreme heads" of the Church of England—disagreed and tried to silence them. James I viewed the Puritans' demands as a challenge to his authority and threatened to "harry them out of the land." Some Puritans, known as **separatists**, were convinced that the Church of England would never change and left it to form their own congregations. One such group, mainly artisans and middling farmers from the village of Scrooby, in Nottinghamshire, became the core of Plymouth Colony.

The Scrooby separatists, seeking a religious environment more tolerant of their beliefs, left England in 1607–1608, settling for more than a decade in Holland. There they worshiped in peace, but many of them struggled to make a living and feared that their children were being tempted by the worldly pleasures of Dutch city life. Some of the Scrooby separatists contemplated moving to America. They gained the backing of the Plymouth Company, which was eager to make another colonization attempt after the Sagadahoc failure. Called **Pilgrims** because they thought of themselves as spiritual wanderers, they were joined by other separatists and by nonseparatist "strangers" hired to help get the colony started. In all, 102 men, women, and children set sail on the *Mayflower* in September 1620.

After a long and miserable voyage, they landed near Massachusetts Bay. Since this was about 200 miles north of the land their charter permitted them to settle, some of the "strangers" claimed that they were no longer legally bound to obey the expedition's separatist leaders. The leaders responded by drafting the **Mayflower Compact** and urging all adult males to sign it. The Compact set out the terms for governing the new colony, and became the first document to establish self-government in North America.

The Pilgrims settled at Plymouth, the site of a Wampanoag village recently depopulated by disease. William Bradford, a Pilgrim leader and Plymouth's governor for many years, would later note that they were surprised to find abandoned cornfields, a clearing "where lately a house had been," Indian graves, and baskets of corn buried underground. Although it helped feed them for a while, this corn was not enough to prevent the Pilgrims from suffering their first winter through a terrible "starving time" that left nearly half of them dead.

When two natives, Squanto and Samoset, emerged from the woods the next spring and began speaking English, the surviving Pilgrims marveled at them as "special instruments sent of God." Samoset had learned English from traders, and Squanto had learned it in England, where he lived for a time after being kidnapped by a sea captain. The two men approached the Pilgrims on behalf of Massasoit, the Wampanoag leader. Although suspicious of the newcomers, the Wampanoags were too few to threaten them and thought the Pilgrims might be useful allies against Wampanoag enemies, such as the Narragansetts, who had escaped the recent epidemics.

In 1621, the Wampanoags and the Pilgrims signed a treaty of alliance, although each side (working through translators) understood its terms differently. The Pilgrims assumed that Massasoit had submitted to the superior authority of King James, whereas Massasoit assumed that the agreement treated himself and the English king as equal partners. Despite frequent disputes caused by English assertion of authority over the Wampano-ags, the two groups enjoyed relatively peaceful relations for nearly half a century.

Economic ties strengthened the alliance. The Indians taught the English how to plant corn and traded corn with them for manufactured goods. The Pilgrims also exchanged corn with other Indians to the north for furs, which they shipped back to England to help pay off their debts to English investors. In the autumn of 1621, Indians and Pilgrims gathered for a feast celebrating the settlers' first harvest—an event Americans still commemorate as the first Thanksgiving.

Plymouth remained small, poor, and weak. It never grew to more than seven thousand settlers and never produced more than small shipments of furs, fish, and timber to sell in England. It took the Pilgrims more than twenty years to repay their English creditors. Yet because of the idealistic visions of the founders of Plymouth Colony, who saw in the New World a chance to escape religious persecution and create peaceful communities and pure churches, it has become an important symbol in American history. It was soon overshadowed, however, by the larger and more powerful colony of Massachusetts Bay.

Historians and archaeologists have reconstructed what the English settlement at Plymouth Colony may have looked like in 1627. Trained interpreters, such as the man working in the garden here, offer visitors information about early New England life. When colonists cut down large sections of forest for wood to build their houses and fences, they reduced the hunting lands available to local Indians.

Massachusetts Bay Colony and Its Offshoots

The Puritans who settled Massachusetts shared many of the Pilgrims' beliefs—with one important exception. They insisted that the Anglican Church *could* be reformed and so were not separatists. When they went to New England, it was to create godly churches to serve as models for English reform. And England, they believed, was in more desperate need of reformation than ever.

Charles I, who became king in 1625, opposed Puritans more forcefully than his father had and supported changes in Anglican worship that recalled Catholic practices. England at the time was also suffering from economic troubles—including crop failures and a depression in the wool industry—that many Puritans saw as signs of God's displeasure with their country, intended to encourage them to move to the New World.

In 1629, a group of Puritan merchants received a royal charter for a joint-stock enterprise, the Massachusetts Bay Company, to set up a colony north of Plymouth. They chose John Winthrop, a prosperous Puritan lawyer, as their leader. In the spring of 1630, a fleet of eleven ships carried about a thousand men, women, and children across the Atlantic.

Before Winthrop's ship landed, he preached a lay sermon, called "A Model of Christian Charity," to his fellow passengers, describing his vision of the society they were about to create. The governor reminded them of their goal "to do more service to the Lord." They should "love one another with a pure heart" and place the good of all above private ambitions. Winthrop argued that the Lord had made them his chosen people—and that as a result, "we shall be as a city upon a hill, the eyes of all people are upon us." If they failed to live up to God's expectations, he would punish them, and the spectacle of their failure would allow their enemies "to speak evil of the ways of God." With this mingled encouragement and threat ringing in their ears, the emigrants set about establishing their colony. Within a few months of their landing, they founded Boston and six adjoining towns.

Winthrop described the settlers' mission in New England as a **covenant**, or contract, with God, binding them to meet their religious obligations in return for God's favor. The settlers also created covenants to define their duties to one another. When they founded towns, colonists signed covenants agreeing to live together in peace. The settlers of Dedham, for example, agreed to "walk in a peaceable conversation with all meekness of spirit," seeking "the good of each other." Worshipers in the church each town was required by law to have likewise wrote covenants binding themselves to live in harmony.

The desire for peace and purity could breed intolerance. Settlers closely scrutinized their neighbors for signs of unacceptable behavior. Standards for church membership were strict; only those who could prove they were saints by describing their conversion experiences were admitted. But the insistence on covenants and conformity also created a remarkably stable society, far more peaceable than Virginia's.

That stability was enhanced by the development of representative government. Colony leaders in effect translated the charter of the Massachusetts Bay Company into a plan of government, a process completed by 1634. The **General Court**, which initially included only the shareholders of the joint-stock company, was transformed into a two-house legislature. Freemen—adult males who held property and were church members—had the right to elect representatives (two per town) to the lower house, as well as eighteen members (called "assistants") to the upper house. They also chose a governor and a deputy governor.

Between 1630 and 1642—when the outbreak of the English Civil War halted emigration—at least thirteen thousand settlers came to New England and established dozens of towns. The progress of settle-

John Winthrop (1588–1649) served as the Massachusetts Bay Colony's governor for most of its first two decades. Throughout his life, Winthrop—like many fellow Puritans—struggled to live a godly life in a corrupt world.

Courtesy, American Antiquarian Society.

ment was generally untroubled in coastal Massachusetts, but when colonists moved into the distant Connecticut River Valley, tensions with Indians grew rapidly. These erupted in 1637 in the brief, tragic conflict called the **Pequot War.**

English settlers from Massachusetts first arrived in the Connecticut Valley in the mid-1630s. The migration accelerated in 1636 when the Reverend Thomas Hooker led part of his congregation from Cambridge, Massachusetts, to what soon became Hartford. The new arrivals found themselves in a dangerous situation. Dutch traders already in the region had been dealing exclusively with the Pequot Indians as partners. In 1633, however, they built an outpost near the site of Hartford and invited other Indian groups to trade with them. The Pequots, suffering terribly from a recent smallpox epidemic, resented losing their special trading rights and began fighting the Dutch. Initially, they saw the new English settlers as potential allies against the Dutch. But when the settlers demanded Pequot submission to English authority as the price of an alliance, they turned against them too in a struggle to retain their control over the land and trade of eastern Connecticut.

The English settlers formed alliances with the Narragansetts and Mohegans, who were both rivals of the Pequots. Together they overwhelmed the Pequots in an astonishingly bloody war. In May 1637, English forces surrounded a Pequot village inhabited mainly by women and children, located on the Mystic River. They set it ablaze and shot anyone who tried to escape. Between three hundred and seven hundred Pequots died, a toll that shocked the settlers' Indian allies, who protested that English-style warfare was "too furious, and slays too many men" (see "American Views: Miantonomo's Plea for Indian Unity").

The English, for their part, marveled that God had given them "so speedy a victory over so proud and insulting an enemy." After the surviving Pequots had fled or been sold into slavery, many more settlers moved to Connecticut, which soon declared itself a separate colony. In 1639, the settlers adopted the **Fundamental Orders**, creating a government similar to that of Massachusetts, and the English government granted them a royal charter in 1662.

Massachusetts spun off other colonies as its population expanded in the 1630s and dissenters ran afoul of its intolerant government. Puritan leaders tried to suppress unorthodox religious opinions whenever they emerged, for fear that God would interpret their failure to do so as a breach of their covenant with him. Officials also worried that a lack of religious unity in Massachusetts would lead to constant disputes over matters of faith. Some dissenting colonists, however, refused to be silenced.

Roger Williams, who founded Rhode Island, was one such irrepressible dissenter. Williams was a separatist minister who declared that because Massachusetts churches had not rejected the Church of England, they shared its corruption. He opposed government interference in religious affairs—such as laws requiring settlers to attend worship services—and argued for the separation of church and state. Williams even attacked the Massachusetts charter, insisting that the king had no right to grant Indian lands to English settlers.

Despite his fiery opinions, Williams was an immensely likable man—even Governor Winthrop remained on friendly terms with him and tried to persuade him to change his views. But when Williams refused to be silenced, the General Court sentenced him to banishment, intending to ship him back to England. But in the winter of 1635, Williams slipped away and followed Winthrop's advice to "steer my course to Narragansett Bay." There he and a few followers found refuge among the Narragansett Indians, from whom he purchased land for the village of Providence, founded in 1636. More towns soon sprang up nearby when a new religious crisis, provoked by a woman named Anne Hutchinson, sent additional refugees to Rhode Island from Massachusetts.

Anne Hutchinson arrived in Boston from England with her husband and seven children in 1634. Welcomed by the town's women for her talents as a midwife, she also began to hold religious meetings in her house. During these meetings, she denounced several ministers, who had taught worshipers that there were certain spiritual exercises they could perform that might prepare them for sainthood. Hutchinson insisted that there was nothing humans could do to encourage God to make them saints. She implied that any minister who taught otherwise might not be a saint himself, in which case he had no authority over the true saints in his church.

Many people, including prominent Boston merchants, flocked to Hutchinson's meetings. But her critics believed her to be a dangerous **antinomian** (someone who claimed to be free from obedience to moral law) because she seemed to maintain that saints were accountable only to God and not to any worldly authority. Her opponents also objected to her teaching of mixed groups of men and women. Governor Winthrop complained that such behavior was neither "comely in the sight of God nor fitting for your sex." This comment suggests that Hutchinson's breach of normal gender roles, which placed women subordinate to men, upset him as much as her religious views did. Colony magistrates arrested her and tried her for sedition—that is, for advocating the overthrow of the government.

American Views

MIANTONOMO'S PLEA FOR INDIAN UNITY (1642)

Until European colonization began to force a change in outlook, the native inhabitants of North America never thought of themselves as one people, any more than Europe's residents considered themselves "Europeans." Miantonomo, a Narragansett living in Rhode Island, was one of the first native leaders to call for a unified response to English intrusion. With the gruesome lessons of the Pequot War fresh in his mind, he urged the Montauks of Long Island to put aside their differences with the Narragansetts and join them in opposing the settlers. His appeal, recorded by Lion Gardiner, an English officer during the Pequot War, was uttered in vain. Captured by the English and tried and convicted of the murder of an Indian, Miantonomo was turned over to a Mohegan rival for execution.

❖ **How did Miantonomo describe Indian life before the arrival of the English?**

❖ **What changes occurred as a result of their settlement?**

Brothers, we must be as one as the English are, or we shall all be destroyed. You know our fathers had plenty of deer and skins and our plains were full of game and turkeys, and our coves and rivers were full of fish.

But, brothers, since these Englishmen have seized our country, they have cut down the grass with scythes, and the trees with axes. Their cows and horses eat up the grass, and their hogs spoil our bed of clams; and finally we shall all starve to death; therefore, stand not in your own light, I ask you, but resolve to act like men. All the sachems both to the east and the west have joined with us, and we are resolved to fall upon them at a day appointed, and therefore I come secretly to you, [be]cause you can persuade your Indians to do what you will.

Source: *Steven Mintz, ed.*, Native American Voices: A History and Anthology *(1995), pp. 84–85.*

During her trial, Hutchinson mounted a lively defense. When asked to explain her views, she reminded her opponents of their objections to her teaching and asked them, "Why do you call me to teach the court?" In the end, however, the court found her guilty and banished her from the colony. With many of her followers, she moved to Rhode Island, where Roger Williams had proclaimed a policy of religious toleration. Other followers returned to England or moved north to what became in 1679 the separate colony of New Hampshire.

At the height of the Hutchinson controversy, a group of zealous Puritan emigrants led by the Reverend John Davenport arrived in Boston. Appalled by the religious turmoil, they departed for the coast of Long Island Sound, where they founded New Haven in 1638. Davenport's efforts to impose perfect Puritan conformity in his colony made Massachusetts seem easygoing in comparison. But New Haven failed to thrive, and in 1662, the poor, intolerant, and isolated colony was absorbed into Connecticut.

The Growth of New England

"This plantation and that of Virginia went not forth upon the same reasons," declared one of Massachusetts's founders. Virginians came "for profit," whereas New Englanders emigrated to bear witness to their Puritan faith. They too hoped for economic prosperity but believed that it would come only if God blessed their efforts to create a godly society. Most New England settlers arrived in the brief span between the founding of Massachusetts in 1630 and 1642, when the outbreak of the English Civil War engaged Puritans to stay at home and fight on Parliament's behalf against the king. Unlike the unmarried young men who moved in great numbers to Virginia, most New Englanders settled with their families; this had important implications for the development of New England society.

John and Anne Moulton were representative of many of New England's young immigrant couples. Both 38 years old, they brought five children (aged 3 to 14) with them from England. Like most settlers, the Moultons were neither rich nor poor. John had been a farmer in England and was wealthy enough to pay his family's passage and set himself up on a New England farm. At the time of the voyage, Anne was pregnant with her sixth child and gave birth shortly after arriving in Massachusetts. Three years later, with the family settled in the town of Hampton (now located in New Hampshire), she bore another daughter.

The average family in early New England, like the Moultons, had seven or eight children. Because women and men arrived in nearly equal numbers, young adults easily found spouses and produced more children. Thus the population continued to grow rapidly even when immigration slowed after 1642, so that by 1660, New England's settlers numbered more than 33,000. Again the experience of the Moulton family is instructive. Henry Moulton, John and Anne's eldest son, was 28—younger than many husbands in early Virginia—when he married Sobriety Hilton, a neighbor's daughter. Together they added six more children to New England's population.

New Englanders—and the family ties that knitted their society together—were also largely spared from the diseases that ravaged Virginia's settlers and devastated Indian populations. Henry and Sobriety Moulton, like many of their neighbors, lived into their eighties and saw their grandchildren grow up. It seemed a "marvelous providence of God" to Plymouth's Governor Bradford that so many settlers made it to their seventies and eighties when few of England's adults lived past 60. Longevity strengthened economic security as well as emotional ties. Fathers lived long enough to build prosperous farms to pass along to their sons. And they accumulated herds of livestock and stores of household goods to give to their daughters when they married.

Unlike Chesapeake colonists, who spread out on tobacco lands near navigable rivers, New Englanders clustered in towns. The Massachusetts government strongly encouraged town formation by granting tracts

of land to groups of families who promised to settle together. Once they received a grant, the families in a group divided it among themselves, allotting each family a farm of sufficient size to support all its members. Social distinctions were maintained, however, with people who had had higher standing in England receiving larger farms than those of lower standing. Land that the original families could not yet farm was held "in common" to be distributed to their children as they grew up. Settlers generally remained in their chosen towns for the rest of their lives. Grown children, inheriting parental estates and finding spouses nearby, often settled in the same community as their parents.

Towns—usually made up of fifty to a hundred families—were the focus of New England life, providing the context for religious, political, and economic activity. The importance Puritans placed on worship with fellow Christians helped promote community feeling. Every Sunday, townspeople gathered at the meetinghouse, usually located near the town center, to listen to the minister preach God's word. Here church members heard their neighbors describe their experiences of conversion and decided whether to admit them.

At other times, the meetinghouse served as a town hall, where men assembled to discuss matters ranging from local taxes to making sure that everyone's fences were mended. Massachusetts law required towns with at least fifty families to support a school (so children could learn to read the Bible), and at town meetings, men often wrangled over the choice of a schoolmaster and what salary to pay him. Townsmen tried to reach decisions by consensus in order to preserve harmony. To oversee day-to-day local affairs, men chose five to seven of their most trusted neighbors to serve as **selectmen**. Each town could also elect two men to represent it in the colony legislature. Many a town neglected to do so, however, either because its citizens could not afford to pay the men's expenses or because they lacked interest in outside political affairs.

Economic life likewise centered on the town. New England's stony soil and short growing season offered few ways to get rich, but even "the poorest person . . . hath a house and land of his own, and bread of his own growing." Farmers grew corn and other foods and raised livestock to feed their families, selling or trading what they could not use. Their goal was to achieve what they called **competency**—the possession of enough property to ensure their families' economic independence.

Maintaining competency was a family affair. Without a staple crop like tobacco to sell in an international market, New England farmers lacked resources to hire indentured servants and relied instead on their wives and children for labor. Women cared for children, cleaned, cooked, sewed and mended, milked cows, and tended poultry. Many farmwives made butter and cheese, brewed beer, preserved fruits and vegetables, salted meat, spun yarn, and wove cloth. Although they generally did not perform heavy agricultural work, women helped with planting and harvesting crops and tended gardens near their houses. If their husbands worked as merchants or craftsmen, wives might also help out in the shop.

Children undertook tasks appropriate to their age and sex, beginning work shortly after their fifth birthday. Older siblings cared for younger ones, fetched tools, and minded cattle. Around age 10, girls began learning more complicated housekeeping skills from their mothers, and boys received instruction from their fathers in such tasks as plowing, cutting hay and wood, and caring for livestock. Many children in their early teens performed tasks little different from adult duties. By the time Nathaniel Ingersoll of Salem, Massachusetts, was 11, he already knew how to handle a plow and ox team.

No family could produce all the goods that it needed, so New Englanders regularly traded with their neighbors. A skilled carpenter might erect a house—often larger and sturdier than the ramshackle dwellings of Chesapeake settlers—in return for barrels of salted beef. Men with several sons sent them to help neighbors whose children were too young to work. Midwives delivered babies in return for cheese or eggs. Women nursed sick neighbors, whom they might one day call on for similar help. These sorts of transactions allowed most New Englanders to enjoy a fairly comfortable life, one that many Virginians might have envied.

Without a staple crop like tobacco, New England prospered by exploiting a variety of resources, developing a diversified economy that was less vulnerable to depression than Virginia's. Farmers sent livestock and meat to merchants to be marketed abroad. Fishermen caught thousands of pounds of cod, haddock, and other fish to be sold in Europe. Some of the region's timber found its way abroad, but most of it ended up in shipyards. New Englanders became such skilled shipbuilders and seafaring merchants that by the 1670s, London merchants were complaining about competition from them. England itself had little use for the dried fish, livestock, salted meat, and wood products that New England vessels carried, but enterprising merchants found exactly the market they needed in the West Indies.

The English in the Caribbean

The Spanish claimed all Caribbean islands by right of Columbus's discovery, but during the early seventeenth century, French, Dutch, and English adventurers boldly defied them. By the 1640s, the English occupied Antigua, Barbados, Montserrat, Nevis, and St. Christopher; in 1655, they conquered the Spanish-held island of Jamaica (see Map 2-3). Although a few English efforts, including an attempt to found a Puritan colony on Providence Island off Nicaragua's coast, failed, the West Indies soon became the jewel of England's empire, producing vast wealth from the cultivation of sugar. Caribbean planters created a society totally unlike any of the mainland colonies—not least of all because their prosperity depended on the exploitation of African slaves.

Sugar and Slaves

Like the early Virginians, the first English colonists who came to the West Indies in the 1630s raised tobacco and imported indentured servants to work their fields. By that time, however, tobacco fetched low prices. Moreover, the disease environment of the West Indies proved even harsher than that of the Chesapeake, and settlers died in great numbers. That thousands came anyway during the 1620s and 1630s testified more to their hopes for prosperity than their actual chances of success.

Most New Englanders came in family groups, bringing many children with them. The lace and ribbons on the clothing of the Mason children, depicted in this 1670 portrait, suggest that they came from a well-to-do family. Like many seventeenth-century portraits, this one is rich in symbolism. The cane in David Mason's hand indicates his status as the male heir, while the rose held by his sister Abigail was a symbol of childhood innocence.

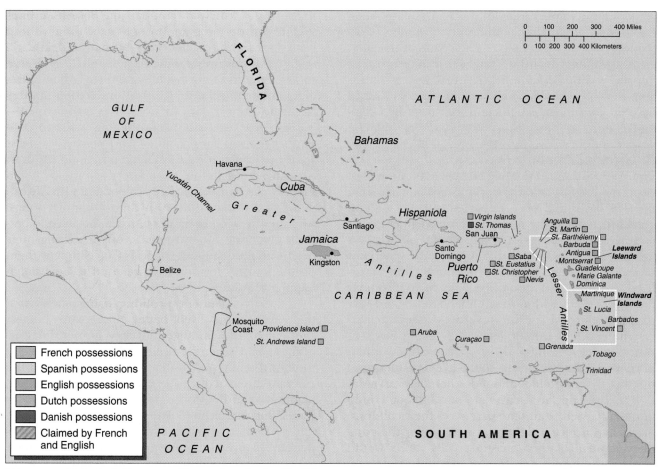

Map 2-3 Principal European Possessions in the Caribbean in the Seventeenth Century
Europeans scrambled for control of Caribbean islands, where they raised sugar cane with slave labor. On many islands, Africans soon formed the majority of the population. In some cases, colonists from one European country settled on lands claimed by a rival power. For instance, English settlers established bases in Belize and on the Mosquito Coast, both of which were claimed by Spain.

But by the 1640s, a Barbados planter boasted of "a great change on this island of late from the worse to the better, praised be God." That change was a shift from tobacco to sugar cane. How the English learned to grow sugar is unclear. Perhaps it was from English visitors to Portuguese sugar plantations in Brazil or from Dutch traders. However they learned, many sugar planters grew astonishingly wealthy. In 1646, a 500-acre plantation on Barbados sold for £16,000—more than the whole island had been worth just a few years before. On average, the estate of a Caribbean sugar planter was worth four times as much as a prosperous Chesapeake plantation.

Sugar rapidly transformed the West Indies. Planters deforested whole islands to raise sugar cane. They stopped planting food crops and raising livestock—thereby creating a demand for lumber and provisions that boosted New England's economy. In 1647, John Winthrop noted that Barbadians "had rather buy food at very dear rates than produce it by labor, so infinite is the profit of sugar works."

The sugar boom also led to a scramble for labor. Planters continued to import white indentured servants, including some kidnapped English and Irish youths, but soon turned to African slaves. The reasons for this decision were complex but hinged on the islands' unhealthy environment and the extremely harsh working conditions on sugar plantations. England could barely meet the demand for workers, and English workers, if they survived, often proved rebellious. English visitors who saw African slaves working on Brazilian plantations considered them more efficient, if more exotic, than English workers. Africans were already used to agricultural work in a tropical climate. And the English would not have to enslave any Africans themselves; they could simply import people who had already been enslaved by other Africans and sold to Dutch or Portuguese traders. The planters' choice has been called an "unthinking decision," but it had an enormous impact on English colonial life, first in the islands and then on the mainland, where slavery would develop later in the seventeenth century (see Chapter 3).

A Biracial Society

The West Indies had the first biracial plantation society in the English colonial world. By 1700, more than 250,000 slaves had been imported into the region, quickly becoming the most numerous segment of its population. In Barbados, for example, black slaves increased from 50 percent to more than 70 percent of the population between 1660 and 1700. Slaves lived in wretched conditions, underfed, poorly dressed, and housed in rough huts. They labored six days a week from sunrise to sunset—except at harvest time, when they toiled seven days a week in round-the-clock shifts. Masters considered them property, often branding them like livestock and hunting them with bloodhounds when they ran away.

Laws declared slavery to be a lifelong condition that passed from slave parents to their children. Slaves had no legal rights and were under the complete control of their masters. Only rarely would masters who killed slaves face prosecution, and those who did and were found guilty were subject only to fines. Slaves, in contrast, faced appalling punishments even for minor offenses. They could be whipped, branded, or maimed for stealing food or

harboring a runaway compatriot. Serious crimes such as murder or arson brought execution without trial. Slaves who rebelled were burned to death.

Astonishingly, slaves managed to preserve some elements of normal life and form communities even under these brutal conditions. When masters began to import African women as well as men—hoping to create a self-reproducing labor force—slaves began to form families and preserve at least some African traditions. They gave their children African names (although masters often gave them English names as well). They celebrated with African music and worked to the rhythm of familiar songs. And they drew on their West African heritage to perform elaborate funeral rituals, often burying their dead with food and other goods to accompany them on the journey to what they believed to be a much happier afterlife.

Some planters, profiting handsomely from their slaves' toil, lived better than many English gentlemen. They indulged in large houses, fine furnishings, and expensive clothing. Even so, many hated the hot, humid West Indian climate and feared the constant threat of disease. After making their fortunes, planters often fled to England, leaving their estates under the care of hired overseers.

But sugar made relatively few white colonists wealthy. Its production required a heavy investment in land, slaves, mills, and equipment. As great planters took vast amounts of land for themselves, freed servants and small farmers struggled to survive. After 1650, many of these poor men, looking for other places to live, headed for the mainland. They

Authentic portraits of West Indian slaves are extremely rare. These sketches of Jamaican slaves show them going about the mundane tasks of daily life.

were soon joined by planters looking for a place to expand their operations once most of the good land on the islands had been brought under cultivation.

form (Carolus) of the king's name. They envisioned it growing from the few English outposts already in the region, established by settlers from New England and the West Indies, into a prosperous, orderly society.

The Proprietary Colonies

The initial burst of English colonization ended in 1640 when England tottered on the brink of civil war. With the accession of Charles II to the English throne in 1660, however, interest in North American colonies revived. Charles II needed to reward the supporters who had remained loyal to him during his long exile in France. One of the easiest ways for him to do so was with grants of huge tracts of American land. Four new colonies—Carolina, Pennsylvania, New Jersey, and New York—resulted from such grants during his reign (1660–1685) (see Map 2-4). All were proprietary colonies, essentially the private property of the people to whom they had been given. Two of them—Carolina and Pennsylvania—like the earlier proprietary colony of Maryland, provided their owners the chance to test idealistic social visions. The origins of New York and New Jersey as English colonies, in contrast, lay not in proprietary visions of social harmony but in the stern reality of military conquest (see the summary table "English Colonies in the Seventeenth Century").

Early Carolina

In 1663, Charles II granted a group of supporters an enormous tract of land stretching from southern Virginia to northern Florida. The proprietors, who included several Barbados planters, called their colony Carolina, after the Latin

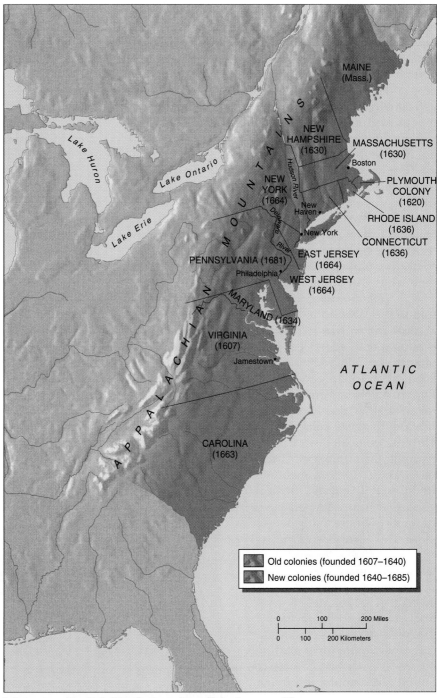

Map 2-4   *English North American Colonies, c. 1685*
After the restoration of Charles II in 1660, several large proprietary colonies joined earlier English settlements in New England and the Chesapeake. By 1685, a growing number of English settlers solidified England's claim to the Atlantic coast from Maine (then part of Massachusetts Bay Colony) to the southern edge of Carolina.

One of the proprietors, Anthony Ashley Cooper, working closely with his secretary, John Locke, devised the **Fundamental Constitutions of Carolina**, a plan to ensure the stability of the colony by balancing property ownership and political rights. It called for the creation of a colonial aristocracy, with three kinds of nobles, who would own two-fifths of the land and wield extensive political power. Below them, a large class of freeholders would own small farms and elect representatives to an assembly. At the bottom of the social order would be slaves.

This plan never went into effect. People moved in from Virginia and the West Indies and settled where they pleased. They even voted in the assembly to reject the Fundamental Constitutions. They also antagonized the Indians in the region, who numbered perhaps fifteen thousand when settlers first arrived. When English traders first appeared, eager to buy deerskins, many Indians had welcomed them. But they grew hostile when some traders began dealing in human flesh, selling guns to some tribes in exchange for captives from rival tribes the traders sold as slaves to the West Indies. Native resentments deepened as settlers moved onto their lands. The result was a deadly cycle of violence.

The colonists at first raised livestock to be sold to the West Indies. But the introduction of rice in Carolina in the 1690s transformed the settlers' economy, making it, as one planter noted, "as much their staple Commodity, as Sugar is to Barbadoes and Jamaica, or Tobacco to Virginia and Maryland." The English had never grown rice, but West Africans had raised it since the 1500s. Considering that rice cultivation in Carolina coincided with an increase in the number of African slaves there, they probably introduced it. Ironically, the profits earned from rice persuaded Carolina planters to invest even more heavily in slave labor.

Carolina society soon resembled the sugar islands from which many of its founders had come. By 1708, there were more black slaves than white settlers in the colony, and two decades after that, blacks outnumbered whites by two to one. Rice farming required a substantial investment in land, labor, and equipment, including dikes and dams for flooding fields. Those who could afford such an investment set themselves up as planters in Car-

olina's coastal rice district, acquiring large estates and forcing poorer settlers to move elsewhere.

Some of these dislocated men went to the northern part of Carolina, where the land and climate were unsuited to rice. There they raised tobacco and produced pitch, tar, and timber products from the region's pine forests. So different were the two regions that the colony formally split into two provinces—North and South Carolina—in 1729.

South Carolina rice planters became some of the wealthiest colonists on the mainland. But their luxurious style of life came at a price. As Carolina began to look "more like a negro country than like a country settled by white people," planters came to dread the prospect of slave rebellion. To avert this nightmare, they enacted slave codes as harsh as those of the sugar islands.

Although John Locke went on to become one of England's most important philosophers, the visionary plan he and Cooper had devised for Carolina disintegrated on contact with American conditions. Carolina would not be a harmonious colony that balanced wealth and power; it evolved instead into a racially divided society founded on the oppression of a black majority and permeated by fear.

Pennsylvania

Even as early Carolina diverged from the plans of its founders, another Englishman dreamed of creating a colonial utopia. William Penn put his plans into action in 1681, when Charles II granted him a huge tract of

Thomas Coram's oil painting (c. 1770) shows the main residence and slave quarters on the Mulberry Plantation near Charleston, South Carolina. The distinctive steep-roofed design of the slave cabins on the left probably reflects African building styles. Slave quarters may not have been located quite as close to the main house as this picture suggests.

SUMMARY

ENGLISH COLONIES IN THE SEVENTEENTH CENTURY

Colony	Date of Founding	Established Religion	Economy	Government
Virginia	1607	Anglican	Tobacco	Royal (after 1625)
Plymouth	1620	Puritan	Mixed farming	Corporate
St. Christopher	1624	Anglican	Sugar	Royal
Barbados	1627	Anglican	Sugar	Royal
Nevis	1628	Anglican	Sugar	Royal
Massachusetts (including present-day Maine)	1630	Puritan	Mixed farming, fishing, shipbuilding	Corporate
New Hampshire	1630 (first settlement, annexed to Mass. 1643–1679; royal colony after 1679)	Puritan	Mixed farming	Corporate (royal after 1679)
Antigua	1632	Anglican	Sugar	Royal
Monserrat	1632	Anglican	Sugar	Royal
Maryland	1634	None (Anglican after 1692)	Tobacco	Proprietary
Rhode Island	1636	None	Mixed farming	Corporate
Connecticut	1636	Puritan	Mixed farming	Corporate
New Haven	1638	Puritan	Mixed farming	Corporate
Jamaica	1655 (captured from Spanish)	Anglican	Sugar	Royal
Carolina	1663	Anglican	Rice	Proprietary
New York	1664 (captured from Dutch)	None	Mixed farming, furs	Proprietary (royal after 1685)
New Jersey	1664	None	Mixed farming	Proprietary
Pennsylvania	1681	None	Wheat, mixed farming	Proprietary

land north of Maryland as payment for a royal debt owed to Penn's father. Penn intended his colony to be a model of justice and peace, as well as a refuge for members of the Society of Friends, or **Quakers**, a persecuted religious sect to which Penn himself belonged.

The Society of Friends was one of many radical religious groups that emerged in England during the civil war. Like the separatists, Quakers abandoned the Church of England as hopelessly corrupt. But they went even further in their beliefs. Rejecting predestination, they maintained that every soul had a spark of grace and that salvation was possible for all who heeded that "Inner Light." They also rejected trained clergy and elaborate church rituals as unnecessary to salvation. Instead of formal religious services, Quakers held meetings at which silence reigned until someone, inspired by the Inner Light, rose to speak.

Quaker beliefs had disturbing social and political implications. Although they did not advocate complete equality of the sexes, Quakers granted women spiritual equality with men, allowing them to preach, hold separate prayer meetings, and exercise authority over "women's matters." Arguing that social distinctions were not the work of God, Quakers refused to defer to their betters. People of lower social rank were expected to remove their hats in the presence of superiors, but Quakers would not do so. And instead of the formal *you,* Quakers addressed superiors with the informal *thee* and *thou.* Because their faith required them to renounce the use of force, Quakers also refused to perform military service, which their enemies considered tantamount to treason.

When English authorities began harassing Quakers, William Penn (who was himself jailed briefly) conceived his plan for a New World refuge. He aimed to launch a "holy experiment," a harmonious society governed by brotherly love. Knowing that Quakers were unwelcome in the existing colonies—Massachusetts had hanged four of them—Penn looked elsewhere. His aristocratic background gave him advantages that other Quakers, who were mainly of humble origins, lacked. Using his father's connection with the king, he acquired the land that became Pennsylvania ("Penn's Woods") and recruited settlers from among Europe's oppressed peoples and persecuted religious sects. By 1700, eighteen thousand emigrants had left England, Wales, Scotland, Ireland, and various German provinces for the new colony.

Many came in families and settled in an area occupied by the Delaware Indians, whose numbers, though still substantial, had recently been reduced by disease and warfare. The "holy experiment" required colonists to live "as Neighbours and friends" with the Indians as well as with one another. Penn aimed to accomplish this by paying Indians for land and regulating trade. As long as Penn remained in control of the colony, relations between the settlers and the Indians were generally peaceful—so much so that refugee Indians from nearby colonies moved into Pennsylvania. Relations between Penn and the settlers, however, were less cordial.

In the **Frame of Government**, his constitution for Pennsylvania, Penn remained true to his Quaker principles with a provision allowing for religious freedom. But true to his aristocratic origins, he designed a legislature with limited powers and reserved considerable authority for himself. When Penn returned to England after a brief stay in the colony (1682–1684), the settlers immediately began squabbling among themselves. The governor and council—both appointed by Penn—fought with elected members of the assembly. Penn's opponents—many of whom were fellow Quakers—objected to his proprietary privileges, including his control of foreign trade and his collection of fees from landholders. Settlers on the lower Delaware River, which the crown had added to Penn's colony to give its port city, Philadelphia, access to the sea, gained autonomy for themselves with their own legislature, in effect creating an unofficial colony that later became Delaware.

A disappointed Penn lamented that the settlers had become "so brutish." He had spent his fortune on his beloved colony, only to die in debt with his hopes for a harmonious society dashed. Settlers continued to fight among themselves, and with Penn's heirs, after his death. A flood of increasingly aggressive immigrants undermined peaceful relations with the Indians, forcing many natives to abandon their homelands and move west.

By 1720, Pennsylvania's ethnically and religiously diverse population numbered more than thirty thousand. William Penn had marveled early on that the "earth by God's blessing has more than answered our expectation." Indeed, his colony had some of the richest farmland along the Atlantic coast and was soon widely known as the "best poor man's country in the world." Growing wheat and other crops, the settlers lived mostly on scattered farms rather than in towns. From the thriving port of Philadelphia—which William Penn had carefully designed to be a "green countrie town"—ships carried much of the harvest to markets in the West Indies and southern Europe. Penn's "holy experiment" in social harmony may have failed, but as a thriving colony, Pennsylvania itself succeeded handsomely.

New Netherlands Becomes New York

The proprietary colonies of New York and New Jersey originated as the Dutch colony of New Netherlands. By the early seventeenth century, the Dutch Republic had become the most powerful trading nation in Europe, with thousands of ships plying the world's oceans. New Netherlands was one of many outposts in its far-flung empire, which included others in the West Indies, Africa's Gold Coast, India, and Formosa (Taiwan). Eager to supplant this rival, the English fought a series of wars with the Dutch in the 1650s and 1660s and gained control of New Netherlands in 1664.

The first Dutch colonists arrived in North America in 1624 to set up a permanent settlement at Fort Orange (Albany) in the as yet unclaimed region between New France and English Virginia. Although Dutch traders ranged as far south as the lower Delaware and east into the Connecticut Valley, the heart of the colony was the Hudson River Valley from New Amsterdam (founded 1625) on Manhattan Island up to Fort Orange. The Dutch established a profitable trade with the Iroquois, who were eager to exchange furs for European tools and weapons.

The **Dutch West India Company**, the trading enterprise that established and governed New Netherlands, also tried to attract settlers in order to provision trading posts. In the 1630s, the company offered large landed estates (called **patroonships**), located mainly along the Hudson River, to wealthy Dutchmen willing to sponsor new emigrants. Few such estates were created, however, because most would-be patroons would not agree to company-imposed limits on their rights. In addition, few Dutchmen wanted to emigrate only to rent land from patroon landlords. At its maximum, the settler population of New Netherlands reached perhaps ten thousand.

What they lacked in numbers the colonists made up for in divisiveness. Ethnic differences prevented them from developing a sense of community. In 1643, a French Jesuit visitor reported hearing at least eighteen languages on the streets of New Amsterdam. Among the colony's Dutch, German, French, English, Swedish, Portuguese, and African settlers were Calvinists, Lutherans, Quakers, Catholics, Jews, Muslims, and people of other faiths. Scattered in villages from Albany to the Atlantic, the colonists often lived isolated and insecure lives.

The Dutch West India Company, more interested in

making profits than keeping order, dispatched a series of inept but aggressive governors who made this unstable situation worse, mainly by provoking conflict with Indians. Although New Netherlands generally maintained good relations with its Iroquois trading partners at Fort Orange (Albany) on the upper Hudson River, it had far less friendly dealings with other Indian peoples along the lower Hudson, around New Amsterdam (New York City). In one particularly gruesome instance in 1645, Governor Willem Kieft ordered a massacre at an encampment of Indians who had refused to pay tribute. A horrified Dutch witness described Indian children being "thrown into the river, and when the fathers and mothers endeavoured to save them, the soldiers would not let them come on land, but made both parents and children drown." He saw victims "with their hands, some with their legs cut off, and some holding their entrails in their arms." Ten years later, Governor Peter Stuyvesant antagonized Susquehannock Indians along the Delaware River by leading Dutch forces in the seizure of a small Swedish colony where the Susquehannocks had traded.

These actions provoked retaliatory raids by the Indians, weakening a colony that increasingly looked like a poor investment to company officials back in Europe. Though profitable, the fur trade did not match the riches to be found in other parts of the Dutch empire. When an English fleet appeared off the coast in 1664 during one of the Anglo-Dutch wars, Governor Stuyvesant, in command of just 150 soldiers, surrendered without firing a shot.

This earliest known depiction of New Amsterdam (published 1651) on the tip of Manhattan island testifies to the town's slow growth. It contained only a few dozen houses and a windmill located outside a fort. The European ships in the background, as well as the Indian canoes in front, indicate the importance of trade to the Dutch colony.

The Hartger's View, New Amsterdam, 1626–1628. Line engraving, 3¼ × 4¾ in. Museum of the City of New York, 29.100.792. The J. Clarence Davies Collection.

Charles II made his brother James, duke of York, proprietor of this new English possession, which was now renamed New York. James immediately created another colony, New Jersey, when he granted some of the land to a group of his supporters. New Jersey's proprietors struggled to control the diverse people already living there and fighting among themselves. At one point the colony split in two parts, East and West Jersey, which reunited to become a single royal colony in 1702 when the frustrated proprietors surrendered their rights to the king.

New York, which James retained for himself, was the most valuable part of the former Dutch colony. It included the port of New York City (the former New Amsterdam) and the Hudson Valley with its fur trade. James, who succeeded his brother to the English throne in 1685, encouraged Dutch colonists to remain on rather generous terms and promoted immigration from England to strengthen the colony and gain income from land sales. By 1700, the settlers numbered twenty thousand.

For nearly twenty years after its takeover by the English, New York lacked something all other English colonies had—a representative assembly. The Dutch had never created one, and James saw no reason to change that policy, despite the friction it created with his colonists. Particularly after neighboring New Jersey and Pennsylvania created their own assemblies, however, New Yorkers pressed their proprietor to follow suit. Only in 1683, when it became clear that New York might lose population to the new colony of Pennsylvania, did James relent and create the assembly that brought New York into line with the other English colonies.

Conclusion

During the seventeenth century, France and England joined Spain as colonial powers in North America. Far to the north, New France's small and scattered settlements clung to the St. Lawrence River Valley. The profits from the fur trade encouraged the French to maintain friendly relations with their Indian allies and ensured that French kings would monitor the colony's affairs and invest in its defense. English colonization, by contrast, was a far more haphazard process. English kings granted charters—sometimes to joint-stock companies (Virginia, Plymouth, Massachusetts), sometimes to proprietors (Maryland, Carolina, New York, New Jersey, Pennsylvania)—and let the colonies develop more or less on their own. England had no equivalent in the seventeenth century to the imperial bureaucracies Spain and France created to manage their New World holdings.

The result was a highly diverse set of English colonies stretching from the Maine coast to the Caribbean. Settlers adjusted to different environments, developed different economies and labor systems, and worshiped in different churches. In many places—South Carolina, New York, Pennsylvania, the West Indies—the majority of settlers were not even of English origin. What held these colonies together—besides their establishment under English charters and their enmity to New Spain and New France—was an overlay of common English institutions of government. By the mid-1680s, all the colonies had legislatures that provided for self-government. All likewise developed laws and judicial institutions based on English models.

The planting of French and English colonies not only ended Spain's monopoly of settlement in North America but also challenged the Indians' hold on the continent. Forced to deal with a rising tide of settlers and often to choose sides between European antagonists, native peoples struggled to adapt to rapidly changing circumstances. Transplanted Europeans adapted too, not only in their dealings with native peoples but also in finding and controlling the supply of laborers they needed to make their colonies prosper. For English colonists, this meant the adoption of slavery, an institution that did not exist in England itself. For millions of Africans, the result was forced migration to the New World.

Review Questions

1. The early settlers of New France and Virginia included few women. What effects did this have on the development of each colony?

2. Which English settlements were proprietary colonies? Did they share any common characteristics? What plans did the various proprietors have for their colonies, and to what extent were those plans put into effect?

3. When Virginia's settlers first arrived, they encountered a numerous and powerful confederation of Powhatan Indians. New England's colonists, in contrast, began settlement after epidemics had drastically reduced the local native population. In what ways did the presence or absence of Indians affect each region's early history?

4. In both Massachusetts and Pennsylvania, religion figured prominently as a motive for settlement. What were the religious beliefs of the settlers in each colony, and how did those beliefs help shape each colony's development?

5. Three colonial regions—the Chesapeake, the West Indies, and Carolina—developed economies

dependent on staple crops. What were those crops? In what ways did staple crop agriculture shape society in each region?

Recommended Reading

Anderson, Virginia DeJohn. *New England's Generation: The Great Migration and the Formation of Society and Culture in the Seventeenth Century* (1991). Examines the experiences of nearly seven hundred emigrants to New England and explores the ways in which the composition of the settler population shaped early New England society.

Dunn, Richard S. *Sugar and Slaves: The Rise of the Planter Class in the English West Indies, 1624–1713* (1972). The authoritative account of British settlement in the West Indies and the development of the slave labor system.

Eccles, W. J. *The Canadian Frontier, 1534–1760* (rev. ed., 1983). Provides a comprehensive overview of French settlement in Canada.

Morgan, Edmund S. *American Slavery, American Freedom: The Ordeal of Colonial Virginia* (1975). This vividly written account of the founding of Virginia and the development of an unfree labor system remains the best study of an early American colony.

Wood, Peter H. *Black Majority: Negroes in Colonial South Carolina from 1670 through the Stono Rebellion* (1974). This study of the founding of South Carolina emphasizes the contributions of the black slaves who eventually comprised a majority of the colony's settlers.

Additional Sources

New France
Eccles, W. J. *Essays on New France* (1987).
Innis, Harold A. *The Fur Trade in Canada: An Introduction to Canadian Economic History* (1962).

Chesapeake Society
Carr, Lois Green, Menard, Russell R., and Walsh, Lorena S. *Robert Cole's World: Agriculture and Society in Early Maryland* (1991).
Horn, James. *Adapting to a New World: English Society in the Seventeenth-Century Chesapeake* (1994).
Main, Gloria. *Tobacco Colony: Life in Early Maryland, 1650–1720* (1982).
Rutman, Darrett, and Rutman, Anita. *A Place in Time: Middlesex County, Virginia, 1650–1750* (1984).

Tate, Thad W., and Ammerman, David L., eds. *The Chesapeake in the Seventeenth Century: Essays on Anglo-American Society* (1979).

New England
Demos, John. *A Little Commonwealth: Family Life in Plymouth Colony* (1970).
Hall, David D. *Worlds of Wonder, Days of Judgment: Popular Religious Belief in Early New England* (1989).
Innes, Stephen. *Creating the Commonwealth: The Economic Culture of Puritan New England* (1995).
Morgan, Edmund S. *Puritan Dilemma: The Story of John Winthrop* (1958).
Ulrich, Laurel Thatcher. *Good Wives: Image and Reality in the Lives of Women in Northern New England, 1650–1750* (1982).

The Proprietary Colonies
Dunn, Richard S., and Dunn, Mary Maples, eds. *The World of William Penn* (1986).
Goodfriend, Joyce D. *Before the Melting Pot: Society and Culture in Colonial New York City, 1664–1730* (1992).
Lemon, James T. *The Best Poor Man's Country: A Geographical Study of Early Southeastern Pennsylvania* (1972).
Levy, Barry. *Quakers and the American Family: British Settlement in the Delaware Valley* (1988).
Sirmans, M. Eugene. *Colonial South Carolina: A Political History, 1663–1763* (1966).

Where to Learn More

❖ **Jamestown Festival Park, Williamsburg, Virginia.** A museum here contains indoor and outdoor exhibits on the site of the first permanent English colony in North America. The library holds some material on early settlers and Virginia Indians; in addition, there are films and videotapes about early Virginia.

❖ **St. Mary's City, Maryland.** Visitors to this site of the first permanent settlement under the Calvert family may tour the area and view exhibits and living history programs that describe life in early Maryland.

❖ **Plimoth Plantation, Plymouth, Massachusetts.** A living history museum, Plimoth Plantation re-creates colony life in the year 1627. There are reproductions of the English village and a Wampanoag settlement. Visitors may also see a replica of the *Mayflower.*

❖ **Pennsbury Manor, Morrisville, Pennsylvania.** Here is a reconstruction of William Penn's seventeenth-century plantation. The site includes furnished buildings and restored gardens. There are also interpreters to inform visitors about agricultural life in early Pennsylvania.

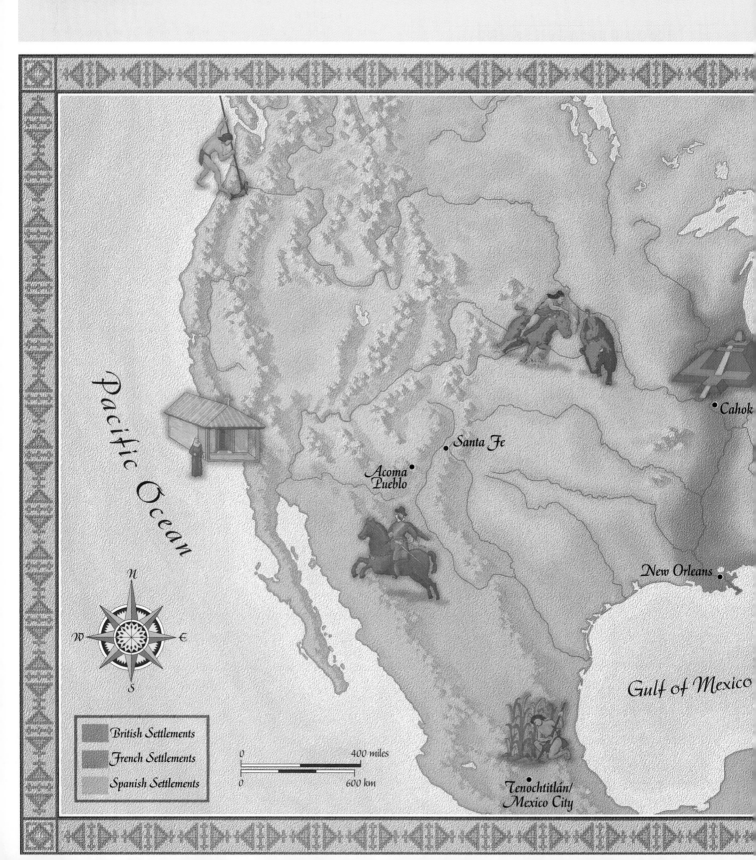

3 THE CREATION OF NEW WORLDS

Pacific Ocean

Santa Fe

Acoma
Pueblo

Cahok

New Orleans

Gulf of Mexico

Tenochtitlán/
Mexico City

British Settlements

French Settlements

Spanish Settlements

0   400 miles

0   600 km

CHAPTER OUTLINE

KEY TOPICS

❖ Patterns of contact between Native Americans and French, Spanish, and English colonists
❖ The development of slavery and other unfree labor systems in early America
❖ The formation of African-American communities
❖ Causes and consequences of European immigration to America

*S*ometime before the spring of 1712, a Carolina slave named Harry took a terrible chance. His master, fed up with Harry's "roguery," had sold him to a new master in Virginia. But before he could be sent there, Harry ran away.

This took great courage, for laws in both Virginia and Carolina prescribed mutilation and even death for recaptured runaway slaves. Harry then made the equally desperate decision to seek refuge among the Tuscarora Indians. Rather than sheltering him, the Tuscaroras might just as easily have killed him or returned him to his master for a reward.

But Harry was lucky, for he had skills that made him valuable to the Tuscaroras. He knew how to design and construct forts and helped the Indians build a stronghold to protect themselves. From this structure, the Tuscaroras could attack the white colonists under whose oppression they too had suffered.

For years, Europeans had occupied the Tuscaroras' land, cheated them in trade, and kidnapped and enslaved them. When yet another group—this time Swiss and German settlers—marched across Tuscarora territory late in 1711, the Indians struck back, raiding frontier towns and killing or capturing their inhabitants. The Carolina government recruited a volunteer force of colonists and Yamasees and other Indian allies and ordered it to search out and destroy Tuscarora settlements.

When these soldiers came near Harry's fort in the spring of 1712, their commander spied it "with a prospective glass and found it strong as well by situation on the river's bank as [by] Workman-

ship." Under Harry's direction, the Indians had dug a deep trench around the fort and surrounded the high earthworks with "large limbs of trees [that] lay confusedly about" to make entrance difficult. They also arranged "large reeds and canes to run into people's legs" as they attacked the walls. The commander had never seen "such subtill contrivances for Defence."

Although the fort withstood a siege of nearly two months, the colonial forces ultimately prevailed. Most of the surviving Tuscaroras fled north to join the powerful Iroquois nations. Others "scattered as the wind scatters the smoke." Harry's fate is unknown.

This episode reveals three important features of the new society that was developing in England's Carolina colony. First, it had an astonishingly diverse population that included such Native American peoples as the Tuscaroras, Yamasees, Creeks, and Catawbas; Africans brought directly from Gambia, Guinea, and Angola or by way of the West Indies; and Europeans from England, Scotland, Ireland, Barbados, German provinces, and Swiss cantons. Second, the interactions among these peoples ranged from cooperation to outright violence. And third, what governed their interactions was a struggle for the control of resources, including trade goods, land, and labor. For slaves like Harry, the struggle was over nothing less than the most fundamental resource, control of one's own life—freedom.

In many ways, the history of North America in the seventeenth and eighteenth centuries is the history of early Carolina writ large. From the southwestern deserts to the Canadian forests to the Atlantic coastal plain, diverse peoples met to trade, work, feast, worship, and fight. Their interactions, which varied from place to place and over time, created not one but many New Worlds.

Indians and Europeans

Between 1650 and 1750, a rising tide of immigrants—European and African, willing and unwilling—irrevocably altered the lives of North America's native population. By 1750, Indians had become a minority north of the Rio Grande. But despite their growing numbers, the colonists were concentrated in certain areas and did not yet dominate the entire

continent. Indians living along the northern Pacific coast, for instance, met their first white men—Russian fur traders—only in the 1740s. In contrast, other native peoples—the Pueblos of the Southwest, the Hurons of Canada, and the Algonquians of the Atlantic seaboard—had by this time dealt with European colonists for a century or more.

The character of the relationship between Indians and Europeans depended on more than

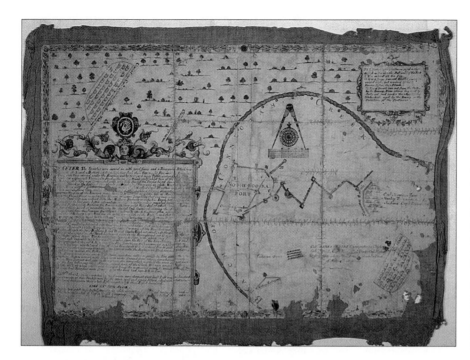

Runaway slaves occasionally found shelter among the Tuscarora Indians and, in return, helped the Indians defend their lands against white encroachment. The fort depicted here may have been constructed with help from runaway slaves during the brief Tuscarora War (1711–1713). About one-fifth of the Tuscarora population was killed or enslaved in the conflict, leading to the tribe's surrender and the migration of many of the survivors to New York.

relative population size and the length of time they had been in contact. It was also shaped by the intentions of the newcomers—whether they came to trade, to settle, or to gain converts—and the responses of particular Native American groups as each struggled to preserve its own culture. The result was a variety of regionally distinctive New World communities. Many of the strategies Native Americans developed as they adapted to new conditions and tried to counter the intrusions of settlers would persist into the twentieth century.

The Web of Trade

Europeans eager to trade with Indians first had to enter into alliances with them. Indians refused to trade with enemies or strangers and demanded that Europeans prove their friendship by offering gifts and military aid as well as trading goods. French traders in Canada adapted best to this practice. They brought gifts and prepared feasts for their native partners, obliging the Indians, in turn, to offer the furs that the French wanted. One seventeenth-century observer described the French governor giving the Hurons barrels of hatchets and arrowheads, in part "to waft their canoes gently homewards, [in] part to draw them to us next year." Each year the French acquired thousands of pelts and the Indians got iron tools, kettles, cloth, beads, and—eventually—guns.

Indians could not have known that trading with Europeans would lead gradually to the destruction of their way of life. One reason for this tragic

outcome was that contact with traders exposed Indians to deadly European diseases (see Figure 3-1). The Huron population declined by half in just six years between 1634 and 1640. Indians trading with the Dutch in New Netherlands in the 1650s insisted that they had once been "ten times as numerous as they now are," but "their population had been melted down" by smallpox.

Trade also undermined self-sufficiency, making many Indian groups dependent on Europeans and others for essential goods. Before the French arrived, for instance, the Micmacs in easternmost Canada supported themselves mainly by fishing. But after becoming partners of the French around 1610, they devoted themselves to trapping beaver year round, relying on others—mainly the French and New England Indians—for food. Micmac potters and basketmakers neglected to practice their crafts once their people began using French-made kettles and other goods. Only after they had trapped virtually all the beavers on their lands did the Micmacs realize the dangers of dependence. Abandoned by the French, who turned instead to the Hurons, the once prosperous Micmacs barely survived.

Other groups would suffer a similar fate over the next century and more, growing accustomed to goods they could not produce on their own and facing hardship should their European partners withdraw from trade. "The Cloaths we wear, we cannot make ourselves," a Carolina Cherokee used to woolen garments observed in 1753. "We cannot

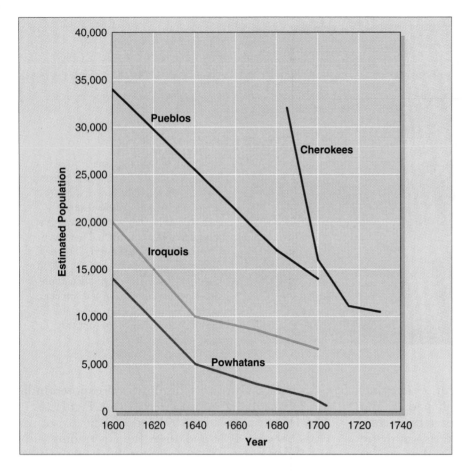

Figure 3-1 Estimated Populations
of Selected Indian Peoples,
1600–1730
*Indian populations shrank dramatically
due to diseases brought by Europeans
from the Old World. By about 1750,
native peoples had become a minority of
the inhabitants of America north of the
Rio Grande.*

Sources: *Daniel Richter, The Ordeal of the
Longhouse (1992); Helen Rountree,
Pocahontas's People (1990); David Weber,
The Spanish Frontier in North America
(1992); Peter Wood, et al., eds., Powhatan's
Mantle (1989).*

make our Guns. . . . Every necessary Thing in Life we must have from the white People."

Another destructive aspect of European trade lay in its effect on warfare. Before European contact, most Indian bands living north of the Rio Grande made war not to destroy their enemies or seize their lands but rather to seek revenge for violent acts committed against their own pseople. Chiefs led expeditions to ambush the enemy, kill a few men, and take prisoners—some of whom might be adopted to replace victims of earlier fights. But after the Europeans arrived, Indians began to fight each other for economic advantage, and the hostilities became far more deadly. Rivalries among French, English, and Dutch traders led to conflicts among their Indian partners. The **Beaver Wars**, a long struggle between the Hurons and the Iroquois that began in the 1640s, illustrate the ferocity of such contests.

Because the French had already made the Hurons their trading partners, Dutch merchants in the Hudson River Valley seeking to break into the fur trade turned to the **Iroquois League**. Composed of five separate Indian nations—the Mohawks, Oneidas, Onondagas, Cayugas, and Senecas—the League had

formed around 1450, long before the arrival of the first Europeans. For almost two hundred years it had functioned as a religious organization to preserve peace among the five nations and strengthen them in their conflicts with other Indian peoples. Envious of the Hurons' access to French trade goods, the Iroquois agreed to supply the Dutch with furs in return for similar goods.

To satisfy the European demand for furs, the Hurons and Iroquois both hunted beaver at an unsustainable rate, a wasteful practice previously unknown among them. By the 1630s, they had killed nearly all the beavers on their own lands and began to look elsewhere for furs. The Hurons cleared new fields to increase their harvest of corn, trading the surplus for furs with Indians living north of the Great Lakes where beavers were still abundant. The Iroquois, however, began to raid Huron trading parties and then to attack Huron villages.

The Iroquois triumphed in the resulting conflict largely because the Dutch readily supplied them with guns while the French were reluctant to arm the Hurons. In the end, the Hurons were destroyed. Thousands were killed or captured, and many others

This eighteenth-century engraving illustrates, in idealized form, the way Indian peoples traded furs for European goods. The barrel may have contained kettles or other metal ware packed in sawdust, while the bale to the left probably held cloth.

fled westward. A French traveler reported seeing no Hurons in "districts which, not ten years ago, I reckoned to contain eight or ten thousand men. . . . A little farther on, were but the shells of cabins abandoned to the fury of the enemy,—those who had dwelt in them having fled into the forest."

Conflicts among native peoples became deadlier once Indians acquired European arms. This 1657 engraving depicts a Huron warrior carrying a gun and wearing a type of armor made of tightly-laced sticks—which would have provided little protection from a musket ball.

The cycle of warfare did not end with the destruction of the Hurons. After their victory, the Iroquois, to maintain control over the fur supply, went on to challenge Indian nations near the Great Lakes and in the Ohio Valley. Seeking iron kettles more durable than earthenware pots, cloth that was lighter and more colorful than animal skins, and guns that were deadlier than bows and arrows, Indians who traded with Europeans changed their lives in ways that suited European needs as much as their own. For the Indians, no less than the Europeans, this was indeed a new world.

Occupying the Land

The French and Dutch came to North America mainly to trade. The English, in contrast, came mainly to settle and had a correspondingly different impact on the native peoples on whom they intruded. Trading colonies relied on Indian partners to supply them with furs and so maintained friendly relations with them out of self-interest. The European population of the trading colonies also stayed fairly low. Even after the devastation of disease, Indians outnumbered Europeans in New France and New Netherlands. As late as 1650, there were just 657 French people in Canada (compared to perhaps ten thousand Hurons) and only three thousand Europeans in New Netherlands. By the same year, in contrast, there were more than fifty thousand Europeans and two thousand Africans in England's North American colonies.

The influx of settlers into the English colonies, as always, exposed native peoples to European diseases. To Puritan New Englanders, it looked as if the Lord was "sweeping away great multitudes of the natives . . . that he might make room for us there." So swift was the decline in native populations—and

CHRONOLOGY

1440s	Portuguese enter slave trade in West Africa.
c. 1450	League of the Iroquois formed.
1610–1614	First war between English settlers and Powhatan Indians.
1619	First Africans arrive in Virginia.
1622–1632	Second war between English settlers and Powhatan Indians.
1637	Pequot War in New England.
1640s	Slave labor begins to dominate in the West Indies.
	First phase of the Beaver Wars.
1651	First "praying town" established at Natick, Massachusetts.
1661	Maryland law defines slavery as lifelong, inheritable status.
1670	Virginia law defines status of slaves.
1675–1676	King Philip's War in New England.
1676	Bacon's Rebellion in Virginia.
1680	Pueblo Revolt in New Mexico.
1680s	Second phase of Beaver Wars begins.
1690s	Shift from white indentured servants to black slaves as principal labor force in the Chesapeake.
1701	Iroquois adopt policy of neutrality toward French and English.
1711–1713	Tuscarora War in Carolina.
1713	Beginnings of substantial Scottish, Scots-Irish, and German immigration to colonies.
1715–1716	Yamasee War in Carolina.
1720s	Black population begins to increase naturally in English mainland colonies.
1732	Georgia established.
1739	Stono Rebellion in South Carolina.
1741	Slave conspiracy discovered in New York City.
1750	Slavery legalized in Georgia.
1760–1775	Peak of European and African immigration to English colonies.

so rapid the influx of Europeans—that in coastal Massachusetts and eastern Virginia, colonists outnumbered Indians by 1650.

Largely because of the colonists' desire for land, violence between Europeans and Indians occurred with greater regularity in the English colonies than in New France or New Netherland. The wars between Virginia's settlers and the Powhatan Indians and the Pequot War in New England, discussed in Chapter 2, were early examples of the many conflicts that marked the history of English colonization.

The first English settlers assumed that there was plenty of land for everyone. Coming from an England where all good farming land had been cultivated for centuries, colonists thrilled at the sight of what they saw as vast unoccupied territory. "The Indians are not able to make use of the one fourth part of the Land," declared one New England settler. Another insisted that the natives "do but run over the grass, as do also the foxes and wild beasts" and that therefore the "spacious and void" land was free for the taking.

But the settlers misunderstood how Indians used their territory. Eastern Algonquian peoples moved frequently to take advantage of the land's diversity. They cleared areas for villages and planting fields, which native women farmed until the soil grew less fertile. Then they moved to a new location, allowing the former village site to return to forest. In ten to twenty years, they or their descendants might return to that site to clear and farm it again. Indians often built villages near the seacoast or rivers so they could fish and use reeds and grasses for weaving. In the winter, village communities broke up into small bands to hunt in the forest for deer and other animals.

Thus what the colonists considered "vacant" lands were in fact either being used for nonfarming activities or recovering from human occupation in order to be farmed in years to come. Settlers who built towns on abandoned Indian village sites deprived the Indians of these future planting fields. Colonists who cut down the forests reduced native hunting grounds. Indians tolerated such intrusions for a while, but competition from the rapidly increasing settlers threatened their survival.

Disputes between Europeans and Indians frequently arose from misunderstandings about the definition of land ownership and property rights. Indian villages claimed sovereignty over a certain territory, and their members collectively exercised their rights to use the land for farming, fishing, hunting, and gathering. No Indian claimed individual ownership of a specific tract of land. Europeans, of course, did, and for them, ownership conferred on an individual the exclusive right to use or sell a piece of land.

These differences created problems whenever Indians transferred land to settlers. The settlers assumed that they had obtained complete rights to the land, whereas the Indians assumed that they had given the settlers not the land itself but only the *right to use it*. Often they thought they had given only the right to share the land and that they themselves would not have to leave. The Indians soon learned what the English meant by a land sale, however, because it was the English understanding that ultimately prevailed, enforced in the settlers' courts under the settlers' laws.

Many of the settlers' agricultural practices also strained their relations with the Indians. When settlers cut down forests, they destroyed Indian hunting lands. When they dammed rivers, they disrupted Indian fishing practices. When they surrounded their fields with log fences and stone walls, they made trespassers of natives who crossed them. Colonial laws prohibited Indians from burning parts of the forest—something they had done each year to destroy underbrush and make the woods suitable for hunting and travel—because settlers feared that fires might spread to their houses, barns, fields, and haystacks. Yet the colonists felt free to let their cattle and pigs loose to graze in the woods and meadows, where they could wander into unfenced Indian cornfields and damage the crops.

As their numbers grew, the settlers gradually displaced Indian inhabitants, acquiring their lands in various ways. Some colonial leaders, such as Roger Williams in Rhode Island and William Penn of Pennsylvania, insisted on buying it. But even purchasers who tried to be fair encountered difficulties. Indians owned their land collectively, so only their leaders had the authority to negotiate sales, but settlers sometimes bought land from individual Indians who had no right to sell it. Because land transfers were often arranged through interpreters and recorded in English, Indians frequently misunderstood the terms of sale. And even Indian groups that had willingly sold land to begin with grew resentful as colonists approached them again and again for more. Finally, native peoples were often forced to sell land to settle debts they had run up with English creditors.

Settlers occasionally obtained land by fraud. In 1734, for instance, James Logan of Pennsylvania produced what he insisted was a copy of a deed from 1686 by which the Delaware Indians had transferred a large tract of land to William Penn. Although Logan did not have the original deed and there was no reference to it in the colony's land records, the Delawares eventually had to give up the territory. Increasingly during the eighteenth century, as colonists moved farther inland and beyond the reach of officials who might have tried to stop them, some simply settled on Indian lands without any legal pretense at all and appealed to colonial governments for help when the Indians objected. Land speculators amplified this kind of unrest on the edges of settlement as they sought to acquire land as cheaply as possible and sell it for as much as they could.

Finally, the settlers often seized Indian lands in the aftermath of war, as befell, among many others, the Pequots in 1637 in Connecticut and, in Carolina, the Tuscaroras in 1713 and the Yamasees in 1715. In each case, settlers moved onto land left vacant as native peoples were killed, captured, and dispersed by colonial forces. Sometimes colonial leaders contrived for some Indian groups to help them displace others. During the Pequot War, Narragansetts had aided Connecticut settlers' efforts to oust the Pequots. Carolina colonists enlisted the help of the Yamasees against the Tuscaroras and then turned to the Cherokees to help them against the Yamasees.

In the end, all these methods produced the same result. The English experience in the conquest of Ireland shaped the settlers' attitudes toward Native Americans. They viewed the Indians, like the Irish, as savages with whom it would be better not to mix. Like the English plantations in Ireland, English settlements in North America separated newcomers from natives. Colonists built communities on lands bought or taken from natives and then discouraged them from living there. In New France and New Spain, Europeans and Indians mingled more freely and even intermarried, but in the English colonies, separation prevailed.

Priests and Preachers

In addition to trade and settlement, religion played a powerful role in shaping relations between Native Americans and Europeans in early colonial North America. The three major New World empires—those of Spain, France, and England—competed for Indians' souls as well as their lands and riches.

Catholic missionaries—mainly Franciscan priests—were the driving force behind Spain's

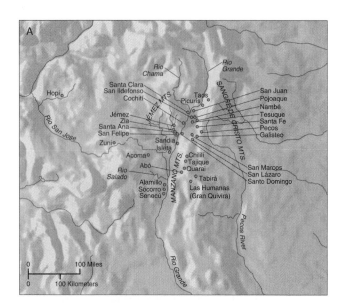

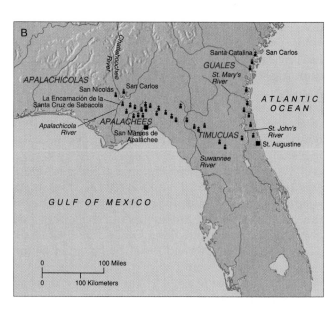

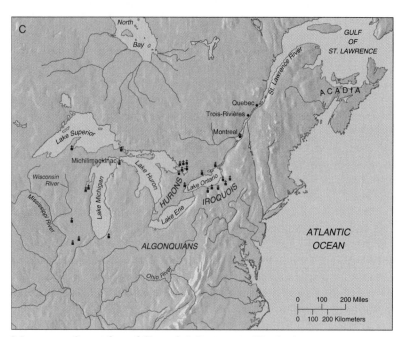

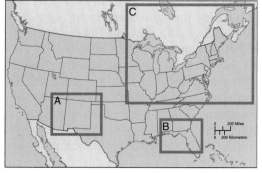

Map 3-1   Spanish and French Missions in North America
*Spanish Franciscans in New Mexico (A) and Florida (B) and French Jesuits in New France
(C) devoted considerable effort to converting native peoples to Catholic Christianity.*

efforts to assert control over its colonies of New Mexico and Florida (see Map 3-1). Spain needed both regions more for strategic than economic reasons. Its bases in Florida helped protect Spanish ships bearing treasure from the mines of Mexico and Peru and discouraged the southward spread of English settlement. New Mexico similarly served as a buffer between the silver mines of northern Mexico and roaming Plains Indians. Neither colony

attracted many settlers, however, because neither appeared to offer much opportunity for wealth. When Franciscan missionaries proposed to move in, Spanish officials—eager to back up their claims with a more visible Spanish presence—agreed and even provided financial support.

Franciscans settled near native villages in both New Mexico and Florida in order to convert their inhabitants to Christianity. The priests wore their finest vestments and displayed religious paintings and statues, trying to impress the Indians with European goods and Catholic ceremonies. They gave away bells, knives, scissors, cloth, and food. According to one Franciscan in New Mexico, these gifts functioned as bait, bringing Indians to the missions "like fish to the fish hook." The natives believed that accepting these gifts obliged them to listen to the priests' Christian message and help them build houses and churches.

After brief religious instruction, the missionaries convinced many Indians to accept baptism into the Catholic Church and with it the promise of salvation and a heavenly afterlife. Although many of these conversions were doubtless genuine, they also had practical motivations. They often followed epidemics that devastated native villages but spared the Spanish, leading many Indians to wonder if the Christian God might indeed be more powerful than their own gods. In New Mexico, the Spanish offered Pueblo converts protection against raids from their Apache rivals and access to Franciscan storehouses in times of famine. Ironically, the corn in the storehouses often came from the Indians' own fields, collected by the Spanish as tribute.

Many Indians did not understand that baptism would commit them to a new way of life. The Franciscans insisted that converts completely abandon native beliefs, which they despised as devil worship. The missionaries sought to "civilize" the new converts by making them adopt Spanish food, clothing, and work routines. Priests in New Mexico, objecting to the ease with which Pueblo marriages could be dissolved, tried to enforce lifelong unions. Punishments for violating the new code were severe and in rare cases led to their victims' deaths.

By the mid-seventeenth century, Spanish missionaries claimed to have baptized tens of thousands of Indians. But many converts blended Christianity with native religion, adding Jesus, Mary, and the Catholic saints to the list of Indian gods and accepting missionaries as counterparts to native priests. In New Mexico, certain Pueblo name-giving ceremonies resembled Christian baptism so closely that the meanings of the two rites could be mixed. Guale Indians in Florida replaced their shell necklaces with religious medals—but that did not necessarily mean that they had fully accepted Christianity. Many converts were **mestizos**—people of mixed Indian and Spanish descent—who occupied a difficult position between two cultures and often practiced native rituals in secret. Some groups, such as the Zuni and Hopi peoples, rejected Christianity

This Jesuit missionary, wearing his distinctive Catholic vestments, is baptizing an Indian in New France. French Jesuits proved to be more tolerant than most European missionaries in allowing Indian converts to retain at least some of their own customs.

altogether. In the end, the spread of Christianity in the Spanish borderlands was not as complete as the Franciscans claimed.

French priests in Canada also tried to convert Indians to Catholicism. Jesuit missionaries lived among the native peoples, often at great distances from French settlements. Like the Franciscans, they tried to impress potential converts with the rituals and material objects of their religion. Priests also amazed Indians with such "magical" items as clocks and magnets and with their ability to predict eclipses and to read and write. Algonquian peoples had no written language and marveled when missionaries silently exchanged information by writing notes. "All this serves to gain their affections, and to render them more docile when we introduce the admirable and incomprehensible mysteries of our Faith," explained one priest, for the Indians would then "accept without reply what we say to them."

French missionaries also resorted to economic pressure. They convinced merchants to sell guns only to converted Indians and to offer them other trade goods at a discount. In New France, as in New Mexico, native conversions usually followed epidemics, which undermined the survivors' faith in their own religion. And as in the Spanish colonies, newly baptized Indians in New France often did not fully understand Christianity. But the Jesuits were generally more tolerant than the Franciscans of native ways. "One must be careful before condemning a thousand things among their customs," warned one priest, because to do so would "greatly offend minds brought up and nourished in another world."

The Protestant English were less successful than the Catholic Spanish and French at attracting Native American converts. Puritans frowned on the rituals and religious objects that drew Indian converts to Catholicism. And with its emphasis on the direct study of scripture, Protestantism required that potential converts learn to read.

Beginning in the 1650s, Puritan ministers in New England, such as John Eliot, established several **praying towns**, communities where Indians lived apart from settlers to learn Protestant Christianity and English ways. The few residents attracted to these towns, however, were mostly the remnants of groups otherwise destroyed by disease. Efforts at conversion in the Anglican southern colonies were even less successful. Anglican missionaries did not even begin work until the eighteenth century and then often felt that the settlers needed religious instruction more urgently than the Indians. In the 1730s and 1740s, German Moravians—members of a Protestant group that stressed personal piety—managed to convert some Indians in western Pennsylvania. On the whole, however, settlers in the English colonies preferred to isolate Indians rather than convert them.

After the First Hundred Years

After nearly a century of European settlement, violent confrontations between colonists and Indians erupted in all three North American empires. The cause and progress of each of these deadly encounters—**King Philip's War** in New England, **Bacon's Rebellion** in Virginia, the **Pueblo Revolt** in New Mexico, and the resumption and conclusion of the Beaver Wars in New France—reflected distinctive features of English, Spanish, and French patterns of colonization.

King Philip's War, which broke out in 1675, was sparked by the growing frustration of the Wampanoags—the Indians who had befriended the Pilgrims more than half a century before—with the land-hungry settlers whose towns now surrounded them. Massasoit's younger son, Metacom—called King Philip by the English—now led the

Nearly a century after King Philip's War, Paul Revere engraved this portrait of the Wampanoag leader to accompany a new edition of a history of that conflict. Note that Philip is shown in European-style dress and has the weapons of war—a gun and a tomahawk—nearby. Behind him are angry warriors. These bellicose images suggest that the antagonism produced by New England's fiercest war lingered among the colonists for generations.

Wampanoags and was struggling to preserve their independence against the incursions of the colonists, who now numbered more than fifty thousand. He had little reason to trust the colonists. His older brother and predecessor as sachem had died mysteriously while being questioned by colonial officials about rumors of an Indian conspiracy. Philip himself had been accused of plotting against the settlers and then forced to sign a treaty submitting to English authority.

In the spring of 1675, a colonial court found three Wampanoags guilty of murdering a Christian Indian who had warned the English of Wampanoag preparations for war. Despite Philip's protest, the court sentenced the men to be hanged. This enraged the Wampanoags, convincing them that they had to strike back against the English before it was too late. Only "a small part of the dominion of my ancestors remains," declared Philip. "I am determined not to live until I have no country."

Philip's forces attacked outlying villages in Plymouth Colony, moved into the Connecticut River Valley, and then turned eastward again to strike towns within 20 miles of Boston. As the Narragansetts and other groups joined the uprising, Philip successfully eluded the combined forces of Massachusetts, Connecticut, and Plymouth for months. By the summer of 1676, however, the Indians were exhausted, weakened by disease and food shortages. Philip moved into western New England, where his men clashed with the powerful Mohawks, long-standing enemies of the Wampanoags and allies of English fur traders in New York. Philip died in an ambush in August 1676, and the war ended soon after.

At least a thousand colonists and perhaps three thousand Indians died in King Philip's War. One out of every sixteen male colonists of military age was killed, making this the deadliest conflict in American history in terms of the proportion of casualties to total population. The Indians succeeded in forcing back the line of settlement—it would be forty years before colonists again occupied land they had first claimed before the war—but lost what remained of their independence in New England. The victorious English sold many native survivors, including Philip's wife and young son, into slavery in the West Indies. Others they employed in marginal jobs or confined in one of the few remaining praying towns. Philip's head, impaled on a stake, was left for decades on the outskirts of Plymouth as a grisly warning of the price to be paid for resisting colonial expansion.

As King Philip's War raged in New England, a bloody conflict erupted in Virginia that had a similarly devastating effect on that colony's remaining native population. Frustrated by shrinking economic opportunities in eastern Virginia, where established planters controlled all the good land, many settlers, including wealthy new arrivals as well as poor, recently freed indentured servants, moved to Virginia's western frontier. There they came into conflict with the region's resident Indians. In the summer of 1675, a group of frontier settlers attacked the Susquehannocks in order to seize their lands. The Indians struck back the next winter, prompting Nathaniel Bacon, a young, wealthy planter who had only recently arrived in Virginia, to lead the settlers in a violent campaign against all Indians, even those at peace with the colonial government. Governor William Berkeley ordered Bacon and his men to stop their attacks. They defied him and marched on Jamestown, turning a war between settlers and Indians into a rebellion of settlers against the colonial authorities.

The rebels believed that Berkeley and the colonial government represented the interests of established tobacco planters who wanted to keep men like themselves from emerging as potential competitors. Desperate because of the low price of tobacco, they demanded lower taxes and easier access to land—meaning, in effect, the right to take land from the Indians. Berkeley offered to build forts—at great expense—along the frontier to protect the settlers from the Indians, but the rebels were not interested in protection. What they wanted was help exterminating the Indians. They captured and burned the colonial capital at Jamestown, forcing Berkeley to flee. Free to direct their aggression against Indians once more, they burned Indian villages and massacred or enslaved the inhabitants. Trying to appease the rebels, the House of Burgesses passed measures allowing them to seize lands belonging to Indians who had left their villages without permission—even though it was to escape the rebels that many Indians had fled. The assembly also legalized the enslavement of Indians.

By the time troops arrived from England to put down the rebellion, Bacon had died of a fever and most of his men had drifted home. Berkeley arrested and hanged twenty-three rebels, but the real victims of the rebellion were Virginia's Indians. The remnants of the once powerful Powhatans lost their remaining lands and either moved west or lived in poverty on the edges of English settlement. In the wake of the rebellion, hatred of Indians became a permanent feature of frontier life in Virginia, and government officials emerged more eager to spend money "for extirpating all Indians" than for maintaining peaceful relations with them.

The Pueblo Revolt against Spain's colony of New Mexico in 1680 had an outcome very different from that of the conflicts between settlers and Indians in England's colonies. Nearly twenty thousand Pueblo Indians in New Mexico had grown increasingly restless under the harsh rule of only 2,500 Spaniards. A prolonged drought that began in the 1660s only increased their distress. Corn harvests dwindled, and many people starved. The Apaches, who had once traded with the Pueblos for corn, now

One of the many pueblos scattered along the Rio Grande valley, Taos served as Popé's headquarters at the start of the Pueblo Revolt in August 1680. Within a few weeks, the Indians drove the Spanish from New Mexico and destroyed most of their settlements. The Spanish did not return until 1693.

raided their storehouses instead, and Spanish soldiers could not stop them.

The spark that ignited the revolt, however, was an act of religious persecution. Spanish officials unwisely chose this troubled time to stamp out all remaining traces of Pueblo religion. In 1675, the governor arrested forty-seven native religious leaders on charges of sorcery. The court ordered most of them to be publicly whipped and released but sentenced four of them to death.

Led by Popé, one of the freed leaders, the outraged Pueblos organized for revenge. A growing network of rebels emerged as Spanish soldiers marched into Pueblo villages and destroyed kivas, the underground chambers that Indians used for religious ceremonies. By the summer of 1680, Popé—working from the village of Taos in northern New Mexico—had at his command a force of seventeen thousand rebels drawn from twenty Pueblo villages. On August 10, the rebels attacked the Spanish settlements. Popé urged them to "break up and burn the images of the holy Christ, the Virgin Mary and the other saints, the crosses, and everything pertaining to Christianity" and ordered Indian converts to "plunge into the rivers and wash themselves" to remove the taint of baptism. Within a few weeks, the rebels had destroyed or damaged every Spanish building and killed more than four hundred Span-

iards, including twenty-one of the colony's thirty-three missionaries. By October, all Spaniards had fled New Mexico.

They did not return for thirteen years. By then, internal rivalries had split the victorious Pueblo coalition and Popé had been overthrown as leader. Even so, the Spanish now understood the folly of pushing the Indians too far. Fearful of inciting another rebellion, officials reduced demands for tribute, and the Franciscans eased their attacks on Pueblo religion. This spirit of accommodation opened a new century of relatively peaceful relations.

The Iroquois experience in the last phase of the Beaver Wars threatened to parallel that of the Indians of New England or Virginia rather than that of the Pueblos in New Mexico. What began as a struggle between the Iroquois and western native peoples for control of the fur trade blossomed into a larger conflict as it was absorbed into the imperial rivalry between England and France. Although the Iroquois suffered devastating losses similar to those inflicted on the Indians in the English colonies, they did not similarly suffer a loss of independence. The key to Iroquois survival in the war's aftermath was the adoption of a position of neutrality between the European powers.

Looking for new trading partners to replace the Hurons, the French turned in the 1680s to the Ottawas, Wyandots, and other Indian peoples living near the Great Lakes. But the Iroquois had begun to raid these same peoples for furs and captives, much as they had attacked the Hurons in the first phase of the Beaver Wars in the 1640s. They exchanged the furs for European goods with English traders, who had replaced the Dutch as their partners after the conquest of New Netherland. Many of the captives were adopted into Iroquois families, replacing victims of warfare and disease. When the French moved into the Great Lakes territory, the Iroquois objected to their attempt to "have all the Bevers" for themselves.

The French attacked the Iroquois to prevent them and their English allies from extending their influence in the west. In June 1687, a combined force of French and Christian Indian soldiers invaded the lands of the Senecas, the westernmost of the five nations of the Iroquois League. The soldiers burned villages and cornfields and looted Seneca cemeteries. The Iroquois retaliated by besieging a French garrison at Niagara, where nearly two hundred soldiers starved to death, and killing hundreds of colonists in attacks on French villages along the St. Lawrence River.

The French participated much more directly and suffered greater losses in this renewal of the Beaver Wars than they had in the fighting of the 1640s. In 1689, France and England went to war in Europe, and the struggle between them and their Indian allies for control of the fur trade in North America became part of a larger imperial contest between the two countries. The European powers made peace in 1697, but calm did not immediately return to the Great Lakes region.

The conflict was even more devastating for the Iroquois. The English, still solidifying their control over their new colony of New York, provided minimal military assistance, and the Iroquois suffered heavy casualties. Perhaps a quarter of their population died from disease and warfare by 1689. The devastation encouraged Iroquois diplomats to find a way to extricate themselves from future English-French conflicts. The result, in 1701, was a pair of treaties, negotiated separately with Albany and Montreal, that recognized Iroquois neutrality and, at least for a few decades, prevented either the English or the French from dominating the western lands.

Each of these late-seventeenth-century conflicts between Indians and Europeans reflected the particular characteristics of each colonial power and the native peoples they were seeking to dominate. English settlers fought with Wampanoags, Powhatans, and Susquehannocks for control of land, and the losers were the outnumbered Indians. Spanish colonists clashed with Pueblos over religion, and the more numerous natives won a temporary victory and a long-run accommodation with the Spanish Catholic minority. French soldiers battled with the Iroquois over control of the fur trade until both sides agreed to an uneasy truce. In each case, nearly a century of contact culminated in a struggle that revealed how difficult, if not impossible, it was to reconcile European and native interests.

Africans and Europeans

Many more Africans than Europeans came to the New World during the colonial period. By the eighteenth century, according to an English observer, Africans had become "the strength and sinews of this western world." Virtually all of them arrived as slaves; thus the history of African experience in America is inseparable from the history of slavery and the slave trade. The evolution of slavery, its impact on both black and white lives, and most of all the creation of a new African-American identity are essential parts of the story of the formation of New World societies.

The Evolution of Slavery in the New World

Europeans in the New World were thrilled to find that land was abundant and quite cheap by European standards. They were perplexed, however, by the unexpectedly high cost of labor. In Europe, the reverse had been true. There land was expensive but labor cheap because competition for jobs among large numbers of workers pushed wages down.

Colonial workers commanded high wages because there were so few of them compared to the supply of land waiting to be developed. Making matters worse, few settlers wanted to work for others when they could get farms of their own. The scarcity and high cost of labor created a major problem for colonial employers, leading some to turn to enslaved Africans as a solution.

The development of slavery in the colonies was not inevitable. Europeans had owned slaves (both white and black) long before the beginning of American colonization, but slaves formed a small—and shrinking—minority of European laborers. By the fifteenth century, slavery had all but disappeared in northern Europe, except as punishment for serious crimes. English laws in particular protected the personal freedom of the king's subjects in important ways.

Slavery persisted longer in southern Europe and the Middle East. In both regions, religion influenced who was enslaved. Because neither Christians nor Muslims would hold as slaves members of their own faiths, Arab traders turned to sub-Saharan Africa to find slaves who did not belong to either religion. Eventually the Arabic word for slave—`abd—became a synonym for "black man." By the fifteenth century, a durable link between slave status and black skin had been forged in European minds.

When Spanish and Portuguese adventurers needed workers to develop newly colonized Atlantic islands and New World lands, they considered slavery the best solution. Masters exercised complete control over slaves and paid them no wages. Slavery's advantages induced English colonists to adopt it in America even though it was unknown as a system of labor at home.

It was Indians, however, not Africans, whom the Europeans first forced into slavery in the Americas. Columbus's enslavement of Caribbean islanders marked the beginning of this process. Spaniards held some native peoples as slaves in all their New World colonies, as did the Portuguese in Brazil. English colonists condemned Indian enemies captured in wartime to slavery as punishment for their opposition to English rule. And in early Carolina, English traders saw an opportunity to profit by enslaving Indians without any judicial niceties. They encouraged Indians "to make War amongst themselves to get Slaves" whom the traders could buy and then resell to West Indian and local planters.

Native American slaves, however, could not fill the settlers' labor needs. Everywhere disease and harsh working conditions reduced their numbers. English colonists also discovered practical reasons not to enslave Indians. When traders incited Indian wars to gain slaves, bloodshed often spread to English settlements. Enslaved Indian men refused to perform agricultural labor, which they considered women's work. Because they knew the land better than the colonists, Indians could easily escape and make their way back to their own people. As a result, although the Indian slave trade persisted in the English colonies through the eighteenth century (and there were still Indian slaves even in the nineteenth century), by 1700 it had given way to a much larger traffic in Africans.

The first to bring Africans to the Americas were the Spanish and Portuguese, who used them to replace or supplement the dwindling numbers of Indian slaves toiling in silver mines and on sugar plantations. English colonists, less familiar with slavery, adopted it more slowly. West Indian planters were the first to do so on a large scale in the 1640s, following the Portuguese example in using black slaves to grow sugar. In most other English colonies, however, a preference for white laborers or different economic conditions either postponed or prevented slavery's widespread adoption.

Black slaves first arrived in Virginia in 1619 when a Dutch trader sold "20. and odd Negroes" in Jamestown. But they did not form a significant portion of the colony's population until the end of the century (see Figure 3-2). For decades, tobacco planters saw no reason to switch from white indentured servants—whose labor they legally controlled for four to seven years—to slaves. Servants were cheap, available, and familiar; slaves were expensive, difficult to obtain, and exotic. Beginning in the 1680s, however, planters in the Chesapeake colonies

of Virginia and Maryland began to shift from servants to slaves.

Two related developments caused this change. First, white indentured servants became harder to find. Fewer young English men and women chose to emigrate as servants after 1660 because an improving economy in England provided more jobs for them at home. Virginia's white population tripled between 1650 and 1700, however, rapidly increasing the number of planters now competing for a shrinking supply of laborers. Planters also faced competition from newer colonies. Places like Pennsylvania and New Jersey instituted relatively generous land policies, attracting many immigrant laborers away from the longer-settled colonies of the Chesapeake region.

Second, even as white servants grew scarcer, African slaves became more available, largely due to changes in the slave trade. Before the 1660s, Dutch and Portuguese merchants dominated the trade and mainly supplied the profitable West Indian market. Beginning in 1674, however, England's Royal African Company started to ship slaves directly from Africa to buyers in the Caribbean and on the mainland. The supply of slaves surged after 1698, when the Royal African Company lost its special trading rights and many English merchants—and New Englanders—entered the fiercely competitive trade.

Chesapeake planters eventually found reasons besides availability to prefer slaves to servants. Although more expensive than servants, slaves were a better long-term investment. Because slave status passed from slave mothers to their children, buying both men and women gave planters a self-reproducing labor force. Runaway black slaves were more easily recaptured than escaped servants, who blended into the white population. And unlike indentured servants, slaves were slaves for life. They would not someday compete as planters with their former masters or, like Nathaniel Bacon's followers, pose a threat to order if they failed to prosper.

Chesapeake planters had already come to see white servants as possessions, whose labor could be bought and sold like any other commodity. This attitude doubtless eased the gradual transition in the 1680s and 1690s to the much harsher system of slavery. In Carolina, of course, the introduction of slavery was not gradual at all. Slaves arrived there right from the start, brought in the 1670s by colony founders accustomed to slavery in Barbados. By 1720, slavery was firmly embedded in all the southern colonies except sparsely settled North Carolina. In that year, one-third of Virginia's settlers—and nearly three-quarters of South Carolina's—were black.

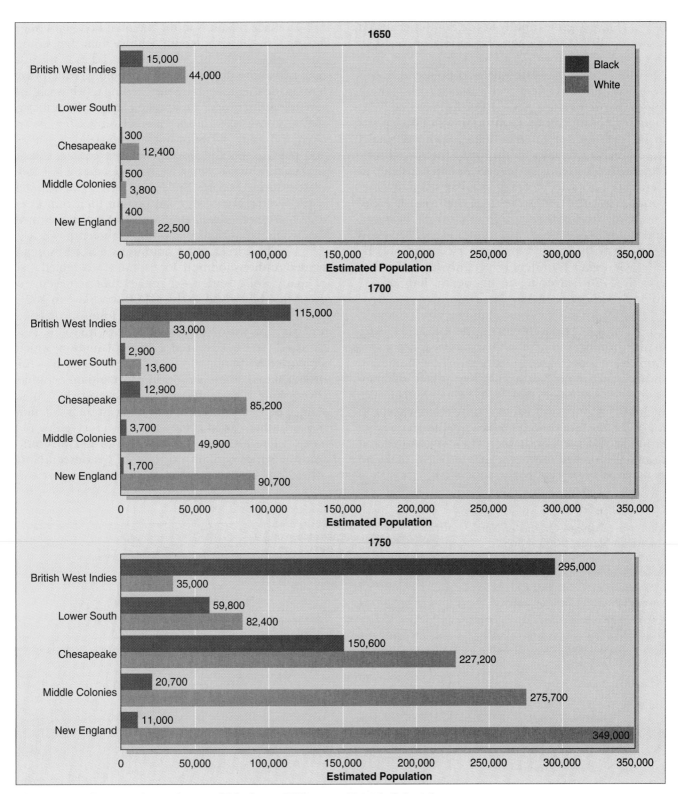

Figure 3-2 *Estimated Population of Blacks and Whites in British Colonial Regions, 1650–1750*

Settler populations increased rapidly in all colonial regions, but the racial composition varied. By 1750, blacks overwhelmingly predominated in the West Indies and were quite numerous in the southern colonies; north of Maryland, however, their numbers remained small.

Source: *John J. McCusker and Russell Menard,* The Economy of British America, 1607–1789 *(1985).*

Slavery grew rapidly in the South because it answered the labor needs of planters engaged in the commercial production of tobacco and rice. The demand for slaves became so powerful that it destroyed James Oglethorpe's plan to keep them out of the new colony of Georgia, founded in 1732. Oglethorpe and other sponsors intended Georgia to be a refuge for English debtors, who normally were jailed until they could repay their creditors. Oglethorpe's idea was to send debtors instead to Georgia to produce exotic goods like silk and wine, benefiting both themselves and the English economy. Only rice turned a profit in Georgia, however, and colonists insisted that they needed slaves to keep up with South Carolina's rice planters. By 1750, Georgia's founders reluctantly legalized slavery; by 1770, slaves made up nearly half of the colony's settlers.

Far fewer slaves lived in the northern colonies. They were too expensive for northern farmers—who mainly produced food for their families, not staple crops for an international market—to use profitably. Instead slaves in the North generally worked as domestic servants, craftsmen, and day laborers, often in cities such as New York and Boston. As a result, except in areas of Long Island, where slaves grew wheat on large farms, and Rhode Island, where they raised cattle and racehorses, only in northern cities did slaves make up as much as 20 percent of the population.

Race relations in the mainland colonies were less rigid in the seventeenth century than they would later become. Before 1700, slaves did not form a majority of the population in any colony, which may have made them seem less threatening to whites. Most seventeenth-century Chesapeake planters did not own slaves. Those who did often held only a few slaves along with white servants. In these households, whites and blacks lived and worked in close contact. Black slaves and white servants ran away together and cooperated during Bacon's Rebellion. In some areas, free blacks—often slaves who had bought their own freedom—prospered in an atmosphere of racial tolerance that would be unthinkable by the eighteenth century.

The career of an ambitious black Virginian named Anthony Johnson, for example, resembled that of many white settlers—a remarkable achievement given that he arrived in the colony as a slave in 1621. Once freed (by unknown means), Johnson married and, with his wife, Mary, raised at least four children. By 1651, he had acquired a large plantation, which supported his family and provided estates for his children. He took his neighbors to court and on occasion successfully sued white settlers. He even bought a slave. The Johnsons impressed many in their community with their "hard labor and known service."

The historical records that preserved Johnson's activities contain no trace of his descendants after 1706. The reasons for this silence are unclear,

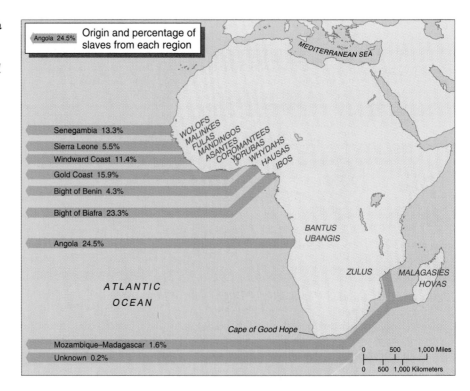

Map 3-2   African Origins of North American Slaves, 1690–1807
Nearly all slaves in English North America were West Africans. Most had been captured or purchased by African slave traders, who then sold them to European merchants.

Source: *After Philip Curtin,* The Atlantic Slave Trade: A Census *(1969), tab. 45, p. 157.*

This late eighteenth-century engraving, showing European slave traders on the coast of Africa, graphically illustrates the first step in the wrenching and dehumanizing process of enslavement.

but by then slavery had become the dominant labor system in the Chesapeake. Tobacco planters no longer welcomed free blacks, fearing that they might encourage slaves to escape. In 1699, Virginia's assembly had passed a law requiring newly freed blacks to leave the colony. The Johnsons had already moved to Maryland, but that colony offered little refuge. Johnson's descendants may have moved again—or perhaps even slipped back into slavery as the institution tightened its hold on the colonial South.

Even in the seventeenth century, few whites, if any, claimed blacks as their equals. After 1700, however, the condition of blacks swiftly deteriorated. Laws now defined slavery as lifelong and hereditary according to the condition of the mother and identified slave status with black skin. Other measures deprived black persons, slave or free, of basic civil rights. They could not vote, testify in court against whites, hold property, congregate in public places, or travel without permission. Interracial marriages, never common, were now prohibited as "shameful Matches."

Colonists resorted to these **slave codes**—which essentially reduced human beings to the status of property—largely because of fears generated by a rising black population. In 1720, a South Carolina planter predicted that slaves would soon rise up against their masters because blacks were "too numerous in proportion to the White Men there." The changing composition of the slave labor force also created tensions.

Most seventeenth-century slaves came to the southern colonies by way of the West Indies or New Netherlands, where they had acquired some familiarity with Europeans and perhaps a few words of English. But after 1700, slave traders brought cargoes of what colonists called "outlandish" slaves directly from Africa. Worried planters commented on the strange appearance and behavior of these people, with whom they could barely communicate. Their uneasiness, of course, scarcely compared to the Africans' harrowing experience of being torn away from the only world they knew and carried off to an unknown fate.

The Shock of Enslavement

European traders did not themselves enslave Africans. Instead, they relied on other Africans to capture slaves for them, tapping into a preexisting African slave trade and helping expand it beyond previous bounds. With the permission of local rulers, Europeans built forts and trading posts (called "factories") on the West African coast and bought slaves from African traders (see Map 3-2). African rulers occasionally enslaved and sold their own people as punishment for crimes, but most slaves were seized by one group from another. Attracted by European cloth, iron, liquor, guns, and other goods, West Africans fought increasingly among themselves to secure captives and began to send raiding parties to kidnap individuals from the interior.

People of all social ranks ended up on the slave ships. Some had already lived as slaves in Africa;

others had been prominent members of their villages. In 1730, Mandingo tribesmen captured Job ben Solomon, an accomplished Arabic scholar of the Fula tribe of Senegal, and sold him to English traders. Unlike the vast majority of slaves, Job made it back to Africa four years later (see "American Views: Job becomes a Slave" on page 82). Even some members of African royal families ended up in shackles. In the end, slavery reduced all Africans, regardless of their social origins, to the same degraded status.

Once captured, slaves marched in chains to the coast, to be confined in cages called "barracoons" until there were enough to fill a ship. Captains examined them to ensure their fitness and branded them like cattle with a hot iron. The slaves then boarded canoes to be ferried to the ships. Desperation overwhelmed some of them, who, according to an English captain, jumped "out of the canoos . . . into the sea, and kept under water till they were drowned, to avoid being taken up and saved."

Slaves brought safely to the ships suffered through a horrendous six- to eight-week-long ocean voyage known as the **Middle Passage**. Captains wedged men below decks into spaces about 6 feet long, 16 inches wide, and 30 inches high. Women and children were packed even tighter. They occasionally came up on deck for fresh air, where in a ceremony called "dancing the slaves," sailors, with whips in hand, commanded them (often shackled in irons) to dance and sing for exercise. Most of the time, slaves remained below decks, where the hot and humid air grew foul from the vomit, blood, and excrement in which the terrified victims lay. No wonder that sailors sometimes heard a "howling melancholy noise" coming from below. Some slaves went insane. Others tried to commit suicide by jumping overboard or starving themselves. Captains force-fed those who refused to eat, however, prying their mouths open and pouring food in through a funnel. On many voyages, between 5 and 20 percent of the slaves perished from disease, but captains had usually packed the ships tightly enough to make a profit selling the rest.

Those who survived the dreadful voyage had to endure the fear and humiliation of sale. Sometimes buyers rushed aboard ship in a scramble to choose slaves. Planters generally preferred males and often sought slaves from particular ethnic groups. South Carolina slave owners thought that Coromantees and Whydahs from the Gold Coast and Senegambia were good workers but that Angolans had "a lazy disposition." Ship captains also sold slaves

The Fortunate Slave: An Illustration of African Slavery in the Early Eighteenth Century by Douglas Grant (1968). From Some Memoirs of the Life of Job by Thomas Bluett (1734). Photo by Precision Chromes Inc., NYPL.

Captured by Mandingo enemies and sold to a Maryland tobacco planter, Job ben Solomon accomplished the nearly impossible feat of returning to Africa as a free man. By demonstrating his talents as a Muslim scholar, including his ability to write the entire Koran from memory, he astonished his owners and eventually convinced them to let him go home.

at public auctions, where eager purchasers poked them, looking for signs of disease. The terrified Africans often thought they were about to be eaten.

African-American Families and Communities

Only 5 percent of all Africans brought to the New World ended up in the mainland English colonies; the vast majority went to New Spain, Brazil, or the West Indies (see Figure 3-3). Black communities developed slowly in early America. In the northern colonies, most slaves lived alone or in pairs with their master's family. Only in the cities, where slaves were more numerous, could they have regular contact with other blacks. More slaves lived in the South, but until the eighteenth century they were dispersed among a much larger white population. Slave numbers grew after 1700, but much of the increase consisted of African immigrants. These people thought of themselves and their fellows not as Africans but as Ibos and Fulas, Yorubas and Wolofs, with different languages, religions, and customs. They needed time to develop a new sense of community.

As bad as slavery was in North America, in one important way it was less terrible than slavery in the West Indies. On the sugar islands, many more slaves died—worked to death in a hot, disease-ridden environment—than were born, so the slave population grew only because of the constant importation of Africans. Conditions in the southern colonies, however, were less harsh, and by about 1750, more slaves there were **creoles** (American-born) than African natives. Creoles lived longer than African immigrants, and creole women usually bore twice as many children as African-born mothers. The mainland slave population therefore began to grow by natural increase and more closely resembled a normal population of men and women, children and elders.

Creole slaves grew up without personal memories of Africa, so African ethnic differences seemed less important to them. Language was no longer a barrier, for most creoles knew some English and spoke dialects they had created by mixing English and African words and speech patterns. The ability to communicate helped them develop a new identity as African-Americans that mingled aspects of their African heritage and a common experience of slavery.

Kinship ties, crucial to West Africans' sense of identity, remained important to American slaves. Maintaining those ties, however, was not always under the slaves' control. Slave families were fragile units, subject to the whims of masters who did not recognize slave marriages as legal, who could break up families by sale at any time, and who could take slave women as sexual partners at will. Even so, slaves managed to form families that preserved and modified African traditions.

Households headed by mothers, common in West Africa, reappeared in America. Slave fathers often belonged to different masters than their wives and children and had to live apart from their families. Some slave husbands, like West African men, took more than one wife (a practice masters allowed because it led to more slave children). Slave parents gave their children African names, often secretly adding them to the "official" names given by masters. These names had specific meanings, such as Quasheba for a girl born on Sunday or Sambo for a second son. American-born slave parents continued to use the names, although often without regard to their original meanings, as reminders of their African heritage.

In Virginia and South Carolina, where by 1750 some plantations supported village-sized populations of slaves, communities preserved other elements of West African culture. Carolina slaves followed West African practice by building their houses of "tabby," a mixture of lime and seashells. Also following West African practice, the houses were sometimes constructed on a circular plan. Potters and basketmakers used African designs in their work. Slaves raised African food plants (millet, yams, sesame seeds) in their gardens. They also made music, performed dances, and told folk tales derived from African models.

Labor, however, consumed most of a slave's waking hours. Some slaves worked as domestic servants, but the vast majority were field hands. On tobacco plantations, slaves toiled in gangs supervised by overseers. Rice planters allowed their workers

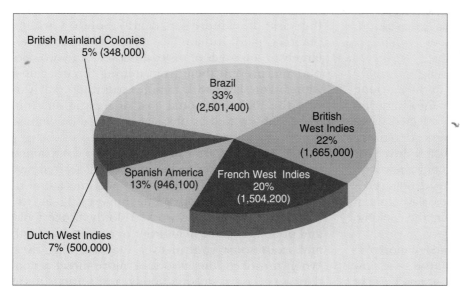

Figure 3-3 Destination of Slaves Imported from Africa to the Americas between 1451 and 1810
Approximately 7.5 million Africans were brought as slaves to the Americas before 1810. The vast majority went to the Caribbean, Mexico, and South America, where they toiled in mines and on sugar plantations.
Source: *Philip Curtin*, The Atlantic Slave Trade: A Census *(1969)*, p. 268.

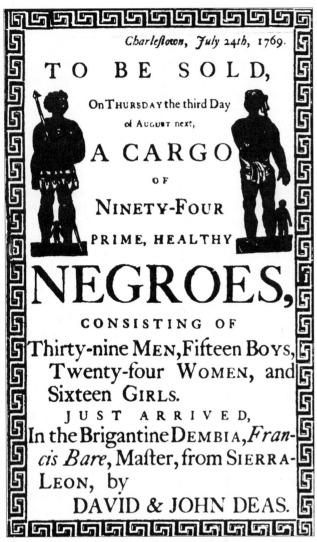

This 1769 broadside advertised the arrival of a cargo of West African slaves in Charleston, South Carolina. By that date, slaves made up over two-thirds of the colony's settlers. Note that nearly equal numbers of men and women have been imported. This practice would eventually contribute to the formation of slave families and communities.

more flexibility, assigning them tasks in the morning and permitting them free time after they were finished. On large plantations, masters selected slaves to be trained as shoemakers, weavers, or tailors. These specialized occupations, like that of driver (or head worker), usually went to men. Only a few slave women—nurses, cooks—avoided the drudgery of field work. And after a day in the fields, slave women had to take care of their families, doing the cooking, child care, washing, and housework.

Family ties made a life in bondage more tolerable. The growth of slave communities—a slow process beginning only in the 1750s—gave a sense of belonging and dignity to people whose masters treated them as outcasts. Yet family and community ties also made it much more difficult for slaves to risk escape or contemplate rebellion. The master could use his power to break up families as a tool to ensure compliant behavior. In effect, every slave child was his hostage.

Over time, masters gradually realized that their economic welfare and even their physical survival depended on the cooperation, or at least the submission, of their slaves, and this encouraged them to improve their treatment of their slaves. By the end of the colonial period, many masters had begun describing themselves as "fathers" to their slave "children." Few slaves, however, saw the relationship in the same benevolent light.

Resistance and Rebellion

Slaves on ships anchored off the Guinea Coast waiting to leave for America sometimes mutinied. These rebellions, fought against great odds, rarely succeeded. But the powerful desire for freedom and the spirit of resistance they represented remained strong among Africans and their descendants in America.

Running away from a master was a desperate act, but hundreds of slaves did just that. Few runaways shared the mistaken impression of some new arrivals in eighteenth-century Virginia that they could "find the Way back to their own Country." But deciding where else to go posed a problem. Escape out of the South did not bring freedom because slavery was legal in every colony. Some runaways went to Florida, where after 1733 Spanish officials enticed them with promises of freedom. Others tried to survive on their own in the woods or join the Indians, a choice that carried the risk of capture or death. South Carolina planters paid Indians to catch escaped slaves, largely to sow seeds of distrust between the two peoples and prevent them from joining forces against whites. For slaves with families, running away carried the high emotional cost of separation from loved ones as well as physical danger. Many chose other ways to resist their bondage.

Landon Carter of Virginia, who complained that his slaves "seem to be quite dead hearted and either cannot or will not work," was the target of forms of resistance more subtle, but every bit as real, as running away. Slaves worked slowly, broke tools, and pretended to be ill in order to conserve strength and exert some control over their working lives. When provoked, they also took more direct action, damaging crops, stealing goods, and setting fire to

This eighteenth-century painting from South Carolina records the preservation of certain African traditions in American slave communities. The dance may be Yoruba in origin, while the stringed instrument and drum were probably modeled on African instruments.

their masters' barns, houses, and fields. Slaves with knowledge of poisonous plants occasionally tried to kill whites, although the penalty for being caught was to be burned to death.

The most serious, as well as the rarest, form of resistance was organized rebellion. South Carolinians and coastal Virginians, who lived in regions where blacks outnumbered whites, had a particular dread of slave revolt. Rebellions, however, required complete secrecy, careful planning, and access to weapons, which made them extremely hard to organize. No slave rebellion succeeded in the British colonies. Rumors usually leaked out before any action had been taken, prompting severe reprisals against the alleged conspirators. In Charleston, South Carolina, rumors of a planned uprising in 1740 led to the torture and execution of fifty blacks. The following year, thirty-five alleged rebels (including four whites—one a tavernkeeper and another allegedly a Spanish priest) were executed in New York City.

Two slave revolts did occur in the colonial period, however, and instilled lasting fear in whites. In 1712 in New York City, where blacks made up perhaps 20 percent of the population, about twenty slaves set a building on fire and killed nine white men who came to put it out. The revolt was quickly suppressed. The court tried forty-three rebels and sentenced twenty-four to death. Their punish-

ments revealed the extent of white terror: thirteen were hanged, three burned at the stake, one starved to death, and one was broken on the wheel. Six committed suicide before execution.

The **Stono Rebellion**, colonial America's largest slave uprising, occurred in South Carolina in 1739. It began when about twenty slaves—including several recently arrived Angolans—broke into a store and armed themselves with stolen guns. As the rebels marched southward along the Stono River, their ranks grew to perhaps a hundred. Heading for freedom in Spanish Florida, they boldly attacked white settlements along the way. White troops (with Indian help) defeated the rebels within a week, but tensions remained high for months. The death toll, in the end, was about two dozen whites and perhaps twice as many blacks. Planters boasted that they "did not torture one Negroe, but only put them to an easy death," although one settler claimed that white soldiers "Cutt off their heads and set them up at every Mile Post they came to."

In the wake of the Stono Rebellion, South Carolina's assembly passed a comprehensive Negro Act, requiring stricter supervision of slave activities. Other measures encouraged more white immigration to offset the colony's black majority. But the colony continued to rely on the labor system that generated so much fear and brutality. In South Carolina, as in the rest of the southern colonies, planters considered slavery indispensable to their economic survival and would not willingly give it up. Their slaves, in turn, obeyed when necessary, resisted when possible, and kept alive the hope that freedom would one day be theirs.

Nonslave Labor in Early America

Slavery was one of several responses to the scarcity of labor in the New World. It took hold mainly in areas where the profits from growing export crops such as

American Views

JOB BECOMES A SLAVE (1730)

Job ben Solomon was no ordinary slave. Born in Senegal to a family of Muslim clerics, he was captured by a rival African tribe, sold to an English slaver, and set to work on a Maryland plantation. He tried and failed to escape but astonished his jailers by writing a letter in Arabic describing his plight. The letter made its way to James Oglethorpe, an official of the Royal African Company as well as founder of Georgia, who bought Job and brought him to England. Englishmen marveled at Job's learning, which he demonstrated by writing the entire Koran from memory. Job was entertained all over London and even presented to King George, but he begged to go home. In 1734, he finally returned to Africa—an unprecedented accomplishment for an American slave. Thomas Bluett, a Maryland colonist who met Job while he was in jail, wrote and published an account of Job's experiences.

❖ **How did Job come to be captured in Africa?**

❖ **What humiliations did he suffer as a result of his enslavement?**

❖ **Does this account demonstrate any evidence of bias on the part of its English author?**

In February, 1730, Job's father hearing of an English ship at Gambia River, sent him, with two servants to attend him, to sell two Negroes, and to buy paper, and some other necessaries; but desired him not to venture over the river, because the country of the Mandingoes, who are enemies to the people of Futa, lies on the other side. Job . . .

intended to go farther. Accordingly having agreed with another man, named Loumein Yoas, who understood the Mandingoe language, to go with him as his interpreter, he crossed the River Gambia, and disposed of his Negroes for some cows. As he was returning home, he stopped for some refreshment at the house of an old acquain-

---

sugar, rice, and tobacco were sufficient to offset the high purchase price of slaves and where a warm climate permitted year-round work. Elsewhere, Europeans found other means to acquire and manage laborers. Indentured servitude, forced labor, tenancy, and the extension of credit all aimed at limiting the freedom of some people in order to make them work for others.

Indian Workers in New France and the Spanish Borderlands

The French and Spanish colonies relied more heavily on native laborers than the English did. The fur trade in New France was in effect a way for the French to harness Indian labor. French officials promised military support and French merchants extended credit in order to get native hunters to trap beavers and bring

them furs. By supplying Indians with trade goods in advance, merchants obligated them to bring in furs as payment. One year's hunting, in short, paid the previous year's debts. If unsuccessful hunters tried to ignore or postpone payment, merchants refused to give them any more of the trade goods on which they had come to depend. Extending credit in this way allowed the French to control native workers without having to subjugate them.

The Spanish used more direct means to control Indian labor, employing three main methods: *encomienda*, *repartimiento*, and *rescate*. *Encomiendas*, granted to influential Spaniards in New Mexico, gave them the right to collect tribute—usually in the form of corn, blankets, and animal hides—from a specific group of natives. The tribute was not supposed to include forced labor but often did. Some Spaniards required native men to

tance; and the weather being hot, he hung up his arms in the house, while he refreshed himself. . . . It happened that a company of the Mandingoes, who live upon plunder, passing by at that time, and observing him unarmed, rushed in, to the number of seven or eight at once, at a back door, and pinioned Job, before he could get to his arms, together with his interpreter, who is a slave in Maryland still. They then shaved their heads and beards, which Job and his man resented as the highest indignity; tho' the Mandingoes meant no more by it, than to make them appear like Slaves taken in war. On the 27th of February, 1730, they carried them to Captain Pike at Gambia, who purchased them; and on the first of March they were put on board. . . .

[Job was sold to a Maryland planter] who put him to work in making tobacco; but he was soon convinced that Job had never been used to such labour. He every day showed more and more uneasiness under this exercise, and at last grew sick, being no way able to bear it; so that his master was obliged to find easier work for him, and therefore put him to tend the cattle. Job would often leave the cattle, and withdraw into the woods to pray; but a white boy frequently watched him, and whilst he was at his devotion would mock him, and throw dirt in his face. This very much disturbed Job, and added considerably to his other misfortunes; all which were increased by his ignorance of the English language, which prevented his complaining, or telling his case to any person about him.

Source: *Philip D. Curtin, ed.,* Africa Remembered: Narratives by West Africans from the Era of the Slave Trade *(1967), pp. 39–41.*

work on their farms and ranches and native women to become domestic servants. Excessive demands for tribute fueled Indian anger during the Pueblo Revolt, and when the Spaniards returned to New Mexico in 1693, they did not reimpose the *encomienda* system.

In New Mexico and Florida, the *repartimiento*—a mandatory draft of native labor for public projects—set Indians to work building forts, bridges, and roads. Laws stated that native workers should be paid and limited the length of service, but the Spanish often ignored these provisions and sometimes forced Indians to work on their private estates. Spaniards also acquired laborers by ransoming captives that Indian tribes seized from one another, a practice called *rescate* ("ransom"). These "freed" Indians usually became servants in Spanish households, often for years. Some families welcomed them as foster members, but others mistreated them or even sold them into slavery.

These methods of labor control depended on two factors: the existence of sizable Indian communities and Spanish military force. Native villages provided plenty of workers as well as existing structures of government that the Spanish could use to collect tribute and organize gangs of workers. At the same time, Spanish soldiers ensured that the Indians—who outnumbered the colonists—obeyed orders. Even the Franciscans relied on military support to control native workers in the missions.

Laborers in the English Colonies

In the English colonies, slavery was just the most oppressive extreme in a spectrum of practices designed to exert control over workers and relieve

SUMMARY

PRINCIPAL COLONIAL LABOR SYSTEMS, 1750

	Colony	Labor System
New England	Massachusetts	Family farms
	Connecticut	Family farms
	New Hampshire	Family farms
	Rhode Island	Family farms
Middle Colonies	New York	Family farms, tenancy
	Pennsylvania and Delaware	Indentured servitude, tenancy, family farms
	New Jersey	Family farms, tenancy
South	Maryland	Slavery
	Virginia	Slavery
	North Carolina	Family farms, slavery
	South Carolina	Slavery

the problems caused by the easy availability of land and the high cost of labor. Most colonial laborers were, in some measure, unfree (see the summary table "Principal Colonial Labor Systems, 1750").

One-half to two-thirds of all white emigrants to the English colonies arrived as indentured servants, bound by contract to serve masters for a period of years. Tens of thousands of people accepted temporary servitude in return for passage across the Atlantic and the chance for a more prosperous future in America. But indentured servants, though less costly than slaves, carried too high a price for farmers, who mainly raised crops for subsistence rather than sale. Thus servants were most common in the Chesapeake, and to a lesser extent in Pennsylvania, where they produced export crops valuable enough to enable their masters to feed, clothe, and shelter them— and still make a profit.

Slaves replaced white indentured servants in Chesapeake tobacco fields during the eighteenth century. Masters continued to import servants for a while to fill skilled jobs but in time trained the more plentiful slaves to fill those jobs also. Thus by the middle of the eighteenth century, white servitude, although it still existed in the Chesapeake region as well as in Pennsylvania and New York, was in decline as a dominant labor system.

Eighteenth-century Chesapeake planters also availed themselves of another unfree labor source: transported English convicts. Lawmakers in England saw transportation as a way of getting rid of large numbers of serious criminals who might otherwise be executed. Between 1718 and 1775, nearly fifty thousand convicts were sent to the colonies, 80 percent of whom ended up in the Chesapeake. Most were young, lower-class males forced by economic hardship to turn to lives of crime. Although some colonists objected to England's policy of sending its undesirables to America, labor-hungry planters eagerly bought them for seven-year terms at relatively low prices and exploited them ruthlessly. A few convicts eventually prospered in America, but most faced lives as miserable as those they had known in England.

An arrangement similar to indentured servitude—the **redemptioner** system—brought many German families to the colonies in the eighteenth century. Instead of negotiating contracts for service before leaving Europe, as indentured servants did, redemptioners promised to redeem, or pay, the costs of passage on arrival in America. They often paid part of the fare themselves before sailing. If they could not raise the rest of it soon after landing, the ship captain who brought them sold them into servitude. The length of their service depended on how much they still owed. Most Germans went to Pennsylvania, where they hoped to find friends or relatives willing to help them pay off their debt quickly.

Purchasing slaves, servants, or convicts did not make sense for everyone. Colonists who owned undeveloped land faced many tasks—cutting trees, clearing fields, building fences and barns—that brought no immediate profit. Rather than buy expensive laborers to do this, landowners rented undeveloped tracts to propertyless families. Both tenants and landlords benefited from this arrangement. Tenants enjoyed greater independence than servants and could save toward the purchase of their own farms. The landlord secured the labor necessary to transform his property into a working farm, which increased the land's value. He also received an annual rent payment, usually a portion of the tenant's crop, and eventually profited from selling the land—often to the tenant family that had rented it. Tenancy worked best in Pennsylvania, New Jersey, and the Hudson and Connecticut River Valleys, where farmers raised wheat and other grains for the market.

Merchants eager to develop New England's fisheries devised other means to fill their labor needs. Because it was fairly easy to get a farm, few New Englanders cared to take on the difficult and risky job of fishing. Moreover, few could afford the necessary equipment, which included boats, sails, provisions, and salt (used for preserving fish). To recruit suppliers, fish merchants advanced credit to coastal villagers so they could outfit their own boats and become fishermen. To pay off the debt, the fishermen were legally bound to bring their catch to the merchant, who then sold it to Europe and the West Indies. Many fishermen ran up such large debts that they were obliged to continue supplying fish to their creditors, whether they wanted to or not. Toward the end of the seventeenth century, as the rising population of coastal villages lowered the cost of labor, merchants abandoned the credit system and paid fishermen wages instead.

In the northern colonies, the same conditions that made men reluctant to become fishermen deterred them from becoming farm laborers. Men who could have their own farms, observed Massachusetts's governor John Winthrop, "would not be hired at all" to work for someone else, except at very high wages. The cost of servants or slaves exceeded whatever small profit could be made on farms that produced no export crops and could not be worked during cold winter months. So northern farmers turned to the cheapest and most dependable workers they could find—their children.

Children as young as 5 or 6 years old began with simple tasks and moved on to more complex work as they grew older. By the time they were in their late teens, girls knew how to run households and boys knew how to farm. Instead of contracts or outright coercion, fathers used their ownership of property to prolong the time their sons worked for them.

Young men in New England could not marry and set up their own households until they could support a wife and family. New England fathers frequently postponed giving them the necessary property until the sons were in their late twenties. Often sons did not actually own any land until their fathers died and left it to them in their wills. Richard Barker's firm hold over his land in late-seventeenth-century Andover, Massachusetts, kept his six sons from marrying until they were between 25 and 35 years old. Most were well into their forties before Barker died, making them at last the legal owners of land they had been tilling most of their lives.

Thus New England's labor shortage produced strong ties of dependency between generations. Fathers kept their sons working for them as long as possible; sons accepted this arrangement because they had no other way to become independent farmers. They would eventually employ their own children in the same way. As New England's population increased in the eighteenth century and vacant land grew scarcer, the price of labor came down. Some fathers could then afford to hire occasional helpers and loosened their hold on their sons, allowing them to marry in their early twenties.

Property owners in all the English colonies found different ways to control the laborers they so desperately needed. But where property owners saw problems—high wages (often twice what workers in England received) and abundant land (which deterred colonists from working for others when they could have their own farms)—others saw opportunities. For tens of thousands of Europeans, the chance to own or rent a farm or to find steady employment made North America an irresistible magnet, promising a prosperity that was beyond their reach at home.

Transplanted Europeans

European immigrants flooded into America in the seventeenth and eighteenth centuries (see Figure 3-4). Nearly 250,000 Scots-Irish people—descendants of Protestant Scots who had settled in northern Ireland in the sixteenth and seventeenth centuries—came to the colonies after 1718 when their landlords raised rents to intolerable levels. Tens of thousands of immigrants arrived from Scotland during the same period, some seeking economic improvement and some sent as punishment for rebellions against the king in 1715 and 1745. Thousands of Irish Catholics arrived as servants, redemptioners, and convicts. By 1773, the tremendous outflow of Britons to America sparked debate in England over whether emigration should be prohibited lest the British Isles themselves be left empty.

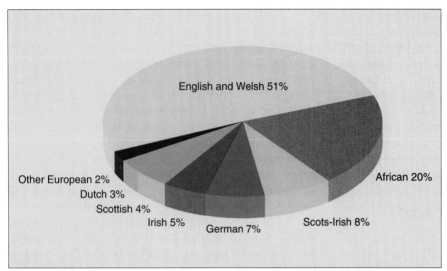

Figure 3-4   *Ethnic Distribution of Non-Indian Inhabitants of British Mainland Colonies, c. 1770*

By the third quarter of the eighteenth century, the colonial population was astonishingly diverse. Only two out of three settlers claimed British ancestry (from England, Wales, Scotland, or northern Ireland), while one out of five was African in origin.

Source: *Adapted from Thomas L. Purvis, "The European Ancestry of the United States Population, 1790," William and Mary Quarterly, 3d series, 41 (1984), p. 98.*

Continental Europe contributed another stream of emigrants, mostly from the German states. Perhaps 100,000 Protestants left the Rhine Valley, where war, economic hardship, and religious persecution had brought misery. Other regions furnished migrants as well. French Protestants (known as Huguenots) began emigrating after 1685, when their faith was made illegal in France, and continued to arrive for decades. Swiss Protestants likewise fled religious persecution. Even a few Poles, Greeks, Italians, and Jews reached the colonies in the eighteenth century.

Many emigrants responded to pamphlets and newspaper articles that exaggerated the bright prospects of life in America. Others studied more realistic accounts from friends and relatives who had already emigrated. One Scot warned his countrymen that at first "poor people will meet with many Difficulties" in North Carolina but they should "take courage and Come to this Country [for] it will be of Benefitt" to their families. Landowners eager for workers sent agents to port towns to recruit new arrivals to become tenants. One happy immigrant wrote to his wife, who remained behind in England, that he had signed a lease for a farm in New York that exempted him from paying rent for the first five years and charged him only 7 pence an acre after that.

Streams of emigrants flowed to places where land was cheap and labor most in demand (see

Map 3-3). Few went to New England, where descendants of the first settlers already occupied the best land. They also avoided areas where slavery predominated—the Chesapeake tidewater region and lowland South Carolina—in favor of the foothills of the Appalachian Mountains from western Pennsylvania to the Carolinas. There, one emigrant declared, a "poor man that will incline to work may have the value of his labour."

This observation, though partly true, did not tell the whole story. Any person who came as a servant, redemptioner, or tenant learned that his master or landlord received much of "the value of his labour." Not all emigrants realized their dreams of becoming independent landowners. The scarcity of labor in the colonies led as easily to the exploitation of white workers as of slaves and Indians. Even so, for many people facing bleak prospects in Europe, the chance that emigration might bring prosperity was too tempting to ignore.

Conclusion

By the middle of the eighteenth century, America offered a strikingly diverse mosaic of peoples and communities. Along the St. Lawrence River, for instance, lay Kahnawake, a village of Mohawks and Abenakis who had adopted Catholicism and French ways under Jesuit instruction. In Andover, Massachusetts, New Englanders tilled fields that their Puritan grandparents had cleared. German immigrants who had forsaken the world in search of spiritual perfection populated the isolated Pennsylvania settlement of Ephrata. The hundred or so slaves on Robert Carter's Virginia plantation at Nomini Hall gathered on Sunday evenings to nurture ties of community with songs and dances, while the master cultivated his very different sense of community with the neighboring planters whom he invited to the great house to sip fine wine.

In North Carolina, Swiss settlers rebuilt the coastal town of New Bern, destroyed during the Tuscarora War, while 100 miles further west, Scottish

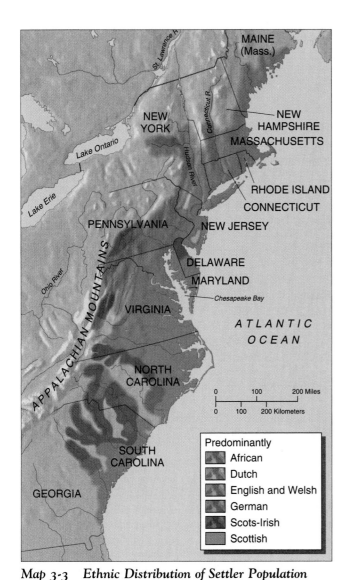

Map 3-3 *Ethnic Distribution of Settler Population in British Mainland Colonies, c. 1755*
Settlers of different ethnic backgrounds tended to concentrate in certain areas. Only New Englanders were predominantly English, while Africans dominated in the Chesapeake tidewater and South Carolina. German, Scottish, and Scots-Irish immigrants often settled in the backcountry.

emigrants cleared land for farms near present-day Fayetteville. Catawba Indians formed new villages in the South Carolina foothills to distance themselves from white settlers. In Mose, Florida, near St. Augustine, runaway slaves farmed and gathered shellfish under the protection of Spanish soldiers. Far to the west, the Spanish, mestizo, and Pueblo residents of Santa Fe warily reestablished ties broken during the Pueblo Revolt.

In these and many other communities, peoples from three continents changed in fundamental ways as they adapted to one another and to American conditions. Indians struggled with the consequences of disease, trade, religious conversion, settlement, and warfare resulting from European immigration. Africans exchanged their traditional ethnic connections for a new identity as African-Americans. English settlers became landowners in unprecedented numbers, and adopted new ways to control laborers, reinventing slavery, unknown in England for centuries. No European settlement in America fully reproduced Old World patterns, and no native village fully preserved the precontact Indian way of life.

For all their divergence from European experience, the North American colonies attracted more and more attention from their home countries as the eighteenth century wore on. Spain, France, and England all recognized the colonies' growing economic power and strove to harness it to block the expansion of their rivals. Everywhere the effort to strengthen imperial ties created ambivalence among colonists. Because they were by far the most numerous, the English settlers' responses were most pronounced. As they saw more clearly the differences between themselves and the English, some colonists began to defend their distinctive habits, while others tried more insistently than ever to imitate English ways. The tension between new and old had, of course, characterized colonial development from the start. What made the eighteenth century distinctive was the many ways in which those tensions worked themselves out.

Review Questions

1. English colonists experienced more frequent, and more violent, conflicts with Indians than the settlers of New France did. Why was this so? What factors affected Indian-white relations in the two colonial regions?

2. Why were Catholic missionaries more successful than Protestants in converting Indians to Christianity in early America?

3. When did Chesapeake planters switch from servants to slaves? What factors contributed to their decision to make this change?

4. By about 1750, more slaves in the mainland British colonies were creoles (American-born) than African-born. What effects did this have on the formation of an African-American community in America?

5. Different labor systems predominated in various regions of British America. How did the economy of each region help determine its labor system?

6. Tens of thousands of European immigrants came to America in the eighteenth century, but they tended to settle only in certain colonial regions. What destinations did they favor and why?

Recommended Reading

Cronon, William. *Changes in the Land: Indians, Colonists, and the Ecology of New England* (1983). This path-breaking study examines the ecological consequences of Indian settlement in New England and of the displacement of Indians by English colonists.

Delage, Denys. *Bitter Feast: Amerindians and Europeans in Northeastern North America, 1600–64* (English ed., 1993). Offering a comprehensive analysis of French, Dutch, and English colonization in northeastern North America, this study focuses on European strategies for trade and economic development and their impact on native peoples.

Jordan, Winthrop. *White over Black: American Attitudes toward the Negro, 1550–1812* (1968). This prizewinning book traces white attitudes toward black people over nearly three centuries of contact, exploring the way in which racial stereotypes contributed to the development of slavery. It is available in an abridged edition as *The White Man's Burden: Historical Origins of Racism in the United States* (1974).

Moore, Brian. *Black Robe* (1985). This powerful novel explores the experiences of a Jesuit missionary among the Indians in seventeenth-century New France.

Nash, Gary B. *Red, White, and Black: The Peoples of Early America* (3d ed., 1991). This important synthesis treats the history of early America as the complex story of interactions between peoples from three major cultures—Native American, European, and African.

Vickers, Daniel. *Farmers and Fishermen: Two Centuries of Work in Essex County, Massachusetts, 1630–1830* (1994). This beautifully written and sophisticated analysis explores the way in which settlers adapted their English experiences to deal with the shortages of labor and capital in New England.

Additional Sources

Indians and Europeans

Axtell, James. *The Invasion Within: The Contest of Cultures in Colonial North America* (1985).

Bourne, Russell. *The Red King's Rebellion: Racial Politics in New England, 1675–1678* (1990).

Cave, Alfred A. *The Pequot War* (1996).

Gutierrez, Ramon. *When Jesus Came, the Corn Mothers Went Away: Marriage, Sexuality, and Power in New Mexico, 1500–1846* (1991).

Hinderaker, Eric. *Elusive Empires: Constructing Colonialism in the Ohio Valley, 1673–1800* (1997).

Jennings, Francis. *The Invasion of America: Indians, Colonialism, and the Cant of Conquest* (1975).

Knaut, Andrew L. *The Pueblo Revolt of 1680: Conquest and Resistance in Seventeenth-Century New Mexico* (1995).

Leach, Douglas Edward. *Flintlock and Tomahawk: New England in King Philip's War* (1958).

Merrell, James H. *The Indians' New World: Catawbas and Their Neighbors from European Contact through the Era of Removal* (1989).

Richter, Daniel. *The Ordeal of the Longhouse: The Peoples of the Iroquois League in the Era of European Colonization* (1992).

Rountree, Helen. *The Powhatan Indians of Virginia: Their Traditional Culture* (1989).

Rountree, Helen. *Pocahontas's People: The Powhatan Indians of Virginia through Four Centuries* (1990).

Salisbury, Neal. *Manitou and Providence: Indians, Europeans, and the Making of New England, 1500–1643* (1982).

Silver, Timothy. *A New Face on the Countryside: Indians, Colonists, and Slaves in South Atlantic Forests, 1500–1800* (1990).

Steele, Ian K. *Warpaths: Invasions of North America* (1994).

Washburn, Wilcomb E. *The Governor and the Rebel: A History of Bacon's Rebellion in Virginia* (1957).

White, Richard. *The Middle Ground: Indians, Empires, and Republics in the Great Lakes Region, 1650–1815* (1991).

Wood, Peter; Waselkov, Gregory; and Hatley, M. Thomas, eds. *Powhatan's Mantle: Indians in the Colonial Southeast* (1989).

Africans in America

Breen, T. H., and Innes, Stephen. *"Myne Owne Ground": Race and Freedom on Virginia's Eastern Shore, 1640–1676* (1980).

Curtin, Philip. *The Atlantic Slave Trade: A Census* (1969).

Davis, David Brion. *The Problem of Slavery in Western Culture* (1966).

Kulikoff, Allan. *Tobacco and Slaves: The Development of Southern Cultures in the Chesapeake, 1680–1800* (1986).

Littlefield, Daniel. *Rice and Slaves: Ethnicity and the Slave Trade in Colonial South Carolina* (1981).

Mannix, Daniel. *Black Cargoes: A History of the Atlantic Slave Trade, 1515–1865* (1962).

Mullin, Gerald W. *Flight and Rebellion: Slave Resistance in Eighteenth-Century Virginia* (1972).

Piersen, William. *Black Yankees: The Development of an Afro-American Subculture in Eighteenth-Century New England* (1988).

Sobel, Mechal. *The World They Made Together: Black and White Values in Eighteenth-Century Virginia* (1987).

Labor Systems and European Immigration

Bailyn, Bernard. *The Peopling of British North America: An Introduction* (1986).

Bailyn, Bernard. *Voyagers to the West: A Passage in the Peopling of America on the Eve of the Revolution* (1986).

DeWolfe, Barbara, ed. *Discoveries of America: Personal Accounts of British Emigrants to America in the Revolutionary Era* (1997).

Dickson, R. J. *Ulster Emigration to Colonial America, 1718–1775* (1966).

Ekirch, A. Roger. *Bound for America: The Transportation of British Convicts to the Colonies, 1718–1775* (1987).

Galenson, David. *White Servitude in Colonial America* (1981).

Innes, Stephen, ed. *Work and Labor in Early America* (1988).

Roeber, A. G. *Palatines, Liberty, and Property: German Lutherans in Colonial British America* (1993).

Salinger, Sharon V. *"To Serve Well and Faithfully": Labor and Indentured Servants in Pennsylvania, 1682–1800* (1987).

Where to Learn More

❖ **Ste. Marie among the Hurons, near Midland, Ontario, Canada.** This site contains a reconstructed Jesuit mission from the seventeenth century. There is a museum with information about seventeenth-century France as well as life among the Huron Indians.

❖ **Taos Pueblo, Taos, New Mexico.** Still a residence for Pueblo Indians, portions of this multi-storied pueblo date from the fifteenth century. This was the site from which Popé directed the beginnings of the Pueblo Revolt in 1680.

❖ **Ephrata Cloister, Ephrata, Pennsylvania.** Founded by German immigrants in the eighteenth century, the Ephrata community attracted religious pietists. The site now contains a museum, buildings that reflect medieval German architectural styles, and a collection of decorative art objects.

❖ **Six Nations Indian Museum, Onchiota, New York.** This museum preserves a rich collection of artifacts relating to Iroquois history and culture. Open to the public in the summer.

❖ **Rhode Island Black Heritage Society, Providence, Rhode Island.** This organization has assembled an archive and museum collection with information about the state's black residents from the colonial period to the present.

4 CONVERGENCE AND CONFLICT, 1660s–1763

British Settlements
French Settlements
Spanish Settlements

0   400 miles
0   600 km

Cahokia

Santa Fe

Acoma Pueblo

New Orleans

Gulf of Mexico

Tenochtitlán/
Mexico City

Atlantic Ocean

Quebec

Albany

Boston
Plymouth

New York

Philadelphia

Jamestown

Roanoke Island

Charleston

Caribbean Sea

KEY TOPICS

❖ Development of closer connections between Britain and the colonies
❖ Rising aspirations of the colonial elite
❖ Religious life in eighteenth-century America
❖ Political developments in England and the colonies
❖ Renewed competition among Britain, France, and Spain in North America
❖ Impact of imperial warfare in North America

*T*he young man came to Williamsburg in the spring of 1763 to take his seat in Virginia's House of Burgesses. He had plenty of time, when not engaged in government business, to attend to his private affairs. His main concern was to arrange for the shipment of tobacco from his plantation to England. But he also found time to write to his tailor, Charles Lawrence of London. "Be pleased to send me," he wrote, "a genteel suit of Clothes made of superfine broad Cloth handsomely chosen," cut to fit a man "Six feet high & proportionably made; if any thing rather Slender than thick for a Person of that height with pretty long arms & thighs." Lawrence could choose the style and color of the suit, and when he was done he should send his bill to Robert Cary, the Virginian's financial agent in London. The colonist then wrote directly to Cary requesting that he send "4 Yards of Silk . . . according to the Inclosed pattern" for a dress for his wife. If the Virginian meant to impress his neighbors with his new suit, it was only fitting that his wife also display her latest London finery.

At the age of 31, this tall and "rather Slender" planter, George Washington, had joined the ranks of Virginia's leaders. In some senses he had come up the hard way. His father had died when Washington was only 11 years old, and most of the family property had gone to his older brother. Because he could not expect to inherit wealth, Washington learned surveying—a useful skill in a colony where land was constantly being divided into new farms. His maps of territory west of the Blue Ridge Mountains helped open up the region, and he became an expert at locating prime lands to buy and resell to the settlers who flooded into the area. When tensions between England and France over rival claims to those western lands flared into war, Washington took up arms to defend England's right. Military service brought him to the attention of Virginia's leaders, even as his economic fortunes

improved. His older brother died and left him the family plantation at Mount Vernon, and in 1759, at age 27, Washington married a wealthy widow, Martha Custis. He thus became one of the richest men in northern Virginia.

By 1763, Washington had spent his whole adult life trying to live, look, and behave like an English country gentleman. He had served his king in battle and had assumed the local political responsibilities expected of a man of his position. He already owned vastly more land than most English gentlemen could dream of, and he prospered from the transatlantic trade that channeled tobacco and other colonial goods into British and European markets. But Washington could not be sure of what an English gentleman looked like. He had to trust his London tailor to know how he should dress.

Throughout British America, colonists who had achieved wealth and power tried, like Washington, to imitate the habits and manners of the English gentry. Their aspirations testified to important developments in the eighteenth century. Prosperity and the demand of a growing population for English manufactures tied the colonies ever more tightly into a trade network centered on the imperial metropolis, London. The flow of goods and information between England and America fueled the desires of Washington and other successful colonists for acceptance as transatlantic members of the English elite. No longer a collection of rough outposts clinging to the Atlantic seaboard, British America was growing in size and sophistication.

These developments in Britain's American colonies brought them to the attention of European statesmen, who increasingly factored North America into their political, diplomatic, and military calculations. Spain and France viewed the growth of British North America as a threat to their own colonial possessions, and they responded aggressively by expanding their territorial claims. With expansion came conflict, and with conflict, war: a series of four imperial wars, which themselves became powerful engines of change in the New World.

Economic Development and Imperial Trade in the British Colonies

The greatest assets that Great Britain could call on in its competition with other European nations were a dynamic economy and a sophisticated financial system that put commerce at the service of the state. In the century after 1690, England became the most advanced economic power in Europe. Although most English subjects remained farmers, more people than ever before engaged in trade and manufacturing. Countless workshops produced the cloth, glassware, paper, pottery, and other goods that appealed to English and North American consumers.

England's leaders came to see colonies as indispensable to the nation's economic welfare. Colonies supplied raw materials unavailable in the mother country, and settlers provided a healthy market for English manufactures. As the eighteenth century progressed, colonial economies grew in tandem with England's. Parliament knitted the colonies into an empire with commercial legislation, while British merchants traded with and extended credit to growing numbers of colonial merchants and planters. Over time, these developments made colonial societies resemble England more closely than ever before and integrated the economies of the colonies with that of the metropolis in a vast transatlantic system.

Washington/Custus/Lee Collection, Washington and Lee University, Lexington, VA.

This, the earliest known portrait of George Washington, was painted by Charles Willson Peale in 1772. It depicts him in his military uniform from the French and Indian War. Military service helped to strengthen Washington's ties with the British Empire.

The Regulation of Trade

England, Holland, and France competed vigorously in the transatlantic trade. To capture a greater share of commercial profits, England pursued a policy of national self-sufficiency in which its American colonies played a key role. Between 1651 and 1733, Parliament passed laws that regulated trade in order to ensure that more wealth flowed into England's treasury than out of it (see the summary table "British Imperial Trade Regulations, 1651–1733"). This governmental intervention in the economy for the purpose of increasing national wealth—called **mercantilism**—aimed to draw the colonies into a mutually beneficial relationship with England.

Parliament enacted four types of mercantilist regulations. The first dealt with ships and their owners and aimed at ending Dutch dominance in England's overseas trade. Beginning with the **Navigation Act of 1651**, all trade in the empire had to be conducted in English or colonial ships, with crews that were at least half Englishmen or colonists. The act stimulated rapid growth in both England's merchant marine and New England's shipping industry. Indeed, shipbuilding and earnings from what was called the "carrying trade" soon became the most profitable sector of New England's economy.

The second type of legislation channeled most colonial trade through England, giving it control over raw materials it would otherwise have to buy from rival nations. Certain colonial goods, called **"enumerated products,"** could be shipped only to England or to another English colony. They initially included tobacco, sugar, indigo, and cotton. Pitch, tar, hemp, rice, molasses, and furs were added later. These laws also required European goods to pass through England before they could be shipped to the colonies. When these goods entered English ports, they were taxed, which made them more expensive and encouraged colonists to buy English-made items.

The third and fourth sorts of regulation further enhanced the advantage of English manufacturers who produced for the colonial market. Parliament subsidized certain goods, including linen,

CHRONOLOGY

1651–1733 Parliament passes series of Navigation Acts to regulate imperial trade.	**1698** First French settlements near mouth of Mississippi River.
1660 Charles II becomes king of England.	**1701** Iroquois adopt policy of neutrality toward France and Britain.
1662 Halfway Covenant adopted by Massachusetts clergy.	**1702–1713** Queen Anne's War in America.
1685 James II becomes king of England.	**1718** Establishment of San Antonio, Texas; New Orleans founded.
1686–1689 Dominion of New England.	**1734–1735** Jonathan Edwards leads religious revival in Northampton, Massachusetts.
1688 Glorious Revolution in England; James II loses the throne.	**1739** Great Awakening begins in Middle Colonies with George Whitefield's arrival.
1689 William and Mary become English monarchs; Leisler's Rebellion begins in New York.	**1744–1748** King George's War in America.
1689–1697 King William's War in America.	**1754–1763** Seven Years' War in America.
1691–1692 Witchcraft trials in Salem, Massachusetts.	**1760s** Spanish begin establishing missions in California.

gunpowder, and silks, to allow manufacturers to undersell European competitors in the colonies. Other laws protected English manufacturers from colonial competition by prohibiting colonists from manufacturing wool, felt hats, and iron on a large scale.

Some tobacco and rice planters—who wanted to ship their crops directly to markets outside England—complained about mercantilist legislation. Nevertheless, the colonies prospered. Between 1650 and 1770, the colonial economy grew twice as fast as England's did. Colonists enjoyed protected markets for their staple crops and low prices on certain English imports. Because the trade laws allowed colonial merchants to operate on equal terms with English traders, they could take full advantage of commercial opportunities within the empire.

Occasionally, merchants evaded these laws by smuggling. New Englanders in particular smuggled sugar products from the French West Indies to avoid paying the high taxes required by the **Molasses Act** of 1733. Customs officials, sent over from England beginning in the 1670s, often failed to stop illegal trade. These officials, whose incomes derived mainly from fines collected from smugglers, generally found it easier to accept bribes and look the other way when a suspicious ship arrived in port. Most colonial trade, however, followed the routes prescribed by law. By not pushing for complete compliance, British officials did not put too much pressure on a system that in fact worked remarkably well.

The Colonial Export Trade and the Spirit of Enterprise

By the mid-eighteenth century, the Atlantic had become a busy thoroughfare of international commerce (see Map 4-1). Between 1700 and 1770, the number of British merchant ships nearly tripled, from 3,300 to 9,400. They, along with colonial vessels, carried goods and people from Great Britain, continental Europe, and West Africa to the British colonies and returned tons of colonial raw materials to the Old World. At the heart of Anglo-American trade lay the highly profitable commerce in staple crops, most of which were produced by slave labor.

West Indian sugar far surpassed all other colonial products in importance (see Figure 4-1 on page 97). By the late 1760s, the value of sugar and sugar by-product exports reached almost £4 million per year—*nearly 50 percent more than the total value of exports from all the other British American colonies combined.* Many West Indian planters, who had long since left their plantations in the hands of overseers and moved back to England, joined with the English merchants who marketed their sugar to lobby Parliament for favorable treatment. Because these planters and merchants—known as the "sugar

SUMMARY

BRITISH IMPERIAL TRADE REGULATIONS, 1651–1733

Name of Act	Key Features
Navigation Act of 1651	• Aimed to eliminate Dutch competition in overseas trade • Required most goods to be carried in English or colonial ships • Required crews to be at least half English
Navigation Act of 1660	• Required all colonial trade to be carried in English ships • Required master and three-quarters of crew to be English • Created list of enumerated goods, such as tobacco and sugar, that could be shipped only to England or another English colony
Staple Act of 1663	• Required products from Europe, Asia, and Africa to be landed in England before being shipped to the colonies
Plantation Duty Act of 1673	• Attempted to reduce smuggling • Required captains of colonial ships to post bond that they would deliver enumerated goods to England or pay the "plantation duty" that would be owed in England
Navigation Act of 1696	• Plugged loopholes in earlier laws • Created vice-admiralty courts in colonies to enforce trade regulations
Woolens Act of 1699	• Forbade export of woolen cloth made in the colonies, to prevent competition with English producers
Hat Act of 1732	• Prohibited export of colonial-made hats
Molasses Act of 1733	• Placed high tax on French West Indian and other foreign molasses imported into colonies to encourage importation of British West Indian molasses

interest"—wielded so much economic power, politicians listened. It was at their insistence that Parliament in 1733 passed the Molasses Act, which taxed sugar products from foreign sources, especially the French West Indies. (Although the act aimed to encourage mainland colonists to buy British sugar and molasses, it in fact only stimulated the ingenuity of New England smugglers.) Parliament removed sugar from the list of enumerated items in 1739, allowing merchants to ship it directly from the islands to southern Europe.

Tobacco from the Chesapeake colonies was the second most valuable staple crop. Exports worth about £750,000 arrived each year in England during the late 1760s. Nearly 90 percent of the crop was later reexported to continental Europe. But persistent low

prices led many tobacco planters, after 1750, to sow some of their land with wheat. This lessened their dependence on tobacco and allowed them to take advantage of the high demand for flour in southern Europe and the West Indies.

Exports of rice and indigo helped make South Carolina planters some of the richest mainland colonists. Most of the rice went to England and the West Indies, although after 1731, Parliament permitted direct shipments to southern Europe. Parliament encouraged indigo production by granting subsidies to growers and placing stiff taxes on foreign indigo. It also subsidized colonial production of naval stores—such as tar, pitch, and turpentine—in order to reduce England's dependence on Swedish suppliers for materials essential to its navy.

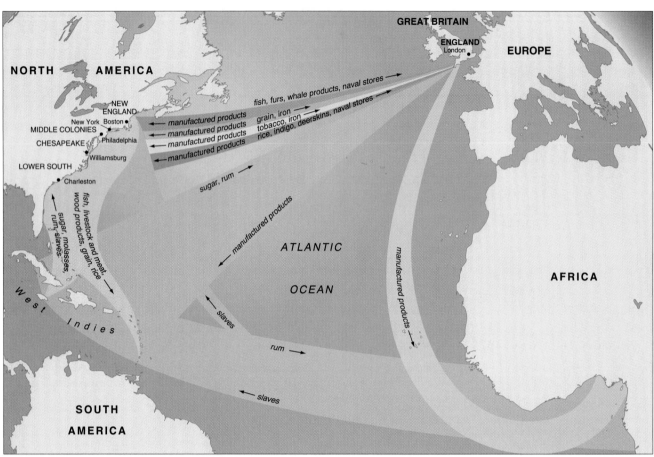

Map 4-1   Anglo-American Transatlantic Commerce
By the eighteenth century, Great Britain and its colonies were enmeshed in a complex web of trade. Britain exchanged manufactured goods for colonial raw materials, while Africa provided the enslaved laborers who produced the most valuable colonial crops.

The export of these items made up a small but important part of the North and South Carolina economies.

Wheat exports from the Middle Colonies boomed after 1750, when a combination of poor harvests and warfare in Europe created strong overseas demand. West Indian planters (though not their slaves) also ate bread made from Pennsylvania flour. Farmers in Great Britain grew enough wheat to supply the domestic market, so there was little demand there for colonial flour. Ships traveling from Philadelphia or New York to English ports instead carried a variety of less valuable goods, including unrefined iron, potash (used in making soap and glass), salted meats, and wood products—naval stores, wooden shingles, and barrel staves.

New England had no staple crop and produced little for export to Great Britain except whale products, such as oil. The region's merchants nevertheless developed a thriving transatlantic trade,

built on their willingness to take risks and grasp whatever opportunities came their way. Realizing that profits could be made from carrying other colonies' goods to market, New Englanders built thousands of vessels and eventually dominated shipping within the empire. Captains sailed from port to port, assembling mixed cargoes. They might set out with a load of salted fish and exchange it for flour in Philadelphia, tar in North Carolina, and tobacco in Virginia and then carry these diverse goods to England to exchange for manufactures. By 1770, New England's earnings from shipping fees, freight charges, and insurance exceeded the total value of its exports.

New England merchants also strengthened trade links to the West Indies that had first been forged in the 1650s. By the mid-eighteenth century, more than half of all New England exports went to the islands: salted meat for planters' dinners, salted fish for slaves, wood for sugar barrels and other

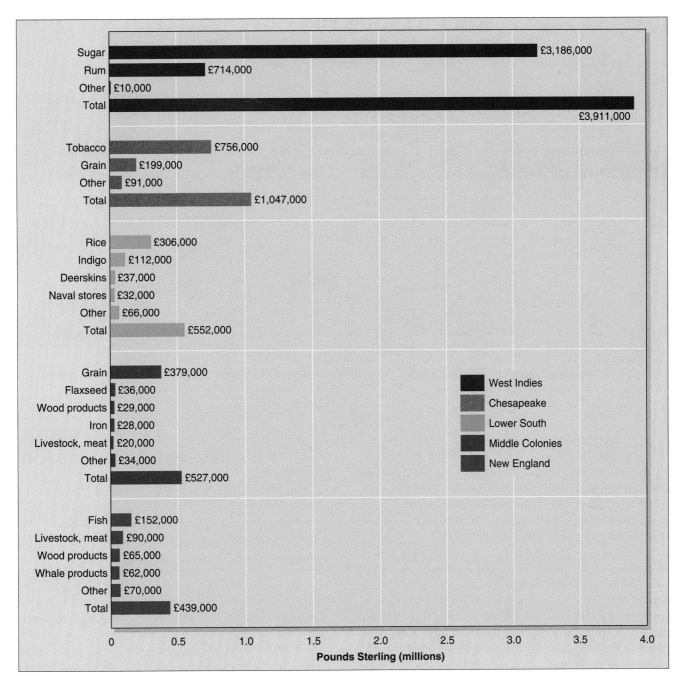

Figure 4-1   Average Annual Value of Colonial Exports by Region, 1768–1772
Staple crops—especially sugar—produced by slave labor were the most valuable items
exported from Britain's North American colonies.

Source: *John J. McCusker and Russell R. Menard, The Economy of British America, 1607–1789, rev.*
ed. (1991).

equipment. Merchants accepted molasses and other sugar by-products in payment, bringing them back to New England to be distilled into cheap rum. Enterprising traders then carried rum to Africa to exchange for slaves. Although English merchants dominated the African slave trade, some New En-glanders profited from it. There were few slaves in New England, and blacks made up less than 3 per-cent of its population in 1760. But because New En-glanders trafficked in slaves and provisioned the West Indies, their commercial economy depended on the institution of slavery too.

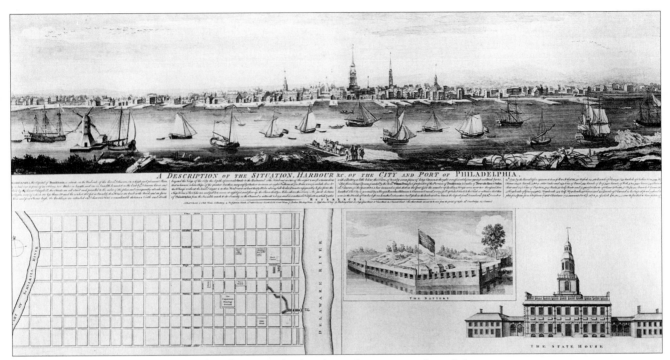

By the 1750s, Philadelphia had emerged as the principal colonial city. Its prosperity depended on its enterprising merchants who traded provisions to Europe and the West Indies and imported dry goods from England.

The Import Trade and Ties of Credit

By the late 1760s, the colonists imported goods worth nearly £4 million each year, almost all of which came from Great Britain. Most imports consisted of manufactured goods, which satisfied a demand for items that could not be produced—at least not cheaply—in America. Bales of English cloth and leather, crates of glassware and pottery, casks of nails and lead shot piled onto the wharves of Philadelphia and New York. Dockworkers emptied ships' holds of wrought iron, brass, and copper, barrels of salt and refined sugar, and bundles of beaverskin hats. Some of these goods—ironware, salt, sugar, hats, linen cloth—were made of materials that had come from the colonies in the first place.

The colonists' consumption of manufactures was vital to British overseas commerce. In terms of value, colonists in fact imported more goods than they exported. This imbalance, however, did not place the colonies as a whole deeply in debt to British suppliers. Earnings from shipping fees, as well as payments from the British government for colonial military expenses, made up most of the difference between imports and exports. The colonial economy may have run an annual deficit of £40,000 by the late 1760s, but that amounted to only about 1 percent of a transatlantic trade worth over £4 million a year.

British merchants extended credit to colonists on generous terms, trying to make it as easy as possible for them to buy British products. Great tobacco planters, of whom Washington was typical, virtually lived on the easy credit that firms like Robert Cary and Company provided. These merchants marketed the planters' tobacco and supplied them with English goods, charging the costs of purchase and transportation against the profits they expected the next year's crop to bring.

Easy credit let planters indulge their taste for fine fabrics and good wine, and many ordered English goods without stopping to worry about how they would pay for them. Gradually, they sank into debt. A Virginian noted in 1766 that no planter would have dared run up a debt of £1,000 in the 1740s, but now "Ten times that sum is . . . spoke of with Indifference." When trade was brisk, and tobacco prices high, neither the planters nor their British creditors worried. But when tobacco prices dropped or an international crisis made overseas trading risky, creditors called in the debts owed to them. At such times, colonial debtors realized how much they

During the eighteenth century, quantities of imported English manufactures began to appear in many colonial houses. This elegant mahogany clothespress, made in England in the 1740s, may have graced the Boston home of Charles Apthorp, once called "the greatest and most noble merchant" in America.

(like Indians involved in European trade) depended on goods and credit supplied by distant merchants.

Becoming More Like England

As colonial commerce grew, so did colonial cities—the connecting points in the economic network tying the colonists to the metropolis. Boston, New York, Philadelphia, and Charleston were as large as many British provincial towns. By 1770, Philadelphia's population had reached 30,000, New York's 25,000, Boston's 16,000, and Charleston's 12,000. A fifth city, Baltimore, was rapidly developing at the best harbor on Chesapeake Bay. Only about 5 percent of all mainland colonists lived in cities, but the influence of urban centers far outweighed their size.

European visitors marveled at America's bustling cities and remarked on their resemblance to England's. One Englishman declared in 1759 that Philadelphia "must certainly be the object of every one's wonder and admiration." Less than eighty years old, it already boasted three thousand houses, impressive public buildings, "handsomely built" streets, two libraries, eight or ten churches, and a college (chartered as the College of Philadelphia in 1755, now the University of Pennsylvania). This same visitor judged Boston to be a "most flourishing" place with "much the air of some of our best country towns in England." Another European traveler enjoyed walking along the tree-lined streets of New York, which "seemed like a garden."

All colonial cities (like England's major ones) were seaports, and Europeans took note of the appearance and activity of their dockyards. Oceangoing ships sailed "right up to the town" of Philadelphia on the Delaware River, according to one observer. Boston had "a very fine wharf, at least half a mile long, undertaken at the expense of a number of private gentlemen" to facilitate shipping. New York had, then as now, one of the world's finest harbors, from which it conducted "a more extensive commerce than any town in the English North American provinces."

Indeed, in their bustle and cosmopolitan atmosphere, colonial cities resembled English provincial cities more than they did the villages and farms of the American countryside. Cities provided all sorts of amenities, including inns, taverns, coffeehouses, theaters, and social clubs. Their populations were much more diverse in ethnic origin and religion. Dr. Alexander Hamilton, a Scottish immigrant, recalled dining at a Philadelphia tavern with "Scots, English, Dutch, Germans, and Irish" and "Roman Catholicks, Church [of England] men, Presbyterians, Quakers, Newlightmen, Methodists, Seventh day men, Moravians, Anabaptists, and one Jew." In addition, the black population in the northern colonies tended to live in cities. By 1750, slaves made up 20 percent of New York City's population, about 10 percent of Philadelphia's, and nearly 9 percent of Boston's.

Colonial cities had much higher proportions of artisans than rural villages did. Perhaps two out of three adult white males living in cities worked at a craft. Many of them—shipbuilders, ropemakers, sailmakers—labored at trades directly related to overseas commerce. Others produced pottery, furniture, paper, glassware, iron tools, and various household items. Colonial products tended to be somewhat cruder and cheaper than British-made goods and often appealed to poorer

Paul Revere, c. 1768–70, Copley, John Singleton, U.S., 1738–1815. Oil on canvas, 35 x 28½ in, (88.9 x 72.3 cm). Gift of Joseph W., William B., and Edward H. R. Revere. Courtesy, Museum of Fine Arts, Boston.

John Singleton Copley's portrait of the silversmith Paul Revere, painted about 1769, depicts one of Boston's most prominent artisans. As colonists grew wealthier, some commissioned portraits for their homes to serve as emblems of their rising social aspirations. Even so, Copley despaired that America would ever provide a suitable market for his artistic talents and he eventually moved to England.

consumers. Yet talented colonists such as the Boston silversmith Paul Revere and the Philadelphia furniture maker John Folwell fashioned goods that would have been prized possessions in any English gentleman's home.

Colonial manufacturing took place not in factories but in workshops often attached to artisans' houses. Artisans managed a work force consisting of their wives and children, along with journeymen or apprentices. Usually teenage boys, apprentices contracted to work for a master for four to seven years in order to learn the "mysteries" of his craft. Like indentured servants, they received no wages but worked for food, clothing, shelter, and a small payment at the end of their service. Once an apprentice finished his training, he became a journeyman, working for a master but now earning wages and saving until he could afford to set up his own shop. Like farmers, colonial artisans valued household inde-

pendence and aimed to limit the time during which they worked for others.

Many artisans flourished in colonial cities. Adino Paddock, for example, moved from the countryside to Boston in 1736 to learn how to make the light carriages known as chaises. By 1758, he had his own shop, and as his business prospered, Bostonians elected him to important local offices. As a gesture of public spirit, Paddock arranged for the transplanting of elm trees on Boston Common, to beautify the city where he had made his fortune, which by 1775 amounted to more than £3,000.

Paddock's rise was more spectacular than most artisans could hope for. Yet many Philadelphia artisans accumulated property worth £50 to £200, enough for a comfortable subsistence. Craft work also offered economic opportunities to city women that were generally unavailable to rural women. Mary Wallace and Clementia Ferguson, for instance, stitched fashionable hats and dresses for New York customers. Nonetheless, even in cities, women's options were limited. Many employed women were widows striving to maintain a family business until sons grew old enough to take over. This was true for printers such as Elizabeth Timothy, who ran the *South Carolina Gazette* after her husband's death in 1739, and Anne Catherine Green, who managed the *Maryland Gazette* for nine years.

Prosperity for urban artisans was by no means guaranteed. Workers at less skilled crafts often earned only a bare living, and ordinary laborers faced seasonal unemployment. The irregular delivery of raw materials idled even the most industrious artisans. Disputes with Indians might deprive urban hatmakers of necessary skins. Silversmiths, tailors, and furniture makers, relying on overseas suppliers of metal, cloth, and exotic woods, suffered when supply ships sank or wars hindered ocean traffic. Makers of luxury goods feared downturns in the economy, for this discouraged nervous customers from purchasing their wares.

Wherever colonists engaged heavily in commerce—in cities or on plantations—the gap between rich and poor widened during the eighteenth century. In 1687, the richest 10 percent of Boston residents owned 46 percent of the taxable property in the town; by 1771, the top tenth held 63 percent of taxable wealth. Similar changes occurred in Philadelphia. In South Carolina and the Chesapeake, many planters added to the already substantial estates they had inherited. This elite group controlled vast amounts of land and slave labor. Over time, it became extremely difficult for newcomers to enter their ranks.

Some observers detected a growing problem of poverty in the colonies. Most cities built workhouses and other shelters for people who could not take care of themselves. Towns collected funds for poor relief in greater amounts than ever before. Even so, poverty had not yet become an entrenched problem. Many poor people were aged or ill, without families to help them. Able-bodied workers forced to accept public relief usually owed their misfortune to temporary downturns in the economy, more often than not the result of

Colonial craftsmen often employed their families, as well as apprentices, in their workshops. This French illustration of a tinsmith's shop depicts a scene that would have been familiar in colonial cities and large towns.

dislocations caused by war. Such was the case in 1757, for example, when Boston's leaders complained that the city's poor relief expenses exceeded those of any comparably sized town "upon the face of the whole Earth." England was then at war with France, and the British commander in chief had halted Boston's overseas trade.

Even in the worst of times, no more than one out of ten white colonists (mainly city-dwellers) depended on public assistance to avoid starvation. Bad as their situation was, it scarcely matched the lot of many English people. As much as one-third of England's population regularly received relief, and the numbers swelled during hard times. Eighteenth-century colonists, on average, enjoyed a higher standard of living than most English or other Europeans. So long as land was available—even if one had to move to the edges of settlement to get it—colonists could at least eke out a bare subsistence, and many did much better.

No one would have mistaken Philadelphia for London or Virginia planters for British lords. Even so, colonial society resembled Great Britain more than ever before. The growth of cities mirrored British urban development. The widening gap between rich and poor convinced many colonists that their society had at last matured from its crude beginnings. Eighteenth-century Britons on both sides of the Atlantic believed that societies ought to be organized hierarchically, with people arranged in ranks from rich to poor according to their abilities and God's design. The more America resembled Britain, many colonists assumed, the more stable and prosperous it would be.

The Transformation of Culture

Despite the convergence of English and colonial society, many influential settlers worried that America remained culturally inferior to Great Britain. Just as Washington trusted a London tailor he had never met to make him a fashionable suit—assuming that Virginia tailors could at best produce a crude copy—other colonial gentlemen tended to see American architecture, fashion, manners, and intellectual life as poor imitations of British models. During the eighteenth century, newly prosperous colonists strove to overcome this provincial sense of inferiority. They built grand houses and filled them with imported goods, cultivated what they took to be the manners of the British gentry, and followed English and European intellectual developments. Some colonial gentlemen even reshaped their religious beliefs to reflect European notions that God played only an indirect role in human affairs.

These elite aspirations, however, were not shared by most settlers. Some Americans may have purchased a few pieces of imported china or a rug to cover a bare floor, but most had little interest in copying the manners of the English elite, and very few altered their spiritual beliefs to fit European patterns. Indeed, religion flourished in eighteenth-century America and, when a tremendous revival swept through the colonies beginning in the 1730s, occupied center stage in American life.

Goods and Houses

Eighteenth-century Americans imported more manufactures from England with every passing year. This did not simply reflect the growth of the colonial population, for the rate at which Americans bought British goods exceeded the rate of population increase. Colonists owned more goods, often of better quality, than their parents and grandparents had possessed.

In the less secure economic climate of the seventeenth century, colonists had limited their purchases of goods, investing instead in land to pass on to their children. But by the eighteenth century, prosperous colonists felt secure enough to buy goods to make their lives more comfortable. Chairs replaced benches, and carpets covered wooden floors. Colonists hung pewter candleholders, mirrors, and perhaps a portrait or two on their walls. At mealtimes, the table might be covered with a damask cloth and set with individual porcelain plates instead of a common wooden dish. Wealthier colonists ate with forks and knives, not just spoons.

Benjamin Franklin described such changes in his own household. Accustomed to eating his breakfast of bread and milk with a pewter spoon from an earthenware bowl, he found it one morning "in a China Bowl with a Spoon of Silver" that had cost "the enormous Sum of three and twenty Shillings." His wife, Deborah, justified the purchase by declaring "that she thought *her* Husband deserved a Silver Spoon & China Bowl as well as any of his Neighbors." Deborah Franklin knew that silver and china, although they served the same function as pewter and earthenware, signified her family's prosperity and good taste. Many colonists likewise acquired such goods to advertise their refined style of life.

By the 1760s, nearly every item that George Washington ordered from his London agent could have been purchased in Philadelphia. But Washington wanted to get the latest English styles and even worried that his agent might take advantage of him by sending goods that were no longer in fashion in England. He once complained that "instead of getting things good and fashionable . . . we often have Articles sent Us that cou[l]d only have been us[e]d by our Forefathers in the days of yore." Washington's desires were hardly unique. One visitor to Maryland, astonished at the speed with which colonists adopted English styles, declared that he was "almost inclined to believe that a new fashion is adopted earlier by the polished and affluent American than by many opulent persons" in London. Colonial shopkeepers regularly assured the "ladies and gentlemen" among their customers that their wares reflected the latest English styles.

Prosperous colonists built grand houses where they lived in greater comfort than ever before. In the seventeenth century, Virginia's governor lived in the finest house in the colony—a four-room dwelling. His eighteenth-century counterpart, however, resided in Williamsburg in the Governor's Palace, an elegant two-storied mansion designed after British architectural styles. By the 1730s, numerous southern planters had built "great houses" with expensive paneling, plasterwork, and marble fireplaces. Others transformed older houses into more stylish residences. Washington extensively remodeled Mount Vernon, adding a second story and extra wings on each side to create a

Only wealthy colonists could afford to build houses with special rooms dedicated to receiving guests. During the eighteenth century, this South Carolina parlor, with its exquisite details and luxurious furnishings, would have been the scene of many fine entertainments.

Courtesy, Winterthur Museum.

home fit for a gentleman. In the northern colonies, merchants built the most impressive houses, often following architectural pattern books imported from England.

These houses were not only larger but also different in design from the homes of less affluent colonists. Most settlers lived in one- or two-room dwellings and thus cooked, ate, and slept in the same chamber. Under such conditions, privacy was virtually unknown. But the owners of great houses could devote rooms to specialized uses. Cooking and other domestic work took place in back or in separate outbuildings. Private bedrooms were located upstairs, allowing first-floor rooms to be used for more public activities. The most distinctive feature of these grand homes was the parlor, an elaborately decorated room used for receiving guests and entertaining them with music, dancing, and card games. Parlor doors often opened onto lawns and formal gardens where guests could stroll and engage in polite conversation.

Prosperous colonists did not build such homes merely to advertise their wealth. They wanted to create the proper setting for a refined way of life, emulating the English gentry in their country estates and London townhouses. They knew that the true measure of their gentility lay not just in where they lived and what they owned but in how they behaved.

Shaping Minds and Manners

Colonists knew that the manners of English gentlefolk set them apart from ordinary people. Many Americans imported "courtesy books," which contained the rules of polite behavior. In previous centuries, such books had prepared princes for life at court and their future duties as kings. Eighteenth-century versions advised would-be gentlemen on how to show regard for social rank, practice personal cleanliness, and respect other people's feelings.

The young George Washington studied such books carefully. At age 13, he copied 110 rules from *Youth's Behaviour, or Decency in Conversation among Men,* including such advice as "In the Presence of Others Sing not to yourself with a humming Noise, nor Drum with your Fingers or Feet" and "In Company of those of Higher Quality than yourself Speak not till you are ask'd a Question then Stand upright put of[f] your Hat and Answer in few words." Many colonists subscribed to English journals such as *The Tatler* and *The Spectator* that printed articles describing good manners.

Women, too, cultivated genteel manners. In Charleston, South Carolina, dozens of girls' boarding schools advertised instruction in "the different branches of Polite Education." Female pupils studied reading, writing, and arithmetic but also learned French, music, dancing, and fancy needlework. This curriculum prepared them for married lives as mistresses of great houses, mothers of future gentlemen and ladies, and hostesses of grand entertainments.

Such entertainments proliferated in the eighteenth century. Invitations to balls, dances, musical performances, and tea parties circulated among well-bred neighbors. One gathering at Robert Carter's Virginia plantation began with an "elegant" dinner at half past four with "several sorts of Wine, good Lemon Punch, Toddy, Cyder, [and] Porter," followed at seven o'clock by dancing and card playing that lasted until nearly midnight. Such occasions excluded ordinary settlers and reinforced elite colonists' sense of themselves as a separate—and better—class of people.

Some aspiring colonial gentlemen adopted more intellectual pursuits. Literacy rates among white colonists were quite high by eighteenth-century standards. In New England, where settlers placed great emphasis on Bible study, about 70 percent of men and 45 percent of women could read and write. Farther south, literacy rates were lower, but still higher than in England, where only a third of all men and even fewer women could read and write. Prominent colonists, intent on developing America's intellectual life, began to participate in a transatlantic world of ideas.

These colonists, however, were more consumers of British and European ideas than producers of an American intellectual tradition. They imported thousands of books, subscribed to British journals, and established libraries in cities such as Philadelphia, Charleston, and New York where borrowing privileges could be purchased for a modest fee. Libraries and private collections contained sermons and other religious writings, classical Greek and Roman texts, political and philosophical works of prominent European thinkers, and mainly British examples of poetry, drama, essays, and novels. Colonists with literary aspirations emulated their favorite writers. Students at Harvard in Cambridge (founded in 1636) modeled their college newspaper on an English periodical, the *Spectator.* In Virginia, William Byrd—the son of an Indian trader who had risen to the rank of gentleman—composed verse in the style of contemporary English poets, and Thomas Jefferson copied out passages from the English novel *Tristram Shandy.* Benjamin Franklin honed his writing skills by rewriting essays from the *Spectator* and comparing his versions to the originals.

Educated colonists were especially interested in the new ideas that characterized what has been called the **Age of Enlightenment.** The European thinkers of the Enlightenment drew inspiration from recent advances in science—such as the English scientist Isaac Newton's explanation of the laws of gravity—that suggested that the universe operated according to natural laws that human reason could discover. They also drew on the work of the English philosopher John Locke, who maintained that God did not dictate human knowledge but rather gave us the power to acquire knowledge through experience and understanding. The hallmark of Enlightenment thought was thus a belief in the power of human reason to improve the human condition.

This optimistic worldview marked a profound intellectual shift. Enlightenment thinkers rejected earlier ideas about God's unknowable will and continued intervention in human and natural events. They instead assigned God a less active role as the creator of the universe, who had set the world running according to predictable laws, and then let nature—and human beings—shape events. Such

ideas inspired a growing international community of scholars to try to discover the laws of nature and to work toward human progress.

Colonial intellectuals sought membership in this scholarly community. A few of them—the Reverend Cotton Mather of Massachusetts, William Byrd, Benjamin Franklin—gained election to the Royal Society of London, the most prestigious learned society in the empire. Most of their scholarly contributions were unimpressive. Byrd, for instance, sent the Royal Society a rather superficial manuscript titled "An Account of a Negro Boy That Is Dappled in Several Places of His Body with White Spots."

Benjamin Franklin, by contrast, achieved genuine intellectual prominence. Even as a youth, Franklin hungered after learning and demonstrated a particular gift for science. His experiments with a kite proved that lightning was electricity (a natural force whose properties were poorly understood at the time) and gained him an international reputation. He also found practical uses for his scientific knowledge. Franklin invented the lightning rod (which prevented fires in wooden buildings by channeling the electrical charge of a lightning bolt into the ground), bifocal spectacles, the iron "Franklin stove" (in which wood burned more efficiently than in fireplaces), and the glass harmonica, an instrument that made him famous among European musicians and composers.

If Franklin's career embodied the Enlightenment ideal of the rational exploration of nature's laws, it also revealed the limited impact of Enlightenment thought in colonial America. Only a few prosperous and educated colonists could afford to pursue their interest in the world of ideas. Franklin himself came from humble origins—his father was a maker of candles and soap—but his success as a printer eventually earned him a "sufficient tho' moderate fortune." Only after retiring from business at age 42 did he purchase the equipment for his electrical discoveries and begin his scientific work, devoting the "leisure during the rest of my life for philosophical studies and amusements." Franklin's equipment was as much a badge of gentlemanly status as George Washington's London-made suit.

Most colonists remained ignorant of scientific advances and Enlightenment ideas. Unlike aspiring gentlemen and ladies, they had little leisure to devote to literature and polite conversation. When they found time to read, they picked up not a courtesy book or the *Spectator* but rather the Bible or perhaps a published sermon. Religion continued to shape the way in which they viewed the world and explained human and natural events.

Painted at about the time Franklin retired from his printing business, this portrait depicts the one-time craftsman as an aspiring gentleman. Wearing a wig and a shirt with ruffled cuffs, Franklin would no longer work with his hands, but would pursue his scientific experiments and other studies.

Robert Feke (1707–1752), Portrait of Benjamin Franklin (1706–1790), c. 1746. Oil on canvas, 127 × 102 cm. Courtesy of the Harvard University Portrait Collection. Bequest of Dr. John Collins Warren, 1856.

Colonial Religion and the Great Awakening

Church steeples dominated the skylines of colonial cities. By the 1750s, Boston and New York each had eighteen churches and Philadelphia boasted twenty. Churches and meetinghouses likewise dominated country towns, though more sparsely in the scattered settlements of the South than in the northern colonies. Often the largest and finest buildings in town, they bore witness to the thriving—and diverse—condition of religion in America.

In all New England colonies except Rhode Island, the Puritan (or Congregationalist) faith was the established religion. The many Congregational churches in the region, headed by ministers trained at Harvard College and Yale (founded 1701), served the majority of its colonists and received financial support from their taxes. Though proud of the Puritan tradition that had inspired New England's origins, ministers and believers nonetheless adapted in important ways to changing social and religious conditions.

The principal adaptation consisted of a move away from strict requirements for church membership. In order to keep their churches pure, New England's founders had required prospective members to give convincing evidence that they had experienced a spiritual conversion. Once admitted, members could receive communion and have their children baptized. By the 1660s, however, fewer colonists sought admission under such strict standards, which left them and their unbaptized children outside of the church. To address this problem, the clergy in 1662 adopted the **Halfway Covenant**, which allowed adults who had been baptized (because their parents were church members), but who had not themselves experienced conversion, to have their own children baptized. The Halfway Covenant gained acceptance only gradually in the following decades. By the 1680s, some ministers made church admission even easier, requiring members only to demonstrate knowledge of the Christian faith and to live godly lives.

The Congregational Church also had gradually to permit a measure of religious toleration in New England. In 1691, Massachusetts received a royal charter granting "liberty of Conscience" to all Protestants, bringing the colony into line with England's religious policy. Anglicans and Baptists eventually won exemptions from paying taxes to support the Congregational Church. At the same time, some Congregationalist preachers began emphasizing personal piety and good works in their sermons, ideas usually associated with Anglicanism. These changes indicated a shift away from the Puritan exclusiveness of New England's early years.

In the South, the established Church of England consolidated its authority in the early eighteenth century but never succeeded in exerting effective control over spiritual life. The bishop of London began appointing agents to oversee church matters, and the Society for the Propagation of the Gospel in Foreign Parts, founded in 1701, attempted to provide ministers for colonial parishes. Even so, these parishes often lacked trained clergy, and those who did emigrate encountered unexpected obstacles.

Many a parson in England could easily ride from one side of his parish to the other in an hour, but Anglican clergymen in the southern colonies served parishes that were vast and sparsely settled. One South Carolina parish, for example, contained 10,400 square miles—and only seven hundred white residents. Ministers also found that influential planters, who had grown used to running parishes when preachers were unavailable, resisted their efforts to take control of churches. Aware that the planters' taxes paid their salaries, many ministers found it easiest simply to preach and behave in ways that offered the least offense. Frontier regions—where few prosperous gentlemen lived—often lacked churches and clergymen. In such places, dissenting religious groups, such as Presbyterians, Quakers, and Baptists, gained followers among people neglected by the Anglican establishment.

No established church dominated in the Middle Colonies of New York, New Jersey, and Pennsylvania. The region's ethnically diverse population and William Penn's policy of religious toleration guaranteed that a multitude of groups would compete for followers. One observer, accustomed to an established church, characterized these conditions as a "soul-destroying whirlpool." Yet religion flourished in the Middle Colonies. By the mid-eighteenth century, the region had more congregations per capita than even New England.

Groups such as the Quakers and the Mennonites, who did not believe in having specially trained ministers, easily formed new congregations in response to local demand. Lutheran and German Reformed churches, however, required European-educated clergy, who were always scarce. Pious laymen held worship services in their homes even as they sent urgent letters overseas begging for ordained ministers. When more Lutheran and Reformed clergy arrived in the 1740s and 1750s,

George Whitefield (who, contemporaries noted, was cross-eyed) enjoyed a remarkable career as a powerful preacher on both sides of the Atlantic. This portrait shows him preaching indoors to a rapt audience. During his tour of the colonies, Whitefield reportedly had a similar effect on crowds of thousands who gathered outdoors to hear his sermons.

they sometimes discovered—like Anglican preachers in the South—that laymen balked at relinquishing control of the churches. Lutheran and Reformed ministers also learned that their professional training alone could not command respect. Their congregations demanded that they be powerful preachers. Because so many other religious alternatives were available, these ministers had to compete for their parishioners' allegiance.

Bewildering spiritual diversity, relentless religious competition, and a comparatively weak Anglican Church all distinguished the colonies from England. Yet in one important way, religious developments during the middle third of the eighteenth century drew the colonies closer to England. A great transatlantic religious revival, originating in Scotland and England, first touched the Middle Colonies in the 1730s. In 1740–1745, it struck the northern colonies with the force of a hurricane, and in the 1760s, the last phase of the revival spread through the South. America had never seen anything like this immense revival, which came to be called the **Great Awakening**.

By 1730, Presbyterians in Pennsylvania had split into factions over several issues, including the disciplining of church members and the requirement that licensed ministers have university degrees. One group, led by an immigrant Scottish evangelist, William Tennent Sr., and his four sons, denounced their opponents as men more interested in regulations than conversion. In the 1730s, Tennent set up the Log College in Neshaminy, Pennsylvania, to train his sons and other young men to be evangelical ministers. What began as a dispute among clergymen eventually blossomed into a broader challenge to religious authority. That challenge gained momentum in late 1739 when one of the most charismatic evangelists of the century, George Whitefield, arrived in the colonies from England.

Whitefield, an Anglican priest, had experienced an uncommonly intense religious conversion while he was still a university student. Already famous in Britain as a preacher of great emotional intensity, he embarked on a tour of the colonies in the winter of 1739–1740. As soon as Whitefield landed in Delaware, his admirers whipped up local enthusiasm, ensuring that he would preach to huge crowds. In Pennsylvania and New Jersey, Whitefield's powerful preaching on the experience of conversion lent support to the Presbyterian faction led by the Tennents and sparked local revivals. Whitefield then moved on to New England, where some communities had already experienced small, local awakenings. In 1734–1735, for instance, the Congregationalist minister Jonathan Edwards had led a revival in Northampton, Massachusetts, urging his parishioners to recognize their sinfulness and describing hell in such a terrifying way that many despaired of their salvation.

Whitefield's tour through the colonies knitted these scattered local revivals into the Great Awakening. Crowds gathered in city squares and open fields to listen to his sermons. Whitefield exhorted his audiences to examine their souls for evidence of the "indwelling of Christ" that would indicate that they were saved. He criticized most ministers for emphasizing good works and "head-knowledge" instead of the emotional side of religion.

Whitefield's open-air sermons scarcely resembled the colonists' accustomed form of worship. Settlers normally gathered with family and neighbors in church for formal, structured services. They sat in pews assigned on the basis of social status, with wealthier members in front and poorer folk in the back. Such worship services reinforced standards of order and community hierarchy. But Whitefield's sermons were highly dramatic performances. He preached for hours in a booming voice, accompanying his words with spirited gestures. Overcome with emotion, he would occasionally dissolve in tears. Thousands of strangers, jostling in crowds that often outnumbered the populations of several villages put together, wept along with him. When the sermon ended, his listeners dispersed, many never to see each other again.

In the wake of Whitefield's visits, Benjamin Franklin noted, "it seem'd as if all the World were growing Religious." Revivals and mass conversions often followed his appearances, to the happy astonishment of local clergy. But their approval evaporated when more extreme revivalists appeared. Gilbert Tennent, William's son, followed Whitefield to Boston and derided the town's ministers as unconverted "dead Drones." James Davenport—a preacher so erratic that many thought him mad—claimed that God gave him the knowledge of other ministers' spiritual state and routinely denounced by name those he "knew" to be damned. Once, in the midst of a sermon urging his audience to rid themselves of all worldly finery, Davenport set an example by tearing off his velvet breeches and throwing them into a bonfire. Officials who valued civic order soon tried to silence such extremists by passing laws that prohibited them from preaching in a town without the local minister's permission.

Disputes between individuals converted in the revivals—called "**New Lights**"—and those who were not ("Old Lights") split churches. New Lights insisted, as the separatist founders of Plymouth once had, that they could not remain in churches with sinful members and unconverted ministers and so left to form new churches. "Formerly the People could bear with each other in Charity when they differ'd in Opinion," lamented one colonist, "but they now break Fellowship and Communion with one another on that Account."

The Awakening came late to the southern colonies, but it was there, in the 1760s, that it produced perhaps its greatest controversy. Many southern converts became Baptists, combining their religious criticism of the Anglicans with a general condemnation of the wealthy planters' way of life. Plainly dressed Baptists criticized the rich clothes, drinking, gambling, and pride of Virginia's gentry. Planters, in turn, viewed Baptists as dangerous people who could not "meet a man upon the road, but they must ram a text of Scripture down his throat." Most of all, they hated the Baptists for their willingness to preach to slaves. More than once, irate gentlemen burst in on Baptist services and beat the preacher senseless.

Although the revivals themselves gradually waned, the Great Awakening had a lasting impact on colonial society. It forged new links between Great Britain and the colonies. Evangelical ministers on both sides of the Atlantic exchanged correspondence. Periodicals such as *The Christian History*—over which Whitefield exercised considerable control—informed British and American subscribers of advances in true religion throughout the empire.

In the colonies, the Awakening led to the founding of new colleges to serve members of different religious denominations. Middle Colony evangelicals founded the College of New Jersey (now Princeton University) in 1746. In the 1760s, New England Baptists established the College of Rhode Island (now Brown University). An evangelical wing of the Dutch Reformed Church founded Queens College (now Rutgers University) in 1766. These colleges drew students from all colonies, not just the local area.

Everywhere, the New Light challenge to established ministers and churches undermined habits of deference to authority. Revivalists urged colonists to think for themselves in choosing which church to join and which minister to follow, not just conform to what the rest of the community did. As their churches fractured, Americans—particularly New Englanders—faced more choices than ever before in their religious lives.

The exercise of religious choice also influenced political behavior. Voters took note of whether candidates for office were New or Old Lights and cast their ballots for men on their own side. In 1766, for instance, Connecticut's New Lights wrested control of the legislature and governorship from Old Lights. Tactics first used to mobilize religious groups—organizing committees, writing petitions and letters—proved useful for political activities as well. Though hardly the intent of Whitefield or other revivalists, the Awakening thus fostered greater political awareness and participation among colonists.

The Colonial Political World

The political legacy of the Great Awakening—particularly the emphasis on individual choice and resistance to authority—corresponded to developments in the colonial political world. For most of the seventeenth century, ties within the empire developed from trade rather than governance. But as America grew in wealth and population, king and Parliament sought to manage colonial affairs more directly than ever before.

In the late seventeenth century, upheavals on both sides of the Atlantic seemed to confirm for both colonists and Englishmen a common interest in protecting the rights and liberties they derived from their shared heritage. The English overthrew King James II, and the people of New England successfully resisted the king's attempt to impose autocratic government in the colonies. But even as colonists and Englishmen asserted their common political culture at the dawn of the eighteenth century, differences in their political practices and ideas slowly began to emerge.

The Dominion of New England and the Limits of British Control

Before 1650, England made little attempt to exert centralized control in North America. Each colony more or less governed itself, and most political activity occurred at the town or county level. Local officials kept the peace, resolved disputes, arranged for public works—schools, roads, bridges—and collected taxes to pay for them. Busy with the routines of daily life, most colonists devoted little time—and even less interest—to politics.

When Charles II became king in 1660, he initially showed little interest in the colonies except as sources of land and government offices with which he could reward his supporters. The grandest prizes, of course, were the great proprietorships, such as Pennsylvania and Carolina, but the creation of a rudimentary imperial bureaucracy also yielded smaller, yet significant, rewards for the king to distribute. With the passage of mercantile regulations governing colonial trade, for example, Parliament required customs officers to administer the imperial trading system and thus created a certain number of jobs.

Charles's brother James, the duke of York, envisioned a more tightly controlled empire. He encouraged Charles to appoint military officers, with strong ties of loyalty to him, as royal governors in America. In 1675, James convinced Charles to create the **Lords of Trade**, a committee of the Privy Council (the group of nobles who served as royal advisers), to oversee colonial affairs.

When James became king in 1685, the whole character of the empire abruptly changed. Seeking to transform it into something much

grander and more susceptible to England's control, James set out to reorganize it along the lines of Spain's empire, combining the colonies into three or four large provinces. He appointed powerful governors to carry out policies that he himself would formulate.

James began in the north, creating the **Dominion of New England** out of eight previously separate colonies stretching from New Hampshire to New Jersey. He chose Sir Edmund Andros, a former army officer, to govern the vast region with an appointive council but no elective assembly. Andros moved to Boston and initially gained some support from merchants excluded from politics by Massachusetts's insistence that only church members could vote. But he eventually antagonized them and other New Englanders by rigidly enforcing the Navigation Acts, limiting towns to just one annual meeting, remodeling the law courts, challenging property titles, and levying taxes without the colonists' consent. He even compelled Boston Puritans to share a meetinghouse with Anglicans.

Events in England ultimately sealed the fate of the Dominion. For years, English Protestants had worried about James's absolutist governing style and his conversion to Catholicism. But their fears increased when in 1688, the queen bore a son to carry on a Catholic line of succession. Parliament's leaders invited James's Protestant daughter, Mary, and her husband, William of Orange, the Stadtholder of the Netherlands, to take over the throne. In November 1688, William landed in England and gained the support of most of the English army. In December, James fled to France, ending a bloodless coup known as the **Glorious Revolution**.

Bostonians overthrew Andros the following April, even before they knew for sure that William was king. Imprisoned for nearly a year, Andros was eventually shipped back to England. Massachusetts colonists hoped that their original charter of 1629 would be reinstated, but a new one was issued in 1691. It made several important changes. Massachusetts now included within its borders what had formerly been Plymouth Colony as well as Maine. Its colonists no longer elected their governor, who would instead be appointed by the English monarch. Voters no longer had to be church members, and religious toleration was extended to all Protestants.

The new charter ended exclusive Puritan control in Massachusetts but also restored political stability. During the three years between Andros's imprisonment and the arrival of a royal governor in 1692, the colony lacked a legally established government. In this atmosphere of uncertainty, a local outbreak of accusations of witchcraft in Salem grew to unprecedented proportions. Colonists, like most Europeans of the time, believed in the existence of witches—humans who acted as Satan's agents and used supernatural powers to hurt their enemies. Over the years, New Englanders had executed a dozen or so accused witches, usually older women. But in the winter of 1691–1692, when several young girls of Salem experienced fits and other strange behavior, hundreds of settlers were accused of witchcraft, and nineteen were hanged. Salem's crisis occurred against a backdrop of local economic change, but it gathered momentum because the courts, which would normally have intervened to settle matters, were unable to function.

The impact of the Glorious Revolution in other colonies likewise reflected distinctive local conditions. In New York, after Andros's deputy left, Jacob Leisler, a rich merchant and militia captain, gained power and ruled in an increasingly dictatorial fashion, persecuting men against whom he held personal grievances. Too slow in relinquishing command to the newly arrived royal governor in 1691, Leisler was arrested for treason and executed. In Maryland, Protestants used the occasion of William and Mary's accession to the throne to lobby for the end of the Catholic proprietorship. They were partly successful. The Calvert family lost its governing powers but retained rights to vast quantities of land. The Anglican Church became the established faith, and Catholics were barred from public office.

The colonists rejected James, not English authority in general. Their motives (especially in New England) largely reflected powerful anti-Catholic sentiment. William's firm Protestantism reassured them, and most colonists assumed that life would return to normal. But the Glorious Revolution in England and the demise of the Dominion had long-lasting effects that shaped political life in England and America for years to come.

The Legacy of the Glorious Revolution

In England, the Glorious Revolution signaled a return to political stability after years of upheaval. English people celebrated the preservation of their rights from the threat of a tyrannical king. In 1689, Parliament passed the Bill of Rights, which justified James's ouster and bound future monarchs to abide by the rule of law. They could not suspend parliamentary laws, collect taxes or engage in foreign wars without Parliament's consent, or maintain a standing army in peacetime. Parliamentary elections and meetings would follow a regular schedule without royal interference. In sum, Parliament claimed to be the crown's equal partner in governing England.

Colonists, too, celebrated the vindication of their rights as Englishmen. They believed that their successful resistance to Andros confirmed that their membership in the empire was founded on voluntary allegiance and not forced submission to the mother country. Observing the similarity between Parliament and the colonial assemblies, they concluded that their own legislatures had a critical role in governance and in the protection of their rights and liberties. On both sides of the Atlantic, representative government had triumphed.

In fact, Parliament claimed full authority over the colonies and did not recognize their assemblies as its equal. For more than a half-century, however, it did not vigorously assert that authority. At the same time, William and his immediate successors lacked James's compulsion to control the colonies. William did make a few changes to imperial administration. In 1696, he replaced the Lords of Trade with a new committee, the **Board of Trade**. This advisory body gathered information from the colonies and recommended policy changes but itself had no executive role. William also approved the **Navigation Act of 1696**, which closed loopholes in earlier laws and created **vice-admiralty courts** in the colonies similar to those of England. Admiralty judges settled maritime disputes and smuggling cases without using juries.

During the first decades of the eighteenth century, Parliament and royal ministers confined their attention to matters of trade and military defense and otherwise left the colonies on their own. The mild imperial rule of this period, later called the era of "salutary neglect," allowed the colonies to grow in wealth, population, and self-government. It also encouraged colonial self-confidence, leading Americans to assume equality with the English as members of the empire.

Diverging Politics in the Colonies and Great Britain

English people on both sides of the Atlantic believed that politics ought to reflect social organization. To illustrate the connection, they often compared the state to a family. Just as fathers naturally headed families,

American Views

BOSTON CELEBRATES A NEW KING (AUGUST 1727)

The first colonial newspaper, the *Boston News-Letter*, appeared in that city in 1704. By the 1720s, Bostonians could choose from three newspapers, and New York and Philadelphia each had one. Published weekly, these papers mainly reported on English and European affairs and often reprinted essays by prominent English political writers. Their pages carried little local news, on the assumption that colonists could learn it by word of mouth. But when truly extraordinary events occurred, such as the accession of a new British monarch, colonial newspapers reported on the local response. The following extract describes Bostonians' reaction to news that George II had become Britain's new king.

❖ **How did Bostonians commemorate the new king's accession?**

❖ **What does this reveal about their attitudes toward George II and British government in general?**

❖ **Who was invited to the "splendid Entertainment," and what does this tell us about the structure of Boston society?**

On Wednesday Morning by order of His Honour William Dummer, Esq., our Lieut. Governour & Commander in chief[,] three Regiments of the Militia and five Troops of horse were under arms in the great street before the State-house, making a very fine appearance. The number of Spectators exceeded the Men in Arms, covering the houses on every side. As

---

adult men led societies. In particular, adult male property holders, who enjoyed economic independence, claimed the right to vote and hold office. Women (who generally could not own property), propertyless men, and blacks had no political role because they, like children, were subordinate to the authority of others. Their dependence on husbands, fathers, masters, or employers—who could influence their political decisions—rendered them incapable of exercising freedom of choice.

States, like families, worked best when all members fulfilled their responsibilities. Rulers ought to govern with the same fairness and benevolence that fathers presumably exercised within their families. When George II became king in 1727, he reassured Parliament of his "constant care" to "secure to All My subjects, the full Enjoyment of their religious and civil Rights." In return for protection, the people owed their rulers the same obedience that children accorded their parents. The House of Commons

responded to George II's assurance of goodwill in 1727 with its own promise of "the highest Returns of Duty, Zeal and Affection to Your Majesty's Person and Government." Such phrases often disguised actual struggles between rulers and people but nevertheless expressed firmly held ideals.

Eighteenth-century people also believed that government should reflect society's hierarchical organization. In England, this idea was embodied in the institutions of monarchy and Parliament. The crown, of course, represented the interests of the royal family. Parliament represented society's two main divisions: the aristocracy in the **House of Lords** and the common people in the **House of Commons**. Americans shared the view that government should mirror social hierarchies but found it much more difficult to put the idea into practice.

American society grew closer to the British model during the eighteenth century but was never identical to it. Thus its political structure would never

soon as the Herauld had said his Amen to God Save the King, the loud and joyful Huzza's of so great a multitude rent the skies, the Regiments made a tripple discharge, the Castle Forts & Ships fir'd their cannon; and a splendid Entertainment follow'd for the Lieut. Governour and his Majesty's Council, Officers, Justices, and the Rev[eren]d Ministers present; with suitable provisions for the Regiments and Troops. The bells rung all the day, and in the Evening the Rejoycing was continued with Fireworks and Bonfires, and the whole Town illuminated in an extraordinary manner, the Windows of each story of the Houses in the principal streets having three or four rows of candles in them. The streets were fill'd all the Evening with the Gentry of both Sexes, who appear'd with much decency and gravity, and with gayety and chearfulness. At nine of the clock a welcome rain, after a time of much heat and drought, put an end to the Ceremony. . . . We pray God, by whom Kings reign, that the royal smiles of His Majesty King George the Second, and the happy influences of his wise and just Government, may ever be falling on all his Majesty's Dominions, and on this loyal and dutiful Province in particular. . . .

Source: New England Weekly Journal *(August 21, 1727)*.

fully mirror that of England. One of the most obvious differences was that America lacked an aristocracy. In England, the members of this tiny privileged minority were easily recognizable by their great wealth, prestigious family lines, leisured lives, and official titles of nobility. British America had elites—mainly rich planters and merchants—but no aristocracy. Such men were often just two or three generations removed from more humble beginnings. Hence the acute anxiety that inspired George Washington and other colonial gentlemen to seek refinement, to gain the automatic recognition that England's more secure elites enjoyed.

In both England and America, land ownership was the prerequisite for political participation, on the grounds that it freed people from dependence on others and gave them a stake in society. In England, this requirement sharply limited participation. By the mid-eighteenth century, only one-tenth of all English heads of households owned all the country's land, and just four hundred great landlords held nearly a quarter of it. Thus only a tiny portion of adult men—perhaps 15 percent—could vote. Landholding in America, however, was much more widespread. By late in life, a large majority of white male farmers owned the land they tilled. The expansion of landholding swelled the ranks of voters. In most colonies, 50 to 75 percent of white men were eligible to vote, although not all exercised this right at election time.

Distinctive social conditions in England and America also gave rise to different notions of political representation. Electoral districts for Parliament came in a confusing mixture of shapes, reflecting their status in past centuries. Once-important towns sent representatives on the basis of their former prominence. Dunwich even retained its right to elect a parliamentary representative long after the city itself had washed into the North Sea. At the same time, rapidly growing cities, such as Manchester, lacked any representative at all. Some English radicals protested this inequity during the eighteenth century. Most of their countrymen, however, accepted the idea of **virtual representation**, which held that representatives served the interests of the nation as a whole, not just the locality from which they came. They assumed that since the colonists held interests in common with English people at home, they were virtually represented in Parliament—just like Manchester's residents.

Since the founding of their colonies, however, Americans had experienced **actual representation**—and believed that elected representatives should be directly responsive to local interests. They were accustomed to sending written instructions to their legislators, informing them how to vote on important issues. Colonial representatives, unlike members of Parliament, resided in their districts. The Americans' experience with actual representation made them extremely skeptical of Parliament's claims to virtual representation. For the first half of the eighteenth century, however, Parliament did not press this claim, and the tensions between the two ideas remained latent.

The most direct political confrontations between England and the colonies instead focused on the role of colonial governors. In every colony except Connecticut and Rhode Island, either the king or proprietors appointed the governors. Their interests thus lay with their English patrons and not the colonies. More important, governors exercised greater powers over the colonial assemblies than the king (after the Glorious Revolution) did over Parliament. Governors could veto laws enacted by the assemblies and initiate legislation in consultation with councilors whom they appointed. They could delay legislative sessions and dissolve the assemblies at will. Governors could also nominate and dismiss colonial judges as they wished.

In practice, several conditions hampered governors' efforts to exercise their legal authority. Many arrived with detailed instructions on how to govern, which limited their ability to negotiate with colonists over sensitive issues. Governors controlled few offices or other prizes with which to buy the allegiance of their opponents. They struggled to dominate assemblies that grew in size as the colonial population expanded. And in several colonies, including Massachusetts and New York, governors relied on the assemblies to appropriate the money for their salaries—a financial dependence that restrained even the most autocratic executive.

In response to the perceived, if not always realized, threat of powerful governors, colonial assemblies asserted themselves as never before. They sent agents (including such prominent figures as Benjamin Franklin) to England to lobby on behalf of colonial interests. Local factions fought for election to the increasingly important legislature, leading to some of the most contentious politics in the British Empire. Governors often stood on the sidelines, either frustrated with their inability to govern or, at times, enlisted on the side of one faction or another.

Decades of struggles with governors led colonists to exalt the assemblies' role as the guarantors of their liberties. In 1738, one Pennsylvanian commentator went so far as to declare that the "necessity of reducing the form of this government to the British mode" by strengthening the executive was a "wicked" design. Most colonists, however, accepted the loose and sometimes contradictory political ties of empire. They assumed that their connections to Britain were voluntary, based on common identity and rights. So long as Parliament treated the Americans as partners in empire and refrained from ruling by coercion, colonists could celebrate British government as "the most perfect combination of human powers in society . . . for the preservation of liberty and the production of happiness."

By the middle of the eighteenth century, the blessings of British government extended to more colonists than ever before. The population of British America grew rapidly and spread out over vast amounts of land. The expansion of British settlement, in turn, alarmed other European powers with American colonies. Both Spain and France launched new settlements as the competition for the continent entered a new and volatile phase.

Expanding Empires

During the first half of the eighteenth century, England, Spain, and France all increased their North American holdings, expanding according to patterns established during the previous century. England's empire continued to expand as a result of the unrelenting growth of its colonial population. Spain and France still relied on missionaries, soldiers, and traders to stake their claims to American territory. In the eighteenth century as in the seventeenth, English settlement generally displaced native peoples. Newly established Spanish and French colonies, however, contained small numbers of Europeans amid much larger populations of Indians. Over time, these empires came into closer contact with one another, intensifying the competition for land, trade, resources, and Indian allies (see Map 4-2).

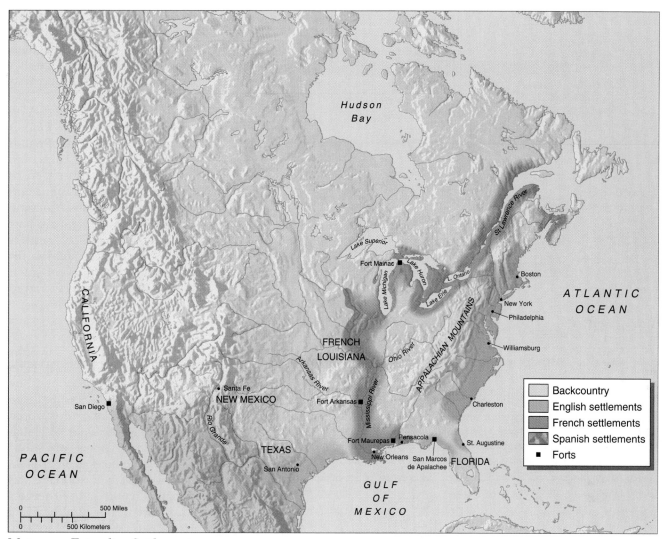

Map 4-2   *Expanding Settlement, c. 1750*
Imperial rivalries drove Spain, France, and England to expand their North American empires in the mid-eighteenth century. Once again, this sparked conflict with native peoples as well as with European competitors.

The English in the Backcountry

Population growth in British North America during the eighteenth century was truly astonishing. Black and white settlers in the mainland colonies numbered 265,000 in 1700; by 1770, they had increased to 2.3 million (see Figure 4-2). Benjamin Franklin predicted in 1750 that if the colonial population continued to grow at this rate, within two hundred years "the greatest Number of Englishmen will be on this Side" of the Atlantic Ocean.

Much of this growth stemmed from natural increase. White families, particularly in the northern colonies, had large numbers of children, most of whom survived to produce many more offspring. Most

women married in their early twenties (a younger age, on average, than European women) and often bore between five and ten children. The descendants of a single couple could, after three or four generations, people small towns. When 80-year-old Judith Coffin, the matriarch of an unusually large Massachusetts family, died in 1705, she had a total of 177 children and grandchildren. By the mid-eighteenth century, even the slave population, first in the Chesapeake and later in the Lower South, began to reproduce itself, although more slowly than the white population.

Immigration also boosted the population, making some regions grow faster than others. Thousands of Scots-Irish and German settlers—and many

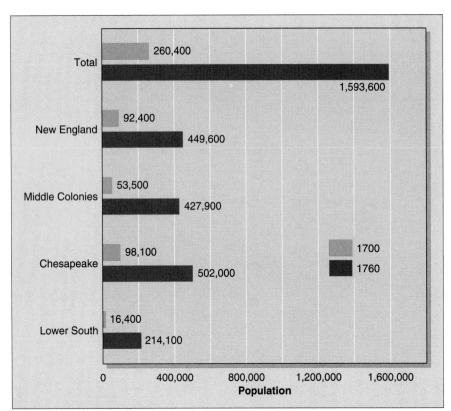

Figure 4-2 *Population Growth in British Mainland Colonies, 1700–1760*
Both natural increase and immigration contributed to a staggering rate of population growth in British North America. Some colonists predicted that Americans would soon outnumber Britain's inhabitants—a possibility that greatly concerned British officials.

Source: John J. McCusker and Russell R. Menard, The Economy of British America, 1607–1789, rev. ed. (1991).

involuntary African immigrants—helped the population of the Lower South increase at nearly twice the rate of New England, which attracted few immigrants (and therefore remained the most thoroughly English of all colonial regions). Pennsylvania absorbed a continuous stream of immigrants. By 1770, it had 240,000 settlers—ten times the number it had in 1710. Indeed, extensive German immigration worried Pennsylvania leaders. Like Benjamin Franklin, they feared that the newcomers would "never adopt our Language or Customs" and would soon "be so numerous as to Germanize us."

Most of the coast from Maine to Georgia was settled by 1760, forcing many immigrants to move inland. Descendants of earlier settlers often joined them, seeking farms that could no longer be had in the more crowded towns of their birth. New Englanders pushed up the Connecticut River Valley and into the hills of western Massachusetts. Settlement in New York followed the Hudson, Mohawk, and Schoharie Rivers deep into the interior. But the

most dramatic expansion occurred in the foothills and valleys of the Appalachian Mountains from Pennsylvania to Georgia, a region known as the **backcountry**.

Between 1730 and 1770, nearly a quarter of a million German, Scots-Irish, and English colonists entered the backcountry. They mainly raised crops and livestock for subsistence on small, isolated farms. Community life developed slowly, in part because backcountry settlers often moved frequently. In addition, a surplus of men among the first settlers delayed the formation of families.

Contemporary observers derided the crudeness of frontier life. William Byrd, a wealthy planter from Virginia's Tidewater, scornfully described one backcountry house as a "castle containing of one dirty room with a dragging door to it that will neither open or shut." Charles Woodmason, an English-born Anglican missionary, was appalled by the sight of settlers who "Live in Logg Cabbins like Hogs" in western Carolina. Most of them, he reported, were "very loose, dissolute, Idle People—Without either Religion or Goodness." Genteel observers offered what they considered the most damaging insult by referring to such settlers as "white Indians."

These comments, though exaggerated, revealed emerging tensions between backcountry settlements and older seacoast communities. Yet many coastal planters—including William Byrd and George Washington—acquired vast tracts of western land with the intent to sell it to these "crude" settlers. During the 1740s and 1750s, scores of Virginia planters, northern merchants, and London investors formed companies whose purpose was to profit from this kind of land speculation. Their interests collided with those of settlers—squatters—who occupied the land without acquiring legal title in the hope that their labor in clearing farms would establish their property rights.

Backcountry settlers often complained that rich eastern planters, who dominated the colonial legislatures, ignored western demands for adequate

This log house, built in Pennsylvania in the early eighteenth century, suggests the sort of dwellings that dotted the back-country. Most such houses would have been smaller than this two-story example. Scandinavian colonists, who settled on the lower Delaware River in the early seventeenth century, introduced log construction to America.

representation. Many western settlers argued that the crudeness of frontier life was only temporary and that they, too, would soon be producing tobacco and other cash crops. Perhaps the best measure of their desire to resemble eastern planters was the spread of slaveholding among prosperous back-country farmers. In one western Virginia county in 1750, only one-fifth of the household heads owned slaves. Just nineteen years later, more than half of them did.

Tensions grew throughout the backcountry as English settlers encroached on Indian lands. Colonists who moved to Pennsylvania's fertile Susque-hanna Valley displaced Delawares, Shawnees, and other native peoples who had sought refuge there from earlier white migrations. In South Carolina, the Catawbas moved to ever more remote sites to keep their distance from white settlers. Indians moving to avoid friction with whites, however, frequently encroached on lands claimed by other tribes—particularly those of the Iroquois Confederacy—leading to conflict among native peoples.

Even where English settlers had not yet appeared, English and Scottish traders could often be found, aggressively pursuing trade with the Indians. Spanish and French observers feared this commercial expansion even more than the movement of settlers. Knowing that the Indians viewed trade as a counterpart to military alliance, they worried that the English, with cheaper and better trade goods, would lure away their native allies. In response, the

Spanish and French expanded their own territorial claims and tried to strengthen relations with Indian peoples.

The Spanish in Texas and California

Spain worried that its existing North American colonies would be overwhelmed by its enemies. Florida had become the target of English raiders from South Carolina, who attacked Spanish missions with the help of local Indians. Years of religious persecution and forced labor encouraged Florida's Indians to oppose the Spanish, but the natives also liked English trade goods—including guns, which Spanish traders were officially prohibited from selling. Spain maintained a precarious hold on coastal bases at St. Augustine, San Marcos de Apalachee, and Pensacola. By the mid-eighteenth century, however, control of Florida's interior effectively passed to Indian bands allied with English (and in the west, French) traders.

In 1700, New Mexico still suffered from the effects of the Pueblo Revolt. Spanish farmers and ranchers slowly moved back up the Rio Grande Valley. Franciscans returned to build fewer missions than before. Fearful of sparking another native revolt, the priests eased their labor demands and avoided outright religious persecution, allowing the Pueblos to retain many of their customs and religious practices. New Mexican officials worried about news brought by Apache hunters that Frenchmen had been seen on the plains. French traders did not reach Santa Fe until 1739, but persistent rumors of their approach fueled Spanish fears that New Mexico would fall into French hands.

To create a buffer zone around their existing colonies, the Spanish moved into Texas and California. Franciscan priests led the way into east Texas, establishing several missions between 1690 and 1720. San Antonio was founded in 1718 to serve as a way station between the Rio Grande and east Texas missions; its fortified chapel, San Antonio de Valero, later became famous as the Alamo. The Spanish advance into Texas, however, met with resistance from the French (who also had outposts on the Gulf Coast) and from the Caddos and other Indians armed with French guns. Efforts to fill east Texas with settlers from Spain, Cuba, and the Canary Islands all failed when Spanish officials could not guarantee their safety. With only 1,800 settlers there as late as 1742, Spain exerted a weak hold on Texas.

Sixteenth-century Spaniards had considered building outposts in California to supply ships traveling between Mexico and the Philippines but failed to

This panel of an eighteenth-century painting by an unknown Mexican artist is representative of a genre of portraits illustrating the categories Spanish colonists developed to designate the offspring of various kinds of mixed marriage. This one, labeled "Español, con India, Mestizo," depicts a Spanish father, an Indian mother, and their mestizo child. The scarcity of European women made mixed marriage common in Spanish colonies. Such unions were exceedingly rare in the English colonies, where cultural preferences and the relative abundance of European women discouraged intermarriage.

do so. The coast could be reached only by a long trek across blazing deserts or a dangerous voyage around Baja California. But Spanish interest revived in the 1760s when it seemed that other European powers—primarily Russia, which had built fur trading posts in Alaska—might occupy California. Largely through the efforts of two men—José de Gálvez, a royal official, and Junípero Serra, a Franciscan priest—the Spanish constructed a string of forts and missions from San Diego north to San Francisco between 1769 and 1776.

They initially encountered little opposition from California's Indians, who lived in small, scattered villages and lacked experience with organized warfare. With no European rivals nearby to com-

pete with them, the Spanish erected an extensive mission system designed to convert and educate Indians and set them to work. Thousands of native laborers farmed irrigated fields and tended horses, sheep, and cattle. They did so under extremely harsh conditions.

According to one observer, Indians who became Christians and settled at the missions endured a fate "worse than that of slaves." The Spanish worked them hard and maintained them in overcrowded, unsanitary dwellings. Native women suffered from sexual exploitation by Spanish soldiers. Epidemics of European diseases swept through the Indian population, reducing it from 300,000 in 1769 to about 200,000 fifty years later. Signs of native resistance met with quick and cruel punishment—including whipping, burning, and execution—so that the Indians would not (as one official later wrote) "come to know their power" over the vastly outnumbered Spanish. (As late as 1790, California had only 990 Spanish residents.) Despite the gruesome consequences, natives staged several revolts during the eighteenth century, but Spanish soldiers usually suppressed them quickly.

Spain's empire grew, even as it weakened, during the eighteenth century. Its scattered holdings north of the Rio Grande functioned as colonies of another colony—Mexico—shielding it from foreign incursion. The scarcity of Spanish settlers, especially women, encouraged racial intermixture in the borderlands and ensured that racial distinctions would never be drawn as sharply there as in the English colonies. From the beginning, Spain's vision of empire had rested not on extensive settlement but on expansive territorial claims backed up by soldiers and missionaries who subjugated native peoples in order to control their labor for Spanish profit. After 1700, however, the limitations of this coercive approach to empire, which had served Spain well for nearly two centuries, became apparent. As their experiences in Florida and Texas vividly demonstrated, the Spanish simply could not compete with the vigorous commercial empires of France and England.

The French along the Mississippi

French expansion followed major waterways—the St. Lawrence River, the Great Lakes, the Mississippi—into the heart of North America. Explorers reached the Mississippi Valley in the 1670s. Within twenty years, French outposts appeared along the Gulf Coast. New Orleans, the capital and main port of French Louisiana, was founded in 1718. Soon forts, trading posts, and villages began to spring up in the continent's interior—a chain of way stations between Canada and the Gulf of Mexico. Military garrisons were strategically located on lakes and rivers: Fort Mainac at the juncture of Lakes Huron and Michigan; Fort Arkansas where the Arkansas and Mississippi Rivers join; Fort Maurepas on the Gulf Coast. Concerned about defending scattered settlements, French officials forbade colonists to move into the interior. But colonists went anyway, building six villages along the Mississippi in a place they called the *Pays des Illinois.*

The first Illinois settlers were independent fur traders (*coureurs de bois,* or "woods runners") unwilling to return to Canada after the French government tried to prohibit their direct trade with Indians. Many found Christian Indian wives and began farming the rich lands along the river. Several hundred emigrants from Canada eventually joined them, including landless sons in search of farms. The settlers, using the labor of their families and of black and Indian slaves, produced profitable surpluses of wheat, corn, and livestock to feed the growing population of New Orleans and the lower Mississippi Valley.

French Louisiana contained a remarkably diverse population of Indian peoples, French soldiers and settlers, German immigrants, and African slaves who, by the 1730s, outnumbered European colonists. Settlers raised some tobacco and indigo as cash crops, but Louisiana's economy depended mainly on the combined efforts of Indians, settlers, and slaves, who farmed, herded, fished, and traded deerskins. Discouraged by the lack of profits, French officials and merchants neglected Louisiana, and even Catholic missionaries failed to establish a strong presence. Substantial European emigration to Louisiana essentially ceased after the 1720s.

But the French approach to empire—in Louisiana as in Canada —had always depended more on Indian alliances than on settlement. Louisiana's principal allies were the Choctaws, whom one military official called "the bulwark of the colony." The Choctaws and other native allies offered trade and military assistance in return for guns, trade goods, French help in fighting English raiders seeking Indian slaves, and occasionally French mediation of Indian disputes.

French expansion along the Mississippi Valley drove a wedge between Florida and Spain's other mainland colonies; it also blocked the westward movement of English settlers. But France's enlarged empire was only as strong as the Indian alliances on which it rested. Preserving good relations was expensive, however, requiring the constant exchange of diplomatic gifts and trade goods. When France ordered Louisiana officials to limit expenses and reduce Indian gifts in 1745, the officials objected that the Choctaws "would ask for nothing better than to have such pretexts in order to resort to the English."

The fear of losing Indian favor preoccupied officials in 1745 because at that moment France's empire in America consisted of two disconnected pieces: New France, centered in the St. Lawrence Valley and the Great Lakes basin, and Louisiana, stretching from New Orleans to the *Pays de Illinois.* Between them lay 1,000 miles of wilderness through which only one thoroughfare passed—the Ohio River. For decades, communication between the two parts of France's North American empire posed no problem because Indians in the Ohio Valley allowed the French free passage through their lands. If that policy ended, however, France's New World empire would be dangerously divided.

A Century of Warfare

The expansion of empires in North America reflected the policies of European states locked in a relentless competition for power and wealth. From the time of the Glorious Revolution, English foreign policy aimed at limiting the expansion of French influence, and this, in turn, resulted in a series of four wars. As the eighteenth century wore on, the conflicts between the two countries increasingly involved their American colonies as well as Spain and its colonies. The outcome of each of the wars in America depended no less on the participation of colonists and Indians than on the policies and strategies of the European powers. The conclusion of the final conflict signaled a dramatic shift in North American history (see the summary table "The Colonial Wars, 1689–1763").

Imperial Conflict and the Establishment of an American Balance of Power, 1689–1738

When he became king of England in 1688, the Dutch Protestant William of Orange was already fighting the **War of the League of Augsburg** against France's Catholic king, Louis XIV. Almost immediately, William brought England into the conflict as a Dutch ally. The war lasted until 1697 and ended—as most eighteenth-century European wars did—in a negotiated peace

SUMMARY

THE COLONIAL WARS, 1689–1763

Name in the Colonies	European Name and Dates	Dates in America	Results for Britain
King William's War	War of the League of Augsburg, 1688–1697	1689–1697	• Reestablished balance of power between England and France
Queen Anne's War	War of Spanish Succession, 1702–1714	1702–1713	• Britain acquired Nova Scotia
King George's War	War of Austrian Succession, 1739–1748	1744–1748	• Britain returned Louisbourg to France • British settlers began moving westward • Weakening of Iroquois neutrality
French and Indian War	Seven Years' War, 1756–1763	1754–1763	• Britain acquired Canada and all French territory east of Mississippi • Britain gained Florida from Spain

that reestablished the balance of power. Little territory actually changed hands, either in this war or in the **War of the Spanish Succession** (1702–1713), which followed it.

In America, these two wars—known to British colonists as **King William's War** and **Queen Anne's War**, after the monarchs on the throne at the time—ended with equal indecisiveness. New France's Indian allies attacked New England's northern frontier with devastating success, as when they destroyed the Massachusetts town of Deerfield in 1704. New Englanders struck back at the exposed settlements of Acadia, which ultimately entered the British Empire as Nova Scotia, and tried unsuccessfully to seize Quebec. Neither war caused more than marginal changes for the colonies in North America. Both had profound effects, however, on the English state and on the Iroquois League.

All European states of the eighteenth century financed their wars by borrowing. But the English were the first to realize that wartime debts did not necessarily have to be repaid during the fol-

lowing peace. The government instead created a **funded debt**. Having borrowed heavily from large joint-stock corporations, the government agreed to use tax revenues to pay interest on those loans but not to pay off the loans themselves. The corporations agreed because the interest payments amounted to a steady form of income that over the long run could amount to more than the original loans. In this way, England became the first European country to harness its national economy efficiently to military ends.

As the debt grew ever larger, more and more taxes were necessary to pay interest on it. Taxes also rose to pay for a powerful navy and a standing army. When the treasury created a larger and more efficient bureaucracy to collect taxes, many Englishmen grew nervous. Their anxiety emerged as a strain of thought known as **Country**, or "**Real Whig**," ideology. Country ideology stressed the threats that a standing army and a powerful state posed to personal liberty. It also emphasized the dangers of taxation to property rights and the need for property holders to retain their right to consent to taxation.

Grassat de Saint-Sauvaur/National Archives of Canada/C-003165.

This eighteenth-century French etching depicts an Iroquois warrior and reflects European notions of Iroquoian ferocity. After 1701 the Iroquois in fact adopted a policy of peace in their dealings with nearby European and native neighbors, although they continued to fight against Indians living farther south.

Real Whig politicians publicized their fears but could not stop the growth of the state. In every successive war, the claims of national interest and patriotism—and the prospect of profit for parties rich enough to lend money to the government—overrode the objections of those who feared the expansion of state power.

In America, the first two imperial wars transformed the role of the Iroquois League. After the English took over New Netherlands in 1664, the Five Nations cultivated trading connections with them and later allied with England during King William's War. But the English offered little help when the French and their Indian allies attacked the Iroquois during that conflict. By 1700, the Iroquois League had suffered such horrendous losses—perhaps a quarter of the population had died from causes related to the war—that its leaders sought an alternative to direct alliance with the British.

With the so-called **Grand Settlement of 1701**, the Iroquois adopted a policy of neutrality with regard to the French and British Empires. Their goal was to refrain from alliances with either European power—which were likely to fight each other again—and instead maneuver between them. The Iroquois' strategic location between New France and the English colonies allowed them to serve as a geographical and diplomatic buffer between the two. Neutral Iroquois diplomats could play the English against the French, gaining favors from one side in return for promises not to ally with the other. This neutralist policy ensured that for nearly fifty years neither England nor France could gain ascendancy in North America.

Iroquois neutrality offered benefits to the Europeans as well as the Indians. The English, for instance, began to negotiate with them for land. The Iroquois claimed sovereignty over much of the country west of the Middle and Chesapeake colonies. To smooth relations with the English, the Iroquois sold them land formerly occupied by Delawares and Susquehannocks. This simultaneously helped satisfy the colonists' land hunger and enrich the Iroquois League.

Meanwhile, a neutral Iroquois League claiming control over the Ohio Valley and blocking English access across the Appalachian Mountains helped the French protect the strategic corridor of the Ohio and Mississippi Valleys that linked Canada and Louisiana. If the English ever established a permanent presence on this strategic corridor, however, the Iroquois would cease to be of use to the French.

The Iroquois remained reasonably effective at keeping the British out of the Ohio Valley until the late 1740s. The next European war, however, altered these circumstances. The French grew increasingly anxious about the future of their empire. At the same time, British strategists brought the North American colonies into their war plans more fully than ever before.

King George's War Shifts the Balance, 1739–1754

What became the third confrontation between Britain and France in Europe, the **War of the Austrian Succession (King George's War** to the British colonists) began as a small war between Britain and Spain in 1739. Its immediate cause was British attempts to poach on trade to Spain's Caribbean colonies. But in 1744, France joined in the war against Britain. An Anglo-French conflict once again erupted in North America.

New Englanders took advantage of the war as yet another chance to attack Canada. This time, their target was the great fortress of Louisbourg on Cape Breton Island, a naval base that dominated the Gulf of St. Lawrence. An expedition from Massachusetts and Connecticut, supported by a squadron of Royal Navy warships, captured Louisbourg in 1745. This success cut Canada off from French reinforcement and resupply. English forces should now have been able to conquer New France.

Instead, politically influential merchants in Albany, New York, chose to continue their profitable trade with the enemy via Lake Champlain, enabling Canada to hold out until the end of the war. When the peace treaty was signed in 1748, Britain, which had fared badly in the European fighting, agreed to return Louisbourg to France. This diplomatic adjustment, routine by European standards, shocked New Englanders. At the same time, New York's illegal trade with the enemy, unremarkable by previous colonial standards, appalled British administrators. They began thinking of ways to prevent such independent behavior in any future war.

King George's War furnished an equal share of shocks for New France, which had suffered more after the conquest of Louisbourg than in any previous conflict. Even before the war's end, aggressive English traders from Pennsylvania began moving west to buy furs from Indians who had once traded with the French. The movements of these traders, along with the appearance of Virginians in the Ohio Valley after 1748, gravely concerned the French.

In 1749, the governor general of New France set out to assert direct control over the region by building a set of forts from Lake Erie to the Forks of the Ohio (the place where the Monongahela and Allegheny Rivers meet to form the Ohio River). This decision signaled the end of France's commitment to Iroquois neutrality. Instead of enjoying their old position as neutral mediators, the chiefs of the Iroquois League now found themselves trapped between empires edging closer to confrontation in the Ohio Valley.

The Iroquois, in fact, had never exerted direct power in the Ohio Country. Their control instead depended on their ability to dominate the peoples who actually lived there—western Senecas, as well as the Delawares and Shawnees, both in theory Iroquois dependents. The appearance of English traders in the valley offering goods on better terms than the French or the Iroquois had ever provided undermined Iroquois dominance.

The Ohio Valley Indians increasingly ignored Iroquois claims of control and pursued their own independent course. One spur to their disaffection from the Iroquois was the 1744 **Treaty of Lancaster**, by which Iroquois chiefs had sold a group of Virginia land speculators rights to trade at the Forks of the Ohio. The Virginians assumed that these trading rights included the right to acquire land for eventual sale to settlers. The Ohio Valley Indians found this intolerable, as did the French. When in 1754 the government of Virginia sent out a small body of soldiers under Lieutenant Colonel George Washington to protect Virginia's claims to the Forks of the Ohio, the French struck decisively to stop them.

Decision: The French and Indian War, 1754–1760

In April 1754, French soldiers overwhelmed a group of Virginians who had been trying to build a small fort at the Forks of the Ohio. They then erected a much larger fort of their own on the spot, Fort Duquesne. The French intended to follow up by similarly ousting Washington's weak, untrained troops, who had encamped further up the Monongahela River. However, at the end of May, Washington's men killed or captured all but one of the members of a small French reconnaissance party. The French decided to teach the Virginians a lesson. On July 3, they attacked Washington at his encampment, Fort Necessity. The next day, with a quarter of his troops killed or wounded, Washington surrendered.

Even before news of these engagements reached Britain, imperial officials worried that the Iroquois might abandon their neutrality for a French alliance. Britain ordered New York's governor to convene an intercolonial meeting in Albany—known as the **Albany Congress**—to discuss matters with the Iroquois. Several prominent colonists, including Governor William Shirley of Massachusetts and Benjamin Franklin, took advantage of the occasion to put forward the **Albany Plan of Union**, which called for an intercolonial union to coordinate colonial defense, levy taxes, and regulate Indian affairs. But the colonies, too suspicious of one another to see their common interests, rejected the Albany Plan. Meanwhile, events in the west took a turn for the worse.

This cartoon, the first to appear in a colonial American newspaper, was printed in the Pennsylvania Gazette *in the spring of 1754. It refers to the plan for a colonial union that was put forward at the Albany Congress. The image alludes to the folk belief that a severed snake could revive if its parts were rejoined before sundown.*

The French expulsion of the Virginians left the Indians of the region, Delawares and Shawnees, with no choice but to ally with the French in what came to be called the **French and Indian War** (see Map 4-3). Soon French and Indian attacks fell like

hammer blows on backcountry settlements from Pennsylvania to the Carolinas. The Iroquois tried to remain neutral, but their neutrality no longer mattered. Europeans were at last contending directly for control of the Ohio Country.

The French and Indian War blazed in America for two years before it erupted as a fourth Anglo-French war in Europe in 1756. Known in Europe as the **Seven Years' War** (1756–1763), it involved fighting in the Caribbean, Africa, India, and the Philippine Islands as well as in Europe and North America. It was unlike any other eighteenth-century conflict not only in its immense scope and expense but also in its decisive outcome.

The war had two phases in North America—one from 1754 to 1758 and the other from 1758 through 1760—that corresponded to shifts in European involvement. During the first phase, the French enjoyed a string of successes as they followed what had been a proven strategy in previous conflicts—guerrilla war. Relying on Indian allies acting together with Canadian soldiers, the French raided English frontier settlements, killing and capturing hundreds of civilians and forcing tens of

Map 4-3 *The French and Indian War, 1754–1763*
Most of the battles of the French and Indian War occurred in the frontier regions of northern and western New York and the Ohio Valley. The influx of settlers into these areas created tensions that eventually developed into war.

thousands more to flee. Then they attacked forti-fied outposts whenever the opportunity appeared. This style of warfare allowed the Canadians' Indian allies—who came from all over the Northeast and the upper Midwest—to act independently in choosing targets and tactics.

The first full campaign of the war, in 1755, saw not only the British colonial frontiers collapsing in terror but also a notable defeat inflicted on the troops Britain had dispatched to attack Fort Duquesne. The British commander in chief, Major General Edward Braddock, with immense self-confidence and no real knowledge of the countryside or his enemy, marched to within 10 miles of Fort Duquesne, only to have his 1,450-man force surrounded by Indians and Canadian militiamen and destroyed. Braddock's defeat set the tone for virtually every military engagement of the next three years and opened a period of demoralization and internal conflict in the British colonies.

Britain responded to Braddock's defeat by sending a new commander in chief with more trained British soldiers. The new commander, Lord Loudoun, tried to set colonial military affairs on a professional footing. He insisted on managing every aspect of the war effort, not only directing the campaigns but also dictating the amount of support, in men and money, that each colony would provide. The colonists, who had plenty of experience with war, had never experienced anything like Loudoun's high-handed style and grew increasingly stubborn in response to it. Colonial soldiers, who had volunteered to serve under their own officers, objected to Loudoun's command. By the end of 1757, a year of disastrous military campaigns, colonial assemblies were also refusing to cooperate.

Britain's aim had been to "rationalize" the war by making it conform to European professional military standards. This approach to warfare required soldiers to advance in formation in the face of massed musket fire without breaking rank. It needed iron discipline, which was enforced—as in the British army—by savage punishments, including hundreds of lashes at the whipping post. Few colonial volunteers met professional standards, and few colonists thought them necessary, especially when British soldiers suffered defeat after defeat at the hands of French and Indian guerrillas. British officers assumed that colonial soldiers were simply lazy cowards. But colonial volunteers, appalled to see men lashed "till the blood came out at the knee" of their breeches, saw British officers as brutal task-masters. They resisted all efforts to impose such discipline on their own units, even to the point of desertion and mutiny.

Despite the astonishing success of their guerrilla tactics, the French, too, began moving toward a more European style of warfare. In the process, they destroyed their strategic and tactical advantages. In 1756, the marquis de Montcalm, a strong proponent of European professional standards of military conduct, assumed command of French forces. In his first battle, the successful siege of Fort Oswego, New York, Montcalm was horrified by the behavior of his Indian allies, which included killing wounded prisoners, taking personal captives, and collecting scalps as trophies. As a result, he came to regard the Indians—so essential to the defense of New France—as mere savages.

Following his next victory, the capture of Fort William Henry, New York, Montcalm conformed to European practice by agreeing that the defeated garrison could go home in return for the promise not to fight again. Montcalm's Indian allies—a thousand or more strong—were not to take prisoners, trophies, or plunder. The tragic result came to be known as the Massacre of Fort William Henry. Understanding themselves to be betrayed by their French allies, the Indians took captives and trophies anyway, killing as many as 185 defenders and taking about 300 captive. This not only outraged the New England colonies (most of the victims were New Englanders) but also alienated the Indians on whom the defense of Canada depended. Ironically, Montcalm's efforts to limit the war's violence—to impose European standards of conduct—prepared the way for the British army and its colonial auxiliaries to win an unlimited victory.

For at the same time that the Europeanization of the war was weakening the French, the British moderated their policies and reached accommodation with the colonists. A remarkable politician came to power in London as England's chief war minister. William Pitt, who as secretary of state directed the British war effort from late 1757 through 1761, realized that friction between the colonists and the commander in chief arose from the colonists' sense that they were bearing all the financial burdens of the war without having any say in how the war was fought. Pitt's ingenious solutions were to promise reimbursements to the colonies in proportion to their contribution to the war effort, to deemphasize the power of the commander in chief, and to replace the arrogant Loudoun with a less objectionable officer.

Pitt's money and measures restored colonial morale. He sent thousands of British soldiers to America to fight alongside tens of thousands of colonial troops. As the Anglo-American forces grew stronger, they operated more successfully, seizing Louisbourg again in 1758. Once more, Canada experienced crippling shortages of supplies, weapons, and trade goods. But this time, unlike in 1745, the Anglo-Americans were united and able to take advantage of the situation. British emissaries persuaded the Delawares and Shawnees to abandon their French alliance, and late in 1758, an Anglo-American force again marched on Fort Duquesne. In command of its lead battalion was Colonel George Washington. The French defenders, abandoned by their native allies and confronted by overwhelming force, blew up the fort and retreated to the Great Lakes.

From this point on, the Anglo-Americans suffered no setbacks and the French won no victories. The war became a contest in which the larger, better-supplied army would triumph. Montcalm, forced back to Quebec, decided to risk everything in a European-style, open-field battle against a British force led by General James Wolfe. At the Battle of Quebec (September 13, 1759), Montcalm lost the gamble—and his life (as did the victorious General Wolfe).

But the French had not yet lost the war. The Anglo-Americans had to hold on to their conquests. The French might still revive their Indian alliances, if only they could be resupplied from France with the weapons and trade goods the Indians demanded. What finally decided the outcome of the war in America was not the Battle of Quebec but two other developments: the Battle of Quiberon Bay in France (November 20, 1759) and the Iroquois' decision to join the Anglo-American side in 1760. The sea battle cost the French navy its ability to operate on the Atlantic, preventing it from carrying the reinforcements and supplies Canada needed to survive. Montcalm's successor could not rebuild the Indian alliances he so desperately needed. At the same time, the Iroquois decision to enter the war on the side of the Anglo-Americans tipped the balance irrevocably against the French. The last ragged, hungry defenders of Canada, surrounded at Montreal by a vastly superior Anglo-American-Iroquoian force, surrendered on September 8, 1760.

The Triumph of the British Empire, 1763

The war pitting Britain against France and Spain (which had entered the fighting as a French ally in 1762) concluded with an uninterrupted series of British victories. In the Caribbean, where every valuable sugar island the French owned eventually came under British control, the culminating event was the surrender of Havana on August 13, 1762. Even more spectacular was Britain's capture of the Philippine capital of Manila on October 5—a victory that literally carried British power around the world.

In his most famous painting, American artist Benjamin West depicted the death of the British general James Wolfe at the Battle of Quebec. He portrays Wolfe as a glorious martyr to the cause of British victory. In the left foreground, West added the figure of an Indian, a "noble savage" who contemplates the meaning of Wolfe's selfless sacrifice of his life.

These conquests created the unshakable conviction that British arms were invincible. An immense surge of British patriotism spread throughout the American colonies. When news of the conquest of Havana reached Massachusetts, bells rang, cannons fired salutes, and bonfires blazed. General John Winslow of Plymouth, a portly man, rejoiced by becoming "so intoxicated as to jump on the table, and break a great number of bowls."

Hostilities ended formally on February 10, 1763, with the conclusion of the **Treaty of Paris**. France regained its West Indian sugar islands—its most valuable colonial possessions—but lost the rest of its North American empire. France ceded to Britain all its claims to lands east of the Mississippi River (except the city of New Orleans) and compensated Spain for the losses it had sustained as an ally by handing over all claims to the Trans-Mississippi West and the port of New Orleans (see Map 4-4). Britain returned Cuba and the Philippines to Spain and in compensation received Florida. Now Great Britain owned everything east of the Mississippi, from the Gulf of Mexico to Hudson's Bay. With France and Spain both humbled and on the verge of financial collapse, Britain seemed preeminent in Europe and ready to dominate in the New World. Never before had Americans felt more pride in being British, members of the greatest empire on earth.

Conclusion

The George Washington who ordered a suit in 1763 was not a revolutionary; on the contrary, he was a man who longed to be part of the elite of the great British Empire. If he feared any threat to his position in that elite, it was not Parliament and the king but the uncomfortably large debts he owed to

Map 4-4 *European Empires in North America, 1750–1763*
Great Britain's victory in the French and Indian War transformed the map of North America. France lost its mainland colonies, England claimed all lands east of the Mississippi, and Spain gained nominal control over the Trans-Mississippi West.

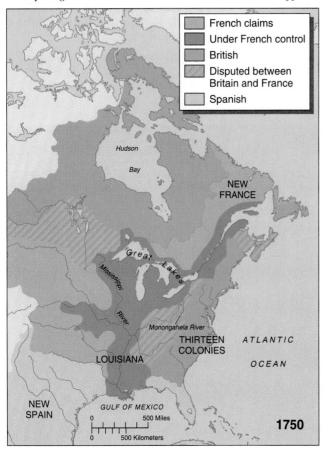

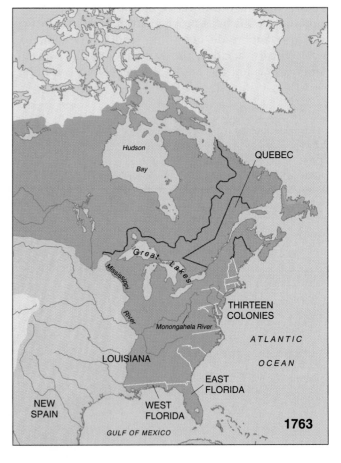

his London agents for the goods he and Martha wanted or perhaps the unruly Baptists who refused to acknowledge the superiority of the great planters. But those worries, though real, were merely small, nagging doubts, shared by most of his fellow planters.

What was more real to Washington was the great victory that the British Empire had just gained over France, a victory that he had helped achieve. With the French eliminated as an imperial power in North America, Washington could look forward to increasing his fortune by speculating in the western lands he knew so well. For Washington, as for virtually all other colonial leaders, 1763 was a moment of great promise and patriotic devotion to the British Empire. It was a time to rejoice in the fundamental British identity and liberty and rights that seemed to ensure that life in the colonies would be better and more prosperous than ever.

Review Questions

1. In what ways did economic ties between Britain and the colonies grow closer in the century after 1660?

2. What did elite colonists think about American society and culture in the eighteenth century? What changes did they want to introduce?

3. What was the Great Awakening, and what impact did it have on colonial society?

4. In what ways were colonial and British political ideas and practices similar? In what ways were they different?

5. Why did England, Spain, and France renew their competition for North America in the eighteenth century?

6. What role did warfare play in North America in the eighteenth century? How would you characterize the role of the Iroquois in these conflicts?

Recommended Reading

Anderson, Fred. *A People's Army: Massachusetts Soldiers and Society in the Seven Years' War* (1984). A sensitive exploration of the wartime experiences of Massachusetts provincial soldiers and their relations with the British army.

Bushman, Richard L. *The Refinement of America: Persons, Houses, Cities* (1992). A sophisticated exploration of the quest for gentility in early America.

Franklin, Benjamin. *Autobiography* (numerous editions). The classic account of Franklin's rise from poor beginnings to prominence in colonial Philadelphia.

Lambert, Frank. *"Pedlar in Divinity": George Whitefield and the Transatlantic Revivals, 1737–1770* (1994). An intriguing study of Whitefield's career as preacher and commercializer of religion in England and America.

McCusker, John J., and Menard, Russell R. *The Economy of British America, 1607–1789* rev. ed. (1991). The most comprehensive study of the economies of each colonial region.

Additional Sources

Colonial Economic Development

Harper, Lawrence A. *The English Navigation Acts: A Seventeenth-Century Experiment in Social Engineering* (1939).

Kammen, Michael. *Empire and Interest: The American Colonies and the Politics of Mercantilism* (1970).

Marshall, Peter, and Williams, Glyn, eds. *The British Atlantic Empire before the American Revolution* (1980).

Walton, Gary M., and Shepherd, James F. *The Economic Rise of Early America* (1979).

Waterhouse, Richard. *A New World Gentry: The Making of a Merchant and Planter Class in South Carolina, 1670–1770* (1989).

Religion, Society, and Culture in Early America

Bonomi, Patricia. *Under the Cope of Heaven: Religion, Society, and Politics in Colonial America* (1986).

Boyer, Paul, and Nissenbaum, Stephen. *Salem Possessed: The Social Origins of Witchcraft* (1974).

Brown, Richard D. *Knowledge Is Power: The Diffusion of Information in Early America, 1700–1865* (1991).

Bushman, Richard L. *From Puritan to Yankee: Character and the Social Order in Connecticut, 1690–1765* (1967).

Butler, Jon. *Awash in a Sea of Faith: Christianizing the American People* (1990).

Demos, John. *Entertaining Satan: Witchcraft and the Culture of Early New England* (1982).

Karlsen, Carol. *The Devil in the Shape of a Woman: Witchcraft in Colonial New England* (1987).

May, Henry. *The Enlightenment in America* (1976).

Westercamp, Marilyn. *Triumph of the Laity: Scots-Irish Piety and the Great Awakening, 1625–1760* (1988).

Wright, Esmond. *Franklin of Philadelphia* (1986).

Colonial and Imperial Politics

Bailyn, Bernard. *The Origins of American Politics* (1968).

Brewer, John. *The Sinews of Power: War, Money, and the English State, 1688–1783* (1989).

Bushman, Richard. *King and People in Provincial Massachusetts* (1985).

Greene, Jack P. *The Quest for Power: The Lower Houses of Assembly in the Southern Royal Colonies, 1689–1776* (1963).

Johnson, Richard. *Adjustment to Empire: The New England Colonies, 1675–1715* (1981).

Jones, J. R. *Country and Court: England, 1658–1714* (1978).

Lovejoy, David S. *The Glorious Revolution in America, 1660–1692* (1972).

Morgan, Edmund S. *Inventing the People: The Rise of Popular Sovereignty in England and America* (1988).

Nash, Gary B. *The Urban Crucible: The Northern Seaports and the Origins of the American Revolution*, abr. ed. (1986).

Plumb, J. H. *The Growth of Political Stability in England, 1675–1725* (1967).

Ritchie, Robert C. *The Duke's Province: A Study of New York Politics and Society, 1664–1691* (1977).

Speck, W. A. *Stability and Strife: England, 1714–1760* (1977).

The Expansion of Empires

Chipman, Donald E. *Spanish Texas, 1519–1821* (1992).

Mancall, Peter. *Valley of Opportunity: Economic Culture along the Upper Susquehanna, 1700–1800* (1991).

Usner, Daniel H., Jr. *Indians, Settlers, and Slaves in a Frontier Exchange Economy: The Lower Mississippi Valley before 1783* (1992).

Weber, David J. *The Spanish Frontier in North America* (1992).

Imperial Warfare

Dowd, Gregory. *A Spirited Resistance: The North American Indian Struggle for Unity, 1745–1815* (1992).

Jennings, Francis. *Empire of Fortune: Crowns, Colonies, and Tribes in the Seven Years' War in America* (1988).

Middleton, Richard. *The Bells of Victory: The Pitt-Newcastle Ministry and the Conduct of the Seven Years' War, 1757–1762* (1985).

Selesky, Harold. *War and Society in Colonial Connecticut* (1990).

Steele, Ian K. *Betrayals: Fort William Henry and the "Massacre"* (1990).

Titus, James. *The Old Dominion at War: Society, Politics, and Warfare in Late Colonial Virginia* (1991).

Where to Learn More

❖ **Mission Parkway, San Antonio, Texas.** Three Spanish missions (Mission Nuestra Señora de la Purisma Concepción, Mission San Francisco de la Espada, Mission San Juan Capestrano) founded in the early eighteenth century are located along this road. Their architecture indicates that they were intended to be fortifications as well as churches.

❖ **Ste. Genevieve Historic District, Ste. Genevieve, Missouri.** This restored site of an early-eighteenth-century French settlement in the *Pays des Illinois* contains many historic buildings open for tours.

❖ **Colonial Williamsburg, Williamsburg, Virginia.** A reconstruction of the capital of eighteenth-century Virginia, this site covers 173 acres and contains many restored and rebuilt structures, including houses, churches, the House of Burgesses, and the Governor's Palace. Many educational and cultural programs are available. Historical interpreters, dressed in period costume, provide information about eighteenth-century Chesapeake life.

❖ **Historical Society of Pennsylvania, Philadelphia, Pennsylvania.** The society preserves many documents and material objects relating to early American, and particularly Philadelphia, history. Its collections include exhibits of paintings, furniture, silver, and costumes.

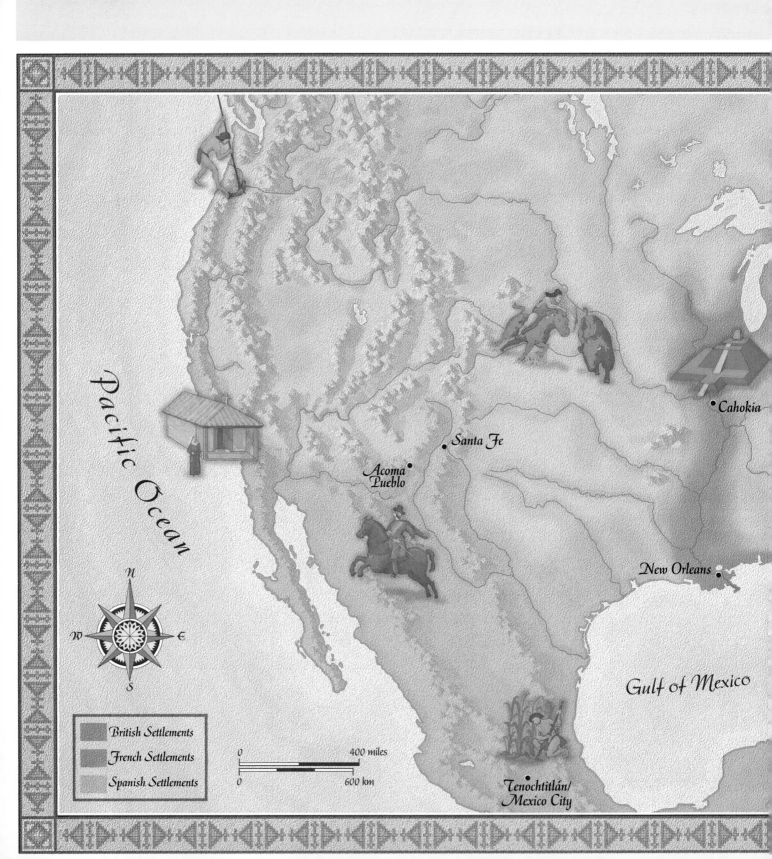

Pacific Ocean

Cahokia

Santa Fe

Acoma
Pueblo

New Orleans

Gulf of Mexico

Tenochtitlán/
Mexico City

British Settlements
French Settlements
Spanish Settlements

0   400 miles

0   600 km

KEY TOPICS

- ❖ British problems and policies in North America after the French and Indian War
- ❖ Native Americans' changing strategic position and their wars with the colonists
- ❖ The American reaction to British attempts to tax the colonies
- ❖ Social tensions and the Regulator movements in North and South Carolina
- ❖ Intercolonial union and resistance to British measures

Boston
Plymouth
New York
Philadelphia
Jamestown
Roanoke Island
Charleston

Atlantic Ocean

Caribbean Sea

*I*n 1774, Christopher Gadsden of South Carolina reportedly announced that "were his wife and all his children in Boston, and they were there to perish by the sword, it would not alter his sentiment or proceeding for American Liberty." He wanted to make an immediate attack on the British troops who then occupied Boston. Except for his impetuosity, Gadsden was a typical member of the American political elite that led the Revolution. Like his peers, he was proud and happy to be a subject of the British monarchy until the 1770s, but like other Americans, he would rebel against the crown. Why they felt compelled to take this drastic step is the subject of this chapter.

A zealot for American rights, Gadsden, the son of a British customs official, had been born in 1724 at Charleston, South Carolina. He had received his schooling in England and Pennsylvania, where he later served as a clerk for a Philadelphia merchant. Chance made him a supply officer aboard a royal naval vessel in the expedition that captured the French fortress of Louisbourg during King George's War (1739–1748). Gadsden then returned to South Carolina and became a merchant. Perhaps he resented the arrogance of people in England who treated colonials as backward provincials, and he doubtless believed that Great Britain subordinated American to British concerns when it returned Louisbourg to France at the end of the war. Many years later, at any rate, he became a leader of American opposition to British taxation.

Until the very eve of independence in 1776, Gadsden and others like him felt immense pride to be British subjects and part of Britain's increasingly powerful empire. They had fought the king's enemies as well as their own in a series of imperial wars and had gloried in British successes. But over the course of the eighteenth century, they had also developed a sense of their identity as Americans. Largely governing themselves through their own legislatures, they believed they enjoyed all the rights of British subjects anywhere.

In the wake of the French and Indian War, British authorities found themselves with a burdensome debt and a vastly increased territory to administer. In response, they attempted to change the way they governed the colonies and for the first time to impose direct taxes on the colonists. Most Americans saw these measures as violations of their rights and opposed them, although they divided over how far to carry their resistance.

Imperial Reorganization

At the close of the French and Indian War, British officials adopted a new and ultimately disastrous course in dealing with America. They tried to fix a relationship between England and the colonies that most Americans would have said was not broken. Why? Simply put, they lacked experience, they misunderstood the situation in America, and they panicked at the magnitude of the problems confronting them.

In 1760, George III succeeded his grandfather, George II, to England's throne. The new king was young and a bit naive. One observer of the king and his chief adviser expressed surprise that "they knew mankind" so little. Despite his inexperience, George III was determined to take an active role in governing his realm. Not surprisingly, he made mistakes. A succession of short-term prime ministers served him throughout the 1760s. The solutions they and the king proposed for the many problems the empire faced in the colonies had one common denominator: They worked mostly to the disadvantage of Americans. As one contemporary critic observed, "A great Empire and little minds go ill together."

British Problems

Britain's empire in 1763 was indeed a great one, and the problems its rulers faced were correspondingly large. Its territories in North America stretched from Hudson's Bay in the north to the Caribbean Sea in the south and from the Atlantic Ocean west to the Mississippi River. Britain also had possessions in the Mediterranean region, Africa, and India. It still faced threats, if diminished ones, from its traditional

European enemies. French territory on the North American mainland had been reduced to two tiny islands in the Gulf of St. Lawrence. But France would be eager for revenge, and French inhabitants in the recently acquired territories might prove disloyal to their new rulers in any future war between the two countries.

Spain was less powerful militarily than France but a more significant presence on the North American mainland. In the territorial settlement at the end of the French and Indian War, it surrendered East and West Florida to Britain but got back its possessions in Cuba and the Philippines that the British had captured. Spain acquired Louisiana from its French ally as compensation for the loss of the Floridas. Shocked by their inability to defend Cuba and the Philippines, Spanish officials stepped up the pace of reforms that they had begun making earlier in the century. Following the more efficient French model of colonial government, they began appointing *intendants* in the colonies. One of the chief responsibilities of these new officials—who were generally Spaniards rather than colonials—was to ensure better tax collection. The crown also expelled the Jesuit order from its dominions because Jesuit priests were too independent of royal control to suit Spanish officials. Spain also strengthened its military forces in much of the empire, including Mexico, which then encompassed Texas, New Mexico, and California, as well as present-day Mexico.

Spain began to establish settlements in California in 1769 (see Chapter 4), but these were too weak and too far from the British colonies on the eastern seaboard to worry authorities in London. British authorities were similarly little concerned about Louisiana, though it was closer and more populated. As for Florida, under British control after 1763, the Spanish authorities evacuated it completely, taking with them not only the free black population of Mose (a settlement of former slaves who had escaped from Georgia and South Carolina) but even the bones of one of the late royal governors.

Protecting and controlling the old and new territories in North America as inexpensively as possible presented British officials with difficult questions. How should they administer the new territories? How should they deal with Indians likely to resist further encroachments on their lands? And perhaps most vexing, how could they rein in the seemingly out-of-control colonists in the old territories?

Permitting most of the new areas to have their own assemblies appeared inadvisable but

Christopher Gadsden of South Carolina was one of the most outspoken advocates of American rights during the revolutionary era. This portrait by Jeremiah Theus was probably commissioned by the colonial legislature to commemorate his attendance at the Stamp Act Congress in 1765.

unavoidable if they were to attract settlers. In the opinion of British authorities, the increasing power of the legislatures had long since "unhinged" the government of the older colonies. They hoped to avoid similar unruliness in the new territories. Indeed, for quite some time they had wanted to roll back the power of the old colonial assemblies. Britain had needed the cooperation of the assemblies during the years of war with France. But now, with France vanquished, imperial officials felt they could crack down on the local governments. Some British statesmen, however, realized a danger in this new approach. With France gone from the continent, Americans would be less dependent on Britain for protection and therefore more inclined to resist unpopular restrictions.

CHRONOLOGY

1759–1761 Cherokee War.	**1766** Stamp Act repealed; Declaratory Act passed.
1760 George III becomes king.	New York Assembly refuses to comply with the Quartering Act.
1761–1762 Writs of Assistance case in Massachusetts.	**1767** Townshend duties imposed.
1763 Peace of Paris ends French and Indian War.	Regulator movements begin in North and South Carolina.
Spanish accelerate imperial reforms.	**1770** Boston Massacre.
British troops remain in America.	Tea duty retained, other Townshend duties repealed.
Proclamation Line of 1763 limits western expansion of colonial settlement.	**1771** North Carolina Regulator movement defeated.
Pontiac's Rebellion begins.	**1772** *Gaspee* burned.
Paxton Boys murder peaceful Indians.	Committees of Correspondence formed.
Virginia Court decides Parson's Cause.	**1773** Boston Tea Party.
1764 Sugar Act passed.	**1774** Coercive Acts passed.
Currency Act passed.	Quebec Act passed.
1765 Quartering Act passed.	First Continental Congress meets and agrees to boycott British imports.
Stamp Act passed.	
Stamp Act Congress meets in New York.	

Resentment against American conduct during the war colored British thinking. Some of the colonies failed to enlist their quota of recruits, and for this the British blamed the local assemblies. Worse yet, some Americans continued to smuggle goods to and from the enemy in the French West Indies during the war. British officials viewed this illicit trade as treasonous.

In any case, smuggling was so common in New England that it cost Britain more to operate the customs service in America than it collected in duties, a situation imperial officials now considered intolerable. England emerged from the war with what was then an immense national debt of approximately £130 million. Interest payments alone accounted for half the government's annual expenditures after the war, and the peacetime budget had doubled since the late 1740s. Alarmed by the unprecedented debt, many Britons concluded that Americans should bear more of the financial burden of running the empire. The colonists certainly appeared prosperous to British soldiers who had served in America. But compared to the English, who paid on average perhaps a third of their income in taxes, many Americans normally rendered no more than 5 percent. An economic recession—triggered by the reduction in spending that followed the war—

put further pressure on British officials to reduce taxes in England.

Dealing with the New Territories

In 1763, the British government took several important steps to deal with the new territories, protect the old colonies, and maintain peace with the Indians. One was to keep a substantial body of troops stationed in America even in peacetime. Another, accomplished in the **Proclamation of 1763**, was to establish civilian governments in East and West Florida (Canada remained under military rule). A third, in the same proclamation, was to temporarily forbid white settlement west of the Appalachian Mountains. The purpose of the **Proclamation Line** restricting white settlement was presumably twofold: to keep whites and Indians apart, preventing fighting between them, and to keep the colonists closer to the coast where they would be easier to control (see Map 5-1). Permanent arrangements for the Mississippi Valley could come later after British officials had time to ponder matters.

Neither the Proclamation Line nor the stationing of troops in America was particularly wise. The Proclamation Line provoked resentment because it threatened to deprive settlers and speculators in the rapidly developing colonies of the land they coveted.

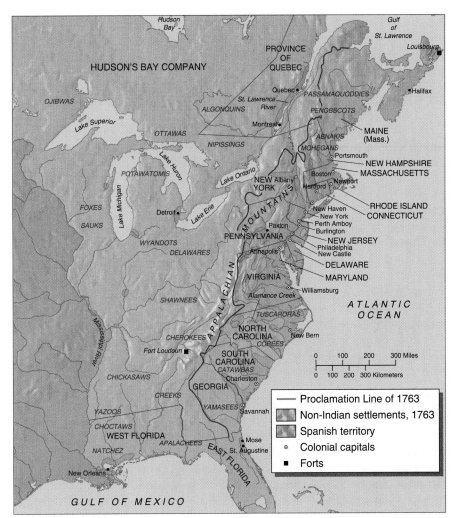

Map 5-1   Colonial Settlement and the Proclamation Line of 1763
This map depicts the regions claimed and settled by the major groups competing for territory in eastern North America. With the Proclamation Line of 1763, positioned along the crest of the Appalachian Mountains, the British government tried to stop the westward migration of settlers under its jurisdiction, and thereby limit conflict with the Indians. The result, however, was frustration and anger on the part of land-hungry settlers.

Some who had moved into the Ohio area were forcefully removed. Other Americans merely ignored the restriction. As for the troops, someone had to pay for them, forcing the British government to take additional measures that further provoked American resentment. These measures included the imposition of direct taxes and the passage of **Quartering Acts** that required colonial assemblies to provide barracks and certain supplies for the troops.

The presence of troops in peacetime alarmed Americans. Imbued with a traditionally English distrust of standing armies, they wondered whether the soldiers were there to coerce rather than protect them. Although the troops were not really meant to be threatening, their presence may have made imperial authorities less cautious in dealing with the colonies. Given their wariness, Americans would doubtless have objected to the troops and the taxes necessary to support them even if the troops had done an exemplary job of protecting the fron-

tiers. But conflicts with Indians cast doubt on their ability to do even that.

Indian Affairs

If Britain confronted complex problems in North America, Native Americans would have said those problems were nothing compared to their own troubles in dealing with the British. Colonial settlers and livestock were displacing Indians from their ancient lands. Free-flowing rum and rampant cheating among traders were making the fur and deerskin trades increasingly violent. Each of the colonies tried to regulate its Indian traders, but the lack of coordination made most of these efforts ineffective.

The British victory over the French and the westward expansion of British territory undermined the Indians' traditional strategies and alignments. British officials no longer found Native American neutrality or military help as important as they once had. Increasingly superfluous as allies and unable to play the European powers off against each other, Native Americans lost much of their former ability to protect themselves by any means short of military resistance. The British took advantage of this increasing vulnerability: Traders exploited the Indians, and settlers encroached on their lands.

Two major Indian wars—one breaking out in the late 1750s during the closing years of the French and Indian War and the other erupting in its aftermath in the early 1760s—challenged British policy toward Native Americans. The first conflict, the **Cherokee War**, took place in the southern Appalachian highlands. Though increasingly vexed by the abuses and encroachments of their white neighbors, the Cherokees had long remained allies of the British. But in 1759, Cherokee warriors returning home from a campaign with the British against the French and their Indian allies in western Pennsylvania may have confiscated horses belonging to Virginia colonists. The colonists attacked the Cherokees, killing some of them. The Cherokees retaliated with attacks on western settlements in all of the southern colonies. In 1760, they captured Fort Loudoun in eastern Tennessee, stuffing the commander's mouth full of dirt and telling him, "Dog, since you are so hungry for land, eat your fill." Three expeditions, manned by British as well as colonial troops, were sent against the Cherokees and eventually subdued them. In 1761, the Cherokees agreed in a treaty to surrender land in the Carolinas and Virginia to the colonists.

The second major conflict, **Pontiac's Rebellion**, broke out in 1763 among Indians in the Great Lakes and Ohio Valley regions formerly claimed by France. Many Native American groups feared that the British planned to exterminate them and take their lands now that the French could no longer help them. They were also resentful that British traders and officials, no longer forced to compete with the French to secure Indian allegiance, had become stingier in their commercial dealings. These concerns helped inspire a united effort to resist the British and revitalize Indian cultures. The spiritual catalyst for this movement was a Delaware leader named Neolin, also known as the Delaware Prophet, who began urging Native Americans to reject European goods and ways. The Pontiac Rebellion itself, named for an Ottawa chief who was one of its principal leaders, began when at least eight major groups joined in attacking British forces and American settlers from the Great Lakes to Virginia in 1763.

Pontiac's Rebellion raged until 1766. During intermittent negotiations, Pontiac cleverly insisted that British possession of the old French forts in western Pennsylvania and Ohio did not give Great Britain title to the area. The French, he maintained, had been there merely as tenants of the Indians, not owners of the land. The British eventually forced the Indians to give up portions of their territory in return for compensation and guarantees that traditional hunting grounds in the Ohio Valley would remain theirs.

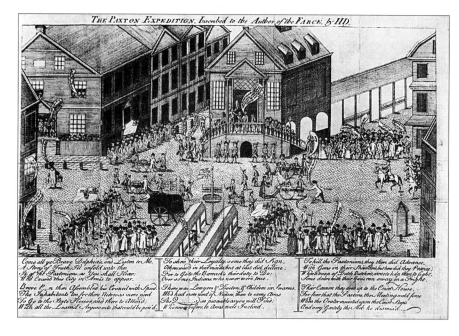

When frontiersmen from Paxton township marched on Philadelphia to demand greater protection against the Indians during Pontiac's Rebellion, Philadelphians prepared to defend themselves. This engraving by Henry Dawkins satirizes the consternation in the city and depicts the governor's representative announcing a peaceful settlement with the Paxton Boys.

At one point during the war, a British commander used germ warfare against the Indians, sending them blankets that smallpox victims had used. Settlers in Paxton township (near modern Harrisburg, Pennsylvania) were equally indiscriminate. Angered by the Pennsylvania Assembly's lack of aggressive action against the Indians, the settlers lashed out at convenient targets, massacring their peaceful neighbors, the Conestogas. Facing arrest and trial for this outrage, the so-called **Paxton Boys** marched toward Philadelphia, threatening the Pennsylvania Assembly. Benjamin Franklin convinced them to disperse. Despite the government's efforts, the Paxton Boys were never effectively prosecuted for their acts.

Pontiac's Rebellion was costly for both sides, claiming the lives of hundreds of Indians and whites. Hoping to prevent such outbreaks, British officials began experimenting with centralized control of Indian affairs during the 1760s. Following the recommendations of the Albany Congress in 1754 (see Chapter 4), they had already created two districts, northern and southern, for the administration of Indian affairs, each with its own superintendent. The Proclamation of 1763, and the line it established restricting further white settlement, gave these superintendents increased responsibility for protecting the Indians against the encroachments of settlers. But they faced daunting obstacles in their efforts to mediate between Indians and colonists. Land-hungry settlers objected to efforts to keep them off Indian lands, and white traders resented restrictions on their activities. Centralized control of the fur and deerskin trades also proved to be expensive for the British government. British authorities therefore permitted several adjustments in the Indian boundary line and in 1768 returned supervision of the Indian traders to the individual colonies. But such tacit recognition of local autonomy conflicted with imperial authorities' plans to restrict the powers of the colonial assemblies.

Curbing the Assemblies

As an episode in Virginia known as the **Parson's Cause** illustrates, British authorities took advantage of opportunities to curb the American legislatures as early as the 1750s. Anglican ministers in Virginia drew tax-supported salaries computed in pounds of tobacco. As a result, when a drought in the mid-1750s caused a sharp rise in tobacco prices, they expected a windfall. The Virginia House of Burgesses, however, restricted their payment to two pennies a pound, below the market value of the tobacco that backed their salaries. Lobbying by the clergy convinced the king to disallow the Two Penny Act, and some Virginia clergymen sued for the unpaid portion of their salaries.

In the most famous of these cases, the Virginia government was defended by Patrick Henry, a previously obscure young lawyer who looked like "a Presbyterian clergyman, used to haranguing the people." Henry gained instant notoriety when he declared that a king who vetoed beneficial acts became a tyrant and thereby forfeited "all right to his subjects' obedience." Given Henry's eloquence, the juries found in favor of the suing minister but awarded him only one penny in damages. This pittance reflected the hostility many Virginians of all denominations felt toward the pretensions of the Anglican clergy.

Meanwhile, still in response to the Two Penny Act, the crown further dismayed Virginians by instructing the colony's governor not to sign any new law that modified existing laws unless it contained a suspending clause making it inoperative until the king approved it. This restriction severely hampered the assembly's ability to respond to emergencies such as the drought. As one Virginian observed, it "put us under the despotic Power of a French or Turkish Government; for what is the real Difference between a French Edict and an English Instruction if they are both equally absolute?" The legislators of the colony, Virginians maintained, had the "Right to enact ANY Law they shall think necessary for their INTERNAL Government."

British authorities also sought to restrict the power of colonial legislatures to issue **legal tender** currency, paper notes that could be used to settle debts. These notes frequently depreciated to only a fraction of their face value in British money. Not surprisingly, British merchants who had to accept them felt cheated and complained. Parliament had responded in 1751 by forbidding further issues of legal tender paper money in New England. In the **Currency Act** of 1764, Parliament extended this restriction to the rest of the colonies, prohibiting all of them from printing their own legal tender paper money. Because the new restrictions came when most colonies were in an economic recession, Americans considered this step an especially burdensome attempt to curtail the assemblies' powers. To deprive them of their paper money was, in the words of one American, "downright Robbery." Worse, however, was yet to come.

The Sugar and Stamp Acts

In 1764, the British prime minister, George Grenville, convinced Parliament—it was not a difficult task—to pass the **American Revenue Act**, commonly known as the **Sugar Act**. The main purpose of this act, as stated in its preamble, was "for improving the revenue of

The last issue of the Pennsylvania Journal *on the day before the Stamp Act was to go into effect. Note the caricature of a stamp in the lower right corner. William Bradford, who printed this paper, was one of the organizers of the Sons of Liberty in Philadelphia.*

this kingdom." To generate funds, the Sugar Act and its accompanying legislation combined new and revised duties on colonial imports with strict provisions for collecting those duties. The act lowered the duty on molasses from the French West Indies from 6 pence a gallon to 3 pence a gallon. Smugglers had long evaded the earlier duty with bribes to customs officials. By lowering the duty and improving its collection, Grenville hoped to capture for the crown what customs officials had been siphoning off for themselves while not excessively increasing the shippers' cost of business.

The Sugar Act legislation also lengthened the list of enumerated products—goods that could be

sent only to England or within the empire—and required that ships carry elaborate new documents certifying the legality of their cargoes. The purpose of the new paperwork was to prevent illegal trade with other countries. A ship's captain, however, could have his entire cargo seized if any of the complicated documents were out of order.

To enforce these cumbersome regulations, the British government continued to use the Royal Navy to seize smugglers' ships, a practice begun during the French and Indian War. It also ordered colonial customs collectors to discharge their duties personally. Previously, the collectors had often lived in England, leaving the work of collection in the colonies to poorly paid deputies who were susceptible to bribes. Finally, Parliament gave responsibility for trying violations of the laws to a new vice-admiralty court in Halifax, Nova Scotia. Vice-admiralty courts had jurisdiction over maritime affairs. Unlike other courts, they normally operated without a jury and were therefore more likely to enforce trade restrictions. For this reason, and because of the remote location of the Halifax court—getting to it would be a hardship—Americans immediately opposed this provision of the Sugar Act. In response, Parliament created three more conveniently located vice-admiralty courts in Boston, Philadelphia, and Charleston, which was not exactly what the colonists had in mind.

In the spring of 1765, Parliament enacted another tax on Americans, the **Stamp Act**. This required that all valid legal documents, as well as newspapers, playing cards, and various other papers, bear a government-issued stamp for which there was a charge. The Sugar Act, though intended to raise revenue, appeared to fall within Britain's accepted authority to regulate commerce; the Stamp Act, by contrast, was the first internal tax (as opposed to an external trade duty) that Parliament had imposed on the colonies. Grenville, a lawyer, realized that it raised a constitutional issue: Did Parliament have the right to impose direct taxes on Americans when Americans had no elected representatives in Parliament? Following the principle of virtual representation—that members of Parliament served the interests of the nation as a whole, not just the locality from which they came—Grenville maintained that it did. Americans, he would find, vigorously disagreed. Nor were they without at least some support in Parliament. Colonel Isaac Barré, a member who had served in the colonies, spoke out against the Stamp Act. In one speech he referred to Americans as "Sons of Liberty," a label Americans soon would adopt for themselves.

American Reactions

The measures Britain took to solve its financial and administrative problems first puzzled, then shocked, and eventually outraged Americans. The colonists had emerged from the French and Indian War believing that they had done their fair share and more toward making Great Britain ruler of the greatest empire the world had yet seen. They expected to be rewarded for their efforts and treated with the respect that they assumed they deserved. They were certain that as British-Americans they shared in the glory and enjoyed all the rights of Englishmen in England. The new restrictions and taxes accordingly hit them like a slap in the face.

Constitutional Issues

To Americans, it was self-evident that the British measures were unfair. It was difficult to contend, however, that the British authorities had no right to impose them. The king and Parliament were considered the sovereign, or highest, authority in the empire. Then as now, the **British Constitution** was not a single written document. It consisted, rather, of the accumulated body of English law and custom, including acts of Parliament. How, then, could the colonists claim that an act of Parliament was unconstitutional?

Constitutional conflict surfaced early in Massachusetts over the issue of **writs of assistance**. These general search warrants, which gave customs officials in America the power to inspect virtually any building suspected of holding smuggled goods, had to be formally renewed at the accession of a new monarch. When George III became king in 1760, Massachusetts merchants—perhaps out of a fondness for smuggling as well as for liberty—sought to block the reissuance of the writs. Their attorney, James Otis Jr., arguing before the Massachusetts superior court, called the writs "instruments of slavery." Parliament, he maintained, lacked the authority to empower colonial courts to issue them. The court, however, did not believe that it could legally agree with him. Otis lost, but "then and there," a future president of the United States, John Adams, would later write, "the child independence was born."

Taxation and the Political Culture

The constitutional issue that most strained the bond between the colonies and the empire was taxation. British measures on other issues annoyed and disturbed Americans, and their cumulative effect helped alienate the colonists from England. But it was outrage over taxation—the most fundamental issue—that would be the midwife of American independence. Because Parliament had customarily refrained from taxing them, Americans assumed that it could not, and because their own assemblies had done it, they believed that those legislatures were in fact their parliaments.

Most Americans, including many who would later side with the British, believed that to deprive them of the right to be taxed only by their own elected representatives was to deny them one of the most basic rights of Englishmen. If taxes were imposed "without our having a legal Representation where they are laid," one American asked, "are we not reduced from the Character of free Subjects to the miserable State of tributary Slaves?"

British subjects everywhere believed that Parliament's exclusive authority to impose taxes on its constituents made Britain the freest country in the world. British officials, who believed in parliamentary sovereignty, counted the colonists among those constituents. Americans, who understood that their interests might conflict with those of England, thought otherwise. Given the selfishness of human nature, they believed that to have governing officials who could do unto them without doing the same to themselves was to risk disaster.

American views on taxation and the role of government reflected the influence of country ideology. As mentioned in Chapter 4, this opposition political philosophy emerged in England in the late seventeenth and early eighteenth centuries partly in response to the development of Britain's powerful standing army and navy. It viewed these forces, and the financial measures needed to support them, as threats to personal liberty. Country ideology proceeded from two basic assumptions: that human beings are selfish and that they need governments to protect them from one another. But country ideology also held that government power, no matter how necessary or to whom entrusted, is inherently aggressive and expansive. According to the English political philosopher John Locke, rulers have the authority to enforce law "only for the public good." When government exceeds this proper function, the people have the right to change it. Only in the last resort does this right justify revolution. The preferable alternative is a system with less disruptive ways of protecting the freedom of the people.

Country ideology stressed that in the English system of government, it was the duty of Parliament, in particular the House of Commons (which represented the people as a whole), to check the executive power of the crown. The House of Commons' control

John Locke (d. 1704), the great English political philosopher whose writings on government influenced American political thinking, as he appeared in a painting now in the National Portrait Gallery in London.

of taxation enabled it to curb tyrannical rulers. When the crown did its job properly, the Commons appropriated the necessary funds; when rulers infringed on the liberty of the people, the Commons restrained them by withholding taxes.

Such important responsibilities required that the people's representatives be men of sufficient property and judgment to make independent decisions. A representative should be "virtuous" (meaning public-spirited), and he should avoid political partisanship, because divisions within the House of Commons could undermine its ability to resist or curb the executive. A representative of the appropriate social status who exhibited the proper behavior deserved the deference of his constituents. They should assume, in other words, that he was more qualified to understand and manage public affairs than they were, and they should accordingly follow his lead. But if he did not measure up, the people should be able to vote him out.

Country ideology appealed to Americans for a number of reasons. In part, colonists were drawn to it as they were to other English fashions. The

works of Alexander Pope, the most widely read English poet of the eighteenth century and a proponent of a version of country ideology, appeared in many colonial libraries. So also did the works of two readable and prolific country ideology publicists, John Trenchard and Thomas Gordon, who collaborated in writing *Cato's Letters* (1720–1724) and the *Independent Whig* (1721). More important, country ideology's suspicion of those in power resonated with American concerns. It suited American politics on the local level, where rivalries and factionalism fostered distrust between those with and without power. And it emboldened the many Americans who feared they had no voice in the decisions of the government in London on matters of vital importance to them. Finally, with its insistence on the important political role of the propertied elite, country ideology appealed to America's local gentry. It suggested that it was their duty, as elected political officials, to safeguard the freedom of their constituents.

These ideas have had an enduring influence on American politics, surfacing even today in the suspicion of Washington and "big government." During the eighteenth century, they predisposed Americans to value local control and to expect the worst from remote governments. In so doing, they helped inspire the American Revolution. Many Americans were ready to attribute any new imperial regulations or taxes to a conspiracy of corrupt British officials to tyrannize them.

Protesting the Taxes

Given this ideological background, the initial American response to the Sugar Act was surprisingly mild. This was because the new taxes it imposed took the form of duties on trade and thus appeared consistent with the earlier Navigation Acts. The actual reaction varied from colony to colony in ways that reflected regional self-interest. The speaker of the legislature in one southern colony commented that it was "much divided" over the effects of the act and would probably not petition against it. In New England, in contrast, the Sugar Act threatened to cut into the profits of the lucrative smuggling trade with the French West Indies. As a result, people there and in other northern colonies were quicker to recognize the act's implications. The legislative body that imposed it—Parliament—and whose constituents in England stood to gain from it, was not accountable to the people on whom it was imposed, the colonists. It was unwise, the New Englanders realized, to allow people to tax you who might thereby lower their own taxes. Parliament would be tempted to shift the tax burden from constituents in England, who could vote, to those in America, who could not. As one alarmed colonist noted, if his fellow Americans submitted to any tax imposed by Parliament, they were dumb and docile donkeys; "*more Sacks, more Sacks,*" or burdens, were coming.

The size of the burden was less important than the principle involved. To Americans steeped in country ideology, direct taxation by London threatened to undercut the elected representatives' power of the purse and thereby remove the traditional first line of defense against a tyrannical executive. Thus all the assemblies eventually passed resolutions flatly maintaining that any parliamentary tax on America, including the Sugar Act, was unconstitutional. Colonists in New York, their assembly stated, "nobly disdain the thought" of claiming to be exempt from taxation by anyone but their own representatives "as a *Privilege.*—They . . . glory in it as their Right." By the end of 1764, New York merchants had joined the artisans and merchants of Boston in a **nonimportation** movement, an organized boycott of British manufactured goods. The goal was to cut into the profits of British employers, inducing them and the workers laid off as a result to bring pressure on the government to back down.

Unlike the Sugar Act, the Stamp Act had an equal impact throughout the colonies, and the response to it was swift and vociferous. Newspapers and pamphlets were filled with denunciations of the supposedly unconstitutional measure, and in taverns everywhere outraged patrons roundly condemned it. "The minds of the freeholders," wrote one observer, "were inflamed . . . by many a hearty damn of the Stamp Act over bottles, bowls and glasses." Parliament, Americans were convinced, did not represent them. Its members did not share their economic interests and would not pay the taxes that they imposed on Americans. Parliament therefore could not legitimately tax Americans.

The colonial legislatures were also quick to condemn the new measure. Virginia's lower house was the first to act, approving Patrick Henry's strong resolutions against the Stamp Act. These were then reprinted in newspapers throughout the colonies, and other legislatures passed similar formal objections.

Shared outrage at the Stamp Act inspired the colonies to join in unified political action. The **Sons of Liberty**, a collection of loosely organized protest groups, put pressure on stamp distributors and British authorities. In August 1765, a Boston crowd led by shoemaker Ebenezer MacIntosh demolished

Samuel Adams, the leader of the Boston radicals, as he appeared to John Singleton Copley in the early 1770s. In this famous picture, thought to be commissioned by another revolutionary leader, John Hancock, Adams points to legal documents guaranteeing American rights.

property belonging to a revenue agent, and another mob sacked Lieutenant Governor Thomas Hutchinson's house. The Sons of Liberty organized similar disturbances in other cities but kept most of them more peaceful with tighter discipline.

Members of the Sons of Liberty included people from all ranks of society. The leaders, however, among them Christopher Gadsden, came mostly from the middle and upper classes. Some of them doubtless joined in the hope of controlling a potential for violence in the movement that threatened their own interests. Indeed, in Charleston, slaves paraded through the streets crying, "Liberty!" much to the dismay of their masters and the rest of the city's white population.

Movement leaders were also concerned that disorderly behavior could discredit the American cause. Even the fiery Samuel Adams, one of the leading organizers of the protest in Boston, would later claim, "I am no friend to *Riots.*" Still, he added, "when the People are oppressed," they will be "discontented, and they are not to be blamed."

Partly as a result of the growing unrest, leaders throughout the colonies determined to meet and agree on a unified response to Britain. As Gadsden observed at the time, "There ought to be no New England men, no New Yorker, etc. known on the Continent, but all of us Americans." Nine colonies eventually sent delegates to the **Stamp Act Congress**, which met in New York City in October 1765. A humorist in the South Carolina legislature, who had opposed sending anyone, observed that the gathering would produce a most unpalatable combination: New England would throw in fish and onions; the middle provinces, flax-seed and flour; Virginia and Maryland, tobacco; North Carolina, pitch, turpentine, and tar; South Carolina, indigo and rice—and Georgia would sprinkle the whole with sawdust. "Such an absurd jumble will you make if you attempt to form [a] union among such discordant materials as the thirteen British provinces," he concluded. A quick-witted member of the assembly shot back that he would not choose his colleague for a cook but that the congress would prepare a dish fit for any king.

It did indeed. The congress adopted the **Declaration of Rights and Grievances**, which denied Parliament's right to tax the colonies, and petitioned both king and Parliament to repeal the Stamp and Sugar acts. Parliament, unwilling to acknowledge this challenge to its authority, refused to receive the colonial petitions.

As protests spread, the stamp distributors got the message and resigned, "for the welfare of the people." In some areas, Americans went about their business as usual without using stamped paper. In other places, they avoided activities that required taxed items. They also stepped up the boycott of British goods that had begun in response to the Sugar Act. British merchants, hurt by this economic pressure, petitioned Parliament for repeal of the Stamp Act, and a new ministry obliged them by rescinding it in March 1766. Modifications in the provisions of the Sugar Act came later in the year.

The Aftermath of Crisis

During the Stamp Act crisis, Benjamin Franklin appeared before Parliament to present American objections to the Stamp and Sugar acts. Some members apparently concluded from his remarks that the colonists would accept port duties but would oppose direct taxes. They were wrong. At this point, Americans were in no mood to accept any tax imposed by Parliament.

Americans in turn misunderstood the **Declaratory Act** that accompanied the repeal of the Stamp Act and was intended to make Parliament's retreat more acceptable to its members. This act stated that Parliament had the right to "legislate for the colonies in all cases whatsoever." Did legislate mean tax? Not necessarily, for taxes were traditionally deemed to be a voluntary gift to the king from the people acting through their own representatives. (This is why money bills, as distinct from other acts, had to originate in the House of Commons.) Americans therefore tended to consider the Declaratory Act a mere face-saving gesture. Unfortunately, it was more than that. As one colonist later observed, it created a "platform for the Invincible Reasoning from the Mouths of four and twenty pounders [cannons]."

A Strained Relationship

Most members of Parliament continued to believe that they represented everyone in the empire and that they could therefore tax people in the colonies as well as in England. Americans believed just as strongly that "in taxing ourselves and making Laws for our own internal government . . . we can by no means allow our Provincial legislatures to be subordinate to any legislative power on earth."

Relations were never quite the same between England and America after the Stamp Act crisis. Each side became ever more suspicious of the other. Americans were convinced that they had forced British authorities to back down and that if need be, they could do it again. Or so they told themselves every March 18, the anniversary of the repeal of the Stamp Act. This date became an occasion for celebration, giving Americans a national holiday before they had a nation.

An exchange between British merchants and their American correspondents in the wake of the Stamp Act's repeal illustrates how far apart Englishmen and Americans had become. The British merchants lectured the Americans, enjoining them "to express filial duty and gratitude to your parent country." To which one Virginia planter tartly replied, "We rarely see anything from your side of the water free from the authoritative style of a master to a schoolboy." This, he observed, was more than "a little ridiculous."

Events likewise testified to enduring tensions between the two sides. When British authorities required Massachusetts to compensate those who had suffered damage in the Stamp Act rioting, the legislature complied but pardoned the rioters. In 1767, an irritated Parliament then passed an act sus-

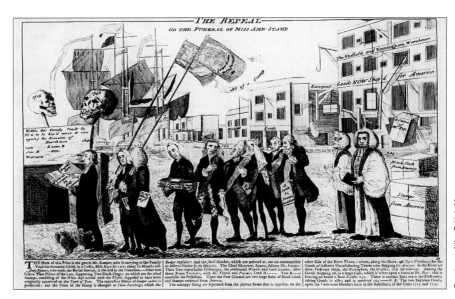

A satirical British engraving from 1766 showing English politicians burying the Stamp Act, "born 1765 died 1766." The warehouses in the background symbolize the revival of trade with America.

pending the New York legislature because it had not complied with the Quartering Act of 1765. This law required colonial assemblies to provide facilities and certain supplies for royal troops. New York finally complied with the act before the suspending act went into effect, and its legislature was not closed. Such incidents boded ill for the hopes of some colonists that a British government that had repealed the Stamp Act would prove cooperative in other ways.

Regulator Movements

In 1766, a committee of the South Carolina legislature appointed to consider "the State of the Province" recommended that it establish courts in the rapidly growing backcountry and petition Parliament for repeal of the Currency Act. These suggestions were prompted by mounting unrest in the southern backcountry. Vigilante groups calling themselves **Regulators** had emerged in North Carolina in response to official corruption and in South Carolina in response to lawlessness. High taxes and high court costs in North Carolina oppressed the colony's western farmers. The Currency Act, because it reduced the amount of money in circulation, compounded their problems, leaving them "crouched beneath their sufferings" and unable to pay their debts and taxes. In South Carolina, the devastation and disruptions of the Cherokee War left a legacy of violence. Outlaws roamed the backcountry stealing livestock and raiding isolated houses. In both colonies, representation in the assemblies did not reflect the growing backcountry population. Western residents thus lacked sufficient influence to make the legislatures responsive to their needs. As a result, the Reg-

ulators did by extralegal action what they couldn't do through legal channels. In North Carolina, they closed courts and intimidated tax officials. In South Carolina, they pursued outlaws and whipped people suspected of harboring them.

The activities of the Regulators brought them into conflict with the local elites and the assemblies in both North and South Carolina. In neither colony did the government move quickly to redress Regulator grievances. British officials, however, only made matters worse. Instead of encouraging the assemblies to increase western representation, the crown did exactly the opposite. As part of its effort to limit the power of colonial legislatures, it forbade them from increasing their size. Americans termed this instruction "perhaps [as] *peculiar* as any that have been given on the continent." As for the shortage of currency, Lord Hillsborough, the secretary of state for the colonies, callously informed North Carolinians that "no Consideration of a possible local inconvenience" would prompt Britain to modify the "sound Principles" of the Currency Act. And instead of approving legislation in South Carolina that would have established courts in the backcountry, British officials disallowed it because it specified that judges would hold their positions contingent on good behavior rather than at the pleasure of the crown.

Thanks to such help from London as well as to their own mistakes, local authorities faced an increasingly serious situation by 1767. In South Carolina, the assembly belatedly reapportioned itself, giving the backcountry some representation, and permitted the crown to dictate the terms of judicial appointments. These and other concessions to western residents narrowly averted bloodshed. But in North Carolina, fighting broke out in 1771. Governor William Tryon lead the local militia against the Regulators who had gathered near Alamance Creek. He ordered the Regulators to disperse or his men would fire. "Fire and be damned," someone replied, and gunfire erupted, killing 29 men and wounding more than 150 on both sides. During the next several weeks, seven Regulators were hanged and six thousand pardoned.

The confrontation in North Carolina was the most serious of its kind, but similar social tensions were apparent in other colonies. To deal with them, colonial leaders had to understand local conditions and be able to act on their knowledge. But at a time when they needed all the wisdom and flexibility at their command, British attempts to reform colonial governments threatened to hamstring them. Worse yet, London was once again trying to tax Americans.

The Townshend Crisis

British authorities had not given up the idea of taxing the colonies with the repeal of the Stamp Act in 1766. They had merely backed off temporarily. Little over a year later, Parliament passed a new collection of taxes, the Townshend duties. Another crisis ensued, lasting until an American boycott of British goods forced repeal of most of the new duties. The relatively quiet period that followed ended when Britain made a serious attempt to enforce compliance with the one duty still on the books, the duty on tea.

Townshend's Plan

Charles Townshend became the leading figure in Britain's government in 1767. A former member of the Board of Trade, he felt himself knowledgeable about the colonies. He was also sensitive to the political winds in Parliament, where many members still wanted to tax Americans. The legislation that bears his name, the **Townshend Duty Act**, was intended to help defer the cost of government in America. It imposed new duties, or external taxes, which Townshend thought the colonists were willing to accept, but no direct, or internal, taxes like the Stamp Tax. The duties covered a number of items the colonists regularly imported—tea, paper, paint, lead, and glass. To make sure that the duties were collected, British authorities added a new board of

customs commissioners for America and located its headquarters in Boston, the presumed home of many smugglers.

Coming on top of the threatened suspension of the New York legislature, the Townshend Duty Act seemed to portend greater British interference in colonial affairs. To the alarm of the Americans, the new customs officials were far more diligent than their predecessors. One of them, taking advantage of technicalities in the law, entrapped Henry Laurens, a prominent merchant in South Carolina. Other officials went after the wealthy Boston merchant John Hancock, perhaps because he was so openly contemptuous of them. The officials seized Hancock's appropriately named vessel *Liberty* and accused him of smuggling. Hancock may indeed have violated the acts of trade at times, but in this case the accusations were apparently false. The incident sparked a riot in Boston during which a crowd on the waterfront roughed up members of the customs service. British authorities responded in 1768 by sending troops to Boston. The soldiers would remain there amid mounting hostility for the next year and a half.

American Boycott

The Townshend duties, like the stamp tax, provoked resistance throughout the colonies. Rejecting the argument that duties were somehow different from taxes, John Dickinson, a wealthy lawyer who wrote under the pen name "A Farmer in Pennsylvania," reminded everyone that a tax was a tax, whatever its form. The purpose of the taxes—to help pay the costs of government in the colonies, including the salaries of governors and judges—also seemed pernicious. Americans believed it was the role of their own assemblies to raise revenues for these costs. By bypassing the assemblies, the Townshend Act threatened to undermine their authority.

There was no equivalent to the Stamp Act Congress in response to the Townshend Act because British officials (acting through the colonial governors) barred the assemblies from sending delegates to such a meeting. Even so, Americans gradually organized an effective nonimportation movement. When, for example, the governor of Virginia dissolved the House of Burgesses for resolves opposing British measures, the members met on their own in the Raleigh Tavern at Williamsburg and adopted a nonimportation agreement. Once again, vigilant laborers and artisans threatened violators of the general boycott with physical violence, but few disturbances occurred. Many Americans signed subscription lists binding them, with the other signers, to buy only goods made in the colonies and nothing made in Great Britain. Handbills, like one urging "the Sons and Daughters of *LIBERTY*" to shun a particular Boston merchant, brought pressure to bear on uncooperative importers. To avoid imported English textiles, American women spun more thread and wove more cloth at home. Wearing homespun became a moral virtue, a sign of self-reliance, personal independence, and the rejection of "corrupting" English luxuries (see "American Views: Social Status and the Enforcement of the Nonimportation Movement").

The nonimportation movement forged a sense of common purpose among all who participated in it—men and women, southern planters and northern artisans alike—giving them the sense of belonging to a larger community of fellow Americans. Although it was at this point more an imagined community than a political community, it was real enough and large enough to reduce imports from Britain by 40 percent after only one year.

Because Britain had increased its exports to Europe since the Stamp Act crisis, it took longer than before for the nonimportation movement to have an effect on its economy (see Figure 5-1). Still, the troubles in America contributed to the king's decision to appoint a new prime minister, Lord North. Thinking—and even looking—remarkably alike, George III and North complemented each other. Whereas North had a propensity to panic in crises, the king could be steadfast—indeed, some would say, stubborn. At the king's insistence, North would remain prime minister until 1782. In 1770, he was prepared to concede that the Townshend duties had been counterproductive because they interfered with British trade. But when Parliament repealed most of them, it left the duty on tea. This symbolic equivalent of the Declaratory Act served to assert Parliament's continuing right to tax the colonies.

The Boston Massacre

Ironically, on the same day that North proposed that Parliament rescind most of the Townshend duties— March 5, 1770—British troops fired on American civilians in Boston. This incident, which came to be known as the **Boston Massacre**, resulted from months of increasing friction between townspeople and the British troops stationed in the city. The townspeople complained that the soldiers insulted them, leered

Mr. and Mrs. Thomas Mifflin of Philadelphia. A prominent merchant and radical opponent of British policy toward the colonies, Mifflin and his wife were visiting Boston in 1773, when John Singleton Copley painted them. Working at a small loom, Sarah Morris Mifflin weaves a decorative fringe. She no doubt did the same during the nonimportation movement against the Townshend duties, thereby helping to make importation of such goods from England unnecessary.

John Singleton Copley, *Mr. and Mrs. Mifflin*. Courtesy of The Historical Society of Pennsylvania.

at women, and competed for scarce jobs. Samuel Adams recounted these real and imagined misdeeds in a column called "A Journal of the Times" that he circulated to other American cities. The hostility was so great, complained a British officer, that "twenty" soldiers could be "knocked down in the Streets" and nothing be heard of it, but if a Bostonian "meets with no more than just a Kick for an Insult to a Soldier, the Town is immediately in an Alarm."

The Boston Massacre occurred when angry and frightened British soldiers fired on a crowd that was pelting them with sticks and stones. Five men died, including Crispus Attucks—"that half Indian, half negro and altogether rowdy," as someone once called him—who has since become the most celebrated casualty of the incident. To preserve order, the troops withdrew from the city. But the damage had been done.

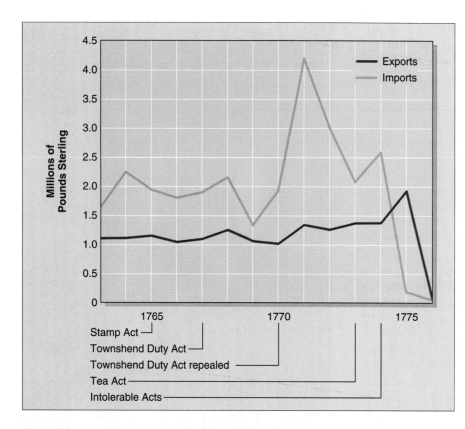

Figure 5-1 Value of American Exports to and Imports from England, 1763–1776
This figure depicts the value of American exports to and imports from England. The decrease of imports in 1765–1766 and the even sharper drop in 1769 illustrate the effect of American boycotts in response to the Stamp Act and Townshend duties.

Source: *U.S. Bureau of the Census, Historical Statistics of the United States, Colonial Times to 1970, Bicentennial Edition, Part 1 (1975).*

The "Quiet Period"

Chastened a bit, both British authorities and American patriots pulled back from the brink. The troops remained on an island in Boston harbor, not in the city itself. With the repeal of the Townshend duties, the nonimportation movement faded. Some organizers tried to keep it going until Britain repealed the remaining duty on tea, but most Americans began using imported goods again.

In the so-called **Quiet Period** that followed, no general grievance united all Americans. But in almost every colony, issues continued to simmer. In Massachusetts and South Carolina, for example, the royal governors temporarily moved the meeting places of the legislatures to small towns miles away from the capital, "for the sole Purpose," as the Declaration of Independence would later charge, "of fatiguing them into compliance" with British measures.

Local circumstances produced a more spectacular confrontation in Rhode Island. The crew of a British revenue schooner, the *Gaspee*, had been patrolling Narragansett Bay, seizing smugglers and, it was said, stealing livestock and cutting down farmers' fruit trees for firewood. Local residents understandably considered such behavior "piratical." Thus when the *Gaspee* ran aground while chasing some

American ships, Rhode Islanders got even. Led by John Brown, a local merchant, they boarded the vessel, shot its captain in the buttocks, putting him and his crew ashore, and burned the ship. The British government appointed a commission of inquiry with instructions to arrest the culprits and send them to England for trial. Despite its offer of a reward for information about the incident, the commission learned nothing. The British attempt to stamp out smuggling in the colonies was so heavy-handed that it offended the innocent more than it frightened the guilty.

Such incidents, and in particular the British threat to send Americans to England for trial, led American leaders to resolve to keep one another informed about British actions. Twelve colonies established **committees of correspondence** for this purpose. Leaders in Boston established similar committees in Massachusetts. There would soon be plenty for these organizations to do, for Boston was about to become the scene of a showdown between imperial authority and colonial resistance.

The Boston Tea Party

During the Quiet Period, Americans drank smuggled (and therefore untaxed) Dutch tea. The British East India Company, which had the exclu-

The Boston Massacre, March 5, 1770, in an engraving by Paul Revere. Copied from an earlier print, Revere's widely circulated version shows—somewhat inaccurately—well organized soldiers firing on helpless civilians; the names of the dead, including Crispus Attucks, appear below.

sive right to distribute tea in the British Empire, suffered as a result. Partly for this reason, and partly because of unexpectedly high expenses in India, the company stood on the verge of bankruptcy. With the **Tea Act of 1773**, Lord North came to the company's aid. The act permitted the company to ship tea from its warehouses in Britain without paying the duty normally collected there. The idea was to make its tea more competitive in price with the Dutch product and thereby to induce Americans to buy it and at the same time to pay the old Townshend duty. The company selected a few merchants to act as its exclusive agents in the colonies. These merchants stood to reap substantial profits from their position.

When the colonists heard of this plan, they responded with an anger that surprised British officials. For some, the anger may have been motivated by jealousy at being excluded from the tea trade. What outraged most Americans, however, was the attempt to seduce them into paying the tax on tea. Thousands decided not to touch the tea. Newspapers discussed its dangers to the body as well as to the body politic and offered recipes for substitutes. "To

their great honor," according to the newspapers, many women rejected the tea and put pressure on others to do likewise, while schoolboys collected and burned tea leaves.

Thomas Hutchinson, who had been lieutenant governor of Massachusetts during the Stamp Act riots, was now the colony's royal governor. Two of his sons were among those chosen to be the East India Company's agents. In most other cities, threats from the Sons of Liberty had convinced the captains of the tea ships to return to England without landing their cargo. Hutchinson, however, was determined to have the tea landed in Boston, and he barred the tea ships there from leaving. As a result, violence once again erupted in the city.

When the Sons of Liberty realized they could not force the ships to leave, they decided on dramatic action. On December 16, 1773, Samuel Adams reportedly told a large gathering at Old South Meeting House that it "could do nothing more to preserve the liberties of America." This remark was apparently a prearranged signal for what came to be known as the **Boston Tea Party**. War whoops immediately answered him from the street outside, and a well-organized band of men disguised as Indians raced aboard the tea ship *Dartmouth*, broke open 342 chests of tea, and systematically heaved the contents in the harbor. In a similar action in 1774, residents of Annapolis, Maryland, forced some merchants to burn their own ship when it arrived with duties tea.

The Intolerable Acts

The destruction of property in the Boston Tea Party shocked many Americans. British officials reacted even more strongly. Their mounting irritation at colonial complaints, the nonimportation movement, and popular demonstrations culminated in rage at this latest defiance of British authority. Bostonians, they believed, were troublemakers whose lawless destruction of the tea was only their most recent outrage.

The response in Parliament was to pass a series of repressive measures known as the **Coercive Acts**. The first of these, effective June 1, 1774, was the **Boston Port Act**, which closed the port of Boston to all incoming and outgoing traffic until the East India Company and the crown received payment for the dumped tea and its duties. The **Administration of Justice Act**, which followed, declared that an official who killed a colonist while performing his duties could be tried in England

American Views

SOCIAL STATUS AND THE ENFORCEMENT OF THE NONIMPORTATION MOVEMENT

Many Americans enthusiastically supported the nonimportation movement called in response to the Townshend Duty Act crisis of the late 1760s. A few, however, openly opposed it. Among these was William Henry Drayton of South Carolina, who objected to the composition of the committee that had been chosen to enforce the nonimportation agreement in his region. The committee included artisans and shopkeepers, men whom Drayton claimed should have no role in public affairs. Their education prepared them only "to cut up a beast in the market to the best advantage, to cobble an old shoe in the neatest manner, or to build a necessary house [outhouse]," not to make public policy. As the following document makes clear, they emphatically disagreed with him. Drayton was later to reverse himself and actively support the Continental Association's ban on importing British goods in 1775. "The people" wanted it, he would later explain, and "it was our duty, to satisfy our constituents; as we were only servants of the public [at large]."

❖ **Who makes policy in the United States today?**

❖ **What qualifications do you think they should have?**

❖ **How do your answers to these questions differ from Drayton's? From the "Mechanics"?**

❖ **How would you explain Drayton's later switch?**

The Mechanics of the General Committee to William Henry Drayton

The gracious Giver of all good things, has been pleased to bestow a certain principle on mankind, which properly may be called *common sense:* But, though every man hath a natural right to a determined portion of this ineffable ray of the Divinity, yet, to the misfortune of society, many persons fall short of this most necessary gift of God; the want of which cannot be compensated by all the learning of the schools.

The *Mechanicks* pretend to nothing more, than having a claim from nature, to their share in this inestimable favour, in common with *Emperors and Kings,* and, were it safe to carry the compari-

son still higher, they would say with William-Henry Drayton himself; who, in his great condescention, has been pleased to allow us a place amongst human beings: But whether it might have happened from an ill construction of his sensory, or his upper works being damaged by some rough treatment of the person who conducted his birth, we know not; however so it is, that, to us, he seems highly defective in this point, whatever exalted notions he may entertain of his own abilities.

By attending to the dictates of *common sense,* the *Mechanicks* have been able to distinguish between RIGHT and WRONG; in doing which indeed no great merit is claimed, because every man's own feelings will direct him thereto, unless

(where he would almost certainly receive sympathetic treatment) rather than in Massachusetts. The third measure, the **Massachusetts Government Act**, drastically modified that colony's charter of 1691. Under the old document, the legislature had elected members to the governor's council; henceforth, the crown would appoint them. And appointed, rather than elected, sheriffs would now name juries. In addition, the Massachusetts Government Act limited the number of town meetings

he obstinately, or from a pertinacious opinion of his own superior knowledge, shuts his eyes, and stoickally submits to all the illegal encroachments that may be made on his property, by an ill-designing and badly-informed ministry.

Mr. Drayton may value himself as much as he pleases, on his having had a liberal education bestowed on him, tho' the good fruits thereof have not hitherto been conspicuous either in his public or private life: He ought however to know, that this is not so absolutely necessary to these, who move in the low sphere of *mechanical* employments. But still, though he pretends to view them with so contemptuous and oblique an eye, these men hope, that they are in some degree useful to society, without presuming to make any comparisons between themselves and him, except with regard to *love for their country;* for he has amply shewn, that an attachment of this sort is not *one* of his *ruling* passions. Nor does he appear in the least to have regarded the peace and good order of that community of which he is a member; otherwise he would not wilfully, and without any cause, have knocked his head against ninety-nine out of every hundred of the people, not only in this province, but *of all North-America,* not one of whom bore him any malice, nor yet do, though they may entertain what opinions they please, with respect to his want of patriotism, from his having proved a Felo de se [murderer of himself] in this point.

After an avowal of principles, incompatible with the essential rights of freemen under the English constitution, surely, no parish in this province, will ever think it prudent, to trust their interests in such hands, for the time to come? Besides, who can say he ever shewed any capacity for business, when he was honoured with a seat in the House of Assembly? . . .

Mr. Drayton may be assured, that so far from being ashamed of our trades, we are in the highest degree thankful to our friends, who put us in the way of being instructed in them; and that we bless God for giving us strength and *judgment* to pursue them, in order to maintain our families, with a decency suitable to their stations in life. Every man is not so lucky as to have a fortune ready provided to his hand, either by his own or his wife's parents, as has been his lot; nor ought it to be so with all men; and Providence accordingly hath wisely ordained otherwise, by appointing the greatest part of mankind, to provide for their support by manual labour; and we will be bold to say, that such are the most useful people in a community. . . .

We are, Yours, &c.
MECHANICKS of the COMMITTEE.
October 3d, 1769.

Source: *South Carolina Gazette, October 5, 1769; reprinted in* The Letters of Freeman, etc.: Essays on the Nonimportation Movement in South Carolina Collected by William Henry Drayton, *ed. Robert M. Weir (1977), pp. 111–114.*

that could be held without the governor's prior approval. In another measure, the British government made its commander in chief in America, General Thomas Gage, the governor of Massachusetts and in the Quartering Act of 1774 declared that the troops under his command could be lodged in virtually any uninhabited building.

On the same day that Parliament enacted these measures, it also passed the **Quebec Act.** This statute enlarged the boundaries of Quebec south to

The Boston Tea Party, December 16, 1773. To prevent payment of the tax on tea shipped to America by the British East India Company in 1773, the Sons of Liberty disguised themselves as Indians and threw the tea overboard.

the Ohio River and stipulated that it be governed by an appointed governor and council but no elected assembly (see Map 5-2). The act also provided for the trial of civil cases without a jury, recognized the Catholic Church, and continued the privileges the church had enjoyed under the French. The colonists linked the Quebec Act with the Coercive Acts and labeled them the **Intolerable Acts**. Some historians now believe that although it was not their intention, the willingness of British authorities to accommodate French traditions may have kept some of Quebec's inhabitants loyal to the crown during the American Revolution.

The Road to Revolution

Americans throughout the colonies considered the Intolerable Acts so threatening that they organized another gathering, the **First Continental Congress**, to respond to them. Congress renewed the nonimportation movement and took measures to enforce it strictly. These measures widened the gap between those who supported British authorities and those who opposed them.

American Response to the Intolerable Acts

Americans found the territorial, administrative, and religious provisions of the Quebec Act deeply disturbing. As one royal governor observed, "The securing of lands for the rising Generation is a matter of great importance to a poor and provident Man with a large family." The Quebec Act, however,

Map 5-2 The Quebec Act of 1774
The Quebec Act enlarged the boundaries of the Canadian province southward to the Ohio River and westward to the Mississippi, thereby depriving several colonies of claims to the area granted to them by their original charters.

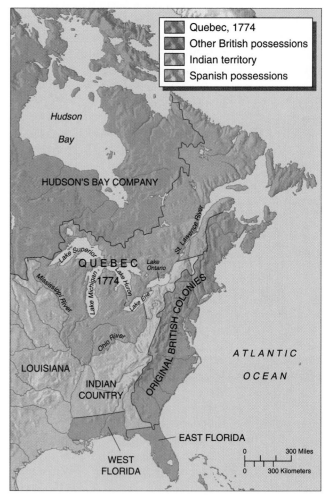

gave Canada jurisdiction over lands in the area north of the Ohio River claimed by Connecticut, Pennsylvania, and Virginia. This deprived settlers of their hoped-for homesteads and land speculators of their hoped-for profits, angering both. As for the administrative provisions of the act—appointed government, no assemblies, no jury for civil cases—Americans feared they signaled what Britain had in store for them.

Americans had similar fears about the religious provisions of the Quebec Act. During the 1760s, some Anglican clergymen had sought to have a bishop appointed for America. Most Americans, including Anglicans, opposed this proposal, however. They were convinced that the creation of such an office would strengthen the Anglican Church at the expense of other denominations, weaken local control of religious affairs, and require the payment of additional taxes. Many Americans believed that British authorities had scrapped the idea. The Quebec Act's concessions to Canadian Catholics, however, seemed to resurrect it in more ominous form. As one Virginian had observed, the hierarchical organization of the Anglican Church was "a Relick of the Papal Incroachments" on English law. The Quebec Act accordingly "gave a General Alarm to all Protestants," whose ministers throughout the continent warned their congregations that they might be "bound by Popish chains."

American reaction to the religious provisions of the Quebec Act may have been exaggerated, but some features of the Coercive Acts were cause for real concern. The Boston Port Act arbitrarily punished innocent and guilty Bostonians alike. The Administration of Justice Act—which some with vivid imaginations dubbed the "Murder Act"—seemed to declare an open season on colonists, allowing crown officials to kill them without fear of punishment. The Massachusetts Government Act raised the more realistic fear that no colonial charter was safe. A Parliament that had stripped the Massachusetts legislature of an important power might equally decide to abolish the lower houses of all the colonies.

Nightmarish scenarios filled the colonial newspapers. One clergyman observed that the terms of the Coercive Acts were such that if someone were to "make water" on the door of the royal customs house, an entire colonial city "might be laid in Ashes." He undoubtedly knew that he exaggerated, but his words embodied real fear and anger, and many other Americans shared his feel-

ings. Trying to make an example of Boston, British authorities had taken steps that united Americans as nothing had ever done before (see the summary table "New Restraints and Burdens on Americans, 1759–1774").

The First Continental Congress

Massachusetts wanted to respond to the Intolerable Acts with an immediate renewal of the nonimportation movement. Leaders in other colonies wanted to organize a more coordinated response and called for another meeting like the Stamp Act Congress. The colonies accordingly agreed to send delegates to a meeting in Philadelphia that came to be called the First Continental Congress. Royal governors attempted to prevent the meeting by barring the legislatures from naming delegates, so the colonies called extralegal public meetings for the purpose. In the end, all the colonies except Georgia were represented.

The First Continental Congress met at Carpenter's Hall in Philadelphia from September 5 to October 26, 1774, with fifty-five delegates present at one time or another. All were leading figures in their home colonies, but only a few knew members from elsewhere. Each colony had one vote, irrespective of the size of its delegation. Some of the more conservative participants favored a compromise with Britain. The speaker of the Pennsylvania Assembly, Joseph Galloway, introduced a measure reminiscent of the Albany Plan of Union. It called for creation of an American "grand council" that would have veto power over parliamentary legislation dealing with America. His plan failed in the Congress by one vote. Instead, those who favored stronger measures—like Samuel Adams and his cousin John, Patrick Henry, and Christopher Gadsden—prevailed. They persuaded most of their colleagues to endorse the **Suffolk Resolves**, which had been passed at a meeting held in Suffolk County (the site of Boston). These resolves denounced the Coercive Acts as unconstitutional, advised the people to arm, and called for general economic sanctions against Britain. The wording was so forceful that one British official told an American, "If these Resolves of your people are to be depended on, they have declared War against us; they will not suffer any sort of Treaty."

The Continental Association

Congress created the **Continental Association** to organize and enforce sanctions against the British. As a first step, the Association pledged Americans

SUMMARY

NEW RESTRAINTS AND BURDENS ON AMERICANS, 1759–1774

	Restraints on Legislative Action	Restraints on Territorial Expansion	Restraints on Colonial Trade	Imposition of New Taxes
1759	Royal instructions restrict the ability of the Virginia assembly to pass timely legislation.			
1762			Writs of assistance issued.	
1763		Proclamation Line keeps white settlement east of the Appalachians.	Peacetime use of the navy and new customs officials to enforce Navigation Acts.	
1764	Currency Act limits the colonial legislatures' ability to issue paper money.		Vice-admiralty courts strengthened for Sugar Act.	Sugar Act imposes taxes for revenue (modified 1766).
1765				Quartering Act requires assemblies to provide facilities for royal troops. Stamp Act imposes internal taxes on legal documents, newspapers, and other items, 1765 (repealed 1766).
1767	Royal instructions limit the size of colonial assemblies.		Vice-admiralty courts strengthened for Townshend duties. American Customs Service established in Boston.	Townshend duties imposed on some imported goods in order to pay colonial officials. (All but tax on tea repealed, 1770.)
1773				Tea Act reduces duty and prompts Boston Tea Party.
1774 (Intolerable Acts)	Massachusetts Government Act limits town meetings, changes legislature, and violates Massachusetts charter.	Quebec Act enlarges Quebec at expense of colonies with claims in the Ohio River Valley.	Boston Port Act closes harbor until East India Company's tea is paid for.	Quartering Act of 1774 declares that troops could be lodged in virtually any uninhabited building in Boston.

to cut off imports from Britain after December 1, 1774. If the dispute with Britain was not resolved by September 1775, the Association called for barring most exports to Britain and the West Indies. Voters in every district throughout the colonies were to choose committeemen to enforce the terms of the Association. All who violated them were to be considered "enemies of American liberty." Their names were to be published, and associators (people agreeing to the Association) would "break off all dealings" with them.

      Congress also issued a declaration of rights and grievances summarizing its position. The declaration condemned most of the steps taken by British authorities since 1763. One resolution in the declaration, however, "cheerfully" consented to trade regulations for the good of the whole empire. Finally, the Congress sent addresses to the people of America, to the inhabitants of Great Britain, and to the king. The address to the king asked him to use his "royal authority and interposition" to protect his loyal subjects in America. The words were significant, for protection and allegiance were considered the reciprocal duties of a sovereign and his people. After agreeing to convene again on May 10, 1775, if its grievances had not been redressed by then, the First Continental Congress adjourned.

      The deliberations and actions of the First Continental Congress revealed division as well as agreement among its delegates. All of the delegates believed that the Coercive Acts were unconstitutional, but they differed over how to resist them. Only a minority was prepared to take up arms against Britain. Most representatives tried to protect the interests of their own colonies. Those from Virginia and Maryland, for example, insisted that the embargo on exports not begin until planters had finished shipping the current tobacco crop. Even more alarming, some South Carolina delegates, in an early example of the sectional stubbornness that would culminate nearly a century later in the U.S. Civil War, threatened to walk out of the meeting unless the nonexportation agreement omitted rice, most of which went to northern Europe by way of Britain. To placate the Carolinians, northerners agreed to the exemption. Gadsden was disgusted with his self-serving South Carolina colleagues. Their actions, he felt, betrayed the spirit of united purpose Patrick Henry had spoken of stirringly earlier in the Congress: "The distinctions between Virginians, Pennsylvanians, New Yorkers and New Englanders are no more. I am not a Virginian, but an American."

Williams Burg, "The Alternative," 1775. Hand-colored print. Size: H. 13¾, W. 19. Courtesy, Winterthur Museum.

In response to the Coercive Acts of 1774, the First Continental Congress called upon Americans to join in a Continental Association that pledged them to cut off commercial dealings with Britain. This print, published in London the following year, suggests what might happen to Virginians who failed to sign up. A bag of feathers and barrel of tar hang from the gallows in the background.

Political Divisions

In the wake of the First Continental Congress, Americans were forced to take sides for and against the Continental Association. As some were uniting against Britain, others were pulling away from their countrymen and supporting the crown.

      The difference between the groups was not yet over independence for the colonies. At this point, not even such well-known radicals as Adams and Gadsden were advocating that. Throughout the pre-Revolutionary period, most colonists hoped and expected that imperial authorities would change their policy toward America. English history, Americans believed, was full of instances in which the resolute opposition of a free people forced oppressive ministries and tyrannical kings to back down. They were confident that it could happen again.

What Americans were divided over was the extent of Parliament's authority over them and the degree to which they could legitimately challenge its authority. As British officials failed, with the passing of time, to accommodate American views of their rights, Americans began in increasing numbers to challenge London's power over them. The experience of James Wilson, a Pennsylvania lawyer, illustrates this shift. In *Considerations on the Nature and Extent of the Legislative Authority of the British Parliament* (published in 1774), Wilson writes that he set out to find a reasonable dividing line between those areas in which Parliament had legitimate authority over the colonies and those in which it did not. But the more he thought, the more he became convinced "that such a line does not exist" and that there can be "no medium between acknowledging and denying that power in all cases." Wilson therefore concluded that Parliament had no authority at all over the colonies, that the colonies' only legal governing bodies were their own assemblies, and that their only link to the British Empire was through the king, to whom colonists owed allegiance. British authorities and their American supporters strongly disagreed, insisting that Parliament had complete authority over the colonies.

During 1774 and early 1775, as the British-American confrontation grew more heated, lively debates raged in newspapers and pamphlets, and the colonists became increasingly polarized. In the last months before the outbreak of the American Revolution, the advocates of colonial rights began to call themselves **Whigs** and condemned their opponents as **Tories**. These traditional English party labels dated from the accession of the Catholic James II to England's throne in the late seventeenth century. The Tories had supported his accession; the Whigs had opposed it. By calling themselves Whigs and their opponents Tories (**loyalist** was a more accurate label), the advocates of colonial rights cast themselves as champions of liberty and their enemies as defenders of religious intolerance and royal absolutism. It was of course unfair to suggest, as some zealous Whigs did, that all who supported the British government believed in "passive obedience and non-resistance." But unfair or not, the Tory label stuck.

Conclusion

All Americans, Whigs and loyalists alike, had considered themselves good British subjects. Even Whigs had therefore been slow to recognize how different their society really was from that of England. Americans, who included many new immigrants, were a more diverse and more democratic people than the English. A considerably larger percentage of them could participate in government, and for all practical purposes they had been governing themselves for a long time.

Perhaps because they came from a more rigid and aristocratic society, it was British officials who first realized the different character of American society. Their perception of this difference led them to fear that Americans might reject British controls. But the steps they took to prevent this from happening had the opposite effect.

From Britain's perspective, the measures it took in the wake of the French and Indian War were a reasonable response to its administrative and financial problems in the colonies. Taken one by one from the colonists' perspective, however, they were felt as a rain of blows that finally impelled them to rebel. A list in roughly chronological order of only the most important measures suggests why: strict enforcement of restrictions on colonial trade, new restrictions on the powers of the colonial assemblies, new restrictions on access to western lands, taxation for the first time by Parliament, use of British troops to enforce some of these steps, and drastic modification of the Massachusetts government in violation of its charter rights.

No wonder that Americans, whose political ideology had already made them wary of governmental power, believed that they were the victims of a conspiracy in London to deprive them of their liberty. That Parliament should be a party to this presumed conspiracy particularly shocked and offended them. Because it was the representative body in the government, Americans had long considered it their "friend," though they were certain that it was not composed of *their* representatives.

Yet Americans probably should not have been surprised at Parliament's role. After the Glorious Revolution, virtually the only institutional limitation on Parliament was Parliament itself. That the most powerful part of the British government should concern itself with the empire after 1763 seemed only natural in Britain; that its American counterparts should defend their own rights seemed only reasonable in America. The American assemblies, after all, had modeled themselves on Parliament. Indeed, both Parliament and the colonial assemblies were doing what similar bodies throughout Europe were also doing at roughly the same time—asserting their powers and defending their liberties against encroachments from above and below.

The attempts to protect their accustomed autonomy first brought the colonial assemblies into conflict with Parliament. Asserting their rights led the individual colonies to cooperate more among themselves. This in turn led to increasingly widespread resistance, then to rebellion, and finally to revolution. Moving imperceptibly from one stage to the next, Americans grew conscious of their common interests and their differences from the English. They became aware, as Benjamin Franklin would later write, of the need to break "through the bounds, in which a dependent people had been accustomed to think, and act" so that they might "properly comprehend the character they had assumed."

In the Boston Tea Party, working men had joined with members of the elite in a dramatic act of defiance. Although no one knows for certain why they all dressed as Indians, it is probably more than just an interesting coincidence that they did. Indians were the true Native Americans and a traditional symbol of the New World. Those who would forge a new political world would have to risk much, even, as it turned out, life itself.

Review Questions

1 How did the British victory and French withdrawal from North America after the French and Indian War affect the relations between Native Americans and whites? Between British authorities and Americans?

2. What was the relationship between the French and Indian War and changes in British policy toward America? What problems were British officials trying to solve in 1763? What difficulties confronted Americans in 1763? How did the expectations of American and British authorities differ in 1763? Why were the new policies offensive to Americans?

3. How was stationing British troops in America related to British taxation of the colonists? Why did the colonists consider taxation by Parliament an especially serious threat to their freedom as well as to their pocketbooks?

4. How did Americans oppose the new measures? Who participated in the various forms of resistance? How effective were the different kinds of resistance? What were the effects of American

resistance to British measures on their own sense of identity as Americans? What were the effects on their own internal politics?

5. What led to the meeting of the First Continental Congress? What steps did the Congress take? What did it expect to achieve? What were the differences between Whigs and Tories?

Recommended Reading

Bernard Bailyn, *The Ideological Origins of the American Revolution*, 2nd ed. (1992). A clear and illuminating account of how the colonists' ideas about politics prepared them to resist British measures.

Edward Countryman, *The American Revolution* (1985). A brief, readable general history of the Revolutionary period that focuses on the involvement of the common people.

Robert A. Gross, *The Minutemen and Their World* (1976). An example of "history from the bottom up," this book provides a close look at the Minutemen of Concord from the late colonial period through the Revolution.

Edmund S. Morgan and Helen M. Morgan, *The Stamp Act Crisis: Prologue to Revolution* (1963, 1995). The classic account of the most important pre-Revolutionary crisis, beautifully written.

Samuel Eliot Morison, ed., *Sources and Documents Illustrating the American Revolution, 1764–1788, and the Formation of the Federal Constitution* (1965). The most readily available and conveniently used collection of documents (mostly official) from the era of the American Revolution.

Additional Sources

Imperial Reorganization

John R. Alden, *John Stuart and the Southern Colonial Frontier: A Study of Indian Relations, War, Trade, and Land Problems in the Southern Wilderness, 1754–1775* (1944, 1966).

Thomas C. Barrow, *Trade and Empire: The British Customs Service in Colonial America, 1660–1775* (1967).

Colin Bonwick, *The American Revolution* (1991).

John Brooke, *King George III* (1972).

Gregory Dowd, *A Spirited Resistance: The North American Indian Struggle for Unity, 1745–1815* (1992).

Tom Hatley, *The Dividing Paths: Cherokees and South Carolinians through the Era of Revolution* (1993).

Paul Langford, *A Polite and Commercial People: England, 1727–1783* (1989).

Howard H. Peckham, *Pontiac and the Indian Uprising* (1947).

John Shy, *Toward Lexington: The Role of the British Army in the Coming of the American Revolution* (1965).

J. Russell Snapp, *John Stuart and the Struggle for Empire on the Southern Frontier* (1996).

Jack M. Sosin, *Whitehall and the Wilderness: The Middle West in British Colonial Policy, 1760–1775* (1961).

David J. Weber, *The Spanish Frontier in North America* (1992).

Richard White, *The Middle Ground: Indians, Empires, and Republics in the Great Lakes Region, 1650–1815* (1991).

American Reactions

Timothy H. Breen, *Tobacco Culture: The Mentality of the Great Tidewater Planters on the Eve of the Revolution* (1985).

Richard D. Brown, *Revolutionary Politics in Massachusetts: The Boston Committee of Correspondence and the Towns, 1772–1774* (1970).

Richard M. Brown, *The South Carolina Regulators* (1963).

Robert M. Calhoon, *Dominion and Liberty: Ideology in the Anglo-American World, 1660–1801* (1994).

H. Trevor Colbourn, *The Lamp of Experience: Whig History and the Intellectual Origins of the American Revolution* (1965).

Edward Countryman, *A People in Revolution: The American Revolution and Political Society in New York, 1760–1790* (1981).

Marc Egnal, *A Mighty Empire: The Origins of the American Revolution* (1988).

Robert A. Ekirch, *"Poor Carolina": Politics and Society in Colonial North Carolina, 1729–1776* (1981).

Jack P. Greene, *Negotiated Authorities: Essays in Colonial Political and Constitutional History* (1994).

Dirk Hoerder, *Crowd Action in Revolutionary Massachusetts, 1765–1780* (1977).

Merrill Jensen, *The Founding of a Nation: A History of the American Revolution, 1763–1776* (1968).

Rachel N. Klein, *Unification of a Slave State: The Rise of the Planter Class in the South Carolina Backcountry, 1760–1808* (1990).

Bernhard Knollenberg, *Origin of the American Revolution, 1759–1766* (1960).

Stephen G. Kurtz and James H. Hutson, eds., *Essays on the American Revolution* (1973).

Benjamin W. Labaree, *The Boston Tea Party* (1964).

Pauline Maier, *From Resistance to Revolution: Colonial Radicals and the Development of American Opposition to Britain, 1765–1776* (1972).

Pauline Maier, *The Old Revolutionaries: Political Lives in the Age of Samuel Adams* (1980).

Edmund S. Morgan, *The Birth of the Republic, 1763–1789* 3rd ed. (1992).

Gary B. Nash, *The Urban Crucible: The Northern Seaports and the Origins of the American Revolution* (1986).

John P. Reid, *Constitutional History of the American Revolution: The Power to Tax* (1987).

Richard A. Ryerson, *"The Revolution Is Now Begun": The Radical Committees of Philadelphia, 1765–1776* (1978).

Peter D. C. Thomas, *The Townshend Duties Crisis: The Second Phase of the American Revolution, 1767–1773* (1987).

Carl Ubbelohde, *The Vice-Admiralty Courts and the American Revolution* (1960).

Robert M. Weir, *"The Last of American Freemen": Studies in the Political Culture of the Colonial and Revolutionary South* (1986).

James P. Whittenburg, "Planters, Merchants, and Lawyers: Social Change and the Origins of the North Carolina Regulation," *William and Mary Quarterly*, 34 (1977), 214–238.

Hiller B. Zobel, *The Boston Massacre* (1970).

The Road to Revolution

David Ammerman, *In the Common Cause: American Response to the Coercive Acts of 1774* (1974).

Carl Bridenbaugh, *Mitre and Sceptre: Transatlantic Faiths, Ideas, Personalities, and Politics, 1689–1775* (1962).

Wallace Brown, *The Good Americans: The Loyalists in the American Revolution* (1969).

Robert M. Calhoon, *The Loyalists in Revolutionary America, 1760–1781* (1973).

J. C. D. Clark, *The Language of Liberty, 1660–1832: Political Discourse and Social Dynamics in the Anglo-American World* (1994).

William H. Nelson, *The American Tory* (1961).

Jack N. Rakove, *The Beginnings of National Politics: An Interpretive History of the Continental Congress* (1979).

Where to Learn More

❖ **Charleston, South Carolina.**   Many buildings date from the eighteenth century. Local officials stored tea in one of them —the Exchange—to prevent a local version of the Boston Tea Party.

❖ **Philadelphia, Pennsylvania.**   Numerous buildings and sites date from the eighteenth century. Independence National Historical Park, between Second and Sixth streets on Walnut and Chestnut streets, contains Carpenter's Hall, where the First

Continental Congress met, and the Pennsylvania State House (now known as Independence Hall), where the Declaration of Independence was adopted.

❖ **Boston, Massachusetts.** Many important buildings and sites in this area date from the seventeenth and eighteenth centuries. They include Faneuil Hall (Dock Square), where many public meetings took place prior to the Revolution, and the Old State House (Washington and State streets), which overlooks the site of the Boston Massacre.

❖ **Fort Michilimackinac National Historic Landmark, Mackinaw City, Michigan.** Near the south end of the Mackinac Bridge, the present structure is a modern restoration of the fort as it was when Pontiac's Rebellion took a heavy toll of its garrison.

Pacific Ocean

Cahokia

Santa Fe

Acoma
Pueblo

New Orleans

Gulf of Mexico

Tenochtitlán/
Mexico City

N
W   E
S

British Settlements
French Settlements
Spanish Settlements

0   400 miles

0   600 km

KEY TOPICS

❖ Mounting tensions between Britain and America and the outbreak of fighting
❖ Organizing for war and declaring independence
❖ The contending forces
❖ The major military campaigns of the Revolution
❖ The alliance with France and the transformation of the Revolution into a worldwide conflict
❖ The peace settlement
❖ The effect of the war on American society

*I*t was May 1780, during some of the darkest days for the American Revolution. Charleston, South Carolina, was soon to fall to an advancing British army. A German officer—a professional mercenary soldier—serving with the British army saw a wounded American sergeant who had been shot and captured after venturing far in front of his unit. Asked why he had been so foolhardy, the American replied that he had been promised an officer's commission if he would successfully scout the enemy lines. His captors told him that he was mortally wounded. "He quietly lay down like a brave man," wrote the German officer, and managed to say, "Well, then, I die for my country and for its just cause." Someone handed him a glass of wine, which he "drank . . . down with relish," and he died.

American independence would be won by the dogged courage of ordinary soldiers like this nameless man. Like him, many fought in hopes of an immediate reward. And also like him, they risked death because they believed in their country's cause.

Between 1774 and 1783, the thinking of those Americans who challenged British authority changed dramatically. As late as 1774, they were still seeking self-government within the British Empire. After 1776, they were struggling for full independence from their once-revered mother country. To be sure, however, most of them, asked what was their country, would have named their home state, and asked what was their cause, would have replied, simply, "Liberty."

American political identity emerged in part from a new ideology of republicanism that combined a New Whig distrust of central authority with a belief in a government rooted in the public spirit of a virtuous citizenry. Clinging fervently to this ideology, Americans relied at the outset of the war on the efficacy of a zealous citizens' militia to defeat the British army. But as the war grew fiercer, they learned that they could prevail only by developing an equally professional fighting force of their own. With vital French assistance, the new American army overcame the enemy. But eight long years of warfare strained and in some ways profoundly altered the fabric of American society.

The Outbreak of War and the Declaration of Independence, 1774–1776

After the Boston Tea Party, both the British and the Americans knew they were approaching a crisis. A British officer in Massachusetts commented in late 1774 that "it is thought by every body here" that British forces would soon have "to take the field." "The people in general are very enraged," he explained, and some would "defend what they call their Liberties," to the death. Many Americans also expected a military confrontation but continued to hope that the king would not "reason with us only by the roar of his Cannon."

Mounting Tensions

In May 1774, General Thomas Gage, the commander in chief of the British army in America, replaced Thomas Hutchinson as governor of Massachusetts. After Gage dissolved the Massachusetts legislature, the General Court, it defied him by assembling anyway. Calling itself the **Provincial Congress**, the legislature in October 1774 appointed an emergency executive body, the **Committee of Safety**, headed by John Hancock, which began stockpiling weapons and organizing militia volunteers. Some localities had already provided for the formation of special companies of **Minute Men**, who were to be ready at "a minutes warning in Case of an alarm."

After the First Continental Congress created the Continental Association in the fall of 1774, local committees formed in several colonies to enforce the association's boycott of British goods. The purpose of the boycott, as with the earlier nonimportation movements, was to create enough economic distress in England to force the British government to change its policies. The local committees, however, were strict and often violent in their enforcement of the boycott, sometimes assaulting suspected loyalists and destroying their property. The increasingly polarized atmosphere, combined with the drift toward military confrontation, drove a growing wedge between American loyalists and the **patriot** anti-British American Whigs.

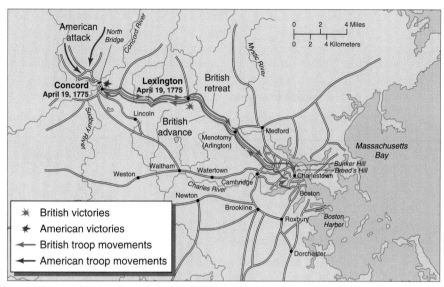

Map 6-1   *The Battles of Lexington and Concord*
This map shows the area around Boston, Massachusetts, where in April 1775 British and American forces fought the first military engagements of the Revolution.

The Loyalists' Dilemma

Loyalists and Whigs began to part company in earnest during the fall and winter of 1774–1775 as the threat of war mounted. Much like other Americans, loyalists came from all walks of life and all social classes. Most were farmers, though office-holders and professionals were more numerous among them than in the population at large. Many recent immigrants to the colonies, as well as some locally unpopular minorities (Scots in the South, Anglicans in New England), also remained loyal because they felt the crown offered them some protection against more established Americans. Most loyalists felt, in short, that they had something to lose—including their honor—if America broke with Britain. During the War for Independence, about 19,000 American men would join British provincial units and fight to restore royal authority. (This compares with the perhaps 200,000 who served in some military capacity on the rebel side.) Including those who did not actually fight, the loyalists numbered close to half a million men and women—some 20 percent of the colonies' free population. Of these, up to 100,000 would leave with the British forces at the end of the war.

British Coercion and Conciliation

Britain held parliamentary elections in the fall of 1774, but if Americans hoped the outcome would change the government's policy toward them, they were disappointed. Few British voters paid much attention to colonial affairs or to opposition criticism of Prime Minister Lord North's handling of them. As one member of Parliament later noted, a robbery near London "would make more conversation than all the distur-

bances of America." North's supporters won easily. Angry and alarmed at the colonists' challenge to Parliament's sovereignty, they took a hard line. Under North's direction, Parliament resolved in February 1774 that Massachusetts was in rebellion, and prohibited the New England colonies from trading outside the British Empire, or sending their ships to the North Atlantic fishing grounds. Similar restrictions on most of the other colonies soon followed.

Meanwhile, in a gesture of appeasement, Parliament endorsed Lord North's **Conciliatory Proposition** pledging not to tax the colonies if they would voluntarily contribute to the defense of the empire. British authorities, however, would decide what was a sufficient contribution. Parliament, as a result, would remain sovereign and the colonial legislatures strictly subordinate to it.

Had it specified a maximum colonial contribution and had it been offered ten years earlier, the colonists might have found the Conciliatory Proposition acceptable. Now it was too late. North's government, in any case, had already sent orders to General Gage to take decisive action against the Massachusetts rebels. These orders triggered the first clash between British and American forces.

The Battles of Lexington and Concord

Gage received his orders on April 14, 1775. On the night of April 18, he assembled seven hundred men on the Boston Common and marched them toward the little towns of Lexington and Concord, some 20 miles away (see Map 6-1). Their mission was to arrest

CHRONOLOGY

1775 **April 19:** Battles of Lexington and Concord.

May 10: Second Continental Congress meets.

June 17: Battle of Bunker Hill.

December 31: American attack on Quebec.

1776 **January 9:** Thomas Paine's *Common Sense*.

July 4: Declaration of Independence.

September 15: British take New York City.

December 26: Battle of Trenton.

1777 **January 3:** Battle of Princeton.

September 11: Battle of Brandywine Creek.

October 17: American victory at Saratoga.

Runaway inflation begins.

Continental Army winters at Valley Forge.

1778 **February 6:** France and the United States sign an alliance.

June 17: Congress refuses to negotiate with British peace commissioners.

July 4: George Rogers Clark captures British post in the Mississippi Valley.

December 29: British capture Savannah.

1779 **June 21:** Spain declares war on Britain.

Americans devastate the Iroquois country.

September 23: John Paul Jones captures the British ship *Serapis*.

1780 **May 12:** Fall of Charleston, South Carolina.

October 7: Americans win Battle of Kings Mountain.

Nathanael Greene takes command in the South.

1781 **January 17:** Americans defeat British at Battle of Cowpens.

March 15: Battle of Guilford Court House.

October 19: Cornwallis surrenders at Yorktown.

1783 **March 15:** Washington quells the Newburgh "Conspiracy."

September 3: Peace of Paris signed.

November 21: British begin evacuating New York.

---

rebel leaders Samuel Adams and John Hancock (then staying in Lexington) and to destroy the military supplies the Committee of Safety had assembled at Concord. Patriots in Boston got wind of the troop movements and sent out riders—one of them the silversmith Paul Revere—to warn their fellows. Adams and Hancock escaped.

When the British soldiers reached Lexington at dawn, they found about seventy armed militiamen drawn up in formation on the village green. Their precise intentions are not clear. Outnumbered ten to one, they probably did not plan to begin a fight. More likely, they were there in a show of defiance, to demonstrate that Americans would not run at the sight of a superior British force.

Months of mounting tension exploded on the Lexington green. A British major ordered the militia to disperse. They were starting to obey when a shot cracked through the dawn stillness. No one now knows who fired. The British responded with a volley that killed or wounded eighteen Americans. Samuel Adams, still within hearing range and thrilled at the thought of American resistance, sup-

posedly exclaimed to Hancock, "O! what a glorious morning is this."

The British troops pressed on to Concord and burned what few supplies the Americans had not been able to hide. When their rear guard came under patriot fire at Concord's North Bridge, the British panicked. As they retreated to Boston, patriot Minute Men and other militia harried them from both sides of the road. By the time the column reached safety, 273 British soldiers were either dead, wounded, or missing. The four thousand Americans who had shot at them along the way suffered nearly 100 dead, wounded, and missing.

News of the fighting at the **Battles of Lexington and Concord** spread quickly. Patriots in Providence, Rhode Island, knew of it by evening of the Wednesday on which it occurred. Rumors of the fighting had already reached New York by the time an express rider confirmed them at noon the following Sunday. The Philadelphia newspaper *Pennsylvania Packet* carried the story on Monday. Williamsburg's *Virginia Gazette* printed an account on May 4, only two weeks after the event. South Carolinians knew by May

The Battle of Lexington, April 19th, 1775. OH:13 3/4 in.; OW:19 in. Courtesy, Winterthur Museum.

This dramatic engraving of the first battle of the American Revolution at Lexington, Massachusetts, on April 19, 1775, is not the photographic work of an eyewitness to events but a close approximation to it. Ralph Earl, a painter, and Amos Doolittle, an engraver, walked over the battlefields at Lexington and Concord a few days after the engagement, interviewed spectators and participants, and collaborated in producing four large engravings that depicted the events with considerable accuracy. This scene from the first plate shows British troops firing on the American militia at Lexington.

9 and Georgians probably soon after. The speed with which distant colonies heard about the outbreak of fighting suggests both the importance Americans attached to it and the extraordinary efforts patriots made to spread word of it. Everywhere, news of Lexington and Concord spurred Whigs into action.

The shots fired that April morning would, in the words of the nineteenth-century Concord philosopher and poet Ralph Waldo Emerson, be "heard round the world." They signaled the start of the American Revolution. And that revolution helped inspire the French Revolution in 1789 and other revolutions in Europe and Latin America.

The Second Continental Congress, 1775–1776

By the time the Second Continental Congress convened in Philadelphia on May 10, 1775, it had a war on its hands. After Gage's troops had limped back into Boston from Lexington and Concord, patriot militia surrounded the city and laid siege to it. On the day Congress met, militia forces from Vermont under Ethan Allen and from Massachusetts under Benedict Arnold overwhelmed the British garrison at **Fort Ticonderoga** at the southern end of Lake Champlain. Rebel forces elsewhere seized arms and ammunition from royal storehouses.

Assuming leadership of the rebellion, Congress in the succeeding months became, in effect, a national government. It called for the patchwork of local forces to be organized into the **Continental Army**, authorized the formation of a navy, established a post office, and authorized the printing of paper **continental dollars** to meet its expenses. Denying Parliament's claim to govern the colonies but not yet ready to declare themselves independent, the delegates sought to preserve their ties to Britain by expressing loyalty to the crown. In the **Olive Branch Petition**, addressed to George III on July 5, they asked the king to protect his American subjects from the military actions ordered by Parliament. The following day, Congress approved the **Declaration of the Causes and Necessity of Taking Up Arms**, asserting the resolve of American patriots "to die freemen, rather than to live slaves." And at the end of the month, it formally rejected North's Conciliatory Proposition.

Commander in Chief George Washington

To take command of the patriot forces around Boston—the newly named Continental Army—Congress turned to George Washington. John Adams, a Whig leader from Massachusetts, first nominated Washington. Selecting the Virginian, Adams realized, would help transform a local quarrel in New England into a continental conflict involving all of British North America. Adams and his fellow delegates also expected Washington's leadership to help attract recruits from Virginia, which was then the most populous colony. Washington claimed, despite (or perhaps because of) his experience in the French and Indian War, to feel inadequate to the task, but by attending Congress in military uniform he seemed to be volunteering for it.

He was the ideal person for the job. Some of his contemporaries had quicker minds and broader educations; Washington, however, was blessed with good judgment, a profound understanding of both the uses and the limitations of power, and a quiet air of authority. In short, he had the gift of command. He soon also realized that the fate of the patriot cause depended on the survival of the army. Early in the war, he almost suffered catastrophic military defeat at least twice, but he learned from his mistakes and thereafter did not risk lives unnecessarily. The troops in turn revered him. In a crisis, wrote a man who served under him, "his likeness was worth more . . . than the British would have given for his person"—presumably a great deal.

This engraving of Washington and his family, including two of his wife's grandchildren from her first marriage and a waiting-man, dates from the 1790s, but the artist, Edward Savage, presented Washington in his uniform as Commander of the Continental Army. Note the authoritative manner in which Martha Washington points to the map. The African-American was probably William Lee, who would be singled out in Washington's last will and testament for his loyalty and "faithful services during the Revolution."

Early Fighting

General Gage, finding himself besieged in Boston after the fighting at Lexington and Concord, decided to seize and fortify territory south of Boston, where his cannons could command the harbor. But the Americans seized high ground first, entrenching themselves on Breeds Hill north of town. On June 17, 1775, Gage sent 2,200 well-trained soldiers to drive the 1,700 patriot men and boys from their new position. The British succeeded, but at great cost. In three assaults, they suffered more than a thousand casualties. The Americans, who retreated when they ran short of gunpowder, lost just under four hundred dead or wounded. One glum British officer observed afterward that another such victory "would have

ruined us." Misnamed for another hill nearby, this encounter has gone down in history as the **Battle of Bunker Hill** (see Map 6-2).

Washington, who arrived in Boston after the battle, took command of the American forces there in early July. Months of standoff followed, with neither side able to dislodge the other. During the winter of 1775–1776, however, the Americans dragged some sixty cannons—the largest weighed as much as a ton— 300 miles through snow and over mountains from Fort Ticonderoga to Boston. In March 1776, Washington mounted the newly arrived guns overlooking Boston harbor, putting the British in an indefensible position. The British then evacuated Boston—which really had no strategic value for them—and moved their troops to Halifax, Nova Scotia. New England was for the moment secure for the patriots.

Initial fighting in the South also went well for the patriots. Virginia's last royal governor, Lord Dunmore, fled the capital, Williamsburg, and set up a base in nearby Norfolk. Promising freedom to slaves who joined him, he succeeded in raising a small force of black and white loyalists. On December 9, 1775, he sent these men, with some British marines, to attack a much larger force of nine hundred Virginia and North Carolina patriots at **Great Bridge**, near Norfolk. As it advanced up a long causeway, Dunmore's little band was slaughtered. It was, one British officer accurately commented, an "extravagant Folly." On February 27, a force of loyalist Scots suffered a similar defeat at **Moore's Creek Bridge** in North Carolina. In June 1776, patriot forces successfully repulsed a large British expedition sent to capture Charleston, South Carolina.

In contrast, an attempt to win Canada to the Whig side met with disaster. Two American armies attacked Canada in late 1775. One, under Richard Montgomery, marched up the Hudson River Valley and quickly captured Montreal. The other, under Benedict Arnold, approached through the Maine wilderness in the face of great hardships. The two forces linked up outside heavily fortified Quebec. Because they expected many of their troops to leave for home when their enlistments expired on January 1, 1776, Arnold and Montgomery felt compelled to attack the city on December 31. The premature attack failed, and most of the Americans who participated in it were captured. The **Siege of Quebec** dragged on into the spring, when a British

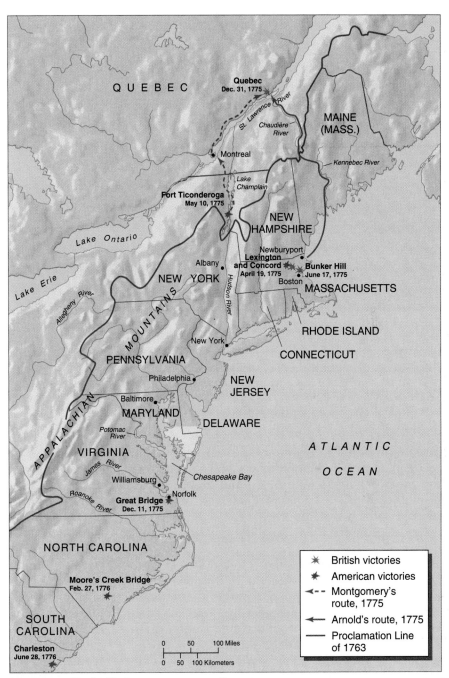

Map 6-2   Early Fighting, 1775–1776
As this map clearly reveals, even the earliest fighting occurred in widely scattered areas, thereby complicating Britain's efforts to subdue the Americans.

fleet relieved it and fresh troops forced the Americans back to Lake Champlain. Canada remained a British province.

Independence

The stunning American successes in New England and the South in late 1775 and early 1776 bolstered the patriots' confidence. During the same

The Battle of Bunker Hill, June 17, 1775. Painted by John Trumbull, who witnessed the battle from the other side of Boston harbor, this dramatic depiction of the fighting in which Major General Joseph Warren of the Massachusetts militia lies dying was completed a decade after the events. The African-American who appears on the far right was the servant of a lieutenant from Connecticut; another African-American not clearly shown, Peter Salem, was reported to have fired one of the shots that killed Major John Pitcairn, who had led the British troops at the battle of Lexington.

period, attempts to promote an Anglo-American reconciliation failed, and the antagonism between the two sides deepened. More and more, Whigs began to think seriously of declaring full independence from Britain.

In August 1775, King George III rejected Congress's Olive Branch Petition. Instead, he issued a proclamation declaring the colonies in rebellion and denying them his protection. In December, Parliament barred all exports from the American colonies. These aggressive actions, especially the king's, persuaded many colonists to abandon their loyalty to the crown. Some, however, continued to search for a formula that would permit them to remain within the British Empire.

At this critical moment, a ne'er-do-well Englishman, recently arrived on American soil, gave the cause of independence a powerful boost. Thomas Paine was by trade a corsetmaker—and twice a fired tax collector. He was also a man of radical ideas that he expressed in a direct style in the everyday English of ordinary people on both sides of the Atlantic. This combination made him a powerful polemicist for the American cause. Benjamin Franklin, in London as a lobbyist for the colonies, recognized Paine's talent and gave him letters of introduction when he sailed for America in 1774. In his pamphlet **Common Sense**,

published in Philadelphia in January 1776, Paine denounced King George and made the case for independence. He ridiculed the absurdity of "supposing a continent to be perpetually governed by an island." America, he maintained, would be better off on every count if it were independent. The king, Paine said bluntly, was "the Royal Brute" whose tyranny should be thrown off. This assertion, which not long before would have shocked even Whigs, seemed self-evident now in light of the king's rejection of the Olive Branch Petition. Simple common sense, Paine concluded, dictated that "'TIS TIME TO PART."

Common Sense, which promptly sold more than 100,000 copies throughout the colonies, helped predispose Americans toward independence. Tactical considerations also led patriot leaders toward a formal separation from Great Britain. Such a move would make it easier for America to gain desperately needed aid from foreign countries, especially from England's ancient enemy, France. Declaring independence would also give the local political elites leading the resistance to British rule a solid legal basis for their newly claimed authority. The revolutionary committees and provincial congresses that were governing the colonies and exercising local power were emergency, extralegal institutions. As the crisis dragged on, their uncertain legal foundation caused confusion and invited challenge. By the spring of 1776, many Americans demanded permanent, legitimate governments to replace both crumbling British authority and these emergency resistance organizations. Accordingly, most of the American states (as the rebellious colonies now called themselves) either instructed or permitted their delegates in Congress to vote for independence.

On June 7, 1776, Virginian Richard Henry Lee introduced in Congress a resolution stating that the united colonies "are, and of right ought to be, free and independent States." Postponing a vote on the issue, Congress appointed a committee to draw up a declaration of independence. The committee turned to a young Virginian named Thomas Jefferson to compose the first draft. "You can write ten times better than I," John Adams told Jefferson. On June 28, after making revisions in Jefferson's proposed text, the committee presented the document to Congress. In the debate that followed, the South Carolina, Pennsylvania, and New York delegations initially opposed independence. As it became clear that the majority favored it, the Pennsylvania and South Carolina delegations switched sides, and the New York delegation decided to abstain. A few delegates—including the notable patriot leaders John Dickinson and Robert Morris of Pennsylvania—clung to the hope of maintaining loyal ties to the crown. But when Congress voted on the resolution for independence on July 2, 1776, it was approved unanimously by all voting delegations. After further tinkering with the wording, Congress officially approved the **Declaration of Independence** on July 4, 1776.

Congress intended the declaration to be a justification for America's secession from the British Empire. Jefferson later maintained that he did not write any more than what everyone was thinking. The political theory that lies behind the declaration is known as the **contract theory of government**. Developed by the late seventeenth-century English philosopher John Locke and others, the contract theory maintains that legitimate government rests on an agreement between the people and their rulers. The people are bound to obey their rulers only so long as the rulers offer them protection. Jefferson's prose, however, transformed what might have been a bland, legalistic rehash of the contract theory into one of history's great statements of human rights.

The Declaration of Independence consists of a magnificently stated opening assumption, two premises, and a powerful conclusion. The opening assumption is that all men are created equal, that they therefore have equal rights, and that they can neither give up these rights nor allow them to be taken away. The first premise—that people establish governments to protect their fundamental rights to life, liberty, and property—is a restatement of contract theory. (With a wonderful flourish reflecting the Enlightenment's optimism about human potential, Jefferson changed "property" to "the pursuit of happiness.") The second premise is a long list of charges meant to prove that George III had failed to defend his American subjects' rights. This indictment, the heart of the declaration, justified the Americans' rejection of their hitherto legitimate ruler. Then followed the dramatic conclusion: that

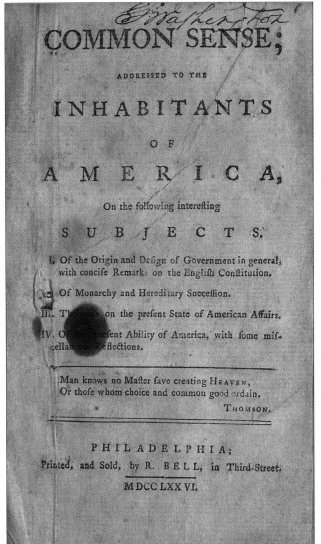

Title page to Thomas Paine's *Common Sense*. Philadelphia, R. Bell, 1776. Inscribed: "G. Washington." Boston Athenaeum.

George Washington's personal copy of Common Sense. *Thomas Paine's stirring argument in favor of American independence. Within a month of its publication in January 1776, Washington observed that "the sound doctrine and unanswerable reasoning" of Paine's pamphlet, given further acts of British cruelty, would soon persuade Americans that separation from England was the proper course.*

Americans could rightfully overthrow King George's rule and replace it with something more satisfactory to them.

Historians have spilled oceans of ink debating Jefferson's use of the expression "all men." Almost certainly he was thinking in the abstract and meant "humanity in general." In practice, of course, many people were excluded from full participation in eighteenth-century American society. Women had no formal political rights and limited legal rights. Propertyless white and free black men

Thomas Jefferson, author of the Declaration of Independence and future president of the United States. Mather Brown, an American artist living in England, painted this picture of Jefferson for John Adams while the two men were in London on diplomatic missions in 1786. A companion portrait of Adams that Jefferson ordered for himself also survives. Brown's sensitive portrait of a thoughtful Jefferson is the earliest known likeness of him.

had similarly restricted rights, and slaves enjoyed no rights at all. (Although himself a slaveowner, Jefferson was deeply troubled by American slavery. He had wanted to include a denunciation of the slave trade among the charges against George III in the Declaration of Independence, but Congress took it out, believing that to blame the king for this inhumane business would appear hypocritical.) But if the words "all men are created equal" had limited practical meaning in 1776, they have ever since confronted Americans with a moral challenge to make good on them.

Republicanism

Americans reacted to news of the Declaration of Independence with mixed emotions. There was rejoicing as orators read the declaration to great crowds. Soldiers fired noisy salutes, and candles lit up the windows of public buildings at night. But even

many who favored independence worried about the future. How would Americans govern themselves? What would they put in place of the former royal government? Monarchy, after all, was the normal form of government in the eighteenth century. A handful of Americans even thought briefly about replacing George III with an American king from one of Europe's other ruling houses. There seemed to be no good candidates, however. And in any case, most Whigs, animated by the political ideology known as **republicanism**, thought a republican government was better suited to American society.

John Adams once complained that republicanism was too shadowy a concept to define, and indeed it was a complex, changing body of ideas, values, and assumptions. Closely related to country (New Whig) ideology, republicanism was derived from the political ideas of classical antiquity, Renaissance Europe, and early modern England. It held that self-government—either directly by the citizens of a country or indirectly by their elected representatives—provided a more reliable foundation for the good society and individual freedom than rule by kings. Thus drawing on contract theory, as in the Declaration of Independence, republicanism called for government by consent of the governed. Drawing on country ideology, it was suspicious of excessively centralized government and insistent on the need for virtuous, public-spirited citizenry. The benefits of monarchy depended on the variable abilities of monarchs; the character of republican government depended on the virtue of the people. Republicanism therefore helped give the American Revolution a moral dimension.

But other than a state that was not ruled by a hereditary king, what was a republic? And what were the chances that one would survive? Every educated person knew, of course, that ancient Rome and Athens had been republics. Classical political theory, beginning with the ancient Greek thinkers Plato and Aristotle, had insisted that republics could endure only as long as their citizens remained virtuous and self-sacrificing. Once individual citizens, greedy for wealth and power, began fighting among themselves, a republic would certainly collapse. A failed republic would give way to the despotism of one-man rule or to oligarchy—rule by a narrow clique of rich men—or, worst of all, to the "mob rule" of ignorant and violent common people. Europe's three surviving republics in the eighteenth century—the Netherlands, Switzerland, and Venice—seemed to bear out this dismal picture. All were rather corrupt and uninspiring societies, and none of them was at all democratic.

But Americans had at hand a more recent example of a republic than ancient Athens or Rome, one more closely linked to their own history than the republics of eighteenth-century Europe. During the English Civil War of the mid-seventeenth century, English Puritans had for a time replaced the monarchy with a republican "Commonwealth," dedicated to advancing the "common weal," or common good. Most eighteenth-century Americans thought of the Puritan Commonwealth as a misguided product of fanaticism that had ended in a military dictatorship. However, some New Englanders, spiritual descendants of the Puritans, considered the Commonwealth to have been a noble experiment. To them, the American Revolution offered another chance to establish a republic of the godly.

"When the mere Politician weighs the Danger or Safety of his Country," warned one clergyman, "he computes them in Proportion to its Fortresses, Arms, Money, Provisions, Numbers of Fighting Men, and its Enemies." But, the clergyman continued, the "Christian Patriot" calculates them "by its Numbers of Sinful or praying People, and its Degrees of Holiness or Vice." Such language recalled the Great Awakening; it reached beyond the upper classes who had been directing resistance to the British and mobilized ordinary people for what their ministers repeatedly assured them was a just war against sin and despotism. Out of this fusion of republican theory (with which only the educated were familiar) and the religious heritage that all Americans understood, a common belief developed that Americans must have "resolution enough to forego Self gratification" and be willing to stake their all "upon the prospect of Securing freedom and happiness to future Generations."

A View of Boston published in Germany about 1776. This excessively imaginative depiction shows a very European-looking city in which the spire of Old South Congregational Church in the center of the picture is barely recognizable. But the etching is notable because the windows of the buildings were cut out and covered with translucent waxed or oiled paper. So when a candle was placed behind the picture, the buildings appeared to be illuminated from within, as they actually were in American cities on the anniversary of the repeal of the Stamp Act, the announcement of the Declaration of Independence, and other celebrations.

1776 Town. Size: H. 11⅛ in., W. 16⅞ in. Courtesy, Winterthur Museum.

The Combatants

At the outset of the American Revolution, republican fervor produced a spontaneous eruption of patriotism that to skeptical foreign observers looked like religious fanaticism. The experience of Lancaster, Pennsylvania, where more men responded to a call for volunteers than were then needed, leaving disappointed men behind, was shared elsewhere. But this enthusiastic flocking to the colors eventually waned, and in any case, its results were often unsatisfactory.

Republican theory mistrusted professional armies as the instruments of tyrants. A free people, republicans insisted, relied for defense on their own patriotism. When individual or community rights were in danger, free men should grab their muskets from over the fireplace, assemble as the local militia, take care of the problem, and go home. But militiamen, as one American general observed, had trouble coping with "the shocking scenes of war" because they were not "steeled by habit or fortified by military pride." In real battles, they often proved unreliable. Americans therefore faced a hard choice: develop a professional army or lose the war. In the end, they did what they had to do. While state militias continued to offer support, it was the disciplined forces of the Continental Army that won the crucial battles. To be sure, when the war was over, Americans tried to forget about their professional troops; in American mythology, it was the "embattled farmers"—Minute Men at Lexington and Concord, swamp fighters in the South—who had won independence. But long before the struggle was over, toughened Continental soldiers knew better.

Professional Soldiers

Drawing on their colonial experience and on republican theory, the new state governments first tried to meet their military needs by relying on the militia and by creating new units based on short-term enlistments. Officers, particularly in the North, were often elected, and their positions depended on personal popularity. As a result, their orders sometimes sounded more like requests than commands, and rules were lax. Discipline became a major problem in both the militia and the new state units, and often volunteers had barely received basic training before their term of duty ended and they returned home.

Washington tightened things up in the new Continental Army. Eventually, he prevailed on Congress to adopt stricter regulations and to require enlistments for three years or the duration of the war. His consistent aim was to turn the Continental Army into a disciplined force that could defeat the British in the large engagements of massed troops characteristic of eighteenth-century European warfare. Guerrilla fighters shooting from behind trees like "savages" had their place in the American war effort, but they could never win a decisive, formal battle. And only such a "civilized" victory would impress the other European powers and establish the legitimacy of the United States.

Many soldiers of fortune, as well as a few idealists, offered their services to American representatives in Europe. So many came to the United States that both Washington and Congress soon regarded most of them as nuisances. But several proved especially valuable in helping Washington forge a professional army. France's 19-year-old Marquis de Lafayette was one of the youngest, wealthiest, and most idealistic. Two Poles, Tadeusz Kosciuszko, an engineer, and Kazimierz Pulaski, a cavalry commander mortally wounded at the Battle of Savannah in 1779, also rendered good service. Johann Kalb, a bogus baron from Germany, became a general and died heroically at Camden, South Carolina, in 1780. Most useful of all, probably, was "Baron" von Steuben. His title, like Kalb's, was bogus, but he had genuine experience in the Prussian army, continental Europe's best. And if he was boastful—he once claimed that he could have a command obeyed from Maine to Georgia—he knew how to get along with American soldiers by explaining the reasons for his orders. He became the Continental Army's drillmaster, and thanks partly to him, Washington's troops increasingly came to resemble their disciplined European counterparts.

The enemy British troopers—and the nearly thirty thousand German mercenaries (Americans called them "Hessians") whom the British government also employed—offered Americans the clearest model of a professional army. British regulars were not (as Americans, then and later, assumed) the "dregs of society." Most enlisted men did come from the lower classes and from economically depressed areas, but many also had skills. British officers usually came from wealthy families or had simply purchased their commissions. Only in rare cases did a man rise from the enlisted ranks to commissioned officer status.

Most British troops carried the "Brown Bess" musket. With bayonet attached, it was almost 6 feet long and weighed over 16 pounds. It fired a lead ball slightly more than ½ inch in diameter, which *might* hit its target at up to 100 yards. Skilled troops could get off more than two rounds per minute under combat conditions. In battle, soldiers usually stood close together in lines or squares. They were expected to withstand bombardment without flinching, fire on command in volleys, charge with the bayonet, and use their heavy musket stock (the wooden end) to crush the skulls of any wounded enemy they strode over.

Military life was tough. On the march, seasoned troops carrying 60-pound packs, normally covered about 15 miles a day but could go 30 miles in a "forced" march. In all weather conditions, they wore heavy woolen uniforms dyed bright red for visibility on smoke-filled battlefields (hence their nickname "Redcoats"). In their barracks, British soldiers doubled up in a bed slightly over 4 feet wide; in the field, they were often wet, crawling with lice, and hungry. Under the best conditions, they mainly ate beef or salt pork and bread. They were frequently undernourished, however, and many more died of disease than of injury in battle. Medical care was, by modern standards, primitive: Treatments for illness included bleeding and purging (induced vomiting and diarrhea). Serious arm or leg wounds usually meant amputation, without antiseptics or anesthetics. But unless a man were extraordinarily lucky, a body wound or amputation usually proved fatal. If loss of blood or infection did not kill him immediately, tetanus probably would later.

Severe discipline held soldiers in line. Striking an officer or deserting could bring death; lesser offenses usually incurred a beating. Several hundred lashes, "well laid on" with the notorious cat-o'-nine-tails (a whip with multiple cords, each ending in a nasty little knot or a metal ball), were not uncommon.

Soldiers amused themselves with gambling (despite regulations against it) and drinking. As one foreign officer serving with the British lamented, America was a terrible country where one drank "to get warm, or to get cool, or . . . because you get no letters." Perhaps two-thirds of the Redcoats were illiterate, and they all suffered from loneliness and boredom. Camaraderie and a legendary loyalty to their regiments sustained them.

After the winter of 1777–1778, conditions in the Continental Army came to resemble those of the British army. Like British regulars, American recruits tended to be low on the social scale. They included young men without land, indentured servants, some criminals and vagrants—in short, men who lacked better prospects. The chances for talented enlisted men to win an officer's commission were greater in the Continental Army than the British army. As a German prisoner of war observed, American troops tended to be taller than their British counterparts. And despite their ragged uniforms, they carried themselves like soldiers. Indeed, Continental soldiers frequently had little more than "their ragged shirt

flaps to cover their nakedness," and more than once their bare marching feet left bloody tracks in the snow.

Both British and American authorities had trouble supplying their troops. Both sides suffered from bureaucratic inefficiencies, but the fundamental problems of each were different. The British had plenty of hard-coin money with a stable value, which many American merchants and farmers were happy to take in payment for supplies. But the British had to rely mostly on supplies shipped to them from the British Isles. The Continental Army, in contrast, had to pay for supplies in paper money, both continental dollars and state-issued currency, whose value sank steadily as the war progressed. After 1780, the burden of provisioning the Continental Army fell on the states, which did little better than Congress had done. Unable to obtain sufficient supplies, the army sometimes provoked resentment by threatening to seize them by force. This in turn increased the public's republican distrust of its own professional army.

Feeling themselves outcasts from an uncaring society, the professional soldiers of the Continental Army developed a community of their own. The soldiers were "as strict a band of brotherhood as Masons," one later wrote, and their spirit kept them together in the face of misery. They groused, to be sure—sometimes alarmingly. In May 1780, Connecticut troops at Washington's camp in Morristown, New Jersey, staged a brief mutiny. A more serious mutiny erupted on January 1, 1781, when armed units from Pennsylvania stationed in New Jersey marched to Philadelphia demanding their arrears in pay. The Pennsylvania Executive Council met part of the soldiers' demands, but some of the men left the service. Washington ordered subsequent mutinies by New Jersey and Pennsylvania troops suppressed by force.

Occasionally, American officers let their disgruntlement get out of hand. The most notorious such case was that of Benedict Arnold, a general who compiled a distinguished record during the first three years of the war but then came to feel himself shabbily treated by Congress and his superiors. Seeking better rewards for his abilities, he offered to surrender the strategic fort at West Point (which he commanded) to the enemy; before he could act, however, his plot was discovered, and he fled to the British, serving with them until the end of the war. Among Americans, his name became a synonym for *traitor*.

What was perhaps the most serious expression of army discontent—one that threatened the future of republican institutions and civilian

Ye Foil'd, Ye Baffled Brittons This Behold   To fave their Country and Promote its Weal
Nor longer urge your Pardons,Threats or Gold; Difdaining Bribes to wound a righteous Caufe
See in each virtuous face Patr'otic Zeal   While ANDRE falls a victim to the Laws.

This print Ye Foil'd, Ye Baffled Brittons, *shows the capture of Major John Andre, the British agent who acted as the go-between for British authorities and the American General Benedict Arnold, who planned to turn over the American fortress at West Point to them. Probably published in Salem, Massachusetts, this print may have been the first depiction of events surrounding Arnold's shocking defection. The three militiamen who captured Andre, who was later hanged as a spy, reportedly refused a bribe for his release. The strange facial expressions of all the participants were probably the artist's crude attempt to indicate surprise.*

government in the United Sates—occurred in March 1783, after the fighting was over. At the time, Washington's troops were stationed near Newburgh, New York, waiting to disband and for Congress to decide how to settle up with them. During the war, Congress had promised officers a pension of half pay for life (the custom in Great Britain), but now many veterans demanded instead full pay for six years. When Congress failed to grant real assurances that *any* pay would be forthcoming, hotheaded young officers called a meeting that could have led to an armed uprising and military coup. General Washington, who had scrupulously deferred to civilian authority throughout the war,

asked permission to address the gathering and, in a dramatic speech, subtly warned the men of all that they might lose by insubordination. A military coup would "open the flood Gates of Civil discord" and "deluge" the nation in blood; loyalty now, he said, would be "one more distinguished proof" of their patriotism. With the fate of the Revolution and the honor of the army hanging in the balance, the movement collapsed. It is still not clear whether the organizers had a military takeover in mind. Some officers and politicians behind the "conspiracy" were probably only bluffing, using the threat of a discontented army to frighten the states into granting Congress the power (which it then lacked) to levy taxes so it would have the funds to pay the army. If so, they may not have realized the potential harm they threatened. In any case, the Continental Army thereafter disbanded without further serious incidents.

Women in the Contending Armies

Women accompanied many units on both sides, as was common in eighteenth-century warfare. A few were prostitutes. Some were officers' wives or mistresses, but most were the married or common-law consorts of ordinary soldiers. These women "camp followers" cooked and washed for the troops, occasionally helped load artillery, and provided most of the nursing care. A certain number in a company were subject to military orders and were authorized to draw rations and pay.

The role of these women found its way into American folklore in the legend of Molly Pitcher (probably Mary Ludwig Hays, the wife of a Continental artillery sergeant), who heroically carried water to gunners to cool them and their overheated guns at the Battle of Monmouth Court House in 1778. Numberless, nameless other women accompanying the troops also found themselves under fire. A British officer fighting in New York, for example, reported discovering three American bodies, one a woman with cartridges in her hands. A few women even managed to serve in the Continental Army's ranks. One was discharged only when she was hospitalized for illness and her sex was discovered.

Black and Native American Participation in the War

Early in the war, some royal officials sought to recruit black slaves into the loyalist forces with a promise of freedom. Such was the case with Lord Dunmore, for example, whose black and white troops met disaster at Great Bridge in some of the earliest fighting of the war. Unfortunately for the British, these offers proved counterproductive, frightening and enraging potentially loyalist slaveowners and driving them to the Whig side. Thus it was not until June 30, 1779, that the British commander in chief, Sir Henry Clinton, promised to allow slaves who fled from rebel owners to join the royal troops to "follow . . . any Occupation" they wished. Hedged as this promise of freedom was, news of it spread quickly among the slave communities, and late in the war enough blacks flocked to the British army in South Carolina and Georgia to make feeding and housing them a serious problem.

This depiction of the death of Jane McCrea with Esopus (now Kingston, New York) burning in the background was part of a satirical cartoon published in London in 1778 to criticize the British conduct of the war. Jane McCrea, who was tomahawked by Indian allies of the British during General Burgoyne's invasion of the Hudson River Valley, was to be married to a British officer. A force sent northward up the Hudson River burned Esopus but failed to relieve Burgoyne who surrendered at Saratoga.

The British shared the racial prejudices of many Americans, however, and despite their efforts to recruit African-Americans, were reluctant to arm them. Instead, the British put most of the ex-slaves to work as agricultural or construction workers (many of the free and enslaved blacks accompanying American troops were similarly employed). A few relatively well equipped black British dragoons (mounted troops), however, saw some combat in South Carolina, much to the horror of local Whigs. Some of these troops formed the nucleus of the postwar First and Second British West India Regiments.

Approximately five thousand African-Americans fought against the British and for American independence, hundreds of them in the Continental Army. Many were freemen from Massachusetts and Rhode Island (see "American Views: An African-American Revolutionary War Veteran Petitions for His Pension"). Several free blacks served among the defenders at Bunker Hill, and at least one distinguished himself sufficiently for his commander to commend him as "an experienced officer as well as an excellent soldier."

Farther south, a young Carolina patriot repeatedly but vainly tried to convince the South Carolina assembly to raise and arm black troops. (On the contrary, the legislature eventually voted to give slaves confiscated from loyalists to white volunteers as a reward for their service in the state regiments.) It is therefore scarcely surprising that, as one Whig put it, many blacks were "a little Toryfied," especially in the South.

Many Indians also favored the British. To Native Americans, the key issue of the American Revolution, as well as in most disputes with whites,

American Views

AN AFRICAN-AMERICAN VETERAN OF THE REVOLUTIONARY WAR PETITIONS FOR HIS PENSION

Rhode Island made a greater effort to recruit African-American soldiers than any other state. Indeed, three-quarters of the Rhode Island regiment that helped defeat Cornwallis at Yorktown was African-American, and a French officer who saw the Continental troops pass in review reported that it was "the most neatly dressed, the best under arms, and the most precise in its maneuvers." In theory at least, African-Americans were supposed to receive all the benefits to which other soldiers were entitled, including pensions. Thus when in 1832 Congress passed the first general pension act authorizing yearly payments to anyone who had served six months or more in any military unit, a number of African-Americans were eligible. Jehu Grant was one of them. Like many others who applied, he sought to document his military service by a narrative of his activities during the war. Few such accounts are as poignant as Grant's, whose letter inquiring about the fate of his application is reproduced here. Because he signed with his mark, one can infer that the original document was not in his own handwriting.

❖ **How did Grant enter the army, and what did he do while in it?**

❖ **How did he obtain his freedom, and what did he do later in life?**

❖ **Do you see any connection between the war service of men like Grant and the decision of the Rhode Island legislature to end slavery in 1784?**

Hon. J. L. Edwards, Commissioner of Pensions:

Your servant
begs leave to state that he forwarded to the War Department a declaration founded on the Pension Act of June 1832 praying to be allowed a pension (if his memory serves him) for ten months' service in the American army of the Revolutionary War. That he enlisted as a soldier but was put to the service of a teamster in the summer and a waiter in the winter. In April 1834 I received a writing from Your Honour, informing me that my "services while a fugitive from my master's service was not embraced in said Act," and that my "papers were placed on file." In my said declaration, I just mentioned the cause of leaving my master, as may be seen by a reference thereunto, and I now pray that I may be permitted to express my feelings more fully on that part of my said declaration.

was simple. As a Cherokee chief told Virginians, "Remember that *the difference is about our land.*" British Indian agents had frequently protected Native Americans against advancing settlers, and Native Americans generally feared that an American victory would sweep away any restraint on whites' westward movement. Many Indian peoples, including the Cherokees, therefore decided that it was in their interest to back the British. Their aid mainly took the form of attacks on white frontier settlements. Usually they did not tell the British in advance what they were planning to do. Thus in one notorious incident, an Indian attack in the Hudson River Valley resulted in the mistaken scalping of Jane McCrae, the fiancée of a British officer. Whig propagandists exploited this tragedy to the fullest.

I was then grown to manhood, in the full vigor and strength of life, and heard much about the cruel and arbitrary things done by the British. Their ships lay within a few miles of my master's house, which stood near the shore, and I was confident that my master traded with them, and I suffered much from fear that I should be sent aboard a ship of war. This I disliked. But when I saw liberty poles and the people all engaged for the support of freedom, I could not but like and be pleased with such [a] thing (God forgive me if I sinned in so feeling). And living on the borders of Rhode Island, where whole companies of colored people enlisted, it added to my fears and dread of being sold to the British. These considerations induced me to enlist into the American army, where I served faithful about ten months, when my master found and took me home. Had I been taught to read or understand the precepts of the Gospel, "Servants obey your masters," I might had done otherwise, notwithstanding the songs of liberty that saluted my ear, [and] thrilled through my heart. But feeling conscious that I have since compensated my master for the injury he sustained by my enlisting, and that God has forgiven me for so doing, and that I served my country faithfully, and

that they having enjoyed the benefits of my service to an equal degree for the length [of] time I served with those generally who are receiving the liberalities of the government, I cannot but feel it becoming me to pray Your Honor to review my declaration on file and the papers herewith amended.

A few years after the war, Joshua Swan, Esq., of Stonington purchased me of my master and agreed that after I had served him a length of time named faithfully, I should be free. I served to his satisfaction and so obtained my freedom. He moved into the town of Milton, where I now reside, about forty-eight years ago. After my time expired with Esq. Swan, I married a wife. We have raised six children. Five are still living. I must be upward of eighty years of age and have been blind for many years, and, notwithstanding the aid I received from the honest industry of my children, we are still very needy and in part are supported from the benevolence of our friends. With these statements and the testimony of my character herewith presented, I humbly set my claim upon the well-known liberality of government.

Most respectfully your humble servant
Jehu Grant
his mark

Source: *John C. Dann, ed.*, The Revolution Remembered: Eyewitness Accounts of the War for Independence, *pp. 27–28.*

Because they could not control the Indians, the British regarded their native allies as a liability as well as an asset and seldom made unrestricted use of them.

Most Native Americans, however, tried at first to remain neutral, and some important groups aided the Americans. Pulled and pushed by both sides, the Iroquois Confederation split. The Mohawks and most of the other Iroquois nations, under the leadership of Thayendanegea—known as Joseph Brant to the English and Americans—sided with the British. The Oneidas and the Tuscaroras, however, joined the Americans. Some small Indian groups, like the Catawbas of South Carolina, who lived in the midst of white settlements, also cooperated with the Americans.

The War in the North, 1776–1777

The Revolutionary War can be divided into three phases. In the first, from the outbreak of fighting in 1775 to 1778, most of the important battles took place in New England, New York, New Jersey, and Pennsylvania. During these years, the Americans faced the British alone. But in 1778, France entered the war on the American side, opening the second phase of the war. Fighting in the second phase would rage from 1778 to 1781 mainly in the South, at sea, and on the western frontier. The third phase of the war, from late 1781 to 1783, saw little actual fighting. With American victory assured, attention shifted to the diplomatic maneuvering leading up to the Treaty of Paris (1783), which ended the war and recognized American independence.

The British Army Hesitates

During the first phase of the war, the British concentrated on subduing New England, the hotbed of what they saw as "rebellious principles." Replacing General Gage, the government appointed Sir William Howe as commander in chief of British forces and his brother, Richard Howe, as admiral of the naval forces in North American waters. New York City had been the headquarters of the British army during the late colonial period, and the Howes decided to make it their base of operations. To counter this move, Washington had moved his forces to New York in the spring of 1776. In August 1776, the Howes landed troops on Long Island and in the **Battle of Brooklyn Heights** quickly drove the American forces deployed there from Brooklyn Heights and back to Manhattan Island (see Map 6-3).

Following instructions to negotiate peace as well as wage war, Richard Howe then met with three envoys from Congress on Staten Island on September 11, 1776. The Howes were prepared to offer fairly generous terms but could not grant independence. The Americans would accept nothing less. So despite a fine meal of cold meat and wine, the meeting produced no substantive negotiations.

In the ensuing weeks, British forces overwhelmed Washington's forces, driving them out of Manhattan and then, moving north, clearing them from the area around the city at the **Battle of White Plains**. But the Howes were hesitant to deal a crushing blow, and the Americans were able to retreat across New Jersey into Pennsylvania. The American cause seemed lost, however; Congress fled from Philadelphia to Baltimore, and the Continental Army almost melted away. The enlistments for most of his troops expired on January 1, and Washington realized that without a success, he would soon have no army left.

On Christmas Eve, he led his forces back across the icy Delaware from Pennsylvania and, in the **Battle of Trenton**, launched an unorthodox surprise attack on a garrison of Hessian mercenaries at Trenton, New Jersey, on the morning of December 26. Still in the midst of their Christmas celebrations, the Hessians quickly surrendered. A week later, in the **Battle of Princeton**, Washington overwhelmed a British force at Princeton, New Jersey. Thereafter, Washington withdrew to winter quarters in Morristown, New Jersey, and the Howes made no further effort to pursue him. Both sides suspended operations until the spring.

"These are the times that try men's souls." So wrote Tom Paine—briefly a volunteer in the Continental Army—of these difficult months. "The summer soldier and the sunshine patriot will, in this crisis, shrink from the service of his country; but he that stands it NOW, deserves the love and thanks of man and woman."

The victories at Trenton and Princeton boosted morale and saved the American cause. But why did the Howes not annihilate the Continental Army while they had the chance? Perhaps, as a favorite Whig ditty had it, it was because Sir William Howe was "snug" abed with his mistress in New York. More significantly, the Howe brothers themselves were not entirely in favor of the war. Seeking to restore peace as well as end the rebellion, they wanted to regain loyal subjects, not alienate them. But if they had inflicted a crushing defeat on the Americans, they would have risked making them permanent enemies of British rule. In short, the British had sound political reasons for not beating the Americans too thoroughly. By the time it later became apparent that this cautious strategy was not working and the Howes were replaced with more aggressive commanders, the British had lost their best chance to win the war.

The Year of the Hangman

Contemporaries called 1777 the Year of the Hangman because the triple sevens suggested a row of gallows. Living up to its ominous name, it was indeed a crucial year for the American cause.

The British began the year by mounting a major effort to end the rebellion. Their strategy was to send a force south from Canada down the Hudson River to link up with the Howes in New York City, separate New England from the rest of the states, and

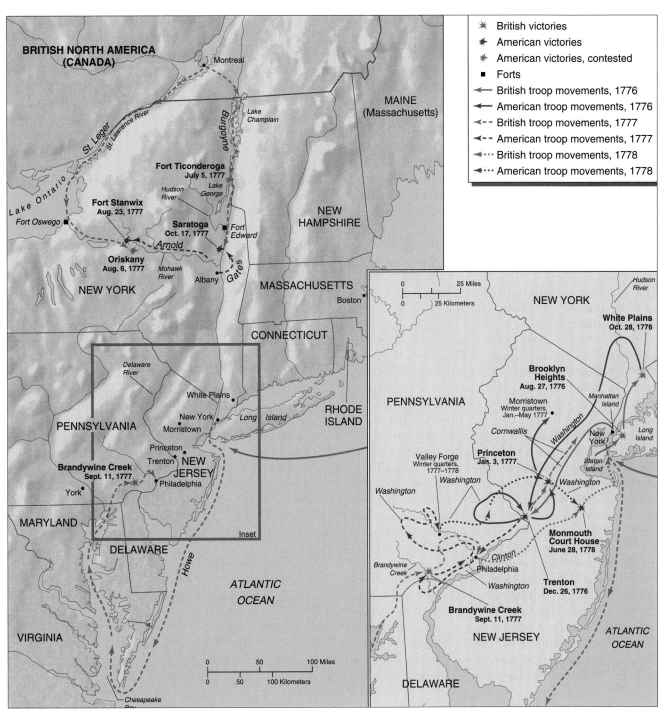

Map 6-3   The War in the North, 1776–1777
Most of the fighting between the British and Americans during the first part of the war occurred in the North, partly because British authorities assumed that the New England colonies were the most rebellious.

then crush the rebellion in that most recalcitrant region. Unfortunately, there was no effort to coordinate strategy between the forces advancing from Canada and the forces under the command of the Howes in New York. Thus in the end, poorly planned,

poorly executed, and unsupported from the South, the campaign ended in disaster for the British.

Some five thousand Redcoats and three thousand German mercenaries assembled in Canada during the winter of 1776–1777. Ravaged by disease, the troops were unable to bury their dead until the frozen ground thawed in the spring. (To amuse himself, the officer in charge of the morgue arranged the dead around a room in lifelike poses, which did nothing to calm the nerves of survivors.) Under the command of the jaunty, high-living, and popular "Gentleman Johnny" Burgoyne, the army finally set off in June with 1,500 horses hauling its heavy artillery and ponderous supply train. A second, smaller column, supported by an Indian force under Joseph Brant, set out to the west to capture an American fort near Oriskany, New York, and then join up with Burgoyne's main force.

Crossing Lake Champlain, Burgoyne's army made a splendid spectacle. Indians in lightly bobbing canoes led the way, followed by row after row of boats filled with uniformed regulars resplendent in the bright sunshine. On July 5, Burgoyne's army recaptured Fort Ticonderoga, but success eluded him after that.

Trouble began as the troops started moving overland through the woods at the southern end of the lake. Forced to clear away huge trees in its path felled by American axmen, the army crawled along at only 2 or 3 miles a day. Early in August, the column under Colonel Barry St. Leger that had been sent west from the Montreal area failed to capture the American fort near Oriskany and turned back to Canada. Burgoyne's Indian allies under Joseph Brant likewise went home. Promised reinforcements never arrived. Ten days later, a Whig militia force wiped out a force of eight hundred men that Burgoyne had sent into Vermont to round up badly needed horses.

By October 1777, Burgoyne's army was down to less than six thousand men and facing disaster. A force of nearly three thousand Continentals and nine thousand militia, commanded by General Horatio Gates, had now assembled to confront the British. The Americans exerted relentless pressure on the harassed and dispirited invaders. Unable to break through the American lines, Burgoyne surrendered to Gates following the **Battle of Saratoga** on October 17, 1777.

Burgoyne's defeat was a stunning reversal for the British. It also gave the American cause a significant boost in the eyes of foreign observers. It would prove an important factor in convincing the French, in particular, eager for a way to strike back at their old enemy, the British, to recognize America as an ally and join the fighting on the American side.

While Burgoyne was making his way to disaster, William Howe, rather than moving north to support him, was making plans to destroy Washington's army and capture Philadelphia. In July 1777, Howe's troops sailed from New York to Chesapeake Bay and from there marched on Philadelphia from the south. They met Washington's army on the banks of **Brandywine Creek**, near the Pennsylvania-Delaware border. An American teenager who fought for the first time that day recalled that some men stiffened their courage by drinking a concoction of liquor and gunpowder. The young man himself could not stomach it, but it may have worked for some of his companions. They put up a good fight before giving way with a loss of 1,200 killed or captured (twice as many as the British).

Howe occupied Philadelphia, and his men settled down in comfortable winter quarters. Congress fled to York, Pennsylvania, and the Continental Army established its own winter camp outside Philadelphia, at **Valley Forge**. Here Washington was joined by his wife, Martha, in a small stone farmhouse, surrounded by the log huts that his men built for themselves.

The Continental Army's miserable winter at Valley Forge has become legendary in American history. Suffering from cold, disease, and starvation, as many as 2,500 soldiers died. Meanwhile, some Congressmen and a few unhappy officers intrigued unsuccessfully to replace Washington with Gates as commander in chief. Yet despite the suffering of the troops, the Continental Army managed, over the course of the winter, to transform itself into a disciplined professional army. Under the watchful eye of General von Steuben, the soldiers drilled endlessly. Just before the encampment broke up in the spring, they put on an impressive demonstration of their new skills, including a precisely timed wave of massed musket volleys. Pleased observers felt that Washington at last had an army capable of meeting the British on equal terms. With the coming of spring, American prospects improved dramatically.

The War Widens, 1778–1781

Since late 1776, Benjamin Franklin and a team of American diplomats had been in Paris negotiating French support for the patriot cause. In the winter of 1777–1778, aware that a Franco-American alliance was close, Parliament belatedly tried to end the rebellion by giving the Americans everything they wanted except independence itself. A peace commission sailed to America with authorization to grant the former colonies full autonomy, including the exclusive right to tax themselves, in return for a resumption of allegiance to the crown. But France and the

United States concluded an alliance on February 6, 1778, and news of it reached America before the British commission arrived. Seeing independence within reach, Congress refused to negotiate.

Foreign intervention would transform the American Revolution into a virtual world war, engaging British forces in heavy fighting not only in North America but also in the West Indies and India. In the end, had it not been for French assistance, the American side probably would not have won the clear-cut victory it did.

The United States Gains an Ally

If the American victory at Saratoga had persuaded the French that the United States had a viable future, Washington's defeat at Brandywine Creek suggested it was a fragile one. Hoping to get even with their old enemy, Britain, the French had already been secretly supplying some aid to the United States. They now became convinced that they needed to act quickly lest further reverses force the Americans to agree to a reconciliation with Britain. The agreements they signed with the United States included both a commercial treaty and a military alliance. Both sides promised to fight together until Britain recognized the independence of the United States, and France pledged not to seek the return of lands in North America.

French entry into the war was the first step in the consolidation of a formidable alliance of European powers eager to see Britain humbled and to gain trading rights in the former British colonies. In turn, France persuaded Spain to declare war on Britain in June 1779. Unlike France, Spain never recognized the independence of the United States and would give it only minimal financial aid. Spain did, however, contribute important logistical support. Much of the salt used to preserve American soldiers' provisions came from Spanish possessions. American agents also purchased other supplies in Spanish New Orleans, and American privateers used New Orleans as a base. More important, the Spanish fleet augmented the naval power of the countries arrayed against Great Britain.

Meanwhile, Catherine the Great of Russia suggested that European powers form a **League of Armed Neutrality** to protect their trade with the United States and other warring countries against British interference. Denmark and Sweden soon joined; Austria, the Netherlands, Portugal, Prussia, and Sicily eventually followed. Britain, however, quickly went to war with Holland, ostensibly over another issue (to avoid war with the League), but really to cut off Dutch trade with the United States.

Great Britain thus found itself nearly completely isolated and even, briefly, threatened with invasion. In the spring of 1779, a joint Franco-Spanish fleet tried to ferry fifty thousand French troops across the English Channel but was foiled by a storm. These threats did not frighten the British leaders into suing for peace. On the contrary, they inspired a wave of patriotism that swelled enlistments in the armed forces. But facing challenges on a worldwide scale, British officials were forced to make several important changes in policy and strategy.

Accordingly, as early in the spring of 1778, the British replaced the Howes with a tough new commander, Sir Henry Clinton, instructing him to detach some of his troops to attack the French West Indies. To replace them, Clinton sought closer cooperation with Britain's Indian and loyalist allies. Knowing he now faced a serious French threat, Clinton began consolidating his forces. He evacuated Philadelphia and pulled his troops slowly back across New Jersey to New York.

On June 28, 1778, Washington caught up with the British and engaged them at the **Battle of Monmouth Court House**. The day was hot and the battle hard-fought. For a while, it looked as if the now well-trained Americans might win, but a mix-up in orders cost Washington the victory. This inconclusive battle proved to be the last major engagement in the North for the rest of the war. Clinton withdrew to New York, and Continental troops occupied the hills along the Hudson Valley north of the city. The war shifted to other fronts.

Fighting on the Frontier and at Sea

Native Americans called Kentucky "a dark and bloody ground," a designation that took on added meaning when Indians began raiding the territory in 1777 on British instructions. The nerve center for coordinating these attacks was the British post of Detroit, and the Americans accordingly made plans to capture it. Two expeditions from Pittsburgh in 1778 failed completely. A third, under Virginian George Rogers Clark, although it never reached Detroit, was more successful (see Map 6-4). In July 1778 Clark's force of 175 frontiersmen captured three key British settlements in the Mississippi Valley (**Kaskaskia**, Cahokia, and Vincennes). The latter fell to the British, but Clark soon recaptured it. These successes may have strengthened American claims to the West at the end of the war.

Blood also ran on the Pennsylvania and upstate New York frontiers. In the summer of 1778, a British force of one hundred loyalists and five hundred Indians struck settlers in north-central

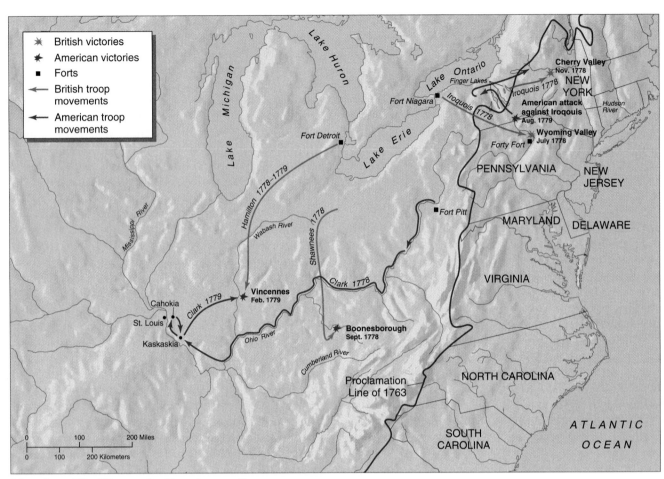

Map 6-4   The War on the Frontier, 1778–1779
*Significant battles in the Mississippi Valley and the frontiers of the seaboard states added to the
ferocity of the fighting and strengthened some American claims to western lands.*

Pennsylvania's **Wyoming Valley**. After the Americans'
Forty Fort surrendered on July 4, raiders killed the
wounded and fleeing defenders. A similar mix of
attackers in November 1778 burned farmsteads and
slaughtered civilians at **Cherry Valley**, New York.
Both raids became the stuff of legends and stimulated equally savage reprisals against the Indians.
Congress authorized an expedition against the Iroquois, and in the late summer of 1779, more than
four thousand Continental soldiers and state militia
swept through the Finger Lakes region of New York,
destroying forty-one Indian villages.

    Anglo-American clashes at sea had begun in
1775, shortly after the Battles of Lexington and Concord, and would continue until the end of the war as
Americans struggled to break the British navy's blockade. Great Britain was the preeminent sea power of
the age, and the United States never came close to
matching it, in either the number or the size of its
ships. But Congress did its best to challenge the

British at sea. In 1775, it authorized the construction
of thirteen frigates—medium-sized, relatively fast
ships, mounting thirty-two guns—as well as the purchase of several merchant vessels for conversion to
warships. In contrast, the Royal Navy in 1779 had
more than a hundred large and heavily armed "ships
of the line." The Americans therefore engaged in
what was essentially a guerrilla war at sea. Their naval
flag, appropriately, pictured a rattlesnake and bore
the motto "Don't Tread on Me."

    The country's first naval hero, Scottish-born
John Paul Jones, was primarily a hit-and-run raider.
Originally named only John Paul, he had gone to
sea at age 12. He took the name Jones as an alias
after he killed a fellow sailor during a mutiny. In
the colonies by chance when the war broke out, this
adventurer offered his services to Congress. As commander of the new frigate *Ranger*, it was Jones who
brought news of the American victory at Saratoga to
France in early 1777. After delivering the news—

which helped Franklin clinch the alliance with France—Jones raided the British coast, inspiring local panic.

Franklin helped secure Jones an old French merchant ship, which he outfitted for war and renamed the *Bon Homme Richard* in honor of Franklin's famous *Poor Richard's Almanac*. After capturing seventeen enemy vessels, he encountered the formidable H.M.S. *Serapis* in the North Sea on September 23, 1779. Completely outgunned, Jones brought the *Bon Homme Richard* close enough to make his small arms fire more effective. Asked by the British if he was surrendering, Jones gave the legendary reply, "I have not yet begun to fight." Lashing the two ships together, Jones and his men battled the crew of the *Serapis* for more than four hours, much of it by moonlight. Finally, the *Serapis* surrendered. Jones's crew took possession of the British vessel and left the crippled *Bon Homme Richard* to sink.

Congress and the individual states supplemented America's naval forces by commissioning individual sea captains to outfit their merchant vessels with guns and act as privateers. In effect legalized pirates, these privateers preyed on British shipping. They sold the goods they seized and divided the proceeds among their crews according to rank. The crews of captured vessels became prisoners of war. Successful privateering could bring wealth but required stealth and speed. One particularly fast vessel cruised off New York towing a buoy to make itself look like a lumbering merchantman under full sail. Once within range of a potential prize, the crew cut away the buoy and took the cannons out from under wraps. Such tactics paid off. Some two thousand American privateers captured more than six hundred British ships and forced the British navy to spread itself thin doing convoy duty.

The Land War Moves South

During the first three years of the war, the British had made little effort to mobilize what they believed to be considerable loyalist strength in the South. In 1778, however, facing a threat from France and with their forces in the North concentrated and inactive, they gave southern loyalists a key role in a new strategy for subduing the rebellion. After first sending Redcoats sweeping through a large area, they would leave behind a Tory militia to reestablish loyalty to the crown and suppress local Whigs. The British hoped by this strategy to recapture everything from Georgia to Virginia; they would deal with New England later.

The British southern strategy began to unfold in November 1778, when General Clinton dispatched

This engraving, published in London in 1779, shows an apocryphal incident during the battle in which John Paul Jones's ship Bon Homme Richard *defeated the British* Serapis. *During the fighting, Jones supposedly shot an American sailor who attempted to lower the ship's flag as a sign of surrender; actually Jones only knocked him down with a pistol. Legend (and the artist) may have confused this incident with another earlier one—while Jones was still a Scotsman (note the bonnet)—in which Jones did kill a mutineer.*

Paul Jones Shooting a Sailor. Color engraving from the Olds Collection #366, no negative number. Collection of The New-York Historical Society.

3,500 troops to take control of Georgia (see Map 6-5). Meeting only light resistance, they quickly seized **Savannah** and Augusta. Indeed, enough inhabitants seemed happy to have the British back that the old colonial government was restored under civilian control. After their initial success, however, the British did suffer some serious setbacks. The Spanish entered the war and seized British outposts on the Mississippi and Mobile Rivers. And in February 1779, at the **Battle of Kettle Creek**, South Carolina's Whig militia decimated a loyalist militia contingent that was trying to fight its way from the North Carolina backcountry to Georgia to join up with British troops.

But the Americans could not beat the British army. In late September and early October 1779, a combined force of 5,500 American and French troops, supported by French warships, laid siege to Savannah. Moving too slowly to encircle the city, they allowed British reinforcements to get through. Then,

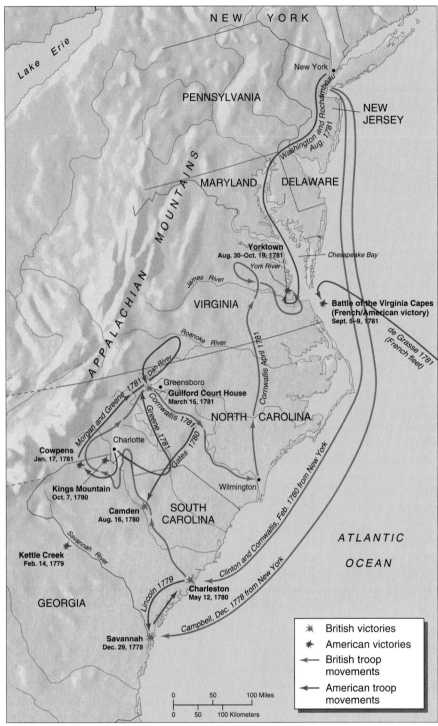

Map 6-5 *The War in the South, 1778–1781*
During the latter part of the war, most of the major engagements occurred in the South. British forces won most of the early ones, but could not control the immense territory involved and eventually surrendered at Yorktown.

The way was now open for the British to attack Charleston, the military key to the Lower South. In December 1779, Clinton sailed through storm-battered seas from New York to the Carolina coast with about nine thousand troops. In the **Battle of Charleston**, he encircled the city, trapping the patriot forces inside. On May 12, 1780, more than five thousand Continentals and militia laid down their arms—the worst American defeat of the war and the largest single loss of United States troops to a foreign army until the surrender of American forces in the Philippines to Japan in 1942.

The British were now poised to sweep all the South before them. Local Whigs, thinking the Revolution over, offered little resistance to Redcoats striking into the Carolina backcountry. At the South Carolina–North Carolina border, British troops under Colonel Banastre Tarleton overwhelmed a detachment of 350 Virginia Continentals trying to retreat homeward after coming too late to Charleston's aid. When the Continentals offered to surrender, Tarleton slaughtered most of them. So complete did the British success seem that Clinton tried to force the American troops whom he had taken prisoner to resume their duties as British subjects and join the loyalist militia. Thinking that matters were now well in hand, Clinton sailed back to New York, leaving the southern troops under the command of Lord Cornwallis.

Clinton's confidence that the South had returned securely to the loyalist camp was premature. Atrocities like Tarleton's slaughter of the Virginians inflamed anti-British feelings. And Clinton's decision to force former rebels into the loyalist militia backfired, infuriating real loyalists—who saw their enemies getting off lightly—as well as Whigs. Atrocities and reprisals mounted on both sides as Whigs continued to defy

impatient to get their ships away from the hurricane-prone coast, the French forced the Americans to launch a premature assault on the city on October 9. The assault failed, and the French sailed off.

SUMMARY

IMPORTANT BATTLES OF THE REVOLUTIONARY WAR

	Battle	*Date*	*Outcome*
Early Fighting	Lexington and Concord, Massachusetts	Apr. 19, 1775	Contested
	Fort Ticonderoga, New York	May 10, 1775	American victory
	Breeds Hill ("Bunker Hill"), Boston, Massachusetts	June 17, 1775	Contested
	Great Bridge, Virginia	Dec. 9, 1775	American victory
	Quebec, Canada	Dec. 31, 1775	British repulse American assault
	Moore's Creek Bridge, North Carolina	Feb. 27. 1776	American victory
The War in the North	Brooklyn Heights, New York	Aug. 27, 1776	British victory
	White Plains, New York	Oct. 28, 1776	British victory
	Trenton, New Jersey	Dec. 26, 1776	American victory
	Princeton, New Jersey	Jan. 3, 1777	American victory
	Brandywine Creek, Pennsylvania	Sept. 11, 1777	British victory (opened way for British to take Philadelphia)
	Saratoga, New York	Sept. 19 and Oct. 17, 1777	American victory (helped persuade France to form an alliance with United States)
	Monmouth Court House, New Jersey	June 28, 1778	Contested
The War on the Frontier	Wyoming Valley, Pennsylvania	June and July 1778	British victory
	Kaskaskia and Cahokia, Illinois; Vincennes, Indiana	July 4, 1778–Feb. 23, 1779	American victories strengthen claims to Mississippi Valley
	Cherry Valley, New York	Nov. 11, 1778	British victory
The War in the South	Savannah, Georgia	Dec. 29, 1778	British victory (took control of Georgia)
	Kettle Creek, Georgia	Feb. 14, 1779	American victory
	Savannah, Georgia	Sept. 3–Oct. 28, 1779	British victory opened way for British to take Charleston
	Charleston, South Carolina	Feb. 11–May 12, 1780	British victory
	Camden, South Carolina	Aug. 16, 1780	British victory
	Kings Mountain, South Carolina	Oct. 7, 1780	American victory
	Cowpens, South Carolina	Jan. 17, 1781	American victory
	Guilford Court House, North Carolina	Mar. 15, 1781	Contested
	Yorktown, Virginia	Aug. 30–Oct. 19, 1781	American victory (persuaded Britain to end the war)

British authority. "Tarleton's Quarter" and "a Georgia parole" (a bullet in the back) became Whig euphemisms for "take no prisoners."

American Counterattacks

In the summer of 1780, Congress dispatched a substantial Continental force to the South under General Horatio Gates, the hero of Saratoga. Local patriots flocked to join him. But Gates was reckless. Pushing through North Carolina, his men tried to subsist on green corn. Weakened by diarrhea, they blundered into Cornwallis's British army near **Camden**, South Carolina, on August 16, and suffered a complete rout. More than one thousand Americans were killed or wounded and many captured. Gates—transformed from the hero of Saratoga to the goat of Camden—fled to Hillsborough, North Carolina.

American morale revived on October 7, 1780, when "over mountain men" (militia) from Virginia, western North and South Carolina, and what is today eastern Tennessee inflicted a defeat on the British at **Kings Mountain**, South Carolina. And in December 1780, Nathanael Greene replaced the discredited Gates, bringing competent leadership to the Continentals in the South.

The daring and resourceful Greene realized he would need an unorthodox strategy to defeat Cornwallis's larger army of seasoned professional troops. He divided his forces, keeping roughly half with him in northeastern South Carolina and sending the other half westward under General Daniel Morgan. Cornwallis ordered Tarleton to pursue Morgan's troops, who retreated northward until they reached an open area in South Carolina called Hannah's Cowpens. There Morgan rallied his men, reportedly inspiring them with the sight of his scarred back; he had been flogged by order of a British court martial during the French and Indian War. At the **Battle of Cowpens** on January 17, 1781, Morgan cleverly posted his least reliable troops, the militia, in the front line, telling them to run after firing two volleys. When Tarleton attacked, the militia fired and withdrew. Thinking that the American ranks had broken, the Redcoats charged—straight into devastating fire from Morgan's Continentals. Tarleton escaped, but his reputation for invincibility had been destroyed.

Cornwallis now badly needed a battlefield victory. Burning his army's excess baggage, he set off in hot pursuit of Greene and Morgan, who had rejoined forces. The Continentals had the advantage of knowing the country, which was laced with rain-swollen rivers. Greene's officers often arranged to have boats

waiting at the deeper crossings. Finally, on February 13, 1781, Greene's tired men crossed the Dan River into Virginia, and Cornwallis gave up the chase, marching his equally exhausted Redcoats southward. To his surprise, Cornwallis now found himself pursued—though cautiously, to be sure—by Greene. On March 15, the opposing forces met at **Guilford Court House** (near present-day Greensboro, North Carolina) in one of the war's bloodiest battles. At one point, with the two sides tangled in hand-to-hand combat, the Americans drove the British back. To blunt the onslaught, Cornwallis fired grapeshot directly into the melee, mowing down friend and foe alike. Thanks to such tactics, the British still held the field at the end of the day. But, as one Englishman observed, "another such victory would destroy the British Army." Cornwallis had to retreat to the coastal town of Wilmington, North Carolina, to rest and regroup. Abandoning his most seriously wounded men, he carried the rest back in ambulance wagons, their broken bones poking through their wounds as they bounced along rutted roads.

By the late summer of 1781, British fortunes were waning in the Lower South. The Redcoats held only the larger towns and the immediately surrounding countryside. With their superior staying power, they won most major engagements, but these victories brought them no lasting gain. As General Greene observed of the Americans, "We fight, get beat, and rise and fight again." When the enemy pressed him too hard, Greene retreated out of reach, advancing again as the British withdrew.

Patriot guerrilla forces, led by such colorful figures as "Swamp Fox" Francis Marion, disrupted British communications between their Charleston headquarters and outlying garrisons. The loyalist militias that the British had hoped would pacify the countryside proved unequal to the task. Whig militiamen had often driven out any loyalists before a British sweep. And those who did welcome the British found themselves the targets of Whig retaliation once the Redcoats had left. Thus although Greene never whipped the Redcoats outright, his campaign was a strategic success. The British could not hold what they had taken; the Americans had time on their side.

Disappointed and frustrated, Cornwallis decided to conquer Virginia to cut off Greene's line of supply and to destroy Whig resolve. British forces, including units commanded by turncoat Benedict Arnold, had already been raiding the state. Cornwallis marched north to join them, reaching Yorktown, Virginia, during the summer of 1781.

The final military show-down of the war was at hand. By now, five thousand French soldiers were in America ready to fight alongside the Continentals, and a large French fleet in the West Indies had orders to support an attack on the British in North America. Faking preparations for an assault on British-occupied New York, the Continentals (commanded by Washington) and the French headed for the Chesapeake. Cornwallis and his six thousand Redcoats soon found themselves besieged behind their fortifications at **Yorktown** by 8,800 Americans and 7,800 French. A French naval victory gave the allies temporary command of the waters around Yorktown. Cornwallis had nowhere to go, and Clinton—still in New York—could not reinforce him quickly enough. On October 19, 1781, the British army surrendered. The defeated men filed between rows of American and French troops to lay down their arms while a British band played mournfully a tune reputedly called "The World Turned Upside Down." When he learned the news in London, the British prime minister, Lord North, took it like "a ball in his breast." "It is all over," he groaned.

The surrender of Lord Cornwallis at Yorktown on October 19, 1781, led to the British decision to withdraw from the war. Cornwallis, who claimed to be ill, absented himself from the ceremony and is not in the picture. Washington, who is astride the horse under the American flag, designated General Benjamin Lincoln (on the white horse in the center) as the one to accept the submission of a subordinate British officer. John Trumbull, who painted The Battle of Bunker Hill *and some three hundred other scenes from the Revolutionary War, finished this painting while he was in London about fifteen years after the events depicted. A large copy of the work now hangs in the rotunda of the United States Capitol in Washington, D.C.*

Surrender of Lord Cornwallis at Yorktown, by John Trumbull (American, 1756–1843). Oil on canvas, 20⅞ x 30⅞ in.

The American Victory, 1782–1783

The British surrender at Yorktown marked the end of major fighting in North America, though skirmishes continued for another year. In April 1782, the Royal Navy defeated the French fleet in the Caribbean, strengthening the British bargaining position. George III had insisted on continuing the war for so long because he feared that conceding American independence would threaten British rule in Canada and the West Indies. But the majority in Parliament now felt that enough men and money had been wasted trying to keep the Americans within the empire. In March 1782, the king accepted Lord North's resignation and appointed Lord Rockingham as prime minister, with a mandate to make peace.

The Peace of Paris

The peace negotiations, which took place in Paris, were lengthy. The Americans demanded independence, handsome territorial concessions—Franklin, the senior American negotiator, asked for all of Canada—and access to the rich, British-controlled fishing grounds in the North Atlantic. The new British prime minister, Lord Shelburne (Rockingham had died in 1782), was inclined to be conciliatory. By making concessions, he hoped to help British merchants recover their lost colonial trade. The French had achieved their objective—to weaken the British—and now wanted out of an increasingly costly world-wide war. Spain had not yet won its most important goal, the recovery of British-held Gibraltar, and thus gave the Americans no support at all.

The American negotiators, Franklin, John Adams, and John Jay, masterfully threaded their way among these conflicting interests. With good reason, they feared that the French and Spanish would strike

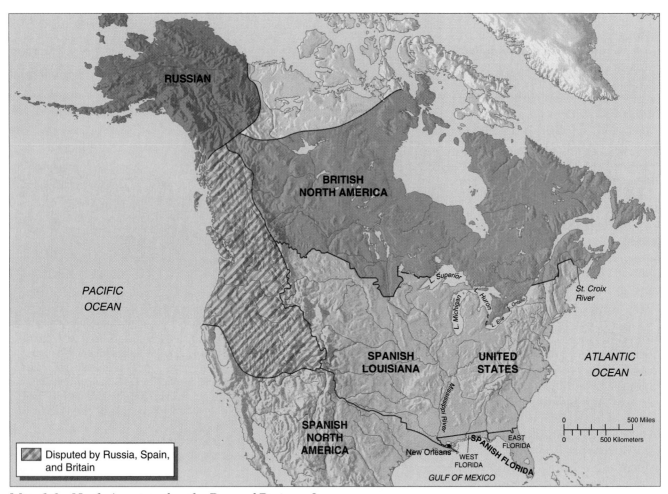

Map 6-6 North America after the Peace of Paris, 1783
*The results of the American Revolution redrew the map of North America, confining Britain
to Canada and giving the United States most of the area east of the Mississippi River, though
Spain controlled its mouth for most of the next twenty years.*

a bargain with the British at the expense of the United States—one that might, for example, confine the new country to a narrow coastal strip or allow Britain to retain areas such as New York City and Charleston, which its troops still occupied. As a result, the Americans disregarded Congress's instructions to avoid making peace unilaterally. Instead, they secretly worked out their own arrangements with the British that would meet Shelburne's objective of restoring Anglo-American commercial ties. On November 30, 1782, the negotiators signed a preliminary Anglo-American treaty of peace. Its terms were embodied in the final **Peace of Paris**, signed by all the belligerents on September 3, 1783.

The Peace of Paris gave the United States nearly everything it sought except Canada (which was never really a serious issue). Great Britain acknowl-

edged that the United States was "free, sovereign and independent." The northern boundary of the new nation extended west from the St. Croix River (which separated Maine from Nova Scotia) past the Great Lakes to what were thought to be the headwaters of the Mississippi River (see Map 6-6). The Mississippi itself—down to just north of New Orleans—formed the western border. Spain acquired the provinces of East and West Florida from Britain. This territory included a substantial chunk of present-day Louisiana, Mississippi, Alabama, and Georgia. It blocked the United States from access to the Gulf of Mexico and would be a source of diplomatic friction for years.

Several provisions of the treaty addressed important economic issues. Adams, on behalf of his fellow New Englanders, insisted on a provision granting American fishermen access to the waters off eastern Canada. The treaty also required that British forces, on quitting American soil, were to leave behind all American-owned property, including slaves. Another provision declared existing debts between citizens of Britain and the United States still valid, giving British merchants hope of collecting on their American accounts. Congress was to "recommend" that the states restore rights and property taken from loyalists during the war. Nothing was said about the slave trade, which Jay had hoped to ban.

The Components of Success

The War for Independence was over. In December 1783, the last British transports put to sea with troops evacuated from New York. Despite the provisions of the peace treaty and the objections of southern planters, about three thousand African-Americans went with them. General Guy Carleton, who had replaced Clinton as commander in chief after Yorktown, agreed to keep a list of these blacks, but he refused to renege on British promises of freedom for slaves who fled rebel owners. (Carleton's list survived and has recently been published.)

Washington's Continental Army had already disbanded in the summer of 1783 (but not, as we have seen, before a dispute over pay came close to provoking a military coup). On December 4, the American commander said an emotional farewell to his officers at New York City's Fraunces Tavern, and on December 23, at Annapolis, Maryland, he resigned his commission to Congress. Like the legendary citizen-soldier Cincinnatus, who after defending the ancient Roman Republic gave up his power and went back to plowing his land, Washington went home to Mount Vernon. By now he had won the respect of friend and foe alike. Only a natural genius, Britons said, could have accomplished what he did. How else could one explain the victory of ragtag provincials over the world's greatest military and naval power?

Washington's leadership was only one of the reasons why the Americans won the Revolutionary War. French assistance played a crucial role. Some historians even contend that without the massive infusion of French men and money in 1781, the Revolution would have failed. The British also contributed heavily to their own downfall. Their fatal mistakes included bureaucratic inefficiency, hesitant command, and, worst of all, overconfidence. British authorities consistently underestimated the enormous difficulty of waging war 3,000 miles from home in an era of slow and uncertain communications. The people they sought to conquer were sparsely distributed over an area that stretched more than 1,500 miles from Maine to Georgia. There was no natural center whose capture would severely cripple the rest of the country. British forces occupied, at one time or another, most of the important seaports and state capitals—Boston, New York, Philadelphia, Charleston, and Savannah—but patriot forces driven from these centers could simply regroup in another location. Finally, Great Britain had tried to solve a political problem by military means. An occupying army is far more likely to alienate people than secure their goodwill.

Yet it took 175,000 to 200,000 soldiers—Continentals and militia troops—to prevent Great Britain from recovering the colonies. Of these, some 7,000—like the nameless soldier recalled at the beginning of this chapter—died in battle for their "country and for its just cause." Perhaps 10,000 more succumbed to disease while on active duty, another 8,500 died while prisoners of war, and nearly 1,500 were reported missing in action. More than 8,000 were wounded and survived. Those who served in the Continental Army, probably more than half of all who fought, served the longest and saw the most action. Their casualty rate—30 to 40 percent—may have been the highest of any war in which the United States has been engaged.

War and Society, 1775–1783

Regular combatants were not the only ones to suffer during the struggle for independence. Eight years of warfare also produced profound dislocations throughout American society. Military service wrenched families apart, sporadic raids by each side brought the war home to vast numbers of people, and everyone endured economic disruptions. As a forge of nationhood, the Revolution tested all Americans, whatever their standing as citizens.

The Women's War

Everywhere women had to see their husbands, sons, brothers, and fiancés go off to fight and die. Like Mary Silliman in Connecticut, they waited, trying to stay calm until they knew "what tidings God" had for them. At first, with spirits still running high, Mary's letters to her husband, Selleck, reveal an affectionate lightheartedness. "These cold nights make me shudder for you," she wrote, adding "Oh, King George, what hardships does thy tyranny put thy late subjects to!" Selleck responded with similarly suggestive banter. Later the couple's letters grew less playful. Mending his coat after a battle, Mary found a spent British musket ball that had been deliberately deformed to make it harder to remove from a wound, and she lost whatever ambivalence she had felt about independence. Then her husband was captured. The daily round of domestic duties helped to keep her going, but his extended absence increased her burdens and enlarged her responsibilities.

Such circumstances elevated women's domestic status. Couples began referring to "our"—not "my" or "your"—property. Wives frequently grew more knowledgeable about a family's financial condition than long-absent husbands. "What shall I do my Dearest? I wish I had Your Advice," wrote Selleck Silliman to his wife after he had been released from captivity.

Women also assumed new public roles during the conflict. Some nursed the wounded. More wove cloth for uniforms. The Ladies' Association of Philadelphia was established in 1780 to demonstrate women's patriotism and raise money to buy shirts for the army. Though women might not be able to march "to glory by the same path as the Men," wrote the association's founder, "we should at least equal and sometimes surpass them in our love for the public good." Similar associations formed in other states.

Despite their increasing private responsibilities and new public activities, however, it did not occur to most women to encroach very far on traditional male prerogatives. When John Adams's wife,

Abigail, urged him and the Second Continental Congress to "Remember the Ladies," she was not expecting equal political rights. What she wanted, rather, was some legal protections for women and recognition of their value and need for autonomy in the domestic sphere. "Remember," she cautioned, "all Men would be Tyrants if they could." Why not, then, make it impossible for "the vicious and lawless" to abuse them with impunity? "I will never consent to have our sex considered in an inferior point of light," she wrote.

Republican ideology, responding to the changing status of women, assigned them a role that was at once exalted and subordinate. It was their job to nurture wise, virtuous, and public-spirited men. It would be this view of women that would prevail in the post-Revolutionary era.

Effect of the War on African-Americans and Native Americans

In the northern states, where slavery was already economically marginal and where blacks were welcome as volunteers in the Continental Army, the Revolutionary War helped bring an end to slavery, although it remained legal there for some time (see Chapter 7). In the South, however, slavery was integral to the economy, and white planters viewed it as crucial to their postwar recovery. Thus although British efforts to recruit blacks brought freedom to thousands and temporarily undermined slavery in the South, the war ultimately strengthened the institution, especially in the Carolinas and Georgia. Of the African-Americans who left with

American soldiers at Yorktown in 1781 as drawn by a young officer in the French army, Jean-Baptiste-Antoine de Verger. The African-American on the left is an infantryman of the First Rhode Island Regiment; the next a musketeer, the third, with the fringed jacket, a rifleman. The man on the right is a Continental artilleryman, holding a lighted match used to fire cannons.

the British at the end of the war, many, both slave and free, went to the West Indies. Others settled in Canada, and some eventually went back to Africa, where Britain established the colony of Sierra Leone for them.

Survivors among the approximately thirteen thousand Native Americans who fought for the British did not have the option of leaving with them at the end of the war. How many died during the war is not known, but certainly many did. Their families and their communities also paid a high price. The Americans repeatedly invaded the Cherokees' homeland in the southern Appalachian Mountains and ravaged the Iroquois country in western New York. They also attacked the Shawnees of Ohio. Where they went, death and desolation followed. As one Cherokee chief reported, so many frontiersmen fell on his people that "there was no withstanding them, they dyed their hands in the blood of many of our Women and children, burnt seventeen towns, destroyed all our provisions," and spread famine across the land.

With the peace treaty of 1783, Britain surrendered its territory east of the Mississippi, shocking and infuriating the Native Americans living there. They had not surrendered, and none of them had been at the negotiations in Paris. The Iroquois told a British commander that if the English really "had basely betrayed them by pretending to give up their Country to the Americans without their Consent, or Consulting them, it was an Act of Cruelty and injustice that Christians only were capable of doing." With the Americans now claiming their country by conquest, the Revolutionary War was a disaster for most Native Americans.

Economic Disruption

The British and American armies both needed enormous quantities of supplies. This heavy demand disrupted the normal distribution of goods and drove up real prices seven- or eightfold. The widespread use of depreciating paper money by the American side amplified this rise in prices and triggered severe inflation.

When the British did not simply seize what they needed, they paid for it in hard currency—gold and silver. American commanders, in contrast, had to rely on paper money because Congress and the states had almost no hard currency at their disposal. The continental dollar, however, steadily declined in value, and by March 1780, Congress was forced to admit officially that it was worthless. (The popular

expression "not worth a continental" suggests that the public had long since reached this conclusion.) Thus not surprisingly, American farmers and merchants, whatever their political opinions, sometimes sold food to the British while their own forces went hungry.

Necessity, not folly, drove Congress and the states to rely on the printing press. Rather than alienate citizens by immediately raising taxes to pay for the war, the states printed paper money supposedly redeemable by future tax revenues. Because the quantity of this paper money rose faster than the supply of goods and services, prices skyrocketed and the value of the money plunged. By April 1779, as Washington commented, "a wagon load of money will scarcely purchase a wagon load of provisions." Savvy people tried to spend money before its value could drop further, whereas those who had salable commodities like grain tended to hoard them in the hope that the price would go even higher. Prices also climbed much faster than wages, leaving many working people impoverished. As always happens in times of severe inflation, people resorted to bartering and demanded price-fixing laws. But often there was nothing to barter, and price controls never worked for long.

The rampant inflation was demoralizing and divisive. Lucky speculators and unscrupulous profiteers grew rich while ordinary and patriotic people suffered. These conditions sparked more than thirty protest demonstrations. In October 1779, frustrated Philadelphia militiamen marched on the house of a local Whig leader, demanding better enforcement of price controls. The confrontation left six people dead but otherwise achieved little. Freebooters—rovers in search of plunder—sailed Long Island Sound in boats with names like *Retrieve My Losses,* ostensibly to harry the British but all too often to trade with them.

As usual, war and its deprivations brought out both the best and the worst in human nature. In September 1781, turncoat Benedict Arnold led a British raid against New London and Groton, Connecticut. Not only did the demoralized local militia fail to help the garrison at one of the American forts as the British overran and slaughtered them, but they also took advantage of the chaos to plunder the towns themselves, leaving wounded survivors to their own devices. Similarly shameful incidents were repeated elsewhere.

The successful outcome of the war and the stable peace that followed suggest that most

Americans somehow managed to cope. But during the last years of the conflict, their economic and psychological reserves ran low. The total real wealth of private individuals declined by an average of 0.5 percent annually from 1774 to 1805, even with the returning prosperity of the 1790s. Such statistics suggest the true economic cost of the War for Independence. And the atrocities committed on both sides provide nearly as accurate an indicator of the conflict's psychological cost.

The Price of Victory

Most American and British commanders tried to keep hostilities "civilized"—if such a characterization can ever be applied to a war—but even so, discipline sometimes broke down among regular troops. Controlling militias or civilians acting on their own was even more difficult, demonstrating once again that civil wars and guerrilla struggles often rank among the worst of human conflicts. Residents of contested areas near British-occupied cities such as New York and Charleston lived in almost constant danger. Their plight emerges starkly from an incident in New Jersey in 1779. A roving Tory band knocked on the door of a Whig militiaman. Entering his house, they announced that he was a dead man. Drinking his liquor and terrorizing his wife, they fell to arguing about how to execute him until one of the intruders resolved the dispute by shooting him. Whigs could be equally brutal. Late in the war, British sympathizers in the Lower South compiled a list of more than three hundred loyalists who had been massacred by Whigs—some, the survivors claimed, while they slept.

Although the British were probably the worse offenders, both sides burned, plundered, and murdered. One can see the results in a returning refugee's description of the area around Beaufort, South Carolina, in the early 1780s:

> All was desolation. . . . Robberies and murders are often committed on the public roads. The people that remain have been peeled, pillaged, and plundered. Poverty, want, and hardship appear in almost every countenance . . . , and the morals of the people are almost entirely extirpated.

Not surprisingly, Americans were in a hypercritical mood as the war ended. They had suffered so much that, as one northerner observed, if "God Almighty placed [the archangel] Gabriel at the head of our affairs, they would find fault with his administration."

Conclusion

Despite the devastation and divisiveness of the war, many people in Europe and the United States were convinced that it represented something momentous. The *Annual Register,* an influential British magazine reflecting respectable opinion, commented accurately in 1783 that the American Revolution

> has already overturned those favourite systems of policy and commerce, both in the old and in the new world, which the wisdom of the ages, and the power of the greatest nations, had in vain endeavored to render permanent; and it seems to have laid the seeds of still greater revolutions in the history and mutual relations of mankind.

Americans, indeed, had fired a shot heard round the world. Thanks in part to its heavy investment in the American Revolution, France suffered a grave financial crisis in the late 1780s. This in turn ushered in the political crisis that culminated in the French Revolution of 1789. The American Revolution helped inspire among French people (including soldiers returning from service in America) an intense yearning for an end to arbitrary government and undeserved social inequalities. Liberty also proved infectious to thousands of German troops who had come to America as mercenaries but elected to stay as free citizens after the war was over. Once prosperous but distant provinces of a far-flung empire, the North American states had become an independent confederation, a grand experiment in republicanism whose fate mattered to enlightened men and women throughout the Western world. In his written farewell to the rank and file of his troops at the end of October 1783, Washington maintained that "the enlarged prospects of happiness, opened by the confirmation of our independence and sovereignty, almost exceed the power of description." He urged those who had fought with him to maintain their "strong attachments to the union" and "prove themselves not less virtuous and useful as citizens, than they have been persevering and victorious as soldiers." The work of securing the promise of the American Revolution, Washington knew, would now shift from the battlefield to the political arena.

Review Questions

1. Who were the loyalists, and how many of them were there? What attempts did the British and Americans make in 1775 to avert war? Why did these steps fail?

2. What actions did the Second Continental Congress take in 1775 and 1776? Why did it choose George Washington as the commander of its army? Why was he a good choice?

3. Why did Congress declare independence in July 1776? How did Americans justify their claim to independence?

4. What was republicanism, and why was the enthusiasm that it inspired insufficient to win the war?

5. What were the chief characteristics of the British and American armies?

6. Why were most of the early battles fought in the northern states? Why did the British not crush the Americans immediately? Why did France decide to enter the war as an ally of the United States? What effect did French entry into the war have on British strategy?

7. Why did the initial British victories in the South not win the war for them? Why did the United States ultimately win? What did it obtain by winning?

8. What were the effects of the war on American society? What impact did it have on the status of women? On the lives of African-Americans? Native Americans? What was the price of victory—for the victors and for the vanquished? What were the immediate results of the American victory?

Recommended Reading

Joy D. Buel and Richard Buel Jr., *The Way of Duty: A Woman and Her Family in Revolutionary America* (1984). This is a readable and unusually full biography of Mary Fish of Connecticut, who lived from 1736 to 1818. Her experiences during the Revolutionary War while her husband, Selleck Silliman, was a prisoner of the British have become the subject of a good movie, *Mary Silliman's War* (1993).

Stephen Conway, *The War of American Independence, 1775–1783* (1995). This short, accessible account emphasizes the degree to which the American Revolution was the first modern war.

John C. Dann, ed., *The Revolution Remembered: Eyewitness Accounts of the War for Independence* (1980). This collection of seventy-nine narratives by veterans seeking pensions for their Revolutionary War service is sometimes poignant and frequently illuminating.

Robert Graves, *Sergeant Lamb's America* (1940, 1962). Based on the real Sergeant Lamb's account of his experiences during the Revolutionary War, this historical novel represents a distinguished English literary figure's attempt to understand what he believed to be "the most important single event of modern times." A sequel, *Proceed, Sergeant Lamb* (1941), continues Lamb's story.

John S. Pancake, *1777, the Year of the Hangman* (1977). This lively account of Britain's blunders in a crucial year of the war is full of good anecdotes even if it cannot always explain the behavior of decision makers.

John Shy, *A People Numerous and Armed: Reflections on the Military Struggle for American Independence* (1990). This collection of essays on various aspects of the American Revolution by a perceptive military historian is full of interesting ideas.

Russell F. Weigley, *The Partisan War: The South Carolina Campaign of 1780–1782* (1970). This short, stimulating account of the American recovery of the Lower South takes "the perspective of our recent insights into unconventional war" and the communist victory in Vietnam.

Additional Sources

The Outbreak of War and the Declaration of Independence

Robert M. Calhoon, *The Loyalists in Revolutionary America, 1760–1781* (1973).

David H. Fischer, *Paul Revere's Ride* (1994).

James T. Flexner, *Washington: The Indispensable Man* (1984).

Eric Foner, *Tom Paine and Revolutionary America* (1976).

Ronald Hamowy, "Jefferson and the Scottish Enlightenment: A Critique of Garry Wills's *Inventing America*," *William and Mary Quarterly* (1979), pp. 503–523.

Don Higginbotham, *The War of American Independence: Military Attitudes, Policies, and Practice, 1763–1789* (1971).

Robert Middlekauff, *The Glorious Cause: The American Revolution, 1763–1789* (1982).

Merrill D. Peterson, *Thomas Jefferson and the New Nation: A Biography* (1970).

Garry Wills, *Inventing America: Jefferson's Declaration of Independence* (1978).

The Combatants

George A. Billias, ed., *George Washington's Generals* (1964).

George A. Billias, ed., *George Washington's Opponents: British Generals and Admirals in the American Revolution* (1969).

William M. Fowler Jr., *Rebels under Sail: The American Navy during the Revolution* (1976).

Sylvia R. Frey, *The British Soldier in America: A Social History of Military Life in the Revolutionary Period* (1981).

Charles P. Neimeyer, *America Goes to War: A Social History of the Continental Army* (1996).

Charles Royster, *A Revolutionary People at War: The Continental Army and American Character, 1775–1783* (1979).

Robert K. Wright, *The Continental Army* (1984).

The War in the North

Ira D. Gruber, *The Howe Brothers and the American Revolution* (1972).

Lee B. Kennett, *The French Forces in America, 1780–1783* (1977).

Benjamin Quarles, *The Negro in the American Revolution* (1961).

Steven Rosswurm, *Arms, Country, and Class: The Philadelphia Militia and "Lower Sort" during the American Revolution, 1775–1783* (1987).

William C. Stinchcombe, *The American Revolution and the French Alliance* (1969).

The War Widens

Sylvia R. Frey, *Water from the Rock: Black Resistance in a Revolutionary Age* (1991).

Barbara Graymont, *The Iroquois in the American Revolution* (1972).

Ronald Hoffman, Thad W. Tate, and Peter J. Albert, eds., *An Uncivil War: The Southern Backcountry during the American Revolution* (1985).

James H. O'Donnell, *Southern Indians in the American Revolution* (1973).

Paul H. Smith, *Loyalists and Redcoats: A Study in British Revolutionary Policy* (1964).

Theodore Thayer, *Nathanael Greene: Strategist of the American Revolution* (1960).

Anthony F. C. Wallace, *The Death and Rebirth of the Seneca* (1969).

Franklin Wickwire and Mary Wickwire, *Cornwallis: The American Adventure* (1970).

The American Victory

Jonathan R. Dull, *A Diplomatic History of the American Revolution* (1985).

Piers Mackesy, *The War for America, 1775–1783* (1964).

James K. Martin and Mark E. Lender, *A Respectable Army: The Military Origins of the Republic, 1763–1789* (1982).

Richard B. Morris, *The Peacemakers: The Great Powers and American Independence* (1965).

Howard H. Peckham, *The Toll of Independence: Engagements and Battle Casualties of the American Revolution* (1974).

The War and Society

Wallace Brown, *The Good Americans: The Loyalists in the American Revolution* (1969).

Richard Buel Jr., *Dear Liberty: Connecticut's Mobilization for the Revolutionary War* (1980).

Colin G. Calloway, *The American Revolution in Indian Country: Crisis and Diversity in Native American Communities* (1995).

Graham Russell Hodges, ed., *The Black Loyalist Directory: African Americans in Exile after the American Revolution* (1996).

Ronald Hoffman and Peter J. Albert, eds., *Women in the Age of the American Revolution* (1989).

Linda Kerber, *Women of the Republic: Intellect and Ideology in Revolutionary America* (1980).

Adrian C. Leiby, *The Revolutionary War in the Hackensack Valley: The Jersey Dutch and the Neutral Ground, 1775–1783* (1962).

Mary Beth Norton, *Liberty's Daughters: The Revolutionary Experience of American Women, 1750–1800* (1980).

Alfred F. Young, ed., *The American Revolution: Explorations in the History of American Radicalism* (1976).

Where to Learn More

❖ **Independence National Historical Park, Philadelphia, Pennsylvania.** Independence Hall, where Congress adopted the Declaration of Independence, is the most historic building in Philadelphia.

❖ **Kings Mountain National Military Park and Cowpens National Battlefield, South Carolina.** Situated approximately 20 miles apart, these were the sites of two battles in October 1780 and January 1781 that turned the tide of the war in the South. Both have museums and exhibits.

❖ **Minute Man National Historical Park, Lexington and Concord, Massachusetts.** There are visitors' centers at both Lexington and Concord with explanatory displays. Visitors may also follow the self-guided Battle Road Automobile Tour.

❖ **Saratoga National Historical Park, New York.** The park preserves and commemorates the American victory that led to French entry into the war. There is a museum with artifacts from the battlefield. Both the explanatory displays and the topography of the area make this an especially illuminating site.

❖ **Valley Forge National Historical Park, Valley Forge, Pennsylvania.** Reconstructed huts convey a sense of life in the Continental Army camp at Valley Forge during the hard winter of 1777–1778.

❖ **Yorktown Battlefield, Colonial National Historical Park, Yorktown, Virginia.** The park commemorates the great American victory here. Excellent exhibits and an observation deck enable visitors to understand the siege; they may also follow a road that winds through the 4,500-acre park.

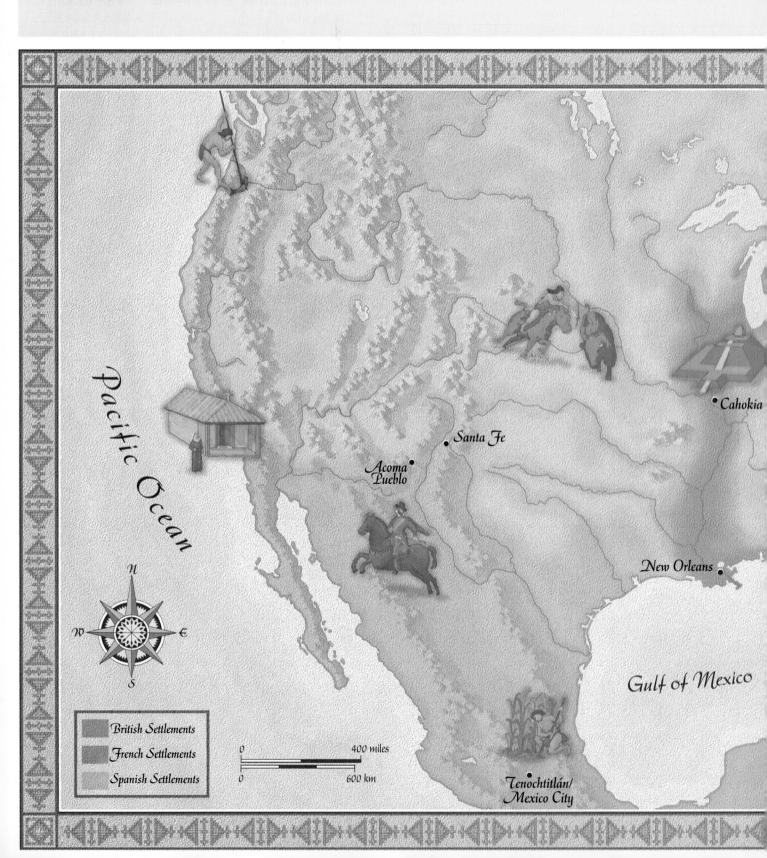

Pacific Ocean

Cahokia

Santa Fe

Acoma Pueblo

New Orleans

Gulf of Mexico

Tenochtitlán/ Mexico City

British Settlements
French Settlements
Spanish Settlements

0   400 miles
0   600 km

Charleston

Atlantic Ocean

Caribbean Sea

CHAPTER OUTLINE

KEY TOPICS

- ❖ Republicanism and the political philosophy of the new state constitutions
- ❖ Internal problems in the United States under the Articles of Confederation
- ❖ Efforts of Britain and Spain to exploit the weaknesses of the United States after the Revolution
- ❖ The movement for a stronger national government
- ❖ The drafting and ratification of the United States Constitution

"*Instead* of a due reverence to authority, and submission to government . . . have you not endeavored . . . to overturn all government and order, to shake off all restraints, human and divine, to give up yourselves wholly to the power of the most restless, malevolent, destructive, tormenting passion?" With these harsh words, Chief Justice William Cushing of Massachusetts denounced the debt-ridden farmers who had taken arms against the state government—and the merchants and creditors who controlled it—during **Shays's Rebellion** of 1786–1787.

Led by Daniel Shays, a former captain in the Continental Army, the rebels were protesting legislative policies that had saddled them with high taxes, left them vulnerable to the loss of their farms when they couldn't pay the taxes or repay other debts, and blocked increases in the supply of currency that would have provided them with economic relief. State forces stamped out Shays's Rebellion early in 1787, but the insurrection triggered waves of agrarian protest in other states, convincing many Americans that the republic stood on the brink of lawlessness.

More so than any other domestic disturbance in the 1780s, Shays's Rebellion dramatized the ideological, social, and economic ferment of America's first republic, its earliest years, which began in a burst of optimism following the victory over the British at Yorktown in 1781. The rebellion underscored, in particular, the clashing, if not contradictory, meanings that newly independent Americans attributed to the concept of liberty. Conservatives such as Cushing—mainly large landowners, wealthy merchants and lawyers, and men of high social standing—equated liberty with the right of the individual to pursue wealth and amass property. They sought a society founded on the rule of law and contract that would provide a stable foundation for an expanding economy.

Ordinary farmers, artisans, and small producers, in contrast, understood liberty more in terms of the traditional right of communities to defend their interests against the threat of moneyed and aristocratic elites. Denounced as radicals by their opponents, the Shaysites viewed themselves as the true conservatives, the preservers of republican liberties won in the Revolution against aristocratic elitists who they claimed had taken control of the Massachusetts government, shut out the popular voice, and victimized the true republicans, the common people who lived off their own labor.

During the Revolutionary War, the states had engaged in an unprecedented period of constitution writing. In 1781, they ratified the Articles of Confederation, the first attempt at a political union of the states. The years that followed were a period of trial and error marked by a running debate over the meaning of liberty and the extent of power that could safely be entrusted to a national government. A host of regional conflicts and economic problems like those that sparked Shays's Rebellion emerged, and the nation found itself caught between the need for more central power and the desire of states to protect their sovereignty. By the end of the 1780s, influential leaders favoring a strong national government had lost confidence in the Articles of Confederation and began working to replace them. They succeeded with the enactment and ratification of the Constitution of the United States in 1788. Their success brought an end to America's first republic under the Confederation government.

The New Order of Republicanism

As royal authority collapsed during the Revolution, various provincial congresses and committees assumed power in each of the former colonies. The Continental Congress, seeking to build support for the war effort, was concerned that these new institutions should have a firm legal and popular foundation. In May 1776, the Congress called on the colonies to form new state governments "under the authority of the people."

This call reflected the political philosophy of republicanism that animated the Revolution (see Chapter 6). To Americans, republicanism meant first and foremost that legitimate political authority derives from the people. It is they who are sovereign, not the king or the aristocracy. The people should elect the officials who govern them, and those officials should represent the interests of the people who elected them. Another key aspect of republicanism was the revolutionary idea that the people could define and limit governmental power through written constitutions.

Thus for many Americans, the Congress's call reflected the root purpose of the Revolution—to banish aristocratic tyranny and reconstruct government in the states on republican principles. But if those principles included the idea that legitimate government flowed from the people, it was not always clear just who "the people" included.

Although Shays's Rebellion was crushed, this uprising of debt-ridden farmers shocked many Americans into accepting the need for a stronger national government.

Defining the People

When news of the peace treaty with Britain reached New Bern, North Carolina, in June 1783, the citizens held a grand celebration. As reported by Francisco de Miranda, a visiting Spanish officer, "There was a barbecue [a roast pig] and a barrel of rum, from which the leading officials and citizens of the region promiscuously drank with the meanest and lowest kind of people, holding hands and drinking from the same cup. It is impossible to imagine, without seeing it, a more purely democratic gathering."

For Miranda, this boisterous mingling of all citizens as seeming equals confirmed the central tenet of republicanism, the belief that the people were sovereign. But republicanism also taught that political rights should be limited to those who owned private property because the independent will required for informed political judgment required economic self-sufficiency. This in effect restricted political participation to propertied white men. Virtually everyone else—propertyless white men, servants legally bound to others, women, blacks (most free blacks and all slaves), and Native Americans—was denied political rights during the Revolutionary era.

Because the ownership of property was relatively widespread among white men, some 60 to 85 percent of adult white men could participate in politics—a far higher proportion than elsewhere in the world of the eighteenth century. The greatest con-

centration of the remaining 25 percent or so shut out of the political process were unskilled laborers and mariners living in port cities. In Philadelphia, for example, half the population of taxable adult men and women in the 1780s reported no taxable property. The city's working poor still included indentured servants, bound by contract to give personal service for a fixed time. The walking poor—vagrants and transient—might be jailed by local authorities, confined to workhouses, or hired out in public auctions for fixed terms of labor. Those who incurred debts they were unable to pay faced imprisonment.

The Revolution did little to change the traditional patriarchal assumption that politics and public life should be the exclusive domain of men. Women, according to republican beliefs, were part of the dependent class and belonged under the control of propertied men—their husbands and fathers. Under common law (the customary, largely unwritten law that Americans had inherited from Britain), women surrendered their property rights at marriage unless they made special arrangements to the contrary. Legally and economically, husbands had complete control over their wives. As a result, argued Theophilus Parsons of Massachusetts in 1778, women were, as a matter of course, "so situated as to have no wills of their own."

To be sure, some women saw in the political and social enthusiasm of the Revolution an opportunity to protest the most oppressive features of their subordination. "I won't have it thought that because we are the weaker sex as to bodily strength we are

CHRONOLOGY

1776 States begin writing the first constitutions.

1777 Articles of Confederation proposed.

1781 Articles ratified.

1783 Americans celebrate independence and the peace treaty with Britain.

1784 Onset of the postwar depression.
Spain closes the Mississippi.
Separatist plots in the West.
Treaty of Fort Stanwix.

1785 Land Ordinance of 1785.
States begin to issue more paper money.
Treaty of Fort McIntosh.

1786 Shays's Rebellion breaks out.
Jay-Gardoqui Treaty defeated.
Annapolis Convention.

1787 Constitutional Convention at Philadelphia.
Northwest Ordinance.

1788 Constitution ratified and goes into effect.
Publication of *The Federalist.*

capable of nothing more than domestic concerns," wrote Eliza Wilkinson of South Carolina. Men, she lamented, "won't even allow us liberty of thought and that is all I want." Such protests, however, had little enduring effect. Most women were socialized to accept that their proper place was in the home with their families.

Gender-specific language—including terms like "men," "Freemen," "white male inhabitants," and "free white men"—explicitly barred women from voting in almost all state constitutions of the 1770s. Only the New Jersey constitution of 1776 defined **suffrage**—the right to vote—in gender-free terms, extend-

With the exception of New Jersey, where women meeting the property qualifications were eligible to vote, the state constitutions of the Revolutionary era prohibited women from voting.

ing it to all adults "worth fifty pounds." As a result, until 1807, when the state legislature changed the constitution, propertied women, including widows and single women, enjoyed the right to vote in New Jersey.

The Revolution otherwise did bring women a few limited gains. They benefited from slightly less restrictive divorce laws and gained somewhat greater access to educational and business opportunities, changes that reflected the relative autonomy of many women during the war when their men were off fighting. The perception of women's moral status also rose. As the Philadelphia physician Benjamin Rush argued in his *Thoughts upon Female Education* (1787), educated and morally informed women were needed to instruct "their sons in the principles of liberty and government."

The Revolution had a more immediate impact on the lives of many African-Americans, triggering the growth of free black communities and the development of an African-American culture. Changes begun by the Revolution were the main factor in the tremendous increase of free blacks from a few thousand at midcentury to more than 100,000 by 1800 (see Figure 7-1). One key to this increase was a shift in the religious and intellectual climate. Revolutionary principles of liberty and equality and evangelical notions of human fellowship convinced many whites for the first time to challenge black slavery. In 1784, Virginia Methodists condemned slavery as "contrary to the Golden Law of God on which hang all the Laws and Prophets, and the unalienable Rights of Mankind, as well as every Principle of Revolution." As many whites grew more hostile to slavery, blacks began to seize opportunities for freedom that emerged from the disruptions of the war and the needs of both sides for military manpower.

Upwards of fifty thousand slaves, or one in ten of those in bondage, gained their freedom as a result of the war. One route was through military service, which generally carried a promise of freedom. When the British began raising black troops, the Americans followed suit. All of the states except Georgia and South Carolina recruited black regiments. Some five thousand blacks served in the Continental armies, and they, like their counterparts in British units, were mostly slaves. Most slaves who gained freedom during the war, however, were those who fled their owners and made their way to the port cities of the North.

By making slave property generally less secure, the Revolution encouraged many masters to free their slaves. Once freed, blacks tried to break all the bonds of their former servitude. "Negro Soloman," his former owner griped, "now free, prefers to mould bricks rather than serve me." A Delaware mistress felt rejected when a slave she had freed spurned her offer of employment with a friend and found her own job. "I cannot help think," she sourly noted, that "it is too generally the case with all those of colour to be ungrateful." As the number of free blacks increased, those still enslaved grew bolder in their efforts to gain freedom. "Henny," warned a

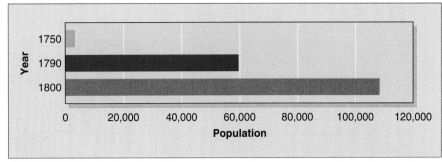

Figure 7-1   *Growth of the Free Black Population between 1750 and 1800*
Gradual emancipation in the North, the freeing of many slaves by their owners in the South, and the opportunities for freedom offered by the Revolution all contributed to an explosive growth in the free population of African-Americans in the second half of the eighteenth century.

Source: A Century of Population Growth in the United States, 1790–1900, (1909) p. 80. Data for 1750 estimated.

Maryland slaveowner in 1783, "will try to pass for a free woman as several have lately been set free in this neighbourhood."

If the control mechanisms of slavery experienced some strain in the South during the Revolution, in the North, where slaves were only a small percentage of the population, they crumbled. Most northern states ended slavery between 1777 and 1784. New York followed in 1799 and New Jersey in 1804. Nonetheless, although a majority of northern whites now agreed that slavery was incompatible with the Revolution's commitment to **natural rights** (the inherent human rights to life and liberty) and human freedom, they refused to sanction a sudden emancipation. The laws ending slavery in most of the northern states called only for the children of slaves to be freed, and only when they reached adulthood.

Northern blacks had to struggle to overcome white prejudice. Although black males were allowed to vote if they met the property qualifications, most were poor and held little property. Facing discrimination in jobs and housing, barred from juries, and denied a fair share of funds for schools, urban blacks had to rely on their own resources. With the help of the small class of property holders among them, they began establishing their own churches and self-help associations.

The impact of the Revolution on Native Americans was almost entirely negative (see Chapter 6). Most Indian peoples stayed neutral during the war or fought for the British. Just as the Americans sought to shake off British control, so the Indians—especially the western tribes and most of the Iroquois Confederation—sought to free themselves from American dominance. The British defeat was thus a

Phillis Wheatley was an acclaimed African-American poet. Kidnapped into slavery as a child in Africa, she was a domestic slave to the Wheatley family of Boston when her first poems were published in 1773.

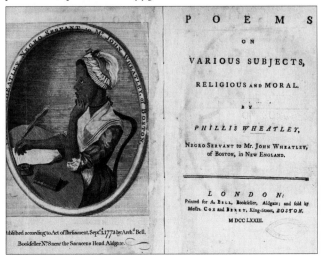

Sweeping chimneys, a dirty, dangerous job, was one of the few employment opportunities open to northern free blacks in the early republic.

double blow, depriving the Indians of a valuable ally and exposing them to the wrath of the victorious patriots. "The minds of these people appear as much agitated as those of the unhappy Loyalists," observed a British officer late in the war of the pro-British southern Indians; "they have very seriously proposed to abandon their country and accompany us [in an evacuation], having made all the world their enemies by their attachment to us."

The state governments, as well as the Confederation Congress, now treated Indian lands after the Revolution as a prize of war to be distributed to white settlers. Territorial demands on the Indians escalated, and even the few tribes that had furnished troops for the American cause lost control over most of their homelands. White Americans did not consider Native Americans to be part of their republican society. With the exception of Massachusetts, the states denied voting and legal rights to the Indians within their borders.

The State Constitutions

"Oppose everything that leans to aristocracy, of power in the hands of the rich and chief men exercised to the oppression of the poor." So the voters of Mecklenburg County, North Carolina, instructed their delegates to the state's constitutional convention in 1776. These instructions reflect a basic premise embodied in the new state constitutions of the Revolutionary period: Power had to be checked to ensure individual liberty and safeguard against tyranny.

Ten new state constitutions were in place by the end of 1777. In Connecticut and Rhode Island,

the new constitutions simply amended the existing colonial charters, which already provided for extensive self-rule, by dropping all references to royal authority. Massachusetts, the only state to hold elections for a special constitutional convention, ratified its constitution in 1780.

All of these constitutions were written documents, a striking departure from the English practice of treating a constitution as a collection of customary rights and practices that had evolved over time. In the American view, a constitution was a formal expression of the people's sovereignty, a codification of the powers of government and the rights of citizenship that functioned as a fundamental law to which all public authority was held accountable.

Because Americans had come to associate tyranny with the privileges of royal governors, all the new state constitutions cut back sharply on executive power. Annual elections were now the norm for governors, who were also made subject to **impeachment**—charges of misconduct, resolved at a public trial—and limited in the number of terms they could serve. Most important, for it struck at what patriots felt was the main source of executive domination and corruption, governors lost control over **patronage**, the power to appoint executive and judicial officials.

As the new constitutions curbed the power of governors, they increased that of the legislatures, making them the focal point of government. Colonial assemblies had been in the forefront of popular opposition to British authority, and the state legislatures that succeeded them were now seen as the most trustworthy defenders of individual liberty. The new constitutions expanded the power of the legislatures to appoint officials and to oversee military and financial matters. To make the legislatures more expressive of the popular will, the new constitutions included provisions that lowered property requirements for voting and officeholding, mandated annual elections, increased the number of seats in the legislatures, and made representation more proportional to the geographical distribution of population. Upper houses were made independent of the executive office and opened to popular election as opposed to the colonial practice of having their members appointed by the governor.

Americans knew that legislatures, too, could act tyrannically, as they believed Britain's Parliament had done. So in a final check on arbitrary power, each state constitution eventually included some form of a **bill of rights** that set explicit limits on the power of government to interfere in the lives of citizens. The Virginia Declaration of Rights, written by the planter George Mason and adopted in June 1776, set the precedent for this notable republican feature. By 1784, the constitutions of all thirteen states had provisions guaranteeing religious liberty, freedom of the press, and a citizen's right to such fair legal practices as trial by jury.

The new constitutions weakened but did not always sever the traditional tie between church and state for the support of religion. Many Americans held, as the Massachusetts Constitution of 1780 put it, that "the happiness of a people, and the good order and preservation of civil government, essentially depend upon piety, religion, and morality." Reflecting this belief, many states, notably in New England, levied taxes for the support of religion. The states of New England also continued to maintain Congregationalism as the established, or state-supported, religion while allowing dissenting Baptists and Methodists to use funds from the compulsory religious taxes to support their ministers. The "common people," explained the Baptist leader Isaac Backus, insisted that they had "as good a right to judge and act for themselves in matter of religion as civil rulers or the learned clergy."

The mid-Atlantic states lacked the religious uniformity of New England. The region had several prominent denominations—Quaker, Episcopalian, Presbyterian, Dutch Reformed, and Lutheran—and none was able to dominate the others. This pluralism checked legislative efforts to impose religious taxes or designate any denomination as the **established church.** In the South, where many Anglican (or Episcopalian) clergymen had been Tories, the Anglican Church lost its former established status. Thomas Jefferson, in Virginia's religious freedom law of 1786, went so far as to assert that "our civil rights have no dependence on our religious opinions any more than on opinions in physics or geometry."

Although in general the executive lost power and the legislative gained power under the new state constitutions, the actual structure of each state government reflected the outcome of political struggles between those holding a radical vision of republicanism and those holding a conservative vision. The democratically inclined radicals wanted to open government to all male citizens. The conservatives, fearing "mob rule," wanted to limit government to an educated elite of substantial property holders. Although they agreed that government had to be derived from the people, most conservatives, like Jeremy Belknap of New Hampshire, thought that the people had to be "taught . . . that they are not able to govern themselves."

In South Carolina, where conservative planters gained the upper hand, the constitution mandated property qualifications that barred 90 percent of the state's white males from holding elective public office. In contrast, Pennsylvania had the most democratic and controversial constitution. Many of Pennsylvania's conservatives had discredited themselves during the Revolution by remaining neutral or loyal to the crown. The Scots-Irish farmers and Philadelphia artisans who stepped into the resulting political vacuum held an egalitarian view of republicanism. The constitution they pushed through in 1776 gave the vote to all free males who paid taxes regardless of wealth and eliminated property qualifications for officeholding. In addition, the constitution concentrated power in a **unicameral** (single-house) **legislature,** eliminating both the office of governor and the more elite upper legislative house. To prevent the formation of an entrenched class of officeholders, the constitution's framers also required legislators to stand for election annually and barred them from serving more than four years out of seven.

The constitutions of the other states, although not as bold in their democratic reforms as Pennsylvania's, typically enhanced the political influence of ordinary citizens more than the constitution of South Carolina did. Unlike the colonial assemblies, the new **bicameral** (two-house) **legislatures** included substantially more artisans and small farmers and were not controlled by men of wealth. The proportion of legislators who came from a common

American Views

A FRENCH OBSERVER DESCRIBES A NEW SOCIETY

In 1782, J. Hector St. John Crèvecoeur, a Frenchman who had lived and traveled in British North America, published his impressions of America. The following selection from his *Letters from an American Farmer* captures the striking optimism and sense of newness that he found. More so than any other literary work, the *Letters* stamped the new American republic, especially in the minds of Europeans, as the home of the world's freest and most equal people.

❖ **What is Crèvecoeur's image of America? Do you believe it was overly optimistic?**

❖ **Why does Crèvecoeur put such emphasis on the absence of titles and great disparities of wealth?**

❖ **Just what was so *new* about America to Crèvecoeur?**

❖ **Why did Crèvecoeur ignore African slaves in his definition of the American? What happened to Native Americans in his account of the making of the American?**

I wish I could be acquainted with the feelings and thoughts which must agitate the heart and present themselves to the mind of an enlightened Englishman when he first lands on this continent. . . . He is arrived on a new continent; a modern society offers itself to his contemplation, different from what he had hitherto seen. It is not composed, as in Europe, of great lords who possess everything and of a herd of people who have nothing. Here are no aristocratical families, no courts, no kings, no bishops, no ecclesiastical dominion, no invisible power giving to a few a very visible one, no great manufactures employing thousands, no great refinements of luxury. The rich and the poor are not so far removed from each other as they are in Europe. Some few towns excepted, we are all tillers of the earth, from Nova Scotia to West Florida. We are a people of cultivators scattered over an immense territory, communicating with each other by means of good roads and navigable rivers, united by the silken bands of mild government, all respecting the laws without dread-

background—those with property valued under £200—more than tripled to 62 percent in the North and more than doubled in the South from the 1770s to the 1780s.

This growing political equality was accompanied by demands that those in government be more responsive to the people. Summing up the prevailing view among Americans about the proper basis for government, William Hooper of North Carolina wrote in 1776, "Rulers must be conceived as the creatures of the people, made for their use, accountable to them, and subject to removal as soon as they act inconsistent with the purposes for which they were formed."

The Articles of Confederation

Once the Continental Congress decided on independence in 1776, it needed to create a legal basis for a permanent union of the states. John Dickinson of Pennsylvania, a reluctant supporter of independence, presented a draft plan for such a union as early as the summer of 1776. Dickinson favored a strong central government to prevent the collapse of the social order that he feared might follow the overthrow of imperial rule. Congress, however, fundamentally altered Dickinson's original plan to recognize the sovereign power of the individual states. According to the key provision of the **Articles of Confederation** that Congress finally submitted to the

ing their power, because they are equitable. We are all animated with the spirit of an industry which is unfettered and unrestrained, because each person works for himself. . . . A pleasing uniformity of decent competence appears throughout our habitations. The meanest of our loghouses is a dry and comfortable habitation. Lawyer and merchant are the fairest titles our towns afford; that of a farmer is the only appellation of the rural inhabitants of our country. It must take some time ere he can reconcile himself to our dictionary, which is but short in words of dignity and names of honour. . . . We have no princes for whom we toil, starve, and bleed; we are the most perfect society now existing in the world. Here man is free as he ought to be, nor is this pleasing equality so transitory as many others are. Many ages will not see the shores of our great lakes replenished with inland nations, nor the unknown bounds of North America entirely peopled. . . .

The next wish of this traveller will be to know whence came all these people. They are a mixture of English, Scotch, Irish, French, Dutch, Germans, and Swedes. From this promiscuous breed, that race now called Americans have arisen. . . .

What, then, is the American, this new man? He is either an European or the descendant of an European; hence that strange mixture of blood, which you will find in no other country. . . . *He* is an American, who, leaving behind him all his ancient prejudices and manners, receives new ones from the new mode of life he has embraced, the new government he obeys, and the new rank he holds. He becomes an American by being received in the broad lap of our Alma Mater. Here individuals of all nations are melted into a new race of men, whose labours and posterity will one day cause great changes in the world.

Source: J. Hector St. John Crèvecoeur, Letters from an American Farmer and Sketches of Eighteenth-Century America, ed. Albert E. Stone (1986), pp. 66–70.

states more than a year later, in November 1777, "Each State retains its sovereignty, freedom and independence, and every power, jurisdiction and right, which is not by this confederation expressly delegated to the United States, in Congress assembled." The effect was to create a loose confederation of autonomous states.

The powers the Articles of Confederation delegated to the central government were extremely limited, in effect little more than those already exercised by the Continental Congress. There were no provisions for a national judiciary or a separate executive branch of government. The Articles made Congress the sole instrument of

national authority but restricted it with a series of constitutional safeguards that virtually eliminated any possibility that it could ever threaten the interests of the states. Each state had only one vote in Congress, making each politically equal regardless of its size or population. State legislatures were to choose their congressional delegations in annual elections, and delegates could serve only three years out of six. Delegates were expected to follow the instructions of their state legislatures and could be recalled at any time. Important measures, such as those dealing with finances or war and peace, required approval from a majority of nine state delegations voting in Congress. Amendments to the

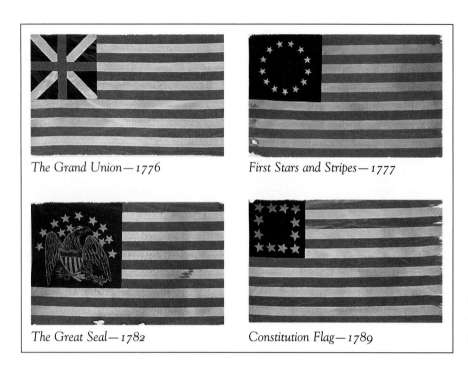

The Grand Union—1776

First Stars and Stripes—1777

The Great Seal—1782

Constitution Flag—1789

This sequence of early U.S. flags reflects the ongoing process of self-definition of the nation that emerged from the Revolution.

Articles of Confederation, including the levying of national taxes, required the unanimous consent of the states.

Congress had authority primarily in the areas of foreign policy and national defense. It could declare war, make peace, conduct foreign affairs, negotiate with Native Americans, and settle disputes between the states. It had no authority, however, to raise troops or impose taxes on its own; it could only ask the states to supply troops and money and hope that they complied.

The central principle behind the Articles was the fear of oppressive, centralized power encroaching on the freedoms for which the Revolution was fought. In the end, as Edward Rutledge, a delegate from South Carolina to the Continental Congress, put it, the new Confederation Congress was vested "with no more Power than is absolutely necessary." "It is *freedom*, Gentlemen, it is *freedom*, & not a choice of the *forms of servitude* for which we contend," resolved the residents of West Springfield, Massachusetts, in instructions to their congressional representatives in 1778.

Most states quickly ratified the Articles of Confederation, but Maryland stubbornly held out until March 1781. Because they needed the approval of all thirteen states, it was not until then that the Articles officially took effect. Surprisingly, given the prevailing deep suspicion of central power, what caused the delay was the demand of some states to give Congress a power not included in the Articles submitted for ratification in 1777.

The issue here concerned the unsettled lands in the West between the Appalachian Mountains and the Mississippi River (see Map 7-1). Some states claimed these lands by virtue of their colonial charter rights, and led by Virginia and Massachusetts, they insisted on maintaining control over these territories. The so-called landless states—those with no claim to the West—insisted that it be set aside as a national domain, a reserve of public land controlled by Congress for the benefit of all the states. Land speculators who had purchased huge blocs of land from the Indians before the Revolution sided with the landless states. Many of them leading politicians, they expected Congress would be more likely to honor their land titles than the individual states.

The British threat to the Chesapeake area in early 1781 finally broke the impasse that had delayed final approval of the Articles. Though retaining control of Kentucky, Virginia gave up its claim in the west to a vast area extending north of the Ohio River. In turn, Maryland, the last holdout among the landless states and now desperate for military aid from Congress, agreed to ratify the Articles. After more than three years of debate and the airing of jealousies among the states, the final cementing of the original Union was decidedly anticlimactic.

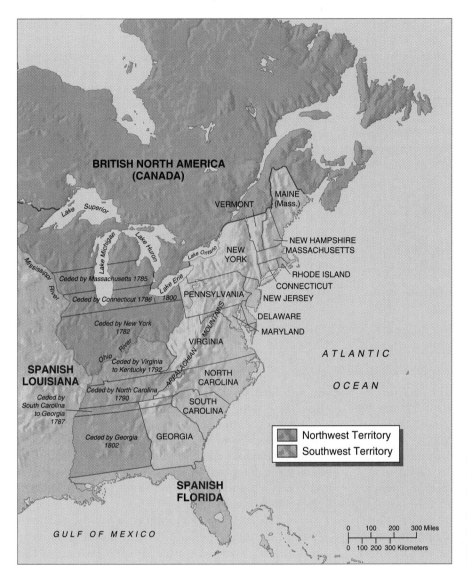

Map 7-1   Cession of Western Lands by the States
Eight states had claims to lands in the West after the Revolution, and their willingness to cede them to the national government was an essential step in the creation of a public domain administered by Congress.

Problems at Home

Neither prosperity nor political stability accompanied the return of peace in 1783. The national government struggled to avoid bankruptcy, and in 1784, an economic depression struck the country. As fiscal problems deepened over the next few years, creditor and debtor groups clashed angrily in state legislatures. When legislatures passed measures that provided relief to debtors at the expense of creditors, the creditors decried what they saw as the interference of ignorant majorities with the rights of private property. Raising the cry of "legislative despotism," the abuse of power by tyrannical lawmakers, they joined their voices to those who early on had wanted the power of the states curbed by a stronger central government. The only solid accomplishment of the Confederation Congress during this troubled period was to formulate an orderly and democratic plan for the settlement of the West under national controls.

The Fiscal Crisis

The Continental Congress and the states incurred heavy debts to finance the Revolutionary War. Unable to impose and collect sufficient taxes to cover the debts and without reserves of gold or silver, they had little choice but to borrow funds and issue certificates or bonds pledging repayment. Congress had the largest responsibility for meeting the war's costs, and to do so it printed close to $250 million in paper notes backed only by its good faith. By the end of the war in 1781, these Continental dollars were nearly worthless, and the

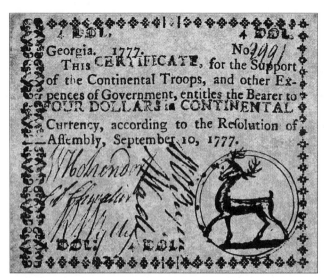

Issued in 1777, this Georgia four-dollar banknote was an example of the type of paper money used to finance the Revolutionary War.

national debt—primarily certificates issued by the Continental Loan Office—stood at $11 million. As Congress issued new securities to settle claims by soldiers and civilians, this sum rose to $28 million within just a few years.

Congress never did put its tottering finances on a sound footing, and its fiscal problems ultimately discredited the Articles of Confederation in the eyes of the **nationalists,** a loose bloc of congressmen, army officers, and public creditors who wanted to strengthen the Confederation at the expense of the states. The nationalists first began to organize in the dark days of 1780 and 1781 when inflation was rampant, the army was going unpaid, Congress had ceased paying interest on the public debt, and the war effort itself seemed in danger of collapsing. Galvanized by this crisis, the nationalists rallied behind Robert Morris, a Philadelphia merchant appointed as superintendent of finance for the Confederation government.

Morris sought to enhance national authority through a bold program of financial and political reform. He began by securing a charter from Congress in 1781 for the Bank of North America, the nation's first commercial bank. Located in Philadelphia and partly owned by private investors, the bank had close connections to the Confederation government. Morris wanted it to serve as a national institution, and he used it to hold government funds, make loans to the government, and issue bank notes—paper money that could be used to settle debts and pay taxes owed to the United States.

Morris was able to resume some specie payments, and he temporarily brought order and economy to the nation's finances. As a result of his reforms, he came to be called the "financier of the Revolution." Nonetheless, he was blocked in his efforts to gain the taxing power that was essential for restoring the shattered credit of the Confederation government.

Morris's larger objective—central to the aims of the nationalists—was to create a "bond of union" by having Congress assume payment of the entire national debt. Settling this debt would lead the propertied classes—the people who had financed the war and held the debt—to identify their economic self-interest with the effective exercise of power by the national government.

But to achieve this political goal, Morris had to gain for Congress what it had always lacked: the power to tax. In 1781, he proposed a national impost, or tariff, of 5 percent on imported goods. Because this was a national tax, it required an amendment to the Articles of Confederation and the consent of all thirteen states. Twelve of the states quickly ratified the impost amendment, but Rhode Island—critically dependent on its own import duties to finance its war debt—rejected it, sending it down to defeat. When a revised impost plan was considered two years later, New York blocked its passage.

These failures doomed Morris's financial reforms. He left office in 1784, and in the same year the Bank of North America severed its ties to the national government and became a private corporation in Pennsylvania. Morris remained committed to the nationalist cause and would see his ideas resurface under the financial programs of Treasury Secretary Alexander Hamilton in the 1790s (see Chapter 8).

The failure of the impost tax was one of many setbacks that put the nationalists temporarily on the defensive. With the conclusion of peace in 1783, confidence in state government returned, taking the edge off calls to invest the central government with greater authority. The states continued to balk at supplying the money requisitioned from them by Congress and denied Congress even limited authority to regulate foreign commerce. Most ominously for the nationalist cause, the states began to assume responsibility for part of the national debt. By 1786, New Jersey, Pennsylvania, Maryland, and New York had absorbed one-third of the debt by issuing state bonds to their citizens in exchange for national securities. As Morris had warned in 1781, such a policy entailed "a principle of disunion . . . which must be ruinous."

Without the power to tax, Congress was a hostage to the sovereignty of the individual states with no real authority over the nation's economic affairs. When the economy plunged into a severe depression in 1784, it could only look on helplessly.

Economic Depression

During the Revolutionary War, Britain closed its markets to American goods. After the war, the British continued this policy, hoping to keep the United States weak and dependent. In the summer of 1783, they excluded Americans from the lucrative trade with the British West Indies. Before the Revolution, this trade in foodstuffs and timber with the sugar islands had been the primary means by which the colonists had built up the credits they needed to offset their imports from Britain.

Meanwhile, British merchants were happy to satisfy America's pent-up demand for consumer goods after the war. A flood of cheap British imports inundated the American market, and coastal merchants made them available to inland traders and shopkeepers by extending easy credit terms. In turn, these local businessmen sold the goods to farmers and artisans in the interior. Ultimately, however, the British merchants required payment in hard currency, gold and silver coins. Without access to its former export markets, America's only source of hard currency was foreign loans obtained by Congress and what money the French army had spent during the war. This was soon exhausted as America's trade deficit with Britain—the excess of imports over exports—ballooned in the early 1780s to £5 million (see Figure 7-2).

The result was an immense bubble of credit that finally burst in 1784, triggering a depression that would linger for most of the rest of the decade. As merchants began to press debtors for immediate payment, prices collapsed (they fell more than 25 percent between 1784 and 1786), and debtors were unable to pay. The best most could hope for was to avoid bankruptcy.

Small farmers everywhere had trouble paying their taxes. In 1786, James Swan of Massachusetts wrote of farmers in his state: "There is no family that does not want some money for some purposes, and the little which the farmer carries home from market, must be applied to other uses, besides paying off the [tax] collector's bills." Rural shopkeepers often could not move goods unless they agreed to barter them for farm produce. Abigail Dwight, who ran a small store in western Massachusetts, reported in 1785 that "most of these People sell on credit for To-Morrow at large—for very little Cash stirring this way—to be pay'd for in old Horses—cows some Boards—cabbages—turnips—Potatoes etc."

In the cities, wages fell 25 percent between 1785 and 1789, and workers began to organize. They called for tariffs to protect them from cheap British imports and for legislative measures to promote American manufacturers. In the countryside, farmers faced a wave of lawsuits for the collection of debts and the dread possibility of losing their land. "To be

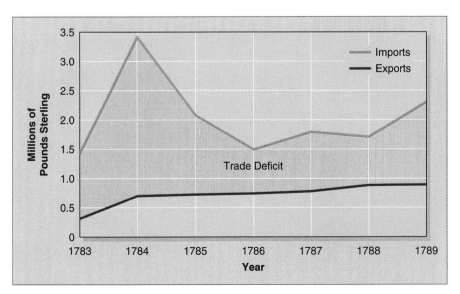

Figure 7-2 *American Exports to and Imports from Britain between 1783 and 1789*
During the 1780s, the United States imported far more from Britain than it exported there. The resulting huge trade deficit drained the country of gold and silver and was a major factor in the credit crisis that triggered an economic depression in the middle of the decade.
Source: *U.S. Bureau of the Census,* Historical Statistics of the United States: Colonial Times to 1970, *Part 2, (1975) p. 1176.*

tenants to *landlords,* we know not who," protested the farmers of Conway, Massachusetts, "and pay rent for lands, *purchased with our money,* and converted from howling *wilderness,* into fruitful fields, by the *sweat of our brows,* seems . . . truly shocking."

With insufficient money in circulation to raise prices and reverse the downturn, the depression fed on itself. Congress was powerless to raise cash and was unable to pay off its old debts, including what it owed to the Revolutionary soldiers. Many state governments made things worse by imposing heavy taxes payable in the paper money they had issued during the Revolution. The result was further to reduce the amount of money in circulation, which increased deflationary pressures, forcing prices still lower.

Britain's trade policies caused particular suffering among New England merchants. No longer protected under the old Navigation Acts as British vessels, American ships were now barred from most ports in the British Empire. Incoming cargoes from the West Indies to New England fell off sharply, and the market for whale oil and fish, two of New England's major exports, dried up. The economy of the mid-Atlantic region held up somewhat better, but even there the loss of the provisioning trade to the British West Indies in grains, livestock, and dairy products cut into the income of merchants and farmers and forced layoffs among artisans who serviced the shipping trade.

In the southern states, British policies compounded the problem of recovering from the physical damage and labor disruptions inflicted by the war. Some 10 percent of the region's slaves had fled during the war, and production levels on plantations fell in the 1780s. Chesapeake planters needed a full decade to restore the prewar output of tobacco, and a collapse in tobacco prices in 1785 left most of them in the same chronic state of indebtedness that had plagued them on the eve of the Revolution.

Farther south, in the Carolina lowcountry, the plantation economy was crippled throughout the 1780s. War damage had been extensive, and planters piled up debts to purchase additional slaves and repair their plantations and dikes. In spite of these investments, rice production was slow to recover. Burdened by new British duties on American rice, planters saw their rice exports fall by 50 percent. Small farmers in the pine barrens of North Carolina likewise had to adjust to the loss of their formerly protected British market for naval stores—tar, pitch, and turpentine.

By the late 1780s, the worst of the depression was over and an upturn was under way in the mid-Atlantic states. Food exports to continental Europe were on the rise, and American merchants were developing new trading ties with India and China. Commercial treaties with the Dutch, Swedes, and Prussians also opened up markets that had been closed to the colonists. Nonetheless, a full recovery had to await the 1790s.

The depression of the 1780s was the culmination of a decade of painful adjustment that followed the wrenching of the American economy from its traditional moorings within the British trading empire. A stagnant economy and burdensome debt combined with a growing population (there were 50 percent more Americans in 1787 than there had been in 1775) to reduce living standards. With more

Depicted here in a folding fan, the Empress of China *was the first American ship to undertake an extensive trading voyage to China. Sailing out of New York in February 1784, the* Empress of China *returned on May 11, 1785, and netted a profit of $37,000 for the investors who had financed the voyage. Building trading contracts to new markets in Asia and Europe helped the United States break its economic dependence on England.*

losers than winners, economic conflict dominated the politics of the states during the Confederation period.

The Economic Policies of the States

The depression had political repercussions in all the states. Britain was an obvious target of popular anger, and merchants poorly positioned to adjust to the postwar dislocations of trade led a campaign to slap retaliatory duties on British ships and special taxes on the goods they carried. Likewise artisans and workers, especially in the North, pushed for tariff barriers against cheap British goods as a way to encourage domestic manufacturing and protect their jobs and wages. Most northern states imposed anti-British measures, but these varied from state to state, limiting their impact and producing squabbles when goods imported in one state were shipped to another.

State legislatures in the North responded to the protests of artisans by passing tariffs, but the lack of a uniform, national policy doomed their efforts. Shippers evaded high tariffs by bringing their cargoes in through states with no tariffs or less restrictive ones. States without ports, like New Jersey and North Carolina, complained of economic discrimination. When they purchased foreign goods from a neighboring shipping state, they were forced to pay part of the tariff cost, but all the revenue from the tariff accrued only to the importing state. James Madison neatly summarized the plight of these states when he noted that "New Jersey, placed between Philadelphia and New York, was likened to a cask tapped at both ends; And North Carolina, between Virginia and South Carolina, to a patient bleeding at both Arms."

Tariff policies also fed sectional tensions between northern and southern states that undermined efforts to confer on Congress the power to regulate commerce. The agrarian states of the South, which had little in the way of manufacturing to protect, had different interests than the states of the North. With the exception of Virginia, they favored free trade policies that encouraged British imports. Southern planters were also happy to take advantage of the low rates charged by British ships for transporting their crops to Europe; by doing so, they put pressure on northern shippers to reduce their rates.

The bitterest divisions exposed by the depression of the 1780s, however, were not between states but between debtors and creditors within states. As the value of debt securities the states had issued to raise money dropped during the Revolutionary War, speculators bought them up for a fraction of their

face value and then put pressure on the states to raise taxes and repay the debts in full in hard currency. Wealthy landowners and merchants likewise supported higher taxes and the rapid repayment of debts in hard currency. Arrayed against these creditor groups by the mid-1780s was a broad coalition of debtors comprised of middling farmers, small shopkeepers, artisans, laborers, and people who had overextended themselves speculating in western land. The debtors wanted the states to issue paper money that they could use instead of hard money—gold and silver—to pay their debts. The paper money would have an inflationary effect, raising wages and the prices of farm commodities and reducing the value of debts contracted in hard currency. The townspeople of Atkinson, New Hampshire, expressing the feelings of many hard-pressed rural areas, put the issue this way: "For want of a suitable medium of trade the Citizens of this State are altogether unable to pay their public taxes, or private debts, or even to support the train of needless and expensive lawsuits, which alone would be an insupportable burden."

This was the economic context in which Shays's Rebellion exploded in the fall of 1786. Farm foreclosures and imprisonments for failure to pay debts had skyrocketed in western Massachusetts. Facing a collapse in farm prices and an impoverishing burden of debt, farmers petitioned the state legislators for economic relief. They complained of heavy taxes and the shortage of money and demanded legislation that would temporarily prohibit creditors from seizing farms and processing suits for debt. When the creditor and seaboard interests in the legislature refused to pass any relief measures, some two thousand farmers took up arms against the state government. Following Daniel Shays, a former Revolutionary War officer, they shut down the courts and hence the legal machinery for collecting debts in three counties in western Massachusetts. When they marched on the state arsenal in Springfield, alarmed state officials raised troops to crush the uprising.

Outside of western Massachusetts, discontented debtors generally stopped short of armed resistance. Whereas the Shaysite rebels had felt betrayed by a state government that had rejected their demands, debtor interests elsewhere were often successful in changing the monetary policy of their states. In 1785 and 1786, seven states enacted laws for new paper money issues. In most cases, the result was a qualified success. Controls on the supply of the new money kept it from depreciating rapidly, so its inflationary effect was mild. It was used chiefly to provide loans to farmers so they could meet their tax or mortgage payments. Combined with laws that prevented or delayed creditors from seizing property from debtors to satisfy debts, the currency issues helped keep a lid on popular discontent.

The most notorious exception to this pattern of fiscal responsibility was in Rhode Island, already nicknamed "Rogue's Island" for the sharp trading practices of its merchants. A rural party that gained control of the Rhode Island legislature in 1786 pushed through a currency law that flooded the state with paper money that could be used to pay all debts. Creditors who balked at accepting the new money at face value were subject to heavy penalties. Shocked, they went into hiding or left the state entirely, and merchants denounced the law as outright fraud.

The actions of the debtor party in Rhode Island alarmed conservatives everywhere, confirming their fears that legislative bodies dominated by common farmers and artisans rather than, as before the Revolution, by men of wealth and social distinction, were dangerous. One South Carolina conservative declared that he could see nothing but an "open and outrageous . . . violation of every principle of justice" in paper money and debt relief laws. Conservatives, creditors, and nationalists alike now spoke of a democratic tyranny that would have to be checked if the republic were to survive and protect its property holders.

Congress and the West

The Treaty of Paris and the surrender of charter claims by the states gave Congress control of a magnificent expanse of land between the Appalachian Mountains and the Mississippi River. This was the first American West. In what would prove the most enduring accomplishment of the Confederation government, Congress set forth a series of effective provisions for its settlement, governance, and eventual absorption into the Union.

Congress took several steps to establish its jurisdiction in the West. Asserting for the national government the right to formulate Indian policy, Congress negotiated a series of treaties with the Indians beginning in 1784 for the abandonment of their land claims in the West. By threatening to use military force, congressional commissioners in 1784 coerced the Iroquois Confederation of New York to cede half of its territory to the United States in the Treaty of Fort Stanwix. Similar tactics in 1785 resulted in the Treaty of Fort McIntosh in which the northwestern tribes ceded much of their land in Ohio. Against the opposition of states intent on grabbing Indian lands for themselves, Congress resolved in 1787 that its treaties were binding on all the states.

And anxious for revenue, Congress insisted on payment from squatters who had filtered into the West before provisions had been made for land sales.

The most pressing political challenge was to secure the loyalty of the West to the new and fragile Union. To satisfy the demands of settlers for self-government, Congress resolved as early as 1779 that new states would be carved out of the western domain with all the rights of the original states. An early plan for organizing the territories, the **Ordinance of 1784,** was largely the work of Thomas Jefferson. In it, he proposed to create ten districts or territories—even suggesting such whimsical names for them as Assenissipia and Cherronesus—each of which could apply for admission as a state when its population equaled that of the free inhabitants in the least populous of the existing states. Jefferson also proposed that settlers be permitted to choose their own officials, and he called for the prohibition of slavery in the West after 1800. Shorn of its no-slavery features, the ordinance passed Congress but was never put into practice.

As settlers and speculators began pouring into the West in 1784, however, Congress was forced to move quickly to formulate a policy for conveying its public land into private hands. If it couldn't regulate land sales and pass on clear titles, Congress would, in effect, have surrendered its claim to govern. One way or another, settlers were going to get their land, but a pell-mell process of private acquisitions in widely scattered settlements threatened to touch off costly Indian wars, deprive the national government of vitally needed revenue, and encourage separatist movements. The members of Congress had to act on national land policy, warned a western Pennsylvanian, or else "lose the only opportunity they ever will have of extending their power and influence over this new region."

Congress responded with the **Land Ordinance of 1785.** The crucial feature of this seminal legislation was its stipulation that public lands be surveyed in a rectangular grid pattern before being offered for sale (see Figure 7-3). By requiring that land first be plotted into townships of thirty-six uniform sections of 640 acres each, the ordinance adopted the New England system of land settlement, an approach that promoted compact settlements and produced undisputed land titles. In sharp contrast was the typical southern pattern whereby settlers picked out a piece of land in a large tract ahead of a precise survey and then fought each other in the courts to secure legal title. In an effort to avoid endless litigation, Congress opted for a policy geared to order and regularity.

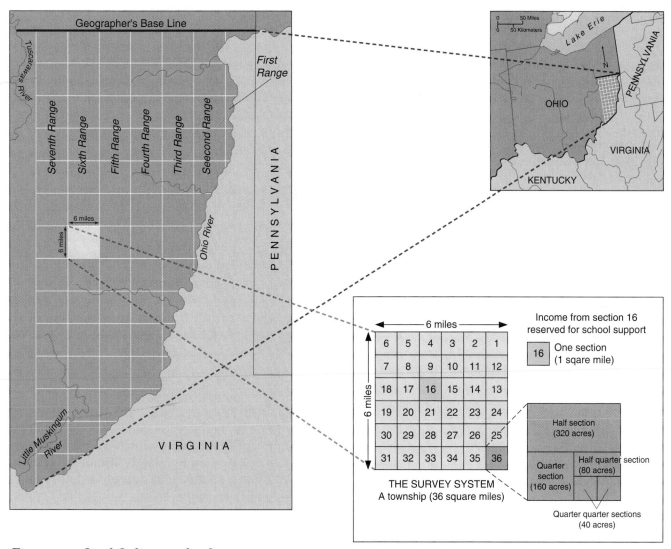

Figure 7-3   Land Ordinance of 1785
The precise uniformity of the surveying system initiated in the Land Ordinance of 1785 created a
rectangular grid pattern that was the model for all future land surveyed in the public domain.

Congress also attempted to attract a certain type of settler to the West by offering the plots of 640 acres at the then hefty sum of no less than $640, or $1 per acre, payable in hard currency or its equivalent. The goal here was to keep out the shiftless poor and reserve the West for enterprising and presumably law-abiding farm families who could afford the entry cost. Concerned about westerners' reputation for lawlessness and afraid that the primitive living conditions might cause them to lapse into savagery, Congress also set aside the income from the sale of the sixteenth section in each township for the support of public schools. Support for education, as a congressional report of 1783 put it, would help provide for "security against the increase of feeble, disorderly and dispersed settlements in those remote

and extended territories [and] against the depravity of manners which they have a tendency to produce."

Before any land sales occurred under the Ordinance of 1785, impatient settlers continued to push north of the Ohio River and claim homesteads as squatters. They clashed both with local Indian tribes and the troops sent by Congress to evict them. Impatient itself with the slow process of surveying, Congress sold off a million and a half acres to a group of New England speculators organized as the Ohio Company. The speculators bought the land with greatly depreciated loan office certificates that had been issued to Revolutionary War veterans, and their cost per acre averaged less than 10 cents in hard money. They now pressed their allies in Congress to establish a governmental structure for the West that would protect their investment by bringing the unruly elements in the West under control.

Both Congress and speculators wanted political stability and economic development in the West and a degree of supervision for settlers commonly viewed in the East as "but little less savage than the Indians." What was needed, wrote James Monroe of Virginia, were temporary controls—made acceptable by the promise of eventual statehood—that "in effect" would place the western territories under "a colonial government similar to that which prevail'd in these States previous to the revolution." The **Northwest Ordinance of 1787,** the most significant legislative act of the Confederation Congress, filled this need, creating a political structure for the territories and a phased process for achieving statehood that neatly blended public and private interests.

According to the ordinance, controls on a new territory were to be strictest in the early stage of settlement, when Congress would appoint a territorial government consisting of a governor, a secretary, and three judges. When a territory reached a population of five thousand adult males, those with 50 acres of land or more could elect a legislature. The actions of the legislature, however, were subject to an absolute veto by the governor. Once a territory had a population of sixty thousand, the settlers could draft a constitution and apply for statehood "on an equal footing with the original states in all respects whatsoever."

Unlike Jefferson's Ordinance of 1784, which called for ten states, the Northwest Ordinance of 1787 stipulated that only three to five states were to be formed out of the Northwest. This was because the admission of new states would weaken the control over Congress that the original thirteen states wanted to maintain for themselves as long as possible. Although less democratic in many respects than Jefferson's plan in mandating a period of outside control by Congress, the 1787 ordinance did provide greater protection for property rights as well as a bill of rights guaranteeing individual freedoms. Most significant, it prohibited slavery.

Southern congressmen agreed to the slavery ban in part because they feared that planters in the new states would compete with them in the production of slave-produced staples such as tobacco. More important, however, they expected slavery to be permitted in the region south of the Ohio River that was still under the administrative authority of Virginia, North Carolina, and Georgia in the 1780s. Indeed, slavery was allowed in this region when the **Southwest Ordinance of 1790** brought it under national control, a decision that would have grave

consequences in the future sectionalization of the United States.

Although the Northwest Ordinance applied only to the national domain north of the Ohio River, it provided the organizational blueprint by which all future territory was brought into the Union. It went into effect immediately and set the original Union on a course of dynamic expansion through the addition of new states.

Diplomatic Weaknesses

In the international arena of the 1780s, the United States was a weak and often ridiculed nation. Under the Articles of Confederation, Congress had the authority to negotiate foreign treaties but no economic or military power to enforce their terms. Unable to regulate commerce or set tariffs, it had no leverage with which to pry open the restricted trading empires of France, Spain, and most important, Britain.

France and the United States, allies during the Revolutionary War, remained on friendly terms after it. The United States even had a favorable trade balance with France, selling more there than it bought. Britain, however, treated its former colonies with contempt, and Spain was likewise openly antagonistic to the new nation. Both Britain and Spain sought to block American expansion into the trans-Appalachian West. And a dispute with Spain over the West produced the most serious diplomatic crisis of the period, one that spilled over into domestic politics, increasing sectional tensions between northern and southern states and leading many to question the country's chances of survival.

Impasse with Britain

The Confederation Congress was unable to resolve any of the major issues that poisoned Anglo-American relations in the 1780s. Key among those issues were provisions in the peace treaty of 1783 that concerned prewar American debts to the British and the treatment of Loyalists by the patriots. Britain used what it claimed to be America's failure to satisfy those provisions to justify its own violations of the treaty. The result was a diplomatic deadlock that hurt American interests in the West and in foreign trade.

Article 4 of the peace treaty called for the payment of all prewar debts at their "full value in sterling money"—that is, in gold or silver coin. Among the most numerous of those with outstanding debts to British creditors were tobacco planters in the Chesapeake region of Virginia and Maryland. During the Revolution, the British army had carried off and freed many of the region's slaves without compensating the planters. Still angry, the planters were in no mood to repay their debts. Working out a scheme with their respective legislatures, they agreed only to pay the face value of their debts to their state treasuries in state or Continental paper money. Since this money was practically worthless, the planters in effect repudiated their debts.

During the Revolution, all the states had passed anti-Loyalist legislation, and many state governments had seized Loyalists' lands and goods, selling them to raise revenue for the war effort. Upwards of 100,000 Loyalists fled to Canada and England, and their property losses ran into millions of dollars. Articles 5 and 6 of the peace treaty pledged Congress to "recommend" to the states that they stop persecuting Loyalists and restore confiscated Loyalist property. But wartime animosities remained high, ebbing only gradually as the 1780s wore on. Despite the pleadings of John Jay, the secretary for foreign affairs in the Confederation government, the states were slow to rescind their punitive legislation or allow the recovery of confiscated property.

Combined with the matter of the unpaid debts, the continued failure of the states to make restitution to the Loyalists gave the British a convenient pretext to hold on to the forts in the West that they had promised to relinquish in the Treaty of Paris. Their refusal to abandon the forts, which extended from Lake Champlain in upstate New York westward along the Great Lakes, was part of an overall strategy to keep the United States weak, divided, and small. The continued British presence in the region effectively shut Americans out of the fur trade with the Indians. It also insulted the sovereignty of the United States and threatened the security of its northern frontier. In 1784, exasperated New Yorkers warned Congress that unless the British were forced to leave, New York would "be compelled to consider herself as left to pursue her own Councils, destitute of the Protection of the United States." Elsewhere, the British, spurred on by Canadian officials, encouraged secessionist movements in the Northwest and sought out Indian allies to fight for a possible buffer state south of the Great Lakes that would keep Americans hemmed in along the Atlantic seaboard.

Throughout the 1780s, the British also explored the possibility of entering into an economic alliance with Vermont. Created in 1777 out of land claimed by both New York and New Hampshire, Vermont proclaimed itself an independent republic, free from the control of the British Parliament and the American Congress. Ethan Allen and his brothers Ira

and Levi held the power in Vermont politics, and their ambitious schemes for profiting from the sale of such raw materials as lumber and naval stores depended on a favorable treaty with Britain. The Allen brothers initiated a series of negotiations with the British in the 1780s in which they offered a treaty of friendship in exchange for recognition of Vermont's independence and trading privileges within the British Empire. The British were tempted but held back for fear of unduly antagonizing the United States. (Most Vermonters were strongly pro-American in their loyalties, and in 1791, after settlement of the disputed land claims, Vermont joined the Union as the fourteenth state.)

Although concerned by British provocations in the West and fears that the British would convert Vermont into a client state, American officials viewed Britain's retaliatory trade policies as the gravest threat to American security and prosperity. John Adams, the American minister to London, sought in vain to counter Britain's anti-American economic policies. "I may reason till I die to no purpose," Adams reported to Jay in June 1785, and he complained that he was treated as a complete "cypher."

Adams soon concluded that the British would never lift their trading and shipping restrictions until forced to do so by a uniform American system of discriminatory duties on British goods. The problem was that a uniform policy was impossible to achieve under the Articles of Confederation. Retaliatory navigation acts by individual states did little good because they left the British free to play one state off another. Adams could denounce Parliament as a "parcel of sots" for restricting American trade, but only with a strong, centralized government could Americans fashion a navigation system that would command Britain's respect.

Spain and the Mississippi River

At the close of the Revolutionary War, Spain reimposed barriers on American commerce within its empire. Anxious to maintain as large a buffer zone as possible between its Louisiana and Florida possessions and the restless Americans, Spain also refused to recognize the southern and western boundaries of the United States as specified in the treaty with Britain in 1783, holding out instead for a more northerly border (see Map 7-2). And of greatest consequence, it denied the claim of the United States to free navigation of the entire length of the Mississippi River.

The Mississippi question was explosive because on its resolution hinged American settlement and control of the entire western region south

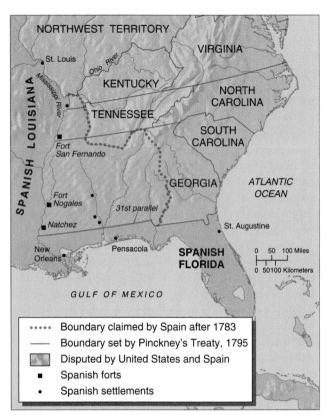

Map 7-2 *Disputed Territory in the West after the Treaty of Paris*
Throughout the 1780s, Spain asserted title to a large area in the West south of the Ohio River.

of the Ohio River. Southerners were rapidly moving into this area, and the slave South expected to gain new support for an alliance against the commercial North as new slave states were created south of the Ohio. Free navigation of the Mississippi was essential to the realization of these expectations. Only with access to the Mississippi and the commercial right of deposit at New Orleans—that is, the right to transfer cargoes to oceangoing vessels—could the region's farmers, then mostly in what would become Tennessee and Kentucky, profitably reach national and international markets.

In the wake of the Revolution, the settlers of Kentucky, which was still part of Virginia, and Tennessee, which was still part of North Carolina, flirted with the idea of secession. According to a 1785 report, settlers in Kentucky felt they did "not at present enjoy a greater portion of liberty [under Virginia] than an American colony might have done a few years ago had she been allowed a Representation in the British Parliament." Impatient to secure both political independence and the economic benefits that would come with access to the Mississippi, the separatists were not particular about whom they dealt

with. They became entangled in a web of diplomatic intrigue that included the Spanish, the Indians, and American authorities east of the mountains.

Spain sought to trade on the divided loyalties of American speculators and frontier settlers to its advantage, employing some of them as spies and informers. Led by General James Wilkinson in Kentucky, these agents encouraged separatist plots and talk of a western confederation under Spanish protection. Spain likewise sought to exploit divisions among Indian groups. When the Confederation government and the state of Georgia negotiated treaties with southern Indians to open up land for white settlement, the Spanish responded by recruiting Indian groups into an alliance system of their own. The staunchest of the Spanish allies were the Creeks, a tribe of some five thousand warriors led by Alexander McGillivray, son of a trader father and a half-French, half-Creek mother.

Spain stepped up pressure on the West in the summer of 1784 when it closed the Mississippi River within Spanish territory to American trade. Hoping now to benefit from American weakness, Spain also opened negotiations for a long-term settlement with the United States. The Spanish negotiator, Don Diego de Gardoqui, offered a deal that cleverly played the interests of the North against those of the South and West. In exchange for an American agreement to surrender claims to navigate the Mississippi for thirty years, Gardoqui proposed to grant the United States significant trading concessions in the Spanish Empire that would open new markets and new sources of hard money to the financially pressed merchants of the northeastern states. John Jay, his American negotiating partner, reluctantly accepted the offer.

When Jay released the terms of the proposed treaty with Spain in 1786, Congress erupted in angry debate. Southerners, who had taken the lead in the settlement of the West, accused Jay of selling out their interests. The treaty threatened the agrarian alliance they hoped to forge with the West, increasing the odds that the West would break from the East and go its own way. Vowing that they would not surrender the West, southern congressmen united to defeat the treaty. Nine states' votes were required for ratification under the Articles, and Jay's treaty could gain only seven—all in the North.

The regional antagonisms exposed by the Jay-Gardoqui talks heightened the alarm over the future of the republic provoked by Shays's Rebellion earlier in 1786. The Union had never appeared more fragile or Congress under the Articles of Confederation so powerless to resolve its differences. South-

This portrait, sketched in about 1790 by John Trumbull, is the only known likeness of Alexander McGillivray, a Creek leader who effectively played off Spanish and American interests in the Southeast to gain a measure of independence for the Creeks in the 1780s.

erners openly calculated the value of remaining in a Union seemingly dominated by the commercial North, and Westerners warned that unless they were upheld on the Mississippi issue, they would consider themselves "relieved from all Federal Obligations and fully at Liberty to exact alliances & Connections wherever they find them." As the sense of crisis deepened in 1786, the nationalists grew in influence and numbers. Led by Alexander Hamilton of New York and James Madison of Virginia, they now argued that only a radical political change could preserve the republic and fulfill the promise of its greatness.

Toward a New Union

In June 1786, a worried John Jay wrote to General George Washington that he was "uneasy and apprehensive; more so than during the war. Then we had a fixed object. . . . The case is now altered; we are going and doing wrong, and therefore I look forward to evils and calamities, but without being able to guess at the instrument, nature, or measure of them." Other nationalists fully shared Jay's forebodings.

Everywhere they saw unsolved problems and portents of disaster: unpaid debts, social unrest, squabbling states, sectional hostilities, the uncertain status of the West, blocked channels of trade, foreign intrigues, and a paralyzing lack of centralized authority and purpose. They feared that the republic's very survival was now at stake.

In September 1786, delegates from several states met at the **Annapolis Convention,** in Annapolis, Maryland, seeking to devise a uniform system of commercial regulation for the country. While there, a group of nationalist leaders called on all the states to send delegates to a convention at Philadelphia "to devise such further provisions as shall appear to them necessary to render the constitution of the Federal Government adequate to the exigencies of the Union." The leaders who met at the **Constitutional Convention** in Philadelphia forged an entirely new framework of governance, the **Constitution of the United States,** that called for a federal republic with a powerful and effective national government. In 1788, after a close struggle in state ratifying conventions, the Constitution was adopted.

The Road to Philadelphia

The road to Philadelphia began at Mount Vernon, George Washington's estate in Virginia. Commissioners from Maryland and Virginia met there in March 1785 to resolve jurisdictional and navigational disputes over the Potomac River and Chesapeake Bay, waters shared by both states. Washington had a personal stake in hosting the conference, for he was president of the Potomac Company, a newly formed group of investors hoping to build a series of canals linking the Potomac River with the Shenandoah and Ohio Valleys. The meeting went so well that the participants invited representatives from Delaware and Pennsylvania to join them at a conference in Annapolis the following year to formulate policies for interstate commerce on the waterways that linked the Chesapeake region and the Ohio Valley. James Madison then broadened the scope of the Annapolis Conference to include representatives from all thirteen states for a general discussion of how best to promote and regulate interstate trade.

Only nine states decided to send delegates to the Annapolis Convention, and those from only five had actually arrived when the nationalists, at the prompting of Madison and Hamilton, abruptly adjourned the meeting. They then called on the states and Congress to approve a full-scale constitutional convention for Philadelphia in May 1787.

The timing of the call for the Philadelphia Convention could not have been better. During the fall and winter of 1786, the agrarian protests unleashed by Shays's Rebellion in Massachusetts spilled over into other states. For many Americans, especially those with wealth to protect, Shays's Rebellion dramatized the need for change. Coupled with talk of a dismemberment of the Union in the wake of the Jay-Gardoqui negotiations, the agrarian unrest strengthened the case of the nationalists for more centralized authority.

All the states except Rhode Island, which wanted to retain exclusive control over its own trade, sent delegates to Philadelphia. The fifty-five men who attended the convention represented an extraordinary array of talent and experience. Chiefly lawyers by training or profession, most of them had served in the Confederation Congress, and more than one-third had fought in the Revolution. Extremely well educated by the standards of the day, the delegates were members of the intellectual as well as the political and economic elite. As a group, they were far wealthier than the average American. Most had investments in land and the public securities of the United States. At least nineteen owned slaves. Their greatest asset as a working body was their common commitment to a nationalist solution to the crisis of confidence they saw gripping the republic. Strong supporters of the Articles of Confederation mostly refused to attend, perhaps because, as Patrick Henry of Virginia remarked, they "smelt a rat."

The Convention at Work

When it agreed to the Philadelphia Convention, Congress authorized only a revision of the Articles of Confederation. Almost from the start, however, the delegates set about replacing the Articles altogether. Their first action was to elect George Washington unanimously as the convention's presiding officer, gaining credibility for their deliberations from his prestige. The most ardent nationalists then immediately seized the initiative by presenting the **Virginia Plan.** Drafted by James Madison, this plan replaced the Confederation Congress with a truly national government organized like most state governments, with a bicameral legislature, an executive, and a judiciary.

Two features of the Virginia Plan stood out. First, it granted the national Congress power to legislate "in all cases in which the separate states are incompetent" and to nullify any state laws that in its judgment were contrary to the "articles of Union." Second, it made representation in both houses of Congress proportional to population. This meant that the most populous states would have more votes in Congress than the less populous states, giving them effective control of the government. In short, Madison sought

Washington's role as a presiding officer of the Constitutional Convention was essential to the nationalists in securing popular support for the new Constitution.

to all but eliminate the independent authority of the states while also forcing the smaller states to defer to the more populous ones in national affairs.

Delegates from the small states countered with the **New Jersey Plan,** introduced on June 15 by William Paterson. This plan kept intact the basic structure of the Confederation Congress—one state, one vote—but otherwise amended the Articles by giving the national government the explicit power to tax and to regulate domestic and foreign commerce. In addition, it gave acts of Congress precedence over state legislation, making them "the supreme law of the respective states."

The New Jersey Plan was quickly voted down, and the convention remained deadlocked for another month over how to apportion state representation in the national government. The issue was finally resolved on July 16 with the so-called **Great Compromise.** Based on a proposal by Roger Sherman of Connecticut, the compromise split the differences between the small and large states. Small states were given equal footing with large states in the Senate, or upper house, where each would have two votes. In the lower house, the House of Representatives, the number of seats was made proportional to population, giving larger states the advantage. The Great Compromise also settled a sectional dispute over representation between the free (or about to be free) states and slave states. The southern states wanted slaves counted for apportioning representation in the House but excluded from direct tax assessments. The northern states wanted slaves counted for tax assessments but excluded for apportioning representation. To settle the issue, the Great Compromise settled on an expedient, if morally troubling, formula: Free residents were to be counted precisely; to that count would be added three-fifths "of all other persons," excluding Indians not taxed. Thus the slave states gained additional political representation while the states in the North received assurances that the owners of nonvoting slaves would have to bear part of the cost of any direct taxes levied by the new government.

The Great Compromise ended the first phase of the convention, which had focused on the general framework of a stronger national government. In its next phase, the convention debated the specific powers to be delegated to the new government. It was at this point that the sectional cleavage between North and South over slavery and other issues came most prominently to the fore. As Madison had warned in late June, "the great division of interests" in the United States would arise from the effect of states "having or not having slaves."

The sectional clash first erupted over the power of Congress to regulate commerce. At issue was whether Congress could regulate trade and set tariffs by a simple majority vote. Southerners worried that a northern majority would pass navigation acts favoring northern shippers and drive up the cost of sending southern commodities to Europe. To counter this threat, delegates from the Lower South demanded that a two-thirds majority be required to enact trade legislation. Suddenly, the central plank in the nationalists' program—the unified power to force trading concessions from Britain—was endangered. A frustrated Madison urged his fellow southerners to remember that "as we are laying the foundation of a great empire, we ought to take a permanent view of the subject."

In the end, Madison had his way; the delegates agreed that enacting trade legislation would require only a simple majority. In return, however, southerners exacted concessions on the slavery issue. When planters from South Carolina and Georgia made it clear they would agree to join a new Union only if they could continue to import slaves, the convention abandoned a proposal to ban the foreign slave trade. Instead, following the lead of Roger Sherman of Connecticut, who argued that emancipation sentiment would eventually lead to abolition of slavery anyway, antislavery New Englanders reached a compromise with the delegates from the Lower South: Congress would be barred from acting against the slave trade for twenty years. In addition, bowing to the fears of planters that Congress could use its taxing power to undermine slavery, the convention denied Congress the right to tax exports from any state. And to alleviate southern concerns that slaves might escape to freedom in the North, the new Constitution included an explicit provision calling on any state to return "persons held to Service or Labour" in another.

After settling the slavery question in late August, the convention had one last significant hurdle to clear: the question of the national executive. For months the delegates had gone around in circles debating how presidents should be elected, how long they should serve, and what their powers should be. But in early September, eager to wrap matters up and close to exhaustion after working through a long, hot summer, they moved quickly to resolve these issues.

In large part because of their confidence in General Washington, whom nearly everyone expected to be the first president, the delegates fashioned a chief executive office with broad discretionary powers. The prerogatives of the president included the rank of commander in chief of the armed forces, the authority to conduct foreign affairs and negotiate treaties, the right to appoint diplomatic and judicial officers, and the power to veto congressional legislation. The president's term of office was set at four years, with no limits on how often an individual could be reelected.

Determining how to elect the president proved a thorny problem. The delegates envisioned a forceful, energetic, and independent executive insulated from the whims of an uninformed public and the intrigues of the legislature. As a result, they rejected both popular election and election by Congress. The solution they hit upon was the convoluted system of an "electoral college." Each state was left free to determine how it would choose presidential electors equal to the number of its representatives and senators. These electors would then cast votes to select a president. If no candidate received a majority of the electoral votes, the election would be turned over to the House of Representatives, where each state would have one vote.

After a style committee polished the wording in the final draft of the Constitution, thirty-nine of the forty-two delegates still in attendance signed the document on September 17. The Preamble, which originally began with a list of the states, was reworded at the last minute to begin simply: "We the people of the United States, in order to form a more perfect Union . . ." This subtle change had significant implications. By identifying the people, and not a collection of states, as the source of authority, it emphasized the national vision of the framers and their desire to create a government quite different from a confederation of states.

Overview
of the Constitution

Although not as strong as the most committed nationalists would have liked, the central government outlined in the Constitution was to have far more powers than those entrusted to Congress under the Articles of Confederation (see the summary table "The Articles of Confederation and the Constitution Compared.") The Constitution's provision for a strong, single-person executive had no precedent in the Articles. Nor did the provision for a Supreme Court. The Constitution vested this Court, as well as the lower courts that Congress was empowered to establish, with the judicial power of the United States. In addition, the Constitution specifically delegated to Congress the powers to tax, borrow and coin money, regulate commerce, and raise armed forces that the Confederation government had lacked.

Most of the economic powers of Congress came at the expense of the states, which were prohibited from passing tariffs, issuing money, or—in an obvious reference to the debtor relief legislation in the 1780s—enacting any law that infringed on the contractual rights of creditors to collect money from debtors. Further curbing the sovereignty of the states was a clause stipulating that the Constitution and all national legislation and treaties were to be "the supreme law of the land." This clause has subsequently been interpreted as giving the central government the power to declare state laws unconstitutional

A no-nonsense realism, as well as a nationalist outlook, infused the Constitution. Its underlying political philosophy was that, in Madison's wonderful phrase, "ambition must be made to counter ambition." Madison and the other members of the national elite who met at Philadelphia were convinced that self-interest, not disinterested virtue, motivated political behavior. As proof, they cited what to them was the sorry record of the state governments in protecting property rights and promoting social order. In their view, these governments

SUMMARY

THE ARTICLES OF CONFEDERATION AND THE CONSTITUTION COMPARED

	Articles	Constitution
Sovereign power of the central government	No power to tax or raise armies	Power granted on taxes and armed forces
Source of power	Individual states government	Shared through federalism between states and the national
Representation in Congress	Equal representation of states in a unicameral Congress	A bicameral legislature with equal representation of the states in the Senate and proportional representation in the House
Amendment process	Unanimous consent of the states	Consent of three-fourths of the states
Executive	None provided for	Office of the president
National judiciary	None provided for	Established the Supreme Court

were failures because they had been captured by unrestrained majorities corrupted by the selfishness of competing interest groups. Accepting interest group politics as inevitable and seeking to prevent a tyrannical majority from forming at the national level, the architects of the Constitution designed a central government in which competing blocs of power counterbalanced one another.

The Constitution placed both internal and external restraints on the powers granted to the central government. The functional division of the government into executive, legislative, and judicial branches, each with ways to keep the others from exercising excessive power, created an internal system of checks and balances. For example, the Senate's authority to approve or reject presidential appointments and to ratify or reject treaties was a curb on the powers of the executive. The president commanded the armed forces, but only Congress could declare war. The president could veto congressional legislation, but Congress could override that veto with a two-thirds vote. To pass in the first place, legislation had to be approved by both the House of Representatives, which, with its membership proportional to population, represented the interests of the people at large, and the Senate, which represented the interests of the states. And as an ultimate check against executive abuse of power, Congress could indict, convict, and remove from office a president who tried to set himself above the law.

Although the Constitution did not explicitly grant it, the Supreme Court soon claimed the right to invalidate acts of Congress and the president that it found to be unconstitutional. This power of **judicial review** provided another check against legislative and executive authority. To guard against an arbitrary federal judiciary, the Constitution empowered Congress to determine the size of the Supreme Court and to indict and remove federal judges appointed by the president.

The external restraints on the central government were to be found in the nature of its relationship to the state governments. This relationship was based on **federalism,** the division of power between local and central authorities. By listing specific powers for Congress, the Constitution implied that all other powers were to be retained by the states. Thus while strengthening the national government, the Constitution did not obliterate the sovereign rights of the states, leaving them free to curb the potential power of the national government in the ambiguous areas between national and state sovereignty.

This ambiguity in the federalism of the Constitution was both its greatest strength and its greatest weakness. It allowed both nationalists and advocates of states' rights to support the Constitution. But the issue of slavery, left unresolved in the gray area between state and national sovereignty, would continue to fester, sparking sectional conflict over the extent of national sovereignty that would plunge the republic into civil war three-quarters of a century later.

The Struggle over Ratification

The realism the Philadelphia delegates displayed in the drafting of the Constitution extended to the procedure they devised for implementing it. Knowing full well that they had exceeded their instructions by proposing an entirely new government, not an amended version of the Articles, and aware that the Articles' requirement of unanimous consent by the state legislatures to any amendment would result in certain defeat, they boldly bypassed both Congress and the state legislatures.

The last article of the Constitution stipulated that it would go into effect when it had been ratified by at least nine of the states acting through specially elected popular conventions. Influenced by the nationalist sentiments of many of its members, one-third of whom had attended the Philadelphia Convention, and perhaps weary of its own impotence, Congress accepted this drastic and not clearly legal procedure, submitting the Constitution to the states in late September 1787.

The delegates in Philadelphia had excluded the public from their proceedings. The publication of the text of the Constitution lifted this veil of secrecy and touched off a great political debate. Although those who favored the Constitution could most accurately have been defined as nationalists, they referred to themselves as **Federalists,** a term that helped deflect charges that they favored an excessive centralization of political authority. By default, the opponents of the Constitution were known as **Antifederalists,** a negative-sounding label that obscured their support of the state-centered sovereignty that most Americans associated with federalism. Initially outmaneuvered in this way, the Antifederalists never did mount an effective campaign to counter the Federalists' output of pamphlets, speeches, and newspaper editorials (see the summary table "Federalists versus Antifederalists").

The Antifederalists did attract some men of wealth and social standing. Three of them—Elbridge Gerry of Massachusetts and George Mason and Edmund Randolph of Virginia—had been delegates at Philadelphia but refused to sign the Constitution. They feared that the new national government would swallow up the state governments.

Most Antifederalists, however, were backcountry farmers, men with mud on their boots who lived far from centers of communication and market outlets for their produce. They distrusted the social and commercial elite, and many Antifederalists saw in the Constitution a sinister plot by this elite "to lord it over the rest of their fellow citizens, to trample the poorer part of the people under their feet that they may be rendered their servants and slaves." The Antifederalists clung to the belief that only a small republic, one composed of relatively homogeneous social interests, could secure the voluntary attachment of the people necessary for a free government. They argued that a large republic, such as the one framed by the Constitution, would inevitably become tyrannical because it was too distant and removed from the interests of common citizen-farmers.

However much the Antifederalists attacked the Constitution as a danger to the individual liberties

SUMMARY

FEDERALISTS VERSUS THE ANTIFEDERALISTS

	Federalists	Antifederalists
Position on the Constitution	Favored the Constitution	Opposed the Constitution
Position on the Articles of Confederation	Felt the Articles had to be abandoned	Felt the Articles needed only to be amended
Position on the power of the states	Sought to curb the power of the states with a new central government	Felt the power of the states should be paramount
Position on the need for a bill of rights	Initially saw no need for a bill of rights in the Constitution	Saw the absence of a bill of rights in the proposed Constitution as a threat to individual liberties
Position on the optimum size of the republic	Believed a large republic could best safeguard personal freedoms	Believed only a small republic formed on common interests could protect individual rights
Source of support	Commercial farmers, merchants, shippers, artisans, holders of the national debt	State-centered politicians, most backcountry farmers

and local independence that they believed the Revolution had been fought to safeguard, they were no political match for the Federalists. They lacked the social connections, access to newspapers, and self-confidence of the more cosmopolitan and better-educated Federalists. In addition, the Federalists could more easily mobilize their supporters, who were concentrated in the port cities and commercial farming areas along the coast.

With talent, intellect, and political savvy on their side, the Federalists skillfully built on the momentum for change that had developed out of the crisis atmosphere of 1786. They successfully portrayed the Constitution as the best opportunity to erect a governing structure capable of preserving and extending the gains of the Revolution.

Conservatives shaken by Shays's Rebellion lined up behind the Constitution. So too did groups—creditors, merchants, manufacturers, urban artisans, commercial farmers—whose interests would be promoted by economic development. The enhanced powers of the national government held out the promise of protecting the home market from British imports, enlarging foreign markets for American exports, promoting a stable and uniform currency, and raising revenues to pay off the Revolutionary War debt.

In the early stages, the Federalists scored a string of easy victories (see Map 7–3). Delaware ratified the Constitution on December 7, 1787, and within a month, so too had Pennsylvania, New Jersey, Georgia, and Connecticut. Except for Pennsylvania, these were small, sparsely populated states that stood to benefit economically or militarily from a stronger central government. The Constitution carried in the larger state of Pennsylvania because of the Federalists' strength in the commercial center of Philadelphia.

The Federalists faced their toughest challenge in the large states that had generally been more successful in going it alone during the 1780s. One of the most telling arguments of the Antifederalists in these and other states was the absence of a bill of rights in the Constitution. The framers had felt it unnecessary to include such an explicit protection of individual rights in a document intended to specify the powers of a national government and had barely discussed a bill of rights in Philadelphia. Realizing the importance of the issue, and citing Article 5 of the Constitution, which provided for an amendment process, the Federalists promised to recommend amending the Constitution with a bill of rights once it was ratified. By doing so, they split the ranks of the Antifederalists in Massachusetts. After the Federalists gained the support of two venerable heroes of the Revolution, John Hancock and Sam Adams, the Massachusetts convention approved the Constitution by a

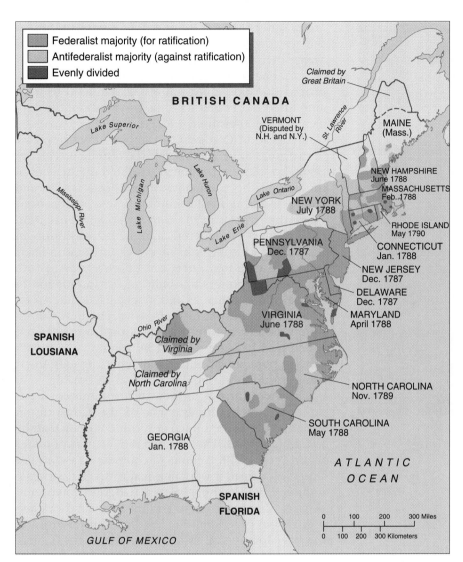

Federalist majority (for ratification)
Antifederalist majority (against ratification)
Evenly divided

Map 7-3   The Ratification Vote on the Constitution

Aside from some frontier districts exposed to possible foreign attack, the strongest support for the Constitution came from coastal and interior areas tied into a developing commercial economy.

Source: *After Norman K. Risjord,* America: A History of the United States, *2nd ed. (1988), p. 170.*

close vote in February 1788. To win over Hancock, the Federalists had played on his vanity, suggesting that they would back him for a top national post. Adams was convinced to back the Federalists by demonstrations of Boston artisans in favor of national tariff protection.

The major hurdles remaining for the Federalists were Virginia, the most populous state, and the strategically located New York. Technically, the Constitution could have gone into effect without them once Maryland, South Carolina, and New Hampshire had ratified it, bringing the total number of states to ratify to the required nine. But without Virginia, which ratified on June 25, and New York, which followed a month later, the new Union would have been weak and the Federalist victory far from assured.

To eke out victory in these crucial states, the Federalists drew on their pragmatism and persuasiveness. As in Massachusetts, they were helped by their promise of a bill of rights. And for the New York

campaign, Madison, Jay, and Hamilton wrote an eloquent series of eighty-five essays known collectively as **The Federalist** to allay fears that the Constitution would so consolidate national power as to menace individual liberties. In the two most original and brilliant essays in *The Federalist,* essays 10 and 51, Madison turned traditional republican doctrine on its head. A large, diverse republic like the one envisaged by the Constitution, he reasoned, not a small and homogeneous one, offered the best hope for safeguarding the rights of all citizens. This was because a large republic would include a multitude of contending interest groups, making it difficult for any combination of them to coalesce into a tyrannical majority that could oppress minority rights. With this argument Madison had developed a political rationale by which Americans could have both an empire and personal freedom.

North Carolina and Rhode Island did not ratify until after the new government was functioning.

Although physically frail, James Madison, shown here in a portrait made in about 1815, was a formidable thinker whose essays in The Federalist *endure as a lasting contribution to political theory.*

North Carolina joined the Union in 1789 once Congress submitted the amendments that comprised the Bill of Rights. The obstinate Rhode Islanders stayed out until 1790, when Congress forced them in with a threat of commercial reprisal.

Conclusion

In freeing themselves from British rule, Americans embarked on an unprecedented wave of constitution making that sought to put into practice abstract principles of republicanism that held that political power should derive from the people. Between 1776 and 1780, Americans developed a unique system of constitutionalism. They proclaimed the supremacy of constitutions over ordinary legislation; detailed the powers of government in a written document; provided protection for individual freedoms in bills of rights; and fashioned a process for framing governments through the election of delegates to a special constitutional convention and the popular ratification of the work of that convention. In all of these

areas, Americans were pioneers in demonstrating to the rest of the world how common citizens could create their own governments.

The curbs on centralized power that characterized the state constitutions also applied to what amounted to the first national constitution, the Articles of Confederation. Indeed, the inability of the Confederation Congress to exercise effective power in the areas of taxation and foreign trade was a crippling flaw that thoroughly discredited the Articles in the eyes of the nationalist-minded leaders who had emerged during the Revolution. These leaders overthrew the Articles at the Constitutional Convention in 1787 and engineered a peaceful revolution in securing the ratification of the Constitution. Their victory in creating a new central government with real national powers was built on the foundation of constitutional concepts and mechanisms that Americans had laid down in their states The new Constitution did rest on the consent of the governed, and it endured because it could be amended to reflect shifts in popular will and to widen the circle of Americans granted the rights of political citizenship.

Accepting as a given that self-interest drove political action, the framers of the Constitution designed the new national government to turn ambition against itself. They created rival centers of power that forced selfish factions to compete in a constant struggle to form a workable majority. That struggle occurred both within the national government and between that government and the states in the American system of federalism. The Constitution thus set the stage for an entirely new kind of national politics.

Review Questions

1. How would you define republicanism? Do you believe that Americans today still believe in the basic tenets of republicanism?

2. What was so unprecedented about the new state constitutions, and what principles of government did they embody?

3. What were the problems of the economy in the 1780s, and why did clashes between debtors and creditors become so divisive? Do you think that an economic recovery could have been achieved under the Articles of Confederation?

4. Do you feel that the diplomatic weaknesses of the United States under the Articles were as serious as its internal problems? What were the sources of those weaknesses, and what threat did they pose for national unity?

5. What sorts of men drafted the Constitution in 1787, and how representative were they of all Americans? What explains the differences between the Federalists and Antifederalists? Do you think they shared the same vision of what they wanted America to become? How widespread was the popular backing for the Constitution, and what accounts for its ratification?

Recommended Readings

J. Hector St. John Crèvecoeur, *Letters from an American Farmer and Sketches of Eighteenth-Century America,* ed. Albert E. Stone (1986). This modern reprint of Crèvecoeur's work provides an accessible account of Americans and their living conditions in the late eighteenth century.

Merrill Jensen, *The New Nation: A History of the United States during the Confederation, 1781–1787* (1948). This work makes the strongest case for the Articles as a tentative success that was overturned in a conservative reaction that exaggerated threats to social order.

Richard B. Morris, *The Forging of the Union, 1781–1789* (1987). The best-balanced synthesis of the 1780s, this book documents the creative statesmanship of the leaders of the Constitutional Convention.

Gordon Wood, *The Creation of the American Republic, 1776–1787* (1969). This masterful study is indispensable for understanding the transformation in American republicanism between the winning of independence and the ratification of the Constitution.

Additional Sources

The New Order of Republicanism

Willi Paul Adams, *The First American Constitutions: Republican Ideology and the Making of the State Constitutions* (1980).

Ruth H. Block, *Visionary Republic: Millennial Themes in American Thought, 1756–1800* (1985).

Sylvia R. Frey, *Water from the Rock: Black Resistance in a Revolutionary Age* (1991).

Linda Kerber, *Women of the Republic* (1980).

Donald Lutz, *Popular Consent and Popular Control: Whig Political Theory in the Early State Constitutions* (1980).

J. R. Pole, *Political Representation in England and the Origins of the American Republic* (1966).

Gordon Wood, *The Radicalism of the American Revolution* (1992).

Problems at Home

Joseph L. Davis, *Sectionalism in American Politics, 1774–1787* (1977).

Robert A. Gross, ed., *In Debt to Shays: The Bicentennial of an Agrarian Rebellion* (1992).

Ronald L. Hoffman and Peter Albert, eds., *Sovereign States in an Age of Uncertainty* (1981).

Jackson Turner Main, *Political Parties before the Constitution* (1973).

Peter S. Onuf, *The Origins of the Federal Republic* (1983).

Diplomatic Weaknesses

Charles T. Ritcheson, *Aftermath of Revolution: British Policy toward the United States, 1783–1795* (1969).

Richard W. Van Alstyne, *The Rising American Empire* (1980).

Arthur P. Whitaker, *The Spanish-American Frontier, 1783–95* (1962 reprint).

Toward a New Nation

Charles Beard, *An Economic Interpretation of the Constitution* (1913).

Roger H. Brown, *Redeeming the Republic: Federalists, Taxation, and the Origins of the Constitution* (1993).

Christopher M. Duncan, *The Anti-Federalists and Early American Political Thought* (1995).

Michael Allen Gillespie and Michael Lienesch, eds., *Ratifying the Constitution* (1989).

Jackson Turner Main, *The Anti-Federalists: Critics of the Constitution, 1781–1788* (1961).

Forrest McDonald, *Novus Ordo Seclorum: The Intellectual Origins of the Constitution* (1985).

Richard B. Morris, *Witness at the Creation* (1985).

Where to Learn More

❖ **South Street Seaport Museum, New York City, New York** Maritime commerce was the lifeblood of the postrevolutionary economy. The artifacts and the exhibits here offer a fine introduction to the seafaring world of the port city that became the nation's first capital in the new federal Union.

❖ **Independence National Historical Park, Philadelphia, Pennsylvania** Walks and guided tours through this historic district enable one to grasp much of the physical setting in which the delegates to the Constitutional Convention met.

❖ **Northern Indiana Center for History, South Bend, Indiana** The permanent exhibition on the St. Joseph River valley of northern Indiana and southern Michigan explains the material world of this region and how it changed as first Europeans and then Americans mingled and clashed with the Native American population.

WE THE PEOPLE

1789

*B*y the 1780s, Americans were a separate, independent people. Having freed themselves from British rule, they built on what they believed was their birthright of English liberties to create the world's largest republic of self-governing citizens. They saw themselves as the inheritors of both the British republican tradition and Britain's North American empire. As George Washington said in 1783, when independence had been secured, Americans were now "the lords and proprietors of a vast tract of continent." But who did Washington and the nation's other founders have in mind when they spoke of "Americans"? And if Americans were the lords, who were the subjects?

The language the founders of the United States had used to justify their revolution against Britain and to define their new republican society was expansive and universalistic. It spoke of human equality and the people's right to consent to their government. "All men are created equal," wrote Jefferson in the Declaration of Independence. And the framers of the Constitution emphasized the need for a government based on the consent of the governed when they wrote in the Preamble, "We the people of the United States, in order to form a more perfect Union . . . and secure the blessings of liberty . . . do ordain and establish this Constitution."

But initially at least, the beneficiaries of these ideals were almost exclusively white male propertyholders of English or European descent. Other Americans—including African-Americans, Native Americans, women, and propertyless white men—were mostly excluded from the rights and privileges of citizenship in the new American republic.

When the Constitution was written, nine out of ten African-Americans were enslaved. Most whites accepted black slavery. As John Jay reported to an English abolitionist, "Very few among them even doubted the propriety and rectitude of it." Whites didn't consider granting rights to slaves as part of the American political order, and they treated the small minority of free blacks as second-class citizens with no claim to equality. The racial character of slavery in North America implicitly linked a white skin to freedom and a black skin to bondage and servitude.

As for Native Americans, they were the subjects Washington had in mind when he spoke of Americans as "lords" of the North American continent. Except as isolated individuals willing to accept white notions of private property, Indians were not allowed an equitable part in the new republic. The state and federal governments vied with one another to dispossess them of their land and push them farther west.

Women, despite their contribution to patriot victory, remained outside the political sphere of republican citizenship. The ingrained legal and cultural assumptions that kept them dependent on their husbands and fathers survived the Revolution largely intact. Republican ideology granted them only the indirect political responsibility of raising their children to be virtuous citizens.

The ideals of freedom and equality that emerged from the American Revolution, however, transcended the barriers of race and gender that kept all but propertyholding white males from enjoying full political rights in 1789. The ideals remained a kind of moral imperative, a reminder of the unfulfilled promise of the Revolution. In succeeding generations, more and more excluded groups would turn to those ideals in their struggle to be included to make "We the people" stand for all Americans.

Pacific Ocean

Portland

Sacramento

San Francisco

Salt Lake City

Santa Fe

San Antonio

Galveston

Omaha

Kansas City

Chicago

St. Louis

Memphis

Vicksburg

New Orleans

Gulf of Mexico

Mexico City

Antebellum Transportation Systems

———— Railroads, c. 1850
———— Canals
———— Cumberland Road
———— Stagecoach routes
------- Trails

Territorial Expansion

Thirteen original colonies, 1776

Westward expansion to 1783

Louisiana Purchase, 1803

Red River Basin, 1818

Florida, 1819

Annexation of Texas, 1845

Oregon Territory, 1846

Mexican cession, 1848

Gadsden Purchase, 1853

N
W   E
S

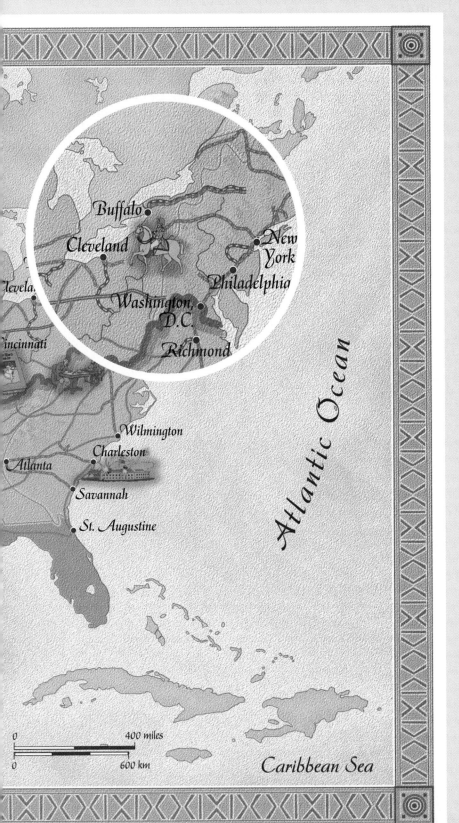

KEY TOPICS

- ❖ Regional diversity of the United States in 1789
- ❖ Laying the foundations of American government during Washington's first term
- ❖ Hamilton's financial policies
- ❖ The emergence of parties during Washington's second term
- ❖ The Adams administration and the election of 1800

*W*hen George Washington arrived in New York on April 23, 1789, for his inauguration as the first president of the United States, he struck many people as anything but presidential. As he took the oath of office a week later, he seemed to one observer "to have forgot half of what he was to say for he made a dead pause and stood for some time, to appearance, in a vacant mood." During his address to the assembled dignitaries he appeared "agitated and embarrassed more than he ever was by the leveled Cannon or pointed Musket. He trembled, and several times could scarce make out to read."

The president's shakiness reflected the shaky start of the country's new government. Two states, North Carolina and Rhode Island, had not yet ratified the Constitution and were still outside the federal Union. The newly elected members of Congress felt no urgency to assume their duties. They had been scheduled to meet in New York on March 4, 1789, to count the ballots of the electoral college and officially confirm Washington's election, but only one-quarter of them had arrived by then. A month would go by before the minimum needed to count the ballots could be mustered. Washington, his dignity ruffled by this show of congressional disinterest, dallied at Mount Vernon until formally notified of his election.

He had every reason to dread taking on the burden of the presidency. As head of the new national government, he would put at risk the legendary status he had achieved during the Revolution. Most Americans intensely feared centralized authority, which is why the framers deliberately left the word *national* out of the Constitution. Washington somehow had to establish loyalty to a new government whose main virtue in the eyes of many was the very vagueness of its defined powers.

The Constitution had created the framework for a national government, but pressing problems demanded the fleshing out of that framework. The government urgently needed revenue to begin paying off the immense debt incurred during the Revolution. It also had to address unstable conditions in the West, the territories between the Appalachians and the Mississippi. Remote from the seat of federal power and wooed by the British in the Old Northwest and the Spanish in the lower Mississippi Valley, western settlers wavered in their loyalties. The government would have to tie those people to the Union more tightly. Ultimately, the key to solving these and other problems was to establish the new republic's legitimacy. Washington and his supporters had to inspire popular backing for the government's right to exercise authority.

The realities of governing would soon shatter the nonpartisan ideal that had prevailed among the backers of the Constitution. By the end of Washington's first term, two political parties had begun to emerge. The **Federalist party**, which included Washington and his successor, John Adams, favored a strong central government. The opposition party, the **Jeffersonian Republicans**, took shape as a result of differences over financial policy and the response to the French Revolution. Led by Thomas Jefferson, the Republicans were distrustful of excessive central power. These first American political parties are not to be confused with the Federalists and Antifederalists of the ratification debate.

The Federalists, who governed through 1800, succeeded in showing a doubting world ruled by kings and queens that the American experiment in republican government could work. But as inheritors of a political tradition that equated parties with factions—temporary coalitions of selfish private interests—the Federalists doubted the loyalty of the Republicans. When the Federalists under President Adams attempted to suppress the Republicans, the stage was set for the critical election of 1800. Jefferson's victory in that election ended both Federalist rule and the republic's first major internal crisis.

This tapestry shows respectful crowds greeting Washington as he entered New York City for his inauguration as president.

Washington's America

Who were the Americans whom Washington was called on to lead? There is no easy answer. In 1789, as now, Americans identified and grouped themselves according to many factors, including race, sex, class, ethnicity, religion, and degree of personal freedom. Geographical factors, including climate and access to markets, further divided them into regions and sections. The resulting hodgepodge sorely tested the assumption—and it was never more than an assumption in 1789—that a single national government could govern Americans as a whole (see Figure 8-1).

The Uniformity of New England

The national census of 1790 counted nearly 4 million Americans, one in four of whom lived in New England. Although often viewed as the most typically "American" part of the young nation, New England in fact was rather atypical. It alone of the nation's formative regions had largely shut itself off from outsiders. Puritan notions of religious liberty that prevailed in the region extended only to those who subscribed to the Calvinist orthodoxy of the dominant Congregationalist church. Geography conspired with this religious exclusiveness to limit population diversity. New England's poor soils and long, cold winters made it an impractical place to cultivate cash crops like the tobacco and rice of the South. As a result, New England farmers had little need of imported white indentured servants or black slaves. Family members, helped by neighbors and the occasional hired hand, provided the labor on New England farms.

Puritan values and a harsh environment thus combined to make New England the most religiously and ethnically uniform region in the United States. Most of the people living there were descended from English immigrants who had arrived in the seventeenth century. Small pockets of Quakers, Baptists, and Catholics had gained the legal right of worship by the 1720s, but Congregationalism remained the official, state-supported religion in Connecticut and Massachusetts. Blacks and Indians together barely constituted 3 percent of New England's population. The few remaining Indians lived on reservations of inferior land, which they usually left only to find work as servants or day laborers.

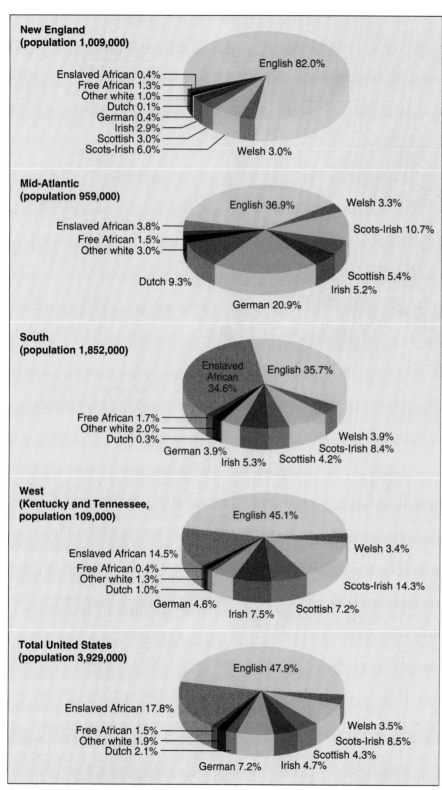

Figure 8-1   Ethnic Breakdown of the United States in 1790, by Region
*Unique racial and ethnic patterns shaped each of the nation's four major regions in
1790. New England was most atypical in its lack of racial or ethnic diversity.*

Source: The Statistics of the Population of the United States, *comp. Francis A. Walker (1872),
pp. 3–7; Thomas L. Purvis, "The European Ancestry of the United States Population, 1790,"*
William and Mary Quarterly, *41 (1984), p. 98.*

New Englanders found slavery incompatible with the natural rights philosophy that had emerged during the Revolution and abolished it in the 1780s. Slavery had, in any case, always been marginal in New England's economy. Owning slaves as domestic servants or artisans had been a status symbol for wealthy urban whites in Boston, Portsmouth, and Newport. As a result, about 20 percent of New England's small African-American population lived in cities, in contrast to the white population, 90 percent of which lived in the countryside. Freed slaves and their descendants tended to remain in the cities, where jobs were easier for them to find than in rural areas.

Women outnumbered men in parts of New England in 1789. This pattern—not found in other parts of the country—was the result of the pressure of an expanding population and the practice of dividing family farms among male heirs. As farms in the older, more densely settled parts of New England were divided into ever-smaller lots, many young men migrated west in search of cheap, arable land. They first pushed into the hilly regions of northern New England and then, by the 1790s, through the Mohawk River Valley into New York. Thus by 1789, women formed a slight majority in Connecticut, Massachusetts, and Rhode Island.

Despite their superior numbers, women in New England, as elsewhere, remained subordinate to men. Even so, the general testing of traditional authority that accompanied the Revolution led some New England women to question male power. The Massachusetts poet Judith Sargent Murray, for example, published essays asserting that women were the intellectual equals of men. Murray was the first woman to

CHRONOLOGY

1789 Inauguration of Washington.	Suppression of the Whiskey Rebellion in western Pennsylvania.
Congress establishes the first federal departments.	**1795** Jay's Treaty with Britain ratified.
French Revolution begins.	Treaty of Greenville with Ohio Indians.
1790 Hamilton submits the first of his financial reports to Congress.	**1796** Pinckney's Treaty with Spain ratified.
1791 Bill of Rights ratified.	Washington's Farewell Address.
Congress charters the Bank of the United States.	John Adams elected president.
1792 St. Clair's defeat along the Wabash.	**1797** Beginning of the Quasi-War with France.
Reelection of Washington.	**1798** XYZ Affair.
1793 France goes to war against Britain, Spain, and Holland.	Alien and Sedition Acts.
Genêt Mission.	Provisional army and direct tax.
Washington issues Proclamation of Neutrality.	Virginia a nd Kentucky Resolutions.
1794 Ohio is opened with the victory of General Anthony Wayne at the Battle of Fallen Timbers.	**1799** Fries's Rebellion in Pennsylvania.
	1800 Franco-American Accord.
	Thomas Jefferson elected president.

argue publicly in favor of equal educational opportunities for young women, and she boldly asserted that women should learn how to become economically independent.

Republican ideology, emphasizing the need of women to be intellectually prepared to raise virtuous, public-spirited children, also led reformers in New England to seek equal access for women to education. In 1789, Massachusetts became the first state to allocate funds specifically for girls' elementary education. And beginning in the 1780s, wealthy residents of eastern cities set up private academies for women that would later provide the foundation for women's higher education. Liberalized divorce laws in New England also allowed a woman to seek legal separation from an abusive or unfaithful spouse.

In other respects, politics in New England remained rooted in the Puritan past. Age, property, and reputation determined one's standing in a culture that valued a clearly defined social order. The moral code that governed town life promoted curbs on individual behavior for the benefit of the community as a whole. With their notions of collective liberty, New Englanders subscribed to a version of republicanism that favored strong government, setting themselves apart from most other

Americans, who embraced a more individualistic idea of liberty and a republicanism suspicious of government power. New Englanders perceived government as a divine institution with a moral responsibility to intervene in people's lives. Acting through town meetings, they taxed themselves for public services at rates two to four times higher than in the rest of the country. Their courts were also far more likely than those elsewhere to punish individuals for crimes against public order (like failing to observe the Sabbath properly) and sexual misconduct.

The Pluralism of the Mid-Atlantic Region

The states of the mid-Atlantic region—New York, New Jersey, and Pennsylvania—were the most ethnically and religiously diverse in the nation. People of English descent comprised somewhat less than 40 percent of the population. Other major ethnic groups included the Dutch and Scots-Irish in New York and Germans and Scots-Irish in New Jersey and Pennsylvania. With ethnic diversity came religious diversity. Transplanted New Englanders, who brought their Congregationalism and Yankee twang with them when they settled Long Island and

Francis Guy, Tontine Coffee House, c. 1797. Oil on canvas. Courtesy Collection of the New York Historical Society.

This painting of about 1797 captures the bustle of commercial activity in New York at the end of the eighteenth century. The large building to the left is the Tontine Coffee House, the site of insurance offices and the Stock Exchange.

northern New Jersey, made up about 40 percent of New York's ethnic English population. Among others of English descent, Anglicans predominated in New York and Quakers in New Jersey and Pennsylvania. The Dutch, concentrated in the lower Hudson Valley, had their own Dutch Reformed Church, and most Germans were either Lutherans or **pietists**, such as Mennonites and Moravians, who stressed personal piety over theological doctrine. The Presbyterian Scots-Irish settled heavily in the backcountry.

This mosaiclike pattern of ethnic and religious groupings was no accident. In contrast to Puritan New England, the Middle Colonies had offered freedom of worship to attract settlers. In addition, economic opportunities for newcomers were much greater than in New England. The soil was better, the climate was milder, and market outlets for agricultural products were more abundant. These conditions made the mid-Atlantic region the nation's first breadbasket. It produced surpluses of wheat, flour, and corn that were shipped out of New York and Philadelphia, the two largest cities in North America by 1790. Commercial agriculture fed urban growth and created a greater demand for labor in both rural and urban areas than in New England. The influx of Germans and Scots-Irish into the region in the eighteenth century occurred in response to this demand.

The demand for labor had also been met by importing African slaves. Blacks, both free and enslaved, made up 5 percent of the mid-Atlantic

population in 1790, and as in New England, they were more likely than whites to live in the maritime cities. New York had more slaveholders in 1790 than any other American city except Charleston, South Carolina. About 40 percent of white families in the city's nearby rural outposts of Queens, Brooklyn, and Staten Island owned slaves, a rate as high as in Maryland and South Carolina.

Despite its considerable strength in the port cities and adjacent rural areas, slavery was never an economically vital institution in most of the mid-Atlantic region. The region's major cash crop, wheat, required seasonal labor, which did not warrant tying up capital in slaves. Commercial agriculture did not rest on a slave base, nor did it produce a politically powerful class of planters. As a result, slavery in the mid-Atlantic region gave way to the demands for emancipation inspired by the natural rights philosophy of the Revolution.

Pennsylvania in 1780, New York in 1799, and New Jersey in 1804 each passed laws of gradual emancipation. These laws did not free adult slaves but provided that children born of a slave mother were to be freed at ages ranging between 18 and 28. Soon after the laws were passed, however, adult slaves began hastening their own freedom. They ran away, set fires, and pressured their owners to accept cash payments in return for a short, fixed term of labor service. But even as they gained their freedom, African-Americans had to confront enduring white racism. The comments of one white New Yorker suggest what they were up against. "We may sincerely advocate the freedom of black men," he wrote, "and yet assert their moral and physical inferiority."

The diversity of the mid-Atlantic region created a complex political environment. Competing cultural and economic interests prevented the kind of broad consensus on the meaning of republicanism that had emerged in New England. Some mid-Atlantic groups favored a strong central government to foster economic development and maintain traditional authority. Others wanted to keep government weak so as to foster a republican equality that would promote individual freedom.

Those who supported strong government included mercantile and financial leaders in the cities and commercial farmers in the countryside. These people tended to be Anglicans, Quakers, and Congregationalists of English descent. Those opposing them and favoring a more egalitarian republicanism tended to come from the middle and lower classes. They included subsistence farmers in the backcountry and artisans and day laborers in the cities. Most were Scots-Irish Presbyterians, but they also included Dutch Calvinists and German Lutherans. Fiercely independent and proud of their liberties, they resented the claims of the wealthy to political authority. They resisted government aid to business as a form of political corruption that unfairly enriched those who were already economically powerful.

The Slave South and Its Backcountry

In the South—the region from Maryland and Delaware to Georgia—climate and soil conditions favored the production of cash staples for world markets. Cultivating these crops required backbreaking labor that white immigrants preferred to avoid. As Thomas Jefferson put it, "In a warm climate no man will work for himself, who can make another labor for him." Southern planters relied on the coerced labor of African slaves, whose numbers made the South the most populous region in the country.

Just under 40 percent of all Southerners were slaves, but their concentration varied within the region. They were a majority in the Chesapeake Tidewater region, where slave ownership was widely distributed among white tobacco planters, including small and middling growers as well as the few great plantation owners. Farther south, in the tidal swamps of the South Carolina and Georgia lowcountry, where draining and clearing the land required huge inputs of labor, blacks outnumbered whites five to one. Slave ownership there was more concentrated than in the Tidewater. Large planters, the richest men in the country, worked hundreds of slaves in the production of rice, indigo, and sea-island cotton. Because yellow fever and malaria plagued the Carolina lowcountry, whites avoided the area, and the death rate among slaves was very high.

Slaves were less numerous in the Piedmont, or foothill, region of the South that lies between the coastal plain and the Appalachian highlands. Although sons of Tidewater planters had expanded tobacco production with slave labor into the Piedmont of Virginia and South Carolina, this was predominantly an area of nonslaveholding farmers. They relied on family labor to raise livestock, corn, and wheat. In the southern mountains, sloping to the southwest from the Blue Ridge in Virginia, the general absence of marketable crops diminished the demand for slave labor.

The free black population in the South had grown rapidly during the 1780s. Thousands of slaves fled behind British lines to win their freedom, and patriots freed others as a reward for enlisting in their forces. The Revolutionary values of liberty and equality also led many slave owners to question the morality of slavery. Legislatures in the Upper South passed laws making it financially easier than before for masters to manumit (free) their slaves. In Virginia alone, ten thousand slaves were manumitted in the 1780s. Slavery remained the foundation of the southern economy, however, and whites feared competition from freed blacks. As a result, no southern state embarked on a general program of emancipation, and slavery in the region survived the turbulence of the Revolutionary era.

Economic conditions in the South, where the raw poverty of the backcountry offset the great wealth of the lowcountry, stamped the region's politics and culture. Tidewater planters were predominantly Anglican and of English descent. Piedmont farmers were more likely to be Scots-Irish Presbyterians and Baptists. More evangelical in their religion, and with simpler habits and tastes, the backcountry Baptists denounced the lowcountry planters for their luxury and arrogance. The planters retaliated by trying unsuccessfully to suppress the backcountry evangelicals.

The planters were indeed proud, domineering, and given to ostentatious displays of their wealth. An English traveler observed that Virginia planters "are haughty and jealous of their liberties, impatient of restraint, and can scarcely bear the thought of being controlled by any superior power." Planters understood liberty to mean the power of white males, unchecked by any outside authority, to rule over others. The only acknowledged check on this power was the planter's sense of duty, his

These drawings from about 1800 show the stages in the preparation of tobacco for marketing. Commercial-grade tobacco had to be selected by hand (c), air-cured in a shed (d), stored in a public warehouse (e), and inspected (f) before it was ready to be shipped to a buyer.

obligation to adhere to an idealized code of conduct befitting a gentleman and a man of honor.

   Backcountry farmers also jealously guarded their liberties. "They are," noted a late-eighteenth-century traveler, "extremely tenacious of the rights and liberties of republicanism. They consider themselves on an equal footing with the best educated people of the country, and upon the principles of equality they intrude themselves into every company." Backcountry farmers shared with the planters a disdain for government and restraints on the individual. But they opposed the planters' belief in a social hierarchy based on wealth and birth that left both poor whites and black slaves in a subordinate position.

The Growing West

Between the Appalachian Mountains and the Mississippi River stretched the most rapidly growing region of the new nation, the West. Land-hungry settlers poured across the mountains once the British recognized the American claim to the region in the Treaty of Paris. During the 1780s, the white population of the West exploded from less than 10,000 to 200,000. The region's Native American population was, in contrast, about 150,000.

Although Indians and whites struck many friendships and mutually advantageous ties, their relations were more generally marked by tension and sporadic violence. An example illustrates the often cruel ferocity of their conflicts. When James Boone, the eldest son of the fabled Daniel Boone, who had blazed the first trail for whites into Kentucky, was captured, tortured, and killed by a band of Indians, a group of whites sought vengeance. They lured some Mingo Indians into their camp, got them drunk, and then killed and scalped them. According to one account, they strung up a pregnant Mingo woman, "sliced open her belly with a tomahawk, and impaled her unborn child on a stake."

Indians strongly resisted white claims on their lands. A confederation of tribes in the Ohio Valley, led by the Miamis and supplied with firearms by the British in exchange for furs, kept whites out of the Old Northwest territory, the area north of the Ohio River. South of the Ohio, white settlements were largely limited to Kentucky and Tennessee. In what is today Alabama and Mississippi, the Creeks and their allies blocked American expansion.

Most white migrants in Kentucky and Tennessee were the young, rural poor from the seaboard slave states. The West offered them the opportunity to claim their own farms and gain economic independence free from the dominance of planters and the economic competition of slave labor. But planters also saw the West as a land of opportunity. The planters of Tidewater Virginia were especially likely to speculate in vast tracts of western land. And many planters' sons migrated to the West with a share of the family's slaves to become planters in their own right. This process laid the foundation for the extension of slavery into new regions. As early as 1790, slaves made up more than 10 percent of the population of Tennessee and Kentucky.

Life in the western settlements was harsh and often cruel. Mortality was high, especially among infants. Travelers from the East described settlers living in crudely built log cabins with squalid, filthy interiors infested with fleas and lice. Easterners also found an appallingly casual acceptance of violence in the West. Men commonly settled disputes in knife-slashing, eye-gouging brawls.

Isolation and uncertainty haunted frontier life. The Appalachians posed a formidable barrier to social and economic intercourse with the East. Few

A frontier log cabin, such as this, was a squalid, rough-hewn structure that could be built in a day with the help of neighbors.

settlers had the labor resources, which chiefly meant slaves, to produce an agricultural surplus for shipment to market down the Ohio and Mississippi Rivers. Most farmers lived at a semisubsistence level. Many of them, mostly Scots-Irish, did not own the land they cultivated. These **squatters**, as they were called, occupied the land hoping someday to obtain clear title to it.

In Kentucky, squatters, aligned with a small class of middling landowners, spearheaded the movement for political separation from Virginia that gained statehood for the territory in 1792. (In similar fashion, white settlers in Vermont established their independence from New York and New Hampshire and gained statehood in 1791.) The settlers wanted to break the control that Tidewater planters had gained over most of the land and lucrative government offices in Kentucky. In their minds, planters, office-holders, land speculators, and gentlemen of leisure were all part of an aristocracy tied to the distant government in Richmond and intent on robbing them of their liberty. As one proponent of statehood proudly announced, "I never was a frend to larned men for I see it is those sort of fokes who always no how to butter thare own bred and care not for others."

Despite the movement in Kentucky for statehood, the ultimate political allegiance of the West was uncertain in 1790. Westerners wanted the freedom to control their own affairs and outlets for their crops. Apparently, they were willing to strike a deal with any outside power offering to meet these needs. The British, contrary to the terms of the Treaty of Paris, had not abandoned their military posts in the Old Northwest. Using their military position and close ties with the Indians as leverage, the British encouraged separatist movements north of the Ohio River.

Spain posed a more serious threat. It rejected the American claim to the 31st parallel as the southern boundary of the United States and asserted that most of the area south of the Ohio and east of the Mississippi was Spanish territory. Most important, Spain controlled New Orleans and hence the main outlet on the Mississippi River for western produce. Washington had warned in 1784 that the political loyalties of the West wavered "on a pivot," and the future of the region loomed as a major test for his administration.

Forging a New Government

The Congress that assembled in New York from 1789 to 1791 faced a challenge scarcely less daunting than that of the Constitutional Convention of 1787. It had to give form and substance to the framework of the new national government outlined in the Constitution. Executive departments had to be established, a federal judiciary organized, sources of revenue found, terms of international trade and foreign policy worked out, and a commitment to add a bill of rights to the Constitution honored.

Staunch supporters of the new government had easily carried the first national elections in 1788 and enjoyed large majorities in both houses of Congress. These people brought superb administrative talents to the task of governing. Many, however, were clumsy politicians and unsympathetic to the egalitarian sensibilities of the electorate. By 1792, they faced growing political opposition.

"Mr. President" and the Bill of Rights

The first problem for Washington and Congress was to decide just how the chief executive of the new republic should be addressed. Vice President John Adams of Massachusetts and his like-minded colleagues in the Senate wanted a title with dignity, something that imparted proper respect both for the office and for national political authority. They preferred "His Highness." In a debate that tied up Congress for a month, the more democratically inclined members of the House argued that such a title smacked of a longing for monarchical rule. Adams and the others grudgingly agreed to accept "Mr. President."

Whatever his title, Washington was intent on surrounding the presidency in a halo of respectability. Dismayed by the hordes of visitors and office-seekers who immediately invaded his rented mansion in New York, he set down strict rules for his interactions with the public. He met with visitors twice a week for an hour and bowed with republican deference to the people but refused to shake hands. He traveled outside New York in a luxurious coach pulled by six horses, and at all times he carried himself with stern reserve. After a dinner with the president, one senator remarked that "as usual the company was as grave as at a funeral."

While Washington was laying down guidelines for presidential etiquette, Congress got down to business. James Madison, now a representative from Virginia, early emerged as the most forceful leader in the House. He pushed for speedy action on the Bill of Rights, which the Federalists had promised to add to the Constitution during the ratification debate. To allay the fears of Antifederalists that the Constitution granted too much power to the national government, the Federalists had promised to consider amendments that protected both individual rights and liberties and the rights of states. But Madison, concerned not to have the new government immediately hobbled by concessions to states, astutely kept the focus of the amendments on personal liberties. He submitted nineteen amendments, and Congress soon settled on twelve. Ten of these amendments, known collectively as the Bill of Rights, were ratified by the states and became part of the Constitution as of December 15, 1791.

The Bill of Rights has been one of the most enduring legacies of the first Congress. The first eight amendments are concerned mostly with individual rights. They guarantee religious freedom, freedom of expression, and the safeguarding of individuals and their property against arbitrary legal proceedings. Only three amendments speak of state interests. Citing the necessity of a "well regulated militia" for "the security of a free State," the Second Amendment guarantees "the right of the people to keep and bear Arms." This assured the states that they could rely on their militias for protection against federal tyranny. The Ninth and Tenth Amendments stipulate that the powers not granted to the national government in the Constitution are retained by the people and the states.

The Bill of Rights broadened the government's base of popular support. Once Congress submitted the amendments to the states for ratification, North Carolina (1789) and Rhode Island (1790) overcame their lingering objections and joined the Union. The Bill of Rights also assured Americans that the central government would not try to impose on them a uniform national culture.

Departments and Courts

In the summer of 1789, Congress authorized the first executive departments: the State Department for foreign affairs, the Treasury for finances, and the War Department for the nation's defense. These departments already existed under the Articles of Confederation, and the only debate about them concerned the extent of presidential control over the officials who would head them. The Constitution gave the president the right to nominate public officials but required the consent of the Senate to confirm their appointments. The Constitution was silent, however, on whether or not the president could dismiss an official without the Senate's consent. Congress decided that the president could do so, setting an important precedent that bolstered presidential power. Department heads would now be closely bound to the president. As a group, they would evolve into the **cabinet**, the president's chief advisory body.

Greater controversy attended the creation of the federal judiciary. The Constitution called for

"one Supreme Court" but left it up to Congress to authorize lower federal courts. The framers were deliberately vague about the federal judiciary because Antifederalists and proponents of states' rights did not want national courts enforcing a uniform judicial system. National courts, they argued, would be far removed from the people and would act as engines of oppression.

The **Judiciary Act of 1789** represented an artful compromise that balanced the concerns of the Antifederalists and states' rights advocates with the concerns of nationalists who strongly opposed leaving matters of national law up to state courts. It created a hierarchical national judiciary based on thirteen federal district courts, one for each state. Appeals from these courts were to be heard in one of three circuit courts, and the Supreme Court was to have the final say in contested cases. In a major concession to the Antifederalists, however, the act limited jurisdiction in federal courts to legal issues stemming from the Constitution and the laws and treaties of the national government. The distinctive legal systems and customs of the states remained intact. State courts would continue to hear and rule on the vast majority of civil and criminal cases.

Revenue and Trade

The government's most pressing need was for revenue. Aware that Congress under the Articles of Confederation had been crippled by its inability to secure a reliable source of income, Madison acted to put the finances of the new federal government on a firm footing. Nearly everyone agreed that the government's chief source of income should be a tariff on imported goods and tonnage duties (fees based on cargo capacity) on ships entering American ports. The United States imported most of its manufactured goods, as well as many raw materials, and foreign-owned ships accounted for nearly half of entering tonnage.

The **Tariff Act of 1789** was designed primarily to raise revenue, not to protect American manufacturers by keeping out foreign goods with high duties. It did, however, seek to protect a few industries thought vital to the economic health of the nation. Thus it levied a duty of 5 percent on most imported goods but imposed tariffs as high as 50 percent on a limited number of items such as steel, salt, cloth, and tobacco. The debate on the Tariff Act provoked some sectional sparring. In general, manufacturers, who were concentrated in the North, wanted high tariffs for protection against foreign competition. In contrast, farmers and southern planters wanted low tariffs to keep down the cost of the manufactured goods they purchased.

Madison originally hoped to use tonnage duties not only to raise revenue but also to strike at foreign nations that had not signed a commercial treaty with the United States. He had in mind specifically Great Britain. Since the Revolution, Britain had kept its trading empire closed to American merchants while at the same time exploiting the United States as a market for its manufactured goods. In contrast, France, America's ally during the Revolution, had a commercial treaty with the United States that recognized the American position on equal trading relations and the rights of neutral shippers during war.

Madison wanted to punish the British with a duty of 60 cents per ton on British ships entering American ports, twice the proposed duty on French ships. He hoped to dislodge the British from their dominant position in American markets and open up overseas trade for American and French shippers.

Madison's duties were in effect a declaration of economic warfare against Britain, but they failed to pass Congress, defeated by an unlikely coalition of sectional interests. Southerners voted against them because they feared their result would be to give New England merchants a monopoly on the carrying trade and raise the cost of shipping tobacco to Europe. But northern merchants, presumably the beneficiaries of the duties, also opposed them. They were leery of disrupting their profitable trade with Britain, especially with the economic slump of the 1780s abating. The **Tonnage Act of 1789**, as finally passed, treated all foreign ships equally. Foreign-owned and foreign-built ships were to pay a duty of 50 cents a ton; foreign-owned but American-built ships were to pay a duty of 30 cents a ton. The duty for American ships was only 6 cents a ton.

Hamilton and the Public Credit

The Treasury was the largest and most important new department. To its head, Alexander Hamilton of New York, fell the task of bringing order out of the nation's ramshackle finances. The basic problem was the huge debt left over from the Revolution. With interest going unpaid, the debt was growing, and by 1789, it had reached $52 million. Most of this, about $40 million, was held by Americans in the form of securities and certificates issued during the Revolution. Foreigners, mostly French and Dutch, held another $12 million. In addition, state governments had debts totaling close to $25 million. Until the government set up and honored a regular schedule for paying interest, the nation's public credit would be worthless. Unable to borrow, the government would collapse.

Courtesy of the Art Commission of the City of New York, City Hall.

As shown in this full-length painting by John Trumbull, Hamilton projected an assured, aggressive self-confidence as a public statesman.

More than any other individual, Hamilton imparted energy and purpose to the Washington administration. He was ambitious, egotistical, and overbearing. When he spoke of the people, he usually did so with a sneer. But he also had a brilliant financial mind and a sweeping vision of national greatness. He was convinced that the economic self-interests of the wealthy and well-born offered the only sound foundation for the success of the new government.

Born illegitimate in the West Indies in 1755 and orphaned at the age of 13, Hamilton craved power and social connections. Friends impressed with his potential sent him as a teenager to New York City for an education at Kings College (now Columbia University). An eager patriot, he served as Washington's personal aide during the Revolution. Washington's backing enabled him to marry into a wealthy New York family. He now had an entry into the world of the social and economic elite, and he parlayed it into a flourishing legal practice and a rising political career. With no ancestral loyalties to any individual state, he brought an unabashed nationalism to Washington's cabinet. And with a conviction born of his own rise that wealth and power were synonymous, he made no apologies for trying to link the interests of the government with those of the wealthy.

At the request of Congress, Hamilton prepared a series of reports on the nation's finances and economic condition. In the first, issued in January 1790, Hamilton proposed a bold plan to address the Revolutionary War debt. The federal government, he maintained, should fund the national debt at full face value. To do this, he proposed exchanging the old debt, including accrued interest, for new government bonds bearing interest at about 4 percent. In addition, Hamilton maintained that the federal government should assume the remaining war debt of the state governments. The intent of this plan was to give the nation's creditors an economic stake in the stability of the new nation and to subordinate state financial interests to those of the central government.

In his second report, issued in December 1790, Hamilton called for an excise tax (a tax on the production, sale, or consumption of a commodity) on distilled whiskey produced within the United States. The purpose of the tax was to raise additional revenue for interest payments on the national debt. It would also establish the government's authority to levy internal taxes on its citizens.

The third report, which followed quickly after the second, recommended the chartering of a national bank, the Bank of the United States. Hamilton patterned his proposed bank after the Bank of England and intended it to meet a variety of needs. Jointly owned by the federal government and private investors, it would serve as the fiscal (financial) and depository agent of the government and make loans to businesses. Through a provision that permitted up to three-fourths of the value of bank stock to be purchased with government bonds, the bank would create a market for public securities and hence raise their value. Most important, the bank would provide the nation with a stable currency. At the time, the country had only three private banks and specie—hard currency in the form of gold and silver coins—was scarce. The government needed a reliable source of money, as did the economy as a whole. Hamilton proposed to allow the Bank of the United States to issue money in the form of paper banknotes that would be backed by a small reserve of specie and the security of government bonds. His goal was both to strengthen the economy and to consolidate the power of the national government.

Hamilton's final report, issued in December 1791, recommended government actions to promote industry. Looking, as always, to the British model of economic development, he argued that the United States would never become a great power until it diversified its largely agrarian economy. As long as the nation imported most of its manufactured goods, Hamilton warned, it would be no more than a second-rate power. Moreover, American manufacturers, saddled with both high labor costs and primitive technology, would remain at a severe competitive disadvantage unless they received government assistance. Hamilton advocated aid in the form of **protective tariffs** (high tariffs meant to make imported goods more expensive than domestic goods) for such industries as iron, steel, and shoemaking—which had already begun to establish themselves—and direct subsidies to assist with start-up costs for other industries. Hamilton believed that such "patronage," as he called it, would ultimately foster interregional economic dependence. An industrializing Northeast, for example, would depend on the South and West for foodstuffs for its workers and raw materials for its factories. In turn, farmers and planters would buy manufactured goods from the Northeast. Thus in Hamilton's vision, manufacturing, like a national currency, would be a great national unifier.

Reaction and Opposition

The breadth and boldness of Hamilton's program invited opposition. For many people, it reflected a vision of the nation that challenged their deeply held beliefs about the purpose and meaning of the American Revolution. Opposition began to emerge with the first report on the public credit, and quickly solidified along economic, ideological, and sectional lines.

About half of the members of Congress owned some of the nation's debt, and nearly all of them agreed with Hamilton that it should be paid off. Some opponents, however, were concerned that Hamilton's plan was unfair. Hard times had forced most of the original holders of the debt—by and large, ordinary citizens—to sell their certificates to speculators at a fraction of their face value. Should the government, asked Madison, reward speculators with a windfall profit when the debt was paid back in full and forget about the true patriots who had sustained the Revolution in its darkest hours?

Others objected on republican grounds that Hamilton had no intention of actually eliminating the government's debt. He envisioned instead a permanent debt, with the government making regular interest payments as they came due. The debt, in the form of government securities, would serve as a vital prop for the support of moneyed groups. One congressman saw this as a violation of "that great principle which alone was the cause of the war with Great Britain . . . that taxation and representation should go hand in hand." Future generations, he argued, would be unfairly taxed for a debt incurred by the present generation.

Opposition to Hamilton's proposal to have the federal government assume state debts reflected sectional differences. With the exception of South Carolina, the southern states had already paid back a good share of their war debts. Thus Hamilton's plan stood to benefit the northern states disproportionately. Because Hamilton had linked the funding of the national debt with the assumption of state debts, southern opposition to assumption threatened funding as well. Tensions mounted as the deadlock continued into the summer of 1790. Frustrated over southern intransigence, New Englanders muttered about seceding. Southerners responded in kind. A Virginia senator charged that disunion would be a small price to pay to escape "the rule of a fixed insolent northern majority."

Tempers cooled when a compromise was reached in July. Southerners agreed to accept funding in its original form because, as Hamilton correctly noted, it would be impractical, if not impossible, to distinguish between the original and current holders of the national debt. Assumption passed after Hamilton cut a deal with Virginians James Madison and Thomas Jefferson. In exchange for southern support of assumption, Hamilton agreed to line up northern votes for locating the nation's permanent capital on the banks of the Potomac River, where it would be surrounded by the slave states of Maryland and Virginia. The package was sweetened by extra grants of federal money to states with small debts.

Hamilton's alliance with Madison and Jefferson proved short-lived, dissolving when Madison led the congressional opposition to Hamilton's proposed bank. Madison and most other Southerners viewed the bank as evidence of a willingness to sacrifice the interests of the agrarian South in favor of the financial and industrial interests of the North. They feared that the bank, with its power to dispense economic favors, would re-create in the United States the kind of government corruption and privilege they associated with Great Britain. They argued that the Constitution did not explicitly authorize Congress to charter a bank or any other corporation.

The bank bill passed Congress on a vote that divided on sectional lines. Madison's objections, however, left Washington concerned that the bank might not be constitutional. He sought the cabinet's opinion, provoking the first great debate over how the Constitution should be interpreted. Thomas Jefferson, the secretary of state, sided with Madison and for the first time openly clashed with Hamilton. Taking a **strict constructionist** position, he argued that all powers the Constitution had not expressly delegated to the national government were reserved to the states under the Tenth Amendment. Hamilton, in a brilliant rejoinder, argued that Article 1, Section 8 of the Constitution, which declares that Congress has the right to "to make all laws which shall be necessary and proper" to exercise its powers and those of the federal government, gives Congress implicit authority beyond its explicitly enumerated powers. With this **broad constructionist** position, he won Washington to his side.

With Washington's signature on the bill, Hamilton's bank was chartered for twenty years. Congress also passed a hefty 25 percent excise tax on distilled liquor. Little, however, of Hamilton's plan to promote manufacturing survived the scrutiny of the agrarian opposition. Tariff duties were raised moderately in 1792, but no funds were forthcoming to accelerate industrial development.

The Emergence of Parties

By the end of Washington's first term, Americans were dividing into two camps. On one side stood those who still called themselves Federalists. These were the supporters of Hamilton's program—speculators, creditors, merchants, manufacturers, and commercial farmers. They were the Americans most fully integrated into the market economy and in control of it. Concentrated in the North, they included New England Congregationalists and mid-Atlantic Episcopalians (former Anglicans), members of the more socially prestigious churches. In both economic and cultural terms, the Federalists were drawn from the more privileged segments of society.

Jefferson and Madison shrewdly gave the name *Republican* to the party that formed in opposition to the Federalists, thus identifying it with individual liberties and the heritage of the Revolution. The Republicans accused Hamilton and the Federalists of attempting to impose a British system of economic privilege and social exploitation. The initial core of the party consisted of southern planters and backcountry Scots-Irish farmers. These were

SUMMARY

FEDERALIST PARTY VERSUS REPUBLICAN PARTY

Federalists	Republicans
Favored strong central government	Wanted to limit the role of the national government
Supported Hamilton's economic program	Opposed Hamilton's economic program
Opposed the French Revolution	Generally supported the French Revolution
Supported Jay's Treaty and closer ties to Britain	Opposed Jay's Treaty and favored closer ties to France
In response to the threat of war with France, proposed and passed the Direct Tax of 1798, the Alien and Sedition Acts, and legislation to enlarge the size of the army	Opposed the Alien and Sedition Acts and the enlarged army as threats to individual liberties
Drew strongest support from New England; lost support in the mid-Atlantic region after 1798	Drew strongest support from the South and West

Americans outside the market economy or skeptical of its benefits. They feared that the commercial groups favored by Hamilton would corrupt politics in their pursuit of power and foster commerce and manufacturing at the expense of agriculture. The Republicans were committed to an agrarian America in which power remained in the hands of farmers and planters.

In 1792, parties were still in a formative stage. The political divisions that had appeared first in Congress and then spread to Washington's cabinet did not yet extend very deeply into the electorate. Washington remained aloof from the political infighting and was still seen as a great unifier. Unopposed, he was reelected in 1792. However, a series of crises in his second term deepened and broadened the incipient party divisions. By 1796, rival parties were contesting the presidency and vying for the support of an increasingly politically organized electorate.

The French Revolution

The French Revolution began in 1789, and in its early phase, most Americans applauded it. France had been an ally of the United States during the Revolutionary War and now seemed to be following the example of its American friends in shaking off monarchical rule. By 1792, however, the French Revolution had turned violent and radical. Its supporters confiscated the property of aristocrats and the church, slaughtered suspected enemies, and executed the king, Louis XVI. In early 1793, republican France was at war against Britain and the European powers.

The excesses of the French Revolution and the European war that erupted in its wake touched off a bitter debate in America. Federalists drew back in horror from France's new regime. They insisted that the terror unleashed by the French was far removed from the reasoned republicanism of the American Revolution. As the Federalist *Gazette of the United States* argued: "The American Revolution, it ought to be repeated, was not accomplished as the French has been, by massacres, assassinations, or proscriptions." For the Republicans, the French remained the standard-bearers of the cause of liberty for common people everywhere. Jefferson admitted that the French Revolution was tarnished by the loss of innocent lives, "but rather than it should have failed, I would have seen half the earth desolated." He was convinced that "the liberty of the whole earth was depending on the issue in the contest."

When the new French ambassador, Edmond Genêt arrived in the United States in April 1793—just as the debate in America over the French Revolution was heating up—Franco-American relations reached a turning point. The two countries were still bound to one another by the Franco-American Alliance of 1778. The alliance required the United States to assist France in the defense of its West Indian colonies and to open American ports to French privateers if France were attacked.

Chapter 8

American Views

THE GRASS-ROOTS POLITICS OF A DEMOCRATIC-REPUBLICAN ORGANIZATION

The Democratic-Republican societies that sprang up in sympathy with the French Revolution modeled themselves after the U.S. Revolutionary committees of the 1770s. Their members drew up constitutions, elected officers, issued resolutions and memorials, and drank toast after toast to the memory of the patriots who secured American independence. Above all, they insisted on the need for the constant vigilance of an informed citizenry to protect republican liberties against government encroachment. The following selection is from the constitution of the Democratic Society in Addison County, Vermont.

❖ What moral principles does the society associate with republican government? What duties of citizenship does it outline? What does the society mean by a "strictly republican government"?

❖ What explains the society's suspicion of public officials? Why does it stress the need for an informed citizenry? How does the society hope to safeguard popular liberties? How practical do you feel this program would be in the United States today?

❖ Why did the Federalists oppose these ideas on popular government? How would they construe the nature of liberty and republican government differently?

We, the undersigned, compact and associate ourselves into a Society . . . to promote the political ends expressed in the following articles, which shall be considered constitutional of our Society.

We make no apology for thus associating ourselves . . . to consider . . . and publish our sentiments, on the political interests, constitution and government of our country; this is a right, the disputation of which reflects on political freedom, and wears an appearance peculiarly absurd, proceeding from the tongue or pen of an American.

We declare the following . . . to be some of our political sentiments, and principles of government, . . .—That all men are naturally free, and possess equal rights. —That all legitimate government originates in the voluntary and social compact of the people. —That no rights of the people are surrendered to their rulers, as a price of protection and government. —That the constitution and laws of a country are the expressions of the general will of the body of the people or nation, that all officers of government are the ministers & servants of the people, and, as such, are amenable

Genêt, it soon became clear, hoped to embroil the United States in the French war against the British. He commissioned American privateers to attack British shipping and tried to enlist an army of frontiersmen to attack Spanish possessions in Louisiana and Florida.

Genêt's actions, as well as the enthusiastic receptions that greeted him as he traveled from Charleston to Philadelphia (chosen in 1790 as the temporary national capital), forced Washington to call a special cabinet meeting. The president feared that Genêt would stampede Americans into the European war, with disastrous results for the nation's finances. The bulk of America's foreign trade was with the British, and tariff duties on British imports were the main source of revenue to pay for Hamilton's assumption and funding programs. Hamilton urged Washington to declare American neutrality in the European war, maintaining that the president could commit the nation

to them, for all their conduct in office. —That it is the right, and becomes the duty of a people, as a necessary means of the security and preservation of their rights, and the future peace and political happiness of the nation, to exercise watchfullness and inspection, upon the conduct of all their public officers; to approve, if they find their conduct worthy of their high and important trusts— and to reprove and censure, if it be found otherwise. That frequent elections, directly from the body of the people, of persons, to important offices of trust, have an immediate tendency to secure the public power; that compensations for public service ought to be reasonable (and even moderate, when the debts and exigencies of a nation require it) and a reward only for actual service; that a public debt (and a financial funding system to continue the same) is a burthen upon a nation, and ought . . . to be reduced and discharged; that an increase of public officers, dependent on the executive power, [is] a foolish copying of ancient corrupt and foreign governments and courts, where the equal rights of men are trampled under the feet of kings and lords; and a

standing army—are all highly dangerous to liberty; and that the constitution, laws, and government of a country are always of right, liable to amendation and improvement.

We are concerned that the present political state of our country calls for the rational, wise and vigilant attention of its citizens. . . . It shall be the objects . . . of this society to study the Constitution, to avail ourselves of the journals, debates, and laws of Congress and such other publications as may be judged necessary to give information as to the proceedings of Congress and the departments of government and also of the conduct of individual officers in the discharge of their trusts. . . . And on information, we will speak; and upon deliberation, we will write and publish our sentiments. A steady zeal and firmness for the liberties of our country, and a strictly republican government, in pursuing our enquiries, & in passing our resolutions, shall be severely guided by the reason and temperance, which a sense of moral obligation, and the dread of ignorant popular convulsions, demand. . . .

Source: *Philip S. Foner, ed.*, The Democratic-Republic Societies, 1790–1800: A Documentary Sourcebook of Constitutions, Declarations, Addresses, Resolutions, and Toasts (*1976*).

to neutrality on his own authority when Congress, as was then the case, was not in session. Hamilton also wanted to suspend the military and commercial treaties of 1778 with France and refuse diplomatic recognition of Genêt. Jefferson, although he too wanted to avoid war, opposed Hamilton on these issues. Disputing Washington's power to act on his own, Jefferson maintained that the warmaking powers of Congress reserved for it alone the right to issue a declaration of neutrality.

Washington steered a middle course. He granted Genêt a formal (but cold) reception and took no action to suspend the Franco-American treaties. But he accepted Hamilton's argument on his authority to declare neutrality and issued a proclamation on April 22, 1793, stating that the United States would be "friendly and impartial toward the belligerent powers."

Despite this proclamation, Genêt continued meddling. He finally exceeded Washington's patience in the summer of 1793 when he grandly announced that he would take his case directly to the American people and force a cowardly administration to stand up for French rights. Washington was on the verge of forcing his recall to France in August when news arrived that a new and more radical French government had decided to bring Genêt back as a political prisoner. The president graciously permitted Genêt to remain in America as a private citizen. Had he returned to France, he would have faced almost certain execution.

Genêt quickly faded from public view, but American politics became more open and aggressive in the wake of his visit. Pro-French enthusiasm lived on in a host of grass-roots political organizations known as the Democratic-Republican societies. Nearly forty of these societies formed in 1793 and 1794. As their name suggests, these societies reflected a belief that democracy and republicanism were one and the same. This was a new concept in American politics. Democracy had traditionally been equated with anarchy and mob rule. The members of the new societies argued to the contrary that only democracy—meaning popular participation in politics and direct appeals by politicians to the people—could maintain the revolutionary spirit of 1776 because the people were the only true guardians of that spirit. As a letter writer to the Newark *Gazette* put it:

> It must be the mechanics and farmers, or the poorer class of people (as they are generally called), that must support the freedom which they and their fathers purchased with their blood—the nobility will never do it—they will be always striving to get the reins of government into their own hands, and then they can ride the people at pleasure.

The Democratic-Republican societies attacked the Washington administration for failing to assist France, and they expressed the popular feeling that Hamilton's program favored the rich over the poor. For the first time, Washington himself was personally assailed in the press.

The core members of the societies were urban artisans whose egalitarian views shocked the Federalists. They expected deference, not criticism and political activism, from the people. In their view, the Democratic-Republicans were rabble-rousers trying to dictate policy to the nation's natural leaders. The Federalists harshly condemned the emergence of organized political dissent from below, but in so doing they only enhanced the popular appeal of the growing Republican opposition.

Securing the Frontier

Control of the West remained an elusive goal throughout Washington's first term. Indian resistance in the Northwest Territory prevented whites from pushing north of the Ohio River. The powerful Miami Confederacy routed two ill-trained American armies in 1790 and 1791. The 1791 encounter, which took place on the banks of the Wabash River in western Ohio, was the worst defeat an American army ever suffered in frontier fighting. More than nine hundred soldiers were killed or wounded, and the commander, General Arthur St. Clair, was lucky to survive. The southern frontier was quieter, but the Spanish continued to use the Creeks and Cherokees as a buffer against American penetration south of the Tennessee River.

By 1793, many western settlers felt abandoned by the national government. They believed that the government had broken a promise to protect them against Indians and foreigners. Much of the popularity of the Democratic-Republican societies in the West fed off these frustrations. Westerners saw the French, who were at war with Britain and Spain, as allies against the foreign threat on the frontier, and they forwarded resolutions to Congress embracing the French cause. These resolutions also demanded free and open navigation on the Mississippi River. This, in the minds of Westerners, was their natural right. Without it, they would be forever impoverished. "If the interest of Eastern America requires that we should be kept in poverty," argued the Mingo Creek society of western Pennsylvania, "it is unreasonable from such poverty to exact contributions. The first, if we cannot emerge from, we must learn to bear, but the latter, we never can be taught to submit to."

Submission to national authority, however, was precisely what the Federalists wanted from both the Indians and the western settlers. St. Clair's humiliating defeat in 1791 prompted a reorganization of the War Department. By the summer of 1794, Washington's administration felt prepared to move against the Indians. This time, it sent into the Ohio region not the usual ragtag crew of militia and unemployed city dwellers but a force built around veterans from the professional army. The commander, General Anthony Wayne, was a savvy, battle-hardened war hero.

On August 4, 1794, at the **Battle of Fallen Timbers**, near present-day Toledo, Wayne's army dealt a decisive blow to the Ohio Indians. The British, who had promised full support for an independent Indian country north of the Ohio River,

This painting by an officer on General Wayne's staff shows Little Turtle, a Miami chief, speaking through an interpreter to General Wayne (with one hand behind his back) during the negotiations that led to the Treaty of Greenville.

backed off for fear of provoking a war with the United States. The Indians had little choice but to submit to the peace terms Wayne demanded. In the **Treaty of Greenville**, signed in August 1795, twelve tribes ceded most of the present state of Ohio to the U.S. government in return for an annual payment of $9,500. The Ohio country was now open to white settlement (see Map 8-1).

The Whiskey Rebellion

Within a few months of Wayne's victory at Fallen Timbers, another American army was on the move. The target this time was the so-called whiskey rebels of western Pennsylvania, who were openly resisting Hamilton's excise tax on whiskey. This tax had always been unpopular among western farmers. The high cost of transport across the mountains made it unprofitable for them to sell their grain in the east. But by distilling corn or rye into whiskey, they reduced it enough in bulk to lower transportation costs and earn a profit. Hamilton's excise tax wiped out these profits.

Hamilton was determined to enforce the tax and assert the supremacy of national laws. Although resistance to the tax was widespread, he singled out the Pennsylvania rebels. It was easier to send an army into the Pittsburgh area than the Carolina mountains. Washington, moreover, was convinced that the Democratic-Republican societies of

western Pennsylvania were behind the defiance of federal authority there. He welcomed the opportunity to chastise these organizations, which he identified with the dangerous doctrines of the French Revolution.

Washington called on the governors of the mid-Atlantic states to supply militia forces to crush the **Whiskey Rebellion**. The 13,000-man army that assembled at Harrisburg and marched into western Pennsylvania in October 1794 was larger than any Washington had commanded during the Revolution. But the rebellion, as Jefferson sardonically noted, "could never be found." The army met no resistance and expended considerable effort rounding up twenty prisoners. Two men were found guilty of treason, but Washington pardoned both. Still, at Hamilton's insistence, the Federalists had made their point: When its authority was openly challenged, this national government was prepared to use military force to compel obedience.

The Whiskey Rebellion starkly revealed the conflicting visions of local liberty and national order that divided Americans of the early republic. The non-English majority on the Pennsylvania frontier—Irish, Scots-Irish, German, and Welsh—justified resistance to the whiskey tax with the same republican ideology that had fueled the American Revolution. Mostly poor farmers, artisans, and laborers, they appealed to notions of liberty, equality, and

Map 8-1   Indian Land Cessions, 1784–1800
The persistent pressure of white settlers and the military forces of the new national government forced Native Americans to cede huge tracts of their western lands.

freedom from oppressive taxation that were deeply rooted in backcountry settlements from Maine to Georgia. In putting down the Pennsylvania rebels, Washington and Hamilton acted on behalf of more English and cosmopolitan groups in the East who valued central power as a check on any local resistance movement that might begin unraveling the still fragile republic.

Treaties with Britain and Spain

Much of the unrest in the West stemmed from the menacing presence of the British and Spanish on the nation's borders. Washington's government had the resources to suppress Indians and frontier dissidents but lacked sufficient armed might to push Spain and especially Britain out of the West.

The British, embroiled in what they saw as a life-or-death struggle against revolutionary France, clamped a naval blockade on France and its colonies in the Caribbean in the fall of 1793. They also supported an uprising of slaves on the French island of Saint-Domingue (present-day Haiti), enraging southern planters fearful that slave rebellions might spread to the United States. The French countered by opening their colonial trade, which had been closed to outsiders during peacetime, to neutral shippers. American merchants stepped in and reaped profits by supplying France. The British retaliated by seizing American ships involved in the French trade. They further claimed the right to search American ships and impress, or forcibly remove, sailors they suspected of having deserted from the British navy. News of these provocations reached America in early 1794 and touched off a major war scare. Desperate to avert a war, Washington sent John Jay, the chief justice of the United States, to London to negotiate an accord.

Jay brought a weak hand to the negotiating table. Britain had enormous military resources, the United States only a small army and navy. What is more, tariffs on British trade were the main source of revenue for the United States government. But the British, too, benefited from their trade with the United States, and they wanted to keep the United States neutral.

From the American point of view, the resulting agreement, known as **Jay's Treaty**, was flawed but acceptable. Jay had to abandon the American insistence on the right of neutrals to ship goods to nations at war without interference (meaning in this case the right of the United States to continue trading with France without British harassment). He also had to grant Britain "most favored nation" status, giving up the American right to discriminate against British shipping and merchandise. And he had to reconfirm the American commitment to assure that pre-Revolutionary debts owed by Americans to the British would be repaid in full. In return for these major concessions, Britain pledged to compensate American merchants for the ships and cargoes it had seized in 1793 and 1794, to abandon the six forts it still held in the American Northwest, and to grant the United States limited trading rights in India and the British West Indies.

Signed in November 1794, Jay's Treaty caused an uproar in the United States when its terms became known in March 1795. Southerners saw in it another sellout of their interests. It required them to pay their prewar debts to British merchants but was silent about the slaves Britain had carried off during the Revolution. And the concessions Britain did make seemed to favor the North, especially New England merchants and shippers. Republicans, joined now by urban artisans, were infuriated that Jay had stripped them of their chief weapon—economic retaliation—for breaking free of British commercial dominance. The Senate ratified the treaty in June 1795, but only because Washington backed it.

Jay's Treaty, combined with a string of French victories in Europe in 1795, convinced Spain to adopt a more conciliatory attitude toward the United States. With France apparently gaining the upper hand in the war, Spain was anxious to shift its allegiance from Britain to France. But it saw the Jay treaty as the beginning of an Anglo-American alliance and decided to reach an agreement with the United States before it changed sides lest the United States and Britain combine forces to challenge its American possessions. In the **Treaty of San Lorenzo** (also known as **Pinckney's Treaty**) of 1795, Spain accepted the American position on the 31st parallel as the northern boundary of Spanish Florida and granted American farmers the right of free transit through the port of New Orleans.

The First Partisan Election

Two terms in office were more than enough for Washington. The partisan politics that emerged during his second term—and its expression in an increasingly partisan press—disgusted him. The first opposition newspaper, the *National Gazette*, appeared in 1791, and the number of newspapers more than doubled within a decade. Circulated and discussed in taverns and coffeehouses, newspapers helped draw ordinary Americans into the political process. An outgrowth of the Revolution's appeal to popular sovereignty, this democratization of political involvement in turn created a basis for two-party politics. It also produced a form of cultural warfare that left gentlemen of wealth and refinement, including the leaders of the Federalist party, on the defensive. No symbol of traditional authority, including Washington, was safe from challenge. Although he remained silent in public, Washington complained bitterly to friends that his

NEWS! NEWS!!

AARON OLIVER, *Post-Rider*,

WISHES to inform the Public, that he has extended his Route ; and that he now rides thro' the towns of *Troy, Pittstown, Hoosick, Mapletown*, part of *Bennington* and *Shaftsbury, Petersburgh, Stephentown, Greenbush* and *Schodack.*

All commands in his line will be received with thanks, and executed with punctuality.

He returns his sincere thanks to his former customers ; and intends, by unabated diligence, to merit a continuance of their favours.

O'er ruggid hills, and vallies wide,
He never yet has fail'd to trudge it :
As steady as the flowing tide,
He hands about the NORTHERN BUDGET.
June 18, 1799.

Post-riders such as Aaron Oliver were the principal means of relaying information in the early republic. Relays of riders in the 1790s delivered the mail from Boston to New York in three and one-half days.

political opponents had maligned him "in such exaggerated and indecent terms as could scarcely be applied to a . . . notorious defaulter, or even a common pickpocket."

Washington announced his decision to retire from public life in his Farewell Address of September 1796, less than two months before the presidential election. He intentionally delayed the announcement to minimize the time the Republicans would have to prepare for the campaign. Washington devoted most of his address to a denunciation of partisanship. He invoked the republican ideal of disinterested, independent statesmanship as the only sure and virtuous guide for the nation. The sectional and pro-French or pro-British bias of partisanship particularly worried him. He warned against any permanent foreign alliances and cautioned that the Union itself would be endangered if parties continued to be characterized "by geographical discriminations—*Northern* and *Southern, Atlantic* and *Western*—whence designing men may endeavor to excite a belief that there is a real difference of local interests and views."

Confirming Washington's fears, the election of 1796 was the first openly partisan election in American history. John Adams was the Federalist candidate and Thomas Jefferson the Republican candidate. Each was selected at a **party caucus**, a meeting of party leaders.

Adams won despite Alexander Hamilton's interference, which inadvertently almost threw the election to Jefferson. Now a private citizen in New York, Hamilton wanted to be the power behind the throne in any new Federalist administration. Uncomfortable with Adams, he connived to have Thomas Pinckney of South Carolina, the other Federalist running with Adams, win the election. The Constitution did not originally call for electors to cast separate ballots for president and vice president. Rather, they cast two votes; the highest vote getter who received a majority became president, and the second highest became vice president. Nor were the electors, nearly half of whom in 1796 were chosen by state legislatures, under any obligation to cast a party ticket. In short, the Constitution was written with absolutely no thought of organized partisan competition for the presidency. Taking advantage of this weakness, Hamilton convinced some of the South Carolina electors to drop Adams from their ballots. He expected that with the solid support of the New England electors for both Adams and Pinckney, Pinkney would be elected president and Adams vice president. But the scheme backfired. When New Englanders learned of it, they refused to vote for Pinckney. As a result, Adams came in first with seventy-one votes, but Jefferson came in second with sixty-eight. Thanks to Hamilton, Adams entered office with his chief rival as vice president and a politically divided administration.

Despite the election's confused outcome, the sectional pattern in the voting was unmistakable. Only the solid support of regional elites in New England and the mid-Atlantic states enabled the Federalists to retain the presidency. Adams received all the northern electoral votes, with the exception of Pennsylvania's. Jefferson was the overwhelming favorite in the South.

The Last Federalist Administration

The Adams administration got off to a rocky start from which it never recovered. The vice president was the leader of the opposition party; key members of the cabinet, which Adams had inherited from Washington, owed their primary loyalty to Hamilton; and the French, who saw Adams as a dupe of the British, instigated a major crisis that left the threat of war hanging over the entire Adams presidency. Adams had been a lawyer before the Revolution; he was a veteran of both Continental Congresses, had been a diplomat in Europe for a decade, and had served as Washington's vice president for eight years. But despite this extraordinarily rich background in public affairs, he was politically naive. Scrupulously honest but quick to take offense, he lacked the politician's touch for inspiring personal loyalty and crafting compromises based on a realistic recognition of mutual self-interest. But putting the interests of the country before those of his party, he almost single-handedly prevented a nearly certain war with France and a possible civil war at home. The price he paid was a badly split Federalist party that refused to unite behind him when he sought reelection in 1800.

The French Crisis and the XYZ Affair

An aggressive coalition known as the Directory gained control of revolutionary France in 1795 and denounced the Jay treaty as evidence of an Anglo-American alliance against France. When Jefferson and the pro-French Republicans lost the election of 1796, the Directory turned openly hostile. In short order, the French annulled the commercial treaty of 1778 with the United States, ordered the seizure of American ships carrying goods to the British, and declared that any American sailors found on British ships, including those forcibly pressed into service,

would be summarily executed. By the time Adams had been in office barely three months, the French had already confiscated more than three hundred American ships.

In the fall of 1797, Adams sent three commissioners to Paris in an effort to avoid war. The French treated the three with contempt. Having just conquered the Netherlands and detached Spain from its British alliance, France was in no mood to compromise. Through three intermediaries—identified by Adams only as X, Y, and Z when he informed Congress of the negotiations—the French foreign minister demanded a large bribe to initiate talks and an American loan of $12 million.

In April 1798, the Senate published a full account of the insulting behavior of the French in what came to be called the **XYZ Affair**. The public was indignant, and war fever swept the country. The Federalists, who had always warned against the French, enjoyed greater popularity than they ever had or ever would again. Congress acted to upgrade the navy, which had languished since the Revolutionary War. Funds were provided to build and arm forty new ships. Responsibility for naval affairs, formerly divided between the Treasury and War Departments, was consolidated in a new Department of the Navy. By the fall of 1798, American ships were waging an undeclared war against the French in Caribbean waters, a conflict that came to be known as the **Quasi-War**.

The Federalists in Congress, dismissing Republican objections, also voted to create a vastly expanded army. They tripled the size of the regular army to ten thousand men and authorized a special provisional

With the horrors of the French Revolution forming a backdrop, this cartoon depicts France as a five-headed monster demanding a bribe from the three Americans sent by Adams. The Federalists hoped that such anti-French sentiments would lead to an open war.

army of fifty thousand. Congress put the provisional army under Washington's command, but he declined to come out of retirement except for a national emergency. In the meantime, he insisted that Hamilton be appointed second in command and given charge of the provisional army's field operations. To pay for both the expanded army and the naval rearmament, the Federalists pushed through the **Direct Tax of 1798**, a levy on the value of land, slaves, and dwellings.

Crisis at Home

The thought of Hamilton in charge of a huge army convinced many Republicans that their worst nightmares were about to materialize. One congressman shuddered that "the monarchy-loving Hamilton is now so fixed, as to be able, with *one-step*, to fill the place of our present commander in chief." Adams shared such fears. He was furious that Hamilton had been forced on him as commander of the provisional army. Years later, he wrote that "the British faction was determined to have a war with France, and Alexander Hamilton at the head of the army and *then* Pres. of U.S. Peace with France was therefore *treason* against their fundamental maxims and reasons of State." As the Republicans immediately sensed and Adams came to realize, Hamilton's supporters, known as the **High Federalists**, saw the war scare with France as an opportunity to stamp out dissent, cement an alliance with the British, and strengthen and consolidate the powers of the national government.

The Federalists passed four laws in the summer of 1798, known collectively as the **Alien and Sedition Acts**, that confirmed the Republicans' fears.

Three of these acts were aimed at immigrants, especially French and Irish refugees who voted for the Republicans. They convinced hundreds of immigrants to flee the country to avoid possible arrest. The **Alien Enemies Act** empowered the president to deport foreigners from countries at war with the United States. The more sweeping **Alien Friends Act** authorized the president to expel any alien resident he suspected of subversive activities. The **Naturalization Act** extended the residency requirement for American citizenship (and hence the right to vote) from five to fourteen years.

The most dangerous of the four acts in the minds of Republicans was the **Sedition Act**, a measure that made it a federal crime to engage in any combination or conspiracy against the government or to utter or print anything "false, scandalous and malicious" against the government. Federalist judges were blatantly partisan in their enforcement of the Sedition Act. Twenty-five individuals, mostly Republican editors, were indicted under the act, and ten were convicted. The most celebrated case involved Matthew Lyon, a Republican congressman from Vermont. Indicted for publishing a letter criticizing President Adams, he was reelected to Congress in December 1798 while still in jail.

Facing a Congress and a Supreme Court dominated by the Federalists, Jefferson and Madison turned to the safely Republican legislatures of Kentucky and Virginia for a forum from which to attack the constitutionality of the Alien and Sedition Acts. Taking care to keep their authorship secret, they each drafted a set of resolutions—Jefferson for

This contemporary cartoon shows Republican Matthew Lyon, on the right with the fire tongs, fighting against Roger Griswold, a Connecticut Federalist. This brawl in Congress on February 15, 1798, revealed the depth of the feeling that now divided the Republicans and Federalists.

the Kentucky legislature and Madison for the Virginia legislature—that challenged the entire centralizing program of the Federalists. In doing so, they produced the first significant articulation of the southern stand on **states' rights**.

The resolutions—adopted in the fall of 1798—proposed a compact theory of the Constitution. They asserted that the states had delegated specific powers to the national government for their common benefit. It followed that the states reserved the right to rule whether the national government had unconstitutionally assumed power not granted to it. If a state decided that the national government had exceeded its powers, it could "interpose" its authority to shield its citizens from a tyrannical law. In a second set of resolutions, the Kentucky legislature introduced the doctrine of **nullification**, the right of a state to render null and void a national law it deemed unconstitutional.

Jefferson and Madison hoped that these resolutions would rally voters to the Republican party as the defender of threatened American liberties. Yet not a single additional state seconded them. In the end, what aroused popular rage against the Federalists was not legislation directed against aliens and subversives but the high cost of Federalist taxes.

The Direct Tax of 1798 fell on all owners of land, dwellings, or slaves and provoked widespread resentment. Enforcing it required an army of bureaucrats—more than five hundred for the state of Pennsylvania alone. In February 1799, in the heavily German southeastern counties of Pennsylvania, a group of men led by an auctioneer named John Fries released tax evaders from prison in Bethlehem. President Adams responded to **Fries's Rebellion** with a show of force, but the fiercest resistance the soldiers he sent to Pennsylvania encountered was from irate farm wives, who doused them with hot water. Fries and two other men were arrested, convicted of treason, and sentenced to be executed (Adams later pardoned them). But the Federalists had now lost much of their support in Pennsylvania.

The End of the Federalists

The events in Pennsylvania reflected an air of menace that gripped the country as the campaign of 1800 approached. The army was chasing private citizens whose only crime in the eyes of many was that they were honoring their Revolutionary heritage by resisting hateful taxes. Federal soldiers also roughed up Republican voters at polling places. No wonder Adams later wrote that "the army was as unpopular as if it had been a ferocious wild beast let loose upon the nation to devour it." Southern Republicans talked in private of the possible need to resist Federalist

Short and pudgy, Adams had little of Hamilton's physical presence as a natural leader. But he had a first-rate mind and the political courage to place the nation's needs above those of his Federalist party when he peacefully ended the Quasi-War with France.

tyranny by force and, failing in that, to secede from the Union. Hamilton and the High Federalists saw in the Kentucky and Virginia resolutions "a regular conspiracy to overturn the government." Reports that Virginia intended to strengthen its militia heightened their anxieties, and they proposed to meet force with force. Speaking of Virginia, Hamilton said that "the government must not merely defend itself, it must attack and arraign its enemies."

No one did more to defuse this charged atmosphere than President Adams. The Federalists depended for their popular support on the expectation of a war with France, which as late as 1798 had swept them to victory in the congressional elections. Still, Adams refrained from asking for a declaration of war. The United States had been successful in the Quasi-War against France. By early 1799, French ships had been forced out of the Caribbean and American coastal waters. And in Europe, the tide of war had turned against the French. As a result, Adams believed that the French would now be more open to conciliation. Of greater importance, Adams recognized that war with France could trigger a civil war at home. Hamilton and the High Federalists, he realized, would use war as an excuse to crush the Republican opposition in Virginia. Fearful of Hamilton's intentions and unwilling to run the risk of militarizing the government and saddling it with a huge war debt, Adams broke with his party and decided to reopen negotiations with France in February 1799.

The **Franco-American Accord of 1800** that resulted from Adams's initiative released the United States from its 1778 alliance with France. It also obligated the United States to surrender all claims against the French for damages done to American shipping during the Quasi-War. The negotiations in Paris dragged on through the election of 1800, but for the Hamiltonian Federalists, the political damage had already been done. The prospect of peace with France deprived them of their trump card in the election. The Republicans could no longer be branded as the traitorous friends of an enemy state. The enlarged army, with no foe to fight, became a political embarrassment, and the Federalists dismantled it. Although rumors of possible violence continued to circulate, the Republicans grew increasingly confident that they could peacefully gain control of the government.

The Federalists nonetheless ran a very competitive race in 1800. Adams's peace policy bolstered his popularity. And because American merchants had profited from supplying both sides in the European war, the country was enjoying a period of prosperity that benefited the president and his party. The Federalists put on a show of unity when they nominated Adams and Charles C. Pinckney of South Carolina as their presidential candidates at their party caucus. But the wounds opened by Adams's decision to broker a peace with France continued to fester. Hamilton and his friends felt that Adams had betrayed them, and Hamilton wrote a scathing attack on the president in a letter that fell into the hands of Aaron Burr, a crafty politician from New York whom the Republicans had teamed up with Jefferson for the presidential election. Burr published the letter, airing the Federalists' squabblings in public.

The Federalists, hampered by party disunity, could not counter the Republicans' aggressive organizational tactics. They found it distasteful to appeal to common people. One party member lamented that the Republicans sent spokesmen "to every class of men, and even to every individual man, that can be gained. Every threshing floor, every husting, every party at work on a house-frame or raising a building, the very funerals are infected with bawlers or *whisperers against government.*"

Wherever they organized, the Republicans attacked the Federalists as monarchists plotting to undo the gains of the Revolution. The Federalists responded with emotional appeals that depicted Jefferson as a godless revolutionary whose election would usher in a reign of terror. "The effect," intoned the Reverend William Linn, "would be to destroy religion, introduce immorality, and loosen all bonds of society."

Attacks like Linn's reflected the fears of Calvinist preachers that a tide of disbelief was about to submerge Christianity in the United States. Church attendance had declined in the 1790s, particularly among men, and perhaps no more than one in twenty Americans was a member of any church. **Deism**, an Enlightenment religious philosophy popular among the leaders of the Revolutionary era, was making inroads among common citizens as well. Deists viewed God as a kind of master clockmaker who created the laws by which the universe runs but otherwise leaves it alone. They rejected revelation for reason, maintaining that the workings of nature alone reveal God's design. In 1794, the famed pamphleteer Thomas Paine, in *The Age of Reason*, denounced churches as "human inventions set up to terrify and enslave mankind, and monopolize power and profit."

These developments convinced Calvinist ministers, nearly all of them Federalists, that the atheism of the French Revolution was infecting American republicanism. They lashed out at the Republicans, the friends of the French Revolution, as perverters of religious and social order. Jefferson, a deist known for his free thinking in religion, bore the brunt of their attack in 1800.

The Republicans won the election by mobilizing voters through strong party organizations. Voter turnout in 1800 was twice what it had been in the early 1790s, and most of the new voters were Republicans. The Direct Tax of 1798 cost the Federalists the support of commercial farmers in the mid-Atlantic states. Artisans in port cities had already switched to the Republicans in protest over Jay's Treaty, which they feared left them exposed to a flood of cheap British imports. Adams carried New England and had a smattering of support elsewhere. With New York added to their solid base in the South and the backcountry, the Jeffersonians gained an electoral majority (see Map 8-2).

Party unity among Republican electors was so strong that Jefferson and Burr each received seventy-three electoral votes. Consequently the election was thrown into the House of Representatives, which, until the newly elected Congress was seated, was still dominated by Federalists.

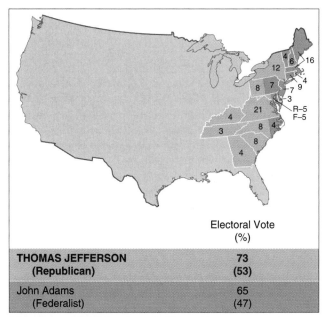

Electoral Vote
(%)

THOMAS JEFFERSON (Republican)	73 (53)
John Adams (Federalist)	65 (47)

Map 8-2   *The Election of 1800*
The sharp erosion of Federalist strength in New York and Pennsylvania after 1798 swung the election of 1800 to the Republicans.

Hoping to deny Jefferson the presidency, the Federalists in the House backed Burr. They believed that he was untainted by the Revolutionary virus that made Jefferson seem so dangerous, even though Hamilton, who faced Burr as a political rival in New York, sought to convince them otherwise. The result was a deadlock that persisted into the early months of 1801. Pennsylvania and Virginia mobilized their state militias, a clear message that the Republicans were prepared to use force against what Jefferson termed any "legislative usurpation" of the people's will as expressed in the election. On February 16, 1801, the Federalists yielded. Informed through intermediaries that Jefferson would not dismantle Hamilton's fiscal system, enough Federalists cast blank ballots to give Jefferson the majority he needed for election. The Twelfth Amendment to the Constitution, ratified in 1804, prevented a similar impasse from arising again by requiring electors to cast separate ballots for president and vice president.

Conclusion

In 1789, the American republic was little more than an experiment in self-government. The Federalists provided a firm foundation for that experiment. Hamilton's financial program, neutrality in the wars

of the French Revolution, and the diplomatic settlement with Britain in Jay's Treaty bequeathed the young nation a decade of peace and prosperity.

Federalist policies, however, provoked strong opposition rooted in conflicting economic interests and contrasting regional views over the meaning of liberty and government in the new republic. Federalist leadership initially depended on a coalition of regional elites in New England, the mid-Atlantic region, and the slave districts of the South. Each of these elites favored the establishment of effective national power, though often for different reasons. Merchants in Congregationalist New England were concerned mainly with reviving their British trading connections and reversing what they saw as the social and moral decline of the 1780s. Quaker and Episcopal businessmen and commercial farmers in the middle states wanted a central government to promote economic development at home and expand markets aboard. Southern slaveholders, hoping to expand into the West, needed a national government strong enough to secure the trans-Appalachian region.

The Federalist coalition split during Washington's second term when southern planters joined urban artisans and backcountry Scots-Irish farmers in opposing Jay's Treaty and the commercially oriented program of the Federalists. When Quaker and German farmers in the mid-Atlantic states defected from the Federalists over the tax legislation of 1798, three of the four regions in Washington's America now lined up behind the Republicans. The new Republican majority was united by their belief that the actions of the New England Federalists—the expansion of the army, the imposition of new taxes, and the passage of the Alien and Sedition Acts—threatened individual liberty and regional autonomy. Non-English groups and farmers south of New England turned to the Republicans as the upholders of these threatened freedoms.

The openly partisan politics of the 1790s surprised the country's founders, who equated parties with the evils of factionalism. They had not foreseen that parties would forge a necessary link between the rulers and the ruled and create a mechanism by which group values and regional interests could be given a political voice. Party formation climaxed in the election of 1800, when the Republicans ended the Federalists' rule. The Republicans won by embracing the popular demand for a more egalitarian social and political order.

To the credit of the Federalists, they relinquished control of the national government peacefully. The importance of this precedent can scarcely be exaggerated. It marked the first time in modern political history that a party in power handed over the government to its opposition. It now remained to be seen what the Republicans would do with their newfound power.

Review Questions

1. What was distinctive about the four regions of the United States in 1790? What were the common values and goals that brought white Americans together?

2. What were the major problems confronting the Washington administration, and how effectively were they resolved?

3. Who were the Federalists and the Republicans, and how did they differ over the meaning of liberty and the power of the national government? What were the major steps in the formation of two distinct parties in the early United States?

4. Why did regional differences tend to pit the North against the South by the late 1790s?

5. How did the XYZ Affair lead to a political crisis in the United States? Why did the Federalists believe that they would benefit from a war against France?

6. Jefferson called his election in 1800 the "revolution of 1800." What do you think he meant? Would you agree with him?

Recommended Reading

Stanley Elkins and Eric McKitrick, *The Age of Federalism* (1993). A magisterial work of narrative history that includes brilliant sketches of the major political actors in the 1790s.

James T. Flexner, *George Washington and the New Nation, 1783–1793* (1969) and *George Washington: Anguish and Farewell, 1793–1799* (1972). These two volumes stand out for their readable and informative account of Washington's political career after the Revolution.

Richard Hofstadter, *The Idea of a Party System, 1780–1840* (1969). This book combines political and intellectual history in a graceful account of how Americans gradually came to accept political parties as a legitimate expression of the popular will.

Seymour Lipset, *The First New Nation: The United States in Historical and Comparative Perspective* (1963).

This work draws on insights from political sociology to show what was unique and enduring in America's pioneering role as a new nation with a written constitution.

John C. Miller, *The Federalist Era, 1789–1801* (1960). This older work is still of great value for its relatively brief and well-balanced overview of the Washington and Adams administrations.

Additional Sources

Washington's America

Reginald Horseman, *The Frontier in the Formative Years, 1783–1815* (1970).

Robert McColley, *Slavery and Jeffersonian Virginia* (1964).

Gary B. Nash, *Forging Freedom: The Formation of Philadelphia's Black Community, 1720–1840* (1988).

Billy G. Smith, *The "Lower Sort": Philadelphia's Laboring People, 1750–1800* (1990).

Laurel Thather Ulrich, *A Midwife's Tale: The Life of Martha Ballard, Based on Her Diary, 1785–1812* (1990).

Daniel Vickers, *Farmers and Fishermen: Two Centuries of Work in Essex County, Massachusetts, 1630–1850* (1994).

Anthony F. C. Wallace, *The Death and Rebirth of the Seneca* (1970).

Betty Wood, *Women's Work, Men's Work: The Informal Slave Economies of Lowcountry Georgia* (1995).

Forging a New Government

Marcus Cunliffe, *George Washington: Man and Monument* (1958).

Ralph Ketcham, *Presidents above Party: The First American Presidency, 1789–1829* (1984).

Richard H. Kohn, *Eagle and Sword: The Federalists and the Creation of the Military Establishment in America, 1783–1802* (1975).

Glenn A. Phelps, *George Washington and American Constitutionalism* (1993).

Gerald Stourzh, *Alexander Hamilton and the Idea of Republican Government* (1970).

Leonard D. White, *The Federalists: A Study in Administrative History* (1948).

The Emergence of Parties

Joyce Appleby, *Capitalism and a New Social Order: The Republican Vision of the 1790s* (1984).

Richard Buel Jr., *Securing the Revolution: Ideology in American Politics, 1789–1815* (1972).

William N. Chambers, *Political Parties in a New Nation: The American Experience, 1776–1809* (1963).

Noble E. Cunningham Jr., *The Jeffersonian Republicans: The Formation of Party Organization, 1789–1801* (1957).

Alexander De Conde, *Entangling Alliance: Politics and Diplomacy under George Washington* (1958).

Thomas P. Slaughter, *The Whiskey Rebellion: Frontier Epilogue to the American Revolution* (1986).

Alfred F. Young, *The Democratic Republicans of New York: The Origins, 1763–1797* (1967).

The Last Federalist Administration

Manning Dauer, *The Adams Federalists* (1953).

Stephen G. Kurtz, *The Presidency of John Adams: The Collapse of Federalism, 1795–1800* (1957).

Roger Sharp, *American Politics in the Early Republic: The New Nation in Crisis* (1993).

Daniel Sisson, *The American Revolution of 1800* (1974).

James M. Smith, *Freedom's Fetters: The Alien and Sedition Laws and American Civil Liberties*, rev. ed. (1966).

William Stinchcombe, *The XYZ Affair* (1980).

Where to Learn More

❖ **Cincinnati Historical Society, Cincinnati, Ohio.** Collections include written and visual materials on the history of the Old Northwest Territory.

❖ **Federal Hall National Memorial, New York, New York.** This museum and historic site holds artifacts relating to President Washington's inauguration.

❖ **Hamilton Grange National Memorial, New York, New York.** The home of Alexander Hamilton contains materials on his life.

❖ **Adams National Historic Site, Quincy, Massachusetts.** This site preserves buildings and manuscripts associated with four generations of the Adams family.

9 | THE TRIUMPH AND COLLAPSE OF JEFFERSONIAN REPUBLICANISM, 1800–1824

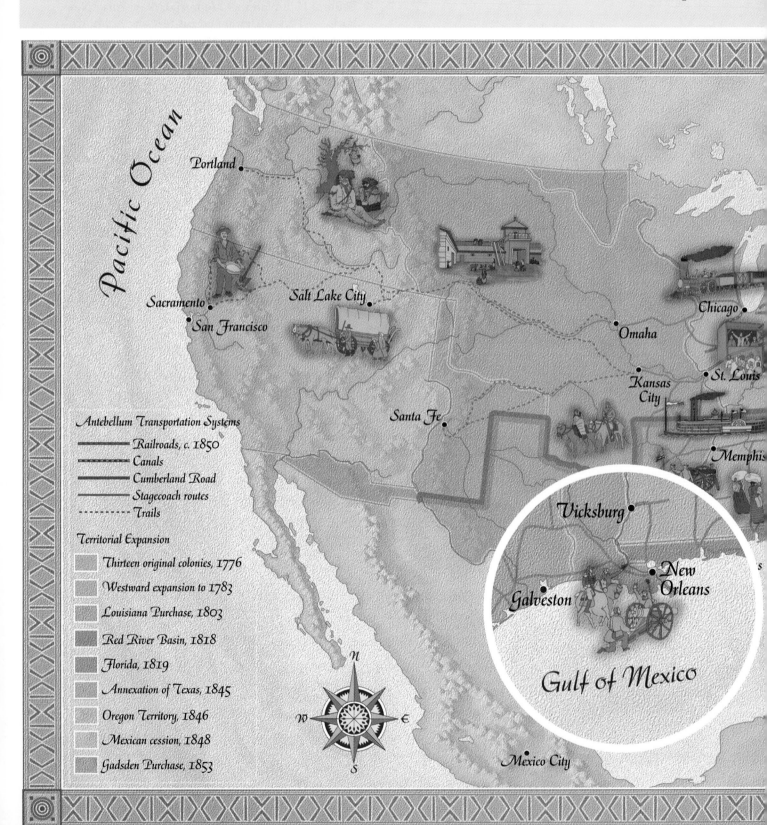

Antebellum Transportation Systems
- Railroads, c. 1850
- Canals
- Cumberland Road
- Stagecoach routes
- Trails

Territorial Expansion
- Thirteen original colonies, 1776
- Westward expansion to 1783
- Louisiana Purchase, 1803
- Red River Basin, 1818
- Florida, 1819
- Annexation of Texas, 1845
- Oregon Territory, 1846
- Mexican cession, 1848
- Gadsden Purchase, 1853

Pacific Ocean

Portland

Sacramento
San Francisco

Salt Lake City

Santa Fe

Omaha

Kansas City

Chicago

St. Louis

Memphis

Vicksburg

Galveston

New Orleans

Gulf of Mexico

Mexico City

N
W   E
S

Quebec

Boston

Buffalo

Cleveland

New York

Philadelphia

Cincinnati

Washington, D.C.

Richmond

Wilmington

Charleston

Atlanta

Savannah

St. Augustine

Atlantic Ocean

Caribbean Sea

0   400 miles

0   600 km

KEY TOPICS

❖ The domination of the Republicans and the collapse of the Federalist party
❖ The territorial expansion of the United States to the west and the south
❖ The growth of nationalism and of sectional rivalry
❖ The first national crisis over slavery
❖ The collapse of the Republican party

255

"*I* have nothing more to offer than what George Washington would have had he been taken by the British officers and put to trial. I have ventured my life in endeavoring to obtain the liberty of my countrymen, and am a willing sacrifice to their cause." The condemned prisoner who uttered these words was a slave, one of twenty-seven who were executed by Virginia authorities for their suspected role in Gabriel's Rebellion of 1800. Gabriel Prosser, a slave blacksmith, had organized one thousand slaves for an attack on Richmond. By seizing arms and capturing key points in the city, Gabriel hoped to spark a general uprising of slaves and whites sympathetic to their cause. Planned for the night of August 30, 1800, the rebellion was first postponed because of torrential rain that washed out a vital footbridge and then betrayed by slave informers.

Gabriel's Rebellion exposed the contradictory and potentially explosive nature of the Revolution's heritage of liberty and equality. As a Virginia Federalist remarked of the rebellion: "A doctrine [of liberty] which, however intelligible and admissible, in a land of freemen, is not only unintelligible and inadmissible, but dangerous and extremely wicked in this country, where every white man is a master, and every black man a slave." For all the anti-Republican partisanship behind this statement, it nonetheless confirms that Gabriel did draw on the Revolution's call for freedom from oppression. Aware of the divisions in the white power structure opened by the bitter clashes between Federalists and Republicans, he expected that his uprising would enlist the support of white artisans anxious to overturn the control of merchants and planters. Where he erred was in not grasping that nearly all whites were determined to apply the libertarian principles of the Revolution only to themselves.

The Jeffersonian democracy that Gabriel wanted to fuse into black Revolutionary activity was emphatically for whites only. Jefferson, himself a large-scale planter who could not conceive of whites and blacks living peacefully in a postemancipation society, headed a party that valued the white farmer as the ideal republican citizen. Jefferson believed that only such citizens had the propertied independence and sturdy self-sufficiency necessary to value the public good over private gain. His republic would escape the social hierarchy of corrupt Europe by filling North America with farm families of white yeomen. These families would feed Europeans with their agricultural surpluses and accept in exchange most of the manufactured goods they needed to improve their standard of living. Westward expansion and free and open trade with the outside world were the keys to Jefferson's empire of liberty.

To an extraordinary extent, Jefferson and his Republican successors, James Madison and James Monroe, succeeded in promoting the growth and independence of the United States in the first quarter of the nineteenth century. Expansionist policies to the south and west more than doubled the size of the republic and fueled the westward spread of slavery. A war against Britain in 1812–1814, if less than a military success, nonetheless freed Americans to look inward for economic development.

At the height of Republican success during the Era of Good Feelings just after the War of 1812, the Federalist party collapsed. Without an organized opposition to enforce party discipline among themselves, the Republicans soon followed the Federalists into political oblivion. The nation's expansion produced two crises—a financial panic and a battle over slavery in Missouri—that shattered the façade of Republican unity. By the mid-1820s, a new party system was emerging.

Jefferson's Presidency

Thomas Jefferson believed that a true revolution had occurred in 1800, a peaceful overthrow of the Federalist party and its hated principles of government consolidation and military force. In his eyes, the defeat of the monarchical Federalists reconfirmed the true political legacy of the Revolution by restoring the republican majority to its rightful control of the government.

Unlike the Hamiltonian Federalists, whose commercial vision of America accepted social and economic inequalities as inevitable, the Jeffersonians wanted a predominantly agrarian republic based on widespread economic equality for white yeomen families. Without such equality, Jefferson was convinced that the privileged few would threaten the people's liberties. Contemporary political thought held that all societies went through stages of economic development that ended in the consolidation of power and suppression of liberties by a wealthy minority. Jefferson hoped to break that cycle through territorial expansion that would add enough land to maintain self-reliant farmers as the guardians of republican freedoms. In the Jeffersonian vision, Americans would never sink into the dependence of impoverished factory labor.

When Jefferson moved into the White House in 1801, Washington was still a wilderness capital with a population that barely reached four thousand people.

Jefferson's first administration was a solid success. A unified Republican party reduced the size and scope of the federal government, allowed the Alien and Sedition Acts to lapse, and celebrated the Louisiana Purchase. An enfeebled Federalist party weakly opposed Jefferson's reelection in 1804. His second term, however, was a bitter disappointment, marked by the massive unpopularity of Jefferson's embargo on American foreign trade. The embargo, designed to compel warring Britain and France to recognize American rights as a neutral shipper, failed at home and abroad. As a result, Jefferson left his successor, James Madison, a divided party, a revived Federalism, and an unresolved crisis in foreign affairs.

Reform at Home

Jefferson set the style and tone of his administration from the beginning. He was the first president to be inaugurated in Washington, D.C., and his inauguration was as unpretentious as the raw and primitive capital city itself. Then little more than a scraggly collection of huts, a few boardinghouses, and unfinished public buildings, Washington lacked, one senator ruefully noted, "only houses, wine cellars, learned men, amiable women, and other trifles to make our city perfect." Jefferson walked from his lodgings to the Capitol building to be sworn in. His dress was neat but shorn of gentlemanly refinements such as a

wig. After giving notice that an unadorned style of republican egalitarianism would now replace the aristocratic formalities of the Federalists, Jefferson emphasized in his inaugural address the overwhelming commitment of Americans to the "republican form" of government and affirmed his own support of civil liberties as an American principle.

A poor public speaker, Jefferson sent written messages to Congress to avoid having to read them in person. This change from Federalist policy both eliminated the impression of a monarch addressing his subjects and played to Jefferson's formidable skills as a writer. He replaced the stiff formalism of receptions for presidential visitors with more relaxed weekly meetings. Presidential dinners became notorious among society and the diplomatic corps for their breezy disregard of aristocratic etiquette and hierarchical seating arrangements. Jefferson welcomed dinner guests at a circular table. Still, he served fine food and wine, and he used these dinners to cultivate party ties that enabled him to steer favored legislation through Congress.

The cornerstone of Republican domestic policy was retrenchment, a return to the frugal, simple federal establishment the Jeffersonians believed was the original intent of the Constitution. Determined to root out what they viewed as the corruption and patronage of a government bloated by the power-grasping Federalists, the Republicans

CHRONOLOGY

1801 Thomas Jefferson is inaugurated, the first Republican president.

John Marshall becomes chief justice.

1802 Congress repeals the Judiciary Act of 1801.

1803 *Marbury* v. *Madison* sets the precedent of judicial review by the Supreme Court.

Louisiana Purchase.

1804 Vice President Aaron Burr kills Alexander Hamilton in a duel.

Judges John Pickering and Samuel Chase impeached by Republicans.

Jefferson is reelected.

1806 Britain and France issue orders restricting neutral shipping.

Betrayal of the Burr conspiracy.

1807 *Chesapeake* affair.

Congress passes the Embargo Act.

1808 Congress prohibits the African slave trade.

James Madison elected president.

1809 Repeal of the Embargo Act.

Passage of the Nonintercourse Act.

1810 Macon's Bill No. 2 reopens trade with Britain and France.

United States annexes part of West Florida.

Georgia state law invalidated by the Supreme Court in *Fletcher* v. *Peck*.

1811 Battle of Tippecanoe and defeat of the Indian confederation.

Charter of the Bank of the United States expires.

1812 Congress declares war on Britain.

American loss of Detroit.

Madison reelected.

1813 Perry's victory at Battle of Put-in-Bay.

Battle of the Thames and death of Tecumseh.

1814 Jackson crushes the Creeks at the Battle of Horseshoe Bend.

British burn Washington, D.C., and attack Baltimore.

Macdonough's naval victory on Lake Champlain turns back a British invasion.

Hartford Convention meets.

Treaty of Ghent signed.

1815 Jackson routs British at the Battle of New Orleans.

1816 Congress charters the Second Bank of the United States and passes a protective tariff.

James Monroe elected president.

1817 Rush-Bagot Treaty demilitarizes the Great Lakes.

1818 Anglo-American Accords on trade and boundaries.

Jackson's border campaign in Spanish East Florida.

1819 Trans-Continental Treaty between United States and Spain.

Beginning of the Missouri controversy.

Financial panic sends economy into a depression.

Dartmouth College v. *Woodward* upholds the charter rights of corporations.

McCulloch v. *Maryland* upholds constitutionality of the Bank of the United States.

1820 Missouri Compromise on slavery in the Louisiana Purchase.

Monroe reelected.

1823 Monroe Doctrine proclaims Western Hemisphere closed to further European colonization.

1825 John Quincy Adams elected president by the House of Representatives.

began with fiscal policy. Jefferson's secretary of the treasury was Albert Gallatin, a native of Switzerland who emerged in the 1790s as the best financial mind in the Republican party. He convinced Jefferson that the Bank of the United States was essential for financial stability and blocked efforts to dismantle it. Unlike Hamilton, however, Gallatin thought that a large public debt was a curse, a drag on productive capital and an unfair burden on future generations. He succeeded in reducing the national debt from $83 million in 1800 to $57 million by 1809.

Gallatin's conservative fiscal policies shrank both the spending and taxes of the national government. The Republicans eliminated all internal taxes, including the despised tax on whiskey. Slashes in the military budget enabled government expenditures to stay below the level of 1800. The army was cut back to three thousand men, and the navy was virtually eliminated, except for the six frigates completed during the Quasi-War with France. Jefferson's defense strategy called for gunboats and coastal fortifications. If the country were invaded, he would rely on the militia, citizen soldiers commanded by professional officers to be trained at the newly established (1802) military academy at West Point. The cuts in military spending combined with soaring revenues from customs collections left Gallatin with a surplus in the budget that he could devote to debt repayment.

Jeffersonian reform targeted the political character, as well as the size, of the national government. Of the six hundred officeholders appointed by Washington and Adams, Jefferson estimated that only six were Republicans. He moved to break the Federalist stranglehold on federal offices and appoint officials with sound Republican principles. Arch-Federalists, those Jefferson deemed guilty of misusing their offices for openly political reasons, were immediately replaced, and Republicans filled other posts opened up by attrition. By the time Jefferson left the presidency in 1809, Republicans held nearly all the appointive offices.

Jefferson moved most aggressively against the Federalists in the judiciary. Just days before they relinquished power, the Federalists passed the **Judiciary Act of 1801**. This act created sixteen new circuit courts; added nearly two hundred federal marshals, attorneys, and clerks; and reduced the size of the

Dolly Madison, the engaging young wife of James Madison, Jefferson's secretary of state, served as the unofficial social hostess in the White House during the administration of Jefferson, a widower.

Supreme Court from six justices to five by stipulating that the next vacancy was not to be filled. The Jeffersonians were enraged. The Federalists already monopolized all federal judgeships, and this last-minute legislation both enlarged the judiciary and packed it with more Federalists appointed by Adams, the outgoing president. To add insult to injury, the Federalists had even tried to ensure that Jefferson would be unable to appoint a Republican to the Supreme Court when the first opening occurred.

The Republicans fought back. Now dominant in Congress, they quickly repealed the Judiciary Act of 1801, replacing it with a measure that eliminated the new judgeships and restored the size of the Supreme Court to six members, each with responsibility for one of the circuit courts. Frustrated Federalists now turned to John Marshall, a staunch Federalist appointed chief justice of the United States by President Adams in 1801, in the hope that he would rule that Congress had acted unconstitutionally in removing the recently appointed federal judges. Marshall moved carefully to avoid an open confrontation. He was aware that the Republicans contended that Congress and the president had at least a coequal right with the Supreme Court to decide constitutional questions.

The issue came to a head in the case of ***Marbury* v. *Madison*** (1803), which centered on Secretary of State James Madison's refusal to deliver a commission to William Marbury, one of Adams's "midnight appointments" as a justice of the peace for the District of Columbia. Marshall held that although Marbury had a legal right to his commission, the Court had no jurisdiction in the case. The Court ruled that the section of the Judiciary Act of 1789 granting it the power to order the delivery of Marbury's commission was unconstitutional because it conferred on the Court a power not specified in Article 3 of the Constitution on cases of original jurisdiction. Stating that it was "emphatically the province and duty of the judicial department to say what the law is," Marshall created the precedent of judicial review, the power of the Supreme Court to rule on the constitutionality of federal law. Although not invoked again until the Dred Scott decision of 1857, this doctrine was of pivotal importance for the future of the Court. Marshall had brilliantly turned a threatening situation into a success for the judiciary.

Marshall's assertion of the Court's power deepened Republican suspicions of judicial tyranny. Demanding popular election for all judges, radical Republicans rejected the entire notion of an appointed judiciary. Jefferson did not want to go that far, but he felt strongly that judges should be accountable to the popular will.

At the urging of the radicals, congressional Republicans brought formal charges against two

Shown here is one of the many councils held by Lewis and Clark with Native Americans. In addition to mapping the Louisiana Purchase Territory and finding an overland trail to the Pacific Ocean, Lewis and Clark were also instructed to form military and economic alliances with Indians to help Americans gain control of the British-dominated fur trade in the Trans-Mississippi West.

notorious Federalist judges. One of them, John Pickering, a district judge from New Hampshire and a mentally unstable alcoholic, was convicted and removed from office. The other was bigger game, Justice Samuel Chase of the Supreme Court, the most obnoxious Federalist still in a position of national power. For all his blatant partisanship, however, Chase was clearly sane, and he escaped conviction in the Senate in early 1805 when the Republicans failed to show he was guilty of "high crimes and misdemeanors," the constitutionally defined grounds for removal from office. His acquittal ended the Republican offensive against the judiciary.

The Louisiana Purchase

In foreign affairs, fortune smiled on Jefferson during his first term. The European war that had almost sucked in the United States in the 1790s subsided. Britain and France agreed on a truce in 1802. Meanwhile, Jefferson, despite his distaste for a strong navy, ordered a show of force in the Mediterranean to punish the Barbary pirates who were preying on

American shipping and taking American sailors hostage.

For years, the North African states of Morocco, Algeria, Tunis, and Tripoli had demanded cash tribute from foreigners as the price for allowing trade in the Mediterranean. Jefferson stopped the payments in 1801, and when the attacks on American shipping resumed, he retaliated by sending warships and marines to the Mediterranean. The tribute system continued until 1815, but thanks to the success of U.S. forces in Tripoli, Jefferson got much better terms.

The Anglo-French peace was a mixed blessing for the United States. Although it removed any immediate threat of war, the return of peace also enabled Spain and France to reclaim their colonial trade in the Western Hemisphere. American shippers were thus deprived of the windfall profits they had earned while dominating that trade during the European war. Of greater long-range concern, the new military ruler of France, Napoleon Bonaparte, was now free to develop his plans for reviving the French empire in America. In a secret treaty with Spain in 1800, Napoleon reacquired for France the Louisiana Territory, a vast, vaguely defined area stretching between the Mississippi River and the Rocky Mountains.

Sketchy, unconfirmed reports of the treaty reached Jefferson in the spring of 1801, and he was immediately alarmed. He had long believed that Spain, proud but militarily impotent, would be powerless to stem the spread of the expanding American population into its territories in western North America. Indeed, Spanish military officials in Louisiana had repeatedly called in vain for military reinforcements to block the Americans, this "new and vigorous people . . . advancing and multiplying in the silence of peace." France, for its part, was a formidable opponent. French control of the Mississippi Valley, combined with the British presence in Canada, threatened to hem in the United States and deprive Jefferson's farmers of their empire for liberty.

Jefferson was prepared to reverse the traditional foreign policy of his party to eliminate this threat. He opened exploratory talks with the British on an Anglo-American alliance to drive the French out of Louisiana. Looking toward the possibility of war, he also strengthened American forces in the Mississippi Valley and secured congressional approval for the Lewis and Clark expedition through upper Louisiana. Although best known for its scientific discoveries, this expedition was designed initially as a military mission.

Jefferson applied diplomatic and military pressure to induce Napoleon to sell New Orleans and a small slice of coastal territory to its east to the United States. This was his main objective: to possess New Orleans and control the mouth of the Mississippi River, outlet to world markets. To his surprise, Napoleon suddenly decided in early 1803 to sell all of the immense Louisiana Territory to the Americans (see Map 9-1).

Map 9-1   *The Louisiana Purchase and the Lewis and Clark Expedition*
The vast expanse of the Louisiana Purchase was virtually unknown territory to Americans before the Lewis and Clark expedition gathered a mass of scientific information about it.

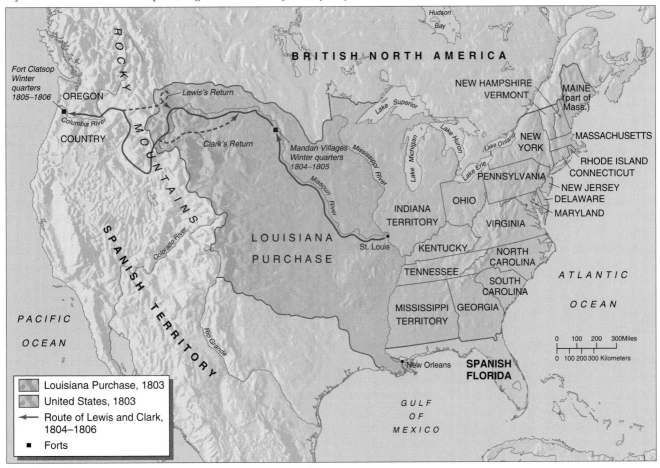

Napoleon's failure to reconquer St. Domingue (modern-day Haiti) was instrumental in his about-face on plans for a revived French empire in America. He had envisioned the rich sugar island of St. Domingue as the jewel of his new empire and intended to use the Louisiana Territory as a granary to supply the island with foodstuffs. During the upheavals of the French Revolution, the slaves on the island, led by Toussaint L'Ouverture, rebelled in a bloody and successful bid for independence. They fought fanatically against the large army Napoleon sent to reassert French control on the island. Black resistance and mosquito-borne yellow fever killed fifty thousand French soldiers by March 1803.

Without firm French control of St. Domingue, Louisiana was of little use to Napoleon. Moreover, resolutions passed in the U.S. Congress threatening an American attack on New Orleans made it likely that Napoleon would have to fight to keep Louisiana. With a renewed war against Britain looming, he had better use for his troops in Europe and wanted to keep Americans neutral in the next round of the Anglo-French war. For $15 million (including about $4 million in French debts owed to American citizens), he offered to part with the whole of Louisiana. The cost to the United States was about 3½ cents per acre.

Jefferson, the strict constructionist, now turned pragmatist. Despite the lack of any specific authorization in the Constitution for the acquisition of foreign territory or the incorporation as American citizens of the fifty thousand French and Spanish descendants then living in Louisiana, he accepted Napoleon's deal. The **Louisiana Purchase** doubled the size of the United States and offered seemingly endless space to be settled by yeoman farmers.

Jefferson was willing, as the Federalists had been when they were in power, to stretch the Constitution to support his definition of the national good. Conversely, it was now the Federalists, fearful of a further decline in their political power, who relied on a narrow reading of the Constitution in a futile attempt to block the Louisiana acquisition.

Florida and Western Schemes

The magnificent prize of Louisiana did not satisfy Republican territorial ambitions. Still to be gained were river outlets on the Gulf Coast essential for the development of plantation agriculture in Alabama and Mississippi. As Secretary of State Madison later bluntly explained, "The free navigation of these rivers was inseparable from the very existence of the United States." The boundaries of the Louisiana Pur-

chase were so vague that Jefferson felt justified in claiming Spanish-held Texas and the Gulf Coast eastward from New Orleans to Mobile Bay, including the Spanish province of West Florida. Against stiff Spanish opposition, he pushed ahead with his plans to acquire West Florida. This provoked the first challenge to his leadership of the party.

Once it was clear that Spain did not want to sell West Florida to the United States, Jefferson accepted Napoleon's offer to act as a middleman in the acquisition. Napoleon's price was $2 million. He soon lost interest in the project, however, and Jefferson lost prestige in 1806 when he pushed an appropriations bill through Congress to pay for Napoleon's services. Former Republican stalwarts in Congress denounced the bill as bribe money and staged a party revolt against the president's devious tactics.

Jefferson's failed bid for West Florida emboldened Westerners to demand that Americans seize the territory by force. In 1805 and 1806, Aaron Burr, Jefferson's first vice president, apparently had just such a land grab in mind. Burr had been suspect in the party since his dalliance with the Federalists in 1800 when he sought the presidency. Burr further cut his ties to the Republican party when he lent a sympathetic ear to Federalist talk of disunion.

A minority of die-hard Federalists, centered in Massachusetts and known as the Essex Junto, feared that incorporation of the vast territory of the Louisiana Purchase into the United States would leave New England powerless in national affairs. Picking up on states' rights themes first used by Jefferson in the Kentucky Resolutions, they concocted a plan for a northern confederacy. New York was central to their scheme. Rebuffed by Hamilton, they turned to Burr and backed him in the New York gubernatorial race of 1804. Burr lost, largely because Hamilton denounced his character. The enmity between the two men reached a tragic climax in July 1804, when Burr killed Hamilton in a duel at Weehawken, New Jersey. Facing murder charges in New Jersey and New York, Burr fled to the West and lined up followers for a separatist plot.

The Burr conspiracy remains mysterious. Burr was undoubtedly eager to pry land loose from the Spanish and Indians, and he may have been thinking of carving out a separate western confederacy in the lower Mississippi Valley. Whatever he had in mind, he blundered in relying on General James Wilkinson as a coconspirator. Wilkinson, the military governor of the Louisiana Territory and also a double agent for Spain, betrayed Burr. Jefferson made extraordinary efforts to secure a conviction, but Burr was acquitted when tried for treason in 1807. He was saved by the

Portrait of Aaron Burr by John Vanderlyn (1775–1850). Painting, oil on canvas, 28⁹⁄₁₆ × 22. Framed: H. 33¼, W. 26⅝.

Suave, ambitious, and immensely persuasive, Aaran Burr was seemingly always at the center of a political storm.

insistence of Chief Justice Marshall that the Constitution defined treason only as the waging of war against the United States or the rendering of aid to its enemies. Moreover, the direct testimony of two witnesses to an "overt act" of treason was necessary for conviction. Lacking such witnesses, the government failed to prove its case, and Burr was acquitted.

Embargo and a Crippled Presidency

Concern about a possible war against Britain in 1807 soon quieted the uproar over Burr's trial. After Britain and France resumed their war in 1803, the United States became enmeshed in the same thicket of neutral rights, blockades, ship seizures, and impressment of American sailors that had almost dragged the country into war in the 1790s. British decrees and French countermoves placed neutral shippers in a no-win situation. Britain proclaimed a blockade of the European continent, which was controlled by Napoleon, and confiscated the cargoes of ships attempting to run the blockade. Napoleon retaliated with seizures of ships that adhered to the blockade by submitting to British searches and accepting the British-imposed licensing system for trading with Europe. Caught in the middle, but eager

to supply both sides, was the American merchant marine, the world's largest carrier of neutral goods.

American merchants and shippers had taken full advantage of the magnificent opportunities opened up by the European war. The flush years from 1793 to 1807 witnessed a tripling of American ship tonnage, and the value of exports soared fives time over. For all the restrictive efforts of the French and the British, American merchants succeeded in trading with anyone they pleased. They dominated trade not only between Britain and the United States but also between the European continent and the French and Spanish colonies in the West Indies. Profits were so great that merchants even made money when only one-third of their ships evaded the blockades.

The ***Chesapeake* incident** in June 1807 nearly triggered an Anglo-American war. When the commander of the U.S. frigate *Chesapeake* refused to submit to a British search in coastal waters off Norfolk, the British ship *Leopard* opened fire. Three Americans were killed in the broadside, eighteen were wounded, and four others (one of whom was subsequently hanged) were impressed as alleged deserters from the Royal Navy. Although some Federalists were convinced that "our rogue of a President will glory in a war with England," Jefferson resisted the popular outcry for revenge. Instead, he barred American ports to British warships and called for monetary compensation and an end to impressment.

Apart from offering a belated apology and a promise of reparations, the British were unmoved by Jefferson's response. Still, Jefferson desperately wanted to avoid war, not only because the country was woefully unprepared but also because he passionately believed that international law should resolve disputes between nations. In a last burst of the idealism that had animated the republicanism of the Revolution, Jefferson resorted to a trade embargo as a substitute for war. The **Embargo Act of 1807**, an expression of Jefferson's policy of "peaceable coercion," prohibited American ships from clearing port to any nation until Britain and France repealed their trading restrictions on neutral shippers.

The basic premise of the embargo went back to the thinking of Thomas Paine during the Revolution, mainly that Europe was so dependent on American-supplied foodstuffs and raw materials that any cutoff of that supply would force Europe to do America's bidding. This premise was not so much wrong as unrealistic. The embargo did hurt Europe, but the people who first felt the pain were British textile workers and slaves in the colonies, hardly those who wielded the levers of power. Meanwhile, politically

LOOK ON THIS PICTURE,   AND ON THIS.

_____ *See what a grace was seated on this brow:* _____
_____ *An eye like Mars to threaten and command,* _____
_____ *A combination, and a form, indeed,*
Where every God did seem to set his seal,
To give the world assurance of a man: _____

HERE IS _____

_____ *like a mildew'd ear,*
Blasting his wholesome brother _____

Vide Hamlet.

THIS WAS _____

New-York, June, 1807.

Federalists attacked Jefferson throughout his presidency as an unworthy heir to Washington.
This 1807 cartoon links Washington with the virtues of law, order, and religion and associates
Jefferson with the evil falsehoods of the Enlightenment and the French Revolution.

influential landlords and manufacturers benefited from short-term shortages by jacking up prices.

The American export trade and its profits dried up with Jefferson's self-imposed blockade. Except for manufacturers, who now had the American market to themselves, nearly all economic groups suffered under the embargo. Especially hard hit were New England shippers and merchants, and they accused the Republicans of near-criminal irresponsibility for forcing a depression on the country. Jefferson responded to these criticisms and to widespread violations of the embargo with a series of enforcement acts. These acts put real teeth into the embargo

and consolidated executive powers far beyond what the Federalists themselves had been able to achieve while in power.

As the embargo tightened and the 1808 election approached, Federalism revived. In New England, governors echoed the states' rights arguments that the Republicans had first employed against the Adams administration. Running against Jefferson's handpicked successor, Secretary of State Madison, the Federalist Charles C. Pinckney of South Carolina tripled his electoral vote over that of 1804. Madison won only because he carried the South and the West, the heartland of Republican support.

Before Madison took office, the Republicans abandoned Jefferson's embargo. Britain and France had remained defiant, and at home the embargo had become an intolerable political burden. The embargo ended on March 3, 1809, and was immediately replaced by the **Nonintercourse Act**, a measure that prohibited American trade only with Britain and France. At the president's discretion, trade could be reopened with either nation after it lifted its restrictions on American shipping.

Madison and the Coming of War

Frail-looking and short, Madison struck most contemporaries as an indecisive and weaker version of Jefferson. He never did succeed in escaping from his predecessor's shadow. Nor did he succeed as president in keeping America at peace. Yet in intellectual toughness and resourcefulness he was at least Jefferson's equal. He failed because of an inherited foreign policy that was partly of his own making as Jefferson's secretary of state. The Republicans' idealistic stand on neutral rights was ultimately untenable unless backed up by military and political force. Madison concluded as much when he decided on war against Britain in the spring of 1812.

The failure of economic sanctions imposed in fits and starts against Britain and France left Madison with war as his only means of enforcing American standards of international behavior. A war against America's old enemy also promised to restore unity to a Republican party increasingly divided over Madison's peaceful diplomacy. What was at stake for Madison was not just the defense of America's economic independence but the legacy of republicanism itself, now under attack by the monarchists in Britain and their presumed American friends in the resurgent Federalist party. Thus did Madison and his fellow Republicans push for a war they were eager to fight but unprepared to wage.

The Failure of Economic Sanctions

Early in his administration, Madison convinced himself that the impasse in Anglo-American relations was about to be broken. Britain benefited from the Nonintercourse Act at the expense of France. Unlike the embargo, which kept American vessels at home, nonintercourse permitted ship clearances. Once at sea, American ships were kept away from France and steered to England by the strong British navy. Perhaps in recognition of this unintended consequence

of the new American policy, the British began to relax their restrictions on neutral shipping, known as the **Orders in Council**, in favor of U.S. commerce. At the same time, the British minister in Washington, David Erskine, reached an agreement with Madison that called for completely rescinding the Orders in Council as they applied to the United States. In return, Madison pledged to terminate nonintercourse against Britain while maintaining it against France.

Madison set June 10, 1809, as the date for the resumption of Anglo-American trade. Unfortunately, Erskine had exceeded his instructions, and the Madison-Erskine agreement was disavowed as soon as news of it reached London. Although Madison reimposed sanctions on Britain in August, he was left looking the fool.

Given Madison's obvious floundering, Congress stepped in with its own policy in 1810. **Macon's Bill No. 2** threw open American trade to everyone but stipulated that if either France or England lifted its restrictions, the president would resume trading sanctions against the other. A concession to mercantile interests in both New England and the Mid-Atlantic states, Macon's bill also bought Madison time before he had to decide between war or submission to the British Orders in Council. Thanks to Napoleon's duplicity, however, that time was short.

Napoleon made an offer in August 1810 that Madison felt he had to accept. The French emperor promised to withdraw his decrees against American shipping on the condition that if Britain did not follow suit, Madison would force the British to respect American rights. Madison took the bait. He was under no illusion as to Napoleon's honesty, but he was desperate to apply pressure on the British to match the apparent French concessions. To Madison's chagrin, Napoleon's offer was an utter fraud. French seizures of American ships continued. By the time his duplicity became clear, Napoleon had already succeeded in worsening Anglo-American tensions. In November 1810, Madison reimposed nonintercourse against Britain, putting the two nations on a collision course.

The Frontier and Indian Resistance

Mounting frustrations in the South and West also pushed Madison toward a war against Britain. Nearly 1 million Americans lived west of the Appalachian Mountains in 1810, a tripling of the western population in just a decade. Cheap, fertile land and markets for crops down the Ohio and Mississippi River systems drew farm families from the East. Farm prices, including those for the southern staples of cotton and tobacco, plunged when Jefferson's embargo shut off exports, and they stayed low after the embargo was lifted. Blame for the persistent agricultural depression focused on the British and their stranglehold on overseas trade after 1808. As a glut of American goods piled up in English ports, prices remained depressed.

Western settlers blamed the British for inspiring Indian attempts to resist them. After the *Chesapeake* incident enflamed relations with the United States, the British did try to cement alliances with Indians in the Old Northwest, reviving the strategy of using them as a buffer against any American move on Canada. However, it was the unceasing demand of Americans for ever more Indian land, not any British incitements, that triggered the **pan-Indian resistance movement** that so frightened western settlers on the eve of the War of 1812. Many Native Americans were also determined to lash back at such white attitudes as those expressed about the Miami Indians by an Ohioan in 1810: "We never permit them to be troublesome, for if any of them displease us, we take them out of doors and kick them a little, for they are like dogs, and so will love you the better for it."

In the Treaty of Greenville (1795), the American government had promised that any future acquisitions of Indian land would have to be approved by all native peoples in the region. Nonetheless, government agents continued their former tactics of playing one group against another and of dividing groups from within by lavishing money and goods on the more accommodationist Christianized Indians. By such means, William Henry Harrison, the governor of the Indiana Territory, procured most of southern Indiana in the **Treaty of Vincennes** of 1804. Two extraordinary leaders, the Shawnee chief Tecumseh and his brother, the Prophet Tenkswatawa, channeled Indian outrage over this treaty into a movement to unify tribes throughout the West for a stand against the white invaders.

The message of pan-Indianism was unwavering: White encroachments had to be stopped and tribal and clan divisions submerged in a return to native rituals and belief systems. As preached by Tecumseh and the Prophet, Indian land could be saved and self-respect regained only through racial solidarity and a spiritual rebirth. Tenkswatawa had undergone such a rebirth when he saved himself from alcoholism, and much of the passion he brought to preaching reflected his own sense of redemption. With the assistance of Tecumseh, Tenkswatawa established the Prophet's Town in 1808. At the confluence of the Wabash and Tippecanoe Rivers in north-central Indiana, this encampment

The Prophet Tenskwatawa was the spiritual leader of the pan-Indian movement that sought to revitalize native culture and block the spread of white settlement in the Old Northwest.

became headquarters of an intertribal confederation. As he tried to explain to the worried Governor Harrison, his goals were peaceful. He admonished his followers, "[Do] not take up the tomahawk, should it be offered by the British, or by the long knives: do not meddle with any thing that does not belong to you, but mind your own business, and cultivate the ground, that your women and your children have enough to live on."

That ground, of course, was the very reason the Indians could not live in peace and dignity. The whites wanted it and would do anything to get it. In November 1811, Harrison marched an army to Prophet's Town and provoked the **Battle of Tippecanoe**. The Indian encampment was on land claimed by the U.S. government in the Treaty of Fort Wayne (1809). Tecumseh was absent, off on a recruiting mission among the southern tribes, and without his restraining influence, impetuous young braves attacked Harrison's army. Losses were heavy on both sides, but Harrison regrouped his forces, drove the surviving Indians away, and burned the abandoned town. Harrison's victory came at a high cost. Tecumseh now joined forces with the British, leaving the frontier more unsettled than ever.

While Harrison's aggressiveness was converting fears of a British-Indian alliance into a self-fulfilling prophecy, expansionist-minded Southerners struck at Britain through Spain, now its ally against Napoleon. With the covert support of President Madison, American adventurers staged a bloodless revolt in Spanish West Florida extending to the Pearl River, the present Gulf Coast boundary between Louisiana and Mississippi. They raised the American flag and declared their independence. This "republic" was quickly recognized by the U.S. government and annexed as part of Louisiana in 1811. Spanish possession of the rest of Florida still galled southern planters anxious to remove the territory as a sanctuary for fugitive slaves.

Hatred of Native Americans, expansionist pressures, the lingering agricultural depression, and impatience with the administration's policy of economic coercion all pointed in the same direction—a war against Britain coupled with an American takeover of British Canada and Spanish Florida. This was the rallying cry of the **War Hawks**, the forty or so prowar congressmen swept into office in 1810. Generally younger men from the South and West, the War Hawks were led by Henry Clay of Kentucky. Along with other outspoken nationalists such as John C. Calhoun of South Carolina, Clay played a key role in building congressional support for Madison's growing aggressiveness on the British issue.

Decision for War

In July 1811, Madison issued a Proclamation calling Congress into an early session on November 4. By the time of the announcement, Madison had probably accepted the inevitability of war against Britain. Deceived by Napoleon and dismissed by the British as the head of a second-rate power, Madison had run out of diplomatic options and was losing control of his party.

When Congress met, Madison tried to lay the groundwork for war. Although he did not rule out a peaceful settlement, he called for military preparations and stressed his "deep sense of the crisis." In January 1812, the authorized size of the army was increased from 10,000 to 35,000 men. Still, fewer than 7,000 men were actually under arms throughout the spring, and Congress refused to enlarge the navy. The Republican-controlled Congress also balked at raising taxes to pay for a war that seemed ever more likely. In opposing Madison, many Republicans cited their party's traditional view of high taxes and a strong military as the tools of despots.

Madison secretly asked Congress on April 1 for a sixty-day embargo, a move designed to give American merchant ships time to return safely to their home ports. On June 1, he sent a war message to Congress in which he laid out the stark alternative of submission or resistance to the British control of American commerce (see "American Views: Madison's War Message of June 1, 1812"). Madison was now convinced that British commercial restrictions were not just a defensive measure aimed at France but an aggressive attempt to reduce the United States to the permanent status of colonial dependent.

For Madison and most other Republicans, the impending conflict was a second war for independence. Free and open access to world markets was certainly at stake, but so was national pride. The arrogant British policy of impressment was a humiliating affront to American honor and headed the list of grievances in Madison's war message.

A divided Congress declared war on Britain. The vote in the House on June 4 was seventy-nine in favor and forty-nine opposed; on June 17, the Senate concurred, nineteen to thirteen. The vote split along regional, economic, and party lines. Support for the war was strongest in regions whose economies had been damaged the most by the British blockades and control of Atlantic commerce. Thus the South and the West, trapped in an agricultural depression and anxious to eliminate foreign threats at their frontiers, favored war. Conversely, mercantile New England, a region that had, ironically, prospered as a result of British interference with ocean commerce, opposed the war.

The votes that carried the war declaration came from northern Republicans, who saw the impending struggle as a defense of America's experiment in self-government. Nine-tenths of the congressional Republicans voted for war, but not a single Federalist did so. For the Federalists, the real enemy was France, which had actually seized more American ships than the British. From their strongholds in coastal New England, the Federalists condemned the war as a French-inspired plot and predicted it would end in financial ruin.

The Federalists' anger increased when they learned that the British had been prepared to yield on one of the most prominent issues in the coming of war. On June 23, the British government revoked for one year its Orders in Council against the United States. A poor harvest and the ongoing economic pressure exerted by Madison had finally caused hard times in England and produced a policy reversal of placating the Americans. This concession, however, did not address impressment or

American Views

MADISON'S WAR MESSAGE OF JUNE 1, 1812

Mounting tensions between the United States and Britain during the Jefferson and Madison administrations climaxed in the War of 1812. Madison's war message to Congress summarized the Republican case for a declaration of war and cited a number of grievances. Central to the thinking of the Republicans was the belief that Americans could establish their own identity and independence only by standing up to British aggressions and escaping the status of a British dependency.

❖ What factors did Madison stress in asking for a declaration of war?

❖ What influence of the War Hawks can you find in the war message?

❖ How did Madison argue that the goal of the British was to gain a monopoly on trade and injure the commercial interests of the United States?

❖ Why did many Americans view the War of 1812 as a second war for American independence?

Without going back beyond the renewal in 1803 of the war in which Great Britain is engaged, and omitting unrepaired wrongs of inferior magnitude, the conduct of her Government presents a series of acts hostile to the United States as an independent and neutral nation.

British cruisers have been in the continued practice of violating the American flag on the great highway of nations, and of seizing and carrying off persons sailing under it, not in the exercise of a belligerent right founded on the law of nations against an enemy, but of a municipal prerogative over British subjects. . . .

Thousands of American citizens, under the safeguard of public law and of their national flag, have been torn from their country and from everything dear to them; have been dragged on board ships of war of a foreign nation and exposed, under the severities of their discipline, to be exiled to the most distant and deadly climes, to risk their lives in battles of their oppressors, and to be the melancholy instruments of taking away those of their own brethren.

Against this crying enormity, which Great Britain would be so prompt to avenge if committed against herself, the United States have in vain exhausted remonstrances and expostulations. . . .

British cruisers have been in the practice

monetary compensation, and news of it did not reach America until August. For Madison, it was too little too late, and he remained committed to war.

The War of 1812

The Republicans led the nation into a war it was unprepared to fight (see Map 9-2). Still, the apparent vulnerability of Canada to invasion made it possible to envision an American victory. Canada was thinly populated, poorly defended, and exposed to a potentially huge American army of militiamen. Yet bungled American invasions verged on tragicomedy, and British-Canadian forces and their Indian allies stymied American advances. For much of the war, Britain was preoccupied with Napoleon in Europe. When free to concentrate on the American sideshow in 1814, the British failed to secure naval control of the Great Lakes, their minimal strategic objective, and their counterinvasions of the United States bogged down. By the fall of 1814, both sides were eager for an end to the military stalemate.

also of violating the rights and peace of our coasts. They hover over and harass our entering and departing commerce. . . .

Under pretended blockades, without the presence of an adequate force and sometimes without the practicability of applying one, our commerce has been plundered in every sea, the great staples of our country have been cut off from their legitimate markets, and a destructive blow aimed at our agricultural and maritime interests. . . .

It has become, indeed, sufficiently certain that the commerce of the United States is to be sacrificed, not as interfering with the belligerent rights of Great Britain; not as supplying the wants of her enemies, which she herself supplies; but as interfering with the monopoly which she covets for her commerce and navigation. She carries on a war against the lawful commerce of a friend that she may the better carry on a commerce with an enemy. . . .

In reviewing the conduct of Great Britain toward the United States our attention is necessarily drawn to the warfare just renewed by the savages on one of our extensive frontiers—a warfare

which is known to spare neither age nor sex and to be distinguished by features peculiarly shocking to humanity. It is difficult to account for the activity and combinations which have for some time been developing themselves among tribes in constant intercourse with British traders and garrisons without connecting their hostility with that influence and without recollecting the authenticated examples of such interpositions heretofore furnished by the officers and agents of the Government. . . .

We behold, in fine, on the side of Great Britain a state of war against the United States, and on the side of the United States a state of peace toward Great Britain.

Whether the United States shall continue passive under these progressive usurpations and these accumulating wrongs, or, opposing force to force in defense of their national rights, shall commit a just cause into the hands of the Almighty Disposer of Events . . . is a solemn question which the Constitution wisely confides to the legislative department of the Government. . . .

Source: *William Appleman Williams, ed.*, The Shaping of American Diplomacy: Readings and Documents in American Foreign Relations *(1956)*.

Internal dissent endangered the Union almost as much as British troops did. The war exacerbated Federalist disenchantment with southern dominance of national affairs. Nearly all Federalists believed that pro-French fanatics and slaveholding agrarians in the Republican party had consistently sacrificed the commercial interests of New England. A minority of Federalists were convinced that New England could never regain its rightful place in shaping national policy and was prepared to lead a secession movement. Although blocked by party moderates at the **Hartford Convention** in 1814, the

secessionists tarred Federalism with the brush of treason. Consequently, the Republicans, the party that brought the country to the brink of a military disaster, emerged from the war more powerful than ever.

Setbacks in Canada

The outbreak of the **War of 1812** unleashed deep emotions that often divided along religious lines. From their strongholds in the Congregationalist churches in New England, the Federalists preached that all true Christians opposed a war "against the nation from which we are descended, and which for

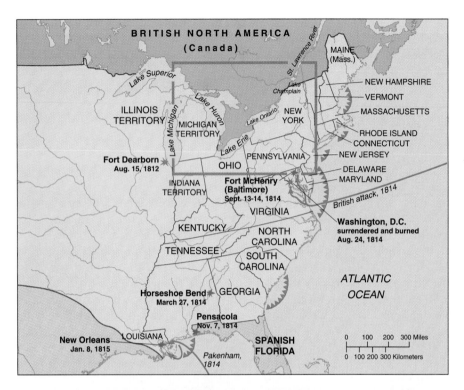

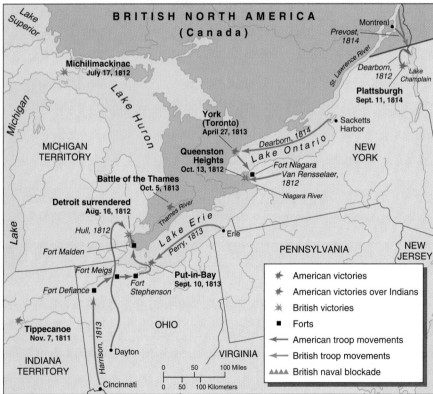

Map 9-2   The War of 1812

Most of the battles of the War of 1812 were fought along the Canadian-American border, where American armies repeatedly tried to invade Canada. Despite the effectiveness of the British naval blockade, the American navy was successful in denying the British strategic control of the Great Lakes. Andrew Jackson's smashing victory at the Battle of New Orleans convinced Americans that they had won the war.

many generations has been the bulwark of the religion we profess." Such antiwar sentiments, however, outraged the Baptists and Methodists, the largest and most popularly rooted denominations. They believed, as resolved by the Georgia Baptist Association in 1813, that the British government was "corrupt, arbitrary, and despotic" and that the war was "just, necessary, and indispensable."

Fiercely loyal to Madison, who had championed religious freedom in Virginia, these Methodists and Baptists harbored old grudges against the established churches of both Britain and New England for suppressing their religious rights. Especially for the Baptists, the war became something of a crusade to secure civil and religious liberties against their traditional enemies. For Spencer Houghton Cone, a lieutenant in a company of sharpshooters and a future president of the National Baptist Convention, service in the war seemed "as much the duty of the Christian as the honor of the soldier."

Madison hoped to channel this Christian, anti-British patriotism into the conquest of Canada. Two out of three Canadians were native-born Americans who, it was assumed, would welcome the U.S. Army with open arms. Only five thousand British troops were initially stationed in Canada, and Canadian militia were outnumbered nine to one by their American counterparts. No wonder that Madison and his advisers felt that Canada was ripe for the taking, "a mere matter of marching," as Jefferson put it.

Canada was also the only area where the United States could strike directly against British forces. Although officially a war fought to defend America's neutrality on the high seas, the

War of 1812 was largely a land war. The United States simply did not have enough ships to do more than harass the powerful British Navy. Against sixteen ships in the U.S. Navy, only seven of which were top-of-the-line frigates (warships), the British could deploy more than two hundred vessels.

By seizing Canada, Madison also hoped to weaken Britain's navy and undercut its navigation system. Madison had been convinced that withholding American foodstuffs and provisions from the British West Indies would quickly force the British to yield to American economic pressure. But the British turned to Canada as an alternative source of supplies. Madison hoped to close off that source. And if, as Madison expected, Napoleon denied the British access to the naval stores of the Baltic region in Europe, an American monopoly on Canadian lumber would cripple British naval power. Facing such a threat, the British would have to end the war on American terms.

Madison's strategic vision was clear, but its execution was pathetic. Three offensives against Canada in 1812 were embarrassing failures. In the first, in July, General William Hull crossed into Canada from Detroit and invited Canadians to join the American cause. He found few takers. Meanwhile, Fort Michilimackinac fell, and Tecumseh's warriors cut Hull's communications. Hull hurried back to Detroit only to surrender his army on August 16 to the smaller British-Indian force.

The loss of Detroit, preceded a day earlier by the abandonment of Fort Dearborn (present-day Chicago) and the massacre of its inhabitants, exposed western settlements to the full fury of frontier warfare. Americans in the Indiana Territory fled outlying areas for the safety of forts in the interior. The acting territorial governor scarcely exaggerated when he proclaimed, "Our former frontiers are now wilds and our inner Settlements have become frontiers." By the end of the year, the British controlled half of the Old Northwest.

Farther east, the Americans botched two offensives in 1812. In October, an American thrust across the Niagara River was defeated when a New York state militia refused to cross the river to join the regular army troops on the Canadian side. This left the isolated forces under General Stephen Van Rensselaer an easy prey for the British at the **Battle of Queenston Heights**. Then the long-delayed third offensive, north from Lake Champlain, turned into a bloodless fiasco. It was aimed at Montreal, the center of British operations in Canada. General Henry Dearborn, the leader of the expedition, turned back in late November when he discovered,

as Van Rensselaer had, that his militia would not leave their state.

Republican expectations of victory in Canada had been wishful thinking. Most Canadians fought against, not with, the Americans. Reliance on state militias for the bulk of the forces proved disastrous. Poorly trained and equipped militias, when they did show up for battle, could not match the discipline of British soldiers or the fighting skills of their Native American allies. Nor was American generalship on a par with that of the British. Primitive land communications made the movement and coordination of troops a nightmare. New England, the obvious base for operations against the strategically critical St. Lawrence River Valley, the entry point for all British

Fearful of an American invasion, Canadian authorities ordered American residents expelled at the beginning of the War of 1812.

POLICE.

WHEREAS authentic intelligence has been received that the Government of the United States of America did, on the 18th instant, declare War against the United Kingdom of Great Britain and Ireland and its dependencies, Notice is hereby given, that all Subjects or Citizens of the said United States, and all persons claiming American Citizenship, are ordered to quit the City of Quebec, on or before TWELVE o'clock at Noon, on WEDNESDAY next, and the District of Quebec on or before 12 o'clock at noon on FRIDAY next, on pain of arrest.   ROSS CUTHBERT, C. Q. S. & Inspector of Police.

The Constables of the City of Quebec are ordered to assemble in the Police Office at 10 o'clock to-morrow morning, to receive instructions.

Quebec, 29th June, 1812.

Cut off from their American customers during the War of 1812, some British businessmen hoped to recoup their losses once hostilities ended by making bandanas for the American souvenir market that celebrated American victories in the war.

Western Victories and British Offensives

American forces fared better in 1813. Motivation remained high because, as noted by Major Isaac Roach of an artillery regiment, many Americans believed that "it had become a jest and byword in England that this country could not be kicked into war." In September, the navy won a major engagement on Lake Erie that opened up a supply line in the western theater. Commodore Oliver Hazard Perry attacked the British fleet in the **Battle of Put-in-Bay**, on the Southwestern shore of the lake, and forced the surrender of all six British ships. The victory signaled General William Henry Harrison to launch an offensive in the West.

With the loss of Lake Erie, the British were forced to abandon Detroit. Harrison caught up with the British garrison and their Indian allies on the banks of the Thames River in southern Ontario. Demonstrating bold leadership and relying on battle-tested western militias, Harrison won a decisive victory. Tecumseh, the most visionary of the Indian warriors, was killed, and the backbone of the Indian resistance broken. The Old Northwest was again safe for American settlement.

The **Battle of the Thames** ended British plans for an Indian buffer state. But by 1814, Britain had bigger goals in mind. A coalition of European powers forced Napoleon to abdicate in April 1814, thus freeing Britain to focus on the American war. It now seemed poised to break the military stalemate with a clear-cut victory.

British strategy in 1814 called for two major offensives, an invasion south from Montreal down Lake Champlain in upstate New York and an attack on Louisiana aimed at seizing New Orleans with a task force out of Jamaica. Meanwhile, diversionary raids along the Mid-Atlantic Coast were to pin down American forces and undermine morale. The overall objective was nothing less than a reversal of America's post-1783 expansion. If the invasions succeeded, the British would have been in a strong position to force a southward adjustment of the Canadian-

supplies and reinforcements, withheld many of its state forces from national service. Consequently, the invasions were piecemeal, ineffective forays launched from western areas where anti-British and anti-Indian sentiment ran high.

All the Republicans had to show for the first year of the war were morale-boosting but otherwise insignificant naval victories. In individual combat between ships, the small American navy acquitted itself superbly. Early in the war, American privateers harassed British merchant vessels, but the easy pickings were soon gone. British squadrons ships redeployed to protect shipping, and other warships kept up a blockade that stifled American commerce.

Military setbacks and antiwar feelings in much of the Northeast hurt the Republicans in the election of 1812. Madison won only narrowly. Federalists and other disaffected Northerners rallied behind DeWitt Clinton, an antiadministration Republican from New York. The now familiar regional pattern in voting repeated itself. Madison swept the electoral vote of the South and West. He ran poorly in the Northeast and won only because his party held on to Pennsylvania.

American boundary and to claim the Louisiana Purchase territory.

The British attacks could hardly have come at a worse time for the Madison administration. The Treasury was nearly bankrupt. Against the wishes of Treasury Secretary Gallatin, Congress had refused to preserve the Bank of the United States when its charter expired in 1811. Lacking both a centralized means of directing wartime finances and any significant increase in taxes, the Treasury was forced to rely on makeshift loans. These loans were poorly subscribed, largely because the cash-rich New England banks refused to loan money to the government. Inflation also became a problem when state banks, no longer restrained by the controls of a national bank, overissued paper money in the form of bank notes.

As the country's finances tottered toward collapse, political dissent in New England was reaching a climax. In 1814, the British extended their blockade of American commerce northward to include New England. Federalist merchants and shippers, who had earlier profited from their illegal trade with the British, now felt the economic pinch of the war. Cries for resistance against "Mr. Madison's war" culminated in a call issued by the Massachusetts legislature for a convention to consider "a radical reform of the national compact." The convention was scheduled for December in Hartford, Connecticut.

The darkest hour came in August 1814. A British amphibious force occupied and torched Washington, D.C. in retaliation for an American raid on York (now Toronto), the capital of Upper Canada. The defense of Washington was slipshod at best, and a local inhabitant can be excused for scribbling on a wall: "The capital and the Union lost by cowardice." Still, the British actions stiffened American resistance, and the failure of a follow-up attack on Baltimore deprived the British of any strategic gain. Baltimore's defenses held, stirring Francis Scott Key, a young lawyer who viewed the bombardment from a British prisoner-of-war ship, to write "The Star Spangled Banner." Fittingly in this strange war, the future national anthem was set to the tune of a British drinking song.

The Chesapeake campaign was designed to divert American attention from the major offensive General George Prevost was leading down the shores of Lake Champlain. Prevost commanded the largest and best-equipped army the British had yet assembled. His opponent was Commodore Thomas Macdonough, one of several young, talented regional commanders Madison appointed late in the war. On September 11, at the **Battle of Plattsburgh**, Macdonough smashed a British fleet on Lake Champlain. Having counted on that fleet to protect his supply lines, Prevost retreated to Canada.

The tide had turned. When news of the setbacks at Baltimore and especially Plattsburgh reached England, the foreign office scaled back the demands it had been making on American negotiators at peace talks in the city of Ghent, in present-day Belgium. The British were ready for peace, but one of their trump cards had yet to be played—the southern offensive against New Orleans. The outcome of that campaign could still upset whatever was decided at Ghent.

The Treaty of Ghent and the Battle of New Orleans

By the fall of 1814, the British were eager to get on with redrawing the map of post-Napoleonic Europe, restoring profitable relations with America, and reducing their huge

This contemporary woodcut shows Washington burning on the night of August 2, 1814, after British troops torched government buildings. Among the losses were both the records and the library of Congress.

war debt. The British negotiators at Ghent agreed to a peace treaty on terms the Americans were delighted to accept. The **Treaty of Ghent**, signed on Christmas Eve, 1814, simply restored relations to their status at the start of the war. No territory changed hands, and nothing was said about impressment or the rights of neutrals.

The ink had barely dried on the Treaty of Ghent when the British government sent reinforcements to General Edward Pakenham, the commander of the Louisiana invasionary force. By this action, the British indicated that they were not irrevocably committed to the peace settlement, which, though signed, could not be formally ratified until weeks had passed while it was sent across the Atlantic. The British had always held that the Louisiana Purchase was fraudulent (they insisted that Louisiana was never Napoleon's to sell), and they were prepared to install a new government in Louisiana if Pakenham succeeded. Far from being an anticlimax to a war that was already over, the showdown between British and American forces at the **Battle of New Orleans** in January 1815 had immense strategic significance for the United States.

The hero of New Orleans, in song and legend, was Andrew Jackson. A planter-politician from Tennessee, Jackson rose to prominence during the war as a ferocious Indian fighter. The Creeks of Alabama and Georgia, much like the Shawnees farther north, had undergone a religious revival that culminated in a military effort to drive American settlers out of their tribal homelands. As a general in the Tennessee militia, Jackson crushed Indian resistance in the Old Southwest at the Battle of Horseshoe Bend in March 1814. He then forced the vanquished Creeks to cede two-thirds of their territory to the United States.

After his Indian conquests, Jackson was promoted to general in the regular army and given command of the defense of the Gulf Coast. In November 1814, he seized Pensacola in Spanish Florida to deny the British its use as a supply depot and then hurried to defend New Orleans. The overconfident British frontally attacked Jackson's lines on January 8, 1815. The result was a massacre. Artillery fire laid down by French-speaking cannoneers from New Orleans accounted for most of the carnage. More than two thousand British soldiers were killed or wounded. American casualties totaled twenty-one.

Strategically, Jackson's smashing victory at New Orleans ended any possibility of a British sphere of influence in Louisiana. Politically, it was a deathblow to Federalism. At the Hartford Convention in

December, party moderates had forestalled talk of secession with a series of proposed constitutional amendments designed to limit southern power in national affairs. At the top of their list was a demand for eliminating the three-fifths clause by which slaves were counted for purposes of congressional representation. They also wanted to require a two-thirds majority in Congress for the admission of new states, declarations of war, and the imposition of embargoes. These demands became public as Americans were rejoicing over the Treaty of Ghent and Jackson's routing of the British. Set against the revived nationalism that marked the end of the war, the Federalists now seemed to be parochial sulkers who put regional interests above the national good. Worse yet, they struck many Americans as quasi-traitors who had been prepared to desert the country in the face of the enemy. As a significant political force, Federalism was dead.

The Era of Good Feelings

In 1817, on the occasion of a presidential visit by James Monroe, a Boston newspaper proclaimed the **Era of Good Feelings**, an expression that nicely captured the spirit of political harmony and sectional unity that washed over the republic in the immediate postwar years. National pride surged with the humbling of the British at New Orleans, the demise of the Federalists lessened political tensions, and the economy boomed. The Republicans had been vindicated, and for a short time they enjoyed de facto status as the only governing party.

At the end of Madison's presidency and in the first administration of his successor, James Monroe of Virginia, the Republicans embarked on a program of economic nationalism that would have pleased Alexander Hamilton. In foreign policy, they moved aggressively to stake out American leadership in the Western Hemisphere. A series of decisions handed down by the Supreme Court also reinforced the postwar nationalism. In 1819, however, an economic depression and a bitter controversy over slavery shattered the harmony. The nationalist tide set in motion by the end of the war had run its course, and the Republicans divided on sectional and economic issues.

Economic Nationalism
The War of 1812 had taught the Republicans to appreciate old Federalist doctrines on centralized

national power. In his annual message of December 1815, Madison outlined a program of economic nationalism that was pushed through Congress by Henry Clay and John Calhoun, the most prominent of the new generation of young, nationalist-minded Republicans.

The first order of business was creating a new national bank. Reliance on state banks for wartime financing had proved a major mistake. The banks lacked sufficient capital reserves or, as occurred in New England, held them back. Demand for credit was met by a flood of state bank notes that fell in value because there was insufficient gold and silver to back them. Many banks suspended specie payments for their notes, and inflation was a persistent problem. After the British burned Washington, the Treasury was temporarily bankrupt, and throughout the war it could borrow only at high interest rates. Fiscal stability required the monetary coordination and restraint that only a new Bank of the United States could provide.

Introduced by Calhoun, the Bank bill passed Congress in 1816. Modeled after Hamilton's original Bank and also headquartered in Philadelphia, the **Second Bank of the United States** was capitalized at $35 million, making it by far the nation's largest bank. Its sheer size, when combined with its official status as the depository and dispenser of the government's funds, gave the Bank tremendous power over the economy. It also enjoyed the exclusive privilege of being able to establish branches in any state.

After moving to repair the fiscal damage of the war, the Republicans then acted to protect what the war had fostered. Embargoes followed by three years of war forced American businessmen to manufacture goods they previously had imported. This was especially the case with iron and textile goods long supplied by the British. In 1815 and again in 1816, the British inundated the American market with cheap imports, a tactic openly designed to strangle American industry in its infancy. This challenge to the nation's economic independence united most Republicans against their traditional antagonist in foreign affairs. In retaliation, they passed the **Tariff of 1816**, the first protective tariff in American history. The act levied duties of 20 to 25 percent on manufactured goods that could be produced in the United States.

Revenue from the tariff and $1.5 million from the Bank of the United States, a cash payment in return for its charter, were earmarked for internal improvements (roads and canals). The push for federal subsidies for transportation projects came from the War Department and the West. The lack of a road system in the trans-Appalachian region had severely hampered troop movements during the war. Also, as settlers after the war moved onto lands seized from the pro-British Indians, western congressmen demanded improved outlets to eastern markets.

In early 1817, an internal improvements bill passed Congress. Despite the soaring rhetoric of John Calhoun, the bill's sponsor, seeking to "bind the republic together with a perfect system of roads and canals," President Madison remained unmoved. Though in agreement with the bill's objectives, he was convinced that the Constitution did not permit federal financing of primarily local projects. He vetoed the bill just before he left office.

Congressional passage of Calhoun's internal improvements bill marked the pinnacle of the Republicans' economic nationalism. Frightened by the sectional disunity of the war years, a new generation of Republicans jettisoned many of the ideological trappings of Jefferson's original agrarian party. Their program was a call for economic, and therefore political, unity. Such unity was to be achieved through a generous program of national subsidies consisting of tariffs for manufacturers in the Northeast and transportation funds for planters and farmers in the South and West. The new national bank would provide a uniform currency and credit facilities for the internal exchange of raw materials and manufactured goods.

Support for this program was strongest in the Mid-Atlantic and western states, the regions that stood to gain the most economically. Opposition centered in the Southeast, notably among die-hard proponents of states' rights in the old tobacco belt of Virginia and North Carolina, and in New England, a region not only well served already by banks and a road network but also anxious not to be politically overshadowed by the rising West. This opposition took on an increasingly hard edge in the South as the Supreme Court outlined an ever more nationalist interpretation of the Constitution.

Judicial Nationalism

The nationalist perspective championed by Republicans after the war had long been upheld in the Supreme Court under Chief Justice John Marshall. A Virginia Federalist whose nationalism was forged during his service in the Revolutionary War, Marshall dominated the Court throughout his tenure (1801–1835) by his forceful personality and the logical power of his nationalist convictions. The defining principles of Marshall's jurisprudence were the authority of the Supreme Court in all matters of

John Marshall by Chester Harding (1792–1886). Oil on canvas, 1830. Boston Athenaeum.

This 1830 painting shows Chief Justice John Marshall in the full robes of his office. Marshall's leadership molded the Supreme Court into an effective instrument of the national government.

constitutional interpretation and the sanctity of contractual property rights.

In *Fletcher* **v.** *Peck* (1810), the Court overturned a Georgia law by ruling that it violated the prohibition in the federal Constitution against any state "impairing the obligation of contracts." The Georgia legislature had voided a land grant made by an earlier legislature on grounds of massive fraud. Fraud had occurred, but Marshall held that the original land grant constituted a legal contract that could not be broken.

Out of the political limelight since the Burr trial in 1807, the Court was thrust back into it by two controversial decisions in 1819. The first involved Dartmouth College and the attempt by the New Hampshire legislature to amend its charter in the direction of greater public control over this private institution. In **Dartmouth College v. Woodward**, the Court ruled that Dartmouth's original royal charter of 1769 was a contract protected by the Constitution. Hence the state of New Hampshire could not alter that charter without the prior consent of the college. By so sanctifying charters or acts of incorporation as contracts, the Court prohibited states from interfering with the rights and privileges they had bestowed on private corporations.

The second important decision in 1819, **McCulloch v. Maryland**, rested on a positive assertion of national power over the states. The case involved the Bank of the United States. Many state bankers were jealous of the privileges of the national bank, and this resentment was shared by legislators who viewed the Bank's branches as an infringement on the states' economic sovereignty. In 1818, the Maryland legislature placed a heavy tax on the branch of the Bank of the United States established in Baltimore (and on all other banks in the state established without legislative authority). James McCulloch, the cashier of the Baltimore branch, refused to pay the tax. This set up a test case that involved two fundamental legal issues: Was the Bank itself constitutional, and could a state tax federal property within its borders?

A unanimous Court, in language similar to but even more sweeping than that used by Alexander Hamilton in the 1790s, upheld the constitutional authority of Congress to charter a national bank and thereby regulate the nation's currency and finances. As long as the end was legitimate "within the scope of the Constitution," Congress had full power to use any means not expressly forbidden by the Constitution to achieve that end. As for Maryland's claim of a constitutional right to tax a federal agency, Marshall stressed that "the power to tax involves the power to destroy." Surely, he reasoned, when the people of the United States ratified the Constitution, they did not intend the federal government to be controlled by the states or rendered powerless by state action. Here was the boldest statement to date of the loose or "implied powers" interpretation of the Constitution and a ringing rebuke to the compact theory of the Union outlined by Southerners in the Virginia and Kentucky Resolutions and picked up by disgruntled Federalists in New England.

Toward a Continental Empire

Marshall's legal nationalism paralleled the diplomatic nationalism of John Quincy Adams, secretary of state from 1817 to 1825. A former Federalist and the son of the second president, Adams broke with the Federalist party over its refusal to support an expansionist policy, and he had held several diplomatic posts under the Madison administration. Adams made few friends as a negotiator. A British statesman once described him as "doggedly and systematically repulsive." Still, he was an effective diplomat. Convinced in his Puritan soul that God and nature had ordained that America stretch from the Atlantic to the Pacific as a beacon of liberty to the world, Adams used whatever tactics were necessary to realize that vision.

SUMMARY		
TERRITORIAL EXPANSION UNDER THE REPUBLICANS		
Benchmark	**Year**	**Land Area of United States and Its Territories (square miles)**
Republicans gain power	1801	864,746
Louisiana Purchase	1803	1,681,828
Trans-Continental Treaty	1819	1,749,462

Adams shrewdly exploited the British desire for friendly and profitable relations after the War of 1812. The British wanted access to American cotton and foodstuffs in exchange for manufactured goods and investment capital. The United States wanted more trading opportunities in the British Empire and a free hand to deal with Spain's disintegrating empire in the Americas.

The **Rush-Bagot Agreement** of 1817 signaled the new pattern of Anglo-American cooperation. The agreement strictly limited naval armaments on the Great Lakes, thus effectively demilitarizing the border. The **Anglo-American Accords** of the following year resolved a number of issues left hanging after the war. Of great importance to New England, the British once again recognized American fishing rights off Labrador and Newfoundland. The boundary of the Louisiana Territory abutting Canada was set at the 49th parallel, and both nations agreed to the joint occupation of Oregon, the territory in the Pacific Northwest that lay west of the Rocky Mountains.

Having secured the northern flank of the United States, Adams was now free to deal with the South and West. Adams wanted all of Florida and an undisputed American window on the Pacific. The adversary here was Spain. Much weaker than it had been in the eighteenth century and heavily involved in trying to suppress independence movements in its South American possessions, Spain could resort only to delaying tactics in trying to hold off the tenacious Adams. The negotiations remained deadlocked until Andrew Jackson gave Adams the leverage he needed.

In March 1818, Jackson led his troops across the border into Spanish Florida. He destroyed the encampments of the Seminole Indians, seized two Spanish forts, and executed two British subjects on the grounds that they were dealing arms to the Seminoles for raids on the Alabama-Georgia frontier. Despite later protestations to the contrary, Jackson had probably exceeded his orders. He might well have been censured by the Monroe administration had not Adams taken the offensive by lecturing Spain that Jackson was acting in the defense of American interests and warning that he might be unleashed again.

Spain yielded to the American threat in the **Trans-Continental Treaty of 1819** (see Map 9-3). The United States annexed East Florida, and Spain recognized the prior American seizures of West Florida in 1810 and 1813. Adams secured an American hold on the Pacific Coast by drawing a boundary between the Louisiana Purchase and the Spanish Southwest that ran stepwise up the Sabine, Red, and Arkansas Rivers to the Continental Divide and then due west along the 42nd parallel to the Pacific. Spain renounced any claim to the Pacific Northwest; the United States in turn renounced its shaky claim to Texas under the Louisiana Purchase and assumed $5 million in Spanish debts to American citizens.

Adams' success in the Spanish negotiations turned on the British refusal to threaten war or assist Spain in the wake of Jackson's highhanded actions in Florida. Spanish possessions and the lives of two British subjects were worth little when weighed against the economic advantages of retaining close trading ties with the United States. Moreover, Britain, like the United States, had a vested interest in developing trade with a Latin American market now opened up by the loss of Spain's former imperial

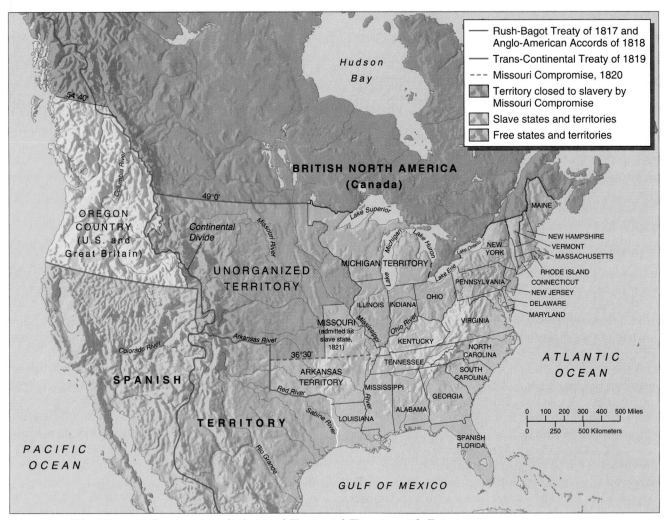

Map 9-3   The Missouri Compromise of 1820 and Territorial Treaties with Britain and Spain, 1818–1819
Treaties with Britain and Spain in 1818 and 1819 clarified and expanded the nation's boundaries. Britain accepted the 49th parallel as the boundary between Canada and the United States in the Trans-Mississippi West to the Oregon Country; Spain ceded Florida to the United States and agreed to a boundary stretching to the Pacific between the Louisiana Purchase territory and Spanish possessions in the Southwest. Sectional disputes over slavery led to the drawing of the Missouri Compromise line of 1820 that prohibited slavery in the Louisiana Territory north of 36°30'.

monopoly. Recognizing this common interest, George Canning, the British foreign minister, proposed in August 1823 that the United States and Britain issue a joint declaration opposing any European attempt to recolonize South America or to assist Spain in regaining its colonies.

President Monroe rejected the British overture, but only at the insistence of Adams. Canning's offer had a string attached to it: a mutual pledge by the British and Americans not to annex former Spanish territory. But Adams was confident that within a

generation, the United States would acquire California, Texas, and perhaps Cuba as well. He wanted to maintain the maximum freedom of action for future U.S. policy and avoid any impression that America was beholden to Britain. Thus originated the most famous diplomatic statement in early American history, the **Monroe Doctrine**.

In his annual message to Congress in December 1823, Monroe declared that the Americas "are henceforth not to be considered as subjects for future colonization by any European power." In turn,

Monroe pledged that the United States would not interfere in the internal affairs of European states. With its continental empire rapidly taking shape and new Latin American republics to be courted, the United States was more than willing to proclaim a special position for itself as the guardian of New World liberties.

The Breakdown of Unity

For all the intensity with which he pursued his continental vision, John Quincy Adams worried, as he confided to a congressman in early 1819, that "the greatest danger of this union was in the overgrown extent of its territory, combining with the slavery question." His words were prophetic. A sectional crisis flared up in 1819 over slavery and its expansion when the territory of Missouri sought admission to the Union as a slave state. Simultaneously, a financial panic ended postwar prosperity and crystallized regional discontent over banking and tariff policies. Party unity cracked under these pressures, and each region backed its own presidential candidate in the wide-open election of 1824.

The Panic of 1819

From 1815 to 1818, Americans enjoyed a wave of postwar prosperity. European markets were starved for American goods after a generation of war and trade restrictions, and farmers and planters met that demand by expanding production and bringing new land into cultivation. The availability of public land in the West on easy terms of credit sparked a speculative frenzy, and land sales soared. State banks and, worse yet, the Bank of the United States fed the speculation by making loans in the form of bank notes far in excess of their ability to redeem those notes in hard currency. Before the bubble burst, cotton prices doubled to 30 cents a pound, real estate values became wildly inflated, and Westerners owed the federal government $21 million for the payment of public lands, a debt greater than the value of all western farm goods.

European markets for American cotton and food supplies returned to normal by late 1818. In January 1819, cotton prices sank in England, and the **Panic of 1819** was on. Cotton was the most valuable American export, and expected returns from the staple were the basis for an intricate credit network anchored in Britain. The fall in cotton prices triggered a credit contraction that soon engulfed the overextended American economy. Commodity prices fell across the board, and real estate values collapsed, especially in and around western cities.

A sudden shift in policy by the Bank of the United States virtually guaranteed that the economic downturn would settle into a depression. The Bank stopped all loans, called in all debts, and refused to honor drafts drawn on its branches in the South and West. Hardest hit by these policies were farmers and businessmen in the West, a region that had piled up debt in the expectation that the income generated by postwar prosperity would return a tidy profit to those who had mortgaged their economic futures. Bankruptcies mushroomed as creditors forced the liquidation of farms and real estate. For Westerners, the Bank of the United States now became "the Monster," a ruthless institution controlled by eastern aristocrats who callously destroyed the hopes of farmers.

Southern resentment over the hard times brought on by low cotton prices focused on the tariff. Planters charged that the Tariff of 1816 unfairly raised their costs and amounted to an unconstitutional tax levied for the sole benefit of northern manufacturers. Unreconstructed Jeffersonians, now known as the Old Republicans, spearheaded a sharp reaction against the South's flirtation with nationalist policies in the postwar period. Taking their cue from John Taylor, a Virginia planter and agrarian philosopher, they demanded a return to strict states' rights doctrines. They saw an ominous pattern of unchecked and unconstitutional federal power emerging in the form of high tariffs, the judicial nationalism of the Supreme Court, and northern efforts to interfere with slavery in Missouri. If Northerners, they asked, could stretch the Constitution to incorporate a bank or impose a protective tariff, what could prevent them from emancipating the slaves?

The Missouri Compromise

Until 1819, slavery had not been a major divisive issue in American politics. The Northwest Ordinance of 1787, which banned slavery in federal territories north of the Ohio River, and the Southwest Ordinance of 1790, which permitted slavery south of the Ohio, represented a compromise that had allowed slavery in areas where climate and soil conditions favored slave-based agriculture. What was unforeseen in the 1780s, however, was the explosive demand for slave-produced cotton generated by the English textile industry in the early nineteenth century. At the republic's founding in 1787, slavery was identified with the declining tobacco economy of the South Atlantic states, and many Americans felt, perhaps wishfully, that the institution would gradually wither away.

By 1819, all hopes for the natural death of slavery were gone. Kentucky, Tennessee, Louisiana, Mississippi, and Alabama had all been added to the Union as slave states since 1787. Florida had just been annexed and surely would be another slave state. A thriving cotton market was underwriting slavery's expansion across the South, and even Missouri, a portion of the Louisiana Purchase that Northerners initially assumed would be inhospitable to slavery, had fallen under the political control of slaveholders.

The Missouri issue pushed northern resentment over the spread of slavery and the southern dominance of national affairs under the Virginia presidents beyond the boiling point. In February 1819, James Tallmadge, a Republican congressman from New York, introduced an amendment in the House mandating a ban on future slave importations and a program of gradual emancipation as preconditions for the admission of Missouri as a state. Missourians, as well as Southerners in general, rejected the **Tallmadge Amendment** as completely unacceptable. They argued that states had absolute sovereignty in the drafting of their constitutions and that any attempt by Congress to set conditions for statehood was unconstitutional. Nonetheless, a solid phalanx of northern congressmen supported the amendment.

Without a two-party system in which each of the parties had to compromise to protect its intersectional interests, voting followed sectional lines. The northern-controlled House passed the amendment, but it was repeatedly blocked in the Senate, where these were eleven free and eleven slave states. The debates were heated, and Southerners spoke openly of secession if Missouri were denied admission as a slave state.

The stalemate over Missouri persisted into the next session of Congress. Finally, Speaker of the House Henry Clay engineered a compromise in March 1820. Congress put no restrictions on slavery in Missouri, and the admission of Missouri as a slave state was balanced by admitting Maine (formerly part of Massachusetts) as a free state. In return for their concession on Missouri, northern congressmen demanded a prohibition on slavery in the remainder of the Louisiana Purchase north of the 36°30' parallel, the southern boundary of Missouri (see Map 9-3 on page 278). Except for the Arkansas Territory and what would become the Indian Territory of Oklahoma, the Louisiana Purchase was closed to slavery in the future.

The compromise almost unraveled when Missouri submitted a constitution the next November that required the state legislature to bar the entry of free blacks. This mandate violated the guarantee in the U.S. Constitution that "the citizens of each State shall be entitled to all privileges and immunities of citizens in the several States." Many eastern states had granted citizenship to African-Americans, and Missouri's restrictionist policy obviously denied these blacks their constitutional right to move into any other state. Nonetheless, and as Southerners were quick to point out, free as well as slave states discriminated against free blacks in terms of voting and militia service.

The nearly universal belief of whites that blacks were second-class citizens made it possible for Clay to pull off a baldfaced dodge. Missouri's constitution was accepted with the proviso that it "shall never be construed" to discriminate against citizens in other states. In short, with meaningless words that begged the issue of Missouri's defiance of the federal Constitution, the **Missouri Compromise** was salvaged. At the cost of ignoring the claims of free blacks for equal treatment as citizens, the Union survived its first great sectional crisis over slavery.

The Missouri crisis made southern whites realize that they were now a distinct political minority within the Union. More rapid population growth in the North had reduced southern representation in the House to just over 40 percent. Of greater concern was the crystallization in Congress of a northern majority arraigned against the expansion of slavery. Southern threats of secession died out in the aftermath of the Missouri Compromise, but it was an open question whether the sectional settlement really solved the intertwined issues of slavery and expansion or merely sidestepped them for a day of final reckoning.

The Election of 1824

The election of 1820 made Monroe, like both is Republican predecessors, a two-term president. Monroe was the uncontested choice of his party, and the Federalists were too weak to run a candidate. Although Monroe won all but one of the electoral votes, Republican unity was more apparent than real. Voters had no choice in 1820, and without two-party competition, no outlets existed for expressing popular dissatisfaction with the Republicans. Instead, the Republicans split into factions as they began jockeying almost immediately for the election of 1824 (see Map 9-4).

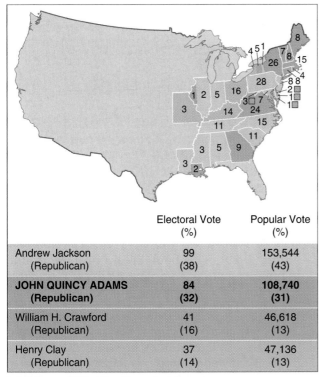

	Electoral Vote (%)	Popular Vote (%)
Andrew Jackson (Republican)	99 (38)	153,544 (43)
JOHN QUINCY ADAMS (Republican)	**84 (32)**	**108,740 (31)**
William H. Crawford (Republican)	41 (16)	46,618 (13)
Henry Clay (Republican)	37 (14)	47,136 (13)

Map 9-4   The Election of 1824
The regional appeal of each of the four presidential candidates in the election of 1824 prevented any candidate from receiving a majority of the electoral vote. Consequently, and as set forth in the Constitution, the House of Representatives now had to choose the president from the three leading candidates. Its choice was John Quincy Adams.

The politics of personality dominated Monroe's second administration. Monroe had no obvious successor, and five candidates competed to replace him. All of them were nominal Republicans, and three were members of his cabinet. Secretary of War John Calhoun soon dropped out. He preferred to accept a nomination as vice president, confident that his turn would come in 1828. The other candidates—Secretary of the Treasury William Crawford from Georgia, Secretary of State John Quincy Adams from Massachusetts, Henry Clay from Kentucky, and Andrew Jackson from Tennessee—each had a strong regional following. As the Republican party fragmented, sectional loyalties were replacing partisan allegiances.

The early favorite was Crawford. He was the "official" party nominee in the sense that he had received the support of the congressional caucus, but most Republicans had boycotted the caucus, by now a useless relic of past party unity. Clay, Jackson, and

Adams were nominated by their state legislatures. None of the candidates ran on a platform, but Crawford was identified with states' rights and Clay and Adams with centralized government. Clay in particular was associated with the national bank, protective tariffs, and federally funded internal improvements, a package of federal subsidies he called the **American System**. Jackson took no stand on any of the issues.

Jackson's noncommittal stance turned out to be a great asset. It helped him project the image of a military hero fresh from the people who was unsullied by any connection with Washington politicians, whom the public associated with hard times and sectional controversies. He was the highest vote getter (43 percent of the popular vote), but none of the four candidates had a majority in the electoral college.

As in 1800, the election was thrown into the House of Representatives. Each state had one vote, and the choice was from among the top three in the electoral college. Clay, who had received the fewest electoral votes, was eliminated. Crawford had suffered a debilitating stroke and was no longer a viable candidate. Thus it came down to Adams or Jackson. Anxious to undercut Jackson, his chief rival in the West, Clay used his influence as speaker of the House to line up support for Adams, a fellow advocate of a strong centralized government.

Adams won the election, and he immediately named Clay as his secretary of state, the office traditionally viewed as a steppingstone to the presidency. Jackson and his followers were outraged. They smelled a "corrupt bargain" in which Clay had bargained away the presidency to the highest bidder. Vowing revenge, they began building a new party that would usher in a more democratic era of mass-based politics.

Conclusion

In 1800, the Republicans were an untested party whose coming to power frightened many Federalists into predicting the end of the Union and constitutional government. The Federalists were correct in sensing that their days of power had passed, but they underestimated the ideological flexibility the Republicans would reveal once in office and the imaginative ways in which Jefferson and his successors would wield executive power to expand the size of the original Union. Far from being anarchists and demagogues, the Republicans were shrewd empire builders astute enough to add to their base of political support in the South and West. They also paved the way for the nation to evolve as a democratic republic rather than the more aristocratic republic preferred by the Federalists.

Most Federalists never did learn the art of popular electioneering, and they were too elitist to have any desire to do so. Although foreign policy issues arising out of Jefferson's and Madison's attempts to assert American neutral rights during the Anglo-French war kept the Federalists alive and even briefly revived the party, the British posed the greatest test of Republican leadership. The Republicans chose war rather than surrendering their claims of American rights. Jackson's victory at the Battle of New Orleans ended the war in an American burst of glory, and the Federalists were swept aside by the postwar surge of nationalism.

By the mid-1820s, the Republicans were about to join the Federalists as political dinosaurs. The Republican era ended when the party became a victim of its own success. With no Federalist threat to enforce party discipline, the Republicans lost their organizational strength. Embracing economic nationalism after the war made the party's original focus on states' rights all but meaningless. Ideologically and organizationally adrift, the party split into regional coalitions in the wake of the Missouri controversy and the panic of 1819. But before it dissolved, the party left as its most enduring legacy the foundations of a continental empire.

Review Questions

1. What changes did the Republicans bring to the federal government? How did their policies differ from those of their Federalist predecessors?

2. Why were the Republicans so intent on expanding the boundaries of the United States, and why did the Federalists oppose an expansionist program?

3. What factors accounted for the Federalists' inability to regain national power after they lost the election of 1800?

4. What external and internal factors drew the United States into war against Britain? Could this war have been avoided?

5. What accounted for the difficulties of the United States in waging the War of 1812, and why was the war widely viewed as a great American victory? How did the war lead to an increasing pattern of diplomatic cooperation between the United States and Britain?

6. What explains the upsurge of nationalism that underlay the Era of Good Feelings? Why were the Republicans unable to maintain their party unity after 1819?

Recommended Reading

George Dangerfield, *The Era of Good Feelings* (1952). This masterful account of America in the years just after the War of 1812 is particularly strong on the reasons behind and the consequences of the new Anglo-American cooperation in foreign policy.

Donald R. Hickey, *The War of 1812: A Forgotten Conflict* (1989). This book breaks no new ground but presents a complete and very readable account of all aspects of the war.

Drew R. McCoy, *The Elusive Republic: Political Economy in Jeffersonian America* (1980). This gracefully written study examines how attitudes on economic development influenced Jeffersonian notions of republicanism and were central to the Republicans' stand on free trade.

Peter S. Onuf, ed., *Jeffersonian Legacies* (1993). This collection of essays presents the latest thinking on the extraordinary range of Jefferson's activities.

Marshall Smelser, *The Democratic Republic, 1801–1815* (1968). This book gives a sound overview of the Jefferson and Madison administrations. Smelser portrays Jefferson as a political moderate adept in wielding power and offers a spirited defense of Madison's record as a war president.

Gore Vidal, *Burr* (1973). This superbly, entertaining novel satirically brings to life the leading personalities of Jefferson's America.

William Earl Weeks, *John Quincy Adams and American Global Empire* (1992). Weeks presents Adams as a cynical, tough-minded negotiator utterly driven by his vision of an American continental empire. Though questioning his tactics, Weeks confirms Adams' reputation as America's greatest secretary of state.

Additional Sources

Jefferson's Presidency

Lance Banning, *The Jeffersonian Persuasion: Evolution of a Party Ideology* (1978).

Doron S. Ben-Atar, *The Origins of Jeffersonian Commercial Policy and Diplomacy* (1993).

Noble E. Cunningham Jr., *The Jeffersonian Republicans in Power: Party Operations, 1801–1809* (1963).

Alexander De Conde, *This Affair of Louisiana* (1976).

Richard E. Ellis, *The Jeffersonian Crisis: Courts and Politics in the Early Republic* (1971).

David Hackett Fischer, *The Revolution of American Conservation: The Federalist Party in the Era of Jeffersonian Democracy* (1965).

Forrest McDonald, *The Presidency of Thomas Jefferson* (1976).

James Sterling Young, *The Washington Community, 1800–1828* (1966).

Madison and the Coming of War

Roger H. Brown, *The Republic in Peril* (1964).

Gregory Evans Dowd, *A Spirited Resistance: The North American Indian Struggle for Unity, 1745–1815* (1992).

R. David Edmunds, *The Shawnee Prophet* (1983) and *Tecumseh and the Quest for Indian Leadership* (1984).

Drew R. McCoy, *The Last of the Fathers: James Madison and the Republican Legacy* (1989).

Bradford Perkins, *Prologue to War: England and the United States, 1805–1812* (1961).

Robert A. Rutland, *Madison's Alternatives: The Jeffersonian Republicans and the Coming of War, 1805–1812* (1975).

The War of 1812

James M. Banner, *To the Hartford Convention: The Federalists and the Origins of Party Politics in the Early Republic, 1789–1815* (1967).

Harry L. Coles, *The War of 1812* (1965).

William Gribbin, *The Churches Militant: The War of 1812 and American Religion* (1973).

Reginald Horsman, *The War of 1812* (1969).

J. C. A. Stagg, *Mr. Madison's War: Politics, Diplomacy, and Warfare in the Early Republic, 1783–1830* (1983).

Steven Watts, *The Republic Reborn: War and the Making of Liberal America* (1987).

The Era of Good Feelings

Samuel Flagg Bemis, *Johns Quincy Adams and the Foundations of American Foreign Policy* (1949).

Noble E. Cunningham Jr., *The Presidency of James Monroe* (1996).

Shaw Livermore, *The Twilight of Federalism: The Disintegration of the Federalist Party, 1815–1830* (1962).

Ernest R. May, *The Making of the Monroe Doctrine* (1975).

Glover Moore, *The Missouri Compromise, 1819–1921* (1953).

Murray N. Rothbard, *The Panic of 1819: Reactions and Policies* (1962).

G. Edward White, *The Marshall Court and Cultural Change, 1815–1835* (1991).

Where to Learn More

❖ **Fort McHenry National Monument, Baltimore, Maryland.**   This historic site preserves the fort that was the focal point of the British attack on Baltimore and contains a museum with materials on the battle and the writing of "The Star-Spangled Banner."

❖ **Tippecanoe Battlefield Museum, Battle Ground, Indiana.**   This museum includes artifacts from the Indian and white settlement of Indiana and visual materials on the Battle of Tippecanoe of 1811.

❖ **Monticello, Charlottesville, Virginia.**   The architecturally unique home of Thomas Jefferson and the headquarters for his plantation serves as a museum that provides insights into Jefferson's varied interests.

❖ **Montpelier, Montpelier Station, Virginia.**   The museum here was the home of James Madison, and it includes material on his life as a politician and planter.

❖ **Perry's Victory and International Peace Memorial, Put-in-Bay, Ohio.**   At the site of Perry's decisive victory on Lake Erie in 1813 now stands a museum that depicts the role of the Old Northwest in the War of 1812.

10 THE JACKSONIAN ERA, 1824–1845

Pacific Ocean

Portland

Sacramento

San Francisco

Salt Lake City

Omaha

Kansas City

St. Louis

Chicago

Louis

Santa Fe

Memphis

emphi

Vicksburg

San Antonio

Galveston

New Orleans

Gulf of Mexico

Mexico City

Antebellum Transportation Systems

Railroads, c. 1850
Canals
Cumberland Road
Stagecoach routes
- - - - - Trails

Territorial Expansion

Thirteen original colonies, 1776

Westward expansion to 1783

Louisiana Purchase, 1803

Red River Basin, 1818

Florida, 1819

Annexation of Texas, 1845

Oregon Territory, 1846

Mexican cession, 1848

Gadsden Purchase, 1853

N
W E
S

Quebec

Boston

Buffalo

Cleveland

New York

Philadelphia

Cincinnati

Washington, D.C.

Richmond

Wilmington

Charleston

Atlanta

Savannah

St. Augustine

Atlantic Ocean

0   400 miles

0   600 km

Caribbean Sea

KEY TOPICS

❖ The rise of new political parties: Jacksonian Democrats and Whigs
❖ The disfranchisement of free blacks and women
❖ Birth of Whig party
❖ The Second Great Awakening
❖ The Bank War
❖ The growing conflict over slavery

"*P*olitics at the present time are the all-engrossing topic of discourse" observed a New Englander in the fall of 1828. "In the ballroom, or at the dinner table, in the Stagecoach & in the tavern; even the social chitchat of the tea table must yield to the everlasting subject." The republic had seen spirited presidential elections before, notably the Jefferson-Adams contest of 1800, but something was clearly new in 1828. Whether measured by the vulgar personal attacks launched by a partisan press, the amount of whiskey and beef consumed at political barbecues, or the huge increase in voter turnout for president, this election marked the entrance of ordinary Americans onto the political stage.

Jefferson's world, one in which refined gentlemen were entrusted with office as their just due, had been left behind by the 1820s. As Jefferson lamented shortly before his death in 1826, he and the other founders of the republic were "left alone midst a new gener[ation] whom we know not, and who know not us." This "new generation" impatiently pushed for greater political and social equality. Ongoing democratization in American politics had expanded the number and potential power of the voters, and professional politicians realized that party success now depended on reaching and organizing this enlarged electorate. The "Jacksonian Democrats," named for their leader, Andrew Jackson, were the first party to learn this fundamental lesson. Trumpeting Andrew Jackson as the friend of the common

man and the foe of aristocratic privilege, they won a landslide victory in 1828 and held national power through the 1830s. The Jacksonians promised to protect farmers and workers from the monied elite, whom they portrayed as the enemies of equality and the corruptors of public morality.

By the mid-1830s, the Whig party had formed in opposition to the Jacksonians. The Whigs offered an ordered vision of American progress and liberty, anchored in the use of governmental power to expand economic opportunities and promote morality. By embracing electoral techniques of popular appeal first used by the Democrats, the Whigs captured the presidency in 1840. Their triumph heralded a new party system, one based on massive voter turnouts and two-party competition in every state.

The luckless Whigs failed to capitalize on their victory in 1840. Their newly elected president, William Henry Harrison, died shortly after entering office, and Vice President John Tyler, his successor, blocked the Whigs' economic program. Spurned by the Whigs as a traitor, Tyler then reopened the explosive question of slavery and territorial expansion by pushing the annexation of the independent republic of Texas, where slavery was legal.

The Democrats regained power in 1844 by skillfully exploiting the Texas issue, but they set an ominous precedent. Debates over the expansion of slavery became embedded in the political system, and the greatest strength of the mass-based parties—their ability to tap and unleash popular emotions—now became their greatest weakness. The slavery issue began to take on a life of its own beyond the control of party leaders. The seeds of the Civil War were being sown.

The Egalitarian Impulse

Political democracy, defined as the majority rule of white males, was far from complete in early-nineteenth-century America. Acting on the belief that only property owners with a stake in society should have a voice in governing it, the landed and commercial elites of the Revolutionary era erected legal barriers against the full expression of majority sentiments. These barriers—property requirements

for voting and officeholding, the prevalence of appointed over elected offices, and the overrepresentation of older and wealthier regions in state legislatures—came under increasing attack after 1800 and were all but eliminated by the 1820s.

As politics opened to mass participation, a democratization movement in American religion also gathered momentum. Popular styles of religious leadership and worship erupted in a broad reaction against the formalism and elitism of the dominant

This early nineteenth-century painting of a polling place in Philadelphia illustrates the growing involvement of common Americans in politics. As suffrage broadened and more Americans came out to vote, elections became more heated and emotional.

Protestant churches. The same egalitarian impulse drove these twin democratic revolutions, and both movements represented an empowerment of the common man. Popular movements now spoke the language of the average man and appealed to his quest for republican equality. (Women would have to wait longer.) John Quincy Adams and his followers never understood the more democratic America of the 1820s. As a result, they were easily routed in the election of 1828 by those who did—the **Jacksonian Democrats**.

The Extension of White Male Democracy

In 1816, Congress voted itself a hefty pay raise. Ever since the First Congress in 1789, the salary of representatives and senators had been $6 per day plus travel expenses. Inflation had so cheapened this pay scale that many government clerks now earned more than members of Congress. Thus a pay raise to an annual salary of $1,500 seemed prudent and justified. The public thought otherwise. The citizens of Saratoga, New York, typified the popular response when they resolved that Congress was guilty of "wanton extravagance" and "a daring and profligate trespass against . . . the *morals* of the *Republic.*" The outcry stunned the politicians, who found themselves deluged with protests decrying their greed.

So sharp was the reaction against the Salary Act of 1816 that 70 percent of the members of Congress were turned out of office at the next election. Congress quickly repealed the salary increase, but not before John C. Calhoun spoke for many in Congress when he plaintively asked, "Are we bound in all cases

to do what is popular?" The answer was apparently yes. As Richard M. Johnson of Kentucky noted, "The presumption is, that the people are always right."

The people had spoken in 1816, and the politicians got the message. The uproar over the Salary Act marked a turning point in the transition from the deferential politics of the Federalist-Republican period to the egalitarianism of the Jacksonian era. The public would no longer passively accept decisions handed down by local elites or established national figures. As a result of demands for a greater popular voice in government, the pace of democratization quickened noticeably after the War of 1812.

Individual states, not the federal government, defined who could vote. Six states—Indiana, Mississippi, Illinois, Alabama, Missouri, and Maine—entered the Union between 1816 and 1821, and none of them required white male voters to own property. Meanwhile, proponents for suffrage liberalization won major victories in the older eastern states. Constitutional conventions in Connecticut in 1818 and Massachusetts and New York in 1821 eliminated property requirements for voting. By the end of the 1820s, universal white male suffrage was the norm everywhere except Rhode Island, Virginia, and Louisiana.

Broadening the suffrage was part of a general democratization of political structures and procedures in the state governments. Representation in most state legislatures was made more equal by giving more seats to newer, rapidly growing regions in the backcountry. States removed or reduced property qualifications for officeholding. The selection of local officials and, in many cases, judges was taken out of

CHRONOLOGY

1826 Disappearance of William Morgan.	**1834** Whig party begins to organize.
1827 Emergence of the Anti-Masons, the first third party.	**1836** Texas War of Independence and establishment of the Republic of Texas.
1828 Andrew Jackson elected president.	Congress passes first gag rule on abolitionist petitions.
John Calhoun writes *The South Carolina Exposition and Protest.*	Van Buren elected president.
1830 Congress passes the Indian Removal Act.	**1837** Panic of 1837 sets off a depression.
1831 William Lloyd Garrison starts publication of *The Liberator.*	**1840** Independent Treasury Act passes.
Nat Turner leads a slave uprising in Virginia.	William Henry Harrison elected as first Whig president.
1832 Jackson vetoes bill for rechartering the Second Bank of the United States; Bank War begins.	**1841** John Tyler succeeds to presidency on death of Harrison.
South Carolina nullifies the Tariffs of 1828 and 1832.	**1842** United States and Britain sign the Webster-Ashburton Treaty.
Jackson reelected.	**1844** Polk elected president.
1833 Congress passes the Force Act and the Compromise Tariff.	Gag rule repealed.
American Anti-Slavery Society established.	**1845** Texas admitted to the Union.

the hands of governors and executive councils and given to the voters in popular elections. With the end of oral or "stand-up" voting, the act of casting a ballot became more private and freer from the intimidation of influential neighbors. Written ballots were the norm by the 1820s. Most significant for national politics, voters acquired the power to choose presidential electors. In 1800, only two states had provided for a statewide popular vote in presidential elections. By 1824, most did so, and by 1832 only South Carolina still clung to the practice of having the state legislature choose the electors (see Map 10-1).

Several currents swelled the movement for democratic reform. Limiting voting rights to those who owned landed property seemed increasingly elitist when economic changes were producing new classes—workers, clerks, and small tradesmen—whose livelihoods were not tied directly to the land. At the same time, the middling and lower ranks of society demanded the ballot and access to offices to protect themselves from the commercial and manufacturing interests, who benefited most from economic change. Propertyless laborers in Richmond argued in an 1829 petition that "virtue [and] intelligence are not among the products of the soil. Attachment to property, often a sordid sentiment,

is not to be confounded with the sacred flame of patriotism."

Of greatest importance, however, was the incessant demand that all white men be treated equally. Seth Luther, an advocate for workers' rights, insisted that "we wish nothing, but those equal rights, which were designed for us all." The logical extension of the ideology of the American Revolution, with its leveling attacks against kings and aristocrats, this demand for equality made republicanism by the 1820s synonymous with simple majority rule. If any white male was the equal of any other, regardless of wealth or property holdings, then only the will of the majority could be the measure of a republican government.

As political opportunities expanded for white males, they shrank for women and free blacks. In the state constitutions of the Revolutionary era, free blacks who met the minimum property requirements usually had the same voting rights as white males. New Jersey's constitution of 1776 was exceptional in also granting the suffrage to single women and widows who owned property. By the early 1800s, race and gender began to replace wealth and status as the basis for defining the limits of political participation. Thus when New Jersey's new constitution

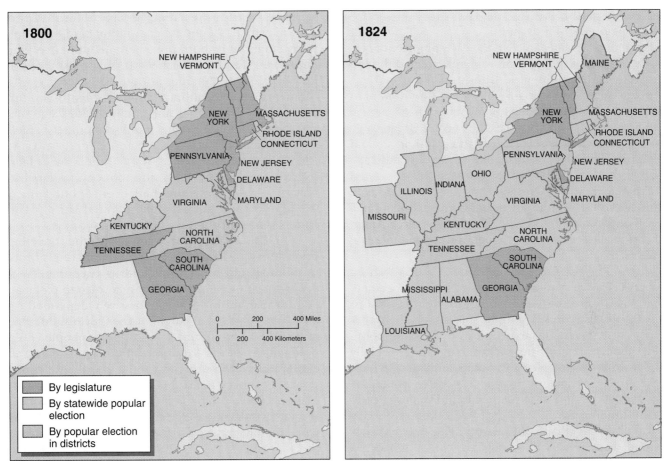

Map 10-1   Methods of Electing Presidential Electors, 1800 and 1824
The Constitution permits each state legislature to choose the method of electing presidential electors for its state. In 1800 the legislatures in most states appointed the electors. By 1824 most states had adopted more democratic systems in which electors pledged to specific presidential candidates were selected by popular vote in statewide elections.
Source: *U.S. Bureau of the Census,* Historical Statistics of the United States, Colonial Times to 1957 *(1960), p. 681.*

in 1807 broadened suffrage by requiring only a simple taxpaying qualification to vote, it specifically denied the ballot to women and free blacks. In state after state, the same constitutional conventions that embraced universal suffrage for white males deprived blacks of the vote or burdened them with special property qualifications. Moreover, none of the ten states that entered the Union from 1821 to 1861 allowed black suffrage. African-Americans protested in vain. "Foreigners and aliens to the government and laws," complained New York blacks in 1837, "strangers to our institutions, are permitted to flock to this land and in a few years are endowed with all the privileges of citizens; but we *native* born Americans . . . are most of us shut out." By the 1850s, blacks could vote only in certain New England states.

The linkage of democracy with white manhood was not accidental. Advocates of greater democratization explicitly argued that only white males had the rational intelligence and love of liberty necessary to be entrusted with political rights. Women were too weak and emotional, blacks too lazy and lascivious. (For the political role that women and blacks did create for themselves, see Chapter 14.) In denouncing distinctions drawn on property as artificial and demeaning, the white egalitarians simultaneously erected new distinctions based on race and sex that were supposedly natural and hence immutable. Thus personal liberties were now to be guarded not by propertied gentlemen but by all white men, whose equality ultimately rested on assumptions of their shared political superiority over women and non-whites.

The Popular Religious Revolt

In religion as well as politics, ordinary Americans demanded a greater voice in the early nineteenth century. Insurgent religious movements rejected the formalism and traditional Calvinism of the Congregational and Presbyterian churches, the dominant Protestant denominations in Washington's America. In a blaze of fervor known as the **Second Great Awakening**, evangelical sects led by the Methodists and Baptists radically transformed the religious landscape between 1800 and 1840. A more popularly rooted Christianity moved outward and downward as it spread across frontier areas and converted marginalized and common folk. By 1850, one in three Americans was a regular churchgoer, a dramatic increase since 1800.

The Baptists and Methodists, both of whom spun off numerous splinter groups, grew spectacularly and were the largest religious denominations by the 1820s. The key to their success was their ability to give a religious expression to the same popular impulse behind democratic reform. Especially in the backcountry of the South and West, where the first revivals occurred, itinerant preachers reshaped religion to fit the needs and values of ordinary Americans.

Evangelical Christianity emphasized personal, heartfelt experience that would produce a spiritual rebirth. Preaching became a form of theater in which scenes of damnation and salvation were acted out by both preacher and audience. The emotional force unleashed at the mass revivals known as camp meetings astounded observers, who often resorted to military comparisons to capture the sense of mass agony and ecstasy. "The scene that then presented itself to my mind was indescribable," recalled James Finley of the camp meeting at Cane Ridge, Kentucky, in 1801. "At one time I saw at least five hundred swept down in a moment, as if a battery of a thousand guns had been opened upon them, and then immediately followed shrieks and shouts that rent the very heavens."

The evangelical religion of the traveling preachers was democratic in its populist rejection of traditional religious canons and its encouragement of organizational forms that gave a voice to plebeian culture. Salvation no longer passively depended on an implacable God as taught by the Calvinist doctrine of individual predestination. Ordinary people could now actively choose salvation, and this possibility was exhilarating. "Why, then, I can be saved!" exclaimed Jesse Lee upon hearing a Methodist preacher in Massachusetts. "I have been taught that only a part of the race could be saved, but if this man's singing be true, all may be saved." Evangelical churches bound the faithful into tightly knit communities that

The Second Great Awakening originated on the frontier. Preachers were adept at arousing emotional fervor, and women in particular responded to the evangelical message of spiritual equality open to all who would accept Christ into their lives.

expressed and enforced local values and standards of conduct. Their hymns borrowed melodies from popular music and were accompanied by fiddles and other folk instruments.

Evangelicalism was a religion of the common people, and it appealed especially to women and African-Americans. The revivals converted about twice as many women as men. Excluded from most areas of public life, women found in the evangelical message of Christian love and equality a spiritual ethic that enhanced their own sense of well-being. Church membership offered them, as the wife of a Connecticut minister explained, a welcome release from "being treated like beasts of burden [and] drudges of domineering masters." In the first flush of evangelical excitement, female itinerant preachers spread the gospel up and down the East Coast. By thus defying social convention, these women offered a model of independent action. Other women organized their own institutions within denominations still formally controlled by men. Women activists founded and largely directed hundreds of church-affiliated charitable societies and missionary associations.

Evangelicalism also empowered black Americans. African-American Christianity experienced its first sustained growth in the generation after the Revolutionary War. As a result of their uncompromising commitment to convert the slaves, the Baptists and Methodists led the way. They welcomed slaves at their revivals, encouraged preaching by blacks, and, above all else, advocated secular and spiritual equality. Many of the early Baptist and Methodist preachers directly challenged slavery. In converting to Methodism, one slave stated that "from the sermon I heard, I felt that God had made all men free and equal, and that I ought not be a slave." Perceiving in it the promise of liberty and deliverance, the slaves received the evangelical gospel in loud, joyous, and highly emotional revivals. They made it part of their own culture, fusing Christianity with folk beliefs from their various African heritages.

For all its liberating appeal to women and blacks, evangelicalism was eventually bound by limits of race and gender in much the same way as the democratic reform movement. Denied positions of authority in white-dominated churches and resentful of white opposition to integrated worship, free blacks in the North founded their own independent churches. As increasing numbers of planters embraced evangelicalism after the 1820s, southern evangelical attacks on slavery first grew muted and then were replaced by a full-blown religious defense of slavery. Just as southern Protestant ministers rested their proslavery case on the biblical sanctioning of human bondage, they also used the Old Testament patriarchs to shore up the position of fathers as the unquestioned authority figures in their households, the masters of slaves, women, and children. Many popular religious sects in the North also used a particular reading of the Bible to exalt the independence of white males at the expense of the dependence of everyone else.

In religion as well as politics, white men still held the power in Jacksonian America. Still, the Second Great Awakening removed a major intellectual barrier to political democracy. Traditional Protestant theology—whether Calvinist, Anglican, or Lutheran—viewed the mass of humanity as sinners predestined to damnation and hence was loath to accept the idea that those same sinners, by majority vote, should make crucial political decisions. In rejecting this theology, ordinary Americans made a fundamental breakthrough in intellectual thought. "Salvation open to all" powerfully reinforced the legitimacy of "one man, one vote."

The Rise of the Jacksonians

The Jacksonian Democrats were the first party to mold and organize the democratizing impulse in popular culture. At the core of the Jacksonian appeal was the same rejection of established authority that was the hallmark of the secular and religious populists. Much like the revivalists and the democratic reformers, the Jacksonians also fashioned techniques of communication that tapped into the hopes and fears of ordinary Americans. In so doing, they built the first mass-based party in American history.

In Andrew Jackson the new **Democratic party** that formed between 1824 and 1828 had the perfect candidate for the increasingly democratic temperament of the 1820s. Born of Scots-Irish ancestry on the Carolina frontier in 1767, Jackson was a self-made product of the southern backcountry. Lacking any formal education, family connections, or inherited wealth to ease his way, he relied on his own wits and raw courage to carve out a career as a frontier lawyer and planter in Tennessee. He won fame as the military savior of the republic with his victory at the Battle of New Orleans. Conqueror of the British, the Spanish, and the Indians, all of whom had blocked frontier expansion, he achieved incredible popularity in his native South. His strengths and prejudices were those most valued by the restless, mobile Americans to whom he became a folk hero.

This 1845 painting captures the heroic, forceful side of Andrew Jackson that made him so appealing to many voters.

As a presidential candidate, Jackson's image was that of the antielitist champion of the people. "Take for your President a man from your own body, untainted by the corruption of a court and uninitiated in Cabinet secrets," urged a New Jersey Jackson convention in 1824. Jackson lost the election of 1824, but his defeat turned out to be a blessing in disguise. The wheeling and dealing in Congress that gave the presidency to John Quincy Adams enveloped that administration in a cloud of suspicion from the start. It also enhanced Jackson's appeal as the honest tribune of the people whose rightful claim to the presidency had been spurned by intriguing politicians in Washington. His supporters now claimed that the people, as well as Jackson, had been swindled by the "corrupt bargain" between Adams and Clay.

Moreover, the ill-fated Adams presidency virtually destroyed itself. Though the same age as Jackson, Adams seemed frozen in an eighteenth-century past in which gentlemanly statesmen were aloof from the people and disdainfully refused to turn to them for support. Uncomfortable with the give-and-take of politics or the very idea of building a coalition to support himself, Adams was out of touch with the political realities of the 1820s.

Just how out of touch was revealed when Adams delivered his first annual message to Congress in 1825. He presented a bold vision of an activist federal government promoting economic growth, social advancement, and scientific progress. Such a vision might have received a fair hearing back in 1815, when postwar nationalism was in full stride. In 1825, it amounted to political suicide. Postwar nationalism had dissolved into sectional bickering and burning resentments against banks, tariffs, and the political establishment, blamed for the hard times after the Panic of 1819. The Jacksonians charged that an administration born in corruption now wanted to waste the people's money by promoting more corruption and greed. They also pounced on Adams's political gaffe of urging Americans not to "proclaim to the world that we are palsied by the will of our constituents." Besides being depicted as the tool of the northeastern monied interests, Adams was attacked as an arrogant aristocrat contemptuous of the common man.

Little of Adams's program passed Congress, and his nationalist vision drove his opponents into the Jackson camp. Southern planters jumped onto the Jackson bandwagon out of fear that Adams might use federal power against slavery; more Westerners joined because Adams revived their suspicions of the East. The most important addition came from New York, where Martin Van Buren had built the **Albany Regency**, a tightly disciplined state political machine.

Van Buren was a new breed of politician, a professional who made a business out of politics. The son of a tavern keeper, he quickly grasped as a young lawyer how politics could open up career opportunities. The discipline and regularity of strict party organization gave him and others from the middling ranks a winning edge in competition against their social betters. In battling against the system of family-centered wealth and prestige on which politics had previously been based, Van Buren redefined parties as something good in and of themselves. Indeed, he and his followers argued that parties were indispensable instruments for the successful expression of the popular will against the dominance of elites.

As shown in this scene from the rural Midwest, election day was an occasion for the male community to gather together in a festive mood to cast ballots, exchange views, and debate with candidates seeking their vote.

State leaders such as Van Buren organized the first national campaign that relied extensively on new techniques of mass mobilization. In rallying support for Jackson against Adams in 1828, they put together chains of party-subsidized newspapers and coordinated a frantic schedule of meetings and rallies. Grass-roots Jackson committees reached out to the voters by knocking on their doors, pressing party literature into their hands, dispensing mass-produced medals and buttons with a likeness of Jackson, and lavishly entertaining all who would give them a hearing. Politics became a folk spectacle as torchlight parades awakened sleepy towns and political barbecues doled out whiskey and food to farmers from the surrounding countryside.

The election of 1828 centered on personalities, not issues. This in itself was a victory for Jackson's campaign managers, who proved far more skillful in the new presidential game of image making then their Adams counterparts, now known as the National Republicans. Although both sides tried to depict the other's candidate as morally unfit to rule, the Jackson men were more in tune with a public

sentiment that identified Adams's call for a strong government with special privileges for the favored few. Thus for many voters, Adams personified a discredited elite and Jackson the voice of the people.

Jackson carried every state south and west of Pennsylvania in 1828 and polled 56 percent of the popular vote (see Map 10-2). Voter turnout shot up to 55 percent from the apathetic 25 percent of 1824. Adams ran well only in New England and in commercialized areas producing goods for outside markets. Aside from the South, where he was virtually untouchable, Jackson's appeal was strongest among ordinary Americans who valued their local independence and felt threatened by outside centers of power beyond their control. He rolled up heavy majorities from Scots-Irish farmers in the Baptist-Methodist evangelical belt of the backcountry and from unskilled workers with an Irish Catholic background. To these voters, Jackson was a double hero, for he had defeated their hated British enemy and promised to do the same to the Yankee capitalists of the Northeast and all the elitist politicians. Democracy, they were convinced, had at last come to presidential politics.

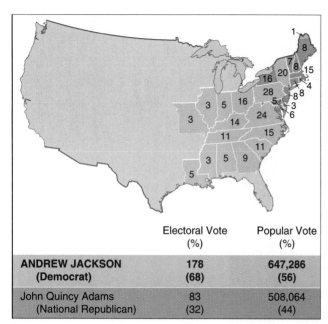

	Electoral Vote (%)	Popular Vote (%)
ANDREW JACKSON (Democrat)	**178** **(68)**	**647,286** **(56)**
John Quincy Adams (National Republican)	83 (32)	508,064 (44)

Map 10-2   The Election of 1828
Andrew Jackson won a decisive victory in 1828 by sweeping the South and West and making major inroads in the Northeast.

Jackson's Presidency

Once in office, Jackson proved to be the most forceful and energetic president since Jefferson. Like a military chieftain tolerating no interference from his subordinates, Jackson dominated his presidency with the sheer force of his personality. At one time or another, his administration angered southern planters, frightened eastern bankers and commercial interests, and outraged New England reformers. Nonetheless, Jackson remained popular because he portrayed himself as the embodiment of the people's will.

The Jacksonians had no particular program in 1828, and Jackson shrewdly had avoided taking a stand on divisive issues. Apart from removing Indians to areas west of the Mississippi River, Jackson's first term was notable primarily for its political infighting. Two political struggles that came to a head in 1832–1833—the **Bank War** and the **nullification crisis**—stamped the Jacksonians with a lasting party identity. By destroying the Second Bank of the United States and rejecting the attempt of South Carolina to nullify (or annul) a national tariff, Jackson firmly established the Democrats as the enemy of special privilege, the friend of the common man, and the defender of the Union. Consequently, even when Jackson stepped down in 1836, the Democrats were so identified with the interests of the people

that they were able to elect Van Buren, who had none of Jackson's personal magnetism or broad appeal.

The Jacksonian Appeal

Jackson's inauguration struck many conservatives as ushering in a vulgar new order in national affairs. A vast crowd poured into Washington to applaud their hero. They cheered loudly when Jackson took his oath of office and then rushed to the White House for a postinauguration reception. Any semblance of order broke down as they pressed in on waiters trying to serve them refreshments. Bowls of liquor-laced punch went flying, and glass and china crashed to the floor as a seeming mob surged through the White House. "But it was the People's day," reported one conservative onlooker, "and the People's President and the People would rule. God grant that one day or other, the People do not put down all rule and rulers."

Ordinary Americans identified with Jackson as with no earlier president, and he convinced them that he was using his office as the instrument of their will. Although led by wealthy planters and entrepreneurs who were hardly average Americans, the Jacksonians skillfully depicted themselves as the champions of the common man against the aristocratic interests who had enriched themselves through special privileges granted by the government. Thus Jackson proclaimed his task as one of restoring the federal government to the ideal of Jeffersonian republicanism, in which farmers and artisans could pursue their individual liberty free of any government intervention that favored the rich and powerful.

Jackson began his assault on special privilege by proclaiming a reform of the appointment process for federal officeholders. Accusing his predecessors, especially Adams, of having created a social elite of self-serving bureaucrats, he vowed to make government service more responsive to the popular will. He insisted that federal jobs required no special expertise or training and proposed to rotate honest, hard-working citizens in and out of the civil service.

Jackson's reform of the federal bureaucracy had more style than substance. He removed only about one-fifth of the officeholders he inherited, and most of his appointees came from the same relatively high status groups as the Adams people. But by providing a democratic rationale for government service, he opened the way for future presidents to move more aggressively against incumbents. Thus emerged the **spoils system**, in which the victorious party gave government jobs to its supporters and removed the appointees of the defeated party. This was a powerful technique for building party strength because it tied party loyalty to the reward of a federal appointment.

When Jackson railed against economic privilege, he most often had in mind Henry Clay's American System. Clay's program called for a protective tariff, a national bank, and federal subsidies for internal improvements; his goal was to bind Americans together in an integrated national market. To the Democrats, Clay's system represented government favoritism at its worst, a set of costly benefits at the public's expense for special-interest groups who corrupted politicians in their quest for economic power. In 1830, Jackson found the perfect opportunity to strike a blow for the Democratic conception of the limited federal role in economic development. He vetoed the Maysville Road Bill, which would have provided federal money for a road to be built entirely within Kentucky. He declared the bill unconstitutional on the grounds that it benefited only the citizens of Kentucky and not the American people as a whole. Moreover, since the Maysville project was within Clay's congressional district, Jackson had the added delight of embarrassing his most prominent political enemy.

On the issue of internal improvements, as well as bureaucratic reform, the Democrats placed party needs ahead of ideology. Jackson's Maysville veto did not rule out congressional appropriations for projects deemed beneficial to the general public. This pragmatic loophole gave Democrats all the room they needed to pass more internal improvement projects during Jackson's presidency than during all of the previous administrations together. Having built a mass party, the Democrats soon discovered that they had to funnel federal funds to their constituents back home.

Any support Jackson might have lost among market-minded entrepreneurs and farmers in the West by his Maysville veto was more than made up by the popularity of his Indian removal policy. Jackson's strongest base of support was in the West and South, and by driving Native Americans from these regions, he more than lived up to his billing as the friend of the common (white) man.

The inauguration of Andrew Jackson in 1829 brought out an unprecedented mob of well-wishers anxious for a glimpse of the new president.

Indian Removal

Some 125,000 Indians lived east of the Mississippi when Jackson became president. The largest concentration was in the South, where five Indian confederations—the Cherokees, Creeks, Choctaws, Chickasaws, and Seminoles—controlled millions of acres of land in what soon would become the great cotton frontiers of southwestern Georgia and central Alabama and Mississippi. That, of course, was the problem: Native Americans held land that whites coveted for their own economic gain.

Pressure from the states to remove the Indians had been building since the end of the War of 1812. It was most intense in Georgia. In early 1825, Georgia authorities finalized a fraudulent treaty that ceded most of the Creek Indians' land to the state. When Adams tried to obtain fairer terms for the Creeks in a new treaty, he was brazenly denounced in Georgia, which based its case for grabbing Indian territory on the inviolability of states' rights. Georgia dared Adams to do something about it; not willing to risk an armed confrontation between federal and state authorities, Adams backed down.

In 1828, Georgia moved against the Cherokees, the best organized and most advanced (by white standards) of the Indian confederations. By now a prosperous society of small farmers with their own written alphabet and schools for their children, the Cherokees wanted to avoid the fate of their Creek neighbors. In 1827, they adopted a constitution declaring themselves an independent nation

Sequoyah, a Cherokee scholar, developed an alphabet for the Cherokee language that enabled his people to publish a tribal newspaper in both Cherokee and English.

with complete sovereignty over their land. The Georgia legislature reacted by placing the Cherokees directly under state law, annulling Cherokee laws and even their right to make laws, and legally defining the Cherokees as tenants on land belonging to the state of Georgia. By also prohibiting Indian testimony in cases against whites, the legislature stripped the Cherokees of any legal rights. They were now easy prey for whites, who scrambled onto Cherokee land after gold was discovered in northern Georgia in 1829. Alabama and Mississippi followed Georgia's lead in denying Indians legal rights.

Thus the stage was set for what Jackson always considered the most important measure of his early administration, the **Indian Removal Act**. Jackson had no qualms about allowing state officials to override federal protection of Native Americans. He had long considered the federal policy of negotiating with the Indians as sovereign entities a farce. But it was awkward politically for the president to declare that he had no intention of enforcing treaty obligations of the U.S. government. The way out of this dilemma was to remove Native Americans from the center of the dispute. In his first annual message, Jackson sided with state authorities in the South and advised the Indians "to emigrate beyond the Mississippi or submit to the laws of those States." This

advice enabled Jackson to pose as the friend of the Indians, the wise father who would lead them out of harm's way and save them from rapacious whites.

Congress acted on Jackson's recommendation in the Indian Removal Act of 1830. The act appropriated $500,000 for the negotiation of new treaties under which the southern Indians would surrender their territory and be removed to land in the trans-Mississippi area (primarily present-day Oklahoma). Although force was not authorized and Jackson stressed that removal should be voluntary, no federal protection was provided for Indians harassed into leaving by land-hungry whites. Ultimately, Jackson did deploy the U.S. Army, but only to round up and push out Indians who refused to comply with the new removal treaties.

And so most of the Indians left the eastern United States—the Choctaws in 1830, the Creeks and Chickasaws in 1832, and the Cherokees in 1838 (see Map 10-3). The government was ill-prepared to supervise the removal. The private groups who won the federal contracts for transporting and provisioning the Indians were those who had entered the lowest bids; they were a shady lot interested only in making a quick buck. Thousands of Indians, perhaps as many as one-fourth of those who started the trek, died on the way to Oklahoma, the victims of cold, hunger, disease, and the general callousness of whites they met along the way. "It is impossible to conceive the frightful sufferings that attend these forced migrations," noted a Frenchman who observed the Choctaw removal. It was indeed, as recalled in the collective memory of the Cherokees, a **Trail of Tears**.

Tribes that organized resistance to removal were attacked by white armies. Federal troops joined local militias in 1832 in suppressing the Sauk and Fox Indians of Illinois and Wisconsin in what was called **Black Hawk's War**. More of a frantic attempt by the Indians to reach safety on the west bank of the Mississippi than an actual war, this affair ended in the slaughter of five hundred Indian men, women, and children by the white troops and their Sioux allies. The Seminoles held out in the swamps of Florida for seven years between 1835 and 1842 in what became the longest Indian war in American history. Their resistance continued even after their leader, Osceola, was captured while negotiating under a flag of truce.

Jackson forged ahead with his removal policy despite the opposition of eastern reformers and Protestant missionaries. Aligned with conservatives concerned by Jackson's cavalier disregard of federal treaty obligations, they came within three votes of defeating the removal bill in the House of Representatives. Jackson ignored their protests (see "American Views: Memorial and Protest of the Cherokee

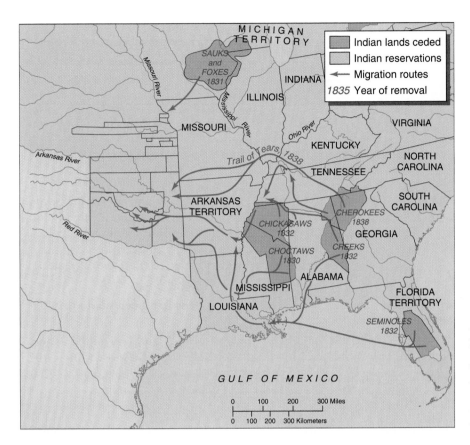

Map 10-3   Indian Removals
The fixed policy of the Jackson administration and pressure from the states forced Native Americans in the 1830s to migrate from their eastern homelands to a special Indian reserve west of the Mississippi River.

Nation, 1836") as well as the legal rulings of the Supreme Court. In *Cherokee Nation* v. *Georgia* (1831) and *Worcester* v. *Georgia* (1832), the Court ruled that Georgia had violated the U.S. Constitution in extending its jurisdiction over the Cherokees. Chief Justice Marshall defined Indian tribes as "dependent domestic nations" subject only to the authority of the federal government. Marshall may have won the legal argument, but he was powerless to enforce his decisions without Jackson's cooperation. Aware that Southerners and Westerners were on his side, Jackson ignored the Supreme Court rulings and pushed Indian removal to its tragic conclusion.

The Nullification Crisis

Jackson's stand on Indian removal did not cost him any essential political support. Indeed, it confirmed the impression of many of his followers that on issues of centralized power, Jackson could be trusted to take the states' rights position. The most sensitive issue involving the power of the national government concerned tariffs. When states' rights forces in South Carolina, known as the nullifiers, directly challenged Jackson in the early 1830s over tariff policy, they precipitated the most serious sectional crisis since the Missouri debates of 1819–1820.

For all his talk of states' rights when it came to Indian policy, Jackson now revealed that on the issue of majority rule in the Union, he was an ardent nationalist. He won the showdown with South Carolina and established the nationalist credentials of his Democratic party. In reaction to his strong stand, however, the solid front of Democratic power in the South began to crack.

After the first protective tariff in 1816, rates increased further in 1824 and then jumped to 50 percent in 1828 in what was denounced as the "Tariff of Abominations." Southerners were especially angry over the last tariff because it had been contrived by northern Democrats to win additional northern support for Jackson in his presidential campaign. The outcry was loudest in South Carolina, an old cotton state losing population to the West in the 1820s, as cotton prices remained low after the Panic of 1819. What fueled antitariff sentiment was not just the economic argument that high tariffs worsened the agricultural depression in the state by raising the cost of manufactured goods purchased by farmers and planters and lowering the foreign demand for agricultural exports. Protective tariffs were also denounced as an unconstitutional extension of national power over the states; many southern planters feared that it was only a prelude to forced emancipation.

South Carolina was the only state where African-Americans made up the majority of the population. Slaves were heavily concentrated in the

American Views

MEMORIAL AND PROTEST OF THE CHEROKEE NATION, 1836

Of the major tribes in the Southeast, the Cherokees fought longest and hardest against the Jacksonian policy of Indian removal. Led by their principal chief, John Ross, the son of a Scot and a mixed-blood Cherokee woman, they submitted the following protest to Congress against the fraudulent 1835 Treaty of New Echota forced on them by the state of Georgia. Although clearly opposed by an overwhelming majority of the Cherokees, this treaty provided the legal basis for the forced removal of the Cherokee people from Georgia to the Indian Territory.

❖ **On what legal grounds did the Cherokees base their protest? What pledges had been made to them by the United States government?**

❖ **What did the Cherokees mean when they said they had been "taught to think and feel as the American citizen"? If the Cherokees had become "civilized" by white standards, why did most whites still insist on their removal?**

❖ **Why would President Jackson have allowed white intruders to remain on land reserved by treaties for the Cherokees?**

❖ **Do you feel that the Cherokees were justified in believing that they had been betrayed by the American government?**

The undersigned representatives of the Cherokee nation, east of the river Mississippi, impelled by duty, would respectfully submit . . . the following statement of facts: It will be seen, from the numerous treaties between the Cherokee nation and the United States, that from the earliest existence of this government, the United States, in Congress assembled, received the Cherokees and their nation into favor and protection; and that the chiefs and warriors, for themselves and all parts of the Cherokee nation, acknowledged themselves and the said Cherokee nation to be under the protection of the United States of America, and of no other sovereign whatsoever: they also stipulated,

marshes and tidal flats south of Charleston, the lowcountry district of huge rice plantations. Here blacks outnumbered whites ten to one in the summer months, and rice planters dreaded the possibility of a massive slave uprising. After major slave rebellions had been narrowly averted in 1822 and 1829, planters believed that slave unrest was being fed by the growing agitation over slavery in the North and in England. In the summer of 1831, the **Nat Turner slave revolt** in Virginia seemed to confirm their worst fears. Fifty-five whites were slain before the uprising was crushed. The revolt and renewed talk of emancipation would be "nothing to what we shall see," warned the South Car-

olina planter James Hamilton Jr., "if we do not stand manfully at the Safety Valve of Nullification."

Led by the lowcountry planters, the antitariff forces in South Carolina controlled state politics by 1832. They called themselves the nullifiers, a name derived from the constitutional theory developed by Calhoun in an anonymous tract of 1828 titled *The South Carolina Exposition and Protest.* Pushing to its logical extreme the states' rights doctrine first outlined in the Kentucky and Virginia Resolutions of 1798, Calhoun argued that a state, acting through a popularly elected convention, had the sovereign power to declare an act of the national government

that the said Cherokee nation will not hold any treaty with any foreign power, individual State, or with individuals of any State: that for, and in consideration of, valuable concessions made by the Cherokee nation, the United States solemnly guaranteed to said nation all their lands not ceded, and pledged the faith of the government, that "all white people who have intruded, or may hereafter intrude, on the lands reserved for the Cherokees, shall be removed by the United States, and proceeded against, according to the provisions of the act, passed 30th March, 1802," entitled "An act to regulate trade and intercourse with the Indian tribes, and to preserve peace on the frontiers." It would be useless to recapitulate the numerous provisions for the security and protection of the rights of the Cherokees, to be found in the various treaties between their nation and the United States. The Cherokees were happy and prosperous under a scrupulous observance of treaty stipulations by the government of the United States, and from the fostering hand extended over them, they made rapid advances in civilization, morals, and in the arts and sciences. Little did they anticipate, that when taught to think and feel as the American citizen, and to have with him a common interest, they were to be *despoiled by their guardian,* to become strangers and wanderers in the land of their fathers, forced to return to the savage life, and to seek a new home in the wilds of the far west, and that without their consent. An instrument purporting to be a treaty with the Cherokee people, has recently been made public by the President of the United States, that will have such an operation, if carried into effect. This instrument, the delegation aver before the civilized world, and in the presence of Almighty God, is fraudulent, false upon its face, made by unauthorized individuals, without the sanction, and against the wishes, of the great body of the Cherokee people. Upwards of fifteen thousand of those people have protested against it, solemnly declaring they will never acquiesce....

Source: *U.S. Congress,* Executive Documents *(1836).*

null and inoperative. Once a state nullified a law, it was to remain unenforceable within that state's borders unless three-fourths of all the states approved a constitutional amendment delegating to the national government the power that was challenged. If such an amendment passed, the nullifying state had the right to leave the Union.

Calhoun, who had been elected vice president in 1828, openly embraced nullification only after he had broken with Jackson. When Calhoun's wife and friends snubbed Peggy Eaton, the wife of Jackson's secretary of war, on the grounds that she was a "loose woman" who had driven her first husband to suicide, Jackson was convinced that Calhoun was plotting to discredit his administration. He believed that the South Carolinian wanted "to coerce me to abandon Eaton, and thereby bring on me disgrace for having appointed him, and thereby weaken me in the affections of the nation, and open the way to his preferment or my ruin." Then, in what finalized the break, friends of Van Buren, who was secretary of state, leaked the information that Calhoun, while secretary of war under President James Monroe, had favored censuring Jackson for his 1818 raid into Spanish Florida. Deceived by Calhoun as to his role in the affair, Jackson felt betrayed and vowed political revenge.

An outcast in Jackson's administration by 1830, Calhoun also faced the danger of losing control of his political base in South Carolina. Unless he publicly identified himself with nullification, his leadership of the state would be threatened. With Calhoun's approval, a South Carolina convention in November 1832 nullified the tariffs of 1828 and 1832 (a compromise tariff that did not reduce rates low enough to satisfy the nullifiers). The convention decreed that customs duties were not to be collected in South Carolina after February 1, 1833.

Calhoun always insisted that nullification was not secession. He defended his doctrine as a constitutional means of protecting minority rights within a Union dominated by a tyrannical national majority. Jackson rejected such reasoning as the talk of a scheming disunionist. He considered nullification a dangerous and nonsensical perversion of the Constitution, and he vowed to crush any attempt to block the enforcement of federal laws. He told a congressman from South Carolina that "if a single drop of blood shall be shed there in opposition to the laws of the United States, I will hang the first man I can lay my hand on engaged in such treasonable conduct, upon the first tree I can reach."

In January 1833, Jackson asked for and received from Congress full authorization in the Force Act to put down nullification by military force. Simultaneously, he worked to defuse nullification by supporting a new tariff that would cut duties by half within two years. Because Jackson's opponents in Congress did not want him to get political credit for brokering a compromise, they pushed through their own tariff measure. The Compromise Tariff of 1833 lowered duties to 20 percent but extended the reductions over a ten-year period. Up against this combination of the carrot and the stick, the nullifiers backed down. In a final act of defiance, they nullified the Force Act.

Jackson reacted swiftly and decisively when challenged by the nullifiers. His stand established the principle of national supremacy grounded in the will of the majority. Despite his victory, however, states' rights doctrines remained popular both in the South and among many northern Democrats. South Carolina had been isolated in its stand on nullification, but many Southerners, and especially slaveholders, agreed that the powers of the national government had to be strictly limited. Their quarrel with the nullifiers was one of tactics, not objectives. Moreover, by dramatically affirming his right to use force against a state in defense of the Union, Jackson drove many planters out of the Democratic party. In the shock waves set off by the nullification crisis, a new anti-Jackson coalition began to form in the South.

The Bank War

What amounted to a war declared by Jackson against the Bank of the United States became the centerpiece of his presidency and a defining moment in the shaping of the Democratic party. The Bank War erupted in 1832 when Jackson was presented with draft legislation for the early rechartering of the national bank. His thunderous veto kept banking and currency issues in the forefront of national politics for the remainder of the decade.

Like most Westerners, Jackson distrusted banks. As a result of the scarcity of gold and silver coins and the absence of any paper currency issued and regulated by the national government, money consisted primarily of notes issued as loans by private and state banks. These bank notes fluctuated in value in accordance with the reputation and creditworthiness of the banks that issued them. In the credit-starved West, banks were particularly unreliable, for many of them were "wildcat" operations that made a quick profit by issuing notes without the specie (gold or silver reserves) to redeem them and then skipping town when they were on the verge of being found out. Even when issued by honest bankers, notes often could not be redeemed at face value because of market conditions. All of this struck many Americans, and especially farmers and workers, as inherently dishonest. They wanted to be paid in "real" money, gold or silver coin, and they viewed bankers as parasites who did nothing but fatten their own pockets by manipulating paper money.

The largest and most powerful bank was the Bank of the United States, and citizens who were wiped out or forced to retrench drastically by the Panic of 1819 never forgave the Bank for saving itself at the expense of its debtors. Still, under the astute leadership of a new president, Nicholas Biddle of Philadelphia, the Bank performed especially well in the 1820s. Prosperous times had returned, and the Bank underwrote the economic expansion with its healthy credit reserves and stable banknotes. By 1832, the Bank was as popular as it ever would be.

Beginning with his first annual message, Jackson had been making noise about not rechartering the Bank, at least in its present form. Searching for an issue to use against Jackson in the presidential campaign of 1832, Clay then forced Jackson's hand. Clay convinced Biddle to apply to Congress for a new charter, even though the current charter would not expire until 1836. Confident of congressional approval, Clay reasoned that he had Jackson trapped. If Jackson went along with the new charter, Clay could take credit for the measure. If he vetoed it, Clay could attack Jackson as the enemy of a sound banking system.

Clay's clever strategy backfired. Jackson turned on Clay and the Bank with a vengeance. As he told his heir apparent, "The bank, Mr. Van Buren, is trying to kill me, *but I will kill it!*" Jackson and his advisers realized that the Bank was vulnerable as a symbol of privileged monopoly, a monstrous institution that deprived common Americans of their right to compete equally for economic advantage. Moreover, many of these advisers were also state bankers and local developers who backed Jackson precisely because they wanted to be free of federal restraints on their business activities. On July 10, 1832, Jackson vetoed the rechartering bill for the Bank in a message that appealed both to state bankers and to foes of all banks. He took a ringing "stand against all new grants of monopolies and exclusive privileges, against any prostitution of our Government to the advancement of the few at the expense of the many."

The business community and eastern elites in general lashed out at Jackson's veto as the demagogic ravings of an economic fool. For Biddle, the veto message had "all the fury of a chained panther, biting the bars of his cage." In rejecting Jackson's claims that the Bank had fostered speculative and corrupt financial practices, the pro-Bank forces had

the better of the economic argument. But Jackson won the political battle, and he went to the people in the election of 1832 as their champion against the banking aristocracy. Although his support was no stronger than in 1828, he easily defeated Clay, the candidate of the short-lived **National Republican party** that had also backed Adams in 1828.

Having blocked the rechartering of the Bank when Congress failed to override his veto, Jackson then set out to destroy it. He claimed that the people had given him a mandate to do so by reelecting him in 1832. He finally found a secretary of the treasury (his first two choices refused) who agreed to sign the order removing federal deposits from the Bank in 1833. Drained of its lifeblood, the deposits, the Bank was reduced by 1836 to seeking a charter as a private corporation in the state of Pennsylvania. In the meantime, the government's monies were deposited in "pet banks," state banks controlled by loyal Democrats.

Jackson won the Bank War, but he left the impression that the Democrats had played fast and loose with the nation's credit system. The economy overheated in his second term. High commodity prices and abundant credit, both at home and abroad, propelled a buying frenzy of western lands. Prices soared, and inevitably the speculative bubble had to burst. When it did, the Democrats would be open to the charge of having squandered the people's money by shifting deposits to reckless state

"General Jackson caricature slaying the many-headed monster," 1836. Courtesy of Collection of The New-York Historical Society.

This Democratic cartoon portrays Jackson as the champion of the people attacking the Bank of the United States, a many-headed monster whose tentacles of corruption spread throughout the states.

bankers who were part of a corrupt new alliance between the government and private economic interests. Jackson was out of office when the **Panic of 1837** hit; Van Buren, his successor, paid the political price for Jackson's economic policies.

Van Buren and Hard Times

Like John Adams and James Madison, Martin Van Buren followed a forceful president who commanded a strong popular following. Fairly or not, he would come out, as they did, second best in any comparison with his predecessor. Where Jackson forged ahead regardless of consequences, Van Buren tended to hang back, carefully calculating all the political angles. This trait served him poorly as president.

Facing a sharp economic downturn, Van Buren appeared indecisive and unwilling to advance a bold program. When the rise of a radical abolitionist movement in the North revived sectional tensions over slavery, he awkwardly straddled the middle of the divisive issue. Van Buren's difficult position was made worse by his cautious political style. In the end, he undermined himself by failing to offer a compelling vision of just what he wanted his presidency to be.

The Panic of 1837

Van Buren was barely settled into the White House when the nation was rocked by a financial panic. For over a decade, the economy had benefited from a favorable business cycle. Easy credit and the availability of territories opened up by Jackson's Indian removal policy generated a stampede to buy land in the West. Government land sales ballooned from under 4 million acres in 1833 to 20 million acres by 1836. As in 1817 and 1818, Americans piled up debt on the assumption that the good times would never end. A banking crisis in 1837 painfully reintroduced economic reality.

Even as it expanded, the American economy had remained vulnerable to disruptions in the supply of foreign capital and the sale of agricultural exports that underpinned prosperity. The key foreign nation was Britain, a major source of credit and demand for exports. In late 1836, the Bank of England tightened its credit policies. Concerned with the large outflow of specie to the United States, it raised interest rates and reduced the credit lines of British merchants heavily involved in the American trade. Consequently, the British demand for cotton fell and with it the price of cotton (see Figure 10-1). Because cotton, as the leading export, was the main security for most loans issued by American banks and mercantile firms, its drop in value set off a chain reaction of contracting credit and falling prices. When panic-stricken investors rushed to the banks to redeem their notes in specie, the hard-pressed banks suspended specie payments.

The shock waves hit New Orleans in March 1837 and spread to the major New York banks by May. What began as a bank panic soon dragged down the entire economy. Bankruptcies multiplied, investment capital dried up, and business stagnated. State governments, which had borrowed lavishly in the heady optimism of the boom years to finance canals and other internal improvements, slashed their budgets and halted all construction projects. Nine states in the South and West defaulted (stopped making payments) on their bonds. Workers in the shoe, textile, mining, and construction industries suddenly found themselves without jobs. As unemployment mounted and workers mobilized mass protest meetings in eastern cities, conservatives feared the worst. "Workmen thrown out of employ by the hundred daily," nervously noted a wealthy merchant in New York City in May 1837. He half expected that "we shall have a revolution here."

After a brief recovery in 1838, another round of credit contraction drove the economy into a depression that did not bottom out until 1843. In the manufacturing and commercial centers of the Northeast, unemployment reached an unheard-of 20 percent. The persistence of depressed agricultural prices meant that farmers and planters who had incurred debts in the 1830s faced the constant threat of losing their land or their slaves. Many fled west to avoid their creditors.

The Independent Treasury

Although the Democrats bore no direct responsibility for the economic downturn, they could not avoid the charge of having brought on the depression. Their political opponents, now coalescing as the **Whig party**, pinned the blame on Jackson's destruction of the Bank of the United States, which they claimed had undermined business confidence. In their view, Jackson had then compounded his error by trying to force a hard-money policy on the state banks that had received federal deposits. The "pet banks" were required to replace small-denomination bank notes with coins or hard money. This measure, it was hoped, would protect the farmers and workers from being paid in depreciated bank notes.

Jackson had taken his boldest step against paper money when he issued the **Specie Circular** of

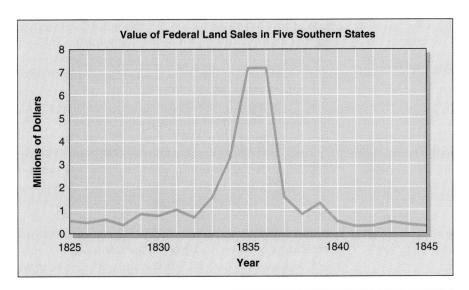

Value of Federal Land Sales in Five Southern States

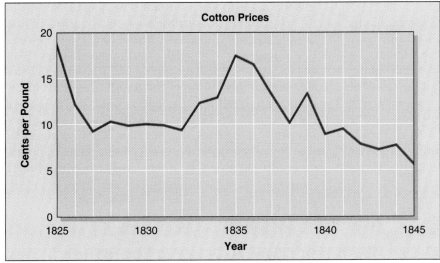

Cotton Prices

Figure 10-1   Cotton Prices and the Value of Federal Land Sales in Five Southern States, 1825–1845
Because the U.S. economy was heavily dependent on cotton exports as a source of credit, the collapse of cotton prices—and a corresponding plunge in the sale of federal land after a speculative run-up in the newer cotton regions of the South—triggered a financial panic in the late 1830s.

Source: *Douglas C. North*, The Economic Growth of the United States, 1790–1860 (1966), *tab. A-X, p. 257.*

1836, which stipulated that henceforth large blocks of public land could be bought only with specie. Aimed at breaking the speculative spiral in land purchases, the Specie Circular likely contributed to the Panic of 1837 by requiring the transfer of specie to the West for land transactions just when eastern banks were strapped for specie reserves to meet demands on their own bank notes. Bankers and speculators denounced Jackson for unwarranted governmental interference with the natural workings of the economy and blundering into a monetary disaster.

Conservative charges of Democratic irresponsibility were overblown, but the Democrats were caught on the horns of a dilemma. By dramatically politicizing the banking issue and removing federal monies from the national bank, the Democrats had in effect assumed the burden of protecting the people from the paper aristocrats in the banking and business community. Once they shifted treasury receipts to selected state banks, they had to try to regulate these banks. Otherwise they would be accused of creating a series of little "monsters" and feeding the paper speculation they so decried. But any regulatory policy contradicted the Democratic commitment to limiting governmental power. A restrictive policy, especially one aimed at replacing bank notes with specie, was bound to upset business interests and drive them out of the Democratic party. Worse yet, even the "pet banks" joined in the general suspension of specie payments when the Panic of 1837 hit. Thus the banks favored by the Democrats proved themselves unworthy of the people's trust.

The only way out of the dilemma was to make a clean break between the government and banking. Van Buren reestablished the Democrats' tarnished image as the party of limited government when he came out for the **Independent Treasury System**. Under this plan, the government would dispense with banks entirely. The Treasury would conduct its business only in gold and silver coin and would store its specie in regional vaults or subtreasuries. First proposed in 1837, the Independent Treasury System finally passed Congress in 1840 on the heels of a second wave of bank failures.

The Independent Treasury System made more political than economic sense. It restored the ideological purity of the Democrats as the friends of honest money, but it prolonged the depression. Specie locked up in government vaults was unavailable for loans in the private banking system that could expand the credit needed to revive the economy. The end result was to reduce the money supply and put even more downward pressure on prices.

Uproar over Slavery

In 1831, the year that Nat Turner led a slave uprising in Virginia, William Lloyd Garrison of Boston inaugurated a radical new phase in northern attacks on slavery with the publication of his abolitionist paper *The Liberator.* The abolitionists embraced the doctrine of *immediatism,* an immediate moral commitment to begin the work of emancipation. Inspired by the wave of religious revivals sweeping the North in the late 1820s, they seized on slavery as the greatest sin of all. With the righteous wrath of evangelical minis-

ters, they called upon all Americans to recognize their Christian duty of ending a system of human bondage that deprived the enslaved of their God-given right to be free moral beings. (For more on the abolitionists, see Chapter 14.)

Although some planters were outraged by the abolitionists from the start, most southern whites ignored them until 1835, the year that the abolitionists launched a propaganda offensive. Taking advantage of technological improvements in the printing industry, they produced over a million pieces of antislavery literature, much of which was sent to the South through the U.S. mails. Alarmed whites vilified the abolitionists as fanatics intent on enticing the slaves to revolt. Abolitionist tracts were burned, and, with the open approval of Jackson, southern postmasters violated federal law by censoring the mails to keep out antislavery materials.

Unable to receive an open hearing in the South, the abolitionists now focused on Congress. Beginning in 1836 and continuing through Van Buren's presidency, hundreds of thousands of antislavery petitions, some of them with thousands of signatures, flooded into Congress. Most of them called for the abolition of slavery in the District of Columbia. Southern congressmen responded by demanding that free speech be repressed in the name of southern white security. The enemy, they were convinced,

The abolitionists relied heavily on printed literature in spreading their antislavery message, and their printing presses were a prime target for destruction by the anti-abolitionist mobs that arose in the North.

was fanaticism, and nearly all agreed with Francis Pickens of South Carolina that they must "meet it and strangle it in its infancy." The strangling took the form of the **gag rule**, a procedural device whereby antislavery petitions were automatically tabled with no discussion.

The gag rule first passed in 1836 and was renewed in a series of raucous debates through 1844. Only the votes of some three-fourths of the northern Democrats enabled the southern minority to have its way. With Van Buren's reluctant support, the gag rule became a Democratic party measure, and it identified the Democrats as a prosouthern party in the minds of many Northerners. Ironically, while Van Buren was attacked in the North as a lackey of the slave interests, he was damned in the South, if only because he was a nonslaveholder from the North, as being unsafe on the slavery issue. In short, tensions over slavery and the economy seemingly doomed Van Buren to be cast as a vacillating president fully trusted by neither section.

	SUMMARY	
THE SECOND PARTY SYSTEM		
	Democrats	**Whigs**
Ideology	Favor limited role of federal government in economic affairs and in matters of individual conscience; support territorial expansion	Favor government support for economic development and controls over individual morality; opposed or indifferent to expansion
Voter support	Mainly subsistence farmers, unskilled workers, and Catholic immigrants	Mainly manufacturers, commercial farmers, skilled workers, and northern evangelicals
Regional strength	South and West	New England and Upper Midwest

The Rise of the Whig Party

The early opponents of the Democrats were known as the National Republicans, a label that captured the nationalist vision of former Jeffersonian Republicans who adhered to the economic program of Henry Clay and John Quincy Adams. The Bank War and Jackson's reaction to nullification shook loose pro-Bank Democrats and many southern states' righters from the original Jacksonian coalition, and these groups joined the opposition to Jackson. By 1834, the anti-Jacksonians started to call themselves Whigs, a name associated with the eighteenth-century American and British opponents of monarchical tyranny. The name stuck because of the party's constant depiction of Jackson as King Andrew, an executive tyrant who ran roughshod over congressional prerogatives and constitutional liberties.

By 1840, the Whigs had mastered the techniques of political organization and mobilization pio-

neered by the Democrats in the late 1820s. They ran William Henry Harrison, their own version of a military hero, and swept to victory. The **second party system** of intense national competition between Whigs and Democrats was now in place (see the summary table "The Second Party System"). It would dominate politics until the rise of the antislavery Republican party in the 1850s.

The Party Taking Shape

The Whig party was born in the congressional reaction to Jackson's Bank veto and his subsequent attacks on the national bank. Led by the unlikely trio of Henry Clay and Daniel Webster, nationalists from the West and New England, and John C. Calhoun, a states' righter from the South, the congressional opposition accused Jackson of demagogic appeals to the poor against the rich. What upset them, apart from the specific content of Jackson's policies, was how he enforced his will. Jackson wielded his executive power like a bludgeon. Whereas all earlier presidents together had used the veto only ten times, Jackson did so a dozen times. He openly defied the Supreme Court and Congress, be it on Indian or banking policy, and unlike any of his predecessors, he took his case directly to the people. To his opponents, Jackson was threatening to undermine the constitutional system of checks and balances and bypass the established leadership of public-spirited gentlemen who had hitherto ruled on behalf of the people.

Local and state coalitions of the Whigs sent an anti-Jackson majority to the House of Representatives in 1835. The most powerful of these coalitions was in New York, where a third party, the **Anti-Masons**, joined the Whigs. The party had originated in western New York in the late 1820s as a grass-roots response to the sudden disappearance and presumed murder of William Morgan, an itinerant artisan who threatened to expose the secrets of the Order of Freemasons. An all-male order steeped in ritual and ceremony, the Masons united urban and small-town elites into a tightly knit brotherhood of personal contacts and mutual aid. When efforts to investigate Morgan's disappearance ran into a legal dead end, rumors spread that the Masons constituted a vast conspiracy that conferred special privileges and legal protection on its exclusive members. To combat this "monster," farmers and townspeople flocked to the new Anti-Masonic party. They sought, in the words of an 1831 Anti-Masonic address, "equal rights and equal privileges among the freemen of the country."

Western New York, an area of religious fervor ignited by revivals and of rapid economic change with the opening of the Erie Canal in 1825, provided fertile ground for the growth of the new party. With close ties to rural landlords and town creditors, the Masons were highly vulnerable to the charge of economic favoritism. In addition, the evangelicals characterized the Masons' secret rituals as a desecration of the Christian faith. The Anti-Masons were thus the first party to combine demands for equal opportunity with calls for the moral reform of a sinful society.

Despite spreading into New England and the neighboring mid-Atlantic states, the Anti-Masons were unable to sustain themselves as a separate party. Their presidential candidate in 1832, William Wirt of Maryland, won only Vermont. Recognizing that the opponents of the Anti-Masons were usually the entrenched local interests of the Democratic party, shrewd politicians, led by Thurlow Weed and William Seward of New York, took up the movement and absorbed most of it into the anti-Jackson coalition. They thus broadened the Whigs' mass base and added an egalitarian message to their appeal.

By 1836, the Whigs were strong enough to mount a serious challenge for the presidency. However, they still lacked an effective national organization that could unite their regional coalitions behind one candidate. They ran three candidates—Webster of Massachusetts, William Henry Harrison of Ohio, and Hugh Lawson White of Tennessee—and some Whigs hoped that the regional popularity of these candidates would siphon off enough votes from Van Buren to throw the election into the House of Representatives. The strategy, if such it can be called, failed. Van Buren won an electoral majority by holding on to the populous mid-Atlantic states and improving on Jackson's showing in New England. Still, the Whigs were encouraged by the results. Compared to Jackson, Van Buren did poorly in what had been the overwhelmingly Democratic South. He lost Tennessee and Georgia and barely carried the popular vote elsewhere. The South was now open to further Whig inroads.

Whig Persuasion

The Whigs, like the Democrats, based their mass appeal on the claim that they could best defend the republican liberties of the people. Whereas the Democrats attributed the threat to those liberties to privileged monopolies of government-granted power, the Whigs found it in the expansive powers of the presidency as wielded by Jackson and in the party organization that put Jackson and Van Buren into office. In 1836, the Whigs called for the election of "a president of the *nation*, not a president of party." Underlying this call was the persistent Whig belief that parties undermined individual liberties and the public good by fostering and rewarding the selfish interests of the party faithful. Although the Whigs dropped much of this ideology when they themselves matured as a party, they never lost their fear of the presidency as an office of unchecked, demagogic power. They always insisted that Congress should be the locus of power in the federal system.

If the Whigs were more reluctant than the Democrats to accept political change in the form of mass-based parties, they were quicker to embrace economic change in the form of banks and manufacturing corporations. Building on ideas that originated with the Clay-Adams core of the party, most Whigs viewed governmental power as a positive force to promote economic development. They favored encouraging the spread of banking and paper money, chartering corporations, passing protective tariffs to support American manufacturers, and opening up new markets for farmers through government-subsidized transportation projects. Such policies, they held, would widen economic opportunities for more and more Americans and provide positive incentives for material self-improvement.

The Whigs' economic program appealed mostly to Americans who were benefiting from economic change or expecting to do so. They drew heavily from commercial and planting interests in the South. They were also the party of bankers, manufacturers, small-town entrepreneurs, farmers prospering from the market outlets of canals and railroads, and skilled workers who valued a high tariff as protection from the competition of goods produced by cheap foreign labor. These Whig groups also tended to be native-born Protestants of New England or Yankee ancestry, particularly those caught up in the religious revivals of the 1820s and 1830s. The strongest Whig constituencies comprised an arc of Yankee settlement stretching from rural New England through central New York and around the southern shores of the Great Lakes.

Whether as economic promoters or evangelical reformers, Whigs believed in promoting social progress and harmony through an interventionist government. The Whigs favored such social reforms as prohibiting the consumption of alcohol; preserving the sanctity of the Protestant Sabbath through bans on business activities on Sundays; caring for orphans, the physically handicapped, and the mentally ill in state-run asylums and hospitals; and teaching virtuous behavior and basic knowledge through a centralized system of public education. Whig ideology blended economic, social, and spiritual reform into a unified message of uplift. An activist government would provide the economic opportunities and moral guidance for a harmonious, progressive society of freely competing individuals whose behavior would be shaped by the evangelical norms of thrift, sobriety, and self-discipline.

Much of the Whigs' reform impulse was directed against non-English and Catholic immigrants, those Americans whom the Whigs believed most needed to be taught the virtues of self-control and disciplined work habits. Not coincidentally, these groups—the Scots-Irish in the backcountry, the Reformed Dutch, and Irish and German Catholics—were the most loyal Democrats. They resented the aggressive moralism of the Whigs and the legislative attempts to interfere with their drinking habits and Sunday amusements. These Democrats were typically subsistence farmers on the periphery of market change or unskilled workers forced by industrial change to abandon their hopes of ever opening their own shops. They equated an activist government with special privileges for the economically and culturally powerful and identified with the Democrats' demand for keeping the government out of the economy and individual religious practices.

The Election of 1840

One of the signs of the Whigs' maturing as a party was their decision in 1840 to place victory above principle. Because of the lingering economic depression, Democratic rule had been discredited for many voters. Aside from the Independent Treasury Act and legislation establishing a ten-hour workday for federal employees, the Van Buren administration had no program to combat the Whig charge of helplessness in the face of economic adversity. The natural choice for the Whigs against Van Buren in 1840 was seemingly Henry Clay running on his American System to revive the economy with governmental aid. Yet the power brokers in the party dumped Clay, who represented the ideological heart and soul of the Whigs, for their version of a military hero popular with the people, William Henry Harrison of Ohio.

Harrison had run surprisingly well as one of the Whigs' regional candidates in 1836 and had revealed a common touch with the voters that the Whigs generally lacked. Unlike Clay, he was untainted by any association with the Bank of the United States, the Masonic Order, or slaveholding. As the victor at the Battle of Tippecanoe and a military hero in the War of 1812, he enabled Whig image makers to cast him in Jackson's former role as the honest, patriotic soldier worthy of the people's trust. In a decision that came back to haunt them, the Whigs geographically balanced their ticket by selecting John Tyler, a planter from Virginia, as Harrison's running mate. Tyler was

This cotton banner used by the Whigs in the campaign of 1840 celebrated their ticket as the friends of common Americans who had been raised in a log cabin.

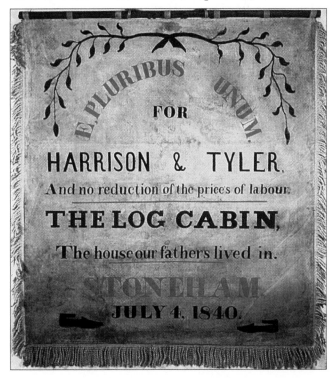

an advocate of states' rights and a former Democrat who had broken with Jackson over the Force Bill.

The Democrats inadvertently gave the Whig campaign a tremendous boost. A Democratic editor wisecracked that "Old Granny" Harrison (he was 67) was such a simpleton that he would like nothing better than to retire to a log cabin with a government pension and a barrel of hard cider. Pouncing on this sneer, the Whigs created a Harrison who never was—a yeoman farmer of humble origins and homespun tastes whose rise to prominence was a democratic model of success for other Americans to follow. Thus Harrison, who was descended from the Virginia slave-holding aristocracy, became a symbol of the common man, and the Whigs were finally able to shed their aristocratic image. Indeed, they pinned the label of the dandified and elitist aristocrat on Van Buren. "Martin Van Ruin," as effectively portrayed by the Whigs, squandered public revenue on effete luxuries and was concerned only with the spoils of office.

The Whigs beat the Democrats at their own game of mass politics in 1840. They reversed the roles and symbolism of the Jackson-Adams election of 1828 and seized the high ground as the party of the people. In a further adaptation of earlier Democratic initiatives, the Whigs put together a frolicking campaign of slogans, parades, and pageantry. Politics became a carnival in which voters were shamelessly wooed with food, drink, and music in huge rallies

Map 10-4   *The Election of 1840*
Building upon their strength in the commercializing North, the Whigs attracted enough rural voters in the South and West to win the election of 1840.

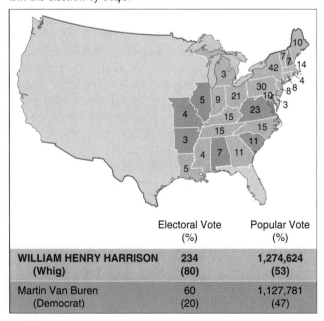

	Electoral Vote (%)	Popular Vote (%)
WILLIAM HENRY HARRISON (Whig)	**234 (80)**	**1,274,624 (53)**
Martin Van Buren (Democrat)	60 (20)	1,127,781 (47)

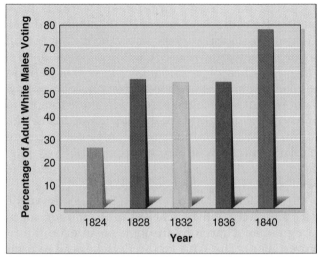

Figure 10-2   *Voter Turnout in Presidential Elections, 1824–1840*
The creation of mass-based political parties dramatically increased voter turnout in presidential elections. Voting surged in 1828 with the emergence of the Jacksonian Democratic Party, and again in 1840 when the Whig Party learned to appeal to the mass electorate.
Source: *Richard P. McCormick, "New Perspectives on Jacksonian Politics" in* The Nature of Jacksonian America, *ed. Douglas T. Miller (1972), p. 103.*

complete with live animals and gigantic buckskin balls that were triumphantly rolled from one rally to another. Clay muttered with some disgust that he regretted the need "of appealing to the feelings and passions of our Countrymen, rather than to their reasons and their judgments." Nonetheless, such hoopla was now essential for electoral victory.

The Whigs gained control of both Congress and the presidency in 1840. Harrison won 53 percent of the popular vote, and for the first time the Whigs carried the South (see Map 10-4). With the arrival of politics as mass spectacle, the turnout surged to an unprecedented 78 percent of eligible voters, a whopping increase over the average of 55 percent in the three preceding presidential elections (see Figure 10-2). The Whigs claimed most of the new voters and were now fully competitive with the Democrats in all parts of the nation. As the new majority party, they finally had the opportunity, or so they thought, to implement their economic program.

The Whigs in Power

Although the Whigs had been noncommittal on their plans during the campaign of 1840, it was common knowledge that Clay would move quickly on Whig economic policies by marshaling his forces in Congress and trying to dominate a pliant Harrison. Harrison's death from pneumonia in April 1841, barely a month after his inauguration, ruined Clay's plans. Tyler, Harrison's successor, was a particularly rigid states' rights ideologue who betrayed party expectations by blocking the key pieces of Clay's program. The Whigs reacted by reading Tyler out of the party.

In 1843, Tyler latched on to the annexation of the slaveholding Republic of Texas as an issue that might get him back into the good graces of the Democratic party and establish his own successful record as president. At the end of his administration, Tyler did succeed in securing the annexation of Texas, but his main accomplishment was to shift the focus of national politics from economic issues to sectional ones of territorial expansion. Running on an expansionist platform, the Democrats regained the presidency in 1844.

Harrison and Tyler

Perhaps the Democrats had been right that Harrison was too old for the demands of the presidency. He fumed that "I am *bothered almost* to death with visitors. I have not time to attend to my person, *not even to change my shirt*, much less to attend to the *public* business." Still, for all his grumblings, he was the type of president the Whigs wanted. He had pledged to follow the dictates of party leaders in Congress and defer to the judgment of his cabinet. Bowing to Clay's demands, he agreed to call Congress into special session to act on Whig party measures. Thus his death was a real blow to Whig hopes of establishing the credibility of their party as an effective agent for positive change.

Just how serious that blow was soon became apparent when Tyler became president, the first vice president to succeed on the death of a president. Tyler was cut from quite different cloth from Harrison. This stiff, unbending planter subscribed to a states' rights agrarian philosophy that put him at odds with the urban and commercial elements of the Whig party even in his home state of Virginia. Clay's economic nationalism struck him as a program of rank corruption that surrendered the constitutional rights of the South to power-hungry politicians and manufacturers in the North. Clay refused to cultivate Tyler's prickly pride with soothing gestures, and he forged ahead with the party agenda—the repeal of the Independent Treasury System and its replacement by a new national bank, a protective tariff, and the distribution of the proceeds of the government's public land sales to the states as funds for internal improvements.

A Democratic observer predicted in mid-May 1841 that "the Whigs will be very much disappointed by the course which the President will feel himself constitutionally bound to pursue." Tyler used the negative power of presidential vetoes to stymie the Whig program. He twice vetoed bills to reestablish a national bank. The second veto led to the resignation of the cabinet he had inherited from Harrison, save for Secretary of State Daniel Webster, who was in the midst of negotiations with the British. Enraged congressional Whigs then expelled Tyler from the party.

A now desperate Clay sought to salvage what was left of his American System. He lined up southern votes for the distribution of federal funds to the states by agreeing to a ceiling of 20 percent on tariff rates. Westerners were won over by Clay's support for the Preemption Act of 1841, a measure that allowed squatters—settlers on public land that had not yet been surveyed and put on the market—to purchase with noncompetitive bids up to 160 acres of land at the minimum government price of $1.25 per acre. This act was popular in the West because squatters no longer had to match the bids of speculators at government land sales.

Clay's legislative wizardry got him nowhere. When the Whigs passed a higher tariff in 1842 with a provision for distribution, Tyler vetoed it and forced them to settle for a protective tariff with no distribution. In the end, Clay had no national bank, no funds for internal improvements, and only a slightly higher tariff. Although Clay's leadership of the Whigs was strengthened, Tyler had deprived that leadership of meaning by denying the Whigs the legislature fruits of their victory in 1840.

The Texas Issue

Constrained by his states' rights view to playing a largely negative role in domestic policy, Tyler was a much more forceful president in foreign policy, an area in which the Constitution gives the chief executive considerable latitude. In 1842, Webster wrapped up his negotiations with the British. The **Webster-Ashburton Treaty** of that year settled a long-standing dispute over the boundary between British Canada and Maine and parts of the Upper Midwest. An agreement was also reached to cooperate in suppressing the African slave trade. Webster now resigned from the cabinet to join his fellow Whigs, allowing Tyler to follow a prosouthern policy of expansion that he hoped would gain him the Democratic nomination for the presidency in 1844. His goal was the annexation of Texas.

Texas had been a slaveholding republic since 1836, when rebellious Americans, joined by some *tejanos* (Texans of Mexican descent), declared their independence from Mexico. Jackson extended diplomatic recognition before leaving office, but he refused the new nation's request to be annexed to the United States out of fear of provoking a war with Mexico, which did not recognize Texan independence. But he was also aware that the addition of Texas, a potentially huge area for the expansion of plantation slavery, would inflame sectional tensions and endanger Van Buren's chances in the upcoming presidential election. In private, however, he urged Texans to seize harbors on the Pacific Coast from Mexican control and thus make annexation more attractive to the commercial interests of the Northeast.

For the sake of sectional harmony, party leaders sidestepped the Texas issue after 1836. Spurned by the Whigs and anxious to return to the Democrats, Tyler renewed the issue in 1843 to curry favor among southern and western Democrats. He replaced Webster as secretary of state with a proannexationist Virginian, Abel P. Upshur, and secretly opened negotiations with the Texans. After Upshur's death in an accidental explosion on the battleship *Princeton*, Calhoun, his successor, completed the negotiations and dramatically politicized the slavery issue. Calhoun made public his correspondence with Richard Pakenham, the British minister in Washington. In his letter, Calhoun accused the British of seeking to force emancipation on Texas in return for economic aid and a British-brokered Mexican recognition of Texan independence. These British efforts, warned Calhoun, were just the opening wedge in a master plan to block American expansion and destroy slavery in the South. After pointedly defending slavery as a benign institution, Calhoun concluded that the security and preservation of the Union demanded the annexation of Texas.

The Pakenham letter hit the Senate like a bombshell, and antislavery Northerners were now convinced that the annexation of Texas was a slaveholders' conspiracy to extend slavery and swell the political power of the South. In June 1844, the Senate rejected Calhoun's treaty of annexation by a two-to-one margin. All but one Whig senator voted against it. Still, the issue was hardly dead. Thanks to Tyler and Calhoun, Texas dominated the election of 1844.

The Election of 1844

The Whig and Democratic National Conventions met in the spring of 1844 in the midst of the uproar over Texas. Both Clay, who had the Whig nomination locked up, and Van Buren, who was the strong favorite for the Democratic one, came out against immediate annexation. Clay's stand was consistent with Whig fears that territorial expansion would disrupt the party's plans for ordered economic development by leading to a breakdown of political and cultural controls. But Van Buren's anti-Texas stand cost him his party's nomination. In a carefully devised strategy, western and southern Democrats united to deny him the necessary two-thirds vote of convention delegates. A deadlocked convention turned to James K. Polk of Tennessee, a confirmed expansionist who had received the blessing of Jackson, the party's patriarch.

To counter the charge that they were a prosouthern party, the Democrats ran in 1844 on a platform that linked Oregon to Texas as territorial objectives. Oregon had first attracted public attention during the Tyler presidency. Glowing reports from Protestant missionaries of the boundless fertility of Oregon's Willamette Valley triggered a migration to the new promised land on the shores of the Pacific by midwestern farm families still reeling from the Panic of 1837. At the same time, the report of a naval expedition sent to explore the Pacific aroused the interest of New England merchants in using Oregon as a jumping-off point for expanded trade with China.

Some six thousand Americans were in Oregon by the mid-1840s, and demands mounted, especially from northern Democrats, that the United States abandon its 1818 agreement of joint occupation with the British and lay exclusive claim to Oregon as far north as the 54°40' parallel, the border with Russian-owned Alaska. These were bold, even reckless, demands since the actual area of American settlement in Oregon was south of the Columbia River, itself well south of even the 49th parallel. Nonetheless, the Polk Democrats seemed to endorse them when they asserted an American claim "to the whole of the Territory of Oregon."

Polk's expansionist program united the Democrats and enabled them to campaign with much more enthusiasm than in 1840. Acquiring Texas and Oregon not only held out the economic hope of cheap, abundant land to debt-burdened farmers in the North and planters in the South but also played on the anti-British sentiments of many voters. In contrast, the Whig campaign was out of focus. Clay sensed that his opposition to the immediate annexation of Texas was hurting him in the South, and he started to hedge by saying that he would accept Texas if the conditions were right. This wavering, however, failed to stem the defection of proslavery southern Whigs to the Democrats and cut into his support among antislavery Whigs in the North. Clay lost to Polk by less than 2 percent of the popular vote.

Tyler claimed Polk's victory as a mandate for the immediate annexation of Texas. He knew that it would still be impossible to gain the two-thirds majority in the Senate necessary for the approval of a treaty. Thus he resorted to the constitutionally unprecedented expedient of a joint resolution in Congress inviting Texas to join the Union. By the narrow margin of twenty-seven to twenty-five, the Senate concurred with the House in favor of annexation. Tyler signed the joint resolution on March 1, 1845.

Although Tyler had failed to secure the Democratic nomination in 1844, he had gained Texas. He also had the satisfaction of getting revenge against the Whigs, the party that had disowned him. Texas, more than any other issue, defeated Clay and the Whigs in 1844.

Conclusion

The Jacksonian era ushered in a revolution in American political life. Responding to a surge of democratization that was in full swing by the 1820s, politicians learned how to appeal to a mass electorate and to build disciplined parties that channeled popular desires into distinctive party positions. In the two decades after 1824, voter participation in national elections tripled, and Democrats and Whigs competed on nearly equal terms in every region.

Although the origins of a national political culture can be traced back to the Federalists and Jeffersonian Republicans, politics did not fully enter the mainstream of American life until the rise of the second party system of Democrats and Whigs. The election of 1824 revived interest in presidential politics, and Jackson's forceful style of leadership highlighted the presidency as the focal point of American politics. Professional politicians soon mastered the art of tailoring issues and images to reach the widest popular audience. Voters in favor of government aid for economic development and a social order based on Protestant moral controls turned to the Whigs' program of an economically and morally activist government. Conversely, the Democratic position, stressing personal liberty, appealed to individuals who saw an activist government as a threat to their economic and cultural equality.

The national issues around which the Democrats and Whigs organized and battled down to 1844 were primarily economic. As long as this was the case, party competition tended to diffuse sectional tensions

This Democratic attack on the Whig ticket in 1844 reveals the skill of politicians in exploiting themes from rural folk culture for partisan purposes. The banner suggests that the Whig candidates were cynically portraying themselves as ordinary folks and really had nothing new to offer.

and strengthen a national political culture. Slavery in the form of the Texas question replaced the economy as the decisive issue in the election of 1844. Once this shift occurred and party appeals began to focus on the place of slavery in American society, an escalating politics of sectionalization was set into motion. Within a decade, the slavery issue would rip apart the second party system.

Review Questions

1. Explain the democratic movements of the early nineteenth century. What role did race and gender play in these movements?

2. What distinguished Jackson's presidency from those of his predecessors? How did he redefine the role of the president?

3. How was the Bank War central to the development of the Democratic and Whig parties? Why did the political debates of the 1830s focus on financial issues?

4. In terms of ideology and voter appeal, how did the Democrats and Whigs differ? How did each party represent a distinctive response to economic and social change?

5. How would you describe the changes in American politics between 1824 and 1840, and what accounted for these changes?

6. How did the annexation of Texas emerge as a political issue in the early 1840s? Why were the Democrats more in favor of territorial expansion than the Whigs?

Recommended Reading

Lee Benson, *The Concept of Jacksonian Democracy: New York as a Test Case* (1964). This study challenges the traditional linkage of the Jacksonian Democrats and reform and argues that ethnicity and religion were the most important factors influencing voter preferences.

Daniel Feller, *The Jacksonian Promise: America, 1815–1840* (1995). This up-to-date survey emphasizes the optimism and innovation of the Jacksonian era.

Marvin Meyers, *The Jacksonian Persuasion* (1960). This gracefully written work explores the beliefs of the Jacksonians and concludes that their agrarian values made them fearful of economic change.

Edward Pessen, *Jacksonian America* (1985). This revisionist work argues that Democrats and Whigs, for all their talk of democratic change, were driven primarily by the goal of acquiring office as an end in itself.

Robert V. Remini, *The Life of Andrew Jackson* (1988). This lively account of Jackson's career was written by his most noted biographer.

Arthur Schlesinger Jr., *The Age of Jackson* (1945). This remains the enduring statement of the democratic impulse behind the Jackson movement.

Charles Sellers, *The Market Revolution: Jacksonian America, 1815–1846* (1991). This boldly conceived work places responses to market change at the center of the era's political development.

Alexis de Tocqueville, *Democracy in America*, ed. Phillips Bradley, 2 vols. (1945). This often-quoted work is a classic still popular for its first-hand depiction of Jacksonian society and institutions.

Harry Watson, *Liberty and Power: The Politics of Jacksonian America* (1990). Watson has produced a very readable and concise synthesis of Jacksonian politics.

Additional Sources

The Egalitarian Impulse
Jon Butler, *Awash in a Sea of Faith: Christianizing the American People* (1990).

Mary W. M. Hargreaves, *The Presidency of John Quincy Adams* (1985).

Nathan O. Hatch, *The Democratization of American Christianity* (1989).

Merrill D. Peterson, ed., *Democracy, Liberty, and Property: The State Constitutional Conventions of the 1820s* (1966).

Chilton Williamson, *American Suffrage from Property to Democracy, 1760–1860* (1960).

Jackson's Presidency
Donald B. Cole, *The Presidency of Andrew Jackson* (1993).

Angie Debo, *And Still the Waters Run: The Betrayal of the Five Civilized Tribes* (1940; reprint, 1972).

Richard E. Ellis, *The Union at Risk: Jacksonian Democracy, States' Rights, and the Nullification Crisis* (1987).

William W. Freehling, *Prelude to Civil War: The Nullification Controversy in South Carolina, 1816–1836* (1966).

Robert V. Remini, *Andrew Jackson and the Bank War* (1967).

Michael Paul Rogin, *Fathers and Children: Andrew Jackson and the Subjugation of the American Indian* (1975).

John William Ward, *Andrew Jackson: Symbol for an Age* (1955).

Van Buren and Hard Times

John M. McFaul, *The Politics of Jacksonian Finance* (1972).

Reginald Charles McGrane, *The Panic of 1837* (1924).

Roger Sharp, *The Jacksonians versus the Banks: Politics in the States after the Panic of 1837* (1970).

Peter Temin, *The Jacksonian Economy* (1969).

Major L. Wilson, *The Presidency of Martin Van Buren* (1984).

The Rise of the Whig Party

John Ashworth, *"Agrarians" and "Aristocrats": Party Political Ideology in the United States, 1837–1846* (1983).

Daniel Walker Howe, *The Political Culture of the American Whigs* (1979).

Lawrence Frederick Kohl, *The Politics of Individualism: Parties and the American Character in the Jacksonian Era* (1989).

Richard P. McCormick, *The Second American Party System* (1966).

Merrill Peterson, *The Great Triumvirate: Webster, Clay, and Calhoun* (1987).

The Whigs in Power

William R. Brock, *Parties and Political Conscience* (1979).

Frederick Merk, *Slavery and the Annexation of Texas* (1972).

Robert J. Morgan, *A Whig Embattled* (1954).

Norma Louis Peterson, *The Presidencies of William Henry Harrison and John Tyler* (1990).

Robert V. Remini, *Henry Clay: Statesman for the Union* (1991).

Where to Learn More

❖ **Rice Museum, Georgetown, South Carolina.** Rice planters were the leaders of the nullification movement, and the interpretive materials here on the history of rice cultivation help one understand how slave labor was employed to produce their great wealth.

❖ **The Hermitage, Hermitage, Tennessee.** This was the plantation home of Andrew Jackson. The site includes a museum with artifacts of Jackson's life.

❖ **Martin Van Buren National Historic Site, Kinderhook, New York.** The site preserves Lindenwald, Van Buren's home after he left the presidency, and includes a library with materials on Van Buren and his political era.

❖ **The Alamo, San Antonio, Texas.** Originally a Franciscan mission, the Alamo was converted into a fort during the Texas War of Independence. The massacre of its defenders in 1836 by Santa Anna's army gave birth to the rallying cry for Texas independence, "Remember the Alamo."

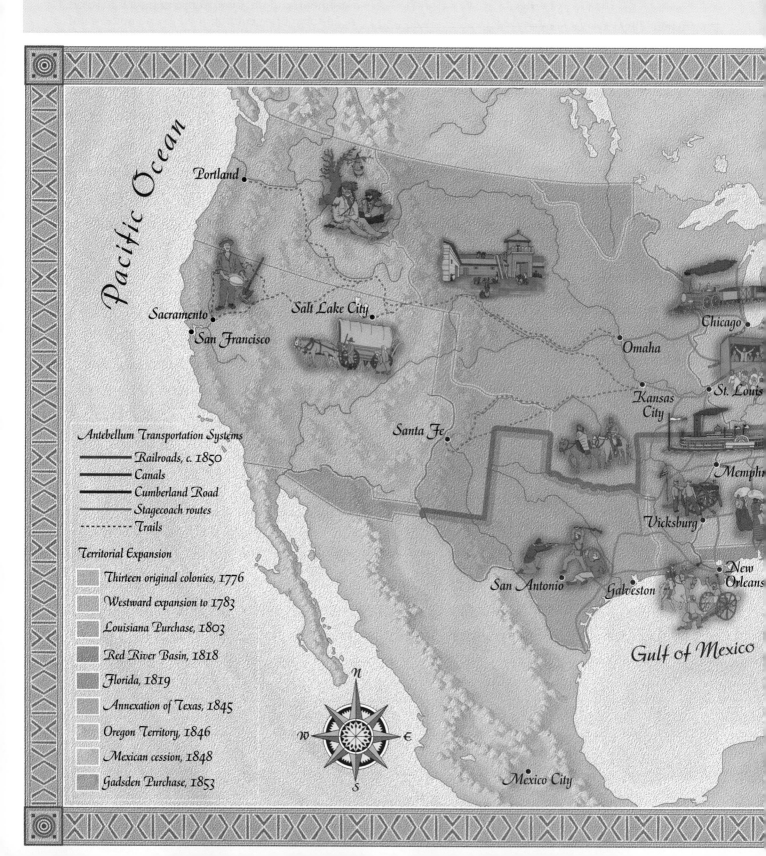

Pacific Ocean

Portland

Sacramento

San Francisco

Salt Lake City

Chicago

Omaha

St. Louis

Kansas City

Santa Fe

Memphis

Vicksburg

San Antonio

Galveston

New Orleans

Gulf of Mexico

Mexico City

Antebellum Transportation Systems

— Railroads, c. 1850
— Canals
— Cumberland Road
— Stagecoach routes
----- Trails

Territorial Expansion

Thirteen original colonies, 1776
Westward expansion to 1783
Louisiana Purchase, 1803
Red River Basin, 1818
Florida, 1819
Annexation of Texas, 1845
Oregon Territory, 1846
Mexican cession, 1848
Gadsden Purchase, 1853

N
W E
S

Boston
Buffalo
Clevela
Cincinnati
New York
Philadelphia
Wilmington
Charleston
Atlanta
Savannah
St. Augustine

Atlantic Ocean

0   400 miles
0   600 km

Caribbean Sea

KEY TOPICS

❖ The increasing industrialization of the U.S. economy between 1815 and 1850
❖ The effect of the transportation revolution on the pattern and direction of American commerce
❖ The growth of cities and the emergence of both a new middle-class society and a lower class of working poor
❖ Massive immigration starting in the 1840s, mainly from Ireland and Germany, providing a new labor force essential to industrialization
❖ New wealth and the increasing inequalities among the rich, the middle class, and the working classes
❖ The emergence of poorly paid, unskilled labor and the decline of the old artisan-mechanic class

315

"Oh, that I had wings!" wished Lucy Larcom as she leaned out a window in the factory at Lowell, Massachusetts, on a warm June afternoon in the 1830s. Like thousands of other young women from New England's farms, she had gone to work in the new textile mills and had become part of the nation's first large industrial work force. Larcom entered the mill when she was 11, glad to be able to relieve her widowed mother of the cost of her upkeep, and now she enjoyed the independence that came with earning her own wages. But mill work was a mixed blessing. Larcom "never cared much for machinery" and hated its noisy clatter, and she resented "being shut in to daily toil so early" in the morning. She recalled that "sometimes the confinement of the mill became very wearisome," and her "whole stifled being would cry out" for freedom. Still, she was there of her own choosing, and she conceded that the discipline of the mill had taught her

self-control. "Perhaps," she mused, "I could have brought myself into the limitations of order and method in no other way."

Larcom's ambivalence typified the reaction of Americans to the wrenching social and economic changes of the Jacksonian era from 1820 to 1850. Factories were new institutions with authoritarian work rules that deprived workers of their accustomed freedoms and radically altered the self-directed rhythm of farm and artisan work. Yet the factories were just one sign of the quickening pace of economic development and social dislocation after 1820. Cities grew rapidly—indeed, at the fastest relative rate in American history. Urbanization also brought new production patterns and increasingly separated one's home from one's place of work. New middle and working classes evolved in response to such changes. These class changes were most pronounced in the Northeast, which can serve as a window through which to view the transformation of the nation's economy and social structure up to the middle of the nineteenth century.

The Transportation Revolution

In 1820, the American economy was little changed from the days of Washington's presidency. Four in five people worked in agriculture, and manufacturing played a minor role in overall economic activity. Over the next three decades, however, America joined England as a world leader in industrialization. By 1850, manufacturing accounted for one-third of total commodity output, and nonfarm employment had more than doubled to 45 percent of the labor force.

The most direct cause of this rapid and sustained surge in manufacturing was the growth of the home market, the increasing consumption within the United States of the goods the country was producing. The improvements in moving people, raw materials, and finished goods that were key to this growth are collectively known as the **transportation**

revolution. Dramatically lower transportation costs and faster shipping times opened up new markets for farmers and manufacturers alike and provided an ongoing incentive for expanding production (see Table 11-1). As physical barriers to economic development fell, agricultural and manufactured goods could be exchanged more efficiently. The economy as a whole benefited, and the growing home market continually stimulated the development of American manufacturing.

Canals and Steamboats

The nation had no system of transportation in 1820. The states had chartered turnpike companies to build improved roads, graded with crushed stone, for overland transportation. Some 4,000 miles of these toll roads had been built by 1820, mostly in the Northeast, but their economic impact was marginal. They made travel more comfortable for passengers on stagecoaches between coastal cities, but they were still too slow and expensive for transporting bulky

TABLE 11.1	IMPACT OF THE TRANSPORTATION REVOLUTION ON TRAVELING TIME		
Route	1800	1830	1860
New York to Philadelphia	2 days	1 day	Less than 1 day
New York to Charleston	More than 1 week	5 days	2 days
New York to Chicago	6 weeks	3 weeks	2 days
New York to New Orleans	4 weeks	2 weeks	6 days

freight. It cost just as much to haul heavy goods by horse-drawn wagons 30 miles into the interior as to ship them 3,000 miles across the Atlantic Ocean. West of the Appalachian Mountains, where the need for improved transportation was the greatest, roads were mostly stump-strewn, muddy trails through forests and swamps.

Water transportation was much cheaper, but it was limited to the coast or navigable rivers. Only farmers located near a city or a river grew surplus crops for sale in an outside market. Rivers were the arteries of commerce in the West, and their southerly flow directed western farm surpluses down the Ohio and Mississippi river systems toward New Orleans. Flatboats (rafts with a deck and a steering device) could carry heavy loads with the current but were useless for upriver traffic. Although keelboats could be poled upstream, they were slow and expensive.

Steamboats provided the first transportation breakthrough. American entrepreneur-inventors had been tinkering with the design of steamboats since John Fitch launched the first one on the Delaware River in 1787, and in 1807, Robert Fulton demonstrated their commercial practicality when he sent the *Claremont* 150 miles up the Hudson River from New York City to Albany. In 1815, the *Enterprise* carried a cargo upriver from New Orleans to Pittsburgh.

Steamboats revolutionized western river transport. By the 1820s, they had reduced the cost and the time of upriver shipments by 90 percent. Engineering changes that lightened their weight and broadened their hulls for a more shallow draft made them ideal for the western rivers and many of their tributaries. By the 1840s, more than five hundred steamboats were plying western waters. More and more farmers could now reap the economic benefits of exporting corn, pork, and other regional foodstuffs. Because freight rates for upstream cargoes dropped much more than those for downriver traf-

fic, western produce now purchased substantially more in outside goods.

Steamboats greatly expanded trade between the South and the West. But because no natural waterways ran on an east-west axis across the mountains, western trade did not start to flow eastward until the completion of the Erie Canal in 1825, the first and most successful of the artificial waterways designed to link eastern seaboard cities with western markets (see Map 11-1).

The Erie Canal originated in the desire of New York City merchants to reach the agricultural markets of the Old Northwest. Prodded by Governor DeWitt Clinton, the New York legislature agreed to fund the project in 1817. This was a daring and expensive undertaking. The United States had barely 100 miles of canals, none longer than 28 miles. The Erie Canal was to stretch 364 miles from Albany to Buffalo, a small port on Lake Erie. Its construction— the excavation of massive amounts of earth, the building of locks to raise and lower the water level for boats, and the clearing and grading of towpaths for the horses and mules that pulled boats along the 40-foot-wide band of water—was the greatest engineering feat of its era.

The completion of the Erie ultimately depended on the backbreaking labor of Irish immigrants, who comprised the bulk of its work gangs. They worked for less than $10 a month, part of which (at their insistence) was paid in whiskey in a daily ration of 12 to 20 ounces. The workers lived in camps built by the canal contractors. Sickness, especially fevers and cholera, was a constant danger. One thousand workers contracted a fever in the marshes around Syracuse in the summer of 1819, and many of them died.

Conditions for workers on the Erie promoted a violent culture of brawling and drinking that fed ethnic stereotypes of the Irish as drunken brutes. The reality, as an Irishman working on the Chesapeake and Ohio Canal a decade later tried to explain, was that "if

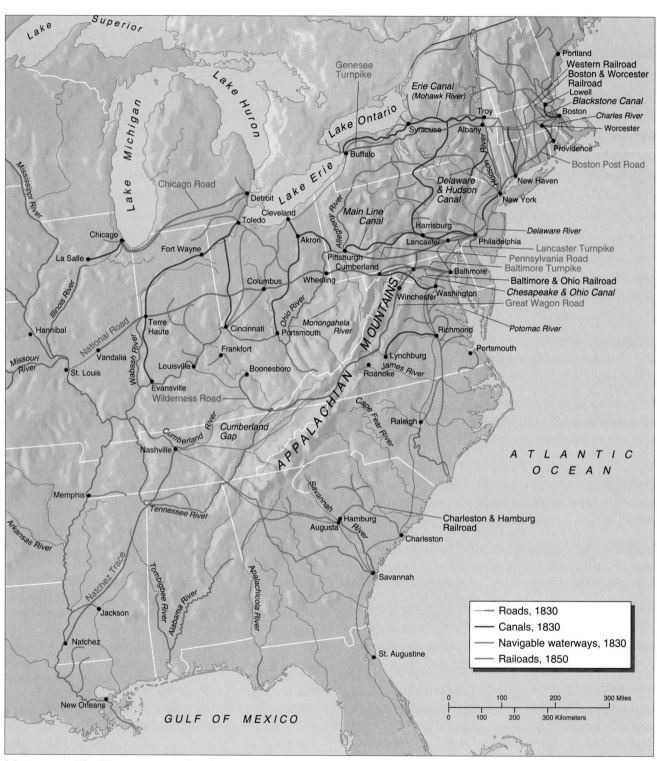

Map 11-1   *The Transportation Revolution*

By 1830, a network of roads, canals, and navigable rivers was spurring economic growth in the first phase of the Transportation Revolution. By 1850, railroads, the key development in the second phase of the Transportation Revolution, were opening up additional areas to commercial activity.

CHRONOLOGY

1790 Samuel Slater opens the first permanent cotton mill in Rhode Island.

1793 Eli Whitney patents the first cotton gin.

1807 Robert Fulton's steamboat, the *Clermont*, makes its pioneering voyage up the Hudson River.

1811 Construction begins on the federally financed National Road at Cumberland, Maryland.

1814 The Boston Associates opens its Waltham mill, the first textile factory to mechanize all phases of production.

1817 Construction on the Erie Canal begins.

1819–1823 Economic depression.

1824 In *Gibbons* v. *Ogden*, the Supreme Court strikes down a state monopoly over steamboat navigation.

1825 Erie Canal is completed.

1828 The Baltimore and Ohio, the most important of the early railroads, is chartered.

1834 Female workers at the Lowell Mills stage their first strike.
National Trades Union is formed.

1837 In *Charles River Bridge* v. *Warren Bridge*, the Supreme Court encourages economic competition by ruling that presumed rights of monopolistic privileges could not be used to block new economic enterprises.

1839–1843 Economic depression.

1842 Massachusetts Supreme Court in *Commonwealth* v. *Hunt* strengthens the legal right of workers to organize trade unions.

1845 Potato famine in Ireland sets off a mass migration of Irish to the United States.

1847 Cyrus McCormick opens his main reaper factory in Chicago.

---

the same number of the laboring class of any other country on the face of the globe, were collected on the line of the Canal, at least as many excesses would be committed by them, as by my hard working generous countrymen." Still, the stereotypes stuck, and when New York City celebrated the completion of the canal in 1825, the Irish were excluded from the festivities.

The Erie was an immediate success. It reduced the cost of sending freight from Buffalo to New York City by more than 90 percent and redirected the southerly flow of farm surpluses in the Great Lakes region to lake ports that sent it east across the Erie. As early as 1827, New York City leapfrogged Philadelphia and Baltimore as the leading exporter of flour, and by the mid-1840s, the Erie was pulling in more western trade than was being sent south to New Orleans on the Mississippi River. Profits from the Erie were so high that the construction cost of $7 million was paid off in just 12 years.

The Erie's success touched off a boom in canal building. Pennsylvania and Maryland launched plans for competing canals to the West, and other states soon joined them. More than 3,000 miles of canals were in place by 1840, but no canal matched the spectacular success of the Erie. Geography gave it a unique advantage. It ran through the only

natural break in the Appalachian Mountains, the Mohawk Valley of central New York. Other major east-west canals across the Appalachians, such as Pennsylvania's Main Line Canal, were more difficult and more expensive to construct. And they could never overcome the tremendous advantage of the Erie's head start in fixing trading patterns along its route.

The Panic of 1837 abruptly ended the canal boom. Financing dried up, and states abandoned canal projects that had left them heavily in debt. Still, the canal boom had greatly accelerated economic growth. Three broad networks of canals existed by 1840. One set linked seaboard cities on the Atlantic with their agricultural hinterlands, another connected the mid-Atlantic states with the Ohio River Valley, and a third funneled western grain to ports on the Great Lakes. Canals and steamboats enlarged the profitable marketing radius of all kinds of goods and expanded the volume of interregional trade. A unified national market was starting to take shape.

Railroads

Railroads were the last and ultimately the most important link in the transportation improvements that spurred economic development in Jacksonian America. Unlike the canals, which seemed to blend

This 1829 painting shows how the Erie Canal blended into the rural landscape of western New York. Although derided by skeptics as "Clinton's Big Ditch," the Erie was an economic success from the very beginning, and the tonnage carried on the Erie continued to grow until it reached a peak in 1880.

into nature and complement the age-old advantages of water transport, railroads struck Americans as a radically new technology that overturned traditional notions of time and space. "What an object of wonder!" exclaimed Christopher Columbus Baldwin of Massachusetts when he saw his first railroad car in 1835. "I cannot describe the strange sensation produced on seeing the train of cars come up. And when I started in them . . . it seemed like a dream."

Americans remembered most the speed and noise from their first encounter with the railroads. Moving at 15 to 20 miles per hour—four times as fast as a canal boat and twice the speed of a stagecoach—the railroads of the 1830s seemed to annihilate distance. After riding on the Western Railroad in Massachusetts, Caroline Fitch of Boston described her trip as a "lightning flash." The hissing of steam engines, squealing of iron wheels on iron rails, and gusts of air rushing into open rail cars made early rail travel an adventure; passengers felt like daring pioneers on a new technological frontier.

The railroads that were a source of such wonder emerged from humble beginnings in late-eighteenth-century England. The first were horse-drawn wagons on wooden poles hauling coal from mines to British seaports. Cast-iron rails permitted much heavier loads to be hauled, and rapid technological advances gave birth to steam locomotives. In 1825, the same year the Erie Canal was completed, the world's first general-purpose steam-powered railroad, the Stockton and Darlington, opened in En-

gland. Businesspeople in the eastern cities of the United States, fearful that the canal would give New York a monopoly on the western trade, were quick to see the commercial promise of rail transport.

The construction of the first American railroads—the Baltimore and Ohio, the Boston and Worcester, and the Charleston and Hamburg—began in the late 1820s, and they all pushed outward from seaboard cities eager to connect to the western market. The Baltimore and Ohio was to cross the Appalachians and connect Baltimore with Wheeling, Virginia, on the Ohio River. Too far east to benefit from the Erie Canal, Boston merchants saw the Boston and Worcester as a link between New England and the eastern terminus of the Erie at Albany. By 1841, Boston had a rail connection to Albany. The Charleston enterprise sought to divert the lucrative cotton trade of the Carolina interior away from Savannah, Georgia. At its completion in 1833, the Charleston and Hamburg, with 136 miles of track, was the world's longest railroad.

Experimentation and innovation marked the first decade of railroad construction. American engineers received in-the-field training as they coped with problems posed by rough, mountainous terrain. They learned how to use crushed rock to cushion rails pounded by iron wheels. Stronger and sturdier iron T-rails replaced wooden rails overlaid with an iron strip. The swivel or bogie truck, loosely jointed forward wheels that turned with the curve of the track, controlled trains on sharp bends.

Express companies in the late 1830s began running special trains in the East. By the mid-1850s, regular express service was established between New York and Chicago.

By 1840, U.S. rail mileage had drawn even with that of canals and was twice as extensive as the total for all of Europe. Although canals and steamboats were responsible for the greatest drop in freight rates in pre–Civil War America, competition from the railroads soon overshadowed them. Canals suffered from freezing in winter and low water in summer. The railroads were faster and more dependable and had more flexible schedules. They could serve landlocked areas beyond the reach of river and canal networks. Above all, they were more efficient. As early as 1840, a railroad could move four times as much freight as a canal for the same cost in labor and capital.

After a pause during the depression from 1839 to 1843, the railroads became the most dynamic booster of interregional trade. Whereas the canal network stopped expanding after 1840, the railroads tripled their mileage in the 1840s. Revenues from freight traffic exceeded those from passenger travel for the first time in 1849. By then, trunk lines built westward from Atlantic Coast cities had reached the Great Lakes and the Ohio Valley and were about to enter the Mississippi Valley. Short lines were being consolidated into larger systems. New York and Pennsylvania took the lead in developing trunk lines to the west.

Although the 1850s were the greatest decade of pre–Civil War rail construction, the rail network in place by midcentury was already altering the North-South sectional balance. Originating from the commercial cities of the Northeast, the major lines ran on an east-west axis that reinforced the shift in regional trade that the Erie Canal had begun. Before the coming of canals and railroads, the bulk of western trade went downriver to New Orleans. By the early 1850s, this traditional trading pattern had been reversed, and most western produce went east. Moving in the opposite direction were northern-born settlers, manufactured goods, and cultural values that increasingly unified the free states east of the Mississippi into a common economic and cultural unit. The Northeast and the Old Northwest were becoming just the North. Significantly, no direct rail connection linked the North and the South.

Government and the Economy

Both national and state government played an active part in the economy. The first major road to the West, the National Road, was a federal project. Begun in 1811, it ran from Cumberland, Maryland, to Vandalia, Illinois, by 1850. In the burst of economic nationalism after the War of 1812, Congress twice voted funds for a network of roads and canals. However, the constitutional objections and vetoes of Presidents Madison and Monroe prevented the federal government from developing a national system of transportation. Still, it was widely accepted that government should promote and regulate economic growth for the benefit of its citizens, and the constitutional scruples that held back the federal government did not apply to the individual states.

Following the lead of New York with the Erie Canal, state governments provided some 70 percent of the funding for canals. High construction costs made private investors leery of risking their scarce capital in such long-term transportation projects. Moreover, publicists for the state construction and ownership of canals argued that these transportation facilities should not be used "to pamper the cupidity and enrich the purses of our capitalists." The

SUMMARY

CHANGES PROMOTING GROWTH IN THE TRANSFORMED ECONOMY

Sector	1815	1850
Travel and transportation	By foot and horse-drawn wagon	Cheaper and faster with canals, steamboats, and railroads opening up new markets
Population	Overwhelmingly native-born, rural, and concentrated east of the Appalachian Mountains	Four times larger as a result of natural increase and surge of immigration after 1840; settlement of West and growth of cities
Wage labor	Native-born, primarily women and children in manufacturing	Expanding as rural poor and immigrants enter the manufacturing work force
Power	Water-driven mills	Steam-driven engines
Farming	Subsistence-oriented; surplus sold in localized markets	Commercialized agriculture spreading in response to improvements in transportation
Manufacturing	Small-scale production in household units and artisan shops	Large-scale production in eastern cities and factories

popular fear, as expressed by John Sergeant of Pennsylvania, was that the private owners of canals would "monopolize their benefits in perpetuity" and thereby deprive the people of part of their sovereign power. Similar arguments also induced the states to invest in the early railroads. Although the Panic of 1837 reduced their financial assistance, about half of all railroad capital before the Civil War came from the state governments.

Over time, the federal government assumed a larger role in assisting the railroads. Initially, it provided engineers for railroad surveys. Congress also lowered tariff duties on iron used in rail construction, which saved the railroads $6 million between 1830 and 1843. The most significant aid offered by Congress was grants of public land that totaled 20 million acres by 1860. Such grants had helped finance canal construction in Ohio and Indiana, and the precedent for railroads was set in 1850 when intense lobbying from southern and western congressmen secured a major grant to build the Illinois Central and the Mobile and Ohio Railroads. The Illinois Central raised the massive funds it needed for

construction by mortgaging the federal lands it had received. Such federal subsidies through grants of public land were the chief means for financing the transcontinental railroads after the Civil War.

Government also encouraged economic growth through legislative and judicial actions. State courts and legislatures after the War of 1812 began to confer new rights and powers on private enterprises that had incorporated as transportation companies. Investors in these corporations received the protection of limited liability. If the corporation went bankrupt, the investors' personal assets were safe from creditors; their potential loss was limited to their direct financial stake in the company. Second, these corporations acquired the power of eminent domain, the legal right to purchase whatever land they needed for their rights-of-way. State courts upheld these enhanced legal powers. Thus farmers who did not want to sell their land for a right-of-way had no legal recourse. The courts ruled that a greater good—the development of the economy through transportation improvements—took precedence over the private property rights of an individual.

By the 1830s, the states were making it easier for businesses to incorporate. The older view of the corporation as a privileged quasi-public institution entrusted with a communal responsibility gave way to the modern notion of the corporation as a private business that should receive no special government favors. A corporate charter had been viewed as a privilege, and each one required a special act of the legislature. As the economy expanded, incorporation was increasingly seen as a democratic right of business enterprise. Most states now enacted uniform provisions for receiving a charter that conferred no special powers as a public agency. Incorporation became an administrative process. The number of corporations grew rapidly under these new laws, and two-thirds of them were in transportation.

The proliferation of corporate charters produced legal clashes between older and newer economic interests. Artisans whose livelihoods were threatened by the spread of factories objected that incorporation "puts means into the hands of inexperienced capitalists to take from us the profits of our art which cost us so many years of labour to obtain." When railroads brought in outside goods that undersold local producers, farmers and artisans in Massachusetts accused the corporations of having delivered "the business and profits of general transportation into the hands of the capitalists." Their fears were well founded: "Scores of deserted villages in various sections of the Commonwealth bear witness to the wasting and blasting effects of this growing monopoly."

At stake also was the ability of new entrepreneurs to compete against the monopoly privileges granted to many of the early corporations. Two decisions of the Supreme Court helped open up the economy to competition. In *Gibbons* v. *Ogden* (1824), the Court overturned a New York law that had given Aaron Ogden a monopoly on steamboat service between New York and New Jersey. Thomas Gibbons, Ogden's competitor, had a federal license for the coastal trade. The right to compete under the national license, the Court ruled, took legal precedence over Ogden's monopoly. The decision prevented states from restricting trade within their jurisdictions and affirmed the supremacy of the national government to regulate interstate commerce.

A new Court, presided over by Chief Justice Roger B. Taney, Jackson's former secretary of the treasury (John Marshall had died in 1835), struck a bolder blow against monopoly in the landmark case of *Charles River Bridge* v. *Warren Bridge* in 1837. Taney ruled in favor of the Warren Bridge Company by deciding that the older Charles River Bridge Company had not received a monopoly from Massachusetts to collect tolls across the Charles River. Any uncertainties in the charter rights of corporations, reasoned Taney, should be resolved in favor of the broader community interests that would be served by free and open competition. His decision divested corporations of any implied charter privileges that could put a monopolistic brake on economic progress.

The Rise of Cities

When Washington became president, Philadelphia, with a population just over forty thousand, was the nation's largest city. Barely one in twenty Americans lived in an urban area (defined as a place with a population of 2,500 or more). By the 1820s, cities had begun to grow more rapidly than rural areas. At midcentury, more than one in seven Americans was a city-dweller, and the nation had ten cities whose population exceeded fifty thousand (see Map 11-2).

The transportation revolution triggered this surge in urban growth. The cities that prospered and grew were those with access to the expanding network of cheap transport on steamboats, canals, and railroads. This network opened up the rural interior for the purchase of farm commodities by city merchants and the sale of finished goods by urban importers and manufacturers. Increased commercial activity tied to interregional trade was the primary source of economic growth in the largest cities until the 1840s. Manufacturing did not begin to play a major role until the late stages of pre–Civil War urbanization. A huge influx of immigrants after the mid-1840s and simultaneous advances in steam engines provided the cheap labor and sources of power that increasingly made cities focal points of manufacturing production.

The Port Cities

America's largest cities in the early nineteenth century were its Atlantic ports: New York, Philadelphia, Baltimore, and Boston. As late as the 1820s, these four cities held more than half the total urban population. Small in size—it took only half an hour to walk entirely across any one of them in 1800—these cities packed together merchants, artisans, and laborers near the waterfronts that were their economic lifeblood. "The carters were driving in every direction," an Englishman wrote of the New York City waterfront in 1806, "and the sailors and labourers upon the wharfs, and on board the vessels, were moving their ponderous burthens from place to place. The merchants and their clerks were busily

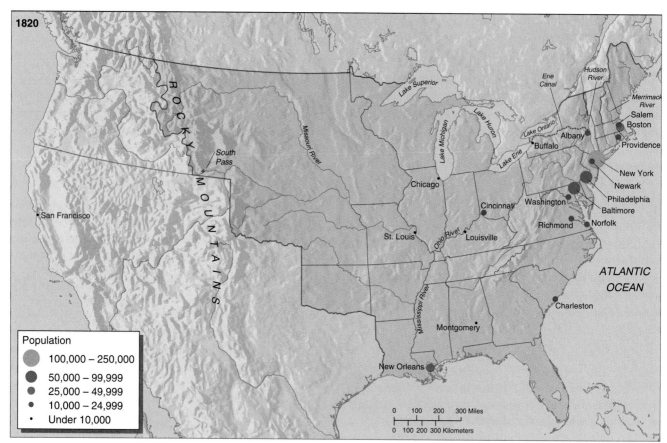

Map 11-2   *The Growth of Cities, 1820–1860*
In 1820 most cities were clustered along the Atlantic seaboard. By 1860, new transportation outlets—canals and railroads—had fostered the rapid growth of cities in the interior, especially at trading locations with access to navigable rivers or to the Great Lakes. Much of this growth occurred in the 1850s.
Source: Statistical Abstract of the United States

engaged in their counting-houses, or upon the piers. . . . Everything was in motion; all was life, bustle, and activity."

These Atlantic seaports all benefited from the increased trade promoted by the transportation revolution, but only New York experienced phenomenal growth. By 1810, New York had become the largest American city, and its population exceeded eight hundred thousand by the 1850s. One-third of the nation's exports and more than three-fifths of its imports passed through New York between 1820 and 1860. No wonder poet Walt Whitman trumpeted this metropolis as "the great place of the Western Continent, the heart, the brain, the focus, the main spring, the pinnacle, the extremity, the no more beyond of the new world."

Nature had blessed New York with incomparable advantages. Its harbor, the finest on the East Coast, gave oceangoing ships direct, protected access to Manhattan Island, and from there the Hudson

River provided a navigable highway flowing 150 miles north to Albany, deep in the state's agricultural interior. No other port was so ideally situated for trade. The entrepreneurial moxie of New York City merchants, the most forward-looking of all mercantile groups, enhanced these natural advantages. In 1817, the merchants established the Black Ball Line, the first line of packet ships that ran on a regular schedule for moving cargoes, passengers, and mail across the Atlantic. The city's merchants also convinced the state legislature to finance the Erie Canal, which guaranteed the ongoing commercial preeminence of the port of New York.

The Erie Canal gave New York City merchants a lucrative gateway to the West. The city benefited not only from the increased volume of western foodstuffs sent east across the canal and down the Hudson River for export to Europe but also from the swelling flow of finished goods shipped out of New York for sale in the West. Western families with

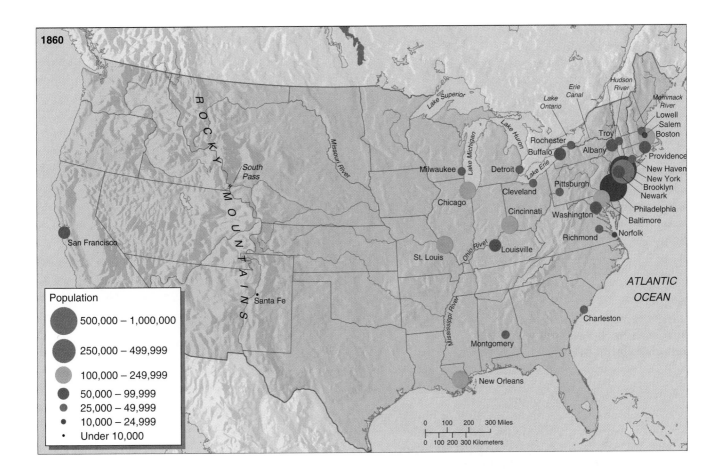

access to the Erie Canal became increasingly specialized economically. New markets for the sale of agricultural surpluses encouraged them to concentrate on cash crops, and profits from the sale of these crops were spent on finished goods that no longer had to be produced within the household. One measure of this trend was that families in upstate New York had virtually stopped making their own textiles by the 1850s. The rise in the disposable income of farmers generated a demand for the textiles, shoes, and other consumer goods that the Erie Canal brought in. These goods came out of New York, but most were not manufactured in the city. Nonetheless, the jobs created by handling these goods and the profits derived from supplying the western market solidified the city's position as the nation's most dynamic economic center.

New Yorkers plowed the profits of this commerce into local real estate—which soared in value fiftyfold between 1823 and 1836—and into financial institutions. The New York Stock Exchange, founded in 1817, became the country's main clearinghouse for stocks, and the city's banks brought together the capital that made New York the country's chief financial center. Agents for the city's mercantile and finan-

cial interests used this capital to offer advantageous terms by which New York captured much of the southern trade and dominated commerce with South America.

Commercial rivals in other port cities could not keep pace with New York. They launched their own canal and railroad ventures to penetrate the West, but none developed a hinterland as rich or extensive as New York's. Boston and Baltimore were also handicapped by the decline in their West Indian trade after the War of 1812, and Philadelphia lagged behind New York in financing international connections. Still, these cities continued to grow and at midcentury remained the nation's largest cities behind New York.

As they grew, the Atlantic ports pioneered new forms of city transportation. Omnibuses (horse-drawn coaches carrying up to twenty passengers) and steam ferries were in common use by the 1820s. The first commuter railroad, the Boston and Worcester, began service in 1838. The greatest advance in moving people within cities came with the introduction of horse-drawn street railway lines in the 1850s. These moved at speeds of about 6 miles an hour, overcoming some of the limitations of the "walking cities" of the early nineteenth century. Cities began to spread outward as cheaper, faster ways of traveling to work became available.

Living conditions improved more slowly. An expanding population strained limited housing resources, and at least one in four families shared a dwelling with others. The first slums appeared, the most notorious of which was the Five Points district of New York City. In 1842, the English novelist Charles Dickens described this area of tenement houses, brothels, and saloons as "these narrow ways, diverging to the right and left, and reeking everywhere with dirt and filth."

Small, flimsy wooden structures, often crammed into a back alley, housed the working poor in cramped, fetid conditions. Indoor plumbing was not available until the 1830s and then only as a luxury for the wealthy. Backyard privies, supplemented by chamber pots, were the standard means of disposing of human wastes. These outhouses overflowed in heavy rain and often contaminated private wells, the source of drinking water. Garbage and animal wastes simply accumulated on streets, scavenged by roving packs of hogs. Rudimentary systems for disposing of sewage and for piping in water from the countryside began to emerge in the 1840s but were inadequate for urban needs.

These conditions—a densely packed population in a poorly drained, garbage-strewn setting—made cities unhealthy. Mortality rates were much higher than in rural areas, and the death rate in New York City was double that of London. Stagnant pools of water bred mosquitoes that carried yellow fever, and contaminated water supplies produced frequent epidemics of cholera and typhus. Despite these deplorable standards in public health, the cities continued to grow.

Interior Cities

The fastest-growing cities were in the interior. Their share of the urban population quadrupled from 1800 to 1840. Some of these cities were specifically designed as new manufacturing centers, and others were favorably located to tap into the expanding transportation network. Both sets of cities had a fran-

This abandoned brewery in the Five Points district of New York City was home in the 1840s to as many as one thousand of New York's poor. The Ladies Home Missionary Society took over the building and had it torn down in 1852.

tic sense of newness. Rochester, New York, a village that the opening of the Erie Canal rapidly transformed into a major flour-milling center, amazed one English visitor in 1827 with its spontaneous energy. "The very streets," he observed, "seemed to be starting up of their own accord, ready-made, and looking as fresh as new, as if they had been turned out of the workmen's hands but an hour before—or that a great boxful of new houses had been sent by steam from New York, and tumbled out on the half-cleared land."

Pittsburgh, at the head of the Ohio River, was the first western city to develop a manufacturing sector to complement its exchange function. Situated among the extensive coalfields of western Pennsylvania, Pittsburgh had access to a cheap fuel that provided the high heat needed to manufacture iron and glass. It emerged after the War of 1812 as America's best-known and most polluted manufacturing city. "It is surrounded," noted the French traveler Michel Chevalier in the 1830s, "with a dense, black smoke which, bursting forth in volumes from the foundries, forges, glass-houses, and the chimneys of all the factories and houses, falls in flakes of soot upon the dwellings and persons of the inhabitants. It is, therefore, the dirtiest town in the United States."

Cincinnati, downstream on the Ohio, soon became as famous for its hogs as Pittsburgh was for its soot. "Porkopolis," as it was called, was the West's first meatpacking center. Industries in animal by-products, such as soap, candles, shoes, and boots, gave the city a diversified manufacturing base that kept it in the forefront of western urban growth. In contrast, Louisville, at the falls of the Ohio, remained more of a distribution point and slipped from the top rank of western cities after 1840. New Orleans, the largest city in the West, kept its rank because of its unique location at the mouth of the Mississippi, the only outlet to the Atlantic for western produce before the Erie Canal began drawing trade toward the Great Lakes. Still, because its economic base remained heavily concentrated on the export of cotton, New Orleans grew more slowly in the late antebellum period.

By the 1840s, St. Louis and the Great Lakes ports of Buffalo, Cleveland, Detroit, Milwaukee, and Chicago were the dynamic centers of western urbanization. St. Louis, just below the merger of the Missouri and the Mississippi Rivers, serviced American trade with the trans-Mississippi West. This trade blossomed once the Trans-Continental Treaty of 1819 eliminated Spanish claims to the Missouri Country. Outfitters used St. Louis as the jumping-off point for the fur trade up the middle Missouri and through the South Pass of the Rocky Mountains to rendezvous points with trappers and Native Americans in Wyoming. The city was also the eastern end of the Santa Fe Trail, a corridor of Anglo-Mexican trade that stretched across the southern plains to Santa Fe, New Mexico. St. Louis tripled in population in the 1830s, and it continued to surge after 1840 as a result of the city's importance in receiving and distributing goods for the upper Mississippi Valley. By midcentury, St. Louis was developing rail connections that linked it to the Great Lakes cities in a great transportation arc that shuttled goods and services east and west.

The success of the Erie Canal in reorienting western trade northward was the impetus behind the spectacular growth of the ports on the Great Lakes. Buffalo led the way in the 1820s, and a decade later, Cleveland and Detroit were also booming. They were soon joined by the Lake Michigan ports of Chicago and Milwaukee. The Great Lakes served as an extension of the Erie Canal, and cities on the lakes where incoming and outgoing goods had to be unloaded for transshipment benefited enormously. They attracted settlers and soon evolved into regional economic centers serving the surrounding agricultural communities. They also aggressively promoted themselves into major rail hubs and thus reaped the economic advantages of being at the juncture of both water and rail transport.

The combined populations of Cleveland, Detroit, Milwaukee, and Chicago increased twenty-five-fold between 1830 and 1850. The only other cities experiencing such phenomenal rates of growth were the new industrial towns. The densest cluster of these was in rural New England along the fall line of rivers, where the rapidly falling water provided cheap power to drive industrial machinery. Each town supported a cluster of factories and machine shops and was tied to a transportation network that brought in raw cotton for the textile mills from the mercantile centers of Boston and Providence and shipped out the finished goods.

The most famous of these new factory cities was Lowell, Massachusetts. Indeed, it became a must stop for foreign visitors. Lowell was America's first large-scale, planned manufacturing city. Founded in 1822 by Boston businessmen, Lowell was built around the falls of the Merrimack River. Within a decade, rural fields had been transformed into a city of eighteen thousand people. Multistoried brick factories surrounded by detached housing for the supervisory staff and large boardinghouses for the workers dominated the landscape and defined the city's industrial functions. The overall impression was one of bustling but well-ordered productive activity. "Everywhere one hears the noise of hammers, of spindles, of bells calling the hands to their work or dismissing them from their tasks, of coaches and six arriving or starting off, of the blasting of rocks to make a millrace or to level a road," noted Michel Chevalier in the mid-1830s; "it is the peaceful hum of an industrious population whose movements are regulated like clockwork." Lowell's success, like that of the Erie Canal, became a model for others to follow, and by 1840, New England led the North in both urbanization and industrialization.

Immigration

After improved transportation and a quickened economic pace provided the initial impetus for urban growth, a surge of immigrants swelled the size of the cities after the 1830s. At midcentury, most of the population in New York was foreign-born, and in all the port cities of the Northeast, immigrants dominated the manufacturing work force.

In the half-century after the Revolution, immigration to the United States had slowed to a trickle. Before 1825, it was well under ten thousand newcomers per year. It then jumped in the 1830s to over fifty thousand per year and soared to 140,000 in the 1840s and 280,000 in the 1850s. Most of these immigrants were Irish and Germans who settled in the Northeast (see Figure 11-1).

Lowell was the nation's leading textile center and the second largest city in Massachusetts by 1850. The building with the cupola and the structure with dormers and chimneys were part of the mill complex. The two detached buildings were boardinghouses for the young women who worked in the mills.

In the 1840s, economic and political upheavals in Europe spurred mass migration, mostly to America. No group suffered more than the Catholic peasants of Ireland. Dominated by their Protestant English landlords, these peasants eked out a subsistence as tenants on tiny plots of land. The potato was practically their only source of food, and when a potato blight wiped out the crop in 1845 and 1846, mass starvation ensured. In the next five years, about 1 million Irish died of malnutrition and disease, and another 1.5 million fled, many to America.

The Irish, like other immigrants, followed the main ocean trade routes to the New World. Most of these routes centered on New York, where two-thirds of all immigrants arrived in the 1840s and 1850s. As the poorest and most desperate of the immigrants, the Irish clustered in the ports. They had no money to buy land or move west unless they joined construction gangs for canals and railroads. Without marketable skills, they had to take the worst and lowest-paying jobs: ragpickers, porters, day laborers, and unskilled factory hands. Wives and daughters became laundresses and maids for the urban middle class.

The living conditions of the urban Irish were deplorable. Packed into dark cellars, unventilated attics, and rank tenements, their mortality rates were frightful. Still, cash wages and access to food made the American city enviable, compared to the prospect of starvation in Ireland. The message the Irish sent home was that for all its hardships, life was better in the New World than in the Old. Urging her parents to join her, Margaret McCarthy, an Irish domestic servant, wrote in 1850 that New York was a place "where no man or woman ever Hungerd or ever will and where you will not be Seen Naked . . . where you would never want or be at a loss for a good Breakfast and Dinner."

German immigrants were second in number only to the Irish by the 1850s. They came to America to escape poor harvests and political turmoil. These immigrants were relatively better off then their Irish counterparts. Far more of them had owned property as farmers, artisans, and shopkeepers, and hence they had the capital to purchase land in the West and the skills to join the ranks of small businesspeople in the cities. They were also more likely than the Irish to have entered the country through

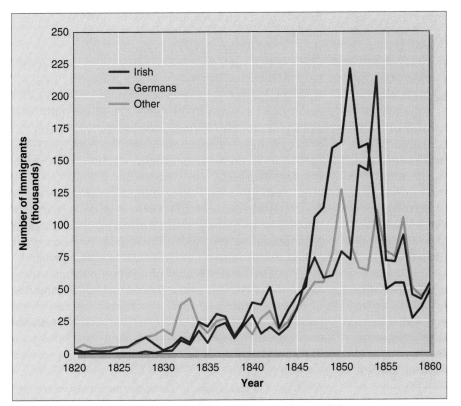

Figure 11-1   *Immigration to the United States, 1820–1860*
The potato famine in Ireland and economic and political unrest on the Continent led to a surge in immigration in the 1840s. The pace slackened in the mid-1850s when economic conditions in Europe improved.
Source: *U.S. Bureau of the Census,* Historical Statistics of the United States, Colonial Times to 1957 (1960), p. 57.

ethnic composition of the working class, especially in the cities of the Northeast. And their cheap labor provided the final ingredient in the expansion of industrialization that began after the War of 1812.

The Industrial Revolution

Manufacturing was the most dynamic growth sector in the American economy after 1815. Once the transportation revolution removed the physical barriers that had blocked the flow of goods, agriculture and manufacturing emerged as separate, specialized economic activities. Each fed on the other as home markets developed for the products of farms and factories. Regions, as well as individuals, had an incentive to specialize in goods that they could produce most efficiently with their labor and capital. Specialization in the scale of production, the organization of work, and the utilization of labor was also occurring. When these changes were combined with power-driven machinery in the new factories, the very meaning of the word *manufacturing* changed. Whereas before the 1820s it referred to the making of things by hand, it now came to mean the production of goods by machines in factories.

The Northeast led America's industrial revolution. In 1815, this region had the largest cities, the most developed capital markets, the readiest access to the technological skills of artisans, and the greatest supply of available labor. The first large-scale factories, the textile mills, were erected in New England in the 1820s, and for the next thirty years, the United States had the most rapidly developing industrial economy in the world.

Early Stages

The household and the small workshop were the sites of manufacturing in Jefferson's America. Household manufacturers accounted for about two-thirds of all clothing worn in the United States and

Baltimore or New Orleans, southern ports engaged in the tobacco and cotton trade with continental Europe. From there they fanned out into the Mississippi and Ohio Valleys.

Compared to the Irish, more German immigrants settled in rural areas, but they also tended to congregate in the cities. With the Irish, they made up over half of the population of St. Louis by the 1850s and were close to a majority in the other large cities of the Midwest and Northeast. With their diversified skills, the Germans found ample economic opportunities in the fast-growing cities and a setting in which to build tightly knit ethnic communities for mutual support. Centered around neighborhoods of German-speaking shops, churches, schools, and benevolent societies, these communities published their own newspapers and met most of the immigrants's cultural and economic needs.

About four in five of the 4.2 million immigrants from all nations who arrived from 1840 to 1860 settled in the New England and mid-Atlantic states. Their sheer numbers transformed the size and

a sizable percentage of such consumer items as shoes, hats, and soap. Because of the high cost of transportation in the pre-canal age, markets for manufactured items were localized, and the overwhelmingly rural population had to produce most of the goods it consumed. Informal trading networks in which labor and services were bartered for needed finished goods made farming communities, if not individual farm families, largely self-sufficient. Wider markets for household manufactures began to develop in the late eighteenth century with the coming of the **putting-out system**. Local merchants furnished ("put out") raw materials to rural households and paid at a piece rate for the labor that converted those raw materials into manufactured products. The supplying merchant then marketed and sold these goods.

In the cities and larger towns, most manufacturing was done by artisans, skilled craftsmen who were also known as mechanics. Working in their own shops and with their own tools, they produced small batches of finished goods. They made clothing and shoes, built houses, butchered carcasses, set type for printing, and turned out metal and wood products to order. Making up close to half of the population in the seaport cities, artisans and their families fed, clothed, and housed the urban population.

All artisans had a specific skill that set them above common laborers. For example, some knew how to gauge when a forge was just hot enough for working hand-wrought iron, and others could lay down and level the frame of a house without blueprints. These skills came from hands-on experience and craft traditions that were handed down from one generation to the next. With no written manuals or technical specifications to follow, artisans had to become highly adept at visualizing physical relationships in three dimension.

Artisanal skills were the "mysteries of the craft," and they were taught by master craftsmen to the **journeymen** and **apprentices** who lived with them and worked in their shops. Journeymen had learned the skills of their craft but lacked the capital to open their own shops. Before establishing their own businesses, they saved their earnings and honed their skills while working for a wage under a master. Apprentices were adolescent boys legally sent by their fathers to live with and obey a master craftsman in return for being taught a trade. By the terms of the contract, known as an **indenture**, the master also provided for the apprentice's schooling and moral upbringing. Although nothing was guaranteed in the craft hierarchy, an apprentice could reasonably expect to be promoted to journeyman in his late

teens and begin advancement toward his **competency**, a secure income from an independent trade that would enable him to support a family.

The artisanal trades dictated a way of life bound by self-regulated rules and values. Artisans controlled entry into their trades and the process of production from start to finish. They set their own work rules and were their own bosses. The independence of their crafts and the satisfaction derived from their work were the basis of their self-identity as workers and citizens. "The Mechanics are a class [of] men," proudly wrote "Peter Single" in the *Mechanic's Free Press* of Philadelphia, "who compose that proportion of the population of our country, on whom depends its present and future welfare; from them emanates her glory, her greatness and her power."

The factory system of production that undercut both household and artisanal manufacturing was in its infancy before 1815, but it had several advantages. First, by uniting the different phases of industrialization in one setting, the factories could produce goods far more quickly and cheaply per worker

As revealed in this portrait of the blacksmith Pat Lyon, the self-image of artisans was closely related to the pride and dignity they derived from their craft work.

than artisans or rural households. Factories subdivided the specialized skills of the artisan into a series of semiskilled tasks, a process foreshadowed by the putting-out system. Second, they pulled workers out of families and shops and put them under systematic controls. And in the final stage of industrialization, they boosted workers' productivity through the use of power-driven machinery. The earliest factories turned out cotton and woolen textiles; the most technologically advanced of the early factories was founded in 1790 by Samuel Slater in Providence, Rhode Island.

Britain pioneered the technological advances that drove early industrialization. The secrets of this technology, especially the designs for the machines that mechanized textile production, were closely guarded by the British government. Despite attempts to prohibit the emigration of artisans who knew how this machinery worked, some British mechanics got to the United States. Slater was one of them, and he took over the operation of a fledging mill started by Moses Brown, a Quaker merchant. With his knowledge of how to build water-powered spinning machinery, Slater converted the mill into the nation's first permanent cotton factory.

Slater's factory, and those modeled after it, manufactured yarn that was put out to rural housewives to be woven into cloth. The first factory to mechanize the operations of spinning and weaving and turn out finished cloth was incorporated in Waltham, Massachusetts in 1813 by the Boston Associates, a group of wealthy merchants. The Waltham factory signaled the future direction of the textile industry. It was heavily capitalized, relied on the latest technology, and recruited its work force from rural farm families.

A rudimentary factory system was in place by 1815. The first real spurt of factory building came with the closing off of British imports during the Embargo and the War of 1812. Hundreds of new cotton and woolen mills were established from 1808 to 1815. But the great test of American manufacturing came after 1815 when peace with Britain brought a flood of cheap British manufactured goods. If factories were to continue to grow, American manufacturers had to reach more consumers in their home market and overcome the British advantage of lower labor costs.

Sources of Workers in Manufacturing

The economy was at a crossroads in 1815. Its growth during the early national period had been heavily dependent on transatlantic trade, but future growth would have to come from within as capital and resources were diverted from carrying goods to producing them. As we have seen, the Erie Canal opened markets at home for American manufacturers. To expand significantly, however, the factories needed abundant sources of cheap labor.

Industrial labor was more expensive in America than in England, where the high cost of land forced the peasantry into the cities to find work. In contrast, land was cheap and plentiful in the United States, and Americans preferred the independence of farm work to the dependence of factory labor. Consequently, the first mill workers were predominantly children. Early mill owners recruited their work force from poor, rural families, especially large ones. For example, the mills that advertised in the *Massachusetts Spy* in the 1820s called for families "of five or six children each." The owners set up the father on a plot of company-owned land, provided piecework for the mother, and put the children to work in the mills.

Although this so-called **Rhode Island system** of family employment sufficed for small mills, it was inadequate for the larger, more mechanized factories that were built in New England after the War of 1812. These mill owners needed more workers to operate their textile machinery than could be found among poor families near the mill. Following a plan pioneered at the Waltham mill, they recruited single, adolescent daughters of farmers from across New England as their laborers.

The **Waltham system** of recruitment succeeded. Throughout the 1820s and 1830s, most mill hands in New England were young farm daughters. They were the most expendable members of large rural families, whose farms could not compete with cheap western foodstuffs. As Jemima Sanborn explained when she went into the mills in Nashua, New Hampshire, they left home because of "the hard times to get a living off the farm for so large a family." Although factory wages were low (a little over a dollar per week after deductions for room and board), they were higher than what these young women could earn doing piecework in the home or hiring out as domestics. The wages also brought a liberating degree of financial independence. "When they felt the jingle of silver in their pockets," recalled Harriet Hanson Robinson of her fellow workers at Lowell in the 1830s, "there for the first time, their heads became erect and they walked as if on air." No longer directly dependent on their male-dominated families for support, these women could now spend their personal time as they pleased.

Based on what they had heard of conditions in British factories, most Americans associated mill towns with morally depraved, impoverished workers.

Shown here working at power looms under the supervision of a male overseer, young single women comprised the bulk of the labor force in the first textile factories of New England.

To overcome parental fears of sending their daughters into such an unwholesome environment, New England manufacturers set up paternalistic moral controls. Single female workers had to live in boardinghouses owned or subsidized by the company. Curfews were imposed, visitors were screened, church attendance was mandatory, and special cultural activities were arranged for the mill hands.

Despite this paternalism, the mill women still worked long hours for low wages. Six days a week from dawn to dusk, the operatives tended clattering, fast-moving machinery in a work environment kept humid to minimize the snapping of threads in the machines. The market for mill cloth was very competitive, and the owners responded by slashing wages and speeding up work. In 1834 and 1836, the female hands at Lowell "turned out" to protest wage reductions in demonstrations that were the largest strikes in American history up to that time. Drawing on the republican heritage of the Revolution, they insisted that "as our fathers resisted unto blood the lordly avarice of the British ministry, so we, their daughters, will never wear the yoke which has been prepared for us" (see "American Views: Proclamation of Striking Women Workers, Lowell, 1834").

After the economic downturn of the late 1830s, conditions in the mills got worse. By the mid-

1840s, however, laborers who would work longer for less pay than their Yankee predecessors were available. The Irish, desperate for work, sent their children into the mills at an earlier age than Yankee farm families had, and these workers stayed longer—they did not leave after two or three years of building up a small dowry for marriage, as many New Englanders did. The Irish soon began to replace the Yankee women in the mills. In the mid-1830s, some 95 percent of the textile operatives in New England were native-born and mostly women; by the early 1850s, more than half were Irish women.

South of New England in the mid-Atlantic region, immigrants played a larger role in the formative stages of industrialization. The farm population here was more prosperous than in New England, and fewer young women were available for factory work. Consequently, manufacturers had to rely on foreign-born labor. As early as 1820, about half of the factory workers in the mid-Atlantic states were immigrants. Many of them were the Irish, who drifted into the factories after working on the canals.

The rise in immigration after the 1820s was crucial for urban manufacturing. The port cities lacked usable water power but did have a large and cheap pool of immigrant labor. This was a decisive advantage. By drawing on this pool, manufacturers

American Views

PROCLAMATION OF STRIKING WOMEN WORKERS, LOWELL, 1834

In February 1834, eight hundred women operatives staged the first work stoppage at the textile mills in Lowell, Massachusetts. They were protesting a proposed cut in their wages. Part of a wave of labor unrest in the mid-1830s, the striking workers in Lowell marched, temporarily shut down the mills, and outlined their grievances and demands in a formal protest. Although the strike lasted less than a week and failed to reverse the wage cuts, it revealed that women workers were as militant as their male counterparts in their quest for economic independence and justice.

❖ **How did the women link their struggle with that of the patriots in the American Revolution? Whom were they referring to when they spoke of "Tories in disguise"?**

❖ **How would wage cuts threaten the economic independence and social equality that these women valued?**

❖ **How did the strikers reject the benevolent paternalism the mill owners tried to impose on them? How did they step outside the bounds of proper "womanly" behavior?**

❖ **What "bondage" did these women want to avoid?**

Our present object is to have union and exertion, and we remain in possession of our unquestionable rights. We circulate this paper wishing to obtain the names of all who imbibe the spirit of our Patriotic Ancestors, who preferred privilege to bondage, and parted with all that renders life desirable and even life itself to procure independence for their children. The oppressing hand of avarice would enslave us, and to gain their object, they gravely tell us of the pressure of the time, this we are already sensible of, and deplore it. If any are in want, the Ladies will be compassionate and assist them; but we prefer to have the disposing of our charities in our own hands; and as we are free, we would remain in possession of what kind Providence has bestowed upon us, and remain daughters of freemen still. . . .

Let oppression shrug her shoulders,
And a haughty tyrant frown,
And little upstart Ignorance,
In mockery look down.
Yet I value not the feeble threats
Of Tories in disguise,
While the flag of Independence
O'er our noble nation flies.

Resolved, That we will not go back into the mills to work unless our wages are continued . . . as they have been.
Resolved, That none of us will go back, unless they receive us all as one.
Resolved, That if any have not enough money to carry them home they shall be supplied.

Source: *Boston* Evening Transcript, *February 18, 1834, as cited in Thomas Dublin,* Women at Work: The Transformation of Work and Community in Lowell, Massachusetts, 1826–1860 *(1979).*

could increase the volume of production while driving down the cost. A few skilled workers supervised the most difficult part of production, and semiskilled or unskilled workers performed by hand the specialized tasks into which the rest of the manufacturing process had been subdivided.

Especially in finished consumer goods, such as the clothing and leather industries, where low-paid workers could stitch cloth or sole a shoe, urban manufacturing became labor-intensive, depending more heavily on workers than on investment in machines and other capital. Shops were enlarged, or work was contracted out at piece rates. New York and Philadelphia, followed by Boston in the 1840s, thus built up a diversified manufacturing sector in consumer goods.

Except in New England textile factories and the smaller factories and shops in the seaboard cities, native-born males were the largest group of early manufacturing workers. They dominated the production of boots and shoes, an industry that employed twice as many workers in Massachusetts as cotton textiles in the 1850s. Native-born men also supplied most of the labor in the small manufacturing centers that sprang up in the medium-sized cities of the interior. They came from the surrounding countryside and were mostly the younger sons of poor farm families who no longer had enough land to pass on to all of the heirs. Unable or unwilling to go west, they sought work at a neighboring factory, usually as unskilled laborers.

As late as 1840, women, including those working at home, made up about half of the manufacturing work force and one-quarter of the factory hands. These proportions declined by midcentury as immigrant males and displaced sons of poor American farmers became the fastest-growing source of manufacturing laborers. Regardless of their sex, few of these workers brought any specific skills to their jobs, and hence they had little bargaining power. Economic necessity forced them to accept low wages and harsh working conditions. The sheer increase in their numbers, as opposed to any productivity gains from technological innovations, accounted by 1850 for two-thirds of the gains in manufacturing output.

The Role of Technology

Technological backwardness was the last major barrier American manufacturers overcame. Significant gains in productivity could be achieved only by applying the latest industrial technology to mechanize production. In closing the technological gap with Britain, manufacturers first relied on the trade secrets brought to America by British mechanics such

as Samuel Slater. This smuggled knowledge was essential for starting up the textile industry, but elsewhere the versatile, practical skills of American mechanics provided the impetus for technological innovation.

Mechanics, especially in the countryside, had an extensive range of skills. The Dominy family of Easthampton, Long Island, for example, worked with wood and iron, built grist mills, and made clocks and watches. Mechanics understood how machines worked and were great tinkerers. They experimented with new designs, improved old ones, and patented inventions that found industrial applications outside their own crafts. Oliver Evans, a wagonmaker in the Delaware Valley, developed machinery for a highly automated flour mill in the 1780s. In the 1830s, two mechanics in Connecticut who made axes built a machine that pressed and forged hot metal into dies, devices that cut metal into special forms. A skilled worker could use their machines to expand his daily production of ax heads twenty-five times over.

The most famous early American invention was the cotton gin. Eli Whitney, a Massachusetts Yankee who had turned out knives and blades at a forge on his father's farm as a teenager, built the first prototype in 1793 while working as a tutor on a Georgia plantation. By cheaply and mechanically removing the seeds from cotton fibers, the cotton gin spurred the cultivation of cotton across the South.

Whitney also pushed the idea of basing production on interchangeable parts. After receiving a federal contract to manufacture muskets, he designed new milling machines and turret lathes that transformed the technology of machine tool production. The federal arsenal at Harpers Ferry, Virginia, developed machine tools that could manufacture standardized, interchangeable parts. The new techniques were first applied in 1815 to the manufacture of wooden clocks and by the 1840s to sewing machines, farm machinery, and watch parts. What became famous in the 1850s as the **American system of manufacturing**—low-cost, standardized mass production, built around interchangeable parts stamped out by machines—was characteristic of only about twenty industries, mostly those in metal cutting. Nonetheless, it was America's unique contribution to the industrial revolution.

As the pace of technological innovation accelerated after 1840, so did the growth of manufacturing. Indeed, the 1840s registered the highest rate of expansion in the manufacturing sector of the economy in the nineteenth century. The adoption of the stationary steam engine in urban manufacturing fueled much of this expansion.

Large cities had always offered manufacturers the advantages of concentrated pools of labor and capital, cheap transportation and trading services, and ready access to urban consumers. But these advantages were largely offset by the lack of water power to drive machinery. Thus urban manufacturing initially rested on an extensive division of labor and the hiring of more workers to expand production. This pattern began to reverse in the 1840s when high-pressure steam engines enabled power-driven industry to locate in the port cities of the Northeast.

Steam power and more mechanized manufacturing also benefited the booming cities in the Great Lakes corridor of the Old Northwest. With limited access to water power, early manufacturing in the West was confined to the processing of farm goods—milling corn and wheat, tanning leather, packing meat, and rendering animal by-products into soap and candles. By turning to steam power and new machine tools, western manufacturers after 1840 enlarged their region's industrial base and created a new industry, the mass production of agricultural implements. The McCormick reaper factory in Chicago was one of the world's most modern industrial facilities by the 1850s. Steam-powered conveyer belts moved parts through the factory in an assembly-line system of production. The West was the center of the farm machinery industry, and the region produced 20 percent of the nation's manufacturing output by the 1850s.

By freeing industry to locate near centers of population and driving the trains that reached areas untouched by rivers or canals, steam power was beginning to transform the American landscape by the mid-nineteenth century. However, most of the change evident in the countryside by 1850 was the product of preindustrial technologies and the aftermath of impounding water for factory use.

The most obvious change involved the clearing of the land. About one-fifth of the original forest cover in the United States east of the Mississippi was gone by 1850. Most of this loss resulted from agricultural use. Clear-cutting, firing, and girdling—killing a tree by removing its bark in a continuous strip—were the cheapest ways to hack out a farm in the wilderness. The initial result was a bleak landscape of stumps and scorched trunks. Wood that was not needed for farmhouses, fences, and fuel found a ready market in the cities and factories, where it was both the primary energy source and the basic building material.

As the land was being cleared and carved into private farms, the lakes and streams continued to be viewed as public property and became dumping grounds for agricultural and industrial wastes.

The dyes and chemical sulfates used in tanneries and in clothing and textile production were released into water supplies. By 1840, the woolens industry alone was discarding some 18,000 tons of grease (which clings to raw wool and is removed in fulling mills) into rivers and streams. Water supplies were being polluted long before any sustained industrialization. What did change with the coming of large factories dependent on water power was the greater degree of private control over water resources and the extent of the ecological impact.

The Boston Associates, the merchant group that built the Waltham-Lowell system of textile mills in New England, illustrate how corporate capital was transforming water from a resource into a private commodity. To provide their mills with a steady, reliable source of water, one that would not be affected by the whims of nature, the Associates constructed a series of dams and canals that extended to the headwaters of the Merrimack River in northern New Hampshire. Inevitably, the ecology of the region under control changed. The level of lakes was altered, the flow of rivers interrupted, the upward migration of spawning fish blocked, and the foraging terrain of wild game flooded. Farmers protested when their fields and pastures were submerged, but lawyers for the Boston Associates successfully argued that water, like any other natural resource, should be treated as a commodity that could contribute to economic progress. Legal battles over water rights led to judicial decisions that cleared the way for the incorporation of nature by other business endeavors. Increasingly, the law treated nature as an economic resource to be engineered and bought and sold.

Growing Inequality and New Classes

As the economy expanded after 1815 and the industrial revolution began to take hold, per capita income doubled in the first half of the century. Living standards for most Americans improved. Houses, for those who could afford them, became larger and better furnished and heated. Food was more plentiful and varied, and factory-made consumer goods made domestic life easier and more comfortable.

There was a price to be paid, however, for the benefits of economic growth. In 1800, fully 90 percent of the free work force was self-employed, primarily as independent farmers and artisans. By midcentury, a permanent wage-earning class and a middle class of nonmanual, salaried employees had emerged. Half of the adult white males were now propertyless. Wealth had become more concentrated, and extremes of wealth and poverty eroded the Jeffersonian ideal of a republic of independent proprietors who valued liberty because they were economically free.

The Old Rich

The gap between the rich and the poor widened considerably in the early phases of industrialization (see Figure 11-2). In 1800, the richest 10 percent of Americans owned 40 to 50 percent of the national wealth. By the 1850s, that share was about 70 percent. The richest 1 percent alone saw their share more than double to 30 percent. Most of this increase occurred after 1815 when industrial development accelerated, and the most glaring discrepancies in wealth appeared in the large cities.

Owners of capital and income-producing property were most successful in generating wealth in the Atlantic seaports. By 1840, the wealthiest 1 percent of the population in New York City, Brooklyn, Philadelphia, and Boston held 40 percent of all tangible property (land, buildings, and other real estate), and their share of intangible assets (bonds, mortgages, and other paper investments) was undoubtedly much higher. The same pattern existed elsewhere. In all American cities by the 1840s, the top 10 percent of the population owned over 80 percent of urban wealth.

Most of the urban rich at midcentury had been born wealthy, the offspring of old-money families who had married and invested wisely. To be sure, there were popular stories of a rise from rags to riches, and many of them focused on John Jacob Astor. Born poor in Germany, he amassed a fortune of $25 million in the fur trade and was the richest man in New York by 1845. But for every Astor, twenty Americans benefited from inherited wealth and family connections to stay in the ranks of the very rich. Indeed, less than 10 percent of this class emerged from a background of even middling wealth.

The urban rich created their own society. As one of them noted, it was a society "characterised by a spirit of exclusiveness and persecution unknown in any other country. Its gradations not being regulated according to rank and titles, selfishness and conceit are its principal elements; and its arbitrary distinctions the more offensive, as they principally refer to fortune." The urban wealthy belonged to exclusive clubs, attended lavish balls and dinners, were waited on by a retinue of servants in their mansions, and generally recoiled from what they considered the "mob government" ushered in by the Jacksonian

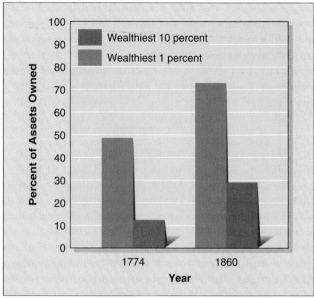

Figure 11-2   Growth in Wealth Inequality, 1774–1860
The two benchmark years for the gathering of data on the nationwide distribution of wealth are 1774 and 1860. Specialized studies on regions and sub-regions indicate that wealth inequality increased most sharply from the 1820s to 1850, the period that coincides with early industrialization.
Source: *Jeffrey G. Williamson and Peter H. Lindert,* American Inequality: A Macroeconomic History *(1980), p. 38.*

Democrats. This aristocracy of wealth tried to use their riches as a shield from the democratic changes in the larger society around them, and they were a constant reminder of how unequal the distribution of wealth had become in the so-called age of the common man.

The New Middle Class

Although the rich increased their share of the economic pie during the Jacksonian era, that pie also grew larger. The economy was now growing three times faster than in the eighteenth century, and incomes were rising. New employment opportunities opened up, especially in nonmanual work. Most of these jobs were in northern cities and bustling market towns, where the need was greatest for office and store clerks, managerial personnel, sales agents, and independent retailers. The result by midcentury was a new middle class superimposed on the older one of independent farmers, artisans, shopkeepers, and professionals.

Cities provided the setting where members of the new middle class began to forge a distinctive identity, one that set them apart from the wealthy above them and the working poor beneath them. The apparent separation of work and home constituted the first step in this evolving sense of class consciousness. The preindustrial household, whether in the city or the countryside, had combined living and working arrangements in a set of personal relations controlled by the male head of the household. Master craftsmen, for example, directed the work of journeymen and apprentices who lived in their households. As the market revolution advanced, the workplace increasingly became a specialized location of production or selling. Middle-class fathers left for their jobs in the morning, while mothers governed households that were primarily residential units.

As homes lost many of their productive functions, they became places of material comfort for the rising middle class. Growing quantities of consumer goods—pianos, carpets, draperies, mirrors, oil lamps, and ornate furniture—filled their homes. Stoves replaced open fireplaces as the main source of heat, and plumbing eliminated outdoor privies. More rooms offered greater privacy, and visitors were now entertained in a parlor.

New status symbols accompanied middle-class prosperity. Having servants, the single largest field of employment in the cities, became a badge of domestic respectability. Shunned as degrading by most native-born white women, these low-paying jobs were filled by African-American and young immigrant (especially Irish) women. Work had not left the middle-class home; instead, it was disguised as the "domestic duties" of middle-class wives and scorned as the servile labor of persons said to lack the capacity for female virtue.

Etiquette books for the middle class propagated ideals of civility and explained the proper behavior needed to win social acceptance. They laid down rules for presenting oneself in public and in the home. "Don't drum with your fingers on chair, table, or window-pane. Don't hum a tune. The

This scene, entitled The Tea Room *by Henry Sargent in his 1821 painting, depicts how the wealthy elite in Boston used their social gatherings to set themselves apart as an elegantly cultured class.*

instinct for making noise is a survival of savagery," warned one adviser. Above all, they stressed decorum and self-restraint. Spitting and tobacco chewing, male activities that continued among the working classes, were condemned as boorish.

Besides seeking guidance from etiquette manuals on achieving respectability, the middle class also tried to shape its behavior by the tenets of evangelical religion. Revivals swept northern cities in the late 1820s. Charles G. Finney led the most dramatic and successful ones in the cities along the Erie Canal in upstate New York. Finney preached that salvation was available to those who willed it, but only by disciplining themselves to lead a Christian life could the converted hope to avoid backsliding into damnation.

Family Group. Davis, Joseph H., M. and M. Karolik Collection. Courtesy, Museum of Fine Arts, Boston.

This pen-and-watercolor drawing of a middle-class family in 1832 illustrates how the home, as it lost its productive functions, became idealized as a center of domestic refinement and material comfort.

Moral self-determination was at the heart of northern evangelicalism, and the new middle class eagerly embraced the ethic of self-control as a moral guide for making sense of the social and economic changes that were transforming their lives.

"A self-indulgent Christian is a contradiction," insisted Finney. Both economic and moral success depended on the virtues of sobriety, self-restraint, and hard work. Aggressiveness and ambition at work were not necessarily sinful so long as businessmen reformed their own moral lives and helped others do the same. This message was immensely reassuring to employers and entrepreneurs in the urban middle class, for it confirmed and sanctified their own pursuit of economic self-interest. It also provided them with a religious inspiration for attempting to exert moral control over their communities and employees.

Merchants, manufacturers, and professionals were the first to be converted by Finney's preaching, and these business leaders, along with their wives and daughters, were in the forefront of evangelical reform. **Temperance**—the prohibition of alcoholic beverages—was the greatest of the evangelically inspired reforms, and abstinence from alcohol became the most telling evidence of middle-class respectability. (For more on reform, see Chapter 14.)

Evangelicalism also shaped middle-class conceptions of womanhood and the home. In a reversal of traditional Calvinist doctrine, the evangelical ministers of the northern middle class enshrined women as the moral superiors of men. Though considered weak and passive, women were also held to be uniquely pure and pious. Women, who easily outnumbered men at Sunday services and weeknight prayer meetings, were now responsible for converting their homes into loving, prayerful centers of domesticity. "There is a ministry that is older and deeper and more potent than ours," wrote a liberal Presbyterian clergyman; "it is the ministry that presides over the crib and impresses the first gospel influence on the infant soul."

This sanctified notion of motherhood accompanied new views of childhood. Evangelical preachers softened the Calvinist doctrine of infant damnation for children who died before baptism. Ideas about infant depravity gave way to conceptions of young children as "little immortal beings," pure and innocent, though potentially corruptible. The primary task of motherhood now became the Christian nurturing of the souls entrusted to their care. "My Children how will they get along through this World of sin and vanity?" worried Mercy Flynt Morris. "It is my duty to warn them against those vices and try to instill into their minds the importance of seeking an interest in Christ—without which they will be miserable."

These changing images of women and children reflected and reinforced shifting patterns of family life. Families became smaller as the birthrate fell by 25 percent in the first half of the nineteenth century. The decline was greatest in the urban middle class after 1820. Sexual abstinence and male withdrawal before ejaculation, not mechanical methods of contraception, explain most of this decline. Advice literature, to say nothing of wives anxious to avoid the medical risks of too-frequent pregnancies, urged men to curb their sexual desires, and middle-class fathers now had an economic incentive to do so. Children were no longer an economic asset as they had been as workers on a family farm. Middle-class couples consciously limited the size of their families, and women stopped having children at a younger age.

Beginning in the 1820s, ministers and female writers elevated the family role of middle-class women into a **cult of domesticity**. This idealized conception of womanhood insisted that the biological differences of God's natural order determined separate social roles for men and women. Characterized as strong, aggressive, and ambitious, men naturally belonged in the competitive world of business and politics. Women's providential task was to preserve religion and morality in the home and family. Held to be innately weak, nurturing, and selfless, only they possessed the moral purity necessary for rearing virtuous children and preserving the home as a refuge from the outside world.

Middle-class women thus became the moral rulers of families that were smaller and more child-centered then those of the eighteenth century. Parents were able to devote more care and financial resources to child rearing. Middle-class children lived at home longer than children had in the past and received more schooling than working-class children. Sons learned to be self-directed men who could take advantage of the educational or professional opportunities their parents had provided for them.

The middle class defined itself in terms of character, not occupational or economic status. Unlike the wealthy, whose riches were inherited, members of the middle class believed that their property was the

product of hard work and self-denial. They also saw themselves as the industrious Americans whose moral fortitude and discipline enabled them to escape the clutches of poverty, the fate of those who were presumed to be lazy and undisciplined.

The Working Classes

The economic changes that produced a new middle class also fundamentally transformed the working class. In preindustrial America, the working class was predominantly native-born and of artisan origins. By midcentury, most urban workers were immigrants or the children of immigrants and had never been artisans in a skilled craft (see Figure 11-3). The size of the industrial work force had grown tremendously, especially in the cities, and was so diverse that contemporaries spoke of it in the plural as the "working classes."

Job skills, sex, race, and ethnicity all divided workers after 1840. Master craftsmen were the most highly skilled and best-paid members of the labor force. Initially, they were in the best positions to take advantage of the growth in manufacturing. However, as industrialization proceeded, the unity of the old artisan class splintered. Ambitious master craftsmen

Figure 11-3 New York City Working Class, 1855
Especially in the large eastern cities, a new working class of wage laborers dominated by immigrants emerged by the 1850s.
Source: *Richard B. Stott*, Workers in the Metropolis: Class, Ethnicity, and Youth in Antebellum New York City *(1990), p. 92.*

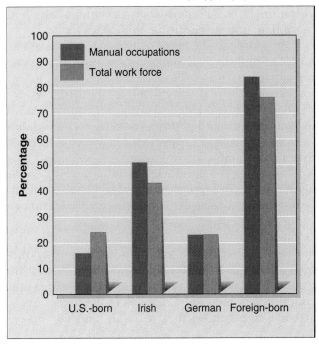

with access to capital ignored craft traditions to rise into the ranks of small businessmen and manufacturers. They expanded output and drove down the cost of production by contracting out work at piece wages and hiring the cheapest workers they could find. The result was to transform the apprentice system into a system of exploited child labor.

By the 1830s, most journeymen were becoming a class of permanent wage earners with little prospect of opening their own shops. Threatened by declining status and income and ever more dependent on a wage for their survival, they denounced the new industrial relations as a "system of mental and physical slavery." To protect their liberties from what they considered a new aristocracy of manufacturers, they organized workingmen's political parties in the 1830s. These parties were broadly reformist and centered in eastern cities. At the top of their list of reforms were free public education, the abolition of imprisonment for debt, and a ten-hour workday. This independent political action was short-lived. The depression of 1839–1843 forced mechanics to concentrate on their economic survival, and the Democrats siphoned off many of their political leaders.

Journeymen also turned to trade union activity in the 1820s and 1830s to gain better wages, shorter hours, and enhanced job security. Benefiting from a strong demand for their skills, workers in the building trades organized the first unions. They were soon followed by shoemakers, printers, and weavers, workers in trades where pressure on urban journeymen was the most intense. Locals from various trades formed the National Trades Union, the first national union, in 1834. The new labor movement launched more than 150 strikes in the mid-1830s.

Although the Panic of 1837 decimated union membership, the early labor movement did achieve two notable victories. First, by the late 1830s, it had forced employers to accept the ten-hour day as the standard for most skilled workers. Second, in a landmark decision handed down in 1842, the Massachusetts Supreme Court ruled in **Commonwealth** v. **Hunt** that a trade union was not necessarily subject to laws against criminal conspiracies and that a strike could be used to force employers to hire only union members. Legally at least, organized labor now had more room to maneuver.

Even at the height of their strength in the mid-1830s, when they may have organized up to one-quarter of the labor force in the larger cities, the trade unions had little to offer unskilled workers and common laborers. The unions were the defenders of artisanal rights and virtues, and they ignored workers whose jobs had never had craft status. As massive immigration merged with industrialization after 1840, this basic division between workers widened. On one side was the male, Protestant, and native-born class of skilled artisans, a group under constant pressure as immigrants poured into the cities and as technological innovation and the division of labor undercut their former control over production. Artisans by midcentury accounted for only 20 percent of the manual workers in the large eastern cities, and two-thirds of these artisans were foreign-born.

On the other side was the working-class majority of factory laborers and the unskilled. These workers were predominantly immigrants and women who worked for a wage as domestic or factory hands. On average, they earned less than $500 a year, about half what skilled workers earned. Their financial survival rested on a family economy in which all members contributed whatever they could earn. The seasonal nature of manual jobs added to the uncertainties of working-class life in cramped tenements, and the tensions frequently exploded in domestic violence.

Artisans continued to think of themselves as independent craftsmen who had little in common with the growing mass of unskilled, foreign-born, and mostly Catholic workers. Indeed, increasingly fearing these workers as a threat to their job security and Protestant values, American-born artisans joined **nativist** organizations in the 1840s that sought to curb mass immigration from Europe and limit the political rights of Catholic immigrants. Ethnic workers viewed temperance as business-class meddling in their lives. In contrast, successful native-born workers tended to embrace the evangelical, middle-class ideology of temperance and self-help. The greatest unity achieved by labor was the nearly universal insistence of whites that blacks be confined to the most menial jobs.

Gender also divided workers. Working-class men shared the dominant ideology of female dependence. They demanded women's services at home and measured their own status as husbands by their ability to keep their wives and daughters from having to work. Beginning in the 1830s, male workers argued that their wages would be higher if women were barred from the work force. A report of the National Trades Union in 1836 cited women's "ruinous competition to male labor." It insisted that a woman's "efforts to sustain herself and family are actually the same as tying a stone around the neck of her natural protector, Man, and destroying him with the weight she has brought to his assistance."

This painting, c. 1829, captures the boisterous disorder and cramped living conditions of the Five Points slum area in New York City.

Because they equated earning wages with manliness and accepted conventional ideas that woman's proper place was in the home, male workers helped lock wage-earning women into the lowest-paying and most exploited jobs. Of the 25,000 women in 1860 working in manufacturing in New York City, two-thirds were in the clothing trades. Many were seamstresses working at home fifteen to eighteen hours a day for starvation wages of less than $100 a year. Over half of them were the sole breadwinners in their households.

"If we do not come forth in our defence, what will become of us?" asked Sarah Monroe of New York City in the midst of a strike by seamstresses in 1831. Women tried to organize as workers, but the male labor movement refused to lend much support. The men tried to channel the discontent of women workers into "proper female behavior" and generally restricted their assistance to pushing for legislation that would limit the hours worked by women and children, a stand that enhanced their male image as protectors of the family. Unable to break free from a gendered notion of domesticity, male workers continued to view women as providers at home and competitors in the workplace.

Conclusion

In 1820, the United States seemed an unlikely candidate for sustained industrialization. Manufacturing activity was a footnote in its agricultural economy. Cheap land was still abundant, and most Americans dreaded the prospect of wage labor in a factory setting. Yet with surprising speed, transportation improvements, technological innovations, and expanding markets drove the economy on a path toward industrialization. As part of this process, wealth inequality increased, old classes were reshaped, and new ones formed. These changes were sharpest in the Northeast, where capital, labor, and expanding urban markets spurred the acceleration of manufacturing.

By 1850, most of the work force in the Northeast was no longer employed in agriculture. In New York, the nation's largest city, wage laborers made up 80 percent of the working population. Still, most Americans dreamed of a life of economic independence on a family farm. This was the great appeal of the West, the nation's fastest-growing region in the first half of the nineteenth century.

Review Questions

1. Why were improvements in transportation so essential to the growth of the economy after 1815? What were the nature and scope of these improvements?
2. What factors contributed to the rapid growth of cities in the Jacksonian era, and what types of cities grew the fastest?
3. What is an industrial revolution, and how can we explain the surge in manufacturing in the United States from 1815 to 1850?
4. Why did economic growth widen the gap between the rich and the poor?
5. How did the class structure change in the first half of the nineteenth century, and how would you characterize the differences between the middle class and manufacturing wage laborers at mid-century?

Recommended Reading

Jeanne Boydston, *Home and Work: Housework, Wages, and the Ideology of Labor in the Early Republic* (1990). This provocative work shows how issues of gender shaped the emergence of a market for labor and influenced the very notion of work itself.

Thomas C. Cochran, *Frontiers of Change: Early Industrialism in America* (1981). This engagingly written narrative argues for the importance of cultural factors in the rise and scope of manufacturing in the United States before 1850.

Brooke Hindle and Steven Lubar, *Engines of Change: The American Industrial Revolution, 1790–1860* (1986). This comprehensive overview is particularly strong in explaining the role of technological innovation in the American industrial revolution.

Jack Larkin, *The Reshaping of Everyday Life, 1790–1840* (1988). This is a very readable depiction of how social and economic changes were reflected in the rhythms and customs of daily life in the first half of the nineteenth century.

Walter Licht, *Industrializing America: The Nineteenth Century* (1995). This smoothly written survey interprets industrialization as both a product and a promoter of economic and social change.

Douglass C. North, *The Economic Growth of the United States, 1780–1860* (1966). North makes an elegant case for viewing the export trade, especially in cotton, as the dynamic element driving antebellum economic growth.

George R. Taylor, *The Transportation Revolution, 1815–1860* (1951). A solid economic history, this classic study persuasively argues that improvements in transportation were the catalyst for the transformation of the nineteenth-century economy.

Additional Sources

The Transportation Revolution

Albert Fishlow, *American Railroads and the Transformation of the Ante-Bellum Economy* (1965).

Carter Goodrich, *Government Promotion of American Canals and Railroads, 1800–1890* (1960).

Louis Hartz, *Economic Policy and Democratic Thought: Pennsylvania, 1776–1860* (1948).

Erik F. Hiates, James Mak, and Gary M. Walton, *Western River Transportation: The Era of Early Internal Development, 1800–1860* (1975).

Morton J. Horowitz, *The Transformation of American Law, 1780–1860* (1977).

Ronald E. Shaw, *Canals for a Nation: The Canal Era in the United States, 1790–1860* (1990).

Peter Way, *Common Labour: Workers and the Digging of North American Canals, 1780–1860* (1993).

The Rise of Cities

Kathleen Neils Conzen, *Immigrant Milwaukee, 1836–1860* (1976).

Oscar Handlin, *Boston's Immigrants: A Study of Acculturation*, rev. ed. (1959).

Marcus L. Hansen, *The Atlantic Migration, 1607–1860* (1940).

Edward K. Spann, *The New Metropolis: New York, 1840–1857* (1981).

Christine Stansel, *City of Women: Sex and Class in New York, 1789–1860* (1986).

Richard C. Wade, *The Urban Frontier* (1964).

The Industrial Revolution

Robert F. Dalzell, *Enterprising Elite: The Boston Associates and the World They Made* (1987).

Thomas Dublin, *Women at Work: The Transformation of Work and Community in Lowell, Massachusetts, 1826–1860* (1979).

Lucy Larcom, *A New England Girlhood* (1889; reprint, 1977).

Merritt Roe Smith, *Harpers Ferry Armory and the New Technology: The Challenge of Change* (1977).

Theodore Steinberg, *Nature Incorporated: Industrialization and the Waters of New England* (1991).

Anthony F. C. Wallace, *Rockdale: The Growth of an American Village in the Early Industrial Revolution* (1978).

Growing Inequality and New Classes

Stuart M. Blumin, *The Emergence of the Middle Class: Social Experience in the American City, 1760–1900* (1989).

Paul E. Johnson, *A Shopkeeper's Millennium: Society and Revivals in Rochester, New York, 1815–1837* (1978).

Bruce Laurie, *Artisans into Workers: Labor in Nineteenth-Century America* (1989).

Edward Pessen, *Riches, Class, and Power before the Civil War* (1973).

David Roediger, *The Wages of Whiteness: Race and the Making of the American Working Class* (1991).

Mary Ryan, *Cradle of the Middle Class: The Family in Oneida County, New York, 1790–1865* (1981).

Sean Wilentz, *Chants Democratic: New York City and the Rise of the American Working Class, 1790–1865* (1984).

Where to Learn More

❖ **Baltimore Center for Urban Archaeology, Baltimore, Maryland.**   Operated by Baltimore City Life Museums, the center has a large collection of artifacts depicting urban life in the eighteenth and nineteenth centuries and a working archaeological library.

❖ **Hanford Mills Museum, East Meredith, New York.** This museum preserves and interprets water-powered machinery and explains the role played by local mills in the community life of the nineteenth century.

❖ **Arabia Museum, Kansas City, Missouri.**   This private museum has a fascinating exhibit of the contents of a steamboat that sank on the Missouri River in 1856. The exhibit reveals the abundance and variety of consumer goods that were being shipped to river towns in the Midwest in the 1850s.

❖ **Slater Hill Historic Site, Pawtucket, Rhode Island.** The Sylvanus Brown House of 1758, the Slaren Mill of 1793, and the Wilkinson Mill of 1810 are on the site. An extensive library and holdings provide insight into the social and economic world of the early industrial revolution.

❖ **Erie Canal Museum, Syracuse, New York.**   The museum houses extensive collections on the building and maintenance of the Erie Canal, and its photo holdings visually record much of the history of the canal.

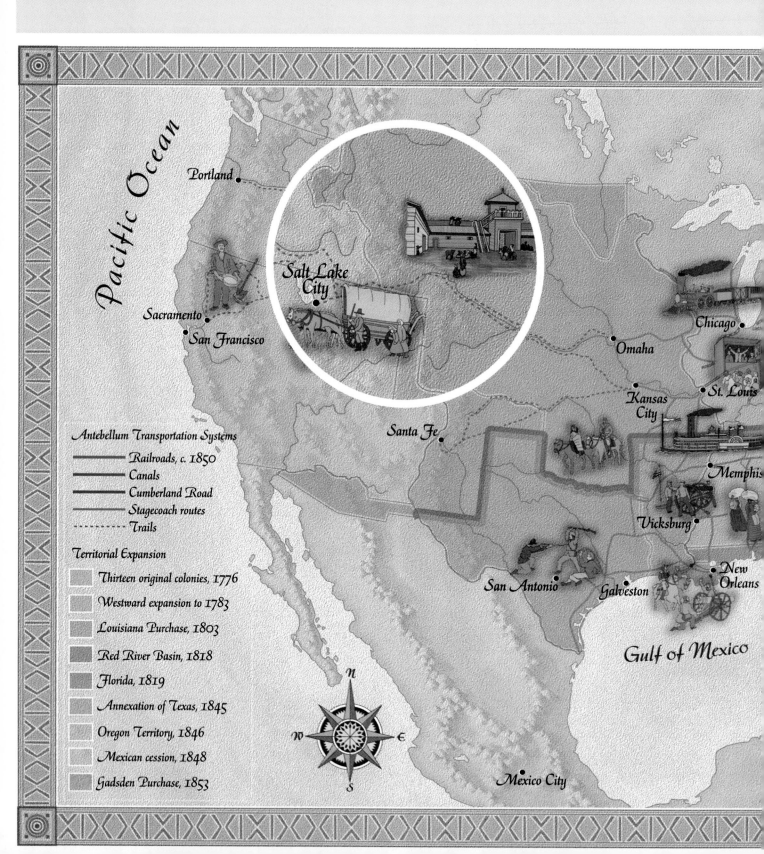

Pacific Ocean

Portland

Salt Lake City

Sacramento

San Francisco

Santa Fe

Omaha

Kansas City

Chicago

St. Louis

Memphis

Vicksburg

San Antonio

Galveston

New Orleans

Gulf of Mexico

Mexico City

Antebellum Transportation Systems

Railroads, c. 1850
Canals
Cumberland Road
Stagecoach routes
Trails

Territorial Expansion

Thirteen original colonies, 1776
Westward expansion to 1783
Louisiana Purchase, 1803
Red River Basin, 1818
Florida, 1819
Annexation of Texas, 1845
Oregon Territory, 1846
Mexican cession, 1848
Gadsden Purchase, 1853

N
W E
S

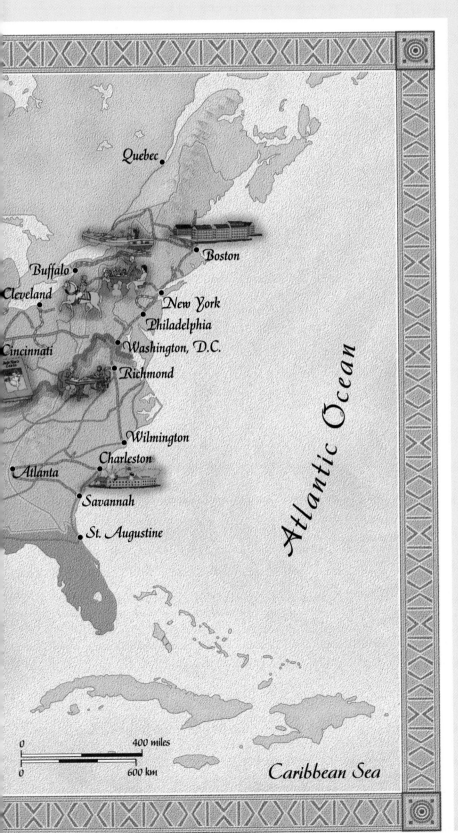

Quebec

Boston

Buffalo

Cleveland

New York

Philadelphia

Cincinnati

Washington, D.C.

Richmond

Wilmington

Charleston

Atlanta

Savannah

St. Augustine

Atlantic Ocean

| 0 | | 400 miles |
| 0 | | 600 km |

Caribbean Sea

KEY TOPICS

❖ Western migration spurred by economic and demographic pressures in the East after the War of 1812

❖ The development of free commercial agriculture tied to eastern markets and increased industrialization and urbanization of the Old Northwest

❖ The development of a plantation economy based on cotton and slavery in the Old Southwest

❖ Manifest Destiny and westward expansion, relegating Native Americans and Mexican-Americans to subjugated status

❖ U.S. annexation of Texas and the wresting of the Southwest and California from Mexico

"*O*ut in Oregon, I can get me a square mile of land," exclaimed a Missourian to his wife in 1843. "I am done with this country. Winters it's frost and snow to freeze a body; summers the overflow from the Old Muddy drowns half my acres. Taxes take the yield of them that's left. What say, Maw . . . it's God's country." And so it proved to be for Peter Burnett. He moved his family to Oregon and then to California, where he became the first governor of the new state, acquired through war with Mexico.

Burnett's family was among the first of the some 300,000 Americans who traveled the Oregon Trail by 1860 and eventually made the United States a nation that spanned the continent. These overlanders, as they came to be known, were part of a restless surge of white settlement that eventually saw more than fifty thousand Americans a year migrate west of the Appalachians after the War of 1812. After moving into the Old Northwest and Old Southwest—the American West of the early nineteenth century—

migrants headed beyond the Mississippi River in the 1840s. The edge of settlement pushed into the Louisiana Purchase territory and across a huge area of plains, desert, mountains, and ocean coast that had seen few American settlers before 1840.

The broad expanse of the trans-Mississippi region had become the new American West by mid-century. The West became a meeting ground of people from diverse cultures as Anglo-Americans came into contact and conflict with Plains Indians and the Mexican-Americans of the Southwest. Convinced of the superiority of their political and cultural values, Anglo-Americans asserted a God-given right to spread across the continent and impose their notions of liberty and democracy on peoples whose land they coveted. In the process, they defeated and subjugated those who stood in their way.

Manifest Destiny was the label for this presumed providential right, and it provided a justification for the aggressively expansionist Democratic administration of James K. Polk that came to power in 1845. The most dramatic result of these policies was the Mexican War of 1846–1848, which made California and the present-day Southwest part of the American continental empire.

The Agricultural Frontier

The U.S. population ballooned from 5.3 million in 1800 to more than 23 million by 1850. The population grew about 33 percent per decade, and four-fifths of this extraordinary gain was from natural increase—the surplus of births over deaths. As the population expanded, it shifted westward. Fewer than one in ten Americans lived west of the Appalachians in 1800; by 1850, about half did (see Map 12-1).

The tremendous amount of land available for settlement accounted for both phenomena. Through purchase and conquest, the land area of the United States more than tripled in the first half of the nineteenth century. Here was space where Americans could raise the large families of a rural society in which, on average, six to eight children

survived to adolescence. Millions of fertile acres lured eastern families ever westward to the next agricultural frontier.

Declining soil fertility and rising population pressure in the rural East generated the impetus behind these migrations. A common desire for greater economic opportunity, however, resulted in two distinct western societies by the 1840s. North of the Ohio River, in the Old Northwest, free labor and family farms defined the social order. South of the Ohio was the Old Southwest, a society dominated by slave labor and the plantation.

The Crowded East

Looking back at his rural youth, Omar H. Morse recalled, "My Parents were in very limited circumstances financially yet blessed with a large family of children which is a poor man's capital though capital of this kind is not considered very available in case of financial Depression." Born in 1824 in the

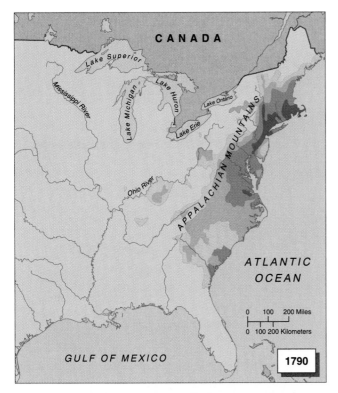

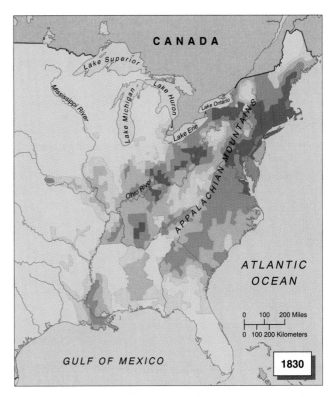

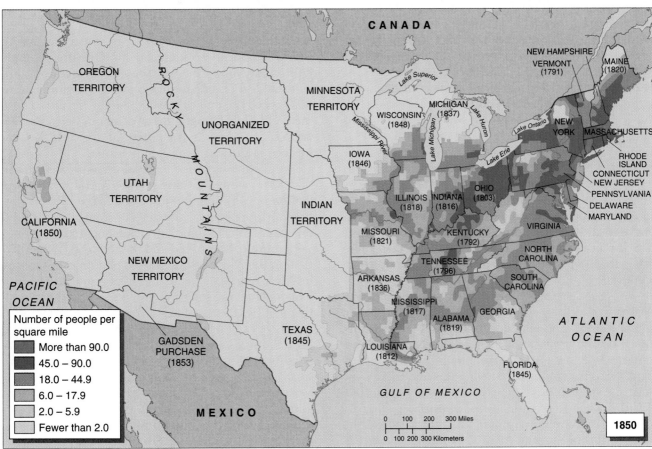

Map 12-1   *The Westward Shift of the United States Population, 1790–1850*
With a speed that was unimaginable in 1790, the United States quickly became a continental nation that stretched from the Atlantic to the Pacific by 1850. Particularly dramatic was the population growth in what became the Midwest.

CHRONOLOGY

1803–1806	Lewis and Clark travel up the Missouri River in search of a water route to the Pacific.
1816	Settlers surge into the trans-Appalachian region.
1821	Mexico gains its independence from Spain.
	Santa Fe Trail opens.
	Stephen F. Austin establishes the first American colony in Texas.
1824	Rocky Mountain Fur Company begins the rendezvous system.
1830	Congress creates the Indian Territory.
1834	Protestant missions are established in Oregon.
	Santa Anna seizes power in Mexico.
1836	Texas wins its independence from Mexico.

1837	Smallpox epidemic hits the Plains Indians.
1842	First large parties of migrants set out on the Oregon Trail.
1845	United States annexes Texas.
	Democrats embrace Manifest Destiny.
1846	Mexican War breaks out.
	United States and Britain reach an agreement in Oregon.
1847	Mormons begin settlement of Utah.
1848	Oregon Territory is organized.
	Treaty of Guadalupe Hidalgo ends the Mexican War.
1851	Fort Laramie Treaty with the Plains Indians is signed.

upstate New York village of Hastings, Morse was typical of the hard-pressed eastern youth who moved west after the War of 1812. With no prospect of inheriting land from his father and tired of taking orders as a farm hand for temporary wages, he moved in the 1840s to Wisconsin, where he found what he thought was "the most beautiful spot of country on God's green Earth." Even after this fresh start, bad luck and too many debts prevented Morse from ever achieving landed independence. He lost three farms and eventually settled in Minnesota, where he worked at odd jobs and built houses. Heading west did not guarantee economic success, but it was the best option open to land-starved easterners who dreamed of leaving a productive farm to their children.

By the early nineteenth century, land was scarce in the East, especially in New England. After generations of population growth and subdivisions of landholdings to male heirs, most New England communities no longer had enough arable land to satisfy all the young men who wanted their own farms. Even recently opened areas such as Vermont felt the pressure of rural overpopulation.

Land was more productive and expensive farther south, in the mid-Atlantic states. Keyed to the major export crop of wheat, agriculture was more commercialized than in New England, and economic inequality was thus higher. Successful farmers became wealthy by specializing in wheat and hiring the rural poor to work their fields. One-third to one-half of the young men in the commercialized agricultural districts of New Jersey and Pennsylvania were landless by the end of the eighteenth century. These men and their families, many of whom were recently arrived Scots-Irish and German immigrants, led the western migration from Pennsylvania.

The pressure to move west was greatest in the slave states along the eastern seaboard. Although population density here was just two-thirds of that in New England, ordinary whites faced even more limited prospects of economic advancement. Landholdings were more concentrated and the soil more exhausted than in the Northeast. Repeated plantings of tobacco in Virginia and Maryland and of cotton farther south had depleted the soil throughout much of the region. In the Chesapeake states, established planters with extensive capital and labor resources shifted to wheat production or bought out their nonslaveholding neighbors. Tenants who wanted their own land and small farmers tired of competing against slave labor were forced west across the mountains. They were joined by the sons of planters. Despite marriages arranged to keep land within the wealthy families, there was no longer enough good land left to carve out plantations for all the younger sons.

By the early 1800s, the young and the poor in the rural East faced limited opportunities for social mobility and economic independence. They had every incentive to head west, where fertile land was abundant, accessible, and, at $2 to $3 per acre, far cheaper than in the East. Land was the basis of wealth and social standing, and its ownership separated the independent from the dependent, the rooted from the rootless. According to the principles of Jeffersonian democracy, the independent farmer was the backbone of the republic, the virtuous citizen who made republican government possible. "Those who labor in the earth," Jefferson wrote in 1785, "are the chosen people of God . . . whose breasts He has made his peculiar deposit for substantial and genuine virtue."

The western settler, observed a traveler on the Missouri frontier in the 1820s, wanted "to be a freeholder, to have plenty of rich land, and to be able to settle his children around him." Government policy under the Jeffersonian Republicans and Jacksonian Democrats attempted to make it easier to reach these goals. Central to the land policy of the federal government after 1800 was the conviction that political liberties rested on the broadest possible base of land ownership. Thus public policy and private aspirations merged in the belief that access to land was the key to preserving American freedom.

When Jefferson took office in 1801, the minimum price for public land was $2 per acre, and a block of 320 acres had to be purchased at one time. By the 1830s, the price of public land was down to $1.25, and the minimum purchase was only 80 acres. Congress also protected squatters, who had settled on public land before it was surveyed, from being outbid by speculators at a land sale. The Preemption Act of 1841 guaranteed the right to purchase up to 160 acres at the minimum price of $1.25 when the public auction was held.

The Old Northwest

The number of Americans who settled in the heartland of the Old Northwest—Ohio, Indiana, and Illinois—rose tenfold from 1810 to 1840. Ohio had already entered the Union in 1803; Indiana joined in 1816, Illinois in 1818. The end of the War of 1812 and the abandonment by the British of their former Indian allies opened up the region to a flood of migrants.

Travelers passing through the Ohio Valley just after the war were astonished by the number of Americans trekking west. Wagonloads of migrants bounced along turnpikes to disembark on the Ohio River at Pittsburgh and Wheeling, where they bought flatboats to carry them down the Ohio to the interior river valleys. Moving north across the Ohio were families from the hill country of Virginia and Kentucky. These two streams of migrants, one predominantly northern and the other southern, met in the lower Midwest and viewed each other as strangers. Lucy Maynard, a New Englander living in south-central Illinois, noted that her neighbors were "principally from Indiana and Kentucky, some from Virginia, all friendly but very different from our people in their manners and language and every other way."

The Old Northwest was less a melting pot in which regional cultures merged than a mosaic of settlements in which the different values and folkways of regional cultures from throughout the East took root and expanded. Belts of migration generally ran along a line from east to west as settlers sought out soil types and ecological conditions similar to those they had left behind. Thus the same North-South cultural differences that existed along the Atlantic seaboard in 1800 were to be found half a century later in the Mississippi Valley.

A transplanted Yankee culture from New England and upstate New York spread over the upper Midwest—northern Ohio, Indiana, and Illinois, as well as Michigan and Wisconsin. These westerners were Whiggish in their politics, tended to be

Clearing the land and erecting a log cabin were the first steps in creating a farm on the western frontier.

antislavery, and valued a communal sense of responsibility that regulated moral behavior and promoted self-improvement. The highland Southerners who settled the lower Midwest—southern Ohio, Indiana, and Illinois, as well as Kentucky—were Democrats: They fiercely distrusted any centralized authority, political or moral, and considered Yankees intolerant do-gooders. Holding the balance of cultural and political power were the migrants from Pennsylvania and New Jersey, who were accustomed to ethnic diversity and the politics of competing economic groups. They settled principally in central Ohio, Indiana, and Illinois. By emphasizing economic growth and downplaying the cultural politics that pitted Yankees against Southerners, they built a consensus around community development.

Much as they had done in the East, the early settlers practiced a diversified agriculture to feed and shelter their families. The first task was to clear the land and sow a crop of corn, a hardy grain that required little care. Wild game and livestock left to forage in the woods supplemented the corn-based diet.

It took about ten years of backbreaking labor to create an 80-acre farm in heavily wooded sections. The Northwest Ordinance of 1787 had barred slavery north of the Ohio, so settlers had to do the work themselves or hire farm hands. The work of women was essential for the success of the farm and the production of any salable surplus. Wives and daughters helped tend the field crops, milked cows and churned butter, and produced the homespun cloth that, along with their dairy goods, found a market in the first country stores on the frontier. Charlotte Webb Jacobs, from the Sugar

Creek community on the Illinois prairie, proudly recalled, "I made everything that we wore; I even made my towels and table cloths, sheets and everything in the clothing line."

Because outside labor was scarce and expensive, communities pooled their efforts for such tasks as raising a cabin. Groups of settlers also acted as a cooperative unit at public land auctions. Local associations known as **claims clubs** enforced the extralegal right of squatters to enter noncompetitive bids on land they had settled and improved. Members of the clubs physically intimidated speculators who refused to step aside until local settlers had acquired the land they wanted.

The high cost of hauling goods to outside markets kept the early frontier economy at a level barely above crude self-sufficiency. Any surplus was sold to newcomers moving into the area or bartered with local storekeepers for essentials such as salt, sugar, and metalwares. This relative self-sufficiency, however, soon gave way to a more commercially oriented agriculture when steamboats, canals, and railroads opened up vast new markets (see Chapter 11). Western lands were at least twice as fertile as those in the East, and farmers could now profit from their bountiful yields.

The first large market was in the South, down the corridor of the Ohio and Mississippi Rivers, and the major staples were corn and hogs. By the 1830s, the Erie Canal and its feeder waterways in the upper Midwest began to reorient much of the western farm trade to the Northeast. Wheat, because of its ready marketability for milling into flour, became the major cash crop for the northern market.

Cyrus McCormick pioneered the development of horse-drawn mechanical reapers. Shown here demonstrating his reaper to potential customers, McCormick helped revolutionize American agriculture with labor-saving machinery that made possible far larger harvests of grain crops.

Wheat production skyrocketed when settlers overcame their initial reluctance to farming in a treeless terrain and moved into the prairies of Indiana and Illinois in the 1840s. New plows—a cast-iron one patented by Jethro Wood in 1819 and a steel version developed by John Deere in 1837—helped break the thick prairie sod. The plows were soon followed by horse-drawn mechanical harvesters and equipped with a self-rake reaper that enabled family farmers to harvest vastly more wheat by the 1840s. Traditional harvesting methods that relied on a worker using a scythe with a cradle frame were slow and relatively expensive. An experienced worker could cut no more than 2 acres a day. The same worker with the new machinery could harvest 12 acres a day, and the per-acre cost of labor fell dramatically. Once railroads provided direct access to eastern markets, the Midwest became the nation's breadbasket.

Although southern cotton was the raw material that fueled New England textile factories in the first stages of industrialization, the commercialization of agriculture in the West also contributed to the growth of eastern manufacturing. The productivity of western farms supplied eastern manufacturers with inexpensive raw materials for processing into finished goods. By flooding national markets with corn and wheat, western produce not only supplied eastern workers with cheap food but also forced noncompetitive eastern farmers either to move west or to work in factories in eastern cities. In turn, the West itself became an ever-growing market for eastern factory goods. For example, nearly half of the nation's iron production in the 1830s was fashioned into farm implements.

In the 1820s, the farm economy of the Old Northwest was just emerging from semisubsistence and depended on the southern trade. Thirty years later, at midcentury, the Old Northwest had become part of a larger Midwest whose economy was increasingly integrated with that of the Northeast. Settlers continued to pour into the region, and three additional states—Michigan (1837), Iowa (1846), and Wisconsin (1848)—joined the Union.

The combination of favorable farm prices and steadily decreasing transportation costs generated a rise in disposable income that was spent on outside goods or invested in internal economic development. A network of canals and railroads was laid down, and manufacturing cities grew out of towns that were aggressively promoted and favorably situated by water or rail transport. There was still room for subsistence farming, but the West north of the Ohio was now economically specialized and socially diverse.

The Old Southwest

"The *Alabama Feaver* rages here with great violence and has *carried off* vast numbers of our Citizens," wrote a North Carolina planter in 1817 about the westward migration from his state. "I am apprehensive, if it continues to spread as it has done, it will almost depopulate the country." The planter, James Graham, had reason to be concerned. About as many people migrated from the old slave states in the East to the Old Southwest as those states gained by natural increase in the 1820s and 1830s. By 1850, more than 600,000 whites born in Maryland, Virginia, and the Carolinas lived in slave states to the south and west, and many of them had brought their slaves with them. Indeed, from 1790 to 1860, more than 800,000 slaves were moved from the South Atlantic region into the Old Southwest.

Soaring cotton prices after the War of 1812 and the smashing of Indian confederations during the war, which opened new lands to whites, propelled the first surge of migration into the Old Southwest. High cotton prices, which peaked at 30 cents a pound before plunging in the Panic of 1819, drew planters to western Tennessee and the Black Belt, a crescent-shaped band of rich, black loamy soil arcing westward from Georgia through central Alabama and Mississippi.

Migration surged anew in the 1830s when cotton prices were again high and the Chickasaws and Choctaws had been forced out of the incredibly fertile Delta country between the Yazoo and Mississippi Rivers (see Chapter 10). The 1840s brought Texas fever to replace the Alabama fever of the 1810s, and a steady movement to the Southwest rounded out the contours of the cotton South. In less than thirty years, six new slave states—Mississippi (1817), Alabama (1819), Missouri (1821), Arkansas (1836), Florida (1845), and Texas (1845)—joined the Union (see the summary table "Westward Expansion and the Growth of the Union, 1815–1850").

The southwestern frontier attracted both slaveholding planters and small independent farmers. The best known, though a minority, were the planters and their sons. They had the capital or the credit to acquire the best lands and the slave labor to make those lands productive. In abandoning the light, sandy, and overworked soils of eastern plantations for the far richer alluvial and prairie soils of the Old Southwest, these slaveholders were responding both to the need for fresh land and to the extraordinary demand for short-staple cotton. As one North Carolina planter put it, Alabama would be a "garden of plenty" compared to the "old-fields and empty corn-houses" of his native state.

Short-staple cotton could be grown anywhere with a minimum of 210 consecutive frost-free days. The crop, however, was of minor commercial importance before Eli Whitney's gin (and its numerous imitators) in the 1790s eliminated the problem of removing the sticky, green seeds from the fiber, an essential step in preparing the cotton to be spun and woven into cloth. The cotton gin was fifty times faster than hand separation. Meanwhile, the mechanization of the British textile industry had created a seemingly unquenchable demand for raw cotton. No place in the world was better positioned to meet that demand than the American South. Most important, a slave labor force was available to work the land. Led by the booming output of the new plantations in the Old Southwest, the South increased its share of world cotton production from 9 percent in 1800 to 68 percent in 1850.

Thanks to cotton and slavery, aggressive, hard-driving planters loomed large in the Old Southwest. But far more typical settlers on the southern frontier were small independent yeomen farmers, who generally owned no slaves. They usually settled in the valleys, on the ridges, and in the hill country. They often soon sold out to neighboring planters and headed west. Many of them shared the belief of the yeoman farmer Gideon Linecum "in the pleasure of frequent change of country."

The yeomanry moved onto the frontier in two waves. The first consisted of stockmen-hunters, a restless, transient group who spread from the pine barrens in the Carolina backcountry to the coastal plain of eastern Texas. They prized unfettered independence and measured their wealth in the livestock left to roam and fatten on the sweet grasses of uncleared forests. They were quick to move on when farmers, the second wave, started to clear the land for crops.

Like the stock herders, the yeoman farmers valued self-sufficiency and the leisure to hunt and fish. In pursuit of these goals, they practiced a diversified agriculture aimed at feeding their families. Corn and pork were the mainstays of their diet, and both could readily be produced as long as there was room for the open-range herding of swine and growing patches of corn and small grains. The more ambitious farmers, usually those who owned one or two slaves, grew some cotton, but most preferred to avoid the economic risks of cotton production. The yeoman's chief source of labor was his immediate family, and to expand that labor force to produce cotton meant going into debt to purchase slaves. That debt could easily cost the yeoman his farm if market prices for cotton fell.

Measured by per capita income, and as a direct result of the profits from slave-produced cotton on virgin soils, the Old Southwest was a

The internal slave trade was the primary means by which the slaves of the Upper South were brought into the plantation markets of the Old Southwest. Shown below are professional slave traders driving a chained group of slaves, known as a coffle, to perspective buyers in the Lower South.

SUMMARY

WESTWARD EXPANSION AND THE GROWTH OF THE UNION, 1815–1850

New Free States	New Slave States	Territories (1850)
Indiana, 1816	Mississippi, 1817	Minnesota
Illinois, 1818	Alabama, 1819	Oregon
Maine, 1820	Missouri, 1821	New Mexico
Michigan, 1837	Arkansas, 1836	Utah
Iowa, 1846	Florida, 1845	
Wisconsin, 1848	Texas, 1845	
California, 1850		

wealthier society than the Old Northwest in 1850. Moreover, in the short term, the settlement of the Old Southwest was also more significant for national economic development. Cotton accounted for more than half the value of all American exports after the mid-1830s. More than any other commodity, cotton paid for American imports and underpinned national credit. But southern prosperity was not accompanied by the same economic development and social change that marked the Old Northwest. Compared to the slave West in 1860, the free-labor West was twice as urbanized, and far more of its work force was engaged in nonagricultural pursuits.

The Southwest Ordinance, enacted by Congress in 1790, opened all territories south of the Ohio River to slavery. Slaves, land, and cotton were the keys to wealth on the southern frontier, and agricultural profits were continually plowed back into more land and slaves to produce more cotton. In contrast, prosperous farmers in the Old Northwest lacked the slaves needed to work additional acres. Hence they were much more likely to invest their earnings in promotional schemes designed to attract settlers whose presence would raise land values and increase business for local merchants and entrepreneurs. As early as the 1840s, rural communities in the Old Northwest were supporting bustling towns that offered jobs in trade and manufacturing on a scale far sur-

passing anything in the slave West. By the 1850s, the Midwest was almost as urbanized as the Northeast had been in 1830, and nearly half the labor force no longer worked on farms.

The Old Southwest remained overwhelmingly agricultural. Once the land was settled, the children of the first generation of slaveholders and yeomen moved west to the next frontier rather than compete for the good land that was left. Relatively few newcomers took their place. By the 1850s, Kentucky, Tennessee, Alabama, and Mississippi—the core states of the Old Southwest—were all losing more migrants than they were gaining; that is, discounting for natural increase, more people were leaving these states than entering.

The Frontier of the Plains Indians

Few white Americans had ventured west of the Mississippi by 1840. What scanty knowledge there was of this huge inland expanse was the result of government-sponsored expeditions. Reports of explorations of the southern Plains by Zebulon Pike in 1806 and Stephen Long in 1819 dismissed the area as the Great American Desert, an arid, treeless landscape with little agricultural potential, fit only for the Indians being removed from the East. The vast plains and plateaus climbing westward to the foothills of the Rocky Mountains in a seemingly endless ocean of grass were unfamiliar and intimidating to farmers accustomed to the wooded, well-watered, humid East.

Moreover, Americans had no legal claim to much of the Trans-Mississippi West—or merely the paper title of the Louisiana Purchase, to which none of the native inhabitants had acquiesced. Beyond Texas and the boundary line drawn by the Trans-Continental Treaty of 1819 lay the northern possessions of Mexico. Horse-mounted Indian tribes dominated by the Sioux were a formidable power on the central Plains northward to the Canadian boundary.

Before the 1840s, Americans lacked the interest, numbers, and concerted military power to control this Far West, held by other peoples. Only fur trappers and traders, who worked with and not against the powerful Sioux, had pushed across the Great Plains and into the Rockies. The 1840s brought a sudden change, a large migration westward that radically altered the ecology of the Great Plains. Farm families trapped in an agricultural depression and enticed by Oregon's bounty turned the trails blazed by the fur traders into ruts on the Oregon Trail, the route that led to the first large settlement of Americans on the Pacific Coast.

Tribal Lands

At least 350,000 Native Americans lived in the plains and mountains of the Trans-Mississippi West in 1840. They were loosely organized into tribal groups, each with its own territory and way of life. Most of them inhabited the Great Plains region that lay north and west of the Indian Territory reserved for eastern tribes in the present state of Oklahoma. The point where the prairies of the Midwest gave way to the higher, drier plains marked a rough division between predominantly agricultural tribes to the east and nomadic, hunting tribes to the west. The Kansas, Osages, and Omahas in what is now Kansas and Iowa and the Arikaras, Mandans, and Hidatsas along the upper Missouri River grew corn, beans, and squash and lived in semipermanent villages, much as woodland Indians had in the East. On the open plains were hunting and raiding peoples, such as the western Sioux, Crows, Cheyennes, and Arapahos.

In the 1830s, the U.S. government set aside a broad stretch of country between the Platte River to the north and the Red River to the south (most of present-day Oklahoma and eastern Kansas) exclusively for Indians. This Indian Territory was reserved for tribes resettled from the East under the Indian Removal Act of 1830 and for village-living groups native to the area. Many government officials envisioned this territory as a permanent sanctuary that would separate Indians from whites and allow them to live in peace on allotments of land granted to individual tribes as compensation for the territory they had ceded to the federal government in earlier treaties. However, even as Congress was debating the idea of a permanent Indian reserve that would be a U.S. government protectorate, the pressure exerted on native peoples in the Mississippi Valley both by raiding parties of Plains Indians and by the incessant demands of white farmers and speculators for more land was rendering a stable Indian-white boundary meaningless.

On the eve of Indian removal in the East, the Sauks, Foxes, Potawatomis, and other Indian peoples inhabited Iowa. The defeat of the Sauks and Foxes in what whites called Black Hawk's War of 1832 opened Iowa to white settlement and forced tribes to cede land. In 1838, Congress created the Territory of Iowa, which encompassed all the land between the Mississippi and Missouri Rivers north of the state of Missouri, and the Indians were now on the verge of being pushed completely out of Iowa. Throughout the upper Mississippi Valley in the 1830s, other groups suffered a similar fate as the number of displaced Indians swelled.

The first to be displaced were farming peoples whose villages straddled the woodlands to the east and the open plains to the west. These border tribes were caught in a vise between the loss of their land to advancing whites and the seizure of their horses and agricultural provisions by Indian raiders from the plains. The Pawnees were among the hardest hit.

By the 1830s, the Pawnees were primarily an agricultural people who embarked on seasonal hunts for game in the Platte River Valley. In 1833, they signed a treaty with the U.S. government in which they agreed to withdraw from south of the Platte in return for subsidies and military protection from the hostile Indians on the plains. Once they moved north of the Platte, the Pawnees were attacked by Sioux who seized control of the prime hunting grounds. Moreover, the Pawnee agricultural villages tempted Sioux raiders seeking provisions and horses. When the desperate Pawnees filtered back south of the Platte, in violation of the treaty of 1833, they were constantly harassed by whites. In vain the Pawnee leaders cited the provisions of the same treaty that promised them protection from the Sioux. Forced back north of the Platte by the U.S. government, the Pawnees were eventually driven out of their Nebraska homeland by the Sioux.

The Sioux were the dominant power on the northern and central Great Plains, more than able to hold their own against white Americans in the first half of the nineteenth century. The Tetons, Yanktons, and Yanktonais comprised the main divisions of the western Sioux. In the eighteenth century, these western Sioux had separated from their woodland kin (known as the Santee Sioux), left their homeland along the headwaters of the Mississippi River, and pushed onto the Minnesota prairies. Armed with guns they had acquired from the French, the western Sioux dominated the prairies east of the Missouri River by 1800.

The Sioux learned to use the horse from the Plains Indians. Introduced to the New World by the

Spanish, horses had revolutionized the lives of native peoples on the Great Plains. As they acquired more horses through trading and raids, the Plains Indians evolved a distinctly new and nomadic culture. Horses made buffalo hunting vastly more productive, they made it easier to transport bulky possessions, and they made possible an aggressive, highly mobile form of warfare. The Sioux were the most successful of all the tribes in melding two facets of the white man's culture, the gun and the horse, into an Indian culture of warrior-hunters.

Although the Sioux frequently fought other tribes, casualties from these encounters were light. The Sioux and other Plains Indians fought not to kill the greatest number of the enemy but rather to dominate hunting grounds and to win individual honor by "counting coup" (touching a live foe). When an Army officer in 1819 urged the Sioux to make peace with the Chippewas, Little Crow, a Santee Sioux, explained why war was preferable: "Why, then, should we give up such an extensive country to save the life of a man or two annually?"

When the United States acquired title to the Great Plains in the Louisiana Purchase of 1803, the western Sioux economy was based on two seasonally restricted systems of hunting. In summer, they hunted buffalo on horse on the plains. In winter, they trapped beaver. In spring, great trading fairs were held in which the western Sioux exchanged their buffalo robes and beaver pelts for goods acquired by the Santee Sioux from European traders.

As the supply of beaver dwindled and the demand for buffalo hides from American and European traders increased in the early 1800s, the Sioux extended their buffalo hunts. In a loose alliance with the Cheyennes and Arapahos, Sioux war parties pushed aside or subjugated weaker tribes to the south and west of the Missouri River basin. The Sioux gained access to new sources for buffalo and raided the village tribes for horses and provisions. Reduced to a dependent status, these tribes were forced to rely on the Sioux for meat and trading goods.

Epidemic diseases brought to the plains by white traders helped Sioux expansion. Because they lived in small wandering bands, the Sioux were less susceptible to these epidemics than the more sedentary village peoples. The Sioux were also one of the first tribes to be vaccinated against smallpox by doctors sent up the Missouri River by the Bureau of Indian Affairs in the early 1830s. Smallpox reached the plains in the 1780s, and a major epidemic in 1837 probably halved the region's Indian population. Particularly hard hit were tribes attempting to resist the Sioux advance. Sioux losses were relatively light and, unlike the other tribes, their population grew.

Some 25,000 strong by 1850, the western Sioux had increased in power and numbers since they first encountered American officials during the

Shown here is a Lakota shirt, c. 1850, that was specially woven for those Sioux warriors who had distinguished themselves in battle. The blue and yellow dyes symbolize sky and earth, and the strands of human hair represent the acts of bravery performed in defense of the Lakota people.

Lewis and Clark Expedition in 1804 and 1805. Even then, Jefferson had cautioned Lewis to cultivate good relations with the Sioux "because of their immense power." Lewis and Clark minced no words when they wrote of the Sioux. "These are the vilest miscreants of the savage race, and must ever remain the pirates of the Missouri, until such measures are pursued by our government as will make them feel a dependence on its will for their supply of merchandise."

Words were one thing, gaining power over the Sioux another. Americans could vilify the Sioux, but they could not force them into dependence in the first half of the nineteenth century. The Sioux continued to extend their influence, and they were shrewd enough to align themselves with the Americans whenever their interests dictated conciliation.

The Fur Traders

"Curiosity, a love of wild adventure, and perhaps also a hope of profit—for times *are* hard, and my best coat has a sort of sheepish hang-dog hesitation to encounter fashionable folk—combined to make me look upon the project with an eye of favour." As best he could recollect, these were the motives that induced Warren A. Ferris, a New York civil engineer, to join the American Fur Company in 1829 at the age of 19 and go west as a fur trapper and mountain man. When Ferris joined up, the American fur trade in the Trans-Mississippi West—and the spirit of adventure it stirred—was at its height. During their golden age in the 1820s and 1830s, the trappers blazed the trails that far greater numbers of white settlers would follow in the 1840s.

The western fur trade originated in the rivalry between British and American companies for profitable furs, especially beaver pelts. Until the early 1820s, the Hudson's Bay Company, a well-capitalized British concern, dominated the trans-Mississippi fur trade. A breakthrough for American interests came in 1824 when two St. Louis businessmen, William Henry Ashley and Andrew Henry of the Rocky Mountain Fur Company, developed the rendezvous system, which eliminated the need for permanent and costly posts deep in Indian territory. In keeping with Indian traditions of periodic intertribal meetings, the rendezvous system brought together trappers, Indians, and traders in a grand annual fair at a designated site in the high mountain country of Wyoming. White trappers and Indians exchanged the animal skins they had gathered in the seasonal hunt for the guns, traps, tobacco, whiskey, textiles, and other trading goods that agents of the fur companies in St. Louis brought to the fair.

The mountain men signed up for two- or three-year stints with the fur companies. Except for the annual fairs, they lived isolated, hard lives in the wilderness. Their closest relations were with Indians, and about 40 percent of the trappers married Indian women, unions that often linked them economically and diplomatically to their bride's tribe.

Living conditions in the wilderness were primitive, even brutal. Mortality rates among trappers ran as high as 80 percent a year. Death often came suddenly from an accidental gunshot wound, an encounter with a grizzly, or an arrow from an Indian whose hunting grounds a trapper had transgressed. Survival required techniques that a "civilized" American would find repellent. Many a trapper avoided death from dehydration by sucking blood from the sliced vein of a horse or drinking the watery contents from the stomach of a buffalo carcass. "Peg-Leg" Smith became a legend for amputating his own leg after it was shattered by a bullet.

For all its dangers, the life of a trapper appealed to unattached young men like Warren Ferris. They were fleeing the confinements, as well as the

The annual rendezvous in Wyoming of fur trappers and traders was a multinational affair in which Anglo-Americans, French Canadians, Mexican-Americans, and Native Americans gathered to trade, drink, and swap stories.

comforts, of white civilization and were as free as they could be. When on a hunt with the Indians, they were part of a spectacle unknown to other white Americans, one that was already passing into history. "Fancy to yourself," Ferris asked readers of his published journals, "three thousand horses of every variety of size and colour, with trappings almost as varied as their appearance . . . ridden by a thousand souls . . . their persons fantastically ornamented. . . . Listen to the rattle of numberless lodgepoles [trailed] by packhorses. . . . Yonder see a hundred horsemen pursuing a herd of antelopes." He was describing the color, bustle, and motion at the start of a hunt with the Salish Indians of Montana in the 1830s, played out on "a beautiful level prairie, with dark blue snow-capped mountains in the distance for the *locale.*"

Such spectacles were increasingly rare after 1840, the year of the last mountain men's rendezvous on the Green River in Wyoming. The most exploitive phase of the fur trade in the 1830s had ravaged the fur-bearing animals and accelerated the spread of smallpox among the tribes. Whiskey, the most profitable item among the white man's trading goods, had corrupted countless Indians and undermined the vitality of tribal cultures.

The mountain men were about to pass into legend, but before they did, they explored every trail and path from the front (or eastern) range of the Rockies to the Pacific. They had gone where no white man had gone before. The main trading corridor of the fur trade—up the lower Missouri to the North Platte and across the plains to the South Pass, a wide plateau crossing the Continental Divide, and into the Wyoming basin— became the main overland route to the West that migrating farm families followed in the 1840s. The mountain men had removed the mystery of western geography, and in so doing they hastened the end of the frontier conditions that had made their unique way of life possible.

The Oregon Trail

The ruts are still there. One can follow them to the horizon in the Platte River Valley of Nebraska and the dry tablelands of Wyoming, Idaho, and Nevada. They were put there by the wheels of wagons hauled by oxen on a jolting 2,000-mile journey across plains, mountains, and deserts from Missouri to Oregon, Utah, and California (see Map 12-2). Some 150,000 Americans made this overland trek in the heyday of the **Oregon Trail** in the 1840s and early 1850s (see Figure 12-1). Most of them walked alongside their wagons. They covered up to 15 miles a day on a trip that lasted close to six months.

Before the 1830s, few Americans had heard of Oregon, and practically none lived there. Under

Map 12-2 Western Overland Trails
The great overland trails to the West began at the Missouri River. The Oregon Trail crossed South Pass in Wyoming and then branched off to Oregon, California, or Utah. The Santa Fe Trail carried American goods and traders to the Mexican Southwest.

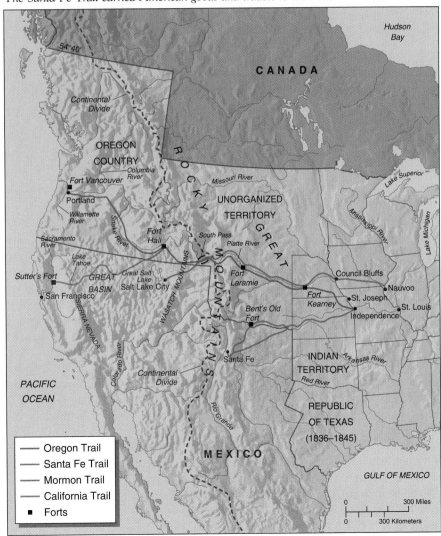

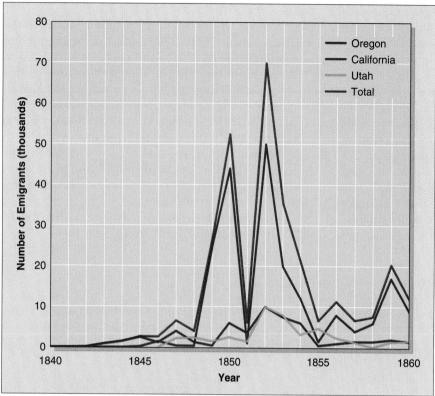

Figure 12.1   *Overland Emigration to the West, 1840–1860*
Emigration to the Trans-Mississippi West steadily increased in the 1840s as farm families moved to Oregon or Utah. After the discovery of gold in California in 1849, California attracted the bulk of the emigrants, many of whom were single men hopeful of striking it rich.

Source: *John D. Unruh Jr.*, The Plains Across: The Overland Emigrants and the Trans-Mississippi West, 1840–60 (1982), pp. 84–85.

ture based on hunting and fishing and become farm laborers for whites. Unlike the trappers, the missionaries sought to change the entire structure of Indian life and beliefs. During a measles epidemic in 1847, the Cayuses killed two of the most prominent missionaries, Marcus and Narcissa Whitman. In retaliation, white Americans, who now numbered more than five thousand, virtually exterminated the Cayuses.

The first large party of overlanders left Independence, Missouri, in 1842 for the Willamette Valley. Independence and St. Joseph in Missouri and, by the 1850s, Council Bluffs in Iowa were the jumping-off points for the Oregon Trail. Each town competed to capture the lucrative trade of outfitting the migrants. There was more than enough trade to go around. Merchants profited from supplying, usually at inflated prices, wagons, mules, oxen, guns, ammunition, and staples like flour, bacon, and sugar.

Most overlanders were young farm families from the Midwest, who had moved at least once before in their restless search for the perfect farm that would keep them out of debt. Indeed, Medorum Crawford said of one family that made the journey to Oregon with him in 1842 and then quickly left for California: "They had practically lived in the wagon for more than twenty years, only remaining in one locality long enough to make a crop, which they had done in every State and Territory in the Mississippi Valley."

Usually the male head of a household made the decision to move. Women regretted giving up ties with kin and friends, which provided security and assistance in their isolated, rural lives. They were well aware of the dangers of childbirth on a long, hard journey. Besides their usual work of minding the children and cooking and cleaning, they would now have to help drive wagons and tend livestock. Still, many women were also optimistic about the journey. "Ho—for California—at last we are on the way," exclaimed Helen Carpenter in 1857, "and with good luck may

an agreement reached in 1818, the Oregon Country was still jointly administered by the United States and Great Britain. Furs—whether beaver pelts or the skins of the Pacific sea otter—had attracted a few American trappers and merchants, but the British-controlled Hudson's Bay Company dominated the region. Protestant missionaries established the first permanent white settlements in the 1830s. Under the leadership of Jason Lee, they set up their missions in the fertile Willamette Valley, south of the Columbia River. Reports of Oregon's fertility that the missionaries sent east sparked the first popular interest in the region, especially among Midwestern farmers stuck in the agricultural depression that followed the Panic of 1837.

While the missionaries were publicizing Oregon and attracting future settlers, they repeatedly failed to convert the Indians to Christianity. With their numbers already thinned by the diseases brought in by the trappers, Oregon tribes such as the Cayuses refused to abandon their traditional cul-

some day reach the 'promised land.'" A study of 159 women's trail diaries indicates that about one-third of the women strongly favored the move, and Margaret Frink undoubtedly spoke for many when she recalled that she "never had occasion to regret the prolonged hardships of the toilsome journey." By adapting to the new conditions of trail life—pitching tents, yoking oxen, cooking over open fires, and gathering buffalo chips (dried dung used for fuel)—women learned skills that would help them start a new life in the West.

The overlanders faced a long, dangerous journey. In the 1840s, some five thousand of the ninety thousand men, women, and children who set out on the Oregon Trail died along the way. Although the overlanders were terrified of encountering Indians, whom they assumed would be hostile, few died from Indian attacks. As long as the wagon trains were just passing through their lands, the Plains Indians left the whites alone. At first they watched with bemused curiosity, and then, as the whites kept coming, they traded game for clothing and ammunition. Indians killed only 115 migrants in the 1840s, and trigger-happy whites provoked most clashes. Disease, especially cholera, was the great killer. Second to disease were accidents, especially drownings when drivers tried to force overloaded wagons across swollen rivers.

Cooperation was the key to a successful overland crossing. Families, not individuals, comprised the basic social unit, and they were part of networks of kin and neighbors who had banded together for the westward journey. The men often drew up a formal, written constitution at the start of the trip spelling out the assignments and work responsibilities of each wagon. Before the trail was well marked, former mountain men hired on as captains to lead the wagon train. Timing was crucial. The wagon train had to leave late enough in the spring to get good grass in Nebraska for the oxen and mules. A wagon train that departed too early risked getting bogged down in spring mud; one that left late risked the

As shown in the drawing by William Henry Jackson, wagon trains of settlers crowded together on the Oregon Trail beginning in the 1840s.

This painting by Alfred James Miller depicts the busy interior of Fort Laramie in 1837.

danger, come autumn, of being trapped in the snows of the Pacific coastal ranges.

"The Oregon fever is raging in almost every part of the Union," proclaimed the *Ohio Statesman* in 1843. Before the fever had run its course, the flow of whites across the continent radically changed the economy and ecology of the Great Plains. Pressure mounted on plant and animal life, and the land could no longer support all the tribes accustomed to living off it. Intertribal warfare intensified as tribes fought for a share of the dwindling supply of buffalo and other game. Far from being separated from whites by a permanent line of division, the Plains Indians now stood astride the main path of white migration to the Pacific.

In response, officials in the Bureau of Indian Affairs organized a great gathering of the tribes in 1851. At this conference they pushed through the **Fort Laramie Treaty**, the first U.S. government attempt to draw boundaries within which to contain the Plains Indians. In exchange for accepting limitations on their movement and for the loss of game, the tribes were to receive annual compensation of $50,000 a year for fifty years (later reduced by the U.S. Senate to ten years).

Most of the Indians at the Fort Laramie conference were the Sioux and their allies. The Sioux viewed the treaty as confirming their dominant power on the Great Plains. When American negotiators tried to restrict Sioux hunting to north of the Platte, the Sioux demanded and received treaty rights to lands south of the Platte as well. "These lands once belonged to the Kiowas and the Crows," argued a western Sioux, "but we whipped those nations out of them, and in this we did what the white men do when they want the lands of the Indians." This was an argument the white man could understand, and the Americans conceded the point.

Two great powers—the Sioux and the U.S. government—reached a standoff at Fort Laramie in 1851. If neither yielded its claims to the Great Plains, war was inevitable. The fighting started in the mid-1850s and climaxed after the Civil War.

The Mexican Borderlands

By the mid-1840s, parties of emigrant Americans were beginning to branch off the main Oregon Trail on their way to Utah and California. These areas were then part of the northern borderlands of Mexico. Mostly a semiarid and thinly populated land of high plateaus, dry basins, and desert bisected north to south by mountain ranges, the borderlands had been part of the Spanish empire in North America. Mexico inherited this territory when it won independence from Spain in 1821. The borderlands covered roughly 1 million square miles; today, they comprise the American Southwest from Texas to California. Mexico's hold on this region was always weak.

It lost Texas in 1837, and in the next decade, the American penetration of Utah and California set the stage for the American seizure of most of the rest in the Mexican War.

The Peoples of the Southwest

Diverse peoples lived in the Southwest. Imperial Spain had divided them into four main groupings: Indians, full-blooded Native Americans who retained their own languages and customs; **mestizos**, those of racially mixed ancestry, usually Spanish and Indian; **criollos**, American-born whites of Spanish ancestry; and Spaniards.

By far the smallest group were the Spaniards. Compared to the English, few Spaniards emigrated to the New World, and most who did were men. Consequently, Spanish males married or lived with native women, and a large class of mestizos emerged. Despite their small numbers, the Spanish, along with the criollos, monopolized economic and political power. This wealthy elite controlled the labor of the mestizos in the predominantly ranching economy of the borderlands. Indians who were part of the mission system set up by Spanish friars also labored for the white minority.

The largest single group in the borderlands were the Indians, about half the population in the 1820s. Most had not come under direct Spanish or Mexican control. Those who had were part of the **mission system**. This instrument of Spanish imperial policy forced Indians to live in a fixed area, to convert to Catholicism, and to work as agricultural laborers.

Spanish missions aimed both to Christianize and "civilize" the Indians, so that they would become loyal imperial subjects. The Spanish forced the mission Indians to abandon their native economies and culture and accept a European definition of civilization that demanded that they live in settled agricultural communities and work under the tight supervision of the friars. The Franciscans established most of the missions. The friars were accompanied by Spanish soldiers and royal officials who built military garrisons known as **presidios**. To this day, surviving presidios and mission churches testify to Spanish rule in the Southwest.

Whether as farmers, hunters, or gatherers, most Indians in the borderlands were still free of white dominance or control in the 1820s. The largest concentration of Indians—some 300,000 when the Spanish friars arrived in the 1760s—was in California. Most of these Indians—the Paiutes, Chumashes, Pomos, Shastas, and a host of smaller tribes—occupied their own distinct ecological zones where they gathered and processed what nature provided. The rivers, forests, and grasslands supplied their material wants. Fish and game were abundant, and wild plants and nuts, especially acorns, provided grain and flour. The Paiutes in the Owens Valley perfected an intricate system for irrigating wild grasses, but only the Yumans along the Colorado River in southeastern California practiced full-scale agriculture. The Spanish marveled at their lush fields of wheat, maize, beans, tobacco, and melons. The Yumans also had an elaborate religion based on an oral tradition of dream songs. (Dream songs remain a distinctive feature of Native American culture.)

The major farming Indians east of California were the Pueblo peoples of Arizona and New Mexico. Named after the adobe or stone community dwellings (*pueblo* is Spanish for "village") in which they lived atop mesas or on terraces carved into cliffs, the Pueblo Indians were a peaceful people closely bound to small, tightly knit communities. Indeed, some of their dwellings, such as those of the Hopis in Arizona or the Acomas in New Mexico, have been continuously occupied for more than five hundred years. Corn and beans were the staples of their irrigation-based agriculture. Formally a part of the Spanish mission system, they had incorporated the Catholic God and Catholic rituals into their own polytheistic religion, which stressed the harmony of all living things with the forces of nature. They continued to worship in their underground sanctuaries known as *kivas*.

Once the Pueblos made their peace with the Spaniards after their great revolt in 1680 (see Chapter 3), their major enemies were the nomadic tribes that lived by hunting and raiding. These tribes outnumbered the Pueblos four to one and controlled most of the Southwest until the 1850s. The horse, which many of the tribes acquired during Spain's temporary retreat from the region during the late seventeenth century in the wake of the Pueblo Revolt, was the basis of their way of life. As the horse frontier spread, the peoples of the southern Plains gained enormous mobility and the means of ranging far and wide for the economic resources that sustained their transformation into societies of mounted warriors.

West of the pueblos around Taos was the land of the Navajos, who herded sheep, raised some crops, and raided other tribes from their mountain fastness. Spilling over onto Navajo lands, the Southern Utes ranged up and down the canyon lands of Utah. The Gila Apaches were the dominant tribe south of Albuquerque and westward into Arizona. To the east in the Pecos River Valley roamed bands of

Mescalero and Jicarillo Apaches. On the broad plains rolling northward from the Texas panhandle and southward into northern Mexico were war parties of Comanches and Kiowas.

The Comanches, a branch of the mountain Shoshonis who moved to the plains when horses became available, were the most feared of the nomadic peoples. They took to the horse as few other people ever had. They were utterly fearless, confident, and masterful horsemen. Their stature as mounted warriors reached mythic proportions. For food and clothing, they relied on the immense buffalo herds of the southern plains. For guns, horses, and other trading goods, they lived off their predatory raids. When the Santa Fe Trail opened in the early 1820s, their shrewdness as traders gave them a new source of firearms that strengthened their raiding prowess.

The three focal points of white settlement in the northern borderlands of Mexico—Texas, New Mexico, and Alta California (as distinguished from Lower, or Baja, California)—were never linked by an effective network of communications or transportation. Navigable rivers were few, and travel was limited to tortuous journeys along Indian and Spanish trails that barely indented the dry and largely barren landscape. Each of these settlements was an isolated offshoot of Hispanic culture with a semiautonomous economy based on ranching and a mostly illegal trade with French, British, and American merchants that brought in a trickle of needed goods.

Neither Spain, which tried to seal off its northern outposts from economic contact with foreigners, nor Mexico, which opened up the borderlands to outsiders, had integrated this vast region into a unified economic or political whole. Indeed, Mexico's most pressing problem in the 1820s was protecting its northern states from the Comanches. To serve as a buffer against the Comanches, the Mexican government in 1821 invited Americans into Texas. The American takeover of Texas had begun.

The Americanization of Texas

The Mexicans faced the same problems governing Texas that the Spanish had. Mexico City was about 1,000 miles from San Antonio, the center of Hispanic settlement in Texas, and communications were slow and cumbersome. The ranching elite of **Tejanos** (Spanish-speaking Mexicans born in Texas) had closer economic ties to American Louisiana than they did to Coahuila, the Mexican state to which Texas was formally attached. These large ranchers had long been smuggling horses and cattle into Louisiana in exchange for manufactured items and tobacco. Markets for farm crops were limited, and the ranchers and a scattered class of tenant farmers produced little surplus food. This low agricultural productivity, combined with the low birthrate among mission Indians, outbreaks of disease, and the generally hostile frontier environment, sharply restricted population growth. Only some five thousand Mexicans lived in Texas in the 1820s.

Sparsely populated and economically struggling, Mexican Texas shared a border with the United States along the Sabine River in Louisiana and the Red River in the Arkansas Territory. The

The paintings of George Catlin are among the best visual sources for understanding the material culture of the Plains Indians. This painting, c. 1834, shows how central was the buffalo in the life of the Commanches, the most powerful tribe on the Southern Plains.

threat that the nearby Americans posed to Mexico's security was obvious to Mexican officials. As one of them early noted with alarm: "If we do not take the present opportunity to people Texas, day by day the strength of the United States will grow until it will annex Texas, Coahuila, Saltillo, and Nuevo León like the Goths, Visigoths, and the other tribes that assailed the Roman Empire." However, attempts to promote immigration into Texas from other parts of Mexico failed. Reasoning that the Americans were going to come in any event, and anxious to build up the population of Texas against Indian attacks, the Mexican government encouraged Americans to settle in Texas by offering huge grants of land in return for promises to accept Mexican citizenship, convert to Catholicism, and obey the authorities in Mexico City.

The first American **empresario**—the recipient of a large grant in return for a promise to bring in settlers—was Stephen F. Austin. He had inherited a huge Spanish grant from his father, Moses Austin, a Missourian who had had business dealings with the Spanish since 1797. After having the grant confirmed by the new Mexican government in 1821, Stephen Austin founded the first American colony in Texas. The Austin grant encompassed 18,000 square miles. Other grants were smaller but still lavish. The empresarios stood to grow wealthy by leasing out land, selling parcels to settlers, and organizing the rest into large-scale farms that produced cotton with slave labor in the bottomlands of the Sabine, Colorado, and Brazos Rivers. For the Americans who followed in their wake, Texas was a dream come true—the chance to acquire good land that was so cheap it was almost free. As early as 1830, eastern and south central Texas were becoming an extension of the plantation economy of the Gulf coastal plain. More than 25,000 whites, with around a thousand slaves, had poured into the region (see "American Views: A Mexican View of the Texans in 1828").

More Americans moved into Texas with slaves than the Mexicans had anticipated. Many settlers simply ignored Mexican laws, especially the Emancipation Proclamation of 1829 that forbade slavery in the Republic of Mexico. In 1830, the Mexican government attempted to assert its authority. It levied the first taxes on the Americans, prohibited the further importation of slaves, and closed the international border to additional immigration. Still, another ten thousand Americans spilled across the border in the early 1830s, and they continued to bring in slaves.

Unlike the empresarios, many of whom became Catholic and married into elite Tejano families, these newcomers lived apart from Mexicans and rejected Mexican citizenship. Cultural tensions escalated. Believing that they belonged to a superior race of liberty-loving white Anglo-Saxons, most of these new arrivals sneered at the Mexicans as a mongrelized race of blacks, Indians, and Spaniards and resented having to submit to their rule. As Protestants, Americans considered Catholicism a despotic, superstitious religion and ignored legal requirements that they accept the Catholic faith.

A clash became inevitable in 1835 when General Santa Anna, elected president of Mexico in 1833, overturned the liberal Mexican constitution of 1824. He established himself as a dictator in 1834, and his dictatorial centralist rule ended any hope of the Americans empresarios and their Tejano allies that Texas might become an autonomous state within a federated Mexico. Skirmishing between Mexican troops and rebellious Texans began in the fall of 1835.

At first, the Anglo-Tejano leadership did not renounce all ties with Mexico. When these leaders drafted a constitution in November 1835, they sought to overthrow Santa Anna, restore the constitution of 1824, and win separate statehood for Texas within a liberal Mexican republic. Santa Anna, however, refused to compromise. When he raised a large army to crush the uprising, he radicalized the rebellion and pushed it to declare complete independence on March 2, 1836. Four days later, a Mexican army of four thousand annihilated the 187 defenders of the

This flag of a volunteer company from New Orleans flew over the Alamo on March 6, 1836, when Santa Anna's troops stormed the mission fortress.

American Views

A MEXICAN VIEW OF THE TEXANS IN 1828

By the late 1820s, Mexico was reassessing its policy of encouraging American immigration to Texas. Concerned over the large numbers and uncertain loyalties of the American settlers, the government appointed a commission in 1827 ostensibly to survey the boundary between Louisiana and the province of Texas. The real purpose of the commission was to recommend policy changes that would strengthen Mexico's hold on Texas. The following excerpt is from a journal kept by José María Sánchez, the draftsman of the boundary commission.

❖ Why was the Mexican government so ineffective in maintaining control over Texas?

❖ What was the appeal of Texas for Americans? How did most of them enter Texas and take up land?

❖ Why did Sánchez have such a low opinion of the Americans in the Austin colony? What did he think of Stephen Austin?

❖ Why did the Mexicans fear that they would lose Texas?

The Americans from the north have taken possession of practically all the eastern part of Texas, in most cases without the permission of the authorities. They immigrate constantly, finding no one to prevent them, and take possession of the *sitio* [location] that best suits them without either asking leave or going through any formality other than that of building their homes. Thus the majority of inhabitants in the Department are North Americans, the Mexican population being reduced to only Bejar, Nacoghoches, and La Bahía del Espíritu Santo, wretched settlements that between them do not number three thousand inhabitants, and the new village of Guadalupe Victoria that has scarcely more than seventy settlers. The government of the state, with its seat at Saltillo, that should watch over the preservation of its most precious and interesting department, taking measures to prevent its being stolen by foreign hands, is the one that knows the least not only about actual conditions, but even about its territory. . . . Repeated and urgent appeals have been made to the

---

Alamo, an abandoned mission in San Antonio. A few weeks later at **Goliad**, another three hundred Texans were killed after they had agreed to surrender (see Map 12-3).

"Remember the Alamo!" and "Remember Goliad!" were powerful rallying cries for the beleaguered Texans. Volunteers from the American South rushed to the aid of the main Texan army, commanded by Sam Houston. A product of the Tennessee frontier and a close friend of Andrew Jackson's, Houston did Jackson proud by catching the overconfident Santa Anna off guard in eastern Texas. Houston's victory in April 1836 at the **Battle of San Jacinto** established the independence of Texas. Captured while trying to flee, Santa Anna signed a treaty in May 1836, recognizing Texas as an independent republic with a boundary on the south and west at the Rio Grande. However, the Nueces River to the north of the Rio Grande had been the administrative border of Texas under Mexican rule. The Mexican Congress rejected the treaty, and the boundary remained in dispute.

Soon forgotten during the ensuing eight years of Texas independence was the support that many Tejanos had given to the successful revolt against Mexican rule. In part because Mexico

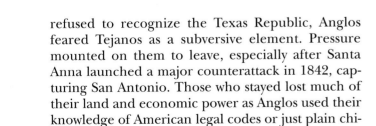

Supreme Government of the Federation regarding the imminent danger in which this interesting Department is of becoming the prize of the ambitious North Americans, but never has it taken any measures that may be called conclusive. . . .

[Sánchez goes on to describe the village of Austin and the American colony founded by Stephen Austin.]

Its population is nearly two hundred persons, of which only ten are Mexicans, for the balance are all Americans from the North with an occasional European. Two wretched little stores supply the inhabitants of the colony: one sells only whiskey, rum, sugar, and coffee; the other, rice, flour, lard, and cheap cloth. . . . The Americans from the North, at least the great part of those I have seen, eat only salted meat, bread made by themselves out of corn meal, coffee, and homemade cheese. To these the greater part of those who live in the village add strong liquor, for they are in general, in my opinion, lazy people of vicious character. Some of them cultivate their small farms by planting corn; but this task they usually entrust to their negro slaves, whom they treat with considerable harshness. Beyond the village in an immense stretch of land formed by rolling hills are scattered the families brought by Stephen Austin, which today number more than two thousand persons. The diplomatic policy of this empresario, evident in all his actions, has, as one may say, lulled the authorities into a sense of security, while he works diligently for his own ends. In my judgment, the spark that will start the conflagration that will deprive us of Texas, will start from this colony. All because the government does not take vigorous measures to prevent it. Perhaps it does not realize the value of what it is about to lose.

Source: *José María Sánchez, "A Trip to Texas in 1828," trans. Carlos E. Castaneda, Southwestern Historical Quarterly, 29 (1926): 260, 261, 271.*

refused to recognize the Texas Republic, Anglos feared Tejanos as a subversive element. Pressure mounted on them to leave, especially after Santa Anna launched a major counterattack in 1842, capturing San Antonio. Those who stayed lost much of their land and economic power as Anglos used their knowledge of American legal codes or just plain chicanery to reduce the Tejanos to second-class citizens.

More difficult to subordinate were the Comanches. While president of Texas, Houston tried to fix a permanent boundary between the Comanches and whites, but Texas pride and the ongoing encroachment of whites on Indian land undercut his efforts. By the early 1840s, Texans and Comanches were in a state of nearly permanent war. Only the force of the federal army after the Civil War ended the Comanches' long reign as the effective rulers of the high, dry plains of northern and western Texas.

The Push into California and the Southwest

Mexican rule in California was always weak. The Sonoran desert and the resistance of the Yuman Indians in southeastern California cut off Mexico

Map 12-3   Texas and Mexico after the Texas Revolt
The Battle of San Jacinto was the decisive American victory that gained the independence of Texas, but the border dispute between Texas and Mexico would not be resolved until the Mexican War a decade later.

from any direct land contact with Alta California. Only irregular communications were maintained over a long sea route. For **Californios**, Californians of Spanish descent, Mexico was literally *la otra banda,* "the other shore." In trying to strengthen its hold on this remote and thinly populated region, the Mexican government relied on a program of economic development. As in Texas, however, Mexican policy had unintended consequences.

The centerpiece of the Mexican program was the secularization of the missions. This policy opened up the landholdings of the Catholic Church to private ownership and released the mission Indians from paternalistic bondage. Small allotments of land were set aside for the Indians, but most returned to their homelands. Those who remained became a source of cheap labor for the rancheros who carved up the mission lands into huge cattle ranches. Thus by the 1830s, California entered its rancho era. The main beneficiaries of this process, however, were not Mexican authorities but the American traders who responded to the economic

opportunities presented by the privatization of the California economy.

New England merchants had been trading in California since the 1780s. What first attracted them were the seal fisheries off the California coast, a source of otter pelts highly prized in the China trade. After the seals had been all but exterminated by the 1820s, Yankee merchants shipped out hides and tallow, a trade fed by the immense cattle resources of the rancheros, to New England for processing into shoes and candles. Ships from New England and New York sailed around Cape Horn to California ports, where they unloaded trading goods. Servicing this trade in California was a resident colony of American agents, some three hundred strong by the mid-1840s.

Whereas Yankees dominated the American colonies in coastal California, the Americans who filtered into the inner valleys of California in the 1830s and 1840s were more representative of the Midwestern farm families who set out on the Oregon Trail. About one in ten of the overland parties took a cutoff on the Trail near Fort Hall on the Snake River that led them across the deserts of northern Nevada to a passage across the Sierra Nevada near Lake Tahoe. At the end of the journey, they dropped down into the fertile Sacramento River Valley. Nearly a thousand Americans had arrived by 1846.

California belonged to Mexico in name only by the early 1840s. The program of economic development had strengthened California's ties to the outside world at the expense of Mexico. American merchants and California rancheros ran the economy, and both groups had joined separatist movements against Mexican rule. Unlike the Californios, who were ambivalent about their future political allegiance, the Americans wanted to be part of the United States and assumed that California would shortly be annexed. With the outbreak of the Mexican War in 1846, their wish became reality.

Except for Utah, the American push into the interior of the Mexican Southwest followed the California pattern of trade preceding settlement. When Mexico liberalized the formerly restrictive trading policies of Spain, American merchants opened up the 900-mile-long **Santa Fe Trail** from Independence, Missouri, to Santa Fe, New Mexico. Starved for mercantile goods, the New Mexicans were a small but highly profitable market. They paid for their American imports with gold, silver, and furs.

Brent's Old Fort, an impregnable adobe structure built on the Arkansas River at the point where the Santa Fe Trail turned to the southwest and Taos, was the fulcrum for the growing economic influence of Americans over New Mexican affairs. Completed in 1832, the fort enabled the Brent brothers from Missouri to control a flourishing and almost monopolistic trade with Indians, trappers, caravans on the Santa Fe Trail, and the large landowners and merchants of New Mexico. This trade pulled New Mexico into the cultural and economic orbit of the United States and undermined what little sovereign power Mexico held in the region.

Although only a few hundred Americans were permanent residents of New Mexico in the 1840s, they had married into the Spanish-speaking landholding elite and were themselves beginning to receive large grants of land. Ties of blood and common economic interests linked this small group of American businessmen with an influential faction of the local elite. American merchants and New Mexican landlords were further united by their growing disdain for the instability of Mexican rule, Santa Anna's dictatorship, and sporadic attempts by Mexico to levy heavy taxes on the Santa Fe trade. Another bond was their concern over the aggressive efforts of the Texans to seize eastern New Mexico. After thwarting a 1841 Texan attempt to occupy Santa Fe, the leaders of New Mexico increasingly looked to the United States to protect their local autonomy. They quickly decided to cooperate with the American army of invasion when the Mexican War got under way. Over the opposition of the clergy and ranchers still loyal to Mexico, this group was instrumental in the American takeover of New Mexico.

At the extreme northern and inner reaches of the Mexican borderlands lay Utah. Dominated by an intermountain depression called the Great Basin, Utah was a starkly beautiful but dry region of alkaline flats, broken tablelands, cottonwood canyons, and mountain ranges. It was home to the Bannocks, Utes, Navajos, Hopis, and small bands of other Indians. Aside from trading ties with the Utes, Spain and Mexico had largely ignored this remote region. Its isolation and lack of white settlers, however, were precisely what made Utah so appealing to the leaders of the Mormons, the Church of Jesus Christ of Latter-day Saints. For the Mormons in the 1840s, Utah became the promised land in which to build a new Zion.

Founded by Joseph Smith in upstate New York in the 1820s, Mormonism grew rapidly within a communitarian framework that stressed hard work and economic cooperation under the leadership of patriarchal leaders. The economic success of close-knit Mormon communities, combined with the righteous zeal of their members, aroused the fears and hostility of non-Mormons. Harassed out of New York,

Ohio, and Missouri, the Mormons thought they had found a permanent home by the late 1830s in Nauvoo, Illinois. But the murder of Joseph Smith and his brother by a mob in 1844 convinced the beleaguered Mormons that they had to leave the settled East for a refuge of their own in the West. In 1846 a group of Mormons migrated to the Great Basin in Utah. Under the leadership of Brigham Young, they established a new community in 1847 at the Great Salt Lake on the western slopes of the Wasatch Mountains. Ten thousand Mormons joined them.

The Mormons thrived in the arid desert. Their intense communitarianism was ideally suited to dispensing land and organizing an irrigation system that coordinated water rights with the amount of land under production. To their dismay, however, they learned in 1848 that they had not left the United States after all. The Union acquired Utah, along with the rest of the northern borderlands of Mexico, as a result of the Mexican War. (For more on the Mormons, see Chapter 14.)

Politics, Expansion, and War

The Democrats viewed their victory in the election of 1844 (see Chapter 10) as a popular mandate for expansion. They had campaigned on a platform that boldly demanded both Texas and the "reoccupation" of Oregon up to 54°40'.

James K. Polk, the new Democratic president, fully shared the expansionist vision of his party. The greatest prize in his eyes was California. Although silent in public on California for fear of further antagonizing the Mexicans, who had never accepted the loss of Texas, Polk made the acquisition of California the cornerstone of his foreign policy. When he was stymied in his efforts to purchase California and New Mexico, he tried to force concessions from the Mexican government by ordering American troops to the mouth of the Rio Grande, far within the territory claimed by Mexico. When the virtually inevitable clash of arms occurred in late April 1846, war broke out between the United States and Mexico.

Victory resulted in the **Mexican Cession of 1848**, which added half a million square miles to the United States. Polk's administration also finalized the acquisition of Texas and reached a compromise with the British on the Oregon Territory that recognized American sovereignty in the Pacific Northwest up to the 49th parallel. The United States was now a nation that spanned a continent.

Manifest Destiny

With a phrase that soon entered the nation's vocabulary, John L. O'Sullivan, editor and Democratic politician, proclaimed in 1845 America's "manifest destiny to overspread and to possess the whole of the continent which Providence has given us for the development of the great experiment of Liberty and federated self-government entrusted to us." Central to Manifest Destiny was the assumption that white Americans were a special people. Part of that sense of specialness was religiously inspired and dated back to the Puritans' belief that God had appointed them to establish a New Israel cleansed of the corruption of the Old World. Evangelical revivals in the early nineteenth century then added an aggressive sense of urgency to America's presumed mission to spread the benefits of Protestantism and Christian civilization. Protestant missionaries, as in Oregon, were often in the vanguard of American expansion.

What distinguished the special American mission as enunciated by Manifest Destiny was its explicitly racial component. Between 1815 and 1850, the term *Anglo-Saxon*, originally loosely applied to English-speaking peoples, acquired racial overtones, in keeping with the then current interest of European and American scientists in defining, classifying, and ranking human races (with themselves, of course, at the top). Caucasian Anglo-Saxon Americans, as the descendants of ancient Germanic tribes that purportedly brought the seeds of free institutions to England, were now said to be the foremost race in the world. Only they, it was argued, had the energy, industriousness, and innate love of liberty to establish a successful free government. This superior racial pedigree gave white Americans the natural right as a chosen people to expand westward, carrying the blessings of democracy and progress.

Advocates of Manifest Destiny insisted that American expansion would be irresistible and peaceful. They were not warmongers calling for conquest. Still, the doctrine was undeniably a self-serving justification for what other peoples would see as territorial aggrandizement. Certainly, that was true of the Mexican-Americans and Native Americans who lost land and cultural independence as they were brought under American control. Manifest Destiny and popular stereotypes lumped Indians and Mexicans together as inferior peoples. An emigrant guide of 1845 spoke of the Mexican Californians as "scarcely a visible grade in the scale of intelligence, above the barbarous tribes by whom they are surrounded." For Waddy Thompson, an American minister to Mexico in the early 1840s, the Mexicans in general were "lazy, ignorant, and, of course, vicious and dishonest." This alleged Mexican inferiority was attributed to racial intermixture with the Indians, who, it was said, were hopelessly unfit for civilization.

Manifest Destiny was closely associated with the Democratic party. For Democrats, spread-eagle expansionism would counterbalance the debilitating effects of industrialization and urbanization. As good Jeffersonians, they stressed the need for more land to realize the ideal of a democratic republic rooted in the virtues and rough equality of independent farmers. For their working-class Irish constituency, the Democrats touted the broad expanses of the West as the surest means to escape the misery of wage slavery. It was no coincidence that O'Sullivan was a Democrat or that he feared that the spread of factories would produce an impoverished class of workers in America as it had in England.

As a manifesto for expansion, Manifest Destiny captured the popular imagination when the country was still mired in a depression after the Panic of 1837. The way out of the depression, according to many Democrats, was to revive the export trade to soak up the agricultural surplus. Thomas Hart Benton, a Democratic senator from Missouri, was the leading spokesman for the vast potential of an American trade with India and China, a trade to be secured by American possession of the harbors on the Pacific Coast.

The Mexican War

Once in office, Polk proved far more conciliatory with the British than with the Mexicans. Despite a stridently anti-British tone in his annual message to Congress in December 1845, Polk was willing to compromise on Oregon because he dreaded the possibility of a two-front war against both the Mexicans and the British. Mexico had severed diplomatic ties with the United States over the annexation of Texas (see Chapter 11), and a war could break out at any time.

In the spring of 1846, after Polk had abrogated the agreement on the joint occupation of Oregon, the British offered a compromise that they had earlier rejected. They agreed to a boundary at the 49th parallel if they were allowed to retain Vancouver Island in Puget Sound. Polk sent the offer to the Senate, which quickly approved it in June 1846. British-American trade continued to flourish, Mexico lost a potential ally, and most important, Polk could now concentrate on the **Mexican War** that had erupted a month earlier.

Unlike Oregon, where he backed off from extravagant territorial claims, Polk refused to budge on the American claim (inherited form the Texans, when the United States annexed Texas in 1845) that the Rio Grande was the border between Texas and Mexico. The Mexicans insisted that the Nueces River, 100 miles to the north of the Rio Grande, was the border, at it had been when Texas was part of Mexico. An immense territory was at stake, for the headwaters of the Rio Grande were in northern New Mexico, and a boundary on the Rio Grande would more than double the size of Texas.

Citing rumors of a Mexican invasion, Polk sent 3,500 troops under General Zachary Taylor to the Nueces River in the summer of 1845. Polk also stepped up his efforts to acquire California. He instructed Thomas Larkin, the American consul in Monterey, California, to inform the Californios and Americans that the United States would support them if they revolted against Mexican rule. Polk also secretly ordered the U.S. Pacific naval squadron to seize California ports if war broke out with Mexico. Polk's final effort at peaceful expansion was the Slidell mission in November 1845. He sent John L. Slidell to Mexico City to offer $30 million to purchase California and New Mexico and to secure the Rio Grande boundary.

When Polk learned that the Mexican government had refused to receive Slidell, he set out to draw Mexico into a war that would result in the American acquisition of California. In early 1846, he ordered General Taylor to advance to the Rio Grande, deep in the disputed border region. Taylor blockaded the mouth of the Rio Grande (an aggressive act even if the river had been an international boundary) and built a fort on the northern bank across from the Mexican town of Matamoros. The Mexicans attacked and were repulsed on April 24.

Even before the news reached Washington, Polk had decided on war, on the grounds that the Mexican government had unjustifiably refused to sell territory to the United States and had fallen behind on debt payments owed to American citizens. Informed of the clash between Mexican and American troops in early May (it took ten days for the news to reach Washington), he sent a redrafted war message to Congress on May 9 asserting that Mexico "has invaded our territory, and shed American blood on American soil." Congress declared war on May 13, 1846.

The war was a stunning military success for the United States (See Map 12-4). The Mexicans fought bravely, but they lacked the leadership, modern artillery, and naval capacity to check the American advances. By the end of 1846, Polk had gained his objectives in the Mexican borderlands. An army sent west under Colonel Stephen W. Kearny occupied New Mexico. The conquest was relatively

This daguerreotype (an early form of a photograph) is one of the few extant views of Americans volunteering for the Mexican War. Shown here are volunteers in 1846 from Exeter, New Hampshire.

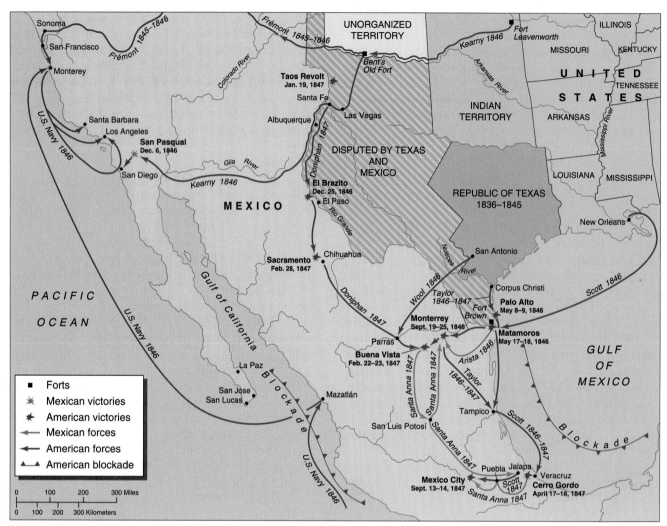

Map 12-4   The Mexican War
Victories under General Zachary Taylor in northern Mexico secured the Rio Grande as the boundary between Texas and Mexico. Colonel Stephen Kearny's expedition won control of New Mexico, and reinforcements from Kearny assured the success of American troops landed by the Pacific Squadron in gaining Alta California for the United States. The success of General Winfield Scott's amphibious invasion at Vera Cruz and his occupation of Mexico City brought the war to an end.

bloodless because most of the local elite cooperated with the American authorities. Sporadic resistance was largely confined to poorer Mexicans and the Pueblo Indians, who feared that their land would be confiscated. The largest uprising, one that was ruthlessly suppressed, was the **Taos Revolt** in January 1847, led by Jesús Trujillo and Tomasito, a Pueblo chieftain. A sympathetic observer described the rebels as "those who defend to the last their country and their homes."

Kearny's army then moved to Tucson and eventually linked up in southern California with pro-American rebels and U.S. forces sent ashore by the Pacific squadron. As in New Mexico, the stiffest resis-

tance came from ordinary Mexicans and the Spanish-speaking Indians.

Despite the loss of its northern provinces, Mexico refused to concede defeat. After Taylor had established a secure defensive line in northeastern Mexico with a victory at Monterrey in September 1846 and repulsed a Mexican counterattack at Buena Vista in February 1847, Polk directed General Winfield Scott to invade central Mexico. Following an amphibious assault on Vera Cruz in March 1847, Scott captured Mexico City in September.

After a frustrating delay while Mexico reorganized its government, peace talks finally got under way and concluded in the **Treaty of Guadalupe**

Hidalgo, signed on February 2, 1848. Mexico surrendered its claim to Texas north of the Rio Grande and ceded Alta California and New Mexico (including present-day Arizona, Utah, and Nevada). The United States paid $15 million, assumed over $3 million in claims of American citizens against Mexico, and agreed to grant U.S. citizenship to Mexicans resident in its new territories.

Polk had gained his strategic goals, but the cost was thirteen thousand American lives (most from diseases such as measles and dysentery), fifty thousand Mexican lives, and the poisoning of Mexican-American relations for generations. The war also, as will be seen in Chapter 15, heightened sectional tensions over slavery and weakened the political structure that was vital to preserving the Union.

Conclusion

Americans were an expansionist people. Though not necessarily proof of Manifest Destiny, their surge across the continent between 1815 and 1850 was fully in keeping with their restless desire for independence on a plot of land. Population pressure on overworked farms in the East impelled much of this westward migration, but by the 1840s, expansion had seemingly acquired a momentum all its own, one that increasingly rejected the claims of other peoples to the land.

Far from being a process of peaceful, evolutionary, and democratic change, as was once thought, expansion involved the spread of slavery, violent confrontations, and the uprooting and displacement of native peoples. By 1850, the earlier notion of reserving the trans-Mississippi West as a permanent Indian country had been abandoned. The Sioux and Comanches were still feared by whites, but their final subjugation was not far off. The derogatory stereotypes of Mexican-Americans that were a staple of both popular thought and expansionist ideology showed clearly that American control after the Mexican War would relegate Spanish-speaking people to second-class status.

However misleading and false much of it was, the rhetoric of Manifest Destiny did highlight a central truth. A broad, popular base existed for expanding across the continent. As the Mexican War made clear, the United States was now unquestionably the dominant power in North America. The only serious threat to its dominance in the near future would come from inside, not outside, its continental domain.

Review Questions

1. What accounted for the westward movement of Americans? How did the presence or absence of slavery affect developmental patterns in the new settlements?

2. How was the West of the Plains Indians transformed after 1830 as peoples migrated both within the region and into it from various directions? Why were the Sioux so powerful, and how did they interact with other Native Americans and the U.S. government?

3. Who lived in the Mexican borderlands of the Southwest, and why was it so difficult for Mexican authorities to maintain effective control of the region? What role did trade play in the American penetration of the Southwest?

4. What did Americans mean by Manifest Destiny? Why was territorial expansion so identified with the Democratic party?

5. Who was responsible for the outbreak of the Mexican War? Were Mexicans the victims of American aggression?

Recommended Reading

Ray Allen Billington, *The Far Western Frontier, 1830–1860* (1956). This is still a useful survey and an excellent example of an older approach to the West from the perspective of whites entering the region with their values of freedom and individualism.

Richard Brandon, *The Last Americans: The Indian in American Culture* (1974). This beautifully written, panoramic account looks at Indian cultures and their interactions with the spread of white settlement.

Patricia Nelson Limerick, *The Legacy of Conquest: The Unbroken Past of the American West* (1987). This forcefully argued work overturns many stereotypes and places the federal government and cultural antagonisms at the center of western history.

D. W. Meinig, *The Shaping of America, Vol. 2: Continental America, 1800–1867* (1993). Meinig's comprehensive work offers a distinctive interpretation of continental expansion from the perspective of historical geography.

Frederick Merk, *Manifest Destiny and Mission in American History* (1963). This book is valuable not only for its revisionist look at the appeal of Manifest Destiny in the 1840s but also for its insights into how a sense of mission influenced American foreign policy in the future.

Clyde A. Milner II, Carol A. O'Connor, and Martha A. Sandweiss, eds., *The Oxford History of the American West* (1994). The essays in this comprehensive collection summarize much of the best work in the modern rethinking of the history of the American West.

Albert K. Weinberg, *Manifest Destiny: A Study of Nationalist Expansion in American History* (1957). This remains the most complete study of the ideas that flowed into the concept of Manifest Destiny.

Richard White, *"Its Your Misfortune and None of My Own": A History of the American West* (1991). This outstanding work draws on cultural and environmental approaches to show how complex and often unequal relationships among a host of peoples shaped the history of the West.

Additional Sources

The Agricultural Frontier

Joan E. Cashin, *A Family Venture: Men and Women on the Southern Frontier* (1991).

Andrew R. L. Cayton and Peter S. Onuf, *The Midwest and the Nation: Rethinking the History of an American Region* (1990).

John Mack Faragher, *Sugar Creek: Life on the Illinois Prairie* (1986).

Paul W. Gates, *The Farmer's Age: Agriculture, 1815–1860* (1962).

John Hebron Moore, *The Emergence of the Cotton Kingdom in the Old Southwest: Mississippi, 1770–1860* (1987).

Malcolm J. Rohrbough, *The Trans-Appalachian Frontier: People, Societies, and Institutions, 1775–1850* (1978).

The Frontier of the Plains Indians

Malcolm Clark Jr., *Eden Seekers: The Settlement of Oregon, 1810–1862* (1981).

Barnard De Voto, *Across the Wide Missouri* (1947).

William H. Goetzmann, *Exploration and Empire: The Explorer and Scientist in the Winning of the American West* (1966).

Julie R. Jeffrey, *Frontier Women: The Trans-Mississippi West, 1840–1880* (1979).

John H. Moore, ed., *The Political Economy of the North American Indians* (1993).

John Unruh, *The Plains Across: The Overland Emigrations and the Trans-Mississippi West, 1840–1860* (1979).

Richard White, *The Roots of Dependency: Subsistence, Environment, and Social Change among the Choctaws, Pawnees, and Navajos* (1983).

The Mexican Borderlands

Rudolfo Acuña, *Occupied America: A History of Chicanos* (1988).

Paul D. Lack, *The Texas Revolutionary Experience: A Political and Social History, 1835–1836* (1992).

Howard R. Lamar, *The Far Southwest, 1846–1912* (1966).

Janet Lecompte, *Pueblo, Hardscabble, Greenhorn: The Upper Arkansas, 1832–1856* (1978).

George Harwood Phillips, *Indians and Intruders in Central California, 1769–1849* (1993).

Andres Tijerina, *Tejanos and Texas under the Mexican Flag, 1821–1836* (1994).

David J. Weber, *The Mexican Frontier, 1821–1846: The American Southwest under Mexico* (1982).

Politics, Expansion, and War

Richard Griswold del Castillo, *The Treaty of Guadalupe Hidalgo: A Legacy of Conflict* (1990).

John S. D. Eisenhower, *So Far from God: The U.S. War with Mexico* (1989).

Thomas R. Hietala, *Manifest Design: American Aggrandizement in Late Jacksonian America* (1985).

Reginald Horsman, *Race and Manifest Destiny: The Origins of American Racial Anglo-Saxonism* (1981).

Robert W. Johannsen, *To the Halls of Montezuma: The Mexican War in the American Imagination* (1985).

David M. Pletcher, *The Diplomacy of Annexation: Texas, Oregon, and the Mexican War* (1973).

Charles G. Sellers, *James K. Polk: Continentalist, 1843–1846* (1966).

Where to Learn More

❖ **Indian Pueblo Cultural Center, Albuquerque, New Mexico.**   This center provides an excellent orientation to the culture, crafts, and community life of the Pueblo and Southwestern Indians. It also includes much material on archaeological findings.

❖ **Museum Association of American Frontier and Fur Trade, Chadron, Nebraska.**   The library in the museum holds archives, maps, and some photographs dealing with the western fur trade.

❖ **Indian Museum of North America, Crazy Horse, South Dakota.**   This is one of the best sources for learning of the culture of the Teton Sioux and other American and Canadian tribes on the Great Plains. Holdings include outstanding examples of Indian art and artifacts.

❖ **Living History Farms, Des Moines, Iowa.** This site includes several working farms, operated as they were at different points in the nineteenth century, as well as a mid-twentieth-century farm. A vintage town with a general store, church, and other buildings has also been re-created.

❖ **Scotts Bluff National Monument, Gering, Nebraska.** Scotts Bluff was a prominent landmark on the Oregon Trail, and the museum exhibits here have interpretive material on the trail and the western phase of expansion.

❖ **Conner Prairie, Noblesville, Indiana.** The museum and historic area re-create a sense of life on the Indiana frontier during the period of the Old Northwest.

❖ **Fort Union National Monument, Watrous, New Mexico.** Fort Union was a nineteenth-century military post, and the holdings and exhibits in the museum relate to frontier military life and the Santa Fe Trail.

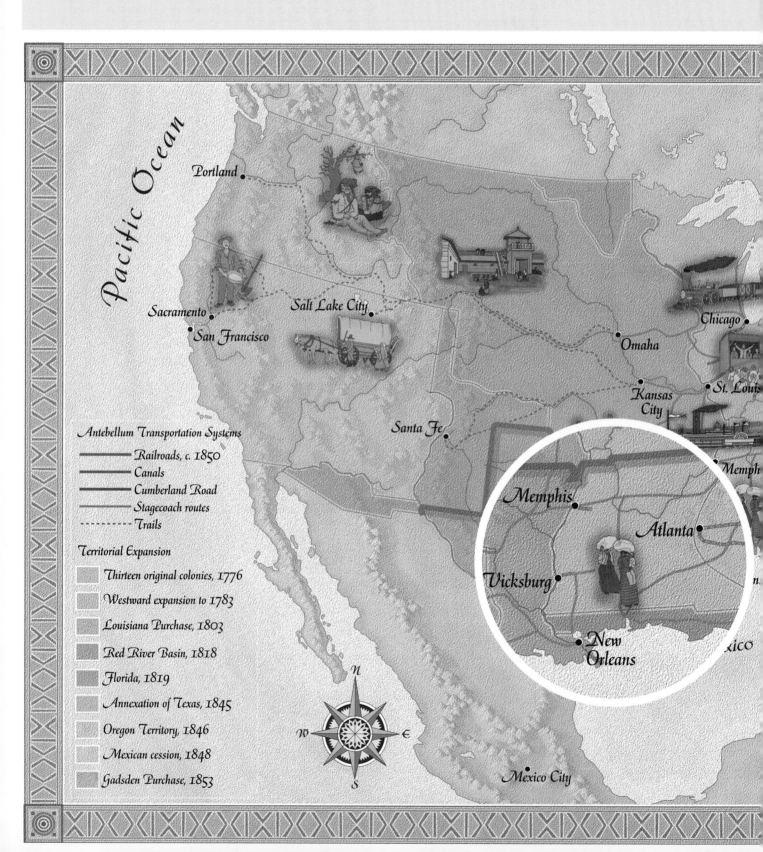

Pacific Ocean

Portland

Sacramento
San Francisco

Salt Lake City

Chicago

Omaha

St. Louis

Kansas City

Santa Fe

Memphis

Antebellum Transportation Systems

Railroads, c. 1850
Canals
Cumberland Road
Stagecoach routes
Trails

Territorial Expansion

Thirteen original colonies, 1776
Westward expansion to 1783
Louisiana Purchase, 1803
Red River Basin, 1818
Florida, 1819
Annexation of Texas, 1845
Oregon Territory, 1846
Mexican cession, 1848
Gadsden Purchase, 1853

Memphis

Atlanta

Vicksburg

New Orleans

Mexico City

N
W · E
S

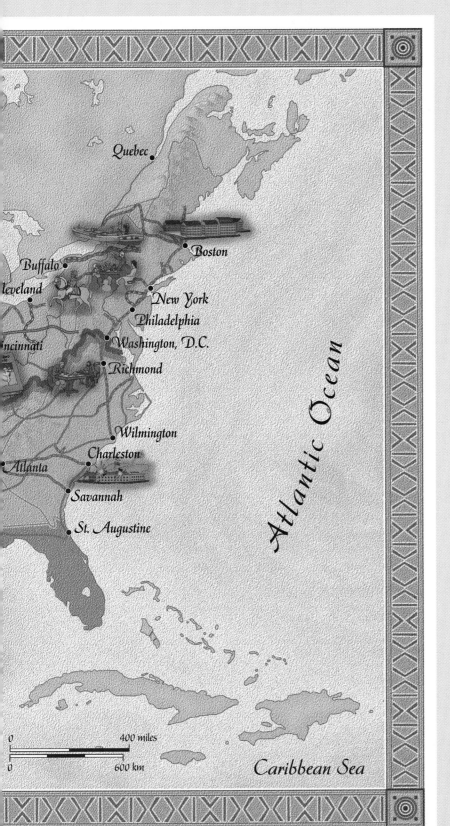

KEY TOPICS

❖ How the increasing demand for cotton made slavery highly profitable in the Lower South
❖ The decline of slavery after 1800 in the increasingly diversified economy of the Upper South
❖ Slave culture and slave resistance
❖ The divisions of free white society
❖ The southern defense of slavery in response to increasing attacks from northern abolitionists

"*T*his morning I had a difficulty with Matt. I tied him up and gave him a gentle admonition in the shape of a good whipping. I intended to put him in jail and keep him there until I sold him, but he seemed so penitent & promised so fairly & the other negroes promising to see that he would behave himself in future that I concluded that I would try him once more." Thus did David Golightly Harris, an upcountry South Carolina farmer who owned ten slaves, casually record in his journal for January 8, 1858, his punishment of a recalcitrant slave.

Harris was an upstanding, God-fearing member of his community, and few of his neighbors would have protested the "good whipping" he had laid on Matt's back. This was the slave South, and white Southerners routinely inflicted pain on slaves to control them and coerce them into productive labor. After all, as an overseer on a large plantation informed a northern visitor in the 1850s, "they'd never do any work at all if they were not afraid of being whipped."

Slavery, and the physical coercion on which it rested, increasingly defined the South as a distinctive region of the antebellum United States. Indeed, only the widespread presence of slaves south of Pennsylvania and the Ohio River enables us to speak of "the" South before the Civil War. For despite the region's geographical and cultural diversity, black slavery created a bond among whites and cast the South in a common mold.

Not only did slavery make the South distinctive, but it was also the source of the region's immense agricultural wealth, the foundation on which planters built their fortunes, the basis for upward mobility by ambitious whites, and the means by which whites controlled the large black minority. As both a powerful symbol and the frightening embodiment of the horrors of being unfree, slavery made southern whites acutely sensitive to the need to protect their own personal liberties, not the least of which was, paradoxically, the right to enslave African-Americans. White males were quick to take offense at any challenge to their honor or independence. A code of honor for planters demanded an apology or vindication in a duel for any insult, whether real or perceived. Precisely because slavery was so deeply embedded in southern life and customs, white leadership reacted to mounting attacks on slavery after 1830 with an ever more defiant defense of the institution. That defense in turn reinforced a growing sense of sectionalism among southern whites, the belief that their values divided them from their fellow citizens in the Union.

Economically and intellectually, the Old South developed in stages. The South of 1860 was geographically much larger and more diverse than it had been in 1800, but it was also more uniformly committed to a single cash crop, cotton. Demand for cotton had exploded as the industrial revolution made the mass production of textiles possible. New England mill owners were now as dependent on slavery as southern planters were. Cotton became king, as contemporaries put it, and it provided the economic basis for southern sectionalism. During the reign of King Cotton, however, regional differences emerged between the Lower South, where the linkage between cotton and slavery was strong, and the Upper South, where slavery was relatively less important and the economy was more diversified. Though the lives of whites and African-Americans in this slave society were starkly different, southern whites also came to believe that they were different from the rest of the nation, giving rise to the proslavery defense that was to deepen sectional divisions.

The Lower South

South and west of South Carolina in 1800 stretched some of the best cotton land in the world. A long growing season, adequate rainfall, navigable rivers, and untapped fertility gave the Lower South—consisting in 1850 of South Carolina, Georgia, Florida, Alabama, Mississippi, Louisiana, and Texas—incomparable natural advantages for growing cotton. Ambitious southern whites exploited these advantages by extending slavery after 1800 to the newer cotton lands

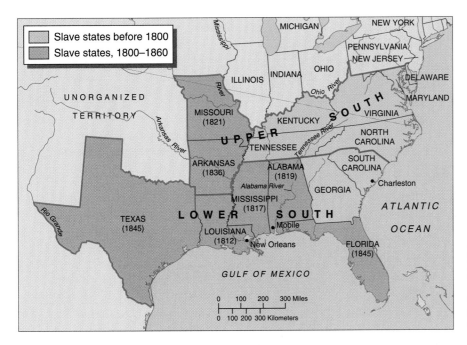

Map 13-1   The Spread of Slavery: New Slave States Entering the Union, 1800–1850
Seven slave states entered the Union after 1800 as cotton production shifted westward.

that opened up in the Lower South (see Map 13-1). Cotton production and slavery thus went hand in hand.

Cotton and Slaves

Before 1800, slavery was associated with the cash crops of tobacco, rice, and sea island (or long-staple) cotton. Tobacco, the mainstay of the colonial Chesapeake economy, severely depleted the soil. Its production had stagnated after the Revolutionary War when it lost its formerly protected markets in Britain. Rice and long-staple cotton, named for its long, silky fibers, were profitable but geographically limited to the humid sea islands and tidal flats off the coast of South Carolina and Georgia. Like sugar cane, introduced into Louisiana in the 1790s, they required a huge capital investment in special machinery, dikes, and labor.

Upland, or short-staple, cotton faced none of these constraints, once the cotton gin removed the technical barrier to its commercial production. It could be planted far inland, and small farmers could grow it profitably because it required no additional costs for machinery or drainage systems. As a result, after the 1790s, the production of short-staple cotton boomed. Moreover, like the South's other cash crops, upland cotton was well suited for slave labor because it required fairly continuous tending throughout most of the year. Once the harvest was in—a time when northern agricultural workers were laid off—the slaves cleared land, cut wood, and made repairs. The long workyear maximized the return on capital invested in slave labor.

Despite the care required, the cultivation of cotton left plenty of time for slaves to grow food. The major grain in the southern diet was corn, which nicely complemented the labor cycle of cotton. Corn needed little attention while cotton was being harvested and could be planted earlier or later than cotton during the long growing season. Surplus corn could be fed to hogs and converted into pork. Because almost all cotton farms and plantations also raised corn and hogs, the South virtually fed itself.

The linkage of cotton and slaves was at the heart of the plantation system that spread westward after the War of 1812. From its original base in South Carolina and Georgia, the cotton kingdom moved into the Old Southwest and then into Texas and Arkansas. As wasteful agricultural practices exhausted new lands, planters moved to the next cotton frontier farther west. Cotton output exploded from 73,000 bales (each bale weighed close to 500 pounds) in 1800 to over 2 million bales by midcentury, thanks to the fertility of virgin land and technological changes, such as improved seed varieties and steam-powered cotton gins (see Figure 13-1). Slave labor accounted for more than 90 percent of cotton production.

Plantations, large productive units specializing in a cash crop and employing at least twenty slaves, were the leading economic institution in the Lower South. Planters were the most prestigious social group, and, though less than 5 percent of white families were in the planter class, they controlled more than 40 percent of the slaves, cotton output, and total agricultural wealth. Most had inherited or

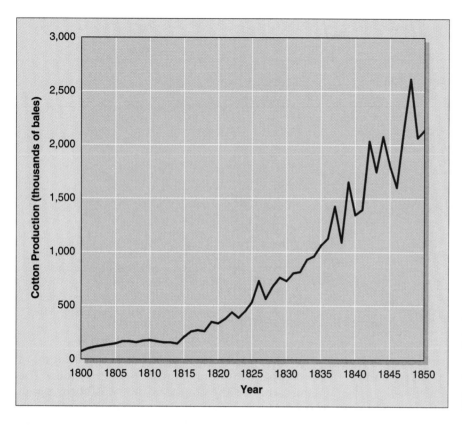

Figure 13-1 U.S. Cotton Production, 1800–1850
Cotton production spiraled upward after 1800, and the South became the world's leading supplier.
Source: *U.S. Bureau of the Census, Historical Statistics of the United States (1960).*

married into their wealth, but they could stay at the top of the South's class structure only by continuing to profit from slave labor.

Plantations were generally more efficient producers of cotton than small farms. Planters had the best land because only they commanded the labor resources to exploit the wet bottomlands, drain the swamps, or clear the raw jungle in the Mississippi Delta. They were also more likely than farmers to belong to agricultural reform societies that made them aware of superior varieties of seed or the most progressive techniques of cultivation. Most important, the ownership of twenty or more slaves enabled planters to use gangs to do both routine and specialized agricultural work. This **gang system**, a cruder version of the division of labor that was being introduced in northern factories, permitted a regimented pace of work that would have been impossible to impose on free agricultural workers. Teams of field hands, made up of women as well as men, had to work at a steady pace or else feel the lash. They were supervised by white overseers and black drivers, slaves selected for their management skills and agricultural knowledge.

By 1850, the plantations of the Lower South were larger and more specialized than elsewhere in the South, and the wealth of their owners was more ostentatiously displayed. More clusters of slave cabins,

overseers' quarters, and cotton gins dotted the countryside. The few towns were little more than a haphazard collection of plain wooden houses scattered around a tavern, country store, and blacksmith's shop.

The harvest was the busiest time on a cotton plantation. Working in gangs, and often supervised by a slave driver, the field hands were assigned a daily quota of cotton to pick.

CHRONOLOGY

1790s Large-scale conversions of slaves to Christianity begin.	**1831–1832** Virginia legislature debates and rejects gradual emancipation.
1793 Eli Whitney patents the cotton gin.	**1832** Thomas R. Dew publishes the first full-scale defense of slavery.
1800 Gabriel Prosser leads a rebellion in Richmond, Virginia.	**1837–1845** Slavery issue divides Presbyterians, Methodists, and Baptists into separate sectional churches.
1808 Congress prohibits the African slave trade.	
1811 Slaves rebel in Louisiana.	**1845** Florida and Texas, the last two slave states, are admitted to the Union.
1816–1819 First cotton boom in the South.	**1850s** Cotton production doubles.
1822 Denmark Vesey's Conspiracy fails in Charleston, South Carolina.	**1857** Hinton R. Helper publishes *The Impending Crisis of the South.*
1831 Nat Turner leads a rebellion in Southampton County, Virginia.	

"During two days' sail on the Alabama River from Mobile to Montgomery," noted a traveler in 1860, "I did not see so many houses standing together in any one spot as could be dignified with the appellation of village."

The plantation districts of the Lower South stifled the growth of towns and the economic enterprise they fostered. Planters, as well as ordinary farmers, strove to be self-sufficient. The most significant economic exchange—exporting cotton—took place in international markets and was handled by specialized commission merchants in Charleston, Mobile, and New Orleans. The Lower South had amassed great wealth, but most outsiders saw no signs of progress there.

The Profits of Slavery

Slavery was profitable on an individual basis. Most modern studies indicate that the average rate of return on capital invested in a slave was about 10 percent a year, a rate that at least equaled what was available in alternative investments in the South or the North. Not surprisingly, the newer regions of the cotton kingdom in the Lower South, with the most productive land and the greatest commitment to plantation agriculture, consistently led the nation in per capita income.

The profitability of slavery ultimately rested on the enormous demand for cotton outside the South. This demand grew at about 5 percent a year in the first half of the nineteenth century. Although cotton prices fluctuated like those of any other commodity in an unregulated market, demand was so strong that prices held steady at around 10 cents a pound in the 1850s even as southern production of cotton doubled. Textile mills in Britain were always the largest market, but demand in continental Europe and the United States grew even faster after 1840.

Southern law defined slaves as chattel, the personal property of their owners, and their market value increased along with the profitability of slavery. Prices for a male field hand rose from $250 in 1815 to $900 by 1860. Prices at any given time varied according to the age, sex, and skills of the slave, as well as overall market conditions, but the steady appreciation of prices for slaves meant that slave owners could sell their human chattel and realize a profit over and above what they had already earned from the slaves' labor. This was especially the case with slave mothers; the children they bore increased the capital assets of their owners. Slave women of childbearing age were therefore valued nearly as much as male field hands. The domestic slave trade brought buyers and sellers of slaves together. Slaves flowed from the older areas of the Upper South to the newer plantation districts in the Lower South. Indeed, when Congress ended the African slave trade in 1808 and it became difficult to smuggle in significant numbers of African slaves, planters in the Deep South had to depend on internal trade for the bulk of their labor supply. This trade was extensive: more than 800,000 slaves were moved between regions in the South from 1790 to 1860, and professional slave traders transported at least 60 percent of them. Drawing on lines of credit from banks, the traders paid cash for slaves, most of whom they bought from plantations in the Upper South. By selling these slaves in regional markets where demand had driven up the price, they turned a tidy profit.

The sheer size of the internal slave trade indicates just how profit-driven slave owners were. Few of them hesitated to break up slave families for sale when market conditions were right. About half of all slave sales separated family members. Slave children born in the Upper South after 1820 stood a one-in-three chance of being sold during their lifetime.

Most of the profits from slave labor and sales went into buying more land and slaves. As long as slaves employed in growing cash staples returned 10 percent a year, slave owners had little economic incentive to shift their capital resources into man-

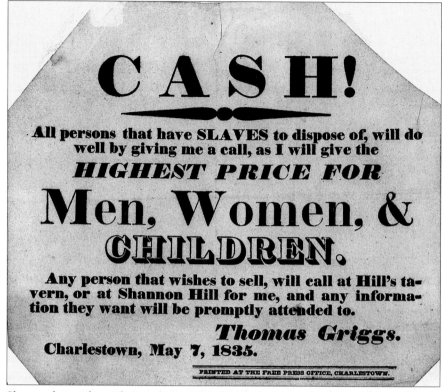

Slave traders such as Thomas Griggs offered cash for slaves whom they sold at a higher price in the booming cotton regions of the Lower South.

ufacturing or urban development. The predictable result was that industrialization and urbanization fell far behind the levels in the free states, creating what outsiders came to decry as southern "backwardness." The South had one-third of the nation's population in 1860 but produced by value only 10 percent of the nation's manufacturing output. Fewer than one in ten Southerners lived in a city, compared to more than one in three Northeasterners and one in seven Midwesterners.

Nowhere was the indifference of planters to economic diversification more evident than in the Lower South, which had the smallest urban population and the fewest factories. Planters here were not opposed to economic innovations that promised greater profits, but they feared social changes that might undermine the stability of slavery. Urbanization and industrialization both entailed such risks.

Most planters suspected that the urban environment weakened slavery. An editorial in the New Orleans *Crescent* charged that slaves in the city were "demoralized to a deplorable extent, all owing to the indiscriminate license and indulgence extended them by masters, mistresses, and guardians, and to the practice of *forging passes,* which has now become a regular business in New Orleans." For a white

person, a "demoralized" slave was one who behaved as if free. Urban slaves, though scarcely free, enjoyed a degree of personal and economic independence that blurred the line between freedom and servitude.

Urban slaves were artisans, semiskilled laborers, and domestics, and unlike their rural counterparts, they usually lived apart from their owners. They had much more freedom than field hands to move around, interact with whites and other blacks, and experiment with various social roles. Many of them, especially if they had a marketable skill, such as carpentry or tailoring, could hire out their labor and retain some wages for themselves after reimbursing their owners. In short, the direct authority of the slave owner was less clear-cut in the town than in the country.

Urban slavery declined from 1820 to 1860 as slaves decreased from 22 percent to 10 percent of the urban population. This decline reflected both doubts about the stability of slavery in an urban setting and the large profits that slave labor earned for slave owners in the rural cotton economy.

The ambivalence of planters toward urban slavery also characterized their attitudes toward industrial slavery and indeed to industrialization itself. If based on free labor, industrialization risked promoting an antislavery class consciousness among manufacturing laborers that would challenge the property rights of slave owners. William Gregg, the owner of a large cotton mill in upcountry South Carolina, showed that these fears were overblown when he built a company town in the 1840s that kept his white workers under tight, paternalistic controls. Still, many planters considered free workers potential abolitionists.

But the use of slaves as factory operatives threatened slave discipline because an efficient level of production required special incentives. "Whenever a slave is made a mechanic, he is more than half freed," complained James Hammond, a South Carolina planter. Elaborating on Hammond's fears, a Virginian noted of slaves that he had hired out for industrial work: "They were worked hard, and had too much liberty, and were acquiring bad habits. They earned money by overwork, and spent it for whisky, and got a habit of roaming about and *taking care of themselves;* because, when they were not at work in the furnace, nobody looked out for them."

The anxieties of planters over industrialization and their refusal to shift capital from plantation agriculture to finance it ensured that manufacturing played only a minor economic role in the Lower South. Planters supported industrialization only as an adjunct, not an alternative, to the plantation economy. Thus planters did invest in railroads and factories, but their holdings remained concentrated in land and slaves. They augmented their income by renting slaves to manufacturers and railroad contractors but were quick to recall these slaves to work on the plantations when needed.

No more than 5 percent of the slaves in the Lower South ever worked in manufacturing, and most of these were in rural enterprises serving local markets too small to interest northern manufacturers. Ever concerned to preserve slavery, planters would not risk slave discipline or the profits of cotton agriculture by embracing the unpredictable changes that industrialization was sure to bring.

The Upper South

Climate and geography distinguished the Upper South from the Lower South. The eight slave states of the Upper South lay north of the best growing zones for cotton. The northernmost of these states—Delaware, Maryland, Kentucky, and Missouri—bordered on free states and were known as the Border South. The four states south of them—Virginia, North Carolina, Tennessee, and Arkansas—constituted a middle zone. Slavery was entrenched in all these states, but it was less dominant than in the cotton South.

The key difference from which others followed was the suitability of the Lower South for growing cotton with gangs of slave labor. Except for prime cotton districts in middle Tennessee, eastern Arkansas, and parts of North Carolina, the Upper South lacked the fertile soil and long growing season necessary for the commercial production of cotton, rice, or sugar (see Map 13-2). Consequently, the demand for slaves was less than in the Lower South. Two-thirds of southern whites lived in the Upper South in 1860, but they held only 45 percent of all slaves. Percentages of slave ownership and of slaves in the overall population were roughly half those in the cotton South.

While the Lower South was undergoing a cotton boom after the War of 1812, the Upper South

Map 13-2 Cotton and Other Crops in the South, 1860
Most of the Upper South was outside the cotton belt where the demand for slave labor was greatest.

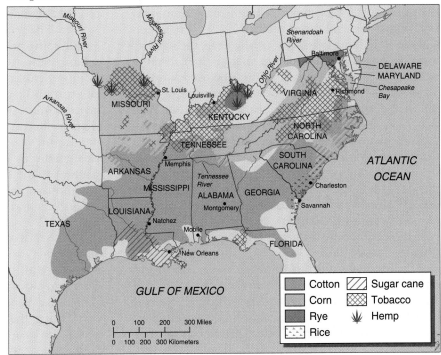

was mired in a long economic slump from which it did not emerge until the 1850s. The improved economy of the Upper South in the late antebellum period increasingly relied on free labor, a development that many cotton planters feared would splinter southern unity in defense of slavery.

A Period of Economic Adjustment

To inhabitants and visitors alike, vast stretches of the Upper South presented a dreary spectacle of exhausted fields and rural depopulation in the 1820s and 1830s. The soil was most depleted where tobacco had been cultivated extensively. Even where the land was still fertile, farmers could not compete against the agricultural commodities that the fresher lands of the Old Southwest produced. Land values fell as whites dumped their property and headed west. "Emigration is here raging with all the strength of fanaticism," wrote a Virginian in 1837, "and nothing else can be talked of but selling estates, at a great sacrifice, and '*packing off*' for the '*far west.*'"

Agricultural reform emerged in the 1830s as one proposed solution to this economic crisis. Its leading advocate was Edmund Ruffin, a Virginia planter who tirelessly promoted the use of marl (shell deposits) to neutralize the overly acidic and worn-out soils of the Upper South. He also called for deeper plowing, systematic rotation of crops, and upgrading the breeding stock for animal husbandry.

Ruffin's efforts, and those of the agricultural societies and fairs spawned by the reform movement, met with some success, especially in the 1840s when the prices of all cash staples fell. Still, only a minority of farmers ever embraced reform. These were generally the well-educated planters who read the agricultural press and could afford to change their farming practices. The landscape of Ruffin's beloved Virginia Tidewater still provoked travelers to remark, as one did in the early 1850s, "I've heard 'em say out West that old Virginny was the mother of statesmen— reckon she must be about done, eh? This 'ere's about the *barrenest* look for a mother ever I see."

Although soil exhaustion and wasteful farming persisted, agriculture in the Upper South had revived by the 1850s. A rebound in the tobacco market accounted for part of this revival, but the growing profitability of general farming was responsible for most of it.

Particularly in the Border South, the trend was toward agricultural diversification. Farmers and planters lessened their dependence on slave labor or on a single cash crop and practiced a thrifty, efficient agriculture geared to producing grain and livestock for urban markets. Western Maryland and the

Shenandoah Valley and northern sections of Virginia grew wheat, and in the former tobacco districts of the Virginia and North Carolina Tidewater, wheat, corn, and garden vegetables became major cash crops.

Expanding urban markets and a network of internal improvements facilitated this transition to general farming. Both of these developments were outgrowths of the movement for industrial diversification launched in the 1820s in response to the heavy outflow of population from the Upper South. Although not far advanced by northern standards, urbanization and industrialization in the Upper South were considerably greater than in the Lower South. The region had twice the percentage of urban residents of the cotton South, and it contained the leading manufacturing cities in the slave states—St. Louis, Baltimore, and Louisville. By 1860, the Upper South accounted for three-fourths of the South's manufacturing capital and output and nearly all of its heavy industry. Canals and railroads linked cities and countryside in a denser transportation grid than in the Lower South.

With an economy more balanced among agriculture, manufacturing, and trade than a generation earlier, the Upper South at midcentury was gradually becoming less tied to plantation agriculture and slave labor. The rural majority increasingly prospered by growing foodstuffs for city-dwellers and factory workers. The labor market for railroad construction and manufacturing work was strong enough to attract northern immigrants and help reduce the loss of the native-born population that had migrated to other states.

The economic adjustment in the Upper South converted the labor surplus of the 1820s into a labor scarcity by the 1850s. "It is a fact," noted Edmund Ruffin in 1859, "that labor is greatly deficient in all Virginia, and especially in the rich western counties, which, for want of labor, scarcely yet yield in the proportion of one tenth of their capacity." Ruffin's commitment to agricultural reform was exceeded only by his devotion to slavery. Like many planters in the cotton states, he feared that free labor was about to replace scarce and expensive slave labor in Virginia and much of the Upper South.

The Decline of Slavery

Slave owners tended to exaggerate all threats to slavery, and Ruffin was no exception. But slavery was clearly growing weaker in the Upper South by the 1850s (see Figure 13-2). The decline was most evident along the northern tier of the Upper South where the proportion of slaves to the overall population fell steadily after 1830. By 1860, slaves in the

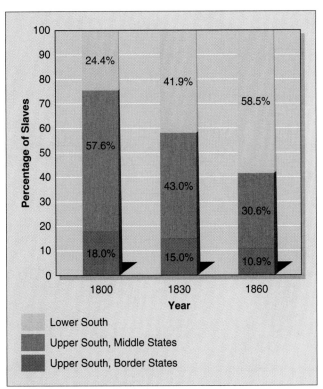

Figure 13-2   *The Changing Regional Pattern of Slavery in the South, 1800–1860*
As the nineteenth century progressed, slavery increasingly became identified with the cotton-growing Lower South.

Border South had dropped to 2 percent of the population in Delaware, 13 percent in Maryland, 19 percent in Kentucky, and 10 percent in Missouri. In Virginia from 1830 to 1860, slaves fell from 39 to 31 percent of the population.

Elsewhere in the Upper South, slavery was more or less holding its own by the 1850s. Tobacco and cotton planters in North Carolina and Tennessee continued to rely heavily on slave labor, but most small farmers were indifferent, if not opposed, to the institution. Only in Arkansas, whose alluvial lands along the Mississippi River offered a new frontier for plantation agriculture, was slavery growing rapidly. Slaves, however, still made up only 25 percent of the population of Arkansas in 1860 and were confined mainly to the southeastern corner of the state. Geographically dominated by the Ozark Highlands, Arkansas was best suited to general farming.

The region's role as a slave exporter to the Lower South hastened the decline of slavery in the Upper South. In every decade after 1820, the internal slave trade drained off about 10 percent of the slaves in the Upper South, virtually the entire natural increase. Slave traders initially made most of their purchases in Virginia and Maryland, but by the 1850s, they were also active in the Carolinas, Kentucky, and Missouri. New Orleans, Memphis, and Natchez, Mississippi, were the major western distribution points for the slaves, who were sent west both by sea and by land.

Selling slaves to the Lower South shored up the economic stake of the Upper South in slavery at a time when the institution was barely profitable there. The sale of surplus slaves was a windfall for planters whose slaves had become an economic burden. This same windfall gave planters the capital to embark on agricultural reform and shift out of tobacco production. Investment capital in the Upper South was not flowing into slave property but into economic diversification that expanded urban manufacturing. Both of these structural changes increasingly put slavery at a competitive disadvantage against free labor.

The wheat, small grains, and fodder crops that replaced tobacco in much of the Upper South did not require the nearly continuous attention of a work force. Unlike tobacco, wheat needed intensive labor only at planting and during the short harvest. Thus as planters abandoned tobacco, they kept fewer slaves and relied on seasonal and cheap agricultural workers to meet peak labor demand.

The cheapness and flexibility of free labor made it better suited than slave labor for general farming. This was what urban manufacturers wanted in their labor supply—workers who could be hired and fired at a moment's notice. Despite the successful use of slaves in tobacco manufacturing and at the large Tredegar Iron Works in Richmond, immigrant workers displaced slaves in most of the factories in the Border South. By 1860, slaves made up just 1 percent of the population in St. Louis and Baltimore, the South's major industrial cities.

Slavery was in economic retreat across the Upper South after 1830. There were still plantation districts with large concentrations of slaves, and slave owners retained enough political power to defeat all challenges to their property interests. Nevertheless, the gradual turn to free labor was unmistakable. Although slavery was safe for the immediate future, agitation for emancipation had begun in the cities of the Border South.

Ties of kinship, not slavery per se, were now the strongest bonds among whites in the Upper South. As Alfred Iveson, a Georgia planter, noted with alarm in 1860: "Those border States can get along without slavery. Their soil and climate are appropriate to white labor; they can live and flourish without African slavery; but the cotton States cannot."

The Collection of Jay P. Altmayer.

Richmond, Virginia, was a major market for slave sales in the Upper South. Shown above are slaves at an auction as their owners wait for bids from the slave traders.

Slave Life and Culture

Nearly 4 million slaves lived in the South by 1860, more than a fivefold increase since the ratification of the Constitution. This population gain was overwhelmingly due to an excess of births over deaths, although as many as fifty thousand Africans may have been smuggled into the country until about 1860 despite the ban on the African slave trade that took effect in 1808.

Almost all southern slaves were thus native-born by the mid-nineteenth century. They were not Africans but African-Americans, and they shared the common fate of bondage. By resisting an enslavement they could not prevent, they shaped a culture of their own that eased their pain and raised their hopes of someday being free. They managed to retain their dignity despite the humiliations to which they were subjected. In their family life and religious beliefs, slaves found the strength to sustain themselves under nearly intolerable circumstances.

Work Routines and Living Conditions

Being treated as a piece of property to be worked for a profit and bought and sold when financially advantageous to one's owners—this was the legal and eco-

nomic reality that all slaves confronted. Each southern state had its own **slave codes**, laws defining the status of slaves and the rights of masters; the codes gave slave owners near-absolute power over their human property.

"The right of personal liberty in the slave is utterly inconsistent with the idea of slavery," wrote Thomas R. R. Cobb of Georgia in a legal treatise on slavery. The slave codes, accordingly, severely restricted the lives of slaves. Slaves could not own property, make contracts, possess guns or alcohol, legally marry (except in Louisiana), leave plantations without the owner's written permission, or testify against their masters or any other white person in a court of law. Many states also prohibited teaching a slave to read or write. The law assumed that the economic self-interest of masters in their slave property gave slaves adequate legal protection against injuries inflicted by others. The murder of a slave by a master was illegal, but in practice the law and community standards looked the other way if a disobedient slave was killed while being disciplined.

The slave codes penalized any challenge to a master's authority or any infraction of plantation rules. Whippings were the most common authorized punishment: twenty lashes on the bare back for leaving a plantation without a pass, one hundred lashes for writing a pass for another slave, and so on. Striking a master, committing arson, or conspiring to rebel were punishable by death.

The owner, as expressed in the Alabama Slave Code of 1852, had "the right to the time, labor and services of the slave." This of course was the whole purpose of owning a slave. Most masters recognized that it was good business sense to feed, clothe, and house their slaves well enough to ensure productive labor and to encourage a family life that would enable the slave population to reproduce itself. Thus planters' self-interest probably improved the living standards for slaves in the first half of the nineteenth century, and the slave population grew at a rate only slightly below that of southern whites.

However, planters rarely provided more than the bare necessities. The slaves lived mainly on rations of cornmeal and salt pork. Together with vegetables they grew on small garden plots that many planters permitted and occasional catches of game and fish, this diet provided ample calories but often insufficient vitamins and nutriments to protect slaves (as well as the many poor whites who ate the same diet) against such diseases as beriberi and pellagra. Intestinal disorders were chronic, and dysentery and cholera were common. About 20 percent of the slaves on a typical plantation were sick at any given time. Infant mortality was twice as high among slaves as among whites in 1850; so was mortality among slave children up to age 14. According to one study, the life expectancy for slaves at birth was 21 to 22 years, roughly half that for whites.

Planters furnished slaves with two sets of coarse clothing, one for summer and one for winter. Their housing, typically a 15-by-15-foot one-room cabin for five or six occupants, provided little more than basic shelter against the elements. "They were built of logs," a traveler noted of slave cabins in South Carolina, "with no windows—no opening at all, except the doorway, with a chimney of sticks and mud; with no trees about them, no porches, or shades, of any kind. Except for the chimney . . . I should have conjectured that it had been built for a powder-house, or perhaps an ice-house—never for an animal to sleep in."

Small and unadorned, slave cabins emphasized not only the planters' desire to minimize housing costs but also their determination to treat slaves as a regimented, collective population. Large planters placed these cabins in a row, an arrangement that projected precision and undifferentiated order. Slaves expressed their own individuality by furnishing their cabins with handmade beds and benches and by pushing for the right to put in gardens.

The diet and housing of most slaves may have been no worse than that of the poorest whites in both the North and the South, but their workload was undoubtedly heavier. Just over half of the slave population at midcentury was concentrated on plantation units with twenty or more slaves, and most of these slaves worked as field hands in gang labor. Overseers freely admitted that they relied on whippings to make slaves work in these gangs.

Most plantation slaves toiled at hard, physical labor from sunup to sundown. The work was more intense and sustained than that of white farmers or white factory hands. The fear of the whip on a bare back set the pace. At daybreak, recalled Solomon Northrup of his enslavement on a Louisiana plantation, "the fears and labors of another day begin; and until its close there is no such thing as rest. [The slave] fears he will be caught lagging through the day; he fears to approach the gin-house with his basket-load of

This row of former slave cabins, c. 1870, housed the slaves on the Kingsley plantation of Florida.

cotton at night; he fears, when he lies down, that he will over-sleep himself in the morning."

Some 15 to 20 percent of plantation slaves were house servants or skilled artisans who had lighter and less regimented workloads than field hands. Some planters used the prospect of transfer to these relatively privileged positions as an incentive to field hands to work harder. Extra rations, time off on weekends, passes to visit a spouse on a nearby plantation, and the right to have a garden plot were among the other incentives planters used to keep labor productivity high. However, what a planter viewed as a privilege benevolently bestowed, slaves quickly came to see as a customary right that they expected planters to observe. Despite the power of the whip, if planters failed to respect these "rights," slave morale would decline and the work routine would be interrupted.

Nearly three-fourths of the slaves worked on plantations and medium-sized farms. Most of the remainder—those in units with fewer than ten slaves—worked on small farms in close contact with the master's family. Their workloads were more varied and sometimes less taxing than those of plantation hands, but these slaves were also more directly exposed to the whims of an angry owner and were less likely to live in complete family units. Holdings of a few slaves or small farms scattered across the countryside meant that husbands and wives often lived on different farms, and the owners of only a few slaves were more vulnerable than planters to market downturns that could force them to sell their slaves and thus further divide families.

One in ten slaves worked outside the plantations and farms. They labored at jobs that most native whites generally shunned. Extractive industries, such as mining and lumbering, relied heavily on these slaves, and every southern industry employed some slaves. The Tredegar Iron Company in Richmond, the largest iron foundry in the South, used slaves as

Especially on large plantations, slave nursemaids cared for the young children in the white planter's family.

From the Collection of the Louisiana State Museum.

its main work force after 1847, partly to curb strikes by its white workers. Racial tensions often flared in southern industry, and when the races worked together, skilled whites typically insisted on being placed in supervisory positions over the slaves.

Digging coal as miners or shoveling it as stokers for boilers on steamboats, laying down iron for the railroads or shaping hot slabs of it in a foundry, industrial slaves worked at least as hard as field hands. Compared to plantation slaves, however, they had more independence off the job and greater opportunities to earn money of their own. Since many of them had to house and feed themselves, they could also enjoy more time free from direct white scrutiny. By undertaking extra factory work, known as "overwork," industrial slaves could earn $50 or more a month, money that could be used to buy goods for their families or, in rare cases, to purchase their freedom.

Families and Religion

The core institution of slave life was the family. Except in Louisiana, southern law did not recognize slave marriages, but masters permitted, even encouraged, marital unions to raise the morale of their labor force and increase its value by producing marketable children. Slaves embraced their families as a source of loving warmth and strength in a system that treated them as commodities.

Despite all the obstacles arrayed against them, many slave marriages produced enduring commitments and a supportive moral code for family members. Most slave unions remained intact until death or, more likely, the sale of a spouse ended the partnership. Close to one-third of slave marriages were broken up by sales or forced removals. A slave bitterly recalled that "the separation of slaves in this way is little thought of. A few masters regard their union as sacred, but where one does, a hundred care nothing about it."

Both parents were present in about two-thirds of slave families, the same ratio as in contemporary peasant families in western Europe. Although the father's role as protector of and provider for his wife and children had no standing under slavery, most slave fathers struggled to help feed their families by hunting and fishing, and they risked death or a terrible beating to defend their wives from sexual abuse by the overseer or master. Besides their field labor, slave mothers had all the burdens of pregnancy, caring for children, laundering, and preparing meals. After escaping from slavery, Sojourner Truth told how she placed her babies in a basket hanging from a tree while she worked in the field and had older children care for them.

No anguish under slavery was more heart-rending than that of a mother whose child was sold away from her. "Oh, my heart was too full!" recalled Charity Bowery on being told that her boy Richard was sold. "[My mistress] had sent me away on an errand, because she didn't want to be troubled with our cries. I hadn't any chance to see my poor boy. I shall never see my poor boy. I shall never see him again in this world. My heart felt as if it was under a great load."

Charity Bowery's experience was hardly unique. Slave parents had to suppress the rage they felt at their powerlessness to protect their children from the cruelties of slavery. Slave accounts are full of stories of children running in vain to their parents to save them from a whipping at the hands of a white. Most parents could only teach their children the

skills of survival in a world in which whites had a legal monopoly on violence. The most valuable of these skills was the art of hiding one's true feelings from whites and telling them what they wanted to hear. As a perceptive traveler noted: "When therefore a white man approaches [the slaves] with inquiries concerning their condition, they are at once put upon their guard, and either make indefinite and vague replies, or directly contradict their real sentiments."

Extensive kinship ties provided a support network for the vulnerable slave family. Thickest on the older and larger plantations, these networks included both blood relatives and other slaves who influenced the life of the family. Children were taught to address elders as "Aunt" and "Uncle" and fellow slaves as "sister" and "brother." Parents thus helped prepare their children for the day when the family might be divided. If separated from a parent, a child could turn to relatives or the larger slave community for care and assistance.

Slaves followed West African customs by prohibiting marriage between cousins and by often naming their children after departed grandparents. They also drew on an African heritage kept alive through folklore and oral histories to create a religion that fit their needs. The ancestors of nineteenth-century slaves brought no common religion with them when they were taken to the New World. However, beliefs common to a variety of African religions survived. Once slaves began to embrace Christianity in the late eighteenth-century, they blended these beliefs into an African Christianity.

In keeping with African traditions, the religion of the slaves fused the natural and spiritual worlds, accepted the power of ghosts over the living, and relied on an expressive form of worship in which the participants shouted and swayed in rhythm with the beat of drums and other instruments. Associated with reverence for ancestors, dance was sacred in Africa. Spirituals, the religious songs of the slaves, were sung in a dance known in America as the "ring shout." Moving counterclockwise and stamping their feet to establish a beat for the music, slaves blended dance and song in a religious ceremony that helped them endure oppression and sustain their self-confidence.

By most estimates, no more than 20 percent of the slaves ever converted to Christianity. Those who did convert found in Christianity a message of deliverance rooted in the liberation of Moses's people from bondage in Egypt. The Jesus of the New Testament spoke to them as a compassionate God who had shared their burden of suffering so that all peoples could hope to find the Promised Land of love and justice. By blending biblical imagery into their spirituals, the slaves expressed their yearning for freedom: "Didn't my Lord deliver Daniel/Then why not every man?"

The initial exposure of slaves to Christianity usually came from evangelical revivalists, and slaves always favored the Baptists and Methodists over other denominations. The evangelical message of universal spiritual equality confirmed the slaves' sense of personal worth. Less formal in both their doctrines and organization than the Presbyterians and Episcopalians, the evangelical sects allowed the slaves more leeway to choose their own preachers and engage in the physical activism and the call-and-response pattern that characterized slave religion. Perhaps because they baptized by total immersion, which evoked the purifying power of water so common in African religions, the Baptists gained the most slave converts.

Most planters were pragmatic about encouraging Christianity among their slaves. Like every other aspect of the slave's life, they favored it only if they could control it. Thus while many planters allowed blacks to preach at religious services on their plantations, they usually insisted that whites be present. Worried that abolitionist propaganda might attract the slaves to Christianity as a religion of secular liberation, some planters in the late antebellum period tried to convert their slaves to their own version of Christianity. They invited white ministers to their plantations to preach a gospel of passivity and obedience. The Christianity they wanted for their slaves centered on Paul's call for servants to "obey in all things your Masters."

Although most slaves viewed the religion of their owners as hypocritical and the sermons of white ministers as propaganda, they feigned acceptance of the religious wishes of their masters. They attended the special slave chapels some masters built and sat in segregated galleries in white churches on Sunday mornings. But in the evening, out of sight of the master or overseer, they held their own services in the woods and listened to their own preachers. As much as they could, the slaves hid their religious life from whites. In creating a spiritual life for themselves, many slaves experienced religion as a rebirth that gave them the inner strength to endure their bondage. As one of them recalled, "I was born a slave and lived through some hard times. If it had not been for *my God*, I don't know what I would have done."

Resistance

Open resistance to slavery was futile. The persistently disobedient slave would be sold "down river" to a harsher master or, in extreme cases, killed. The fate of Richard, Charity Bowery's boy who was sold away from her, typified that of the openly defiant slave. He resisted the efforts of his new owner in Alabama to break his will. When the owner threatened to shoot him if he did not consent to being whipped, Richard replied, "Shoot away, I won't come to be flogged." The master shot and killed him.

Although the odds of succeeding were infinitesimal, slaves as desperate as Richard did plot rebellions. Four major uprisings occurred in the nineteenth century. The first, **Gabriel Prosser's Rebellion** in 1800, involved about fifty armed slaves around Richmond, though perhaps as many as one thousand slaves knew about Prosser's plans. The failure to seize a key road to Richmond and a warning to whites by a slave informer doomed the rebellion before it got under way. State authorities executed Prosser and twenty-five of his followers.

A decade later, in what seems to have been a spontaneous bid for freedom, several hundred slaves in the river parishes (counties) above New Orleans marched on the city. Poorly armed, they were no match for the U.S. Army troops and militiamen who stopped them. More than sixty slaves died, and the heads of the leading rebels were posted on poles along the Mississippi River to warn others of the fate that awaited rebellious slaves.

The most carefully planned slave revolt, *Denmark Vesey's Conspiracy*, like Prosser's, failed before it got started. Vesey, a literate carpenter and lay preacher in Charleston who had purchased his freedom with the money he had won in a lottery, planned the revolt in the summer of 1822. Vesey drew on biblical passages, antislavery sentiments in Congress he had gleaned from newspaper reports on the Missouri Compromise debates, and the successful revolt of slaves in Haiti to inspire his followers. He tried to steel the courage of his coconspirators by telling them that his chief lieutenant, Gullah Jack, a conjurer, or voodoo doctor, would cast spells on their enemies. He assigned teams of rebels specific targets, such as the municipal guardhouse and arsenal. Once Charleston was secured, the rebels apparently planned to flee to Haiti. The plot collapsed when two domestic servants betrayed it. White authorities responded swiftly and savagely. They hanged thirty-five conspirators, including Vesey, and banished thirty-seven others. After destroying the African Methodist Episcopal Church where Vesey had preached and the conspirators had met, they tried to seal off the city from subversive outsiders by passing the Negro Seamen's Act, which mandated the imprisonment of black sailors while their ships were berthed in Charleston.

One slave revolt, **Nat Turner's Rebellion** in Southampton County, Virginia, did erupt before it could be suppressed. Turner was a literate field hand driven by prophetic visions of black vengeance

After eluding his white pursuers for two months, Nat Turner, the leader of the South's most famous slave revolt, was accidentally captured on October 30, 1831.

against white oppressors. Like Vesey, he was well versed in the Bible. Convinced by what he called "signs in heaven" that he should "arise and prepare myself and slay my enemies with their own weapons," he led a small band of followers on a murderous rampage in late August 1831. The first white to be killed was Joseph Travis, Turner's owner, known for his lenient treatment of slaves. In the next two days, sixty other whites were also killed. An enraged posse, aided by slaves loyal to the whites, captured or killed

most of Turner's party. Turner hid for two months before being apprehended. He and more than thirty other slaves were executed, and panicky whites killed more than a hundred other slaves.

Slaves well understood that the odds against a successful rebellion were insurmountable. They could see who had all the guns. Whites were also more numerous. In contrast to the large black majorities in the slave societies of the West Indies and Brazil—majorities made possible only by the continuous and heavy importation of African slaves—slaves in the American South made up only one-third of the population in the nineteenth century. Slaves lacked the numbers to overwhelm whites and could not escape to mountain hideaways or large tracts of jungle. Mounted patrols of whites were part of the police apparatus of slavery, and their surveillance limited organized rebellion by slaves to small, local affairs that were quickly suppressed.

Nor could many slaves escape to freedom. Few runaways made it to Canada or a free state. Whites could stop any blacks and demand to see papers documenting their freedom or right to travel without a master. The **Underground Railroad**, a secret network of stations and safe houses organized by Quakers and other antislavery whites and blacks, provided some assistance. However, fellow slaves or free blacks, especially those in the cities of the Border South, provided the only help most runaways could count on. Out of more than 3 million slaves in the 1850s, only about a thousand a year permanently escape (see "American Views: A Letter from an Escaped Slave to His Former Master").

After fleeing from slavery in Maryland in 1849, Harriet "Moses" Tubman, standing on left, risked reenslavement by returning to the South on several occasions to assist other slaves in escaping. She is photographed here with some of those she helped free.

American Views

A LETTER FROM AN ESCAPED SLAVE TO HIS FORMER MASTER

In 1859, Jackson Whitney was one of six thousand fugitive slaves living in Canada, a sanctuary of freedom beyond the reach of the Fugitive Slave Act of 1850. Like most fugitives, he was male, and he had been forced to leave his family behind in Kentucky. His letter, as well as other direct testimony by African-Americans about their experiences and feelings while enslaved, gives us information about slavery that only the slaves could provide.

❖ **How would you characterize the tone of Whitney's letter? How did he express his joy at being a free man?**

❖ **How did Whitney feel that he had been betrayed by Riley, his former owner? What did Whitney mean by the phrase "a slave talking to 'massa' "? How did he indicate that he had been hiding his true feelings as a slave?**

❖ **How did Whitney contrast his religious beliefs and those of Riley? How did he expect Riley to be punished?**

❖ **What pained Whitney about his freedom in Canada, and what did he ask of Riley?**

March 18, 1859

Mr. Wm. Riley, Springfield, Ky. —Sir: I take this opportunity to dictate a few lines to you, supposing you might be curious to know my whereabouts. I am happy to inform you that I am in Canada, in good health, and have been here several days. Perhaps, by this time, you have concluded that robbing a woman of her husband, and children of their father does not pay, at least in your case; and I thought, while lying in jail by your direction, that if you had no remorse or conscience that would make you feel for a poor, broken-hearted man, and his worse-than-murdered wife and child, . . . and could not by any entreaty or permission be induced to do as you promised you would, which was to let me go with my family for $800—but contended for $1,000, when you had promised to take the same you gave for me (which was $660.) at the time you bought me, and let me go with my dear wife and children! but instead would render me miserable, and lie to me, and to your neighbors . . . and when you was at Louisville trying to sell me!

The few who made it to the North did so by running at night and hiding during the day. The most ingenious resorted to clever stratagems. Henry "Box" Brown arranged to have himself shipped in a box from Richmond to Philadelphia. Ellen Craft, a light-skinned slave who could pass as white, disguised herself as a male slaveholder accompanied by his dark-skinned servant (her husband, William). What could have been a fatal flaw in their plan as they traveled from Savannah to Philadelphia—their inability to write and hence sign their names or document their assumed identities—was overcome by having Ellen pose as a sickly, rheumatic master whose right hand had to be kept bandaged.

Running away was common, but most runaways fled no farther than to nearby swamps and woods. Most voluntarily returned or were tracked down by bloodhounds within a week. Aside from protesting a special grievance or trying to avoid punishment, these slaves usually wanted to visit a spouse or loved one. Occasionally, runaways could strike a bargain of lenient treatment in return for faithful ser-

then I thought it was time for me to make my feet feel for Canada, and let your conscience feel in your pocket. —Now you cannot say but that I did all that was honorable and right while I was with you, although I was a slave. I pretended all the time that I thought you, or some one else had a better right to me than I had to myself, which you know is rather hard thinking. —You know, too, that you proved a traitor to me in the time of need, and when in the most bitter distress that the human soul is capable of experiencing; and could you have carried out your purposes there would have been no relief. But I rejoice to say that an unseen, kind spirit appeared for the oppressed, and bade me take up my bed and walk—the result of which is that I am victorious and you are defeated.

I am comfortably situated in Canada, working for George Harris [another fugitive slave from Kentucky who had bought a farm in Canada]. . . .

There is only one thing to prevent me being entirely happy here, and that is the want of my dear wife and children, and you to see us enjoying ourselves together here. I wish you could realize the contrast between Freedom and Slavery;

but it is not likely that we shall ever meet again on this earth. But if you want to go to the next world and meet a God of love, mercy, and justice, in peace; who says, "Inasmuch as you did it to the least of them my little ones, you did it unto me"— making the professions that you do, pretending to be a follower of Christ, and tormenting me and my little ones as you have done—[you] had better repair the breaches you have made among us in this world, by sending my wife and children to me; thus preparing to meet your God in peace; for, if God don't punish you for inflicting such distress on the poorest of His poor, then there is no use of *having any* God, or *talking* about one. . . .

I hope you will consider candidly, and see if the case does not justify every word I have said, and ten times as much. You must not consider that it is a slave talking to 'massa' now, but one as free as yourself.

I subscribe myself one of the *abused* of America, but one of the *justified* and *honored* of Canada.

Jackson Whitney

Source: *John W. Blassingame, ed.*, Slave Testimony: Two Centuries of Letters, Speeches, Interviews, and Autobiographies (*1977*).

vice in the future. Most were severely punished. Such temporary flights from the master's control siphoned off some of the anger that might otherwise had boiled over in violent and self-destructive attacks on slave owners. All planters had heard about the field hand who took an ax to an overseer, the cook who poisoned her master's family, or the house servant who killed a sleeping master or mistress.

Slaves resisted complete domination by their masters in less overt ways. They maintained a rich oral tradition in which folktales, such as those based on Brer Rabbit, enabled them to mock powerful whites by identifying themselves with apparently defenseless animals who used wit and cunning to outsmart their stronger enemies. Slave owners routinely complained of slaves malingering at work, abusing farm animals, losing tools, stealing food, and committing arson. None of these acts challenged the system of slavery itself. Such resistance was beyond the power of the slaves. Subversive protests confirmed slaves' sense of their humanity and value as a people. By resisting dehumanization, slaves endured with dignity and self-respect.

Free Society

The abolitionists and the antislavery Republican party of the 1850s portrayed the social order of the slave South as little more than haughty planters lording it over shiftless, poor whites. The reality was considerably more complex. Planters, who set the social tone for the South as a whole, did act superior, but they were a tiny minority and had to contend with an ambitious middle class of small slaveholders and a majority of nonslaveholding farmers. Some landless whites on the margin of rural society fit the stereotype of poor whites, but they were easily outnumbered by self-reliant farmers who worked their own land. Southern cities, though small by northern standards, provided jobs for a growing class of free workers who increasingly clashed with planters over the use of slave labor.

These same cities, notably in the Upper South, were also home to the nation's largest concentration of free blacks. Though restricted in their freedom, these blacks competed with whites for jobs, and their very freedom contradicted the racial defense of slavery. Pressure was mounting on them by the 1850s to leave the South or be enslaved. The free society in the South was surely more diverse than its antislavery critics charged, but overriding racism bonded most whites together to defend the prerogatives of white supremacy.

The Slaveholding Minority

The white-columned plantation estate approached from a stately avenue of shade trees and framed by luxuriant gardens remains the most popular image of the slave South. In fact, such manorial estates were utterly unrepresentative of the lifestyle of the typical slaveholder. Only the wealthiest planters could live in such splendor, and they comprised less than 1 percent of southern white families in 1860. Yet displayed in their homes and grounds, their wealth and status were so imposing that they created an idealized image of grace and grandeur that has obscured the cruder realities of the slave regime.

Only in the rice districts of the South Carolina lowcountry and in the rich sugar parishes and cotton counties of the Mississippi Delta were large planters more than a small minority of the slaveholding class, let alone the general white population. Families of the planter class—defined as those who held a minimum of twenty slaves—constituted only around 3 percent of all southern families in 1860. Fewer than one out of five planter families—less than 1 percent of all families—owned more than fifty slaves. Far from exhibiting their wealth in displays of conspicuous consumption, most planters lived in drab log cabins. "The planter's home is generally a rude ungainly structure, made of logs, rough hewn from the forest; rail fences and rickety gates guard its enclosures," complained a speaker to the Alabama

Colonel James A. Whiteside and his family were among the small elite of southern whites who enjoyed the wealth and ease of life on a large plantation. Reflecting the ideal of patriarchy, this portrait, c. 1858, projects the colonel as a figure of power and authority.

SUMMARY

STRUCTURE OF FREE SOCIETY IN THE SOUTH, C. 1860

Group	Size	Characteristics
Large planters	Less than 1 percent of white families	Owned fifty or more slaves and plantations in excess of one thousand acres; the wealthiest class in America
Planters	About 3 percent of white families	Owned twenty to forty-nine slaves and plantations in excess of one hundred acres; controlled bulk of southern wealth and provided most of the political leaders
Small slaveholders	About 20 percent of white families	Owned fewer than twenty slaves, and most often less than five; primarily farmers, though some were part of a small middle class in towns and cities
Nonslaveholding whites	About 75 percent of white families	Most were yeomen farmers who owned their own land and stressed production for family use; one in five owned neither slaves nor land and squatted on least desirable land where they planted some corn and grazed some livestock; in cities they worked as artisans or, more typically, day laborers
Free blacks	About 3 percent of all free families	Concentrated in the Upper South; hemmed in by legal and social restrictions; most were tenants or farm laborers; about one-third lived in cities and generally were limited to lowest-paying jobs

horticultural society in 1851. "We murder our soil with wasteful culture because there is plenty of fresh land West—and we live in tents and huts when we might live in rural palaces."

Most planters wanted to acquire wealth, not display it. They were acquisitive and restless, eager to move on and abandon their homes when the allure of profits from a new cotton frontier promised to relieve them of the debts they had incurred to purchase their slaves. The sheer drive and penny-pinching materialism of these planters on the make impressed Tyrone Power, an Irish actor who visited the South in the 1830s. The slaveholders he saw carving plantations out of the wilderness were "hardy, indefatigable, and enterprising to a degree; despising and condemning luxury and refinement, courting labour, and even making a pride of the privations which they, without any necessity, continue to endure with their families."

Most planters expected their wives to help supervise the slaves and run the plantation. Besides raising her own children, the plantation mistress managed the household staff, oversaw the cooking and cleaning, gardened, dispensed medicine and clothing to the slaves, and often assisted in their religious instruction. When guests or relatives came for an extended visit, the wife had to make all the special arrangements that this entailed. On the occasions when the master was called off on a business or political trip, she kept the plantation accounts. In many respects, she worked harder than her husband.

Planter wives often complained in their journals and letters of their social isolation from other white women and the physical and mental toil of managing slaves. Still, they enjoyed a wealth and status unknown to most southern women and only rarely questioned the institution of slavery. Their deepest anger stemmed from their humiliation by husbands who kept slave mistresses or sexually abused slave women, a practice far from uncommon.

Bound by their duties as wives not to express this anger publicly and unwilling to renounce the institution that both victimized them and benefited them, the white women in the plantation household tended to take their frustrations out on the black women whose alleged promiscuity they blamed for the sexual transgressions of white males. "Sometimes white mistresses will surmise that there is an intimacy between a slave woman & the master," recalled a former slave, "and perhaps she will make a great fuss & have her whipped, & perhaps there will be no peace until she is sold."

Despite the tensions and sexual jealousies that it aroused in white families, the ownership of slaves was the surest means of social and economic advancement for most whites. Most slave owners, however, never attained planter status. Nine in ten slave owners in 1860 owned fewer than twenty slaves, and fully half of them had fewer than five. Many whites also rented a few slaves on a seasonal basis.

Generally younger than the planters, small slaveholders were a diverse lot. About 10 percent were women, and another 20 percent or so were merchants, businessmen, artisans, and urban professionals. Most were farmers trying to acquire enough land and slaves to enter the ranks of planters. To keep costs down, they often began by purchasing children, the cheapest slaves available, or a young slave family, so that they could add to their slaveholdings as the slave mother bore more children.

Other slaveholding farmers had inherited their slaves and were trying to regain their fathers' planter status. Partible inheritance—the equal division of property among the children—was the norm in the nineteenth-century South. Except among the richest planter families, this division of the family property reduced the sons to modest slaveholders who had to struggle to achieve their own plantations.

Small slaveholders enjoyed scant economic security. A deadly outbreak of disease among their slaves or a single bad crop could destroy their credit and force them to sell their slaves to clear their debts. Owners of fewer than ten slaves stood a fifty-fifty chance within a decade of dropping out of the slaveholding class. Nor could small holders hope to compete directly with the planters. In any given area suitable for plantations, they were gradually pushed out as planters bought up land to raise livestock or more crops. In general, only slave owners who had established themselves in business or the professions had the capital reserves to rise into the planter elite.

Especially in the Lower South, owning slaves was a necessary precondition for upward mobility, but it was hardly a sufficient one. Slaveholders who failed to advance had nonetheless acquired a badge of social respectability. As a Baptist opponent of slavery put it, "Without slaves a man's children stand but poor chance to marry in reputation." Aside from conferring status, owning a few slaves could relieve a white household of much hard domestic labor. "I

wish to God every head of a family in the United States had one [slave] to take the drudgery and menial service off his family," proclaimed Andrew Johnson of Tennessee in the U.S. Senate. Thanks to slavery, even average whites in the South could aspire to some relief from endless toil.

The White Majority

Three-fourths of southern white families owned no slaves in 1860. Although most numerous in the Upper South, nonslaveholders predominated wherever the soil and climate were not suitable for plantation agriculture. Most of them were yeoman farmers who worked their own land with family labor.

These farmers were quick to move when times were bad and their land was used up, but once settled in an area, they formed intensely localized societies. These societies reinforced the authority of fathers and husbands over their families as the model of Christian discipline necessary for a well-ordered community. The community extended 5 to 10 miles around the nearest country store or county courthouse. Networks of kin and friends provided labor services when needed, fellowship in evangelical churches, and staple goods that an individual farm could not produce. Social travel and international markets, so central to the lives of planters, had little relevance in the farmers' community-centered existence. The yeomanry aimed to be self-sufficient and limited market involvement to the sale of livestock and an occasional cotton crop that could bring in needed cash.

Yeoman farmers jealously guarded their independence, and in their tight little worlds of face-to-face relationships, they demanded that planters treat them as social equals. Ever fearful of being reduced to dependence on any private or public power, they tried to avoid debt and wanted to limit government authority. Rather than risk financial ruin by buying slaves on credit to grow cotton, they grew food crops and depended on their sons and, when needed, their wives and daughters to work the fields. Far longer than most northern farmers, and in part because poor transportation facilities raised the cost of manufactured goods, they continued to make their own clothes, shoes, soap, and other consumer items.

Nonslaveholding farmers from the mountains and planters on the bottomlands rarely mixed, and their societies developed in isolation from each other. In areas where there were both small farms and scattered plantations, the interests of the yeomen and the planters were often complementary. Planters provided local markets for the surplus grain and livestock of nonslaveholders and, for a small fee, access

A yeoman farmstead in New Braumfels, Texas. The yeomanry strove for self-sufficiency by growing food crops and grazing livestock.

to grist mills and gins for grinding corn and cleaning cotton. They lent small sums to poorer neighbors in emergencies or to pay taxes. The yeomen staffed the slave patrols and became overseers on the plantations. Both groups sought to protect property rights from outside interference and to maintain a system of racial control in which white liberties rested on black degradation.

When yeomen and planters did clash, it was usually over economic issues. Large slaveholders needing better credit and marketing facilities gravitated toward the Whig party, which called for banks and internal improvements. Nonslaveholding farmers, especially in the Lower South, tended to be Democrats who opposed banks and state-funded economic projects. They considered bankers grasping outsiders who wanted to rob them of their economic independence, and they suspected that state involvement in the economy only led to higher taxes and increased the public debt. These partisan battles, however, rarely boiled over into a debate about the merits of slavery. As long as planters deferred to the egalitarian sensibilities of the yeomen by courting them at election time and promising to safeguard their liberties, the planters were able to maintain broad support for slavery across class lines.

Around 15 percent of rural white families owned neither land nor slaves. These were the so-called poor whites, stigmatized by both abolitionists and planters as lazy and shiftless. The abolitionists considered these whites a kind of underclass who proved that slavery so degraded the dignity of labor

that many whites shunned all work and lapsed into a wretched poverty. For the planters, they were a constant nuisance and a threat to slave discipline. Planters habitually complained that these poor whites demoralized the slaves by showing that a person could survive without steady labor. They were also blamed for enticing the slaves into trading stolen plantation property for guns and alcohol.

Some of the landless whites did live down to the negative stereotype ironically drawn of them by both opponents and proponents of slavery. Still, the label of "poor white trash" is misleading. Most of them were resourceful and enterprising enough to supply themselves with all the material comforts they wanted. Back in the swamps and pine barrens shunned by planters and yeomen alike, they squatted on a few acres of land, put up crude cabins for shelter, planted some corn, and grazed livestock in the surrounding woods. Aided by the mild southern climate, they had all the corn and pork they could eat. Not having to do steady work for survival, they hunted, fished, and took orders from no one. Although poor by most standards, they were also defiantly self-reliant.

Nonslaveholders were a growing majority in southern cities, and their numbers were growing fastest among the working classes. These urban workers shared no agricultural interests or ties with the planters. Nor were most of them, especially in the unskilled ranks, southern-born. Northerners and immigrants dominated the urban work force.

Free workers, especially Irish and German immigrants, increasingly replaced slaves in urban labor markets. These white workers bitterly resented competition from black slaves, and their demands to exclude slaves from the urban workplace reinforced planters' belief that cities bred abolitionism. When urban laborers protested against slave competition in the 1850s, planters singled them out as the non-slaveholders most likely to attack slavery.

Free Blacks

A few southern blacks—6 percent of the total in 1860—were "free persons of color" and constituted 3 percent of the free population in the South (see Figure 13-3). These free blacks occupied a precarious and vulnerable position between degraded enslavement and meaningful freedom. White intimidation and special legal provisions known as **black codes** (found throughout the North as well) denied them nearly all the rights of citizenship. Because of the legal presumption in the South that all blacks were

slaves, they had to carry freedom papers, official certificates of their freedom. They were shut out of the political process and could not testify against whites in court. Many occupations, especially those involved in the communication of ideas, such as the printing trades, were closed to them.

Every slave state forbade the entry of free blacks, and every municipality had its own rules and regulations that forced them to live as an inferior caste. In Charleston, for example, a free black could not smoke a cigar or carry a cane in public. Any sign of upward mobility or intimation of equal standing with whites was ruthlessly suppressed. Whites had the right of way, and a free black who bumped into a white on the street was likely to be flogged.

More than four-fifths of the free blacks lived in the Upper South. Most of them were the offspring of slaves freed by private manumissions between 1780 and 1800 when a slump in tobacco markets and the

Figure 13-3 *Slave, Free Black, and White Population in Southern States, 1850*
Except for Texas, slaves by 1850 comprised over 40 percent of the population in every state of the Lower South. The small population of free blacks was concentrated in the Upper South.

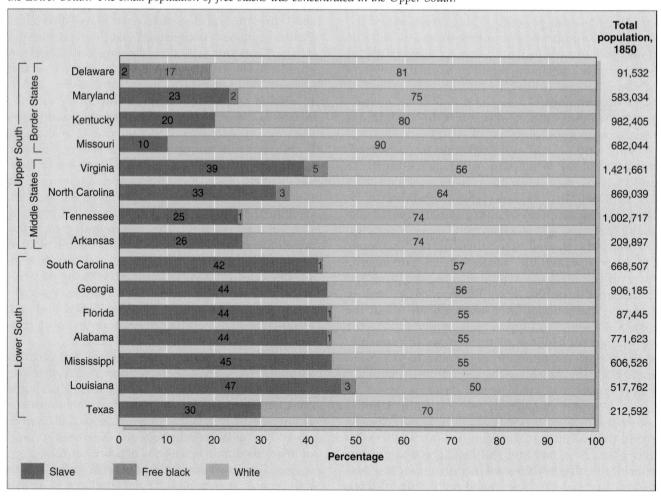

Revolutionary War creed of natural rights had loosened slavery in the Chesapeake region. Manumissions dropped sharply after 1810, the result of heightened white anxieties over slave security after Prosser's Rebellion and the rising demand for slaves in the Lower South. From 1810 to 1860, only 13 percent of blacks in the Upper South were free.

As in the North, legal barriers and white prejudice generally confined these free blacks to the poorest-paying and most menial work. A handful of blacks became independent farmers, but most rural blacks were farm laborers or tenants. The best economic opportunities came in the cities, where some blacks found factory jobs and positions in the skilled trades. Because the South had a general shortage of skilled labor, free blacks with the necessary skills could earn a respectable income as carpenters, barbers, shoemakers, tailors, and plasterers. Indeed, the percentage of blacks in the skilled trades was generally higher in the South than in the North. Highly skilled blacks, such as Thomas Day, widely recognized as the finest cabinetmaker in North Carolina, could command a premium in wages from white employers.

One-third of free blacks in the Upper South lived in cities, a much higher proportion than among whites. Cities offered blacks not only jobs but also enough social space to found their own churches and mutual-aid associations. Especially after 1840, urban African-American churches proliferated, and they were at the center of black community life. These

A free black wood sawyer. The skilled trades offered among the best economic opportunities for free blacks in the South.

churches sponsored Sunday schools and day schools that were about the only means of education open to black people. Despite white opposition to black schools, the demand for schooling persisted. A "good education," declared a black schoolmaster in Baltimore, "is the *sine qua non* as regards the elevation of our people."

Less than 2 percent of the blacks in the Lower South were free in 1860. Given the greater profitability of slavery there, manumissions were rare. Most of the Lower South's free blacks descended from black emigrants who fled the revolutionary unrest in Haiti in the 1790s. These refugees were artisans, shopkeepers, and farmers who settled primarily in Charleston and New Orleans. Able to secure a solid economic footing, their descendants inherited more wealth than any other free blacks in the United States. Free blacks in the Lower South were more likely than those in the Upper South to have a marketable skill, and two-thirds of them lived in cities.

A light skin also enhanced the social standing of free blacks among color-conscious whites in the Lower South. Nearly 70 percent of free blacks in 1860 were mulattoes, and from their ranks came nearly all of the very small number of black planters. Mulattoes could count on greater white patronage, and they monopolized the best jobs available to free blacks. A mulatto elite emerged in Charleston, Mobile, and New Orleans that carefully distanced itself from most blacks, slave or free. In New Orleans, where the tradition of racially mixed unions dated back to French and Spanish rule, mulattoes put on lavish "octoroon balls" attended by free women of color and white men. Even here, however, the mulatto elite remained suspended between black and white worlds that never fully accepted them as one of their own.

Despite the tendency toward a three-tiered racial hierarchy in the port cities of the Lower South, whites still insisted on making a racial dichotomy between white and black the overriding social division in the South. As the racial defense of slavery intensified in the 1850s, more calls were made for laws to banish or enslave free blacks. Arkansas passed such a law in 1859, and similar bills were proposed in the Florida, Tennessee, Mississippi, and Missouri legislatures. Even Maryland, which had the largest free-black population, held a referendum in 1859 on whether to reenslave its free blacks. Only the opposition of nonslaveholders heavily dependent on the cheap labor of free blacks defeated the referendum.

Despised and feared by whites as a subversive element in a slave society, free blacks across the South were daily reminded that their freedom rested on the whims of the white majority. As white attitudes turned uglier in the late antebellum period, that freedom was less secure than ever.

The Proslavery Argument

In the early nineteenth century, white Southerners made no particular effort to defend slavery. They saw no need to do so because the institution was not under heavy outside attack. If pressed, most whites would have called slavery a necessary evil, an unfortunate legacy from earlier generations that was needed to maintain racial peace with so many blacks living in their midst.

The 1830s marked a turning point. The twin shocks of Nat Turner's Rebellion and the onset of the abolitionist crusade in the North unleashed mobs of whites who stifled any open criticism of slavery in the Lower South. Southern whites also began to reassess how they justified slavery, both to the outside world and to themselves. By the 1850s, politicians, intellectuals, and evangelical ministers were defending slavery as a positive good, an institution ordained by God as the foundation of southern prosperity, white democracy, and Christian instruction for heathen Africans. They portrayed slavery as a mild, paternalistic, and even caring institution.

The most obvious problem with this view of slavery was that it described the institution as its defenders wanted it to be and not as it was. However comforting this benign portrayal of slavery may have been to individual slaveholders, it failed to convince the abolitionists or the southern dissenters who condemned slavery on moral and economic grounds.

Evangelical Protestantism dominated southern religious expression by the 1830s, and its ministers took the lead in combating abolitionist charges that slavery was a moral and religious abomination. Except for a radical minority of antislavery evangelicals in the Upper South, a group largely silenced or driven out by the conservative reaction following Nat Turner's

uprising, the southern churches had always supported slavery. This support grew more pronounced and articulate once the abolitionists stepped up their attacks on slavery in the mid-1830s.

Because southern evangelicals accepted the Bible as God's literal word, any support for chattel servitude in the Bible reinforced the proslavery cause. The patriarchs of Israel owned slaves. Slavery was practiced throughout the Roman world at the time of Christ, and his apostles urged obedience to all secular laws, including those governing slavery. Through a selective reading of the Bible, the proslavery ideologues found abundant evidence to proclaim that slavery was fully in accord with the moral law of God.

Southern evangelicals also turned to the Bible to support their argument that patriarchal authority—the unquestioned power of the father—was the basis of all Christian communities. Part of that authority extended over slaves, and slavery thus became a matter of family governance, a domestic institution in which Christian masters of slaves, unlike capitalist masters of free "wage slaves" in the North, accepted responsibility for caring for their workers in sickness and old age. Far from being a moral curse, slavery was part of God's plan to Christianize an inferior race and teach its people how to produce raw materials that benefited the world's masses.

The growing commitment of southern evangelicals to slavery as a positive good clashed with the antislavery position and the generally more liberal theology of northern evangelicals. In 1837, differ-

As this 1841 cartoon reflects, a staple of proslavery propaganda was to contrast the allegedly contented and healthy lot of slaves with that of starving factory workers exploited by the system of wage labor.

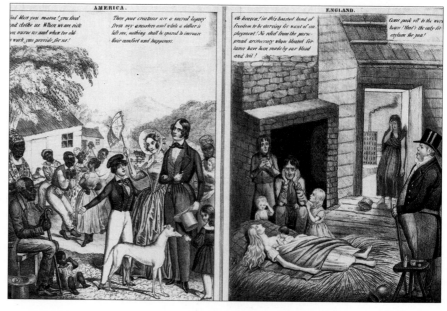

ences over slavery and theology formally split the Presbyterians along sectional lines. In 1844, and as a direct result of the slavery issue, the Methodist Episcopal Church, the nation's largest, divided into northern and southern churches. The Baptists did the same a year later. These religious schisms foreshadowed the sectionalized political divisions of the 1850s; they also severed one of the main emotional bonds between northern and southern whites.

The religious defense of slavery was central to the slaveholding ethic of paternalism that developed after 1830. By the 1850s, planters commonly described slaves as members of an extended family who were treated better than free workers in the North. This language often reflected the psychological need of planters to feel appreciated, even loved, as caring parents by their slave dependents. Some evangelical masters tried to act as moral stewards to their slaves and to curb the worst features of their bondage. Led by Charles Colcock Jones, a minister and planter in the Georgia lowcountry, they founded religious missions to the slaves and sought reforms, such as legal measures that would prevent the separation of slave families. Such slaveholders, however, were a minority, and efforts to reform slavery failed largely because masters would accept no limits on their power to control and work their slaves as they saw fit.

The crusade to sanctify slavery won few converts outside the South. Most northern churches did not endorse abolitionism but did have moral qualms about slavery. In a particularly stinging rebuke to southern church leaders in the 1850s, black abolitionists succeeded in having slaveholders barred from international religious conventions.

More common than the biblical defense of slavery was the racial argument that blacks were unfit to live as a free people among whites. Drawing in part on the scientific wisdom of the day, the racial defense alleged that blacks were naturally lazy and inherently inferior to whites. If freed, so went the argument, they would steal from whites and sexually assault their women. Only the controls of slavery enabled the races to coexist in the South.

Slavery as a necessary means of racial control was a central theme in Thomas R. Dew's *Review of the Debates in the Virginia Legislature of 1831 and 1832,* the first major justification of slavery by a Southerner. Dew, a Tidewater planter, was responding to a proposal for gradual emancipation that had been introduced into the Virginia legislature. Although the plan was defeated (largely because the eastern plantation counties were overrepresented in the legislature), upper-class conservatives such as Dew were alarmed by the potentially dangerous class division that had

opened up between slaveholders and nonslaveholders. He tried to unite whites on the issue of race.

The racial argument resonated powerfully among whites because nearly all of them, including those otherwise opposed to slavery, dreaded emancipation. The attitude of a Tennessee farmer, as recorded by a northern traveler in the 1850s, was typical: "He said he'd always wished there hadn't been any niggers here . . ., but he wouldn't like to have them free." Unable to conceive of living in a society with many free blacks, most whites could see no middle ground between slavery and the presumed social chaos of emancipation.

The existence of *black* slavery also had egalitarian implications for the nonslaveholding majority of whites. Slavery supposedly spared southern whites from the menial, degrading labor that northern whites had to perform. Moreover, because slaves lacked political rights, champions of slavery argued that black bondage buttressed the political liberties of all white males by removing from politics the leveling demands of the poor and propertyless for a redistribution of wealth.

Despite its apparent success in forging white solidarity, the racial argument could be turned on its head and used to weaken slavery. Most northern whites were about as racist as their southern counterparts, but they were increasingly willing to end slavery on the grounds that the stronger white race should assist weaker blacks to improve themselves as free persons. In short, nothing in the internal logic of racist doctrines necessitated enslaving blacks. That same logic, however, encouraged some southern whites to challenge the economic prerogatives of slaveholders. Why, for example, should any whites, as members of the master race, be forced into economic competition against skilled slave artisans? Why should not all nonagricultural jobs be legally reserved for whites? Doctrines of black inferiority could not prevent white unity from cracking when the economic interests of nonslaveholders clashed with those of planters.

Conclusion

Slavery and the biracial social order of whites and a large black minority defined the South as a distinctive region. The spread of plantation agriculture across the Lower South after 1830 deepened the involvement of southern whites in cotton and slavery. At the same time, an abolitionist movement in the North morally attacked slavery and demanded that it be abolished. As southern interests became more enmeshed in an institution that outsiders condemned, religious and intellectual leaders portrayed slavery as a Christian institution and a positive good necessary for white democracy and harmonious race relations. Proslavery ideologues stridently described the South as separate from and superior to the rest of the nation.

The proslavery argument depicted a nearly ideal society blessed by class and racial harmony. In reality, social conditions in the slave South were far more contradictory and conflict-ridden. Slaves were not content in their bondage. They hungered for freedom and sustained that dream through their own forms of Christianity and the support of family and kin. Relations between masters and their slaves were antagonistic, not affectionate, and wherever the system of control slackened, slaves resisted their owners.

Nor did all whites accept slavery as a labor arrangement that was in their best interests. Racial slavery divided as well as united southern whites, and economic inequality among them grew after 1830. The publication in 1857 of Hinton Rowan Helper's *Impending Crisis of the South*, a scathing indictment by a white North Carolinian of how slavery stunted economic opportunities for average whites, was a vivid reminder that the proslavery argument had not converted all whites.

During the 1850s, the size of the slaveholding class fell from 31 percent of white families in the South to 25 percent. Slaveowners were a shrinking minority, and slavery was in decline throughout the Upper South. In the Border South, free labor was replacing slavery as the dominant means of organizing economic production. In these states, slavery was a vulnerable institution. Planters were not fooled by the public rhetoric of white unity. They knew that slavery was increasingly confined to the Lower South and that elsewhere in the South, white support for it was gradually eroding.

Facing the threat of outside interference with slavery and internal white disloyalty, planters feared the double-edged challenge to their privileged positions. By the 1850s, many of them were concluding that the only way to resolve their dilemma was to make the South a separate nation.

Review Questions

1. What factors accounted for the tremendous expansion of cotton production in the South? How was this expansion linked to slavery and westward movement?

2. What differentiated the Upper South from the Lower South? What role did slavery play in each region after 1815?

3. How would you characterize the life of a plantation slave? Why were religion and family such key features of the world that slaves built for themselves? What evidence is there of resistance and rebellion among the slaves?

4. How did most nonslaveholding whites live? What values did they prize most highly? Why did most nonslaveholders accept slavery or at least not attack it directly?

5. What was the position of free blacks in southern society? How were their freedoms restricted?

6. How did southern whites attempt to defend slavery and reconcile it with Christianity?

Recommended Reading

Shearer Bowman, *Masters and Lords: Mid-19th Century U.S. Planters and Prussian Junkers* (1993). This fascinating study in comparative history portrays southern planters as agrarian capitalists.

Clement Eaton, *The Growth of Southern Civilization, 1790–1860* (1961). Although dated, this remains a useful and readable introduction to the broad themes in the development of the Old South.

William W. Freehling, *The Road to Disunion: Secessionists at Bay, 1776–1854* (1990). A fine introduction to the social diversity of the Old South, this work is especially strong in exploring the tensions over slavery between the Upper South and the Lower South.

Eugene D. Genovese, *Roll Jordan Roll: The World the Slaveholders Made* (1974). This richly textured study of slavery is an excellent source for the interaction between masters and slaves. Genovese argues that paternalistic relations of dependent rights and obligations characterized slavery.

James Oakes, *The Ruling Race* (1982). This relatively short but provocative history of the slave-owning class stresses the restless, acquisitive nature of the small slave owners, the most typical holders of slaves.

Kenneth M. Stampp, *The Peculiar Institution* (1956). This work, which has aged well, is still the best one-volume history of southern slavery and leaves no doubt that slavery was both brutal and profitable.

Charles S. Sydnor, *The Growth of Southern Sectionalism, 1819–1848* (1948). This is the most thorough account of how the South moved from its nationalist stance in the early nineteenth century toward increasing sectional self-consciousness.

Bertram Wyatt-Brown, *Southern Honor: Ethics and Behavior in the Old South* (1982). This book is valuable for its insights into the culture of the planter class and the notions of honor that structured social relations among all whites.

Additional Sources

The Lower South

Robert W. Fogel and Stanley Engerman, *Time on the Cross: The Economics of American Negro Slavery* (1974).

Lacy K. Ford Jr., *Origins of Southern Radicalism: The South Carolina Upcountry, 1800–1860* (1988).

Stephanie McCurry, *Masters of Small Worlds* (1995).

Joseph P. Reidy, *From Slavery to Agrarian Capitalism in the Cotton Plantation South* (1992).

J. Mills Thornton III, *Politics and Power in a Slave Society* (1978).

Gavin Wright, *The Political Economy of the Cotton South* (1978).

The Upper South

David F. Allmendinger, *Ruffin: Family and Reform in the Old South* (1990).

Fred Arthur Bailey, *Class and Tennessee's Confederate Generation* (1987).

David W. Crofts, *Old Southampton: Politics and Society in a Virginia County, 1834–1869* (1992).

Barbara J. Fields, *Slavery and Freedom on the Middle Ground: Maryland during the Nineteenth Century* (1985).

Robert Tracey McKenzie, *One South or Many? Plantation Belt and Upcounty in Civil War Era Tennessee* (1994).

Michael Tadman, *Speculators and Slaves: Masters, Traders, and Slaves in the Old South* (1989).

Slave Life and Culture

John W. Blassingame, *The Slave Community: Plantation Life in the Antebellum South* (1972).

Charles B. Dew, *Bond of Iron: Master and Slave at Buffalo Forge* (1994).

Herbert G. Gutman, *The Black Family in Slavery and Freedom, 1750–1925* (1974).

Peter Kolchin, *Unfree Labor: American Slavery and Russian Serfdom* (1987).

Roderick A. McDonald, *The Economy and Material Culture of Slaves* (1993).

Robert Starobin, *Industrial Slavery in the Old South* (1970).

Richard C. Wade, *Slavery in the Cities* (1964).

Free Society

Ira Berlin, *Slaves without Masters: The Free Negro in the Antebellum South* (1974).

Charles C. Bolton, *Poor Whites of the Antebellum South* (1994).

Victoria E. Bynum, *Unruly Women: The Politics of Social and Sexual Control in the Old South* (1992).

Bill Cecil-Fronsman, *Common Whites: Class and Culture in Antebellum North Carolina* (1992).

Elizabeth Fox-Genovese, *Within the Plantation Household: Black and White Women of the Old South* (1988).

J. William Harris, *Plain Folk and Gentry in a Slave Society* (1985).

Frank Owsley, *Plain Folk in the South* (1949).

The Proslavery Argument

David L. Bailey, *Shadow on the Church: Southwestern Evangelical Religion and the Issue of Slavery, 1783–1860* (1985).

George M. Fredrickson, *The Black Image in the White Mind* (1971).

Eugene D. Genovese, *The Slaveholders' Dilemma: Freedom and Progress in Southern Conservative Thought, 1820–1860* (1992).

W. S. Jenkins, *Pro-Slavery Thought in the Old South* (1935).

Donald G. Mathews, *Religion in the Old South* (1977).

Mitchell Snay, *Gospel of Disunion: Religion and Separatism in the Antebellum South* (1993).

Where to Learn More

❖ **Appalachian Museum of Berea College, Berea, Kentucky.** This museum is an excellent source for understanding the lifestyles and material culture of the nonslaveholding farmers in the Appalachian highlands.

❖ **Museum of African-American Culture, Columbia, South Carolina.** This museum provides a wealth of material on the culture of nineteenth-century blacks, including the free black population in the South.

❖ **Cottonlandia Museum, Greenwood, Mississippi.** The library and museum depict the history of cotton in the Mississippi Delta. Special collections include some Native American artifacts.

❖ **Jarrell Plantation, Juliette, Georgia.** This state historic site consists of a fifteen-building farm complex that conveys a good sense of the physical dimensions of a nineteenth-century Georgia plantation.

❖ **Meadow Farm Museum, Richmond, Virginia.** The archives and museum are especially strong on southern farm life in the mid-nineteenth century.

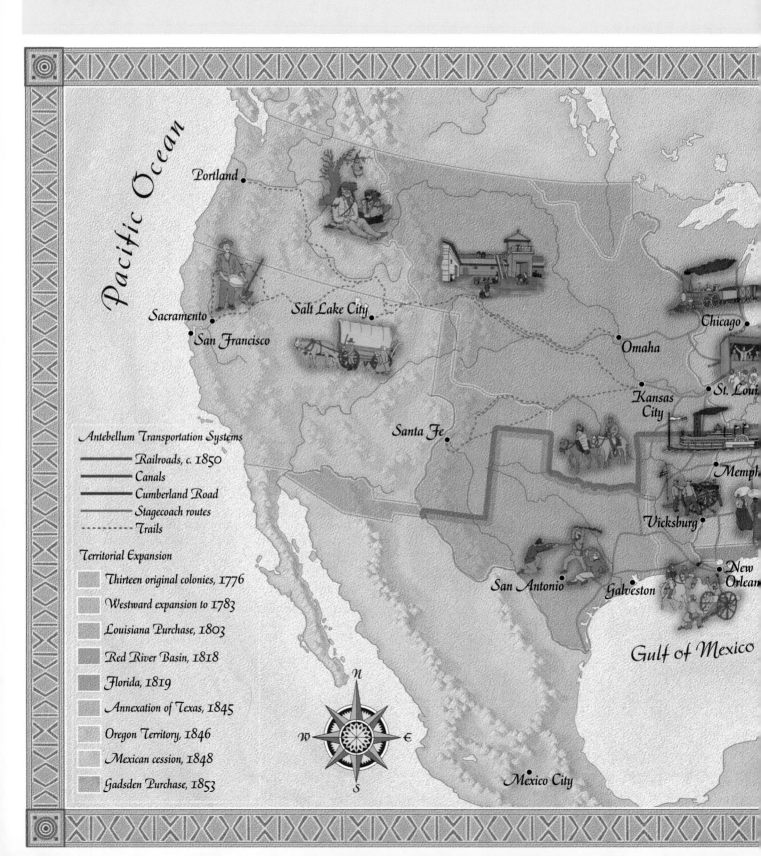

Pacific Ocean

Portland

Sacramento
San Francisco

Salt Lake City

Chicago

Omaha

St. Loui

Kansas City

Santa Fe

Memph

Antebellum Transportation Systems
—— Railroads, c. 1850
—— Canals
—— Cumberland Road
—— Stagecoach routes
----- Trails

Vicksburg

Territorial Expansion
Thirteen original colonies, 1776
Westward expansion to 1783
Louisiana Purchase, 1803
Red River Basin, 1818
Florida, 1819
Annexation of Texas, 1845
Oregon Territory, 1846
Mexican cession, 1848
Gadsden Purchase, 1853

San Antonio
Galveston
New Orlean

Gulf of Mexico

N
W   E
S

Mexico City

KEY TOPICS

❖ The rise of the reform movement after the War of 1812
❖ The spread of reform from moral to social issues in the 1820s
❖ The development of regimented institutions—penitentiaries, asylums, workhouses—for criminals, the poor, and the insane
❖ The growth of abolitionist agitation and sentiment in the North
❖ Women's crucial role in the reform movements and the rise of an organized women's rights movement

"*Would* to God this [Fourth of July] were truly—what it is not, though lying lips declare it to be—the JUBILEE OF FREEDOM! That Jubilee cannot come, so long as one slave is left to grind in his prison-house. It will come only when liberty is proclaimed throughout ALL the land, unto ALL the inhabitants thereof." The abolitionist William Lloyd Garrison issued this call for freeing the slaves in a speech on July 4, 1839. He had been instrumental in organizing an antislavery movement in the 1830s that branded slavery as a sin, an unconscionable blot on America as a Christian nation. The abolitionists demanded in the name of Christian morality and human rights that all Americans commit themselves to the immediate end of slavery.

Abolitionism was the most radical extension of the reform impulse after the War of 1812 that swept many Americans into organized movements for individual improvement and social betterment. This reform impulse was strongest in the North in areas where traditional social and economic relations were undergoing wrenching changes as a market revolution accelerated the spread of cities, factories, and commercialized farms. These were also the areas where the emotional fires of evangelical revivals burned the hottest.

The religious message of the Second Great Awakening provided a framework for responding to change. New within mainstream Protestantism was the belief that anyone who sought salvation could attain it, not just those whom God had predestined to be saved. Evangelicalism taught that in both the spiritual and secular realms, individuals were accountable for their own actions. Through Christian activism, individuals could strive toward moral perfectibility. Social evils, and the sinful consequences of change, could be cleansed if only good Christians would help others find the path of righteousness.

The first wave of reform after the War of 1812 focused on changing individual behavior and targeted drinking, gambling, sexual misconduct, and Sabbath-breaking. By the 1830s, a second phase of reform turned to institutional solutions for crime, poverty, and social delinquency, largely untouched by voluntary moral suasion. One group of reformers, the abolitionists, aimed to reshape the very structure of American society through their moral crusade to eliminate slavery.

Women, especially those from the evangelical middle class, were active in both these phases of reform. They gained self-confidence and organizational experience from their reform activities, and some of them began to question their subordinate place in public life. Abolitionism, more than any other reform movement, radicalized many women. In identifying with the plight of blacks under slavery, female abolitionists drew parallels with their own lack of power in a male-dominated society. Coming primarily from an abolitionist background, women reformers founded a women's rights movement in the 1840s. They organized the Seneca Falls Convention of 1848, which called for extending the full rights and privileges of citizenship to women.

Women's demands that abolitionist societies treat them as equals split the abolitionist movement by 1840. Abolitionists who opposed Garrison and his support of women's rights broke away and formed an independent political party. These anti-Garrisonian abolitionists set out to win northern voters over to the antislavery stance. This was the first stage in the evolution of the politics of sectionalism that dominated national affairs in the 1850s.

Reform and Moral Order

American society was being transformed after 1815. The growth of cities, the spread of industrialization, and the vast westward migration accelerated in the generation after the War of 1812. Former restraints of family, church, and community that had once produced a sense of social order and public morality seemed to be breaking down. Religious leaders and wealthy businessmen in the East saw evidence of disorder and unchristian wickedness all around them in the more fluid, materialistic society that was emerging. In their eyes, infidelity flourished on the frontier, licentiousness was rampant in the cities, and the evils of

*The second major structure from right in the illustration above is the Bible House, the head-
quarters of the American Bible Society on Nassau Street in New York City. The Bible House
was the distribution point for hundreds of thousands of Bibles printed on the technologically
most advanced steam-powered presses.*

drink were causing workers to forsake God and their
families. Alarmed by what they perceived as a widespread breakdown in moral authority, they sought to
impose moral discipline on their fellow Americans.

These eastern elites, aided by their wives and
daughters, created a network of voluntary, church-
affiliated reform organizations known collectively as
the **benevolent empire**. Revivals in the 1820s and
1830s then broadened the base of reform to include
the newly evangelicalized middle class in northern
cities and towns. From this class emerged the temperance crusade, the largest reform movement in
pre–Civil War America.

The Benevolent Empire

For the Reverend Lyman Beecher, the American condition in 1814 presented "a scene of destitution and
wretchedness." From his Presbyterian pulpit in Litch-
field, Connecticut, and then in Boston, he became
the leader of a clerical drive to restore moral leadership to America. Like other clergy with whom he
created the benevolent empire, Beecher was driven
by a profound fear of disorder.

The America these ministers valued was one
of respectable churchgoers whose behavior conformed to Puritan and Federalist standards of freedom as defined and ordered by an educated clergy.
Such a morally homogeneous America, feared
Beecher, was being fragmented and corrupted by mass
emigration to the unchurched West and by challenges
to religious orthodoxy from populist sects. At risk was
not only Beecher's vision of a Christian republic but

also the stability of the Union itself. Beecher believed
that only religion, as preached by "pious, intelligent,
enterprising ministers through the nation," could provide the order that would preserve the Union and
place it under "the moral government of God."

Evangelical businessmen in the seaboard cities
backed Beecher's call to restore moral order. Worried
by the increasing number of urban poor, wealthy merchants contributed vital financial support. From its origins in the Plan of Union between Congregationalists
and Presbyterians in 1801 to merge forces for western
missions, the network of reform associations grew to
include the American Board of Commissioners for
Foreign Missions (1810), the American Bible Society
(1816), the American Sunday School Union (1824),
the American Tract Society (1825), and the American
Home Missionary Society (1826). Based on British
models of reform, the memberships of these moral
agencies was cross-denominational. The constant pros-
elytizing of the itinerant revivalists of the Second Great
Awakening fed their growth and prepared the way for
a national marketplace for spirituality that emerged
in the 1820s.

The reform societies were radical innovators
in adapting the Second Great Awakening's techniques
of organization and communication. The key, as the
revivalist Charles G. Finney explained, was to find the
best measures to persuade the people to "vote in the
Lord Jesus Christ as the governor of the Universe."
Instead of relying on sporadic, individual efforts, the
Christian reformers sent out speakers on regular
schedules along prescribed routes. They developed

CHRONOLOGY

1817 American Colonization Society is founded.

1820s Shaker colonies grow.

1825 Robert Owen begins his utopian experiment at New Harmony, Indiana.

1826 American Temperance Society launches its crusade.

1829 David Walker publishes *Appeal to the Colored Citizens of the World.*

1830 Joseph Smith founds the Church of Jesus Christ of Latter-day Saints.

1830–1831 Evangelical revivals are held in northern cities.

1831 William Lloyd Garrison begins publishing *The Liberator.*

1832 New England Anti-Slavery Society is founded.

1833 Slaves in the British Empire are emancipated. American Anti-Slavery Society is organized.

1834 New York Female Moral Reform Society is founded.

1836 Congress passes gag rule.

1837 Horace Mann begins campaign for school reform as secretary of the Massachusetts Board of Education.

Antiabolitionist mob kills Elijah P. Lovejoy.

1838 Sarah Grimké publishes *Letters on the Equality of the Sexes and the Condition of Women.*

1840 Abolitionists split into Garrisonian and anti-Garrisonian societies.

Political abolitionists launch the Liberty party.

1841 Brook Farm is established.

Dorothea Dix begins her work to improve conditions for the mentally ill.

1846–1848 Mormons migrate to the West.

1847 John Humphrey Noyes establishes the Oneida Community.

1848 Seneca Falls Convention outlines a program for women's rights.

---

organizations that maintained a constant pressure for reform. National and local boards of directors supervised the work of salaried managers, who inspired volunteers to combat sin among the unconverted.

Sooner even than the politicians, religious reformers grasped how technological advances in printing and papermaking enabled them to reach an increasingly literate mass audience. Steam presses and stereotype plates halved the cost of printing and dramatically increased its speed. The American Bible Society was the first to exploit this revolution in the print media. Between 1790 and 1830, the number of religious newspapers grew from fourteen to more than six hundred. By then, religious presses were churning out more than 1 million Bibles and 6 million tracts a year. These publications were mass-distributed by traveling agents and heavily promoted in national advertising campaigns. For the evangelicals, the printed word became the God-given means of spreading the gospel. As the *Christian Herald* editorialized in 1823, "Preaching of the gospel is a Divine institution—'printing' is no less so. . . . The PULPIT AND THE PRESS are inseparably connected."

While the largest and most nationally organized of the Protestant voluntary associations focused on missionary activity, especially on the western frontier and in the slums of eastern cities, a host of local societies were more concerned with stamping out individual vices. These societies of ministers and concerned laity were self-appointed moral watchdogs for their local communities. Their purpose, as summed up by a Massachusetts group, the Andover South Parish Society for the Reformation of Morals, was "to discountenance [discourage] immorality, particularly Sabbath-breaking, intemperance, and profanity, and to promote industry, order, piety, and good morals." These goals linked social and moral discipline in a broad sweep of benevolence that appealed both to pious churchgoers concerned about godlessness and profit-oriented businessmen eager to curb their workers' unruly behavior.

The reformers tried to instill these goals in the young through Sunday schools. With volunteers drawn largely from the teenage daughters of evangelical businessmen, these interdenominational schools combined elementary education with the teaching of the Bible and Christian principles. The American Sunday School Union was both a coordinating agency for local efforts and a publishing house for books and periodicals. By 1832, nearly 10 percent of all American children aged 5 to 14 were attending one of eight thousand Sunday schools.

The boldest expression of the drive to enhance Christian power was the **Sabbatarian movement**. Traditionally, Protestants had devoted Sunday to worship and Bible reading. But the accelerated pace of business activity by the 1820s, as well as the growth of popular forms of entertainment, such as theater, dancing, and music, intruded on the Sabbath. In 1828, evangelicals led by Lyman Beecher formed the **General Union for Promoting the Observance of the Christian Sabbath**.

The immediate goal of the General Union was the repeal of a law passed by Congress in 1810 directing post offices to deliver mail on Sunday, a law that to Christian reformers symbolized the moral degeneracy into which the republic had fallen. Its broader mission was to enforce local statutes that shut down business and leisure activities on Sundays. The Sabbatarians considered such statutes no less "necessary to the welfare of the state" than "laws against murder and polygamy." To their opponents, such laws were "repugnant to the rights of private property and irreconcilable with the free exercise of civil liberty."

The Sabbatarian crusade soon burned itself out. It suffered a crippling setback in 1829 when Congress rejected petitions demanding an end to Sunday mails. Insisting on the separation of church and state, the Democratic Congress upheld the postal law of 1810. At the local level, the Sabbatarians outraged canal operators, hotel keepers, tavern owners, and other businessmen who would lose their Sunday trade. Workingmen sought out allies in the Democratic party to resist a moral crusade that threatened their one day of recreation in a six-day workweek. Southern evangelicals held back for fear that the reformers' blend of moral and political activism might raise the sensitive issue of slavery. Even religious conservatives in New England felt that the Sabbath purists had gone too far. The most pressing religious needs, insisted these Calvinist ministers, were to enforce discipline within the churches and to safeguard theological doctrine.

The General Union disbanded in 1832, but it left an important legacy for future reform movements. On the one hand, it developed techniques that converted the reform impulse into direct political action. In raising funds, training speakers, holding rallies, disseminating literature, lobbying for local Sunday regulations, and coordinating a petition to Congress, the Sabbatarians created an organizational model for other reformers to follow in mobilizing public opinion and influencing politicians. On the other hand, the failure of the Sabbatarians revealed that heavy-handed attempts to force the "unconverted" to follow Christian standards of conduct were self-defeating. A new approach was needed that encouraged individuals to reform themselves without coercive controls. It soon emerged in the temperance movement.

The Temperance Movement

The greatest reform movement, in both immediate impact and the number of people involved, was temperance, the drive against drinking alcohol. The success of temperance rested on what Lyman Beecher called "a new moral power." Dismayed by popular resistance to the coercive moralism of the first wave of Christian reform, evangelicals like the Reverend John Chester concluded in 1821 that "you cannot coerce a free people that are jealous to fastidiousness of their rights." Therefore, reform had to rest on persuasion, and it had to begin with the voluntary decision of individuals to free themselves from sin. The electrifying new teaching that anyone could gain salvation through self-will was the central message of the dramatic religious revivals that gathered up mass converts from the business and middle classes in the late 1820s and the 1830s. For these evangelicals, the self-control to renounce alcohol became the key to creating a harmonious Christian society of self-regulating citizens.

The early temperance movement was led by former Federalists in New England who sought to substitute moral leadership for their declining political authority. Their impact was limited, and they aimed at little more than getting people to moderate their intake of alcohol. Temperance then shifted tone and organization in the mid-1820s. In 1826, evangelicals founded the **American Temperance Society** in Boston and took control of the movement. They were inspired by Beecher's *Six Sermons on Temperance*, a stirring call for voluntary associations dedicated to the belief that "the daily use of ardent spirits, in any form, or in any degree" was a sin. They now sought a radical change in American attitudes toward alcohol and its role in social life.

The temperance forces faced a daunting challenge. American consumption of alcohol increased after 1800, reaching an all-time high by 1830 of 7.1 gallons of pure alcohol per year for every American aged 14 and over (about three times present-day levels). Alcoholic beverages were plentiful and

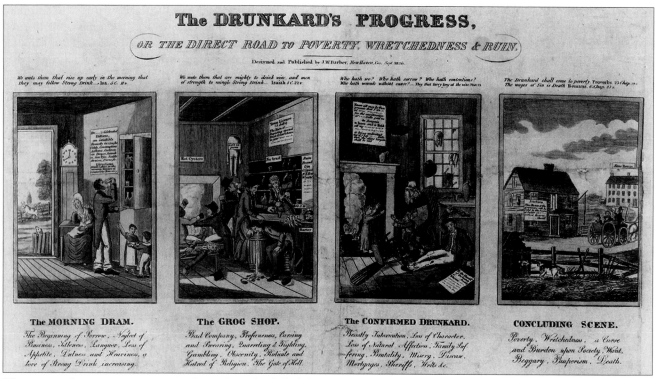

These scenes from a temperance tract depict the evils of alcohol.

cheaper than tea or coffee. "Liquor at that time," recalled a carpenter, "was used as commonly as the food we ate." An English observer in 1819 was shocked to discover that "you cannot go into hardly any man's house without being asked to drink wine, or spirits, even *in the morning.*"

Drinking was more than a casually accepted activity in pre-1830 America. It was a bond of male fellowship, forged wherever men gathered in groups. Taverns easily outnumbered churches as centers of community sociability, especially for the men who met in them to swap stories and to test their manliness in games of chance, physical brawling, and blood sports like dogfights and cockfighting. Alcohol flowed freely when courts were in session and during election rallies and militia musters. It was used to pay both common laborers and the itinerant preachers on the early Methodist circuit. Masters and journeymen shared a drink as a customary way of taking a break from work. No wedding, funeral, or meeting of friends was complete without alcohol. Indeed, not to offer a drink to guests was simply inhospitable.

For the temperance crusade to succeed, old forms of cultural and social behavior had to be abandoned and new ones learned. The reformers had to demonize alcohol and then banish it from the household and workplace. They had to finance a massive

propaganda campaign and link it to an organization that could mobilize and energize thousands of people. They built such a mass movement by merging temperance into the network of churches and lay volunteers that the benevolent empire had developed and by adopting the techniques of revivals to win new converts.

Evangelical reformers denounced intemperance as the greatest sin of the land, worse even than slavery and the horrors of the African slave trade. In the words of the Reverend Herman Humphrey, it deprived "its victims of the means of grace. . . . If there is any evil which hardens the heart faster, or fills the mouth with 'cursing and bitterness' sooner, or quickens hatred [of] God and man into a more rapid and frightful maturity, I know not what it is." Alcohol became the master symbol for all that was wrong in America—crime, poverty, insanity, broken families, boisterous politicking, Sabbath-breaking— and all that threatened the dawning of a Christian age of progress and prosperity.

This message, with its dark overtones of damnation but bright assurances of salvation through self-discipline, was thundered from the pulpit and the public lectern. Thanks to the generous financial subsidies of such wealthy benefactors as Stephen Van Rensselaer and Edward Delavan of New York, it was also broadcast in millions of tracts printed on the latest high-speed presses. This technologically advanced campaign of mass persuasion spread the temperance message and prepared the way for the revivalistic gathering in of converts. As in the revivals, temperance rallies combined emotionally charged sermons with large, tearful prayer meetings to evoke guilt among sinners, who would then seek release by taking the pledge of abstinence.

The temperance crusade was stunningly successful. Within a decade, more than five thousand local chapters and statewide groups were affiliated with the American Temperance Society. A million members had pledged abstinence by 1833. The movement, though national, was always strongest in the Northeast, where New England and New York alone claimed 72 percent of all temperance societies in the mid-1830s. Most of the converts came from the upper and middle classes. Businessmen welcomed temperance as a model of self-discipline in their efforts to regiment factory work. Young, upwardly mobile professionals and petty entrepreneurs, worried about both their religious salvation and their success in the competitive marketplace, learned in temperance how to be thrifty, self-controlled, and more respectable and creditworthy. Many of them presumably agreed with the *Temperance Recorder* that "the enterprise of this country is so great, and competition so eager in every branch of business . . ., that profit can only result from . . . *temperance.*"

Women were indispensable to the temperance movement. What women called "the slavery of intemperance" in the home gave them an immediate stake in the movement. Lacking legal protection against abusive husbands who drank away the family resources, women had a compelling reason to join the crusade against drinking, a predominantly male activity. Women comprised 35 to 60 percent of the members in local temperance societies, but their greatest role was not in the public arena but at home. As the moral protectors of the family, they pressured their husbands to take the teetotaler's pledge and stick by it, raised sons to shun alcohol, and banished liquor from their homes. By the 1840s, temperance and middle-class domesticity had become synonymous.

Temperance made its first significant inroads among the working classes when the economic depression of 1839–1843 created widespread hardships in eastern cities. Joining together in what they called **Washington Temperance Societies**, small businessmen and artisans, many of them reformed drunkards, carried temperance into working-class districts. The Washingtonians gained a considerable following by insisting that workers could survive the

depression only if they stopped drinking and adopted the temperance ethic of frugality and self-help. Their wives organized auxiliary societies and pledged to enforce sobriety and economic restraint at home.

Annual per capita consumption of alcohol by adults fell from over 7 gallons in 1830 to less than 2 gallons by 1845, a telling measure of the temperance movement's success. In 1851, Maine passed the first statewide prohibition law. Other northern states followed suit, but antitemperance coalitions soon overturned most of these laws outside New England. Nonetheless, alcohol consumption remained at the low level set in the 1840s. For temperance, at least, moral suasion proved able to change individual behavior.

Backlash against Benevolence

Many Americans were indifferent or hostile to the benevolent empire's do-gooding. Some of the harshest critics came out of the populist revivals of the early 1800s. Free-Will Baptists, Universalists, Disciples of Christ, and many Methodist sects spurned the entire program of the Christian reformers—its missions, Sabbath regulations, Sunday schools, tract societies, and vast network of well-financed local organizations. They considered such a program a conspiracy of orthodox Calvinists from old-line denominations to impose social and moral control on behalf of a religious and economic elite. The goal of the "orthodox party," warned the Universalist *Christian Intelligencer,* was the power of "governing the nation"; the societies they formed "are but so many strings . . ., the ultimate design of which is to draw them into power."

The fears of elite dominance that leaders of these populist sects expressed sprang from more than resentment of the financial and organizational resources of the wealthier and more prestigious Presbyterians and Congregationalists, the mainstays of benevolent reform. These fears also revealed a profound mistrust of the emerging market society.

In contrast to the evangelical reformers, drawn from the well-educated business and middle classes who were benefiting from economic change, most evangelical members of the grass-roots sects and followers of the itinerant preachers were unschooled, poor, and hurt by market fluctuations that they could not control. Often they were farmers forced by debt to move west or artisans and tradesmen displaced by new forms of factory production and new commercial outlets. Socially uprooted and economically stranded, they found a sense of community in their local churches and resisted control by wealthier, better-educated outsiders. Above all, they clung to

SUMMARY

THE REFORM IMPULSE

Type	Objects of Reform	Means	Example	Origin
Moral reform	Individual failings such as drinking, sexual misconduct, Sabbath-breaking	Mass distribution of literature, speaker tours, lobbying	American Temperance Society	1810s–1820s
Institutional reform	Crime, poverty, delinquency	Penitentiaries, asylums, almshouses, state-supported schools	Massachusetts Board of Education	1830s
Utopian societies	Selfish materialism of society	New, highly structured communities	Shakers	1820s
Abolition	Slavery	Petition and mailing campaigns	American Anti-Slavery Society	1830s
Women's rights	Legal subordination of women	Lobbying, petition campaigns	Seneca Falls Convention	1840s

beliefs that shored up the threatened authority of the father over his household.

The importance of women in evangelical reform challenged patriarchal authority. Middle-class evangelicalism in the Northeast was becoming feminized with the elevation of women to the status of moral guardians of the family (see Chapter 10) and agents of benevolent reform outside the household. This new social role for women was especially threatening—indeed, galling—for men who were the causalities of the more competitive economy. Raised on farms where the father had been the unquestioned lawgiver and provider, these men attacked feminized evangelicalism for undermining their paternal authority, and they rejected the middle-class values of progress and human perfectibility that seemed to mock their own failure and lost economic independence. They found in Scripture an affirmation of the patriarchal power that any man, no matter how poor or economically dependent, could exercise over his wife and children.

The **Church of Jesus Christ of Latter-day Saints** (also known as the **Mormon Church**) represented the most enduring religious backlash of economically struggling men against the aggressive efforts of reforming middle-class evangelicals. Joseph Smith, who established the church in upstate New York in

1830, came from a New England farm family uprooted and impoverished by market speculations gone sour. He and his followers were alienated not only from the new market economy but also from what they saw as the religious and social anarchy around them. Most of the early converts to Mormonism were young men in their twenties who had not yet established themselves in northern rural society.

Based on Smith's divine revelations as set forth in *The Book of Mormon* (1830), their new faith offered them a sanctuary as a biblical people and a release from social and religious uncertainties. Like Smith, they had been confused, even angered, by the competing voices of revival ministers and the fragmenting of a father-centered rural world. They believed that the mainstream evangelical churches had corrupted Christ's original gospel and fallen under the sway of the haughty rich by identifying salvation with worldly success. "This generation abounds in ignorance, superstition, selfishness, and priest-craft," charged the Mormon John Whitmer; "for this generation is truly led by . . . hireling priests whose God is the substance of the world's goods."

For rural families seeking security from individualism and economic dislocation, Mormonism provided both a theology and an economic and gender organization that defended communal beliefs centered on male authority. Mormonism assigned complete spiritual and secular authority to men. Unlike the female-dominated evangelicalism, men led their families into Mormonism. Only through subordination and obedience to their husbands could women hope to gain salvation.

To be a Mormon was to join a large extended family that was part of a shared enterprise. Men bonded their labor in a communal economy to benefit all the faithful. A law of tithing, instituted in 1841, required Mormons to give 10 percent of their property to the church upon conversion and 10 percent of their annual income thereafter. Driven by a strong sense of social obligation, the Mormons tried to replace selfish individualism with economic cooperation. By emphasizing the needs of the community as they strove to build their kingdom of God on earth, the Mormons forged the most successful alternative vision in antebellum America to the individualistic Christian republic of the benevolent reformers. (For the Mormons' role in the westward movement, see Chapter 12.)

Institutions and Social Improvement

Although evangelical Protestantism was its mainspring, antebellum reform also had its roots in the European Enlightenment. Enlightenment thinkers broke with Calvinist dogma by insisting that reason could lead to an understanding of the physical world and improve the human condition. Like the evangelicals inspired by religious optimism, other reformers drawing on Enlightenment doctrines of progress had unbounded faith in social improvement. They saw in America an unlimited potential to fashion a model republic of virtuous, intelligent citizens.

Studies published in the 1820s that documented increasing urban poverty, crime, and teenage delinquency created a sense of urgency for many reformers. They interpreted these studies as evidence that the family, community, and religion—the traditional shapers of American character—were now failing to rear virtuous, productive citizens. New public institutions that would provide the poor and the socially deviant with a morally wholesome environment free from corrupting influences were needed. Guided by the Enlightenment belief that environmental conditions shaped human character, reformers created a new system of public schooling in the North. They also prodded state legislatures to fund penitentiaries for criminals, asylums for the mentally ill, reformatories for the delinquent, and almshouses for the poor.

As reformers were implementing new institutional techniques for shaping individual character after 1820, a host of utopian communities sprang up. These communities also tapped into an impulse for human betterment, but they attempted to stand outside of society and reform it by the moral force of their example. These utopian groups typically rejected either private property or families based on monogamous marriage. To replace these accepted social relations, they offered a communitarian life designed to help a person reach perfection. Most of these communities were short-lived because their experiments in new forms of social and economic organization were far too radical for all but a handful of Americans.

School Reform

"An ignorant people always has been and always will be a degraded and oppressed people—they are always at the mercy of the corrupt and designing," cautioned Philadelphia school officials in their annual report for 1836. They warned that "if we fail by Education to awake—guide—confirm the moral energies of our people, we are lost!" Such alarm signified the urgency with which reformers approached public education. Secular revivalists as much as they were institutional innovators, the school reformers embarked on a crusade to save America from ignorance and vice.

Before the 1820s, schooling in America was an informal, haphazard affair that nonetheless met the basic needs for reading, writing, and arithmetic skills of an overwhelmingly rural population. New England, largely because of the Puritans' insistence that the Bible should be accessible to all, pioneered in publicly supported common schools in the seventeenth century, but even there, attendance and tax support were irregular until well into the nineteenth century. Private tutors and academies for the wealthy, a few charitable schools for the urban poor, and rural one-room schoolhouses open for a few months a year comprised formal education at the primary level. Still, except for isolated areas in the backcountry, literacy rates in America were among the highest in the Western world, and most parents supported schooling that was under local control and equipped their children for work in a rural society.

The first political demands for free tax-supported schools originated with the **Workingmen's movement** in eastern cities in the 1820s. Decrying what the Philadelphia Working Men's Committee in 1830 described as "a monopoly of talent, which consigns the multitude to comparative ignorance, and secures the balance of knowledge on the side of the rich and the rulers," workers called for free public schooling. In pushing for what they called "equal republican education," they were also seeking to guarantee that all citizens, no matter how poor, could achieve meaningful liberty and equality. However, the stiff resistance of wealthier property holders who refused to be taxed to pay for the education of working-class children blocked most of their proposals.

The breakthrough in school reform came in New England, where the disruptive forces of industrialization and urbanization were felt the earliest. Increasing economic inequality, growing numbers of Irish Catholic immigrants, and the emergence of a mass democracy based on nearly universal white male suffrage convinced reformers of the need for state-supported schools. Appealing to both the hopes and the fears of urban businessmen and the middle class, the reformers enlisted support for a system of "universal education" designed to restore civic virtue, train the masses in the responsibilities of political citizenship, and close the dangerous class divisions that were emerging.

In 1837, the Massachusetts legislature established the nation's first state board of education. The head of the board for the next twelve years was Horace Mann, a former Whig politician and temperance advocate who now tirelessly championed educational reform. Mann demanded that the state government assume centralized control over Massachusetts schools. He preached standardization and professionalism. All schools should have the same standards of compulsory attendance, strict discipline, common textbooks, professionally trained teachers, and graded, competitive classes of age-segregated students.

Once this system was in place, Mann promised that schools would become "the great equalizer of the conditions of men—the balance-wheel of the social machinery." Poverty would no longer threaten social disruption because the ignorant would have the knowledge to acquire property and wealth. Education, Mann stated, "does better than disarm the poor of their hostility against the rich; it prevents being poor." Trained in self-control and punctuality, youths would be able to take advantage of economic opportunities and become intelligent voters concerned with the rights of property. The children of Catholic immigrants, hapless victims of vice and superstition to most Protestants, would learn Protestant morality and thrift and become productive citizens. These children, wrote the Boston reformer Samuel Bates, must be "liberalized, Americanized."

For all its optimism, Mann's program faced stiff opposition in Massachusetts and everywhere else

where it was attempted. Democrats in the Massachusetts legislature denounced it as "a system of centralization and of monopoly of power in a few hands, contrary in every respect, to the true spirit of our democratical institutions." The laboring poor, who depended for economic survival on the wage income that their children could contribute to the family economy, resisted compulsory attendance laws and a longer school year. Farmers fought to maintain local control over schooling and to block the higher taxes needed for a more comprehensive and professionalized system. The Catholic Church protested the thinly veiled attempts of the reformers to indoctrinate all students in the moral strictures of middle-class Protestantism. Failing to get a share of state revenues, Catholics followed the lead of Bishop John Hughes of New York City and began building at great expense their own parochial schools.

Despite the cries of tyranny they provoked, Mann and his allies prevailed in most of the industrializing states. Ethnic and religious differences divided their opponents, and the educational reformers received strong support from the professional and business constituencies of the Whig party. Manufacturers hoped that the schools would turn out a more obedient and punctual labor force, and the more skilled and more prosperous workers saw in free public education a means of upward mobility for their children.

Most important for its political success, school reform appealed to the growing northern urban middle class. In the rhetoric of the reformers, state-supported education was to be the indispensable foundation for creating a harmonious society of individuals with the self-restraint necessary to improve themselves continually. Opposing both the "vicious passions" of the poor and the "idle luxury" of the rich, schools would instill the moral and economic discipline that the middle class deemed essential for a progressive and ordered society. Teaching morality and national pride was central to the educational curriculum, and from the popular McGuffey Readers used as a classroom text, students learned such lessons as "God gives a great deal of money to some persons, in order that they may assist those [who] are poor."

Out of the northern middle class also came the young female teachers who increasingly staffed elementary schools. As part of Mann's reforms for graded classes, school discipline was to rest less on corporal punishment and more on rewarding good behavior. Presumed by their nature to be more nurturing than men, women now had an entry into teaching, the first profession open to them. Besides

Pencil/Watercolor, 13½ × 18⅛ in. M. and M. Karolik Collection of American Paintings, 1815–1865, Courtesy of Museum of Fine Arts, Boston.

The sewing table on the right in this painting, Girls' Evening School, *from about 1840, indicates how notions of women's domestic sphere limited the educational opportunities available for young women in the mid-nineteenth century. Still, women trained in female academies and seminaries increasingly displaced men as teachers in public schools.*

the superior moral qualities they supposedly brought to teaching young children, women could also be hired far more cheaply than men: School boards assumed that they would accept low wages while waiting to be married.

Just over 50 percent of the white children between 5 and 19 years of age in the United States were enrolled in school in 1850—the highest percentage in the world at the time. School attendance varied by class and region. Working-class parents were quicker to pull their children out of school at an early age than higher-income middle-class parents. Planters continued to rely on private tutors or academies for their children, and southern farmers saw little need for public education. As a result, the slave states, especially in the Lower South, lagged behind the rest of the nation in providing for common schools.

Prisons, Workhouses, and Asylums

The transformation of the common schools was part of a wider reform effort after 1820 that sought to improve society through specialized institutions of moral reformation. Up to this time, Americans had depended on voluntary efforts to cope with crime, poverty, and social deviance. Convinced that these efforts were now inadequate, reformers turned to public authorities to establish a host of new institutions—penitentiaries, workhouses, mental hospitals, orphanages, and reformatories—to deal with social problems.

All these public institutions reflected a new attitude toward conditions that had been regarded as inevitable and irreversible. Eighteenth-century Americans viewed crime, poverty, and deviance as a natural part of a divinely sanctioned order—and they expected good Christians to respond with charity and the wicked to suffer for their sinfulness. Virtually no one, for example, ever thought of rehabilitating criminals. Prisons were simple structures whose only purpose was to hold criminals before they were fined, whipped, mutilated, or executed in a public ritual that drew large crowds of festive onlookers. But the institutional reformers of the Jacksonian era believed that criminals, as well as the poor and other deviants, could be morally redeemed.

Having abandoned ideas of innate depravity, the reformers believed that people's environments shaped their character for good or evil. The Boston Children's Friend Society was devoted to the young, "whose plastic natures may be molded into images of perfect beauty, or . . . perfect repulsiveness." Samuel Gridley Howe, a prison reformer, proclaimed: "Thousands of convicts are made so in consequence of a faulty organization of society. . . . They are thrown upon society as a sacred charge; and that society is false to its trust, if it neglects any means for their reformation." The means of reformation, confidently asserted advocates for moral rehabilitation, were to be found in the properly ordered environment of new institutions. Here, discipline and moral character would be instilled in criminals and other deviants

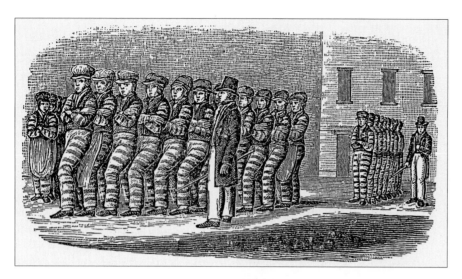

This scene of prisoners lined up in military order in the courtyard of the New York State prison in Auburn illustrates the regimented routine of order and discipline reformers thought would reshape the character of prison inmates.

who lacked the self-control to resist the corrupting vices and temptations that pervaded society.

Reformers had particularly high expectations for the penitentiary systems pioneered in Pennsylvania and New York in the 1820s. As two French observers noted in the early 1830s, "The penitentiary system . . . to them seems the remedy for all the evils of society." Unlike earlier prisons, the penitentiaries were huge, imposing structures that isolated the prisoners from each other and the outside world. Inmates in the New York system worked together in gangs during the day, but under the Pennsylvania plan, each prisoner was held in solitary confinement.

The penitentiaries were the institutional expression of the new philosophy of prisoner rehabilitation. No longer were criminals to be brutally punished or thrown together under inhumane conditions that perpetuated a cycle of moral depravity. Now, cut off from all corrupting influences, forced to learn that hard work teaches moral discipline, and uplifted by religious literature, criminals would be guided toward becoming law-abiding, productive citizens. For its proponents, the penitentiary became "a grand theatre, for the trial of all new plans in hygiene and education, in physical and moral reform."

The same philosophy of reform provided the rationale for asylums to house the poor and the insane. The number of transient poor and the size of urban slums increased as commercial capitalism uprooted farmers from the land and undercut the security of craft trades. Recognizing that families and local authorities could not cope with rising poverty, state governments in the Northeast began to intervene in the 1820s by building workhouses. Believing that the poor, much like criminals, had only themselves to blame, public officials and their evangelical

allies prescribed a therapeutic regimen of discipline and physical labor to cure the poor of their moral defects. The structured setting for that regimen was the workhouse.

What the poor needed, reformers were convinced, was a wholesome environment to promote moral regeneration. The custodians of the workhouses banished drinking, gambling, and idleness. Under the workhouse rules in New York, officers could "rightly exercise . . . a measure of moral force upon the will of these persons, to induce them to do that which their own uncultivated understanding might oppose." They were to administer their duties "with strictness—severity." Their prime responsibility was to supervise the inmates in a tightly scheduled daily routine built around manual labor. Once purged of their laziness and filled with self-esteem as the result of work discipline, the poor would be released to become useful members of society.

Public insane asylums offered a similar order for the mentally ill. Reformers associated insanity with the excessive disorder of society. People, it was felt, faced too many choices in a highly mobile, materialistic, and competitive society, and that drove some of them insane. Reformers predicted that the insane could be cured by a highly structured and institutionally managed environment. Following the lead of New York and Massachusetts in the 1830s, twenty-eight states had established mental hospitals by 1860. These facilities set rigid rules and work assignments to teach patients how to order their lives.

Much of the public commitment to the mentally ill resulted from the crusading efforts of Dorothea Dix, a Massachusetts schoolteacher. In the early 1840s she discovered that the insane in her home state were dumped into jails and almshouses, where they suffered filthy, inhumane treatment. She found the insane "confined . . . in *cages, closets, cellars, stalls, pens! Chained, naked, beaten with rods,* and *lashed into obedience.*" Horrified, Dix lobbied state legislatures across the nation for the next twenty years to improve treatment for the mentally ill.

The reformers acted out of humanitarian concerns, and they did provide social deviants with cleaner and safer living conditions. But their penitentiaries and asylums succeeded more in classifying and segregating their inmates than in reforming them. Freedom was too easily identified with tractability and submission to routine, and regimentation turned out not to be the best builder of character. What reformers praised as enlightened discipline, others denounced as a cruel new form of control. Witnessing the rigorous control of every movement of the isolated prisoners at the Eastern State Penitentiary in Philadelphia, English novelist Charles Dickens declared "this slow and daily tampering with the mysteries of the brain to be immeasurably worse than any torture of the body."

Institutionalization did not produce model citizens. After early successes, rates of recovery in mental hospitals dropped. Penitentiaries, reformatories, and workhouses failed to eliminate or noticeably check poverty, crime, and vice. Refusing to question their basic premise that repressive institutions could enhance individual responsibility, reformers abandoned their environmental explanations for deviance. By midcentury, they were defining deviants and dependents as permanent misfits who suffered from ingrained character defects. The asylums remained, but stripped of their earlier optimism, they became little more than holding pens for the outcasts of society.

Utopian Alternatives

The quest for human perfectibility that underlay the reformers' early idealism found its ultimate expression in the utopian community movement in the antebellum North. Unlike the reformers, who aimed to improve the existing order by guiding individuals to greater self-discipline, the utopians sought perfection by withdrawing from society and its confining institutions. A radically new social order, not an improved old one, was their goal.

Though following different religious and secular philosophies of communitarian living, all the utopians wanted to fashion a more rational and personally satisfying alternative to the competitive materialism of antebellum America. Robert Owen, a proponent of utopian **socialism**, promised to create a new order where "the degrading and pernicious

practices in which we are now trained, of buying cheap and selling dear, will be rendered unnecessary" and "union and co-operation will supersede individual interest." Nearly all their communities sought to transform the organization and rewards of work, thus challenging the prevailing dogmas about private property. The more radical communities experimented with new roles for women by redefining family life and rejecting prevailing conventions of marriage and gender roles.

The most successful utopian communities were religious sects whose reordering of both sexual and economic relations departed most sharply from middle-class norms. The largest of these sects were the **Shakers**. At their height in the 1830s, Shaker communities, mostly in the North, attracted some six thousand followers.

Named for the convulsive dancing that was part of their religious ceremonies, the Shakers traced their origins to the teachings of Ann Lee ("Mother Ann"). An illiterate factory laborer in mid-eighteenth-century England and the anguished mother of four dead children, Lee had a revelation in 1770 that the Second Coming of Christ was about to occur and would express itself in a womanly form, that of Mother Ann herself, the embodiment of the female side of God. Fired by another vision in 1774, Lee led eight of her followers to America, where, after her death in 1784, her disciples established the first Shaker community in New Lebanon, New York.

The Shakers prohibited sexual intercourse and individual ownership of property. As preached by Mother Ann, sexual passion and private property enslaved women as wives and mothers and enriched the wealthy at the expense of the poor. Organized around a doctrine of celibate **communism**, Shaker communities held all property in common, and the sexes worked and lived apart from each other. Dancing during religious worship brought men and women together and provided an emotional release from enforced sexual denial. As an early Shaker leader explained, "There is evidently no labor which so fully absorbs all the faculties of soul and body, as real spiritual devotion and energetic exercise in sacred worship." Leadership rested with elders and eldresses, who exercised authority over their gender-defined spheres of community life. In worldly as well as spiritual terms, women enjoyed an equality in Shaker life that the outside world denied them. For this reason, twice as many women as men joined the Shakers.

No longer sustained after 1850 by fresh converts spun off by the revivals of mainstream evangelicalism, the Shakers gradually dwindled. Their rule of celibacy meant, of course, that they could propagate themselves only by recruiting new members. Viewed as eccentric outsiders by contemporaries, the Shakers today are best remembered for the beautiful simplicity of the furniture they made in their workshops.

John Humphrey Noyes founded another utopian community that offered women a liberating alternative to the burdens of monogamous marriage and constant childbearing. A graduate of Dartmouth who studied for the ministry at Yale, Noyes carried evangelical notions of perfectionism to their logical extreme. He preached that the millennium ushering in the Second Coming of Christ was already under way and that the converted could lead lives free from sin. Believing that marriage, the selfish "exclusive possession of one woman to one man," was the main barrier to perfection, he proposed instead "complex marriage," the mutual love of all the saved for each other. Despite the notoriety that swirled around this apparent call for free love and adultery, Noyes was not advocating the abandonment of sexual restraints. His ideal of physical love was sexual intercourse without male orgasm, and his goal was a religious society in which cooperative arrangements between men and women regulated child care and the distribution of property.

After he had been drummed out of the ministry for his radical teachings, Noyes established the **Oneida Community** in upstate New York in 1847. He attracted over two hundred followers with his perfectionist vision of plural marriage, community nurseries, group discipline, and common ownership of property. The profits from the patent on an animal trap and the sale of products from its workshops gave the community a secure economic base, and it flourished for thirty years. Charged with adultery, Noyes fled to Canada in 1879. The Oneida Community, reorganized in 1881 as a joint-stock company in the United States and committed thereafter to conventional sexual mores, survived into the twentieth century.

In contrast with the Shaker and Oneida communities and a host of other experiments anchored by religious perfectionism, secular variants of utopianism met with little success. Secular utopians aspired to perfect social relations through the rational design of

The clean, functional lines of Shaker furniture reflect the stress on order and usefulness in Shaker communities.

planned communities. Bitter critics of the social evils of industrialization, they tried to construct models for a social order free from poverty, unemployment, and inequality. They envisioned cooperative communities that balanced agricultural and industrial pursuits in a mixed economy that recycled earnings to the laborers who actually produced the wealth.

Despite their high expectations, nearly all the planned communities ran into financial difficulties and soon collapsed. The pattern was set by the first of the controversial socialist experiments, **New Harmony** in Indiana, the brainchild of the wealthy Scottish industrialist and philanthropist Robert Owen. Within two years of its founding in 1825, New Harmony fell victim to inadequate financing and internal bickering. The economic misery of the depression of the 1840s revived interest in utopian ventures and helped popularize the ideas of Charles Fourier, a French utopian who proposed to restore dignity to labor and end poverty by dividing society into phalanxes, cooperative units of workers who lived communally. Scores of **Fourierist communities** were set up, but few survived into the 1850s.

About the only secular cooperative that gained lasting fame was **Brook Farm** in West Roxbury, Massachusetts (today part of Boston). Established in 1841, Brook Farm was a showcase for the transcendentalist philosophy of Ralph Waldo Emerson. A former Unitarian minister in Boston who turned to lecturing and writing after leaving the ministry, Emerson taught that intuition and emotion could grasp a truer ("transcendent") reality than the senses alone could. The Boston intellectuals drawn to Brook Farm in the 1840s saw it as a refuge from the pressures and coarseness of commercial society, a place where they could realize the Emersonian ideal of spontaneous creativity. Although disbanded after six years as an economic failure, Brook Farm inspired intellectuals such as Nathaniel Hawthorne, who briefly lived there. In turn, his writings and those of other writers influenced by **transcendentalism** flowed into the great renaissance of American literature in the mid-nineteenth century, an outpouring of work that grappled with Emersonian themes of individualism and the reshaping of the American character.

In an 1837 address at Harvard titled "The American Scholar," Emerson had called for a distinctly national literature devoted to the democratic possibilities of American life. "The literature of the poor, the feelings of the child, the philosophy of the street, the meaning of household life, are the topics of the time," he proclaimed. Writers soon responded to Emerson's call.

Walt Whitman, whose *Leaves of Grass* (1855) foreshadowed modern poetry in its use of free verse, shared Emerson's faith in the possibilities of individual fulfillment, and his poems celebrated the democratic variety of the American people. David Henry Thoreau, Emerson's friend and neighbor, embodied the transcendentalist fascination with nature and self-discovery by living in relative isolation for sixteen months at Walden Pond, near Concord, Massachusetts. His *Walden, or Life in the Woods* (1854) became an American classic for its account of how self-reliance could free a person from the fetters and artificialities of "civilized" society. "I went to the woods," he wrote, "because I wished to . . . confront only the essential facts of life, and see if I could not learn what it had to teach, and not, when I came to die, discover that I had not lived."

Hawthorne and Herman Melville, the greatest novelists of the American renaissance, did not share the optimism of Emerson, Whitman, and Thoreau in the democratic promise of unrestrained individualism. Both of these writers focused on the existence of evil and the human need for community. In *The Scarlet Letter* (1850) and *The House of the Seven Gables* (1851), Hawthorne probed themes of egoism and pride to reveal the underside of the human soul. Melville's *Moby Dick* (1851) depicted the consequences of a competitive individualism unchecked by a social conscience. In his relentless pursuit of the great white whale, Captain Ahab destroys himself and his crew.

Much of the initial appeal of utopian communities rested on the same concerns over the splin-

tering and selfishness of antebellum society that Hawthorne and Melville expressed. Although the works of these novelists have endured, the utopian experiments quickly collapsed. They offered economic security and social harmony to buttress a threatened sense of community, but the acquisitiveness and competitive demands of the larger society exerted a stronger pull on most Americans. Without a strong, authoritarian leader, or the cohesiveness of a disciplined religious vision that freed women from traditional restraints, the utopians soon returned to the society they had tried to leave.

Women's Role in Reform

Women played a central role in the major reform movements. They first entered reform through benevolent and missionary societies in the early 1800s. These women's organizations, whose members were predominately upper-class, were concerned with the spiritual welfare of the poor and the widowed. Influenced by the Second Great Awakening, middle-class women turned to reform in the 1820s. Many of them staffed societies that continued the earlier benevolent pattern of relying on moral suasion and deferring to the existing political and social order. Others, however, were more openly reformist.

A second phase of women's reform by the 1830s began to question the assumptions of a male-dominated society. Women founded or joined new organizations that took up the causes of prostitutes and slaves, previously shunned as outside the scope of respectable reform. These reformers were aggressive activists who boldly sought political support by lobbying and petitioning. They increasingly challenged the limited role American life allotted to women. Those most determined to demand fundamental change came from the abolitionist crusade.

Reform and Women's Sphere

An idealized image of "true womanhood" emerged in the commercializing Northeast after 1815. Often labeled the cult of domesticity (see Chapter 11), this image limited women's social role to home and family. Ministers, male moralists, and many women writers redefined femininity to encompass the virtues of piety, purity, and submissiveness. Because of their allegedly unique virtues, women's natural place was at home, morally training and uplifting their families. This became the role model for all respectable women.

The first phase of women's reform represented an extension of this domestic ideal for women. Assumptions about the unique moral qualities of women as Christian mothers justified and even encouraged women's assuming the role of "social mother" by organizing on behalf of the orphaned and the widowed. Founded in 1797, the **Society for the Relief of Poor Widows with Small Children** in New York typified these early approaches to reform. The women in the society came from socially prominent families. Motivated by religious charity and social duty, they visited poor women and children, dispensed funds, and set up work programs. However, they limited their benevolence to the "deserving poor"—socially weak but morally strong people who had suffered personal misfortune. They screened out all who were thought to be unworthy.

The revivalist call in the 1820s for moral action inspired middle-class women to join voluntary female groups. They founded maternal associations, where they prayed and fasted for the moral strength to save the souls of their children. Other associations sponsored revivals, visited the poor, established Sunday schools, and distributed Bibles and religious tracts. These reformers widened the public role of women, but their efforts also reinforced cultural stereotypes of women as nurturing helpmates who deferred to males as the wielders of economic and political power.

A New Militancy

A second type of women's reform developed in the 1830s. Although most women still favored conservative reform—teaching Sunday school, doing missionary work among the poor, and administering charity—new, more confrontational organizations emerged. Women from the broad middle ranks of society now flocked to various moral reform and antislavery groups that aggressively pushed for an expanded female role in setting public policy.

Unlike their benevolent counterparts, the reformers in the 1830s challenged male prerogatives and moved beyond moral suasion. The crusade against prostitution exemplified the new militancy. Women seized leadership of the movement in 1834 with the founding of the New York Female Moral Reform Society. This was an exclusively female organization that replaced the New York Magdalen Society, a male-dominated group forced to disband when its first report scandalized the city fathers with its exposé of "kept women and ruined servant girls." Far from trying to spare men from embarrassment, the female reformers used their society to publicize the names of the male patrons at the city's brothels. Through the society's journal, *Advocate for Moral Reform,* they identified male greed and licentiousness as the causes for the fallen state of women. They blamed male businessmen for the low wages that forced some women to resort to prostitution and denounced lustful men for engaging in "a regular crusade against [our] sex."

In 1839, this attack on the sexual double standard became a national movement with the establishment of the **American Female Moral Reform Society**. With 555 affiliates throughout the evangelical heartland of the North, this new national association shifted from moral pressure to legal sanctions. Female activists mounted a lobbying campaign that, unlike earlier efforts, bypassed prominent men and reached out to a mass audience for signatures. By the 1840s, such unprecedented political involvement enabled women to secure the first state laws criminalizing seduction and adultery.

Newer women's groups formed after 1830 that focused on poverty also developed a more radical critique of American society and its male leadership. The **Boston Seamen's Aid Society**, founded in 1833 by Sarah Josepha Hale, a widow with five children, soon rejected the benevolent tradition of distinguishing between the "respectable" and the "unworthy" poor. After opening workshops to train poor women as seamstresses and laundresses, Hale discovered that her efforts to guide them toward self-sufficiency flew in the face of the low wages and substandard housing that trapped her clients in poverty. She concluded in 1838 that "it is hardly possible for the hopeless poor to avoid being vicious." Even more shocking to the benevolent establishment and its financial backers in the business community, Hale attacked male employers for exploiting the poor. "Combinations of selfish men are formed to beat down the price of female labor," she wrote in her 1836 annual report, "and then . . . they call the diminished rate the market price."

The Appeal of Abolitionism

The rising concern of female reformers in the 1830s over the inequities of a male-controlled power structure and the injustices inflicted on women and children found its greatest expression in abolitionism. "From the beginning," noted the Boston abolitionist Lydia Maria Child in 1838, "women, by paying their money, have become members of anti-slavery societies and conventions in various free states." As Christian wives and mothers, they could identify with the plight of the black family under slavery. Abolitionist literature emphasized the anguish of families broken up by the slave trade and the sexual degradation of female slaves forced to submit to their owners' lust.

The black artist Patrick Reason made this engraving in 1835. White female abolitionists identified strongly with his image of the chained female slave.

The most powerful abolitionist depiction of slavery showed a chained female slave imploring, "Am I not a woman and a sister?" In a male-governed society in which husbands could abuse their wives with legal impunity and gain custody of the children after a divorce, such images of slavery spoke with special force to northern white women.

Women established their own antislavery societies in the 1830s as auxiliaries to the national organization run and dominated by men. Initially, their gender-segregated role was limited to raising funds, circulating petitions, and visiting homes to gain converts. Their contributions as unpaid volunteers were indispensable in spreading the antislavery message. Often operating out of local churches, women were grass-roots organizers of a massive petition campaign that the abolitionists launched in the mid-1830s. Women signed more than half of the antislavery memorials sent to Congress. "There would be but few abolition petitions if the ladies . . . would let us alone," complained a Mississippi congressman.

Most women accepted, or at least did not openly question, their restricted role within the antislavery movement. That role subordinated them to male power and limited their activities to those deemed proper for women. Some antislavery women, however, found in abolitionism a liberating message of individualism and equality that spoke to them as oppressed members of society. For these women, abolitionism was a bridge to feminism, a bold effort to make women the political and social equals of men.

Abolitionism and Women's Rights

Abolitionism emerged from the same religious impulse that energized reform throughout the North. Like other reformers, the abolitionists came predominantly from evangelical, middle-class families, particularly those of New England stock, and they were also committed to a moral crusade that would free individual consciences and rid the nation of sin. What distinguished the abolitionists was their insistence that slavery was *the* great national sin, mocking American ideals of liberty and Christian morality.

Starting with a core of antislavery Quakers and free blacks, abolitionism began as a moral protest against the gradualist approach and white supremacist assumptions of the **American Colonization Society**, the main antislavery group in the decade after the War of 1812. Under the early leadership of William Lloyd Garrison, the abolitionists uncompromisingly attacked not only slaveholders but also all others whose moral apathy helped support slavery.

After provoking a storm of protest in both North and South, the abolitionist movement split in 1840. Crucial in this division was Garrison's support of women's rights. Most abolitionists broke with him and founded their own antislavery organization. Female abolitionists took the lead in organizing a separate women's rights movement.

The anti-Garrison abolitionists treated slavery as a political question that could be addressed through political means. Although this new approach diluted the moral intensity of the original abolitionist message, it enabled the abolitionists to begin mobilizing a constituency of voters that would soon push slavery to the center of national politics.

Rejecting Colonization

As slavery expanded westward in the early nineteenth century, white Americans of all classes and all regions believed that they could not live peacefully side by side with large numbers of emancipated blacks in a free republic. Most whites were convinced that emancipation would lead either to a race war or the debasement of their superior status through racial interbreeding. This paralyzing fear of general emancipation, rooted in pervasive racism, long shielded slavery from sustained attack. Only free blacks in the North advocated slavery's immediate end. Organized antislavery activities by whites slackened once Congress prohibited the African slave trade in 1808, and most of it was confined to deeply religious farmers in the subsistence districts of the Upper South.

SUMMARY

TYPES OF ANTISLAVERY REFORM

Type	Definition	Example
Gradualist	Accepts notions of black inferiority and attempts to end slavery gradually by purchasing the freedom of slaves and colonizing them in Africa	American Colonization Society
Immediatist	Calls for immediate steps to end slavery and denounces slavery and racial prejudice as moral sins	Abolitionists
Political antislavery	Recognizes slavery in states where it exists but insists on keeping slavery out of the territories	Free-Soilers

In 1817, antislavery reformers from North and South founded the American Colonization Society. Slaveholding politicians from the Upper South, notably Henry Clay, James Madison, and President James Monroe, were the leading organizers of the society, whose goal was to promote emancipation by sending freed blacks to Africa. Gradual emancipation followed by the removal of blacks from America was the only solution that white reformers could imagine for ridding the nation of slavery and avoiding a racial bloodbath. Their goal was to make America all free and all white.

Although the American Colonization Society clung to its program until the Civil War, it had no real chance of success. No form of emancipation, however gradual, could appeal to slave owners who could profit from the demand for their slaves in the Lower South. Moreover, the society could never afford to purchase the freedom of any significant number of slaves. Blacks already free accounted for nearly all of those the society transported to its West African colony, Liberia. At the height of its popularity in the 1820s, the society colonized only fourteen hundred blacks. During that same decade, the American slave population increased by 700,000.

Free African-Americans were the harshest critics of colonization. They bitterly attacked the colonizers' central assumption that free blacks were unfit to live as free citizens in America. Typical of the colonizers' racist thinking was the claim by Henry Clay in 1827 that the "free coloured" were the "most vicious" of all Americans. "Contaminated themselves, they extend their vices to all around them, to the slaves and to the whites." The annual report of the American Colonization Society in 1824 approvingly quoted a New England minister who said of the free black: "You cannot raise him from the abyss of his degradation. You may call him free . . . but you cannot bleach him into the enjoyment of freedom."

Confronted with this wall of racial prejudice, free blacks condemned colonization as a scheme to prop up slavery by ridding the nation of the slaves' natural allies in the black population. Most American blacks were native-born, and they considered themselves Americans with every right to enjoy the blessings of republican liberty. As a black petition in 1817 stated, banishment from America "would not only be cruel, but in direct violation of the principles, which have been the boast of this republic."

A black protest meeting in 1817 at Philadelphia's Bethel Church began black resistance to colonization. Organizing through their own churches in northern cities, free blacks founded some fifty abolitionist societies, offered refuge to fugitive slaves, and launched the first African-American newspaper in 1827, *Freedom's Journal*. David Walker, a free black who had moved from North Carolina to Massachusetts, was the Boston agent for the *Journal*, and in 1829 he published his ***Appeal to the Colored Citizens of the World***. A searing indictment of white greed and hypocrisy, the *Appeal* vented the rage of blacks at their oppression. Rejecting colonization, Walker insisted that "America is more our country, than it is the whites'—we have enriched it with our *blood and tears*," and he warned white Americans that "wo, wo, will be to you if we have to obtain our freedom by fighting."

Walker's *Appeal* shocked white America, especially after copies of it were found in the possession of slaves. As if in response to his call for revolutionary resistance by the enslaved, Nat Turner's Rebellion exploded in the summer of 1831 (see Chapter 13). The nation seemed on the brink of bloody slave uprisings. Both alarmed and inspired by the increased tempo of black militancy, a small group of antislavery whites abandoned all illusions about colonization and embarked on a radically new approach for eradicating slavery.

Abolitionism

The leading figure in early abolitionism was William Lloyd Garrison. A Massachusetts printer, Garrison found his life's cause in 1829 when he became coeditor of an antislavery newspaper in Baltimore. Before the year was out, Garrison was arrested and convicted of criminal libel for his editorials against a Massachusetts merchant engaged in the domestic slave trade. He spent seven weeks in jail before a wealthy New York City philanthropist paid his $100 fine. Recognizing that his lack of freedom in jail paled against that of the slave, Garrison emerged with an unquenchable hatred for slavery. Returning to Boston, he launched his own antislavery newspaper, **The Liberator**, in 1831. A year later, he was instrumental in founding the New England Anti-Slavery Society.

Garrison instilled the antislavery movement with moral urgency. As militant as the free blacks who comprised the bulk of the early subscribers to *The Liberator*, he thundered, "If we would not see our land deluged in blood, we must instantly burst asunder the

William Lloyd Garrison, the driving force behind early abolitionism, stamped the movement with an uncompromising moral intensity.

shackles of the slaves." Repudiating the gradualism and racial prejudice of the colonizers, he committed abolitionism to the twin goals of immediatism—an immediate moral commitment to end slavery—and racial equality.

Only by striving toward these goals, he insisted, could white America ever hope to end slavery without massive violence. Slaveholders, as well as all other whites, had to realize that the work of emancipation needed to begin immediately as a moral imperative owed to those who were equal in the eyes of God. For black freedom to be meaningful and not the shameful mockery imposed on free blacks by white prejudice, whites had to accept black equality before the law as a goal that would hasten the end of slavery.

The demand of the abolitionists for the legal equality of blacks was as unsettling to public opinion as their call for immediate, uncompensated emancipation. Most whites believed that only they could—or should—exercise the rights of freedom and equality. Whiteness had become a visible badge of one's fitness for republican citizenship, and discriminatory laws, aptly described by abolitionist Lydia Maria Child as "this legalized contempt of color," restricted the political and civil liberties of free blacks in every state. Denied the vote outside New England, segregated in all public facilities, prohibited from moving into several western states, and excluded from most jobs save menial labor, free blacks everywhere were walled off as an inferior caste unfit for equality (see "American Views: Appeal of a Female Abolitionist").

As he promised in the first issue of *The Liberator*, Garrison was harsh and uncompromising in denouncing slavery and advocating black rights. But without the organizational and financial resources of a national society, the message of the early Garrisonians rarely extended beyond free black communities in the North. The success of British abolitionists in 1833 when gradual, compensated emancipation was enacted for Britain's West Indian colonies inspired white and black abolitionists to gather at Philadelphia in December 1833 and form the **American Anti-Slavery Society**. Sixty-two delegates attended the meeting, one-third of them Quakers. Most of the remainder were evangelical businessmen and ministers from other reform movements.

Arthur and Lewis Tappan, two wealthy merchants from New York City, provided financial backing, and Theodore Dwight Weld, a young evangelical minister, fused abolitionism with the moral passion of religious revivalism. Weld brought abolitionism to the West in 1834 with the revivals

American Views

APPEAL OF A FEMALE ABOLITIONIST

Lydia Maria Child's *Appeal,* published in Boston in 1833, was a landmark in abolitionist literature for both the thoroughness of its attack on slavery and its refutation of racist ideology and discrimination. This condemnation of racial prejudice was the most radical feature of abolitionist ideology. It directly challenged the deeply held beliefs and assumptions of nearly all white Americans, in the North as well as the South. Racism and slavery, as Child shows in this excerpt from her *Appeal,* fed off one another in the national curse of slavery.

❖ **How does Child argue that northern whites must bear some of the responsibility for perpetuating slavery?**

❖ **What arguments does Child make against racial discrimination in northern society?**

❖ **What did Child mean when she wrote that "the Americans are peculiarly responsible for the example they give"? Do you agree with her?**

❖ **How does Child deal with the charge that the abolitionists threatened the preservation of the Union?**

While we bestow our earnest disapprobation on the system of slavery, let us not flatter ourselves that we are in reality any better than our brethren of the South. Thanks to our soil and climate, and the early exhortations of the Quakers, the *form* of slavery does not exist among us; but the very *spirit* of the hateful and mischievous thing is here in all its strength. . . . Our prejudice against colored people is even more inveterate than it is at the South. The planter is often attached to his negroes, and lavishes caresses and kind words upon them, as he would on a favorite hound: but our cold-hearted, ignoble prejudice admits of no exception—no intermission.

The Southerners have long continued habit, apparent interest and dreaded danger, to palliate the wrong they do; but we stand without excuse. . . . If the free States wished to cherish the system of slavery forever, they could not take a more direct course than they now do. Those who are kind and liberal on all other subjects, unite with the selfish and the proud in their unrelenting efforts to keep the colored population in the lowest state of degradation; and the influence they unconsciously exert over children early infuses into their innocent minds the same strong feelings of contempt. . . .

The state of public feeling not only makes it difficult for the Africans to obtain information, but it prevents them from making profitable use of what knowledge they have. A colored man, how-

he preached at Lane Theological Seminary in Cincinnati. The "Lane rebels," students gathered by Weld, fanned out as itinerant agents to seek converts for abolitionism throughout the Yankee districts of the rural North. Weld's *American Slavery as It Is: Testimony of a Thousand Witnesses,* a massively documented indictment of slavery, became a best-seller in 1839. Abolitionist women, notably Angelina Grimké, Weld's wife and the daughter of

a South Carolina planter, contributed much of the research.

Revivalistic exhortations were just one of the techniques the abolitionists exploited to mobilize public opinion against slavery. They spread their message through rallies, paid lecturers, children's games and toys, and the printed word. Drawing on the experience of reformers in Bible and tract societies, the abolitionists harnessed steam printing to the cause

ever intelligent, is not allowed to pursue any business more lucrative than that of a barber, a shoeblack, or waiter. These, and all other employments, are truly respectable, whenever the duties connected with them are faithfully performed; but it is unjust that a man should, on account of his complexion, be prevented from performing more elevated uses in society. Every citizen ought to have a fair chance to try his fortune in any line of business, which he thinks he has ability to transact. Why should not colored men be employed in the manufactories of various kinds? If their ignorance is an objection, let them be enlightened, as speedily as possible. If their moral character is not sufficiently pure, remove the pressure of public scorn, and thus supply them with motives for being respectable. All this can be done. It merely requires an earnest wish to overcome a prejudice, which . . . is in fact opposed to the spirit of our religion, and contrary to the instinctive good feelings of our nature. . . . When the majority heartily desire a change, it is effected, be the difficulties what they may. The Americans are peculiarly responsible for the example they give; for in no other country does the unchecked voice of the people constitute the whole of government. . . .

The strongest and best reason that can be given for our supineness on the subject of slavery, is the fear of dissolving the Union. The Constitution of the United States demands our highest reverence. . . . But we must not forget that the Constitution provides for any change that may be required for the general good. The great machine is constructed with a safety valve, by which any rapidly increasing evil may be expelled whenever the people desire it.

If the Southern politicians are determined to make a Siamese question of this also—if they insist that the Union shall not exist without slavery—it can only be said that they join two things, which have no affinity with each other, and which cannot permanently exist together. —They chain the living and vigorous to the diseased and dying; and the former will assuredly perish in the infected neighborhood.

The universal introduction of free labor is the surest way to consolidate the Union, and enable us to live together in harmony and peace. If a history is ever written entitled "The Decay and Dissolution of the North American Republic," its author will distinctly trace our downfall to the existence of slavery among us.

Source: *Lydia Maria Child,* An Appeal in Favor of That Class of Americans Called Africans, *ed. Carolyn L. Karcher (1996).*

of moral suasion. They distributed millions of anti-slavery tracts, and by the late 1830s, abolitionist sayings appeared on posters, emblems, song sheets, and even candy wrappers.

The abolitionists focused their energies on mass propaganda because they saw their role as social agitation. Their problem was the moral apathy of whites regarding slavery. To break through that apathy and change public opinion, they described slavery in horrific terms of absolute moral and physical degradation so that whites could identify as fellow human beings with the plight of the slave. This strategy convinced some whites to work for racial justice and the speedy end of slavery. By 1840, nearly 200,000 Northerners belonged to two thousand local affiliates of the American Anti-Slavery Society. Most whites, however, remained unmoved, and some violently opposed the abolitionists.

Antiabolitionist mobs in the North went on a rampage in the mid-1830s (see Figure 14-1). They disrupted antislavery meetings, beat and stoned speakers, destroyed printing presses, burned the homes of the wealthy benefactors of the movement, and vandalized free black neighborhoods in a wave of terror that drove blacks from several northern cities. Although Garrison and Weld, the most frequent targets of mob violence, escaped with their lives, Elijah P. Lovejoy, an abolitionist editor in Illinois, was killed by a mob in 1837. By attacking slavery and appealing to women and children, the abolitionists had challenged the social and economic leadership of local elites, especially those with profitable ties to the slave economy of the South. These elites often incited the mobs, whose fury expressed the anxieties of semiskilled and common laborers that they might lose their jobs if freed slaves moved north.

There were few abolitionists to lynch in the South. The hostility to abolitionism there took the form of burning and censoring antislavery literature, offering rewards for the capture of leading abolitionists to stand trial for inciting slave revolts, and tightening up slave codes and the surveillance of free blacks. Meanwhile, Democrats in Congress yielded to slaveholding interests in 1836 by passing a gag rule that automatically tabled antislavery petitions. Citing the fear of slave revolts in the South and the need for national harmony, Congress was now on record as infringing on the constitutional right of Americans to petition their representatives for the redress of grievances.

The hostility and violence abolitionism provoked convinced Garrison and some of his followers that American institutions and values were fundamentally immoral. In 1838, Garrison helped found the **New England Non-Resistant Society,** dedicated to the belief that a complete moral regeneration, based on renouncing force in all human relationships, was necessary if America were ever to live up to its Christian and republican ideals. The Garrisonian nonresistants rejected all coercive authority, whether expressed in human bondage, clerical support of slavery, male dominance in the patriarchical family, the racial oppression of blacks, or the police power of government. The logic of their stand as Christian **anarchists** drove them to denounce all formal political activities and even the legitimacy of the Union, based as it was on a pact with slaveholders.

Garrison's opponents within the abolitionist movement accused him of alienating the public by identifying the antislavery cause with radical attacks on traditional authority. Garrison's support for the growing demand of antislavery women to be treated

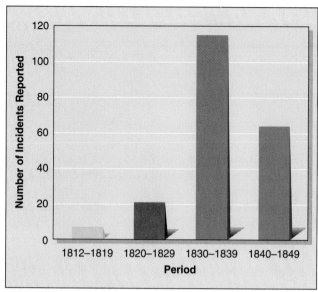

Figure 14-1   Mob Violence and the Abolitionists
Civil disturbances resulting in attacks on individuals or property increased sharply in the 1830s. The abolitionist campaign to flood the country with antislavery literature triggered much of this surge. Nearly half of the mob activity in the 1830s was directed against the abolitionists.

Source: *Leonard L. Richards, "Gentlemen of Property and Standing":* Anti-Abolitionist Mobs in Jacksonian America *(1970).*

as equals in the movement brought the factional bickering to a head in 1840 and split the American Anti-Slavery Society. In turn, the opposition of most male abolitionists to the public activities of their female counterparts provoked a militant faction of these women into founding their own movement to achieve equality in American society.

The Women's Rights Movement

The participation of thousands of women in antislavery and moral reform work led to the first organized movement for women's rights. Feminism grew out of abolitionism because of the parallels many women drew between the exploited lives of the slaves and their own subordinate status in northern society. Considered biologically inferior to men, women were denied the vote, deprived of property or control of any wages after marriage, and barred from most occupations and advanced education. "In striving to cut [the slave's] irons off, we found most surely that *we* were manacled *ourselves,*" argued Abby Kelley, a Quaker abolitionist.

The participation of women in abolitionism always aroused opposition, especially from conservative clergy convinced that women had no place in a movement that stirred fears of social instability and racial mixing. The issue came to a head in 1837 when

Angelina and Sarah Grimké, South Carolinians born into the planter aristocracy, attracted large crowds of men and women to their antislavery lectures in New England. The Grimké sisters had moved north because of their opposition to slavery and had become Quakers. Coming from the planter class with firsthand experience of the evils of slavery, they attracted large audiences on the abolitionist lecture circuit. But by publicly lecturing to a "promiscuous" (mixed) audience of men and women, they defied restrictions on women's proper role and enraged the Congregational clergy of Massachusetts. Harshly criticized for their unwomanly behavior, the Grimkés publicly responded with an indictment of the male patriarchy and the shocking assertion that "men and women are *created equal*! They are both moral and accountable beings and whatever is right for man to do is right for woman." The clergy had unintentionally triggered the opening salvo in the campaign of women for equal citizenship.

Now more sensitive than ever to the injustice of their assigned role as men's submissive followers, antislavery women demanded an equal voice in the abolitionist movement. Despite strong opposition from many of his fellow male abolitionists, Garrison helped Abby Kelley win a seat on the business committee of the American Anti-Slavery Society at its convention in 1840. Her election ended any hope of healing the division between the Garrisonian and anti-Garrisonian abolitionists. The anti-Garrisonians walked out of the convention and formed a separate organization in 1840, the **American and Foreign Anti-Slavery Society.**

What was rapidly becoming known as the "woman question" also disrupted the 1840 World Anti-Slavery Convention in London. The refusal of the convention to seat the American female delegates was the final indignity that transformed the discontent of women into a self-conscious movement for women's equality. Two of the excluded delegates, Lucretia Mott and Elizabeth Cady Stanton, vowed to build an organization to "speak out for *oppressed* women."

Their work went slowly. The early feminists were overshadowed by the abolitionist crusade. Dependent on the abolitionists for most of their followers, the feminists were unable to do more than hold local meetings and sponsor occasional speaking tours. Many women sympathetic to the movement held back lest they be shunned in their communities. A minister's wife in Portsmouth, New Hampshire, spoke for many of these women when she wrote to a feminist friend, "There are but few here who think of women as anything more than slave or a plaything, and they think I am different from most women."

In 1848, Stanton and Mott were finally able to call the first national convention ever devoted to women's rights at Seneca Falls, in upstate New York. The **Seneca Falls Convention** issued the **Declaration of Sentiments**, a call for full female equality. Modeled directly on the Declaration of Independence, it identified male patriarchy as the source of women's oppression and demanded the vote for women as a sacred and inalienable right of republican citizenship. This call for suffrage raised the prospect of women's self-determination as independent citizens.

The Seneca Falls agenda defined the goals of the women's movement for the rest of the century. The call for the vote met the stiffest opposition, and

Elijah Lovejoy, an abolitionist editor, was shot dead in November 1837, when a mob in Alton, Illinois, burned the warehouse where he had stored his printing press.

male legislators refused to budge. The feminists' few successes before the Civil War came in economic rights. By 1860, fourteen states had granted women greater control over their property and wages—most significantly under New York's Married Women's Property Act of 1860. Largely the result of the intense lobbying of Susan B. Anthony, the act established women's legal right to their own wage income and to sue fathers and husbands who tried to deprive them of their wages.

Despite these initial steps in dismantling legal and economic discrimination against women, the feminist movement did not attract broad support. Most women found in the doctrine of separate spheres a reassuring feminine identity that they could express either at home or in benevolent and reform societies. Within the reform movement as a whole, women's rights were always of minor concern. The abolitionists, those most likely to provide the feminists with a receptive audience, remained focused on emancipation.

Political Antislavery

Most abolitionists who had broken with Garrison in 1840 believed that emancipation could best be achieved by moving abolitionism into the mainstream of American politics. Political abolitionism had its roots in the petition campaign of the late 1830s. Congressional efforts to suppress the discussion of slavery backfired when John Quincy Adams, the former president who had become a Massachusetts congressman, resorted to an unending series of parliamentary ploys to get around the gag rule. A failure as president, Adams became a hero to antislavery Northerners, a champion of the constitutional right to petition Congress for redress of grievances. Northern whites who had shown no interest in abolitionism as a moral crusade for blacks now began to take a stand against slavery when the issue involved the civil liberties of whites and the overwhelming political power of the South. By the hundreds of thousands, they signed abolitionist petitions in 1837 and 1838 to protest the gag rule and block the admission of Texas as a slave state.

In 1840, anti-Garrison abolitionists tried to turn this new antislavery constituency into an independent political party. They formed the **Liberty party** and ran for the presidency James G. Birney, a former slaveholder converted by Weld to abolitionism. Birney failed to draw even 1 percent of the total popular vote, but pockets of antislavery strength appeared in rural areas of the North dominated by evangelical New Englanders. These districts elected several antislavery congressmen, most of whom were Whigs forced by the Liberty party to take a stronger antislavery position to win the evangelical vote.

The Liberty party condemned racial discrimination in the North, as well as slavery in the South, and won the support of most black abolitionists. "To it," recalled Samuel Ward of New York, "I devoted my political activities; with it I lived my political life." Black abolitionists had organized state conventions in the North pressing black demands for political and civil equality. In 1843, a national African-American convention in Buffalo endorsed the Liberty party.

This political activism was part of a concerted effort by blacks to assert their own leadership in an antislavery movement that rarely treated them as equals. Frederick Douglass was their most dynamic spokesman. After escaping from slavery in 1838, Douglass became a spellbinding lecturer for abolitionism and in 1845 published his classic autobiography, *Nar-*

The Seneca Falls Convention helped inspire women to organize on their own behalf. Shown here is a meeting in 1860 of women strikers in Lynn, Massachusetts.

After escaping to freedom in 1838, Frederick Douglass became a commanding figure in the abolitionist movement. His speeches denouncing slavery were fiery and eloquent.

rative of the Life of Frederick Douglass, an American Slave. Increasingly dissatisfied with Garrison's Christian pacifism and his stand against political action, Douglass broke with Garrison in 1847 and founded a black abolitionist newspaper, **The North Star**. The break became irreparable in 1851 when Douglass publicly denied the Garrisonian position that the Constitution was a proslavery document. If properly interpreted, Douglass insisted, "the Constitution is a *glorious liberty document*," and he called for a political war against slavery.

That war had started in the 1840s with the Liberty party. Although the party elected only one of its candidates to Congress (Gerrit Smith of New York), it kept slavery in the limelight of national politics. A small but vocal bloc of antislavery politicians, many of whom owed their election to the vote of Liberty men, emerged in Congress. Led by Joshua R. Giddings, an antislavery Whig from Ohio, these congressmen began to popularize the frightening concept of "the **Slave Power**"—a vast conspiracy of planters and their northern lackeys that had seized control of the federal government and was plotting to spread slavery and subvert any free institutions that

opposed it. As proof, they cited the gag rule shutting off debate on slavery and the campaign of the Tyler administration to annex slaveholding Texas.

The notion of the Slave Power originated in abolitionist propaganda and was the basis of the Liberty party's appeal to northern white voters. Typical of that appeal were the claims of the Michigan Liberty party in 1843 that slavery was "not only a monstrous legalized system of wickedness . . . but an overwhelming political monopoly . . . which has thus tyrannically subverted the constitutional liberties of more than 12,000,000 of nominal American freemen." Moreover, the Liberty party blamed the depression of 1839–1843 on the "withering and impoverishing effect of slavery on the free States." Planters, it was charged, had reneged on their debts to northern creditors and manipulated federal policies on banking and tariffs to the advantage of the South.

The specter of the Slave Power made white liberties and not black bondage central to northern concerns about slavery. This redefined the evil of slavery to appeal to the self-interests of northern whites who had rejected the moral appeals of the Garrisonians. Whites who had earlier been apathetic now began to view slavery as a threat to their rights of free speech and self-improvement through free labor untainted by the degrading competition of slave labor.

Birney again headed the Liberty party ticket in 1844, but he ran only marginally stronger than in 1840. Nonetheless, the image of the Slave Power predisposed many Northerners to see the expansionist program of the incoming Polk administration as part of a southern plot to secure more territory for slaveholders at the expense of northern farmers. Northern fears that free labor would be shut out of the new territories won in the Mexican War provided the rallying cry for the Free-Soil party of 1848, an antislavery party that foreshadowed the more powerful Republican party of the late 1850s.

Conclusion

The reform impulse driving social movements arose as a religious response to the unsettling pace of social and economic change in the decades after the War of 1812. From its beginnings in the benevolent societies of upper-class conservatives concerned with social order and the need to uphold traditional Protestant morality, the reform impulse spiraled outward into a growing critique of American institutions and values. The new evangelical Protestantism promised that human perfectibility was possible if individuals strove to free themselves from sin. Influenced by this promise, the northern middle class embraced reform causes that sought to improve human character. Temperance, the most widely accepted of these causes, changed American drinking habits and established sobriety as the cultural standard for respectable male behavior. And although benevolent efforts based on volunteerism and moral suasion continued, middle-class reform also emphasized institutional solutions for what now were defined as the social problems of ignorance, crime, and poverty.

The most radical of the reform movements focused on women's equality and the elimination of slavery. Denied entry into politics and business, women found in reform work an outlet for their religious and social concerns and an affirmation of their sense of self. The women's rights movement emerged out of their involvement in reform, especially in abolitionism. By directly challenging the underlying values that kept women and blacks in positions of social inferiority, feminism and abolitionism threatened to upset the structure of American society. Both movements triggered a backlash from the more conservative majority. This backlash prevented women from gaining legal and political equality, the major demand of the feminists, and convinced most abolitionists that they had to switch from moral agitation to political persuasion.

The most effective approach of the political abolitionists in widening the antislavery appeal was their charge that a Slave Power conspiracy threatened the freedoms of northern whites. This image of an evil Slave Power would shape northern responses to the Mexican War and in the 1850s would mobilize northern whites against the expansion of slavery into the western territories.

Review Questions

1. What was the religious impulse behind the first wave of reform? What innovations in reaching a mass audience did the benevolent reformers pioneer?

2. How did reform movements begin to change by the 1830s? Why did temperance become the greatest and most successful reform?

3. What accounts for the initial optimism of the institutional reformers? What problems were they reacting to, and how did they expect to solve them?

4. What drew women into reform? Why did many of them feel a special affinity for abolitionism?

5. Why was abolitionism the most radical reform of all?

6. What was the Slave Power, and what role did it play in the growth of the political antislavery movement?

Recommended Reading

Robert H. Abzug, *Cosmos Crumbling: American Reform and the Religious Imagination* (1994). Abzug provides a fresh look at antebellum reform by using the lives of individual reformers to show how Protestant Christianity inspired a rethinking of American values in a period of rapid economic change.

Whitney R. Cross, *The Burned-Over District: The Social and Intellectual History of Enthusiastic Religion in Western New York, 1800–1850* (1950). This enormously influential work was the first to examine the linkages between the economic transformation of rural society and revivalistic waves of reform.

David Brion Davis, ed., *Antebellum American Culture* (1979). This superb collection of source materials covers all facets of the commitment to reform and institutional change.

Steven Mintz, *Moralists and Modernizers: America's Pre–Civil War Reformers* (1995). This recent survey demonstrates how both the fears and possibilities of change influenced the impulse of reform.

James Brewer Stewart, *Holy Warriors: The Abolitionists and American Slavery* (1976). Stewart provides the best overview of abolitionism and what distinguished it from the mainstream of the reform tradition.

Alice F. Tyler, *Freedom's Ferment: Phases of American Social History to 1860* (1944). Tyler offers a useful and accessible narrative treatment of the varieties of antebellum reform.

Ronald A. Walters, *American Reformers, 1815–1860* (1978). Although superseded by later works in its discussion of the role of women, this remains the most insightful treatment of the entire range of antebellum reform.

Additional Sources

Reform and Moral Order

Charles I. Foster, *An Errand of Mercy: The Evangelical United Front* (1960).

Mark Y. Hanley, *Beyond a Christian Commonwealth: The Protestant Quarrel with the American Republic, 1830–1860* (1994).

Carroll Smith-Rosenberg, *Religion and the Rise of the American City* (1971).

W. J. Rorabaugh, *The Alcoholic Republic* (1979).

Kenneth H. Winn, *Exiles in a Land of Liberty: Mormons in America, 1830–1846* (1989).

Peter J. Wosh, *Spreading the Word: The Bible Business in Nineteenth-Century America* (1994).

Institutions and Social Improvement

Gerald N. Grob, *Mental Institutions in America: Social Policy to 1875* (1973).

Carl J. Guarneri, *The Utopian Alternative: Fourierism in Nineteenth-Century America* (1991).

Adam Jay Hirsch, *The Rise of the Penitentiary* (1992).

Carl F. Kaestle, *Pillars of the Republic: Common Schools and American Society, 1780–1860* (1983).

Michael B. Katz, *In the Shadow of the Poorhouse: A Social History of Welfare in America* (1986).

David Rothman, *The Discovery of the Asylum: Social Order and Disorder in the New Republic* (1971).

Stephen J. Stein, *The Shaker Experience in America* (1992).

Women's Role in Reform

Norma Basch, *In the Eyes of the Law: Women, Marriage, and Property in Nineteenth-Century New York* (1982).

Barbara I. Berg, *The Remembered Gate: Origins of American Feminism: The Woman and the City, 1800–1860* (1978).

Nancy F. Cott, *The Bonds of Womanhood: "Woman's Sphere" in New England, 1780–1835* (1977).

Ann Douglas, *The Feminization of American Culture* (1977).

Barbara Leslie Epstein, *The Politics of Domesticity: Women, Evangelicalism, and Temperance in Nineteenth-Century America* (1981).

Lori D. Ginzberg, *Women and the Work of Benevolence: Morality, Politics, and Class in the 19th-Century United States* (1990).

Nancy A. Hewitt, *Women's Activism and Social Change: Rochester, New York, 1822–1872* (1984).

Abolitionism and Women's Rights

Ellen Du Bois, *Feminism and Suffrage: The Emergence of an Independent Women's Movement, 1848–1869* (1978).

Debra G. Hansen, *Strained Sisterhood: Gender and Class in the Boston Female Anti-Slavery Society* (1993).

Leon F. Litwack, *North of Slavery: The Negro in the Free States, 1790–1860* (1961).

John R. McKivigan, *The War against Proslavery Religion: Abolitionism and the Northern Churches, 1830–1865* (1984).

Jane H. Pease and William H. Pease, *They Who Would Be Free: Blacks' Search for Freedom, 1830–1861* (1974).

C. Peter Ripley et al., eds., *Witness for Freedom: African-American Voices on Race, Slavery, and Emancipation* (1993).

Philip J. Staudenraus, *The African Colonization Movement, 1816–1865* (1961).

Jean Fagan Yellin and John C. Van Horne, eds., *The Abolitionist Sisterhood: Women's Political Culture in Antebellum America* (1993).

Where to Learn More

❖ **Black Freedom Trail, Boston, Massachusetts.** This walking trail includes many of the sites in antebellum Boston that figured prominently in the African-American struggle for freedom.

❖ **Historic New Harmony, New Harmony, Indiana.** The tours and museum holdings at this preserved site offer a glimpse into the communal living that Robert Owen tried to promote in his utopian plan.

❖ **Oberlin College Library, Oberlin, Ohio.** Oberlin was a hotbed of reform agitation, and the tracts, broadsides, photographs, and other memorabilia here are especially rich on the activities of white evangelical and black abolitionists.

❖ **Shaker Museum at Sabbathday Lake, Poland Spring, Maine.** The exhibits, artifacts, and archives are a superb source for understanding the history and material culture of the Shakers and other radical religious sects.

❖ **Women Right's Historical Park, Seneca Falls, New York.** The park provides an interpretive overview of the first women's rights convention and includes among its historical sites the restored home of Elizabeth Cady Stanton.

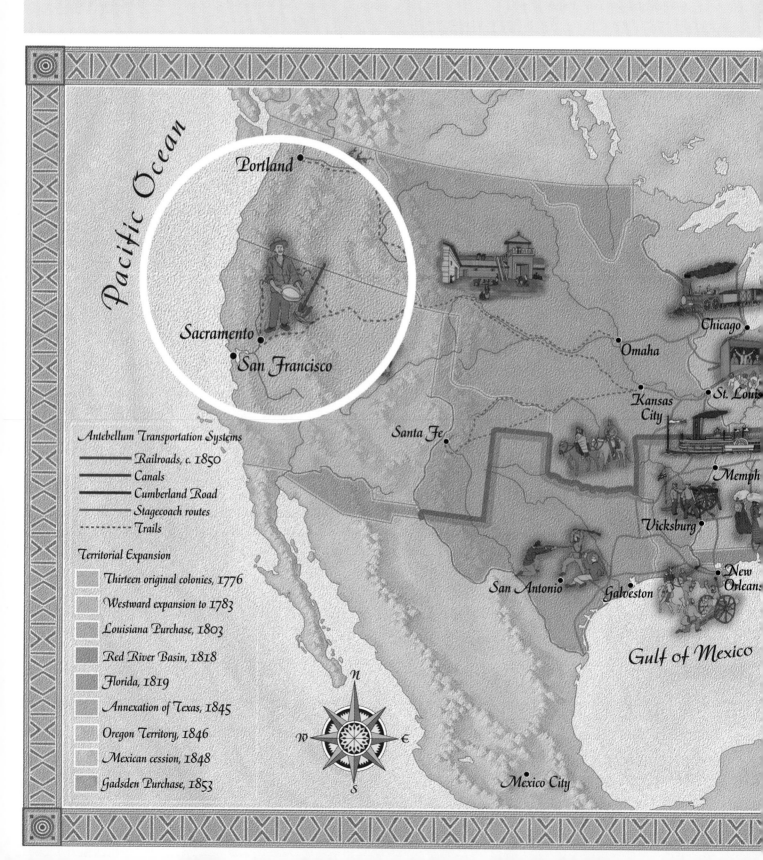

Antebellum Transportation Systems

——— Railroads, c. 1850
——— Canals
——— Cumberland Road
——— Stagecoach routes
- - - - - Trails

Territorial Expansion

Thirteen original colonies, 1776

Westward expansion to 1783

Louisiana Purchase, 1803

Red River Basin, 1818

Florida, 1819

Annexation of Texas, 1845

Oregon Territory, 1846

Mexican cession, 1848

Gadsden Purchase, 1853

KEY TOPICS

❖ The controversy over slavery in the territories and the attempt to resolve it

❖ The causes and consequences of political realignment in the 1850s

❖ Why Lincoln was elected in 1860

❖ The secession crisis and why the political system could not fix it

George N. Sanders, the American consul in London, held a dinner party on the eve of George Washington's birthday in 1854. He invited seven European revolutionaries who sat around the heavy oak table, lighted to brilliance by three ornate chandeliers and set with fine china, crystal, and silver. The party dined on Virginia ham and Carolina sweet potatoes and talked about America. The guests marveled at how the United States remained both united and committed to democracy—to rule by the consent of the governed.

Yet within six years, the United States would break apart. Northerners and Southerners accused each other of violating the country's commitment to democracy. And unable to reconcile their differences through the political process, they went to war.

For Northerners, democracy meant majority rule and the supremacy of the central government over the states. For Southerners, it meant the protection of minority rights (although not, of course, the rights of black slaves) and the supremacy of the states over the central government. These conflicting views were as old as the Constitution itself. James Madison, the Virginian whose genius guided the Constitutional Convention of 1787, had foreseen the difficulty of balancing majority will and minority rights in a democratic society. He believed that the federal government would protect individual rights by balancing the competing claims of states and interest groups. The national government, he wrote, functioned as "a disinterested and dispassionate umpire in disputes between different passions and interests in the State." Suppose, however, that a numerical majority hostile to a geographic, religious, or ethnic minority won control of the national government. Who or what would protect the minority?

The collapse of governments was familiar to European revolutionaries. But the United States had seemed different. Americans had governed themselves for more than eighty years. They had spread across a continent and absorbed millions of newcomers from Europe without compromising their political traditions. They reveled in their diversity and bigness. Why did the nation fall apart?

In a word, slavery. The issue transformed the national government from umpire to advocate, from a force for harmonizing disparate interests to a pulpit for articulating basic differences. The nation, as Abraham Lincoln put it, could not exist half slave and half free.

But slavery had existed on the American continent since the colonial period. Colonists north and south held slaves. The Constitution acknowledged slavery's existence. And the Missouri Compromise of 1820 had apparently resolved for all time how slavery would be extended into the territories. Why did slavery become the issue that would not go away?

The answer lies in the events of the late 1840s and the 1850s. There were signs of slavery's explosive potential before then: the debate over the Missouri Compromise, the nullification controversy, and the battles in Congress over abolitionist mailings and petitions. But by the late 1840s, the periodic clashes between northern and southern congressmen over issues relating to slavery were becoming more frequent and more difficult to resolve. In the coming years, several developments—including white Southerners' growing consciousness of themselves as a minority, the confounding of political issues and moral questions, and the rise of the Republican party—would aggravate sectional antagonism. But the flash point that first brought it to the fore was the issue of slavery in the territories acquired from Mexico.

Slavery in the Territories

Whatever its boundaries over the years, the West symbolized the hopes and dreams of white Americans. It was the region of fresh starts, of possibilities. To exclude slavery from the western territories was to exclude white Southerners from pursuing their vision of the American dream. Exclusion meant, an Alabamian declared, "that a free citizen of Massachusetts was a better man and entitled to more privileges than a free citizen of Alabama." Northern politicians disagreed. They argued that exclusion preserved equality—the equality of all white men and women to live and work without competition from slave labor or rule by despotic slaveholders. The issue of slavery in the territories became an issue of freedom for both sides.

From the late 1840s until 1861, northern and southern leaders attempted to fashion a solution to the problem of slavery in the territories. Four proposals dominated the debate:

- ❖ Outright exclusion
- ❖ Extension of the Missouri Compromise line to the Pacific
- ❖ Popular sovereignty—allowing the residents of a territory to decide the issue
- ❖ Protection of the property of slaveholders (meaning their right to own slaves) even if few lived in the territory

The first major debate on these proposals occurred during the early days of the Mexican War and culminated with the Compromise of 1850.

The Wilmot Proviso

In August 1846, David Wilmot, a Pennsylvania Democrat, offered an amendment to an appropriations bill for the Mexican War. The language of the **Wilmot Proviso** stipulated that "as an express and fundamental condition to the acquisition of any territory from the Republic of Mexico . . . neither slavery nor involuntary servitude shall ever exist in any part of said territory." This language deliberately reflected Thomas Jefferson's Northwest Ordinance of 1787, which prohibited slavery in the Old Northwest. The proviso did not apply to Texas, which had become a state before the war began.

Wilmot had, he explained, no "morbid sympathy for the slave" but merely wanted an area where "my own race and own color can live without the disgrace [of] association with negro slavery." By thus linking the exclusion of slavery in the territories to freedom for whites, he hoped to generate support across the North regardless of party and even in some areas of the Upper South.

Linking freedom for whites to the exclusion of slaves infuriated Southerners. It implied that the mere proximity of slavery degraded whites and that Southerners were therefore a degraded people, unfit to join other Americans in the territories. Georgia's Whig senator, Robert Toombs, issued a warning that reflected the feelings of many Southerners. "I do not hesitate to avow before this House and the Country, and in the presence of the living

God, that if, by your legislation, you seek to drive us from the territories of California and New Mexico, purchased by the common blood and treasure of the whole people . . . , thereby attempting to fix a national degradation upon half the states of this Confederacy, *I am for disunion.*"

Northern congressmen ignored such threats. Now a majority in the House of Representatives (because the population of the northern states was greater than that of the southern states), they passed more than fifty versions of the proviso between 1846 and 1850. In the Senate, however, where each state had equal representation, the proviso was consistently rejected and never became law.

The proviso debate sowed distrust and suspicion between Northerners and Southerners. Congress had divided along sectional lines before, but seldom had divisions become so personal. The leaders of both the Democratic and Whig parties, disturbed that the issue of slavery in the territories could so monopolize Congress and poison sectional rela-

A military man with no political experience prior to his election as President in 1848, Zachary Taylor's steadfast stand against slavery in the territories acquired from Mexico surprised many who assumed that the Louisiana slaveholder would favor slavery's extension. Taylor's sudden death in July 1850 opened the way for the Compromise of 1850.

tions, sought to defuse the issue as the presidential election of 1848 approached.

The Election of 1848

Both Democrats and Whigs wanted to avoid identification with either side of the Wilmot Proviso controversy, and they selected their presidential candidates accordingly. The Democrats nominated Michigan senator Lewis Cass, a veteran party stalwart whose public career stretched back to the War of 1812. Cass understood the destructive potential of the slavery issue. In 1847, he suggested that territorial residents, not Congress, should decide slavery's fate. This solution, **popular sovereignty**, had a do-it-yourself charm: Keep the politicians out of it and let the people decide. Cass was deliberately ambiguous, however, on *when* the people should decide. The timing was important. If residents could decide only when applying for statehood, slavery would be legal up to that point. The ambiguity aroused more fears than it allayed.

The Whigs were silent on the slavery issue. Reverting to their winning 1840 formula of nominating a war hero, they selected General Zachary Taylor of Mexican War fame. If the Whigs were looking for someone with no political record, they found him in the squat and craggy-faced Taylor. Taylor belonged to no party and had never voted. He was also inarticulate to the point of unintended humor. In one address, he intoned: "We are at peace with all of the world, and seek to maintain . . . amity with the rest of mankind." If one had to guess his views, his background provided some clues. He lived in Louisiana in the Lower South, he owned a one-hundred-slave plantation, and his now-deceased daughter had married Jefferson Davis, currently Mississippi's staunch proslavery senator.

Taylor's background disturbed many antislavery northern Whigs. These **Conscience Whigs** along with remnants of the old Liberty party and a scattering of northern Democrats bolted their parties and formed the **Free-Soil party**. The name reflected the party's vow to keep the territories free. Its slogan—"Free soil, free speech, free labor, free men"—was a catalog of white liberties that the South had allegedly violated over the previous decade.

The Free-Soilers' appeal centered on their opposition to slave labor in the territories. Free labor, they believed, could not compete with bonded labor. Slavery condemned the white worker to unemployment, poverty, and eventually a condition little better than slavery itself. The party nominated former president Martin Van Buren. The old New

Yorker, who had remained active in state politics, had little hope of winning. But he could wield some influence if he were to prevent one of the major party candidates from winning a majority of electoral votes, thereby throwing the election into the House of Representatives.

Chalking up one out of seven northern votes, Van Buren ran strongly enough in eleven of the fifteen northern states to deny the winning candidate in those states a majority of the votes cast. But he could not overcome Taylor's strength in the South. Taylor was elected, giving the nation its first president from the Lower South.

The Compromise of 1850

Taylor had little time to savor his victory. Gold had been discovered in California in January 1848, and in little more than a year, eighty thousand people, most of them from the North, had rushed into the territory. These **Forty-Niners**, as they were called, included free blacks as well as slaves brought into the gold fields by their southern masters. Open hostility flared between white prospectors and their black competitors. When the territory's new residents began asking for statehood and drafted a state constitution, the document contained no provision for slavery. The constitution reflected antiblack rather than antislavery sentiment. Keeping California white shielded residents against social and economic interaction with blacks. "Free" in the context of territorial politics became a synonym for "whites only."

Miners in the California gold fields, 1849. Labor competition prompted white miners to favor the exclusion of blacks—and slavery—from California.

CHRONOLOGY

1846 Wilmot Proviso is submitted to Congress but is defeated.

1848 Gold is discovered in California.

Whig party candidate Zachary Taylor defeats Democrat Lewis Cass and Free-Soiler Martin Van Buren for the presidency.

1850 California applies for statehood.

President Taylor dies; Vice President Millard Fillmore succeeds him.

Compromise of 1850 is passed.

1851 Harriet Beecher Stowe publishes *Uncle Tom's Cabin.*

1852 Democrat Franklin Pierce is elected president in a landslide over Whig candidate Winfield Scott.

Whig party disintegrates.

1853 National Black Convention called in Rochester, New York, to demand repeal of the Fugitive Slave Act.

1854 Ostend Manifesto is issued.

Kansas-Nebraska Act repeals the Missouri Compromise.

Know-Nothing and Republican parties are formed.

1855 Civil war erupts in "Bleeding Kansas."

William Walker attempts a takeover of Nicaragua.

1856 "Sack of Lawrence" occurs in Kansas; John Brown makes a retaliatory raid at Pottawatomie Creek.

Democratic congressman Preston Brooks of South Carolina canes Massachusetts senator Charles Sumner in the U.S. Senate.

Democrat James Buchanan is elected president over Republican John C. Frémont and American (Know-Nothing) candidate Millard Fillmore.

1857 Supreme Court issues *Dred Scott* decision.

Kansas territorial legislature passes the proslavery Lecompton Constitution.

Panic of 1857 begins.

Hinton Rowan Helper publishes *The Impending Crisis.*

1858 Senatorial candidates Abraham Lincoln and Stephen A. Douglas hold series of debates in Illinois.

1859 John Brown's Raid fails at Harpers Ferry, Virginia.

1860 Constitutional Union party forms.

Democratic party divides into northern and southern factions.

Republican candidate Abraham Lincoln is elected president over southern Democratic candidate John C. Breckinridge, northern Democratic candidate Stephen A. Douglas, and Constitutional Unionist candidate John Bell.

South Carolina secedes from the Union.

1861 The rest of the Lower South secedes from the Union.

Crittenden Plan and Tyler's Washington peace conference fail.

Jefferson Davis assumes presidency of the Confederate States of America.

Lincoln is inaugurated.

Fort Sumter is bombarded; Civil War begins.

Several Upper South states secede.

If Congress accepted the residents' request for statehood, California would enter the Union as a free state. The Union at the time consisted of fifteen free states and fifteen slave states. The admission of California would tip the balance and give free states a majority in the Senate. California, with its rapidly growing population, would also add to the sixty-one-vote majority the North enjoyed in the House of Representatives. New Mexico (which then included most of present-day New Mexico, Arizona, small parts of Nevada, and Colorado) appeared poised to follow suit and enter the Union as the seventeenth free state. Southerners saw their political

power slipping away. Northern leaders saw an opportunity to stop the extension of slavery and reduce southern influence in the federal government.

When Congress confronted the issue of California statehood in December 1849, partisans on both sides began marshaling forces for what promised to be a long and bitter struggle. Because nine Free-Soil candidates had won seats in the House of Representatives, neither Whigs nor Democrats held a majority there. South Carolina senator John C. Calhoun understood that only a politically unified South could protect its interests. He urged southern congressmen to ignore party ties and unite behind a plan he proposed to gain federal protection for slavery in the territories. Most southern Whigs ignored Calhoun and waited to hear from President Taylor before abandoning him and their party. The snub did not deter Calhoun and his Democratic party supporters in the South from issuing a call for a southern convention in Nashville for June 1850. The implication was clear: If Congress did not resolve the California statehood issue to the South's satisfaction, some southern leaders were prepared to consider secession.

On the other side, the supporters of the Wilmot Proviso hoped to build a northern coalition dedicated to excluding slavery from the territories and reducing southern political power. Some hoped to go further and spark a liberation movement in the South. One Ohio congressman threatened: "We will establish a cordon of free states that shall surround you; and then we will light up the fires of liberty on every side until they melt your present chains and render all your people free." Such rhetoric enraged and frightened Southerners.

No one, at first, knew where Taylor stood. Although a political novice, the president was not stupid. Recognizing his lack of political experience, he selected Whig senator William H. Seward of New York as his adviser. Seward, a committed antislavery man, was one of the most hated politicians in the South; Taylor, a slaveholder from Louisiana, was distrusted by many northern members of his party. This odd match provided the first insight into the president's thinking on California.

He supported, it turned out, a version of popular sovereignty and favored allowing California and the other territories acquired from Mexico to decide the slavery issue for themselves. Under normal circumstances, the residents of a new territory organized a territorial government under the direction of Congress. When the territory's population approached thirty thousand or so, residents could draft a constitution and petition Congress for statehood. California already easily exceeded the population threshold. Taylor proposed bypassing the territorial stage—and congressional involvement in it—and having California and New Mexico admitted as states directly. (Before his inauguration in March 1849, he had already privately encouraged people in both territories to write state constitutions and to request admission.) The result would be to bring both into the Union as free states.

Although Seward no doubt encouraged him in it, Taylor's position was his own. The president was

a nationalist and a strong believer in Manifest Destiny. He did not oppose slavery, but he abhorred the slavery issue because it threatened his vision of a continental empire. He was thus willing to forgo the extension of slavery into the territories. Southerners were certain to object strongly. But the president had a chilling message for them: "Whatever dangers may threaten [the Union] I shall stand by it and maintain it in its integrity."

Southerners resisted Taylor's plan, and Congress deadlocked on the territorial issue. Henry Clay then stepped forward with his last great compromise. To break the impasse, Clay urged that Congress should take four steps:

❖ Admit California as a free state, as its residents clearly preferred

❖ Allow the residents of the New Mexico and Utah territories to decide the slavery issue for themselves too

❖ End the slave trade in the District of Columbia

❖ Pass a new fugitive slave law to enforce the constitutional provision stating that a person "held to Service or Labor in one state . . . escaping into another . . . shall be delivered upon Claim of the party to whom such Service or Labor may be due."

Clay's proposal provoked a historic Senate debate in February 1850, featuring America's three most prominent statesmen—Clay, Calhoun, and Daniel Webster—together for the last time. The emaciated Calhoun, who would be dead in two months, had to be carried into the Senate chamber. Too weak to read his remarks, he passed them to Virginia senator James M. Mason. Calhoun argued that the compromise did not resolve the slavery issue to the South's satisfaction, and he proposed to give Southerners in Congress the right to veto legislation in Congress as a way to safeguard their minority rights. Webster stood up to support the compromise, at deep political peril to himself. His Massachusetts constituents detested the fugitive slave provision, which gave southern slaveholders the right to "invade" northern states to reclaim escaped slaves. Webster declared that he came to the debate "not as a Massachusetts man, nor as a Northern man, but as an American." He would swallow the fugitive slave law to save the Union.

After a tumultuous six-month debate that lasted into the summer of 1850, the Senate rejected the compromise. Calhoun had died at the end of

Debate over the Compromise of 1850 brought together three of the Senate's greatest orators and statesmen for the last time, as depicted in this idealized rendering: Henry Clay (speaking), John C. Calhoun (standing third from right), and Daniel Webster (seated at left with his head in his hand).

March 1850, even before the debate ended. The 73-year-old Clay, exhausted, left Washington to recover his health. He would die less than two years later. Webster, estranged from fellow northern Whigs, left the Senate and went to his grave a few months after Clay.

President Taylor, who had vowed to veto any compromise, died unexpectedly of a stomach ailment after overindulging in cherries and milk in the hot sun at a July 4 celebration in Washington. Vice President Millard Fillmore, a pro-Clay New Yorker, assumed the presidency after Taylor's death. Compared with Taylor, who stormed around the White House daring Southerners to attempt secession, Fillmore was a back-room man, quiet, at home with the cigar-and-brandy crowd, and effective with the deal. Fillmore let it be known that he favored Clay's package and would sign it if passed.

Although the Senate had rejected the compromise, Illinois senator Stephen A. Douglas kept it alive. A small man with a large head that made him mushroomlike in appearance, Douglas epitomized the promise of American life for men of his generation. A native Vermonter, he migrated first to New York, then to Illinois as a teenager, read law, and developed a voracious appetite for politics. By the age of 28, he had already served as state legislator, chairman of the state Democratic party, and judge of the state supreme court. He envisioned an urban,

industrial West linked to the East by a vast railroad network eventually extending to the Pacific. Above all, Douglas professed an unbending nationalism. To him, according to his biographer, "the Union was sacred, the symbol of all human progress." After his election to Congress in 1842, the "Little Giant," as his constituents affectionately called him, developed a reputation as an astute parliamentarian and a tenacious debater.

Like Webster, Douglas feared for the Union if the compromise failed. Realizing that it would never pass as a package, he proposed to break it up into its components and hold a separate vote on each. With a handful of senators voting for all parts, and with different sectional blocs supporting one provision or another, Douglas engineered a majority for the compromise, and Fillmore signed it (see Map 15-1).

The **Compromise of 1850** was not a compromise in the sense of opposing sides consenting to certain terms desired by the other. The North gained California but would have done so in any case. Southern leaders looked to the West and saw no slave territories awaiting statehood. Their future in the Union appeared to be one of numerical and economic decline, and the survival of their institutions seemed doubtful. They gained the **Fugitive Slave Act**, which reinforced their right to seize and return to bondage slaves who had fled to free

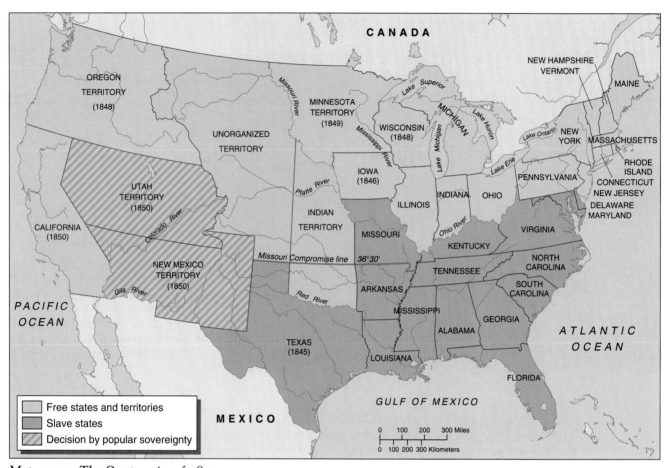

Map 15-1   *The Compromise of 1850*
Given the unlikely prospect that any of the western territories would opt for slavery, the compromise sealed the South's minority status in the Union.

territory, but it was slight consolation. One Lower South senator termed it "useless." Because most slaves who escaped to the North did so from neighboring slave states, the law affected mainly the states of the Upper South. Few slave owners from the Lower South would bear the expense and uncertainty of chasing an escaped slave into free territory. And the North's hostile reception to the law made Southerners doubt their commitment to the compromise.

Response to the Fugitive Slave Act

The Fugitive Slave Act was ready-made for abolitionist propaganda mills and heart-rending stories. A few months after Congress passed it, a Kentucky slaveholder visited Madison, Indiana, and snatched a black man from his wife and children, claiming that the man had escaped nineteen years earlier. Blacks living in northern communities feared capture, and some escaped across the Canadian border. Several northern cities and states vowed

resistance, but except for a few publicized cases, northern authorities typically cooperated with southern slave owners to help them retrieve their runaway property. The effect of the act on public opinion, however, was to polarize North and South even further.

The strongest reaction to the act was in the black communities of the urban North. Previously, black abolitionists in the North had focused on freeing slaves in the South. The Fugitive Slave Act brought the danger of slavery much closer to home. No black was safe under the new law. Mistaken identity, the support of federal courts for slaveholders' claims, and the presence of informants made reenslavement a real possibility. The lives that 400,000 northern blacks had constructed, often with great difficulty, appeared suddenly uncertain.

Northern blacks formed associations to protect each other and repel—violently, if necessary—any attempt to capture and reenslave fellow blacks.

Boston's black leaders created the **League of Freedom**. Chicago blacks organized the **Liberty Association**, with teams assigned to "patrol the city, spying for possible slave-hunters." Similar associations appeared in Cleveland and Cincinnati. Black leader Frederick Douglass, an escaped slave himself, explained the need for such organizations: "We must be prepared . . . to see the streets . . . running with blood . . . should this law be put into operation." Some blacks left the United States. In October 1850, two hundred blacks left Pittsburgh for Ontario, Canada, vowing that "they would die before being taken back into slavery." As many as twenty thousand blacks may have found their way across the border during the 1850s in response to fears over capture and reenslavement. Another solution was proposed by Martin Delany, a prominent black abolitionist. He argued for the establishment of a black homeland at several potential sites in Central or South America or on the west coast of Africa. "Go we must," he wrote in 1852. "To remain here in North America and be crushed to the earth in vassalage and degradation, we never will."

During the early 1850s, blacks across the North gathered in conventions to demand the repeal of the Fugitive Slave Act. Frederick Douglass convened the **National Black Convention** in Rochester, New York, in July 1853, at which he established a national council of black leaders to address issues of political and civil rights. Although the council was short-lived, it reflected a growing militancy among northern blacks. Less than a year later, for example, a black New York City woman schoolteacher defied that city's public transit segregation ordinance and succeeded in pressing state legislators to strike down the law.

On several occasions, northern blacks fought to defend their rights. In September 1851, Edward Gorsuch, a Maryland slaveholder, went to Christiana, Pennsylvania, where two of his escaped slaves were living. A fugitive slave named William Parker had organized the town's black community to defend against such an incident. Gorsuch located the two fugitives in a house occupied by Parker and a dozen other armed black men. Another fifty blacks and some whites arrived and surrounded Gorsuch, his son, two relatives, two neighbors, and a federal marshal. Gunfire erupted, wounding both Gorsuch and his son. As the elder Gorsuch lay on the ground, a group of black women "rushed from the house with corn cutters and scythe blades [and] hacked the bleeding and lifeless body."

How much of this militancy filtered down to slaves in the South is difficult to say. Slavehold-

ers noted an increase in black resistance during the early 1850s. A white Virginian noted in 1852 that "it is useless to disguise the fact, its truth is undeniable, that a greater degree of insubordination has been manifested by the negro population within the last few months, than at any previous period in our history as a state." Southerners often concocted tales of slave plots and unrest during times of national distress. But even if the Virginia writer exaggerated, his concern reflected genuine southern anxiety.

Uncle Tom's Cabin

Sectional controversy over the Fugitive Slave Act was relatively modest compared to the firestorm abolitionist writer Harriet Beecher Stowe ignited with the publication of a novel about southern slavery. *Uncle Tom's Cabin*, which first appeared in serial form in 1851, moved many northern whites from the sidelines of the sectional conflict to more active participation.

Stowe grew up in a remarkable family. Her father was Lyman Beecher, the prominent evangelical reformer. In Beecher's view, evangelical Christianity erased the line between public and private. Personal and societal salvation were closely connected; one could not occur without the other. In 1832, he became president of Lane Theological Seminary and moved his large family from New England to Cincinnati. He hoped, as he put it, to save the West from "Catholics and infidels." In Cincinnati, he became an active opponent of slavery.

Beecher instilled a sense of righteous indignation in his offspring. All six of his sons became ministers. Two of his three daughters, Catharine and Harriet, became accomplished nonfiction writers specializing in family and domestic advice books. Harriet married Calvin Stowe, a biblical scholar, who held views similar to Beecher's.

What first drew Harriet Beecher Stowe to the subject of slavery was her concern about its impact on family life in the South. It was not until the passage of the Fugitive Slave Act, however, that abolition became a major focus in her life. Even then, her views on blacks remained ambivalent. She did not, like William Lloyd Garrison, advocate racial equality. She supported abolition, but she also believed America should be a white person's country. Like the antislavery whites who had founded the colonization movement, she thought it would be best for both races if freed slaves, after sufficient exposure to "civilization" from white evangelicals, were repatriated to Africa. As she wrote at the conclusion of *Uncle Tom's Cabin*: "Let the church of the North receive

Harriet Beecher Stowe, the daughter of a prominent Northern evangelist, catapulted to international fame with the publication of Uncle Tom's Cabin. *The novel helped raise the debate over slavery from a political to a moral level.*

these poor sufferers until they have attained to somewhat of a moral and intellectual maturity, and then assist them in their passage to those shores where they may put in practice the lessons they have learned in America."

Slavery was an abstract concept to most white Northerners. Stowe's challenge was to personalize it in a way that would make them see it as an institution that not just oppressed blacks but destroyed families and debased well-meaning Christian masters as well. Stowe herself had little experience of the South, no more than four hours spent on a Kentucky plantation. But she was familiar with the accounts of black abolitionists and counted Frederick Douglass among her friends.

At the beginning of *Uncle Tom's Cabin*, a Kentucky slave owner is reluctantly forced by financial ruin to sell some of his slaves. Among them are the son of two mulatto slaves, George and Eliza Harris, and an older slave, Tom. Eliza escapes across the ice-choked Ohio River, clutching her son to her breast as slavecatchers and their bloodhounds pursue them.

Tom submits to sale to a New Orleans master. When that master dies, Tom is sold to Simon Legree, who owns a plantation on the Red River in Louisiana. Legree is vicious and sadistic—the only major slaveholding character in the book whom Stowe portrays in this manner. Tom, a devout Christian, remains loyal and obedient until Legree asks him to whip another slave. When Tom refuses, Legree beats him to death. Legree, incidentally, is from Vermont.

Stowe offered not abstractions but characters who seemed real. She aimed to evoke strong emotions in the reader. The broken family, the denial of freedom, and the Christian martyr were emotional themes. The presence of mulattoes in the book testified to widespread interracial and extramarital sex, which Northerners, then in the midst of a religious revival, viewed as an abhorrent sin destructive to family life. And the depiction of southern masters struggling unsuccessfully with their consciences focused public attention on how slavery subverted Christianity.

Uncle Tom's Cabin created a sensation in the United States and abroad. The book sold ten thousand copies in its first week and 300,000 within a year. By the time of the Civil War, the book had sold an unprecedented 3 million copies in the United States and tens of thousands more in Europe. Stowe's book gave slavery a face; it changed people's moral perceptions about the institution in an era of deep Protestant piety; it was a Sermon on the Mount for a generation of Northerners seeking witness for their Christianity and a crusade on behalf of their faith. It transformed abolitionism, bringing a movement whose extreme rhetoric many Northerners had previously viewed with disapproval to the edge of respectability.

For Southerners, *Uncle Tom's Cabin* was a damnable lie, a political tract disguised as literature. One Southerner denounced the book as a "criminal prostitution of the high functions of the imagination to the pernicious intrigues of sectional animosity." Some Southerners retaliated with crude plays and books of their own. In these versions of slavery, no slave families were broken up, no slaves were killed, and all masters were models of Christian behavior. Few Northerners, however, read these southern responses. The writers penned them more to convince fellow Southerners that slavery was necessary and good than to change opinions in the North.

Northern blacks embraced *Uncle Tom's Cabin*. Frederick Douglass's National Black Convention resolved that the book was "a work plainly marked by the finger of God" on behalf of black people. Some blacks hoped that the popularity of *Uncle Tom's Cabin* would highlight the hypocrisy of northern whites who were quick to perceive evil in the South but were often blind to discrimination against African-Americans in the North. Despite reactions to Stowe's book, however, blacks continued to face voting restrictions, segregation, and official harassment in most northern cities.

The Election of 1852

While the nation read and reacted to *Uncle Tom's Cabin*, a presidential election campaign took place. The Compromise of 1850 had divided the Whigs deeply. Northern Whigs perceived it as a capitulation to southern slaveholding interests and refused to support the renomination of President Millard Fillmore. Many southern Whigs, angered by the suspicions and insults of their erstwhile northern colleagues, abandoned the party. Although the Whigs nominated Mexican War hero and Virginian Winfield Scott for president, few southern Whigs viewed the nonslaveholding general as a friend of their region.

The Democratic party entered the campaign more united. Despite reservations, both northern and southern wings of the party announced their support for the Compromise of 1850. Southern Democrats viewed the party's nominee, Franklin Pierce of New Hampshire, as safe on the slavery issue despite his New England heritage. Pierce satisfied Northerners as a nationalist devoted to the idea of Manifest Destiny. He belonged to **Young America**, a mostly Democratic group that advocated extending American influence into Central and South America and the Caribbean with an aggressive foreign policy. His service in the Mexican War and his good looks and charm won over doubters from both sections.

Given the disarray of the Whigs and the relative unity of the Democrats, the election results were predictable. Pierce won overwhelmingly with 254 electoral votes to Scott's 42. But Pierce's landslide victory could not obscure the deep fissures in the American party system. The Whigs, although they would continue to run local candidates through the rest of the 1850s, were finished as a national party. And the Democrats, despite their electoral success, emerged frayed from the election. In the Lower South, conflicts within the party between supporters and opponents of the Compromise of 1850 had overshadowed the contests between Democrats and Whigs. Southern Democrats had wielded great influence at the party's nominating convention and dominated party policy, clouding its prospects in the North. During the election, much of the party's support in the North had come from the first-time votes of mainly Catholic immigrants. But the growing political influence of Catholics alarmed evangelical Protestants of both parties, thus adding religious bigotry to the divisive issues undermining the structure of the national parties.

As Franklin Pierce took office in March 1853, it seemed that the only thing holding Democrats together was the thirst for political patronage. Even before the presidential election, Indiana Free-Soiler George W. Julian had observed that the Whigs and the Democrats "are at this time pitted against each other in a mere scramble for place and power." The low voter turnout in the 1852 election—Whig participation declined by 10 percent and Democratic participation by 17 percent, mostly in the Lower South—reflected public apathy and disgust at the prevailing party system. As the slavery issue confronted the nation with the most serious challenge it had faced since its inception, American voters were losing faith in their parties' ability to govern and in each other.

Political Realignment

Franklin Pierce, only 48 when he took office, was one of the youngest presidents in American history. He hoped to duck the slavery issue by focusing on Young America's dreams of empire. During the 1840s, the nationalist appeal of Manifest Destiny had helped elect Democrat James K. Polk to the presidency and had bolstered support for the Mexican War. Americans were still susceptible to nationalist fervor. For all their sectional, religious, ethnic, and racial differences, they shared a common language and political institutions. New technologies like the railroad and the telegraph were working to bind them together physically as well. The country was optimistic, and its possibilities for advancement seemed limitless. As Florida senator Stephen R. Mallory claimed, "It is no more possible for this country to pause in its career, than for the free and untrammeled eagle to cease to soar." But President Pierce's attempts to forge national sentiment around an aggressive foreign policy failed. And his administration's inept handling of a new territorial controversy in Kansas forced him to confront the slavery debate.

As Missouri senator Thomas Hart Benton, a Democrat, had realized during the debates over the Wilmot Proviso in 1848, no matter what policies a president pursued, Congress and the American people would interpret them in the light of their impact, real or potential, on slavery. The issue, said Benton, was like the plague of frogs that God had inflicted on the Egyptians to convince them to release the Hebrews from bondage. "You could not look upon the table but there were frogs, you could not sit down at the banquet but there were frogs, you could not go to the bridal couch and lift the sheets but there were frogs!" So it was with "this black question, forever on the table, on the nuptial couch, everywhere!"

Franklin Pierce lacked the skilled leadership the times demanded. Troubled by alcoholism, worried about his chronically ill wife, and grief-stricken over the death of three young sons, including one in a train wreck, Pierce presided weakly over the nation and increasingly deferred to proslavery interests in his policies.

Young America's Foreign Misadventures

Pierce's first missteps occurred in pursuit of Young America's foreign ambitions. The administration turned a greedy eye toward Spanish-ruled Cuba, just 90 miles off the coast of Florida. Spanish authorities were harassing American merchants exporting sugar from Cuba and the American naval vessels protecting the merchants' ships. Southerners supported an aggressive Cuba policy, seeing the island as a possible new slave state. And nationalists saw great virtue in replacing what they perceived as a despotic colonial regime with a democratic government under the guidance of the United States.

In October 1854, three American diplomats met in Ostend, Belgium, to discuss Cuba. It is not clear whether Pierce approved or even knew of their meeting, but the diplomats believed that they had the administration's blessing. One of them, the American minister to Spain, Pierre Soulé of Louisiana, was especially eager for the United States to acquire Cuba. The group composed a document on Cuba called the **Ostend Manifesto** that claimed that the island belonged "naturally to the great family of states of which the Union is the Providential Nursery." The implication was that Spain's control of Cuba was unnatural. The United States would offer to buy Cuba from Spain, but if Spain wouldn't sell, the authors warned, "by every law, human and Divine, we shall be justified in wresting it from Spain."

The Ostend Manifesto caused an uproar and embarrassed the Pierce administration when it became public. In the polite world of nineteenth-century diplomacy, it was a significant breach of etiquette. Other nations quickly denounced it as a "buccaneering document" and a "highwayman's plea." It provoked a similar reaction in the United States, raising suspicions in the North that the South was willing to provoke a war with Spain to expand the number of slaveholding states.

Meanwhile, the Pierce administration's aggressive foreign policy encouraged private citizens to pursue Young America's goals in Latin America. Such was the case of self-styled "General" William Walker and his private army, "the immortals." Newspaper reporters loved the diminutive Walker, whose exploits provided excellent copy. The popular press called him "the grey-eyed man of destiny." Walker moved from Tennessee to California, and in 1853, after gathering arms and men, he invaded Mexican-owned Baja California and proclaimed a republic. Before he could establish a permanent government and legalize slavery, the Mexican authorities tossed him out. Undaunted, Walker and his followers plunged into the civil war that had erupted in Nicaragua in May 1855. He gained control of the country by the end of the year, proclaimed himself president, and invited southern slaveholders to take up residence. The Pierce administration immediately recognized Walker's government; the people of Nicaragua did not. Backed by other Central American countries, they fought to oust the little general. Congressional pressure forced the Pierce administration to cool its support for Walker, and his financial resources dried up. His foes overthrew him in 1857, and he fled Nicaragua on an American naval vessel. After two more abortive attempts at conquest in Central America, he was executed by a Honduran firing squad in 1860.

These and other setbacks frustrated Pierce's hope that foreign adventures would mute the angry debate over slavery. Instead, the proslavery overtones of the Cuban fiasco and Walker's open courting of southern support sharpened sectional conflict. As Pierce was fumbling in foreign policy, Senator Stephen A. Douglas of Illinois was developing a national project that also promised to draw the country together—the construction of a transcontinental railroad and the settling of the land it traversed. The result was worse conflict and the first outbreak of sustained sectional violence.

Stephen Douglas's Railroad Proposal

Douglas, like many Westerners, wanted a transcontinental railroad. He himself had a personal stake in railroad building in that he owned some Chicago real estate and speculated in western lands. Railroads and the people and business they carried drove up property values. But beyond personal gain, Douglas, the supreme nationalist, understood that a transcontinental railroad would tie the nation together. Not only would it physically link East and West, but it would also help spread American democracy. In short, a transcontinental railroad made good economic and political sense.

Douglas had in mind a transcontinental route extending westward from Chicago through the Nebraska Territory. Unfortunately for his plans, Indians already occupied this region, many of them on land the U.S. government had set aside as Indian Territory and barred to white settlement. "How," Douglas complained, "are we to develop, cherish, and protect our immense interests and possessions on the Pacific with a vast wilderness 1,500 miles in breadth, filled with hostile savages, and cutting off all direct communication?" Removing the "Indian barrier" and establishing white government were "first steps," in the senator's view, toward a "tide of emigration and civilization."

Once again, and not for the last time, the federal government responded by reneging on earlier promises and forcing Indians to move. In 1853, President Pierce sent agents to convince the Indians in the northern part of the Indian Territory to cede land for the railroad. Commissioner of Indian Affairs George A. Manypenny, who oversaw the negotiations, commented that "by alternate persuasion and force some of these tribes have been removed, step by step, from mountain to valley, and from river to plain, until they have been pushed halfway across the continent."

With the Indian "obstacle" removed, Douglas sought congressional approval to establish a government for the Nebraska Territory. But southern senators defeated his proposal. They objected to it not only because it called for a northern rather than southern route for the transcontinental railroad but also because the new territory lay above the Missouri Compromise line and would enter the Union as yet another free state. Bowing to southern pressure, Douglas rewrote his bill and resubmitted it in January 1854. He predicted that the new bill would "raise a hell of a storm." He was right.

The Kansas-Nebraska Act

Douglas's Kansas-Nebraska Bill split the Nebraska Territory into two territories, Kansas and Nebraska, with the implicit understanding that Kansas would become a slave state and Nebraska a free state. Consistent with Douglas's belief in popular sovereignty,

it left the actual decision on slavery to the residents of the territories. But because it allowed Southerners to bring slaves into an area formerly closed to slavery, it repealed the Missouri Compromise (see Map 15-2).

Northerners of all parties were outraged. The Missouri Compromise had endured for thirty-four years as a basis for sectional accord on slavery. Now it was threatened, northern leaders charged, by the South's unquenchable desire to spread slavery and expand its political power. In defense of the bill, Douglas claimed that it was unlikely that a majority in either territory would vote for slavery. But a group of northern leaders of Douglas's own Democratic party countered vehemently that repealing the Missouri Compromise was more than a political maneuver. Using language indicative of the way religious and conspiratorial imagery had infected political debate, transforming it into a contest of good against evil, of liberty against oppression, they said it was "a gross violation of a sacred pledge," "a criminal betrayal of precious rights," and "part and parcel of an atrocious plot" to make a free territory a "dreary region of despotism, inhabited by masters and slaves." President Pierce, however, backed the bill, assuring the support of enough northern Democrats to secure it a narrow margin of victory. The **Kansas-Nebraska Act** was law.

In August 1854, shortly after Congress adjourned, Douglas left Washington for his home in Chicago, to rest and mend political fences. He did not enjoy a pleasant journey home. "I could travel," he later recalled, ". . . by the light of my own effigy on every tree we passed." Arriving in Chicago, he addressed a large, hostile crowd outside his hotel balcony. As he departed, he lost his temper and blurted, "It is now Sunday morning. I'll go to church; you can go to hell."

"Bleeding Kansas"

Because of its fertile soil, favorable climate, and location adjacent to the slave state of Missouri, Kansas was the most likely of the new territories to support slavery. As a result, both Southerners and antislavery Northerners began an intensive drive to recruit settlers and establish a majority there. Speaking for the antislavery forces, William H. Seward said in the Senate, "We will engage in competition for the virgin soil of Kansas, and God give this victory to the side which is strong in numbers as it is in right." South Carolina editor Robert Barnwell Rhett accepted the challenge, urging fellow Southerners to "send men to Kansas, ready

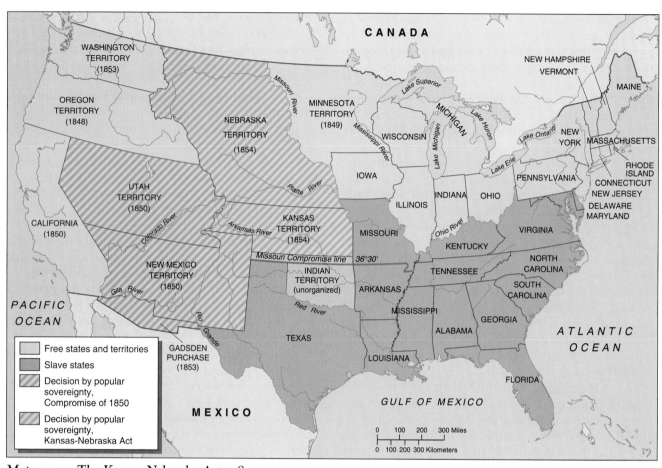

Map 15-2   The Kansas-Nebraska Act, 1854
*The Kansas-Nebraska Act of 1854, which divided the Nebraska Territory in two and repealed
the Missouri Compromise, reopened the incendiary issue of slavery in the territories.*

to cast in their lot with the proslavery part there
and able to meet Abolitionism on its own issue, and
with its own weapons."

    As proslavery residents of Missouri poured
into Kansas, antislavery organizations funded and
armed their own migrants. In March 1855, proslavery forces, relying on the ineligible votes of Missouri residents, fraudulently elected a territorial
legislature. This legislature promptly passed a series
of harsh measures, including a law mandating the
death penalty for aiding a fugitive slave and
another making it a felony to question slaveholding
in Kansas. For good measure, the proslavery majority expelled the few free-staters elected to the
assembly. In response, free-staters established their
own government in Topeka and vowed to make
Kansas white.

    A sporadic civil war erupted in Kansas in
November 1855 and reached a climax in the spring
of 1856. Journalists dubbed the conflict "**Bleeding
Kansas.**" On May 21, a group of proslavery officials

attacked free-state stronghold Lawrence, subjecting
it to a heavy artillery barrage. No one was killed, but
the town suffered substantial damage. Eastern newspapers, exaggerating the incident, called it "**the sack
of Lawrence.**" Three days later, antislavery agitator
John Brown, originally from Connecticut, went with
several sympathizers to Pottawatomie Creek south of
Lawrence in search of proslavery settlers. Armed with
razor-sharp broadswords, they split the skulls and
hacked the bodies of five men.

    Kansans were not the only Americans bleed-
ing over slavery. Five days before the "sack of
Lawrence," Massachusetts senator Charles Sumner
delivered a longwinded diatribe, "The Crime Against
Kansas," full of personal insults against several Southerners, especially elderly South Carolina senator
Andrew P. Butler. Two days after Sumner's outburst,
and a day after the story of the sack of Lawrence
appeared in the newspapers, Butler's cousin, South
Carolina congressman Preston Brooks, entered a
mostly vacant Senate chamber where Sumner sat

Armed Missourians cross the border into Kansas to vote illegally for a proslavery government in 1855.

working on a speech. Seeking to defend his cousin's honor, Brooks raised his walking cane and beat Sumner over the head. Bloody and unconscious, the senator slumped to the floor. He recovered but did not return to the Senate for over three years. His empty chair offered Northerners' mute confirmation of their growing conviction that Southerners were despotic. Southerners showered Brooks with new walking canes.

Know-Nothings and Republicans

The Sumner incident, along with the Kansas-Nebraska Bill and the civil war in Kansas, further polarized North and South, widening sectional divisions within the political parties. Some northern Democrats distanced themselves from their party and looked for political alternatives; northern Whigs seized on changing public opinion to form new coalitions; and free-soil advocates gained new adherents. From 1854 to 1856, Northerners moved into new political parties that altered the national political landscape and sharpened sectional conflict.

Although the slavery issue was mainly responsible for party realignment in the North, other factors played a role as well. Nearly 3.5 million immigrants entered the United States between 1848 and 1860, the greatest influx in American history in proportion to the total population. Some of these newcomers, especially the Germans, were escaping failed democratic revolutions in Europe. They were predominantly middle-class Protestants who, along with fewer German Catholics and Jews, settled mostly in the cities, where they established

shops and other businesses. More than 1 million of the immigrants, however, were poor Irish Roman Catholics fleeing their homeland to avoid starvation.

The Irish immigrants made their homes in northern cities, at the time in the midst of Protestant revivals and reform. They also competed for jobs with native-born Protestant workers. Because the Irish would work for lower wages, the job competition bred animosity and sometimes violence. Culturally, the Irish held different views on keeping the Sabbath, and they preferred to send their children to separate sectarian schools. But it was their Roman Catholic religion that most concerned some urban Protestants. These Protestants associated Catholicism with despotism and immorality, the same evils they attributed to Southerners. For their part, the Irish made it clear that they had little use for Protestant reform, especially temperance and abolitionism. The clash of cultures would soon further disturb a political environment increasingly in flux over the slavery issue.

Democrats wooed the Irish newcomers. The champions of individual rights against intrusive government and meddling reformers, they supported the strict separation of church and state. Evangelical Protestants, especially those who were not Democrats, took a different view. They believed that the assertion of individual rights led to chaos and had to be countered by evangelically led reform. And reform required government action on a wide variety of issues, from drinking to slavery to economic policy. To the reformers, every political issue had moral overtones. Those who disagreed with them were not

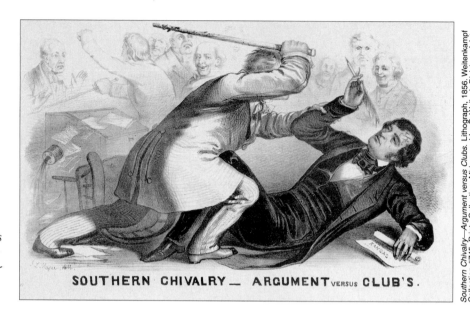

Southern Chivalry—Argument versus Clubs. Lithograph, 1856. Weitenkampf Collection #745, Prints Collection: Miriam and Ira D. Wallach Division of Art, Prints and Photographs, The New York Public Library, Astor, Lenox, and Tilden Foundations.

A typical Northern view of South Carolina's Representative Preston S. Brooks attacking Massachusetts Senator Charles Sumner in 1856 for Sumner's intemperate speech against Brooks's relative, Senator Andrew P. Butler. The incident reinforced sectional antagonism.

SOUTHERN CHIVALRY — ARGUMENT VERSUS CLUB'S.

merely political opponents but obstacles to the creation of a righteous society.

New parties emerged from this cauldron of religious, ethnic, and sectional strife. Anti-immigrant, anti-Catholic sentiment gave rise to the **Know-Nothing party**, which began as a secret organization in July 1854. Its name derived from the reply that members gave when asked about the party: "I know nothing." Although strongest in the North, Know-Nothing chapters blossomed in several southern cities that had experienced some immigration since 1848, among them Richmond, Louisville, New Orleans, and Savannah. The party's members in both North and South were mostly former Whigs. In addition to their biases against Catholics and foreigners, the Know-Nothings shared a fear that the slavery issue could destroy the Union. But because attempts to solve the issue seemed only to increase sectional tensions, the Know-Nothings hoped to ignore it.

Know-Nothing candidates fared surprisingly well in local and congressional elections during the fall of 1854, carrying 63 percent of the statewide vote in Massachusetts and making strong showings in New York and Pennsylvania. In office, Know-Nothings achieved some notable reforms. In Massachusetts, where they pursued an agenda similar to that of the Whigs in earlier years, they secured administrative reforms and supported public health and public education programs.

The Know-Nothings' anti-Catholicism, however, overshadowed their reform agenda. In several states and cities, they passed legislation barring Catholics from public office and unsuccessfully sought to increase the time required for an immigrant to become a citizen from one year to twenty-one years. The Know-Nothings also fostered anti-Catholic violence such as a bloody election day riot that erupted in Louisville, Kentucky, in 1855.

Ethnic and religious bigotry were weak links to hold together a national party. Southern and northern Know-Nothings soon fell to quarreling among themselves over slavery, despite their vow to avoid it, and the party split. Many northern Know-Nothings soon found a congenial home in the new **Republican party**.

The Republican party formed in the summer of 1854 from a coalition of antislavery Conscience Whigs and Democrats disgusted with the Pierce administration's Kansas policy. The Republicans supported many of the same kinds of reforms as the Know-Nothings, and like them, the Republicans also supported strong state and national governments to promote those reforms. Most Republicans were likewise native-born white Protestants, and some shared the Know-Nothing's anti-immigrant, anti-Catholic bias. But the overriding bond among Republicans was their opposition to the extension of slavery in the territories. Unlike the Know-Nothings, the Republicans confronted the slavery issue head on.

Reflecting its opposition to slavery, the Republican party was an antisouthern sectional party. The overwhelming majority of its members were Northerners. Northern Whig merchants and entrepreneurs who joined the party were impatient with southern obstruction in Congress of federal programs for economic development, such as a transcontinental railroad, harbor and river improvements, and high tariffs to protect American industries (located mostly in the North) from foreign competition. In a bid to keep slavery out of the territories, the Republicans favored limiting homesteads in the West to 160 acres. Not incidentally, populating the territories with northern whites would ensure a western base for the new party.

The Republicans found strong backing in Horace Greeley's *New York Tribune*. Greeley, a New Englander who arrived in New York in 1831 had emerged by the mid-1840s as one of the nation's most influential journalists. He was convinced that a society founded on free white labor had made his success possible, and he attacked the South at every opportunity. New York was the nation's financial and commercial center and controlled its lines of communication, giving Greeley an enormous advantage in the sectional propaganda war. Greeley, perhaps more than anyone, burned Kansas into the northern consciousness with his paper's colorful, if often exaggerated, reporting of events there. Newspapers tied to political parties were common during the nineteenth century, but the *Tribune*'s slashing style and blaring headlines, both innovations, attracted thousands of new readers and inflamed northern and southern public opinion.

Heightened sectional animosity laced with religious and ethnic prejudice fueled the emergence of new parties and the weakening of old political affiliations in the early 1850s. Accompanying the political realignment were diverging views on the proper role of government. As the nation prepared for the presidential election of 1856, the Democrats had become a party top-heavy with Southerners; the Know-Nothings splintered along sectional lines; some Whigs remained active under the old party name, mainly on the state and local levels in North and South; and the Republican party was becoming an important political force in the North and, to Southerners, the embodiment of evil.

The Election of 1856

The presidential election of 1856 proved one of the strangest in American history. The Know-Nothings and the Republicans faced a national electorate for the first time. The Democrats were deeply divided over the Kansas issue. Rejecting both Pierce and Douglas, they turned instead to a longtime insider, James Buchanan. This Pennsylvanian's major asset

was that he had been absent from the country the previous three years as ambassador to Great Britain and was thus untainted by the Kansas controversy. The members of the increasingly powerful southern wing of the party supported him because he had cooperated with them during his more than thirty years in Congress. Northerners accepted him primarily because of his clean slate on Kansas and because he hailed from a state crucial to a Democratic victory.

The Republicans passed over their most likely candidate, the New York senator and former Whig William H. Seward. Instead, they followed a tried-and-true Whig precedent and nominated a military hero, John C. Frémont, a handsome, dark-haired soldier of medium height and medium intelligence. His wife, Jessie Benton, the daughter of Missouri senator Thomas Hart Benton, was his greatest asset. In effect, she ran the campaign and wisely encouraged her husband to remain silent.

The Know-Nothings split into the "South Americans" and the "North Americans." The South Americans nominated Millard Fillmore, although he was not a Know-Nothing. The North Americans eventually and reluctantly embraced Frémont, despite the widespread but mistaken belief that he was a Roman Catholic.

Openly reviling what they called the "Black Republican party," Southerners threatened disunion if Frémont won. Virginia governor Henry A. Wise declared that Frémont's election "would be an open, overt proclamation of public war." Georgia's fire-eating Senator Robert Toombs concurred, warning that "the election of Frémont would be the end of the Union, and ought to be."

Buchanan claimed to be the only national candidate on the ballot. Writing to a colleague before the election, he stated, "I consider that all incidental questions are comparatively of little importance . . . when compared with the grand and appalling issue of Union or Disunion." Voters agreed, for Buchanan bested Frémont in the North and Fillmore in the South to win the presidency.

The overall result pleased Southerners, but the details left them uncomfortable. Buchanan won by carrying every southern state and the Lower North—Pennsylvania, New Jersey, Illinois, Indiana, and California. But Frémont, a political novice running on his party's first national ticket, carried eleven free states, and the rest he lost by scant margins to Buchanan. It was a remarkable showing for a two-year-old party. In the South and border states, Fillmore managed more than 40 percent of the vote and carried Maryland, despite bearing the standard of a fragmented party.

Buchanan, who brought more than a generation of political experience to the presidency, would need every bit and more. He had scarcely settled into office when two major crises confronted him: a Supreme Court decision that challenged the right of Congress to regulate slavery in the territories and renewed conflict over Kansas.

The *Dred Scott* Case

Dred Scott was a slave owned by an army surgeon based in Missouri. In the 1830s and early 1840s, he had traveled with his master to the state of Illinois and the Wisconsin Territory before returning to Missouri. In 1846, Scott sued his master's widow

Dred Scott and his wife Harriet are portrayed here with their children as an average middle-class family, an image that fueled Northern opposition to the Supreme Court's 1857 decision that denied both Scott's freedom and his citizenship.

for freedom on the grounds that the laws of Illinois and the Wisconsin Territory barred slavery. After a series of appeals, the case reached the Supreme Court.

Chief Justice Roger Taney of Maryland, joined by five other justices of the nine-member Supreme Court (five of whom came from slave states), dismissed Scott's suit two days after Buchanan's inauguration in March 1857. There is evidence that Buchanan had urged the Court to issue a sweeping ruling on slavery in the territories that would set the question to rest once and for all. Although Buchanan apparently did not suggest which way he wanted the Court to rule, such contact between the executive and the judicial branches of government concerning a pending case was inappropriate. In any case, Taney's opinion, far from settling the sectional debate over slavery, deepened it.

Taney's opinion contained two bombshells. First, using dubious logic and failing to take into account the status of blacks in several northern states, he argued that blacks were not citizens of the United States. Because Scott was not a citizen, he could not sue. In reaching this conclusion, Taney noted that the framers of the Constitution had never intended citizenship for slaves. The framers, according to Taney, respected a long-standing view that slaves were "beings of an inferior order . . . so far inferior that they had no rights which the white man was bound to respect."

Second, Taney held that even if Scott had standing in court, his residence in the Wisconsin Territory did not make him a free man. This was because the Missouri Compromise, which was still in effect in the 1840s, was, in Taney's view, unconstitutional. (The Wisconsin Territory lay above the compromise line.) The compromise, the Chief Justice explained, deprived citizens of their property (slaves) without the due process of law granted by the Fifth Amendment to the U.S. Constitution. In effect, Taney ruled that Congress could not bar slavery from the territories.

Black Americans reacted bitterly to the ***Dred Scott* decision**. Throughout the struggle of black abolitionists to free their compatriots in the South, they had appealed to the basic American ideals of freedom, liberty, and self-determination. Now Taney was saying that these ideals did not apply to blacks. Throughout the urban North, blacks held meetings to denounce the decision. One gathering in Philadelphia in April 1857 resolved "that the only duty the colored man owes to a constitution under which he is declared to be an inferior and degraded being . . .

is to denounce and repudiate it." A statewide black convention in Ohio objected in even stronger language: "If the Dred Scott dictum be the true . . . law of the land, then are the founders of the American Republic convicted by their descendants of base hypocrisy, and colored men absolved from all allegiance to a government which withdraws all protection." The gap between American ideals and the application of those ideals to black Americans had never been wider or more apparent.

The decision also shocked Republicans. The right of Congress to ban slavery from the territories, which Taney had apparently voided, was one of the party's central tenets. Republicans responded by ignoring the implications of the decision for the territories while promising to abide by it so far as it affected Dred Scott himself. Once in office, Republicans vowed, they would seek a reversal. This position allowed them to attack the decision without appearing to defy the law.

The *Dred Scott* decision boosted Republican fortunes in the North even as it seemed to undercut the party. Fears of a southern Slave Power conspiracy, which some had dismissed as fanciful and politically motivated, now seemed justified. If Congress could not ban slavery from the territories, Republicans asked, how secure was the right of states to ban slavery within their borders? A small group of slaveholders, they charged, was holding nonslaveholding whites hostage to the institution of slavery.

The Lecompton Constitution

Establishing a legitimate government in Kansas was the second major issue to bedevil the Buchanan administration. The president made a good start, sending his friend and fellow Pennsylvanian Robert Walker (then a resident of Mississippi) to Kansas as territorial governor to oversee the election of a constitutional convention in June 1857. Walker, though sickly, was a man of integrity.

The violence had subsided in Kansas, and prospects had grown for a peaceful settlement. But free-staters, fearing that the slavery forces planned to stuff the ballot box with fraudulent votes, announced a boycott of the June election. As a result, proslavery forces dominated the constitutional convention, which was held in Lecompton. And Walker, although a slaveholder, let it be known that he thought Kansas would never be a slave state. He thus put himself at odds with proslavery residents from the outset.

Walker convinced the free-staters to vote in October to elect a new territorial legislature. The returns gave the proslavery forces a narrow victory, but Walker discovered irregularities. In McGee, Kansas, twenty voters somehow had cast twelve hundred votes for proslavery candidates. And in Oxford, a community of a mere six houses, 1,601 names appeared on the voting rolls, all in the same handwriting and all copied from the Cincinnati city directory. Walker threw out these returns, and the free-staters took control of the territorial legislature for the first time.

Undeterred, the proslavery forces drafted a proslavery constitution at the constitutional convention in Lecompton. Buchanan, who had promised Southerners a proslavery government in Kansas, dismissed Walker before he could rule on the **Lecompton Constitution**, then ignored the recommendation of Walker's successor that he reject it. He submitted the Lecompton Constitution to the Senate for approval even though it clearly sidestepped the popular sovereignty requirement of the Kansas-Nebraska Act.

As with the Kansas-Nebraska Act, many Northerners were outraged by the Lecompton Constitution. The proslavery Kansans behind the constitution had a record of fraud, and Buchanan's own appointee had advised him against it. Northern Democrats facing reelection refused to support a president of their own party and, though the constitution passed in the Senate, Democratic opposition killed it in the House. Among Lecompton's opponents was Stephen A. Douglas, who justified his vote with an impassioned defense of popular sovereignty, which the president and proslavery Kansans had openly defied.

Douglas knew that the *Dred Scott* decision and Buchanan's support of the Lecompton Constitution would help the Republicans and hurt him and his fellow northern Democrats in the 1858 congressional elections. The **Panic of 1857**, a severe economic recession that lingered into 1858, also worked to the advantage of the Republicans. The Democratic administration did nothing as unemployment rose, starvation stalked the streets of northern cities, and homeless women and children begged for food and shelter. Republicans claimed that government intervention—specifically, Republican-sponsored legislation to raise certain tariffs, give western land to homesteaders, and fund transportation projects—could have prevented the panic. The Democrats' inaction, they said, reflected the southern Slave Power's insensitivity to northern workers.

Southerners disagreed. The panic had scarcely touched them. Cotton prices were high, and few southern banks failed. Cotton seemed indeed to be king. The financial crisis in the North reinforced the southern belief that northern society was corrupt and greedy. The Republicans' proposed legislative remedies, in their view, would enrich the North and beggar the South.

Such were the issues confronting Douglas as he returned home to Illinois in the summer of 1858 to begin his reelection campaign.

The Lincoln-Douglas Debates

Douglas faced a forceful opponent. The Republicans had nominated Abraham Lincoln, a 49-year-old lawyer and former Whig congressman. The Kentucky-born Lincoln had risen from modest circumstances to become a prosperous lawyer in the Illinois state capital of Springfield. His marriage to wealthy and well-connected Mary Todd helped both his law practice and his pocketbook. After one term in Congress from 1847 to 1849, he returned to his law practice but maintained his interest in politics. Strongly opposed to the extension of slavery into the territories, he considered joining the Republican party after the passage of the Kansas-Nebraska Act. Lincoln had developed a reputation as an excellent stump speaker with a homespun sense of humor, a quick wit, and a self-deprecating style that fit well with the small-town residents and farmers who composed the majority of the Illinois electorate.

But substance counted more than style with Illinois voters. Most of them opposed the extension of slavery into the territories, but generally not out of concern for the slaves. Illinois residents, like most Northerners, believed in white supremacy. What they wanted was to keep the territories free for white people. Few voters would support dissolving the Union over the slavery issue. Douglas, who knew his constituents well, branded Lincoln a dangerous radical for warning, in a biblical paraphrase, that the United States, like "a house divided against itself," could not "endure permanently half slave and half free."

Lincoln could not allow the charge of radicalism to go unanswered. Little known beyond the Springfield area, he also had to find a way to gain greater exposure. So in July 1858, he challenged Douglas to a series of debates across the state. Douglas was reluctant to provide exposure for his lesser-known opponent, but he could not reject Lincoln's offer outright lest voters think he was dodging his challenger. He agreed to debates in seven of the state's nine congressional districts.

The **Lincoln-Douglas debates** were defining events in American politics. Farmers rode into market towns like Ottawa, Galesburg, Alton, and Freeport, bringing their families and picnic baskets. They settled in their wagons or on the ground under trees to hear the two great debaters confront each other on the most troubling issue of the day. What a sight it must have been, the stubby-legged, animated, barrel-chested Little Giant engaging the gangly, deliberate former rail-splitter, Abe Lincoln.

The debates put the differences between Lincoln and Douglas, Republicans and Democrats, and North and South into sharp focus. At Freeport, Lincoln asked Douglas to reconcile popular sovereignty, which Douglas had long championed, with the *Dred Scott* decision, which seemed to outlaw it by prohibiting a territorial legislature from excluding slavery before statehood. Douglas replied with what became known as the **Freeport Doctrine**. Slavery, he argued, could exist in a territory only if residents passed a law to protect it. Without such a law, no slaveholders would move in, and the territory would be free. Thus if residents did nothing, there could be no slavery in the territory.

For Douglas, slavery was not a moral issue. What mattered was what white people wanted. If they wanted slavery, fine; if they did not, fine also.

Lincoln and many Republicans had a very different view. For them, slavery *was* a moral issue. As such, it was independent of what the residents of a territory wanted. In the final Lincoln-Douglas debate, Lincoln turned to his rival and explained:

The Lincoln-Douglas debates in 1858 mesmerized, entertained, infuriated, and inspired the citizens of Illinois. Part of the attraction was the physical contrast between the Rail Splitter and the Little Giant. But also, as the black man trapped in the fence indicates, the debates highlighted the differences between Republicans and Northern Democrats over the extension of slavery in the territories.

The real issue in this controversy . . . is the sentiment on the part of one class that looks upon the institution of slavery *as a wrong*, and of another class that *does not* look upon it as a wrong. . . . The Republican party . . . look upon it as being a moral, social and political wrong . . . and one of the methods of treating it as a wrong is to *make provision that it shall grow no larger*. . . . That is the real issue. . . . It is the eternal struggle between these two principles—right and wrong—throughout the world.

Abolitionists and evangelicals had been saying much the same thing. But Lincoln was calm and nonaccusatory, his measured words more like a conversation than a sermon. And people listened.

Lincoln tempered his moralism with practical politics. He took care to distance himself from abolitionists, asserting that he abided by the Constitution and did not seek to interfere where slavery existed. Privately, however, he prayed for its demise. Nor did he agree, publicly at least, with abolitionist calls for racial equality. Several times during the debates he noted "a physical difference between the white and black races" that would "forever forbid the two races living together on terms of social and political equality." At the Springfield debate, he echoed the wishes of most white Illinoisans when he declared, "What I would most desire would be the separation of the white and black races." Indeed, he had once advocated sending freed slaves to Africa. Slavery was immoral, but inequality was not. The Republican party was antislavery, but it did not advocate racial equality.

Illinois voters retained a narrow Democratic majority in the state legislature, which reelected Douglas to the U.S. Senate. (State legislatures elected senators until 1913, when the Seventeenth Amendment provided for direct election by the people.) But Douglas alienated southern Democrats with his strong defense of popular sovereignty and lost whatever hope he had of becoming the standard-bearer of a united Democratic party in 1860. Lincoln lost the senatorial contest but won national respect and recognition.

Despite Lincoln's defeat in Illinois, the Republicans made a strong showing in the 1858 congressional elections across the North. The increased Republican presence and the sharpening sectional divisions among Democrats portended a bitter debate over slavery in the new Congress. Americans were viewing issues and each other more than ever before in sectional terms. *Northern* and *Southern* took on meanings that expressed a great deal more than geography.

The Road to Disunion

The unsatisfying Compromise of 1850, the various misadventures in the Caribbean and Central America, and the controversies over Kansas and the *Dred Scott* case convinced many Northerners that Southerners were conspiring with the federal government to restrict their political and economic liberties. Southerners interpreted the response to these same events as evidence of a northern conspiracy to gain increased power in the federal government and reduce the South's political and economic influence. There were no conspiracies, but with so little goodwill on either side, hostility predominated. Slavery, above all, accounted for the growing divide.

When abolitionist John Brown, who had avenged the "sack of Lawrence" in 1856, led a raid against a federal arsenal at Harpers Ferry, Virginia, in 1859 in the vain hope of sparking a slave revolt, he brought the frustrations of both sides of the sectional conflict to a head. The presidential election campaign of 1860 began before the uproar over the raid had subsided. In the course of that contest, one of the last nationally unifying institutions, the Democratic party, broke apart. The election of Abraham Lincoln, an avowedly sectional candidate, triggered a crisis that defied peaceful resolution.

Although the crisis spiraled into a civil war, this outcome did not signal the triumph of sectionalism over nationalism. Ironically, in defending their stands, both sides appealed to time-honored nationalist and democratic sentiments. Southern secessionists believed they were the true keepers of the ideals that had inspired the American Revolution. They were merely re-creating a more perfect Union. It was not they, but the Republicans, who had sundered the old Union by subverting the Constitution's guarantee of liberty. Lincoln similarly appealed to nationalist themes, telling Northerners that the United States was "the last best hope on earth."

Northerners and Southerners both appealed to nationalism and democracy but applied different meanings to those concepts. These differences underscored how far apart the sections had grown. When Southerners and Northerners looked at each other, they no longer saw fellow Americans; they saw enemies.

SUMMARY

SOUTH AND NORTH COMPARED IN 1860

	South	North
Population	Biracial: 35 percent African-American	Overwhelmingly white: less than 2 percent African-American
Economy	Growing though relatively undiversified; 84 percent of work force in agriculture	Developing through industrialization and urbanization; 40 percent of workforce in agriculture
Labor	Heavily dependent on slave labor, especially in Lower South	Free wage labor
Factories	15 percent of national total	85 percent of national total; concentrated in the Northeast
Railroads	Approximately 10,000 miles of track; primarily shorter lines, with fewer links to trunk lines	Approximately 20,000 miles of track; more effectively linked in trunk lines connecting east and west
Literacy	17 percent illiteracy rate for free population	6 percent illiteracy rate

North-South Differences

Behind the ideological divide that separated North and South lay real and growing social and economic differences (see the summary table "South and North Compared in 1860"). As the North became increasingly urban and industrial, the South remained primarily rural and agricultural. The urban population of the free states increased from 10 to 26 percent between 1820 and 1860. In the South, in the same period, it increased only from 5 to 10 percent. Likewise the proportion of the northern work force in agriculture declined from 68 percent to 40 percent between 1800 and 1860, whereas in the South it increased from 82 percent to 84 percent. Northern farmers made up for the decline in farm workers by relying on machinery instead. In 1860, the free states had twice the value of farm machinery per worker as the slave states had.

The demand for farm machinery in the North reflected growing demand for manufactured products in general. The need of city-dwellers for ready-to-wear shoes and clothing, household iron products, processed foods, homes, workplaces, and public amenities boosted industrial production in the North. In contrast, in the South, the slower rate of urbanization, the lower proportion of immigrants, and the region's labor-intensive agriculture kept industrial development modest. The proportion of manufacturing capital invested in the South declined from 31 to 16 percent between 1810 and 1860. In 1810, per capita investment in industrial enterprises was 2.5 times greater in the North than in the South; in 1860, it was 3.5 times greater.

The rate of urban and industrial growth in the North was greater than anywhere else in the world in the early nineteenth century. As a result, the South inevitably suffers by comparison. Even when compared to the West, however, the South was falling behind. The South and West had about the same levels of manufacturing investment and urban population in the 1850s, but the rate of growth was even greater in the West than in the North. What is more, a vast railroad network linked the West to the Northeast rather than the South (see Map 15-3).

More subtle distinctions between North and South became evident as well by midcentury. Southerners tended to be more violent than Northerners. The slave states had a higher homicide rate than the free states, and more Southerners carried weapons. Southern values stressed courtesy, honor,

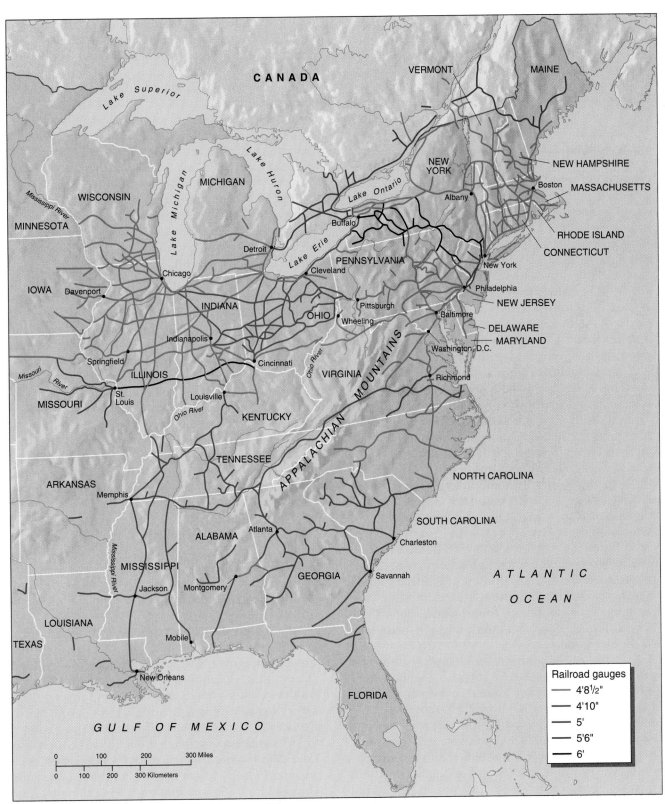

Map 15-3   Railroads in the United States, 1860
A vast network of railroads honeycombed the North and West by 1860. While the South made considerable progress in railroad construction during the 1850s, its lines had many different gauges and it lacked suitable connections to the West.

and courage. Southerners were more inclined to military service than Northerners. They had proportionately more cadets enrolled in the United States Military Academy at West Point; more than 60 percent of the volunteer soldiers for the Mexican War hailed from the South; and, excluding West Point and the Naval Academy at Annapolis, seven of the nation's eight military colleges were located in the South.

The South had a high illiteracy rate, nearly three times greater than the North—eight times greater if southern blacks are included. The "ideology of literacy," as one historian called it, was not as widespread in the South as in the North. Northerners, for example, supported far more public schools and libraries than Southerners. In the South, education was barred by law to slaves and limited for most whites. Many white leaders viewed education more as a privilege for the well-to-do than a right for every citizen. A South Carolinian wrote in the 1850s that "it is better that a part should be fully and highly educated and the rest utterly ignorant."

Evangelical Protestantism attracted increasing numbers in both North and South, but its character differed in the two regions. The Methodist Church divided along sectional lines over slavery in 1844, and the Baptists split the following year. The Presbyterians splintered in 1837 over mainly doctrinal issues, but the rupture became complete in 1861. In the North, evangelical Protestants viewed social reform as a prerequisite for the Second Coming of Christ. As a result, they were in the forefront of most reform movements. Southern evangelicals generally defended slavery. Just as southern politics stressed individual rights, southern religion emphasized individual salvation over social reform. Northern churches hunted sinners outside their congregations (and often found them in Southerners); southern churches confined their preaching to their members.

Slavery accounted for many of the differences between the North and the South. Investment in land and slaves limited investment in manufacturing. The availability of a large slave labor force reduced the need for farm machinery and limited the demand for manufactured products. Slaves were relatively immobile. They did not migrate to cities in massive numbers as did northern farmers. Nor could they quickly fill the labor demands of an expanding urban economy. Agriculture usually took precedence.

Slavery also divided northern from southern churches. And it accounted for the contrast between the inward, otherworldly emphasis of southern the-

ology and the reformist theology of northern evangelicals. Southerners associated black slavery with white freedom; Northerners associated it with white degradation.

Slavery contributed to the South's martial tradition and its lukewarm attitude toward public education. Fully 95 percent of the nation's black population lived in the South in 1860, 90 percent of them slaves. As a result, the South was a region on edge. Fearful of revolt, especially in the 1850s, when rumors of slave discontent ran rampant, whites felt compelled to maintain patrols and militias in constant readiness. The South was also determined to keep slaves as ignorant as possible. Educated slaves would be susceptible to abolitionist propaganda and more inclined to revolt.

The South's defense of slavery and the North's attack on it fostered an array of stereotypes that exaggerated the real differences between the sections. Like all stereotypes, these reduced individuals to dehumanized categories. They encouraged the people of each section to view those of the other less as fellow Americans than as aliens in their midst.

Southerners saw Northerners as crass and materialistic but themselves as generous and compassionate. Northerners saw Southerners as brutal and backward, themselves as progressive and temperate. Southerners perceived themselves as honorable and chaste and saw Northerners as corrupt and loose-living. Northerners saw Southerners as perverse and lazy, themselves as righteous and hardworking. The South, according to Southerners, was the land of moonlight and magnolias (an image actually originated in the North), while the North was the region of muggings and mudslinging. Northerners saw Southerners as lords of the lash and themselves as angels of mercy.

Ironically, although slavery increasingly defined the character of the South in the 1850s, a growing majority of white Southerners did not own slaves. Slavery nonetheless implicated nonslaveholders in ways that assured their support for it. By satisfying the demand for labor on large plantations, it relieved many rural whites from serving as farm hands and enabled them to work their own land. Slaveholders also recruited nonslaveholders to suppress slave violence or rebellion. It was nonslaveholders, for example, who often manned patrols and militia companies. Some nonslaveholders hoped to purchase slaves someday. Many dreamed of migrating westward to the next cotton frontier where they might find greater opportunity to own land and slaves. This dream not only bound white Southerners together on slavery but also prompted their strong support for southern access to the western territories. Finally, regardless of a white man's social or economic status, he shared an important feature with the largest slaveholder: As long as racial slavery existed, the color of his skin made him a member of a privileged class that could never be enslaved.

While white Southerners were more united on slavery than on other issues, their defense of slavery presented them with a major dilemma. It left them vulnerable to moral condemnation because in the end, slavery was morally indefensible. By the 1850s, most western nations had condemned and abolished the institution. And because Northerners controlled the flow of information through the popular newspapers and the national network of communications, credit, and commerce, Southerners were likely to find themselves increasingly isolated. A minority in their own country and a lonely voice for a despised institution that was for them a significant source of wealth, Southerners were understandably jittery.

John Brown's Raid

Shortly after he completed his mayhem at Pottawatomie Creek, John Brown left Kansas and approached several New England abolitionists for funds to continue his private war in the territory. By 1857, Brown had become a rustic celebrity in New England. He had dined at Ralph Waldo Emerson's home, had tea with Henry David Thoreau, and discussed theology with the abolitionist minister Theodore Dwight Weld. Brown's frontier dress, rigid posture, reticent manner, and piercing eyes gave him the appearance of a biblical prophet. After several failed businesses, more than twenty lawsuits for nonpayment of debts, and a brush with horse rustling, he had at last found his life's calling: He had become a moderately successful fund raiser for his own violent frontier exploits.

But when Brown returned to Kansas in late 1857, he discovered that peace had settled over that troubled territory. Residents now cared more about making money than making war. Leaving Kansas for the last time, he went east with a new plan. He proposed to attack and capture the federal arsenal at Harpers Ferry, Virginia, a small town near the Maryland border. The assault, Brown imagined, would spark a slave uprising in the area, eventually spreading to the rest of the state. With funds from his New England friends, he equipped a few dozen men and hired an English army officer to train them.

When Brown outlined his scheme to Frederick Douglass, the noted black abolitionist warned him against it. But his white New England friends were less cautious, and a group of six prominent abolitionists (the **"Secret Six"**) gave Brown additional funds for his project.

Brown and his "army" moved to a Maryland farmhouse in the summer of 1859 to train and

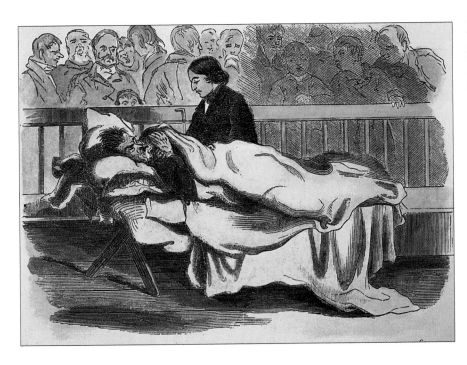

John Brown, wounded during his raid on the federal arsenal at Harpers Ferry, lies on a cot during his trial for murder and treason in Charlestown, Virginia in 1859.

complete planning for the raid. On the night of October 16, 1859, he and twenty-two followers captured the federal arsenal at Harpers Ferry and waited for the slaves to rally to his banner. Meanwhile, the townspeople alerted outside authorities. The Virginia militia and a detachment of United States Marines under the command of Colonel Robert E. Lee arrived and put a quick end to **John Brown's Raid**. They wounded Brown and killed or captured most of his force.

Brown had launched the operation without provisions and at a site from which escape was impossible. Although the primary goal of the attack had been to inspire a slave insurrection, no one had bothered to inform the local slaves. And despite the secret nature of the expedition, Brown had left behind a mountain of documents at the Maryland farmhouse. He had tried to conquer the state of Virginia with twenty-two men and an ill-conceived plan. Was he crazy? As the *Boston Post* editorialized after the raid, "John Brown may be a lunatic, [but if so] then one-fourth of the people of Massachusetts are madmen."

Although the *Post* may have exaggerated, the editorial reflected an article of faith among many abolitionists that, given the signal, slaves would immediately throw off their chains, slaughter their masters, and join a rebellion. But even those slaves in the area who knew of the raid understood the odds against Brown and had the good sense not to join him. As Abraham Lincoln observed, "It was not a slave insurrection. It was an attempt by white men to get up a revolt among slaves, in which the slaves refused to participate."

The raid, though foolish and unsuccessful, played on Southerners' worst fears of slave rebellion, adding a new dimension: Here was an attack engineered not from within the South but from the North. Some southern whites may have dismissed the ability or even the desire of slaves to mount revolts on their own, but they less easily dismissed the potential impact of outside white agitators.

Brown's raid amplified southern dismay over a recent defection of one of their own. In 1857, Hinton Rowan Helper, a nonslaveholding white from North Carolina, had published *The Impending Crisis*, in which he argued that slavery harmed nonslaveholding southern whites. Republicans had printed 100,000 copies of an abridged version of Helper's book, adding such provoking captions as "The Stupid Masses of the South" and "Revolution—Peacefully if we can, Violently if we must." Southerners lumped John Brown's Raid with the distribution of Helper's book as evidence of a conspiracy to defame and threaten the South.

The state of Virginia tried Brown on the charge of treason to the state. Brown, recovering from his wounds, attended most of the trial on a stretcher. The trial was swift but fair. The jury sentenced Brown to hang. Throughout his brief imprisonment and trial, Brown maintained a quiet dignity that impressed even his jailers. The governor of Virginia spoke admirably of him as "a man of clear head, of courage, fortitude, and simple ingenuousness." Speaking to the court after his sentencing, Brown suggested that he was God's agent in a holy war: "I believe that to have interfered as I have done . . . in behalf of [God's] despised poor, is no wrong, but right. Now, if it is deemed necessary that I should forfeit my life for the furtherance of the ends of justice, and mingle my blood further with the blood of my children and with the blood of millions in this slave country whose rights are disregarded by wicked, cruel, and unjust enactments, I say, let it be done."

Some Northerners compared Brown's execution with the death of a religious martyr. Abolitionist William Lloyd Garrison asked readers of *The Liberator* to "let the day of [Brown's] execution . . . be the occasion of such a public moral demonstration against the bloody and merciless slave system as the land has never witnessed." When the state of Virginia hanged Brown, church bells tolled across the North. Thoreau compared Brown with Jesus and called the abolitionist "an angel of light." Emerson observed that Brown would "make the gallows glorious like the cross." Writing to Margeretta Mason, wife of Virginia senator James M. Mason, abolitionist Lydia Maria Child asserted that "in this enlightened age, all despotisms ought to come to an end by the agency of moral and rational means. But if they resist such agencies, it is in the order of Providence that they must come to an end by violence." Most Northerners, however, including many Republicans, had condemned the raid. Still, the dignity of Brown's death touched many. Condemning the deed, they nevertheless embraced the cause.

The outpouring of northern grief over Brown's death convinced white Southerners that the threat to their security was not over. The discovery of Brown's correspondence at his Maryland farmhouse further fueled southern rancor, and Southerners increasingly ceased to believe northern disclaimers about the raid. Senator Mason asserted in Congress that "John Brown's invasion was condemned [in the North] only because it failed." Several members of the Secret Six had ties to the Republican party, and Southerners targeted them for special censure. Mississippi senator Jefferson Davis remarked that the Republican party "was organized on the basis of making war" against the South.

John Brown's Raid significantly changed southern public opinion. However much they defended slavery, most Southerners were for the Union. The northern reaction to John Brown's trial and death, however, troubled them. The *Richmond Whig*, a newspaper that had reflected moderate Upper South opinion for decades, observed in early 1860 that "recent events have wrought almost a complete revolution in the sentiments, the thoughts, the hopes, of the oldest and steadiest conservatives in all the southern states. . . . There are thousands upon . . . thousands of men in our midst who, a month ago, scoffed at the idea of a dissolution of the Union as a madman's dream, but who now hold the opinion that its days are numbered, its glory perished."

It was one thing to condemn slavery in the territories but another to attack it violently where it was long established. Southerners now saw in the Republican party the embodiment of John Brown's ideals and actions. So in their view, the election of a Republican president would be a death sentence for the South.

The impact of this shifting sentiment was immediately apparent in Congress when it reconvened three days after Virginia hanged Brown. Debate quickly turned tense and ugly. South Carolina senator James H. Hammond captured the mood well, remarking of his colleagues on the Senate floor that "the only persons who do not have a revolver and a knife are those who have two revolvers." The southern and northern wings of the Democratic party were now almost totally estranged. Southern Democrats seemed concerned only to promote an extreme proslavery agenda rather than to initiate real legislation.

The Election of 1860

An atmosphere of mutual sectional distrust and animosity characterized the campaign for the presidential election of 1860. In April, the Democratic party, the sole surviving national political organization, held its convention in Charleston, South Carolina. The location was not conducive to sectional reconciliation. The city had been a hotbed of nullification sentiment during the 1830s, and talk of disunion had surfaced periodically ever since, especially in the influential *Charleston Mercury*, edited by Robert Barnwell Rhett. At the convention, Charlestonians packed the galleries and cheered for their favorite extremists.

Northern Democrats arrived in Charleston united behind Stephen A. Douglas. Although they constituted a majority of the delegates, they could not muster the two-thirds majority vote necessary to nominate their candidate. Other issues, however, were decided on a simple majority vote, permitting northern Democrats to defeat a platform proposal for a federal slave code in the territories.

Southern extremists who favored secession hoped to disrupt the convention and divide the party. They reasoned that the Republicans would then win the presidency, providing the South with the justification to secede. The platform vote gave them the opportunity they were seeking. Accompanied by spectators' cheers, delegates from five Lower South states—South Carolina, Florida, Mississippi, Louisiana, and Texas—walked out. The Arkansas and Georgia delegations joined them the following day.

Still without a nominee, the Democrats agreed to reconvene in Baltimore in June. This time, the Upper South delegations marched out when Douglas Democrats, in a commanding majority, refused to seat the Lower South delegations that had walked out in Charleston. The remaining delegates nominated Douglas for president. The bolters, who included almost all southern delegates plus a few Northerners loyal to President Buchanan, met in another hall and nominated John C. Breckinridge of Kentucky.

The disintegration of the national Democratic party alarmed those Southerners who understood that it would ensure the election of a Republican president in November. The *Memphis Appeal* warned that "the odium of the Black-Republican party has been that it is *Sectional*." Should Southerners now allow a group of "restless and reckless or misguided men to destroy the national Democratic party?" the *Appeal* asked. Its emphatic answer was "No!"

The *Appeal* reflected the sentiment of many former Whigs, mainly from the Upper South, who would not support Breckinridge and could not support Douglas. Together with Whig allies in the North who had not defected to the Republican party, they met in Baltimore in May 1860 to form the **Constitutional Union** party and nominated John Bell of Tennessee for president.

Sensing victory, the Republicans convened in Chicago. If they could hold the states won by Frémont in 1856, add Minnesota (a new Republican-leaning state), and win Pennsylvania and one of three other Lower North states—Illinois, Indiana, or New Jersey—their candidate would win. These calculations dictated a platform and a candidate who could appeal to the four Lower North swing states where antislavery sentiment was not so strong.

The issue of slavery in the territories had dominated the Republicans' 1856 platform. Now they embraced other issues as well, presenting themselves as the party of sound economy, business, and industry. Delegates enthusiastically cheered a tariff plank calling for the protection of American industry.

In selecting an appropriate presidential nominee, the Republicans faced a dilemma. Senator William H. Seward came to Chicago as the leading Republican candidate. But his immoderate condemnation of Southerners and slavery made moderate northern voters wary of him, yet these were precisely the voters the party needed for victory.

Reservations about Seward benefited Abraham Lincoln. A year after his losing 1858 Senate campaign, he had embarked on a speaking tour of the East at the invitation of influential newspaper editor Horace Greeley. Lincoln's lieutenants at the convention stressed their candidate's moderation and morality, distancing him from both the abolitionists and Seward. Moreover, Chicago was Lincoln's home turf, and he had many friends working for him at the convention. When Seward faltered, Lincoln rose and won the Republican nomination.

True to their Whig heritage, the Republicans staged a colorful campaign featuring drill teams and organized groups of young men called the **Wide Awakes** outfitted in flowing black oilcloth capes. Douglas supporters countered by enrolling teams of "Little Giants." Breckinridge and Bell followed suit, and soon large groups of young men were marching all over the country in support of one candidate or another. The theme was political, but the atmosphere was an odd mix of military parade and religious revival.

The presidential campaign of 1860 actually comprised two campaigns. In the South, the contest was between Breckinridge and Bell; in the North, it was Lincoln against Douglas. Breckinridge and Bell had scattered support in the North, as did Douglas in the South, but in the main this was a sectional election. Lincoln did not even appear on the ballot in most southern states.

Lincoln's strategy was to say practically nothing. He spent the entire campaign in Springfield, Illinois. When he did speak, it was to a reporter or friends but not in a public forum. He discounted southern threats of disunion if he were to become president. Other Republicans dismissed southern talk of secession as well. Republican leaders thought the South too fragmented to unite behind a move as drastic as disunion. "The South," Greeley wrote dismissively, "could no more unite upon a scheme of secession than a company of lunatics could conspire to break out of bedlam."

Douglas campaigned hard, trying to convince the electorate that the Union hung in the balance. Breckinridge, like Lincoln in the North, sought to assure voters that he was not the disunion candidate. And Bell ran a low-key campaign, venturing out of Tennessee infrequently. He reiterated his support of the Constitution and the Union but said little else.

States in those days held gubernatorial elections on different days, even in different months, from the national presidential election. When, in mid-October, Republicans had swept the statehouses in two crucial states, Pennsylvania and Indiana, Douglas made an extraordinary decision, but one consistent with his ardent nationalism. He abandoned his campaign and headed south at great personal peril to urge Southerners to remain in the Union now that Lincoln's election was inevitable.

Lincoln became the nation's sixteenth president with 39 percent of the popular vote (see Map 15-4). Bell won the three Upper South states of Virginia, Kentucky, and Tennessee. Douglas, though second after Lincoln in the popular balloting, won the undivided electoral vote of only one state, Missouri.

Lincoln took most northern states by significant margins and won all the region's electoral votes except three in New Jersey. This gave him a substantial majority of 180 electoral votes. Breckinridge won eleven southern states but received a majority of the popular vote cast in just four. In the South as a whole, his opponents, Bell and Douglas, together reaped 55 percent of the popular vote, confirming Republicans' skepticism about southern determination to secede.

The urban vote in the 1860 election is intriguing. Lincoln fared worst in the larger cities of the North, and urban voters drubbed Breckinridge in the South. City-dwellers tended to vote for the centrist candidates, Douglas and Bell. The close commercial ties of North and South, the tendency

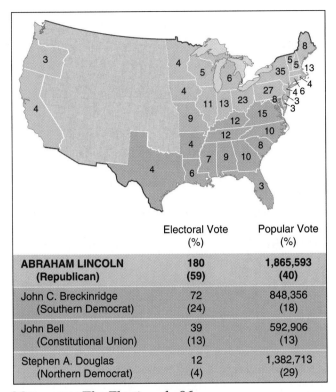

	Electoral Vote (%)	Popular Vote (%)
ABRAHAM LINCOLN (Republican)	**180 (59)**	**1,865,593 (40)**
John C. Breckinridge (Southern Democrat)	72 (24)	848,356 (18)
John Bell (Constitutional Union)	39 (13)	592,906 (13)
Stephen A. Douglas (Northern Democrat)	12 (4)	1,382,713 (29)

Map 15-4 *The Election of 1860*
The election returns from 1860 vividly illustrate the geography of sectionalism.

of immigrants in northern cities to vote Democratic, and the concern of affluent urban residents that disunion could bring economic uncertainty motivated their votes. The owners of large plantations in the South similarly had a strong economic interest in preserving the Union and tended to vote for the southern centrist, Bell. But the United States was still a nation mostly of farms and small towns, and rural communities returned strong majorities for Lincoln in the North and Breckinridge in the South.

Secession Begins

The events following Lincoln's election demonstrated how wildly mistaken were those who dismissed southern threats of secession. Four days after Lincoln's victory, the South Carolina legislature called on the state's citizens to elect delegates to a convention to consider secession. Meeting on December 20, the delegates voted unanimously to leave the Union. By February 1, six other states— Mississippi, Florida, Alabama, Georgia, Louisiana, and Texas—had all held similar conventions and decided to leave the Union (see Map 15-5). Representatives from the seven seceding states met to form a separate country, the **Confederate States of Amer-**

ica. On February 18, Jefferson Davis was sworn in as its president.

The swiftness of secession in the Lower South obscured divisions in most states over the issue. Secessionists barely secured a majority in the Georgia and Louisiana conventions. In Mississippi, Florida, and Alabama, the secessionist majority was more comfortable, but pro-Union candidates polled a significant minority of votes. With Lincoln headed for the White House, the greatest support for secession came from large landowners in counties in which slaves comprised a majority of the population. Support for secession was weakest among small, nonslaveholding farmers.

Secessionists mounted an effective propaganda campaign, deftly using the press to convince voters to elect their delegates to the state conventions. Framing the issue as a personal challenge to every southern citizen, they argued that it would be cowardly to remain in the Union, a submission to despotism and enslavement. Southerners, they maintained, were the true heirs to the spirit of 1776. Lincoln and the Republicans were like King George III and the British—they meant to deny Southerners the right to life, liberty, and the pursuit of happiness. Republicans, the secessionists warned, would turn southern society upside down. They would use the federal government to incite slave rebellions and would drain the economy of the South with their economic legislation. In short, the secessionists presented themselves as the guardians of American democracy and the Republicans as its usurpers.

Unionists, in response, could only offer voters a wait-and-see strategy. By remaining in the Union, they argued, Southerners could extract concessions from the Republicans that would protect their institutions.

Presidential Inaction

Because Lincoln would not take office until March 4, 1861, it was the Buchanan administration that had to cope with the secession crisis during the critical months of December and January. The president's failure to work out a solution with Congress as secession fever swept the Lower South further undermined Unionist forces in the seceding states.

When Buchanan lost the support of northern Democrats over the Lecompton Constitution, he turned to the South for support and filled his cabinet with Southerners. Now, facing the secession crisis, he proposed holding a constitutional convention to amend the Constitution in ways that would satisfy the

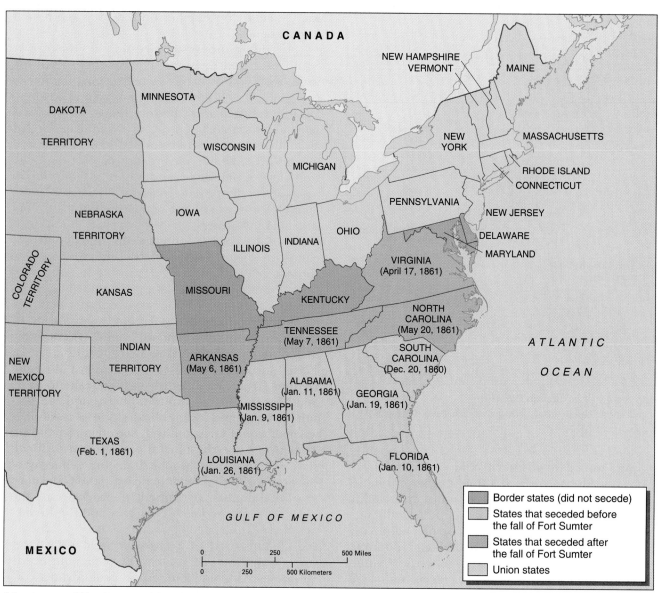

Map 15-5   *The Course of Secession*
Before the firing on Fort Sumter in April 1861, the Confederacy consisted primarily of states in the Lower South. After Sumter, and after President Lincoln called upon them for troops, the Upper South states of Virginia, North Carolina, Tennessee, and Arkansas seceded.

South's' demands on slavery. This outright surrender to southern demands, however, had no chance of passing in Congress.

Thereafter, Buchanan's administration quickly fell apart. As the Lower South states left the Union, their representatives and senators left Washington, and with them went Buchanan's closest advisers and key cabinet officials. Commenting on the emotionally charged atmosphere in the Senate as prominent Southerners gave their farewells and departed, one observer wrote, "There was everywhere

a feeling of suspense, as if, visibly, the pillars of the temple were being withdrawn and the great Government structure was tottering."

Buchanan, a lame duck, bereft of friends and advisers, did little more than condemn secession. He was reluctant to take action that would limit the options of the incoming administration or, worse, tip the balance in the Upper South toward secession. He hoped that waiting might bring an isolated Lower South to its senses and give efforts to mediate the sectional rift a chance to succeed.

Peace Proposals

Kentucky senator John J. Crittenden chaired a Senate committee that proposed a package of constitutional amendments in December 1860 designed to solve the sectional crisis. The central feature of the **Crittenden Plan** was the extension of the Missouri Compromise line through the territories all the way to the state of California. The plan was of marginal interest to the South, however, because it was unlikely to result in any new slave states. And Republicans opposed it because it contradicted one of their basic principles, the exclusion of slavery from the territories. Despite a flood of letters supporting the Crittenden Plan, including a petition from 38,000 citizens of New York City, Republicans successfully bottled it up in Congress and prevented action on it.

Meanwhile, ex-president John Tyler emerged from retirement to lead an effort by the border states—the Upper South and the Lower North—to forge a peace. Delegates from these states responded to Tyler's invitation and met in February 1861 at the Willard Hotel in Washington. But the plan the conference produced differed little from Crittenden's, and it, too, got nowhere in Congress.

Lincoln's Views on Secession

President-elect Lincoln monitored the secession of the Lower South states and the attempts to reach a compromise from his home in Springfield. Although he said nothing publicly, he made it known that he did not favor compromises like those proposed by Crittenden and Tyler. As he put it to a friend, "We have just carried an election on principles fairly stated to the people. Now we are told in advance, the government shall be broken up, unless we surrender to those we have beaten, before we take the offices. . . . If we surrender, it is the end of us, and of the government. They will repeat the experiment upon us. . . . A year will not pass, till we shall have to take Cuba as a condition upon which they will stay in the Union."

Lincoln counted on Unionist sentiment to keep the Upper South from seceding. Like Buchanan, he felt that the longer the Lower South states remained isolated, the more likely they would be to return to the fold. For a while, events seemed to bear him out. In North Carolina, the *Wilmington Herald* responded to South Carolina's secession by asking readers, "Will you suffer yourself to be spit upon in this way? Are you *submissionists* to the dictation of South Carolina . . . are

you to be called cowards because you do not follow the crazy lead of that crazy state?"

One by one, Upper South states registered their support for the Union. North Carolinians went to the polls in February and turned down the call for a secession convention. Also in February, Virginians elected Unionists to their convention by a five-to-one margin, leading a Charleston editor to lament, "Virginia would never secede now." On the other side, a correspondent of Senator Seward rejoiced, "The Gulf Confederacy can count Virginia out of their little family arrangement—*she will never* join them." Tennesseans also refused to call a convention. In Missouri, not one secessionist won election to the state convention. In Kentucky the legislature adjourned without taking any action on a convention or a statewide referendum on secession. And the Maryland legislature, already out of session, showed no inclination to reconvene.

A closer look, however, reveals that there were limits to the Upper South's Unionism. Most voters in the region went to the polls assuming that Congress would eventually reach a compromise based on the Crittenden proposals, Tyler's peace conference, or some other remedy. Leaders in the Upper South saw themselves as peacemakers. As one Virginian explained, "Without submission to the North or desertion of the South, Virginia has that moral position *within the Union* which will give her power to arbitrate between the sections." But what if arbitration failed? Or what if the Lower South states precipitated a crisis that forced the Upper South to choose sides? It was unlikely that the Upper South would abide the use of federal force against its southern neighbors.

Lincoln believed that the slavery issue had to come to a crisis before the nation could solve it. Although he said in public that he would never interfere with slavery in the slave states, the deep moral revulsion he felt toward the institution left him more ambivalent in private. As he confided to a colleague in 1860, "The tug has to come, and better now, than any time hereafter" (see "American Views: Lincoln on Slavery").

Fort Sumter: The Tug Comes

In his inaugural address on March 4, 1861, Abraham Lincoln denounced secession and vowed to uphold federal law but tempered his firmness with a conciliatory conclusion. Addressing Southerners specifically, he assured them, "We are not enemies but friends. . . . Though passion may have strained, it

American Views

LINCOLN ON SLAVERY

In the weeks after the 1860 election, northern and southern leaders sought out President-elect Abraham Lincoln for his views on slavery. Two letters, one to fellow Illinois Republican Lyman Trumbull and the other to Virginia Democrat John A. Gilmer, indicate Lincoln's firm opposition to the extension of slavery into the territories.

❖ **Lincoln's tone is considerably more conciliatory in the letter to Gilmer than in the one to Trumbull. Which one do you think better reflects his intentions?**

❖ **Despite the difference in tone, do you think both say essentially the same thing?**

Springfield, Ills. Dec. 10, 1860
Hon. L. Trumbull
My dear Sir: Let there be no compromise on the question of *extending* slavery. If there be, all our labor is lost, and ere long, must be done again. The dangerous ground—that into which some of our friends have a hankering to run—is Pop[ular] Sov[ereignty]. Have none of it. Stand firm. The tug has to come, & better now, than any time hereafter. Yours as ever,
A. Lincoln

Springfield, Ill. Dec. 15, 1860
Hon. John A. Gilmer:
My dear Sir: . . . I have no thought of recommending the abolition of slavery in the District of Columbia, nor the slave trade among the slave states . . . and if I were to make such recommendation, it is quite clear Congress would not follow it. As to the use of patronage in the slave states, where there are few or no Republicans, I do not expect to inquire for the politics of the appointee, or whether he does or not own slaves. . . . In one word, I never have been, am not now, and probably never shall be, in a mood of harassing the people, either North or South. On the territorial question, I am inflexible. . . . On that, there is a difference between you and us; and it is the only substantial difference. You think slavery is right and ought to be extended; we think it is wrong and ought to be restricted. For this, neither has any just occasion to be angry with the other.
Your obt. Servt.
A. Lincoln

Source: *John G. Nicolay and John Hay, eds.,* Works of Abraham Lincoln, *vol. 6 (1905).*

must not break our bonds of affection. The mystic chords of memory, stretching from every battlefield, and patriot grave, to every living heart and hearthstone, all over this broad land, will yet swell the chorus of the Union, when again touched, as surely they will be, by the better angels of our nature."

Southerners wanted concessions, not conciliation, however. The new president said nothing about slavery in the territories, nothing about constitutional amendments proposed by Crittenden and Tyler, and nothing about the release of federal property in the South to the Confederacy. Even some Northerners hoping for an olive branch were disappointed. As one Ohio editor wrote, Lincoln's policies would "stain the soil and color the waters of the entire continent." But Lincoln was hoping for time—time to get the Lower South states quarreling with one another, time to allow Union sentiment to build in the Upper South; and time to convince Northerners that the Union needed preserving. He did not get that time.

One day after Lincoln's inauguration, Major Robert Anderson (like Lincoln, a native Kentuckian), the commander of **Fort Sumter** in Charleston harbor, informed the administration that he had only four to six weeks' worth of provisions left. Sumter was one of three southern forts still under federal control. Confederate batteries had ringed the fort, and Anderson estimated that only a force of at least twenty thousand troops could run the gauntlet and provision and defend the fort. Anderson assumed that Lincoln would understand the hopeless arithmetic and order him to evacuate Fort Sumter. The commanding general of the army, Winfield Scott, advised the president accordingly, as did many members of his cabinet. Lincoln stalled.

News of Anderson's plight changed the mood in the North. The Slave Power, some said, was holding him and his men hostage. Frustration grew over Lincoln's silence and inaction. The Confederacy's bold resolve seemed to contrast sharply with the federal government's confusion and inertia. "The bird of our country," cracked New York diarist George Templeton Strong, "is a debilitated chicken, disguised in eagle feathers. . . . We are a weak, divided, disgraced people unable to maintain our institutional existence."

By the end of March, nearly a month after Anderson had informed Lincoln of the situation at Fort Sumter, the president finally moved. By this time, northern public opinion and Lincoln's cabinet (with Secretary of State Seward a notable exception) favored an effort to provision Major Anderson.

Seward made a last, desperate attempt to avert armed conflict by drawing on the reservoir of common American nationalism. He suggested that Lincoln trump up charges of Spanish and French aggression in the Caribbean and convene Congress to declare war. Seward hoped his absurd plan would draw seceding states back into the Union to make common cause against Spain and France. Lincoln politely rejected the advice and ordered an expedition to provision Fort Sumter.

The president still hoped to avoid a confrontation. He did not send the troops that Anderson had requested. Instead he ordered unarmed boats to proceed to the fort, deliver the provisions, and leave. Only if the Confederates fired on them were they to force their way into the fort with the help of armed reinforcements. Lincoln notified South Carolina authorities that he intended to do nothing more than "feed the hungry."

At Charleston, Confederate general P. G. T. Beauregard had standing orders to turn back any relief expedition. But President Davis wanted to take Sumter before the provisions arrived to avoid fighting Anderson and the reinforcements at the same time. He also realized that the outbreak of fighting would compel the Upper South to join the Confederacy. But his impatience to force the issue placed the Confederacy in the position of firing, unprovoked, on the American flag and at a man who had become a national hero.

On April 10, Davis ordered Beauregard to demand the immediate evacuation of Fort Sumter. Anderson refused but wondered what the hurry was, considering that his provisions would run out in a few days. The remark gave Beauregard pause and prompted additional negotiations. Anderson did not yield, and before dawn on April 12, 1861, the first Confederate shell whistled down on the fort. After more than a day of shelling, during which more than five thousand artillery rounds struck Fort Sumter, Anderson surrendered. Remarkably, neither side suffered any casualties, a deceptive beginning to an exceptionally bloody war.

When the verdict of Fort Sumter reached President Lincoln, he called on the southern states still in the Union to send troops to put down the rebellion. Refusing to make war on South Carolina, the Upper South states of Virginia, North Carolina, Tennessee, and Arkansas seceded, and the Confederacy expanded to eleven states.

Conclusion

When David Wilmot had submitted his amendment to ban slavery from the territories gained from Mexico, he could not have foreseen that the debate he unleashed would end in civil war just

SUMMARY

THE EMERGING SECTIONAL CRISIS

Event	Year	Effect
Wilmot Proviso	1846	Congressman David Wilmot's proposal to ban slavery from territories acquired from Mexico touched off a bitter sectional dispute in Congress.
Compromise of 1850	1850	Law admitted California as a free state, granted the population of Utah and New Mexico Territories the right to decide on slavery, and established a new and stronger Fugitive Slave Act, all of which "solved" the territorial issue raised by the Wilmot Proviso but satisfied neither North nor South and planted the seeds of future conflict.
Election of 1852	1852	Results confirmed demise of the Whig party, initiating a period of political realignment.
Kansas-Nebraska Act	1854	Law created the Kansas and Nebraska Territories and repealed the Missouri Compromise of 1820 by leaving the question of slavery to the territories' residents. Its passage enraged many Northerners, prompting some to form the new Republican party.
"Bleeding Kansas"	1855–1856	Sometimes violent conflict between pro- and antislavery forces in Kansas further polarized the sectional debate.
Election of 1856	1856	Presidency was won by Democrat James Buchanan of Pennsylvania, but a surprisingly strong showing by the recently formed Republican party in the North set the stage for the 1860 election.
Dred Scott Case	1857	The Supreme Court ruling that slaves were not citizens and that Congress had no authority to ban slavery from the territories boosted Republican prospects in the North.
Lecompton Constitution	1857	Proslavery document, framed by a fraudulently elected convention in Kansas and supported by President Buchanan, further convinced Northerners that the South was subverting their rights.
John Brown's Raid	1859	Unsuccessful attempt to free the South's slaves, this attack on a federal arsenal in Harpers Ferry, Virginia, increased sectional tension.
Election of 1860	1860	Republican Abraham Lincoln won a four-way race for the presidency. The last major national party, the Democrats, disintegrated. Lower South states seceded.
Fort Sumter	1861	Confederate forces attacked the fort in April 1861, Lincoln called for troops, and several Upper South states seceded. The Civil War was underway.

fifteen years later (see the summary table "The Emerging Sectional Crisis"). Northerners and Southerners had lived together in one nation for nearly eighty years. During that time, they had reached accommodations on slavery at the Constitutional Convention of 1787, in the Compromises of 1820 and 1850, and on numerous lesser occasions. But they could not reach agreement during the 1850s. By that time, the slavery issue had become weighted with so much moral and political freight that it defied easy resolution. Throughout the Western world, attitudes toward slavery were changing. Northern evangelical Protestants in the 1840s and 1850s branded slavery a sin and slaveholders sinners. The overwhelming popularity of *Uncle Tom's Cabin* both tapped and fed this sentiment.

Political conflict over slavery coalesced around northern efforts to curtail southern expansion and power and southern attempts to maintain their power and influence in the federal government by planting the institution in the western territories. This conflict eventually helped undo the Compromise of 1850 and turned Stephen A. Douglas's railroad bill into a battle royal over Kansas. Unable to resolve sectional differences over slavery, the Whigs disintegrated and the Democrats divided into northern and southern factions. The Republican party formed from the political debris. Ethnic and religious conflicts further disturbed the political landscape and contributed to party realignment.

Northerners and Southerners eventually interpreted any incident or piece of legislation as an attempt by one side to gain moral and political advantage at the other's expense. Northerners viewed the *Dred Scott* decision, the Lecompton Constitution, and the southern reaction to John Brown's Raid as evidence of a Slave Power conspiracy to deny white Northerners their constitutional rights. Southerners interpreted northern reaction to these same events as evidence of a conspiracy to rob them of security and equality within the Union.

By 1861, the national political parties that had muted sectional animosities were gone, and so were national church organizations and fraternal associations. The ideals that had inspired the American Revolution remained in place, especially the importance of securing individual liberty against encroachment by government. But with each side interpreting them differently, these ideals served more to divide than to unite. Southerners viewed the North in general and the Republican party in particular as threats to their individual liberties. Lincoln's victory, they believed, robbed the national government of its traditional role as "a disinterested and dispassionate umpire." Northerners believed that the South was conspiring to rob them of their individual rights as well and that only a redeemed federal government stood between their freedom and the despotism of the Slave Power. Both sides claimed for themselves the role of guardian of the Revolutionary tradition. Lincoln's election left Northerners feeling vindicated and Southerners feeling vulnerable.

Ironically, as Americans in both sections talked of freedom and self-determination, the black men and women in their midst had little of either. Lincoln went to war to preserve the Union; Davis, to defend a new nation. Slavery was the spark that ignited the conflict, but white America seemed more comfortable embracing abstract ideals than real people. Northerners and Southerners would confront this irony during the bloodiest war in American history—but they would not resolve it.

Review Questions

1. How do you account for the great success of Harriet Beecher Stowe's *Uncle Tom's Cabin*?

2. If you were a Democratic representative from your state to the U.S. Congress in 1854, what would your position be on the Kansas-Nebraska Bill? What if you were a Whig?

3. Discuss the role of evangelical religion in sharpening the sectional conflict between North and South.

4. Between the time he was elected president in November and his inauguration in March, what options did Abraham Lincoln have for resolving the sectional crisis?

5. Northerners and Southerners appealed to the same American ideals in support of their respective positions. Could they both have been correct?

Recommended Reading

William W. Freehling, *The Road to Disunion, Vol. 1: Secessionists at Bay, 1776–1854* (1990). This is a detailed and lively treatment of events and personalities in the years leading up to passage of the Kansas-Nebraska Act.

David M. Potter, *The Impending Crisis, 1848–1861* (1976). This remains the most comprehensive analysis of the coming of the war. It is a balanced account that is especially strong on political events.

Harriet Beecher Stowe, *Uncle Tom's Cabin* (1852; reprint edition 1982, with notes by Kathryn Kish Sklar). Reading this book is essential for understanding why and how it generated so much controversy and intensified sectional antagonisms in the early 1850s.

Additional Sources

Slavery in the Territories

Irving H. Bartlett, *John C. Calhoun: A Biography* (1993).

Eugene H. Berwanger, *The Frontier against Slavery: Western Anti-Negro Prejudice and the Slavery Extension Controversy* (1967).

Lacy Ford Jr., "Inventing the Concurrent Majority: Madison, Calhoun, and the Problem of Majoritarianism in American Political Thought," *Journal of Southern History,* 60 (February 1994): pp. 19–58.

Holman Hamilton, *Prologue to Conflict: The Crisis and Compromise of 1850* (1966).

Joan D. Hedrick, *Harriet Beecher Stowe: A Life* (1993).

Robert E. May, *The Southern Dream of a Caribbean Empire, 1854–1861* (1973).

Merrill Peterson, *The Great Triumvirate: Webster, Clay, and Calhoun* (1987).

Benjamin Quarles, *Black Abolitionists* (1969).

Political Realignment

Tyler Anbinder, *Nativism and Slavery: The Northern Know-Nothings and the Politics of the 1850s* (1992).

Richard J. Carwardine, *Evangelicals and Politics in Antebellum America* (1993).

William J. Cooper Jr., *The South and the Politics of Slavery, 1828–1856* (1978).

Don E. Fehrenbacher, "The New Political History and the Coming of the Civil War," *Pacific Historical Review,* 54 (May 1985): 117–142.

Don E. Fehrenbacher, *Slavery, Law, and Politics: The Dred Scott Case in Historical Perspective* (1981).

Eric Foner, *Free Soil, Free Labor, Free Men: The Ideology of the Republican Party before the Civil War* (1970).

William Gienapp, *Origins of the Republican Party, 1852–1856* (1987).

Michael F. Holt, *The Political Crisis of the 1850s* (1978).

Daniel Walker Howe, "The Evangelical Movement and Political Culture in the North during the Second Party System," *Journal of American History,* 77 (March 1991): 1216–1239.

Robert W. Johannsen, *The Frontier, the Union, and Stephen A. Douglas* (1989).

Robert W. Johannsen, ed., *The Lincoln-Douglas Debates of 1858* (1965).

James A. Rawley, *Race and Politics: "Bleeding Kansas" and the Coming of the Civil War* (1969).

James Brewer Stewart, *Holy Warriors: The Abolitionists and American Slavery* (1976).

J. Mills Thornton, *Politics and Power in a Slave Society: Alabama, 1800–1860* (1978).

Gerald W. Wolff, *The Kansas-Nebraska Bill: Party, Section, and the Coming of the Civil War* (1977).

The Road to Disunion

William L. Barney, *The Road to Secession: A New Perspective on the Old South* (1972).

Bruce Collins, *White Society in the Antebellum South* (1985).

Avery Craven, *The Growth of Southern Nationalism, 1848–1861* (1953).

Daniel W. Crofts, *Reluctant Confederates: Upper South Unionists in the Secession Crisis* (1989).

Richard N. Current, *Lincoln and the First Shot* (1963).

David Donald, *Charles Sumner and the Coming of the Civil War* (1960).

Michael P. Johnson and James L. Roark, eds., *No Chariot Let Down: Charleston's Free People of Color on the Eve of the Civil War* (1984).

John McCardell, *The Idea of a Southern Nation: Southern Nationalists and Southern Nationalism, 1830–1860* (1979).

James M. McPherson, "Antebellum Southern Exceptionalism: A New Look at an Old Question," *Civil War History,* 29 (September 1983): 230–244.

Stephen Oates, *To Purge This Land with Blood: A Biography of John Brown* (1970).

Michael Snay, *Gospel of Disunion: Religion and Separatism in the Antebellum South* (1993).

Kenneth M. Stampp, *America in 1857: A Nation on the Brink* (1990).

Kenneth M. Stampp, *And the War Came: The North and the Secession Crisis, 1860–1861* (1950).

Eric H. Walther, *The Fire-Eaters* (1992).

Where to Learn More

❖ **Harpers Ferry National Historical Park, West Virginia.**   Exhibits interpret John Brown's Raid and re-create some of the atmosphere and structures of the 1850s village and the federal arsenal.

❖ **"A House Divided," mounted by the Chicago Historical Society, Chicago.**   This exhibit depicts the major events of the sectional crisis during the 1850s, the election of 1860, and the coming of the Civil War. It will continue until 2001.

❖ **Fort Sumter National Monument, Charleston, South Carolina.**   This historic site interprets the bombardment of the fort and the events that immediately preceded the Civil War.

16 BATTLE CRIES AND FREEDOM SONGS
THE CIVIL WAR, 1861–1863

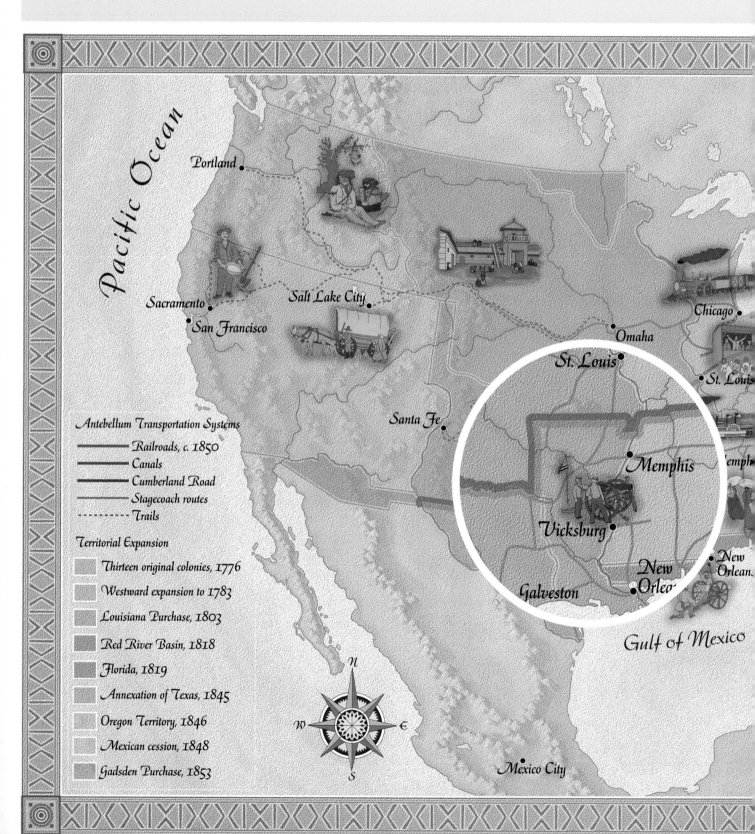

Pacific Ocean

Portland

Sacramento

San Francisco

Salt Lake City

Santa Fe

Chicago

Omaha

St. Louis

St. Louis

Memphis

Memph

Vicksburg

New Orleans

New Orlean.

Galveston

Gulf of Mexico

Mexico City

Antebellum Transportation Systems

Railroads, c. 1850
Canals
Cumberland Road
Stagecoach routes
- - - - - Trails

Territorial Expansion

Thirteen original colonies, 1776

Westward expansion to 1783

Louisiana Purchase, 1803

Red River Basin, 1818

Florida, 1819

Annexation of Texas, 1845

Oregon Territory, 1846

Mexican cession, 1848

Gadsden Purchase, 1853

N
W E
S

CHAPTER OUTLINE

KEY TOPICS

❖ The comparative economic and human resources of the North and South

❖ Confederate and Union military strategies

❖ Changing perceptions of the nature and length of the war

❖ The course of the war through 1863 and the major battles that shifted it in the North's favor

❖ Steps leading to the Emancipation Proclamation

*I*n October 1862, a photographic exhibit opened in New York City. The pictures were by two photographers working for Mathew Brady. Taken a month earlier near Sharpsburg, a small town in western Maryland, they featured gently rolling hills littered with bloated corpses. Until then, most Northerners had experienced the Civil War only distantly through newspaper dispatches. Now Brady's photographers, as a *New York Times* reviewer pointed out, had "done something to bring home to us the terrible reality and earnestness of war. If he has not brought bodies and laid them in our door-yards and along streets, he has done something very like it."

For others, the face of war was more immediate. Kate Cumming, a nurse in a Confederate hospital in Chattanooga, once witnessed a stream of blood cascading from an operating table into a large tub that held a recently severed arm. The blood ran over the bucket, onto the floor, and down the stairs into the kitchen below, where the hospital staff took their meals.

On July 4, 1862, after a bloody weeklong battle, Confederate and Union soldiers laid down their arms to pick berries together. As a Confederate private described it, "Our boys and the Yanks made a bargain not to fire at each other and went out in the field . . . and gathered berries together and talked over peacefully and kindly as if they had not been engaged for the last seven days in butchering each other."

In 1862, a 70-year-old slave woman in Georgia gathered her twenty-two children and grandchildren, seized an abandoned flatboat, and drifted 40 miles down the Savannah River. When a Union vessel rescued the party, "the grandmother rose to her full height, with her youngest grandchild in her arms, and said only, 'My God! Are we free?'"

The Civil War comprised a million such stories and evoked countless emotions. The experiences of many of the people who lived through it have found their way into print. Some fifty thousand books about the war have been published since it ended in 1865, an average of one a day. This outpouring attests to the country's enduring need to understand, explain, and reinterpret its bloodiest conflict. The Civil War preserved the Union, abolished slavery, and killed at least 620,000 soldiers—more than in all other wars the country fought from the Revolution to the Korean conflict. To come to terms with it is to try to reconcile its great accomplishments with its awful consequences.

When the war began, only a minority of Northerners linked the preservation of the Union with the abolition of slavery. By 1863, Union and freedom had become inseparable Federal objectives. The Confederacy fought for independence and the preservation of slavery. But their own ambivalence about slavery and the contempt of outside public opinion eventually led Southerners to emphasize independence. To save their new nation, some Southerners by late 1864 favored abandoning the "peculiar institution."

The Confederate objectives dictated a defensive military strategy; the Union objectives dictated an offensive strategy. But during the war's early years, both sides faced similar problems—raising an army, financing the war effort, mobilizing the civilian population, and marshaling resources. The Confederacy confronted the added burden of starting a government from scratch with relatively fewer resources than the Federals.

At the end of the war's first year, the Confederacy's strong military position east of the Appalachians belied its numerical and economic inferiority. Confederate advances resulted as much from the bungling of Union commanders as from the gallant efforts of the South's own forces. By the end of 1862, Union officers had begun to expose Southern military shortcomings and Federal officials had expanded the North's war aims to include the abolition of slavery. Within a year, the trans-Mississippi portion of the Confederacy capitulated as dissent and despair mounted on the home front.

Mobilization, North and South

Neither side was prepared for a major war. The Confederacy lacked a national army. Each southern state had a militia, but by the 1850s, these companies had become more social clubs than fighting units. Aside from private boats and some captured Federal vessels, the Confederacy also lacked a navy. The Union had a regular army of only sixteen thousand men, most of whom were stationed west of the Mississippi River. Their major concern had been to intervene between white settlers and Indians. The Federal navy had just three ships available for immediate service along the U.S. coast. Its sailors were trained for deep-water operations, not for coastal or inland-waterway maneuvers.

Each government augmented these meager military reserves with thousands of new recruits and developed a bureaucracy to mount a war effort. At the same time, the administrations of Presidents Lincoln and Davis secured the loyalty of their civilian populations and devised military strategies for a war of indeterminate duration. How North and South went about these tasks reflected both the different objectives of the two sides and the distinctive personalities of their leaders, Abraham Lincoln and Jefferson Davis.

War Fever

The day after Major Robert Anderson surrendered Fort Sumter, President Lincoln moved to enlarge his small, scattered army by mobilizing state militias for ninety days. Four states—Virginia, Arkansas, North Carolina, and Tennessee—refused the call and seceded from the Union. The governors of Kentucky and Missouri also declined to send troops, though these states remained in the Union. About one-third of the officer corps in the regular army, including some of the highest-ranking officers,

A rousing send-off for the Union's 7th Regiment in 1861 reflects the optimism and enthusiasm of citizens at the beginning of the war.

CHRONOLOGY

1861 April: Confederates fire on Fort Sumter; Civil War begins.

1861 July: First Battle of Bull Run.

1862 February: Forts Henry and Donelson fall to Union forces.

    March: Peninsula Campaign begins.

    Ironclads *Monitor* and *Virginia* (*Merrimac*) do battle.

    Battle of Pea Ridge, Arkansas.

    Battle of Glorieta Pass, New Mexico.

    April: Battle of Shiloh.

    New Orleans falls to Federal forces.

    May: Union captures Corinth, Mississippi.

    July: Seven Days' Battles end.

    Congress passes the Confiscation Act.

    August: Second Battle of Bull Run.

    September: Battle of Antietam.

    December: Battle of Fredericksburg.

1863 January: Emancipation Proclamation takes effect.

    May: Battle of Chancellorsville; Stonewall Jackson is mortally wounded.

    July: Battle of Gettysburg.

    Vicksburg falls to Union forces.

    Black troops of the 54th Massachusetts Volunteer Infantry Regiment assault Fort Wagner outside Charleston, South Carolina.

    September: Battle of Chickamauga.

    November: Battle of Chattanooga.

---

resigned their commissions to join the Confederacy. Still, Lincoln seemed likely to meet his target of 75,000 troops.

Lincoln's modest ninety-day call-up reflected the general belief, North and South, that the war would end quickly. The *New York Times* predicted that the "local commotion" in the South would be put down "in thirty days." Union general in chief Winfield Scott was more cautious, warning that the war could last as long as ten months. Some Southerners believed that the Yankees would quit after the first battle. "Just throw three or four shells among those blue-bellied Yankees," a North Carolinian boasted, "and they'll scatter like sheep." The North's numerical superiority was inconsequential because "the Yankee army is filled up with the scum of creation and ours with the best blood of the grand old Southland."

Not everyone thought the war would be brief. William T. Sherman, who had recently headed a Louisiana military academy and would become one of the Union's few great commanders, wrote in April 1861, "I think it is to be a long war—very long—much longer than any politician thinks."

Northerners closed ranks behind the president after the Confederacy's attack on Fort Sumter. Leading Democrat Stephen A. Douglas called on the Republican Lincoln to offer his and his party's support. "There can be no neutrals in this war," Douglas said, "*only patriots—or traitors.*" Residents of New York City, where sympathy for the South had probably been greater than anywhere else in the North, now sponsored huge public demonstrations in support of the war effort. One New Yorker exclaimed, "It seems as if we never were alive till now; never had a country till now." The city council appropriated $1 million to raise and equip Union regiments. Vigilance committees intimidated pro-Southern newspapers. And American flags flew everywhere. The *New York Daily Tribune*, an abolitionist paper, made the objective of this patriotic fervor clear: "We mean to conquer [the Southern people]—not merely to defeat, but to conquer, to SUBJUGATE them—and we shall do this the most mercifully, the more speedily we do it. But when the rebellious traitors are overwhelmed in the field, and scattered like leaves before an angry wind, it must not be to return to peaceful and contented homes. They must find poverty at their firesides, and see privation in the anxious eyes of mothers and rags of children."

Southerners were equally eager to support their new nation. A *London Times* correspondent traveling in the South witnessed large crowds with "flushed faces, wild eyes, screaming mouths." They punctuated stirring renditions of "Dixie" with the high-pitched piercing sounds that would later be known as the "rebel yell." Enlistment rallies, wild send-offs at train stations, and auctions and balls to raise money for the troops were staged throughout the Confederacy during the war's early months. As in the North, war fever fired hatred of the enemy. A Louisiana plantation overseer wrote:

> My prayer Sincerely to God is that Every Black Republican in the Hole combined whorl Either man women o chile that is opposed to negro slavery . . . shal be trubled with pestilences & calamitys of all kinds & drag out the Balance of there existence in misry & degradation with Scarsely food & rayment enughf to keep sole & body to geather and O God I pray the to Direct a bullet or a bayonet to pirce the art of every northern Soldier that invades southern Soil.

As war fever gripped North and South, volunteers on both sides rushed to join, quickly filling the quotas of both armies. The Confederates turned away 200,000 eager recruits in June and July for lack of arms and supplies. In the North, Congress responded to the clamor by authorizing the enlistment of 500,000 volunteers.

Most soldiers were motivated by patriotism, a desire to defend their homes and loved ones, and a craving for glory and adventure. A recruitment poster in one Massachusetts town promised "travel and promotion" as well as good pay. Some men succumbed to the pressure of companions and sweethearts. A young Alabamian received a package from his fiancée with a skirt, a petticoat, and a note demanding "Wear these or volunteer!"

The initial enthusiasm, however, wore off quickly. After four months of war, a young Confederate soldier admitted, "I have seen quite enough of a Soldier's life to satisfy me that it is not what it is cracked up to be." A Confederate general observed: "The first flush of patriotism led many a man to join who now regrets it."

The South in particular faced a contradiction between its ideology and the demands of full-scale war. Southerners were loyal to their localities, counties, and states. Southern leaders had been fighting for decades to defend states' rights against national authority. Now these same leaders had to forge the states of the Confederacy into a nation. By early spring 1862, the Confederate government was compelled to order the first general draft in U.S. history. It required three years' service from men between 18 and 35 years of age (a range later expanded to 17 to 50). Several Southern politicians denounced the draft as unconstitutional and coercive. But in 1864, the Confederate Congress added a compulsory reen-

listment provision. At that point, the only way a recruit could get out of the army was to die or desert.

The Confederate draft law allowed several occupational exemptions. Among them was an infamous provision that allowed one white man on any plantation with more than twenty slaves to be excused from service. The reason for the exemption was to assure the security and continued productivity of large plantations, not to protect the privileged, but it led some Southerners to conclude that the struggle had become "a rich man's war but a poor man's fight."

The initial flush of enthusiasm faded in the North as well. Responding to a Federal call for additional troops, some Northern states initiated a draft during the summer of 1862. In March 1863, Congress passed the **Enrollment Act**, a draft law that, like

Several hundred women, disguised as men, made their contribution to the war effort by enlisting. Frances Clalin served with Federal forces in Missouri. Many were found out after suffering wounds or illness.

the Confederate draft, allowed for occupational exemptions. A provision that allowed a draftee to hire a substitute aroused resentment among working-class Northerners. Anger at the draft—as well as poor working conditions—sparked several riots during 1863. But the North was less dependent on conscription than the South. Only 8 percent of Union forces were drafted, compared to 20 percent for the Confederacy.

The comments of many rank-and-file soldiers may give the impression that only people of lesser or modest means fought, but in fact the armies of both sides included men from all walks of life, from common laborers to clerks to bankers. An undetermined number of women, typically disguised as men, also served in both armies. Perhaps as many as three hundred women joined the Union ranks, and about half that number enlisted in the Confederate army. They joined for the same reasons as men: adventure, patriotism, and glory.

The North's Advantage in Resources

The resources of the North—including its population, industrial and agricultural capacity, and transportation network—greatly exceeded those of the South (see Figure 16-1). The 2.1 million men who fought for the Union represented roughly half the men of military age in the North. The 900,000 men who fought for the Confederacy, in contrast, represented fully 90 percent of its eligible population. Irish and German immigrants continued to flow into the North during the war, although at a slower rate than before 1861, and thousands of them enlisted, often as substitutes for native-born Northerners. And nearly 200,000 blacks, most of them ex-slaves from the South, took up arms for the Union. Not until the last month of the war did the Confederacy consider arming slaves.

The Confederacy compensated somewhat for its numerical disadvantage by requiring long tours of duty, which meant that its forces tended to be more experienced than those of the Union. But the Union's greater numbers left the South vulnerable to a war of attrition. As one Confederate veteran explained to a Union veteran several years after the war, "When one of your men got killed, a dozen took his place. When one of our boys died, it was just another good man gone."

At the beginning of the war, the North controlled 90 percent of the nation's industrial capacity. It had seventeen times more cotton and woolen cloth than the South, thirty times more boots and shoes, and thirty-two times more firearms. The North had dozens of facilities for producing the tools to make war material; the South had no such factories and only one munitions plant, the Tredegar Iron Works in Richmond. Northern farms, more mechanized than their Southern counterparts, produced record harvests of meat, grains, and vegetables. Southern farms were also productive, but the South lacked the North's capacity to transport and distribute food efficiently. The railroad system in the North was more than twice the size of the South's. And Northern railroads, with their main lines of a uniform track gauge, were more efficiently interlinked than Southern railroads, which were of several different gauges.

Thanks to the North's abundance of resources, no soldier in any previous army had ever been outfitted as well as the blue-uniformed Union trooper. The official color of the Confederate uniform was gray, although a dust-brown shade was more common. Most Southern soldiers, however, did not wear distinguishable uniforms, especially toward the end of the war. They also often lacked proper shoes or any footwear at all. In winter and

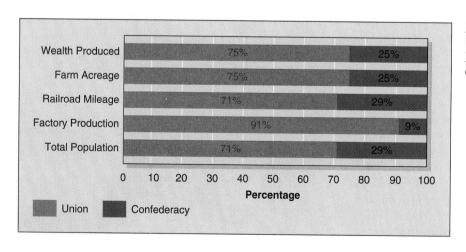

Figure 16-1   A Comparison of the Union and Confederate Control of Key Resources at the Outset of the Civil War.

on certain road surfaces, this shortage was a severe handicap. When Confederate general Robert E. Lee invaded Maryland in 1862, he left behind several thousand barefoot soldiers because they couldn't march on gravel roads.

Still, the South never lost a battle because of insufficient supplies or inadequate weaponry. New foundries opened, and manufacturing enterprises in Augusta, Georgia; Selma, Alabama; and elsewhere joined the Tredegar Iron Works to keep the Confederate armies equipped with the weapons and other supplies they needed to keep fighting. European imports and Northern weapons captured on the battlefield added to the South's reserve. The Confederacy's chief of ordnance—the man responsible for supplying its armies with war materiel—stated confidently in 1863, "We are now in a condition to carry on the war for an indefinite period."

Unstable finances proved more of a handicap to the Confederacy than its relatively low industrial capacity. The Confederate economy—and its treasury—depended heavily on cotton exports. But a Union naval blockade and the ability of textile manufacturers in Europe to find new sources of supply restricted this crucial source of revenue. The imposition of taxes would have improved the Confederacy's finances, but Southerners resisted taxation. They paid what taxes the government could impose—less than 1 percent of Confederate revenues—in nearly worthless state paper money. The government sold interest-bearing bonds to raise money, but as Confederate fortunes declined, so did bond sales. With few other options, the Confederacy financed more than 60 percent of the $1.5 billion it spent on the war with printing-press money. Inflation spiraled out of control, demoralizing civilians.

The Union had more abundant financial resources than the Confederacy, and the Federal government was more successful than the Confederate government at developing innovative ways to meet the great cost of the war. Its first recourse was to borrow money by selling long-term interest-bearing bonds and shorter-term interest-bearing treasury notes. Together these bonds accounted for 66 percent of the $4 billion that the Union raised to wage the war. Secretary of the Treasury Salmon P. Chase astutely hired a private entrepreneur, Jay Cooke, to market the bonds. Cooke mounted extensive newspaper and door-to-door campaigns offering the average citizen a stake in the war effort. Like the Confederacy, the Federal government issued paper money—bills derisively known as "greenbacks"—that was not backed by gold or silver. But the Federal government also offset its expenses with the country's first income tax, which citizens could pay in greenbacks, a move that bolstered the value and credibility of the paper currency. These financial measures eliminated the need for wage and price controls and rationing and warded off ruinous inflation in the North.

Leaders and Governments

Leadership ability, like resources, played an important role in the war. It was up to the leaders of the two sides to determine and administer civilian and military policy, to define the war objectives of each side, and to inspire a willingness to sacrifice in both citizens and soldiers.

Confederate president Jefferson Davis had to build a government from scratch during a war. Abraham Lincoln at least had the benefit of an established governmental structure, a standing army, healthy financial resources, and established diplomatic relations with the nations of Europe.

Davis and Lincoln were both born in Kentucky within a year and 100 miles of each other. Davis, like Lincoln, was born into modest circumstances. His forebears had moved from Philadelphia to Georgia to Kentucky and finally, a few years after Davis's birth, to Louisiana. He attended the military academy at West Point, where he was a mediocre student. He abandoned his military career after seven years of service and married the 16-year-old daughter of General Zachary Taylor. Davis and his bride moved to a plantation in Mississippi, where she soon died of yellow fever. Immersing himself in books and cotton farming, Davis had emerged as a gentleman planter by the 1840s and married Varina Howell in 1845. He returned to military service during the Mexican War, fought well, and used his success to become a senator from Mississippi in 1847. He served as secretary of war under President Franklin Pierce and returned to the Senate in 1857.

Although Davis's career qualified him for the prodigious task of running the Confederacy, aspects of his character compromised his effectiveness. He had a sharp intellect but related awkwardly to people and was not "one of the boys." Colleagues found him aloof. He was inclined to equate compromise with weakness and interpreted any opposition as a personal attack. His wife commented, "If anyone disagrees with Mr. Davis he resents it and ascribes the difference to the perversity of his opponent." Davis was also fatalistic.

According to his wife, when he heard that the Confederate Congress had selected him as president, he spoke of it "as a man might speak of a sentence of death."

Southerners viewed themselves as the genuine heirs of the American Revolution and the true defenders of the United States Constitution. The Confederate Constitution differed in only minor particulars from the Federal document. If the South were to establish itself as a separate country, however, Southerners had to renounce their American identity and develop one of their own. But on what distinctive aspects of Southern life could the Confederacy build such an identity? Slavery was distinctively Southern, but most white Southerners, even if they believed that slavery served their interests, did not own slaves. Southerners had forcefully advanced the ideology of states' rights during the 1840s and 1850s, but with its emphasis on the primacy of state sovereignty over central authority, states' rights too was a weak foundation on which to build a national consciousness.

Could appeals to the defense of slavery or to states' rights, or even just to Southern independence, sustain the loyalty of Southern Unionists who only reluctantly had sided with their states? Of yeomen farmers who had voted against secession and who harbored political and economic resentments against slaveholding planters? Of Southern women who wept through their cheers as they waved good-bye to brothers, husbands, and sons? Of the countless devout Southerners who privately questioned slavery and wondered if the war might be God's final act to rid the South of the sin of human bondage? What would happen when the Confederacy began to lose men, battles, and property? Although Southerners fought for a variety of reasons, protecting their homes and families remained paramount. When these were threatened or destroyed, where would loyalty lie? Did Davis, or anyone else for that matter, possess the skill to hold together a new nation that was more like the nation it had renounced than anything that could replace it?

Structural issues that Lincoln never had to consider compounded Davis's problems. Both Davis and Lincoln made some bad appointments. But Lincoln had the advantage of an established bureaucracy staffed by experienced personnel who could at least partially compensate for incompetent cabinet officials. Davis's appointees had to build departments from nothing. The Confederate secretary of the navy lacked a navy, the postmaster general had no stamps, the secretary of the treasury had no money, and the secretary of state had no diplomatic credentials to

any foreign country. Lincoln could use patronage to loyal Republicans to exert some discipline on his cabinet and the rest of his administration. The Confederacy, however, had no political parties. Davis faced shifting alliances and found it difficult to build a loyal base of support.

Northerners, like Southerners, needed a convincing reason to endure the prolonged sacrifice of the Civil War. For them, the struggle was a distant one, fought mostly on Southern soil far from their homes. Lincoln and other Northern leaders secured support by convincing their compatriots of the importance of preserving the Union. Lincoln eloquently articulated this view, framing the war as more than a military conquest. In a message to Congress on July 4, 1861, he explained that the struggle to preserve the Union was "not altogether for today; it is for a vast future." The president viewed the conflict in global terms, its results affecting the hopes for democratic government around the world. He concluded that the war "embraces more than the fate of these United States. It presents to the whole family of man, the question, whether a constitutional republic . . . can or cannot maintain its territorial integrity, against its own domestic foes."

Lincoln handled disagreement better than Davis did. He defused tense situations with folksy humor, and his simple eloquence captured the imagination of ordinary people, even if it did not persuade his political enemies. Lincoln viewed himself as a man of the people. He was not aloof, like Davis. Friends and critics alike agreed that Lincoln made himself available to them. But even if Jefferson Davis had been a more effective leader than Lincoln, it is unlikely that he could have overcome the odds against him. The key to Southern independence lay less with the Confederacy's president than with its forces on the battlefield.

Lincoln's Fight for the Border States

The secession of Virginia, Arkansas, North Carolina, and Tennessee left four border slave states—Maryland, Delaware, Kentucky, and Missouri—hanging in the balance. Were Maryland and Delaware to secede, the Federal capital at Washington, D.C., would be surrounded by Confederate territory. The loss of Kentucky and Missouri would threaten the borders of Iowa, Illinois, Indiana, and Ohio and remove the Deep South from the threat of imminent invasion. Kentucky's manpower, livestock, and waterways were as important to hold for the Union as they were to gain for the Confederacy. The state also had special symbolic significance as the birthplace of the rival presidents, Lincoln and Davis. Lincoln viewed Kentucky as the key to retaining the three other border states: "I think to lose Kentucky is nearly to lose the whole game. Kentucky gone, we cannot hold Missouri, nor, as I think, Maryland. . . . We would as well consent to separation at once, including the surrender of this capital."

Early reports from the four states were troubling. The governors of Maryland and Delaware, although they did not move to join the Confederacy, politely declined to comply with Lincoln's request for troops. The governors of Kentucky and Missouri responded less politely to the request, firing back angry denunciations of the Federal government.

Maryland's strategic location north of Washington, D.C., rendered its loyalty to the Union vital. Although a majority of its citizens opposed secession, a mob attack on Union troops passing through Baltimore in April 1861 indicated strong pro-Southern sentiment. Lincoln dispatched Federal troops to monitor the fall elections in the state, placed its legislature under military surveillance, and arrested officials who opposed the Union cause, including the mayor of Baltimore. This show of force guaranteed the pro-Union candidate for governor an overwhelming victory and saved Maryland for the Union. Delaware, although nominally a slave state, remained staunchly for the Union.

Missourians settled their indecision by combat. The fighting culminated with a Union victory in March 1862 at the Battle of Pea Ridge, Arkansas. Pro-Confederate Missourians refused to concede defeat and waged an unsuccessful guerrilla war over the next two years.

Kentucky never seceded but attempted to remain neutral at the outset of the war. The Legislature was pro-Union, the governor pro-Southern. Both sides actively recruited soldiers in the state. In September 1861, when Confederate forces invaded Kentucky and Union forces moved to expel them, the state became one of the war's battlegrounds.

Although Virginia went with the Confederacy, some counties in the western part of the state opposed the state's secession and, as early as the summer of 1861, took steps to establish a pro-Union state. In June 1863, West Virginia became the nation's thirty-fifth state.

Strategies and Tactics

To a great extent, the political objectives of each side determined its military strategy. Southerners wanted independence; Northerners fought to preserve the Union. The North's goal required conquest. Federal forces had to invade the South, destroy its armies, and rout its government. Occupying a part of the Confederacy or winning a few battles might reduce the South's ability and will to fight, but as long as there were Confederate armies in the field and a functioning Confederate government, the rebellion would grind on.

The Confederacy, for its part, did not need to conquer the North. Fighting a defensive battle in its own territory, the South had only to hang on until growing Northern opposition to the war or some decisive Northern military mistake convinced the Union to stop fighting.

But the South's strategy had two weaknesses. First, it demanded more patience than the South had shown in impulsively attacking Fort Sumter. Second, the South might not have sufficient resources to draw out the war long enough to swing Northern public opinion behind peace. The question was what would break first, Northern support for the war or Southern ability to wage it?

The Early War, 1861–1862

The North's offensive strategy dictated the course of the war for the first two years. In the West, the Federal army's objectives were to hold Missouri, Kentucky, and Tennessee for the Union, to control the Mississippi River, and eventually to detach the area west of the Appalachians from the rest of the Confederacy. In the East, Union forces sought to capture Richmond, the Confederate capital. The U.S. Navy imposed a blockade along the Confederate coast and pushed into inland waterways to capture Southern ports.

The Confederates defended strategic locations throughout their territory or abandoned them when prudence required. Occasionally taking advantage of surprise or terrain, Southern forces ventured out to engage Union armies. Between engagements, each side sniped at, bushwhacked, and trapped the other.

By the end of 1862, the result remained in the balance. Although Union forces attained some success in the West, Southern armies there remained intact. In the East, where resourceful Confederate leaders several times stopped superior Union forces, Southerners clearly had the best of it.

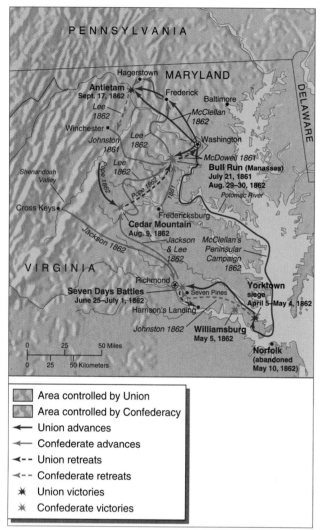

Map 16-1 From First Bull Run to Antietam: The War in the East, 1861–1862
The early stages of the war demonstrated the strategies of both Confederate and Union forces. Federal troops stormed into Virginia hoping to capture Richmond and bring a quick end to the war. Through a combination of poor generalship and Confederate tenacity, they failed. Confederate troops hoped to defend their territory, prolong the war, and eventually win their independence as Northern patience evaporated. They proved successful initially, but, with the abandonment of the defensive strategy and the invasion of Maryland in the fall of 1862, the Confederates suffered a political and morale setback at Antietam.

First Bull Run

By July 1861, the border states appeared more secure for the Union than they had a few months earlier. President Lincoln shifted his attention southward and ordered Union general Irvin McDowell to move Federal forces into Virginia to take Richmond (see Map 16-1). Confronting McDowell 20 miles southwest of Washington at Manassas, an important junction in the

railway that supplied the Confederate capital, was a Confederate army under General P. G. T. Beauregard. Another Confederate force, this one under General Joseph E. Johnston, lay to the west in the Shenandoah Valley. McDowell ordered General Robert Patterson to prevent Johnston from reinforcing Beauregard. Johnston eluded Patterson, however, and boarded his men on trains for Manassas. This was one of the first times trains had been used to move troops during war.

McDowell and Beauregard's armies clashed on July 21 at the **First Battle of Bull Run** (known to the Confederacy as the First Battle of Manassas). The Union forces seemed at first on the verge of winning. But Beauregard's forces, with Johnston's reinforcements, repulsed the assault, scattering not only the Union army but also hundreds of picnickers who had come out from Washington to watch the fight. At the height of the battle, General Barnard Bee of South Carolina called out to Colonel Thomas J. Jackson for assistance. Jackson, a Virginia college professor turned officer, either did not hear Bee or chose to ignore him. In exasperation, Bee shouted, "There stands Jackson—like a damned stone wall!" The rebuke became, in the curious alchemy of battlefield gossip, a shorthand for courage and steadfastness. Jackson's men henceforth called him "Stonewall."

Bull Run dispelled some illusions and reinforced others. It boosted Southerners' confidence and seemed to confirm their boast that one Confederate could whip ten Yankees, even though the opposing armies were of relatively equal strength when the fighting began. The Union rout planted the suspicion in Northern minds that perhaps the Confederates were invincible and destroyed the widespread belief in the North that the war would be over quickly.

The War in the West

While Federal forces retreated in Virginia, they advanced in the West. Two Confederate forts on the Tennessee-Kentucky border, **Fort Henry** on the Tennessee River and **Fort Donelson** on the Cumberland River, guarded the strategic waterways that linked Tennessee and Kentucky to the Mississippi Valley. The forts also defended Nashville, the Tennessee state capital (see Map 16-2). In February 1862, Union general Ulysses S. Grant coordinated a land and river campaign against the forts with Flag Officer Andrew H. Foote, who commanded a force of ironclad Union gunboats.

Grant, recently promoted to brigadier general, had resigned from the military in the 1850s after a mediocre career marked by bouts of excessive drinking. Before rejoining the army, he had worked

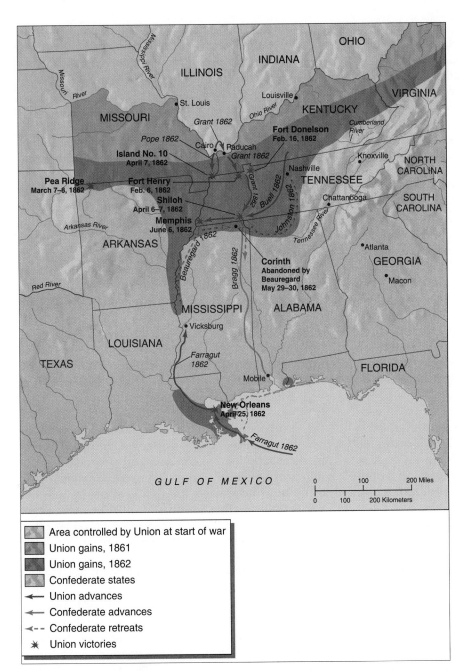

Map 16-2   The War in the West, 1861–1862
Because of the early Union emphasis on capturing Richmond, the war in the West seemed less important to Northerners. But, from a strategic standpoint, the victories at Forts Henry and Donelson, which drove a wedge into southern territory and closed the Confederacy's quickest path to the West from Virginia and the Carolinas, and the capture of New Orleans and its Mississippi River port, were crucial and set the stage for greater Federal success in the West in 1863.

in his family's struggling leather business in Illinois. A plain-looking man with dark brown hair and a beard streaked with gray, he often looked as if he had slept in his uniform. Behind the rumpled appearance lay a flexible military mind that would eventually grasp how the Civil War must be won.

Grant appreciated the strategic importance of river systems in the conquest of the western Confederacy. The Southerners, reflecting their defensive strategy, had concentrated their forces at fixed points. Grant's combined river and land campaign caught them unprepared and outflanked. By Febru-

ary 16, both forts had fallen. The Union victory drove a wedge into Southern territory and closed the Confederacy's quickest path to the West from Virginia and the Carolinas. The Confederacy's only safe link across the Appalachians was now through Georgia. The Confederacy never recovered the strategic advantage in the West after the loss of Forts Henry and Donelson.

Grant next moved his main army south to Pittsburg Landing on the Tennessee River to prepare for an assault on the key Mississippi River port and rail center of Vicksburg. Confederate forces interrupted his planning on April 6, 1862, with a surprise attack on a Federal outpost at **Shiloh Church** near Pittsburg Landing. The raw Federal recruits ran at the first sounds of gunfire, and the Confederates overtook their positions. But the next day, Grant sent in fresh troops and rallied his forces for a fierce counterattack that pushed the Southerners back to Corinth, Mississippi. General Henry W. Halleck, Grant's superior, assumed personal command of the Union troops and captured Corinth in May 1862, but he did not pursue the Confederate army, which slipped away to fight another day.

Federal forces complemented their victories at Shiloh and Corinth with another important success in the western Confederacy. Admiral David G. Farragut, who remained a Unionist even though born in Tennessee, blasted the Confederate river defenses protecting New Orleans and sailed a Federal fleet into the city in April 1862. The result was to open two hundred miles of the Mississippi River, the nation's most vital commercial waterway, to Union traffic. With the fall of Memphis to Union forces in June, Vicksburg remained the only major river town still in Confederate hands.

The fall of New Orleans underscored a major problem with the Confederates' defensive strategy: Their military reserves were stretched too thin to defend their vast territory. The defenses at New Orleans had been weak in part because the troops assigned to them had been shifted north to counter the Union advance in Tennessee.

The Federal offensive in the West had swept into the heart of Dixie. Vicksburg and the rich cottonfields of Mississippi were now vulnerable to Union assault. To the east lay Chattanooga, Tennessee, the last major Confederate bastion protecting Georgia and the eastern Confederacy from Union armies.

Reassessing the War

The fierce fighting at Shiloh wrought unprecedented carnage. Each side suffered more than ten thousand casualties. By the time the smoke had cleared, the soldiers' view of the war had undergone a major transformation. The initial enthusiasm and bravado was replaced by the sober realization that death or capture was a likely outcome and that heroism, courage, and piety did not guarantee survival. A hunger for peace replaced the thirst for battle. "Too shocking too horrible," a Confederate survivor of Shiloh wrote. "God grant that I may never be the partaker in such scenes again. . . . When released from

this I shall ever be an advocate of peace." A Union soldier wrote of "the dead and dying lying in masses, some with arms, legs, and even their jaws shot off, bleeding to death, and no one to wait upon them to dress their wounds."

Landing in a hospital scarcely improved a wounded or ill soldier's chances of survival. Kate Cumming, a nurse at a Confederate hospital in Corinth, wrote of soldiers brought from the battle "mutilated in every imaginable way." The wounded lay packed together on the floor, and Cumming negotiated the rooms with great difficulty to avoid stepping on the dead and dying. Piercing the air were the screams of men undergoing amputations, often with little or no anesthetic. Some pleaded with physicians to kill them and end their misery. Others bore the pain stoically and entrusted last words and letters to nurses, dying with the word "Mother" on their lips.

Women on both sides played a major role in caring for the wounded and sick. As Kate Cumming explained, "In war, the men to fight, and the women to nurse." In the North, members of the **U.S. Sanitary Commission** attempted to upgrade hospital and medical care. This voluntary organization, formed in April 1861, was staffed mainly by women volunteers who collected and distributed medical supplies and clothing and advised on cleaning hospitals and camps. The commission made some headway during the first year of the war, but in the months after Shiloh and with the resumption of fighting in the East, the extent of casualties often overwhelmed the dedicated volunteers. And the bloodiest fighting lay ahead.

Even if a soldier escaped death on the battlefield and survived a hospital stay, he still faced the possibility of death from disease. Roughly twice as many men died from disease than on the battlefield during the Civil War. Heaps of garbage, contaminated food and water, and swarming mosquitoes, flies, and lice created unhealthy camp conditions. Typhoid, commonly and appropriately known as camp fever, claimed the most lives.

Many soldiers turned to religion for consolation in response to the growing carnage. The frequency of camp prayer meetings and revivals increased after Shiloh. Many a recruit carried books with titles such as *Satan's Bait* and *A Mother's Parting Words to Her Soldier Boy* in his knapsack. Soldiers often gathered with their comrades to sing hymns before retiring for the night. Stories circulated of a Bible that stopped a bullet whistling toward a soldier's heart. But veterans knew that a deck of cards did just as well, and they understood that neither Bibles nor cards offered protection against artillery.

Soldiers responded in various ways to constant danger and fear. Some talked or yelled loudly. (The Confederate rebel yell probably served to relieve some of the tension of battle as well as to frighten the enemy.) Others shook so much that they fell down, unable to control their limbs. A few soldiers could not wake up in the morning without being doused with cold water; "they *wanted* to stay out, they couldn't bear to remember all this mess waiting with first light."

The harsh conditions of camp life often strained relations between officers and enlisted men. Volunteers expected the army to follow the same democratic procedures they were used to in civilian life. Companies elected their officers up to the rank of lieutenant and captain, and some regiments elected officers as high as the rank of colonel. Personality rather than ability carried many elections, with incompetence and insubordination the outcome in some cases. Independent young men, unaccustomed to deferring to anyone in civilian life, did not willingly become more docile in the military.

Soldiers also suffered from boredom. Battles rarely lasted more than a day or two. While in camp between engagements, a recruit faced seemingly incessant drilling (loading and firing a rifle required nine separate steps) and heavy chores such as chopping wood and hauling water. Typically, he

Artist Winslow Homer's depiction of the place soldiers spent most of their time: camp. A soldier's life was boredom occasionally interspersed with fierce and deadly combat.

spent what little time remained resting, writing, reading, and eating. To relieve their anxieties, soldiers talked about home and loved ones, upcoming or recent battles, and food. Soldiers also fought the boredom and harsh physical conditions of camp life by singing, playing cards, and competing in sports like footracing and makeshift forms of football and baseball.

Women camp followers cooked, did laundry, and provided sexual services for a price. The two capitals, Washington and Richmond, had notorious vice districts. A Confederate recruit lamented that "almost half of the women in the vicinity of the army, married and unmarried, are lost to all virtue." Both armies experienced soaring rates of venereal disease.

By 1862, the war's carnage and brutality had dispelled any lingering notions of war as a chivalrous enterprise. At a battle in Virginia that year, Stonewall Jackson reprimanded a Confederate general who had ordered his men not to shoot at a Union officer riding before his own men, rallying them on. "This is no ordinary war," Jackson said, "and the brave and gallant Federal officers are the very kind that must be killed. Shoot the brave officers and the cowards will run away and take the men with them." The reluctance of some commanders to pursue retreating armies or to initiate campaigns resulted in part from their recognition of how awful the war really was.

The War in the East

With Grant and Farragut squeezing the Confederacy in the West, Lincoln ordered a new offensive against Richmond in the East that he believed would end the war. Following the defeat at Bull Run, he had shaken up the Union high command and appointed General George B. McClellan to lead what was now called the Army of the Potomac.

A West Point graduate, McClellan had served with distinction in the Mexican War. In 1857, he resigned from the military to pursue a career in business as a railroad official. He was called back into active duty at the outbreak of the Civil War. When he assumed command of the Army of the Potomac, it was no more than a collection of raw recruits and disgruntled veterans. McClellan succeeded in transforming it into a disciplined fighting force. He was well liked by his soldiers, who referred to him affectionately as "Little Mac." McClellan returned their affection, perhaps too much. A superb organizer, he would prove overly cautious on the field of battle.

In March 1862, at the outset of the **Peninsula Campaign**, McClellan moved his 112,000-man army out of Washington and maneuvered his forces by boat down the Potomac River and Chesapeake Bay to the peninsula between the York and James Rivers southeast of the Confederate capital. Union forces took Yorktown, Williamsburg, and Norfolk. The Confederates, commanded by General Joseph E. Johnston, withdrew up the Peninsula toward Richmond, preparing for what most felt would be the decisive battle of the war.

McClellan, moving ponderously up the peninsula, clashed with Johnston's army inconclusively at Seven Pines in late May 1862. Johnston was badly wounded in the clash, and President Davis replaced him with General Robert E. Lee, who renamed the forces under his command the Army of Northern Virginia.

Lee was from a prominent Virginia family long accustomed to power and command. His father, "Light-Horse Harry" Lee, had been a Revolutionary War hero. Lee attended West Point, served with dis-

A career army officer who resigned his commission to serve his state and new country, Confederate General Robert E. Lee's quiet courage and sense of duty inspired his men.

tinction in the Mexican War, and commanded the Federal force that captured John Brown at Harpers Ferry in 1859. In 1831, he married Mary Custis, the granddaughter of George Washington's adopted son. Their gracious home in Arlington, Virginia, had a commanding view of the Potomac and Washington, D.C. Before the war, it had seemed as if Lee would live out his days as a soldier-farmer much like his wife's grandfather.

In 1860, the army posted Lee to Texas, where he watched the secession drama unfold. He opposed secession but was unwilling to take up arms against his native Virginia. Refusing an offer from Winfield Scott to take command of Federal forces, he resigned from the U.S. Army and went with Virginia after it left the Union.

Lee's reserved and aristocratic bearing masked a gambler's disposition. One fellow officer noted, "His name might be Audacity. He will take more chances, and take them quicker than any other general in this country." Under his daring leadership, the Confederacy's defensive strategy underwent an important shift.

As McClellan had been making his way up the peninsula in May, Confederate general Stonewall Jackson had been conducting a brilliant hit-and-run campaign against confused Union troops in the Shenandoah Valley. In an offensive-defensive strategy, Jackson used selective strikes to maneuver the enemy into a vulnerable position and then deliver a decisive blow. It was this aggressive strategy, with its danger of high casualties and its promise of a knockout victory, that Lee persuaded a reluctant President Davis to accept for the confrontation with McClellan.

Jackson's Shenandoah campaign had pinned down Federal troops there, preventing them from reinforcing McClellan in the peninsula. But Lee was able to call on Jackson to reinforce him in the defense of Richmond.

Lee seized the initiative on June 25, 1862, attacking McClellan's right flank. Although inconclusive, the attack pushed the nervous McClellan into a defensive position. For a week, the armies sparred in a series of fierce engagements known collectively as the **Seven Days' Battles**. More than thirty thousand men were killed or wounded on both sides, the deadliest week of the war so far. Although McClellan prevailed in these contests, the carnage so shocked him that he withdrew down the peninsula and away from Richmond. The retreat bitterly disappointed Lincoln, who wanted McClellan to push on to the Confederate capital. The exasperated president ordered

McClellan and the Army of the Potomac back to northern Virginia and placed John Pope at the head of the newly formed Army of Virginia to carry on the fight.

Although Lee had saved Richmond, his troops had suffered frightfully. He had lost one-fourth of his eighty thousand–man army, but he remained convinced of the wisdom of his offensive-defensive strategy. Better coordination between his staff and field commanders, he believed, would have reduced his casualties and inflicted greater damage on the enemy.

Lee and Jackson went to work on John Pope to vindicate their tactics. A series of inconclusive skirmishes, highlighted by Jackson's lightning thrusts at Pope and young J. E. B. Stuart's daring cavalry raid on a Federal base, brought Union and Confederate armies together once more near Manassas Junction. The **Second Battle of Bull Run** was as much a disaster for the Union as the first had been. Lee's generalship completely befuddled Pope and again saved Richmond. With better coordination than they had displayed during the Peninsula Campaign, Lee's forces sustained fewer losses than Pope's army and kept the Federals from moving beyond the positions they held in Virginia at the start of the war. Lee and the Army of Northern Virginia were developing a reputation for invincibility.

Turning Points, 1862–1863

The impressive Confederate victories in the East masked the delicate condition of Southern fortunes. The longer the Confederacy held off Union offensives, the greater the likelihood of securing the South's independence. But the longer the war continued, the higher the probability that the Confederacy's shortcomings in men, finances, and materiel would erode its ability to keep fighting. Lee's offensive-defensive strategy seemed to be working, but it raised the possibility that the Confederacy could exhaust its men and resources before it sealed its independence.

The waning summer months of 1862 brought other concerns to the Davis administration in Richmond. Access to the sea was vital for the South's export economy and its financial well-being. But the Union navy was choking the South's commercial link with Europe.

Davis looked to the nations of Europe for diplomatic recognition as well as for trade. Diplomatic ties would lend legitimacy to the Confederacy's fight for independence. With them might come financial aid, offers to mediate with the North, perhaps even armed intervention against the North. For these same reasons, the Union sought to block recognition. Southern envoys and their Union counterparts sparred in the courts and parliaments of Europe.

But the most important arena of the war remained the battlefield. Diplomatic triumph, financial solvency, and civilian support depended on military success. Having stymied the Union war machine, Lee contemplated a bold move—a thrust into Northern territory to bring the conflict to the North and stoke Northerners' rising hostility to the war. It was a bold plan that might end the war and secure Southern independence—or hasten an otherwise inevitable Union victory.

President Lincoln also harbored a bold plan. Gradually during the spring and summer of 1862, the president had concluded that emancipation of the Confederacy's slaves was essential for preserving the Union. Emancipation would provide Federal forces with both a moral and strategic advantage over their foes. But Lincoln was reluctant to take this step before the Union's fortunes on the battlefield improved. Without a significant victory, emancipation would appear to be an act of desperation.

As the fall of 1862 approached, both Union and Confederate governments prepared for the most significant conflicts of the war to date.

The Naval War

The Union's naval strategy was to blockade the Southern coast and capture its key seaports and river towns. The intention was to prevent arms, clothing, and food from reaching the Confederacy and keep cotton and tobacco from leaving. Destroying the South's ability to carry on trade would also prevent the Confederacy from raising money to purchase the goods it needed to wage war.

Neither side had much of a navy at the outset of the war. With more than 3,000 miles of Confederate coastline to cover, the Union blockade was weak at first. As time passed and the number of ships in the Union navy grew, the blockade tightened. The skyrocketing prices of Southern staples on world markets by 1862 attested to the effectiveness of the Union strategy.

Understandably, the Confederate naval strategy was to break the blockade and defend the South's vital rivers and seaports. The Confederacy attacked the blockade with a variety of weapons. In March 1862, the South refurbished a scuttled Union vessel, the *Merrimac*, with iron plate and renamed it the *Virginia*. The *Virginia* easily destroyed two wooden Union ships blockading Hampton Roads, Virginia. But the Southern advantage was short-lived. The Union navy had outfitted an ironclad of its own, the *Monitor*, and a day after the *Virginia*'s success, the two vessels dueled each other to a draw. Thereafter, the Union navy gained a superiority in ironclads, and the Confederates never seriously threatened the blockade again.

But if the Confederates could not break the blockade, they could evade it. They built several warships to serve as blockade runners and as privateers to attack Union merchant ships. The *Sumter*, under the command of Raphael Semmes, captured eighteen ships in the Caribbean and the Atlantic in 1862. Semmes did even better with his next command, the *Alabama*. In this vessel, he sailed the Atlantic for two years, preying on Union vessels. He seized sixty-four merchant ships and sank a Union warship. The Union cruiser *Kearsarge* finally sent the *Alabama* to the bottom of the Atlantic in June 1864. During the *Alabama*'s rovings, merchants at English ports provided the ship with supplies, fuel, and other support, creating tensions between the Federal and British governments. Although the Confederate navy never seriously threatened Union overseas commerce, insurance rates for Northern merchants rose during the war. And more than seven hundred Union vessels flew the British flag to avoid capture. The Confederate navy also disrupted Federal coastal operations.

Historians disagree about the effectiveness of the Union naval blockade. As late as 1864, the ports of Charleston, Mobile, Wilmington (North Carolina), and Galveston remained in Confederate control and open to blockade runners. The last of these ports did not fall to the Union until January 1865. One estimate suggests that the Union navy captured only one in six blockade runners. The rest succeeded in smuggling in arms, food, and clothing to the Confederacy. With the enormous profits shipowners reaped from blockade running, they could afford to lose some of their ships. Yet high insurance rates and the threat of seizure may have caused some merchants on both sides of the Atlantic to abandon blockade running. In any case, blockade runners were small, light ships, designed for speed and evasion. Their cargo space was small. Larger Southern vessels rarely attempted to slip through the blockade. With limited resources and capital, the Confederacy was heavily dependent on the flow of trade. Any restriction in that flow hurt the Southern cause.

The Diplomatic War

Southerners thought that the recognition of their independence by overseas governments would legitimize their cause in the eyes of the world. They also remembered the crucial role that timely French assistance had played in the American Revolution and hoped for similar support.

Great Britain had several reasons to support the Confederate cause. After two wars and a succession of diplomatic wrangles, it had no great love of the United States. If the country divided, it would pose less of a threat to British economic and territorial ambitions. Also, the aristocratic pretensions of some Southerners appealed to their British counterparts, who viewed the upstart, immigrant-clogged cities of the North with distaste. (One member of Parliament claimed that the Union army was composed of "the scum and refuse of Europe.") Finally, some British textile magnates supported the Confederacy because they feared a drastic reduction in the supply of Southern cotton.

British foreign policy, however, had been antislavery for a quarter century, and the slavery issue turned many Britons against the South. The Union cause had support in high ruling circles, especially from Queen Victoria, as well as from middle-class and working-class Britons. One working-class leader declared the Confederate cause "odious and . . . blasphemous" and hoped for a reunited America that would become "the hope of freedom, and a refuge for the oppressed of every race and of every clime."

Emperor Napoleon III of France, who had imperial designs on Mexico, favored the Confederacy. A restored Union, he thought, would pose a greater threat to his ambitions than a divided one. But Napoleon feared antagonizing the powerful British and would not intervene unilaterally in the Confederate cause.

The Russians were probably the staunchest supporters of the Union abroad. The odd friendship between the Western world's most autocratic country and its most democratic one resulted primarily from political expediency. The Russian tsar, Alexander II, saw the United States as a counterweight to British power. There was also some sympathy for the North's opposition to slavery in Russia, where the tsar had abolished serfdom (a form of slavery) in 1861.

Southerners were convinced that their cotton was so important to the world economy that they could use it as a diplomatic bargaining chip. "You dare not to make war on cotton. . . . Cotton is King." So declared South Carolina senator James H. Hammond in a warning to the North in 1858. A *London Times* correspondent reported that a Southerner told him, "Why, sir, we have only to shut off your supply of cotton for a few weeks and we can create a revolution in Great Britain." But King Cotton was no more successful at coercing the British—who had large cotton reserves and an alternate source of supply in Egypt—into granting recognition to the Confederacy than it was at stopping the North from going to war against the South.

The Davis administration did chalk up some minor diplomatic victories early in the war. Great Britain declared itself neutral and allowed British merchants to sell arms and supplies to both Confederate and Union forces. This policy especially benefited the Confederacy, with its limited arsenal. France followed with a similar concession. Davis almost won a more significant diplomatic victory in November 1861 when a Federal warship overtook the British mail packet *Trent* and, ignoring Britain's neutrality, seized two Confederate diplomats en route to England. The affair outraged the British and pushed Britain and the Union to the verge of war. Lincoln's secretary of state, William Seward, however, advised "one war at a time," and Lincoln agreed. The Confederates were released, and the crisis was defused.

In the end, the Confederacy's hopes for diplomatic recognition depended on its ability to show that it could secure its independence on the battlefield. After Lee's victories in Virginia in the spring of 1862 and his subsequent decision to invade the North, British intervention in the war grew more likely. The British government had more or less decided that if Lee emerged victorious from his planned invasion, it would press for mediation. The United States ambassador to Great Britain, Charles Francis Adams, worried that "unless a very few weeks show some great military result we shall have our hands full in this quarter." William Gladstone, England's future prime minister, believed that Lee would achieve his goal. He concluded that "we may anticipate with certainty the success of the Southern States so far as regards their separation from the North."

Antietam

The alarming arithmetic of the offensive-defensive strategy convinced Lee that the South could not sustain a prolonged conflict. He knew that his army must keep the pressure on Union forces and, if possible, destroy them quickly. Union success in the Mississippi Valley threatened to cut the Confederacy in two and deprive it of the resources of a vast chunk of territory. Within a year, the Confederacy might cease to exist west of the Appalachians. He desperately needed a dramatic victory.

In September 1862, Lee crossed the Potomac into Maryland as his band played "Maryland, My Maryland" for the unimpressed residents. He was on his way to cut off the Pennsylvania Railroad at Harrisburg. Lee established camp at Frederick, scattering his army at various sites, convinced that McClellan and the Army of the Potomac would not attack him.

At this point, luck intervened for the North. At an abandoned Confederate encampment, a Union corporal found three wrapped cigars on the ground, evidently tossed out by a careless Confederate officer. To the corporal's amazement, the wrapping was a copy of Lee's orders for the disposition of his army. But even with this information, "Little Mac" moved so cautiously that Lee had time to gather his and Jackson's regiments and retreat to defensive positions at Sharpsburg, Maryland, along Antietam Creek. There Lee's army of 50,000 men came to blows with McClellan's army of 75,000.

The **Battle of Antietam** saw the bloodiest single day of fighting in American history. About 2,100 Union soldiers and 2,700 Confederates died on the battlefield, and another 18,500, equally divided, were wounded. McClellan squandered his numerical superiority with uncoordinated and timid Union attacks. Although the armies had fought to a tactical draw, the battle was a strategic defeat for the Confederacy. In the battle's aftermath, Lee's troops limped back across the Potomac into Virginia. McClellan did not pursue.

Antietam marked a major turning point in the war. It kept Lee from directly threatening Northern industry and financial institutions. It prompted Britain and France to abandon plans to grant recognition to the Confederacy. And it provided Lincoln with the victory he needed to announce the abolition of slavery.

Emancipation

President Lincoln despised slavery, but he had always maintained that preserving the Union was his primary war goal. "If I could save the Union without freeing any slave I would do it," he wrote to newspaper editor Horace Greeley in August 1862, "and if I could save it by freeing all the slaves I would do it; and if I could save it by freeing some and leaving others alone, I would also do that." An astute politician, Lincoln realized that he had to stress union and equivocate on slavery to keep the Northern public united in support of the war. But from the war's outset, the possibility of emancipation as a war objective was considered in the Republican Congress, within the Union army, and among citizens throughout the Northern states. Northern soldiers, as they moved south, saw slaves building trenches, earthworks, bridges, and roads for the Confederate army as well as working South-

One of the photographs taken by Mathew Brady's photographers at Antietam. By the fall of 1862, any illusions about the romance and adventure of war had dissipated, at least among the competing armies. The outmanned Confederates could ill-afford such heavy casualties as they suffered at Antietam. Although a tactical draw, the battle ended Lee's hope of a Northern invasion and led President Lincoln to issue the Emancipation Proclamation.

ern farms. As a result, pressure grew within the Union army to declare emancipation as a way to deprive the South and the Confederate army of its labor force.

In August 1861, fighting to keep Missouri in the Union, General John C. Frémont broadly interpreted federal legislation allowing Union commanders to confiscate Confederate property and issued a proclamation freeing the state's slaves. Frémont's decree delighted abolitionists but alarmed wavering Unionists in the border states. President Lincoln commanded Frémont to rescind it.

Lincoln said in his inaugural address that he had "no purpose, directly or indirectly, to interfere with the institution of slavery in the states where it exists." Despite the urging of some Republican colleagues, he stood by this pledge and revoked two other emancipation edicts besides Frémont's. By March 1862, however, his moral repugnance toward slavery and the military arguments for abolition led him to propose a resolution, which Congress adopted, supporting the compensated emancipation of slaves. The measure died, however, when Congress failed to appropriate funds for it and border state slaveholders expressed no interest in the plan.

Pressure from Northern civilians, Union soldiers, and Congress for some form of emancipation mounted in the spring of 1862. In response, the Republican Congress prohibited slavery in the territories and abolished slavery in the District of Columbia. The act emancipating the district's slaves called for compensating slave owners and colonizing the freed slaves in black republics such as Haiti and Liberia. Then in July 1862, Congress passed the **Confiscation Act**, which ordered the seizure of land from disloyal Southerners and the emancipation of their slaves.

Although support for emancipation had grown both in the army and among civilians, Lincoln still faced political considerations that dictated against it. Emancipation was still not favored by a majority in the North, especially not in the border states. Lincoln feared a blow to Union military morale, the loss of loyal border states, and a voter backlash in the fall 1862 congressional elections. The thousands of Irish Catholic immigrants who entered the Union army and who had competed with blacks for jobs in Northern cities during the 1850s were especially opposed to emancipation, fearing loss of economic security. Roman Catholic archbishop John Hughes of New York declared that "we Catholics, and a vast majority of our brave troops in the field, have not the slightest idea of carrying on a war that costs so much blood and treasure just to gratify a clique of Abolitionists in the North."

But other considerations favored emancipation. Freeing the slaves would appeal to the strong antislavery sentiment in Britain and gain support for the Union cause abroad. And it would weaken the Confederacy's ability to wage war by removing a crucial source of labor.

By mid-1862, the president had resolved to act on his moral convictions and proclaim emancipation. Taking the advice of Secretary of State Seward, however, he decided to wait for a battlefield victory so that the measure would not appear an act of desperation. Antietam gave the president his opening, narrow though it was, and on September 22, 1862, he announced his intention to issue the **Emancipation Proclamation**, to take effect January 1, 1863, in all states still in rebellion. The proclamation exempted slaves in the border states loyal to the Union and in areas under Federal occupation.

Southerners reacted to the Emancipation Proclamation with outrage. Some viewed it as an invitation to race war and conjured up fears of freed slaves slaying white women and children while their men were at the battlefront. Jefferson Davis, taking a positive view, thought the proclamation would invigorate the Southern war effort. Some observers abroad were skeptical. One London newspaper, noting that emancipation did not apply to all slaves, stated, "The principle is not that a human being cannot justly own another, but that he cannot own him unless he is loyal to the United States." Foreign newspapers and governments questioned the president's sincerity, but the European people supported him. English textile workers who had cause to side with the South because their jobs depended on Southern cotton, supported Lincoln's efforts to "strike off the fetters of the slave."

Northerners generally approved the Emancipation Proclamation. Although abolitionists comprised a minority of the Northern population, most civilians and soldiers accepted emancipation for its military advantages. A private in the Army of the Potomac who had previously expressed serious reservations about emancipation wrote home his support for "putting away any institution if by so doing it will help put down the rebellion." Not all sentiment in the North was so accommodating. Many Democrats opposed the move both for political and personal

Courtesy, Georgia Department of Archives and History.

Throughout the Confederacy, slaves provided valuable support services from building defenses to keeping the railroads running; one of the motives behind the Emancipation Proclamation was to remove or at least limit a vital workforce for the Confederate war effort.

reasons. And some Republicans expressed regret that Lincoln's document was not more sweeping.

But the Emancipation Proclamation represented far more than its qualified words and phrases expressed. "A mighty *act*," Massachusetts governor John Andrew called it. Lincoln had freed the slaves. He and the Union war effort were now tied to the cause of freedom. What began as a war to save the Union had became a holy war of deliverance. Freedom and Union entwined in the public consciousness of the North. As Lincoln noted in his December 1862 message to Congress, "In giving freedom to the slave, we assure freedom to the free." Emancipation also unified the Republican party and strengthened the president's hand in conducting the war.

"Stealing" Freedom

As word of the Emancipation Proclamation raced through the slave grapevine, slaves rejoiced that their long-awaited day of jubilee had arrived. But the proclamation only continued a process that had begun when the first Union armies invaded the

South. In the months before freedom came, many slaves had run away to Union camps, dug Union trenches, and scouted for Federal troops.

Southern masters fought to deter their slaves by severely punishing the families of black men who fled to Union lines. They used the courts and slavecatchers to reclaim runaways. Some Confederate masters protected their investments by removing slaves to Texas or to areas far from Federal forces. And a few slave owners whipped, sold, and even killed their slaves to prevent them from joining Union troops.

But in the end, slaveholders could not stem the tide of slaves fleeing toward the Union lines and freedom. The 1862 Confiscation Act included slaves with other Confederate property as the "contraband" of war and subject to confiscation, a term Union general Benjamin Butler had applied to escaped slaves as early as May 1861. As they helped the Union cause, **contrabands** also sought to help fellow slaves "steal" their freedom. When Union forces occupied part of the Georgia coast in April 1862, for example, March

Even before the Emancipation Proclamation, slaves throughout the South "stole" their free-
dom. After the Proclamation, the trickle of blacks abandoning their masters became a flood, as
they sought freedom behind Union lines.

Haynes, a slave who had worked as a river pilot in Savannah, began smuggling slaves to Union lines. Federal general Quincy Adams Gillmore provided a swift boat for Haynes's missions. In return, Haynes supplied Gillmore with "exact and valuable information" on the strength and location of Confederate defenses.

The former slaves who arrived at Federal camps after emancipation often encountered poor conditions but relished their freedom nonetheless. A Northern missionary in occupied Louisiana wrote in 1863 that he was surrounded by "negroes in uniform, negroes in rags, negroes in frame houses, negroes living in tents, negroes living in rail pens covered with brush, and negroes living under brush piles without any rails, negroes living on the bare ground with the sky for their covering; all hopeful . . . every one pleading to be taught, willing to do anything for learning."

The Emancipation Proclamation accelerated the slaves' flight from bondage. Personally fighting to secure their freedom and liberating those still enslaved became the objective of many, for after 1863, ex-slaves served in increasing numbers in the Union army.

Black Troops in the Union Army

More than 80 percent of the roughly 180,000 black soldiers and 20,000 black sailors who fought for the Union were slaves and free blacks from the South. For the typical Southern black who joined the army, the passage from bondage to freedom

COME AND JOIN US BROTHERS.
PUBLISHED BY THE SUPERVISORY COMMITTEE FOR RECRUITING COLORED REGIMENTS
1210 CHESTNUT ST. PHILADELPHIA.

Once orders were issued allowing the recruitment of black troops, posters like this appeared throughout the North. The illustrations stressed the dignity and manhood of military service, but also showed segregated soldiers and white officers.

came quickly. Making his escape from his master, he perhaps "stole" his family as well. He typically experienced his first days of freedom behind Union lines, where he may have learned to read and write. Finally, he put on the Federal uniform, experiencing as one Southern black volunteer commented, "the biggest thing that ever happened in my life."

As early as August 1862, five thousand African-Americans had enrolled in the Union army in the occupied Sea Islands off South Carolina despite a widely publicized Confederate directive promising to shoot black prisoners of war. This threat was later withdrawn when Union officers declared that they would do the same with Confederate prisoners. The Confederacy, however, held fast to its refusal to parole, or send back, captured black soldiers, a policy that led to the end of prisoner exchanges in early 1863 and contributed to horrible conditions in overcrowded prisoner-of-war camps on both sides.

Initially, the enlistment of blacks in South Carolina encountered opposition in the North. By early 1863, however, public opinion was changing. One reason was that white Northerners realized that the enlistment of African-Americans relieved them

in comparable numbers from military service. President Lincoln strongly advocated enlisting former slaves. In March 1863, he wrote with exaggerated enthusiasm, "The bare sight of 50,000 armed and drilled black soldiers on the banks of the Mississippi would end the rebellion at once."

On the contrary, the appearance of black Union troops infuriated the Confederates. After a battle at Milliken's Bend, Mississippi, in 1863, for example, observers found dead Confederate and black Union soldiers entangled in each other's arms and impaled on one another's bayonets.

But for blacks, the promise of freedom and redemption outweighed the dangers of combat. Black abolitionists campaigned tirelessly for the enlistment of free blacks and fugitive slaves in the Union army. Frederick Douglass, whose son Lewis distinguished himself in the all-black 54th Massachusetts Volunteer Infantry Regiment, explained in early 1863, "Once let the black man get upon his person the brass letters, 'U.S.,' let him get an eagle on his buttons and a musket on his shoulder and bullets in his pockets, and there is no power on earth which can deny that he has earned the right to citizenship in the United States." Other black abolitionists took up the refrain. Sojourner

American Views

LEWIS DOUGLASS ON THE FIGHTING OF THE 54TH MASSACHUSETTS REGIMENT

When the Civil War began, Union officials did not permit African Americans to enlist. But northern blacks successfully pressured the Lincoln administration to reverse that policy and began fighting in all-black units as early as 1862. The excerpt here is a letter from Lewis Douglass (son of black abolitionist Frederick Douglass) of the 54th Massachusetts Regiment to his wife after the failed Union assault on Fort Wagner in South Carolina.

❖ **What motivated northern blacks, all of whom were free, to enlist by the thousands in the Union army?**

July 20 [1863]

My Dear Amelia:

I have been in two fights, and am unhurt. I am about to go in another I believe tonight. Our men fought well on both occasions. The last one was desperate. We charged that terrible battery on . . . Fort Wagner and were repulsed. . . . I escaped unhurt from amidst that perfect hail of shot and shell. It was terrible. . . . This regiment has established its reputation as a fighting regiment. Not a man flinched, though it was a trying time. Men fell all around me. . . . Our men would close up again, but it was no use. . . . How I got out of that fight alive I cannot tell, but I am here. My dear girl, I hope again to see you. I must bid you farewell should I be killed. Remember if I die, I die in a good cause. I wish we had a hundred thousand colored troops. We would put an end to this war.

Your own loving
Lewis

Source: *Carter G. Woodson, ed.,* The Mind of the Negro as Reflected in Letters Written During the Crisis 1800–1860 *(1926).*

Truth, a former slave who saw many of her thirteen children sold into slavery, canvassed northern cities to rally public opinion for the deployment of black troops.

Although blacks were eager to engage the enemy and fought as ably as their white comrades, they received lower pay than whites and performed the most menial duties in camp. Abolitionists and black leaders in the North pressured President Lincoln for more equitable treatment of African-American recruits. When Frederick Douglass complained to Lincoln about the lower pay that black troops received, the president defended the practice, noting that "their enlistment was a serious offense to popular prejudice" and the fact "that they were not to receive the same pay as white soldiers seemed a necessary concession to smooth the way to their employment at all as soldiers."

Despite discrimination, blacks fought valiantly at Port Hudson, Louisiana; near Charleston; and, late in the war, at the siege of Petersburg, Virginia. After hearing of African-American troops fighting Confederate forces nearby, one young white Mississippian wrote in her diary, "It is said the Negro regiments fought there like mad demons." The most celebrated black encounter with Confederate troops occurred in July 1863 during a futile assault by the 54th Massachusetts Regiment on **Fort Wagner** outside Charleston (see "American Views: Lewis Douglass on the Fighting of the 54th

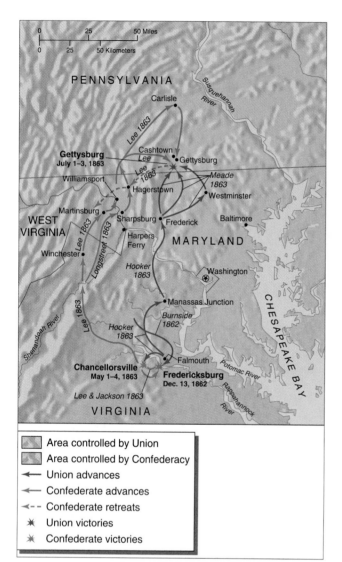

Map 16-3   *From Fredericksburg to Gettysburg: The War in the East, December 1862–July 1863*
By all logic, the increasingly outgunned and out-financed Confederacy should have been showing signs of faltering by 1863. But bungling by Union generals at Fredericksburg and Chancellorsville sustained Southern fortunes and encouraged Robert E. Lee to attempt another Northern invasion.

Massachusetts Regiment"). The Northern press, previously lukewarm toward black troops, heaped praise on the effort. "Through the cannon smoke of that dark night," intoned a writer in the *Atlantic Monthly*, "the manhood of the colored race shines before many eyes that would not see."

If only President Lincoln could find such gallantry among his generals! George McClellan had failed to follow his advantage at Antietam in September 1862, allowing Lee's army to escape to Vir-

ginia and remain a formidable fighting force. And despite Union successes in the West, the Confederate forces massed there remained largely intact.

Fredericksburg and Chancellorsville

In late 1862, after Antietam, the president replaced McClellan with General Ambrose E. Burnside. The new chief of the Army of the Potomac, an imposing physical presence, sported bushy whiskers on his cheeks that came to be known as "sideburns," a transposition of the two parts of his name. Despite his commanding stature, Burnside was shy and insecure. Claiming incompetence, he had twice refused the command. His judgment proved better than Lincoln's.

Moving swiftly against Lee's dispersed army in northern Virginia, Burnside reached the Rappahannock River opposite **Fredericksburg** in November 1862 (see Map 16-3). But the pontoon bridges to ford his 120,000 soldiers across the river arrived three weeks late, giving Lee an opportunity to gather his 78,000 men. On December 13, the Union forces launched a poorly coordinated and foolish frontal assault that the Confederates repelled, inflicting heavy Federal casualties. Burnside, having performed to his own expectations, was relieved of his command, and Major General Joseph Hooker was installed in his place.

The hard-drinking Hooker lacked Burnside's humility but not his incompetence. Resuming the offensive in the spring of 1863, Hooker hoped to outflank Lee. But the Confederate commander surprised Hooker by sending Stonewall Jackson to outflank the Union right. Between May 1 and May 4, Lee's army delivered a series of crushing attacks on Hooker's forces at **Chancellorsville**. Outnumbered two to one, Lee had pulled off another stunning victory—but at a high cost. Lee lost some thirteen thousand men, fewer than Hooker's seventeen thousand. But it was a price the Confederacy could ill afford to pay.

Lee also lost Stonewall Jackson at Chancellorsville. Nervous Confederate sentries mistakenly shot and wounded him as he returned from a reconnoitering mission, and he died a few days later. Known for his lightning strikes at the enemy and his brilliant understanding of the tactics of modern warfare, Jackson had helped Lee win some of the Confederacy's most stunning victories in 1862. Lee recognized the tragedy of Jackson's loss for himself and his country. "Any victory," the Confederate commander wrote, "would be dear at such a price. I know not how to replace him."

Still, Lee appeared invincible. Chancellorsville thrust Lincoln into another bout of despair.

MASTER ABRAHAM LINCOLN GETS A NEW TOY.

"Master Abraham Lincoln gets a new Toy." The "toy" in this case is Major General Joseph Hooker, who, in late 1862, became the latest in a frustrating line of musical-chair generals whom President Lincoln appointed in the hope of achieving a decisive victory over Confederate forces. Not until Grant and Sherman emerged the following year, did the President find generals who were not only willing to fight, but to fight well.

"My God!" he exclaimed in agony, "What will the country say! What will the country say!" Meanwhile, Lee, to take advantage of the Confederacy's momentum and the Union's gloom, planned another bold move. On June 3, 1863, the 75,000-man Army of Northern Virginia broke camp and headed north once again.

Gettysburg

President Lincoln sent the Union Army of the Potomac after Lee. But General Hooker dallied, requested more troops, and allowed the Confederates to march from Maryland into Pennsylvania. An infuriated Lincoln replaced Hooker with George Gordon Meade.

Lee and Meade were personal friends—they had served together during the Mexican War—and the change in command worried the Confederate general. He had counted on the bungling Hooker as his opponent. "General Meade," he commented prophetically, "will commit no blunder in my front."

Meade set out after the Confederate army, which was encamped at Cashtown, Pennsylvania, 45 miles from Harrisburg. That the greatest battle of the war erupted at nearby **Gettysburg** was pure chance. A Confederate brigade left Cashtown to confiscate much-needed shoes in Gettysburg. Meeting Federal cavalry resistance near the town, the brigade withdrew. On July 1, 1863, a larger Confederate force advanced toward Gettysburg to disperse the cavalry and seize the shoes. What the Confederates did not realize was that the entire Army of the Potomac was coming up behind the cavalry (see Map 16-4).

During the first day of battle, July 1, the Confederates appeared to gain the upper hand, forcing Union forces back from the town to a new position on Cemetery Hill. On the second day, the entire Union army was in place, but the Confederates seized the initiative and took several key locations along Cemetery Ridge before Federal forces pushed them back to the previous day's positions. Although the opposing sides had suffered heavy casualties, both armies were intact, and if anything,

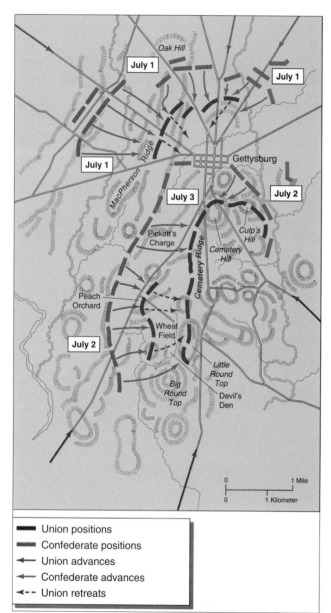

Map 16-4   The Battle of Gettysburg, July 1–3, 1863
In a war that lasted four years, it is difficult to point to the decisive battle. But clearly the outcome during those hot July days at Gettysburg set the tone for the rest of the war. The result was unclear until the final day of battle and, even then, it might have gone either way. Winning by a whisker was enough to propel Union armies to a string of victories over the next year, and throw Confederate forces back on their defenses among an increasingly despairing population. Gettysburg marked the last major Southern invasion of the North.

Lee had the advantage. On July 3, the third day of the battle, Lee made a fateful error. Believing that the center of Meade's line was weak, he ordered an all-out assault against it. The night before, Meade

had remarked to his colleague, Brigadier General John Gibbon, "If Lee attacks tomorrow, it will be in your front. He has made attacks on both our flanks and failed and if he concludes to try it again, it will be on our center." Thus Meade was prepared for Lee's assault.

The next morning, a bright, hot summer day, the Confederates launched an assault on Culp's Hill, only to fall back by noon. The key battle of the day occurred at three in the afternoon at Cemetery Ridge, preceded by a fierce artillery duel. When the Union guns suddenly went silent, the Confederates, thinking they had knocked them out, began a charge led by General George Pickett. As the Confederate infantry marched out with battle colors flying, the Union artillery opened up again, supported by Federal riflemen. They tore apart the charging Southerners. Some managed to reach their objective, a low stone wall at the crest of the hill, but the Federals who held the wall outnumbered them and pushed them back. The Confederates retreated down the gentle slope strewn with their fallen comrades, the hopes of a Southern victory dashed. Half of Pickett's thirteen thousand–man division lay dead or wounded.

At Gettysburg, Lee had violated his own rule never to order a frontal assault. After the battle, he explained, "I believed my men were invincible." By the second day of the battle, he may have been suffering from combat fatigue. He managed only one message to his generals in the field that day. Meade, in contrast, remained in constant touch with his staff. After Pickett's charge, Lee rode among his troops and urged them to brace for a final Union assault. The attack never came. Meade allowed Lee to withdraw into Maryland and cross the Potomac to Virginia.

Gettysburg was the bloodiest battle of the war. The Union suffered 23,000 casualties; the Confederacy, 28,000 (see "American Views: The Horror of Battle"). Yet Lincoln blasted Meade for failing to follow up on his victory. "I do not believe you appreciate the magnitude of the misfortune involved in Lee's escape," he wrote to his general. "He was within your easy grasp, and to have closed upon him would, in connection with our other late successes, have ended the war. As it is, the war will be prolonged indefinitely. . . . Your golden opportunity is gone, and I am distressed immeasurably because of it." Convinced by his aides that Meade would resign when he read the letter, Lincoln never sent it.

Legend (map key):

- Union positions
- Confederate positions
- Union advances
- Confederate advances
- Union retreats

American Views

THE HORROR OF BATTLE

In this excerpt, Union general Carl Schurz describes a field hospital just after the battle of Gettysburg in July 1863. The horrors of the Civil War evoked countless such testimonials. The unprecedented carnage quickly dispelled notions of the romance of war on both sides.

❖ **Why would Schurz, a Republican, depict the hospital scene in such graphic terms?**

At Gettysburg the wounded—many thousands of them—were carried to the farmsteads behind our lines. The houses, the barns, the sheds, and the open barnyards were crowded with moaning and wailing human beings, and still an unceasing procession of stretchers and ambulances was coming in from all sides to augment the number of the sufferers. A heavy rain set in during the day . . . and large numbers had to remain unprotected in the open, there being no room left under roof. I saw long rows of men lying under the eaves of the buildings, the water pouring down upon their bodies in streams.

Most of the operating tables were placed in the open where the light was best, some of them partially protected against the rain by tarpaulins or blankets stretched upon poles. There stood the surgeons, their sleeves rolled up to the elbows, their bare arms as well as their linen aprons smeared with blood, their knives not seldom held between their teeth, while they were helping a patient on or off the table, or had their hands otherwise occupied; around them pools of blood and amputated arms or legs in heaps, sometimes more than man-high.

Carl Schurz

Source: *Carl Schurz*, The Reminiscences of Carl Schurz, *vol. 3 (1907–1908).*

Vicksburg

When Lincoln mentioned "our other late successes" in his letter to Meade, he was referring to another crucial Union victory. On July 4, one day after Pickett's charge at Gettysburg, the city of **Vicksburg**, the last major Confederate stronghold on the Mississippi, surrendered to Ulysses S. Grant.

Grant is often perceived, incorrectly, as a general who ground out victories by dint of his superior numbers, with little finesse and less concern for his troops' safety. "The Butcher," as some called him later, did make mistakes, but he fretted about the lives of his troops as much as any other commander. In his campaigns in the western Confederacy, he demonstrated an ability to use his forces creatively, swiftly, and with a minimum loss of life.

Vicksburg presented Grant with several strategic obstacles (see Map 16-5). The formidable defenses on the city's western edge, which towered over the Mississippi, had thwarted a naval assault by Union admiral David G. Farragut in May 1862. And an assault by William T. Sherman later that year had failed in the labyrinth of swamps, creeks, and woods that protected the city from the north. The only feasible approaches appeared to be from the south and east.

By March 1863, Grant had devised a brilliant plan to take Vicksburg that called for rapid maneuvering and expert coordination. Grant had his twenty thousand Union troops ferried across the Mississippi from the Louisiana side at a point south of Vicksburg. Then he marched them quickly into the interior of Mississippi. Cut off from supplies, they moved

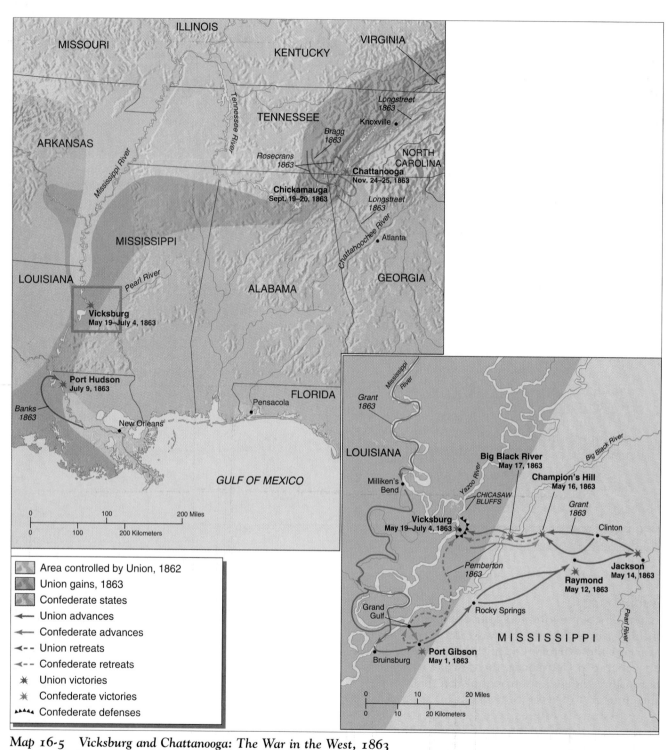

Map 16-5   Vicksburg and Chattanooga: The War in the West, 1863
Devising a brilliant strategy, Union General Ulysses S. Grant took the last major Mississippi River stronghold from Confederate hands on July 4, 1863, dealing a significant economic and morale blow to southern forces. Coupled with the defeat at Gettysburg a day earlier, the fall of Vicksburg portended a bitter finale to hopes for Southern independence. Grant completed his domination of the West by joining forces with several Union generals to capture Chattanooga and push Confederate forces into Georgia setting the stage for the capture of that key southern state by the Federals in 1864.

northeastward, captured the Mississippi state capital at Jackson, and turned west toward Vicksburg. On May 22, 1863, Grant settled down in front of the city, less than 600 yards from Confederate positions. Grant's tight siege and the Union navy's bombardment from the river cut the city off completely. As food stores dwindled, residents were forced to eat mules and rats to survive. Their situation hopeless, General John Pemberton and his thirty thousand–man garrison surrendered on July 4.

Chattanooga

As Grant was besieging Vicksburg in June 1863, Union general William S. Rosecrans, commanding the Army of the Cumberland, advanced on Confederate general Braxton Bragg, whose Army of Tennessee held **Chattanooga**, a "doorway" on the railroad that linked Richmond to the Lower South. The capture of the city would complete the uncoupling of the West from the eastern Confederacy.

Bragg lacked confidence in his men and consistently overestimated the force and cunning of his enemy. At Rosecrans's approach, he abandoned Chattanooga and took up positions at nearby Chickamauga Creek. Recognizing the importance of the pending battle, President Davis ordered Lee to send General James Longstreet and eleven thousand troops to reinforce Bragg.

When the two armies clashed at Chickamauga on September 19, Bragg and Longstreet pushed Rosecrans back to Chattanooga. Union general George Thomas, unaware of Rosecrans's retreat, withstood a furious Confederate onslaught. This feat, which slowed but did not break the Southern advance, earned Thomas the nickname "Rock of Chickamauga." Bragg seized the railroad leading into Chattanooga and bottled up Rosecrans there much as Grant had confined Pemberton at Vicksburg. Both sides had suffered heavily—the Federals with sixteen thousand casualties and the Confederates with eighteen thousand. But the prospect of recovering Chattanooga and capturing an entire Union army banished Confederate concerns about casualties at least for the moment.

Suddenly, the Union's careful strategy for the conquest of the western Confederacy seemed in jeopardy. President Lincoln, determined to hold Chattanooga and deal a heavy blow to the Army of Tennessee, shuffled his command, replacing Rosecrans with Thomas and appointing Grant to head all Union operations in the West.

The Confederate position on the heights overlooking Chattanooga appeared impregnable. But the Confederate camp was plagued by dissension. Some officers openly questioned Bragg's ability. President Davis considered replacing him but had no one else available with Bragg's experience. Instead, he ordered Longstreet (along with one-third of Bragg's army) on a futile expedition against Union forces at Knoxville, Tennessee. Converging on Chattanooga with reinforcements, Union generals Grant, Sherman, and Hooker took advantage of the divided Confederate army to break the siege. In a series of precise and coordinated maneuvers, the four generals captured Confederate positions and forced Bragg's army to retreat into Georgia. The Union now dominated most of the West and faced an open road to the East.

The War in the Trans-Mississippi West

The Confederacy's reverses at Vicksburg and Chattanooga mirrored its misfortunes farther west beyond the Mississippi River. Although a relatively minor theater of war, the territory west of the Mississippi provided supplies and strategic advantages for the Confederate West. Success in the Trans-Mississippi West could occupy Federal troops and relieve pressure from other parts of the Confederacy while allowing food and munitions to reach desperate Southern armies.

The loyalties of Native Americans in the Trans-Mississippi West generally split evenly between the Union and the Confederacy. Three regiments of Cherokee Indians, led by Colonel (later Brigadier General) Stand Watie, fought for the South at the Battle of Pea Ridge in 1862. The Union won the battle and with it control of Missouri and northern Arkansas. Most battles between pro-Union and pro-Confederate Native American forces occurred in the Indian Territory (now Oklahoma).

Texas was critical to Confederate fortunes, both as a source of supply for the East and as a base for the conquest of the Far West. President Davis envisaged a continental Confederacy that included California, with its gold fields and Pacific ports. The ports would give the Confederacy access to Asian trade and, Davis reasoned, weaken the Federal naval blockade.

Texas, however, was far from secure. It suffered from internal dissent and violence on its borders. Texans, like many other Southerners, were ambivalent about secession. As early as 1862, areas of northern Texas, a Unionist stronghold before the war, rebelled against Confederate authorities and were brutally suppressed. Germans in the Fredericksburg–San Antonio area openly defied the Confederacy from 1862 until

SUMMARY

MAJOR BATTLES OF THE CIVIL WAR, 1861–1863

Battle or Campaign	Date	Outcome and Consequences
First Bull Run	July 21, 1861	Confederate victory, destroyed the widespread belief in the North that the war would end quickly, fueled Confederate sense of superiority
Forts Henry and Donelson	Feb. 6–16, 1862	Union victory, gave the North control of strategic river systems in the western Confederacy and closed an important link between the eastern and western Confederacy
Shiloh Church	Apr. 6–7, 1862	Union victory, high casualties transformed attitudes about the war on both sides
Seven Days' Battles	June 25–July 1, 1862	Standoff, halted Union General McClellan's advance on Richmond in the Peninsula Campaign
Second Bull Run	Aug. 29–30, 1862	Confederate victory, reinforced Confederate General Robert E. Lee's reputation for invincibility
Antietam	Sept. 17, 1862	Standoff, halted Lee's advance into the North, eliminated Confederacy's chance for diplomatic recognition, encouraged Lincoln to issue the Emancipation Proclamation
Fredericksburg	Dec. 13, 1862	Confederate victory, revived morale of Lee's army
Chancellorsville	May 2–6, 1863	Confederate victory, Confederate General Stonewall Jackson killed, encouraged Lee to again invade North
Gettysburg	July 1–3, 1863	Union victory, halted Confederate advance in the North, major psychological blow to Confederacy
Vicksburg	Nov. 1862–July 1863	Union victory, closed the key remaining Confederate port on the Mississippi, with Gettysburg, dealt a severe blow to Confederate cause
Chattanooga	Aug.–Nov. 1863	Union victory, solidified Union dominance in the West and cleared the way to Atlanta

the war's end. And the Mexican population in southern Texas supported the Union. On the state's western border, Comanches raided homesteaders at will until late 1864. In the east and along the southern frontier in the lower Rio Grande Valley, Union gunboats and troops disrupted Confederate supply lines. For a time, Texas maintained commercial contact with the rest of the Confederacy through Matamoros, Mexico. But by 1864, with the Union in control of the Mississippi, Texas had lost its strategic importance.

The Confederacy's transcontinental aspirations died early in the war. In March 1862, a Confederate army seeking to conquer the Southwest was overwhelmed by Union forces at the **Battle of Glorieta Pass** in New Mexico. The Southwest from New Mexico to California would remain firmly in Union hands.

Conclusion

By late fall 1863, the Civil War was over in large portions of the former Confederacy. Northern forces controlled the Mississippi River and all the ports along its banks. Federal gunboats patrolled other rivers in the Confederate West, and Union troops garrisoned strategic forts along these waterways.

The Confederacy had also lost the war over slavery in many parts of the South. Tens of thousands of slaves abandoned plantations, farms, and towns to find freedom behind Union lines, depriving the South of their labor. And when many former slaves signed on to fight with Union armies, the South suffered doubly.

Not the least of Union advantages in the fall of 1863 was the ability of President Lincoln to articulate the meaning of the war for soldiers and civilians, for Americans and Europeans. In November, the president was asked to say a few words at the dedication of the federal cemetery at Gettysburg. There, surrounded by a somber scene of fresh graves, Lincoln bound the cause of the Union to that of the country's founders: "Fourscore and seven years ago our fathers brought forth upon this continent a new nation, conceived in liberty and dedicated to the proposition that all men are created equal. Now we are engaged in a great civil war, testing whether that nation, or any nation so conceived and so dedicated can long endure."

Many Confederate leaders had proclaimed, though less eloquently, a similar connection between their government and the Revolutionary generation. But the Emancipation Proclamation allowed Lincoln to make an even broader and bolder claim for the significance of the conflict. A Union victory would not only honor the past but also call forth a new nation, cleansed of its sins, to serve as an inspiration to oppressed peoples around the world. He called on the nation to resolve "that the nation shall, under God, have a new birth of freedom; and that government of the people, by the people, for the people, shall not perish from the earth." Not only did the two-minute Gettysburg Address capture what Union supporters were fighting for, but it also connected their sacrifices to the noble causes of freedom and democratic government.

Without battlefield victories, similar claims by the Davis administration would ring hollow. Historians have often noted how Lincoln articulated the Union cause better than Davis did the Confederate cause. Whatever shortcomings the Southern president suffered as an orator, however, the worsening situation on the battlefield left him little to say. The Confederacy's hopes now rested increasingly on Robert E. Lee and the Army of Northern Virginia. Despite two unsuccessful invasions of the North, Lee remained unbeaten on Southern soil. But time was running out for the general and his government. The incompetence of the Union commanders he had faced so far exaggerated his brilliance. Eventually, Lincoln would find a general to test the Army of Northern Virginia.

The Confederacy also faced an enemy with a seemingly endless reserve of troops and supplies. The North thrived on war and victory, while the South's economy and will faltered with defeat. The outcome of the war was not yet foreordained. The South still had armies in the field, a government in Richmond, and a heart for independence. But the Confederate cause was growing desperate.

Review Question

1. How did the Union and the Confederacy compare in terms of resources, leadership, and military strategies in the period 1861–1863? What impact did these factors have on the course of the war?

2. What was the significance of the battles of Antietam and Gettysburg? In what ways were they turning points in the Civil War?

3. If you were a Confederate general, what would you have done differently at Gettysburg? At Vicksburg?

4. What effects did the Emancipation Proclamation have on both the Union and Confederate causes?

Recommended Reading

Stephen Crane, *The Red Badge of Courage* (1895; reprinted 1984). The Civil War did not inspire great American novels. But this is a notable exception that not only depicts the horrors of combat, but its impact on the soldiers who fought.

Shelby Foote, *The Civil War: A Narrative*, 3 vols. (1958–1974). For a highly readable, if weighty, narrative of the Civil War, these volumes are an excellent choice. Although the account is thin on interpretation and obviously omits recent research on blacks and women in the war, it is a balanced, comprehensive view of the conflict.

James M. McPherson, *Battle Cry of Freedom: The Civil War Era* (1982). This is probably the best account of the war in print. It is more up-to-date than the Foote volumes, and more interpretive. The author draws a number of interesting conclusions on several controversial topics from military strategy to the home front.

Additional Sources

Mobilization, North and South

Richard N. Current, *Lincoln's Loyalists: Union Soldiers from the Confederacy* (1992).

William C. Davis, *"A Government of Our Own": The Making of the Confederacy* (1994).

William C. Davis, *Jefferson Davis: The Man and His Hour* (1991).

David Donald, *Lincoln* (1995).

Paul D. Escott, *After Secession: Jefferson Davis and the Failure of Southern Nationalism* (1978).

Drew Gilpin Faust, *The Creation of Confederate Nationalism: Ideology and Identity in the Civil War* (1988).

George M. Fredrickson, *The Inner Civil War: Northern Intellectuals and the Crisis of Union* (1965).

Archer Jones, *Civil War Command and Strategy: The Process of Victory and Defeat* (1992).

George C. Rable, *The Confederate Republic: A Revolution against Politics* (1994).

Charles Royster, *The Destructive War: William Tecumseh Sherman, Stonewall Jackson, and the Americans* (1991).

The Early War, 1861–1862

Michael Fellman, *Inside War: The Guerrilla Conflict in Missouri during the Civil War* (1989).

Gerald F. Linderman, *Embattled Courage: The Experience of Combat in the American Civil War* (1989).

James M. McPherson, *What They Fought For, 1861–1865* (1994).

Grady McWhiney and Perry Jamieson, *Attack and Die: Civil War Military Tactics and the Southern Heritage* (1982).

Reid Mitchell, *Civil War Soldiers* (1988).

Clarence L. Mohr, *On the Threshold of Freedom: Masters and Slaves in Civil War Georgia* (1986).

Stephen W. Sears, *George B. McClellan: The Young Napoleon* (1988).

Stephen W. Sears, *To the Gates of Richmond: The Peninsula Campaign* (1992).

Turning Points, 1862–1863

Ira Berlin et al., eds., *Freedom: A Documentary History of Emancipation, 1861–1867, Ser. 1, Vol. 1: The Destruction of Slavery* (1985).

Paul D. Casdorph, *Lee and Jackson: Confederate Chieftains* (1992).

Dudley T. Cornish, *The Sable Arm: Negro Troops in the Union Army, 1861–1865* (1966).

LaWanda Cox, *Lincoln and Black Freedom: A Study in Presidential Leadership* (1981).

Paul D. Escott, *Slavery Remembered: A Record of Twentieth-Century Slave Narratives* (1979).

Eric Foner, *Nothing but Freedom: Emancipation and Its Legacy* (1983).

John Hope Franklin, *The Emancipation Proclamation* (1963).

Ernest B. Furgurson, *Chancellorsville, 1863: The Souls of the Brave* (1992).

Louis S. Gerteis, *From Contraband to Freedman: Federal Policy toward Southern Blacks, 1861–1865* (1973).

Joseph T. Glatthaar, *Forged in Battle: The Civil War Alliance, Black Soldiers and White Officers* (1990).

Robert W. Johannsen, *Lincoln, the South, and Slavery: The Political Dimension* (1991).

Alvin M. Josephy Jr., *The Civil War in the American West* (1993).

William S. McFeely, *Grant: A Biography* (1981).

James M. McPherson, *The Negro's Civil War: How American Negroes Felt and Acted* (1965).

Alan T. Nolan, *Lee Considered: General Robert E. Lee and Civil War History* (1991).

Benjamin Quarles, *The Negro in the Civil War* (1953).

Stephen W. Sears, *Landscape Turned Red: The Battle of Antietam* (1983).

David Paul Smith, *Frontier Defense in the Civil War: Texas' Rangers and Rebels* (1992).

Garry Wills, *Lincoln at Gettysburg: The Words That Remade America* (1992).

Where to Learn More

❖ **Museum of the Confederacy, Richmond, Virginia.** This museum has rotating exhibits on various aspects of the Confederate effort during the Civil War, both on the home front and on the battlefield. The Confederate White House, which is open to the public, is next door to the museum.

❖ **Gettysburg National Military Park, Gettysburg, Pennsylvania.** An excellent and balanced interpretation awaits the visitor at this national park. For a similar experience, visit **Antietam National Battlefield, Sharpsburg, Maryland.**

❖ **Various locations.** Many southern states, where most of the war was fought, have historic sites related to battles or significant events such as Manassas National Battlefield Park; Fredericksburg and Spotsylvania County Battlefields; Memorial National Military Park; Shiloh National Military Park; Vicksburg National Military Park; and Chickamauga and Chattanooga National Military Park.

17 THE UNION PRESERVED
THE CIVIL WAR, 1863–1865

Pacific Ocean

Portland

Sacramento
San Francisco

Salt Lake City

Santa Fe

San Antonio

Galveston

Omaha

Kansas City

Chicago

St. Louis

Memphis

Vicksburg

New Orleans

Gulf of Mexico

Mexico City

Antebellum Transportation Systems

— Railroads, c. 1850
— Canals
— Cumberland Road
— Stagecoach routes
------- Trails

Territorial Expansion

Thirteen original colonies, 1776

Westward expansion to 1783

Louisiana Purchase, 1803

Red River Basin, 1818

Florida, 1819

Annexation of Texas, 1845

Oregon Territory, 1846

Mexican cession, 1848

Gadsden Purchase, 1853

N
W E
S

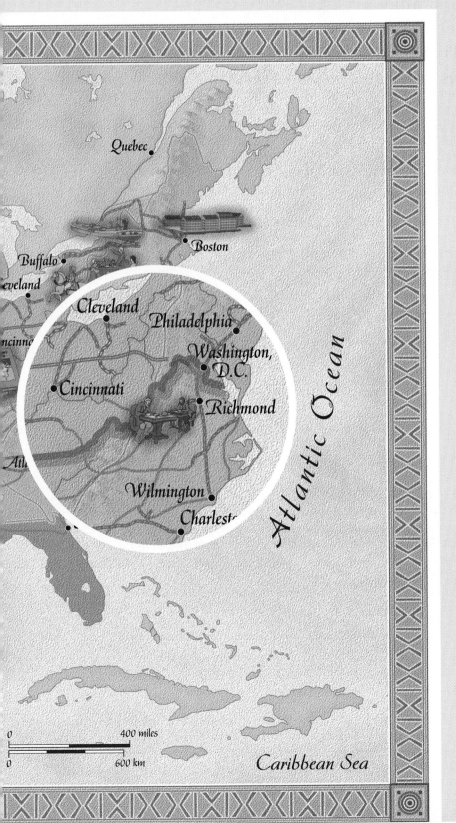

KEY TOPICS

❖ The impact of the war on Northern political, economic, and social life

❖ How military reversals affected Confederate political and economic life and civilian morale

❖ The strategies and campaigns of Union generals Grant and Sherman in 1864 and 1865

❖ The meaning of the Civil War for the nation and its citizens

*C*olonel Alfred Pike of North Carolina and his men trained their rifles on the prisoner. They wanted information, but she refused to talk. Desertion from the Confederate army had increased during 1864, and Pike suspected that she knew the location of several deserters. Exasperated, Pike ordered his men to tie her thumbs together "behind her back & suspend her with a cord tied to her two thumbs thus fastened behind her to a limb so that her toes could just touch the ground." The colonel later reported with satisfaction that the woman "told some truth" after a while.

As this incident reflects, by late in the Civil War, the South was a nation at war with itself. Its people and government were reeling from the impact of defeat. Economic collapse, declining civilian morale, and desertion were undermining the Confederate cause as much as military setbacks were.

In the meantime, the Union juggernaut rolled on. The North's strong economy stoked the war effort. The Lincoln administration formulated aggressive economic and military policies to win the war and secure the peace. The North, too, suffered social and political disruption, but the marvelous elixir of battlefield victory did wonders to allay these ills, if only temporarily.

For black Southerners, the war against slavery was almost over, and another war to secure the fruits of freedom had begun. Disagreement arose between North and South, black and white, Congress and president over what those fruits should be even as the Civil War raged on. The differing perceptions of freedom would haunt the nation for generations.

But for the immediate future, winning the war remained paramount for the Union. As Lincoln and his generals prepared the North's final campaigns, the South hoped General Lee could produce one last miracle.

War Transforms the North

Union successes by 1863 had a profound impact on both sides. For the North, hopes of victory and reunion increased. The Federal government expanded its bureaucracy to wage war efficiently, and a Republican-dominated Congress passed legislation that broadened Federal power and furthered the war effort. The Lincoln administration faced opposition on these measures and on its conduct of the war from within Congress, from the Democratic party, and from state leaders. But it successfully weathered dissent thanks to the president's political skill, the desire of the Republicans to remain in power, and the Union's improving military fortunes. Boosted by Federal economic legislation and wartime demand, the Northern economy boomed. Women entered the work force in growing numbers. But labor unrest and class and racial tensions suggest that prosperity had a price.

Wartime Legislation and Politics

Before the Civil War, the Federal government rarely affected citizens' lives directly. But raising troops, protecting territory, and mobilizing the economy for war required the kind of strong and active central government the Republican party favored. With the departure of the South from the Union, Republicans dominated all branches of the Federal administration. This left them in a position to test the constitutional limits of federal authority.

President Lincoln began almost immediately to use executive authority to suppress opposition to the war effort in the North. Within the first few weeks of the conflict, he ordered raids on telegraph offices in the North and the seizure of telegrams to intercept seditious messages to the South. In one of his most controversial actions, he also issued a temporary suspension of the writ of **habeas corpus**, the constitutional requirement that authorities explain before a court their legal reasons for arresting someone. Habeas corpus protects a defendant against illegal imprisonment. Suspending it allowed authorities

A Republican propaganda piece, painted in 1862, depicting the President dealing with "Copperheads"—the Republican term for northern war dissenters; an Irish Democrat restrains Lincoln, reflecting the Republicans' association of treasonous dissent with Democrats and their Catholic immigrant allies.

to arrest suspected Confederate agents and hold them indefinitely. The Constitution forbids suspension of the writ except "when in cases of Rebellion or Invasion the public Safety may require it." Explaining his extraordinary actions in a July 4, 1861, message to Congress, Lincoln stated, "It became necessary for me to choose whether I should let the government fall into ruin, or whether . . . availing myself of the broader powers conferred by the Constitution in case of insurrection, I would make an effort to save it." Some citizens objected. New England abolitionist Wendell Phillips charged that "Abraham Lincoln sits today a more unlimited despot than the world knows this side of China." But most Republicans supported the president, and Congress approved his action.

Executive sanctions fell particularly hard on the Democratic party. "Disloyalty" was difficult to define in the midst of war. Though many Democrats opposed secession and supported the Union, they challenged the president on the conduct of the war, on emancipation, and on Lincoln's coolness toward peace initiatives. Those opposed to Republican policies formed secret societies in Ohio, Indiana, and Illinois. Republicans, exaggerating the danger of the societies, accused them of plotting to form a Northwest Confederacy. Most of the groups were harmless and operated under the loose guidance of the Democratic party. But a few had ties with Confederate agents. Republicans called these dissenters "Copperheads," after the poisonous snake.

It was hard to know where sympathy for the South ended and active support of the Confederacy began. For some Republicans, the distinction was not worth making. They knew that Confederate agents were active in the North, planning sabotage and obtaining military information, and they suspected that sympathetic Northerners were assisting them.

Federal laws were in place to punish disloyalty, but the courts enforced them poorly. Bypassing Congress and the judiciary in September 1862, Lincoln declared a suspension of habeas corpus for the duration of the war. His decree subjected antiwar protesters and later, draft resisters and persons accused of more serious activities against the administration to arbitrary arrest. Those detained faced military, not civilian, courts and were subject to military punishments. More than fourteen thousand citizens were arrested under Lincoln's decree. Few, however, lived in the North, and few were antiwar critics. Most lived in the border states and were detained for trading with the enemy, defrauding the War Department, draft evasion, blockade running, and guerrilla activities.

In April 1866, a year after the war ended, the U.S. Supreme Court in *Ex parte Milligan* held that Lincoln's declaration was unconstitutional. "Martial rule," the court decided, "can never exist where the courts are open. . . . It is . . . confined to the locality of actual war."

Despite the suspension of habeas corpus, Lincoln compiled a fairly good record for upholding basic American civil liberties. Although the authorities shut down a handful of newspapers temporarily, the administration made no attempt to control the news or subvert the electoral process. Two major elections were held during the war. In the first, the off-year election in 1862, Republicans retained control of Congress but lost several seats to Democrats. In the presidential election of 1864, Lincoln won reelection in a hard-fought contest.

While fellow Republicans sometimes chastised the president for violating civil liberties, mismanaging military command assignments, or moving too slowly on emancipation, they rarely threatened to disrupt the party or the administration over political or philosophical differences. Party discipline, though sometimes tenuous, kept most Republicans behind the administration on crucial issues. Republican governors often found common ground with the Lincoln administration. State governments supported the war to save the Union, and state leaders did not obstruct Lincoln's exercise of his role as commander in chief. Although congressional Republicans grumbled about Lincoln's expansion of executive authority, they did not attempt to override his

CHRONOLOGY

1862 May: Congress passes Homestead Act.

1862 July: Congress passes Federal Land Grant College Act (Morrill Act).

1862 September: President Lincoln suspends the writ of habeas corpus.

1863 February: Congress passes National Banking Act.

1863 July: New York Draft Riot occurs.

1864 May: Battle of the Wilderness.

1864 June: Battle of Cold Harbor.

1864 September: Sherman captures Atlanta.

1864 November: President Lincoln is reelected. Sherman begins his march to the sea.

1865 January: Congress passes Thirteenth Amendment to the Constitution, outlawing slavery (ratified December 1865).

1865 February: Charleston surrenders.

1865 March: Confederate Congress authorizes enlistment of black soldiers.

1865 April: Federal troops enter Richmond. Lee surrenders to Grant at Appomattox Court House. Lincoln is assassinated.

---

executive decrees. In some instances, they passed complementary measures or ratified his actions, as in the Habeas Corpus Act of March 1863. The strength of the Democratic party in the North also reinforced party loyalty among Republicans.

But there was dissent in the Republican party, and it had an effect on national policy. **Radical Republicans** hounded Lincoln from early in his administration, establishing the **Joint Committee on the Conduct of the War** to examine and monitor military policy. Some of them accused Democratic generals, including McClellan, of deliberately subverting the war effort with their poor performance. They also pressed Lincoln for quicker action on emancipation, the enlistment of black troops, and the confiscation of rebel property. The radicals did not, however, sacrifice party unity to ideological purity. They supported the president on most crucial matters.

Lincoln likewise supported his party on an array of initiatives in Congress. Republicans had unsuccessfully pursued some of these before the war. Now, with a Republican president and a comfortable majority in both houses, they enacted them into law. Turning to the settlement of the West, they passed the **Homestead Act** in May 1862. This granted 160 acres of land free to any settler in the territories who agreed to improve the land (by cultivating it and erecting a house) within five years of the grant. In addition to offering a fresh start to farmers whose land elsewhere had played out, the act was a boon for railroad companies. (Congress had passed a similar bill in 1860, but President Buchanan vetoed it.)

Other legislation to boost the nation's economy included the **Land Grant College Act** of 1862, a protective tariff that same year, and the **National Banking Act** of 1863. The Land Grant Act awarded the proceeds from the sale of public lands to the states for the establishment of colleges offering instruction in "agriculture and mechanical arts." (President Buchanan had also vetoed an earlier version of this act.) The tariff legislation protected Northern industry from foreign competition while raising revenue for the Union. It stimulated industrial output, contributing to the surge in manufacturing that began in the North during the Civil War and continued after it. Southern Democrats had vigorously opposed such legislation, fearing that foreign ports would retaliate by raising taxes on Southern cotton.

The National Banking Act of 1863 replaced the bank notes of individual states, which were often backed by flimsy reserves and subject to wild fluctuations in value, with a uniform national currency. It authorized existing and new banks in several cities throughout the country to issue bank notes backed by United States bonds and guaranteed by Washington. The consequences of the act would contribute to financial hardship later in the century, but when it was passed, it brought order to a chaotic monetary system and boosted the creditworthiness of the federal government.

Changes in the disposition of federal lands, the protective tariff, and the establishment of a national banking system presaged the active role the federal government would henceforth play in shaping the nation's economy. These measures helped sustain the Union war effort and enjoyed widespread support. The expansion of government into other areas, however, aroused opposition in some quarters, none more than the draft laws.

Conscription and the Draft Riots

Congress passed the first national conscription law in 1863. Almost immediately, evasion, obstruction, and weak enforcement threatened to undermine it. As military authorities began arresting draft dodgers and deserters, secret societies formed to harbor draftees and instruct them on evasion. In Wisconsin, the governor begged federal officials to send six hundred troops to enforce draft notices.

Conflicts between citizens and federal officials over the draft sometimes erupted in violence. The worst draft riot occurred in New York City in July 1863. Opposition to what many perceived as the Republican's war ran deep in New York, and support for the Democratic party was strong. The city's merchants were hurting from their lost trade in Southern cotton, and its Irish workers feared competition for jobs from freed slaves migrating to the North. Many in New York's large ethnic population found the Protestant morality and anti-immigrant nativism of some Republicans offensive.

The **New York Draft Riot** began when a mostly Irish mob protesting conscription burned the federal marshal's headquarters. Racial and class antagonisms quickly joined antidraft anger as the mob went on a rampage through the city's streets, fighting police, plundering houses of the wealthy, and crying, "Down with the rich!" The rioters hanged two blacks who wandered into their path and burned the Colored Orphan Asylum. City authorities and the police stood by unable or unwilling to stem the riot, which claimed eighty lives. It was finally quelled by army units fresh from Gettysburg, along with militia and naval units. The draft resumed a month later.

The Northern Economy

"The North," one historian has said, "was fighting the South with one hand and getting rich with the other behind its back." After an initial downturn during the uncertain months preceding the war, the Northern economy picked up quickly. High tariffs and massive federal spending soon made up for the loss of Southern markets and the closing of the Mississippi River. Profits skyrocketed for some businesses. The earnings of the Erie Railroad, for example, jumped from $5 million in 1860 to $10 million in 1863. New industries boomed, and new inventions increased manufacturing efficiency. For example, technological advances in the sewing machine industry, which was first commercialized in the 1850s, greatly increased the output of the North's garment factories. Production of petroleum, a lubricant, increased from 84,000 gallons to 128 million gallons during the war.

Despite the loss of manpower to the demands of industry and the military, the productivity

The lynching of a black New Yorker during the Draft Riots in July 1863. The violence against blacks during the riots reflected decades of racial tensions, especially between Irish immigrants and blacks, over jobs and housing.

of Northern agriculture grew during the war. As machines replaced men on the farm, the manufacturers of farm machinery became wealthy. Crop failures in Europe dramatically increased the demand for American grain. Exports of wheat from the United States to Great Britain jumped from less than 25,000 pounds in 1859 to 1.2 million pounds in 1862. "Old King Cotton's dead and buried; brave young Corn is king," went a popular Northern refrain of the day. Northern crops brought in $955 million in 1863 and nearly $1.5 billion a year later. The resulting profits spread throughout the economy as Northerners, according to one disapproving observer, went on a shopping spree "unexampled, even in the history of our wasteful people."

Working people should have benefited from wartime prosperity. With men off to war and immigration down, labor was in short supply. But workers reaped minimal gains. Although wages increased, prices rose more. Declining real wages led to exploitation, especially of women in garment factories.

Workers organized to combat poor working conditions and low wages. The trade union movement, which suffered a serious setback in the depression of 1857, revived. Local unions of shoemakers, carpenters, and miners emerged in 1862 across the North, and so did a few national organizations. Unions divided along racial and gender lines, and some ethnic groups formed their own workers' associations. By 1865, more than 200,000 Northern workers belonged to a labor union.

Employers struck back at union organizing by hiring strikebreakers, usually blacks. Labor conflicts between striking white workers and black strikebreakers sparked riots in New York City and Cincinnati. The racial antagonism accounted in part for workers' opposition to Lincoln's Emancipation Proclamation and for the continued strength of the Democratic party in Northern cities. White workers supported the Democrats because they feared that freed slaves would flood Northern cities as a result of Lincoln's policies, undercutting wages and taking white workers' jobs.

The promise of enormous profits bred greed and corruption as well as exploitation. Illicit trade between North and South was inevitable when cotton could be bought at 20 cents a pound in New Orleans and sold for $1.90 a pound at Boston. Profiteers not only defied the government to trade with the enemy but also sometimes swindled the government outright. Some merchants reaped high profits supplying the army with shoddy goods at inflated prices. A writer for *Harper's Weekly* complained that "soldiers, on the first day's march or in the earliest storm, found their clothes . . . scattering to the wind in

rags." Some Yankee soldiers experienced leaky tents, tainted meat, and wormy grain. With winning the war taking precedence over fiscal prudence, even parties who dealt legitimately with government agencies could expect handsome returns.

Some Northerners viewed the spending spree uneasily. They were disturbed to see older men flaunting their wealth while young men were dying on the battlefield. "The lavish profusion in which the old southern cotton aristocracy used to indulge," wrote an indignant reporter for the *New York World*, "is completely eclipsed by the dash, parade, and magnificence of the new northern shoddy aristocracy. . . . The individual who makes the most money—no matter how—and spends the most money—no matter for what—is considered the greatest man."

Exploited workers likewise resented the "shoddy aristocracy." Speaking at a labor rally in New York City, one man said bitterly of the wealthy people profiting from the war, "Union with them means no more nor less than that they want the war prolonged that they may get the whole of the capital of the country into their breeches pocket and let it out at a percentage that will rivet the chain about your neck."

Comments like these hinted at the deep social and ethical problems that were emerging in Northern society and would become more pronounced in the decades after the Civil War. For the time being, the benefits of economic development for the Union cause outweighed its negative consequences. The thriving Northern economy fed, clothed, and armed the Union's soldiers and kept most civilians employed and well fed. Prosperity and the demands of a wartime economy also provided Northern women with unprecedented opportunities.

Northern Women and the War

More than 100,000 Northern women took jobs in factories, sewing rooms, and arsenals during the Civil War. Stepping in for their departed husbands, fathers, and sons, they often performed tasks previously reserved for men, but at lower pay. The expanding bureaucracy in Washington also offered opportunities for many women. The United States Treasury alone employed 447 women in the war years. And unlike private industry, the federal government paid women and men equally for the same work.

Women also had the opportunity to serve the war effort directly in another profession previously dominated by men—nursing. Physicians and officers, however, although they tolerated women nurses as nurturing morale boosters, thought little of their ability to provide medical care. Women sometimes challenged this condescending view, braving dismissal to confront

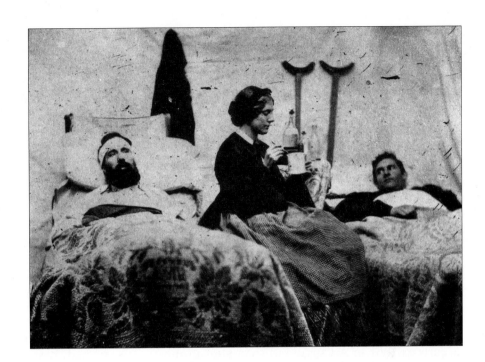

Nurse Ann Bell tends a fallen Union soldier. Although medical practices were primitive and many young men died from poorly treated wounds or disease, the U.S. Sanitary Commission attempted to improve care in Union hospitals during the war. The war helped open nursing as a respectable occupation for women.

the medical-military establishment head-on. Clara Barton, among the most notable nurses of the war, treated soldiers on the battlefield at great peril to her safety and to the consternation of officers. One of them remarked to her, "Miss Barton, this is a rough and unseemly position for you, a woman, to occupy." She shot back, "Is it not as rough and unseemly for these pain-racked men?" The officer temporarily suspended Barton for her candor. A British journalist, impressed by Barton and the thousands of women like her, commented that no conflict in history was so much "a woman's war" as the Civil War.

If the war created opportunities for many women, it also left tens of thousands widowed and devastated. In a society that assumed that men supported women, the death of a husband could be a financial and psychological disaster. Many women were left to survive on meager pensions with few skills they could use to support themselves.

The new economic opportunities the war created for women left Northern society more open to a broader view of women's roles. One indication of this change was the admission of women to eight previously all-male state universities after the war. Like the class and racial tensions that surfaced in Northern cities, the shifting role of women during the Civil War hinted at the promises and problems of postwar life. The changing scale and nature of the American economy, the expanded role of govern-

ment, and the shift in class, racial, and gender relations are all trends that signaled what historians call the "modernization" of American society. Many of these trends began before the war, but the war highlighted and accelerated them.

The Confederacy Disintegrates

Even under the best of conditions, the newly formed political and economic institutions of the Confederacy would have had difficulty maintaining control over the country's class and racial tensions. But as battlefield losses mounted, the Confederacy disintegrated.

Victory is a marvelous glue. Defeat dissolves the bonds that hold a small society like the Confederacy together and exposes the large and small divisions within it. After 1863, defeat infected Confederate politics, ruined the Southern economy, and eventually invaded the hearts and minds of the Southern people. The Davis administration tried to deal with a maddening array of dissenting or indifferent politicians. But the deteriorating military situation and the impending Confederate economic collapse doomed these efforts. The South pinned its waning hopes on its defensive military strategy. If it could prolong the conflict a little longer, perhaps a war-weary North would replace Lincoln and the Republicans in the 1864 elections with a Democratic president and Congress inclined to make peace.

Southern Politics

Dissent plagued Southern politics before the end of the war's first year, and before defeat and privation sapped Confederate morale. Residents of western Virginia mounted a secession movement of their own, declaring themselves for the Union and forming the new state of West Virginia. Several counties in north Alabama, in German-speaking districts in Texas, and throughout the mountains of Tennessee and North Carolina contemplated similar action. Most Southern Unionists supported the war once the fighting began.

But as the war turned against the Confederacy, southerners increasingly turned against each other. Some joined the peace societies that emerged as early as 1861 in Arkansas and soon after in most other Southern states. North Carolinians opposed to the war formed the **Order of the Heroes of America**, whose members not only demonstrated for peace but took control of the Piedmont and mountain sections of the state as well. Other Southerners preferred quieter dissent. They refused to join the army, pay taxes, or obey laws prohibiting trade with the enemy.

States' rights, a major principle of the seceding states, proved an obstacle to the Davis administration's efforts to exert central authority. The governors of Georgia and North Carolina gave the Richmond government particular difficulty, hoarding munitions, soldiers, supplies, food, and money. At one point, Georgia's governor contemplated a separate peace between his state and the United States. Even cooperative governors refused to allow state agents to collect taxes for the Confederacy.

Unlike Abraham Lincoln, Jefferson Davis could not appeal to party loyalty to control dissent because the Confederacy had no parties. Davis's frigid personality, his insistence on attending to minute details, and his inability to accept even constructive criticism gracefully also set him apart from Lincoln and worsened political tensions within the Confederacy. Deteriorating military fortunes after 1863 added significantly to his political problems.

Several parts of the South began clamoring for peace during the fateful summer of 1863. In a tour of his state that year, North Carolina political leader Jonathan Worth heard calls for the overthrow of the Davis administration and a separate peace

with the North. "Every man [I] met," he concluded "was for reconstruction on the basis of the old [U.S.] constitution." By November 1864, the Confederacy suffered as much from internal disaffection as from the attacks of Union armies. Confederate authorities could not suppress civilian unrest in Virginia, North Carolina, and Tennessee, and Union spies operated openly in Mobile, Wilmington, and Richmond.

Divisions among Confederate officials themselves added to the growing disarray of the Davis administration. Some Southern politicians and journalists, long accustomed to an opposition role in national affairs before secession, maintained it after secession in the Confederacy. When Union general George B. McClellan crept toward Richmond in 1862, for example, the *Richmond Examiner* accused the Davis administration of dragging its feet in imposing martial law on the city. "To the dogs with Constitutional questions and moderation!" one editorial screamed. Less than two years later, however, when Davis suspended habeas corpus in several areas threatened by Union armies, the *Examiner* unleashed a tirade against the president for acting unconstitutionally, warning him that he was the people's "servant" and not their "dictator."

Davis and other Confederate leaders might have averted some of these political problems had they succeeded in building a strong sense of Confederate nationalism among soldiers and civilians. They tried several strategies to do so. For example, Davis tried to identify the Confederacy's fight for independence with the American Revolution of 1776. But egalitarian Revolutionary ideals quickly lost their appeal in the face of poverty, starvation, and defeat. Davis also tried to cast the Confederacy as a bastion of freedom standing up to Lincoln's despotic abuse of executive authority, but he, too, eventually invoked authority similar to Lincoln's. Some Southerners saw slavery as the cornerstone of the Confederacy. But Davis understood that identifying the Southern cause too closely with slavery risked alienating foreign governments and dividing Southern whites. Confederate religious leaders sought to distinguish their new nation from the North by referring to Southerners as God's "chosen people." But when Confederate military fortunes declined, religious leaders drew back from such visions of collective favor and stressed the need for individual salvation.

Secession and the early battles gave Southerners a common purpose but not a common nation. The diaries of Southern soldiers reveal devotion to God, state, locality, family, and friends but rarely to the Confederacy. Battlefield and economic reverses diminished what national feeling there was. Planters in the lower Mississippi Valley, for example, quickly succumbed to Union offers of cash for cotton. Desertion increased, and the will to resist Federal troops declined. Worn out, fed up, and homesick, some Confederate soldiers just called it quits.

In a devout society convinced it was fighting a holy war, some Southerners sought some moral failing to account for their mounting losses. Some identified slavery as the culprit. A Confederate leader in South Carolina asked in 1864, "Are we not fighting against the moral sense of the world? Can we hope to succeed in such a struggle?" In a similar vein, a Louisiana woman admitted that "always I felt that moral guilt of it [slavery], felt how impossible it must be for an owner of slaves to win his way into Heaven."

Thoughts about heaven may have come more frequently to white Southerners after 1863 as the Southern economy collapsed and many civilians struggled simply to survive.

The Southern Economy

Defeat came to the South, according to one historian, "not because the government failed to mobilize the South's resources" but "because there was virtually nothing left to mobilize." By 1863, the Confederacy was having a difficult time feeding itself. Destruction of farms by both sides and growing Union control of waterways and rail lines restricted the distribution of food. Speculators held certain commodities off the market to drive up prices, making shortages worse. People ate rats and mules to supplement their meager diets. Lacking access to salt, an essential food preservative, they obtained it by evaporating sea water or by boiling the salt-saturated soil from the floors of smokehouses. Bread riots erupted in Mobile, Atlanta, and Richmond. In Mobile, a group of women marched under banners reading "Bread or Blood" and "Bread and Peace." Armed with hatchets, they looted stores for food and clothing. In a show of grim humor, people in Southern cities held "starvation parties" at which they served only water.

More than one-quarter of Alabama's population was receiving public welfare by the end of the war. "Deaths from starvation have absolutely occurred," a Confederate official in the state informed President Davis in 1864. As the price of medicines skyrocketed, Southerners tried ineffectual home remedies. One

Wartime food shortages, skyrocketing inflation, and rumors of hoarding and price-gouging drove women in several southern cities to protest violently. Demonstrations like the 1863 food riot shown here reflected a larger rending of southern society as Confederate losses and casualties mounted on the battlefield. Some Southern women placed survival and providing for their families ahead of boosting morale and silently supporting a war effort that had taken their men away. Their defection hurt the Confederate cause.

recommended treatment for diphtheria was to smear the patient with lard.

Southern soldiers had marched off to war in neat uniforms with shiny buttons, many leaving behind self-sustaining families. But in August 1863, diarist Mary Chesnut, wife of a Confederate official in Richmond, watched ten thousand men marching near Richmond and commented, "Such rags and tags as we saw now. Most garments and arms were . . . taken from the enemy." The soldiers' families were threadbare as well. The prohibitive cost of new clothing prompted a group of women in northern Georgia to raid a textile mill for calico cloth in 1863. During the winter of 1863–1864, women lined their clothes with rags and newspapers to keep warm. In the devastated areas near battle sites, civilians survived by selling fragments of dead soldiers' clothing stripped off their bodies and by collecting spent bullets and selling them for scrap.

A privileged few avoided such hardship. Mary Chesnut noted the contrast between rich ladies "in their landaus . . . with tall footmen in livery" and the shabbiness of "poor soldiers' wives . . . on the sidewalks."

The predations of both Union and Confederate soldiers further threatened civilians in the South. The women and children left alone on farms and plantations were vulnerable to stragglers and deserters from both armies. One Louisiana woman described how "for more than a year past, lawless men have been permitted to band themselves together, and roam at will . . . insulting, chastising, robbing, burning houses, murdering the families of our soldiers; and in some instances despoiling in the most brutal manner, wives, daughters and sisters of that which is dearer than life itself—their honor."

Southerners also feared that slaves on isolated plantations would rise up against their masters. Most slaves, however, were more intent on escape than revenge. There was no point in murdering the master or his family when freedom was just out the door and down the road to the Union lines. There was no point in sacking the big house when a Union regiment would make short work of the whole plantation and all others around it. Escaped slaves had children, husbands, wives, and other relatives to find and spirit away to Union camps. The business of freedom was too time-consuming to waste on whites. Leave it to God to mete out punishment for the evil of bondage.

Some slaves felt genuine affection for the families they served and stayed on with them even after the war. Some protected whites from Union soldiers and hid valuables for them. But women forced to manage plantations alone could never be sure where their slaves stood. Mary Chesnut wrote in her diary about her mother's butler: "He looks over my head—he scents freedom in the air." As slaves stopped working and abandoned plantations, the women left to run them had to work the fields themselves.

As Confederate casualties mounted, more and more Southern women and children, like their Northern counterparts, faced the pain of grief. Funeral processions became commonplace in the cities and black the color of fashion. With little food, worthless money, and a husband or father gone forever, the future looked bleak.

Southern Women and the War

In the early days of the Civil War, Southern white women continued to live their lives according to antebellum conventions. Magazine articles urged them to preserve themselves as models of purity for men debased by the violence of war. The Southern woman, by her moral example, "makes the confederate soldier a gentleman of honor, courage, virtue and truth, instead of a cut-throat and vagabond," opined one magazine. She would buttress the nation's morale through the wavering fortunes of war. On her shoulders rested "the destinies of the Southern Confederacy," the *Natchez Weekly Courier* declared.

Women flooded newspapers and periodicals with patriotic verses and songs. A major theme of these works, illustrated by the following example from the *Richmond Record* in September 1863, was the need to suppress grief and fear for the good of the men at the front:

The maid who binds her warrior's sash
And smiling, all her pain dissembles,
The mother who conceals her grief
[had] shed as sacred blood as e'er
was poured upon the plain of battle.'

A Virginia woman confided to her diary, "We must learn the lesson which so many have to endure—to struggle against our feelings."

By the time of the Civil War, such emotional concealment had become second nature to Southern white women. They had long had to endure their anguish over their husbands' nocturnal visits to the slave quarters. They were used to the condescension of men who assumed them to be intellectually inferior. And they accepted in bitter, self-sacrificing silence the contradiction between the myth of the pampered leisure they were presumed to enjoy and the hard demands their lives actually entailed.

But some Southern women chafed at their supporting role and, as Confederate manpower and materiel needs became acute, took on new productive responsibilities. Initially, they did so within the domestic context: Women formed clubs to sew flags and uniforms. To raise money for the war effort, they held benefits and auctions and collected jewelry and other valuables.

Soon, however, the needs of the Confederacy drew women outside the home to fill positions vacated by men. They managed plantations. They worked in the fields alongside slaves, and if they had worked there before, they worked harder. They worked in factories to make uniforms and munitions. They worked

Rose O'Neal Greenhow, a Washington, D.C., socialite and widow, was one of several Southern women who spied for their country. Here she is photographed with her daughter in Washington before her deportation to Richmond in 1862. Greenhow drowned off the coast of North Carolina in 1864 as a Union warship ran her blockade runner aground.

in government offices as clerks and secretaries. They taught school. A few, like Belle Boyd and Rose O'Neal Greenhow, spied for the Confederacy. And many, like their Northern counterparts, served as nurses. Eventually, battlefield reverses and economic collapse undermined all these roles, leaving women and men alike struggling simply to survive.

Not all women shared the patriotic fervor that impelled some to toil to support the war effort. As the war dragged on and the Southern economy deteriorated, even the patriots suffered from resentment and doubt. By 1864, many women were helping their deserting husbands or relatives elude Confederate authorities. In Randolph County, North Carolina, for example, two women torched a barn belonging to a state official in charge of rounding up deserters. Incidents like these convinced authorities that women were mainly responsible for the high desertion rate in the last years of the war. A North Carolina official explained that "desertion takes place because desertion is encouraged. . . . And though the ladies may not be willing to concede the

fact, they are nevertheless responsible . . . for the desertion in the army and the dissipation in the country" (see "American Views: Southern Women against the War").

By 1864, Southern white women had tired of the war. What had begun as a sacred cause had disintegrated into a nightmare of fear and deprivation. Some women turned to work, others to protest, and many to religion. Some devoutly religious women concluded that it was God, not the Yankees, who had brought destruction on the South for its failure to live up to its responsibilities to women and children.

The Union Prevails, 1864–1865

Despite the Union's dominant military position after Vicksburg and Gettysburg and the Confederacy's mounting home-front problems, three obstacles to Union victory remained. Federal troops under General William T. Sherman controlled Chattanooga and the gateway to Georgia, but the Confederate Army of Tennessee, commanded by Joseph E. Johnston, was still intact, blocking Sherman's path to Atlanta. Robert E. Lee's formidable Army of Northern Virginia still protected Richmond. And the Confederacy still controlled the rich Shenandoah Valley, which fed Lee's armies and supplied his cavalry with horses. In March 1864, President Lincoln brought General Ulysses S. Grant to Washington and appointed him commander of all Union armies. Grant set about devising a strategy to overcome these obstacles.

Grant's Plan to End the War
Grant brought two innovations to the final campaign. First, he coordinated the Union war effort. Before, the Union's armies in Virginia and the West had operated independently, giving Confederate leaders the opportunity to direct troops and supplies to whichever arena most needed them. Now Grant proposed to deprive them of that option. The Union's armies in Virginia and the Lower South would attack at the same time, keeping steady pressure on all fronts. Second, Grant changed the tempo of the war. Before, long periods of rest had intervened between battles. Grant, with the advantage of superior numbers, proposed nonstop warfare. As he explained, he wanted to "hammer continuously against the armed force of the enemy and his resources, until by mere attrition, if in no other way, there should be nothing left to him but an equal submission with the loyal section of our common country to the constitution and laws of the land."

American Views

SOUTHERN WOMEN AGAINST THE WAR

As Confederate military fortunes deteriorated during and after 1863, food shortages, marauding Yankees and deserters, and widespread poverty plagued the home front. The documents excerpted here reflect the growing desperation of the women left to cope with these conditions, the pressures on soldiers to desert and return to their families, and the inability of public officials to boost sagging Confederate morale.

❖ **Why did some Southern women encourage their husbands to desert?**

❖ **How should Confederate officials have responded to women who wanted their men to return home?**

❖ **What do these documents reveal about their authors' attitude toward Southern independence?**

Letter of Martha Revis to her husband
Marshall, Madison County, North Carolina, July 20, 1863
Dear Husband: I seat myself to drop you a few lines to let you know that me and Sally is well as common, and I hope these few lines will come to hand and find you well and doing well. . . . The people is all turning to Union here since the Yankees has got Vicksburg [on July 4]. I want you to come home as soon as you can after you git this letter. . . . That is all I can think of, only I want you to come home the worst that I ever did. . . . The folks is leaving here, and going North as fast as they can.
Your wife, till death.

Petition from Women of Miller County, Georgia, to President Jefferson Davis
September 8, 1863
Our crops is limited and so short . . . cannot reach the first day of march next . . . our fencing is unanamosly allmost decayed . . . But little of any sort to Rescue us and our children from a unanamus starveation. . . . An allwise god ho is slow to anger and full of grace and murcy and without Respect of persons and full of love and charity that he will send down his fury and judgement in a very grate manar [on] all those our leading men and those that are in power ef thare is no more favors shone to those the mothers and wives. . . . I tell you that with out some grate and speadly alterating in the conduckting of afares in this our little nation god will frown on it and that speadly.

Source: *Paul D. Escott and David R. Goldfield, eds.,* Major Problems in the History of the American South *(1990).*

Although Grant's strategy ultimately worked, several problems and miscalculations undermined its effectiveness. With Sherman advancing in Georgia, Grant's major focus was Lee's army in Virginia. But Grant underestimated Lee. The Confederate general thwarted him for almost a year and inflicted horrendous casualties on his army. Confederate forces under Jubal Early drove off Union forces from the Shenandoah Valley in June 1864, depriving Grant of troops and allowing the Confederates to maintain their supply lines. And the incompetence of General Benjamin Butler, charged with advancing up the James River to Richmond in May 1864 to relieve Lee's pressure on Grant, further eroded Grant's plan. Grant also faced administrative problems. He left General George G. Meade, the victor of Gettysburg, in command of the Army of the Potomac but accompanied the army in its campaign against Lee and directed its movements, undercutting Meade's authority. Finally, he had to contend with disaffection in his officer corps. Many officers in the Army of the Potomac felt enduring loyalty to General George McClellan, whom Lincoln had dismissed in 1862, and considered Grant a mediocrity who had triumphed in the West only because his opposition there had been third-rate.

Lee's only hope was to make Grant's campaign so costly and time-consuming that the Northern general would abandon it before the Southerners ran out of supplies and troops. But despite problems and setbacks, Grant kept relentless pressure on Lee. Tied down in Virginia, the Confederate general was unable to send troops to help slow Sherman's advance in Georgia.

From the Wilderness to Cold Harbor

Grant and Meade began their campaign against Lee in May 1864, crossing the Rapidan River near Fredericksburg, Virginia, and marching toward an area known as the Wilderness (see Map 17-1). Just a year earlier, Lee and Jackson had won a smashing victory at nearby Chancellorsville. Hoping to duplicate that earlier success, Lee attacked the Army of the Potomac, which outnumbered his 118,000 to 60,000, in the thickets of the Wilderness on May 5 and 6 before it could reach open ground. The densely wooded terrain reduced the Union army's advantage in numbers and artillery. Much of the fighting involved in fierce hand-to-hand combat. Exchanges of gunfire at close range set the dry underbrush ablaze. Wounded soldiers, trapped in the fires, begged their comrades to shoot them before they burned to death. The toll was frightful—eighteen

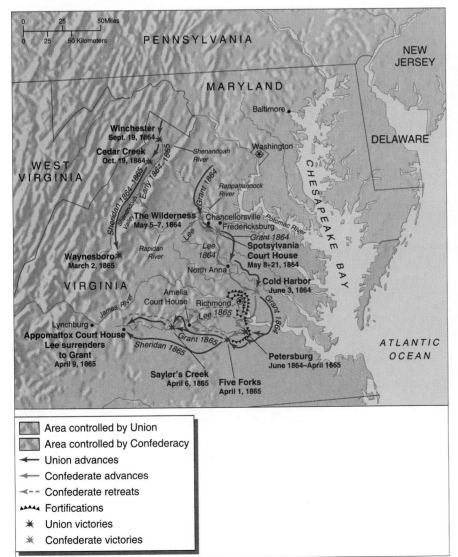

Map 17-1   Grant and Lee in Virginia, 1864–1865
The engagements in Virginia from May 1864 to April 1865 between the two great generals for the Union and the Confederacy proved decisive in ending the Civil War. Although General Lee fared well enough in the Wilderness, Spotsylvania, and Cold Harbor campaigns, the sheer might and relentlessness of Grant and his army wore down the Confederate forces. When Petersburg fell after a prolonged siege on April 2, 1865, Richmond, Appomattox, and dreams of Southern independence soon fell as well.

thousand casualties on the Union side, ten thousand on the Confederate side.

In the past, Union commanders would have pulled back and rested after such an encounter. But Grant startled Lee's army by pushing on. "Surprise and disappointment were the prevailing emotions," one Southerner wrote, "when we discovered after the contest in the Wilderness that General Grant was not going to retire." Lee's offensive in the **Battle of the Wilderness** was his last. From then on, his army was on the defensive against Grant's relentless pursuit.

Marching and fighting, his casualties always higher than Lee's, Grant continued South. Attack-

ing the entrenched Confederate Army at **Spotsylvania**, his army suffered another eighteen thousand casualties to the Confederates' eleven thousand. Undeterred, Grant moved on toward **Cold Harbor**, where Lee's troops again awaited him in entrenched positions. Flinging his army against withering Confederate fire on June 3, he lost seven thousand men in eight minutes.

In less than a month of fighting, the Army of the Potomac had lost 55,000 men. The slaughter undermined Grant's support in Northern public opinion and led peace advocates to renew their quest for a cease-fire. With antiwar sentiment grow-

Union General Ulysses Grant had the pews from a local church moved to a grove of trees where he and his officers planned the following day's assault on Confederate troops at Cold Harbor, Virginia. Grant appears at the left of the photograph, leaning over a bench and studying a map.

ing in the North as the presidential elections approached in November, Lee's defensive strategy seemed to be working.

At this point, Grant decided to change his tactics. Abandoning his march on Richmond from the north, he shifted his army south of the James River to approach the Confederate capital from the rear. Wasting no time, he crossed his army over the James and on June 17, 1864, surprised the Confederates with an attack on **Petersburg**, a critical rail junction 23 miles south of Richmond. It was a brilliant maneuver, but the hesitant actions of Union corps commanders gave Lee time to reinforce the town's defenders. Both armies dug in for a lengthy siege.

In an effort to break the stalemate, Union troops dug a tunnel under the Confederate defenses and filled it with 8,000 pounds of explosive powder. They ignited it on July 30, throwing dirt, men, and guns high into the air and leaving a large crater in the ground. But Union troops were as awed by the explosion as the Confederates. They hesitated in their attack on the breach in the Confederate lines, giving Lee time to rally his forces. The attack failed, the Union lost another four thousand men, and the siege of Petersburg continued.

Atlanta

While Grant advanced on Lee in Virginia, Union forces under William T. Sherman in Georgia engaged in a deadly dance with the Army of Ten-

nessee under the command of Joseph E. Johnston as they began the **Atlanta Campaign**, a scheme to take Atlanta, Georgia (see Map 17-2). Johnston had replaced the incompetent Braxton Bragg after the Confederate debacle at Chattanooga in late 1863. He shared Lee's belief that the Confederacy's best hope lay in a defensive strategy. Hoping to lure Sherman into a frontal assault, Johnston settled his forces early in May at Dalton, an important railroad junction in Georgia 25 miles south of Chattanooga and 75 miles north of Atlanta. The wily Union general declined to attack and instead made a wide swing around the Confederates, prompting Johnston to abandon Dalton, rush south, and dig in again at Resaca to prevent Sherman from cutting the railroad. Again Sherman swung around without an assault, and again Johnston rushed south to cut him off, this time at Cassville.

This waltz continued for two months until Johnston had retreated to a strong defensive position on Kennesaw Mountain, barely 20 miles north of Atlanta. At this point, early in July, Sherman decided to attack, with predictably disastrous consequences. The Union suffered three thousand casualties, the Confederates only six hundred. Sherman would not make such a mistake again. He resumed his maneuvering and by mid-July had forced Johnston into defensive positions on Peachtree Creek just north of Atlanta. President Davis feared that Johnston would let Sherman take Atlanta without a fight

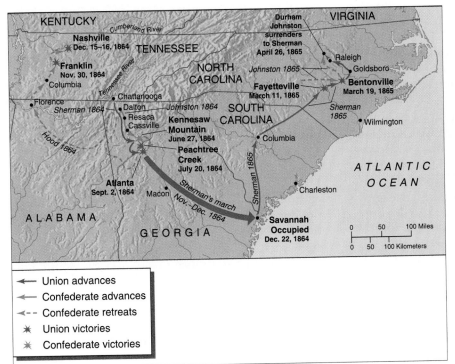

Map 17-2 *The Atlanta Campaign and Sherman's March, 1864–1865* *Sherman, a brilliant tactician who generally refused to be goaded into a frontal assault, "danced" with Confederate General Joseph E. Johnston until an impatient Jefferson Davis replaced Johnston with Hood, and soon, Atlanta was in Federal hands. The fall of Atlanta opened the way to the rest of Georgia, a key supply state for the Confederacy. With orders not to harm the civilian population, Sherman's men took their wrath out on property as they made their way through Georgia and South Carolina.*

SUMMARY

MAJOR BATTLES OF THE CIVIL WAR, 1864–1865

Battle or Campaign	Date	Outcome and Consequences
Wilderness and Cold Harbor	May and June 1864	Both Confederate victories that inflicted huge losses on Grant's army; turned public opinion against Grant but failed to force him to withdraw
Atlanta	May–September 1864	Union victory; Confederacy lost key rail depot and industrial center
Sherman's March	November 1864–March 1865	Nearly unopposed, Sherman's army cut a path of destruction through Georgia and South Carolina, breaking Southern morale
Battles of Franklin and Nashville	November and December 1864	Union victories in Tennessee; effectively destroyed Army of Tennessee
Siege of Petersburg	June 1864–April 1865	Long stalemate ended in Union victory; led to fall of Richmond and surrender of Lee's army at Appomattox Court House

and waltz with the Union general until the sea stopped them both. He dismissed Johnston and installed John Bell Hood of Texas in his place. This was a grave error. Hood, in the accurate view of those who fought for him, had a "lion's heart" but a "wooden head."

In late July, Hood began a series of attacks on Sherman, beginning at Peachtree Creek on July 20, and was thrown back each time with heavy losses. In less than nine days, Hood suffered thirteen thousand casualties, compared to the Union's six thousand. Davis, who three weeks earlier had eagerly sought an offensive, ordered Hood back to defensive positions in Atlanta.

Sherman launched a series of flanking maneuvers around the city in late August that left Hood in danger of being surrounded. The Confederate general had no choice but to abandon Atlanta and save his army. On the night of September 1, Hood evacuated the city, burning everything of military value.

The loss of Atlanta was a severe blow to the Confederacy. Several of the South's major railroads converged at the city, and its industries helped arm and clothe the South's armies. Atlanta's fall also left Georgia's rich farmland at the mercy of Sherman's army.

Most significant, the fall of Atlanta revived the morale of the war-weary North and helped assure Lincoln's reelection in November. The last hope of the Confederacy—that a peace candidate would replace Lincoln and end the war—was fast fading. As the disconsolate editor of the *Richmond Examiner* explained, the "disaster at Atlanta [came] in the very nick of time" to "save the party of Lincoln from irretrievable ruin. . . . It will obscure the prospect of peace, late so bright. It will also diffuse gloom over the South."

The Election of 1864

Before Sherman's victory at Atlanta, Northern dismay over Grant's enormous losses and his failure to take Richmond raised the prospect of a Democratic election victory. Nominating George B. McClellan, former commander of the Union's armies, as their presidential candidate, the Democrats appealed to the voters as the party of peace. They also appealed to the antiemancipation sentiment that was strong in some parts of the North.

The fall of Atlanta and the Union's suddenly improved military fortunes undermined Democratic prospects. Another Union victory three weeks before the elections gave Lincoln a further boost and diminished McClellan's chances. Since September, Union forces under General Philip H. Sheridan had been on the offensive in the Shenandoah Valley. In lightning cavalry raids on farms and supply depots, they destroyed valuable Confederate food reserves. And in a decisive battle on October 19, they overwhelmed the valley's Confederate defenders. Lee had now been deprived of a vital source of supply.

In the voting on November 8, Lincoln captured 55 percent of the popular vote, losing only New Jersey, Delaware, and Kentucky. Republicans likewise swept the congressional elections, retaining control of both the Senate and the House of Representatives.

The Republican victory reinforced the Union commitment to emancipation. A proposed constitutional amendment outlawing slavery everywhere in the United States, not just those areas still in rebellion, had failed in Congress when it was introduced earlier in 1864. Reintroduced after the election, it passed Congress and was ratified as the **Thirteenth Amendment** to the U.S. Constitution in 1865. All ear-

lier amendments related to government powers and functions; this was the first to outlaw a domestic institution previously protected by the Constitution and state law. (Ironically, an earlier Thirteenth Amendment had been proposed to the states by Congress and President Buchanan in March 1861, just before Lincoln took office and the South seceded. This amendment would have prohibited Congress from interfering with slavery wherever it existed. It lapsed when Southerners deserted Congress and the Civil War began.)

Sherman's March to the Sea

After Sherman took Atlanta, Hood withdrew his army toward Tennessee, hoping to lure Union forces away from Georgia. Grant wanted Sherman to go after Hood. But Sherman had a different idea. He proposed to break Confederate resistance once and for all by marching his army to the sea and destroying everything in its path.

Sherman's March got under way on November 15. His force of sixty thousand men encountered little resistance, prompting North Carolina's marveling governor, Zebulon Vance, to comment, "It shows what I have always believed, that the great *popular heart* is not now and never had been in this war!" Sherman entered Savannah on December 22, 1864, and presented the city to Lincoln as a Christmas present. Just a few weeks earlier, Union forces in Tennessee had routed Hood's army at the **Battle of Franklin** and then crushed it entirely at the **Battle of Nashville**. Hood's defeat removed any threat to Sherman's rear.

Vowing to make Georgia howl, Union General William T. Sherman and his army cut a wide swath of destruction through the Confederate bread-basket during the fall of 1864. This painting shows Sherman looking on while his men vandalize a railroad and burn bridges and homes. The effect was both strategic— Georgia was a major source of food and materiel for the faltering Confederacy— and psychological—to further weaken the Southern will to fight.

Fleeing Confederates left Richmond in flames after the fall of Petersburg in April 1865.

Sherman resumed his march in February 1865, heading for South Carolina, the heart of the Confederacy and the state where the Civil War had begun. "The truth is," Sherman wrote a friend, "the whole army is burning with an insatiable desire to wreak vengeance on South Carolina." South Carolinians sent taunting messages promising stiff resistance, but these served only further to provoke Sherman's troops. They pushed aside the small force that assembled to oppose them, wreaked greater destruction in South Carolina than they had in Georgia, and burned the state capitol at Columbia. Sherman sent the colonel of a black regiment to receive the surrender of Charleston and ordered black troops to be the first to take possession of the city. The soldiers marched in singing "John Brown's Body" to the cheers of the city's black population.

Sherman ended his march in Goldsboro, North Carolina, in March 1865 after repelling a surprise Confederate attack at Bentonville led by the restored Joseph E. Johnston and the remnants of the Army of Tennessee. Behind the Union army lay a barren swath 425 miles long from Savannah to Goldsboro. A wave of despair spread through what remained of the Confederacy, and desertions soared in Lee's Army of Virginia.

Arming the Confederacy's Slaves

In a move reflecting their desperation in March 1865, Confederate leaders revived a proposal that they had previously rejected to arm and free slaves.

Slaves had served involuntarily in the Confederate army, and a number of Louisiana free blacks had volunteered for service in Southern ranks early in the war. But this proposal represented a major policy shift. President Davis hoped it would gain the Confederacy not only a military benefit but also diplomatic recognition from countries that had balked because of slavery.

The issue divided Confederate leaders. Confederate general Howell Cobb argued that "if slaves will make good soldiers, our whole theory of slavery is wrong." Others thought it was preferable to abandon slavery than to lose independence. A Confederate congressman from Georgia wrote to a friend in October 1864 that if the South lost the war, slavery was over anyway, and "we and our children will be slaves, while our freed negroes will lord it over us." But if the Confederacy enlisted slaves, it could "win our independence, and have liberty and homes for ourselves and our children."

Not surprisingly, slaves themselves greeted the proposal with little enthusiasm. They might have found service in the Confederate army an acceptable alternative to bondage earlier in the war, but not now, with Union victory imminent. Mary Chesnut recalled in March 1865 that early in the war, when her husband "spoke to his Negroes about it, his head men were keen to go in the army, to be free and get a bounty after the war. Now they say coolly that they don't want freedom if they have to fight for it. That means they are pretty sure of having it anyway."

On March 13, 1865, a reluctant Confederate Congress passed a bill to enlist black soldiers, but without a provision offering them freedom. President Davis and the War Office bypassed the equivocal congressional legislation ten days later, issuing a general order that promised immediate freedom to slaves who enlisted. The war ended before the order could have any effect. The irony was that in the summer of 1864, a majority of Northerners probably would have accepted reunion without emancipation had the Confederacy abandoned its fight.

The Road to Appomattox

With Sherman's triumph in Georgia and the Carolinas and Sheridan's rout of the Confederates in the Shenandoah Valley, Lee's army remained the last obstacle to Union victory. On April 1, Sheridan's cavalry seized a vital railway junction on Lee's right flank, forcing Lee to abandon Petersburg and the defense of Richmond. He tried a daring run westward toward Lynchburg, hoping to secure much-needed supplies and join Johnston's Army of Tennessee in North Carolina to continue the fight.

President Davis fled Richmond with his cabinet and headed toward North Carolina. Union troops occupied the Confederate capital on April 3, and two days later, President Lincoln walked through its streets to the cheers of his army and an emotional reception from thousands of blacks. "I know I am free," shouted one black spectator, "for I have seen Father Abraham and felt him."

Grant's army of 80,000 outran Lee's diminishing force of 35,000 and cut off his escape at **Appomattox Court House**, Virginia, on April 7. Convinced that further resistance was futile, the Confederate commander met Grant on April 9, 1865, in the McLean house at Appomattox Court House to sign the documents of surrender. The Union general offered generous terms, allowing Lee's men to go home unmolested and to take with them horses or mules "to put in a crop." Grant reported feeling "sad and depressed" at "the downfall of a foe who had fought so long and valiantly, and had suffered so much for a cause, though that cause was, I believe, one of the worst for which a people ever fought." Lee rode through the thinned ranks of his troops, who crowded around him in silent tribute, brushing the general's boots and the withers of his horse with their hats.

The fleeing Davis met Joseph E. Johnston at Greensboro, North Carolina, hoping to convince him to continue fighting. But Johnston, like Lee, saw no point in continued bloodshed and surrendered to Sherman near Durham, North Carolina, on April 26. Davis continued south, urging the people to fight on, but the people were tired of the war and ignored him. On May 10, Union cavalry captured Davis and his companions in southern Georgia. On May 26, Texas general Kirby Smith surrendered his trans-Mississippi army, and the Civil War came to an end.

The Death of Lincoln

Washington greeted the Confederate surrender at Appomattox with predictable and raucous rejoicing—torchlight parades, cannon salutes, and crowds spontaneously bellowing "The Star-Spangled Banner." On April 11, President Lincoln addressed a large crowd from the White House balcony and spoke briefly of his plans to reconstruct the South with the help of persons loyal to the Union, including recently freed slaves. At least one listener found the speech disappointing. Sometime actor and full-time Confederate patriot John Wilkes Booth muttered to a friend in the

This photograph of Abraham Lincoln was taken four days before John Wilkes Booth assassinated him in Ford's Theater.

throng, "That means nigger citizenship. Now, by God, I'll put him through. That is the last speech he will ever make."

On the evening of April 14, Good Friday, the president went to Ford's Theater in Washington to view a comedy, *Our American Cousin*. During the performance, Booth shot the president, wounding him mortally, then jumped from from Lincoln's box to the stage shouting "Sic semper tyrannis" ("Thus ever to tyrants") and fled the theater. Union troops tracked him down to a barn in northern Virginia and killed him. Investigators arrested eight accomplices who had conspired with Booth to murder other high officials in addition to Lincoln. Four of the accomplices were hanged. Besides the president, however, the only other official attacked was Secretary of State Seward, who received serious but not fatal knife wounds.

Southerners reacted to Lincoln's assassination with surprisingly mixed emotions. Many saw in the death of the man they had regarded as their bitterest enemy for four years some slight hope of relief for the South's otherwise bleak prospects. But General Johnston and others like him understood Lincoln's influence with the radical elements in the Republican party who were pressing for harsh terms against the South. The president's death, Johnston wrote, was "the greatest possible calamity to the South."

Conclusion

Just before the war, William Sherman had warned a friend from Virginia, "You people of the South don't know what you are doing. This country will be drenched in blood. . . . War is a terrible thing." He was right. More than 365,000 Union soldiers died during the war, 110,000 in battle, and more than 256,000 Confederate soldiers, 94,000 of them in battle. Total casualties on both sides, including wounded, were more than 1 million.

Southern armies suffered disproportionately higher casualties than Northern armies. One in four Confederate soldiers died or endured debilitating wounds, compared to one in ten Federal soldiers. During the first year after the war, Mississippi allocated one-fifth of its budget for artificial limbs. Compounding the suffering of the individuals behind these gruesome statistics was the incalculable suffering—in terms of grief, fatherless children, women who never married, families never made whole—of the people close to them.

The war devastated the South. The region lost one-fourth of its white male population between the ages of 20 and 40. It also lost two-fifths of its livestock and half its farm machinery. Union armies destroyed many of the South's railroads and shattered its industry. Between 1860 and 1870, the wealth of the South declined by 60 percent, and its share of the nation's total wealth dropped from more than 30 percent to 12 percent. The wealth of the North, in contrast, increased by half in the same period.

The Union victory solved the constitutional question about the right of secession and sealed the fate of slavery. The issue that dominated the prewar sectional debate had vanished. Now when politicians intoned in Independence Day orations or campaign speeches about the ideals of democracy and freedom, the glaring reality of human bondage would no longer mock their rhetoric.

For black Southerners, emancipation was the war's most significant achievement. Journalists sponsored by the federal government who recorded the testimony of ex-slaves in the 1930s during the Great Depression, seventy years after emancipation, found their memory of the jubilee as fresh as yesterday. Lincoln entered African-American folklore as a larger-than-life figure. At age 91, Fanny Burdock of Valdosta, Georgia, told a recorder a common tale of seeing Lincoln "coming all dusty and on foot" past her Georgia home.

> We run right to the fence and had the oak bucket and the dipper. When he draw up to us, he so tall, black eyes so sad. Didn't say not one word, just looked hard at all us, every one us crying. We give him nice cool water from the dipper. Then he nodded and set off and we just stood there till he get to being dust then nothing. After, didn't our owner or nobody credit it, but me and all my kin, we knowed. I still got the dipper to prove it.

The Civil War stimulated other changes that grew more significant over time. It did not make the Union an industrial nation, but it taught the effectiveness of centralized management, new financial techniques, and the coordination of production, marketing, and distribution. Entrepreneurs would apply these lessons to create the expanding corporations of the postwar American economy.

Likewise, the war did not revolutionize gender relations in American society, but by opening new opportunities to women in fields such as nursing and teaching, it helped lay the foundation for the women's suffrage movement of the 1870s and 1880s.

For many Americans, especially black and white Southerners, the war was the most important event in their lives. It had a devastating impact on the families and friends of those who died. But it was not responsible for every postwar change in American society, and it left many features of American life intact. The experience of pulling together in a massive war effort, for example, did not soften class antagonisms. European socialist and father of communism Karl Marx hailed Lincoln as a son of the working class and predicted that "as the American War of independence initiated a new era of ascendancy for the middle class, so the American anti-slavery war will do for the working classes." But capitalism, not labor, triumphed during the war. And it was industrialists and entrepreneurs, not working people, who most benefited from the war's bonanza. Lincoln brutally suppressed strikes at defense plants and threw labor leaders into military prisons.

The war to end slavery changed some American racial attitudes, especially in the North. When Lincoln broadened the war's objectives to include the abolition of slavery, he connected the success of the Union to freedom for the slave. At the outset of the Civil War, only a small minority of Northerners considered themselves abolitionists. After the Emancipation Proclamation, every Northern soldier became a liberator. By the end of the war, perhaps a majority of Northerners supported granting freedmen the right to vote and to equal protection under the law, even if they believed (as many did) that blacks were inferior to whites. The courage of black troops and the efforts of African-American leaders to link the causes of reunion and freedom were influential in bringing about this shift.

Most white Southerners did not experience a similar enlightenment. Some were relieved by the end of slavery, but most greeted it with fear, anger, and regret. For them, the freed slaves would be living reminders of the South's defeat and the end of a way of life grounded in white supremacy.

If the Civil War resolved the sectional dispute of the 1850s by ending slavery and denying the right of the Southern states to secede, it created two new equally troubling problems: how to reunite South and North and how to deal with the legacy of slavery. At his last cabinet meeting on April 14, Lincoln gave little indication of how he intended to proceed on these problems. He seemed inclined to be conciliatory, cautioning against reprisals on Confederate leaders and noting the courage of General Lee and his officers. The president said nothing about the rights of freedmen, although earlier statements indicated that he favored suffrage, but not social equality, for African-Americans.

America's greatest crisis had closed. In its wake, former slaves tested their new freedom and the nation groped for reconciliation. The struggle to preserve the Union and abolish slavery had renewed and vindicated the nation's ideals. It was time to savor the hard-fought victories before plunging into the uncertainties of Reconstruction.

Review Questions

1. Compare and contrast the roles played by women, in the North and in the South, during the Civil War, and explain how their actions and activities aided or hindered the war effort of their respective nations.

2. Some historians view the 1864 presidential election as one of the most important elections in American history. Why?

3. Looking back at the Confederacy's position after Gettysburg, defeat seemed inevitable. But even as late as the summer of 1864, many Southerners still believed that they had a fighting chance at independence. Why did they feel this way, and what happened between then and the end of the year to dash such hopes?

4. Given the enormity of the losses in lives and property, it is not surprising that some historians have attributed major changes in American society to the Civil War. But other historians claim that the Civil War's impact has been exaggerated. Analyze and assess what the Civil War did or did not accomplish.

Recommended Reading

Two recent biographies of major Civil War figures provide remarkable insight not only into the men who led the fight on both sides, but on the nature of the war itself, especially the final two years. See Emory M. Thomas, *Robert E. Lee: A Biography* (1995), which presents the enigmatic Confederate leader in a balanced account; and John P. Marszalek, *Sherman: A Soldier's Passion for Order* (1993), another balanced biography that dispels many myths about the mercurial Union general whose march through Georgia became a symbol for a new type of warfare.

Additional Sources

War Transforms the North

Mark E. Neely Jr., *The Fate of Liberty: Abraham Lincoln and Civil Liberties* (1991).

Elizabeth B. Pryor, *Clara Barton: Professional Angel* (1987).

The Confederacy Disintegrates

Stephen V. Ash, *When the Yankees Came: Conflict and Chaos in the Occupied South, 1861–1865* (1995).

Catherine Clinton and Nina Silber, eds., *Divided Houses: Gender and the Civil War* (1992).

Robert F. Durden, *The Gray and the Black: The Confederate Debate on Emancipation* (1972).

Drew Gilpin Faust, "Altars of Sacrifice: Confederate Women and the Narratives of War," *Journal of American History*, 76 (March 1990): 1200–1228.

Mark Grimsley, *The Hard Hand of War: Union Policy Toward Southern Civilians, 1861–1865* (1995).

C. Vann Woodward, ed., *Mary Chesnut's Civil War* (1981).

The Union Prevails

Richard E. Beringer, Herman Hattaway, Archer Jones, and William N. Still Jr., *Why the South Lost the Civil War* (1986).

Albert Castel, *Decision in the West: The Atlanta Campaign of 1864* (1992).

Joseph T. Glatthaar, *The March to the Sea and Beyond* (1985).

Craig L. Symonds, *Joseph E. Johnston: A Civil War Biography* (1992).

Emory Thomas, *The Confederate Nation, 1861–1865* (1979).

Where to Learn More

❖ **Cyclorama, Grant Park, Atlanta, Georgia.** This exhibit vividly depicts the 1864 Battle of Atlanta, complete with "gunfire" and oozing "blood." Interpretive literature at the site helps make sense of the panoramic depiction.

❖ **Appomattox Court House, Appomattox, Virginia.** What historian Bruce Catton termed "a stillness at Appomattox" can be felt at the McLean House in this south central Virginia town. The house is much as it was when Confederate general Robert E. Lee surrendered his forces to Union general Ulysses S. Grant on April 9, 1865. An almost reverential solitude covers the house and the well-maintained grounds today. Other sites related to the last year of the war include Kennesaw Mountain National Battlefield Park, Petersburg National Battlefield, and Richmond National Battlefield Park.

WE THE PEOPLE
1789-1865

*S*elf-government is a difficult business. Like a never-finished painting by an artist sensitive to new themes and ideas, a self-governing nation changes in response to the changing priorities of the people who compose it. The men who gathered in Philadelphia in 1787 began the American experiment in democracy. The Constitution they created was vague enough to satisfy contending parties yet specific enough to provide a framework for government.

Over the next eighty years, the United States experienced remarkable geographic and economic expansion that challenged its constitutional framework. The electorate expanded as states eliminated property qualifications for voting, but suffrage remained restricted to white men. Two major questions that dogged the framers remained persistently troublesome: How should power be distributed between the states and the national government? And how could minority rights be protected in a society predicated on majority rule?

Americans and their political parties often behaved in contradictory ways on these issues. Thomas Jefferson, for example, was a champion of limited government and strict adherence to the terms of the Constitution, but he acted with questionable constitutional authority to secure the Louisiana Purchase and double the country's territory. Andrew Jackson was likewise inconsistent on state versus federal power. He angrily struck down the Bank of the United States, a federal creation, and defied the Supreme Court to allow Georgia to expel the Cherokees from its borders. But he also upheld the federal government's authority against South Carolina's claim that it could nullify federal tariffs.

The rapid territorial expansion of the United States exacerbated tensions over state and federal authority and minority rights that eventually threatened the nation's existence. Bound up with expansion was the question of power over the new lands. The Indians whose land it had been were denied control of it: they were allowed to remain or forced to move at the whim of the government. Control of new land became a pressing issue for white Southerners when, after the Mexican War, the national government sought to prohibit slavery in the territories. With slavery restricted, white Southerners began to see themselves as a disadvantaged minority without power in a nation of majority rule.

That explains how the issue of states' rights and federal power became bound up with the question of minority rights. The framers believed that the Constitution offered protection to minorities. The First Amendment, for example, guaranteed the rights of religious minorities. By protecting minority rights, the Constitution encouraged freedom of thought and expression. Free thinking in turn encouraged innovation and the flourishing of the many religious and other reform movements that emerged in the antebellum period.

But as abolitionists and women's rights advocates pointed out, there was a discrepancy between the status of many Americans and the ideals expressed in the Declaration of Independence and Constitution. The protections of the Constitution did not extend to all. Slaves had no political rights, and other African-Americans, women, and Native Americans had few rights. Little wonder at the panic of white Southerners who saw themselves slipping into the ranks of a dependent minority alongside slaves, Indians, and women.

The Civil War brought to a head the merged disputes about state and federal power and minority rights. Many white Southerners questioned the legitimacy of Abraham Lincoln and his fellow Republicans when they took control of the federal government after the election of 1860. Southerners feared that a party elected by a minority of the nation would, acting in the name of the majority, deprive them of their right to property and mobility. Republicans, in turn, viewed the white overlord South as a threat to the national government and slavery as a denial of its principles.

The ensuing bloody and costly conflict ended slavery and resolved the issue of secession but left open the two major constitutional questions that had dominated the national conversation since the Philadelphia convention. If the war boosted the profile of the federal government over the states, it did not resolve the question of how far the national government could extend its power. Nor did a formula emerge for the guarantee of minority rights. African-Americans, Indians, working people, and women would struggle for such a guarantee during the late nineteenth century, with only partial success. But the struggle affirmed the value and strength of American ideals forged, however imperfectly, a century earlier. The work known as America remained in progress.

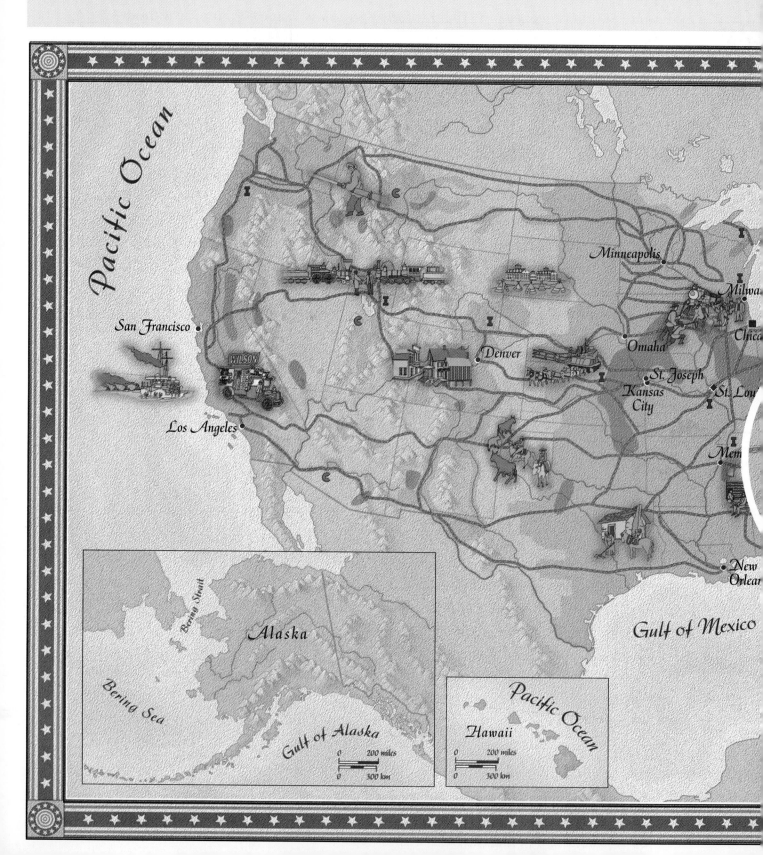

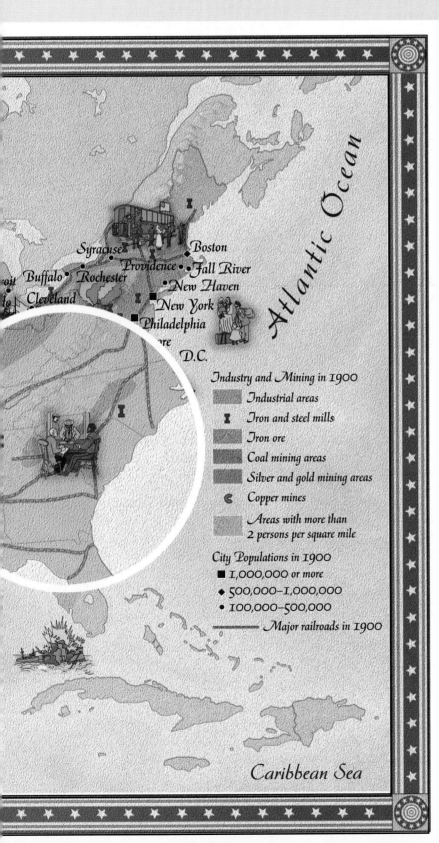

Syracuse
Buffalo • Rochester
Cleveland
Providence • Boston
Fall River
New Haven
New York
Philadelphia
D.C.

Atlantic Ocean

Industry and Mining in 1900

- Industrial areas
- ⊥ Iron and steel mills
- Iron ore
- Coal mining areas
- Silver and gold mining areas
- ☾ Copper mines
- Areas with more than 2 persons per square mile

City Populations in 1900
- ■ 1,000,000 or more
- ◆ 500,000–1,000,000
- • 100,000–500,000
- —— Major railroads in 1900

Caribbean Sea

KEY TOPICS

❖ The clash between African-American aspirations and southern white expectations
❖ Federal government plans to bring the South back into the Union and secure freedom for former slaves
❖ The efforts and results of southern Republican governments to keep the allegiance of blacks and win the support of whites
❖ Why and how Reconstruction ended

*A*s Union general William T. Sherman burned his way through Georgia and South Carolina in late 1864 and early 1865, slaves left their plantations to work for and follow the conquering army. In January 1865, Sherman allowed former slaves to settle on farms abandoned by their masters along the Atlantic coast. Tom Mansart, a former slave, seized this opportunity to stake out a farm near Port Royal, South Carolina. Less than a year later, the federal government returned the land to its previous owner. Mansart found work as a stevedore in nearby Charleston and joined a labor union founded by free blacks before the war. By 1871, he had married and risen to prominence in his community. He was president of his eight-hundred-member union, and his backing helped elect local Republican candidates to office.

The Mansart family's good fortune declined after 1871 as first an economic depression and then racial violence stole their dream. Tom Mansart was killed at the door of his house during the election campaign of 1876, the victim of one of the white mobs roaming through South Carolina to discourage blacks from voting. The federal troops that had been sent to Charleston to maintain an open political process instead fraternized with the city's white leaders.

Tom Mansart's story, as told by African-American leader W. E. B. Du Bois in *The Black Flame* (1957), exemplified both the promise of the Reconstruction era and its eventual betrayal by northern and southern whites. Crossing the threshold of freedom in 1865, southern blacks saw their prospects widening. Rights formerly denied them—to move, to own property, to get an education, to keep their families together, to succeed or fail in their own endeavors—were now theirs. Freedom meant more than a change in status; it marked a rebirth. But by 1877, African-Americans again faced restrictions that, though not as severe as slavery, deprived them of the promised fruits of freedom.

The position of African-Americans in American society was one of the two great issues of Reconstruction. Americans of both sections disagreed about how much freedom to grant the former slaves, almost all of whom lived in the South. The other great issue was how and under what terms to readmit the former Confederate states. The Constitution was silent on the subject. As with the issue of black equality, opinions in both sections varied widely.

The formation of a national consensus on freedom and reunification began with the demands and hopes of three broad groups. One was the Republican party, which controlled the federal government and determined its policies. Most Republicans were unwilling to accept the seceding states back in the Union without an expression of loyalty and a commitment to protecting the rights of freedmen. A second group, the more than 4 million former slaves, demanded voting rights, access to education, and the opportunity to seek economic self-sufficiency. Few northern blacks yet enjoyed all these benefits, and few southern whites could conceive of former slaves possessing them. The third group, southern whites, hoped to restore their shattered lives, fortunes, and dignity. In their vision of a renewed South, blacks remained subservient, and the federal government stopped interfering in southern affairs.

Between 1865 and 1867, under President Andrew Johnson's Reconstruction plan, southern whites pretty much had their way with the former slaves and with their own state governments. Congressional action between 1867 and 1870 attempted to balance black rights and home rule, with mixed results. After 1870, white Southerners gradually regained control of their states and localities, often through violence and intimidation, denying black Southerners their political gains while Republicans in Washington lost interest in policing their former enemies.

By the time the last federal troops left the South in 1877, southern whites had prevailed. The Confederate states had returned to the Union with all of their rights and many of their leaders restored. And the freed slaves remained in mostly subservient positions with few of the rights and privileges enjoyed by other Americans.

Southern Whites and the Ghosts of the Confederacy, 1865

Confederate soldiers—generals and troops alike—returned to devastated homes they could scarcely recognize. General Braxton Bragg returned to his "once prosperous" Alabama home to find *"all, all* was lost, except my debts." Bragg and his wife found temporary shelter in a slave cabin. Yeomen farmers, the backbone of the Confederacy, found uprooted fences, farm animals dead or gone, and buildings destroyed. With no income or savings to soften their plight, they and their families wandered about in a living nightmare, seeking shelter where they could. They lived in morbid fear of vengeful former slaves or the hated Yankee soldiers wreaking more damage. "The demoralization is complete," a Georgia girl noted.

Their cause lost and their society reviled, white Southerners lived through the summer and fall of 1865 surrounded by ghosts—the ghosts of lost loved ones, joyful times, bountiful harvests, self-assurance, and slavery. Defeat shook the basic tenets of their religious beliefs. A North Carolinian cried, "Oh, our God! What sins we must have been guilty of that we should be so humiliated by Thee now!" Some praised God for delivering the South from the sin of slavery. A Virginia woman expressed thanks that "we white people are no longer permitted to go on in such wickedness, heaping up more and more wrath of God upon our devoted heads."

But many other white Southerners refused to accept their defeat as a divine judgment. Instead, they insisted, God had spared the South for a greater purpose. They came to view the war as the Lost Cause and interpreted it not as a lesson in humility but as an episode in the South's journey to salvation. Robert E. Lee became the patron saint of this cause, his poignant nobility a contrast to the crassness of the Yankee warlords. White Southerners would not allow the memory of the bloody struggle to die, transforming it into a symbol of courage against great odds and piety against sin. Eventually, they believed, redemption would come. Not all white Southerners shared this belief. Unionists, many residents of the upland South, and some city-dwellers preferred to look ahead to a new way of life, not to sanctify the past. But this contrasting vision remained a minority one.

Fifteen years after the war, Mark Twain traveled the length of the East Coast. After visiting a gentlemen's club in Boston, he recalled that the conversation had covered a variety of topics, none of which

This engraving shows Southerners decorating the graves of rebel soldiers at Hollywood Memorial Cemetery in Virginia, in 1867. Northern and Southerners alike honored their war dead. But in the South, the practice of commemorating fallen soldiers became an important element in maintaining the myth of the Lost Cause that colored white Southerners' view of the War.

included the Civil War. Northerners had relegated that conflict to history books and moved on. This was not the case in the South. There defeat and destruction demanded rationalization and remembrance. Thus Twain reported that, unlike in the North, gentlemen's talk in Atlanta inevitably wandered to the war and to heroism and sacrifice. "In the South," Twain wrote, "the war is what A.D. is elsewhere: they date from it." Such people would not accept the changes implied by defeat. They would fight to preserve as much of their past as the victors allowed.

Most white Southerners approached the great issues of freedom and reunification with unyielding views. They saw African-Americans as adversaries whose attempts at self-improvement were a direct challenge to whites' beliefs in their own racial superiority. White Southerners saw outside assistance to blacks as another invasion. The Yankees may have destroyed their families, their farms, and their fortunes, but they would not destroy the racial order. The war may have ended slavery, but white Southerners were determined to preserve strict racial boundaries.

More than Freedom: African-American Aspirations in 1865

If blacks could have peered into southern white minds, they would have been stunned. The former slaves did not initially even dream of social equality;

CHRONOLOGY

1863 Lincoln proposes his Ten Percent Plan.

1864 Congress proposes the Wade-Davis Bill.

1865 Sherman issues Field Order No. 15.

Freedmen's Bureau is established.

Andrew Johnson succeeds to the presidency, unveils his Reconstruction plan.

Massachusetts desegregates all public facilities.

Blacks in several southern cities organize Union Leagues.

Former Confederate states begin to pass black codes.

1866 Congress passes Southern Homestead Act, Civil Rights Act of 1866.

Ku Klux Klan is founded.

Fourteenth Amendment to the Constitution is passed (ratified in 1868).

President Johnson goes on a speaking tour.

1867 Congress passes Military Reconstruction Acts, Tenure of Office Act.

1868 President Johnson is impeached and tried in the Senate for defying the Tenure of Office Act.

Republican Ulysses S. Grant is elected president.

1869 Fifteenth Amendment passed (ratified 1870).

1870 Congress passes Enforcement Act.

Republican regimes topple in North Carolina and Georgia.

1871 Congress passes Ku Klux Klan Act.

1872 Freedmen's Bureau closes down.

Liberal Republicans emerge as a separate party.

Ulysses S. Grant is reelected.

1873 Severe depression begins.

Colfax Massacre occurs.

U.S. Supreme Court's decision in the *Slaughter-house* cases weakens the intent of the Fourteenth Amendment.

Texas falls to the Democrats in the fall elections.

1874 White Leaguers attempt a coup against the Republican government of New Orleans.

Democrats win off-year elections across the South amid widespread fraud and violence.

1875 Congress passes Civil Rights Act of 1875.

1876 Supreme Court's decision in *United States* v. *Cruikshank* nullifies Enforcement Act of 1870.

Outcome of the presidential election between Republican Rutherford B. Hayes and Democrat Samuel J. Tilden is contested.

1877 Compromise of 1877 makes Hayes president and ends Reconstruction.

---

far less did they plot the kind of vengeful murder and mayhem whites feared. They did harbor two potentially contradictory aspirations. The first was to be left alone, free of white supervision. Responding to the key question of the time, "What shall we do with the Negro?" former slave and abolitionist Frederick Douglass responded, "Do nothing. . . . Give him a chance to stand on his own legs! Let him alone!" But former slaves also wanted land, voting and civil rights, and education. To secure these, they needed the intervention and support of the white power structure.

In 1865, blacks had reason to hope that their dreams of full citizenship might be realized. They enjoyed a reservoir of support for their aspirations among some Republican leaders. The views of James A. Garfield, Union veteran, U.S. congressman, and future president, were typical of these

Republicans. Commenting on the ratification of the Thirteenth Amendment, Garfield asked, "What is freedom? Is it the bare privilege of not being chained? . . . If this is all, then freedom is a bitter mockery, a cruel delusion."

The first step Congress took beyond emancipation was to establish the Bureau of Refugees, Freedmen, and Abandoned Lands in March 1865. Congress envisioned the **Freedmen's Bureau**, as it came to be called, as a multipurpose agency to provide social, educational, and economic services, advice, and protection to former slaves and destitute whites. Congress also authorized the bureau to rent confiscated and abandoned farmland to freedmen in 40-acre plots with an option to buy. This auspicious beginning to realizing African-American aspirations belied the great disappointments that lay ahead.

Education

The greatest success of the Freedmen's Bureau was in education. The bureau coordinated more than fifty northern philanthropic and religious groups, which in turn established three thousand freedmen's schools in the South serving 150,000 men, women, and children.

Initially, single young women from the Northeast comprised much of the teaching force. One of them, 26-year-old Martha Schofield, came to Aiken, South Carolina, from rural Pennsylvania in 1865. Like many of her colleagues, she had joined the abolitionist movement as a teenager and decided to make teaching her life's work. Her strong Quaker beliefs reflected the importance of Protestant Christianity in motivating the young missionaries. When her sponsoring agency, the Pennsylvania Freedmen's Relief Association, folded in 1871, her school closed. Undaunted, she opened another school on her own, and despite chronic financial problems and the hostility of Aiken's whites, she and the school endured. (Since 1953, her school has been part of Aiken's public school system.)

By the time Schofield opened her own school in 1871, blacks outnumbered whites in the teaching corps of the "colored" schools. The financial troubles of northern missionary societies and declining interest in the freedmen's condition among Northern whites opened opportunities for black teachers. Support for them came from black churches, especially the **African Methodist Episcopal (AME) Church**.

The former slaves crowded into basements, shacks, and churches to attend school. "The children . . . hurry to school as soon as their work is over," wrote a teacher in Norfolk, Virginia, in 1867. "The plowmen hurry from the field at night to get their hour of study. Old men and women strain their dim sight with the book two and half feet distant from the eye, to catch the shape of the letter. I call this heaven-inspired interest."

At the end of the Civil War, roughly 90 percent of southern blacks could not read or write, compared with less than 30 percent of southern whites. Within a decade, the freedmen's schools had reduced illiteracy among the former slaves to below 70 percent. Joseph Wilson, a former slave, attributed the rising literacy rate to "this longing of ours for freedom of the mind as well as the body."

Some blacks went on to one of the thirteen colleges established by the American Missionary Association and black and white churches. Between 1860 and 1880 more than one thousand southern blacks earned college degrees at institutions still serving students today such as Howard University in Washington, D.C., Fisk University in Nashville, Hampton Institute (now University), Tuskegee Institute, and Biddle Institute (now Johnson C. Smith University) in Charlotte.

Pursuing freedom of the mind involved challenges beyond those of learning to read and write. Many whites condemned efforts at "Negro improvement." They viewed the time spent on education as wasted, forcing the former slaves to catch their lessons in bits and pieces between work, often by candlelight or on Sundays. Whites also harassed white female teachers, questioning their morals and motivations and threatening people who rented rooms to them. The *Atlanta Constitution*, in a vicious caricature, suggested that Harriet Beecher Stowe planned to establish a freedmen's school near Atlanta "for the

The Freedmen's Bureau, northern churches, and missionary societies established more than three thousand schools attended by some 150,000 men, women, and children in the years after the Civil War. At first, mostly young white women from the Northeast staffed these schools.

This painting of a mother and daughter reading captures the enduring thirst for education that dramatically reduced illiteracy among African-Americans of the Reconstruction era.

benefit of mulatto children that have been born in the South since its invasion by Yankee school-marms."

After the Freedmen's Bureau folded in 1872 and many of the northern societies that supported freedmen's education collapsed or cut back their involvement, education for southern blacks became more haphazard.

"Forty Acres and a Mule"

Although education was important to the freed slaves in their quest for civic equality, land ownership offered them the promise of economic independence. For generations, blacks had worked southern farms and had received nothing for their labor. An overwhelmingly agricultural people, freedmen looked to farm ownership as a key element in their transition from slavery to freedom. "Gib us our own land and we take care of ourselves," a Charleston slave asserted to a Northern visitor in 1865. "But without land, de ole massas can hire or starve us, as dey please."

Even before the war's end, rumors circulated through black communities in the South that the government would provide each black family with 40 acres and a mule. These rumors were fueled by General

William T. Sherman's **Field Order No. 15** in January 1865, which set aside a vast swath of abandoned land along the South Atlantic coast from the Charleston area to northern Florida for grants of up to 40 acres. The Freedmen's Bureau likewise raised expectations when it was initially authorized to rent 40-acre plots of confiscated or abandoned land to freedmen.

Early indications in various parts of the South suggested that freedmen might realize their hope of land ownership. By June 1865, about forty thousand former slaves had settled on "Sherman land" along the southeastern coast. In 1866, Congress passed the **Southern Homestead Act**, giving blacks preferential access to public lands in five southern states. Two years later, the Republican government of South Carolina initiated a land redistribution program financed by the sale of state bonds. The state used proceeds from the bond sales to purchase farmland, which it then resold to freedmen, who paid for it with state-funded long-term low-interest loans. By the late 1870s, more than fourteen thousand African-American families had taken advantage of this program.

The highest concentration of black land ownership was in the Upper South and in areas of the Lower South with better economic conditions and less white hostility toward blacks. By 1890, one out of three black farmers in the Upper South owned his land, compared to one out of five for the South as a whole. In Virginia, 43 percent of black farmers owned the land they farmed.

Land ownership did not ensure financial success. Most black-owned farms were small and of marginal land quality. The value of these farms in 1880 was roughly half that of white-owned farms. Blacks also had trouble obtaining credit to purchase or expand their holdings. A lifetime of field work left some freedmen without the managerial skills to operate a farm. The hostility of white neighbors and their refusal to lend tools or animals, share work, sell land, or offer advice also played a role in thwarting black aspirations. Black farmers often had the most success when groups of families settled together, as in the farm community of Promise Land in upcountry South Carolina.

The vast majority of former slaves, especially those in the Lower South, never fulfilled their dreams of land ownership. Rumors to the contrary, the federal government never intended to implement a land redistribution program in the South. General Sherman viewed his field order as a temporary measure to support freedmen for the remainder of the war. President Andrew Johnson nullified the order in September 1865, returning confiscated lands to their former owners. Even Republican supporters of black land ownership questioned the constitutionality of seizing privately owned real estate.

Most land redistribution programs that did emerge after the war, including government-sponsored programs, required black farmers to have capital. But in the impoverished postwar economy of the South, it was difficult for them to acquire it.

Republican party rhetoric of the 1850s extolled the virtues and dignity of free labor over the degradation of slave labor. Free labor usually meant working for a wage or under some other contractual arrangement. But unlike slaves, according to the then prevailing view, free laborers could enjoy the fruits of their work and might someday become owners or entrepreneurs themselves. It was self-help, not government assistance, that guaranteed individual success. After the war, many northern whites envisioned former slaves assuming the status of free laborers, not necessarily of independent landowners.

For most officials of the Freedmen's Bureau, who shared these views, reviving the southern economy was a higher priority than helping former slaves acquire farms. They wanted both to get the crop in the field and start the South on the road to a free labor system. They thus encouraged freedmen to work for their former masters under contract and postpone their quest for land. Bureau and military officials lectured former slaves on the virtues of staying home and working "faithfully" in the fields.

At first, agents of the Freedmen's Bureau supervised labor contracts between former slaves and masters. But after 1867, bureau surveillance declined. Agents assumed that both blacks and whites had become accustomed to the mutual obligations of contracts. The bureau, however, underestimated the power of white landowners to coerce favorable terms or to ignore those they did not like. Contracts implied a mutuality that most planters could not accept in their relations with former slaves. As northern journalist Whitelaw Reid noted in 1865, planters "have no sort of conception of free labor. They do not comprehend any law for controlling laborers, save the law of force."

The former slaves had their own views of their proper place in the labor hierarchy. If they could not own land in the short term, they would strive for the best labor arrangement in the meantime. As early as 1862, slaves behind Union lines abandoned the gang system of labor, which they associated with slavery and dependence. In contracts with planters (usually their former masters) after the war, freedmen in most of the South insisted on working the land independently with their families. By contrast, freedmen in the rice districts along the South Atlantic coast retained their task system of labor, which allowed them flexibility and a degree of independence.

Throughout the South in 1865 and 1866, landlords complained of a chronic labor shortage, although few freedmen had left the region. The alleged shortage was the result of former slaves' refusing to work under conditions that resembled slavery. The withdrawal of black women from field work also contributed to the impression of a labor shortage. By staying home to care for their families, black women avoided the economic and sexual exploitation of the slavery era. They also sought to place themselves on an equal social footing with white plantation women, who likewise worked in the home and not in the fields.

Migration to Cities

While some blacks asserted their rights as workers on southern farms, others affirmed their freedom by moving to towns and cities. Even before the war, the city had offered slaves and free blacks a measure of freedom unknown in the rural South. After the war, African-Americans moved to cities to find families, seek work, escape the tedium and supervision of farm life, or simply test their right to move about.

For these same reasons, whites disapproved of black migration to the city. For one thing, it reduced the labor pool for farms. It also gave blacks more opportunities to associate with whites of similar social status, to compete for jobs, and to establish schools, churches, and social organizations, fueling their hopes for racial equality. Whites felt confident that they could fix the freedmen's place in southern society on the farm; the city was another matter.

Between 1860 and 1870, the official African-American population in every major southern city rose significantly. In Atlanta, for example, blacks accounted for one in five residents in 1860 and nearly one in two by 1870.

Some freedmen came to cities initially to reunite with their families. Every city newspaper after the war carried advertisements from former slaves seeking their mates and children. In 1865, the Nashville *Colored Tennessean* carried this poignant plea: "During the year 1849, Thomas Sample carried away from this city, as his slaves, our daughter, Polly, and son. . . . We will give $100 each for them to any person who will assist them . . . to get to Nashville, or get word to us of their whereabouts."

Once in the city, blacks faced two immediate problems: finding a place to live and securing a job. They usually settled for the cheapest accommodations in low-lying areas or on the outskirts of town where building codes did not apply. Rather than developing one large ghetto, as in many northern cities, southern blacks lived in several concentrations in and around cities.

Sometimes armed with a letter of reference from their former masters, blacks went door to door to seek employment. Many found work serving white families—as guards, laundresses, maids—for very low wages. Both skilled and unskilled laborers found work rebuilding war-torn cities like Atlanta. Frederick Ayer, a Freedmen's Bureau agent in Atlanta, reported to a colleague in 1866 that "many of the whites are making most vigorous efforts to retrieve their broken fortunes and . . . rebuild their dwellings and shops. . . . This furnished employment to a large number of colored people as Masons, Carpenters, Teamsters, and Common Workmen."

Most rural blacks, however, arrived in cities untrained in the kinds of skills sought in an urban work force and so worked as unskilled laborers. In both Atlanta and Nashville, blacks comprised more than 75 percent of the unskilled work force in 1870. Their wages were at or below subsistence level. A black laborer in Richmond admitted to a journalist in 1870 that he had difficulty making ends meet on $1.50 a day. "It's right hard," he reported. "I have to pay $15 a month rent, and only two little rooms." His family survived because his wife took in laundry while her mother watched the children. Considering the laborer's struggle, the journalist wondered, "Were not your people better off in slavery?" The man replied, "Oh, no sir! We're a heap better off now. . . . We're men now, but when our masters had us we was only change in their pockets."

Faith and Freedom

Religious faith framed and inspired the efforts of African-Americans to test their freedom on the farm and in the city. Much as southern whites interpreted their destiny in religious terms, blacks found hope for the future in their Christian faith. Southern whites used religion to transform the Lost Cause from a shattering defeat to a premonition of a greater destiny. Blacks, in contrast, saw emancipation as the beginning of an exodus from bondage to the promised land.

Some black churches in the postwar South originated in the slavery era, but most split from white-dominated congregations after the war. Whites deplored blacks' expressive style of worship, and blacks were uncomfortable in congregations that treated them as inferiors. A separate church also reduced white surveillance.

The First African Baptist Church in Richmond originated in a white Baptist congregation founded before the war. An 1846 agreement allowed blacks to hold separate services, but only with a white minister officiating. In 1866, the white pastor resigned, noting that blacks "would naturally and justly prefer a minister of their own color." The white church transferred the deed to blacks that year, and the Reverend James Henry Holmes, a former slave, became their first black pastor. The church flourished under Holmes, paid off its debt, and by the 1870s boasted the largest black congregation in the United States.

The church became a primary focus of African-American life. It gave blacks the opportunity to hone skills in self-government and administration that white-dominated society denied them. Within the supportive confines of the congregation, they could assume leadership positions, render important decisions, deal with financial matters, and engage in politics. The church also operated as an educational institution. Local governments, especially in rural areas, rarely constructed public schools for blacks; churches often served that function. The desire to read the Bible inspired thousands of former slaves to attend the church school.

The church also spawned other organizations that served the black community over the next century. Burial societies, Masonic lodges, temperance groups, trade unions, and drama

The black church was the center of African-American life in the postwar urban South. Most black churches formed after the Civil War, but some, like the First African Baptist Church in Richmond, shown here in an 1874 engraving, traced their origins to before 1861.

clubs originated in churches. By the 1870s, blacks in Memphis had more than two hundred such organizations. They often came together to celebrate such holidays as Independence Day on July 4 and the anniversary of the Emancipation Proclamation on January 1. These commemorations antagonized whites and further divided the black and white communities.

African-Americans took great pride in their churches, which became visible measures of their progress. In Charleston, the first building erected after the war was a black church. The First Colored Baptist Church in Nashville became a landmark for its imposing brick and stone façade. Blacks donated a greater proportion of their earnings to their churches than whites did.

The church and the congregation were a cohesive force in black communities. They supported families under stress from discrimination and poverty. Husbands and wives joined church-affiliated societies together. Their children joined organizations such as the Young Rising Sons and Daughters of the New Testament. The church enforced family and religious values, punishing violaters guilty of such infractions as adultery. Black churchwomen— both working- and middle-class—were especially prominent in the family-oriented organizations.

Most black churches looked inward to strengthen their members against the harsh realities of postbellum southern society. Few ministers dared to engage in or even support protest activities. Some, especially those in the Colored Methodist Episcopal Church, counseled congregants to abide by the rules of second-class citizenship and to trust in God's will to right the wrongs of racism.

Northern-based denominations, however, notably the AME Church, were more aggressive advocates of black rights. AME ministers stressed the responsibility of individual blacks to realize God's will of racial equality.

Henry McNeal Turner, probably the most influential AME minister of his day, helped expand the denomination into the South from its small primarily northern base at the end of the Civil War. The white Southern Methodist church granted the 19-year-old Turner a license to preach in 1853. He served as an itinerant minister for both black and white congregations during the next five years. In 1858, he joined the AME Church and moved north to lead a congregation in Baltimore. Having served as a U.S. Army chaplain, Turner moved to Georgia and evangelized former slaves who thronged to an activist church with black roots. Within five years, the AME Church had grown to 500,000 members, 80 percent of whom lived in the South. Turner entered Georgia politics in the late 1860s and held

several state elective offices. His church elevated him to bishop in 1880.

Turner's career and the efforts of former slaves in the classroom, on the farm, in cities, and in the churches reflect the enthusiasm and expectations with which southern blacks greeted freedom. But the majority of southern whites were unwilling to see those expectations fulfilled. For this reason, African-Americans could not secure the fruits of their emancipation without the support and protection of the federal government. The issue of freedom was therefore inextricably linked to the other great issue of the era, the rejoining of the Confederacy to the Union, as expressed in federal Reconstruction policy.

Federal Reconstruction, 1865-1870

When the Civil War ended in 1865, no acceptable blueprint existed for reconstituting the Union. In 1863, Lincoln proposed to readmit a seceding state if 10 percent of its prewar voters took an oath of loyalty to the Union and it prohibited slavery in a new state constitution. But this **Ten Percent Plan** did not require states to grant equal civil and political rights to former slaves, and many Republicans in Congress thought it was not stringent enough. In 1864, a group of them responded with the **Wade-Davis Bill**, which required a *majority* of a state's prewar voters to pledge their loyalty to the Union and demanded guarantees of black equality before the law. The bill was passed at the end of a congressional session, but Lincoln kept it from becoming law by refusing to sign it (an action known as a pocket veto).

The controversy over these plans reflected two obstacles to Reconstruction that would continue to plague the ruling Republicans after the war. First, neither the Constitution nor legal precedent offered any guidance on whether the president or Congress should take the lead on Reconstruction policy. Second, there was no agreement on what that policy should be. Proposals requiring various preconditions for readmitting a state—loyalty oaths, new constitutions with certain specific provisions, guarantees of freedmen's rights—all provoked vigorous debate.

President Andrew Johnson, some conservative Republicans, and most Democrats believed that because the Constitution made no mention of secession, the southern states had been in rebellion, but had never left the Union, so there was no need for a formal process to readmit them. Moderate and radical Republicans disagreed, arguing that the defeated states had forfeited their rights. Moderates and radicals parted company, however, on the conditions necessary for readmission to the Union. The radicals wanted to treat the former Confederate states as territories—or "conquered provinces"—subject to congressional legislation. Moderates wanted to grant the seceding states more autonomy and limit federal intervention in their affairs while they satisfied the conditions of readmission. No group held a majority in Congress, and legislators sometimes changed their positions (see the summary table "Contrasting Views of Reconstruction").

Presidential Reconstruction, 1865–1867

When the Civil War ended in April 1865, Congress was not in session and would not reconvene until December. Thus the responsibility for developing a Reconstruction policy initially fell on Andrew Johnson, who succeeded to the presidency upon Lincoln's assassination. Johnson seemed well suited to the difficult task. The new president's personal and political background was promising to his Republican colleagues. Johnson was born in humble circumstances in North Carolina in 1808. He learned the tailoring trade and struck out for Tennessee as a teenager to open a tailor shop in the eastern Tennessee town of Greenville. Gaining his edu-

Andrew Johnson. When this photograph was taken in 1865, Johnson had recently ascended to the presidency and enjoyed widespread support within the Republican party and among the general public. However, his lenient policies toward the South and his tolerance of blatant violations of black civil rights turned public opinion against him in the North and provoked a confrontation with Congress.

cation informally, he prospered modestly, purchased a few slaves, and pursued politics as a hobby. His neighbors elected him alderman, mayor, state legislator, congressmen, governor, and then, in 1856, U.S. senator.

Johnson was the only southern senator to remain in the U.S. Senate after secession. This defiant Unionism won him popular acclaim in the North and credibility among Republican leaders, who welcomed him into their party. During the war, as military governor of Tennessee, he solidified his Republican credentials by advocating the abolition of slavery in Tennessee and severe punishment of Confederate leaders. His views landed him on the Republican ticket as the candidate for vice president in 1864. Indiana Republican congressman George W. Julian, who advocated harsh terms for the South and extensive rights for blacks, viewed Johnson's accession to the presidency in 1865 as "a godsend."

Most Northerners and many Republicans approved Johnson's Reconstruction plan when he unveiled it in May 1865. Johnson extended pardons and restored property rights, except in slaves, to Southerners who swore an oath of allegiance to the Union and the Constitution. Southerners who had held prominent positions in the Confederacy, however, and those with more than $20,000 in taxable property had to petition the president directly for a pardon. The plan had nothing to say about the voting rights and civil rights of former slaves.

Northern Democrats applauded the plan's silence on these issues and its promise of a quick restoration of the southern states to the Union. They expected the southern states to favor their party and expand its political power. Republicans, although some of them would have preferred the plan to have provided for black suffrage, approved of the restoration of property rights to whites. This position was consistent with their view of former slaves as laborers, not property owners. Republicans also hoped that Johnson's conciliatory terms might attract some southern whites to the Republican party.

White Southerners, however, were not so favorably impressed with Johnson's plan, and their response turned northern public opinion against the president. On the two great issues of freedom and reunion, white Southerners quickly demonstrated their eagerness to reverse the results of the Civil War. Although most states accepted President Johnson's modest requirements, several objected to one or more provisions. Mississippi and Texas refused to ratify the Thirteenth Amendment, which abolished slavery. Alabama accepted only parts of the amendment. South Carolina declined to nullify its secession ordinance. No southern state authorized black voting. When Johnson ordered special congressional elections in the South in the fall of 1865, the all-

SUMMARY

CONTRASTING VIEWS OF RECONSTRUCTION: PRESIDENT AND CONGRESS

Politician or Group	Policy on Former Slaves	Policy on Readmission of Former Confederate States
President Johnson	Opposed to black suffrage Silent on protection of black civil rights Opposed to land redistribution	Maintained that rebellious states were already readmitted Granted pardons and restoration of property to all who swore allegiance to the United States
Radical Republicans	Favored black suffrage Favored protection of black civil rights Favored land redistribution	Favored treating rebellious states as territories and establishing military districts* Favored limiting franchise to blacks and loyal whites
Moderate Republicans	Favored black suffrage Favored protection of civil rights Opposed land redistribution	Favored some restrictions on white suffrage* Favored requiring states to meet various requirements before being readmitted* Split on military rule

True of most but not all members of the group.

white electorate returned many prominent Confederate leaders to office, including Alexander Stephens, the former vice president of the Confederacy, along with six Confederate cabinet officers, several generals, and more than fifty members of the Confederate Congress.

In late 1865, the newly elected southern state legislatures revised their antebellum slave codes. The updated and renamed **black codes** allowed local officials to arrest blacks who could not document employment and residence or who were "disorderly" and sentence them to forced labor on farms or road construction crews. The codes also restricted blacks to certain occupations, barred them from jury duty, and forbade them to possess firearms. Apprenticeship laws permitted judges to take black children from parents who could not, in the judges' view, adequately support them. Given the widespread poverty in the South in 1865, the law could apply to almost any freed black family. Northerners looking for contrition in the South during the seven months after surrender found no sign of it. Worse, President Johnson did not seem perturbed about this turn of events.

The Republican-dominated Congress reconvened in December 1865 in a belligerent mood. A few

radical Republicans pushed for swift retribution. George W. Julian thundered that he would "indict, convict and hang Jefferson Davis in the name of God; as for Robert E. Lee, unmolested in Virginia, hang him too." His colleague, Benjamin F. Wade, suggested that "if the negroes by insurrection would contrive to slay one-half of the Southern whites, the remaining half would then hold them in respect and treat them with justice." Few in Congress took these statements seriously. Nonetheless, a consensus formed among radical Republicans, who comprised nearly half of the party's strength in Congress, that to gain readmission, a state would have to extend suffrage to blacks, protect freedmen's civil rights, and have its white citizens officially acknowledge these rights. Some radicals also supported the redistribution of land to former slaves, but few pressed for social equality. They envisioned a new South of modest farms, some owned by former slaves, and a Republican party built on an alliance between blacks and white loyalists.

Thaddeus Stevens of Pennsylvania led the radical forces in the House of Representatives, while abolitionist veteran Charles Sumner of Massachusetts rallied radicals in the Senate. Stevens had established himself as a partisan for black political rights in the North as

"Selling a Freeman to Pay His Fine at Monticello, Florida." This 1867 engraving shows how the black codes of the early Reconstruction era in the South reduced former slaves to virtually their pre–Civil War status. Scenes such as this convinced Northerners that the white South was unrepentant and prompted Congressional Republicans to devise their own Reconstruction plan.

early as the 1840s. As a congressman during the Civil War, he pushed Lincoln to free and arm the slaves and later to extend them the right to vote. Stevens dreamed of a South populated by white and black yeoman farmers. With no large plantations and few landless farmers, the South would become an ideal republic, a boon to the rest of the nation instead of a burden. Few shared his vision, and when he died in 1868, a reporter noted that "no man was oftener outvoted." Yet he remained the conscience of the House, a standard of idealism in an age of growing cynicism. His epitaph read in part, "The principle which I advocated through a long life, Equality of Man before his Creator."

Charles Sumner was among the foremost abolitionist politicians before the Civil War. His combative nature won him few friends, even within his own party. As fierce as Stevens in the promotion of black civil and political rights after the war, he also believed that the Reconstruction era offered a "golden moment" to remake the South into an egalitarian region. Sumner died in 1874 as his dream was fading. The last piece of Reconstruction legislation, the Civil Rights Act of 1875, became a posthumous tribute to his uncommon ability to overcome the racial prejudices of the day with a vision of a colorblind society.

But the radicals could not unite behind a program, and it fell to their moderate colleagues to take the first step toward a Congressional Reconstruction plan. The moderates shared the radicals' desire to pro-

tect the former slaves' civil and voting rights. But they would not support land redistribution schemes or punitive measures against prominent Confederates. The moderates' first measure, passed in early 1866, extended the life of the Freedmen's Bureau and provided it with authority to punish state officials who failed to extend to blacks the civil rights enjoyed by whites. But President Johnson vetoed the legislation.

Undeterred, Congress passed the **Civil Rights Act of 1866** in direct response to the black codes. The act specified the civil rights to which all U.S. citizens were entitled. In creating a category of national citizenship with rights that superseded state laws restricting them, the act changed federal-state relations (and in the process overturned the *Dred Scott* decision). President Johnson vetoed the act, but it became law when Congress mustered a two-thirds majority to override his veto, the first time in American history that Congress passed major legislation over a president's veto.

Andrew Johnson's position reflected both his view of government and his racial attitudes. The Republican president remained a Democrat in spirit. Republicans had expanded federal power during the Civil War. Johnson, however, like most Democrats, favored more of a balance between federal and state power. He also shared with many of his white southern neighbors a belief in black inferiority and a view that white plantation owners had conspired to limit the economic and political power of white yeomen like himself. Johnson supported abolition assuming that, once free, blacks would emigrate to Africa. Given the president's views and his inflexible temperament, a clash between him and Congress became inevitable.

To keep freedmen's rights safe from presidential vetoes, state legislatures, and federal courts, the Republican-dominated Congress moved to incorporate some of the provisions of the 1866 Civil Rights Act into the Constitution with an amendment. The **Fourteenth Amendment**, which Congress passed in June 1866, addressed the issues of civil and voting rights and marked a fundamental shift of power from the states to the federal government (see the summary table "Constitutional Amendments and Federal Legislation of the Reconstruction Era"). It guaranteed every citizen

SUMMARY

CONSTITUTIONAL AMENDMENTS AND FEDERAL LEGISLATION OF THE RECONSTRUCTION ERA

Amendment or Legislation	Purpose	Significance
Thirteenth Amendment (passed and ratified in 1865)	Prevented southern states from reestablishing slavery after the war	Final step toward full emancipation of slaves
Freedmen's Bureau Act (1865)	Oversight of resettlement, reflief, education, and labor for former slaves	Involved the federal government directly in assisting the transition from slavery to freedom; worked fitfully to achieve this objective during its seven-year career
Southern Homestead Act (1866)	Provided blacks preferential access to public lands in five southern states	Lack of capital and poor quality of federal land thwarted the purpose of the act
Civil Rights Act of 1866	Defined rights of national citizenship	Marked an important change in federal–state relations, tilting balance of power to national government
Fourteenth Amendment (passed 1866; ratified 1868)	Prohibited states from violating the rights of their citizens	Strengthened the Civil Rights Act of 1866 and guaranteed all citizens equality before the law
Military Reconstruction Acts (1867)	Set new rules for the readmission of ex-Confederate states into the Union and secured black voting rights	Initiated Congressional Reconstruction
Tenure of Office Act (1867)	Required congressional approval for the removal of any official whose appointment had required Senate confirmation	A congressional challenge to the president's right to dismiss Cabinet members that led to President Andrew Johnson's impeachment trial
Fifteenth Amendment (passed 1869; ratified 1870)	Guaranteed the right of all American male citizens to vote regardless of race	The basis for black voting rights
Civil Rights Act of 1875	Prohibited racial discrimination in jury selection, public transportation, and public accommodations	Rarely enforced; Supreme Court declared it unconstitutional in 1883

equality before the law. The two key sections of the amendment prohibited states from violating the civil rights of their citizens, thus outlawing the black codes, and gave states the choice of enfranchising blacks or losing representation in Congress. Some radical Republicans expressed disappointment that the amendment, in a reflection of northern ambivalence on the subject, failed to give the vote to blacks outright.

The amendment also disappointed advocates of woman suffrage, for the first time using the word *male* in the Constitution to define who could vote. Wendell Phillips, a prominent abolitionist, counseled them, "One question at a time. This hour belongs to the Negro." Susan B. Anthony, who had campaigned for the abolition of slavery before the war and helped mount a petition drive that collected 400,000 signatures for the Thirteenth Amendment, formed the **American Equal Rights Association** in 1866 with her colleagues to push for woman suffrage at the state level.

The amendment had little immediate impact on the South. Although enforcement of black codes diminished, white violence against blacks increased. In the 1870s, several decisions by the U.S. Supreme Court would weaken the amendment's provisions. Eventually, however, the Fourteenth Amendment would play a major role in securing the civil rights of African-Americans when the issue reemerged in the 1950s.

President Johnson seemed to encourage white intransigence by openly denouncing the Fourteenth Amendment. In August 1866, at the start of the congressional election campaign, he undertook an unprecedented "swing around the circle" of key northern states to sell his message of sectional reconciliation to the public. Although listeners appreciated Johnson's desire for peace, they questioned his claims of southern white loyalty to the Union. The president's diatribes against the Republican Congress won him followers in those northern states with a reservoir of opposition to black suffrage. But the tone and manner of his campaign offended many as undignified. In the November elections, the Democrats suffered embarrassing defeats in the North as Republicans managed better than two-thirds majorities in both the House and Senate, sufficient to override presidential vetoes. Radical Republicans, joined by moderate colleagues buoyed by the election results and revolted by the president's and the South's intransigence, seized the initiative when Congress reconvened a month after the election.

Congressional Reconstruction, 1867–1870

The radicals' first salvo in their attempt to take control over Reconstruction occurred with the passage over President Johnson's veto of the **Military Recon-**struction Acts**. The measures, passed in March 1867, inaugurated a period known as **Congressional Reconstruction** or Radical Reconstruction. Except for Tennessee, the only southern state to ratify the Fourteenth Amendment (and readmitted to the Union as a result), Congress divided the ex-Confederate states into five military districts, each headed by a general (see Map 18-1). The commanders' first order of business was to conduct voter registration campaigns to enroll blacks and bar whites who had held office before the Civil War and who had supported the Confederacy. The eligible voters would then elect a state constitutional convention to write a new constitution that guaranteed **universal manhood suffrage**. Once a majority of eligible voters ratified the new constitution and the Fourteenth Amendment, their state would be eligible for readmission to the Union.

The Reconstruction Acts fulfilled the radicals' three major objectives. First, they secured the freedmen's right to vote. Second, they ensured the likelihood that southern states would be run by Republican regimes that would enforce the new constitutions, protect former slaves' rights, and maintain the Republican majority in Congress. Finally, the acts set standards for readmission that required the South to accept the consequences of defeat: the preeminence of the federal government and the end of involuntary servitude.

Map 18-1   Congressional Reconstruction, 1865–1877
When Congress wrested control of Reconstruction policy from President Andrew Johnson, it divided the South into the five military districts depicted here. The commanding generals for each district held the authority both to hold elections and decide who could vote.

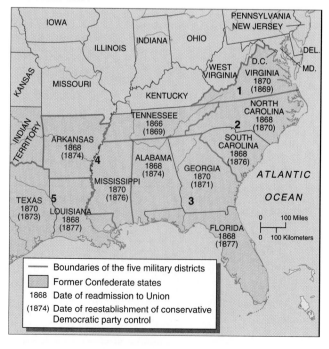

To limit presidential interference with their policies even further, Republicans passed the **Tenure of Office Act**, prohibiting the president from removing certain officeholders without the Senate's consent. Johnson, angered at what he believed was an unconstitutional attack on presidential authority, deliberately violated the act in February 1868. He fired Secretary of War Edwin M. Stanton, a leading radical. The House responded to this defiance of congressional authority by approving, for the only time in American history, articles of impeachment against the president. If convicted in the Senate trial that followed, President Johnson would be removed from office. The Senate voted 35 to 19 to convict, one vote short of the two-thirds necessary to remove Johnson. The seven Republicans who voted against their party had little respect for the president but felt that a conviction would damage the office of the

presidency and erase the constitutional separation of powers. The outcome weakened the radicals' clout in Congress and eased the way for moderate Republican Ulysses S. Grant to gain the party's nomination for president in 1868.

The Republicans viewed the 1868 presidential election as a referendum on Congressional Reconstruction. They supported black suffrage in the South but equivocated on allowing African-Americans to vote in the North (blacks could vote in only eight of the twenty-two northern states). Republicans "waved the bloody shirt," reminding voters of Democratic disloyalty, the sacrifices of war, and the peace only Republicans could redeem. Democrats denounced Congressional Reconstruction as federal tyranny and in openly racist appeals warned white voters that a Republican victory would mean black rule. Grant won the election, but his margin of victory was uncomfortably narrow.

Reflecting growing ambivalence in the North over issues of race and federal authority, New York's Horatio Seymour, the Democratic presidential nominee, probably carried a majority of the nation's white vote. Blacks, voting overwhelmingly for Grant, probably provided him his margin of victory.

The Republicans retained a strong majority in both houses of Congress and managed to pass another major piece of Reconstruction legislation, the **Fifteenth Amendment**, in February 1869. In response to growing concerns about voter fraud and violence against freedmen, the amendment guaranteed the right of American men to vote, regardless of race. Although the amendment provided a loophole allowing states to impose restrictions on the right to vote based on literacy requirements or property qualifications and also failed to address the issue of woman suffrage, it was nonetheless a milestone. It made the right to vote perhaps the most distinguishing characteristic of American citizenship.

The Fifteenth Amendment allowed states to keep the franchise a male prerogative, angering many in the woman

Casting a ballot. Richmond blacks vote for a state constitutional convention in 1867. A key objective of Congressional Reconstruction was to secure the voting rights of freedmen.

Southern Republican Governments, 1867–1870

Away from Washington, the first order of business for the former Confederacy was to draft state constitutions. The documents embodied progressive principles new to the former Confederacy. They mandated the election of numerous local and state offices. Self-perpetuating local elites could no longer appoint themselves or cronies to powerful positions. The constitutions committed southern states, many for the first time, to public education. Lawmakers enacted a variety of reforms, including social welfare, penal reform, legislative reapportionment, and universal manhood suffrage.

The Republican regimes that gained control in southern states promoted vigorous state government and the protection of civil and voting rights. Three diverse Republican constituencies supported these governments. One consisted of native whites, most of them yeomen farmers. Residing mainly in the upland regions of the South and long ignored by lowland planters and merchants in state government, some had supported the Union during the war. The conflict had left many of them devastated. They struggled to keep their land and hoped for an easing of credit and for debt-stay laws to help them escape foreclosure. They wanted public schools for their children and good roads to get their crops to market. Some urban merchants and large planters also called themselves Republicans. Many were Whigs before the war, and a few had been Unionists. They were attracted to the party's emphasis on economic development, especially railroad construction, and would become prominent in Republican leadership after 1867.

Collectively, these native whites were called **scalawags**, a derogatory term derived from the name of the district of Scalloway, on Scotland's Shetland Islands, known for its scraggly livestock. The term was first applied in western New York before the Civil War to an idle person and then to a mischievous one. Although their opponents may have perceived them as a unified group, scalawags held a variety of views. Planters and merchants opposed easy debt and credit arrangements and the use of their taxes to support programs other than railroads or port improvements. Yeomen farmers desperately needed the debt and credit legislation to retain their land. And even though they supported public schools and road building—which would require increased state revenues—they opposed higher taxes.

Northern transplants, or **carpetbaggers**, as their opponents called them, constituted a second group of southern Republicans. The term also had antebellum origins, referring to a suspicious stranger. Cartoonists depicted carpetbaggers as shoddily dressed

Susan B. Anthony and Elizabeth Cady Stanton, shown in a photograph from 1892, were stalwart advocates of woman suffrage. They supported the Fourteenth Amendment despite its silence on woman suffrage, but opposed the ratification of the Fifteenth Amendment because it allowed states to keep the franchise a male privilege.

suffrage movement more than had the Fourteenth Amendment. The resulting controversy severed the ties between the movement and Republican politics. Susan B. Anthony broke with her abolitionist colleagues and opposed the amendment. Fellow abolitionist and woman suffragist Elizabeth Cady Stanton charged that the amendment created an "aristocracy of sex." In an appeal brimming with ethnic and racial animosity, Stanton warned that "if you do not wish the lower orders of Chinese, African, Germans and Irish, with their low ideas of womanhood to make laws for you and your daughters . . . awake to the danger . . . and demand that woman, too, shall be represented in the government!" Such language created a major rift in the nascent women's movement. Women who supported the amendment formed the New England Woman Suffrage Association, challenging Anthony's American Equal Rights Association.

and poorly groomed men, their worldly possessions in a ratty cloth satchel, slinking into a town and swindling the locals before departing with their ill-gotten gains. The reality was far different from the caricature. Thousands of Northerners came south during and after the war. Many were Union soldiers who simply enjoyed the climate and perhaps married a local woman. Most were drawn by economic opportunity. Land was cheap and the price of cotton high. Although most carpetbaggers had supported the Republican party before they moved south, few became politically active until the cotton economy nosedived in 1866. Financial concerns were not all that motivated carpetbaggers to enter politics; some hoped to aid the freedmen.

Carpetbaggers never comprised more than 2 percent of any state's population. Most white Southerners viewed them as an alien presence, instruments of a hated occupying force. They provoked resentment because they seemed to prosper while most Southerners struggled in poverty. And they further estranged themselves from their neighbors by supporting and participating in the Republican state governments that most whites despised. In Alabama, local editors organized a boycott of northern-owned shops. "STARVE THEM OUT!" they wrote. "Don't put your foot in the doors of their shops, offices, and stores. Purchase from true men and patronize those of known Southern sympathies." Because many of them tended to support extending political and civil rights to blacks, carpetbaggers were also often at odds with their fellow white Republicans, the scalawags.

African-Americans constituted the Republican party's largest southern constituency. In three states— South Carolina, Mississippi, and Louisiana—they also constituted the majority of eligible voters. They viewed the franchise as the key to civic equality and economic opportunity and demanded an active role in party and government affairs.

"The Shackle Broken by the Genius of Freedom" is the title of this 1874 lithograph of South Carolina legislator Robert B. Elliott addressing his fellow lawmakers. Born in Boston, educated in England, Elliott served with distinction in Congress and at the state level during Reconstruction.

Blacks began to take part in southern politics even before the end of the Civil War, especially in cities occupied by Union forces. In February 1865, blacks in Norfolk, Virginia, gathered to demand a say in the new government that Union supporters were forming in that portion of the state. In April, they created the Colored Monitor Union club, modeled after Republican party organizations in northern cities, called **Union Leagues**. They demanded "the right of *universal* suffrage" for "*all* loyal men, without distinction of color." Blacks in other southern cities held similar meetings, seeking inclusion in the democratic process in order to protect their freedom. As a member of the Alexandria, Virginia, black Union League argued in August 1865, "The only salvation for us . . . is in the *possession of the ballot.* Give us this, and we will protect ourselves."

Southern whites viewed these developments with alarm but could not at first counter them. Despite white threats, blacks thronged to Union League meetings in 1867, even forging interracial alliances in states such as North Carolina and Alabama. Focusing on political education and recruitment, the leagues successfully mobilized black voters. In 1867, more than 90 percent of eligible black voters across the South turned out for elections. Black women, even though they could not vote, also played a role. During the 1868 presidential campaign, for example, black maids and cooks in the South wore buttons touting the candidacy of Republican presidential nominee Ulysses S. Grant.

Southern blacks were not content just to vote; they also demanded political office. White Republican leaders in the South often took the black vote for granted. But on several occasions after 1867, blacks threatened to run independent candidates, support rival Democrats, or simply stay home unless they were represented among Republican nominees. These demands brought them some success. The number of southern black congressmen in the U.S. House of Representatives increased from two in 1869 to seven in 1873, and more than six hundred blacks, most of them former slaves from plantation counties, were elected to southern state legislatures between 1867 and 1877.

White fears that black officeholders would enact vengeful legislation proved unfounded. African-Americans generally did not promote race-specific legislation. Rather, they supported measures such as debt relief and state funding for education that benefited all poor and working-class people, white and black alike. Like all politicians, however, black officials in southern cities sought to enact measures beneficial to their constituents. In Atlanta, for example, black officeholders had a sidewalk laid in front of a prominent black church and diverted a road scheduled to cut through a black neighborhood. In Richmond, blacks secured an ordinance forbidding the robbing of black graves to supply medical schools with corpses. And they succeeded in having a black police commissioner appointed in Jacksonville, Florida. Gains like these underscored the advantages of suffrage for the African-American community.

During the first few years of Congressional Reconstruction, Republican governments walked a tightrope, attempting to lure moderate Democrats and unaffiliated whites into the party without slighting the black vote. They used the lure of patronage power and the attractive salaries that accompanied public office. In 1868, for example, Louisiana's Republican governor, Henry C. Warmoth, appointed conservative whites to state and local offices, which he divided equally between ex-Confederate veterans and blacks, and repealed a constitutional provision disfranchising former Confederate officials.

Republicans also gained support by expanding the role of state government to a degree unprecedented in the South. Southern Republican administrations appealed to hard-pressed upland whites by prohibiting foreclosure and passing stay laws that allowed farm owners extra time to repay debts. They undertook building programs that benefited both blacks and whites, erecting hospitals, schools, and orphanages. Stepping further into social policy than most northern states at the time, Republican governments in the South expanded women's property rights, enacted legislation against child abuse, and required child support from fathers of mulatto children. In South Carolina, the Republican government provided medical care for the poor; in Alabama, it provided free legal aid for needy defendants.

Despite these impressive policies, southern Republicans were unable to hold their diverse constituency together. Although the party had some success among white yeoman farmers, the liberal use of patronage to attract conservative whites failed to gain it many new adherents. At the same time, it alienated the party's core supporters, who resented seeing their former enemies rewarded with lucrative offices.

The high costs of their activist policies further undermined the Republicans by forcing them to raise state taxes. Small property holders, already reeling from declining staple prices, found the taxes especially burdensome, despite liberal stay laws. Revenues nonetheless could not keep pace with expenditures. In Mississippi—where the Republican governor built a public school system for both blacks and whites, founded a black university, reorganized the state judiciary, built new courthouses and two state hospitals, and pushed through legislation giving blacks equal access to public facilities—the state debt soared to $1.5 million between 1869 and 1873. This was in an era when state budgets rarely exceeded $1 million.

Unprecedented expenditures and the liberal use of patronage sometimes resulted in waste and corruption. Officials charged with selecting railroad routes, appointing lesser officials, and erecting public buildings were well positioned to benefit from their power. Their high salaries offended many in an otherwise impoverished region. Problems like these were not limited to the South. They were pervasive throughout the country in the 1860s and 1870s. The perception of dishonesty was nonetheless damaging to governments struggling to build legitimacy among a skeptical white electorate.

The excesses of some state governments, high taxes, contests over patronage, and conflicts over the relative roles of whites and blacks within the party opened rifts in Republican ranks. Patronage triggered intraparty warfare. Every office secured by a Democrat created a disappointed Republican. Class tensions erupted in the party as economic development policies, favored by former Whigs, sometimes superseded relief and social service legislation supported by small farmers. The failure of Alabama Republicans to deliver on promises of debt relief and land redistribution eroded the significant support the party had enjoyed among upcountry whites. There were differences among blacks too. In the Lower South, divisions that had developed in the prewar era between urban, lighter-skinned free blacks and darker, rural slaves persisted into the Reconstruction era. In many southern states, black clergy, because of their independence from white support and their important spiritual and educational role, became leaders. But most preached salvation in the next world rather than equality in the present, conceding more to whites than their rank-and-file constituents.

Counter-Reconstruction, 1870-1874

Republicans might have survived battles over patronage, differences over policy, and the resentment provoked by extravagant expenditures and high taxes. But they could not overcome racism. Racism killed Republican rule in the South because it deepened divisions within the party, encouraged white violence, and eroded support in the North. Southern Democrats discovered that they could use race baiting and racial violence to create racial solidarity among whites that overrode their economic and class differences. Unity translated into election victories.

Northerners responded to the persistent violence in the South not with outrage but with a growing sense of tedium. They came to accept the arguments of southern whites that it was folly to allow blacks to vote and hold office. Racism became respectable. Noted intellectuals and journalists espoused "scientific" theories that claimed to demonstrate the natural superiority of whites over blacks. These theories influenced the **Liberal Republicans**, followers of a new political movement that splintered the Republican party, further weakening its will to pursue Reconstruction policy.

By 1874, Americans were concerned with an array of domestic problems that overshadowed Reconstruction. A serious economic depression left them more preoccupied with survival than racial justice. Corruption convinced many that politics was part of the nation's problems, not a solution to them. With the rest of the nation thus distracted and weary, southern whites reclaimed control of the South.

The Uses of Violence

Racial violence preceded Republican rule. As African-Americans moved about, attempted to vote, haggled over labor contracts, and carried arms as part of occupying Union forces, they tested the patience of southern whites. In a racial world turned upside down from the white perspective, any assertion of equality from blacks seemed threatening.

Cities, where blacks and whites competed for jobs and where black political influence was most visible, became flashpoints for interracial violence. In May 1866, for example, the collision of two wagons in Memphis, one driven by a white carter, the other by a black carter, touched off three days of white attacks on blacks and black neighborhoods. Forty-six blacks and two whites died in the fray, and five black women were raped. The white mob destroyed black churches, schools, and homes.

White paramilitary groups flourished in the South during the Reconstruction era and were responsible for much of the violence directed against African-Americans. Probably the best known of these groups was the **Ku Klux Klan**. Founded in Tennessee by six Confederate veterans in 1866, the Klan was initially a social club. Prominent ex-Confederates such as General John B. Gordon and General Nathan Bedford Forrest, allegedly the first Grand Wizard of the Klan, saw the political potential of the new organization. Within a year, the Klan had spread throughout the South. In 1867, when blacks entered politics in large numbers, the Klan unleashed a wave of terror against them. Klan night riders in ghostlike disguises intimidated black communities. The Klan directed much of its violence toward subverting the electoral process. One historian has estimated that roughly 10 percent of all black delegates to the 1867 state constitutional conventions in the South became victims of political violence during the next decade.

Not all Klan attacks had political objectives. Klansmen struck against anyone, black or white, whom they believed had violated racial boundaries. A Georgia Klansman murdered a freedman because he could read and write. Klansmen in Florence, South Carolina, killed a black who rented a plantation "because such a thing ought not to be." And in 1868, Klansmen murdered three southern white Republican Georgia state legislators. Membership in the Klan crossed class lines. Race became an issue on which whites, regardless of differing economic interests, could agree.

By 1868, white paramilitary organizations permeated the South. Violence was particularly severe in election years in Louisiana, which had a large and active black electorate. Before the presidential election of 1868, for example, Louisiana whites killed at least seven hundred Republicans, including black leader William R. Meadows, whom whites dragged from his home and shot and beheaded in front of his family. As the election neared, white mobs roamed New Orleans, attacking blacks and breaking up Republican rallies. The violence cut the Republican vote in the state by 50 percent from the previous spring.

Two Alabama Klansmen, shown here in 1868 at the height of the Ku Klux Klan's campaign of political terror. Although Congress outlawed the Klan, political terrorist groups associated with the Democratic party continued the Klan's violent legacy in the 1870s and succeeded in reestablishing white Democratic party rule in the South.

But the most serious example of political violence in Louisiana, if not in the entire South, occurred in Colfax in 1873 when a white Democratic mob attempted to wrest control of local government from Republicans. For three weeks, black defenders held the town against the white onslaught. When whites finally broke through, they massacred the remaining blacks, including those who had surrendered and laid down their weapons.

Racial violence and the combative reaction it provoked both among blacks and Republican admin-

istrations energized white voters. Democrats regained power in North Carolina, for example, after the state's Republican governor enraged white voters by calling out the militia to counter white violence during the election of 1870. That same year, the Republican regime in Georgia fell as well.

Some Republican governments countered the violence successfully for a time. Republican governor Edmund J. Davis of Texas, for example, organized a special force of two hundred state policemen to round up Klan night riders. Between 1870 and 1872, Davis's force arrested six thousand and broke the Klan in Texas. Arkansas governor Powell Clayton launched an equally successful campaign against the Klan in 1869. But other governors hesitated to enforce laws directed at the Klan, fearing that to do so would further alienate whites.

The federal government responded to requests for help from southern Republican administrations with a variety of legislation. One example was the Fifteenth Amendment, ratified in 1869, which guaranteed the right to vote. Another was the **Enforcement Act of 1870**, which enabled the federal government to appoint supervisors in states that failed to protect citizens' voting rights. When violence and intimidation persisted, Congress followed with a second, more sweeping measure, the **Ku Klux Klan Act of 1871**. This law permitted federal authorities, with military assistance, if necessary, to arrest and prosecute members of groups that denied a citizen's civil rights if state authorities failed to do so. The Klan Act was not successful in curbing racial violence, as the Colfax Massacre in 1873 made vividly clear. But with it, Congress, by claiming the right to override state authority to bring individuals to justice, established a new precedent in federal-state relations.

The Failure of Northern Will

The success of political violence after 1871 reflected less the inadequacy of congressional legislation than the failure of will on the part of northern Republicans to follow through on commitments to southern Republican administrations. The erosion of northern support for Congressional Reconstruction began as early as the presidential election of 1868. Republican candidate Ulysses S. Grant's campaign theme that year was "Let Us Have Peace," a reference to the political turmoil in the South.

The commitment to voting rights for southern blacks, widespread among Republicans in 1865 and affirmed in the Fifteenth Amendment passed in 1869, faded as well. American politics in the 1870s seemed more corrupt and less responsible to the electorate than ever before. Scandal abounded. Democratic boss William M. Tweed and his associates transformed **Tammany Hall**, a Democratic Club, into a full-fledged political machine that robbed New York

City of an astounding $100 million. Federal officials allowed private individuals to manipulate the stock market for spectacular gains. Several members of Congress and President Grant's vice president exchanged government favors for railroad stock. And the president's secretary of war was caught selling contracts to firms supplying goods to Indians.

A growing number of Americans attributed the debacle to the expansion of the right to vote. Voting was a privilege to be earned, they maintained, not a basic right of citizenship. And blacks, according to some Republicans, had not earned that right.

The racist assumption behind this view found growing support among intellectuals. Racism gained an aura of scientific respectability in the late nineteenth century. Science was held in high esteem at the time, helping assure public acceptance of the putatively scientific views of the racial theorists. According to those views, some peoples are inherently inferior to others, a natural state of affairs that no government interference can change.

According to white racial theorists, it was folly to grant suffrage to African-Americans because an inferior race (black) could not hold power over a superior race (white). Blacks, because of their race, could not understand the basic principles of democracy. Thus Missouri's Republican senator Carl Schurz looked on with equanimity as white terror toppled Republican regimes in the South in 1872. He urged his colleagues to let affairs run their course and admit that southern black voters and officeholders "*were* ignorant and inexperienced; that the public business *was* an unknown world to them, and that in spite of the best intentions they *were* easily misled." Allowing an unfit people to vote resulted in a "more disastrous process than rebellion," intoned *The Nation*, a leading Republican journal, in 1872. If southern Republican governments depended primarily on their "control over the colored man," they rested on sand. The perpetual turmoil in the South, the extravagances of some Republican southern administrations, and their persistent inability to attract sufficient numbers of whites all reinforced the view that these governments were unnatural.

Blacks were not the only targets of racial theory. Immigrants were also said to derive from inferior races. Their growing numbers coincided with the flourishing of corrupt political machines in northern cities, fueling Republican reservations about an unrestricted franchise. Like blacks, immigrants were held to be incapable of understanding the American electoral process. As one Republican leader observed, "What is bad among ignorant foreigners in New York will not be good among ignorant natives in South Carolina."

Concerns about the quality of the electorate reflected the rising stakes of public office in post–Civil War America. The urban industrial economy boomed in the five years after the war. Engineers flung railroads across the continent. Steam propelled factories to unprecedented levels of productivity and ships to new speed records. Discoveries of rich natural resources such as oil and iron presaged a new age of industrial might. Republicans promoted and benefited from the boom, and it influenced their priorities. Railroad, mining, and lumber lobbyists crowded Washington and state capitals begging for financial and land subsidies and favorable legislation. In an era before conflict-of-interest laws, leading Republicans sat on the boards of railroads, land development companies, and industrial corporations. While the federal government denied land to the freedman, it doled out millions of acres to corporations. Issues of fiscal responsibility, tariffs, and hard money replaced freedom and reunion, moving the Republican party, as *The Nation* explained in 1874, "out of the region of the Civil War."

Not all Republicans approved the party's promotion of economic development. Some questioned the prudence of government intervention in the "natural" operation of the nation's economy. The emerging scandals of the Grant administration led to calls for reform. Republican governments, North and South, were condemned for their lavish spending and high taxes. The time had come to restore good government.

The reform movement attracted an assortment of groups concerned about the size, activism, and expense of government. Business leaders decried the ability of wealthy lobbyists to influence economic decisions. An influential group of intellectuals and opinion makers lamented the inability of politicians to understand "natural" laws. Some reformers expressed alarm at the federal government's increasing intervention in the affairs of the states since the Civil War. And some Republicans joined the reform movement out of fear that Democrats would capitalize on the turmoil in the South and the political scandals in the North to reap huge electoral victories in 1872.

Liberal Republicans and the Election of 1872

Liberal Republicans put forward an array of suggestions to improve government and save the Republican party. They advocated civil service reform to reduce reliance on patronage and the abuses that accompanied office seeking. To limit government and reduce artificial economic stimuli, the reformers called for tariff reduction and an end to federal land grants to railroads. For the South, they recommended a general amnesty for whites and a return to "local self-government" by men of "property and enterprise."

When the Liberals failed to convince other Republicans to adopt their program, they broke with the party. Taking advantage of this split, the Democrats forged an alliance with the Liberals. Together, the Democrats and Liberals nominated journalist Horace Greeley to challenge Ulysses S. Grant for the presidency in the election of 1872. Grant won resoundingly, helped by high voter turnout among blacks in the South. He carried all southern states except Georgia, Tennessee, and Texas. Elsewhere, Republicans again used the tactic of waving the bloody shirt to good effect. It was the Republicans, they declared, who had saved the Union, the Democrats who had almost destroyed it. Greeley had been a staunch Republican during the Civil War and had spent most of his career attacking Democrats. Republicans used his own words against him during the campaign. Many Democratic voters stayed home.

The election suggested that the excesses of the Grant administration had not yet exceeded public tolerance and that the Republican experiment in the South retained some public support. But Greeley had helped the Republicans by running an inept campaign. Within a year, an economic depression, continued violence in the South, and the persistent corruption of the Grant administration would turn public opinion against the Republicans. With this shift, support for Reconstruction and black rights would also fade.

Redemption, 1874–1877

For southern Democrats, the Republican victory in 1872 underscored the importance of turning out larger numbers of whites and restricting the black vote. They accomplished these goals over the next four years with a surge in political violence. Southern Democrats operated in the secure knowledge that federal authorities would not intervene against them. Preoccupied with corruption and economic crisis and increasingly indifferent, if not hostile, to African-American aspirations, most Americans looked the other way. The elections of 1876—on the local, state, and national levels— affirmed the triumph of southern whites. Reconstruction did not end; it was overthrown.

Southern Democrats called their victory "Redemption." The religious metaphor was apt. If the Civil War represented a lost crusade, then the end of Reconstruction symbolized the white South's redemption. Democrats depicted themselves as **Redeemers**, holy warriors who had saved the South from the hell of black Republican rule. Generations of American boys and girls would learn this interpretation of the Reconstruction era, and it would affect race relations for nearly a century.

The Democrats' Violent Resurgence

The violence between 1874 and 1876 differed in several respects from earlier attempts to restore white government by force. Attackers operated more

openly and more closely identified themselves with the Democratic party. Mounted, gray-clad ex-Confederate soldiers flanked Democratic candidates at campaign rallies and "visited" black neighborhoods afterward to discourage blacks from voting. With blacks intimidated and whites already prepared to vote, election days were typically quiet (see "American Views: Black Hopes and White Repression").

Democrats swept to victory across the South in the 1874 elections. "A perfect reign of terror" redeemed Alabama for the Democrats. The successful appeal to white supremacy inspired a massive white turnout to unseat Republicans in Virginia, Florida (legislature only), and Arkansas. Texas had fallen to the Democrats in 1873. Only South Carolina, Mississippi, and Louisiana—states with large black populations—survived the debacle. But the relentless tide of terror would soon overwhelm them as well.

In Louisiana, a group of elite Democrats in New Orleans organized a military organization known as the **White League** in 1874 to challenge the state's Republican government. In September 1874, more than eight thousand White Leaguers staged a coup to overthrow the Republican government of New Orleans. The city's police, commanded by former Confederate general, James Longstreet, and the intervention of nearby federal troops saved the government and prevented a wholesale slaughter. But the incident only inspired White Leaguers to redouble their efforts.

Few Reconstruction politicians endured greater trials than Louisiana Republican Marshall Harvey Twitchell. Born in Vermont, he led black troops during the Civil War and settled in Louisiana after the war. He married the daughter of a prominent plantation owner and launched a successful business career. But with the advent of Congressional Reconstruction, Twitchell entered politics and built a powerful Republican organization in Red River Parish. The hospitable reception he had until then enjoyed in his adopted state quickly evaporated. During the 1874 election campaign, White Leaguers murdered his brother and two brothers-in-law. Two years later, White Leaguers shot him six times in an assassination attempt. Although he lost both arms, he survived. He left Louisiana in 1877, never to return.

The Weak Federal Response

Unrest like that in Louisiana also plagued Mississippi and South Carolina. When South Carolina governor Daniel H. Chamberlain could no longer contain the violence in his state in 1876, he asked the president for help. Although President Grant acknowledged the gravity of Chamberlain's situation, the president would only offer the governor the lame hope that South Carolinians would exercise "better judgment and cooperation" and assist the governor in bringing offenders to justice "without aid from the federal Government."

Congress responded to the violence with the **Civil Rights Act of 1875**. Introduced by Charles Sumner, the bill went through several variations. Congress finally passed a watered-down version after Sumner's death. The act prohibited discrimination against blacks in public accommodations such as theaters, parks, and trains and guaranteed freedmen's rights to serve on juries. It had no provision for voting rights, which Congress presumed the Fifteenth Amendment protected. The only way to enforce the law was for individual blacks to bring grievances related to it before federal courts in the South. Congress did not concern itself with the personal and financial difficulties blacks would face in doing so.

When blacks tested the law by trying to make free use of public accommodations, they were almost always turned away. Some filed suit, with disappointing results. Although a Texas judge fined a Galveston theater $500 for refusing to allow blacks to sit wherever they wanted to, most judges either interpreted the law narrowly or declared it unconstitutional. In 1883, the U.S. Supreme Court pronounced the Civil Rights Act unconstitutional, declaring that only the states, not Congress, could redress "a private wrong, or a crime of the individual."

The Election of 1876 and the Compromise of 1877

Reconstruction officially ended with the presidential election of 1876 in which Democrat Samuel J. Tilden ran against Republican Rutherford B. Hayes. Republicans again waved the bloody shirt, touting their role in preserving the Union during the Civil War, but they ignored Reconstruction. The Democrats hoped that their resurgent strength in the South and a respectable showing in the North would bring them the White House. The scandals of the Grant administration, northern weariness with southern Republican governments, and the persisting economic depression worked in the Democrats' favor.

When the ballots were counted, it appeared that Tilden, a conservative New Yorker respectable enough for northern voters and Democratic enough for white southerners, had won. But despite a majority in the popular vote, disputed returns in three southern states left him with only 184 of the 185 electoral votes needed to win (see Map 18-2). The three states—Florida, South Carolina, and Louisiana—were the last in the South still to have Republican adminstrations.

Both camps maneuvered intensively in the months following the election to claim the disputed votes. Congress appointed a fifteen-member commission to settle the issue. Because the Republicans

controlled Congress, they held a one-vote majority on the commission.

Southern Democrats wanted Tilden to win, but they wanted control of their states more. They were willing to deal. As one South Carolina newspaper editorialized in February 1877, "It matters little to us who rules in Washington, if South Carolina is allowed to have [Democratic governor Wade] Hampton and Home Rule." Hayes had intended to remove federal support from the remaining southern Republican governments anyway. It thus cost him nothing at all to promise to do so in exchange for the contested electoral votes. Republicans also made some vague promises to invest in the southern economy and support a transcontinental railroad along a southern route, but these were secondary. What the South wanted most was to be left alone, and that is what it got. The so-called **Compromise of 1877** installed Hayes in the White House and gave Democrats control of all state governments in the South. Congress never carried through on the economic promises, and southern Democrats never pressed them to.

Southern Democrats emerged the major winners of the Compromise of 1877. President Hayes and

Map 18-2   *The Election of 1876*
The Democrat Samuel J. Tilden won a majority of the popular vote, but eventually fell short of an electoral vote majority when the contested electoral votes of Florida, Louisiana, and South Carolina went to his Republican opponent, Rutherford B. Hayes. The map also indicates the Republicans' failure to build a base in the South after more than a decade of Reconstruction.

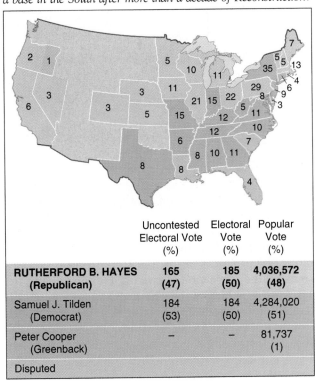

	Uncontested Electoral Vote (%)	Electoral Vote (%)	Popular Vote (%)
RUTHERFORD B. HAYES (Republican)	**165** **(47)**	**185** **(50)**	**4,036,572** **(48)**
Samuel J. Tilden (Democrat)	184 (53)	184 (50)	4,284,020 (51)
Peter Cooper (Greenback)	–	–	81,737 (1)
Disputed			

American Views

BLACK HOPES AND WHITE REPRESSION

The following two extracts frame the Reconstruction era. The first, a memorial that the Colored People's Convention of South Carolina presented to Congress in November 1865, expresses the expectations with which African-Americans greeted emancipation and their hopes for federal protection of their rights. The second is from instructions that a white paramilitary group issued to members on harassing black political meetings before the elections of 1876 in South Carolina. Its remarkable openness about the use of violence to thwart the democratic process reflects the impunity with which southern whites felt they could operate given the absence of the kinds of federal protections the first document called for.

❖ **Why did South Carolina whites find the demands of the Colored People's Convention of South Carolina objectionable?**

❖ **Did the black petitioners demand too much?**

❖ **Given the open admission that the Red Shirts aimed to do violence, or at least intimidate black voters, why didn't the federal government intervene?**

Colored People's Convention of South Carolina Petition to Congress, November 1865

We, the colored people of the State of South Carolina, in Convention assembled, respectfully present for your attention some prominent facts in relation to our present condition, and make a modest yet earnest appeal to your considerate judgment. . . . Conscious of the difficulties that surround our position, we would ask for no rights or privileges but such as rest upon the strong basis of justice and expediency, in view of the best interests of our entire country.

We ask first, that the strong arm of law and order be placed alike over the entire people of this State; that life and property be secured, and the laborer free to sell his labor as the merchant his goods.

We ask that a fair and impartial instruction be given to the pledges of the government to us concerning the land question.

We ask that the three great agents of civilized society—the school, the pulpit, the press—be as secure in South Carolina as in Massachusetts or Vermont.

We ask that equal suffrage be conferred upon us, in common with the white men of this State. This we ask, because "all free governments derive their just powers from the consent of the governed"; and we are largely in the majority in this State, bearing for a long period the burden of onerous taxation, without a just representation. We ask for equal suffrage as a protection for the hostility evoked by our known faithfulness to our country and flag under all circumstances.

---

his successors into the next century left the South alone. In practical terms, the Compromise of 1877 signaled the revocation of civil rights and voting rights for southern blacks. The Fourteenth and Fifteenth Amendments would be dead letters in the South until well into the twentieth century. On the two great issues confronting the nation at the end of the Civil War, reunion and freedom, the white South had won.

It reentered the Union largely on its own terms with the freedom to pursue a racial agenda consistent with its political, economic, and social interests.

The Memory of Reconstruction

Southern Democrats used the memory of Reconstruction to help maintain themselves in power. The Civil War became the glorious Lost Cause, Recon-

We ask that colored men shall not in every instance be tried by white men; and that neither by custom nor enactment shall we be excluded from the jury box.

We protest against any code of black laws the Legislature of this State may enact, and pray to be governed by the same laws that control other men.

Thus we ever pray.

Charleston, S.C., November 24, 1865;
Zion Presbyterian Church

Instructions to South Carolina Red Shirts, 1876

1. That every Democrat in the Townships must be put upon the Roll of the Democratic Clubs. . . .
2. That a Roster must be made of every white and of every Negro in the Townships and returned immediately to the County Executive Committee.
3. That the Democratic Military Clubs are to be armed with rifles and pistols and such other arms as they may command. . . .
12. Every Democrat must feel honor bound to control the vote of at least one Negro, by intimidation, purchase, keeping him away or as each individual may determine, how he may best accomplish it.
13. We must attend every Radical [Republican] meeting that we hear of whether they meet at night or in the day time. Democrats must go in as large numbers as they can get together, and well armed, behave at first with great courtesy and assure the ignorant Negroes that you mean them no harm and so soon as their leaders or speakers begin to speak and make false statements of facts, tell them then and there to their faces that they are liars, thieves and rascals, and are only trying to mislead the ignorant Negroes. . . .
14. In speeches to Negroes you must remember that argument has no effect upon them: they can only be influenced by their fears, superstitions and cupidity. . . . Treat them so as to show them, you are the superior race, and that their natural position is that of subordination to the white man. . . .
16. Never threaten a man individually. If he deserves to be threatened, the necessities of the times require that he should die. . . .

Sources: *Colored People's Convention: Philip S. Foner and George E. Walker, eds.,* Proceedings of the Black State Conventions, 1840–1865, *vol. 2 (1979); Red Shirts: Paul D. Escott and David Goldfield, eds.,* Major Problems in the History of the American South, *vol. 1 (1990).*

struction the story of the Redemption. Whenever southern Democrats felt threatened over the next century, they reminded their white constituents of the "horrors of Reconstruction," the menace of black rule, and the cruelty of Yankee occupiers. The southern view of Reconstruction permeated textbooks, films, and standard accounts of the period. By the 1920s, if not earlier, most Americans believed that the policies of Reconstruction had been misguided and had brought great suffering to the white South. The widespread acceptance of this view allowed the South to maintain its system of racial segregation and exclusion without interference from the federal government.

Not all memories of Reconstruction conformed to this thesis. In 1913, John R. Lynch, a former black Republican congressman from Mississippi,

In his biting 1876 cartoon, "Is This a Republican Form of Government?" noted political cartoonist Thomas Nast condemns northern acquiescence in Reconstruction's violent end.

published *The Facts of Reconstruction* to "present the other side." He hoped his book would "bring to public notice those things that were commendable and meritorious, to prevent the publication of which seems to have been the primary purpose of nearly all who have thus far written upon that important subject." But most Americans ignored his book. Two decades later, a more forceful defense, W. E. B. Du Bois's *Black Reconstruction* (1935), met a similar fate. An angry Du Bois attacked the prevailing view of Reconstruction as "one of the most stupendous efforts the world ever saw to discredit human beings, an effort involving universities, history, science, social life and religion."

The Failure of Reconstruction

Most blacks and whites in 1877 would have agreed on one point. Reconstruction had failed. As Republican governments and black voters succumbed to the southern white reign of terror in the early 1870s, the *Atlanta Constitution* chided blacks for being so pre-

sumptuous as to want to participate in the democratic process. Politics, the *Constitution* intoned, "was not intended . . . for the blacks, but for the whites. . . . This government is still a white man's government, and will remain forever such. The superior intelligence of the white race . . . will for all time secure political ascendancy." The *Constitution* excused the freedman for his delusion, blaming the "infamous carpetbagger and the radical [Republican] party."

If the demise of Reconstruction elicited a sigh of relief from most white Americans, blacks greeted it with frustration. Their dreams of land ownership faded as a new labor system relegated them to a lowly position in southern agriculture. Redemption reversed their economic and political gains and deprived them of most of the civil rights they had enjoyed under Congressional Reconstruction. Although they continued to vote into the 1890s, they had by 1877 lost most of the voting strength and political offices they held. Rather than becoming part of southern society, they were increasingly set apart from it, valued only for their labor.

Still, the former slaves were better off in 1877 than in 1865. They were free, however limited their freedom. Some owned land; some held jobs in cities. They raised their families in relative peace and experienced the spiritual joys of a full religious life. They socialized freely with relatives and friends, and they moved about. But by 1877, the "golden moment"—an unprecedented opportunity for the nation to live up to its ideals by extending equal rights to all its citizens, black and white alike—had passed.

Sharecropping

When they lost political power, blacks also lost economic independence. As the Freedmen's Bureau retreated from supervising farm labor contracts and opportunities for blacks to possess their own land dried up, the bargaining power of black farm laborers decreased and the power of white landlords increased. The faltering southern economy contributed to the loss of labor autonomy as well. Cash wages were at first high enough and rental agreements between tenant farmers and landlords at first fair enough for blacks to be able to buy their own tools and perhaps a few extra acres. But the dramatic decline of cotton prices soon after the war reduced cash surpluses in an already cash-poor region. Unable now to purchase their own animals or tools and lacking cash to buy food and other necessities at local stores, freedmen were forced to barter their crops for credit.

The upshot was that by the late 1870s, most former slaves in the rural South had been drawn into a subservient position in a new labor system called **sharecropping** (see Maps 18-3 and 18-4). The premise of this system was relatively simple: The landlord furnished the sharecroppers a house, a plot of land to work, seed, some farm animals and farm implements and advanced them credit at a store the landlord typically owned. In exchange, the sharecroppers promised the landlord a share of their crop, usually one-half. The croppers kept the proceeds from the sale of the other half to pay off their debts at the store and save or spend as they and their families saw fit. In theory, a sharecropper could save enough to secure economic independence.

But white landlords perceived black independence as both contradictory and subversive. With whites holding the accounts at the store, blacks found that the proceeds from their share of the crop never left them very far ahead. In exchange for extending credit to sharecroppers, store owners felt justified in requiring collateral. but sharecroppers had no assets other than the cotton they grew. So southern states passed **crop lien laws**, which gave the store owner the right to the next year's crop in exchange for this year's credit. If the following year's harvest couldn't pay off the debt, the sharecropper sank deeper into dependence. Some found themselves in perpetual debt and worked as vir-

tual slaves. They could not simply abandon their debts and go to another farm because the new landlord would check their references. Those found to have jumped their debts could end up on a prison chain gang. Not all white landlords cheated their tenants, but given blacks' innocence regarding accounting methods and crop pricing, the temptation to do so was great. Thus weak cotton prices conspired with white chicanery to keep blacks economically dependent.

Sharecropping represented a significant step down from tenancy. Tenants owned their own draft animals, farm implements, and seed. Once they negotiated with a land owner for a fixed rent, they kept whatever profits they earned. Eventually, they could hope to purchase some land and move into the landlord class themselves. But the continued low price of cotton made such mobility less likely during the Reconstruction era. Movement in the opposite direction was more common, especially for whites who owned small farms and could not eke out an income to at least pay taxes on loans. Landowning farmers and their families slid increasingly into tenancy and sharecropping.

Map 18-3   *The Extent of Sharecropping, 1880*
Virtually unknown in 1865, sharecropping took hold in the South during the 1870s. Although both blacks and whites worked as sharecroppers, the labor system became most characteristic for rural blacks.

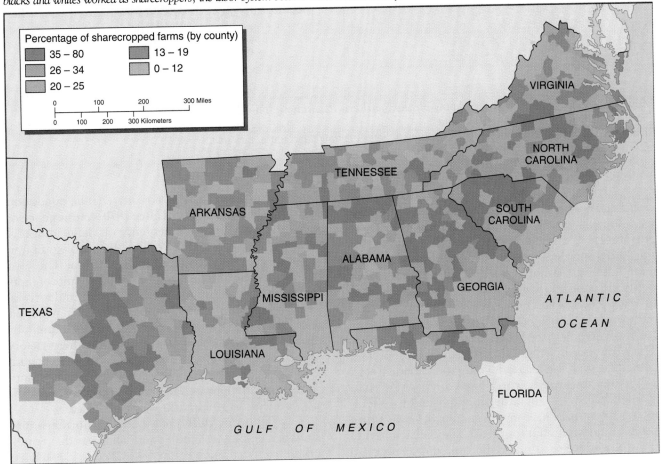

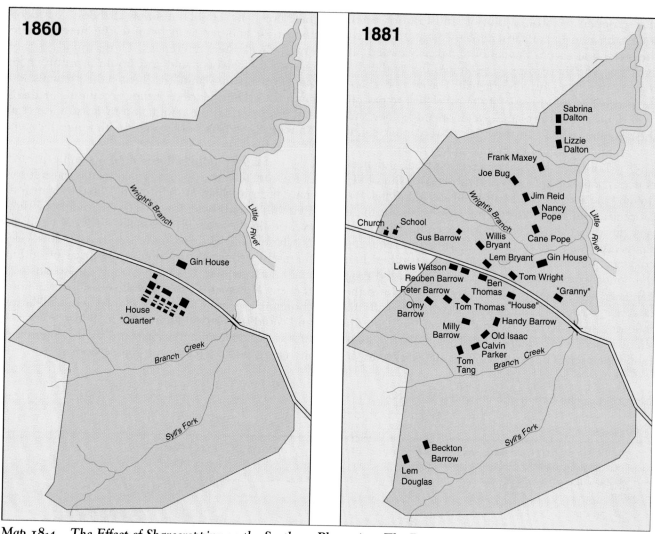

Map 18-4   *The Effect of Sharecropping on the Southern Plantation: The Barrow Plantation, Oglethorpe County, Georgia*
Sharecropping changed the landscape of the plantation South, cutting large estates into small holdings worked by sharecroppers and tenants.

Historians have often depicted the share-cropping system as a compromise between white land-lord and black laborer. But compromise implies a give-and-take between relatively equal negotiators. As northern and federal support for Reconstruction waned after 1870 and southern Democrats regained political control, white power over black labor increased. Blacks had no recourse to federal and state authorities or, increasingly, to the polls as a white reign of terror stripped them of their political rights. The prophecy of one Alabama planter in 1866 had come to pass: "The nigger is going to be made a serf, as sure as you live. It won't need any law for that. Planters will have an understanding among themselves: 'You won't hire my niggers, and I won't hire yours,' then what's left for them? They're attached to the soil, and we're as much their masters as ever."

Northern Republicans offered little opposition to southern labor practices after 1870. A resurgence of labor militancy and the emergence of a large industrial work force caused them to rethink the ideology of free labor they had espoused during the Civil War. They had trouble reconciling their notions of the dignity of inde-pendent labor with the aggressive, hostile, and increas-ingly foreign-born workers who now toiled in northern factories. The gap between worker and entrepreneur had widened between 1860 and 1870. Northern factory owners were now no more interested in encouraging upward mobility for their workers than southern land-lords. Instead, they used the courts and state and local governments to keep workers in their place.

The only difference between northern and southern employers' outlook on labor was that South-erners exercised more control over their workers. What had been a triangular debate—among northern whites, southern whites, and freedmen—had become a lopsided discourse divided along racial rather than sectional lines. In 1876, after a political campaign marked by brazen violence against Republican voters, Wade Hampton, ex-Confederate general and newly elected governor of South Carolina, provided an appropriate summary of labor perspectives in both regions. "The real North," he explained, "never liked Negroes and was not willing to attack slavery. Now that it is gone they are glad and so are we; but they no more than we want to make Negroes their equals. They want good, cheap, profitable labor and so do we."

Segregation

A labor arrangement like sharecropping was not feasible in the fluid labor markets of southern cities. Whites relied instead on racial **segregation** to control urban blacks and keep them in an inferior economic social position. Racial segregation, which had prevailed nationwide before the Civil War, restricted blacks to separate and rarely equal public facilities. After the war, and especially after 1870, it spread rapidly in southern cities. In Richmond by the early 1870s, segregation laws required blacks registering to vote to enter through separate doors and registrars to count their ballots separately. The city's prison and hospitals were segregated. So too were its horse-drawn railways, its schools, and most of its restaurants, hotels, and theaters.

During the same period, many northern cities and states, often in response to protests by African-Americans, were ending segregation. Massachusetts, for example, passed the nation's first public accommodations law in May 1865, desegregating all public facilities. Cities such as New York, Cleveland, and Cincinnati desegregated their streetcars. Chicago, Cleveland, Milwaukee, and the entire state of Michigan desegregated their public school systems. Roughly 95 percent of the nation's black population, however, lived in the South. Integration in the North consequently required whites to give up very little to blacks.

Segregation and exclusion defined the boundaries of black life in the urban South after the war. Barred from juries, excluded from some public facilities, and segregated into inferior accommodations in others, blacks fell into a twilight category of citizenship with few rights and many obligations. As W. E. B. Du Bois said in 1877, "The slave went free; stood a brief moment in the sun; then moved back again toward slavery."

Modest Gains and Future Victories

Southern blacks experienced some advances in the decade after the Civil War, but these owed little to Reconstruction. Black families functioned as economic and psychological buffers against unemployment and prejudice. Black churches played crucial roles in their communities. Self-help and labor organizations offered mutual friendship and financial assistance. All of these institutions existed in the slavery era, although on a smaller scale. And some of them, such as black labor groups, schools, and social welfare associations, endured because comparable white institutions excluded blacks.

Blacks also scored some modest economic successes during the Reconstruction era, mainly from their own pluck. In the Lower South, black per capita income increased 46 percent between 1857 and 1879, compared with a 35 percent decline for whites. Sharecropping, oppressive as it was, represented an advance over forced and gang labor. Collectively, blacks owned more than $68 million worth of property in 1870, a 240 percent increase over 1860, but the average worth of each was only $408. Those who had been free before the war sometimes fared worse after it, especially property-owning free blacks in the Lower South. Urban blacks, especially in the Upper South, fared somewhat better. The overwhelming majority of blacks, however, were landless agricultural laborers eking out a meager income that merchants and landlords often snatched to cover debts.

The Fourteenth and Fifteenth Amendments to the Constitution are among the few bright spots in Reconstruction's otherwise dismal legacy. The Fourteenth Amendment guaranteed former slaves equality before the law; the Fifteenth Amendment protected their right to vote. Both amendments elevated the federal government over the states by protecting freedmen from state attempts to deny them their rights. But the benefits of these two landmark amendments did not accrue to African-Americans until well into the twentieth century. Southern whites effectively nullified the Reconstruction amendments, and the U.S. Supreme Court virtually interpreted them, and other Reconstruction legislation, out of existence.

In the ***Slaughterhouse* cases** (1873), the Supreme Court contradicted the intent of the Fourteenth Amendment by decreeing that most citizenship rights remained under state, not federal, control. In ***United States* v. *Cruikshank*** (1876), the Court overturned the convictions of some of those responsible for the Colfax Massacre ruling that the Enforcement Act applied only to violations of black rights by **states**, not individuals. Within the next two decades, the Supreme Court would uphold the legality of racial segregation and black disfranchisement, in effect declaring that the Fourteenth and Fifteenth Amendments did not apply to African-Americans. The Civil War had killed secession forever, but states' rights enjoyed a remarkable revival.

As historian John Hope Franklin accurately concluded, Reconstruction "had no significant or permanent effect on the status of the black in American life. . . . [Blacks] made no meaningful steps toward economic independence or even stability."

Conclusion

Blacks had entered freedom with many hopes, among the most prominent of which was to be let alone. White southerners, after four bloody years of unwanted attention from the federal government, also longed to be left alone. But they did not include their ex-slaves as equal partners in their vision of solitude. Northerners, too, began to seek escape from the issues and consequences of the war, eventually abandoning their commitment to secure civil and voting rights for southern blacks.

White Southerners robbed blacks of their gains and sought to reduce them again to servitude and dependence, if not to slavery. But in the processs, the majority of whites lost as well. Yeoman farmers missed an opportunity to break cleanly from the Old South and establish a more equitable society. Instead, they allowed the old elites to regain power and gradually ignore their needs. They preserved the social benefit of a white skin at the cost of almost everything else. Many lost their farms and sank into tenancy, leasing land from others. Fewer had a voice in state legislatures or Congress. A new South, rid of slavery and sectional antagonism, had indeed emerged, redeemed, regenerated, and disenthralled. But the old South lingered on in the new like Spanish moss on live oaks.

As federal troops left the South to be redeployed restraining striking workers in the North and suppressing Native Americans on the Great Plains, an era of possibility for American society ended and a new era began. "The southern question is dead," a Charleston newspaper proclaimed in 1877. "The question of labor and capital, work and wages" had moved to the forefront. The chance to redeem the sacrifice of a bloody civil war with a society that fulfilled the promise of the Declaration of Independence and the Constitution for all citizens slipped away. It would take a new generation of blacks a long century later to revive it.

Review Questions

1. Given the devastation in the South after the Civil War and the loss of property, lives, and hope among many white Southerners, do you think they should they have supported black aspirations for civil rights, land, and suffrage? How differently would things have turned out if they had?

2. Some historians have placed a great deal of the blame for Reconstruction's failures on the backs of southern Republicans. Is this fair? Explain your response.

3. By 1874, political violence directed at blacks and at white Republicans in the South was almost routine. Why did the federal government not respond more vigorously to suppress the violence?

4. Blacks did achieve some notable gains during Reconstruction, despite its overall failure. What were those gains?

Recommended Reading

W. E. B. Du Bois, *Black Reconstruction in America, 1860–1880* (1935). This early and long-ignored study by the foremost black scholar of his time refuted the contemporary historical wisdom that Reconstruction was a horror visited on the South by an overbearing federal government and ignorant, willful blacks.

Eric Foner, *Reconstruction: America's Unfinished Revolution, 1863-1877* (1988). The standard work on Reconstruction is notable for its emphasis on the experience and aspirations of black Southerners.

Gaines M. Foster, *Ghosts of the Confederacy: Defeat, the Lost Cause, and the Emergence of the New South, 1865 to 1913* (1987). Foster paints a fine picture of how the memory of the Civil War affected white southerners and their views on Reconstruction policy.

Leon Litwack, *Been in the Storm So Long: The Aftermath of Slavery* (1979). This is an eloquent account of the early days of freedom from the freedmen's perspective, up to 1867.

Whitelaw Reid, *After the War: A Southern Tour, May 1, 1865, to May 1, 1866* (1866). A northern journalist's critical view of southern white defiance during the early days of Reconstruction predicts future difficulties for federal policies and black aspirations.

Albion W. Tourgée, *A Fool's Errand* (1879). The author was an Ohioan who migrated to North Carolina in 1865 to take advantage of economic opportunities in the state and eventually became involved in politics. His frustrations with Reconstruction and his keen analysis of racism are important themes of this novel.

Additional Sources

Southern Whites and the Ghosts of the Confederacy

Dan T. Carter, *When the War Was Over: The Failure of Self-Reconstruction in the South, 1865–1867* (1985).

LaWanda Cox and John Cox, *Politics, Principle, and Prejudice, 1865–1866* (1963).

Black Aspirations beyond Freedom

Ira Berlin et al., *Freedom: A Documentary History of Emancipation, 1861–1867. The Wartime Genesis of Free Labor: The Lower South* (1990).

John Blassingame, *Black New Orleans, 1860-1880* (1973).

Carol R. Bleser, *The Promised Land: The History of the South Carolina Land Commission* (1963).

Edmund L. Drago, *Black Politicians and Reconstruction in Georgia* (1982).

Barbara Fields, *Slavery and Freedom on the Middle Ground: Maryland during the Nineteenth Century* (1985).

Michael W. Fitzgerald, *The Union League Movement in the Deep South: Politics and Agricultural Change during Reconstruction* (1989).

Herbert G. Gutman, *The Black Family in Slavery and Freedom, 1750–1925* (1976).

Gerald Jaynes, *Branches without Roots: The Genesis of the Black Working Class in the American South, 1862–1882* (1986).

Jacqueline Jones, *Labor of Love, Labor of Sorrow: Black Women, Work, and the Family from Slavery to the Present* (1985).

Peter Kolchin, *First Freedom: The Responses of Alabama's Blacks to Emancipation and Reconstruction* (1972).

Howard N. Rabinowitz, *Race Relations in the Urban South, 1865–1890* (1978).

Howard N. Rabinowitz, ed. *Southern Black Leaders of the Reconstruction Era* (1982).

Emma Lou Thornbrough, ed., *Black Reconstructionists* (1972).

William P. Vaughn, *Schools for All: Blacks and Public Education in the South, 1865–1871* (1974).

Joel Williamson, *After Slavery: The Negro in South Carolina during Reconstruction, 1861–1877* (1965).

Federal Reconstruction, 1865–1870

Richard Abbott, *The Republican Party and the South, 1855–1877* (1986).

Herman Belz, *A New Birth of Freedom: The Republican Party and Freedmen's Rights, 1861–1866* (1976).

Michael Les Benedict, *A Compromise of Principle: Congressional Republicans and Reconstruction, 1863–1869* (1974).

Louis S. Gerteis, *From Contraband to Freedmen: Federal Policy toward Southern Blacks, 1861–1865* (1973).

Thomas Holt, *Black over White: Negro Political Leadership in South Carolina during Reconstruction* (1977).

Harold Hyman, *A More Perfect Union: The Impact of the Civil War and Reconstruction on the Constitution* (1973).

Richard Lowe, *Republicans and Reconstruction in Virginia, 1856–1870* (1991).

Peyton McCrary, *Abraham Lincoln and Reconstruction: The Louisiana Experiment* (1978).

William S. McFeely, *Grant: A Biography* (1981).

Carl H. Moneyhon, *Republicanism in Reconstruction Texas* (1980).

Michael Perman, *Reunion without Compromise: The South and Reconstruction, 1865–1868* (1973).

Willie Lee Rose, *Rehearsal for Reconstruction: The Port Royal Experiment* (1964).

James E. Sefton, *Andrew Johnson and the Uses of Constitutional Power* (1980).

Mark W. Summers, *Railroads, Reconstruction, and the Gospel of Prosperity: Aid under the Radical Republicans, 1865–1877* (1984).

Hans Trefousse, *The Radical Republicans: Lincoln's Vanguard for Racial Justice* (1969).

Counter-Reconstruction, 1870–1874

Richard N. Current, *Those Terrible Carpetbaggers: A Reinterpretation* (1988).

Russell Duncan, *Entrepreneur for Equality: Governor Rufus Bullock, Commerce, and Race in Post–Civil War Georgia* (1994).

Michael Perman, *The Road to Redemption: Southern Politics, 1869–1879* (1984).

George C. Rable, *But There Was No Peace: The Role of Violence in the Politics of Reconstruction* (1984).

John G. Sproat, *"The Best Men": Liberal Reformers in the Gilded Age* (1968).

Allen W. Trelease, *White Terror: The Ku Klux Conspiracy and Reconstruction* (1971).

Redemption, 1874–1877

Otto H. Olsen, ed., *Reconstruction and Redemption in the South* (1980).

Keith Ian Polakoff, *The Politics of Inertia: The Election of 1876 and the End of Reconstruction* (1973).

C. Vann Woodward, *Reunion and Reaction: The Compromise of 1877 and the End of Reconstruction* (1951).

The Failure of Reconstruction

Stephen Ward Angell, *Bishop Henry McNeal Turner and African-American Religion in the South* (1992).

John Hope Franklin, *Reconstruction after the Civil War* (1961).

William Gillette, *Retreat from Reconstruction, 1869–1879* (1979).

Betty Lamson, *The Glorious Failure: Black Congressman Robert Brown Elliott and Reconstruction in South Carolina* (1973).

James M. McPherson, *Ordeal by Fire: Reconstruction* (1982).

Michael Perman, *Emancipation and Reconstruction, 1862–1879* (1979).

Roger L. Ransom and Richard Sutch, *One Kind of Freedom: The Economic Consequences of Emancipation* (1977).

James L. Roark, *Masters without Slaves: Southern Planters in the Civil War and Reconstruction* (1977).

Kenneth M. Stampp, *The Era of Reconstruction, 1865–1877* (1965).

Where to Learn More

❖ **Penn Center Historic District, St. Helena Island, South Carolina.** The Penn School was a sea-island experiment in the education of free blacks established by northern missionaries Laura Towne and Ellen Murray in 1862 that they operated until their deaths in the early 1900s. The Penn School became Penn Community Services in 1948, serving as an educational institution, health clinic, and a social service agency.

❖ **Hampton University Museum, Hampton, Virginia.** Hampton University was founded by the Freedmen's Bureau in 1868 to provide "practical" training in the agricultural and mechanical fields for former slaves. In addition to a history of the institution, the museum includes one of the oldest collections of African art in the United States.

❖ **Beauvoir, Biloxi, Mississippi.** The exhibits at Beauvoir, the home of Jefferson Davis, evoke the importance of the Lost Cause for the white survivors of the Confederacy. Especially interesting is the Jefferson Davis Soldiers Home on the premises and the Confederate Veterans Cemetery. Davis spent his retirement years in Beauvoir.

❖ **Valentine Museum, Richmond, Virginia.** This urban history museum was the first to mount a comprehensive exhibit on Reconstruction in 1996. The exhibit is expected to travel to locations around the country beginning in 1997. Contact the Valentine at (804) 649–0711 for the exhibit's itinerary.

APPENDIX

THE DECLARATION OF INDEPENDENCE

When in the course of human events it becomes necessary for one people to dissolve the political bands which have connected them with another and to assume, among the powers of the earth, the separate and equal station to which the laws of nature and of nature's God entitle them, a decent respect to the opinions of mankind requires that they should declare the causes which impel them to the separation.

We hold these truths to be self-evident, that all men are created equal; that they are endowed by their Creator with certain unalienable rights; that among these are life, liberty, and the pursuit of happiness. That, to secure these rights, governments are instituted among men, deriving their just powers from the consent of the governed; that, whenever any form of government becomes destructive of these ends, it is the right of the people to alter or to abolish it, and to institute a new government, laying its foundation on such principles, and organizing its powers in such form, as to them shall seem most likely to effect their safety and happiness. Prudence, indeed, will dictate that governments long established should not be changed for light and transient causes; and, accordingly, all experience hath shown that mankind are more disposed to suffer, while evils are sufferable, than to right themselves by abolishing the forms to which they are accustomed. But when a long train of abuses and usurpations, pursuing invariably the same object, evinces a design to reduce them under absolute despotism, it is their right, it is their duty, to throw off such government and to provide new guards for their future security. Such has been the patient sufferance of these colonies, and such is now the necessity which constrains them to alter their former systems of government. The history of the present King of Great Britain is a history of repeated injuries and usurpations, all having, in direct object, the establishment of an absolute tyranny over these States. To prove this, let facts be submitted to a candid world:

He has refused his assent to laws the most wholesome and necessary for the public good.

He has forbidden his governors to pass laws of immediate and pressing importance, unless suspended in their operation till his assent should be obtained; and, when so suspended, he has utterly neglected to attend to them.

He has refused to pass other laws for the accommodation of large districts of people, unless those people would relinquish the right of representation in the legislature, a right inestimable to them and formidable to tyrants only.

He has called together legislative bodies at places unusual, uncomfortable, and distant from the depository of their public records, for the sole purpose of fatiguing them into compliance with his measures.

He has dissolved representative houses, repeatedly for opposing, with manly firmness, his invasions on the rights of the people.

He has refused, for a long time after such dissolutions, to cause others to be elected; whereby the legislative powers, incapable of annihilation, have returned to the people at large for their exercise; the state remaining, in the meantime, exposed to all the danger of invasion from without and convulsions within.

He has endeavored to prevent the population of these States; for that purpose, obstructing the laws for naturalization of foreigners, refusing to pass others to encourage their migration hither, and raising the conditions of new appropriations of lands.

He has obstructed the administration of justice by refusing his assent to laws for establishing judiciary powers.

He has made judges dependent on his will alone for the tenure of their offices and the amount and payment of their salaries.

He has erected a multitude of new offices and sent hither swarms of officers to harass our people and eat out their substance.

He has kept among us, in time of peace, standing armies, without the consent of our legislatures.

He has affected to render the military independent of, and superior to, the civil power.

He has combined with others to subject us to a jurisdiction foreign to our Constitution and unacknowledged by our laws, giving his assent to their acts of pretended legislation—

For quartering large bodies of armed troops among us;

For protecting them by a mock trail from punishment for any murders which they should commit on the inhabitants of these States;

For cutting off our trade with all parts of the world;

For imposing taxes on us without our consent;

For depriving us, in many cases, of the benefit of trial by jury;

For transporting us beyond seas to be tried for pretended offences;

For abolishing the free system of English laws in a neighboring province, establishing therein an arbitrary government, and enlarging its boundaries, so as to render it at once an example and fit instrument for introducing the same absolute rule into these colonies;

For taking away our charters, abolishing our most valuable laws, and altering, fundamentally, the powers of our governments.

For suspending our own legislatures and declaring themselves invested with power to legislate for us in all cases whatsoever.

He has abdicated government here by declaring us out of his protection and waging war against us.

He has plundered our seas, ravaged our coasts, burnt our towns, and destroyed the lives of our people.

He is, at this time, transporting large armies of foreign mercenaries to complete the works of death, desolation, and tyranny already begun with circumstances of cruelty and perfidy scarcely paralleled in the most barbarous ages, and totally unworthy the head of a civilized nation.

He has constrained our fellow citizens, taken captive on the high seas, to bear arms against their country, to become the executioners of their friends and brethren, or to fall themselves by their hands.

He has excited domestic insurrections amongst us and has endeavored to bring on the inhabitants of our frontiers, the merciless Indian savages, whose known rule of warfare is an undistinguished destruction of all ages, sexes, and conditions.

In every stage of these oppressions, we have petitioned for redress in the most humble terms; our repeated petitions have been answered only by repeated injury. A prince whose character is thus marked by every act which may define a tyrant is unfit to be the ruler of a free people.

Nor have we been wanting in attention to our British brethren. We have warned them, from time to time, of attempts made by their legislature to extend an unwarrantable jurisdiction over us. We have reminded them of the circumstances of our emigration and settlement here. We have appealed to their native justice and magnanimity, and we have conjured them, by the ties of our common kindred, to disavow these usurpations, which would inevitably interrupt our connections and correspondence. They, too, have been deaf to the voice of justice and consanguinity. We must, therefore, acquiesce in the necessity which denounces our separation, and hold them, as we hold the rest of mankind, enemies in war, in peace, friends.

We, therefore, the representatives of the United States of America, in general Congress assembled, appealing to the Supreme Judge of the world for the rectitude of our intentions, do, in the name and by the authority of the good people of these colonies, solemnly publish and declare, that these united colonies are, and of right ought to be, free and independent states: that they are absolved from all allegiance to the British Crown, and that all political connection between them and the state of Great Britain is, and ought to be, totally dissolved; and that, as free and independent states, they have full power to levy war, conclude peace, contract alliances, establish commerce, and to do all other acts and things which independent states may of right do. And, for the support of this declaration, with a firm reliance on the protection of Divine Providence, we mutually pledge to each other our lives, our fortunes, and our sacred honor.

THE CONSTITUTION OF THE UNITED STATES OF AMERICA

We the people of the United States, in order to form a more perfect union, establish justice, insure domestic tranquillity, provide for the common defense, promote the general welfare, and secure the blessings of liberty to ourselves and our posterity, do ordain and establish this Constitution for the United States of America.

Article I

SECTION 1. All legislative powers herein granted shall be vested in a Congress of the United States, which shall consist of a Senate and House of Representatives.

SECTION 2. 1. The House of Representatives shall be composed of members chosen every second year by the people of the several States, and the electors in each State shall have the qualifications requisite for electors of the most numerous branch of the State legislature.

2. No person shall be a representative who shall not have attained to the age of twenty-five years,

and been seven years a citizen of the United States, and who shall not, when elected, be an inhabitant of that State in which he shall be chosen.

3. Representatives and direct taxes[1] shall be apportioned among the several States which may be included within this Union, according to their respective numbers, which shall be determined by adding to the whole number of free persons, including those bound to service for a term of years, and excluding Indians not taxed, three fifths of all other persons.[2] The actual enumeration shall be made within three years after the first meeting of the Congress of the United States, and within every subsequent term of ten years, in such manner as they shall be law direct. The number of representatives shall not exceed one for every thirty thousand, but each State shall have at least one representative; and until such enumeration shall be made, the State of New Hampshire shall be entitled to choose three, Massachusetts eight, Rhode Island and Providence Plantations one, Connecticut five, New York six, New Jersey four, Pennsylvania eight, Delaware one, Maryland six, Virginia ten, North Carolina five, South Carolina five, and Georgia three.

4. When vacancies happen in the representation from any State, the executive authority thereof shall issue writs of election to fill such vacancies.

5. The House of Representatives shall choose their speaker and other officers; and shall have the sole power of impeachment.

SECTION 3. 1. The Senate of the United States shall be composed of two senators from each State, chosen by the legislature thereof,[3] for six years; and each senator shall have one vote.

2. Immediately after they shall be assembled in consequence of the first election, they shall be divided as equally as may be into three classes. The seats of the senators of the first class shall be vacated at the expiration of the second year, of the second class at the expiration of the fourth year, and of the third class at the expiration of the sixth year, so that one third may be chosen every second year; and if vacancies happen by resignation, or otherwise, during the recess of the legislature of any State, the executive thereof may make temporary appointments until the next meeting of the legislature, which shall then fill such vacancies.[4]

3. No person shall be a senator who shall not have attained to the age of thirty years, and been

nine years a citizen of the United States, and who shall not, when elected, be an inhabitant of that State for which he shall be chosen.

4. The Vice President of the United States shall be President of the Senate, but shall have no vote, unless they be equally divided.

5. The Senate shall choose their other officers, and also a president pro tempore, in the absence of the Vice President, or when he shall exercise the office of the President of the United States.

6. The Senate shall have the sole power to try all impeachments. When sitting for that purpose, they shall be on oath or affirmation. When the president of the United States is tried, the chief justice shall preside: and no person shall be convicted without the concurrence of two thirds of the members present.

7. Judgment in cases of impeachment shall not extend further than to removal from office, and disqualification to hold and enjoy any office of honor, trust or profit under the United States: but the party convicted shall nevertheless be liable and subject to indictment, trial, judgment and punishment, according to law.

SECTION 4. 1. The times, places, and manner of holding elections for senators and representatives, shall be prescribed in each State by the legislature thereof; but the Congress may at any time by law make or alter such regulations, except as to the places of choosing senators.

2. The Congress shall assemble at least once in every year, and such meeting shall be on the first Monday in December, unless they shall by law appoint a different day.

SECTION 5. 1. Each House shall be the judge of the elections, returns and qualifications of its own members, and a majority of each shall constitute a quorum to do business; but a smaller number may adjourn from day to day, and may be authorized to compel the attendance of absent members, in such manner, and under such penalties as each House may provide.

2. Each House may determine the rules of its proceedings, punish its members for disorderly behavior, and, with the concurrence of two thirds, expel a member.

3. Each house shall keep a journal of its proceedings, and from time to time publish the same, excepting such parts as may in their judgment require secrecy; and the yeas and nays of the members of either house on any question shall, at the desire of one fifth of those present, be entered on the journal.

[1]See the Sixteenth Amendment.
[2]See the Fourteenth Amendment.
[3]See the Seventeenth Amendment.
[4]See the Seventeenth Amendment.

4. Neither House, during the session of Congress, shall, without the consent of the other, adjourn for more than three days, nor to any other place than that in which the two Houses shall be sitting.

SECTION 6. 1. The senators and representatives shall receive a compensation for their services, to be ascertained by law, and paid out of the Treasury of the United States. They shall in all cases, except treason, felony, and breach of the peace, be privileged from arrest during their attendance at the session of their respective Houses, and in going to and returning from the same; and for any speech or debate in either House, they shall not be questioned in any other place.

2. No senator or representative shall, during the time for which he was elected, be appointed to any civil office under the authority of the United States, which shall have been created, or the emoluments whereof shall have been increased, during such time; and no person holding any office under the United States shall be a member of either House during his continuance in office.

SECTION 7. 1. All bills for raising revenue shall originate in the house of Representatives; but the Senate may purpose or concur with amendments as on other bills.

2. Every bill which shall have passed the House of Representatives and the Senate, shall, before it become a law, be presented to the President of the United States; If he approves he shall sign it, but if not he shall return it, with his objections, to that House in which it shall have originated, who shall enter the objections at large on their journal, and proceed to reconsider it. If after such reconsideration two thirds of that House shall agree to pass the bill, it shall be sent, together with the objections, to the other House, by which it shall likewise be reconsidered, and if approved by two thirds of that House, it shall become a law. But in all such cases the votes of both Houses shall be determined by yeas and nays, and the names of the persons voting for and against the bill shall be entered on the journal of each House respectively. If any bill shall not be returned by the President within ten days (Sundays excepted) after it shall have been presented to him, the same shall be a law, in like manner as if he had signed it, unless the Congress by their adjournment prevent its return, in which case it shall not be a law.

3. Every order, resolution, or vote to which the concurrence of the Senate and the House of Representatives may be necessary (except on a question of adjournment) shall be presented to the President of the United States; and before the same shall take effect, shall be approved by him, or being disapproved by him, shall be repassed by two thirds of the Senate and House of Representatives, according to the rules and limitations prescribed in the case of a bill.

SECTION 8. The Congress shall have the power

1. To lay and collect taxes, duties, imposts, and excises, to pay the debts and provide for the common defense and general welfare of the United States; but all duties, imposts, and excises shall be uniform throughout the United States.

2. To borrow money on the credit of the United States;

3. To regulate commerce with foreign nations, and among the several States, and with the Indian tribes;

4. To establish a uniform rule of naturalization, and uniform laws on the subject of bankruptcies throughout the United States.

5. To coin money, regulate the value thereof, and of foreign coin, and fix the standard of weights and measures;

6. To provide for the punishment of counterfeiting the securities and current coin of the United States;

7. To establish post offices and post roads;

8. To promote the progress of science and useful arts, by securing for limited times to authors and inventors the exclusive right to their respective writings and discoveries;

9. To constitute tribunals inferior to the Supreme Court;

10. To define and punish piracies and felonies committed on the high seas, and offenses against the law of nations;

11. To declare war, grant letters of marque and reprisal, and make rules concerning captures on land and water;

12. To raise and support armies, but no appropriation of money to that use shall be for a longer term than two years;

13. To provide and maintain a navy;

14. To make rules for the government and regulation of the land and naval forces;

15. To provide for calling forth the militia to execute the laws of the Union, suppress insurrections and repel invasions;

16. To provide for organizing, arming, and disciplining the militia, and for governing such part of them as may be employed in the service of the United States, reserving to the States respectively, the appointment of the officers, and the authority of training the militia according to the discipline prescribed by Congress;

17. To exercise exclusive legislation in all cases whatsoever, over such district (not exceeding ten miles square) as may, by cession of particular States, and the acceptance of Congress, become the seat of the government of the United States, and to exercise like authority over all places purchased by the consent of the legislature of the State in which the same shall be, for the erection of forts, magazines, arsenals, dockyards, and other needful buildings; and

18. To make all laws which shall be necessary and proper for carrying into execution the foregoing powers, and all other powers vested by this Constitution in the government of the United States, or any department or officer thereof.

SECTION 9. 1. The migration or importation of such persons as any of the States now existing shall think proper to admit, shall not be prohibited by the Congress prior to the year one thousand eight hundred and eight, but a tax or duty may be imposed on such importation, not exceeding ten dollars for each person.

2. The privilege of the writ of habeas corpus shall not be suspended, unless when in cases of rebellion or invasion the public safety may require it.

3. No bill of attainder or ex post facto law shall be passed.

4. No capitation, or other direct, tax shall be laid, unless in proportion to the census or enumeration herein-before directed to be taken.[5]

5. No tax or duty shall be laid on articles exported from any State.

6. No preference shall be given by any regulation of commerce or revenue to the ports of one State over those of another: nor shall vessels bound to, or from, one State be obliged to enter, clear, or pay duties in another.

7. No money shall be drawn from the treasury, but in consequence of appropriations made by law; and a regular statement and account of the receipts and expenditures of all public money shall be published from time to time.

8. No title of nobility shall be granted by the United States: and no person holding any office of profit or trust under them, shall, without the consent of the Congress, accept of any present, emolument, office, or title, of any kind whatever, from any king, prince, or foreign State.

SECTION 10. 1. No State shall enter into any treaty, alliance, or confederation; grant letters of marque and reprisal; coin money; emit bills of credit; make any thing but gold and silver coin a tender in payment of debts; pass any bill of attainder, ex post facto law, or law impairing the obligation of contracts, or grant, any title of nobility.

2. No State shall, without the consent of the Congress, lay any imposts or duties on imports or exports, except what may be absolutely necessary for executing its inspection laws: and the net produce of all duties and imposts laid by any State on imports or exports, shall be for the use of the treasury of the United States; and all such laws shall be subject to the revision and control of the Congress.

3. No State shall, without the consent of Congress, lay any duty of tonnage, keep troops, or ships of war in time of peace, enter into any agreement or compact with another State, or with a foreign power, or engage in war, unless actually invaded, or in such imminent danger as will not admit of delay.

Article II
SECTION I. 1. The executive power shall be vested in a President of the United States of America. He shall hold his office during the term of four years, and, together with the Vice President, chosen for the same term, be elected, as follows:

2. Each State shall appoint, in such manner as the legislature thereof may direct, a number of electors, equal to the whole number of senators and representatives to which the State may be entitled in the Congress: but no senator or representative, or person holding any office of trust or profit under the United States, shall be appointed an elector.

The electors shall meet in their respective States, and vote by ballot for two persons, of whom one at least shall not be an inhabitant of the same State with themselves. And they shall make a list of all the persons voted for, and of the number of votes for each; which list they shall sign and certify, and transmit sealed to the seat of the government of the United States, directed to the president of the Senate. The president of the Senate shall, in the presence of the Senate and House of Representatives, open all the certificates, and the votes shall then be counted. The person having the greatest number of votes shall be the President, if such number be a majority of the whole number of electors appointed; and if there be more than one who have such majority, and have an equal number of votes, then the House of Representatives shall immediately choose by ballot one of them for President; and if no person have a majority, then from the five highest on the list the said House shall in like manner choose the President. But in choosing the President, the

[5]See the Sixteenth Amendment.

votes shall be taken by States, the representation from each State having one vote; a quorum for this purpose shall consist of a member or members from two thirds of the States, and a majority of all the States shall be necessary to a choice. In every case after the choice of the President, the person having the greatest number of votes of the electors shall be the Vice President. But if there should remain two or more who have equal votes, the Senate shall chose from them by ballot the Vice President.[6]

3. The Congress may determine the time of choosing the electors, and the day on which they shall give their votes; which day shall be the same throughout the United States.

4. No person except a natural born citizen, or a citizen of the United States, at the time of the adoption of this Constitution, shall be eligible to the office of President; neither shall any person be eligible to the office who shall not have attained to the age of thirty-five years, and been fourteen years a resident within the United States.

5. In case of the removal of the President from office, or of his death, resignation, or inability to discharge the powers and duties of the said office, the same shall devolve on the Vice President, and the Congress may by law provide for the case of removal, death, resignation or inability, both of the President and Vice President, declaring what officer shall then act as President, and such officer shall act accordingly until the disability be removed, or a President shall be elected.

6. The President shall, at stated times, receive for his services a compensation which shall neither be increased nor diminished during the period for which he shall have been elected, and he shall not receive within that period any other emolument from the United States, or any of them.

7. Before he enter on the execution of his office, he shall take the following oath or affirmation:—"I do solemnly swear (or affirm) that I will faithfully execute the office of president of the United States, and will to the best of my ability, preserve, protect and defend the Constitution of the United States."

SECTION 2. 1. The President shall be commander in chief of the army and navy of the United States, and of the militia of the several States, when called into the actual service of the United States; he may require the opinion in writing, of the principal officer in each of the executive departments, upon any subject relating to the duties of their respective offices, and he shall have power to grant reprieves and pardons for offenses against the United States, except in cases of impeachment.

2. He shall have power, by and with the advice and consent of the Senate, to make treaties, provided two thirds of the senators present concur; and he shall nominate, and by and with the advice and consent of the Senate, shall appoint ambassadors, other public ministers and consuls, judges of the Supreme Court, and all other officers of the United States, whose appointments are not herein otherwise provided for, and which shall be established by law; but the Congress may by law vest the appointment of such inferior officers, as they think proper, in the President alone, in the courts of laws, or in the heads of departments.

3. The President shall have power to fill up all vacancies that may happen during the recess of the Senate, by granting commissions which shall expire at the end of their next session.

SECTION 3. He shall from time to time give to the Congress information of the state of the Union, and recommend to their consideration such measures as he shall judge necessary and expedient; he may, on extraordinary occasions, convene both houses, or either of them, and in case of disagreement between them with respect to the time of adjournment, he may adjourn them to such time as he shall think proper; he shall receive ambassadors and other public ministers; he shall take care that the laws be faithfully executed, and shall commission all the officers of the United States.

SECTION 4. The President, Vice President, and all civil officers of the United States, shall be removed from office on impeachment for, and conviction of, treason, bribery, or other high crimes and misdemeanors.

Article III

SECTION 1. The judicial power of the United States shall be vested in one Supreme Court, and in such inferior courts as the Congress may from time to time ordain and establish. The judges, both of the Supreme and inferior courts, shall hold their offices during good behavior, and shall, at stated times, receive for their services, a compensation, which shall not be diminished during their continuance in office.

SECTION 2. 1. The judicial power shall extend to all cases, in law and equity, arising under this Constitution, the laws of the United States, and treaties made, or which shall be made, under their authority;—to all cases of admiralty and maritime jurisdiction;—to controversies to which the United

---

[6]Superseded by the Twelfth Amendment.

States shall be a party;[7]—to controversies between two or more States;—between a State and citizens of another State;—between citizens of different States;—between citizens of the same State claiming lands under grants of different States, and between a State, or the citizens thereof, and foreign States, citizens or subjects.

2. In all cases affecting ambassadors, other public ministers and consuls, and those in which a State shall be party, the Supreme Court shall have original jurisdiction. In all the other cases before mentioned, the Supreme Court shall have appellate jurisdiction, both as to law and fact, with such exceptions, and under such regulations as the Congress shall make.

3. The trial of all crimes, except in cases of impeachment, shall be by jury; and such trial shall be held in the State where the said crimes shall have been committed; but when not committed within any State, the trial shall be such place or places as the congress may by law have directed.

SECTION 3. 1. Treason against the United States shall consist only in levying war against them, or in adhering to their enemies, giving them aid and comfort. No person shall be convicted of treason unless on the testimony of two witnesses to the same overt act, or on confession in open court.

2. The Congress shall have power to declare the punishment of treason, but no attainder of treason shall work corruption of blood, or forfeiture except during the life of the person attained.

Article IV

SECTION 1. Full faith and credit shall be given in each State to the public acts, records, and judicial proceedings of every other State. And the Congress may by general laws prescribe the manner in which such acts, records and proceedings shall be proved, and the effect thereof.

SECTION 2. 1. The citizens of each State shall be entitled to all privileges and immunities of citizens in the several States.[8]

2. A person charged in any State with treason, felony, or other crime, who shall flee from justice, and be found in another State, shall on demand of the executive authority of the State from which he fled, be delivered up to be removed to the State having jurisdiction of the crime.

3. No person held to service or labor in one State under the laws thereof, escaping into another,

shall, in consequence of any law or regulation therein, be discharged from such service or labor, but shall be delivered up on claim of the party to whom such service or labor may be due.[9]

SECTION 3. 1. New States may be admitted by the Congress into this Union; but no new State shall be formed or erected within the jurisdiction of any other State, nor any State be formed by the junction of two or more States, or parts of States, without the consent of the legislatures of the States concerned as well as of the Congress.

2. The Congress shall have power to dispose of and make all needful rules and regulations respecting the territory or other property belonging to the United States; and nothing in this Constitution shall be so construed as to prejudice any claims of the United States, or of any particular State.

SECTION 4. The United States shall guarantee to every State in this Union a republican form of government, and shall protect each of them against invasion; and on application of the legislature, or of the executive (when the legislature cannot be convened) against domestic violence.

Article V

The Congress, whenever two thirds of both Houses shall deem it necessary, shall propose amendments to this Constitution, or, on the application of the legislatures of two thirds of the several States, shall call a convention for proposing amendments, which in either case shall be valid to all intents and purposes, as part of this Constitution, when ratified by the legislatures of three fourths of the several States, or by conventions in three fourths thereof, as the one or the other mode of ratification may be proposed by the Congress; Provided that no amendment which may be made prior to the year one thousand eight hundred and eight shall in any manner affect the first and fourth clauses in the ninth section of the first article; and that no State, without its consent, shall be deprived of its equal suffrage in the Senate.

Article VI

1. All debts contracted and engagements entered into, before the adoption of this Constitution, shall be as valid against the United States under this Constitution, as under the Confederation.[10]

2. This Constitution, and the laws of the United States which shall be made in pursuance

---

[7]See the Eleventh Amendment.
[8]See the Fourteenth Amendment, Sec. 1.

[9]See the Thirteenth Amendment.
[10]See the Fourteenth Amendment, Sec. 4.

thereof; and all treaties made, or which shall be made, under the authority of the United States, shall be the supreme law of the land; and the judges in every State shall be bound thereby, any thing in the Constitution or laws of any State to the contrary notwithstanding.

3. The senators and representatives before mentioned, and the members of the several State legislatures, and all executive and judicial officers, both of the United States and of the several States, shall be bound by oath or affirmation to support this Constitution; but no religious test shall ever be required as a qualification to any office or public trust under the United States.

Article VII

The ratification of the conventions of nine States shall be sufficient for the establishment of this Constitution between the States so ratifying the same.

Done in Convention by the unanimous consent of the States present the seventeenth day of September in the year of our Lord one thousand seven hundred and eighty-seven, and of the independence of the United States of America the twelfth. In witness whereof we have hereunto subscribed our names.

Articles in addition to, and amendment of, the Constitution of the United States of America, proposed by Congress, and ratified by the legislatures of the several States, pursuant to the fifth article of the original Constitution.

Amendment I

[First ten amendments ratified December 15, 1791]
Congress shall make no law respecting an establishment of religion, or prohibiting the free exercise thereof; or abridging the freedom of speech, or of the press; or the right of the people peaceably to assemble, and to petition the government for a redress of grievances.

Amendment II

As well regulated militia, being necessary to the security of a free State, the right of the people to keep and bear arms, shall not be infringed.

Amendment III

No soldier shall, in time of peace be quartered in any house, without the consent of the owner, nor in time of war, but in a manner to be prescribed by law.

Amendment IV

The right of the people to be secure in their persons, houses, papers, and effects, against unreasonable searches and seizures, shall not be violated, and no warrants shall issue, but upon probable cause, supported by oath or affirmation, and particularly describing the place to be searched, and the persons or things to be seized.

Amendment V

No person shall be held to answer for a capital or otherwise infamous crime, unless on a presentment or indictment of a grand jury, except in cases arising in the land or naval forces, or in the militia, when in actual service in time of war or public danger; nor shall any person be subject for the same offense to be twice put in jeopardy of life or limb; nor shall be compelled in any criminal case to be a witness against himself, nor be deprived of life, liberty, or property, without due process of law; nor shall private property be taken for public use, without just compensation.

Amendment VI

In all criminal prosecutions, the accused shall enjoy the right to a speedy and public trial, by an impartial jury of the State and district wherein the crime shall have been committed, which district shall have been previously ascertained by law, and to be informed of the nature and cause of the accusation; to be confronted with the witnesses against him; to have compulsory process for obtaining witnesses in his favor, and to have the assistance of counsel for his defense.

Amendment VII

In suits at common law, where the value in controversy shall exceed twenty dollars, the right of trial by jury shall be preserved, and no fact tried by a jury shall be otherwise reexamined in any court of the United States, than according to the rules of the common law.

Amendment VIII

Excessive bail shall not be required, nor excessive fines imposed, nor cruel and unusual punishments inflicted.

Amendment IX

The enumeration in the Constitution of certain rights shall not be construed to deny or disparage others retained by the people.

Amendment X

The powers not delegated to the United States by the Constitution, nor prohibited by it to the States, are reserved to the States respectively, or to the people.

Amendment XI [January 8, 1798]

The judicial power of the United States shall not be construed to extend to any suit in law or equity, commended or prosecuted against one of the United States by citizens of another State, or by citizens or subjects of any foreign State.

Amendment XII [September 25, 1804]

The electors shall meet in their respective States, and vote by ballot for President and Vice President, one of whom, at least, shall not be an inhabitant of the same

State with themselves; they shall name in their ballots the person voted for as President, and in distinct ballots, the person voted for as Vice President, and they shall make distinct lists of all persons voted for as President and of all persons voted for as Vice President, and of the number of votes for each, which lists they shall sign and certify, and transmit sealed to the seat of the government of the United States, directed to the President of the Senate;—The President of the Senate shall, in the presence of the Senate and House of Representatives, open all the certificates and the votes shall then be counted;—The person having the greatest number of votes for President, shall be the President, if such number be a majority of the whole number of electors appointed; and if no person have such majority, then from the persons having the highest numbers not exceeding three on the list of those voted for as President, the House of Representatives shall choose immediately, by ballot, the President. But in choosing the President, the votes shall be taken by States, the representation from each State having one vote; a quorum for this purpose shall consist of a member or members from two thirds of the States, and a majority of all the States shall be necessary to a choice. And if the House of Representatives shall not choose a President whenever the right of choice shall devolve upon them, before the fourth day of March next following, then the Vice President shall act as President, as in the case of the death or other constitutional disability of the President. The person having the greatest number of votes as Vice President shall be the Vice President, if such number be a majority of the whole number of electors appointed, and if no person have a majority, then from the two highest numbers on the list, the Senate shall choose the Vice President; a quorum for the purpose shall consist of two thirds of the whole number of Senators, and a majority of the whole number shall be necessary to a choice. But no person constitutionally ineligible to the office of president shall be eligible to that of Vice President of the United States.

Amendment XIII [December 18, 1865]

SECTION 1. Neither slavery nor involuntary servitude, except as punishment for crime whereof the party shall have been duly convicted, shall exist within the United States, or any place subject to their jurisdiction.

SECTION 2. Congress shall have power to enforce this article by appropriate legislation.

Amendment XIV [July 28, 1868]

SECTION 1. All persons born or naturalized in the United States, and subject to the jurisdiction thereof, are citizens of the United States and of the State wherein they reside. No State shall make or enforce any law which shall abridge the privileges or immunities of citizens of the United States; nor shall any State deprive any person of life, liberty, or property, without due process of law; nor deny to any person within its jurisdiction the equal protection of the laws.

SECTION 2. Representatives shall be apportioned among the several States according to their respective numbers, counting the whole number of persons in each State, excluding Indians not taxed. But when the right to vote at any election for the choice of electors for President and Vice President of the United States, representatives in Congress, the executive and judicial officers of a State, or the members of the legislature thereof, is denied to any of the male inhabitants of such State, being twenty-one years of age, and citizens of the United States, or in any way abridged, except for participating in rebellion, or other crime, the basis of representation there shall be reduced in the proportion which the number of such male citizens shall bear to the whole number of male citizens twenty-one years of age in such State.

SECTION 3. No person shall be a senator or representative in Congress, or elector of President and Vice President, or hold any office, civil or military, under the United States, or under any State, who having previously taken an oath, as a member of Congress, or as an officer of the United States, or as a member of any State legislature, or as an executive or judicial officer of any State, to support the Constitution of the United States, shall have engaged in insurrection or rebellion against the same, or given aid or comfort to the enemies thereof. But Congress may by a vote of two thirds of each House, remove such disability.

SECTION 4. The validity of the public debt of the United States, authorized by law, including debts incurred for payment of pensions and bounties for services in suppressing insurrection or rebellion; shall not be questioned. But neither the United States nor any State shall assume or pay any debt or obligation incurred in aid of insurrection or rebellion against the United States, or any claim for the loss or emancipation of any slave; but all such debts, obligations, and claims shall be held illegal and void.

SECTION 5. The Congress shall have the power to enforce, by appropriate legislation, the provisions of this article.

Amendment XV [March 30, 1870]

SECTION 1. The right of citizens of the United States to vote shall not be denied or abridged by the United States or by any State on account of race, color, or previous condition of servitude.

SECTION 2. The Congress shall have power to enforce this article by appropriate legislation.

Amendment XVI [February 25, 1913]

The Congress shall have power to lay and collect taxes on incomes, from whatever source derived, without apportionment among the several States, and without regard to any census or enumeration.

Amendment XVII [May 31, 1913]

The Senate of the United States shall be composed of two senators from each State, elected by the people thereof, for six years; and each senator shall have one vote. The electors in each State shall have the qualifications requisite for electors of the most numerous branch of the State legislature.

When vacancies happen in the representation of any State in the Senate, the executive authority of such State shall issue writs of election to fill such vacancies: *Provided,* That the legislature of any State may empower the executive thereof to make temporary appointments until the people fill the vacancies by election as the legislature may direct.

This amendment shall not be so construed as to affect the election or term of any senator chosen before it becomes valid as part of the Constitution.

Amendment XVIII[11] [January 29, 1919]

After one year from the ratification of this article, the manufacture, sale, or transportation of intoxicating liquors within, the importation thereof into, or the exportation thereof from the United States and all territory subject to the jurisdiction thereof for beverage purposes is thereby prohibited.

The Congress and the several States shall have concurrent power to enforce this article by appropriate legislation.

This article shall be inoperative unless it shall have been ratified as an amendment to the Constitution by the legislatures of the several States, as provided in the constitution, within seven years from the date of the submission hereof to the States by Congress.

Amendment XIX [August 26, 1920]

The right of citizens of the United States to vote shall not be denied or abridged by the United States or by any State on account of sex.

Congress shall have the power to enforce this article by appropriate legislation.

Amendment XX [January 23, 1933]

SECTION 1. The terms of the President and Vice President shall end at noon on the 20th day of January and the terms of Senators and Representatives at noon on the 3d day of January, of the years in which such terms would have ended if this article had not been ratified; and the terms of their successors shall then begin.

SECTION 2. The Congress shall assemble at least once in every year, and such meeting shall begin at noon on the 3d day of January, unless they shall by law appoint a different day.

SECTION 3. If, at the time fixed for the beginning of the term of president, the President-elect shall have died, the Vice President-elect shall become President. If a President shall not have been chosen before the time fixed for the beginning of his term, or if the President-elect shall have failed to qualify, then the Vice President-elect shall act as president until a President shall have qualified; and the Congress may by law provide for the case wherein neither a President-elect nor a Vice President-elect shall have qualified, declaring who shall then act as President, or the manner in which one who is to act shall be selected, and such person shall act accordingly until a President or Vice President shall have qualified.

SECTION 4. The Congress may by law provide for the case of the death of any of the persons from whom, the House of Representatives may choose a President whenever the right of choice shall have devolved upon them, and for the case of the death of any of the persons from whom the Senate may choose a Vice President whenever the right of choice shall have devolved upon them.

SECTION 5. Sections 1 and 2 shall take effect on the 15th day of October following the ratification of this article.

SECTION 6. This article shall be inoperative unless it shall have been ratified as an amendment to the Constitution by the legislatures of three-fourths of the several States within seven years from the date of its submission.

Amendment XXI [December 5, 1933]

SECTION 1. The Eighteenth Article of amendment to the Constitution of the United States is hereby repealed.

SECTION 2. The transportation or importation into any State, Territory, or possession of the United States for delivery or use therein of intoxicating liquors in violation of the laws thereof, is hereby prohibited.

SECTION 3. This article shall be inoperative unless it shall have been ratified as an amendment to the Constitution by conventions in the several States, as provided in the Consitution, within seven years from the date of the submission thereof to the States by the Congress.

---

[11]Repealed by the Twenty-first Amendment.

Amendment XXII [March 1, 1951]

No person shall be elected to the office of the President more than twice, and no person who has held the office of President, or acted as President, for more than two years of a term to which some other person was elected President shall be elected to the office of the President more than once.

But this article shall not apply to any person holding the office of President when this article was proposed by the Congress, and shall not prevent any person who may be holding the office of President, or acting as President, during the term within which this article becomes operative from holding the office of President or acting as President during the remainder of such term.

This article shall be inoperative unless it shall have been ratified as an amendment to the Constitution by the legislatures of three-fourths of the several States within seven years from the date of its submission to the States by the Congress.

Amendment XXIII [March 29, 1961]

SECTION 1. The District constituting the seat of Government of the United States shall appoint in such manner as the Congress may direct.

A number of electors of President and Vice President equal to the whole number of Senators and Representatives in Congress to which the District would be entitled if it were a State, but in no event more than the least populous State; they shall be in addition to those appointed by the States, but they shall be considered, for the purposes of the election of President and Vice Presient, to be electors appointed by a State; and they shall meet in the District and perform such duties as provided by the twelfth article of amendment.

SECTION 2. The Congress shall have power to enforce this article by appropriate legislation.

Amendment XXIV [January 23, 1964]

SECTION 1. The right of citizens of the United States to vote in any primary or other election for President or Vice President, for electors for President or Vice President, or for Senator or Representative in Congress, shall not be denied or abridged by the United States or any State by reason of failure to pay any poll tax or other tax.

SECTION 2. The Congress shall have power to enforce this article by appropriate legislation.

Amendment XXV [February 10, 1967]

SECTION 1. In case of the removal of the President from office or of his death or resignation, the Vice President shall become President.

SECTION 2. Whenever there is a vacancy in the office of the Vice president, the President shall nominate a Vice President who shall take office upon confirmation by a majority of both Houses of Congress.

SECTION 3. Whenever the President transmits to the President pro tempore of the Senate and the Speaker of the House of Representatives his written declaration that he is unable to discharge the powers and duties of his office, and until he transmits to them a written declaration to the contrary, such powers and duties shall be discharged by the Vice President as Acting President.

SECTION 4. Whenever the Vice president and a majority of either the principal officers of the executive departments or of such other body as Congress may by law provide, transmit to the President pro tempore of the Senate and the Speaker of the House of Representatives their written declaration that the President is unable to discharge the powers and duties of his office, the Vice President shall immediately assume the powers and duties of the office as Acting President.

Thereafter, when the President transmits to the President pro tempore of the Senate and the Speaker of the house of Representatives his written declaration that no inability exists, he shall resume the powers and duties of his office unless the Vice President and a majority of either the principal officers of the executive departments or of such other body as Congress may by law provide, transmit within four days to the President pro tempore of the Senate and the Speaker of the House of Representatives their written declaration that the President is unable to discharge the powers and duties of his office. Thereupon Congress shall decide the issue, assembling within forty-eight hours for that purpose if not in session. If the Congress, within twenty-one days after receipt of the latter written declaration, or, if Congress is not in session, within twenty-one days after Congress is required to assemble, determines by two-thirds vote of both houses that the President is unable to discharge the powers and duties of his office, the Vice President shall continue to discharge the same as Acting President; otherwise, the President shall resume the powers and duties of his office.

Amendment XXVI [June 30, 1971]

SECTION 1. The right of citizens of the United States who are eighteen years of age or older to vote shall not be denied or abridged by the United States or by any State on account of age.

SECTION 2. The Congress shall have power to enforce this article by appropriate legislation.

PRESIDENTS AND VICE PRESIDENTS

1. George Washington (1789)
   John Adams (1789)

2. John Adams (1797)
   Thomas Jefferson (1797)

3. Thomas Jefferson (1801)
   Aaron Burr (1801)
   George Clinton (1805)

4. James Madison (1809)
   George Clinton (1809)
   Elbridge Gerry (1813)

5. James Monroe (1817)
   Daniel D. Thompkins (1817)

6. John Quincy Adams (1825)
   John C. Calhoun (1825)

7. Andrew Jackson (1829)
   John C. Calhoun (1829)
   Martin Van Buren (1833)

8. Martin Van Buren (1837)
   Richard M. Johnson (1837)

9. William H. Harrison (1841)
   John Tyler (1841)

10. John Tyler (1841)

11. James K. Polk (1845)
    George M. Dallas (1845)

12. Zachary Taylor (1849)
    Millard Fillmore (1849)

13. Millard Fillmore (1850)

14. Franklin Pierce (1853)
    William R. King (1853)

15. James Buchanan (1857)
    John C. Breckinridge (1857)

16. Abraham Lincoln (1861)
    Hannibal Hamlin (1861)
    Andrew Johnson (1865)

17. Andrew Johnson (1865)

18. Ulysses S. Grant (1869)
    Schuyler Colfax (1869)
    Henry Wilson (1873)

19. Rutherford B. Hayes (1877)
    William A. Wheeler (1877)

20. James A. Garfield (1881)
    Chester A. Arthur (1881)

21. Chester A. Arthur (1881)

22. Grover Cleveland (1885)
    T. A. Hendricks (1885)

23. Benjamin Harrison (1889)
    Levi P. Morgan (1889)

24. Grover Cleveland (1893)
    Adlai E. Stevenson (1893)

25. William McKinley (1897)
    Garret A. Hobart (1897)
    Theodore Roosevelt (1901)

26. Theodore Roosevelt (1901)
    Charles Fairbanks (1905)

27. William H. Taft (1909)
    James S. Sherman (1909)

28. Woodrow Wilson (1913)
    Thomas R. Marshall (1913)

29. Warren G. Harding (1921)
    Calvin Coolidge (1921)

30. Calvin Coolidge (1923)
    Charles G. Dawes (1925)

31. Herbert C. Hoover (1929)
    Charles Curtis (1929)

32. Franklin D. Roosevelt (1933)
    John Nance Garner (1933)
    Henry A. Wallace (1941)
    Harry S. Truman (1945)

33. Harry S. Truman (1945)
    Alben W. Barkley (1949)

34. Dwight D. Eisenhower (1953)
    Richard M. Nixon (1953)

35. John F. Kennedy (1961)
    Lyndon B. Johnson (1961)

36. Lyndon B. Johnson (1963)
    Hubert H. Humphrey (1965)

37. Richard M. Nixon (1969)
    Spiro T. Agnew (1969)
    Gerald R. Ford (1973)

38. Gerald R. Ford (1974)
    Nelson A. Rockefeller (1974)

39. James E. Carter Jr. (1977)
    Walter F. Mondale (1977)

40. Ronald W. Reagan (1981)
    George H. Bush (1981)

41. George H. Bush (1989)
    James D. Quayle III (1989)

42. William J. B. Clinton (1993)
    Albert Gore (1993)

PRESIDENTIAL ELECTIONS

Year	Number of States	Candidates	Party	Popular Vote*	Electoral Vote[†]	Percentage of Popular Vote
1789	11	GEORGE WASHINGTON	No party designations		69	
		John Adams			34	
		Other Candidates			35	
1792	15	GEORGE WASHINGTON	No party designations		132	
		John Adams			77	
		George Clinton			50	
		Other Candidates			5	
1796	16	JOHN ADAMS	Federalist		71	
		Thomas Jefferson	Democratic-Republican		68	
		Thomas Pinckney	Federalist		59	
		Aaron Burr	Democratic-Republican		30	
		Other Candidates			48	
1800	16	THOMAS JEFFERSON	Democratic-Republican		73	
		Aaron Burr	Democratic-Republican		73	
		John Adams	Federalist		65	
		Charles C. Pinckney	Federalist		64	
		John Jay	Federalist		1	
1804	17	THOMAS JEFFERSON	Democratic-Republican		162	
		Charles C. Pinckney	Federalist		14	
1808	17	JAMES MADISON	Democratic-Republican		122	
		Charles C. Pinckney	Federalist		47	
		George Clinton	Democratic-Republican		6	
1812	18	JAMES MADISON	Democratic-Republican		128	
		DeWitt Clinton	Federalist		89	
1816	19	JAMES MONROE	Democratic-Republican		183	
		Rufus King	Federalist		34	
1820	24	JAMES MONROE	Democratic-Republican		231	
		John Quincy Adams	Independent Republican		1	
1824	24	JOHN QUINCY ADAMS		108,740	84	30.5
		Andrew Jackson		153,544	99	43.1
		William H. Crawford		46,618	41	13.1
		Henry Clay		47,136	37	13.2
1828	24	ANDREW JACKSON	Democrat	647,286	178	56.0
		John Quincy Adams	National Republican	508,064	83	44.0
1832	24	ANDREW JACKSON	Democrat	687,502	219	55.0
		Henry Clay	National Republican	530,189	49	42.4
		William Wirt	Anti-Masonic	33,108	7	2.6
		John Floyd	National Republican		11	

*Percentage of popular vote given for any election year may not total 100 percent because candidates receiving less than 1 percent of the popular vote have been omitted.

[†]Prior to the passage of the Twelfth Amendment in 1904, the electoral college voted for two presidential candidates; the runner-up became Vice-President. Data from Historical Statistics of the United States, Colonial Times to 1957 (1961), pp. 682–683, and The World Almanac.

PRESIDENTIAL ELECTIONS
(continued)

Year	Number of States	Candidates	Party	Popular Vote	Electoral Vote	Percentage of Popular Vote
1836	26	MARTIN VAN BUREN	Democrat	765,483	170	50.9
		William H. Harrison	Whig		73	
		Hugh L. White	Whig		26	
		Daniel Webster	Whig	739,795	14	49.1
		W. P. Mangum	Whig		11	
1840	26	WILLIAM H. HARRISON	Whig	1,274,624	234	53.1
		Martin Van Buren	Democrat	1,127,781	60	46.9
1844	26	JAMES K. POLK	Democrat	1,338,464	170	49.6
		Henry Clay	Whig	1,300,097	105	48.1
		James G. Birney	Liberty	62,300		2.3
1848	30	ZACHARY TAYLOR	Whig	1,360,967	163	47.4
		Lewis Cass	Democrat	1,222,342	127	42.5
		Martin Van Buren	Free Soil	291,263		10.1
1852	31	FRANKLIN PIERCE	Democrat	1,601,117	254	50.9
		Winfield Scott	Whig	1,385,453	42	44.1
		John P. Hale	Free Soil	155,825		5.0
1856	31	JAMES BUCHANAN	Democrat	1,832,955	174	45.3
		John C. Frémont	Republican	1,339,932	114	33.1
		Millard Fillmore	American ("Know Nothing")	871,731	8	21.6
1860	33	ABRAHAM LINCOLN	Republican	1,865,593	180	39.8
		Stephen A. Douglas	Democrat	1,382,713	12	29.5
		John C. Breckinridge	Democrat	848,356	72	18.1
		John Bell	Constitutional Union	592,906	39	12.6
1864	36	ABRAHAM LINCOLN	Republican	2,206,938	212	55.0
		George B. McClellan	Democrat	1,803,787	21	45.0
1868	37	ULYSSES S. GRANT	Republican	3,013,421	214	52.7
		Horatio Seymour	Democrat	2,706,829	80	47.3
1872	37	ULYSSES S. GRANT	Republican	3,596,745	286	55.6
		Horace Greeley	Democrat	2,843,446	*	43.9
1876	38	RUTHERFORD B. HAYES	Republican	4,036,572	185	48.0
		Samuel J. Tilden	Democrat	4,284,020	184	51.0
1880	38	JAMES A. GARFIELD	Republican	4,453,295	214	48.5
		Winfield S. Hancock	Democrat	4,414,082	155	48.1
		James B. Weaver	Greenback-Labor	308,578		3.4
1884	38	GROVER CLEVELAND	Democrat	4,879,507	219	48.5
		James G. Blaine	Republican	4,850,293	182	48.2
		Benjamin F. Butler	Greenback-Labor	175,370		1.8
		John P. St. John	Prohibition	150,369		1.5
1888	38	BENJAMIN HARRISON	Republican	5,447,129	233	47.9
		Grover Cleveland	Democrat	5,537,857	168	48.6
		Clinton B. Fisk	Prohibition	249,506		2.2
		Anson J. Streeter	Union Labor	146,935		1.3

*Because of the death of Greeley, Democratic electors scattered their votes.

PRESIDENTIAL ELECTIONS
(continued)

Year	Number of States	Candidates	Party	Popular Vote	Electoral Vote	Percentage of Popular Vote
1892	44	GROVER CLEVELAND	Democrat	5,555,426	277	46.1
		Benjamin Harrison	Republican	5,182,690	145	43.0
		James B. Weaver	People's	1,029,846	22	8.5
		John Bidwell	Prohibition	264,133		2.2
1896	45	WILLIAM MCKINLEY	Republican	7,102,246	271	51.1
		William J. Bryan	Democrat	6,492,559	176	47.7
1900	45	WILLIAM MCKINLEY	Republican	7,218,491	292	51.7
		William J. Bryan	Democrat; Populist	6,356,734	155	45.5
		John C. Woolley	Prohibition	208,914		1.5
1904	45	THEODORE ROOSEVELT	Republican	7,628,461	336	57.4
		Alton B. Parker	Democrat	5,084,223	140	37.6
		Eugene V. Debs	Socialist	402,283		3.0
		Silas C. Swallow	Prohibition	258,536		1.9
1908	46	WILLIAM H. TAFT	Republican	7,675,320	321	51.6
		William J. Bryan	Democrat	6,412,294	162	43.1
		Eugene V. Debs	Socialist	420,793		2.8
		Eugene W. Chafin	Prohibition	253,840		1.7
1912	48	WOODROW WILSON	Democrat	6,296,547	435	41.9
		Theodore Roosevelt	Progressive	4,118,571	88	27.4
		William H. Taft	Republican	3,486,720	8	23.2
		Eugene V. Debs	Socialist	900,672		6.0
		Eugene W. Chafin	Prohibition	206,275		1.4
1916	48	WOODROW WILSON	Democrat	9,127,695	277	49.4
		Charles E. Hughes	Republican	8,533,507	254	46.2
		A. L. Benson	Socialist	585,113		3.2
		J. Frank Hanly	Prohibition	220,506		1.2
1920	48	WARREN G. HARDING	Republican	16,143,407	404	60.4
		James M. Cox	Democrat	9,130,328	127	34.2
		Eugene V. Debs	Socialist	919,799		3.4
		P. P. Christensen	Farmer-Labor	265,411		1.0
1924	48	CALVIN COOLIDGE	Republican	15,718,211	382	54.0
		John W. Davis	Democrat	8,385,283	136	28.8
		Robert M. La Follette	Progressive	4,831,289	13	16.6
1928	48	HERBERT C. HOOVER	Republican	21,391,993	444	58.2
		Alfred E. Smith	Democrat	15,016,169	87	40.9
1932	48	FRANKLIN D. ROOSEVELT	Democrat	22,809,638	472	57.4
		Herbert C. Hoover	Republican	15,758,901	59	39.7
		Norman Thomas	Socialist	881,951		2.2
1936	48	FRANKLIN D. ROOSEVELT	Democrat	27,752,869	523	60.8
		Alfred M. Landon	Republican	16,674,665	8	36.5
		William Lemke	Union	882,479		1.9
1940	48	FRANKLIN D. ROOSEVELT	Democrat	27,307,819	449	54.8
		Wendell L. Willkie	Republican	22,321,018	82	44.8
1944	48	FRANKLIN D. ROOSEVELT	Democrat	25,606,585	432	53.5
		Thomas E. Dewey	Republican	22,014,745	99	46.0

PRESIDENTIAL ELECTIONS
(continued)

Year	Number of States	Candidates	Party	Popular Vote	Electoral Vote	Percentage of Popular Vote
1948	48	HARRY S. TRUMAN	Democrat	24,105,812	303	49.5
		Thomas E. Dewey	Republican	21,970,065	189	45.1
		J. Strom Thurmond	States' Rights	1,169,063	39	2.4
		Henry A. Wallace	Progressive	1,157,172		2.4
1952	48	DWIGHT D. EISENHOWER	Republican	33,936,234	442	55.1
		Adlai E. Stevenson	Democrat	27,314,992	89	44.4
1956	48	DWIGHT D. EISENHOWER	Republican	35,590,472	457*	57.6
		Adlai E. Stevenson	Democrat	26,022,752	73	42.1
1960	50	JOHN F. KENNEDY	Democrat	34,227,096	303†	49.9
		Richard M. Nixon	Republican	34,108,546	219	49.6
1964	50	LYNDON B. JOHNSON	Democrat	42,676,220	486	61.3
		Barry M. Goldwater	Republican	26,860,314	52	38.5
1968	50	RICHARD M. NIXON	Republican	31,785,480	301	43.4
		Hubert H. Humphrey	Democrat	31,275,165	191	42.7
		George C. Wallace	American Independent	9,906,473	46	13.5
1972	50	RICHARD M. NIXON‡	Republican	47,165,234	520	60.6
		George S. McGovern	Democrat	29,168,110	17	37.5
1976	50	JIMMY CARTER	Democrat	40,828,929	297	50.1
		Gerald R. Ford	Republican	39,148,940	240	47.9
		Eugene McCarthy	Independent	739,256		
1980	50	RONALD REAGAN	Republican	43,201,220	489	50.9
		Jimmy Carter	Democrat	34,913,332	49	41.2
		John B. Anderson	Independent	5,581,379		
1984	50	RONALD REAGAN	Republican	53,428,357	525	59.0
		Walter F. Mondale	Democrat	36,930,923	13	41.0
1988	50	GEORGE BUSH	Republican	48,901,046	426	53.4
		Michael Dukakis	Democrat	41,809,030	111	45.6
1992	50	BILL CLINTON	Democrat	43,728,275	370	43.2
		George Bush	Republican	38,167,416	168	37.7
		H. Ross Perot	United We Stand, America	19,237,247		19.0
1996	50	BILL CLINTON	Democrat	45,590,703	379	49.0
		Bob Dole	Republican	37,816,307	159	41.0
		H. Ross Perot	Reform	7,866,284		8.0

*Walter B. Jones received 1 electoral vote.

†Harry F. Byrd received 15 electoral votes.

‡Resigned August 9, 1974: Vice President Gerald R. Ford became President.

ADMISSION OF STATES INTO THE UNION

State	Date of Admission	State	Date of Admission
1. Delaware	December 7, 1787	26. Michigan	January 26, 1837
2. Pennsylvania	December 12, 1787	27. Florida	March 3, 1845
3. New Jersey	December 18, 1787	28. Texas	December 29, 1845
4. Georgia	January 2, 1788	29. Iowa	December 28, 1846
5. Connecticut	January 9, 1788	30. Wisconsin	May 29, 1848
6. Massachusetts	February 6, 1788	31. California	September 9, 1850
7. Maryland	April 28, 1788	32. Minnesota	May 11, 1858
8. South Carolina	May 23, 1788	33. Oregon	February 14, 1859
9. New Hampshire	June 21, 1788	34. Kansas	January 29, 1861
10. Virginia	June 25, 1788	35. West Virginia	June 20, 1863
11. New York	July 26, 1788	36. Nevada	October 31, 1864
12. North Carolina	November 21, 1789	37. Nebraska	March 1, 1867
13. Rhode Island	May 29, 1790	38. Colorado	August 1, 1876
14. Vermont	March 4, 1791	39. North Dakota	November 2, 1889
15. Kentucky	June 1, 1792	40. South Dakota	November 2, 1889
16. Tennessee	June 1, 1796	41. Montana	November 8, 1889
17. Ohio	March 1, 1803	42. Washington	November 11, 1889
18. Louisiana	April 30, 1812	43. Idaho	July 3, 1890
19. Indiana	December 11, 1816	44. Wyoming	July 10, 1890
20. Mississippi	December 10, 1817	45. Utah	January 4, 1896
21. Illinois	December 3, 1818	46. Oklahoma	November 16, 1907
22. Alabama	December 14, 1819	47. New Mexico	January 6, 1912
23. Maine	March 15, 1820	48. Arizona	February 14, 1912
24. Missouri	August 10, 1821	49. Alaska	January 3, 1959
25. Arkansas	June 15, 1836	50. Hawaii	August 21, 1959

DEMOGRAPHICS OF THE UNITED STATES

POPULATION GROWTH

Year	Population	Percent Increase
1630	4,600	
1640	26,600	478.3
1650	50,400	90.8
1660	75,100	49.0
1670	111,900	49.0
1680	151,500	35.4
1690	210,400	38.9
1700	250,900	19.2
1710	331,700	32.2
1720	466,200	40.5
1730	629,400	35.0
1740	905,600	43.9
1750	1,170,800	29.3
1760	1,593,600	36.1
1770	2,148,100	34.8
1780	2,780,400	29.4
1790	3,929,214	41.3
1800	5,308,483	35.1
1810	7,239,881	36.4
1820	9,638,453	33.1
1830	12,866,020	33.5
1840	17,069,453	32.7
1850	23,191,876	35.9
1860	31,443,321	35.6
1870	39,818,449	26.6
1880	50,155,783	26.0
1890	62,947,714	25.5
1900	75,994,575	20.7
1910	91,972,266	21.0
1920	105,710,620	14.9
1930	122,775,046	16.1
1940	131,669,275	7.2
1950	150,697,361	14.5
1960	179,323,175	19.0
1970	203,235,298	13.3
1980	226,545,805	11.5
1990	248,709,873	9.8

Source: *Historical Statistics of the United States* (1975); *Statistical Abstract by the United States* (1991).
Note: Figures for 1630–1780 include British colonies within limits of present United States only; Native American population included only in 1930 and thereafter.

IMMIGRATION, BY ORIGIN
(in thousands)

Period	Europe	Americas	Asia
1820–30	106	12	—
1831–40	496	33	—
1841–50	1,597	62	—
1851–60	2,453	75	42
1861–70	2,065	167	65
1871–80	2,272	404	70
1881–90	4,735	427	70
1891–1900	3,555	39	75
1901–10	8,065	362	324
1911–20	4,322	1,144	247
1921–30	2,463	1,517	112
1931–40	348	160	16
1941–50	621	355	32
1951–60	1,326	997	150
1961–70	1,123	1,716	590
1971–80	800	1,983	1,588
1981–90	762	3,616	2,738

Source: *Historical Statistics of the United States* (1975); *Statistical Abstract of the United States* (1991).

WORK FORCE

Year	Total Number Workers (1000s)	Farmers as % of Total	Women as % of Total	% Workers in Unions
1810	2,330	84	(NA)	(NA)
1840	5,660	75	(NA)	(NA)
1860	11,110	53	(NA)	(NA)
1870	12,506	53	15	(NA)
1880	17,392	52	15	(NA)
1890	23,318	43	17	(NA)
1900	29,073	40	18	3
1910	38,167	31	21	6
1920	41,614	26	21	12
1930	48,830	22	22	7
1940	53,011	17	24	27
1950	59,643	12	28	25
1960	69,877	8	32	26
1970	82,049	4	37	25
1980	108,544	3	42	23
1990	117,914	3	45	16
1995	124,900	3	46	15

Source: *Historical Statistics of the United States* (1975); *Statistical Abstract of the United States* (1991 and 1996).

RACIAL COMPOSITION OF THE POPULATION
(in thousands)

Year	White	Black	Indian	Hispanic	Asian
1790	3,172	757	(NA)	(NA)	(NA)
1800	4,306	1,002	(NA)	(NA)	(NA)
1820	7,867	1,772	(NA)	(NA)	(NA)
1840	14,196	2,874	(NA)	(NA)	(NA)
1860	26,923	4,442	(NA)	(NA)	(NA)
1880	43,403	6,581	(NA)	(NA)	(NA)
1900	66,809	8,834	(NA)	(NA)	(NA)
1910	81,732	9,828	(NA)	(NA)	(NA)
1920	94,821	10,463	(NA)	(NA)	(NA)
1930	110,287	11,891	(NA)	(NA)	(NA)
1940	118,215	12,866	(NA)	(NA)	(NA)
1950	134,942	15,042	(NA)	(NA)	(NA)
1960	158,832	18,872	(NA)	(NA)	(NA)
1970	178,098	22,581	(NA)	(NA)	(NA)
1980	194,713	26,683	1,420	14,609	3,729
1990	208,704	30,483	2,065	22,354	7,458

Source: U.S. Bureau of the Census, U.S. Census of Population: 1940, vol. II, part 1, and vol. IV, part 1; 1950, vol. II, part 1; 1960, vol. I, part 1; 1970, vol. I, part B; and Current Population Reports, P25-1095 and P25-1104; and unpublished data.

THE ECONOMY AND FEDERAL SPENDING

Year	Gross National Product (GNP) (in billions)	Foreign Trade (in millions) Exports	Imports	Balance of Trade	Federal Budget (in billions)	Federal Surplus/Deficit (in billions)	Federal Debt (in billions)
1790	(NA)	$ 20	$ 23	$ −3	$ 0.004	$+0.00015	$ 0.076
1800	(NA)	71	91	−20	0.011	+0.0006	0.083
1810	(NA)	67	85	−18	0.008	+0.0012	0.053
1820	(NA)	70	74	−4	0.018	−0.0004	0.091
1830	(NA)	74	71	+3	0.015	+0.100	0.049
1840	(NA)	132	107	+25	0.024	−0.005	0.004
1850	(NA)	152	178	−26	0.040	+0.004	0.064
1860	(NA)	400	362	−38	0.063	−0.01	0.065
1870	$ 7.4	451	462	−11	0.310	+0.10	2.4
1880	11.2	853	761	+92	0.268	+0.07	2.1
1890	13.1	910	823	+87	0.318	+0.09	1.2
1900	18.7	1,499	930	+569	0.521	+0.05	1.2
1910	35.3	1,919	1,646	+273	0.694	−0.02	1.1
1920	91.5	8,664	5,784	+2,880	6.357	+0.3	24.3
1930	90.7	4,013	3,500	+513	3.320	+0.7	16.3
1940	100.0	4,030	7,433	−3,403	9.6	−2.7	43.0
1950	286.5	10,816	9,125	+1,691	43.1	−2.2	257.4
1960	506.5	19,600	15,046	+4,556	92.2	+0.3	286.3
1970	992.7	42,700	40,189	+2,511	195.6	−2.8	371.0
1980	2,631.7	220,783	244,871	+24,088	590.9	−73.8	907.7
1990	5,524.5	394,030	494,042	−101,012	1,251.8	−220.5	3,233.3
1995	7,237.5	786,529	891,593	−105,064	1,519.1	−163.9	6,207.0

Source: U.S. Office of Management and Budget, Budget of the United States Government, annual; Statistical Abstract of the United States, 1996.

GLOSSARY

Act for Religious Toleration The first law in America to call for freedom of worship for all Christians. It was enacted in Maryland in 1649 to quell disputes between Catholics and Protestants, but it failed to bring peace.

Actual representation The practice whereby elected representatives normally reside in their districts and are directly responsive to local interests.

Administration of Justice Act One of the **Coercive** or **Intolerable Acts** passed by Parliament in 1774 in response to the **Boston Tea Party.** It provided that British officials accused of capital crimes could be tried in England.

African Methodist Episcopal (AME) Church Religious body founded by blacks for blacks in the North during the early nineteenth century that gained adherents among former slaves in the South after the Civil War.

Age of Enlightenment Major intellectual movement occurring in western Europe in the late seventeenth and early eighteenth centuries. Inspired by recent scientific advances, thinkers emphasized the role of human reason in understanding the world and directing its events. Their ideas placed less emphasis on God's role in ordering worldly affairs.

Alamo Franciscan mission at San Antonio, Texas, that was the site in 1836 of a siege and massacre of Texans by Mexican troops.

Albany Congress Intercolonial congress called in 1754 in Albany, New York, to deal with Iroquois grievances against the English. At the congress, prominent colonists proposed the **Albany Plan of Union.**

Albany Plan of Union Plan put forward in 1754 by Massachusetts Governor William Shirley, Benjamin Franklin, and other colonial leaders, calling for an intercolonial union to manage defense and Indian affairs. The plan was rejected by participants at the **Albany Congress.**

Albany Regency Popular name after 1820 for the state political machine in New York headed by Martin Van Buren.

Alien and Sedition Acts Collective name given to four acts passed by Congress in 1798 that curtailed freedom of speech and the liberty of foreigners resident in the United States.

Alien Enemies Act Law passed by Congress in 1798 authorizing the president in the event of war to deport aliens suspected of endangering the public peace; one of the **Alien and Sedition Acts.**

Alien Friends Act Law passed by Congress in 1798 authorizing the president during peacetime to expel aliens suspected of subversive activities; one of the **Alien and Sedition Acts.**

American and Foreign Anti-Slavery Society Antislavery organization formed in 1840 when a group of moderate abolitionists split off from the **American Anti-Slavery Society** in protest of the radicalism of William Lloyd Garrison and his support of women's rights.

American Anti-Slavery Society The first national organization of abolitionists, founded in 1833. *See also* **American and Foreign Anti-Slavery Society.**

American Colonization Society Organization, founded in 1817 by antislavery reformers, that called for gradual emancipation and the removal of freed blacks to Africa.

American Equal Rights Association Association formed by women's rights activists in 1866 to advocate universal **suffrage** at the state level after the **Fourteenth Amendment** failed to provide federal guarantees for women's voting rights.

American Female Moral Reform Society Organization founded in 1839 by female reformers that established homes of refuge for prostitutes and petitioned for state laws that would criminalize adultery and the seduction of women.

American Revenue Act Commonly known as the **Sugar Act,** law passed in 1764 to raise revenue in the American colonies. It lowered the duty from 6 pence to 3 pence per gallon foreign molasses imported into the colonies and increased the restrictions on colonial commerce.

American System The program of government subsidies favored by Henry Clay and his followers to promote American economic growth and protect domestic manufacturers from foreign competition.

American system of manufacturing A technique of production pioneered in the United States in the first half of the nineteenth century that relied on precision manufacturing with the use of interchangeable parts.

American Temperance Society National organization established in 1826 by evangelical Protestants that campaigned for total abstinence from alcohol and was successful in sharply lowering per capita consumption of alcohol.

Anarchist A person who believes that all government interferes with individual liberty and should be abolished by whatever means.

Anglican Of or belonging to the Church of England, a Protestant denomination.

Anglo-American Accords Series of agreements reached in the British-American Convention of 1818 that fixed the western boundary between the United States and Canada at the 49th parallel, allowed for the joint occupation of the Oregon Country, and restored to Americans fishing rights off Newfoundland.

Annapolis Convention Conference of state delegates at Annapolis, Maryland, that issued a call in September 1786 for a convention to meet at Philadelphia in May 1787 to consider fundamental changes to the **Articles of Confederation.**

Antietam, Battle of Narrow strategic Union victory in the Civil War in September 1862 that turned back the first Confederate invasion of the North and enabled President Lincoln to issue the **Emancipation Proclamation.**

Antifederalist An opponent of the **Constitution** in the debate over its ratification.

Anti-Masons Third party formed in 1827 in opposition to the presumed power and influence of the Masonic order.

Antinomian A person who believes that salvation comes through faith alone and that individuals who are saved obey the spirit within them rather than the moral law.

Appeal to the Colored Citizens of the World Pamphlet published in 1829 by David Walker, a Boston free black, calling for slaves to rise up in rebellion.

Appomattox Town in south-central Virginia where Confederate general Robert E. Lee surrendered to Union general Ulysses S. Grant on April 9, 1865, ending the Civil War.

Apprentice A person, usually a young male, bound by a legal agreement to serve an employer for a specified amount of time in return for training in a craft, trade, or business.

Archaic The period roughly between 8000 and 1500 B.C., during which time Native Americans adapted to a changed continental climate, developed larger communities, and, in several regions, adopted agriculture.

Articles of Confederation Written document setting up the loose confederation of states that comprised the first national government of the United States from 1781 to 1788.

Atlanta Campaign Decisive Civil War campaign in 1864 in which Union general William T. Sherman maneuvered past Confederate general Joseph E. Johnson from northwestern Georgia toward Atlanta until President Davis replaced Johnson with General John B. Hood, who promptly engaged Sherman and lost this vital rail junction to the Union.

Backcountry The western edges of settlement in colonies from Pennsylvania south to the Carolinas. Colonists first began moving to this region in the eighteenth century, developing a society that was at first somewhat cruder than longer-settled eastern communities.

Bacon's Rebellion Violent conflict in Virginia (1675–1676), beginning with settler attacks on Indians but culminating in a rebellion led by Nathaniel Bacon against Virginia's government.

Bank War The political struggle between President Andrew Jackson and the supporters of the **Second Bank of the United States.**

Beaver Wars Series of bloody conflicts, occurring between 1640s and 1680s, during which the Iroquois fought the French and their Indian allies for control of the fur trade in eastern North America and the Great Lakes region.

Benevolent empire Network of reform associations affiliated with Protestant churches in the early nineteenth century dedicated to the restoration of moral order.

Bicameral legislature A legislative body composed of two houses.

Bill of rights A written summary of inalienable rights and liberties.

Black codes Laws passed by states and municipalities denying many rights of citizenship to free blacks. Also, during **Reconstruction,** laws passed by newly elected southern state legislatures to control black labor, mobility, and employment.

Black Death Outbreak of the pneumonic form of bubonic plague in Europe between 1347 and 1351 that killed perhaps a third of Europe's population.

Black Hawk's War Short 1832 war in which federal troops and Illinois militia units defeated the Sauk and Fox Indians led by Black Hawk.

"Bleeding Kansas" Violence between pro- and antislavery forces in Kansas Territory after the passage of the **Kansas-Nebraska Act** in 1854.

Board of Trade Committee set up by King William in 1696 that replaced the Lords of Trade as overseers of colonial affairs. The board gathered information about the colonies and recommended policy changes but had no executive authority.

Boston Massacre Incident that occurred in Boston on March 5, 1770, in which British soldiers fired on a crowd that had been harassing them. Five civilians were killed.

Boston Port Act One of the **Coercive Acts** passed by Parliament in 1774 in response to the **Boston Tea Party**. It closed the port of Boston until townspeople paid for the tea and the duties on it.

Boston Seamen's Aid Society Female reform organization founded in 1833 to assist widows and orphans of sailors.

Boston Tea Party Incident that occurred on December 16, 1773, in which Bostonians, disguised as Indians, destroyed £9,000 worth of tea belonging to the British East India Company in order to prevent payment of the duty on it.

Brandywine Creek, Battle of Revolutionary War engagement on September 11, 1777, in southeastern Pennsylvania in which British forces under Sir William Howe defeated Americans under General Washington, thereby clearing the way for the British occupation of Philadelphia.

British Constitution The principles, procedures, and precedents that governed the operation of the British government. These could be found in no single written document; Parliament and the king made the Constitution by their actions.

Broad constructionist Person who favors reading implied powers into the **Constitution**.

Brook Farm A utopian community and experimental farm established in 1841 near Boston.

Brooklyn Heights, Battle of Revolutionary War battle fought on August 27, 1776, when William Howe landed a large British force on Long Island, New York, outflanked the American defenders, and attacked their rear. Although the Americans suffered heavy casualties, General Washington was later able under cover of darkness to withdraw his forces to Manhattan Island.

Bull Run, First Battle of The first major battle of the Civil War in July 1861; a disaster for Federal forces.

Bull Run, Second Battle of Site of a federal defeat in August 1862 one year after a similar loss at the same place.

Bunker Hill, Battle of Revolutionary War battle actually fought on nearby Breed's Hill, overlooking Boston harbor, on June 17, 1775. It was a costly engagement for the British, who suffered more than a thousand casualties.

Cabinet The body of secretaries appointed by the president to head executive departments and serve as advisers.

Californio A person of Spanish descent in California.

Camden, Battle of Decisive British victory at Camden, South Carolina, on August 16, 1780, with more than one thousand Americans killed or wounded and many captured. A second battle near Camden on April 25, 1781, was more nearly a draw.

Carpetbaggers Northerners who came to the post–Civil War South, initially for economic reasons, and then became involved in Republican politics; a disparaging term.

Chancellorsville Battle ending in a Confederate victory in Virginia in May 1863 during which General Thomas "Stonewall" Jackson was mortally wounded.

Charles River Bridge v. *Warren* Supreme Court decision of 1837 that promoted economic competition by ruling that the broader rights of the community took precedence over any presumed right of monopoly granted in a corporate charter.

Charleston, Battle of Revolutionary War engagement that began on February 11, 1780, when Sir Henry Clinton, leading eight thousand British troops from New York encircled and laid siege to Charleston, South Carolina. On May 12, of that year, 5,400 American defenders under Benjamin Lincoln surrendered in the costliest American defeat of the Revolutionary War.

Chattanooga Site of a series of Civil War campaigns culminating in a smashing Union victory in November 1863 as federal troops broke a Confederate siege of the city and opened the road to Georgia.

Cherokee War Conflict (1759–1761) on the southern frontier between the Cherokee Indians and colonists from Virginia southward. It caused South Carolina to request the aid of British troops and resulted in the surrender of more Indian land to whites.

Cherry Valley   Site of a Revolutionary War incident that occurred on November 11, 1778, when Joseph Brant of the Mohawks and Captain Walter Butler led seven hundred Indians and **Tories** on a raid of a New York valley that left as many as fifty **Whig** settlers dead.

Chesapeake **Incident**   Attack in 1807 by the British ship *Leopard* on the American ship *Chesapeake* in American territorial waters that nearly provoked an Anglo-American war.

Civil Rights Act of 1866   Law that defined national citizenship and specified the civil rights to which all national citizens were entitled.

Civil Rights Act of 1875   Law that prohibited racial discrimination in jury selection, public transportation, and public accommodations; declared unconstitutional by the U.S. Supreme Court in 1883.

Claims club   A group of local settlers on the nineteenth century frontier who banded together to prevent the price of their land claims from being bid up by outsiders at public land auctions.

Coercive Acts   Legislation passed by parliament in 1774; included the **Boston Port Act,** the **Massachusetts Government Act,** the **Administration of Justice Act,** and the **Quartering Act** of 1774.

Cold Harbor   Crossroads 10 miles northeast of Richmond where in June 1864, General Ulysses S. Grant launched a disastrous assault on Confederate positions during the Civil War.

Columbian exchange   The transatlantic exchange of plants, animals, and diseases that occurred after the first European contact with the Americas.

Committees of Correspondence   Committees formed in Massachusetts and other colonies in the pre-Revolutionary period to keep Americans informed about British measures that would affect the colonies.

Committee of Safety   Any of the extralegal committees that directed the Revolutionary movement and carried on the functions of government at the local level in the period between the breakdown of royal authority and the establishment of regular governments under the new state constitutions. Some Committees of Safety continued to function throughout the Revolutionary War.

Common Sense   Influential pamphlet by Thomas Paine. Published in Philadelphia in January 1776, it convinced many Americans that common sense dictated that the colonies should be independent of Great Britain.

Commonwealth v. Hunt   Case in which the Massachusetts Supreme Court in 1842 ruled that labor unions were not inherently criminal conspiracies guilty of restraining trade.

Communism   A social structure based on the common ownership of property.

Competency   In colonial New England, the possession of enough property to maintain a family's independent economic existence.

Compromise of 1850   Congressional solution to the controversy over California's admission to the Union as a free state; it granted the populations of other territories the right to decide on slavery (**popular sovereignty**) and establishing the **Fugitive Slave Act.**

Compromise of 1877   A deal that settled the contested presidential election of 1876 by installing Republican Rutherford B. Hayes in the White House and returning home rule to the South. It formally ended **Reconstruction** and left the fate of the freedmen in the hands of southern whites.

Conciliatory Proposition   Plan proposed by Lord North and adopted by the House of Commons in February 1775 whereby Parliament would "forbear" taxation of Americans in colonies whose assemblies imposed taxes considered satisfactory by the British government. The Continental Congress rejected this plan on July 31, 1775.

Confederate States of America   Nation proclaimed in Montgomery, Alabama, in February 1861 after the seven states of the Lower South seceded from the United States.

Confiscation Act of 1862   Second confiscation law passed by Congress, ordering the seizure of land from disloyal Southerners and the emancipation of their slaves.

Congressional Reconstruction   Name given to the period 1867–1870 when the Republican-dominated Congress controlled **Reconstruction** policy. It is sometimes known as Radical Reconstruction, after the radical faction in the **Republican party.**

Conquistador   Spanish for "conqueror," applied to a Spanish soldier who participated in the conquest and colonization of America.

Conscience Whigs   Primarily northern members of the **Whig party** who opposed the extension of slavery in the territories. When the party disintegrated after 1852, many of these Whigs eventually joined the **Republican party.**

Constitutional Convention   Convention that met in Philadelphia in 1787 and drafted the **Constitution of the United States.**

Constitutional Union party   National party formed in 1860, mainly by former **Whigs,** that emphasized allegiance to the Union and strict enforcement of all national legislation.

Constitution of the United States   The written document providing for a new central government of the United States drawn up at the **Constitutional Convention** in 1787 and ratified by the states in 1788.

Continental Army   The regular or professional army authorized by the Second Continental Congress and commanded by General George Washington during the Revolutionary War. Better training and longer service distinguished its soldiers from the state militiamen.

Continental Association   Agreement, adopted by the **First Continental Congress** in 1774 in response to the **Coercive Acts,** to cut off trade with Britain until the objectionable measures were repealed. Local committees were established to enforce the provisions of the association.

Continental dollars   Paper money issued by the Continental Congress to finance the Revolution. Lacking tax revenues to back it up, this money depreciated rapidly. By mid-1781, it was literally worthless, but it had served its purpose by helping Congress conduct the war for six years.

Contrabands   Slaves who escaped from their masters to Union lines during the Civil War.

Contract theory of government   The belief that government is established by human beings to protect certain rights—such as life, liberty, and property—that are theirs by natural, divinely sanctioned law and that when government protects these rights, people are obligated to obey it. But when government violates its part of the bargain (or contract) between the rulers and the ruled, the people are no longer required to obey it and may establish a new government that will do a better job of protecting them. Elements of this theory date back to the ancient Greeks; John Locke used it in his *Second Treatise on Government* (1682), and Thomas Jefferson gave it memorable expression in the Declaration of Independence, where it provides the rationale for renouncing allegiance to King George III.

Copperhead   A term Republicans applied to Northern war dissenters and those suspected of aiding the Confederate cause during the Civil War.

Country (Real Whig) ideology   Strain of thought first appearing in England in the late seventeenth century in response to the growth of governmental power and a national debt. Main ideas stressed the threat to personal liberty posed by a standing army and high taxes and emphasized the need for property holders to retain the right to consent to taxation.

Coureur de bois French for "woods runner," an independent fur trader in New France.

Covenant A formal agreement or contract. The idea of a covenant became an important organizing principle in early New England. Settlers believed that they made a covenant with the Lord to create a godly society, and in their towns and churches, settlers made covenants whereby they agreed to live and worship in harmony.

Cowpens, Battle of January 17, 1781, engagement in upstate South Carolina during the Revolutionary War involving approximately one thousand men on each side, in which Americans won a resounding victory over the British under Banastre Tarleton, thereby compromising his reputation for invincibility and boosting American morale.

Creole A slave of African descent born in the colonies.

Criollo A person of Spanish descent born in the Americas or the West Indies.

Crittenden Plan Series of measures submitted to Congress in January 1861 by John Crittenden of Kentucky to permit slavery below the **Missouri Compromise** line.

Crop lien laws In the Reconstruction and post-Reconstruction South, laws that gave merchants the right to sharecroppers' future cotton crop in exchange for credit.

Cult of domesticity The belief that women, by virtue of their sex, should stay home as the moral guardians of family life.

Culture area A geographical region inhabited by peoples who share similar basic patterns of subsistence and social organization.

Currency Act Law passed by Parliament in 1764 to prevent the colonies from issuing **legal tender** paper money, which often depreciated.

Dartmouth College **v.** *Woodward* Supreme Court decision of 1819 that prohibited states from interfering with the privileges granted to a private corporation.

Declaration of Independence The document by which the Second Continental Congress announced and justified its decision (reached July 2, 1776) to renounce the colonies' allegiance to the British government. Drafted mainly by Thomas Jefferson and adopted by Congress on July 4, the declaration's indictment of the king provides a remarkably full catalog of the colonists' grievances, and Jefferson's eloquent and inspiring statement of the **contract theory of government** makes the document one of the world's great state papers.

Declaration of Rights and Grievances Resolves, adopted by the **Stamp Act Congress** at New York in 1765, asserting that the **Stamp Act** and other taxes imposed on the colonists without their consent, given through their colonial legislatures, were unconstitutional.

Declaration of Sentiments The resolutions passed at the **Seneca Falls Convention** in 1848 calling for full female equality, including the right to vote.

Declaration of the Causes and Necessity of Taking Up Arms Document, written mainly by John Dickinson of Pennsylvania and adopted on July 6, 1775, by which the Second Continental Congress justified its armed resistance against British measures.

Declaratory Act Law passed in 1766 to accompany repeal of the **Stamp Act** that stated that Parliament had the authority to legislate for the colonies "in all cases whatsoever." Whether "legislate" meant tax was not clear to Americans.

Deism Religious orientation that rejects divine revelation and holds that the workings of nature alone reveal God's design for the universe.

Democratic party Political party formed in the 1820s under the leadership of Andrew Jackson; favored states' rights and a limited role for the federal government, especially in economic affairs.

Denmark Vesey's Conspiracy The most carefully devised slave revolt, named after its leader, a free black in Charleston. The rebels planned to seize control of Charleston and escape to freedom in Haiti, a free black republic, but they were betrayed by other slaves, and seventy-five conspirators were executed.

Direct Tax of 1798 A national tax levied on land, slaves, and dwellings.

Dominion of New England James II's failed plan of 1686 to combine eight northern colonies into a single large province, to be governed by a royal appointee (Sir Edmund Andros) with an appointed council but no elective assembly. The plan ended with James's ouster from the English throne and rebellion in Massachusetts against Andros's rule.

Dred Scott **decision** Supreme Court ruling, in a lawsuit brought by Dred Scott, a slave demanding his freedom based on his residence in a free state and a free territory with this master, that slaves could not be U.S. citizens and that Congress had no jurisdiction over slavery in the territories.

Dutch West India Company Trading enterprise that established and governed the Dutch colony of New Netherlands from its first permanent settlement at Fort Orange in 1624 until it was seized by the English in 1664.

Emancipation Proclamation Decree announced by President Lincoln in September 1862 and formally issued on January 1, 1863, freeing slaves in all Confederate states still in rebellion.

Embargo Act of 1807 Act passed by Congress in 1807 prohibiting American ships from leaving for any foreign port.

Empresario An agent who received a land grant from the Spanish or Mexican government in return for organizing settlements.

Encomienda In the Spanish colonies, the grant to a Spanish settler of a certain number of Indian subjects, who would pay him tribute in goods and labor.

Enforcement Act of 1870 Largely ineffectual law passed in response to growing political violence in the South, enabling the federal government to appoint supervisors where states failed to protect citizen's voting rights.

Enrollment Act A law passed by the U.S. Congress in 1863 during the Civil War subjecting all able-bodied men between the ages of twenty and forty-five to the draft. Its unpopularity contributed to the New York City draft riots later that year.

Enumerated products Items produced in the colonies and enumerated in acts of Parliament that could be legally shipped from the colony of origin only to specified locations, usually England and other destinations within the empire.

Era of Good Feelings The period from 1817 to 1823 in which the disappearance of the **Federalists** enabled the **Republicans** to govern in a spirit of seemingly nonpartisan harmony.

Established church A church supported in part by public taxes.

Fallen Timbers, Battle of Battle fought in northern Ohio in August 1794, in which an American army led by General Anthony Wayne decisively defeated an Indian confederation.

Federalism The sharing of powers between the national government and the states.

Federalist A supporter of the **Constitution** who favored its ratification.

Federalist party Political party organized within the Washington administration by supporters of Alexander Hamilton who favored a strong national government, commercial development, and a pro-British stance in foreign policy.

The Federalist A series of eighty-five essays, written anonymously and individually by Alexander Hamilton, James Madison, and John Jay, published in New York in 1787 and 1788 to rally support for the ratification of the **Constitution.**

Field Order No. 15 Order by General William T. Sherman in January 1865 to set aside abandoned land along the southern Atlantic coast for 40-acre grants to freedmen; rescinded by President Andrew Johnson later that year.

Fifteenth Amendment **Reconstruction** amendment passed by Congress in February 1869 guaranteeing the right of all American male citizens to vote regardless of race.

First Continental Congress Meeting of delegates from most of the colonies held in 1774 in response to the **Coercive Acts.** The Congress endorsed the **Suffolk Resolves,** adopted the **Declaration of Rights and Grievances,** and agreed to establish the **Continental Association** to put economic pressure on Britain to repeal its objectionable measures. The Congress also wrote addresses to the king, the people of Britain, and the American people.

Fletcher v. *Peck* Supreme Court decision of 1810 that overturned a state law by ruling that it violated a legal contract.

Fort Donelson With **Fort Henry,** one of two strategic forts on the Tennessee and Cumberland Rivers; site of a January 1862 Union victory during the Civil War.

Fort Henry With **Fort Donelson,** one of two strategic forts on the Tennessee and Cumberland Rivers; site of a January 1862 Union victory during the Civil War.

Fort Laramie Treaty Treaty of 1851 in which the United States attempted to establish definite boundaries for each of the major Indian tribes on the Central Plains.

Fort Sumter Begun in the late 1820s to protect Charleston, South Carolina, it became the center of national attention in April 1861, when President Lincoln attempted to provision federal troops at the fort, triggering a hostile response from on-shore Confederate forces, opening the Civil War.

Fort Ticonderoga Strategically important fort between Lake George and Lake Champlain in New York State. Benedict Arnold and Ethan Allen, leading respectively forces from Massachusetts and Vermont, captured it, its fifty defenders, and its military stores on May 10, 1775, at the outset of the Revolutionary War.

Fort Wagner Confederate installation guarding the entrance to Charleston harbor during the Civil War and site of a failed Federal assault in July 1863 during which a black Union regiment, the 54th Massachusetts, distinguished itself.

Forty Niners Miners who rushed to California after the discovery of gold in the northern part of the territory in 1848.

Fourierist communities Short-live utopian communities in the 1840s based on the ideas of economic cooperation and self-sufficiency popularized by the Frenchman Charles Fourier.

Fourteenth Amendment Constitutional amendment passed by Congress in April 1866 incorporating some of the features of the **Civil Rights Act of 1866.** It prohibited states from violating the civil rights of its citizens and offered states the choice of allowing blacks to vote or lose representation in Congress.

Frame of Government William Penn's 1682 plan for the government of Pennsylvania, which created a relatively weak legislature and strong executive. It also contained a provision for religious freedom.

Franco-American Accord of 1800 Settlement reached with France that brought an end to the **Quasi-War** and released the United States from its 1778 alliance with France.

Franklin, Battle of Confederate General John B. Hood's disastrous frontal assault on well-entrenched Union positions south of Nashville in November 1864 during the Civil War.

Fredericksburg Site of a Union setback in late 1862 that ended another Federal attempt to march on Richmond during the Civil War.

Freedmen's Bureau Agency established by Congress in March 1865 to provide social, educational, and economic services, advice, and protection to former slaves and destitute whites; lasted seven years.

Freedom's Journal The first African-American newspaper, founded in 1827 by John Russwurm and Samuel Cornish.

Freeport Doctrine Illinois Senator Stephen A. Douglas's statement during the 1858 **Lincoln-Douglas debates** that slavery could exist in a territory only if residents passed a law to protect it and that if residents did not pass such a law, there would be no slavery.

Free Soil party Anti-Southern party centered on keeping slavery out of the territories.

French and Indian War The last of the Anglo-French colonial wars (1754–1763) and the first in which fighting began in North America. The war (which merged with the European conflict known as the **Seven Years' War**) ended with France's defeat and loss of its North American empire.

Fries's Rebellion An armed attempt to block enforcement of the **Direct Tax of 1798** in the eastern counties of Pennsylvania, named for an auctioneer who played a prominent role.

Fugitive Slave Act Law, part of the **Compromise of 1850,** that required that authorities in the North to assist southern slavecatchers and return runaway slaves to their owners.

Fundamental Constitutions of Carolina The complex plan for organizing the colony of Carolina. Drafted in 1669 by Anthony Ashley Cooper and John Locke, its provisions included a scheme for creating a hierarchy of nobles who would own vast amounts of land and wield political power; below them would be a class of freedmen and slaves. The provisions were never implemented by the Carolina colonists.

Fundamental Orders Design for Connecticut government, adopted in 1639, that was modeled on that of Massachusetts Bay, except that voters did not have to be church members.

Funded debt Means by which governments allocate a portion of tax revenues to guarantee payment of interest on loans from private investors. England used this process to begin paying debts incurred during the first two Anglo-French wars, thereby harnessing private capital to serve the nation's military needs.

Gabriel Prosser's Rebellion Slave revolt that failed when Gabriel Prosser, a slave preacher and blacksmith, organized a thousand slaves for an attack on Richmond, Virginia, in 1800. A thunderstorm upset the timing of the attack, and a slave informer alerted the whites. Prosser and twenty-five of his followers were executed.

Gag rule Procedural rule passed in the House of Representatives that prevented discussion of antislavery proposals from 1836 to 1844.

Gang system The organization and supervision of slave field hands into working teams on southern plantations.

Gaspee British revenue schooner burned in Narragansett Bay by Rhode Islanders in 1772. The incident led to the appointment of a British commission of inquiry whose powers prompted Americans to establish **committees of correspondence.**

General Court The legislature of the colony of Massachusetts.

General Union for Promoting the Observance of the Christian Sabbath Reform organization founded in 1828 by Congregationalist and Presbyterian ministers that lobbied for an end to the delivery of mail on Sundays and other Sabbath violations.

Gettysburg Town in Pennsylvania; site of a pivotal Union victory in July 1863 during the Civil War.

Ghent, Treaty of   Treaty signed in December 1814 between the United States and British that ended the **War of 1812.**

Gibbons v. *Ogden*   Supreme Court decision of 1824 involving coastal commerce that overturned a steamboat monopoly granted by the State of New York on the grounds that only Congress had the authority to regulate interstate commerce.

Glorieta Pass   Mountain pass in New Mexico; site of an important Civil War battle in April 1862 that maintained the Southwest under Union Control.

Glorious Revolution   Bloodless revolt that occurred in England in 1688 when parliamentary leaders invited William of Orange, a Protestant, to assume the English throne and James II fled to France. James's ouster was prompted by fears that the birth of his son would establish a Catholic dynasty in England.

Goliad   Town in Texas where Mexican troops put to death over three hundred American prisoners on March 27, 1836, during the Texas War for Independence.

Grand Settlement of 1701   Separate peace treaties negotiated by Iroquois diplomats at Montreal and Albany that marked the beginning of Iroquois neutrality in conflicts between the French and the British in North America.

Great Awakening   Tremendous religious revival in colonial America. Sparked by the tour of the English evangelical minister, George Whitefield, the Awakening struck first in the Middle Colonies and New England in the 1740s and eventually spread to the southern colonies by the 1760s.

Great Bridge   Causeway near Norfolk, Virginia, that on December 9, 1775, was the site of a Revolutionary War battle between Americans and a British force composed mostly of African-Americans and other **Loyalists** who had joined the governor of Virginia, Lord Dunmore. Victory by the Americans enabled them to occupy Norfolk shortly thereafter.

Great Compromise   Plan proposed by Roger Sherman of Connecticut at the 1787 **Constitutional Convention** for creating a national **bicameral legislature** in which all states would be equally represented in the Senate and proportionally represented in the House.

Greenville, Treaty of   Treaty of 1795 in which Indians in the Old Northwest were forced to cede most of the present state of Ohio to the United States.

Guadalupe Hidalgo, Treaty of   Treaty signed in 1848 that ended the **Mexican War;** Mexico surrendered its claim to Texas above the Rio Grande and, in the **Mexican Cession of 1848,** ceded New Mexico and Alta California to the United States in return for a payment of $15 million.

Guilford Court House, Battle of   A fiercely fought Revolutionary War engagement that occurred on March 15, 1781, near modern Greensboro, North Carolina, in which British forces under Lord Cornwallis and Americans commanded by General Nathanael Greene both sustained heavy losses. The British technically won but were forced to withdraw to Wilmington, North Carolina.

Habeas Corpus   Writ that requires arresting authorities to explain the grounds for a person's imprisonment or detention before a court of law.

Halfway Covenant   Plan adopted in 1662 by New England clergy to deal with the problem of declining church membership. It allowed adults who had been baptized because their parents were church members but who had not yet experienced conversion to have their own children baptized. Without the Halfway Covenant, these third-generation children would remain unbaptized until their parents experienced conversion.

Hartford Convention   A meeting of New England **Federalists** in late 1814 in which they protested the **War of 1812** and demanded constitutional changes to protect the commercial interests of New England.

Headright system   Adopted first in Virginia and later in Maryland, a system of land distribution during the early colonial era that granted settlers 50 acres for themselves and another 50 for each "head" (or person) they brought with them to the colony.

High Federalists   Followers of Alexander Hamilton who wanted President John Adams to declare war against France in 1798 and stamp out political dissent within the United States.

Holy Roman Empire   The loose confederation of German and Italian territories under the authority of an emperor that existed from ninth or tenth century until 1806.

Homestead Act   Law passed by Congress in May 1862 providing homesteaders (mainly in the West) with 160 acres of free land in exchange for improving the land (as by cultivating it and erecting a house) within five years of the grant.

House of Burgesses   The legislature of colonial Virginia. First organized in 1619, it was the first institution of representative government in the English colonies.

House of Commons   The lower house of the British Parliament, which included representatives elected by England's propertied class.

House of Lords   The upper house of the British Parliament, where members of the aristocracy were represented.

Impeachment   The formal charging of a public official with improper conduct.

Indenture   A contract binding a person to the legal service of another for a specified period.

Indentured servant   An individual—usually male but occasionally female—who contracted to serve a master for a period of four to seven years in return for payment of the servant's passage to America. Indentured servitude was the primary labor system in the Chesapeake colonies for most of the seventeenth century.

Independent Treasury System   Fiscal arrangement first instituted by President Martin Van Buren in which the federal government kept its money in regional vaults ("pet banks") and transacted its business entirely in hard money.

Indian Removal Act   Legislation passed by Congress in 1830 that provided funds for removing and resettling eastern Indians in the West. It granted the president the authority to use force if necessary.

Intendant   A royally appointed government official in New France.

Intolerable Acts   American term for the **Coercive Acts** and the **Quebec Act.**

Iroquois League   Also known as the League of Five Nations. The union of five nations (Mohawks, Oneidas, Onondagas, Cayugas, and Senecas) formed around 1450. Essentially a religious organization, its purpose was to maintain peace among the five nations and unite them to fight against other enemies. After the Tuscarora War (1713–1715), the Tuscaroras joined the league, thereafter known as the League of Six Nations.

Jacksonian Democrats   See **Democratic party.**

Jay's Treaty   Treaty with Britain negotiated in 1794 in which the United States made major concessions to avert a war over the British seizure of American ships.

Jeffersonian Republicans   See **Republican party.**

John Brown's Raid   New England abolitionist John Brown's ill-fated attempt to free Virginia's slaves with a raid on the federal arsenal at Harpers Ferry, Virginia, in 1859.

Joint Committee on the Conduct of the War Committee created by the Republican-dominated Congress in December 1861 to examine and monitor Civil War military policy, although it ultimately devoted itself more to harassing Democratic officers and promoting the political agenda of **Radical Republican** congressmen.

Joint-stock company Business enterprise in which a group of stockholders pooled their money to engage in trade or to fund colonizing expeditions. Joint-stock companies participated in the founding of the Virginia, Plymouth, and Massachusetts Bay colonies.

Journeyman A person who has completed an apprenticeship in a trade or craft and is now a qualified worker in another person's employ.

Judicial review A power implied in the **Constitution** that gives federal courts the right to review and determine the constitutionality of acts passed by Congress and state legislatures.

Judiciary Act of 1789 Act of Congress that implemented the judiciary clause of the **Constitution** by establishing the Supreme Court and a system of lower federal courts.

Judiciary Act of 1801 Law passed by a **Federalist**-dominated Congress that created new judgships and judicial offices that outgoing President John Adams filled with prominent **Federalists.**

Kansas-Nebraska Act Law passed in 1854 creating the Kansas and Nebraska Territories but leaving the question of slavery open to residents, thereby repealing the **Missouri Compromise.**

Kaskaskia Illinois town on the Mississippi River occupied on July 4, 1778, during the Revolutionary War, by George Rogers Clark, commanding troops from Virginia; Cahokia, Illinois, and Vincennes, Indiana, soon capitulated, though the British later reoccupied Vincennes before Clark recaptured it on February 23, 1779. Clark's operations strengthened American claims to the areas at the end of the war.

Kettle Creek, Battle of Revolutionary War engagement in upstate Georgia on February 14, 1779, in which Americans under General Andrew Pickens defeated a band of about seven hundred Tories from North and South Carolina. This victory boosted American morale and intimidated Tories in the area.

King George's War The third Anglo-French war in North America (1744–1748), part of the European conflict known as the **War of the Austrian Succession.** During the North American fighting, New Englanders captured the French fortress of Louisbourg, only to have it returned to France after the peace negotiations.

King Philip's War Conflict in New England (1675–1676) between Wampanoags, Narragansetts, and other Indian peoples against English settlers; sparked by English encroachments on native lands.

King William's War The first Anglo-French conflict in North America (1689–1697), the American phase of Europe's **War of the League of Augsburg.** Ended in negotiated peace that reestablished the balance of power.

Kings Mountain, Battle of Decisive American Revolutionary War victory in northwestern South Carolina on October 7, 1780, when nine hundred American militia from Virginia, the western Carolinas, and eastern Tennessee annihilated or captured over one thousand **Loyalists,** an important turning point in the southern campaign.

Kiva A Pueblo Indian ceremonial structure, usually circular and underground.

Know-Nothing party Anti-immigrant party formed from the wreckage of the **Whig party** and some disaffected northern Democrats in 1854.

Ku Klux Klan Perhaps the most prominent of the vigilante groups that terrorized blacks in the South during **Reconstruction,** founded by Confederate veterans in 1866.

Ku Klux Klan Act of 1871 Law that held the perpetrators responsible for denying a citizen's civil rights and allowed the federal government to prosecute and send military assistance if states failed to act.

Lancaster, Treaty of Negotiation in 1744 whereby Iroquois chiefs sold Virginia land speculators the right to trade at the Forks of the Ohio. Although the Iroquois had not intended this to include the right to settle in the Ohio Country, the Virginians assumed that it did. Ohio Valley Indians considered this treaty a great grievance against both the English and the Iroquois.

Land Grant College Act Law passed by Congress in July 1862 awarding proceeds from the sale of public lands to the states for the establishment of agricultural and mechanical (later engineering) colleges. Also known as the Morrill Act, after its sponsor, Congressman Justin Morrill of Vermont.

Land Ordinance of 1785 Act passed by Congress under the **Articles of Confederation** that created the grid system of surveys by which all subsequent public land was made available for sale.

Lawes Divine, Morall and Martiall A harsh code of laws in force in Virginia between 1609 and 1621, intended to use military discipline to bring order to the struggling colony.

League of Armed Neutrality Association of European powers (Russia, Denmark, Sweden, Austria, Netherlands, Portugal, Prussia, and Sicily), formed between 1780 and 1782 to protect their rights as neutral traders against British attempts to impose a blockade on its enemies. Britain declared war on the Dutch on December 20, 1780, in an effort to cut off their trade with the United States.

League of Freedom African-American organization formed in Boston in 1851 to protect blacks against the **Fugitive Slave Act.**

Lecompton Constitution Proslavery draft written in 1857 by Kansas territorial delegates elected under questionable circumstances; it was rejected by two governors, supported by President Buchanan, and decisively defeated by Congress.

Legal tender An attribute of money that results from legislation declaring it to be, as in the case of modern United States currency, "legal tender for all debts public and private." Creditors must therefore accept it at face value.

Lexington and Concord, Battles of First skirmishes of the Revolutionary War, April 19, 1775. British forces, determined to destroy American supplies, fired on American militia at Lexington, then pushed on to Concord, where they themselves came under attack. On the long retreat back to Boston, the British suffered 273 dead, wounded, or missing, inflicted by some four thousand American militiamen.

Liberal Republicans Members of a reform movement within the **Republican party** in 1872 that promoted measures to reduce government influence in the economy and restore control of southern governments to local white elites.

The Liberator The best-known and most influential abolitionist newspaper; founded in 1831 by William Lloyd Garrison.

Liberty Association African-American organization formed in Chicago in 1851 that patrolled the city to spot slavecatchers.

Liberty party The first antislavery political party, formed in 1840.

Lincoln-Douglas debates Series of debates in the 1858 Illinois senatorial campaign during which Democrat Stephen A. Douglas and Republican Abraham Lincoln staked out their differing opinions on the issue of slavery in the territories.

Lords of Trade A standing committee of the Privy Council, appointed to oversee colonial affairs; created by Charles II in 1675.

Lost Cause The phrase many white Southerners applied to their Civil War defeat. They viewed the war as a noble cause, but only a temporary setback in the South's ultimate vindication.

Louisiana Purchase   The U.S. purchase from France in 1803 of a huge tract of land between the Mississippi River and the Rocky Mountains.

Loyalist   An American supporter of the British crown during the Revolution. *See also* **Tories.**

Macon's Bill No. 2   Act passed by Congress in 1810 that reopened American trade with Britain and France but stipulated that if either nation lifted its restrictions on American shipping, trading sanctions would be reimposed on the other.

Manifest Destiny   Doctrine, first expressed in 1845, that the expansion of white Americans across the continent was inevitable and ordained by God.

Marbury v. Madison   Supreme Court decision of 1803 that created the precedent of judicial review by ruling as unconstitutional part of the **Judiciary Act of 1789.**

Massachusetts Government Act   Law passed in 1774 in response to the **Boston Tea Party** and directed at Massachusetts; one of the **Coercive** or **Intolerable Acts.** It provided for an appointed rather than an elected upper house of the legislature and restricted the number and kind of town meetings that a community might hold.

Matrilineal   Descriptive of societies in which family descent is traced through the mother's line.

Mayflower Compact   Document creating a civil government for Plymouth Colony. The compact was signed by all adult males before their ship, the *Mayflower,* landed in 1620.

McCulloch v. Maryland   Supreme Court decision of 1819 that established the supremacy of federal over state authority by declaring that states could not tax federal institutions.

Mercantilism   Economic system whereby the government intervenes in the economy for the purpose of increasing national wealth. Mercantilists advocated possession of colonies as places where the mother country could acquire raw materials not available at home.

Mestizo   A person of mixed Spanish and Indian ancestry.

Mexican Cession of 1848   The ceding of New Mexico and Alta California to the United States by Mexico as a result of the U.S. victory in the **Mexican War.** *See also* **Treaty of Guadalupe Hidalgo.**

Mexican War   War fought between the United States and Mexico from May 1846 to February 1848. *See also* **Treaty of Guadalupe Hidalgo; Mexican Cession of 1848.**

Middle Passage   The voyage between West Africa and the New World slave colonies.

Military Reconstruction Acts   The first major legislation in the period known as **Congressional Reconstruction;** passed in March 1867 over President Johnson's veto; divided the ten remaining ex-Confederate states into five military districts each headed by a general who was charged to conduct voter registration drives among blacks and bar whites who had held office before the Civil War and who had supported the Confederacy. The remaining voters would elect a constitutional convention to write a new state constitution that guaranteed **universal manhood suffrage.** If a majority of voters ratified both the new constitution and the **Fourteenth Amendment,** their state would be readmitted into the Union.

Minute Men   Special companies of militia formed in Massachusetts and elsewhere beginning in late 1744. These units were composed of men who were to be ready to assemble with their arms at a minute's notice.

Mission system   Chain of missions established by Franciscan monks in the Spanish Southwest and California that forced Indians to convert to Catholicism and work as agricultural laborers.

Missouri Compromise   Sectional compromise in Congress in 1820 that admitted Missouri to the Union as a slave state and Maine as a free state and prohibited slavery in the **Louisiana Purchase** territory above 36°30′ north latitude.

Molasses Act   Law passed by Parliament in 1733 that taxed sugar products from foreign sources in order to encourage British colonists to buy sugar and molasses only from the British West Indies.

Monmouth Court House, Battle of   Last major Revolutionary War engagement between the main British and American forces in the North; occurred on June 28, 1778, in central New Jersey as the British withdrew from Philadelphia toward their headquarters at New York City. The Americans under General Washington and the British under Sir Henry Clinton each suffered about 350 casualties.

Monroe Doctrine   Declaration by President James Monroe in 1823 that the Western Hemisphere was to be closed off to further European colonization and that the United States would not interfere in the internal affairs of European nations.

Moore's Creek Bridge, Battle of   Revolutionary War engagement that occurred on February 27, 1776, near Wilmington, North Carolina, when an American force of approximately one thousand militia clashed with about eighteen hundred **Loyalists,** most of them Highland Scots. The smashing American victory disrupted British plans for the **Loyalists** to link up with a large British expedition that sailed from Ireland to North Carolina during the winter of 1775–1776.

Mormon Church (Church of Jesus Christ of Latter-day Saints)   Church founded in 1830 by Joseph Smith and based on the revelations in a sacred book he called the Book of Mormon.

Nashville, Battle of   Union General George H. Thomas's destruction of the Confederacy's Army of Tennessee in December 1864 during the Civil War.

National Banking Act   Law passed in 1863 authorizing certain banks to issue bank notes backed by U.S. bonds and guaranteed by Washington. It brought order to a chaotic monetary system and raised the creditworthiness of the federal government.

National Black Convention   A prominent gathering of northern black leaders in 1853, called to protest the Fugitive Slave Act.

National Republican party   Short-lived political party opposed to Andrew Jackson that unsuccessfully ran John Quincy Adams for presidency in 1828 and Henry Clay in 1832.

Nationalists   Group of leaders in the 1780s who spearheaded the drive to replace the **Articles of Confederation** with a stronger central government.

Nativist   Favoring the interests and culture of native-born inhabitants over those of immigrants.

Nat Turner slave revolt   Uprising of slaves in Southampton County, Virginia, in the summer of 1831 led by Nat Turner that resulted in the death of fifty-five whites.

Naturalization Act   Law passed by Congress in 1798 that extended the residency requirement of alien residents for U.S. citizenship from five to fourteen years. One of the **Alien and Sedition Acts.**

Natural rights   Political philosophy that maintains that individuals have an inherent right, found in nature and preceding any government or written law, to life and liberty.

Navigation Act of 1651   First piece of mercantilist legislation passed to regulate colonial commerce. Called for imperial trade to be conducted using English or colonial ships with mainly English crews.

Navigation Act of 1696   Law that closed loopholes in earlier mercantilist legislation and also created **vice-admiralty courts** in the colonies.

New England Non-Resistant Society   Pacifist organization founded by Garrisonian abolitionists in 1838 that was opposed to all authority resting on force.

New Harmony   Short-lived utopian community established in Indiana in 1825, based on the socialist ideas of Robert Owen, a wealthy Scottish manufacturer.

New Jersey Plan   Proposal of the New Jersey delegation at the 1787 **Constitutional Convention** for a strengthened national government in which all states would have equal representation in a **unicameral legislature.**

New Lights   People who experienced conversion during the revivals of the **Great Awakening.**

New Orleans, Battle of   Decisive American **War of 1812** victory over British Troops in January 1815 that ended any British hopes of gaining control of the lower Mississippi River Valley.

New York Draft Riot   Most Irish-immigrant protest against conscription in New York City in July 1863 that escalated into class and racial warfare that had to be quelled by federal troops.

Nonimportation   A tactical means of putting economic pressure on Britain by refusing to buy its exports to the colonies. Initiated in response to the taxes imposed by the **Sugar** and **Stamp Acts,** it was used again against the **Townshend duties** and the **Coercive Acts.** The nonimportation movement popularized resistance to British measures and deepened the commitment of many ordinary people to a larger American community.

Nonintercourse Act   Law passed by Congress in 1809 that prohibited American trade with Britain and France.

The North Star   Antislavery newspaper established by Frederick Douglass in Rochester, New York, in 1847.

Northwest Ordinance of 1787   Legislation passed by Congress under the **Articles of Confederation** that prohibited slavery in the Northwest Territories and provided the model for the incorporation of future territories into the Union as coequal states.

Nullification   A constitutional doctrine holding that a state has a legal right to declare a national law null and void within its borders.

Nullification crisis   Sectional crisis in the early 1830s in which a **states' rights** party in South Carolina attempted to nullify federal law.

Olive Branch Petition   Petition, written largely by John Dickinson and adopted by the Second Continental Congress on July 5, 1775 as a last effort of peace that avowed America's loyalty to George III and requested that he protect them from further aggressions. Congress continued military preparations, and the king never responded to the petition.

Oneida Community   Utopian community established in upstate New York in 1848 by John Humphrey Noyes and his followers.

Order of the Heroes of America   Loosely knit group of pro-Unionists in the Piedmont and mountain sections of North Carolina who demonstrated for peace and sometimes violently opposed Confederate authorities during the Civil War.

Orders in Council   Decrees of the British ministry setting up a naval blockade of Europe and controls over neutral shipping during the Napoleanic Wars.

Ordinance of 1784   Act passed but never put into effect by the Congress under the **Articles of Confederation** that embodied the proposals of Thomas Jefferson for dividing the public domain into states and immediately granting settlers the right of self-government.

Oregon Trail   Overland trail of more than 2,000 miles that carried American settlers from the Midwest to new settlements in Oregon, California, and Utah.

Ostend Manifesto   Message sent by U.S. envoys to President Pierce from Ostend, Belgium, in 1854, stating that the United States had a "divine right" to wrest Cuba from Spain.

Paleo-Indians   The first human inhabitants of the Americas, who crossed the land bridge from Asia perhaps as long as fifty thousand years ago and survived by hunting large mammals.

Panic of 1819   A severe tightening of credit set off by a fall in cotton prices and more restrictive financial policies by the Second Bank of the United States.

Panic of 1837   A sharp contraction in credit and currency triggered by a fall in cotton prices.

Panic of 1857   Banking crisis that caused a credit crunch in the North; it was less severe in the South, where high cotton price spurred a quick recovery.

Pan-Indian resistance movement   Movement calling for the political and cultural unification of Indian tribes in the late eighteenth and early nineteenth centuries.

Paris, Treaty of   Treaty concluded in 1763 to end the **French and Indian War (Seven Years' War).** Its principal feature was France's loss of nearly all of its North American empire, retaining only its West Indian possessions.

Parson's Cause   Series of developments (1758–1763) that began when the Virginia legislature modified the salaries of Anglican clergymen, who complained to the crown and sued to recover damages. British authorities responded by imposing additional restrictions on the legislature. Virginians, who saw this as a threat, reacted by strongly reasserting local autonomy.

Party caucus   A meeting of party leaders to decide questions of policy or to select candidates running for office.

Patriarchal   Descriptive of societies in which fathers are the heads of clans or families, women and children are legally dependent on husbands and fathers, and family descent and inheritance follow the male line.

Patrilineal   Descriptive of societies in which family descent is traced through the father's line.

Patriot   Term usually used to refer to Americans during the Revolutionary period whose resistance to British measures included a willingness to resort to arms and, ultimately, a commitment to American independence. However, many **Loyalists** were also patriotic in their allegiance to Great Britain.

Patronage   The power to appoint individuals to governmental positions.

Patroonship   The grant of a vast estate of land in New Netherlands, offered by Dutch authorities as a way to attract settlers. Very few patroonships were actually created.

Paxton Boys   Frontiersmen from Paxton township (near modern Harrisburg, Pennsylvania) who responded in 1763 to **Pontiac's Rebellion** by massacring nearby Indians; later they marched toward Philadelphia to demand greater military protection for the frontiers.

Peace of Paris   Treaties signed in 1783 by Great Britain, the United States, France, Spain, and the Netherlands that ended the Revolutionary War. First in a preliminary agreement and then in the final treaty with the United States, Britain recognized the independence of the United States, agreed that the Mississippi River would be its western boundary, and permitted it to fish in some Canadian waters. Prewar debts owed by the inhabitants of one country to those of the other were to remain collectible, and Congress was to urge the states to return property confiscated from **Loyalists.** British troops were to evacuate United States territory without removing slaves or other property. In a separate agreement, Britain relinquished its claim to East and West Florida to Spain.

Peninsula Campaign Civil War campaign launched by Union general George B. McClellan in the spring of 1862 with Richmond as its objective; it failed despite superior numbers of Federal troops.

Pequot War Conflict between English settlers (who had Narragansett and Mohegan allies) and Pequot Indians over control of land and trade in eastern Connecticut. Pequots were nearly destroyed in a set of bloody confrontations, including a deadly English attack on a Mystic River village in May 1637.

Petersburg During the Civil War, a key Confederate rail and supply center that guarded the Confederate capital of Richmond 30 miles to the north; besieged by Union forces from June 1864 to March 1865.

Pietists Protestants who stress a religion of the heart and the spirit of Christian living.

Pilgrims Settlers of Plymouth Colony, who viewed themselves as spiritual wanderers.

Pinckney's Treaty Treaty with Spain in 1795 in which Spain recognized the 31st parallel as the boundary between the United States and Spanish Florida and opened the Mississippi River through the port of New Orleans to American shipping.

Plattsburg, Battle of American naval victory on Lake Champlain in September 1814 in the **War of 1812** that thwarted a British invasion from Canada.

Plymouth Company One of two joint-stock companies chartered in 1606 to establish English colonies in America. Composed of merchants from England's western ports, the company organized the founding of Plymouth Colony in 1620.

Pontiac's Rebellion Indian uprising (1763–1766) led by Pontiac of the Ottawas and Neolin of the Delawares. Fearful of their fate at the hands of the British after the French had been driven out of North America, the Indian nations of the Ohio River Valley and the Great Lakes area united to oust the British from the Ohio-Mississippi Valley. They failed and were forced to make peace in 1766.

Popular sovereignty The notion that territorial residents should have the right to decide whether they wanted slavery.

Praying towns Villages established in Massachusetts for Indian converts to Christianity. The inhabitants were expected to follow an English way of life as well as the Puritan religion.

Predestination The belief that God decided at the moment of Creation which humans would achieve salvation.

Presidio A military post established by the Spanish in the Southwest.

Princeton, Battle of Revolutionary War battle fought on January 3, 1777. Eluding the main British forces under Cornwallis, General Washington attacked a British column near Princeton, New Jersey, inflicting heavy losses on them before withdrawing into winter quarters not far away at Morristown. The battles of **Trenton** and Princeton greatly improved **patriot** morale.

Proclamation Line Boundary, decreed as part of the **Proclamation of 1763,** that limited British settlements to the eastern side of the Appalachian Mountains, thereby threatening colonial expansionists and causing resentment. It proved unenforceable.

Proclamation of 1763 Royal proclamation setting the boundary known as the **Proclamation Line.**

Proprietary colony A colony created when the English monarch granted a huge tract of land to an individual or group of individuals, who became "lords proprietor." Many lords proprietor had distinct social visions for their colonies, but these plans were hardly ever implemented. Examples of proprietary colonies are Maryland, Carolina, New York (after it was seized from the Dutch), and Pennsylvania.

Protective tariff A tax on imported goods specifically intended to raise their price high enough to protect domestic producers of those goods from foreign competition.

Provincial Congress An extralegal, Revolutionary representative body that conducted government and waged the Revolution at the state level in the period between the breakdown of royal authority and the establishment of regular legislatures under new state constitutions. Many members of these congresses had been members of the old colonial assemblies; the Massachusetts **General Court** and the Virginia **House of Burgesses,** in fact, transformed themselves into provincial congresses or conventions. (The terms were used interchangeably at first.)

Pueblo Revolt Rebellion in 1680 of Pueblo Indians in New Mexico against their Spanish overlords, sparked by religious conflict and excessive Spanish demands for tribute.

Puritan An individual who believed that Queen Elizabeth's reforms of the Church of England had not gone far enough in improving the church, particularly in ensuring that church members were among the saved. Puritans led the settlement of Massachusetts Bay Colony.

Put-in-Bay, Battle of American naval victory on Lake Erie in September 1813 in the **War of 1812** that denied the British strategic control over the Great Lakes.

Putting-out system System of manufacturing in which merchants furnished households with raw materials for processing by family members.

Quakers Members of the Society of Friends, a radical religious group that arose in the mid-seventeenth century. Quakers rejected formal theology and an educated ministry, focusing instead on the importance of the "Inner Light," or Holy Spirit that dwelt within them. Quakers were important in the founding of Pennsylvania.

Quartering Acts Acts of Parliament requiring colonial legislatures to provide supplies and quarters for the troops stationed in America. Americans considered this taxation in disguise and objected. None of these acts passed during the pre-Revolutionary controversy required that soldiers be quartered in an occupied house without the owner's consent.

Quasi-War Undeclared naval war of 1797 to 1800 between the United States and France.

Quebec Act Law passed by Parliament in 1774 that provided an appointed government for Canada, enlarged the boundaries of Quebec southward to the Ohio River, and confirmed the privileges of the Catholic Church. Alarmed Americans termed this act and the **Coercive Acts** the **Intolerable Acts.**

Quebec, Siege of An attempt during the Revolutionary War by American forces under Richard Montgomery and Benedict Arnold to capture Quebec City during the winter of 1775–1776. In an abortive attack on the city on December 31, 1775, Arnold was wounded and Montgomery killed. The siege failed and Canada remained in British hands, serving as a base for later British expeditions down the Hudson River valley.

Queen Anne's War American phase (1702–1713) of Europe's **War of the Spanish Succession.** At its conclusion, England gained Nova Scotia.

Queenston Height, Battle of Major defeat in October 1812 for an American army attempting to invade Canada along the Niagara frontier during the **War of 1812.**

Quiet Period The apparently calm years (1770–1773) between Britain's repeal of most of the **Townshend duties** and the **Boston Tea Party.** No general grievances against Britain united Americans during this period, though many localized disputes continued.

Radical Republicans A shifting group of Republican congressmen, usually a substantial minority, who favored the abolition of slavery from the beginning of the Civil War and later advocated harsh treatment of the defeated South.

Real Whig ideology See **Country (Real Whig) ideology.**

Reconquista The long struggle (ending in 1492) during which Spanish Christians reconquered the Iberian peninsula from Muslim occupiers, who first invaded in the eighth century.

Reconstruction The era (1865–1877) when the resolution of two major issues—the status of the former slaves and the terms of the Confederate states' readmission into the Union—dominated political debate.

Redeemers Southern Democrats who wrested control of governments in the former Confederacy, often through electoral fraud and violence, from Republicans beginning in 1870.

Redemptioners Similar to **indentured servants,** except that redemptioners signed labor contracts in America rather than in Europe, as indentured servants did. Shipmasters sold redemptioners into servitude to recoup the cost of their passage if they could not pay the fare upon their arrival.

Reformation Sixteenth-century movement to reform the Catholic Church that began with Martin Luther's critique of church practices in 1517. The Reformation ultimately led to the founding of a number of new Protestant Christian religious groups.

Regulators Vigilante groups active in the 1760s and 1770s in the western parts of North and South Carolina. The South Carolina Regulators attempted to rid the area of outlaws; the North Carolina Regulators sought to protect themselves against excessively high taxes and court costs. In both cases, westerners lacked sufficient representation in the legislature to obtain immediate redress of their grievances. The South Carolina government eventually made concessions; the North Carolina government suppressed its Regulator movement by force.

Renaissance Major cultural movement in Europe during the fifteenth and sixteenth centuries that began in the city-states of Italy and spread to other parts of the continent. Sharing a "rebirth" of interest in the classical civilizations of ancient Greece and Rome, many artists of the period produced notable works in painting, sculpture, architecture, writing, and music.

Repartimiento In the Spanish colonies, the assignment of Indian workers to labor on public works projects.

Republicanism A complex, changing body of ideas, values, and assumptions, closely related to **country ideology,** that influenced American political behavior during the eighteenth and nineteenth centuries. Derived from the political ideas of classical antiquity, **Renaissance** Europe, and early modern England, republicanism held that self-government by the citizens of a country, or their representatives, provided a more reliable foundation for the good society and individual freedom than rule by kings. The benefits of monarchy depended on the variable abilities of monarchs; the character of republican government depended on the virtue of the people. Republicanism therefore helped give the American Revolution a moral dimension. But the nature of republican virtue and the conditions favorable to it became sources of debate that influenced the writing of the state and federal constitutions as well as the development of political parties.

Republican party (Jeffersonian) Party headed by Thomas Jefferson that formed in opposition to the financial and diplomatic policies of the **Federalist party;** favored limiting the powers of the national government and placing the interests of farmers and planters over those of financial and commercial groups; supported the cause of the French Revolution.

Republican party Party that emerged in the 1850s in the aftermath of the bitter controversy over the **Kansas-Nebraska Act,** consisting of former **Whigs,** some northern Democrats, and many **Know-Nothings.**

Rescate Procedure by which Spanish colonists would pay ransom to free Indians captured by rival natives. The rescued Indians then became workers in Spanish households.

Rhode Island system During the industrialization of the early nineteenth century, the recruitment of entire families for employment in a factory.

Rush-Bagot Agreement Treaty of 1817 between the United States and Britain that effectively demilitarized the Great Lakes by sharply limiting the number of ships each power could station on them.

Sabbatarian movement See **General Union for Promoting the observance of the Christian Sabbath.**

"Sack of Lawrence" Vandalism and arson committed by a group of proslavery men in Lawrence, the free-state capital of Kansas Territory.

Saint A Puritan who had experienced religious conversion and had been admitted to membership in a Puritan church.

San Jacinto, Battle of Battle fought in eastern Texas on April 21, 1836, in which Texas troops under General Sam Houston overwhelmed a Mexican army and forced its commander, General Santa Anna, to recognize the independence of Texas.

San Lorenzo, Treaty of See **Pinckney's Treaty.**

Santa Fe Trail Overland trail across the Southern Plains from St. Louis to New Mexico that funneled American traders and goods to Spanish-speaking settlements in the Southwest.

Saratoga, Battle of Two engagements (September 19 and October 7, 1777) during the Revolutionary War in the vicinity of Saratoga, New York, that resulted in the surrender on October 17 of 5,700 troops commanded by General John Burgoyne to American forces under General Horatio Gates. This stunning American victory contributed to the French decision to sign an alliance with the United States on February 6, 1778.

Savannah, Battles of Series of Revolutionary War encounters that began when British forces routed American militia and occupied Savannah on December 29, 1778. A French fleet under the Comte d'Estaing and American forces under General Benjamin Lincoln then tried to recapture the city by siege, beginning on September 3, 1779, but an assault on October 9 failed, with heavy casualties. D'Estaing, wounded, departed with this fleet on October 28, leaving the way open for the British attack on **Charleston,** South Carolina.

Scalawags Southern whites, mainly small landowning farmers and well-off merchants and planters, who supported the southern **Republican party** during **Reconstruction** for diverse reasons; a disparaging term.

Second Bank of the United States A national bank chartered by Congress in 1816 with extensive regulatory powers over currency and credit. See also **First Bank of the United States.**

Second Great Awakening Series of religious revivals in the first half of the nineteenth century characterized by great emotionalism in large public meetings.

Second party system The national two-party competition between **Democrats** and **Whigs** from the 1830s through the early 1850s.

Secret Six Group of prominent New England abolitionists who financially supported John Brown's scheme to attack the federal arsenal at Harpers Ferry, Virginia, and foment a slave rebellion in the South.

Sedition Act Law passed by Congress in 1798 that provided fines and imprisonment for anyone found guilty of saying or writing anything false or malicious about the government or one of its officers. One of the **Alien and Sedition Acts.**

Segregation A system of racial control that separated the races, initially by custom but increasingly by law during and after **Reconstruction.**

Selectmen Group of men (usually seven) selected annually to run local affairs in a New England town.

Seneca Falls Convention The first convention for women's equality in legal rights, held in upstate New York in 1848. See also **Declaration of Sentiments.**

Separatist Member of an offshoot branch of Puritanism. Separatists believed that the Church of England was too corrupt to be reformed and hence were convinced that they must "separate" from it to save their souls. Separatists helped found Plymouth Colony.

Seven Days' Battles Weeklong series of fierce engagements in June and July 1862 along Virginia's peninsula that resulted in a Federal retreat during the Civil War.

Seven Years' War Conflict (1756–1763) that pitted France, Austria, and Russia against England and Prussia; in 1762, Spain entered the war on France's side. Often called the first "world war" because fighting occurred in Europe, India, the Philippines, and North America. The American phase was known as the **French and Indian War.**

Shakers The followers of Mother Ann Lee, who preached a religion of strict celibacy and communal living.

Sharecropping Labor system that evolved during and after **Reconstruction** whereby landowners furnished laborers with a house, farm animals, and tools and advanced credit in exchange for a share of the laborers' crop.

Shays's Rebellion An armed movement of debt-ridden farmers in western Massachusetts in the winter of 1786–1787. The rebellion shut down courts and created a crisis atmosphere, strengthening the case of **nationalists** that a stronger central government was needed to maintain civil order in the states.

Sherman's March Three-month army march during the Civil War in late 1864 led by Union general William T. Sherman from Atlanta to Savannah and the sea, destroying property as well as the morale of Georgians.

Shiloh Church Site of a Union victory along the Tennessee-Mississippi border in April 1862 that enabled Federal forces to capture Corinth, Mississippi, an important rail junction, during the Civil War.

***Slaughterhouse* cases** Group of cases resulting in one sweeping decision by the U.S. Supreme Court in 1873 that contradicted the intent of the **Fourteenth Amendment** by decreeing that most citizenship rights remained under state, not federal, control.

Slave codes Sometimes known as "black codes." A series of laws passed mainly in the southern colonies in the late seventeenth and early eighteenth centuries to define the status of slaves and codify the denial of basic civil rights to them. Also, after American independence and before the Civil War, state laws in the South defining slaves as property and specifying the legal powers of masters over slaves.

Slave Power A key concept in abolitionist and northern antislavery propaganda that depicted southern slaveholders as the driving force in a political conspiracy to promote slavery at the expense of white liberties.

Socialism A social order based on public ownership of the means of production.

Society for the Relief of Poor Widows with Small Children Female benevolent organization founded in New York City in 1797 to assist widows and orphans.

Sons of Liberty Secret organizations in the colonies formed to oppose the **Stamp Act.** From 1765 until independence, they spoke, wrote, and demonstrated against British measures. Their actions often intimidated stamp distributors and British supporters in the colonies.

Southern Homestead Act Largely unsuccessful law passed in 1866 that gave blacks preferential access to public lands in five southern states.

Southwest Ordinance of 1790 Legislation passed by Congress that set up a government with no prohibition on slavery in U.S. territory south of the Ohio River.

Specie Circular Proclamation issued by President Andrew Jackson in 1836 stipulating that only gold or silver could be used as payment for public land.

Spoils system The awarding of government jobs to party loyalists.

Spotsylvania, Battle of Another in a series of dogged attacks in Virginia by Union General U.S. Grant and entrenched Confederate positions during May 1864. Despite high casualties and mounting public criticism, Grant continued to push on until the disaster at Cold Harbor later in the month caused him to reconsider his tactics.

Squatters Settlers who moved onto public land before it had been surveyed for sale.

Stamp Act Law passed by Parliament in 1765 to raise revenue in America by requiring taxed, stamped paper for legal documents, publications, and playing cards. Americans opposed it as "taxation without representation" and prevented its enforcement. Parliament repealed it a year after its enactment.

Stamp Act Congress October 1765 meeting of delegates sent by nine colonies, held in New York City, that adopted **Declaration of Rights and Grievances** and petitioned against the **Stamp Act.**

States' rights Favoring the rights of individual states over those claimed by the national government.

Stono Rebellion Uprising in 1739 of South Carolina slaves against whites; inspired in part by Spanish officials' promise of freedom for American slaves who escaped to Florida.

Strict constructionist Person who holds that the national government has only those powers specifically delegated to it in the **Constitution.**

Suffolk Resolves Militant resolves adopted in September 1774 in response to the **Coercive Acts** by representatives from the towns in Suffolk County, Massachusetts, including Boston. They termed the **Coercive Acts** unconstitutional, advised the people to arm, and called for economic sanctions against Britain. The **First Continental Congress** endorsed these resolves.

Suffrage The right to vote in a political election.

Sugar Act See **American Revenue Act.**

Tallmadge Amendment Proposed amendment to the Missouri statehood bill in 1819 that mandated the gradual end of slavery in Missouri.

Taos Revolt Uprising of Pueblo Indians in New Mexico that broke out in January 1847 over the imposition of American rule during the **Mexican War;** the revolt was crushed within a few weeks.

Tariff Act of 1798 Law placing a duty of 5 percent on most imported goods, designed primarily to generate revenue and not to protect American goods from foreign competition.

Tariff of 1816 The first openly protective tariff passed by Congress.

Tea Act of 1773 Act of Parliament that permitted the East India Company to sell tea through agents in America without paying the duty customarily collected in Britain, thus reducing the retail price. Americans, who saw the act as an attempt to induce them to pay the **Townshend duty** still imposed in the colonies, resisted this act through the **Boston Tea Party** and other measures.

Tejano   A person of Spanish or Mexican descent born in Texas.

Temperance   Reform movement originating in the 1820s that sought to eliminate the consumption of alcohol.

Ten Percent Plan   Plan devised by President Lincoln in 1863 as a method for readmitting the seceding states to the Union; required 10 percent of a state's prewar voters to swear allegiance to the Union and a new state constitution that banned slavery. Many congressional Republicans considered this standard too thin to support a general reconstruction of the Union and responded with the **Wade-Davis Bill.**

Tenure of Office Act   Law Congress passed in 1867 prohibiting the president from removing certain officeholders without the Senate's consent; President Andrew Johnson's defiance of the act led to an **impeachment** trial in the Senate that narrowly failed to remove him from office.

Thames, Battle of the   American victory in October 1813 over combined British and Indian forces in southern Ontario during the **War of 1812.**

Thirteenth Amendment   Constitutional amendment ratified in 1865 that freed all slaves throughout the United States.

Tippecanoe, Battle of   American victory in November 1811 over Shawnee Indians at Prophetstown in the Indiana Territory that provoked Indians into warfare along the western frontier.

Tonnage Act of 1789   Duty levied on the tonnage of incoming ships to U.S. ports; tax was higher on foreign-owned ships to favor American shippers.

Tordesillas, Treaty of   Treaty negotiated by the pope in 1494 to resolve the territorial claims of Spain and Portugal. It drew a north-south line approximately 1,100 miles west of the Cape Verde Islands, granting all lands west of the line to Spain and all lands east of the line to Portugal. This limited Portugal's New World empire to Brazil but confirmed its claims in Africa and Asia.

Tories   A derisive term applied to **Loyalists** in America who supported the king and Parliament just before and during the American Revolution. The term derived from late-seventeenth-century English politics when the Tory party supported the Duke or York's succession to the throne as James II. Later, the Tory party favored the Church of England and the crown over dissenting denominations and Parliament.

Townshend Duty Act   Act of Parliament, passed in 1767, imposing duties on colonial tea, lead, paint, paper, and glass. Designed to take advantage of the supposed American distinction between internal and external taxes, the Townshend duties were to help support government in America. The act prompted a successful colonial **nonimportation** movement.

Trail of Tears   The forced march in 1838 of the Cherokee Indians from their homelands in Georgia to the Indian Territory in the West; thousands of the Cherokees died along the way.

Transcendentalism   A philosophical and literary movement centered on an idealistic belief in the divinity of individuals and nature.

Trans-Continental Treaty of 1819   Treaty between the United States and Spain in which Spain ceded Florida to the United States, surrendered all claims to the Pacific Northwest, and agreed to a boundary between the **Louisiana Purchase** territory and the Spanish Southwest.

Transportation revolution   Dramatic improvements in transportation that stimulated economic growth after 1815 by expanding the range of travel and reducing the time and cost of moving goods and people.

Trenton, Battle of   Revolutionary War clash that occurred on December 26, 1776, when General Washington, who had withdrawn his forces into Pennsylvania, recrossed the Delaware River and surprised approximately fourteen hundred Hessians at Trenton, New Jersey, capturing or killing nearly one thousand.

Uncle Tom's Cabin   Novel about slave life in the South by Harriet Beecher Stowe.

Underground Railroad   Support system set up by antislavery groups in the Upper South and the North to assist fugitive slaves in escaping the South.

Unicameral legislature   A legislative body composed of a single house.

Union League   A **Republican party** organization in northern cities that became an important organizing device among freedmen in southern cities after 1865.

United States* v. *Cruikshank   The 1876 case in which the U.S. Supreme Court nullified the **Enforcement Act of 1870,** overturning the convictions of whites accused of violence against blacks in Louisiana and declaring that the **Fifteenth Amendment** did not sanction federal interference in matters that were clearly reserved for the states.

U.S. Sanitary Commission   Private, voluntary medical organization founded in May 1861 and dedicated to tending Union wounded and improving soldier comfort and morale during the Civil War.

universal manhood suffrage   The right of all male U.S. citizens to vote; a key element of **Radical Republican** policy in the South after 1867.

Valley Forge   Area of Pennsylvania approximately 20 miles northwest of Philadelphia where General Washington's continental troops were quartered from December 1777 to June 1778 while British forces occupied Philadelphia during the Revolutionary War. Approximately 2,500 men, about a quarter of those encamped there, died of hardship and disease.

Vice-admiralty courts   Royal courts established in the colonies to handle maritime cases and enforce the Acts of Trade. The enlarged role of these bodies, which operated without juries, was considered a grievance.

Vicksburg   Key Mississippi River port and rail junction that fell in July 1863 to a brilliant Union campaign by Ulysses S. Grant, commander of the Army of Tennessee, during the Civil War.

Vincennes, Treaty of   Treaty of 1804 in which Americans claimed that Indian leaders ceded most of southern Indiana to the United States.

Virginia Company   One of two joint-stock companies chartered in 1606 to establish English colonies in America. Also known as the London Company, it organized the founding of the Virginia Colony. The company went bankrupt in 1624, and a year later Virginia became a royal colony.

Virginia Plan   Proposal of the Virginia delegation at the 1787 **Constitution Convention** calling for a national legislature in which the states would be represented according to population. The national legislature would have the explicit power to veto or overrule laws passed by state legislatures.

Virtual representation   The notion, current in eighteenth-century England, that parliamentary members represented the interests of the nation as a whole, not those of the particular district that elected them.

Wade-Davis Bill   Congressional alternative to Lincoln's **Ten Percent Plan,** passed in 1864; required 50 percent of prewar voters to pledge their loyalty and demanded guarantees for black equality. The president exercised a pocket veto, and it never became law.

Waltham system   During the industrialization of the early nineteenth century, the recruitment of unmarried young women for employment in a factory.

War Hawks Members of Congress, predominately from the South and West, who aggressively pushed for a war against Britain after their election in 1810.

War of 1812 War fought between the United States and Britain from June 1812 to January 1815 largely over British restrictions on American shipping.

War of the Austrian Succession A small conflict between Britain and Spain that began in 1739 and widened into a larger European war in 1740 (lasting until 1748) when the King of Prussia attacked lands claimed by Austria's ruling family. Known in America as **King George's War.**

War of the League of Augsburg Conflict in Europe (1688–1697) that pitted France against Spain, Sweden, the Holy Roman Empire, the Dutch republic, various German principalities, and, in 1689, England. The principal aim was to halt the growing power of France's Louis XIV. In America, this was known as **King William's War.**

War of the Spanish Succession European conflict (1702–1713) that began in a struggle between the king of France and the Holy Roman emperor over claims to the Spanish throne. England, Holland, and the Holy Roman Empire fought France and Spain in a war known in America as **Queen Anne's War.**

Washington Temperance Societies Temperance associations dominated by mechanics and laborers that first formed in Baltimore in 1840.

Webster-Ashburton Treaty Treaty signed by the United States and Britain in 1842 that settled a boundary dispute between Maine and Canada and provided for closer cooperation in suppressing the African slave trade.

Whig party Political party formed in the mid-1830s in opposition to the **Jacksonian Democrats** that favored a strong role for the national government in promoting economic growth.

Whigs the name used by advocates of colonial resistance to British measures during the 1760s and 1770s. The Whig party in England unsuccessfully attempted to exclude the Catholic Duke of York from succession to the throne as James II; victorious in the **Glorious Revolution,** the Whigs later stood for religious toleration and the supremacy of Parliament over the crown.

Whiskey Rebellion Armed uprising in 1794 by farmers in western Pennsylvania who attempted to prevent the collection of the excise tax on whiskey.

White League One of several military organizations operating openly and in concert with the **Democratic party** in the South to thwart black voting rights during **Reconstruction.**

White Plains, Battle of Revolutionary War engagement that took place on October 28, 1776, between General Washington's troops, evacuating New York City, and British forces under Sir William Howe. Washington sustained more than three hundred casualties before withdrawing his troops.

Wide Awakes Group of red-shirted, black-caped young men who paraded through city streets in the North extolling the virtues of the **Republican party** during the 1860 presidential election campaign.

Wilderness, Battle of the Civil War clash between Confederate and Union forces near Chancellorsville in May 1864 marked by fierce hand-to-hand combat in dense woods.

Wilmot Proviso Never-approved amendment to a **Mexican War** appropriations bill that would ban slavery from any territory acquired from Mexico, submitted to Congress by Pennsylvania Democrat David Wilmot.

Workingmen's movement Associations of urban workers who began campaigning in the 1820s for free public education and a ten-hour workday.

Writs of assistance Documents issued by a court of law that gave British officials in America the power to search for smuggled goods wherever they wished. The legality of these writs became an important cause of controversy in Massachusetts in 1761 and 1762.

Wyoming Valley Pennsylvania site where, in June and July 1778, a force comprised of Iroquois Indians and **Tories** under colonel John Butler routed **Patriot** defenders and laid waste to settlements during the Revolutionary War.

XYZ Affair Diplomatic incident in 1798 in which Americans were outraged by the demand of the French for a bribe as a condition for negotiating with American diplomats.

Yorktown, Siege of Final major decisive engagement of the Revolutionary War in which American and French forces under Generals Washington and Rochambeau laid siege to British forces under Lord Cornwallis at Yorktown, Virginia, from August 30 to October 19, 1781. The surrender of approximately eight thousand British troops on October 19 led to the British government's decision to end the war.

Young America Mid-nineteenth-century movement that espoused strong nationalistic views and the desire to expand American influence overseas.

PHOTO CREDITS

CHAPTER 1: The British Library, 3; The Granger Collection, 5; Danny Lehman Photography, 8; Comstock, 9; British Museum, London, 10; National Geographic Society, 14; Lucas Cranach, Martin Luther (1483–1546). Oil on wood. The Granger Collection, 16; University of Toronto—Thomas Fisher Rare Book Library, 18; Peabody Museum, Harvard University, 22; Jerry Jacka Photography, 23; The British Museum, 29

CHAPTER 2: The British Library, 35; Virginia Historical Society, 39; Plymouth Plantation Photo, 45; Courtesy, American Antiquarian Society, 46; Attributed to the Freake–Gibbs Painter American, Active Boston, Mass. ca. 1670 THE MASON CHILDREN: DAVID, JOANNA, AND ABIGAIL, 1670. Oil on canvas, 39 × 42-1/2″. The Fine Arts Museum of San Francisco, Gift of Mr. and Mrs. John D. Rockefeller 3rd, 1979.7.3, 50; Courtesy of National Library of Jamaica, 54; The Hartger's View, New Amsterdam 1626–1628. Line engraving 3-1/4 × 4-3/4″. Museum of the City of New York. 29.100.792. The J. Clarence Davies Collection, 57

CHAPTER 3: The South Carolina Historical Society, 63; National Archives of Canada, 65; Library of Congress, 69; Photo by Tom L. McKnight, 72; The British Museum, 77; The Fortunate Slave: An Illustration of African Slavery in the Early Eighteenth Century by Douglas Grant (1968). From Some Memoirs of the Life of Job by Thomas Bluett (1734). Photo by Precision Chromes Inc., NYPL, 80; Colonial Williamsburg Foundation. Abby Aldrich Rockefeller Folk Art Center, Williamsburg, VA, 81

CHAPTER 4: Washington/Custis/Lee Collection, Washington and Lee University, Lexington, VA, 93; Library Company of Philadelphia, 98; Clothespress. 1730–40. England, London, Mahogany, glass H: 98 in. (249 cm); 45-3/4 in. (116 cm). Gift of Albert Sack, Courtesy, Museum of Fine Arts, Boston, 99; Paul Revere. ca. 1768–70. Copley, John Singleton, U.S., 1738–1815. Oil on canvas, 35 × 28-1/2 in. (88.9 × 72.3 cm.) Gift of Joseph W., William B., and Edward H. R. Revere. Courtesy, Museum of Fine Arts, Boston, 100; The Granger Collection, 101; Courtesy, Winterhur Museum, 102; Robert Feke (1707–1752) Portrait of Benjamin Franklin (1706–1790), c. 1746. Oil on canvas, 127 × 102 cm. Courtesy of the Harvard University Portrait Collection. Bequest of Dr. John Collins Warren, 1856, 104; National Portrait Gallery, London, 106; Grassat de Saint–Sauvaur/National Archives of Canada/C–003165, 119; North Wind Picture Archives, 121

CHAPTER 5: Library of Congress, 131; Library Company of Philadelphia, 134; New York Public Library, 136; National Portrait Gallery, London, 138; Courtesy of The British Museum, 141; Mr. and Mrs. Mifflin, by John Singleton Copley. Courtesy of The Historical Society of Pennsylvania, 143; The Boston Tea Party, 16 December 1773: colored engraving, 1793, the earliest known American depiction of the event, 148; Williams Burg, "The Alternative". 1775, hand-colored print. Size: H. 13-3/4, W. 19. "Courtesy, Winterhur Museum", 151

CHAPTER 6: The Battle of Lexington, April 19th 1775. OH. 13-3/4″ , W. 19″. Courtesy, Winterhur Museum, 161; "The Washington Family". Size: H. 21-5/8″, W. 26-15/16. Courtesy, Winterhur Museum, 162; The Granger Collection, 164; Title page to Thomas Paine's Common Sense, Philadelphia: R. Bell, 1776. Inscribed: "G. Washington". Boston Athenaeum, 165; "1776 Town". Size: H. 11-1/8″, W. 16-7/8. Courtesy, Winterhur Museum, 167; "Mezzotint, 1780–1800. Size: H. 7-3/8″, W. 9-3/4″. Courtesy, Winterhur Museum, 170; Library of Congress, 171; "Paul Jones Shooting a Sailor", color engraving from the Olds Collection #366, no negative number. Collection of the New–York Historical Society, 179; Surrender of Lord Cornwallis at Yorktown, by John Trumbull, (American 1756–1843), oil on canvas 20-7/8 × 30-5/8 inches, 183

CHAPTER 7: The Granger Collection, 195; Corbis–Bettmann, 196; New York Public Library, 198; Gallery of the Republic, 202; Gallery of the Republic, 202; Gallery of the Republic, 202; The Granger Collection, 204; Frick Art Reference Library, 213; The Granger Collection, 220; Courtesy of The Historical Society of Pennsylvania, 206

CHAPTER 8: Tontine Coffee House, by Francis Guy, oil on canvas, c. 1797, Courtesy Collection of The New–York Historical Society, 230; Courtesy of the Arents Collection, New York Public Library, Special Collections, 232; New York Public Library, 233; Courtesy of the Art Commission of the City of New York, City Hall, 236; Chicago Historical Society, 243; The Granger Collection, 246; The Granger Collection, 247; White House Historical Association, 249, Library of Congress, 538

CHAPTER 9: The Granger Collection, 259; By permission of the Houghton Library, Harvard University, 260; Portrait of Aaron Burr, by John Vanderlyn

(1775–1850). Painting, oil on canvas, 28-9/16 × 22. Framed: H. 33-1/4; W. 26-5/8, 263; "Look On This Picture, and On This", Courtesy of Collection of The New–York Historical Society, 264; McCord Museum of Canadian History, 271; National Geographic Society, 272; Library of Congress, 273; John Marshall by Chester Harding (1792–1886), Oil on Canvas, 1830. Boston Athenaeum, 276

CHAPTER 10: John L. Krimmel, painting, 1815. Oil paint, canvas, H. 16-3/8, W. 25-5/8. Courtesy, Winterhur Museum, 287; Thomas Sully, General Andrew Jackson, 1845. Oil on Canvas. In the Collection of The Corcoran Gallery of Art, Washington, D.C., Gift of William Wilson Corcoran, 292; The Granger Collection, 296; General Jackson caricature slaying the many headed monster, 1836. Courtesy of Collection of The New–York Historical Society, 301; The Granger Collection, 304; Smithsonian Institute, 307; Smithsonian Institute, 311

CHAPTER 11: The Granger Collection, 321; Courtesy of Miriam and Ira D. Wallach Division of Art, Prints, and Photographs, The New York Public Library, Astor, Lenox, and Tilden Foundations, 326; Museum of American Textile History, 328; Corbis–Bettmann, 332; "Family Group", Davis, Joseph H., M. and M. Karolik Collection. Courtesy, Museum of Fine Arts, Boston, 338; Brown Brothers, 341

CHAPTER 12: The Granger Collection, 349; Denver Art Museum, 355; The Denver Public Library, Western History Department, 356; Library of Congress, 359; Gallery of the Republic, 363; (EXETER, N.H., (EXETER NEW HAMPSHIRE, VOLUNTEERS LEAVING FOR THE MEXICAN WAR), 1846). Courtesy Amon Carter Museum, Fort Worth, Texas, 369

CHAPTER 13: Collection of The New–York Historical Society, 378; Library of Congress, 380; The Collection of Jay P. Altmayer, 384; Remains of Slave Quarters, Fort George Island, Florida, Photograph from the Bagoe Collection. Courtesy: Collection of the New–York Historical Society, 385; From the Collection of the Louisiana State Museum, 386; James Cameron (1817–1882), "Colonel and Mrs. James A. Whiteside, Son Charles and Servants. Oil on canvas; c. 1858–1859. Hunter Museum of Art, Chattanooga, Tennessee, Gift of Mr. and Mrs. Thomas B. Whiteside, 392; The Collection of Jay P. Altmayer, 397

CHAPTER 14: Girl's Evening School, ca. 1840, U.S. Pencil/Watercolour, 13-1/2 × 18-1/8 in. M. and M. Karolik Collection of American Paintings, 1815–1865, Courtesy of Museum of Fine Arts, Boston, 413; The Granger Collection, 414; Paul Rocheleau, Photographer, 416; The Granger Collection, 421; Lynn Historical Society, 426; The Granger Collection, 425; Frederick Douglas (1817?–95). Oil on canvas, c1844, attr. to E. Hammond. The Granger Collection, 427

CHAPTER 15: Art Resource, 433; California State Library, 434; Southworth, Albert Sands (1811–1894), and Hawes, Josiah Johnson (1808–1901), Harriet Beecher Stowe. Daguerreotype. 4-1/4 in × 3-1/4 in. The Metropolitan Museum of Art, Gift of I.N. Phelps Stokes, Edward S. Hawes, Alice Mary Hawes, and Marion August Hawes, 1937, 440; The Newberry Library, 445; Southern Chivalry—Argument Versus Clubs, lithograph, 1856. Weitenkampf Collection #745, Prints Collection: Miriam and Ira D. Wallach Division of Art, Prints, and Photographs, The New York Public Library, Astor, Lenox, and Tilden Foundations, 446; Library of Congress, 450; The Granger Collection, 455

CHAPTER 16: George Hayward, 1834–1872, Departure of the Seventh Regiment, N.Y.S.M., April 19, 1861, Pencil, watercolor, and Gouache. M. and M. Karolik Collection, Courtesy, Museum of Fine Arts, Boston, 471; Boston Public Library, 473; Winslow Homer (1836–1910), Rainy Day in Camp, 1871, Oil on Canvas, 20 in × 36 in. The Metropolitan Museum of Art, Gift of Mrs. William F. Milton, 1923, 481; Art Resource, 482; Library of Congress, 486; Courtesy, Georgia Department of Archives and History, 488; Chicago Historical Society, 490; Library of Congress, 495

CHAPTER 17: Blythe, David Gilmour (1815–1865) U.S., Lincoln Crushing the Dragon Rebellion, 1862, Oil on Canvas, 18 × 22 in. Courtesy, Museum of Fine Arts, Boston. Bequest of Martha C. Karolik for the M. and M. Karolik Collection of American Paintings, 1815–1865, 505; Corbis–Bettmann, 511; Library of Congress, 513; Library of Congress, 516; The Granger Collection, 519; Library of Congress, 520; Library of Congress, 521

CHAPTER 18: The Granger Collection, 531; The Granger Collection, 533; National Museum of American History, 534; The Granger Collection, 536; The Granger Collection, 540; The Granger Collection, 543; Library of Congress, 545; Library of Congress, 554

INDEX